SOMETHING ABOUT THE AUTHOR®

Something about
the Author *was named
an* **"Outstanding
Reference Source,"**
*the highest honor given
by the American
Library Association
Reference and Adult
Services Division.*

ISSN 0276-816X

SOMETHING ABOUT THE AUTHOR®

**Facts and Pictures about Authors
and Illustrators of Books for Young People**

volume 217

GALE
CENGAGE Learning™

Detroit • New York • San Francisco • New Haven, Conn • Waterville, Maine • London

GALE
CENGAGE Learning

Something about the Author, Volume 217

Project Editor: Lisa Kumar

Editorial: Laura Avery, Pamela Bow, Jim Craddock, Amy Fuller, Andrea Henderson, Margaret Mazurkiewicz, Tracie Moy, Jeff Muhr, Kathy Nemeh, Mary Ruby, Mike Tyrkus

Permissions: Leitha Etheridge-Sims, Jackie Jones

Imaging and Multimedia: Leitha Etheridge-Sims, John Watkins

Composition and Electronic Capture: Amy Darga

Manufacturing: Drew Kalasky

Product Manager: Janet Witalec

For product information and technology assistance, contact us at
Gale Customer Support, 1-800-877-4253.
For permission to use material from this text or product,
submit all requests online at **www.cengage.com/permissions.**
Further permissions questions can be emailed to
permissionrequest@cengage.com

Since this page cannot legibly accommodate all copyright notices, the acknowledgments constitute an extension of the copyright notice.

While every effort has been made to ensure the reliability of the information presented in this publication, Gale, a part of Cengage Learning, does not guarantee the accuracy of the data contained herein. Gale accepts no payment for listing; and inclusion in the publication of any organization, agency, institution, publication, service, or individual does not imply endorsement of the editors or publisher. Errors brought to the attention of the publisher and verified to the satisfaction of the publisher will be corrected in future editions.

EDITORIAL DATA PRIVACY POLICY: Does this publication contain information about you as an individual? If so, for more information about our editorial data privacy policies, please see our Privacy Statement at www.gale.cengage.com.

Gale
27500 Drake Rd.
Farmington Hills, MI, 48331-3535

LIBRARY OF CONGRESS CATALOG CARD NUMBER 62-52046

ISBN-13: 978-1-4144-5377-4
ISBN-10: 1-4144-5377-9

ISSN 0276-816X

This title is also available as an e-book.
ISBN-13: 978-1-4144-6449-7
ISBN-10: 1-4144-6449-5
Contact your Gale sales representative for ordering information.

Printed in the United States of America
1 2 3 4 5 6 7 14 13 12 11 10

Contents

Authors in Forthcoming Volumes vii

Introduction ix

SATA Product Advisory Board xi

Illustrations Index 179

Author Index 213

A

Adams, Diane 1960- 1

Alexander, Alma 1963- 3

Allen, Joy 1948- 5

Arnosky, Jim 1946- 8

Auseon, Andrew 1976- 16

B

Bailey, Linda 1948- 18

Berkes, Marianne 1940(?)- 23

Berman, Rachel 1946- 26

Bernstein, Jonathan 27

Black, Kat 28

Black, Katherine
  See Black, Kat 28

Brown, Calef 29

Burg, Ann E. 1954- 31

C

Cabot, Meg 1967- 33

Cabot, Meggin
  See Cabot, Meg 33

Cabot, Patricia
  See Cabot, Meg 33

Cantrell, Julie 1973- 39

Carroll, Jenny
  See Cabot, Meg 33

Cockcroft, Jason 39

Collins, Pat Lowery 1932- 40

Czekaj, Jef 1969- 44

D

Dadey, Debbie 1959- 46

Daly, James 52

Dillard, Sarah 1961- 53

Dionne, Erin 54

DoCampo, Valeria 1976- 55

Donovan, Gail 1962- 56

Duffy Stone, Heather 57

E

Echeverria-Bis, Olivia 59

Ehrlich, Amy 1942- 59

F

Fantaskey, Beth 1965- 66

Fitzmaurice, Kathryn 68

G

Glatt, Lisa 1963- 70

Goodman, Emily 71

H

Hartinger, Brent 1964- 71

Hazelaar, Cor 76

Henry, Rohan 76

Hoban, Julia 77

Horton, Joan 78

Hromic, Alma A.
  See Alexander, Alma 3

Hughes, Carol 1955- 80

J

Jacobs, Lee
  See Stone, Tanya Lee 158

Javernick, Ellen 1938- 83

Jones, Marcia Thornton 1958- 85

K

Katz, Bobbi 1933- 89

Kelley, Ann 1941- 93

Kelley, Gary 1945- 94

King, Amy
    See King, A.S. 97

King, A.S. 1970- 97

Kleven, Elisa 1958- 98

L

Lee, Huy Voun 1969- 105

Leonhard, Herb 107

Lewis, Kim 1951- 107

Lieshout, Elle van
    See van Lieshout, Elle 165

M

MacDonald, Anne Louise 1955- 112

Macdonald, Wendy 113

Macdonald, Wendy M.
    See Macdonald, Wendy 113

Mantha, John 1960- 115

McCormack, Caren McNelly 117

McDowell, Marilyn Taylor 118

Michalak, Jamie 1973- 119

Mitchell, Saundra 1974(?)- 121

Modesitt, Jeanne 1953- 122

Morozumi, Atsuko 1955- 125

O

Os, Eric van
    See van Os, Erik 167

Osterweil, Adam 1972- 128

P

Potter, Katherine 129

Proimos, James 1955- 131

R

Remkiewicz, Frank 1939- 136

Rich, Naomi 143

Ritchie, Scot 1954- 144

Rui, Paolo 1962- 147

Runyon, Brent 1976- 147

S

Schneider, Elisa
    See Kleven, Elisa 98

Schubert, Dieter 150

Schubert, Ingrid 1953- 154

Siomades, Lorianne 156

Stone, Tanya Lee 1965- 158

Storms, Patricia 1963- 163

Sussman, Michael 1953- 164

Sussman, Michael B.
    See Sussman, Michael 164

V

van Lieshout, Elle 1963- 165

van Os, Erik 1963- 167

W

Walsh, Rebecca 169

Weaver, Will 1950- 171

Weaver, William Weller
    See Weaver, Will 171

Weber, Lisa K. 175

Weingarten, Lynn 175

Weissman, Elissa Brent 176

Z

Zuckerman, Amy 177

Authors in Forthcoming Volumes

Below are some of the authors and illustrators that will be featured in upcoming volumes of *SATA*. These include new entries on the swiftly rising stars of the field, as well as completely revised and updated entries (indicated with *) on some of the most notable and best-loved creators of books for children.

*Tim Bowers ▮ As an illustrator for children's picture books, Bowers has seen his work paired with texts by such noted children's writers as Cynthia Rylant, Margie Palatini, Laura Numeroff, and J. Patrick Lewis. Beginning his career in his native Ohio, Bowers created commercial illustrations, storyboards, and cartoon characters for the advertising industry. Bowers' award-winning illustration projects include Lewis's picture book *First Dog* and the imaginative verse collection *Dogku* by popular novelist Andrew Clements.

Jason Chin ▮ Chin creates illustrations for a variety of children's books, from Atticus Gannaway's *The Silver Sorceress of OZ* to the picture-book adaptation of Simon Winchester's compelling *The Day the World Exploded: The Earthshaking Catastrophe at Krakatoa*. In addition to his illustration projects, Chin's characteristic detailed line-and-watercolor art is a feature of his fanciful environmentally grounded story *Redwoods*.

Rebecca Emberley ▮ The daughter of noted artist and children's author Ed Emberley, Emberley is a prolific illustrator who specializes in creating bilingual concept books such as *My Opposites/ Mis opuestos* for young children. In addition to picture books, she has also collaborated with her father and brother Michael Emberley on *Three: An Emberley Family Sketchbook*, and has rejoined her dad on *There Was an Old Monster* and several other stories.

*Stephen Michael King ▮ Australian author/illustrator King found his creative outlet in illustrating stories after a childhood illness rendered him deaf. In his original picture book *Milli, Jack, and the Dancing Cat* an inhibited artist is drawn out of her shell by a traveling minstrel and his feline partner, while *Emily Loves to Bounce* captures the energy of a playful little girl in its rhyming text. In addition to his own award-winning stories, King also illustrates stories by others, including beloved Australian children's authors Jackie French and Margaret Wild.

Deborah Lytton ▮ Lytton, a singer and actress who appeared for several years on the popular soap opera *Days of Our Lives*, now works as an attorney in addition to writing. In her first novel, *Jane in Bloom*, she explores the aftermath of an idolized older sister's tragic death. Lytton's themes include a family's fall into turmoil and a twelve year old's efforts to cope with grief and shock while also reevaluating what is really important in order to forge her own identity.

*David Parkins ▮ An accomplished artist who lives and works in England, Parkins has garnered recognition for creating the bold, detailed, and energetic illustrations that appear in over ninety picture books for children. Among the long list of works that have benefitted from his diverse illustration styles are stories by Dick King-Smith, Geraldine McCaughrean, Jan Mark, and Richard Platt. In addition to book illustration, Parkins also works as a cartoonist: his satiric renderings have appeared in major London newspapers and he has enjoyed a long association with the popular British comic strip "The Beano."

Ellen Potter ▮ Potter is the author of *Olivia Kidney*, a novel for young readers that was praised by reviewers for its multi-leveled plot and a story that weaves reality with the fantastical. In addition to several sequels featuring the twelve-year-old Olivia, Potter also treats readers to her quirky storytelling in the novels *Pish Posh* and *Slob*, as well as penning the critically acclaimed adult novel *The Average Human*.

Christopher Santoro ▮ Based in Savannah, Georgia, Santoro is a prolific illustrator and author who began illustrating children's books in the late 1970s. In addition to producing interactive toddler board books such as *Open the Barn Door*, he has created colorful art for stories by other authors, such as Dom DeLuise, Lynne Plourde, and Kathleen Krull. Santoro's work has been cited by the prestigious Society of Illustrators as well as by the American Institute of Graphic Arts, and has also appeared in such high-profile periodicals as the *New Yorker*.

*David Stahler, Jr. ▮ Stahler teaches English literature at an independent Vermont high school in addition to being a children's book writer. He made his writing debut with the well-received novel *Truesight*, and expanded that story into a trilogy in *The Seer* and *Otherspace*. Stahler's standalone novels include the young-adult fantasy *A Gathering of Shades* and a teen-themed horror tale titled *Doppelganger*.

*Lisa Yee ▮ An inventive writer and entrepreneur, Yee channeled her boundless energy and sense of fun into a career that eventually established her as co-owner and creative director of a marketing and creative services company. With *Millicent Min, Girl Genius*, Yee achieved equal acclaim as a children's book author specializing in middle-grade fiction. In addition to creating a sequel, *Stanford Wong Flunks Big-Time*, she has continued to broaden her preteen fan base with the novels *Absolutely Maybe* and *Bobby vs. Girls (Accidentally)*.

Introduction

Something about the Author (*SATA*) is an ongoing reference series that examines the lives and works of authors and illustrators of books for children. *SATA* includes not only well-known writers and artists but also less prominent individuals whose works are just coming to be recognized. This series is often the only readily available information source on emerging authors and illustrators. You'll find *SATA* informative and entertaining, whether you are a student, a librarian, an English teacher, a parent, or simply an adult who enjoys children's literature.

What's Inside *SATA*

SATA provides detailed information about authors and illustrators who span the full time range of children's literature, from early figures like John Newbery and L. Frank Baum to contemporary figures like Judy Blume and Richard Peck. Authors in the series represent primarily English-speaking countries, particularly the United States, Canada, and the United Kingdom. Also included, however, are authors from around the world whose works are available in English translation. The writings represented in *SATA* include those created intentionally for children and young adults as well as those written for a general audience and known to interest younger readers. These writings cover the entire spectrum of children's literature, including picture books, humor, folk and fairy tales, animal stories, mystery and adventure, science fiction and fantasy, historical fiction, poetry and nonsense verse, drama, biography, and nonfiction. Obituaries are also included in *SATA* and are intended not only as death notices but also as concise overviews of people's lives and work. Additionally, each edition features newly revised and updated entries for a selection of *SATA* listees who remain of interest to today's readers and who have been active enough to require extensive revisions of their earlier biographies.

Autobiography Feature

Beginning with Volume 103, many volumes of *SATA* feature one or more specially commissioned autobiographical essays. These unique essays, averaging about ten thousand words in length and illustrated with an abundance of personal photos, present an entertaining and informative first-person perspective on the lives and careers of prominent authors and illustrators profiled in *SATA*.

Two Convenient Indexes

In response to suggestions from librarians, *SATA* indexes no longer appear in every volume but are included in alternate (odd-numbered) volumes of the series, beginning with Volume 57.

SATA continues to include two indexes that cumulate with each alternate volume: the Illustrations Index, arranged by the name of the illustrator, gives the number of the volume and page where the illustrator's work appears in the current volume as well as all preceding volumes in the series; the Author Index gives the number of the volume in which a person's biographical sketch, autobiographical essay, or obituary appears in the current volume as well as all preceding volumes in the series.

These indexes also include references to authors and illustrators who appear in *Gale's Yesterday's Authors of Books for Children, Children's Literature Review,* and *Something about the Author Autobiography Series.*

Easy-to-Use Entry Format

Whether you're already familiar with the *SATA* series or just getting acquainted, you will want to be aware of the kind of information that an entry provides. In every *SATA* entry the editors attempt to give as complete a picture of the person's life and work as possible. A typical entry in *SATA* includes the following clearly labeled information sections:

PERSONAL: date and place of birth and death, parents' names and occupations, name of spouse, date of marriage, names of children, educational institutions attended, degrees received, religious and political affiliations, hobbies and other interests.

ADDRESSES: complete home, office, electronic mail, and agent addresses, whenever available.

CAREER: name of employer, position, and dates for each career post; art exhibitions; military service; memberships and offices held in professional and civic organizations.

MEMBER: professional, civic, and other association memberships and any official posts held.

AWARDS, HONORS: literary and professional awards received.

WRITINGS: title-by-title chronological bibliography of books written and/or illustrated, listed by genre when known; lists of other notable publications, such as plays, screenplays, and periodical contributions.

ADAPTATIONS: a list of films, television programs, plays, CD-ROMs, recordings, and other media presentations that have been adapted from the author's work.

WORK IN PROGRESS: description of projects in progress.

SIDELIGHTS: a biographical portrait of the author or illustrator's development, either directly from the biographee—and often written specifically for the *SATA* entry—or gathered from diaries, letters, interviews, or other published sources.

BIOGRAPHICAL AND CRITICAL SOURCES: cites sources quoted in "Sidelights" along with references for further reading.

EXTENSIVE ILLUSTRATIONS: photographs, movie stills, book illustrations, and other interesting visual materials supplement the text.

How a *SATA* Entry Is Compiled

SATA editors examine a wide variety of published sources to gather information for an entry. Biographical and bibliographic sources are consulted, as are book reviews, feature articles, published interviews, and material sometimes obtained from the biographee's family, publishers, agent, or other associates. Whenever possible, the author or illustrator is sent a copy of the entry to check for accuracy and completeness.

Entries that have not been verified by the biographees or their representatives are marked with an asterisk (*).

Contact the Editor

We encourage our readers to examine the entire *SATA* series. Please write and tell us if we can make *SATA* even more helpful to you. Give your comments and suggestions to the editor:

Editor
Something about the Author
Gale, Cengage Learning
27500 Drake Rd.
Farmington Hills MI 48331-3535

Toll-free: 800-877-GALE
Fax: 248-699-8070

Something about the Author Product Advisory Board

The editors of *Something about the Author* are dedicated to maintaining a high standard of excellence by publishing comprehensive, accurate, and highly readable entries on a wide array of writers for children and young adults. In addition to the quality of the content, the editors take pride in the graphic design of the series, which is intended to be orderly yet inviting, allowing readers to utilize the pages of *SATA* easily and with efficiency. Despite the longevity of the *SATA* print series, and the success of its format, we are mindful that the vitality of a literary reference product is dependent on its ability to serve its users over time. As literature, and attitudes about literature, constantly evolve, so do the reference needs of students, teachers, scholars, journalists, researchers, and book club members. To be certain that we continue to keep pace with the expectations of our customers, the editors of *SATA* listen carefully to their comments regarding the value, utility, and quality of the series. Librarians, who have firsthand knowledge of the needs of library users, are a valuable resource for us. The *Something about the Author* Product Advisory Board, made up of school, public, and academic librarians, is a forum to promote focused feedback about *SATA* on a regular basis. The nine-member advisory board includes the following individuals, whom the editors wish to thank for sharing their expertise:

SOMETHING ABOUT THE AUTHOR

ADAMS, Diane 1960-

Personal

Born 1960, in Long Beach, CA; married. *Education:* University of Redlands, B.A. (Spanish); attended Art Center College of Design. *Hobbies and other interests:* Reading, walking dogs, playing golf.

Addresses

Home—Redlands, CA. *E-mail*—dadamsgc@aol.com.

Career

Art and writing teacher. Presenter at schools.

Member

Society of Children's Book Writers and Illustrators.

Awards, Honors

Minnesota Read Aloud Book Award nomination, 2005, and Kansas State Reading Circle Recommended Reading selection, 2006, both for *Zoom!*

Writings

FOR CHILDREN

Zoom! (picture book), illustrated by Kevin Luthardt, Peachtree Publishers (Atlanta, GA), 2005.

I Can Do It Myself!, illustrated by Nancy Hayashi, Peachtree Publishers (Atlanta, GA), 2009.

ILLUSTRATOR

Stephanie Stuve Bodeen, *A Home for Salty,* Friends of San Pablo National Wildlife Refuge (Fremont, CA), 2007.

Sidelights

While growing up in California, Diane Adams enjoyed writing poetry, inspired by the stories of author/illustrator Maurice Sendak, among others. During college, she earned a degree in Spanish at the University of Redlands, and also studied at Pasadena's prestigious Art Center College of Design. Adams took a new direction in her creative career when she expanded her work as an art and writing instructor into the field of children's books. In addition to creating artwork for Stephanie Stuve Bodeen's *A Home for Salty,* Adams has also created stories for the picture books *Zoom!* and *I Can Do It Myself!*

Inspired by Adams' love of roller coasters and featuring artwork by Kevin Luthardt, *Zoom!* depicts one young boy's triumph over his own fears. Encouraged by his eager father, the boy reluctantly agrees to go on the Dino Coaster at the local amusement part. After father

Diane Adams' high-energy picture book Zoom! *features colorful illustrations by Kevin Luthardt.* (Illustration © 2005 by Kevin Luthardt. Reproduced by permission.)

and son reach the top and begin the first huge drop of the roller-coaster ride, "the roles are reversed, with the child obviously thrilled and Dad clearly not," according to *School Library Journal* contributor Grace Oliff. A *Publishers Weekly* critic wrote that Adams captures the attention of young audiences by crafting "singsongy couplets with plenty of heavy-duty action words" to capture the "lurching," "jerking," and "rumbling" of the speeding roller coasters around the track.

Adams teams up with artist Nancy Hayashi to create *I Can Do It Myself!*, a story that focuses on a typical childhood assertion. The story introduces a determined girl named Emily Pearl, whose independent nature makes her confident enough to tackle many challenges. Emily can make her own bed, pour her own juice, make her own sandwiches, and even play a musical instrument while doing acrobatics. However, at bedtime, Emily admits her reliance on others, who can give a loving hug and read a good-night tale. Praising Hayashi's "cheerful watercolors"—which show Emily to be a bit less than the "big girl" she asserts herself to be—Jane Marino added in *School Library Journal* that Adams' rhyming story is "told in a fresh, yet familiar

way." In *Kirkus Reviews* a critic recommended *I Can Do It Myself!* for "one-on-one in-the-lap fun," noting that the mix of story and art will likely elicit "spontaneous giggles . . . at storytime."

Biographical and Critical Sources

PERIODICALS

Booklist, March 15, 2009, Carolyn Phelan, review of *I Can Do It Myself!*, p. 66.
Kirkus Reviews, February 1, 2009, review of *I Can Do It Myself!*
Publishers Weekly, April 11, 2005, review of *Zoom!*, p. 53.
School Library Journal, May, 2005, Grace Oliff, review of *Zoom!*, p. 76; April, 2009, Jane Marino, review of *I Can Do It Myself!*, p. 99.

ONLINE

Diane Adams Home Page, http://www.dianeadams.net (May 31, 2010).*

ALEXANDER, Alma 1963-
[A pseudonym]
(Alma A. Hromic)

Personal

Born July 5, 1963, in Novi Sad, Yugoslavia (now Serbia); married R.A. Deckert (a journalist and editor), June, 2000. *Education:* University of Cape Town, South Africa, M.Sc. (microbiology), 1987.

Addresses

Home—Bellingham, WA. *Agent*—Jill Grinberg Literary Management, 244 5th Ave., Ste. 11, New York, NY 10001-7931.

Career

Writer, editor, and microbiologist. Allergy Society, South Africa, editor of scientific journal; editor for an educational publisher in New Zealand; literary critic.

Awards, Honors

Finalist, Sir Julius Vogel Award, 2002, and Award of Excellence, WordWeaving, both for *Changer of Days;* competition winner, International BBC, 2001, for "The Painting."

Writings

NOVELS

The Embers of Heaven, Harper (New York, NY), 2000.
The Secrets of Jin-Shei, HarperCollins (New York, NY), 2004.
Changer of Days, Eos (New York, NY), 2005.
The Hidden Queen, Eos (New York, NY), 2005.

"WORLDWEAVERS" YOUNG-ADULT FANTASY NOVELS

Gift of the Unmage, Eos (New York, NY), 2007.
Spellspam, Eos (New York, NY), 2008.
Cybermage, Eos (New York, NY), 2009.

AS ALMA A. HROMIC

Houses in Africa (memoir), David Ling Publishing Limited (Auckland, New Zealand), 1995.
The Dolphin's Daughter and Other Stories, Longman (London, England), 1995.
(With husband R.A. Deckert) *Letters from the Fire,* HarperCollins New Zealand (Auckland, New Zealand), 1999.

Author of blogs. Also contributor of short fiction and nonfiction to magazines in South Africa, New Zealand, and the United Kingdom.

Author's work has been translated into Dutch, Italian, and German.

Sidelights

Alma Alexander was born Alma A. Hromic in Yugoslavia, and grew up in various African countries where her father, employed by international aid agencies, was posted. Alexander was trained in microbiology in South Africa, but writing about science overtook her desire for lab and research work. From South Africa, she moved to New Zealand, where she published her first book-length work, *Houses in Africa,* a memoir of the twenty years she spent in Zambia, Swaziland, and South Africa. Under her birth name, she also published a collection of three fables titled *The Dolphin's Daughter and Other Stories.*

In 1999, with the beginning of NATO air strikes against Serbia, Alexander witnessed from afar the destruction of her native town, Novi Sad. From her home in Auckland, New Zealand, she began a series of e-mail correspondences with friend and Florida journalist R.A. Deckert. The result of this correspondence was *Letters from the Fire,* a "cyber-romance novel set in the political context of the NATO bombings," as Margie Thomson described the book in the *New Zealand Herald Review.* Dave is a liberal Florida journalist who is opposed to the war, and Sasha is a Serb living in a city undergoing NATO bombing, and in the book they watch the unfolding of events in Serbia from their separate perspectives. For Vasili Stavropoulos, reviewing *Letters from the Fire* in Australia's *Sydney Morning Herald,* the novel "makes an important contribution to our understanding of the Kosovo crisis, bringing it back from the abstractions of international relations to the minutiae of ordinary life." The fictional romance between Dave and Sasha became a reality when the book's coauthors were married in 2000 and moved to the state of Washington.

The versatile Alexander ventured into fantasy literature in 2001 with *Changer of Days.* The novel tells the story of nine-year-old Anghara Kir Hama, who loses her powerful father and loving mother, and also her royal name and her home at Miranei, mountain capital of the land of Roisinan. She is forced into hiding by her greedy half-brother Sif, who not only steals her kingdom but also seeks her death to secure his hold on the future of the Kir Hama dynasty. Anghara must act with a maturity far beyond her years in order to survive; she develops her special powers of sight as she flees to the safety of Sanctuary, but even there she finds betrayal. Finally escaping to the harsh desert, she finds allies and a new strength to battle Sif. Victoria Strauss, writing on *SF-Site.com,* called *Changer of Days* an "epic fantasy."

Alexander discovered science fiction and fantasy when she was a teen growing up in Africa. Speaking with interviewer Chris Przybyszewski for *SFSite.com,* she noted that once she discovered the works of writers such as Ursula K. LeGuin, Roger Zelazny, and J.R.R.

Tolkien, "I never looked back." The work of LeGuin in particular influenced her 2004 novel, *The Secrets of Jin-Shei.* According to *Booklist* reviewer Nancy Pearl, this "fast-paced, imaginative, and thoroughly engrossing fantasy explores the meaning of friendship and loyalty among eight women."

Set in a mythical Chinese kingdom where mothers pass to their daughters a secret language and the ability to create special friendships, *The Secrets of Jin-Shei* focuses on the young poet Tai, daughter of a seamstress. Tai finds her special friendship, her jin-shei, in the form of the oldest daughter of the emperor, and this friendship changes not only Tai's life but also the fate of the entire realm. Pearl noted that this was the first of Alexander's novels to be published in the United States and prophesied that it "will surely whet readers' appetites for more." A *Kirkus Reviews* critic described *The Secrets of Jin-Shei* as depicting an "ancient sisterhood [whose members] fight, die, and practice sorcery for one another as they struggle to survive." For this critic the novel is "more episodic than epic," but Jennifer Baker, writing in *Library Journal,* had higher praise, calling *The Secrets of Jin-Shei* a "perfect genre-buster: romance, political intrigue, adventure, horror, magic, suspense—and enough anthropological detail to create a believable alternate history." Strauss found the same work both "vivid and involving . . . an exotic journey into the imagination, and a graceful exploration of the heart."

Alexander has also authored "Worldweavers," a fantasy series for teens. The first book in the series, *Gift of the Unmage,* introduces seventeen-year-old Galathea "Thea" Winthrop. Thea is the only person in her family without the ability to do magic, and she attempts to travel back in time in the hope of awakening her magical abilities. In the past, she meets with the ancient Anasazi and she learns that while she does have magical powers, her spiritual self has barred her from accessing them. Thea then sets out to learn why. Praising the book in *Kliatt,* Cara Chancellor called it "an incredibly fresh and unique twist on YA fantasy that blends contemporary ideas and ancient magic with phenomenal skill." *Booklist* writer Ilene Cooper was also impressed, remarking that in *Gift of the Unmage* "Alexander does an exquisite job of showing Thea's growth, her ability to maintain her own counsel." Cheri Dobbs, writing in *School Library Journal,* found that "fans of science fiction, folklore, and fantasy will be intrigued by the directions in which this story goes," and a *Kirkus Reviews* writer stated that Alexander's "combination of suspense, magic and teen angst will appeal to young-adult fans."

In *Spellspam* Thea has recovered her magic and has learned that she can create new worlds using her computer. She has also saved human magic from growing extinct. Now, the students at the academy for magic are receiving spam e-mails with magical qualities. Indeed, when students open e-mails promising to clear up acne,

they become partially invisible. Thea must discover the culprit as the e-mails and their effects become more and more drastic. Like *Gift of the Unmage, Spellspam* was applauded by critics, Chancellor calling it "an incredibly enjoyable tale that blends reality, legend, and magic in one of the freshest fantasy narratives this year." According to *School Library Journal* writer Samantha Larsen Hastings, "Thea is a likable character who struggles with feelings of being different and alone, something many teens can relate to," and a *Kirkus Reviews* contributor remarked that the novel's "energetic plot, well-integrated back story and teen characters will make fans very happy." In *Cybermage,* Thea is again on the case of computer-based magic gone awry.

Discussing her move to young-adult literature in a *Finding Wonderland* online interview, she explained: "I do not, never have done, never will, write 'down' to a level considered appropriate for 'children'. When I myself was one of those children, authors being patronizing and assuming I was ignorant or lazy was one of the top reasons why I would toss a book aside without finishing it. If the author cannot respect me, the reader, then I didn't see why I should reciprocate."

Alexander also added: "I do not believe for a moment that the troubles and trials of someone who happens to be fourteen or fifteen are any less valid or important than a mid-life crisis, and indeed are frequently far MORE important and life-changing than the latter, and my teen characters have choices to make and decisions to wrestle with that are every bit as complex as those that would face—and probably faze—an 'adult' character."

Alexander once noted: "Reading is the first thing that got me interested in writing. As a child I read the way other people breathed or ate—it was as much a part of my existence as my heartbeat. After that, it was just a matter of time. In particular, though, I have to single out the influence of my poet grandfather, who taught me to love language when I was barely a toddler. It was thanks to this man and his beautiful spirit that I felt able to spread my own literary wings. I owe him more than I can possibly say.

"I read widely and voraciously. In the mainstream arena (and I include historical fiction in this bracket), I would single out an eclectic mixture of contemporary and more venerable writers like Louis de Bernieres, Pearl Buck, Howard Spring, Oscar Wilde, Shakespeare, John Galsworthy, Isabel Allende, Sharon Penman, Ivo Andric (Nobel prize winner from Yugoslavia), and a bunch of poets including, but not limited to, Neruda, Rimbaud, Pushkin, and my grandfather (Stevan Mutibaric). In the speculative fiction arena (fantasy and science fiction), I would like to mention Neil Gaiman, Guy Gavriel Kay, Charles de Lint, Judith Tarr, Michael Moorcock, Arthur C. Clarke, Ursula K. Le Guin, and the list goes on. A writer cannot be a writer unless the reading net is cast far and wide.

"My writing process is, in a word, chaotic. I seldom, if ever, write from synopsis and frequently find out what happens next in a story at the time as my readers would—by writing that next scene. I never know what my characters might get up to from one chapter to the next, and I am often utterly taken by surprise when they change the track I thought they were on and pursue their own agendas. Somehow, though, it always works out.

"The most surprising thing I have learned as a writer is that it is possible to live in many worlds and love them all."

Biographical and Critical Sources

BOOKS

Hromic, Alma A., *Houses in Africa,* David Ling Publishing Limited (Auckland, New Zealand), 1995.

PERIODICALS

Booklist, March 1, 2004, Nancy Pearl, review of *The Secrets of Jin-Shei,* p. 136; March 1, 2007, Ilene Cooper, review of *Gift of the Unmage,* p. 73.

Kirkus Reviews, February 1, 2004, review of *The Secrets of Jin-Shei,* pp. 95-96; March 1, 2007, review of *Gift of the Unmage,* p. 215; April 1, 2008, review of *Spellspam*; February 15, 2009, review of "Worldweavers" series.

Kliatt, March 1, 2007, Cara Chancellor, review of *Gift of the Unmage,* p. 6; March 1, 2008, Cara Chancellor, review of *Spellspam,* p. 8; May 1, 2008, Cara Chancellor, review of *Gift of the Unmage,* p. 24.

Library Journal, March 1, 2004, Jennifer Baker, review of *The Secrets of Jin-Shei,* p. 106.

MBR Bookwatch, March 1, 2008, Dylan James, review of *Gift of the Unmage.*

New Zealand Herald, October 2, 1999, Margie Thomson, review of *Letters from the Fire.*

School Library Journal, August 1, 2007, Cheri Dobbs, review of *Gift of the Unmage,* p. 109; July 1, 2008, Samantha Larsen Hastings, review of *Spellspam,* p. 94.

Sydney Morning Herald, December 24, 1999, Vasili Stavropoulos, "We Shall Create a Desert and Call It Peace."

ONLINE

Alma A. Hromic Home Page, http://www.almahromic.com (July 5, 2004).

Alma Alexander Home Page, http://www.almaalexander.com (August 5, 2009).

Finding Wonderland Web log, http://writingya.blogspot.com/ (May 21, 2009), interview with Alexander.

SFSite.com, http://www.sfsite.com/ (April, 2004), Chris Przybyszewski, "A Conversation with Alma Alexander"; (July 5, 2004) Victoria Strauss, review of *The Secrets of Jin-Shei.**

ALLEN, Joy 1948-

Personal

Born 1948; children: four.

Addresses

Home—Cameron Park, CA. *E-mail*—joybug2@aol.com.

Career

Graphic designer and illustrator. Joy Allen Illustrations (designer), Cameron Park, CA, founder, 1997.

Awards, Honors

Silver Angel Award, Excellence in Media, 2002, for *Mud Pie Annie* by Sue Buchanan and Dana Schafer; Oppenheim Toy Portfolio Platinum Award, 2004, for "Hopscotch Hill School" series by Valerie Tripp.

Writings

SELF-ILLUSTRATED

Baby Signs: A Baby-sized Guide to Speaking with Sign Language, Dial Books for Young Readers (New York, NY), 2008.

Always a Princess, G.P. Putnam's Sons (New York, NY), 2009.

Princess Party, G.P. Putnam's Sons (New York, NY), 2010.

ILLUSTRATOR

Beverly Weiler, *Santa's Christmas Tree,* Great Western Publications (Gardena, CA), 1980.

Susan Hood, *Bad Hair Day,* Grosset & Dunlap (New York, NY), 1999.

Jeremiah Gamble, *Hold the Boat!,* Bethany Backyard (Minneapolis, MN), 1999.

Julie Glass, *A Dollar for Penny,* Random House (New York, NY), 2000.

Rich Scharlotte, *Grandma's Gospel,* WaterBrook Press (Colorado Springs, CO), 2000.

J.K. Arden, *Be My Valenslime,* Dutton Children's Books (New York, NY), 2001.

Linda Williams Aber, *Carrie Measures Up!,* Kane Press (New York, NY), 2001.

Sue Buchanan and Dana Schafer, *Mud Pie Annie: God's Recipe for Doing Your Best,* Zonderkidz (Grand Rapids, MI), 2001.

Lisa Schulman, *Unbelievable!,* Hampton-Brown (Carmel, CA), 2001.

Tony Johnston, *My Best Friend Bear,* Rising Moon (Flagstaff, AZ), 2001.

Karen Beaumont, *Being Friends,* Dial Books for Young Readers (New York, NY), 2002.

Jane O'Connor, *Dear Tooth Fairy,* Grosset & Dunlap (New York, NY), 2002.

Sonia W. Black, *Home for the Holidays,* Scholastic, Inc. (New York, NY), 2002.

X.J. Kennedy, *Exploding Gravy: Poems to Make You Laugh,* Little, Brown (Boston, MA), 2002.

Steve Metzger, *I'll Always Come Back!,* Scholastic, Inc. (New York, NY), 2002.

Laura Derico, compiler, *Prayers for a Child's Day,* Standard Pub. (Cincinnati, OH), 2003.

Mary Packard, *Where Is Jake?,* Children's Press (New York, NY), 2003.

Michele Sobel Spirn, *I Am the Turkey,* HarperCollins (New York, NY), 2004.

Mary Packard, *The Very Bad Day,* Children's Press (New York, NY), 2004.

Ellen Olson-Brown, *Ten Stinky Babies,* Tricycle Press (Berkeley, CA), 2005.

David T. Greenberg, *The Book of Boys (for Girls) and the Book of Girls (for Boys),* illustrated by Joy Allen, Little, Brown (Boston, MA), 2005.

Charnan Simon, *Tressa the Musical Princess,* Kindermusik International (Greensboro, NC), 2005.

Alina B. Klein, *Martimus at Midnight,* AuthorHouse (Bloomington, IN), 2006.

Crystal Bowman, *The House in the Middle of Town,* Standard Pub. (Cincinnati, OH), 2007.

Sue Buchanan and Dana Shafer, *Mud Pie Annie,* Zonderkidz (Grand Rapids, MI), 2008.

Lisa Glatt and Suzanne Greenberg, *Abigail Iris: The One and Only,* Walker & Co. (New York, NY), 2009.

Lisa Glatt and Suzanne Greenberg, *Abigail Iris: The Pet Project,* Walker Books for Young Readers (New York, NY), 2010.

Cat Cora, *A Suitcase Surprise for Mommy,* Dial Books for Young Readers (New York, NY), 2011.

Joy Allen's illustration projects include creating artwork for Karen Beaumont's picture book **Being Friends.** (Illustration copyright © 2002 by Joy Allen. Reproduced by permission of Dial Books for Young Readers, a division of Penguin Putnam Books for Young Readers.)

ILLUSTRATOR; "HOPSCOTCH HILL SCHOOL" SERIES

Valerie Tripp, *Bright, Shiny Skylar,* Pleasant Company
(Middleton, WI), 2003.
Valerie Tripp, *Hallie's Horrible Handwriting,* Pleasant
Company (Middleton, WI), 2003.
Valerie Tripp, *Thank You, Logan!,* Pleasant Company
(Middleton, WI), 2003.
Valerie Tripp, *Good Sport Gwen,* Pleasant Company
(Middletown, WI), 2004.
Valerie Tripp, *Teasing Trouble,* Pleasant Company
(Middleton, WI), 2004.
Valerie Tripp, *Lindy's Happy Ending,* Pleasant Company
(Middleton, WI), 2005.
Valerie Tripp, *The One and Only Delaney,* Pleasant Com-
pany (Middleton, WI), 2005.

ILLUSTRATOR; "CAM JANSEN" SERIES

David A. Adler, *Cam Jansen and the Mystery Writer Mys-
tery,* Viking (New York, NY), 2007.
David A. Adler, *Cam Jansen and the Summer Camp Mys-
teries: A Super Special,* Viking (New York, NY), 2007.
David A. Adler, *Cam Jansen and the Green School Mys-
tery,* Viking (New York, NY), 2008.
David A. Adler, *Cam Jansen and the Basketball Mystery,*
Viking Children's Books (New York, NY), 2009.
David A. Adler, *Cam Jansen: The Sports Day Mysteries:
A Super Special,* Puffin Books (New York, NY), 2009.
David A. Adler, *Cam Jansen and the Wedding Cake Mys-
tery,* Viking Children's Books (New York, NY), 2010.

Sidelights

Although she first worked as a graphic designer, Joy
Allen turned to illustration in 1997, and her colorful
images now appear in a wide range of books, from picture books and chapter books to educational materials.
Part of Pleasant Company's "Hopscotch Hill School"
beginning-reader series, *Bright, Shiny Skylar, Teasing
Trouble,* and *Hallie's Horrible Handwriting* pair school
stories by Valerie Tripp with Allen's art, "capture[ing]
. . . the body language of primary-grade children in a
series of brightly colored illustrations," according to
Booklist critic Carolyn Phelan in a review of *Teasing
Trouble.* Her illustrations also bring to life David A.
Adler's "Cam Jansen" chapter-book series. *Dear Tooth
Fairy,* an installment in the "All Aboard Reading" series, features a story by Jane O'Connor along with water color, ink, and charcoal images by Allen that "add
interesting and humorous details," according to *School
Library Journal* critic Marilyn Taniguchi.

Reviewing Allen's work for Julie Glass's *A Dollar for
Penny,* Ilene Cooper noted in *Booklist* that the author's
"jaunty" verses are "illustrated with happy watercolor
artwork that fills the pages." *Abigail Iris: The One and
Only,* part of a series of chapter books by Lisa Glatt
and Susanne Greenberg, focuses on an upbeat third
grader who finds contentment within her bustling family despite sometimes stressful circumstances. The first

Two imaginative little girls have a special day in Allen's self-illustrated
Princess Party. (Copyright © 2009 by Joy Allen. All rights reserved. Reproduced by
permission of G.P. Putnam's Sons, a division of Penguin Putnam Books for Young Readers.)

book in the series, it attracts young readers with what a
Kirkus Reviews critic described as "homespun sketches
and a breezy first-person text." Allen's "appealing black-
and-white . . . drawings show the characters' personalities, attitudes, and emotions," according to Phelan,
while in *School Library Journal* Lucinda Snyder asserted that the book's pen-and-ink drawings "make the
[same] story more accessible for reluctant readers and
help convey the protagonist's charm."

A rhyming story about two friends who are different in
almost every way, *Being Friends* benefits from Allen's
"spirited paintings" which "capture the joy and energy
behind a true childhood friendship," according to
Booklist contributor Kathy Broderick. In *School Library
Journal,* Doris Losey also cited the artist's "expressive,
colorful pastel illustrations," which "offer lots of details
to explore," and a *Kirkus Reviews* writer praised *Being
Friends* as "a delight to look at and . . . a gem for best
friends of any age to share." Another story about friendship, Tony Johnston's *My Best Friend Bear,* captures
the affection bestowed upon a favorite toy through
Allen's "appealing watercolor-and-colored-pencil illustrations," which "do a nice job depicting the special
bond between girl and bear," according to *Booklist* critic
Lauren Peterson.

In both *Princess Party* and *Always a Princess* Allen
pairs her engaging art with an original story that taps
into young girls' fascination with fairy princesses, as

well as their love of the color pink. In *Princess Party* two little girls host a party for their friends and decide that being a princess does not restrict one to party dresses and practicing the social graces: cowgirls and trampoline-jumpers can be princesses too! In *Kirkus Reviews* a contributor noted Allen's "cheery rhyming . . . text" in *Princess Party,* as well as the "sugar-shock of pink" that highlights the book's water color-and-graphite illustrations. Praising the same story for updating the characteristics of a true princess to reflect the reality of real girls, Judith Constantinides predicted in *School Library Journal* that Allen's sparkly covered picture book "should be a winner for the youngest princess-loving set."

Biographical and Critical Sources

PERIODICALS

Booklist, July, 2000, Ilene Cooper, review of *A Dollar for Penny,* p. 2045; May 15, 2001, Lauren Peterson, review of *My Best Friend's Bear,* p. 1758; September 15, 2002, Kathy Broderick, review of *Being Friends,* p. 238; July, 2003, Hazel Rochman, review of *Hallie's Horrible Handwriting,* p. 1903; July, 2004, Carolyn Phelan, review of *Teasing Trouble,* p. 1852; August, 2004, Gillian Engberg, review of *I Am the Turkey,* p. 1945; March 1, 2009, Carolyn Phelan, review of *Abigail Iris: The One and Only,* p. 43.

Horn Book, May-June, 2002, Susan P. Bloom, review of *Exploding Gravy: Poems to Make You Laugh,* p. 341.

Kirkus Reviews, March 1, 2002, review of *Exploding Gravy,* p. 337; April 1, 2002, review of *Being Friends,* p. 486; July, 2004, Carolyn Phelan, review of *Teasing Trouble,* p. 18452; August 15, 2004, review of *I Am the Turkey,* p. 813; January, 2005, Susan Lisim, review of *I Am the Turkey,* p. 98; June 15, 2005, review of *The Book of Boys (for Girls) and the Book of Girls (for Boys),* p. 683; February 1, 2009, review of *Abigail Iris: The One and Only;* July 15, 2009, review of *Princess Party.*

New York Times Book Review, August 11, 2002, review of *Exploding Gravy.*

Publishers Weekly, February 26, 2001, review of *My Best Friend Bear,* p. 84; October 13, 2003, review of *Bright, Shiny Skylar,* p. 80.

School Library Journal, June, 2001, Barbara Auerbach, review of *Carrie Measures Up,* p. 100; August, 2001, Susan Marie Pitard, review of *My Best Friend Bear,* p. 154; July, 2002, Doris Losey, review of *Being Friends,* p. 77; March, 2003, Marilyn Taniguchi, review of *Dear Tooth Fairy,* p. 200; July, 2005, Lynda Ritterman, review of *Lindy's Happy Ending,* p. 84; August, 2005, Catherine Threadgill, review of *The Book of Boys (for Girls) and the Book of Girls (for Boys),* p. 113; March, 2009, Lucinda Snyder, review of *Abigail Iris: The One and Only,* p. 112; November, 2009, Judith Constantinides, review of *Princess Party,* p. 72.

ONLINE

Joy Allen Home Page, http://www.joyallen.us (May 31, 2010).

Joy Allen Web log, http://joyallensblog.blogspot.com (May 31, 2010).*

* * *

ARNOSKY, Jim 1946-

Personal

Born September 1, 1946, in New York, NY; son of Edward J. (a draftsman) and Marie Arnosky; married Deanna L. Eshelman, August 6, 1966; children: Michelle, Amber. *Education:* Attended high school in Pennsylvania. *Hobbies and other interests:* Collecting old fishing tackle and old boats, "not classic boats—just lovely old boats."

Addresses

Home—South Ryegate, VT 05069.

Career

Draftsman in Philadelphia, PA, 1964; Braceland Brothers (printers), Philadelphia, art trainee, 1965-66, creative artist, 1968-72; freelance illustrator and writer, beginning 1972. Presenter in schools. *Exhibitions:* Work included in *Cricket*'s traveling illustrators' exhibitions. *Military service:* U.S. Navy, 1966-68; U.S. Navy Reserves, 1968-72.

Awards, Honors

Christopher Award, and Children's Science Book honorable mention, New York Academy of Sciences, both 1983, both for *Drawing from Nature; Washington Post/Children's Book Guild* nonfiction award, 1988; Eva L. Gordon Award, American Nature Study Society, 1991; Orbus Pictus Honor Book citation, National Council of Teachers of English, 2001, for *Wild and Swampy;* Key Lifetime Achievement Award for Excellence, American Association for the Advancement of Science/Subaru, and American Association of Science Teachers Award, both 2005; several of Arnosky's works have been named Outstanding Science Trade Books by the National Science Teachers Association/Children's Book Council, including *Nearer Nature, Wild and Swampy,* and *Following the Coast.*

Writings

SELF-ILLUSTRATED; FOR CHILDREN

I Was Born in a Tree and Raised by Bees, Putnam (New York, NY), 1977.

Outdoors on Foot, Coward (New York, NY), 1977.

Jim Arnosky (Photograph by Deanna Arnosky. Reproduced by permission.)

Nathaniel, Addison Wesley (Reading, MA), 1978.

A Kettle of Hawks and Other Wildlife Groups, Coward (New York, NY), 1979.

Mudtime and More: Nathaniel Stories, Addison Wesley (Reading, MA), 1979.

Drawing from Nature, Lothrop (New York, NY), 1982, reprinted, Onion River Press (Underhill, VT), 2005.

Freshwater Fish and Fishing, Four Winds (New York, NY), 1982.

Mouse Numbers and Letters, Harcourt (New York, NY), 1982.

Secrets of a Wildlife Watcher, Lothrop (New York, NY), 1983.

Mouse Writing, Harcourt (New York, NY), 1983.

Drawing Life in Motion, Lothrop (New York, NY), 1984.

Watching Foxes, Lothrop (New York, NY), 1984.

Deer at the Brook, Lothrop (New York, NY), 1986.

Flies in the Water, Fish in the Air: A Personal Introduction to Fly Fishing, Lothrop (New York, NY), 1986.

Raccoons and Ripe Corn, Lothrop (New York, NY), 1987.

Sketching Outdoors in Spring, Lothrop (New York, NY), 1987.

Sketching Outdoors in Summer, Lothrop (New York, NY), 1988.

Sketching Outdoors in Autumn, Lothrop (New York, NY), 1988.

Sketching Outdoors in Winter, Lothrop (New York, NY), 1988.

Gray Boy, Lothrop (New York, NY), 1988.

Come out, Muskrats, Lothrop (New York, NY), 1989.

In the Forest, edited by Dorothy Briley, Lothrop (New York, NY), 1989.

Near the Sea: A Portfolio of Paintings, Lothrop (New York, NY), 1990.

Fish in a Flash! A Personal Guide to Spin-Fishing, Bradbury Press (New York, NY), 1991.

Otters under Water, Putnam (New York, NY), 1992.

Long Spikes: A Story, Clarion (New York, NY), 1992.

Sketching Outdoors in All Seasons, Countryman Press (Woodstock, VT), 1993.

Every Autumn Comes the Bear, Putnam (New York, NY), 1993.

All Night near the Water, Putnam (New York, NY), 1994.

I See Animals Hiding, Scholastic (New York, NY), 1995.

Little Champ, Putnam (New York, NY), 1995.

Nearer Nature, Lothrop (New York, NY), 1996.

Rabbits and Raindrops, Putnam (New York, NY), 1997.

Bug Hunter, Random House (New York, NY), 1997.

Animal Tracker, Random House (New York, NY), 1997.

Bird Watcher, Random House (New York, NY), 1997.

Bring 'Em Back Alive!: Capturing Wildlife on Home Video, a Guide for the Whole Family, Little, Brown (Boston, MA), 1997.

Shore Walker, Random House (New York, NY), 1997.

Watching Water Birds, National Geographic Society (Washington, DC), 1997.

Little Lions, Putnam (New York, NY), 1998.

Watching Desert Wildlife, National Geographic Society (Washington, DC), 1998.

Big Jim and the White-legged Moose, Morrow (New York, NY), 1999.

Arnosky's Ark, National Geographic Society (Washington, DC), 1999.

Mouse Letters: A Very First Alphabet Book, Clarion (New York, NY), 1999.

Mouse Numbers: A Very First Counting Book, Clarion (New York, NY), 1999.

Rattlesnake Dance, Putnam (New York, NY), 2000.

A Manatee Morning, Simon & Schuster (New York, NY), 2000.

Beaver Pond, Moose Pond, National Geographic Society (Washington, DC), 2000.

Wild and Swampy, Morrow (New York, NY), 2000.

Raccoon on His Own, Putnam (New York, NY), 2001.

One Whole Day Wolves, National Geographic Society (Washington, DC), 2001.

Mouse Shapes: A Very First Book, Clarion (New York, NY), 2001.

Mouse Colors: A Very First Book, Clarion (New York, NY), 2001.

Wild Ponies, National Geographic Society (Washington, DC), 2002.

Turtle in the Sea, Putnam (New York, NY), 2002.

Field Trips: Bug Hunting, Animal Tracking, Bird Watching, Shore Walking, HarperCollins (New York, NY), 2002.

Armadillo's Orange, Putnam (New York, NY), 2003.

Following the Coast, HarperCollins (New York, NY), 2004.

Beachcombing: Exploring the Seashore, Dutton (New York, NY), 2004.

Under the Wild Western Sky, HarperCollins (New York, NY), 2005.

Hook, Line, and Seeker: A Personal Guide to Fishing, Boating, and Water Wildlife, Scholastic (New York, NY), 2005.

Coyote Raid in Cactus Canyon, Putnam (New York, NY), 2005.

Whole Days Outdoors: An Autobiographical Album ("Meet the Author" series), Richard C. Owen (Katonah, NJ), 2006.

Grandfather Buffalo, G.P. Putnam's Sons (New York, NY), 2006.

Parrotfish and Sunken Ships: Exploring a Tropical Reef HarperCollins (New York, NY), 2007.

Babies in the Bayou, G.P. Putnam's Sons (New York, NY), 2007.

The Brook Book: Exploring the Smallest Streams, Dutton (New York, NY), 2008.

Gobble It Up!: A Fun Song about Eating! (with sound recording), Scholastic Press (New York, NY), 2008.

Wild Tracks!: A Guide to Nature's Footprints, Sterling Pub. Co. (New York, NY), 2008.

Dolphins on the Sand, Dutton (New York, NY), 2008.

Crocodile Safari, Scholastic Press (New York, NY), 2009.

I'm a Turkey!, Scholastic Press (New York, NY), 2009.

Slither and Crawl: Eye to Eye with Reptiles, Sterling Pub. (New York, NY), 2009.

Slow Down for Manatees, G.P. Putnam's Sons (New York, NY), 2009.

The Pirates of Crocodile Swamp, G.P. Putnam's Sons (New York, NY), 2009.

"CRINKLEROOT" GUIDEBOOK SERIES; SELF-ILLUSTRATED

Crinkleroot's Animal Tracks and Wildlife Signs, Putnam (New York, NY), 1979, revised edition published as *Crinkleroot's Book of Animal Tracking,* Bradbury Press (New York, NY), 1989.

Crinkleroot's Guide to Walking in Wild Places, Bradbury Press (New York, NY), 1990.

Crinkleroot's Guide to Knowing the Birds, Bradbury Press (New York, NY), 1992.

Crinkleroot's Guide to Knowing the Trees, Macmillan (New York, NY), 1992.

Crinkleroot's Twenty-five Fish Every Child Should Know, Macmillan (New York, NY), 1993.

Crinkleroot's Twenty-five Birds Every Child Should Know, Macmillan (New York, NY), 1993.

Crinkleroot's Twenty-five Mammals Every Child Should Know, Macmillan (New York, NY), 1994.

Crinkleroot's Twenty-five More Animals Every Child Should Know, Macmillan (New York, NY), 1994.

Crinkleroot's Guide to Knowing Butterflies and Moths, Simon & Schuster (New York, NY), 1996.

Crinkleroot's Guide to Knowing Animal Habitats, Simon & Schuster (New York, NY), 1997.

Crinkleroot's Visit to Crinkle Cove, Simon & Schuster (New York, NY), 1998.

Crinkleroot's Nature Almanac, Simon & Schuster (New York, NY), 1999.

"ALL ABOUT" SERIES; SELF-ILLUSTRATED

All about Alligators, Scholastic (New York, NY), 1994.

All about Owls, Scholastic (New York, NY), 1995.

All about Deer, Scholastic (New York, NY), 1996.

All about Rattlesnakes, Scholastic (New York, NY), 1997.

All about Turkeys, Scholastic (New York, NY), 1998.

All about Turtles, Scholastic (New York, NY), 2000.

All about Frogs, Scholastic (New York, NY), 2002.

All about Sharks, Scholastic (New York, NY), 2003.

All about Lizards, Scholastic (New York, NY), 2004.

All about Manatees, Scholastic (New York, NY), 2008.

ILLUSTRATOR

Melvin Berger and Gilda Berger, *Fitting In: Animals in Their Habitats,* Coward (New York, NY), 1976.

Miska Miles, *Swim, Little Duck,* Atlantic Monthly Press (Boston, MA), 1976.

Miska Miles, *Chicken Forgets,* Atlantic Monthly Press (Boston, MA), 1976.

Miska Miles, *Small Rabbit,* Atlantic Monthly Press (Boston, MA), 1977.

Marcel Sislowitz, *Look: How Your Eyes See,* Coward (New York, NY), 1977.

Berniece Freschet, *Porcupine Baby,* Putnam (New York, NY), 1978.

Berniece Freschet, *Possum Baby,* Putnam (New York, NY), 1978.

Kaye Starbird, *The Covered Bridge House, and Other Poems,* Four Winds (New York, NY), 1979.

Berniece Freschet, *Moose Baby,* Putnam (New York, NY), 1979.

Eloise Jarvis McGraw, *Joel and the Magic Merlini,* Knopf (New York, NY), 1979.

Michael New, *The Year of the Apple,* Addison Wesley (Reading, MA), 1980.

Betty Boegehold, *Bear Underground,* Doubleday (New York, NY), 1980.

Ann E. Weiss, *What's That You Said? How Words Change,* Harcourt (New York, NY), 1980.

A.R. Swinnerton, *Rocky the Cat,* Addison Wesley (Reading, MA), 1981.

Berniece Freschet, *Black Bear Baby,* Putnam (New York, NY), 1981.

Margaret Bartlett and Preston Bassett, *Raindrop Stories,* Four Winds (New York, NY), 1981.

Betty Boegehold, *Chipper's Choices,* Coward (New York, NY), 1981.

Joan Hiatt Harlow, *Shadow Bear,* Doubleday (New York, NY), 1981.

Anne Rockwell, *Up a Tall Tree,* Doubleday (New York, NY), 1981.

Berniece Freschet, *Wood Duck Baby,* Putnam (New York, NY), 1983.

Honoré de Balzac, *A Passion in the Desert,* Creative Education, 1983.

Berniece Freschet, *Raccoon Baby,* Putnam (New York, NY), 1984.

Dale H. Fife, *The Empty Lot,* Sierra Club (San Francisco, CA), 1991.

Bob Dylan, *Man Gave Names to All the Animals,* Sterling (New York, NY), 2010.

Adaptations

A four-part television series, *Drawing from Nature,* featuring Jim Arnosky and based on his books *Drawing from Nature* and *Drawing Life in Motion,* was produced by the Public Broadcasting Service (PBS) in 1987; Crinkleroot, Arnosky's fictional character, has been featured on PBS's *Backyard Safari* series; several of his books have been adapted for educational media.

Sidelights

An inveterate observer of nature and a skilled artist, Vermont-based naturalist, illustrator, and author Jim Arnosky blends his interests and talents to create dozens of picture books about wildlife and nature; his one hun-

dredth title, *Wild Tracks!: A Guide to Nature's Footprints* was released in 2008. While his friendly, informal style is a characteristic of his illustrated fiction, Arnosky primarily writes nonfiction: his unique "how-to" books have received the greatest acclaim due to their ability to inspire children to pursue such outdoor activities as fishing, drawing from nature, appreciating ecosystems, and identifying birds and animal tracks. His popular Crinkleroot character, introduced in his very first children's book, has proven to be a staple for Arnosky, who introduces a multitude of animal facts to young readers through the guise of that grandfatherly woodsman. Arnosky's books on sketching from nature, including *Drawing from Nature* and *Drawing Life in Motion,* also inspired a four-part television series produced by the Public Broadcasting Service.

In his many nonfiction titles, Arnosky details the life cycle of animals from manatees to rattlesnakes, and has been praised by critics for presenting clear explanations and finely detailed drawings. Critics have also frequently observed that, although Arnosky's books initially set out to introduce a particular outdoor activity, their end result is to fully reorient readers to the natural world by presenting new ways of seeing and participating in it. *Booklist* critic Linda Callaghan commented in her review of *Flies in the Water, Fish in the Air: A Personal Introduction to Fly Fishing:* "Blending the beauty of nature with the joy of sport, Arnosky leaves no doubt that fishing is an art form, a reverent pilgrimage in which the respectful and observant are rewarded." Callaghan added that this book is "a pleasure to the eye, the mind, and the soul." Similarly, *School Library Journal* contributor Patricia Homer wrote that Arnosky's *Drawing from Nature* is "a spiritual sharing of ideas and techniques by a gifted wildlife artist" whose "goal seems to be to teach young readers how to see as an artist would, and observe as a naturalist would. He succeeds beautifully."

In 1977, Arnosky introduced the character of Crinkleroot in *I Was Born in a Tree and Raised by Bees.* In this debut book, old Crinkleroot, a forest dweller, takes the reader through four seasons of life in the wild, pointing out bits of that life which most observers would miss. "Crinkleroot is a backwoods gnome who introduces readers to simple nature information and experiences," according to Susan Sprague in her *School Library Journal* review. The subject matter of *I Was Born in a Tree and Raised by Bees* is very inclusive; according to a *Kirkus Reviews* contributor, "Crinkleroot's tour mixes . . . hidden pictures with project suggestions . . . a mini-lecture on interdependence . . . and random notes" on a variety of subjects.

Crinkleroot continues his educational function in several other works, including *Crinkleroot's Guide to Knowing Butterflies and Moths* which *Booklist* reviewer Carolyn Phelan called an "appealing, practical cross between a picture book and field guide." Such books deal with birds, trees, mammals, and tracking, all told by the benevolent, Santa-like woodsman. "Arnosky's text is a felicitous blending of spare, elegant description and homey conversation," noted Margaret A. Bush in a *Horn Book* review of *Crinkleroot's Guide to Walking in Wild Places.* With *Crinkleroot's Guide to Knowing the Birds* "Arnosky has created another wonderful nature guide featuring his lovable woodsman," according to *Booklist* critic Chris Sherman. Reviewing *Crinkleroot's Guide to Knowing Animal Habitats,* Helen Rosenberg wrote in *School Library Journal* that the book is "crammed full of information and delightfully presented with appealing watercolor illustrations." Of *Crinkleroot's Visit to Crinkle Cove,* Rosenberg noted in *Booklist* that "everyone's favorite woodsman and nature guide" takes a different approach. Instead of focusing on one aspect of nature or one animal, he looks at a cross-section and sees how nature is interconnected.

The title character of *Nathaniel* and *Mudtime and More: Nathaniel Stories* reveals a different aspect of Arnosky's personality. The "Nathaniel" books are wordless, featuring line drawings of a farmer/woodsman in a variety of humorous episodic situations. *Nathaniel* was characterized by *School Library Journal* contributor Michele Woggon as "a gentle but silly wilderness resident."

Arnosky's elegant artwork pairs with his informative text in **Arnosky's Ark,** *a picture book published by National Geographic.* (National Geographic Society, 1999. Copyright © 1999 by Jim Arnosky. Reproduced by permission.)

Arnosky observes nature by participating in it through fishing, drawing, boating, or walking. This constant interaction has given him the special connection with na-

Arnosky shares his love of music in his self-illustrated **Gobble It Up!,** *a songbook about good eating.* (Copyright © 2008 by Jim Arnosky. All rights reserved. Reproduced by permission of Scholastic, Inc.)

ture that is apparent to readers of books such as *Field Trips: Bug Hunting, Animal Tracking, Bird Watching, Shore Walking, Beachcombing: Exploring the Seashore, Crocodile Safari,* and *Hook, Line, and Seeker: A Personal Guide to Fishing, Boating, and Water Wildlife.* "I have developed an intimate relationship with my subject matter," he once commented in *Horn Book.* "Through my study of nature I have become convinced that every little thing is part of some whole and that if you look closely enough and think well enough, you will recognize the scheme of things. You may even find a place for yourself in that order. I have found my place. It is outdoors near the earth and its waters, near the birds and beasts."

Hook, Line, and Seeker features the "engaging mixture of personal anecdotes and practical tips" that is characteristic of the author's nature guides, according to *Booklist* contributor John Peters. Other popular fish-related titles from Arnosky include *Freshwater Fish and Fishing, Flies in the Water, Fish in the Air: A Personal Introduction to Fly Fishing,* and *Fish in a Flash! A Personal Guide to Spin-Fishing.* Reviewing the last-named title, *Horn Book* critic Bush wondered, "Who but Jim Arnosky could convey such a sense of excitement and fun in an instructional guide to spin-fishing?" Bush further observed that Arnosky's writing is marked by "a measured economy and with great respect for his subject and audience."

Moving from the water onto dry land, Arnosky leads young readers to a heightened awareness of the natural world through a wide range of instructional books. The nature guide *Field Trips* gives young naturalists helpful suggestions as to what to look for on a nature walk,

what to collect, and how to keep proper notes. As Danielle J. Ford noted in *Horn Book,* "a walk through the woods or along the shore takes on new meaning with the advice provided for novice naturalists in this first-rate guide." In *Crocodile Safari* he takes readers on a tour of Florida's mangrove swamps, and shares some more nature-watching methods in *Secrets of a Wildlife Watcher,* providing "how-to" tips as well as information on animal behavior. In her *Appraisal* review, Carolyn Noah remarked that "Arnosky's delight in wildlife, and the effectiveness with which he conveys it, conspire to lure the young naturalist, book in hand, out into the wild." A quote from physicist Albert Einstein that serves as the epigram to *Secrets of a Wildlife Watcher*—"Joy in looking and comprehending is nature's most beautiful gift"—has been cited by several critics as a singularly well-suited motto for Arnosky's work.

Arnosky's "All About" series also features his characteristic blending of entertainment with instruction. In a spate of books dealing with various animals from rattlesnakes to turtles, Arnosky provides young readers with pertinent information from behavior to structure. *Booklist* reviewer Hazel Rochman commented favorably on *All about Alligators,* the first book in the series, noting that "Arnosky's clear text and handsome watercolors convey a sense of wonder." Susan Oliver, writing in *School Library Journal,* remarked of *All about Deer* that the "author's wonderfully simple and enticing style ensures that children will look at these wild animals with both wonder and understanding." Reviewing *All about Frogs, Horn Book* contributor Betty Carter noted that the "well-organized expository prose lends itself to reading aloud," and *Booklist* reviewer Carolyn Phelan praised the "strong visual presentation and clearly writ-

ten text" in *All about Sharks.* Praising *All about Manatees* for its "wonderfully detailed illustrations, a *Kirkus Reviews* writer added that "the title of both book and series is entirely appropriate, as readers will, in fact, learn all about manatees."

Arnosky also provides excellent introductions to water fowl and desert habitats in his "Watching" books: *Watching Foxes, Watching Water Birds,* and *Watching Desert Wildlife.* Reviewing *Watching Desert Wildlife,* Bush wrote that "Arnosky here makes his first foray into the desert and creates an exquisite introduction to desert wildlife." Other creatures found in the desert can be found in the pages of *Slither and Crawl: Eye to Eye with Reptiles,* which focuses on North American species of snakes, lizards, turtles, and crocodiles. Its informative text is highlighted by field sketches and what *School Library Journal* critic Patricia Manning praised as "outstanding acrylics." Arnosky's large-format paintings "make enticing invitations to budding naturalists to go out and see for themselves," concluded John Peters in his *Booklist* review of *Slither and Crawl.*

The books *Following the Coast, Beachcombing,* and *Parrotfish and Sunken Ships: Exploring a Tropical Reef* were inspired by Arnosky's travels along the Gulf and Atlantic coasts. *Following the Coast,* a record of his annual trip from Florida to Delaware, during which he and his wife catalog and sketch the wildlife they observe, is "a more personal work than most of Arnosky's oeuvre," according to a critic in *Kirkus Reviews.* As *School Library Journal* contributor Susan Oliver noted, the book's "tone is casual and conversational, as the author muses about his experiences and what he's learned about these coastal environments." Taking readers on "a vicarious tour of the treasures found on a typical tropical beach" according to *Booklist* critic Gillian Engberg, *Beachcombing* instructs young readers how to identify sand dollars, coconuts, shark teeth, coral, and other items. As Nancy Call wrote in *School Library Journal,* this book "will appeal to those children who are looking for relaxing fun." Another journey is to be had by readers of *Parrotfish and Sunken Ships,* which explores a unique marine environment off the Florida Keys. The book's "wonderfully realistic paintings" and "clear text . . . successfully draw . . . readers into an underwater world teaming with life," wrote Carole Phillips in her *School Library Journal* review of the book.

Arnosky sometimes weaves nature into fictional stories for younger readers. Geared for older elementary readers, *The Pirates of Crocodile Swamp* finds two brothers living in a troubled family, where their abusive and alcoholic father eventually causes the death of their younger brother. When their father suddenly packs eleven-year-old Sandy and nine-year-old Jack into the family car and drives south to the Florida Keys, the boys are determined to escape from their dad. Gathering together meager supplies, they take a boat and reach a nearby nature preserve, called Crocodile Swamp, where they hope to hide. Once there, Sandy and Jock

meet a local fisherman who relates the lore of the pirates who once inhabited the area. Noting that the novel features the author's "trademark insight into the delights and dangers of the natural . . . world," Walter Minkel added in *School Library Journal* that *The Pirates of Crocodile Swamp* is a "fast-moving" story that will draw readers in due to Arnosky's "direct and gripping" prose and likeable characters. The author's "passion for this part of the world is evident," noted a *Kirkus Reviews* writer in reviewing the novel, and in *Booklist* Todd Morning concluded that the "well-paced and exciting" story reveals "many details about the natural world of the Keys."

In his many picture-book guides for younger children, Arnosky depicts his animal subjects as he observes them in his studies, relying more on his accurate and detailed illustrations than on his sparse and well-chosen words to tell the story of the animal's existence. In *Babies in the Bayou* his rhyming text only hints at each baby animal discussed, encouraging young readers to mine the book's acrylic paintings for clues as to the animal's name. This "technique . . . both encourages readers to interact with the narrative and highlights the lyricism of the [author's] language," in the opinion of a *Kirkus Reviews* writer. *Slow Down for Manatees* is based on a true story about a pregnant manatee that is injured and then cared for until both she and her off-

Arnosky's evocative artwork mirrors a sensitive story in his original picture book **Grandfather Buffalo.** (G.P. Putnam's Sons, 2006. Reproduced by permission of G.P. Putnam's Sons, a division of Penguin Putnam Books for Young Readers.)

spring can be released into the wild. One of several books Arnosky has written about manatees, *Slow Down for Manatees* exhibits "the author's customary attention to environmental detail," according to a *Kirkus Reviews* writer.

Arnosky is often praised for telling animals' stories without romanticizing or humanizing nature's creatures. The raccoons in his picture book *Raccoons and Ripe Corn,* for example, are captivating subjects even though they are not presented as cute or cuddly. "These raccoons are greedy and somewhat destructive, *Booklist* contributor Denise M. Wilms commented. "A close-up of one of them gnawing an ear of corn has an undercurrent of ferocity." In *I'm a Turkey!* he also demonstrates his facility with song, capturing the sounds and energy of the wild turkey in a mix of animated lyrics and paintings. Here the author/illustrator's "sense of humor and fine eye for wildlife detail is evident in every ruffled feather," according to a *Kirkus Reviews* writer. In *Booklist* Carolyn Phelan also enjoyed *I'm a Turkey!,* predicting that the "personality and charm" exuded by the gobbling flock will have young readers "singing turkey, too."

Keeping in mind the emotions of his very youngest readers, Arnosky provides age-appropriate illustrations in many of his pre-reader books. In the "Mouse" series of picture books, for example, the pint-sized protagonist introduces toddlers to letters, numbers, shapes, and colors. *Otters under Water* conveys almost wordlessly the high spirits of two young otters as they frolic in the water under the careful eye of their mother. "Arnosky's watercolor illustrations deftly entice even reluctant, landlocked readers," noted a critic in *Publishers Weekly.* A young armadillo learns to appreciate his neighbors in *Armadillo's Orange.* When the orange that Armadillo uses to mark his burrow rolls away, he relies on the honeybees, snakes, and birds that share the garden to lead him home. According to Diane Foote in *Booklist,* Arnosky's "final image of Armadillo, curled snugly in his burrow, exemplifies the reassurance his story provides." Praised by *School Library Journal* contributor Susan E. Murray as an example of "Arnosky at his best," *Grandfather Buffalo* "is a perfect interplay of poetic text and strong art that is full of love and empathy" as it depicts the bond between an elderly bull buffalo and a newly born calf.

In *Arnosky's Ark* the author "celebrates a century of conservation efforts," according to Shelle Rosenfeld in *Booklist.* In the work, Arnosky profiles thirteen animals that are or were once on the endangered-species list. Another work with an environmental theme is *Turtle in the Sea,* "a useful, enjoyable book for introducing young children to the plight of this animal," noted *School Library Journal* contributor Ellen Heath. In the book, Arnosky focuses on the dangers faced by a female sea turtle, her shell scarred from encounters with a shark, a fisherman's net, and a motorboat. According to a critic in *Kirkus Reviews,* "readers will marvel over Arnosky's characteristic watercolor paintings, which truly bring nature to life."

Arnosky weaves information about nature throughout a fictional story in his self-illustrated picture book **Big Jim and the White-legged Moose.** (Copyright © 1999 by Jim Arnosky. Used by permission of the author.)

A bear that annually visited the area near Arnosky's Vermont home is the subject of *Every Autumn Comes the Bear,* which a *Kirkus Reviews* writer dubbed "real natural history in a lovely book." A mother mountain lion and her young provide the focus for *Little Lions,* a picture book that is "a fine combination of dignity and playfulness," according to Phelan. Another book with roots close to the author/illustrator's home, *Nearer Nature* collects essays chronicling part of a year spent in Vermont. "Arnosky's very special insights, patient observations, and fluent writing make this a book to learn from, delight in, and savor," wrote Diane Tuccillo in a *Voice of Youth Advocates* review. "There are few authors who write this kind of material for a teen audience," Tuccillo further commented. "A treat for the eye and the spirit, [*Nearer Nature*] . . . is a book for the unique young adult who enjoys nature writing."

In his art books, Arnosky's personal approach manifests as an invitation to readers to see and understand nature through his eyes. His award-winning *Drawing from Nature* received accolades from reviewers for its well-presented insights into how a naturalist and artist views his subject matter. Reviewing the companion book, *Drawing Life in Motion, Booklist* critic Denise M. Wilms remarked that Arnosky's text "cultivates an appreciation for careful observation of the natural world." Writing of both volumes in the *Voice of Youth Advocates,* Delia A. Culberson noted that "every page . . . is a lesson not only in the fine art of drawing but also in careful, almost microscopic, observation."

Pursuing his calling as both a naturalist and an author, Arnosky spends most of his days rambling through whatever habitat he is observing for his books. "The life I live is a reward in itself," he remarked in *Horn Book*. "I have no weekdays or weekends. I look forward to every day. Except for family events and rare occasions, my schedule is determined by the activities of the animals I choose to study. Few people are able to follow their instincts as truly as I follow mine. I write about the world I live in and I try to share all I see and feel in my books." As he told *Bookpage* online interviewer Lisa Horak, "I am convinced that if you love the outdoors, natural places, and wildlife, you will grow into a person who will consider those factors no matter what work you do. My job is to foster an appreciation of nature and a curiosity about wildlife. I tell kids what I know and let them decide how to think about it. Hopefully they'll use that knowledge and make a difference."

Biographical and Critical Sources

BOOKS

Authors of Books for Young People, 3rd edition, Scarecrow Press (Lanham, MD), 1990.
Children's Books and Their Creators, edited by Anita Silvey, Houghton Mifflin (Boston, MA), 1995.
Children's Literature Review, Volume 15, Gale (Detroit, MI), 1988.

PERIODICALS

Appraisal, winter, 1980; winter, 1984, Carolyn Noah, review of *Secrets of a Wildlife Watcher,* p. 7.
Booklist, October 1, 1983, Denise M. Wilms, review of *Drawing Life in Motion,* p. 214; July, 1986, Linda Callaghan, review of *Flies in the Water, Fish in the Air: A Personal Introduction to Fly Fishing,* p. 1618; September 1, 1987, Denise M. Wilms, review of *Raccoons and Ripe Corn,* p. 58; October 15, 1992, Chris Sherman, review of *Crinkleroot's Guide to Knowing the Birds,* p. 432; August, 1994, Hazel Rochman, review of *All about Alligators,* p. 2045; May 1, 1996, Carolyn Phelan, review of *Crinkleroot's Guide to Knowing Butterflies and Moths,* p. 1508; March 1, 1998, Carolyn Phelan, review of *Little Lions,* p. 1139; August, 1998, Helen Rosenberg, review of *Crinkleroot's Visit to Crinkle Cove,* p. 2012; August, 1999, Susan Dove Lempke, review of *Big Jim and the White-legged Moose,* p. 2062; November 15, 1999, Shelle Rosenfeld, review of *Arnosky's Ark,* p. 630; February 1, 2000, Kay Weisman, review of *All about Turtles,* p. 1024; November 1, 2000, Denia Hester, review of *Wild and Swampy,* p. 528; January 1, 2001, Stephanie Zvirin, review of *Beaver Pond, Moose Pond,* p. 966; February 1, 2002, Carolyn Phelan, review of *All about Frogs,* p. 942; September 1, 2002, John Peters, review of *Turtle in the Sea,* p. 136; July, 2003, Carolyn Phelan, review of *All about Sharks,* p. 1893; August, 2003, Diane Foote, review of *Armadil-*

lo's Orange, p. 1986; February 15, 2004, Kay Weisman, review of *Following the Coast,* 1054; July, 2004, Gillian Engberg, review of *Beachcombing: Exploring the Seashore,* p. 1848; August, 2005, John Peters, review of *Hook, Line, and Seeker: A Beginner's Guide to Fishing, Boating, and Watching Water Wildlife,* p. 2020; February 1, 2006, Julie Cummins, review of *Grandfather Buffalo,* p. 53; December 1, 2006, Carolyn Phelan, review of *Babies in the Bayou,* p. 58; August, 2007, Randall Enos, review of *Parrotfish and Sunken Ships: Exploring a Tropical Reef,* p. 80; December 1, 2007, Carolyn Phelan, review of *The Brook Book: Exploring the Smallest Streams,* p. 56; April 1, 2008, review of *Wild Tracks!: A Guide to Nature's Footprints,* p. 53; June 1, 2008, Carolyn Phelan, review of *All about Manatees,* p. 83; July 1, 2008, Thom Barthelmess, review of *Dolphins in the Sand,* p. 70; September 1, 2008, Shelle Rosenfeld, review of *Gobble It Up!: A Fun Song about Eating!,* p. 103; December 1, 2008, Hazel Rochman, review of *Crocodile Safari,* p. 61; February 15, 2009, Todd Morning, review of *The Pirates of Crocodile Swamp,* p. 83; April 1, 2009, John Peters, review of *Slither and Crawl: Eye to Eye with Reptiles,* p. 35; October 15, 2009, Carolyn Phelan, review of *I'm a Turkey!,* p. 55.
Horn Book, May-June, 1987, Anita Silvey, review of *Sketching Outdoors in Spring,* p. 355; September-October, 1989, Jim Arnosky, "The Moon in My Net"; November-December, 1990, Margaret A. Bush, review of *Crinkleroot's Guide to Walking in Wild Places,* p. 757; September-October, 1991, Margaret A. Bush, review of *Fish in a Flash!,* pp. 608-609; November-December, 1998, Margaret A. Bush, review of *Watching Desert Wildlife,* p. 751; March-April, 2002, Betty Carter, review of *All about Frogs,* p. 226; July-August, 2002, Danielle J. Ford, review of *Field Trips: Bug Hunting, Animal Tracking, Bird-watching, Shore Walking,* p. 482; March-April, 2008, Danielle J. Ford, review of *The Brook Book,* p. 224.
Kirkus Reviews, December 1, 1976, review of *I Was Born in a Tree and Raised by Bees,* p. 1261; October 15, 1993, review of *Every Autumn Comes the Bear,* p. 1325; January 1, 2002, review of *All about Frogs,* p. 42; March 15, 2002, review of *Field Trips,* p. 405; July 1, 2002, review of *Turtle in the Sea,* p. 948; September 1, 2002, review of *Wild Ponies,* p. 1302; June 1, 2003, review of *Armadillo's Orange* and *All about Sharks,* p. 799; February 1, 2004, review of *Following the Coast,* p. 128; April 1, 2004, review of *Beachcombing,* p. 324; January 1, 2005, review of *Coyote Raid in Cactus Canyon,* p. 47; April 15, 2005, review of *Under the Wild Western Sky,* p. 468; January 1, 2006, review of *Grandfather Buffalo,* p. 37; December 15, 2006, review of *Babies in the Bayou,* p. 1263; August 15, 2007, review of *Parrotfish and Sunken Ships;* January 1, 2008, review of *The Brook Book;* March 15, 2008, review of *Wild Tracks!;* April 15, 2008, review of *All about Manatees;* July 15, 2008, review of *Dolphins on the Sand;* September 1, 2008, review of *Gobble It Up!;* February 1, 2009, reviews of *The Pirates of Crocodile Swamp* and *Crocodile Safari;* August 15, 2009, review of *I'm a Turkey!;* December 1, 2009, review of *Slow Down for Manatees.*
New York Times Book Review, October 9, 1983, Selma J. Lanes, review of *Mouse Writing,* p. 38; September 8,

1985, review of *Watching Foxes,* p. 35; August 30, 1992, Janet Maslin, review of *Crinkleroot's Guide to Knowing the Trees,* p. 19; August 30, 1995, p. 19.

Publishers Weekly, May 29, 1987, Kimberly Olson Fakih, "Watching the Artist Watch Nature," pp. 43-44; August 9, 1999, review of *Arnosky's Ark,* p. 354; June 11, 2001, review of *Raccoon on His Own,* p. 87; December 4, 2006, review of *Babies in the Bayou,* p. 57.

School Library Journal, March, 1977, Susan Sprague, review of *I Was Born in a Tree and Raised by Bees,* p. 128; September, 1978, Michele Woggon, review of *Nathaniel,* p. 129; January, 1983, Patricia Homer, review of *Drawing from Nature,* p. 70; December, 1988, Eleanor K. MacDonald, review of *Sketching Outdoors in Autumn* and *Sketching Outdoors in Winter,* p. 114; September, 1996, Susan Oliver, review of *All about Deer,* p. 195; June, 1997, Helen Rosenberg, review of *Crinkleroot's Guide to Knowing Animal Habitats,* p. 105; May, 2001, Lee Bock, review of *Raccoon on His Own,* p. 108; March, 2002, Ellen Heath, review of *All about Turtles,* p. 206; June, 2002, Susan Scheps, review of *Field Trips,* p. 118; August, 2002, Ellen Heath, review of *Turtle in the Sea,* p. 146; October, 2002, Patricia Manning, review of *Wild Ponies,* p. 140; July, 2003, Grace Oliff, review of *Armadillo's Orange,* p. 86; May, 2004, Susan Oliver, review of *Following the Coast,* p. 128; July, 2004, Nancy Call, review of *Beachcombing,* p. 90; March, 2005, Rosalyn Pierini, review of *Coyote Raid in Cactus Canyon,* pp. 164-165; July, 2005, Robin L. Gibson, review of *Under the Wild Western Sky,* p. 85; February, 2006, Susan E. Murray, review of *Grandfather Buffalo,* p. 92; January, 2007, Judith Constantinides, review of *Babies in the Bayou,* p. 88; September, 2007, Carole Phillips, review of *Parrotfish and Sunken Ships,* p. 180; January, 2008, Christine Markley, review of *The Brook Book,* p. 103; June, 2008, Ellen Heath, review of *Wild Tracks!,* p. 118; September, 2008, Jane Marino, review of *Gobble It Up!,* p. 137; February, 2009, Margaret Bush, review of *Crocodile Safari,* p. 88; March, 2009, Walter Minkel, review of *The Pirates of Crocodile Swamp,* p. 140; June, 2009, Patricia Manning, review of *Slither and Crawl,* p. 103.

Voice of Youth Advocates, October, 1987, Delia A. Culberson, review of *Drawing from Nature* and *Drawing Life in Motion,* p. 183; April, 1997, Diane Tuccillo, review of *Nearer Nature,* p. 50.

ONLINE

Bookpage.com, http://www.bookpage.com/ (November, 1998), Lisa Horak, "Talking Turkey and Then Some: A Naturalist Brings the Wild World to Children."

Jim Arnosky's Wildlife Journal Web site, http://www.jim arnosky.com (June 10, 2010).*

* * *

AUSEON, Andrew 1976-

Personal

Born 1976, in Columbus, OH; married Sarah Zogby; children: Samara Ruth, one other daughter. *Education:* Ohio University, B.A. (creative writing); Vermont College, M.F.A. (creative writing for children and young adults). *Hobbies and other interests:* Travel.

Addresses

Home—Baltimore, MD.

Career

Writer. PhotoAssist, Inc., photo editor, 1999-2003; The History Factory, senior researcher, 2002-04; Words & Numbers, Baltimore, MD, currently editor and staff writer.

Member

Society of Children's Book Writers and Illustrators.

Writings

Funny Little Monkey, Harcourt (Orlando, FL), 2005.

(With David O. Russell) *Alienated,* Aladdin (New York, NY), 2009.

Jo-Jo and the Fiendish Lot, HarperTeen (New York, NY), 2009.

Freak Magnet, HarperTeen (New York, NY), 2010.

Adaptations

Jo-Jo and the Fiendish Lot was adapted for film.

Sidelights

In addition to designing video games, Andrew Auseon also writes quirkily titled novels for teens that include *Funny Little Monkey, Jo-Jo and the Fiendish Lot,* and *Freak Magnet.* His middle-grade novel *Alienated,* in which preteen journalists Gene and Vince discover that a group of space aliens are living quietly under the radar in a Southern California suburb, was a collaboration with David O. Russell. In his novels, Auseon is inspired by the books that captured his imagination as a child, great stories that "conjured magic," as he noted on his home page. "This kind of enchantment is what I'm constantly trying to replicate when I write novels," he added. "I hope to one day capture that magic in one of my own books, create a story that would have made a younger version of me happy."

Described by a *Publishers Weekly* reviewer as a "darkly comic debut," *Funny Little Monkey* introduces readers to mild-mannered Arty Moore. Arty is a mere shadow in contrast to his much-larger and quite intimidating twin brother Kurt. Raised by a single mother, and with a father who serves as a poor role model due to his career as a bank robber, the boys have always found themselves at odds. Now, as a freshman at Millard Fillmore High, Arty's luck seems to be changing when he makes two new friends: the beautiful, wealthy overachiever Leslie Dermott and Kerouac, the ringleader of a rebel-

Cover of Andrew Auseon's debut middle-grade novel Funny Little Monkey. (Meisel, Louis K., illustrator. From a jacket of Funny Little Monkey by Andrew Auseon, copyright © 2005. Reproduced by permission of the author and Houghton Mifflin Harcourt Publishing Company. This material may not be reproduced in any form or by any means without the prior written permission of the publisher and the author.)

lious group of kids. With his friends' help, Arty is able to finally put his bullying brother in his place, while at the same time adjusting to life in high school. The *Publishers Weekly* critic wrote that in *Funny Little Monkey* Auseon "taps into the painful experience of high school, leavened with healthy doses of hyperbole, hope and wry humor," while Susan W. Hunter noted in *School Library Journal* that Arty "steps up and uses an outrageous fabrication to resolve the final crisis in this offbeat coming-of-age story."

Seventeen-year-old Jo-Jo Dyas, the main character in *Jo-Jo and the Fiendish Lot,* is feeling pretty hopeless in the wake of his girlfriend Violet's terrible death and so he decides to end it all. Hiking to a remote area of Baltimore with a gun in hand, Jo-Jo stumbles upon the body of a dead girl lying in a drainage culvert. Oddly, the girl wakes up, introduces herself as Max, and explains that she lives in a colorless limbo known as the Afterlife, where she works as the drummer for a punk band called the Fiendish Lot. When Jo-Jo accidentally kills himself, he joins Max and her band, hoping to lo-

cate Violet in the afterlife. In the process, he finds the opportunity to correct some of the missteps that haunted him in life. In *School Library Journal,* Joyce Adams Burner called *Jo-Jo and the Fiendish Lot* "outrageously inventive" and "darkly humorous," and Daniel Kraus concluded in *Booklist* that "music-obsessed teens will respond to Auseon's firm grasp of the transformative . . . power of a kick-ass rock show."

Also geared for teens, *Freak Magnet* focuses on the living: in particular, on high-school graduate Charlie and his current crush, Gloria. Charlie is working at the local café, and it is love at first sight when Gloria walks through the door. Although the two at first seem too different—Charlie is uninhibited in his opinions while Gloria keeps her thoughts to herself—their friendship grows as the weeks go by. Featuring details "original enough to amuse and move readers," *Freak Magnet* was recommended as a "predictable but undeniably pleasurable" read by *Booklist* critic Daniel Kraus.

Biographical and Critical Sources

PERIODICALS

Booklist, April 15, 2005, Jennifer Hubert, review of *Funny Little Monkey,* p. 1447; January 1, 2009, Daniel Kraus, review of *Jo-Jo and the Fiendish Lot,* p. 70; November 15, 2009, Kimberly Garnick, review of *Alienated,* p. 39.
Bulletin of the Center for Children's Books, December, 2009, Kate Quealy-Gainer, review of *Alienated,* p. 168; April 15, 2010, Daniel Kraus, review of *Freak Magnet,* p. 40.
Columbus Dispatch, November 6, 2005, Nancy Gilson, "Novel Explores Sophomoric Cruelty of High School."
Kirkus Reviews, June 1, 2005, review of *Funny Little Monkey,* p. 632; February 1, 2009, review of *Jo-Jo and the Fiendish Lot;* September 15, 2009, review of *Alienated.*
Publishers Weekly, July 11, 2005, review of *Funny Little Monkey,* p. 94; October 26, 2009, review of *Alienated,* p. 58.
School Library Journal, June, 2005, Susan W. Hunter, review of *Funny Little Monkey,* p. 147; June, 2009, Joyce Adams Burner, review of *Jo-Jo and the Fiendish Lot,* p. 115; January, 2010, James K. Irwin, review of *Alienated,* p. 112.
Voice of Youth Advocates, June, 2005, Jazmine Nazek, review of *Funny Little Monkey,* p. 133; June, 2009, Catherine Gilmore-Clough, review of *Jo-Jo and the Fiendish Lot,* p. 146.

ONLINE

Andrew Auseon Home Page, http://www.andrewauseon. com (June 21, 2010).*

B

BAILEY, Linda 1948-

Personal

Born 1948, in Winnipeg, Manitoba, Canada; married; children: Lia, Tess. *Education:* University of British Columbia, B.A. (English), M.A. (education).

Addresses

Home—Vancouver, British Columbia, Canada. *E-mail*—linda@lindabaileybooks.com.

Career

Writer. Presenter to schools and other organizations.

Member

Canadian Society of Children's Authors, Illustrators, and Performers, Children's Book Centre of Canada, Society of Children's Book Writers and Illustrators, Writers' Union of Canada, Vancouver Children's Literature Roundtable.

Awards, Honors

4-Surrey Book of the Year award, 1993, and Langley Book of the Year Award, 1994, both for *How Come the Best Clues Are Always in the Garbage?;* Ruth Schwartz Award, Arthur E. Ellis Award for best juvenile, Crime Writers of Canada, Silver Birch Award shortlist, and Canadian Library Association Notable Canadian Fiction designation, all 1994, all for *How Can I Be a Detective If I Have to Baby-sit?;* Arthur Ellis Award, 1996, for *How Can a Frozen Detective Stay Hot on the Trail?;* Arthur Ellis Award, CLB Book-of-the-Year honor, and Manitoba Young Readers' Choice honor, all 1996, all for *Who's Got Gertie?;* Arthur Ellis Award, 1997, and Red Cedar Award shortlist, 1999, both for *What's a Daring Detective like Me Doing in the Doghouse?;* Silver Birch Award shortlist, and Our Choice selection, both 2000, and Red Cedar Award shortlist, 2002, all for *How Can a Brilliant Detective Shine in the Dark?;* Silver Birch Award for nonfiction, 2001, for *Adventures in the Middle Ages;* Great Books Award, Canadian Toy Testing Council, 2002, for *The Best Figure Skater in the Whole Wide World;* Atlantic Hackmatack Award for English Nonfiction, Blue Spruce Award shortlist, and Red Cedar Award shortlist, all 2003, all for *Adventures with the Vikings; Child* magazine Best Children's Book Award, 2003, Ontario Blue Spruce Award, CNIB Tiny Torgi Award, and University of Chicago Zena Sutherland Award, all 2004, and Saskatchewan Shining Willow Award and Georgia Picture Storybook Award, both 2005, all for *Stanley's Party;* Atlantic Hackmatack Award for English Nonfiction shortlist, and Red Cedar Award shortlist, both 2004, both for *Adventures in Ancient Greece;* Silver Birch Award shortlist, 2004, and Atlantic Hackmatack Award for English Nonfiction shortlist, 2006, both for *Adventures in Ancient China;* Atlantic Hackmatack Award for English Nonfiction, 2006, for *Adventures in the Ice Age;* Book of the Year Gold Award, *ForeWord* magazine, 2007; Time to Read Award, British Columbia Achievement Foundation, 2007; British Columbia Chocolate Lily Award, 2008; California Young Reader Medal, 2009.

Writings

FOR CHILDREN

Petula, Who Wouldn't Take a Bath, illustrated by Jackie Snider, HarperCollins (Toronto, Ontario, Canada), 1996.

Gordon Loggins and the Three Bears, illustrated by Tracy Walker, Kids Can Press (Toronto, Ontario, Canada), 1997.

When Addie Was Scared, illustrated by sister, Wendy Bailey, Kids Can Press (Tonawanda, NY), 1999.

The Best Figure Skater in the Whole Wide World, illustrated by Alan Daniel and Lea Daniel, Kids Can Press (Toronto, Ontario, Canada), 2001.

Stanley's Party, illustrated by Bill Slavin, Kids Can Press (Toronto, Ontario, Canada), 2003.

Stanley's Wild Ride, illustrated by Bill Slavin, Kids Can Press (Toronto, Ontario, Canada), 2006.

The Farm Team, illustrated by Bill Slavin, Kids Can Press (Toronto, Ontario, Canada), 2006.

Goodnight, Sweet Pig, illustrated by Josee Masse, Kids Can Press (Toronto, Ontario, Canada), 2007.

Stanley at Sea, illustrated by Bill Slavin, Kids Can Press (Toronto, Ontario, Canada), 2008.

Stanley's Beauty Contest, illustrated by Bill Slavin, Kids Can Press (Toronto, Ontario, Canada), 2009.

Stanley's Little Sister, illustrated by Bill Slavin, Kids Can Press (Toronto, Ontario, Canada), 2010.

Author's books have been translated into several language, including Braille.

FOR CHILDREN; "STEVIE DIAMOND" MYSTERY SERIES

How Come the Best Clues Are Always in the Garbage?, illustrated by Pat Cupples, Kids Can Press (Toronto, Ontario, Canada), 1992.

How Can I Be a Detective If I Have to Baby-sit?, illustrated by Pat Cupples, Kids Can Press (Toronto, Ontario, Canada), 1993.

Who's Got Gertie? And How Can We Get Her Back?, illustrated by Pat Cupples, Kids Can Press (Toronto, Ontario, Canada), 1994.

How Can a Frozen Detective Stay Hot on the Trail?, illustrated by Pat Cupples, Albert Whitman (Morton Grove, IL), 1996.

What's a Daring Detective like Me Doing in the Doghouse?, illustrated by Pat Cupples, Albert Whitman (Morton Grove, IL), 1997.

How Can a Brilliant Detective Shine in the Dark?, Kids Can Press (Tonawanda, NY), 1999.

What Is a Serious Detective like Me Doing in Such a Silly Movie?, Kids Can Press (Tonawanda, NY), 2002.

Author's books have been translated into several languages, including French, Chinese, Polish, and Danish.

FOR CHILDREN; "GOOD TIMES TRAVEL AGENCY" SERIES

Adventures in Ancient Egypt, illustrated by Bill Slavin, Kids Can Press (Toronto, Ontario, Canada), 2000.

Adventures in the Middle Ages, illustrated by Bill Slavin, Kids Can Press (Toronto, Ontario, Canada), 2000.

Adventures with the Vikings, illustrated by Bill Slavin, Kids Can Press (Toronto, Ontario, Canada), 2001.

Adventures in Ancient Greece, illustrated by Bill Slavin, Kids Can Press (Toronto, Ontario, Canada), 2002.

Adventures in Ancient China, illustrated by Bill Slavin, Kids Can Press (Toronto, Ontario, Canada), 2003.

Adventures in the Ice Age, illustrated by Bill Slavin, Kids Can Press (Toronto, Ontario, Canada), 2004.

Adaptations

Stanley's Party and *Stanley's Wild Ride* were adapted for videocassette, Nutmeg Media, 2006.

Sidelights

Canadian author Linda Bailey is the creator of the "Stevie Diamond Mystery" and "Good Times Travel Agency" series for middle-grade readers. Other children's books by Bailey include *Gordon Loggins and the Three Bears, The Farm Team, Goodnight, Sweet Pig,* and a series of books that were inspired by Bailey's dog Sophie and focus on a rambunctious pup named Stanley. Reviewing *Stanley at Sea,* a *Kirkus Reviews* writer reflected the appeal of Bailey's stories by predicting that "Stanley's waggish appeal will win over readers young or grown."

Gordon Loggins and the Three Bears, Bailey's send-up of the classic Goldilocks story, finds a boy slipping through a door in the school library bookshelf and ending up starring in the librarian's story-hour tale. The book was described by *Quill & Quire* contributor Anne Louise Mahoney as a "hilarious story [that] will be a big hit with kids who know the classic tale." Praising Josee Masse's illustrations for *Goodnight, Sweet Pig, School Library Journal* contributor Donna Atmur added that Bailey's tale about Hamlette, a piglet that cannot fall asleep, "would also make an excellent bedtime story for restless children."

Pigs also figure in *The Farm Team,* a barnyard tale by Bailey in which Farmer Stolski's animals take on a rival hockey team in a game that makes the winter seem less harsh. An entertaining read-aloud, *The Farm Team*

Josee Masse creates the colorful digitized illustrations that capture the whimsy in Linda Bailey's story for **Goodnight, Sweet Pig!** *(Illustration © 2007 by Josee Masse. Used by permission of Kids Can Press Ltd., Toronto, Ontario, Canada.)*

The adventures of a mischievous dog and his doggie pals play out in Bailey's story and Bill Slavin's art for **Stanley's Wild Ride.** (Illustration © 2006 by Bill Slavin. Used with permission of Kids Can Press Ltd., Toronto, Ontario, Canada.)

also features "action-filled acrylic paintings" by frequent collaborator Bill Slavin that "capture [the story's] . . . drama and humor." The "goofy" images that pair with Bailey's hockey-themed tale attracted similar praise from a *Kirkus Reviews* writer, the critic adding that Bailey's silly sports tale "gets the competitive hum just right, even for a bunch of chickens, sheep and piglets."

Bailey introduces an engaging hound dog in her "Stanley" picture books, which feature Slavin's humorous cartoon art. In *Booklist,* Ilene Cooper dubbed *Stanley's Party* "a well-plotted delight," and Shawn Brommer predicted in *School Library Journal* that Bailey's energetic pooch will make "dog lovers and party animals alike . . . howl with delight." Stanley returns in *Stanley's Wild Ride,* as the pup and his friends dig their way to freedom and then sample a variety of wheeled ve-

hicles that take them on an adventurous tour of the town. Entered into a local dog show in *Stanley's Beauty Contest,* Stanley hopes to win one of the prize dog biscuits, but must resort to more underhanded means to gain the doggy treat when he is upstaged in every event. *Stanley at Sea* finds the mischievous dog lured with his friends into a dingy floating out to sea, his actions captured in illustrations that "positively exude enthusiasm," according to a *Kirkus Reviews* writer. In *Booklist,* Gillian Engberg dubbed *Stanley's Wild Ride* a "well-paced, energetic story" that will have particular appeal among "restless young listeners," and Ieva Bates noted in *School Library Journal* that "Stanley's many fans will love poring over . . . his adventure" in *Stanley's Beauty Contest.*

In *How Come the Best Clues Are Always in the Garbage?,* the first novel in Bailey's "Stevie Diamond Mystery" series, eleven-year-old Stevie and friend Jesse

Kulniki set out to find out who stole the funds of Garbage Busters, an environmental group that is protesting a fast-food restaurant's excessive use of packaging. Joseph J. Rodio, writing in *Catholic Library World*, noted the "humorous insights" into the adult world in Bailey's series opener, as well as her portrayal of the well-developed friendship between the two girls. In *Canadian Children's Literature*, Gisela Sherman praised the quick-paced plot, "great dialogue, comic timing, odd clues and hilarious situations" in *How Come the Best Clues Are Always in the Garbage?*, adding that Bailey's environmental message "fits in naturally."

The "Stevie Diamond Mystery" series continues in *How Can I Be a Detective If I Have to Baby-sit?*, which finds Stevie and Jesse spending a week at a British Columbian reforestation camp, where Stevie's father is working. Although the girls look forward to enjoying the great outdoors, they quickly realize that they were invited along so that they could baby-sit five-year-old Alexander, the camp cook's son. When Stevie and Jesse discover that Alexander's family is in some kind of trouble, their vacation becomes a sleuthing job. Calling *How Can I Be a Detective If I Have to Baby-sit?* "a cut above most detective series for the age group," *School Library Journal* contributor Linda Wicher described the plot as "nimble," and *Booklist* reviewer Chris Sherman called Bailey's story "entertaining" and its heroine "engaging," going on to predict that the novel's fast pace will appeal to young readers.

Stevie and Jesse return in *Who's Got Gertie? And How Can We Get Her Back?*, *How Can a Frozen Detective Stay Hot on the Trail?*, and *What Is a Serious Detective like Me Doing in Such a Silly Movie?* In *Who's Got Gertie?* thirteen-year-old Stevie and Jesse try to locate a missing neighbor, a retired actress, while *How Can a Frozen Detective Stay Hot on the Trail?* finds the sleuthing duo tracking down missing carnivorous plants in chilly Winnipeg, where one of the suspects is Stevie's uncle. *Who's Got Gertie?* was praised by *Quill & Quire* contributor Sarah Ellis, who cited Bailey's successful depiction of "middle-grade-mayhem" and described the novel as "colourful, lively, ephemeral, attention-getting, extravagant, and a crowd pleaser." Janet McNaughton, reviewing *How Can a Frozen Detective Stay Hot on the Trail?* for *Quill & Quire*, praised the author's characterization, plotting, and use of local color, and added that "the mystery works well, too."

What's a Daring Detective like Me Doing in the Doghouse? finds Stevie working at a day-care center for dogs while someone known only as the "Vancouver Prankster" causes all manner of mischief, eventually stealing the Canadian prime minister's underwear. When a stray dog appears to have a connection to the prankster, the girls investigate. In *How Can a Brilliant Detective Shine in the Dark?* a family reunion leads to a lost treasure, a hidden cave, and maybe murder, while *What Is a Serious Detective like Me Doing in Such a Silly Movie?* follows the girls' experiences as part of

the cast of a horror film called *Night of the Neems*. Reviewing the last-named title, Phelan cited Bailey's "flair for crisp dialogue," while *School Library Journal* contributor Tina Zubak wrote of *How Can a Brilliant Detective Shine in the Dark?* that "the book's humor and fast pace make it an enjoyable, old-fashioned who-dunit."

Bailey begins her "Good Times Travel Agency" series with *Adventures in Ancient Egypt*, which introduces twins Josh and Emma Binkerton. Together with tag-along little sister Lizzy, the twins find themselves transported into the past via the pages of a magical travel guide they discover in a strange travel agency. Trapped in the year 2500 B.C., the children discover that the only way to return to their own time is to read the entire travel guide, cover to cover, and a number of interesting adventures occur while they do so. "Bailey delivers not only a fast-paced story but also a fun way to convey information" regarding her ancient setting, noted Shelley Townsend-Hudson in a *Booklist* review of *Adventures in Ancient Egypt*.

Readers are carried along on the Binkerton children's further time-travel adventures in *Adventures in the*

Cover of Bailey's "Stevie Diamond Mystery" series opener How Come the Best Clues Are Always in the Garbage?, *featuring artwork by Pat Cupples.* (Illustration copyright © 1994 by Pat Cupples. Used by the permission of Kids Can Press Ltd., Toronto, Ontario, Canada.)

Middle Ages, Adventures in Ancient Greece, Adventures in Ancient China, Adventures in the Ice Age, and *Adventures with the Vikings,* the last which finds the children stowed away on a Viking ship in 800 A.D. Calling the Binkertons' escapades in *Adventures in Ancient Greece* "as hilarious as they are exciting," *Resource Links* contributor Veronica Allan added that Bailey's novel blends "historical information with fictional adventure in a way that cleverly presents facts" while also "entertaining . . . readers." Praising "the creative pen and ink, watercolour drawings and cartoon captions of Bill Slavin" that bring each series installment "to life," *Resource Links* writer Gail Lennon described *Adventures with the Vikings* as "interesting and innovative" in its approach to teaching about ancient cultures. In *Booklist,* Carolyn Phelan praised the same book as a "brief, accessible introduction to the subject," while Lynda Ritterman wrote in *School Library Journal* that *Adventures in Ancient China* is "both fun and educational" due to Bailey's unique "combination of adventure story and factual material."

Biographical and Critical Sources

PERIODICALS

Booklist, March 15, 1996, Chris Sherman, review of *How Can I Be a Detective If I Have to Baby-sit?,* p. 1264;

Cover of Bailey's Adventures in the Ice Age, *featuring cartoon artwork by Bill Slavin.* (Illustration © 2004 by Bill Slavin. Used by the permission of Kids Can Press Ltd., Toronto, Ontario, Canada.)

November 15, 1999, John Peters, review of *When Addie Was Scared,* p. 632; January 1, 2001, Shelley Townsend-Hudson, review of *Adventures in Ancient Egypt,* p. 941; October 15, 2001, Carolyn Phelan, review of *Adventures with the Vikings,* p. 391; November 1, 2004, Kay Weisman, review of *Adventures in the Ice Age,* p. 477; May 1, 2003, Carolyn Phelan, review of *How Can a Brilliant Detective Shine in the Dark?,* p. 1528; July, 2003, Ilene Cooper, review of *Stanley's Party,* p. 1895; March 1, 2006, Gillian Engberg, review of *Stanley's Wild Ride,* p. 98; October 1, 2006, Carolyn Phelan, review of *The Farm Team,* p. 56.

Books for Keeps, September, 1996, David Bennett, review of *How Come the Best Clues Are Always in the Garbage,* p. 13.

Bulletin of the Center for Children's Books, December, 1997, Deborah Stevenson, review of *Gordon Loggins and the Three Bears,* p. 117; October 4, 2002, review of *What's a Serious Detective like Me Doing in Such a Silly Movie?;* May, 2003, review of *Stanley's Party,* p. 350.

Canadian Book Review Annual, 2004, Christine Linge Macdonald, review of *Adventures in the Ice Age,* p. 544.

Canadian Children's Literature, winter, 1994, Gisela Sherman, review of *How Come the Best Clues Are Always in the Garbage?,* p. 66.

Canadian Review of Materials, February 15, 2003, review of *Adventures in Ancient Egypt;* March 28, 2003, review of *Stanley's Party;* February 15, 2007, Gregory Bryan, review of *Goodnight, Sweet Pig.*

Catholic Library World, December, 1996, Joseph J. Rodio, review of *How Come the Best Clues Are Always in the Garbage?,* p. 55.

Kirkus Reviews, September 15, 2006, review of *The Farm Team,* p. 946; February 1, 2008, review of *Stanley at Sea;* February 1, 2009, review of *Stanley's Beauty Contest.*

Publishers Weekly, February 3, 2003, review of *Stanley's Party,* p. 74; March 5, 2007, review of *Goodnight, Sweet Pig,* p. 59.

Quill & Quire, December, 1994, Sarah Ellis, review of *Who's Got Gertie?,* p. 31; September, 1996, Janet McNaughton, review of *How Can a Frozen Detective Stay Hot on the Trail?,* and Joan Findon, review of *How Come the Best Clues Are Always in the Garbage?,* both p. 74; July, 1997, Anne Louise Mahoney, review of *Gordon Loggins and the Three Bears,* p. 51; September, 2001, review of *The Best Figure Skater in the Whole Wide World,* p. 52; January, 2006, Sherie Posesorski, review of *Stanley's Wild Ride;* January, 2007, Nathan Whitlock, review of *Goodnight, Sweet Pig;* January, 2009, Sarah Ellis, review of *Stanley's Beauty Contest.*

Resource Links, December, 1999, review of *When Addie Was Scared,* p. 2; February, 2000, review of *How Can a Brilliant Detective Shine in the Dark?,* p. 7; December, 2000, review of *Adventures in Ancient Egypt,* pp. 10-11; October, 2001, Gail Lennon, review of *Adventures with the Vikings,* p. 22; December, 2001, Valerie Pollock, review of *The Best Figure Skater in the*

Whole Wide World, p. 2; December, 2002, Veronica Allan, review of *Adventures in Ancient Greece,* p. 36; June, 2003, Isobel Lang, review of *Stanley's Party,* p. 1; October, 2003, Greg Bak, review of *Adventures in Ancient China,* p. 12; June, 2006, Denise Parrott, review of *Stanley's Wild Ride,* p. 2; February, 2007, Evette Berry, review of *The Farm Team,* p. 1; June, 2007, Tanya Boudreau, review of *Goodnight, Sweet Pig,* p. 1.

School Library Journal, May, 1996, p. 110; July, 1996, Linda Wicher, review of *How Can I Be a Detective If I Have to Baby-sit?,* p. 82; December, 2001, Rita Soltan, review of *The Best Figure Skater in the Whole Wide World,* p. 88; June, 2003, Tina Zubak, review of *How Can a Brilliant Detective Shine in the Dark?,* p. 136; July, 2003, Shawn Brommer, review of *Stanley's Party,* p. 87, and Tina Zubak, review of *What's a Serious Detective like Me Doing in Such a Silly Movie?,* p. 123; January, 2004, Lynda Ritterman, review of *Adventures in Ancient China,* p. 110; June, 2006, Suzanne Myers Harold, review of *Stanley's Wild Ride,* p. 98; November, 2006, Blair Christolon, review of *The Farm Team,* p. 84; June, 2007, Donna Atmur, review of *Goodnight, Sweet Pig,* p. 92; April, 2008, Gay Lynn Van Vleck, review of *Stanley at Sea,* p. 102; March, 2009, Ieva Bates, review of *Stanley's Beauty Contest,* p. 106.

Times Educational Supplement, July 5, 1996, review of *How Come the Best Clues Are Always in the Garbage?,* p. R8.

ONLINE

Canadian Society of Children's Authors, Illustrators, and Performers Web site, http://www.canscaip.org/ (May 31, 2010), "Linda Bailey."

Linda Bailey Home Page, http://www.lindabaileybooks.com (May 31, 2010).*

* * *

BERKES, Marianne 1940(?)-

Personal

Born c. 1940; married Roger Berkes; children: Melissa Broker. *Hobbies and other interests:* Music, theatre, travelreading, writing, swimming, boating, walking the beach.

Addresses

Home—Martin County, FL. *E-mail*—Mberkesbooks@aol.com.

Career

Children's book author. Former children's librarian; former educator in New York; Sunshine School, Pawling, NY, founder. Worked as a director of children's theatre.

Marianne Berkes (Photograph courtesy of Dawn Publications.)

Member

International Reading Association, Society of Children's Book Writers and Illustrators (SCBWI-Florida affiliate), National Association for the Education of Young Children, Authors Guild, Florida Oceanographic Coastal Center, Florida Reading Association, Florida Association of Media Educators.*

Awards, Honors

North American Publishing Company Gold Ink Award, Pewter Award, 2002, for *Seashells by the Seashore;* Florida Reading Association (FRA) award, 2004-05, and *Science Books and Films* Best Books designation, both for *Marsh Morning;* Bank Street Best Children's Books designation, 2005; Math and Science Teachers' Choice Gold Award, 2006; National Parenting Publications Gold Award, 2006; Benjamin Franklin Silver Award; Blue Hen Picture Book Award; Maine Chickadee Award nominee; FRA Best Children's Picture Books nomination, 2007, and Indiana Young Hoosier Award nominee 2008, both for *Over in the Ocean: In a Coral Reef;* Benjamin Franklin Gold Award, iParenting Media Award, and International Reading Association Teachers' ChoiceAward 2008, and Charlotte Award nomination, 2010, all for *Over in the Jungle;* iParenting Media Award, and Moonbeam Children's Book Award, both for *Going around the Sun; Foreward* magazine Book of the Year designation, and iParenting Media Award, both 2010, both for *Over in the Arctic.*

Writings

Marsh Music, illustrated by Robert Noreika, Millbrook Press (Brookfield, CT), 2000.

Seashells by the Seashore, illustrated by Robert Noreika, Dawn Publications (Nevada City, CA), 2002.

Marsh Morning, illustrated by Robert Noreika, Millbrook Press (Brookfield, CT), 2003.

Over in the Ocean: In a Coral Reef, illustrated by Jeanette Canyon, Dawn Publications (Nevada City, CA), 2004.

Over in the Jungle: A Rainforest Rhyme, illustrated by Jeanette Canyon, Dawn Publications (Nevada City, CA), 2007.

Going around the Sun: Some Planetary Fun, illustrated by Janeen Mason, Dawn Publications (Nevada City, CA), 2008.

Over in the Arctic: Where the Cold Winds Blow, illustrated by Jill Dubin, Dawn Publications (Nevada City, CA), 2008.

Going Home: The Mystery of Animal Migration, illustrated by Jennifer DiRubbio, Dawn Publications (Nevada City, CA), 2010.

Over in Australia: Animals Down Under, illustrated by Jennifer DiRubbio, Dawn Publications (Nevada City, CA), 2011.

Animalogy, Sylvan Dell Publishing, 2011.

Sidelights

Children's book author Marianne Berkes was an early-childhood educator in New York State prior to moving south in 1990 and becoming a children's librarian in Florida. Since retiring from this job, Berkes has divided her time between writing for children and speaking at schools, libraries, and conferences where she describes the publishing process and reads from her award-winning children's picture books. Her books, which include *Marsh Music, Over in the Jungle: A Rainforest Rhyme,* and *Going Home: The Mystery of Animal Migration,* are noted for their rhyming texts, their focus on nature, and their informative glossaries.

Berkes' *Marsh Music* and *Marsh Morning* are both inspired by the cacophony of sounds the author heard emanating from the pond in the back yard of her Florida home. As the author stated on her home page: "I enjoy writing about things that interest me. . . . And I love to do the research. For example, I have always been fascinated with frogs, and when I moved to Florida, I couldn't believe the variety of sounds that came from the pond in the back of my home. I recorded them. Then, of course, I needed to find out which frog was making which sound; that required a lot of research." Both *Marsh Music* and *Marsh Morning* utilize a rhyming text and are accompanied by lush watercolor illustrations by Connecticut artist Robert Noreika. In *Marsh Music* Berkes transports readers to a Florida marsh after sunset, as a hefty bull frog named Maestro oversees "a symphony of frogs plunking spider webs, playing pod instruments, and making sounds" that teach children the basics of musical tempo, according to *Booklist* contributor Connie Fletcher. In similar fashion, *Marsh Morning* focuses on dawn in the marsh lands and uses both music and metaphor to illustrate the rustling that starts each day. Berkes highlights the varied wildlife in this natural setting, moving her focus from frogs to birds. For curious young naturalists, she includes a glossary of terms and a list of the bird varieties depicted in Noreika's illustrations. *Booklist* reviewer Julie Cummins called *Marsh Morning* "great . . . for budding young birders," while Nancy Cull, writing in *School Library Journal,* dubbed the book "excellent."

In *Seashells by the Seashore* Berkes once again utilizes a rhyming text. This time she focuses on a young girl named Sue as she collects a dozen shells to give to her

Berkes shares her love of the ocean in her picture book Seashells by the Seashore, *featuring paintings by Robert Noreika.* (Dawn Publications, 2002. Robert Noreika, illustrator. Reproduced by permission.)

Berkes' lyrical, nature-themed story in Over in the Arctic **features artwork by Jill Dubin.** (Dawn Publications, 2008. Illustration copyright © 2008 by Jill Dubin. Reproduced by permission.)

grandmother as a birthday present. Watercolor illustrations by Noreika depict Sue as, together with her brother and a friend, she scavenges along the beach in search of colorful shells. As readers turn each page, a sidebar depicts the collection of shells as it grows, each new addition including a descriptive label. *School Library Journal* critic Gay Lynn Van Vleck noted that "Berkes offers ample facts in her rhymes, and gives a short paragraph of information on each type of shell on a spread at the end," creating a book that departs lessons to "young beachcombers."

In *Over in the Ocean: In a Coral Reef* the reef is teeming with all manner of parent creatures and their young offspring, and children can count and clap to the rhythm of "Over in the Meadow" while pufferfish "puff," gruntfish "grunt," and seahorses flutter. The colorful art by Jeanette Canyon is constructed entirely from polymer clay, and in a review for *Kirkus Reviews* a contributor dubbed Canyon's illustrations "eye-popping."

Caynon also created the artwork for Berkes' companion volume, *Over in the Jungle,* and the author continues her musical tour of nature with other artists in *Over in the Arctic: Where the Cold Winds Blow,* illustrated by Jill Dubin, and *Going around the Sun: Some Planetary Fun,* illustrated by Janeen Mason. In *Going around the*

Sun a "rhymed tour of the solar system is framed as a dialogue between Mother Sun and her satellites," explained *Booklist* critic John Peters, while *Over in the Arctic* introduces several different Arctic creatures, including ten that are hiding in Dubin's cut-paper collage illustrations. The layered habitats of the Earth's rainforests are brought to life in *Over in the Jungle,* a book that *School Library Journal* critic Judith Constantinides recommended as "a handsome book on an important subject." In the same periodical, Julie Roach deemed *Over in the Arctic* "a useful introduction" to the polar region, while a *Kirkus Reviews* writer noted Berkes' "easily chanted rhyme" and her imaginative treatment of "standard number-recognition and counting concepts."

As an author and storyteller, Berkes is thrilled when her books inspire children to leave the television set or computer screen and go outside to experience nature for themselves. "Music, nature, and the sea have always been a constant in my life," she once told *SATA.* "My parents were both very musical and loved nature. My father was a boat builder and I grew up on the Long Island Sound in City Island, New York. In the summer, we would often spend a few weeks in the Catskill Mountains, so I had the best of both worlds. I always loved the outdoors and wished more kids today could

have the opportunities I had growing up—to really get out and play in nature. I would ride my bike for hours or hike through the woods with my friends until it was time to come home for supper. I think those experiences really inspired me to write about nature in a lyrical kind of way! I love how, when I read my stories to children, they really get inside the books, each time discovering something new and exciting."

Biographical and Critical Sources

PERIODICALS

Booklist, December 1, 2000, Connie Fletcher, review of *Marsh Music,* p. 716; March 1, 2002, Ellen Mandel, review of *Seashells by the Seashore,* p. 1137; March 15, 2003, Julie Cummins, review of *Marsh Morning,* p. 1328.

Kirkus Reviews, September 1, 2004, review of *Over in the Ocean: In a Coral Reef,* p. 860; August 1, 2008, review of *Over in the Arctic: Where the Cold Winds Blow.*

Palm Beach Post, October 4, 2000, Linda Haase, "Songs of Frogs Inspire Author to Compose Children's Book," p. 6; February, 7, 2003, Jeri Butler, profile of Berkes, p. E1; October 13, 2004, Jeri Butler, "Author's New Book Takes Children under the Sea," p E5.

School Library Journal, April, 2002, Gay Lynn Van Vleck, review of *Seashells by the Seashore,* p. 100; April, 2003, Nancy Call, review of *Marsh Morning,* p. 116; May, 2007, Judith Constantinides, review of *Over in the Jungle: A Rainforest Rhyme,* p. 114; June, 2008, John Peters, review of *Going around the Sun: Some Planetary Fun,* p. 118; September, 2008, Julie Roach, review of *Over in the Arctic,* p. 137.

ONLINE

Marianne Berkes Home Page, http://www.marianneberkes.com (June 1, 2010).

*   *   *

BERMAN, Rachel 1946-

Personal

Born 1946, in New Orleans, LA.

Addresses

Home—Toronto, Ontario, Canada.

Career

Fine artist and illustrator. *Exhibitions:* Work included in exhibits at John Inglis Fine Arts, Toronto, Ontario, Canada, Ingram Gallery, Toronto, and Winchester Galleries, Victoria, British Columbia, Canada.

Awards, Honors

Governor General's Literary Award for Children's Literature Illustration finalist, 2009, for *Bradley McGogg, the Very Fine Frog.*

Illustrator

Glenda Leznoff, *Pigmalion,* Tradewind Books (Boston, MA), 2001.

Tim Beiser, *Bradley McGogg, the Very Fine Frog,* Tundra (Toronto, Ontario, Canada), 2008, Tundra (Plattsburg, NY), 2009.

Sidelights

A self-educated artist and illustrator, Rachel Berman gains inspiration for her evocative artwork from her many travels throughout North America, Europe, and the Middle East. Born in New Orleans, Louisiana, Berman now makes her home in Canada, and her urban-themed paintings are exhibited in major galleries in several of that country's major cities. In 2009 Berman gained recognition for her art when she was nominated for the prestigious Governor General's Award for picture-book illustration for her work on *Bradley McGogg, the Very Fine Frog.*

Featuring a text by Tim Beiser, *Bradley McGogg, the Very Fine Frog* follows a hungry frog as he goes from friend to friend, looking for something to eat. Because he is a frog, Bradley graciously declines friend Mousie's offer of cheese, and Cow's lunch of green grass and clover is equally unappealing. After several more stops

Rachel Berman's illustrations are a highlight of Tim Beiser's story in **Bradley McGogg, the Very Fine Frog.** (Berman, Rachel, illustrator. From an illustration in Bradley McGogg, the Very Fine Frog, by Tim Beiser. Tundra books, 2008. Illustrations copyright © 2008 by Rachel Berman. Reproduced by permission.)

in his unsuccessful search, McGogg returns home to find his hollow-log home full of enough bugs to make a tasty meal. Beiser's "sophisticated" rhyme is matched by Berman's gouache-and-watercolor art, which Linda L. Walkins noted in *School Library Journal* imbues "each animal's face . . . with character and personality." In *Quill & Quire* Sarah Ellis praised Berman's art as "full of personality and emotion," adding that her "gentle setting, rural and mildly Edwardian," gives a not to noted English author//illustrator Beatrix Potter. The artist's "magical images . . . illuminate the text and . . . engage readers in the story in wonderful ways!," asserted Myra Junyk in a review of *Bradley McGogg, the Very Fine Frog* for *Canadian Review of Materials,* the critic going on to recommend the award-winning picture book for featuring "valuable lessons about community, friendship, sharing, individual differences, politeness and diversity."

Another illustration project, Glenda Leznoff's *Pigmalion,* also benefits from Berman's art. In Leznoff's story of a young pig with dreams of performing in a stage production of George "Barnyard" Shaw's *Pigmalion,* Berman contributes water-color illustrations that "refine" the story "with deft gouaches, placing the tale somewhere in the south of France," according to a *Publishers Weekly* critic. Remarking that the artist's "clever" and "stylish illustrations . . . set the story in a bygone era," Valerie Neilsen concluded in the *Canadian Review of Materials* that *Pigmalion* is "just the right length for an enjoyable storytime reading."

Biographical and Critical Sources

PERIODICALS

Canadian Review of Materials, April 15, 2005, Valerie Nielsen, review of *Pigmalion;* November 21, 2008, Myra Junyk, review of *Bradley McGogg, the Very Fine Frog.*
Publishers Weekly, March 11, 2002, review of *Pigmalion,* p. 71.
Quill & Quire, January, 2009, Sarah Ellis, review of *Bradley McGogg, the Very Fine Frog.*
Resource Links, June, 2002, Gillian Richardson, review of *Pigmalion,* p. 3.
School Library Journal, August, 2002, Adele Greenlee, review of *Pigmalion,* p. 160; March, 2009, Linda L. Walkins, review of *Bradley McGogg, the Very Fine Frog,* p. 106.

ONLINE

Artists in Canada Web site, http://www.artistsincanada.com (June 21, 2010), Robert Amos, interview with Berman.*

* * *

BERNSTEIN, Jonathan

Personal

Born in Scotland.

Addresses

Home—Los Angeles, CA.

Career

Screenwriter, author, and journalist.

Writings

Pretty in Pink: The Golden Age of Teenage Movies, St. Martin's Griffin (New York, NY), 1997.
Knickers in a Twist: A Dictionary of British Slang, Canongate (Berkeley, CA), 2006.
Hottie, Razorbill (New York, NY), 2009.
Burning Ambition (sequel to *Hottie*), Razorbill (New York, NY), 2010.

Contributor to periodicals, including *Arena, Entertainment Weekly, New York Times,* London *Observer, Rolling Stone,* and *Spin.*

SCREENPLAYS

(Author of story, with others) *Just My Luck,* Scholastic, Inc. (New York, NY), 2006.
(With others) *Meet the Robinsons,* Buena Vista Pictures (United States), 2007.

Also author of television plays *The Brown Man,* 1993, and *Bait Shop,* 2008. Author of screenplays, including *Max Keeble's Big Move,* 2001, *Larry the Cable Guy: Heath Inspector,* 2006, and *The Spy Next Door,* 2010.

Sidelights

A Los Angeles-based journalist and screenwriter whose credits include the film *Meet the Robinsons,* Jonathan Bernstein entertains teen readers with his fiction debut *Hottie.* In addition to fiction, the Scottish-born Bernstein also presents U.S. readers with an entertaining glossary of Britishisms in *Knickers in a Twist: A Dictionary of British Slang,* and has published articles in a number of high-profile periodicals.

A beautiful, blonde high-school freshman is the focus of *Hottie,* but in Bernstein's novel the typical YA formulas are quickly discarded. Alison Cole feels like she has it all: she is dating a cute surfer boyfriend and she has just been elected president of her class at Beverly Hills High. Then, during a cutting-edge plastic surgery procedure, she is literally zapped by lightning and ends up with super powers. Unfortunately, the ability to shoot fire from one's fingertips quickly erodes Alison's popularity, and when she decides to channel her powers for good she must chose her crime-fighting sidekick from among her less-popular classmates. While Alison comes up against a surprising foe, she also worries over her tumultuous love life, as well as over the cute junior who seems to have it in for her. In a sequel, *Burning*

Ambition, Alison returns, beautifully manicured as usual. This time her goal is to upstage a fifteen-year-old brat who is hoping to use her position as editor-in-chief during Alison's summer internship at *Jen* magazine to pursue Alison's boyfriend.

Comparing Bernstein's quick-moving prose to that in the "Gossip Girls" novels by Cecily von Ziegesar, Amy S. Pattee wrote in *School Library Journal* that *Hottie* is similarly salted with "brand names and Hollywood stars." However, the way they appear in Bernstein's witty prose, these materialistic "details are not aspirational guidelines but more satirical asides," Pattee added. In *Kirkus Reviews* a critic dubbed *Hottie* a "mindlessly fun superhero send-up" and predicted that "seasoned chick-lit readers are bound to enjoy" Bernstein's "Malibu Barbie makeover" of the traditional caped-crusader saga.

Biographical and Critical Sources

PERIODICALS

Kirkus Reviews, January 1, 2009, review of *Hottie.*

Cover of Jonathan Bernstein's teen novel **Hottie,** *which follows the adventures of a teen superhero,* (Cover photograph by Michael Frost, 2008. Cover background illustration courtesy of Shutterstock.com, 2008. Reproduced by permission of Razorbill, a division of Penguin Putnam Books for Young Readers.)

School Library Journal, June, 2009, Amy S. Pattee, review of *Hottie,* p. 116.

ONLINE

Jonathan Bernstein Home Page, http://jonathanbernstein. com (June 25, 2010).
Jonathan Bernstein Web log, http://jonathanbernsteinbook. blogspot.com (June 25, 2010).*

* * *

BLACK, Kat
(Katherine Black)

Personal

Born in Australia; divorced. *Religion:* Roman Catholic.

Addresses

Home—Lynn, MA.

Career

Author and illustrator. Former Web developer; worked in children's book industry for nineteen years, including as designer for Walter Lorraine (publisher).

Member

Society of Children's Book Writers and Illustrators.

Writings

A Templar's Apprentice (book one of "Book of Tormod" series), Scholastic Press (New York, NY), 2009.
(Self-illustrated) *Touchstone Tarot,* Kunati (Clearwater, FL), 2009.

Sidelights

In *A Templar's Apprentice,* Kat Black begins her "Book of Tormod" novel trilogy, drawing middle-grade readers back to Scotland at the turn of the fourteenth century. "The great thing about these kinds of books is the learning process," Black noted in discussing the process of researching and writing historical fiction. "You start out with one fact and in researching it, you're shoved into another and you branch off in a different direction. I never know where the facts will take me but I know somehow they'll all fit in and their spin will make the book even more interesting."

Scotland circa 1300 is a time of crusading knights, and the greatest of these are the Knights Templar. Members of a secret society, the Templar knights in Black's story also have special powers, such as mind control and an ability to know the future. For thirteen year-old Tor-

mod, the Knights Templar are heroic, and when he serves as one of their messengers the young teen soon finds himself apprenticed to a knight named Alexander. In the service of Alexander, Tormod begins to recognize that he also has special powers, and knight and page use their visions of the future to keep safe from a villainous French king and his soldiers. Noting that the "historical setting" in *A Templar's Apprentice* "is well drawn," Eric Norton added in *School Library Journal* that Black incorporates elements of Scottish brogue in the dialogue between Tormod and Alexander. A *Publishers Weekly* contributor dubbed *A Templar's Apprentice* an "impressive debut," adding that the story's "action is frequent and often brutal, but never feels out of place."

Biographical and Critical Sources

PERIODICALS

Bulletin of the Center for Children's Books, February, 2009, April Spisak, review of *A Templar's Apprentice,* p. 234.

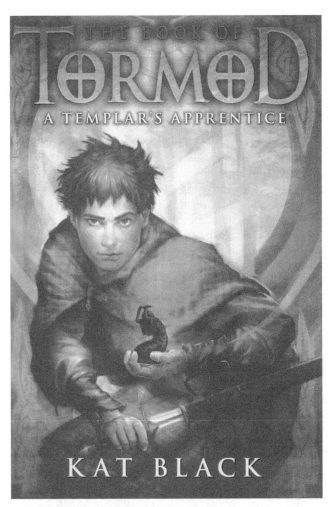

Cover of Kat Black's middle-grade adventure novel **A Templar's Apprentice,** *featuring artwork by Scott M. Fischer.* (Illustration © 2009 by Scott M. Fischer. Reproduced by permission of Scholastic, Inc.)

Kirkus Reviews, January 1, 2009, review of *A Templar's Apprentice.*
Publishers Weekly, March 9, 2009, review of *A Templar's Apprentice,* p. 49.
School Library Journal, May, 2009, Eric Norton, review of *A Templar's Apprentice,* p. 100.

ONLINE

Kat Black Home Page, http://katblackbooks.com (May 31, 2010).
Kat Black Web log, http://kmblack.livejournal.com (June 1, 2010).*

* * *

BLACK, Katherine
See BLACK, Kat

* * *

BROWN, Calef

Personal

Male. *Education:* Art Center College of Design, B.F.A.

Addresses

Home and office—ME. *Agent*—Jennifer Vaughn Artist Agent, 1947 Grant Ave., San Francisco, CA 94133. *E-mail*—calef@calefbrown.com.

Career

Author and illustrator. Freelance illustrator and designer for print and animation. Former instructor at Art Center College of Design and Otis School of Art and Design; presenter at schools.

Writings

SELF-ILLUSTRATED

Polka-Bats and Octopus Slacks: 14 Stories, Houghton Mifflin (Boston, MA), 1998.
Dutch Sneakers and Flea-Keepers: 14 More Stories, Houghton Mifflin (Boston, MA), 2000.
Tippintown: A Guided Tour, Houghton Mifflin (Boston, MA), 2003.
Flamingos on the Roof: Poems and Paintings, Houghton Mifflin (Boston, MA), 2006.
Soup for Breakfast: Poems and Pictures, Houghton Mifflin (Boston, MA), 2008.
Hallowilloween: Nefarious Silliness, Houghton Mifflin Harcourt (Boston, MA), 2010.

ILLUSTRATOR

John Harris, *Greece! Rome! Monsters!,* J. Paul Getty Museum (Los Angeles, CA), 2002.

John Harris, *Pop-up Aesop,* J. Paul Getty Museum (Los Angeles, CA), 2005.

Daniel Pinkwater, *The Neddiad: How Neddie Took the Train, Went to Hollywood, and Saved Civilization,* Houghton Mifflin (Boston, MA), 2007.

Daniel Pinkwater, *The Yggyssey: How Iggy Wondered What Happened to All the Ghosts, Found out Where They Went, and Went There,* Houghton Mifflin (Boston, MA), 2009.

Jonah Winter, *Gertrude Is Gertrude Is Gertrude Is Gertrude,* Atheneum Books for Young Readers (New York, NY), 2009.

Contributor to *Exquisite Corpse Adventure* (online novel), produced by Library of Congress, 2009-10. Contributor to numerous periodicals, including *Business Week, Chicago Tribune, Fortune, Los Angeles Magazine, New Yorker, Rolling Stone, Spin, Sports Illustrated, Time,* and *Yale Medicine.*

Sidelights

Calef Brown originally worked as a freelance illustrator, creating works for such high-profile periodicals as the *New York Times, Rolling Stone,* and *Newsweek.* He became interested in writing and illustrating children's books when the fast-paced, deadline-oriented life of freelancing began to wear thin. As Brown explained in

Calef Brown's poetry collection **Flamingos on the Roof** *pairs his unique paintings with his quirky rhyming verse.* (Copyright © 2006 by Calef Brown. Reprinted by permission of Houghton Mifflin Harcourt Publishing Company. All rights reserved.)

an online interview with Nate Williams for *Illustration Mundo,* his intent in writing for children was to "illustrate something of my own that would have a longer shelf life than the magazine pieces that I was doing." This aim was achieved when his picture book *Polka-Bats and Octopus Slacks: 14 Stories* was published in 1998 and went into five printings. In each of the books he has since created for young children, Brown mixes original poetry with his folk-art inspired illustrations. As he commented to *Illustration Mundo,* his texts are designed to be "read aloud. I want them to be musical—some rhythmic, percussive and lively, others quiet and atmospheric."

Critics have acknowledged Brown's skill both as a writer and an illustrator. In her evaluation of *Flamingos on the Roof: Poems and Paintings* for *Horn Book,* Susan Dove Lempke noted his ability to pair a well-written text with engaging, colorful illustrations and added that the book's "imaginative wordplay is matched by . . . acrylic paintings depicting people and places in unusual hues." A *Kirkus Reviews* critic was impressed by the author/illustrator's ability to create audibly pleasing poetry full of child appeal. Noting that Brown's texts are "composed with a fine ear for consistent rhythms and silly wordplay," the critic concluded that books such as *Flamingos on the Roof* "will tempt readers into repeat visits."

Like *Flamingos on the Roof, Soup for Breakfast: Poems and Pictures* presents what *School Library Journal* contributor Joan Kindig described as a "combination of stylized illustrations and offbeat verse." The volume's fourteen poems range in topic from a grandfather's moustache to a tattletale egret to the value of compassion. A *Kirkus Reviews* writer predicted that the "wacky, wild and sometimes witty collection . . . will not disappoint Brown's many fans," who will enjoy the book's wordplay and fanciful acrylic visuals. In *Publishers Weekly* a critic characterized Brown's illustrations as "somewhere between surreal and folk art," noting his use of "improbable color combinations" and "oddball" characters, while Lempke wrote in *Horn Book* that the work "demonstrates his [Brown's] inventiveness" and "sparks a creative response in the reader." *Soup for Breakfast* is a reminder "that poetry and pictures can exist just for kicks," the *Publishers Weekly* reviewer concluded.

In addition to his original stories, Brown has contributed his whimsical artwork to the equally whimsical texts of authors such as Jonah Winter and Daniel Pinkwater. His "brash and welcoming" acrylic paintings, rendered in what *Booklist* critic Thom Barthelmess described as a suitably "post-impressionistic" style, team with Winter's "infectious, rhythmic" text to make *Gertrude Is Gertrude Is Gertrude Is Gertrude* a "ebullient" picture-book ode to twentieth-century modernist writer Gertrude Stein. While writing that Winter and Brown's "creative, artistic" picture book might be overly sophisticated for a young audience, Susan Scheps added in

Brown continues to dish up a satisfying mix of poetry and art in his self-illustrated picture book Soup for Breakfast. (Copyright © 2008 by Calef Brown. Reprinted by permission of Houghton Mifflin Harcourt Publishing Company. All rights reserved.)

School Library Journal that the text captures the essence of Stein's writing while the brightly colored "avant-garde folk-style paintings include . . . representations of 'modern' paintings" by Picasso, Matisse, and others.

Biographical and Critical Sources

PERIODICALS

Booklist, March 15, 1998, John Peters, review of *Polka-Bats and Octopus Slacks: 14 Stories,* p. 1243; April 1, 2000, Gillian Engberg, review of *Dutch Sneakers and Flea-Keepers: 14 More Stories,* p. 1456; April 15, 2003, Michael Cart, review of *Tippintown: A Guided Tour,* p. 1475; April 15, 2006, Hazel Rochman, review of *Flamingos on the Roof: Poems and Paintings,* p. 44; January 1, 2009, Thom Barthelmess, review of *Gertrude Is Gertrude Is Gertrude Is Gertrude,* p. 78.

Horn Book, May-June, 2006, Susan Dove Lempke, review of *Flamingos on the Roof,* p. 337; March-April, 2009, Susan Dove Lempke, review of *Soup for Breakfast,* p. 208.

Kirkus Reviews, March 15, 2006, review of *Flamingos on the Roof,* p. 286; October 1, 2008, review of *Soup for Breakfast.*

Publishers Weekly, March, 1998, review of *Polka-Bats and Octopus Slacks,* p. 67; April 17, 2000, review of *Dutch Sneakers and Flea-Keepers,* p. 78; April 9, 2001, review of *Polka-Bats and Octopus Slacks,* p. 28; October 7, 2002, review of *Greece! Rome! Monsters!,* p. 73; March 3, 2003, review of *Tippintown,* p. 75; March 20, 2006, review of *Flamingos on the Roof,* p. 55; October 13, 2008, review of *Soup for Breakfast,* p. 54.

School Library Journal, April, 2000, Linda M. Kenton, review of *Dutch Sneakers and Flea-Keepers,* p. 118; May, 2003, Liza Graybill, review of *Tippintown,* p. 108; July, 2006, Susan Scheps, review of *Flamingos on the Roof,* p. 118; February, 2009, Joan Kindig, review of *Soup for Breakfast,* p. 115, and Susan Scheps, review of *Gertrude Is Gertrude Is Gertrude Is Gertrude,* p. 128.

ONLINE

Calef Brown Home Page, http://www.calefbrown.com (June 1, 2010).

Houghton Mifflin Web site, http://www.houghtonmifflin books.com/ (June 1, 2010), "Calef Brown."

Illustration Mundo Web site, http://www.illustrationmundo. com/ (March 31, 2007), Nate Williams, interview with Brown.*

*   *   *

BURG, Ann E. 1954-

Personal

Born 1954, in NY; married; children: one son, one daughter. *Education:* Attended college.

Addresses

Home—Albany, NY.

Career

Writer. Teacher of English for over ten years.

Writings

FOR CHILDREN

Autumn Walk, illustrated by Kelly Asbury, HarperFestival (New York, NY), 2003.

E Is for Empire: A New York State Alphabet, Sleeping Bear Press (Chelsea, MI), 2003.

Times Square: A New York State Numbers Book, illustrated by Maureen K. Brookfield, Sleeping Bear Press (Chelsea, MI), 2005.

Rebekkah's Journey: A WWII Refugee Story, illustrated by Joel Iskowitz, Sleeping Bear Press (Chelsea, MI), 2006.

Kate's Surprise, illustrated by Phyllis Harris, Children's Press (New York, NY), 2007.

Pirate Pickle and the White Balloon, illustrated by Marilyn Janovitz, Children's Press (New York, NY), 2007.

The New York Reader, illustrated by K.L. Darnell, Sleeping Bear Press (Chelsea, MI), 2008.

YOUNG-ADULT NOVELS

All the Broken Pieces, Scholastic Press (New York, NY), 2009.

Sidelights

While growing up in New Jersey, Ann E. Burg gained a passion for reading and writing, a passion she carried into her adult years. In addition to working as an English teacher, Burg also wrote articles in her spare time, then made the break to full-time writer with the support of her family. Her books for children include the verse novel *All the Broken Pieces,* the picture books *Rebekkah's Journey: A WWII Refugee Story* and *Kate's Surprise,* and several illustrated books focusing on Burg's home state of New York that mix educational concepts with interesting facts from history.

Rebekkah's Journey, featuring illustrations by Joel Iskowitz, takes readers back to Oswego, a town in upstate New York, circa 1944, as hundreds of refugees arrived from war-torn Europe and found temporary shelter in an unused army base. Burg describes the experiences of these people, many of them Jewish, through her story of seven-year-old Rebecca and her mother. Confronted by a strange culture and a new language, the two must forge a new life while also working to preserve the traditions that have bound them as a family and as part of a strong culture. Based on interviews with the men, women, and children who experienced this transition, *Rebekkah's Journey* shares "a quiet story" grounded in "long-ago memories," according to *School Library Journal* contributor Heidi Estrin.

Another story of wartime, *All the Broken Pieces* is set in 1977 and focuses on Matt Pin, a boy who is still haunted by memories of his experiences in his Vietnamese village two years after being airlifted out of the war-ravaged region. Now living with his adoptive U.S. family, where he has discovered a passion for baseball and feels welcomed, twelve-year-old Matt is haunted by terrible memories as well as guilt over the fact that his little brother was horribly injured during the terrible or-

deal. "The intensity of the simple words" in Burg's free-verse text will inspire re-reading, encouraging children "to make connections between past and present, friends and enemies," predicted Hazel Rochman in her *Booklist* review of *All the Broken Pieces,* and *Horn Book* contributor Jonathan Hunt wrote that a wartime survivor's "painful memories are adeptly captured" in the book's "fleeting but powerful images." A *Publishers Weekly* contributor wrote that Burg's "spare" text "beautifully evokes [Matt's] . . . emotions . . . as he struggles to come to terms with his past," and a *Kirkus Reviews* writer dubbed *All the Broken Pieces* "a memorable debut" in which Burg's verse narrative conveys "highly charged emotions and heavy content with elegiac simplicity."

Although Burg gears *E Is for Empire: A New York State Alphabet, Times Square: A New York State Numbers Book,* and *The New York Reader* to residents of the Empire State, the colorful format and interesting information make these picture books of interest to readers of all fifty states. In *E Is for Empire,* Burg ranges throughout the largest of the northeastern states, collecting an alphabet's worth of people, places, and things from history, and *Times Square* contains 1-to-12 and 10-to-100 count-downs of fascinating facts about the state. In *The New York Reader* Burg's text pairs with delicate watercolor art by K.L. Darnell. Reviewing *Times Square,* Lisa Gangemi Kropp noted in *School Library Journal* that the "warm watercolor tones" of Maureen K. Brookfield's accompanying illustrations pair well with Burg's collection of "little-known facts" and "brief histories."

Biographical and Critical Sources

PERIODICALS

Booklist, February 15, 2009, Hazel Rochman, review of *All the Broken Pieces,* p. 80.

Horn Book, May-June, 2009, Jonathan Hunt, review of *All the Broken Pieces,* p. 292.

Kirkus Reviews, February 15, 2009, review of *All the Broken Pieces.*

Publishers Weekly, April 13, 2009, review of *All the Broken Pieces,* p. 49.

School Library Journal, January, 2006, Lisa Gangemi Kropp, review of *Times Square: A New York State Number Book,* p. 118; February, 2007, Heidi Estrin, review of *Rebekkah's Journey: A WWII Refugee Story,* p. 85; May, 2009, Heather M. Campbell, review of *All the Broken Pieces,* p. 101.

ONLINE

Sleeping Bear Press Web site, http://www.sleepingbear press.com/ (May 31, 2010), "Ann E. Burg."*

C

CABOT, Meg 1967-
(Meggin Cabot, Patricia Cabot, Jenny Carroll)

Personal

Born February 1, 1967, in Bloomington, IN; daughter of A. Victor (a college professor) and Barbara Cabot; married Ben D. Egnatz (a financial writer), April 1, 1993. *Education:* Indiana University, B.A., 1991.

Addresses

Office—P.O. Box 4904, Key West, FL 33041-4904. *Agent*—Laura Langlie, 275 President St., Ste. 3, Brooklyn, NY 11231.

Career

Writer. New York University, New York, NY, assistant manager of undergraduate dormitory for ten years.

Member

Authors Guild, Authors League of America, Society of Children's Book Writers and Illustrators, Romance Writers of America.

Awards, Honors

Reviewers Choice Award, best British Isles historical romance, *Romantic Times,* 1999, for *An Improper Proposal;* cited among "Top Ten Quick Picks for Reluctant Readers" and Best Book selection, both American Library Association, both 2001, both for *The Princess Diaries;* Edgar Allan Poe Award nomination in young-adult category, Mystery Writers of America, 2003, for *Safe House; The Princess Diaries* voted among 100 best-loved novels, British Broadcasting Corporation's "The Big Read," 2003.

Writings

YOUNG-ADULT FICTION

Nicola and the Viscount, Avon (New York, NY), 2002.
Victoria and the Rogue, Avon (New York, NY), 2003.

Meg Cabot (Reproduced by permission.)

All-American Girl, HarperCollins (New York, NY), 2003.
Teen Idol, HarperCollins (New York, NY), 2004.
Ready or Not (sequel to *All-American Girl*), HarperCollins (New York, NY), 2005.
How to Be Popular, HarperTempest (New York, NY), 2006.
Pants on Fire, HarperCollins (New York, NY), 2007.

Jinx, HarperCollins (New York, NY), 2007.

Airhead, Point (New York, NY), 2008.

Being Nikki (sequel to *Airhead*), Point (New York, NY), 2009.

Runaway (sequel to *Being Nikki*), Point (New York, NY), 2010.

Contributor of short fiction to anthologies, including *13: Thirteen Stories That Capture the Agony and Ecstasy of Being Thirteen,* edited by James Howe, 2003; *Girls' Night In,* Red Dress Ink, 2004; *Friends: Stories about New Friends, Old Friends, and Unexpectedly True Friends,* edited by Ann M. Martin and David Levithan, 2005; *Girls' Night Out,* Red Dress Ink, 2006; *Everything I Needed to Know about Being a Girl I Learned from Judy Blume,* edited by Jennifer O'Connell, 2007; and *Midnight Feast,* HarperCollins UK, 2007. Contributor to *Shelf Discovery: Teen Classics We Never Stopped Reading,* by Lizzie Skurnick, Avon (New York, NY), 2009. Contributor to *Seventeen* magazine. Author, with others, of screenplay for film *The Ice Princess,* produced by Disney.

"PRINCESS DIARIES" YOUNG-ADULT NOVEL SERIES

The Princess Diaries (also see below), HarperCollins (New York, NY), 2000.

Princess in the Spotlight (also see below), HarperCollins (New York, NY), 2001.

Princess in Love (also see below), HarperCollins (New York, NY), 2002.

Princess in Waiting (also see below), HarperCollins (New York, NY), 2003.

Project Princess, HarperTrophy (New York, NY), 2003.

Princess Lessons, HarperCollins (New York, NY), 2003.

Perfect Princess, HarperCollins (New York, NY), 2004.

Princess in Pink, HarperCollins (New York, NY), 2004.

Mia Tells It like It Is (contains *The Princess Diaries* and *Princess in the Spotlight*), Avon Books (New York, NY), 2004.

The Highs and Lows of Being Mia (contains *Princess in Love* and *Princess in Waiting*), Avon Books (New York, NY), 2004.

Princess in Training, HarperCollins (New York, NY), 2005.

Holiday Princess (nonfiction), illustrated by Chesley McLaren, HarperCollins (New York, NY), 2005.

Party Princess, HarperCollins (New York, NY), 2006.

Sweet Sixteen Princess, HarperCollins (New York, NY), 2006.

Valentine Princess, HarperTempest (New York, NY), 2006.

Princess on the Brink, HarperCollins (New York, NY), 2006.

Princess Mia, HarperTeen (New York, NY), 2008.

Forever Princess, HarperTeen (New York, NY), 2009.

(And author of introduction) *Ransom My Heart, by Princess of Genovia Mia Thermopolis,* HarperCollins (New York, NY), 2009.

"MEDIATOR" YOUNG-ADULT NOVEL SERIES

(Under pseudonym Jenny Carroll) *Shadowland,* Pocket Pulse (New York, NY), 2000.

(Under pseudonym Jenny Carroll) *Ninth Key,* Pocket Pulse (New York, NY), 2001.

(Under pseudonym Jenny Carroll) *Reunion,* Pocket Pulse (New York, NY), 2001.

(Under pseudonym Jenny Carroll) *Darkest Hour,* Pocket Pulse (New York, NY), 2001.

Haunted, HarperTrophy (New York, NY), 2003.

Twilight, HarperCollins (New York, NY), 2005.

"1-800-WHERE-R-YOU" YOUNG-ADULT NOVEL SERIES

(Under pseudonym Jenny Carroll) *When Lightning Strikes,* Pocket Pulse (New York, NY), 2001, published under name Meg Cabot, Simon Pulse (New York, NY), 2007.

(Under pseudonym Jenny Carroll) *Code Name Cassandra,* Pocket Pulse (New York, NY), 2001, published under name Meg Cabot, Simon Pulse (New York, NY), 2007.

(Under pseudonym Jenny Carroll) *Safe House,* Pocket Pulse (New York, NY), 2002, published under name Meg Cabot, Simon Pulse (New York, NY), 2007.

(Under pseudonym Jenny Carroll) *Sanctuary,* Pocket Pulse (New York, NY), 2002, published under name Meg Cabot, Simon Pulse (New York, NY), 2007.

Missing You, HarperCollins (New York, NY), 2006.

"AVALON HIGH" YOUNG-ADULT NOVEL SERIES

Avalon High, HarperCollins (New York, NY), 2006.

Avalon High 2: Coronation: Book 1: The Merlin Prophecy (manga), illustrated by Jinky Coronado, HarperCollins (New York, NY), 2007.

Avalon High 2: Coronation: Book 2: Homecoming (manga), illustrated by Jinky Coronado, HarperCollins (New York, NY), 2008.

Avalon High 2: Coronation: Book 3: Hunter's Moon (manga), illustrated by Jinky Coronado, HarperCollins (New York, NY), 2009.

"ALLIE FINKLE'S RULES FOR GIRLS" MIDDLE-GRADE NOVEL SERIES

Moving Day, Scholastic Press (New York, NY), 2008.

The New Girl, Scholastic Press (New York, NY), 2008.

Best Friends and Drama Queens, Scholastic Press (New York, NY), 2009.

Stage Fright, Scholastic Press (New York, NY), 2009.

Glitter Girls and the Great Fake Out, Scholastic Press (New York, NY), 2010.

ADULT NOVELS

The Boy Next Door, Avon (New York, NY), 2002.

She Went All the Way, Avon (New York, NY), 2002.

Boy Meets Girl (sequel to *The Boy Next Door*), Avon (New York, NY), 2004.

Every Boy's Got One (sequel to *Boy Meets Girl*), Avon (New York, NY), 2005.

Size 12 Is Not Fat: A Heather Wells Mystery, Avon (New York, NY), 2006.

Queen of Babble, William Morrow (New York, NY), 2006.

Size 14 Is Not Fat Either: A Heather Wells Mystery, Avon (New York, NY), 2006.

Queen of Babble in the Big City, William Morrow (New York, NY), 2007.

Queen of Babble Gets Hitched, William Morrow (New York, NY), 2008.

Big Boned: A Heather Wells Mystery, Avon (New York, NY), 2008.

Insatiable, Morrow (New York, NY), 2010.

UNDER PSEUDONYM PATRICIA CABOT; ADULT ROMANCE NOVELS

Where Roses Grow Wild, St. Martin's Press (New York, NY), 1998.

Portrait of My Heart, St. Martin's Press (New York, NY), 1998.

An Improper Proposal, St. Martin's Press (New York, NY), 1999.

A Little Scandal, St. Martin's Press (New York, NY), 2000.

A Season in the Highlands (anthology), Pocket Books (New York, NY), 2000.

Lady of Skye, Pocket Books (New York, NY), 2001.

Educating Caroline, Pocket Books (New York, NY), 2001.

Kiss the Bride, Pocket Books (New York, NY), 2002.

Adaptations

The Princess Diaries was adapted for a film starring Julie Andrews, Walt Disney Pictures, 2001. *The Princess Diaries 2: Royal Engagement,* a screenplay by Shonda Rhimes, was based on Cabot's characters, Walt Disney Pictures, 2004. Cabot's book series "1-800-WHERE-R-YOU" was adapted as the Lifetime television network series *1-800-MISSING,* directed by Michael Fresce, 2003. The "Princess Diaries" novels were adapted as audiobooks and released by Listening Library. The "Mediator" novels were adapted as audiobooks and released by Recorded Books, 2006. *Avalon High* was optioned for film by Walt Disney Pictures.

Sidelights

Meg Cabot is a popular writer who is known for her ability to capture the way adolescents think and talk. While Cabot is best known as the author of the "Princess Diaries," novel series, about a Manhattan teen, she also writes stand-alone novels with teen appeal, such as *Teen Idol* and *How to Be Popular,* the latter which *Booklist* reviewer Carolyn Phelan dubbed an "appealing, first-person story of teen yearning, befuddlement, and love." Cabot's "1-800-WHERE-R-YOU" series mixes mystery with a supernatural element, while her other series include the "Avalon High," "All-American

Girl," "Mediator," and "Airhead" books, as well as the middle-grade "Allie Finkle's Rules for Girls" series. "While legions of Meg Cabot imitators get waylaid by brand-name this and 'Oh my God' that, Cabot's voice remains fresh," noted *New York Time Book Review* contributor Lauren Mechling in a review of Cabot's 'tween novel *Moving Day.* "She favors the spill-the-beans-as-you-go style common to teenage fiction, but her material has a spirited fizz that's lacking in many so-called young adult comedies."

In the first volume of Cabot's "Princess Diaries" series, readers meet Mia, an awkward, fourteen-year-old, often histrionic, and sometimes whiney New Yorker. Mia's ordinary troubles—a crush on the most popular boy in school, a flat chest, and an artist mom who is dating Mia's algebra teacher—are magnified the day her father shows up and reveals that he is a prince of Genovia, a small European country. Suddenly, Mia finds herself totally miscast; more ugly duckling than swan, she is nevertheless expected to carry herself like royalty and deal gracefully with the pressures that come from a life in the public eye. Many of her diary entries feature revelations concerning life as a princess, including taking

Cover of the novel that started it all for Cabot: **The Princess Diaries.**
(HarperTeen, 2008. Used by permission of HarperCollins Children's Books, a division of HarperCollins Publishers.)

lessons in how to act like royalty from her imperious grandmère and being followed around by relentless paparazzi. "Readers will relate to Mia's bubbly, chatty voice and enjoy the humor of this unlikely fairy tale," predicted Debbie Stewart in a review of *The Princess Diaries* for *School Library Journal*. While a *Publishers Weekly* critic felt that Cabot's humor descends into "slapstick" on occasion, Chris Sherman wrote in *Booklist* that reading *The Princess Diaries* "is like reading a note from your best friend."

In his *Booklist* review of *The Princess Diaries,* Sherman praised Cabot's accurate rendition of contemporary adolescent slang, as well as her ability to create well-rounded, lovable characters, and concluded with a prediction that teens would "lin[e] up for this hilarious story." Teens did indeed line up, not only for the original novel, but also for the feature-film adaptations of the novel and its engaging sequels. Further "Princess Diaries" novels find Crown Princess Amelia Mignonette Grimaldi Thermopolis Renaldo learning the finer points of acting regal while also coping with the everyday problems of being a teen: namely, homework, annoying relatives, and adolescent romance. *Princess in Love* finds Mia living in New York, attending Albert Einstein High, and wishing she could trade in her current boyfriend, Kenny, for a more suitably princely love interest. A date for the prom with new beau Michael Moscovitz is on her mind in *Princess in Pink,* as a citywide service workers' strike threatens to cancel both the party and Mia's chance to wear her new pink prom dress. Her relationship with Michael has lasting power, despite the stresses caused by her arduous math classes, but in *Princess on the Brink* a brutal pre-calculus class and college-student Michael's impending trip to Japan threaten to take their toll on Mia's love life.

Reviewing *Party Princess* in *Kliatt,* Carol Reich wrote that "Mia may be a drama queen, but she is still lovable and her hilarious diary entries couldn't be more enjoyable." Shelle Rosenfeld also commented favorably on Cabot's teen protagonist, writing in *Booklist* that "Mia's journal entries, filled with pop references . . . , are sure to entertain," while the teen's "romantic expectations . . . contrast humorously with reality checks." Praising the series as "a great bet for reluctant readers," Paula Rohlick added in *Kliatt* that *Princess in Training* ranks as "a particularly enjoyable episode in this irresistible series."

The "Princess Diaries" series winds down with *Valentine Princess, Princess on the Brink,* and *Forever Princess,* while Princess Mia Thermopolis is the purported author of the Cabot-penned historical novel *Ransom My Heart,* which Mia is shown busily writing in *Forever Princess.* With its focus on pressures for sex and holding to one's principles, *Princess on the Brink* was praised by *Booklist* critic Gillian Engberg as a series installment that features "the usual comedy" along with "larger questions about sex and relationships." In addition to showing Mia working on a novel in *Forever*

Princess, Cabot ends her "Princess Diaries" series as the princess reflects on her past and anticipates her future. Physical passion is also the focus of *Ransom My Heart,* but restraint does not necessarily win out in the story of Finnula Crais, a miller's daughter living in rural England, circa 1290. In an attempt to aid her pregnant and unmarried sister Mellana, Finn undertakes the kidnapping of wealthy earl Hugh Fitzstephen, a knight recently returned from the crusades. Although he learns of the young woman's plan, the earl lets the plot succeed, with romance the result. "Both Finnula and Hugh are well-crafted characters with likeable personalities and real depth," noted *School Library Journal* contributor Karen E. Brooks-Reese, the critic dubbing *Ransom My Heart* a "well-researched" novel enhanced by "witty dialogue."

In her inaugural works in the "1-800-WHERE-R-YOU" series, Cabot exhibits the same winning characteristics she uses in her "Princess Diaries" books. In series opener *When Lightning Strikes,* sixteen-year-old at-risk student Jessica Mastriani has been struck by lightning and left with an ability to find missing children. Unfortunately, the government wants the teen to channel her psychic ability to find criminals, and Jessica turns to a handsome biker for help in eluding the federal authorities. "Jessica's thrilling first-person account of her adventure is enhanced by raucously funny teen observations," remarked Roger Leslie in *Booklist.*

Code Name Cassandra finds Jessica—now nicknamed Lighting Girl—attempting to escape the limelight and keep her special ability under wraps, until one of her charges at a summer camp for musically gifted children goes missing. Her gift becomes a curse in *Safe House;* not only does it make Jessica stand out from the other students at Ernest Pyle High School, but she is quickly blamed when a popular cheerleader at school goes missing and winds up dead. Finally accepting that her ability makes her different in *Sanctuary,* the sixteen year old joins government agent Cyrus Krantz in the search for a missing child, while in *Missing You* Jess finally follows her dream of studying music at Juilliard. With her psychic powers now seemingly spent, the former Lightning Girl hopes to lead a normal life . . . that is, until her former hometown beau hunts her down with hopes that she can reunite him with his missing sister.

Cabot again employs a first-person teenage narrator in *Shadowland,* the first book in her "Mediator" series. Like the protagonist of *When Lightning Strikes,* Susannah "Suze" Simon has the mixed blessing of a sixth sense. Her special ability is as a mediator, which means putting ghosts in contact with the living world in order to resolve the conflicts between them. The only problem comes when she actually falls for Jesse, one of her spectral contacts. In *Ninth Key* Suze finds ghosts turning up everywhere, even in the past of her current human love interest, the dishy Tad Beaumont, while Jesse's long-dead fiancée is driven from her grave to haunt the teen mediator in *Darkest Hour.* Paul Slater, a

Cover of Cabot's high-tech chick-lit fantasy Airhead, *which focuses on a hard-core computer gamer.* (Cover photograph © 2009 by Michael Frost. Reproduced by permission of Scholastic, Inc.)

fellow mediator with a jealous streak, becomes a threat in *Haunted,* while in *Twilight* Suze realizes that her powers extend beyond merely bridging the worlds of ghosts and humans. Now she is forced to choose between her own desires and those of her haunted lover.

In a review of *Shadowland* for *Publishers Weekly,* a critic noted that Cabot's "intriguing premise of a sixteen-year-old with a sixth sense may stand more than a ghost of a chance at snaring teen readers." Deeming *Twilight* "a page-turning good time," Stephanie Squicciarini added in *Kliatt* that "humor, suspense, love, and betrayal" all figure in Cabot's supernatural tale, resulting in a novel "that is sure to please."

In another series opener, *Airhead,* Cabot focuses on sixteen-year-old Em Watts, a computer gamer who has little interest in the mind games played by the popular girls in her swanky New York City high school. When a freak accident results in daring transplant surgery that leaves the massively injured Em in the brain-dead body of top teen model Nikki Howard, the teen finds herself controlling a real-life avatar and leaving her former life behind. As the new Nikki attempts to learn the rules of the rich, she also works to navigate her new self into her old role and a new relationship with Christopher, a fellow gamer and Em's secret crush. In *Booklist* Phelan asserted that Cabot injects *Airhead* with "elements of humor and glimmers of compassion for the rich and famous" while also giving voice to readers "who distain . . . pop-culture glamour." A treat for fans, according to a *Publishers Weekly* critic, the novel "dishes up" the well-known Cabot fare: "romance, humor, believable teen dialogue, and even a fantastical twist." Noting the story's mix of "hilarious situations and awkward encounters," *Kliatt* critic Ashleigh Larsen added that *Airhead* combines "witty conversational dialogue" and upbeat themes relevant to real-world teens, and Em's imaginative story continues in *Being Nikki* and *Runaway.*

Cabot's other books for teens include her "Avalon High" novels, three of which are formatted as graphic novels with illustrations by Jinky Coronado. A standalone novel in which a small-town Iowa teen moves east to live with Manhattan relatives who suspect her of witchcraft, *Jinx* was described by *Kliatt* critic Claire Rosser as classic Cabot: an "entertaining, fluffy novel . . . that will have appeal to those who like their chick lit mixed with some magic." Tall tales are the forté of high-school senior Katie Ellison, but efforts to juggle three boyfriends makes the lies spiral out of control in *Pants on Fire,* an "enjoyable read," according to *Booklist* critic Debbie Carton. While Cabot's "boy-crazy" heroine does not exactly earn reader sympathy, readers will find her *Pants on Fire* an "amusing" story that is "as easy to swallow as iced tea on a hot afternoon."

An optimistic nine year old is the star of Cabot's "Allie Finkle's Rules for Girls" series. Geared for preteen readers, the series opens in *Moving Day,* as Allie worries about a move to a new town and a new school. As her worries spark misunderstandings, mishaps, and other unfortunate scrapes with friends and family, Allie attempts to set things right by establishing workable rules for life that have "good intentions and reckless results," according to *School Library Journal* critic Tina Zubak. Cabot's 'tween-friendly *Moving Day* "will surely leave readers looking forward to future installments," according to *Booklist* critic Bina Williams. Allie's story continues in *Stage Fright,* as she opes for the lead in the fourth-grade class play, while *Best Friends and Drama Queens* finds her anticipating the arrival of a new girl named Cheyenne, only to watch as Cheyenne divides the students of Room 209, Pine Heights Elementary, into competitive cliques. In reviewing *Best Friends in Drama Queens,* Phelan praised the young narrator's "fresh voice and believable fourth-grade perspective," and a *Kirkus Reviews* critic dubbed the "irony" of Allie's situation "hilarious and touching."

In her light fiction for teenagers and young adults, Cabot often features journalists and other characters engaged in the writing profession. For example, *Ready or Not* continues the story of high-school student Samantha

Madison, a character first introduced in *All American Girl*, as she pursues her relationship with the son of the president of the United States and ends up on national television because of her views on provocative political and social issues. *Teen Idol* is the story of a small-town girl from the Midwest and her encounter with the teenage movie star who inspires her metamorphosis from anonymous high school advice columnist to social activist. Noting that the novel contains "lots of heart and humor," Rohrlick noted in *Kliatt* that *Ready or Not* showcases Cabot's talent for "creating convincing, down-to-earth teen characters" and draws in young readers by "incorporating lots of pop culture references and amusing lists."

Upon graduating from teenagers into twenty-something adults, Cabot's fans can continue to fuel their addiction to her novels with books featuring more mature protagonists. Among these are *Boy Meets Girl, Queen of Babble,* and the novels in Cabot's "Heather Wells Mystery" series. In *Boy Meets Girl* and its sequels, Cabot expands her journal-entry device by using e-mail, answering-machine messages, and other communications to frame the story of a young career woman whose job in the human relations department of a New York newspaper leads her into one dilemma after another. While inappropriate for younger teens due to their mature content, her romance novels published under the pen name Patricia Cabot have also earned praise for their mix of mystery and romance, as well as for featuring characters whose humor and humanity engage readers' interest and affection. She has also moved into paranormal fiction with *Insatiable,* a novel about a woman who is able to predict death and sometimes even prevent it, until a vampire enters the picture in the person of her current love interest.

In an interview with *Teenreads.com,* Cabot discussed her writing process. "I truly do base ALL my characters on people I know," she admitted, "although I try to disguise them so the people they're based on won't recognize themselves and sue me. I do this by giving them character traits that other people I know have. So no one character is truly based 100 percent on any one person, but a mix of a lot of people." Setting is one of the most important considerations when beginning a novel; as Cabot explained, "where we live does shape our lives, in many ways. I debate long and hard about where I'm going to set a novel, do research on it once I've decided, and try to set it in a place I've actually been (unless of course it's a made-up place). The more details you can add about a setting (so long as they enhance the story), the more realistic your story will seem to readers."

Biographical and Critical Sources

PERIODICALS

Booklist, September 15, 2000, Chris Sherman, review of *The Princess Diaries,* p. 233; May 1, 2001, Roger Leslie, review of *When Lightning Strikes,* p. 1744; April 15, 2004, Shelle Rosenfeld, review of *Princess in Pink,* p. 1436; October 1, 2004, Debbie Carton, review of *Teen Idol,* p. 7; November 15, 2004, Kaite Mediatore, review of *Every Boy's Got One,* p. 560; August, 2005, Cindy Welch, review of *Princess in Training,* p. 2014; September 15, 2005, Abby Nolan, review of *Ready or Not: An All-American Girl Novel,* p. 57; February 1, 2006, Cindy Welch, review of *Avalon High,* p. 43; February 15, 2006, Cindy Welch, review of *Party Princess,* p. 92; May 15, 2006, Carolyn Phelan, review of *Queen of Babble,* p. 22; September 15, 2006, Carolyn Phelan, review of *How to Be Popular,* p. 69; November 15, 2006, Gillian Engberg, reviews of *Size 12 Is Not Fat: A Heather Wells Mystery,* p. 29, and *Size 14 Is Not Fat Either: A Heather Wells Mystery,* p. 35; December 15, 2006, Gillian Engberg, review of *Princess on the Brink,* p. 48; May 1, 2007, Debbie Carton, review of *Pants on Fire,* p. 81; April 15, 2008, Carolyn Phelan, review of *Airhead,* p. 39; June 1, 2008, Bina Williams, review of *Moving Day,* p. 72; November 15, 2008, Carolyn Phelan, review of *Best Friends and Drama Queens,* p. 40; December 15, 2008, Shelley Mosley, review of *Ransom My Heart,* p. 28; October 1, 2009, Carolyn Phelan, review of *Stage Fright,* p. 38.

Horn Book, January-February, 2006, Jeannine M. Chapman, review of *Avalon High,* p. 74; May-June, 2009, Rachel L. Smith, review of *Best Friends and Drama Queens,* p. 292.

Kirkus Reviews, July 1, 2005, review of *Ready or Not,* p. 732; October 15, 2005, review of *Size 12 Is Not Fat,* p. 1108; December 1, 2005, review of *Avalon High,* p. 1272; April 15, 2006, review of *Queen of Babble,* p. 366; August 1, 2006, review of *How to Be Popular,* p. 782; July 15, 2007, review of *Jinx;* December 15, 2008, review of *Forever Princess;* February 1, 2009, review of *Best Friends and Drama Queens.*

Kliatt, May, 2004, Paula Rohrlick, review of *Princess in Waiting,* p. 16; July, 2004, Paula Rohrlick, review of *Teen Idol,* p. 7; May, 2005, Paula Rohrlick, review of *The Princess Diaries, Volume VI: Princess in Training,* p. 8; July, 2005, Paula Rohrlick, review of *Ready or Not,* p. 8; September, 2005, Paula Rohrlick, review of *Teen Idol,* p. 17; January, 2006, Paula Rohrlick, review of *Avalon High,* p. 5; March, 2006, Joanna Solomon, review of *Party Princess,* p. 8, and Stephanie Squicciarini, review of *Twilight,* p. 26; July, 2006, Joanna Solomon, review of *How to Be Popular,* p. 218; September, 2006, Carol Reich, review of *Party Princess,* p. 46; July, 2008, July, 2008, Ashleigh Larsen, review of *Airhead,* p. 8, and Claire Rosser, review of *Jinx,* p. 10.

Library Journal, January 1, 2008, Stacey Hayman, review of *Ransom My Heart,* p. 83.

New York Times Book Review, June 15, 2008, Laura Mechling, review of *Moving Day,* p. 17.

Publishers Weekly, November 30, 1998, review of *Portrait of My Heart,* p. 69; October 18, 1999, review of *An Improper Proposal,* p. 78; October 9, 2000, review of *The Princess Diaries,* p. 88; November 6, 2000, review of *Shadowland,* p. 92; December 11, 2000, re-

view of *Lady of Skye,* p. 68; July 9, 2001, review of *The Princess Diaries,* p. 21; October 29, 2001, review of *Educating Caroline;* November 17, 2003, review of *Boy Meets Girl,* p. 42; August 30, 2004, review of *Teen Idol,* p. 56; November 8, 2004, review of *Every Boy's Got One,* p. 33; August 7, 2006, review of *How to Be Popular,* p. 61; October 9, 2006, review of *Size 14 Is Not Fat Either,* p. 40; May 7, 2007, review of *Pants on Fire,* p. 61; July 30, 2007, review of *Jinx,* p. 84; April 28, 2008, review of *Airhead,* p. 140; October 27, 2008, reviews of *Ransom My Heart,* p. 32, and *Forever Princess,* p. 55.

School Library Journal, October, 2000, Debbie Stewart, review of *The Princess Diaries,* p. 155; August, 2004, Linda Binder, review of *Princess in Pink,* and Ginny Collier, review of *Teen Idol,* both p. 116; February, 2005, Amy Patrick, review of *Twilight,* p. 132; April, 2005, Erin Dennington, review of *Every Boy's Got One,* p. 161; January, 2006, Amy Patrick, review of *Avalon High,* p. 129; April, 2008, Karen E. Brooks-Reese, review of *Ransom My Heart,* p. 152; June, 2008, Tina Zubak, review of *Moving Day,* p. 98.

Voice of Youth Advocates, February, 2005, Luch Schall, review of *Twilight,* p. 488; August, 2005, Patti Sylvester Spencer, review of *Princess in Training,* p. 212; February, 2006, Amy Alessio, review of *Avalon High,* p. 482; April, 2006, Molly Gregerson, review of *Party Princess,* p. 39.

ONLINE

Meg Cabot Home Page, http://www.megcabot.com (June 1, 2010).
TeenReads.com, http://www.teenreads.com/ (August 16, 2006), interview with Cabot.*

* * *

CABOT, Meggin
See CABOT, Meg

* * *

CABOT, Patricia
See CABOT, Meg

* * *

CANTRELL, Julie 1973-

Personal

Born 1973, in LA; married; children: two.

Addresses

Home—Oxford, MS. *Agent*—Greg Johnson, WordServe Literary Group, Inc., 10152 Knoll Circle, Highlands Ranch, CO 80130. *E-mail*—juliepcantrell@bellsouth.net.

Career

Writer for children. *Southern Literary Review,* editor in chief.

Writings

God Is with Me through the Day, Zonderkidz (Grand Rapids, MI), 2009.
God Is with Me through the Night, Zonderkidz (Grand Rapids, MI), 2009.
Into the Free (novel), David C. Cook (CO), 2012.

Biographical and Critical Sources

PERIODICALS

Kirkus Reviews, February 15, 2009, review of *God Is with Me through the Day.*

ONLINE

Julie Cantrell Home Page, http://www.juliecantrell.com (May 30, 2010).
Julie Cantrell Web log, http://juliecantrell.wordpress.com (May 30, 2010).
Zondervan Web site, http://www.zondervan.com/ (May 30, 2010), "Julie Cantrell."*

* * *

CARROLL, Jenny
See CABOT, Meg

* * *

COCKCROFT, Jason

Personal

Born in England; married; wife's name Lisa.

Addresses

Home—Whibye, Yorkshire, England.

Career

Illustrator and author of books for children.

Awards, Honors

Blue Peter Award, 2000, for *A Pilgrim's Progress.*

Writings

SELF-ILLUSTRATED

Counter Clockwise, Katherine Tegen Books (New York, NY), 2009.

ILLUSTRATOR

Elizabeth Laird, *Secret Friends,* Hodder Children's (London, England), 1997.

Helen Cresswell, *The Sea Piper,* new edition, Hodder Children's (London, England), 1997.

Helen Cresswell, *The Little Sea Pony,* new edition, Hodder Children's (London, England), 1997.

Sally Grindley, *Just Grandpa and Me,* Dorling Kindersley London, England), 1998.

Sally Grindley, *A Flag for Grandma,* DK Pub. (New York, NY), 1998.

Helen Cresswell, *The Little Grey Donkey,* new edition, Hodder Children's (London, England), 1998.

Michael Morpurgo, *Tom's Sausage Lion,* new edition, Corgi Yearling (London, England), 1999.

Leon Garfield, *Mr. Corbett's Ghost, and Other Stories,* new edition, Oxford University Press (Oxford, England), 1999.

Pippa Goodhart, *Milly,* Hodder Children's (London, England), 1999.

Geraldine McCaughrean, reteller, *John Bunyan's A Pilgrim's Progress,* Hodder Children's (London, England), 1999, Overlook Press (New York, NY), 2005.

Maggie Pearson, *A Deer from the Hill,* Hodder Children's (London, England), 1999.

Sandra Ann Horn, *The Dandelion Wish,* DK Pub. (New York, NY), 2000.

Cynthia Cotten, *Snow Ponies,* Henry Holt (New York, NY), 2001.

Lynn Plourde, *Thank You, Grandpa,* Dutton (London, England), 2001, Dutton Children's Books (New York, NY), 2003.

Leon Garfield, *Black Jack,* new edition, Oxford University Press (Oxford, England), 2002.

Leon Garfield, *Devil-in-the-Fog,* new edition, Oxford University Press (Oxford, England), 2002.

Judith Nicholls, *Billywise,* Bloomsbury Children's Book (New York, NY), 2002.

Frances Hodgson Burnett, *The Secret Garden,* new edition, foreword by Gillian Cross, Kingfisher (London, England), 2002.

Tony Bradman, *Daddy's Lullaby,* Margaret K. McElderry Books (New York, NY), 2002.

James Riordan, reteller, *Jason and the Golden Fleece,* Frances Lincoln (London, England), 2003.

Angela McAllister, *The Little Blue Rabbit,* Bloomsbury Children's Books (New York, NY), 2003, published as *Blue Rabbit,* Bloomsbury (London, England), 2003.

Miriam Moss, *The Horse Girl,* Frances Lincoln (London, England), 2004.

Tim Bowler, *Blood on Snow,* Hodder Children's (London, England), 2004.

Martin Waddell, *Room for a Little One,* Orchard (London, England), 2004, Margaret K. McElderry Books (New York, NY), 2006.

Marion Rose, *The Christmas Tree Fairy,* Bloomsbury Children's Books (New York, NY), 2005.

Ian Whybrow, *Star Baby,* Orchard (London, England), 2006.

Tim Bowler, *Walking with the Dead,* Hodder Children's (London, England), 2006.

Marni McGee, *A Song in Bethlehem,* Alfred A. Knopf (New York, NY), 2007.

David Self, *Saint Paul,* Lion Children's (Oxford, England), 2009.

Biographical and Critical Sources

PERIODICALS

Publishers Weekly, September 26, 2005, review of *The Christmas Tree Fairy,* p. 87.

School Library Journal, June, 2005, Heide Piehler, review of *John Bunyan's A Pilgrim's Progress,* p. 163.

Voice of Youth Advocates, June, 2009, Diane Colson, review of *Counter Clockwise,* p. 149.*

*   *   *

COLLINS, Pat Lowery 1932-

Personal

Born October 6, 1932, in Los Angeles, CA; daughter of Joseph Michael (an auditor/comptroller) and Margaret (a radio scriptwriter) Lowery; married Wallace Collins (a network engineer), April 18, 1953; children: Christopher, Kimberly, Colleen, Cathlin, Mathias. *Education:* Attended University of California—Los Angeles, 1949, and Immaculate Heart College, 1950; University of Southern California, B.A. (English), 1953; further study at Choinard Art Institute, DeCordova Museum School (Lincoln, MA), and Brandeis University. *Politics:* "Independent." *Religion:* Roman Catholic.

Addresses

Home and office—3 Wauketa Rd., Gloucester, MA 01930-1423. *E-mail*—patlc@comcast.net.

Career

Poet, writer, artist, and illustrator. Child actress in radio. Lesley University, Cambridge, MA, instructor in creative writing at low-residency M.F.A. program. Gives readings; visits schools and conferences and does Skype visits. *Exhibitions:* Work represented in permanent and private collections in the United States and Japan.

Member

Society of Children's Book Writers and Illustrators, Authors Guild, PEN New England (member of Children's Book Caucus), New Hampshire Art Association.

Awards, Honors

First-place winner, *American Health* magazine short-story contest, 1988; fellow in residence, Millay Colony for the Arts, 1990; Best Books for Children citation

Pat Lowery Collins (Photograph by David Stotzer. Reproduced by permission.)

(preschool to grade six category), Bowker, 1990; individual artist's fellowship in fiction, New Hampshire State Council on the Arts, 1991; Children's Book of the Year citation, Child Study Children's Book Committee, 1992, for *I Am an Artist;* Book of the Year citation, Ohio Reading Circle, for *Don't Tease the Guppies;* writer's grant in poetry, Vermont Studio Center, 1997; professional development grant, Massachusetts Cultural Council, 1997; Books for the Teen Age selection, New York Public Library, and Children's Literature Choice citation, both 2000, both for *Signs and Wonders;* Best Children's Book of 2003, and Julia Ward Howe Award for Young Readers, 2004, both Boston Author's Club, both for *The Fattening Hut;* Boston Author's Club award finalist, and Cybils Award nomination, both 2009, and American Library Association Rainbow List selection, 2010, all for *Hidden Voices.*

Writings

FICTION; FOR CHILDREN

My Friend Andrew, illustrated by Howard Berelson, Prentice-Hall (Englewood Cliffs, NJ), 1981.

Tumble, Tumble, Tumbleweed, illustrated by Charles Robinson, Albert Whitman (Niles, IL), 1982.

Taking Care of Tucker, illustrated by Maxie Chambliss, Putnam (New York, NY), 1989.

Waiting for Baby Joe, illustrated by Joan Whinham Dunn, Albert Whitman (Niles, IL), 1990.

Tomorrow, Up and Away, illustrated by Lynn Munsinger, Houghton (Boston, MA), 1990.

I Am an Artist, illustrated by Robin Brickman, Millbrook Press (Brookfield, CT), 1992.

Don't Tease the Guppies, illustrated by Marylin Hafner, Putnam (New York, NY), 1994.

Come Out, Come Out!, illustrated by Dee Huxley, Philomel (New York, NY), 2004.

I Am a Dancer, illustrated by Mark Graham, Millbrook Press (Minneapolis), 2008.

FICTION; FOR YOUNG ADULTS

Signs and Wonders, Houghton (Boston, MA), 1999.

Just Imagine, Houghton (Boston, MA), 2001.

The Fattening Hut, Houghton (Boston, MA), 2003.

Hidden Voices: The Orphan Musicians of Venice, Candlewick Press (Somerville, MA), 2009.

Daughter of Winter, Candlewick Press (Somerville, MA), 2010.

OTHER

The River Shares Its Secret (textbook), Houghton (Boston, MA), 1981.

(Illustrator) Isabel Joshlin Glaser, compiler, *Dreams of Glory: Poems Starring Girls*, Atheneum (New York, NY), 1995.

The Quiet Woman Wakes Up Shouting (poetry chapbook), Folly Cove Books (Gloucester, MA), 1998.

(And illustrator) *Schooner* (nonfiction picture book), Commonwealth Editions (Beverly, MA), 2002.

Contributor to *Ten Times Round,* Ginn (Lexington, MA), 1987; *Mystery Sneaker,* Ginn, 1987; *The 1994 Writer's Handbook;* and *You and Me,* Orchard Books (New York, NY), 1997. Contributor to anthologies, including *Primavera: An Anthology of Writing by Women,* University of Chicago Press (Chicago, IL), 1980. Contributor to periodicals, including *The Writer, Northshore, Small Pond Review, WIND, California Quarterly, ArtsNorth, Yankee, Cricket, US1 Worksheets, My Own Magazine, Parting Gifts, Visions International* and *Ad Hoc Monadnock.*

Sidelights

An artist and author, Pat Lowery Collins has written many poems and books for children, but she may be best known for her dramatic novels for young adults. In teen-focused books such as *Signs and Wonders, Just Imagine,* and *The Fattening Hut,* articulate young women grapple with the transition to adulthood in the face of cultural challenges ranging from poverty to sexual oppression, while Collins captures the energy of close-knit families in picture books such as *Come Out, Come Out!*

Collins grew up in Los Angeles, California, where many of her neighbors included Hollywood film stars and producers. Her mother was a writer of radio plays, and Collins acted in radio plays while growing up. After graduating from Immaculate Heart High School, she attended the University of Southern California, where she earned a degree in English, then married and raised five children with her husband, Wallace Collins. Part-time studies in art culminated in her decision to write and illustrate children's books, a career she began after her children were all busy at school. On her home page, Collins explained that writing for children "was a natural outgrowth of writing poetry" and is "dependent on precise, visual imagery and careful word choices." Her stories are inspired by childhood memories, as well as by the events in her own family. "I began to write young adult novels because many of the main characters that presented themselves to my imagination were teenagers," she added. "Though none of my books appear on the surface to be alike in any way, they share a careful attention to detail and to the sound and rhythm of words and phrases. Each attempts to connect to the reader's own hopes and dreams. . . . My characters, in [both my] fictional picture books and novels, are struggling to succeed or stand out in some way . . . , often against what seem to be impossible odds."

Collins' first book for children, *My Friend Andrew,* is illustrated by Howard Berelson and was published in 1981. Other picture books followed in quick succession: *Taking Care of Tucker,* illustrated by Maxie Chambliss, *Tomorrow, Up and Away,* illustrated by Lynn Munsinger, and *Come Out, Come Out!,* illustrated by De Huxley among them. *I Am an Artist* and *I Am a Dancer* each focus on a child who is dedicated to a creative dream, and both pair a free-verse text with colorful illustrations. Praising *Come Out, Come Out!,* which focuses on a young girl's habit of hiding from her family whenever she is angry, Hazel Rochman wrote in *Booklist* that Collins captures a preschooler's "anger and the sweetness of being missed," and *School Library Journal* contributor Elaine Lesh Morgan described *I Am a Dancer* as "a lovely merging of art and poetry" that conveys "a delightful sense of joyful motion."

Published in 1999, *Signs and Wonders* was Collins' first young-adult novel. The story focuses on fourteen-year-old Taswell, who believes that she is pregnant with "the prophet for the New Millennium." The troubled girl was abandoned by her mother many years ago. Her father has remarried, and her grandmother, Mavis, decides to send Taswell to a convent school because the older woman is too busy to care for her granddaughter. The story is told through the letters Taswell writes to her grandmother, her father and stepmother, and to her guardian angel, Pim. "The epistolary form allows easy access to the protagonist's thoughts," commented a *Publishers Weekly* reviewer, "but not necessarily an easy identification with her." Eventually, the reader comes to realize that Taswell is not actually pregnant but has convinced herself that she is as a way of dealing with her feelings of abandonment. This "inevitable discovery that hers is a hysterical pregnancy . . . is well played," Ilene Cooper wrote in *Booklist.*

Just Imagine is set in a different time period—the Great Depression of the 1930s—but once again a young girl deals with abandonment through her imagination. Mary Francis's family has been split in two. Her mother and younger brother Leland live in Beverly Hills, California, where Leland is trying to become a child star, while Mary Francis and her father have moved with the girl's grandmother to New England. Despite Gram's efforts to take good care of Mary Francis, the girl is still traumatized by the constant fighting within the family. Mary Francis has an interest in spiritualism, and she attempts to "project" her spirit across the country in an attempt to be closer to her mother and to escape the tensions at home. "Juggled between these vastly different realities—her mother's seemingly glamorous life in Hollywood and her father's cold, hard struggle to make a living in Massachusetts—;Mary Francis emerges as an endearing and memorable character," Alison Follos wrote in her *School Library Journal* review of *Just Imagine.*

Winner of the Boston Author's Club's Julia Ward Howe Award, *The Fattening Hut* is a novel in verse in which narrator Helen is a member of a tribal culture which

Cover of Collins' award-winning historical novel **Hidden Voices,** *which takes readers back to the age of Vivaldi.* (Jacket photographs copyright © 2009 by Dougal Waters/Getty Images (girl); copyright © 2009 by Marisa Allegra Williams/iStockphoto (Venice); copyright © 2009 by Anika Salsera/iStockphoto (musical notes). Reproduced by permission of the publisher Candlewick Press, Inc., Cambridge, MA.)

practices female circumcision (female genital mutilation). Now considered old enough to marry, Helen is sent to the fattening hut to be prepared to become a bride. There, she and other young women will eat and eat until they are plump, beautiful, and ready for their arranged marriages. But before they can be married, they must pass through the cutting ceremony. Helen does not know exactly what the cutting ritual entails, but she fears it. Helen is unusually bright and educated for a girl in her culture; her Aunt Margaret was taught to read by the British colonizers of their island, and she passed the skill down to her niece. The woman also encourages the girl in her rebellion, even helping her to escape from the fattening hut. "This is a tough book that expects a lot from its readers," Roxanne Burg commented in *School Library Journal*. However, the process of female circumcision is presented "carefully, with the meaning clear enough but events not graphically depicted—so middle school readers would be able to handle it," Claire Rosser wrote in *Kliatt*.

In writing *Hidden Voices: The Orphan Musicians of Venice,* Collins researched eighteenth-century composer Antonio Vivaldi, even traveling to Venice, Italy, to visit the site of what was once the Ospedale della Pietá, an orphanage for girls exhibiting musical talent and the place where Vivaldi taught music while also creating many of his musical works. Described by *School Library Journal* Renee Steinberg as an "engrossing story," *Hidden Voices* follows talented vocalist Luisa, serious Anetta, and romantic Rosalba, three orphaned teen who live at the Ospedale della Pietá. Destined for life in the Roman Catholic Church, the musically gifted young women long for something more, and their stories are told in alternating narratives that weave together to form what Steinberg described as "a rich story of friendship and self-realization." Noting that the contrasting personalities of the three narrators make *Hidden Voices* "engrossing," a *Kirkus Reviews* writer added that Collins' "fatherly" characterization of the talented Vivaldi "binds the girls and the story together." In *Booklist* Carolyn Phelan had strong praise for the historical novel, writing that, "with its unique setting, vivid musical themes, and sharply realized characters," *Hidden Voices* "is well worth reading." Claire E. Gross found Collins' story to be "languid" and "sprawling," but added in *Horn Book* that the author captures the "subtle psychological damages" of the school's institutionalized setting in her "well-researched evocation of a vibrant period of musical history."

Collins once commented: "The major link between my painting and writing is my abiding interest in people—how they think, what they feel, their expressions, the things that touch their lives—which I may try to capture at one time with words and at another with paint, pencil, or pastel.

"Coming from a family of writers, I always understood that reading is an integral part of learning to be a writer and that the great writers of the past and present are the best teachers of how to use words well and how to craft compelling stories."

Biographical and Critical Sources

BOOKS

Collins, Pat Lowery, *Signs and Wonders,* Houghton (Boston, MA), 1999.

PERIODICALS

Booklist, October 15, 1992, Sheilamae O'Hara, review of *I Am an Artist,* p. 433; June 1, 1994, Kathryn Broderick, review of *Don't Tease the Guppies,* p. 1836; October 1, 1999, Ilene Cooper, review of *Signs and Wonders,* p. 370; April 1, 2001, Karen Simonetti, review of *Just Imagine,* p. 1481; November 1, 2003, Gillian Engberg, review of *The Fattening Hut,* p. 490; February 1, 2005, Hazel Rochman, review of *Come Out, Come Out!,* p. 964; June 1, 2008, Gillian Engberg, review of *I Am a Dancer,* p. 84; April 15, 2009, Carolyn Phelan, review of *Hidden Voices: The Orphan Musicians of Venice,* p. 49.

Horn Book, November-December, 1990, Martha V. Parravano, review of *Waiting for Baby Joe,* pp. 738-739; January, 2000, review of *Signs and Wonders,* p. 74; July-August, 2009, Claire E. Gross, review of *Hidden Voices,* p. 419.

Kirkus Reviews, June 15, 2002, review of *Schooner,* p. 878; September 1, 2003, review of *The Fattening Hut,* p. 1121; April 1, 2009, review of *Hidden Voices.*

Kliatt, September, 2003, Claire Rosser, review of *The Fattening Hut,* pp. 6-7.

Publishers Weekly, November 8, 1999, review of *Signs and Wonders,* p. 68; October 20, 2003, review of *The Fattening Hut,* pp. 55-56.

School Library Journal, April, 1981, Nancy Palmer, review of *My Friend Andrew,* p. 110; March, 1983, A.S.T. Blackburn, review of *Tumble, Tumble, Tumbleweed,* p. 160; March, 1989, Ellen Dibner, review of *Taking Care of Tucker,* p. 156; December, 1992, Alexandra Marris, review of *I Am an Artist,* p. 78; May, 1994, John Sigwald, review of *Don't Tease the Guppies,* p. 90; December, 1995, Marjorie Lewis, review of *Dreams of Glory: Poems Starring Girls,* p. 116; October, 1999, Joel Shoemaker, review of *Signs and Wonders,* p. 148; May, 2001, Alison Follos, review of *Just Imagine,* p. 148; November, 2003, Roxanne Burg, review of *The Fattening Hut,* p. 134; April, 2005, Martha Topol, review of *Come Out, Come Out!,* p. 96; June, 2008, Elaine Lesh Morgan, review of *I Am a Dancer,* p. 120; May, 2009, Renee Steinberg, review of *Hidden Voices,* p. 102.

ONLINE

Houghton Mifflin Web site, http://www.houghtonmifflin. com/ (July 1, 2010), "Pat Lowery Collins."

Pat Lowery Collins Home Page, http://www.patlowerycollins.com (June 1, 2010).

*   *   *

CZEKAJ, Jef 1969-

Personal

Surname pronounced "Check-eye"; born 1969. *Education:* Attended college. *Hobbies and other interests:* Indie rock music.

Addresses

Home—Somerville, MA.

Career

Illustrator and author of comics and children's books. Also works as a disc jockey.

Awards, Honors

Xeric Foundation grant, 2003.

Writings

SELF-ILLUSTRATED

Grampa and Julie: Shark Hunters (originally published in *Nickelodeon Magazine*), Top Shelf Productions (Marietta, GA), 2004.
Hip and Hop, Don't Stop, Disney/Hyperion (New York, NY), 2010.
Cat Secrets, Balzer & Bray (New York, NY), 2011.

Creator of mini-comic "R2-D2 Is an Indie Rocker" (renamed "Hypertruck"). Contributor to comic-book series, including "Bizzarro" and "Coober Skeber 2."

ILLUSTRATOR

Mary K. Corcoran, *The Quest to Digest,* Charlesbridge (Watertown, MA), 2006.
Jacqueline Jules, *Unite or Die: How Thirteen States Became a Nation,* Charlesbridge (Watertown, MA), 2009.
Mary K. Corcoran, *The Circulatory Story,* Charlesbridge (Watertown, MA), 2010.

First published in* Nickelodeon *magazine, Jef Czekaj's "Grampa and Julie: Shark Hunters" comic series was collected in book form in 2004. (Czekaj Press, 2004. Copyright © 1999, 2000, 2001, 2002, 2003, 2004 by Jef Czekaj. Reproduced by permission.)

Sidelights

While his career has evolved into illustrating children's books, Jef Czekaj got his start writing "indie zine" comics such as "R2D2 Is an Indie Rocker" in the mid-1990s. He first won over younger fans as the creator of the "Grampa and Julie: Shark Hunters" comic strip, which ran in *Nickelodeon Magazine* for over a decade. Czekaj's first published book, a collection of the first three years of that popular strip, has been followed by several illustration projects as well as by the original self-illustrated picture books *Hip and Hop, Don't Stop* and *Cat Secrets.*

Czekaj started creating comics in grade school, and his parody strip "Stupidman" was an outgrowth of his love of the *Mad Magazine* style of humor. From there, he turned to online "zines", telling *Reglar Wiglar* online interviewer Chris Auman: "I had seen zines, but had no idea that other people were doing comics in zine form. It was awesome to find out that other people were doing the same thing as me. When I moved to Boston . . . , I was happy to discover there was a vibrant mini-comics scene. That definitely inspired me." Czekaj channeled his passion for indie rock music through his simple line art, leading to "R2D2 Is an Indie Rocker," and eventually to "Gramps and Julie: Shark Hunters."

In *Grampa and Julie: Shark Hunters* Gramps is a world-famous scientist and third-grader Julie is his grand-daughter. Their search for Stephen, the world's largest shark, spans the world—from the ocean floor to outer space—and yields lots of humorous adventures, mention of underpants, and friendships with characters such as D.J. Chicken, ocean monkeys, and the alien residents of Planet Purple. Reviewing the collection for *Kliatt,* George Galuschak predicted the book's popularity among young readers, counseling that the book "contains lots of action and bad jokes, so readers won't be bored." "Czekaj demonstrates a wonderful sense of the absurd" in chronicling Grampa and Julie's "hilarious" exploits, noted Tina Coleman in *Booklist,* and "the adventures [in the graphic novel] are never truly scary."

According to a *Publishers Weekly* critic, *Grampa and Julie: Shark Hunters* is a "charming children's comic [that] overflows with humor, adventure and whimsy."

Czekaj's illustration projects include two biology-based picture books by Mary K. Corcoran: *The Quest to Digest* and *The Circulatory Story,* as well as Jacqueline Jules' quirky history book *Unite or Die: How Thirteen States Became a Nation.* Reviewing *The Quest to Digest* in *School Library Journal,* JoAnn Jonas cited Czekaj's "abundant, humorous cartoons," which capture the science behind "belching, passing gas, and diarrhea." In the "colorful comic-book illustrations" he creates for *Unite or Die* the artist also chronicles the founding of the United States, presenting the exploits of the likes of George Washington and Ben Franklin in "vividly-colored spreads [that] will hold the interest of even middle school students," according to Nancy Baumann, reviewing in the same periodical.

Biographical and Critical Sources

PERIODICALS

Booklist, November 1, 2004, Tina Coleman, review of *Grampa and Julie: Shark Hunters,* p. 478.

Kliatt, May, 2005, George Galuschak, review of *Grampa and Julie,* p. 37.

Publishers Weekly, September 20, 2004, review of *Grampa and Julie,* p. 48.

School Library Journal, September, 2006, JoAnn Jonas, review of *The Quest to Digest,* p. 190; April, 2009, Nancy Baumann, review of *Unite or Die: How Thirteen States Became a Nation,* p. 149.

ONLINE

Jef Czekaj Home Page, http://www.czekaj.com (May 31, 2010).

Jef Czekaj Web log, http://blog.czekaj.com (June 10, 2010).

Newsarama Web site, http://forum.newsarama.com/ (October 6, 2004), Matt Brady, interview with Czekaj.

Reglar Wiglar Web site, http://reglarwiglar.com/ (June 10, 2010), Chris Auman, interview with Czekaj.*

D

DADEY, Debbie 1959-

Personal

Last name is pronounced "Day-dee"; born May 18, 1959, in Morganfield, KY; daughter of Voline (a model maker) and Rebecca (a teacher) Gibson; married Eric Dadey (a chemist), June 11, 1981; children: Nathan, Becky, Alex. *Education:* Western Kentucky University, B.S., M.S.L.S. *Politics:* Democrat. *Religion:* Roman Catholic. *Hobbies and other interests:* Hiking, biking, making crafts, scrapbooking, playing with her children.

Addresses

Home—Furlong, PA.

Career

Author and educator. St. Romuald Elementary School, Hardinsburg, KY, teacher, 1981-83; St. Leo Elementary School, Versailles, KY, teacher, 1983-84; Sayre School, Lexington, KY, began as teacher, became librarian, 1986-90; Tates Creek Elementary School, Lexington, librarian, 1990-92. Freelance writer, Argus Communications, 1989; instructor, University of Kentucky, 1990-92, and Southern Methodist University, 1995-97; writing consultant, Scott County Schools, 1991-92.

Member

International Reading Association (Bluegrass Chapter vice president), Society of Children's Book Writers and Illustrators, National Education Association, Kentucky Education Association, Fayette County Education Association.

Awards, Honors

(With Marcia Thornton Jones) Children's Choice selection, International Reading Association, and Children's Top 100 Books selection, National Education Association, both 1990, both for *Vampires Don't Wear Polka Dots;* (with Jones) Elba Award, 1996, for *Wizards Don't Need Computers;* Best Children's Books of the Year citation, Bank Street College, 2000, and master list inclusion, Kentucky Bluegrass Award, 2001-02, both for *Cherokee Sister;* (with Jones) Milner Award, 2002, for body of work.

Writings

FOR CHILDREN

Buffalo Bill and the Pony Express, illustrated by Mike Gordon, Disney Press (New York, NY), 1994.

My Mom the Frog, Scholastic (New York, NY), 1996.

Shooting Star: Annie Oakley, the Legend, illustrated by Scott Goto, Walker (New York, NY), 1997.

Bobby and the Great, Green Booger ("Bobby" series), illustrated by Mike Gordon, Willowisp Press (St. Petersburg, FL), 1997.

Bobby and the Big Blue Bulldog ("Bobby" series), illustrated by Mike Gordon, Willowisp Press (St. Petersburg, FL), 1998.

Will Rogers: Larger than Life, illustrated by Scott Goto, Walker (New York, NY), 1999.

Cherokee Sister, Delacorte (New York, NY), 2000.

King of the Kooties, illustrated by Kevin O'Malley, Walker (New York, NY), 2001.

Whistler's Hollow, Bloomsbury (New York, NY), 2002.

(With son, Nathan Dadey) *Slime Wars,* illustrated by Bill Basso, Scholastic (New York, NY), 2002.

Swamp Monster in Third Grade, illustrated by Margeaux Lucas, Scholastic (New York, NY), 2002.

(With Nathan Dadey) *Slime Time,* illustrated by Bill Basso, Scholastic (New York, NY), 2004.

Lizards in the Lunch Line, illustrated by Margeaux Lucas, Scholastic, Inc. (New York, NY), 2004.

The Worst Name in Third Grade, illustrated by Tamara Petrosino, Scholastic (New York, NY), 2005.

Great Green Gator Graduation, illustrated by Margeaux Lucas, Scholastic (New York, NY), 2006.

Contributing editor of *Kidstuff* magazine, and of *Writer's Digest,* 1998-2002. Contributor to *Kicks* magazine.

"MARTY" SERIES

Marty the Maniac, illustrated by Mel Crawford, Willowisp Press (St. Petersburg, FL), 1996.

Marty the Mud Wrestler, illustrated by Mel Crawford, Willowisp Press (St. Petersburg, FL), 1997.

Marty the Millionaire, illustrated by Mel Crawford, Willowisp Press (St. Petersburg, FL), 1997.

"ADVENTURES OF THE BAILEY SCHOOL KIDS" SERIES; WITH MARCIA THORNTON JONES

Vampires Don't Wear Polka Dots, illustrated by John Steven Gurney, Scholastic (New York, NY), 1990.

Werewolves Don't Go to Summer Camp, illustrated by John Steven Gurney, Scholastic (New York, NY), 1991.

Santa Claus Doesn't Mop Floors, illustrated by John Steven Gurney, Scholastic (New York, NY), 1991.

Leprechauns Don't Play Basketball, illustrated by John Steven Gurney, Scholastic (New York, NY), 1992.

Ghosts Don't Eat Potato Chips, illustrated by John Steven Gurney, Scholastic (New York, NY), 1992.

Aliens Don't Wear Braces, illustrated by John Steven Gurney, Scholastic (New York, NY), 1993.

Frankenstein Doesn't Plant Petunias, illustrated by John Steven Gurney, Scholastic (New York, NY), 1993.

Genies Don't Ride Bicycles, illustrated by John Steven Gurney, Scholastic (New York, NY), 1993.

Pirates Don't Wear Pink Sunglasses, illustrated by John Steven Gurney, Scholastic (New York, NY), 1993.

Witches Don't Do Back Flips, illustrated by John Steven Gurney, Scholastic (New York, NY), 1994.

Skeletons Don't Play Tubas, illustrated by John Steven Gurney, Scholastic (New York, NY), 1994.

Cupids Don't Flip Hamburgers, illustrated by John Steven Gurney, Scholastic (New York, NY), 1995.

Gremlins Don't Chew Bubble Gum, illustrated by John Steven Gurney, Scholastic (New York, NY), 1995.

Monsters Don't SCUBA Dive, illustrated by John Steven Gurney, Scholastic (New York, NY), 1995.

Zombies Don't Play Soccer, illustrated by John Steven Gurney, Scholastic (New York, NY), 1995.

Dracula Doesn't Drink Lemonade, illustrated by John Steven Gurney, Scholastic (New York, NY), 1995.

Elves Don't Wear Hard Hats, illustrated by John Steven Gurney, Scholastic (New York, NY), 1995.

Martians Don't Take Temperatures, illustrated by John Steven Gurney, Scholastic (New York, NY), 1995.

Gargoyles Don't Drive Buses, illustrated by John Steven Gurney, Scholastic (New York, NY), 1996.

Wizards Don't Need Computers, illustrated by John Steven Gurney, Scholastic (New York, NY), 1996.

Mummies Don't Coach Softball, illustrated by John Steven Gurney, Scholastic (New York, NY), 1996.

Cyclops Doesn't Roller Skate, illustrated by John Steven Gurney, Scholastic (New York, NY), 1996.

Angels Don't Know Karate, illustrated by John Steven Gurney, Scholastic (New York, NY), 1996.

Dragons Don't Cook Pizza, illustrated by John Steven Gurney, Scholastic (New York, NY), 1997.

Bigfoot Doesn't Square Dance, illustrated by John Steven Gurney, Scholastic (New York, NY), 1997.

Mermaids Don't Run Track, illustrated by John Steven Gurney, Scholastic (New York, NY), 1997.

Bogeymen Don't Play Football, illustrated by John Steven Gurney, Scholastic (New York, NY), 1997.

Unicorns Don't Give Sleigh Rides, illustrated by John Steven Gurney, Scholastic (New York, NY), 1997.

Knights Don't Teach Piano, illustrated by John Steven Gurney, Scholastic (New York, NY), 1998.

Hercules Doesn't Pull Teeth, illustrated by John Steven Gurney, Scholastic (New York, NY), 1998.

Ghouls Don't Scoop Ice Cream, illustrated by John Steven Gurney, Scholastic (New York, NY), 1998.

Phantoms Don't Drive Sports Cars, illustrated by John Steven Gurney, Scholastic (New York, NY), 1998.

Giants Don't Go Snowboarding, illustrated by John Steven Gurney, Scholastic (New York, NY), 1998.

Frankenstein Doesn't Slam Hockey Pucks, illustrated by John Steven Gurney, Scholastic (New York, NY), 1998.

Trolls Don't Ride Roller Coasters, illustrated by John Steven Gurney, Scholastic (New York, NY), 1999.

Wolfmen Don't Hula Dance, illustrated by John Steven Gurney, Scholastic (New York, NY), 1999.

Goblins Don't Play Video Games, illustrated by John Steven Gurney, Scholastic (New York, NY), 1999.

Dracula Doesn't Rock and Roll, illustrated by John Steven Gurney, Scholastic (New York, NY), 1999.

Ninjas Don't Bake Pumpkin Pies, illustrated by John Steven Gurney, Scholastic (New York, NY), 1999.

Sea Monsters Don't Ride Motorcycles, illustrated by John Steven Gurney, Scholastic (New York, NY), 1999.

The Bride of Frankenstein Doesn't Bake Cookies, illustrated by John Steven Gurney, Scholastic (New York, NY), 2000.

Robots Don't Catch Chicken Pox, illustrated by John Steven Gurney, Scholastic (New York, NY), 2000.

Vikings Don't Wear Wrestling Belts, illustrated by John Steven Gurney, Scholastic (New York, NY), 2000.

Ghosts Don't Rope Wild Horses, illustrated by John Steven Gurney, Scholastic (New York, NY), 2000.

Wizards Don't Wear Graduation Gowns, illustrated by John Steven Gurney, Scholastic (New York, NY), 2000.

Sea Serpents Don't Juggle Water Balloons, illustrated by John Steven Gurney, Scholastic (New York, NY), 2000.

Swamp Monsters Don't Chase Wild Turkeys, illustrated by John Steven Gurney, Scholastic (New York, NY), 2001.

Aliens Don't Carve Jack-o-Lanterns, illustrated by John Steven Gurney, Scholastic (New York, NY), 2001.

Mrs. Claus Doesn't Climb Telephone Poles, illustrated by John Steven Gurney, Scholastic (New York, NY), 2001.

Leprechauns Don't Play Fetch, illustrated by John Steven Gurney, Scholastic (New York, NY), 2002.

Ogres Don't Hunt Easter Eggs, illustrated by John Steven Gurney, Scholastic (New York, NY), 2002.

Wizards Don't Wear Graduation Gowns, illustrated by John Steven Gurney, Scholastic (New York, NY), 2002

Dracula Doesn't Play Kickball, illustrated by John Steven Gurney, Scholastic (New York, NY), 2004.

Werewolves Don't Run for President, illustrated by John Steven Gurney, Scholastic (New York, NY), 2004.

The Abominable Snowman Doesn't Roast Marshmallows, illustrated by John Steven Gurney, Scholastic (New York, NY), 2005.

Dragons Don't Throw Snowballs, illustrated by John Steven Gurney, Scholastic (New York, NY), 2006.

"BAILEY SCHOOL KIDS JUNIOR CHAPTER-BOOK SERIES; WITH MARCIA THORNTON JONES

Ghosts Do Splash in Puddles, illustrated by Joëlle Dreidemy, Scholastic (New York, NY), 2006.

Reindeer Do Wear Striped Underwear, illustrated by Joëlle Dreidemy, Scholastic (New York, NY), 2006.

Cupid Does Eat Chocolate-covered Snails, illustrated by Joëlle Dreidemy, Scholastic (New York, NY), 2007.

Dragons Do Eat Homework, illustrated by Joëlle Dreidemy, Scholastic (New York, NY), 2007.

Pirates Do Ride Scooters, illustrated by Joëlle Dreidemy, Scholastic (New York, NY), 2007.

Wizards Do Roast Turkeys, illustrated by Joëlle Dreidemy, Scholastic (New York, NY), 2007.

Vampires Do Hunt Marshmallow Bunnies, illustrated by Joëlle Dreidemy, Scholastic (New York, NY), 2008.

"BAILEY SCHOOL KIDS SUPER SPECIALS" SERIES; WITH MARCIA THORNTON JONES

Mrs. Jeepers Is Missing, illustrated by John Steven Gurney, Scholastic (New York, NY), 1996.

Mrs. Jeepers' Batty Vacation, illustrated by John Steven Gurney, Scholastic (New York, NY), 1997.

Mrs. Jeepers' Secret Cave, illustrated by John Steven Gurney, Scholastic (New York, NY), 1998.

Mrs. Jeepers in Outer Space, illustrated by John Steven Gurney, Scholastic (New York, NY), 1999.

Mrs. Jeepers' Monster Class Trip, illustrated by John Steven Gurney, Scholastic (New York, NY), 2001.

Mrs. Jeepers on Vampire Island, illustrated by John Steven Gurney, Scholastic (New York, NY), 2001.

Mrs. Jeepers' Scariest Halloween Ever, illustrated by John Steven Gurney, Scholastic (New York, NY), 2005.

Mrs. Jeeper's Creepy Christmas, illustrated by John Steven Gurney, Scholastic (New York, NY), 2007.

"BAILEY CITY MONSTERS" SERIES; WITH MARCIA THORNTON JONES

The Monsters Next Door, illustrated by John Steven Gurney, Scholastic (New York, NY), 1998.

Howling at the Hauntlys', illustrated by John Steven Gurney, Scholastic (New York, NY), 1998.

Vampire Trouble, illustrated by John Steven Gurney, Scholastic (New York, NY), 1998.

Kilmer's Pet Monster, illustrated by John Steven Gurney, Scholastic (New York, NY), 1999.

Double Trouble Monsters, illustrated by John Steven Gurney, Scholastic (New York, NY), 1999.

Spooky Spells, illustrated by John Steven Gurney, Scholastic (New York, NY), 1999.

Vampire Baby, illustrated by John Steven Gurney, Scholastic (New York, NY), 1999.

Snow Monster Mystery, illustrated by John Steven Gurney, Scholastic (New York, NY), 1999.

The Hauntlys' Hairy Surprise, illustrated by John Steven Gurney, Scholastic (New York, NY), 1999.

Happy Boo Day, illustrated by John Steven Gurney, Scholastic (New York, NY), 2000.

"TRIPLET TROUBLE" SERIES; WITH MARCIA THORNTON JONES

Triplet Trouble and the Talent Show Mess, illustrated by John Speirs, Scholastic (New York, NY), 1995.

Triplet Trouble and the Runaway Reindeer, illustrated by John Speirs, Scholastic (New York, NY), 1995.

Triplet Trouble and the Red Heart Race, illustrated by John Speirs, Scholastic (New York, NY), 1996.

Triplet Trouble and the Field Day Disaster, illustrated by John Speirs, Scholastic (New York, NY), 1996.

Triplet Trouble and the Cookie Contest, illustrated by John Speirs, Scholastic (New York, NY), 1996.

Triplet Trouble and the Pizza Party, illustrated by John Speirs, Scholastic (New York, NY), 1996.

Triplet Trouble and the Class Trip, illustrated by John Speirs, Scholastic (New York, NY), 1997.

Triplet Trouble and the Bicycle Race, illustrated by John Speirs, Scholastic (New York, NY), 1997.

"BARKLEY'S SCHOOL FOR DOGS" SERIES; WITH MARCIA THORNTON JONES

Playground Bully, illustrated by Amy Wummer, Volo (New York, NY), 2001.

Puppy Trouble, illustrated by Amy Wummer, Volo (New York, NY), 2001.

Top Dog, illustrated by Amy Wummer, Volo (New York, NY), 2001.

Ghost Dog, illustrated by Amy Wummer, Volo (New York, NY), 2001.

Snow Day, illustrated by Amy Wummer, Volo (New York, NY), 2001.

Sticks and Stones and Doggie Bones, illustrated by Amy Wummer, Volo (New York, NY), 2002.

Buried Treasure, illustrated by Amy Wummer, Volo (New York, NY), 2002.

Blue Ribbon Blues, illustrated by Amy Wummer, Volo (New York, NY), 2002.

Santa Dog, illustrated by Amy Wummer, Volo (New York, NY), 2002.

Tattle Tails, illustrated by Amy Wummer, Volo (New York, NY), 2002.

Puppy Love, illustrated by Amy Wummer, Volo (New York, NY), 2002.

Puppies on Parade, illustrated by Amy Wummer, Volo (New York, NY), 2003.

"GHOSTVILLE ELEMENTARY" SERIES; WITH MARCIA THORNTON JONES

Ghost Class, illustrated by Jeremy Tugeau, Scholastic (New York, NY), 2002.
Ghost Game, illustrated by Jeremy Tugeau, Scholastic (New York, NY), 2003.
New Ghoul in School, illustrated by Jeremy Tugeau, Scholastic (New York, NY), 2003.
Happy Haunting, illustrated by Jeremy Tugeau, Scholastic (New York, NY), 2003.
Stage Fright, illustrated by Jeremy Tugeau, Scholastic (New York, NY), 2004.
Happy Boo-Day to You!, illustrated by Jeremy Tugeau, Scholastic (New York, NY), 2004.
Ghosts Be Gone!, illustrated by Guy Francis, Scholastic (New York, NY), 2004.
Beware of the Blabbermouth!, illustrated by Guy Francis, Scholastic (New York, NY), 2004.
Class Trip to the Haunted House, illustrated by Guy Francis, Scholastic (New York, NY), 2005.
Frights! Camera! Action!, illustrated by Guy Francis, Scholastic (New York, NY), 2005.
The Treasure Haunt, illustrated by Guy Francis, Scholastic (New York, NY), 2005.
Frighting like Cats and Dogs, illustrated by Guy Francis, Scholastic (New York, NY), 2006.
Guys and Ghouls, illustrated by Guy Francis, Scholastic (New York, NY), 2006.
No Haunting Zone!, illustrated by Guy Francis, Scholastic (New York, NY), 2007.
Red, White, and Boo!, illustrated by Guy Francis, Scholastic (New York, NY), 2007.

"KEYHOLDERS" SERIES; WITH MARCIA THORNTON JONES

This Side of Magic, illustrated by Adam Stower, Starscape (New York, NY), 2009.
The Other Side of Magic, illustrated by Adam Stower, Starscape (New York, NY), 2009.
Inside the Magic, illustrated by Adam Stower, Starscape (New York, NY), 2009.
The Wrong Side of Magic, illustrated by Adam Stower, Starscape (New York, NY), 2010.

OTHER

(With Marcia Thornton Jones) *Story Sparkers: A Creativity Guide for Children's Writers,* Writer's Digest Books (Cincinnati, OH), 2000.

Sidelights

Debbie Dadey has written scores of popular and compelling easy-reader novels for primary-grade and middle-grade readers that blend tongue-in-cheek horror with fast-paced storytelling. Working with Marcia Thornton Jones on such popular series as the "Adventures of the Bailey School Kids," the "Bailey City Monsters," "Barkley's School for Dogs," and the "Keyholders," Dadey has introduced legions of young readers to a jaunty world of gremlins, wizards, pirates, and aliens. Her solo efforts have also produced the "Marty" and "Bobby" books for younger readers, as well as humorous stand-alone titles such as *King of the Kooties* and *My Mom the Frog.* Other of Dadey's solo books, such as *Cherokee Sister* and *Whistler's Hollow,* are for somewhat older readers and of a more serious nature.

"I have always been a daydreamer, sometimes to my teachers' chagrin," Dadey once told *SATA.* "I think anyone who can dream can write. All it takes is the desire and the dream." She began achieving her dream, with the help of Marcia Thornton Jones, when Dadey was working as a librarian at an elementary school where Jones was a teacher. "It was one of those days when the kids didn't seem to be paying attention to anything we had to say," Dadey recalled. "We decided if we grew horns, sprouted fangs, had steam rolling out of our ears, and were fifteen feet tall the kids in our school would really pay attention to us. That's the reason we wrote *Vampires Don't Wear Polka Dots.* It's a story about a tough group of third graders who get an even tougher teacher [Mrs. Jeepers] . . . she might even be a monster or vampire!"

The success of their first book encouraged Dadey and Jones to continue collaborating, and their work was done largely during lunch in their school cafeteria. Memories of summer camp inspired the pair's next book, *Werewolves Don't Go to Summer Camp.* "We had been to short little camps as kids," Dadey explained, adding that the book expands on their rather ordinary experiences to focus on a week-long camp where the counselor is rumored to be a real werewolf.

Leprechauns Don't Play Basketball pits a vampire and a leprechaun against one another right in the middle of an elementary school. "It was interesting because of the research we did into leprechauns and vampires," Dadey and Jones once told *SATA.* "If we write about a certain creature, we always read as much as we can about it. We come up with some interesting tid-bits and try to include them in our stories." While writing *Ghosts Don't Eat Potato Chips,* the two authors "read so many ghost books we had to check under our beds before we went to sleep at night!"

In the forty-fourth book in the series, *Ghosts Don't Ride Wild Horses,* the kids from Bailey School are on a trip to a ghost town. The school outing turns dangerous when the ghost of a cowboy picks on redheaded Eddie, whom the ghost sees as the incarnation of Blackheart Eddie who stole his gold. Can the school kids, including Liza, Melody, and Howie, save their friend? In *Swamp Monsters Don't Chase Wild Turkeys* Melody, Liza, Eddie, and Howie once again find something strange going on at their school. The ecology project coordinator, claiming to be from Australia, actually turns out to be a swamp monster, and the kids at Bailey School are the only thing that can save the town from his evil intentions.

Debbie Dadey and Marcia Thornton Jones team up on **Vampires Don't Wear Polka Dots,** *an easy reader illustrated by John Steven Gurney.*
(Illustration copyright 2007 by Scholastic, Inc. Reproduced by permission of Scholastic, Inc.)

The "Adventures of the Bailey School Kids" proved so popular that Dadey and Jones decided to branch out into companion series. In the "Bailey City Monsters" books Ben and his sister are sure that their new neighbors, the Hauntlys, are actually as creepy as their name implies. The siblings strive, throughout several volumes, to prove that the Hauntlys are in fact monsters and that their hotel, the Hauntly Manor Inn, is a vacation spot for monsters. In the "Ghostville Elementary" series, which includes *Ghost Class, Happy Haunting,* and *Ghosts Be Gone,* a group of young students bravely confronts all manner of school spooks, from ghosts lurking in the school's basement to transparent teachers wandering the elementary school's hallowed halls.

Another series, "Triplet Trouble," is geared for slightly younger readers and features the mischievous Tucker triplets while avoiding the monsters that appear in the "Bailey School Kids" books. Dadey and Jones have also teamed up to write the "Barkley's School for Dogs" books as well as enjoying a change of pace with their "Keyholder" fantasy series. *This Side of Magic,* the first book in the "Keyholder" saga, focuses on fifth graders Penny, Luke, and Natalie, who live in a small town that is surrounded by magical creatures that remain unseen. The town is protected by a magical wall of thorns that

has been crafted of ancient spells, and six "Keyholders" in every generation are entrusted with maintaining the wall. That task now falls to the three friends, who learn of the existence of unicorns, dragons, and talking rodents while also striving to keep the wall strong against the advances of the evil Queen of Boggarts. In *Kirkus Reviews* a writer remarked on the "bright humor" in *This Side of Magic,* and Carolyn Phelan predicted in *Booklist* that the "Keyholder" books "will find a ready audience" of fantasy fans.

Since Dadey has left teaching to write full time, she no longer collaborates with Jones over the lunch table; as they live in different states the authors instead use e-mail and fax. They take turns writing chapters of their fast-selling books, employing what they refer to as the "hot potato" method of writing. Beginning with research on various topics, they then move on to an outline, and then one collaborator begins writing a chapter, forwarding that portion to the other, who then takes the "hot potato" and continues the tale.

In addition to her collaborative efforts, Dadey has also carved out a successful writing career on her own, penning several novels and picture books. Her first solo effort, *Buffalo Bill and the Pony Express,* is a short fictional account of that legend of the Wild West and of the opening of travel and communication routes. Dadey continued to write about Western themes with her picture book *Shooting Star: Annie Oakley, the Legend,* a tall tale about the famous sharp-shooter. In this "spirited yarn," as a contributor for *Publishers Weekly* described the book, Oakley not only out-shoots the grand duke of Russia and shoots candles out with her bullets, but she also manages to shoot craters in the moon and blunt the points of celestial stars. Ilene Cooper noted in a *Booklist* review of *Shooting Star* that Dadey mixes fact and fantasy with a "sassy" tone, and *School Library Journal* critic Shirley Wilton described *Shooting Star* as a "great book for reading aloud or for introducing children to a colorful historical figure."

For *Will Rogers: Larger than Life* Dadey again teams up with the same artist who illustrated *Shooting Star,* Scott Goto, to present an account of the laconic lasso artist who became one of the most beloved humorists of his day. Dadey again blends fact and tall tale in her recounting of Rogers's life, spinning "historical straw into tall-tale gold for a memorable introduction to an American humorist," according to *Booklist* contributor John Peters. Dadey's account has Rogers roping a horse at five years of age and proceeding to plow three hundred acres with his feet, and when he lassos the Earth, the backlash sends him sailing to Mars.

Dadey has also crafted primary-and middle-grade novels that are full of the same sort of fun and irreverent humor that characterize her series work with Jones. Her books about Marty—*Marty the Maniac, Marty the Mud Wrestler,* and *Marty the Millionaire*—as well as her "Bobby" books—*Bobby and the Great, Green Booger*

and *Bobby and the Big Blue Bulldog*—are easy readers for primary grades, as is *My Mom the Frog*. In *My Mom the Frog* young Jason discovers a wart on his hand. His mother, being supportive, promises to buy some medicine for it, and meanwhile gives it a kiss to make it better. The next day, Jason discovers that his mom is missing. When his sister tells him about the old wives' tale that you will turn into a frog if you touch a wart, Jason is soon convinced that his mother has been turned into the frog that he finds on the kitchen floor next to his mother's purse.

King of the Kooties is a humorous tale about bullying, which is "a topic of concern to elementary school children," as Phelan noted in *Booklist*. Nate has a new friend, Donald, who has just become his neighbor and will be in his fourth-grade class this year. However, they will have to share their class with Louisa, a bully who loves to tease and ridicule. Her newest target, it seems, is Donald, whom she calls the Kootie King. The two friends try a number of defenses to ward off Louisa's attacks, including a bribe of cookies, but they finally decide that their best tactic would be to create a good offense. They decide to set up the Kingdom of the Kooties and to establish Louisa as its first princess. A contributor for *Kirkus Reviews* noted that this exploration of "one approach to the age-old problem of bullies" is "never didactic."

More serious in tone and geared for middle-grade readers are *Cherokee Sister* and *Whistler's Hollow*. The former title, set in 1838, is full of "vivid description . . . [which] transport readers back to the 1830s," as Sarah O'Neal wrote in *School Library Journal*. Twelve-year-old Allie's best friend is Leaf, a young Cherokee girl. One Sunday, Allie slips away from church and goes to visit Leaf, where, with her tanned skin and Leaf's buckskin dress, she blends in very well—so well, in fact, that the soldiers who have been sent to remove the Cherokee from their land mistake Allie for one and send her off to a relocation camp for the Trail of Tears. "*Cherokee Sister* took me eight years to write," Dadey told online interviewer Julia Durango in *By the Book*. "It was an education for me because I did a lot of research and rewrote the story so many times. Of course, in that same time period I also did five series."

Adapting a tale from her own grandmother, Dadey follows the trials of a young girl who becomes orphaned after World War I in *Whistler's Hollow*. When her mother dies, eleven-year-old Lillie Mae is sent to the Kentucky farm of a great uncle and aunt by another greedy aunt. These nurturing older relatives raised Lillie Mae's father, who is now missing in action. The young girl hopes against hope that her father will return to claim her, but meanwhile she finds that something is terribly wrong at the farm. There is a terrible smell emanating from the attic, and mysterious sounds come at night. Although her neighbor, Paul, knows the source of the smells and sounds—her great-uncle has a still set up in the attic—Paul convinces her that the house is haunted. To make Lillie Mae's life even more miserable, Paul turns the other children at school against her. While a reviewer for *Publishers Weekly* complained that Dadey's "heavy-handed revelations and forced dialogue exacerbate the feel of melodrama" in the novel, a contributor for *Kirkus Reviews* praised her ability to paint characters in a "few short strokes." Readers will have "no problem identifying with [Lillie Mae's] most universal desire . . . to be connected to people she can love and be loved in return," the critic added, while Alison Grant praised *Whistler's Hollow* in *School Library Journal* as "a quiet, lovely story about extended family, acceptance, and the power of secrets."

Responding to a question from Durango as to whether she might run out of ideas after so many books, Dadey replied, "I have lots of ideas, after all they are all around me." She further noted: "My problem is having enough time to write all the ideas that come to me."

Biographical and Critical Sources

PERIODICALS

Booklist, September 15, 1992, Sheilamae O'Hara, review of *Leprechauns Don't Play Basketball,* p. 148; March 15, 1997, Ilene Cooper, review of *Shooting Star: Annie Oakley, the Legend,* p. 1245; April 1, 1999, John Peters, review of *Will Rogers: Larger than Life,* p. 1419; September 15, 1999, Carolyn Phelan, review of *King of the Kooties,* p. 256; April 1, 2000, Susan Dove Lempke, review of *Cherokee Sister,* p. 1476.

Bulletin of the Center for Children's Books, June, 1997, Elizabeth Bush, review of *Shooting Star,* pp. 353-354; June 1, 2009, Carolyn Phelan, review of *This Side of Magic,* p. 57.

Kirkus Reviews, April 1, 1997, review of *Shooting Star,* p. 552; July 15, 1999, review of *King of the Kooties,* p. 1131; June 1, 2002, review of *Whistler's Hollow,* p. 803; April 1, 2009, review of *This Side of Magic.*

Publishers Weekly, March 24, 1997, review of *Shooting Star,* p. 83; October 4, 1999, review of *King of the Kooties,* p. 75; June 10, 2002, review of *Whistler's Hollow,* p. 61; May 4, 2009, review of *This Side of Magic,* p. 50.

School Library Journal, April, 1997, Shirley Wilton, review of *Shooting Star,* p. 122; September, 1999, Ruth Semrau, review of *Will Rogers,* p. 180; November, 1999, Anne Knickerbocker, review of *King of the Kooties,* p. 112; April, 2000, Sarah O'Neal, review of *Cherokee Sister,* p. 134; July, 2002, Alison Grant, review of *Whistler's Hollow,* p. 118.

ONLINE

By the Book Web site, http://www.geocities.com/julia durango/ (March 13, 2001), Julia Durango, "Debbie Dadey Does It All."

Debbie Dadey and Marcia Thornton Jones Home Page, http://www.baileykids.com (June 1, 2010).

Scholastic Web site, http://www.scholastic.com/ (April 9, 2002), "Debbie Dadey and Marcia Thornton Jones."*

* * *

DALY, James

Personal

Married; wife's name Laura; children: Samantha, Jackson, Charlotte. *Education:* Boston University, B.S. (journalism and economics; cum laude); New England School of Photography, degree; postgraduate study at Harvard University.

Addresses

Home—Alameda, CA.

Career

Educator, journalist, and author. *Wired* (magazine), features editor, c. mid-1990s; *Business 2.0* (magazine), founder, editor in chief, and editorial director, 1997-2001; *Red Herring* (Web site), editor in chief, 2004; *Edutopia* (magazine and Web site) editor, then editorial director; GreatSchools (nonprofit organization), educational director, beginning 2009; 2030 Media (content-creation firm), founder and owner.

Awards, Honors

Numerous awards for journalism.

Writings

(With Amy Zuckerman) *2030: A Day in the Life of Tomorrow's Kids,* illustrated by John Manders, Dutton Children's Books (New York, NY), 2009.

Contributor to periodicals, including *Forbes ASAP, ID, Los Angeles Times, Rolling Stone, San Francisco Chronicle,* and *Writers Digest.*

Sidelights

James Daly is a veteran journalist who specializes in the ways technology impacts both business and education. In addition to heading the editorial staff of several groundbreaking Web sites, he has also founded the successful magazine *Business 2.0* which received several journalism awards under Daly's editorial guidance. His work as editorial director of GreatSchools, a nonprofit organization focusing on expanding the possibilities of contemporary education, brought him into contact with fellow journalist Amy Zuckerman, and their joint interests in technology inspired their book *2030: A Day in the Life of Tomorrow's Kids.*

In *2030* Daly and Zuckerman team up with artist John Manders to inspire young readers with a child's-eye view of the world they will live in as adults. Based on a

wealth of documented articles, reports, interviews, and other research about advances in science and technology, the book pairs a simple text with cartoon illustrations that reveal a future where skateboards hover above the ground, robots clean houses, and wristwatches transmit health data to doctors. *2030* will be a boon to "any librarian who's been stumped by a child's request for a book about . . . 'the real future,'" predicted Carolyn Phelan in her review for *Booklist,* while Steven Engelfried wrote in *School Library Journal* that the coauthors' "breezy narrative" teams with Manders' "fanciful cartoon drawings" to "show a lively and appealing [future] world." As a *Futurist* reviewer quipped of the world set forth in *2030,* while "school will still be in session, . . . most kids will be excited to go."

"Children are the people we create who in turn recreate us," Daly noted on the GreatSchools Web log. "Sometimes those changes are very hard [for adults] to adapt to, but all reveal great things about yourself. Those changes can be subtle, but they are always profound. So take a deep breath and enjoy the ride. Before you know it, their childhood will be gone."

Biographical and Critical Sources

PERIODICALS

Booklist, January 1, 2009, Carolyn Phelan, review of *2030: A Day in the Life of Tomorrow's Kids,* p. 86.
Futurist, January-February, 2010, review of *2030,* p. 57.
Kirkus Reviews, February 1, 2009, review of *2030.*
School Library Journal, March, 2009, Steven Engelfried, review of *2030,* p. 139.

James Daly teams up with fellow journalist Amy Zuckerman and artist John Manders to create the forward-looking picture book 2030. (Illustration copyright © 2009 by John Manders. Reproduced by permission of Dutton Children's Books, a division of Penguin Putnam Books for Young Readers.)

ONLINE

GreatSchools Web log, http://blogs.greatschools.org/ (June 1, 2010), "Jim Daly."
Visions for Tomorrow Web site, http://visionsfortomorrow. net/ (June 10, 2010), "James Daly."*

*   *   *

DILLARD, Sarah 1961-

Personal

Born 1961. *Education:* Attended Wheaton College; Rhode Island School of Design, M.F.A. *Hobbies and other interests:* Skiing, snowshoeing.

Addresses

Office—P.O. Box 453, Waitsfield, VT 05673. *Agent*—Lori Nowicki, Painted Words, 310 W. 97th St., Ste. 24, New York, NY 10025; loripainted-words.com. *E-mail*—sarah@sarahdillard.com.

Career

Author and illustrator.

Writings

SELF-ILLUSTRATED

Follow the Bunny, Price Stern Sloan (New York, NY), 2006.
Perfectly Arugula, Sterling (New York, NY), 2009.

ILLUSTRATOR

Patricia Hruby Powell, *Blossom Tales: Flower Stories of Many Folk,* Moon Mountain Publishing (North Kingstown, RI), 2002.
Beverly Larson, *Touch and Feel Bible Stories,* Kregel Kidzone (Grand Rapids, MI), 2002.
Allia Zobel-Nolan, *Touch and Feel Baby Jesus Is Born,* Kregel Kidzone (Grand Rapids, MI), 2003.
Treesha Runnells, *Five Wishing Stars,* Intervisual Books (Atlanta, GA), 2003.
Treesha Runnells, *Ten Wishing Stars,* Intervisual Books (Atlanta, GA), 2003.
Annie Auerbach, *Traveling in Twos: The Journey to Noah's Ark,* Piggy Toes Press (Atlanta, GA), 2003.
Mindy MacDonald, *Noah's Crew Came 2 by 2,* Multnomah Publishers (Sisters, OR), 2004.
Wendy Wax, *What Do You Say?: Please and Thank You!,* Kindermusik International (Greensboro, NC), 2005.
Sudipta Bardhan-Quallen, *Tightrope Poppy the High-wire Pig,* Sterling Publishing (New York, NY), 2006.
Follow the Bunny, Price Stern Sloan (New York, NY), 2006.

Trisha Speed Shaskan, *If You Were a Divided-by Sign,* Picture Window Books (Minneapolis, MN), 2009.
Trisha Speed Shaskan, *If You Were a Times Sign,* Picture Window Books (Minneapolis, MN), 2009.
Marcie Aboff, *If You Were an Even Number,* Picture Window Books (Minneapolis, MN), 2009.
Marcie Aboff, *If You Were an Inch or a Centimeter,* Picture Window Books (Minneapolis, MN), 2009.
Marcie Aboff, *If You Were an Odd Number,* Picture Window Books (Minneapolis, MN), 2009.
Marcie Aboff, *If You Were a Set,* Picture Window Books (Minneapolis, MN), 2009.
Marcie Aboff, *If You Were a Polygon,* Picture Window Books (Minneapolis, MN), 2010.
Marcie Aboff, *If You Were a Triangle,* Picture Window Books (Minneapolis, MN), 2010.

Also illustrator of *Bear Paints,* Sandvik Innovations; *The Wheels on the Bus,* Reader's Digest Children's Books; and *Alphabet Song and Dance,* Educators Publishing Service.

Sidelights

A painter who works primarily in gouache and watercolor, Sarah Dillard has contributed illustrations to numerous picture books, including stories by Marcie Aboff, Wendy Wax, Patricia Hruby Powell, and Sudipta Bardhan-Quallen. Powell's *Blossom Tales: Flower Sto-*

Sarah Dillard treats young storybook audiences to a high-energy tale in her self-illustrated picture book **Perfectly Arugula.** (Sterling, 2009. Illustration © by Sarah Dillard. All rights reserved. Reproduced by permission.)

ries of Many Folk, one of Dillard's first illustration projects, contains fourteen short narratives from around the globe, including tales from Russia, Sicily, and Japan. "The illustrations are appealing," noted *School Library Journal* contributor Donna L. Scanlon, the critic also praising the "muted jewel tones" in Dillard's paintings. In *Tightrope Poppy the High-wire Pig,* a rhyming tale by Bardhan-Quallen, a young porker hopes to fulfill her dreams of leading an adventurous life by joining the circus. The "cheery illustrations" are a key component of this work, Catherine Threadgill observed in *School Library Journal.*

An uptight party host is the focus of *Perfectly Arugula,* a humorous work featuring an original story by Dillard. When Arugula the hedgehog decides to hold a tea party for her friends, including Basil the raccoon and Pistachio the beaver, she deliberately excludes Fidget, an energetic squirrel who does not share Arugula's sense of decorum. Once the soiree begins, however, Arugula becomes upset by her guests' minor mishaps, such as dropping crumbs on the floor, and her criticisms cast a pall over the proceedings until Fidget makes an unexpected appearance. According to a contributor in *Kirkus Reviews,* "Dillard's crisp illustrations . . . and the . . . design [of *Perfectly Arugula*] mimic 1950s styles with flair."

Biographical and Critical Sources

PERIODICALS

Booklist, April 1, 2002, GraceAnne A. DeCandido, review of *Blossom Tales: Flower Stories of Many Folk,* p. 1330.
Kirkus Reviews, February 1, 2009, review of *Perfectly Arugula.*
School Library Journal, July, 2002, Donna L. Scanlon, review of *Blossom Tales,* p. 110; March, 2006, Catherine Threadgill, review of *Tightrope Poppy the High-wire Pig,* p. 175.

ONLINE

Painted Words Web site, http://www.painted-words.com/ (May 20, 2010), "Sarah Dillard."
Sarah Dillard Home Page, http://www.sarahdillard.com (May 20, 2010).
Sarah Dillard Web log, http://www.sarahdillard.blogspot.com (May 20, 2010).

*   *   *

DIONNE, Erin

Personal

Married; husband a copywriter; children: one daughter. *Education:* B.A.; Emerson College, M.F.A. (creative writing), 1999. *Hobbies and other interests:* Vegetable gardening, Boston Red Sox.

Addresses

Home—Greater Boston, MA. *Agent*—The Cooke Agency, 278 Bloor St., Ste. 305, Toronto, Ontario M4W 3M4, Canada. *E-mail*—erin@erindionne.com; erinmdionne@yahoo.com.

Career

Novelist and educator. Montserrat College of Art, Beverly MA, assistant professor of English.

Member

Society of Children's Book Writers and Illustrators.

Awards, Honors

Susan P. Bloom Discovery Night Award, PEN/New England Children's Book Caucus, 2006, for *Models Don't Eat Chocolate Cookies.*

Writings

Models Don't Eat Chocolate Cookies, Dial Books for Young Readers (New York, NY), 2009.
The Total Tragedy of a Girl Named Hamlet, Dial Books for Young Readers (New York, NY), 2010.

Sidelights

Erin Dionne's middle-grade novel *Models Don't Eat Chocolate Cookies* was a short story before Dionne, a college English professor, decided to workshop the story at the Santa Barbara Writer's Conference. Although the story is fiction, its author does admit to some grounding in real life: when she was in seventh grade Dionne did have to wear a horrible peach bridesmaid's dress during her cousin's wedding, and then there was that day she was really sick during gym class. . . .

In *Models Don't Eat Chocolate Cookies* readers meet quick-witted and somewhat overweight eighth grader Celeste Harris. Propelled by the prodding of her well-meaning aunt Doreen, Celeste suddenly finds herself drawn into the competitive world of plus-size modeling when she is entered as a contestant in the Miss Husky Peach Modeling Challenge. While getting into a slightly more compact shape for the pageant takes up much of her time, the thirteen year old watches as her supposed best friend is lured into the clique of skinny and popular Lively Carson, Celeste's nemesis. Although Celeste at first intends to sabotage her efforts to get into shape for the modeling competition, she realizes that her get-fit plan is also building her confidence and self-esteem. Noting that *Models Don't Eat Chocolate Cookies* will appeal to "teens of all body types," *School Library Journal* contributor Miranda Doyle added that Dionne's "wry, funny tone makes this book a pleasurable read." In *Kirkus Reviews* a critic recommended the novel's

Cover of Erin Dionne's middle-grade novel Models Don't Eat Choco-late Cookies, *which focuses on a teen's effort to qualify for a size-plus modeling contest.* (Dial Books for Young Readers, 2009. Cover photo © by Bill Tru-ran/Alamy. Reproduced by permission of Dial Books for Young Readers, a division of Penguin Putnam Books for Young Readers.)

"engaging" discussion of beauty-pageant culture, and Carolyn Phelan remarked in *Booklist* that Celeste's "wry . . . narrative . . . provides convincing views of middle-school friendships, family dynamics, and . . . personal growth."

Another eighth grader is the star of *The Total Tragedy of a Girl Named Hamlet,* but for Hamlet Kennedy the problem is not her weight; it is her parents' obsession with all things Shakespeare. In addition to suffering a home life straight out of Elizabethan England, Hamlet must now endure the humiliation of having her super-bright seven-year-old sister, Desdemona, attend the same middle school. In a narrative that *School Library Journal* critic Caroline Tesauro dubbed "charming," Hamlet recounts her efforts to aid the disloyal Desde-mona and the pangs of first love while also exhibiting a growing confidence through her starring role in the school's production of Shakespeare's *A Midsummer Night's Dream. The Total Tragedy of a Girl Named Hamlet* is "an excellent choice for middle-school read-ers," concluded Tesauro, and a *Kirkus Reviews* writer

cited the young teen's "good-humored" perspective on life among of the novel's strengths. In Hamlet's "relat-able and engaging" voice, *The Total Tragedy of a Girl Named Hamlet* "will resonate with anyone who has been embarrassed by family or confused by boys," con-cluded a *Publishers Weekly* contributor.

Dionne's advice to budding writers? "Read. A lot," she recommended on her home page. "[Read] everything you can get your hands on. Read stuff you like, but if you find something you don't like, ask yourself 'why?' Reading and asking those questions teaches you what you like in writing and what you think makes a good story. Then, start writing! You can write stories about your favorite characters from books or TV shows . . . , or you can make up your own characters and worlds. But remember: writing takes patience, time, and lots of revision!"

Biographical and Critical Sources

PERIODICALS

Booklist, March 1, 2009, Carolyn Phelan, review of *Mod-els Don't Eat Chocolate Cookies,* p. 39; January 1, 2010, Heather Booth, review of *The Total Tragedy of a Girl Named Hamlet,* p. 84.
Kirkus Reviews, February 1, 2009, review of *Models Don't Eat Chocolate Cookies;* December 15, 2009, review of *The Total Tragedy of a Girl Named Hamlet.*
Publishers Weekly, January 25, 2010, review of *The Total Tragedy of a Girl Named Hamlet,* p. 119.
School Library Journal, April, 2009, Miranda Doyle, re-view of *Models Don't Eat Chocolate Cookies,* p. 132; February, 2010, Caroline Tesauro, review of *The Total Tragedy of a Girl Named Hamlet,* p. 108.

ONLINE

Cynsations Web site, http://cynthialeitichsmith.blogspot. com/ (May 14, 2009), Cynthia Leitich Smith, inter-view with Dionne.
Erin Dionne Home Page, http://www.erindionne.com (May 31, 2010).*

*   *   *

DOCAMPO, Valeria 1976-

Personal

Born 1976, in Buenos Aires, Argentina. *Education:* Uni-versity of Buenos Aires, degree (graphic design and vi-sual communication).

Addresses

Home—Buenos Aires, Argentina. *Agent*—Mela Bolinao, MB Artists, 775 6th Ave., Ste. No. 6, New York, NY 10001; mela@mbartists.com.

Career

Illustrator and educator. University of Buenos Aires, Buenos Aires, Argentina, former instructor in illustration.

Illustrator

Isabel F. Campoy and Alma Flor Ada, *Celebrate Kwanzaa with Boots and Her Kittens,* translated by Joe Hayes and Sharon Franco, Alfaguara/Santillana USA (Miami, FL), 2007.

Eric A. Kimmel, *The Three Little Tamales,* Marshall Cavendish (New York, NY), 2009.

Eric A. Kimmel, *Medio Pollito: A Spanish Tale,* Marshall Cavendish (New York, NY), 2010.

Sarah Lynn, *Tip-tap Pop,* Marshall Cavendish (New York, NY), 2010.

Biographical and Critical Sources

PERIODICALS

Booklist, March 15, 2009, Shauna Yusko, review of *The Three Little Tamales,* p. 68.

School Library Journal, June, 2009, Teri Markson, review of *The Three Little Tamales,* p. 92.

ONLINE

MB Artists Web site, http://www.mbartists.com/ (June 20, 2010), "Valeria DoCampo."*

*   *   *

DONOVAN, Gail 1962-

Personal

Born 1962, in CT; married; children: two daughters. *Education:* Sarah Lawrence College, B.A.; Brown University, M.A. (writing).

Addresses

Home—Portland, ME. *Agent*—Edite Kroll, ekroll@ maine.rr.com. *E-mail*—gdonovan@maine.rr.com.

Career

Author.

Awards, Honors

Best Books for Children designation, New York Public Library, 2009, for *In Memory of Gorfman T. Frog.*

Writings

(Adaptor) Hans de Beer, *Lars and Robby,* illustrated by John Huxtable, Sterling Juvenile (New York, NY), 2003.

(Adaptor with Susan Hill Long) Hans de Beer, *Lars Saves the Day,* illustrated by John Huxtable, Sterling Juvenile (New York, NY), 2004.

(Adaptor with Susan Hill Long) Hans de Beer, *Lars and the Lemmings,* illustrated by John Huxtable, Sterling Juvenile (New York, NY), 2004.

(Adaptor with Susan Hill Long) Hans de Beer, *Little Bear Lost,* illustrated by John Huxtable, Sterling Juvenile (New York, NY), 2004.

In Memory of Gorfman T. Frog, illustrated by Janet Pedersen, Dutton Children's Books (New York, NY), 2009.

Also author of *Sounds on the Go!* and *Sounds on the Farm,* both illustrated by Lauren Ovresat, published by Innovative Kids.

"RAINBOW FISH AND FRIENDS" SERIES; BASED ON THE STORIES BY MARCUS PFISTER

The Copycat Fish, illustrated by David Austin Clar Studio, Night Sky Books (New York, NY), 2001.

A Fishy Story, illustrated by David Austin Clar Studio, Night Sky Books (New York, NY), 2001.

Lost at Sea, illustrated by David Austin Clar Studio, Night Sky Books (New York, NY), 2001.

Ready, Set, Swim!, illustrated by David Austin Clar Studio, Night Sky Books (New York, NY), 2002.

S.O.S., Save Our Shortcut!, illustrated by David Austin Clar Studio, Night Sky Books (New York, NY), 2002.

Scaredy-cat Fish, illustrated by David Austin Clar Studio, Night Sky Books (New York, NY), 2002.

Star of the Sea, illustrated by David Austin Clar Studio, Night Sky Books (New York, NY), 2002.

Follow the Leader, illustrated by David Austin Clar Studio, Night Sky Books (New York, NY), 2003.

Surprise Party, illustrated by David Austin Clar Studio, Night Sky Books (New York, NY), 2003.

Sidelights

Gail Donovan is a Maine-based author who was inspired to begin writing for children while reading to her own two young daughters. Her first writing involved creating stories in the "Rainbow Fish and Friends" series, which is based on the popular characters created by German writer Marcus Pfister. In more recent years, Donovan has also worked with Susan Hill Long to adapt several stories by popular Dutch author Hans de Beer, among them *Lars and Robby, Lars and the Lemmings,* and *Little Bear Lost.* In 2009 she published her first original story, *In Memory of Gorfman T. Frog,* a humorous and sometimes poignant tale illustrated by Janet Pedersen.

A talkative, impatient, and self-centered boy named Joshua Tree Hewitt is the star of *In Memory of Gorfman T. Frog,* and in Donovan's story the boy's discovery of a misshapen frog triggers a range of emotions. After Joshua brings the five-legged amphibian to his fifth-grade class, his fellow students are inspired to learn about the creature. When the frog dies in the boy's

Gail Donovan's touching coming-of-age story comes to life in Janet Pedersen's illustrations for **In Memory of Gorfman T. Frog.** (Illustration copyright © 2009 by Janet Pedersen. Reproduced by permission of Dutton Children's Books, a division of Penguin Putnam Books for Young Readers.)

care, Joshua feels responsible. However, in going to family members for counsel, he learns that other things triggered Gorfman's demise, and he also begins to balance talking with listening to others. Donovan's "plot development is quick," wrote Rachel Artley in her *School Library Journal* review of *In Memory of Gorfman T. Frog,* and Joshua "and his classmates . . . act like typical fifth graders." The "constantly changing focus" in Donovan's narrative "mirror[s] the impulsive nature of the sympathetic main character," according to a *Kirkus Reviews* writer, and in *Booklist* Todd Morning commented that the novel effectively captures the "school world of kids" and combines it with an effective "ecological message."

Biographical and Critical Sources

PERIODICALS

Booklist, February 15, 2009, Todd Morning, *In Memory of Gorfman T. Frog,* p. 90.

Kirkus Reviews, February 1, 2009, review of *In Memory of Gorfman T. Frog.*

School Library Journal, February, 2002, Sharon R. Pearce, reviews of *Lost at Sea, The Copycat Fish,* and *A Fishy Story,* all p. 98; April, 2009, Rachel Artley, review of *In Memory of Gorfman T. Frog,* p. 132.

ONLINE

Gail Donovan Home Page, http://www.gaildonovan.com (May 31, 2010).*

*   *   *

DUFFY STONE, Heather

Personal

Female. *Education:* Earned M.A. (counseling). *Hobbies and other interests:* Traveling.

Addresses

Home—Brooklyn, NY. *Agent*—Jenoyne Adams, Bliss Literary Agency International, 1601 N. Sepulveda Blvd., Ste. No. 389, Manhattan Beach, CA 90266. *E-mail*—hduffystone@gmail.com.

Career

Educator, counselor, and writer. High school counselor and English teacher in New York, NY. Formerly worked for a teen magazine and a literary agency, developed creative writing programs for high schools, and taught at an international school in Italy.

Writings

This Is What I Want to Tell You (novel), Flux (Woodbury, MN), 2009.

Sidelights

In her debut novel *This Is What I Want to Tell You,* high school English teacher and counselor Heather Duffy Stone examines the complicated relationship that exists among Noelle, a sensitive fifteen year old; Noelle's twin brother, Nadio; and their longtime friend Keeley, who begins a secret romance with Nadio. "I wanted to convey the truth of first relationships," Stone remarked to *Kidlit.com* interviewer Mary Kole. Although noting that the work had its origins in a short story about a single mother, Stone added that *This Is What I Want to Tell You* "belongs to the twins. I loved writing both of them—it really fed two sides of my story, and my needs as a writer, but I think I could also appeal to different kinds of readers, too."

Told in alternating chapters from the twins' perspective, *This Is What I Want to Tell You* begins as Keeley returns from a summer in England. Noelle, who has grown resentful of her friend's good fortune, distances herself from Keeley and also engages in a clandestine relationship with Parker, an older boy she meets at a party. Meanwhile, Nadio and Keeley begin dating but elect not to tell Noelle about their romance; the consequences of this decision threaten to destroy the friendship all three teens once shared.

"The story's appeal lies mainly in its unveiling of secrets," observed a *Publishers Weekly* reviewer in a review of *This Is What I Want to Tell You,* "but Stone also offers insight into feelings of jealousy and lust." *Booklist* contributor Daniel Kraus maintained that the author's "central triangle of relationships is both strong and universal, and her details are authentic," while in *Kirkus Reviews* a critic dubbed *This Is What I Want to Tell You* "powerful and engaging and worthy of attention."

Biographical and Critical Sources

PERIODICALS

Booklist, January 1, 2009, Daniel Kraus, review of *This Is What I Want to Tell You,* p. 71.
Kirkus Reviews, February 1, 2009, review of *This Is What I Want to Tell You.*
Publishers Weekly, March 2, 2009, review of *This Is What I Want to Tell You,* p. 64.

ONLINE

Author2Author Web log, http://author2author.blogspot. com/ (October 17, 2008), Lisa Schroeder, interview with Duffy Stone.
Heather Duffy Stone Web log, http://www.heatherduffy stone.com (May 20, 2010).
Kidlit.com, http://kidlit.com/ (April 22, 2009), Mary Kole, interview with Duffy Stone.*

E-F

ECHEVERRIA-BIS, Olivia

Personal
Born in East Los Angeles, CA. *Education:* Attended college.

Addresses
Home—Fresno, CA.

Career
Writer and educator. Fresno Unified School District, Fresno, CA, reading specialist; Fresno City College, lecturer in developmental English. Formerly worked as a fashion designer; Bis & Beau (fashion boutique), Beverly Hills, CA, cofounder with Priscilla Presley, 1973.

Writings
The EGGbees: A Story about Family, illustrated by sister Charmaine Echeverria Gyorkos, Piñata Books (Houston, TX), 2009.

Biographical and Critical Sources

PERIODICALS

Kirkus Reviews, April 1, 2009, review of *The EGGbees: A Story about Family.*
School Library Journal, April, 2009, Mary Elam, review of *The EGGbees,* p. 102.

ONLINE

Charmaine Echeverria Web site, http://www.litaville.com/ (June 1, 2010), "Olivia Echeverria-Bis."*

EHRLICH, Amy 1942-

Personal
Born July 24, 1942, in New York, NY; daughter of Max (a television writer and novelist) and Doris (Rubenstein) Ehrlich; married Henry Ingraham (a college professor), June 22, 1985; children: Joss. *Education:* Attended Bennington College, 1960-62, 1963-65.

Addresses
Home—Barnet, VT.

Career
Writer, editor, and educator. Early jobs for short periods include teacher in day-care center, fabric colorist, and hospital receptionist. Freelance writer and editor for publishing companies; roving editor at *Family Circle* magazine; Delacorte Press, New York, NY, senior editor, 1977-78; Dial Books for Young Readers, New York, NY, senior editor, 1978-82, executive editor, 1982-84; Candlewick Press, Cambridge, MA, vice president, and founding editor-in-chief, 1991-96, editor-at-large, beginning 1996. Vermont College, Montpelier, instructor in writing for children in M.F.A. program.

Member
Authors Guild, PEN.

Awards, Honors
New York Times Outstanding Book of the Year designation, *School Library Journal* Best Book of the Year selection, and American Library Association (ALA) Children's Books of Exceptional Interest citation, all 1972, all for *Zeek Silver Moon; Booklist* Editor's Choice citation, Children's Choice designation, International Reading Association/Children's Book Council (IRA/CBC), Children's Book of the Year selection, Child Study Association, and Pick of the Lists citation, American Booksellers Association (ABA), all 1979, all for *Thumbelina;*

59

Amy Ehrlich (Reproduced by permission.)

IRA/CBC Children's Choice citation, 1997, for *The Everyday Train;* ABA Pick of the Lists citation, Kansas State Reading Circle selection, and *Booklist* Editor's Choice citation, all 1981, all for *Leo, Zack, and Emmie;* ABA Pick of the Lists citation, and *Booklist* Editor's Choice citation, both 1982, both for *The Snow Queen;* ABA Pick of the Lists citation, Child Study Association Children's Book of the Year selection, all 1985, and Kansas State Reading Circle selection, all for *Cinderella;* Children's Book of the Year citation, *Redbook,* 1987, for *The Wild Swans; Booklist* Young-Adult Reviewer's Choice and Best of the Decade citations, and Dorothy Canfield Fisher Award, 1990, all for *Where It Stops, Nobody Knows (Joyride); Booklist* Editor's Choice citation, 1993, for *Parents in the Pigpen, Pigs in the Tub.*

Writings

Zeek Silver Moon, illustrated by Robert Andrew Parker, Dial (New York, NY), 1972.

(Adapter) Dee Brown, *Wounded Knee: An Indian History of the American West* (from Brown's *Bury My Heart at Wounded Knee*), Holt (New York, NY), 1974.

The Everyday Train, illustrated by Martha Alexander, Dial (New York, NY), 1977.

(Reteller) Hans Christian Andersen, *Thumbelina,* illustrated by Susan Jeffers, Dial (New York, NY), 1979, revised edition, Dutton Children's Books (New York, NY), 2005.

(Reteller) Hans Christian Andersen, *The Wild Swans,* illustrated by Susan Jeffers, Dial (New York, NY), 1981, revised edition, Dutton Children's Books (New York, NY), 2008.

Leo, Zack, and Emmie, illustrated by Steven Kellogg, Dial (New York, NY), 1981.

(Reteller) Hans Christian Andersen, *The Snow Queen,* illustrated by Susan Jeffers, Dial (New York, NY), 1982, revised edition, Dutton Children's Books (New York, NY), 2005.

(Adapter) *Annie* (storybook; based on the movie of the same title), Random House (New York, NY), 1982.

Annie Finds a Home, illustrated by Leonard Shortall, Random House (New York, NY), 1982.

Annie and the Kidnappers, Random House (New York, NY), 1982.

(Editor and adapter) *The Random House Book of Fairy Tales,* illustrated by Diane Goode, Random House (New York, NY), 1985.

(Adapter) *The Ewoks and the Lost Children* (storybook from the George Lucas television film), Random House (New York, NY), 1985.

(Reteller) Charles Perrault, *Cinderella,* illustrated by Susan Jeffers, Dial (New York, NY), 1985, reprinted, Dutton Children's Books Children's (New York, NY), 2004.

(Adapter) *Bunnies All Day Long,* illustrated by Marie H. Henry, Dial (New York, NY), 1985.

(Adapter) *Bunnies and Their Grandma,* illustrated by Marie H. Henry, Dial (New York, NY), 1985.

(Adapter) *Bunnies on Their Own,* illustrated by Marie H. Henry, Dial (New York, NY), 1986.

(Adapter) *Bunnies at Christmastime,* illustrated by Marie H. Henry, Dial (New York, NY), 1986.

Leo, Zack, and Emmie Together Again, illustrated by Steven Kellogg, Dial (New York, NY), 1987.

Buck Buck the Chicken, illustrated by R.W. Alley, Random House (New York, NY), 1987.

Emma's New Pony, photographs by Richard Brown, Random House (New York, NY), 1988.

Where It Stops, Nobody Knows (young-adult novel), Dial (New York, NY), 1988, published as *Joyride,* Candlewick Press (Cambridge, MA), 2001.

(Adapter) *Pome and Peel,* illustrated by Laszlo Gal, Dial (New York, NY), 1989.

The Story of Hanukkah, illustrated by Ori Sherman, Dial (New York, NY), 1989.

(Reteller) Brothers Grimm, *Rapunzel,* illustrated by Kris Waldherr, Dial (New York, NY), 1989.

Lucy's Winter Tale, illustrated by Troy Howell, Dial (New York, NY), 1991.

The Dark Card (young-adult novel), Viking (New York, NY), 1991.

Parents in the Pigpen, Pigs in the Tub, illustrated by Steven Kellogg, Dial (New York, NY), 1993.

Maggie and Silky and Joe, illustrated by Robert Blake, Viking (New York, NY), 1994.

(Editor) *When I Was Your Age: Original Stories about Growing Up,* Candlewick Press (Cambridge, MA), 1996.

Hurry up, Mickey, illustrated by Miki Yamamota, Candlewick Press (Cambridge, MA), 1996.

(Editor) *When I Was Your Age, Volume Two: Original Stories about Growing Up,* Candlewick Press (Cambridge, MA), 1999.

Kazam's Magic, illustrated by Barney Saltzberg, Candlewick Press (Cambridge, MA), 2001.

Bravo, Kazam!, illustrated by Barney Saltzberg, Candlewick Press (Cambridge, MA), 2001.

Rachel: The Story of Rachel Carson, illustrated by Wendell Minor, Harcourt (San Diego, CA), 2002.

Willa: The Story of Willa Cather, illustrated by Wendell Minor, Simon & Schuster Books for Young Readers (New York, NY), 2006.

Baby Dragon, illustrated by Will Hillenbrand, Candlewick Press (Cambridge, MA), 2008.

The Girl Who Wanted to Dance, illustrated by Rebecca Walsh, Candlewick Press (Cambridge, MA), 2009.

Sidelights

Amy Ehrlich is a writer and editor whose work for children encompasses both original picture books and critically acclaimed young-adult novels such as the award-winning *Where It Stops, Nobody Knows* and *The Dark Card.* Ehrlich's picture books and early readers are noted for their innovative story lines and language that challenges the reader. She has also retold several classic fairy tales, such as Hans Christian Andersen's *Thumbelina,* Charles Perrault's *Cinderella,* and the Grimm Brothers' *Rapunzel,* prompting critics to remark on her innovative use of language and sympathetic characterizations. As an editor, Ehrlich has compiled *When I Was Your Age: Original Stories about Growing Up,* a mix of fiction and memoir that contains stories of childhood by ten well-known writers for young people.

"I always wanted to write, even from the time I was a young child," Ehrlich once noted in an interview for *SATA.* Such an ambition was natural, for Ehrlich was raised in a writer's household. Her father, Max Ehrlich, was a television writer and novelist. Though a distant father, deeply involved in his own work, he influenced his daughter to follow a writing life. "I did read some of his books," Ehrlich explained, "and I think in a way that had a big influence on me as a writer. He was always proud of my writing." As a young child, Ehrlich made up a story at night in bed, continuing and building on the tale in her imagination each night. She was also a serious reader, absorbing everything from the "Little House" books of Laura Ingalls Wilder to P.L. Travers' *Mary Poppins* and Jean de Brunhoff's engaging character Babar. The first adult novel she tackled was Betty Smith's *A Tree Grows in Brooklyn.* The wonder of books for her was that they "give the reader a very completely drawn alternate reality," as she explained. "I do really believe in the power of the story in books—not only in children's books, but also adult books."

Growing up in New York and Connecticut, Ehrlich did relatively well in school. "Inside I always felt different—alienated and out of step," as she explained. Winning an award for a short story in the ninth grade, she finally felt special in a truly positive sense. Fortunately, she was able to attend a Quaker boarding school in Poughkeepsie, New York. "That was a very good experience because I was in an advanced English class in my senior year, and the teacher was very good," Ehrlich once explained to *SATA.* Also, the entire atmosphere of the school, with its emphasis on academic and intellectual achievement, was a match for Ehrlich and prepared her for the rigors of a college education.

Ehrlich attended Bennington College during the early 1960s but never completed her degree. Throughout the 1960s and early 1970s, she lived a roving life, taking jobs as a teacher in a day-care center, as a fabric colorist, and as a receptionist. Eventually, she gravitated to freelance and part-time work in publishing, writing copy and working with children's books as an editorial assistant. During this time she would generally spend the summers on a farm in Vermont, then return to New York in the fall and find freelance work again.

"I had wanted to write a children's book for a long time and my boss encouraged me to write one," Ehrlich once told *SATA.* "I was writing a lot of copy and she'd always say, 'Oh, your copy's so good—why don't you write a book?'" Ehrlich tried, but had trouble initially finding the right material. Then some friends of hers in California had a baby and Ehrlich wanted to send a little story as a present. "I sat down and started writing this thing. After I got to the second page I realized I

Ehrlich's easy-reading Leo, Zack, and Emmie Together Again *features artwork by Steven Kellogg.* (Illustration copyright © 1981 by Steven Kellogg. Used by permission of Dial Books for Young Readers, a division of Penguin Putnam Books for Young Readers.)

Ehrlich features an unusually tiny hero in **Baby Dragon,** *a picture book featuring tinted line art by Will Hillenbrand.* (Illustration copyright © 2008 by Will Hillenbrand. Reproduced by permission of the publisher Candlewick Press, Inc., Cambridge, MA.)

was writing a book." The text for *Zeek Silver Moon* took a weekend of nonstop work to complete and was published exactly as written. Winner of the *New York Times* Outstanding Book of the Year award, among others, *Zeek Silver Moon* was representative of the manner in which parents were bringing up children at the time, tracing the everyday childhood events of the first five years of a boy's life.

Ehrlich then took a break from books, spending a year in Jamaica. Then in 1973, after returning to the United States, she had a son. "After my son was born," Ehrlich told *SATA*, "my view of life changed dramatically." Moving back to New York City, she continued with her

writing, adapting Dee Brown's *Bury My Heart at Wounded Knee* for young readers. Ehrlich's *Wounded Knee: An Indian History of the American West* presents an overview of the conquest of the Indians of the American West by European settlers, ending with the carnage at the battle of Wounded Knee. A single parent, she also took various editorial jobs, eventually ending up at Dial for six years. In 1977, she published *The Everyday Train,* a picture-book story of a little girl who loves to watch the freight train pass her house each day. Ehrlich's retelling of Hans Christian Andersen's story in *Thumbelina* also garnered a favorable response, as did her *Leo, Zack, and Emmie,* an easy-to-read title about how the new girl in Leo and Zack's class affects their

friendship. There followed more retellings, based on both fairy tales and movies, as with Ehrlich's "Annie" books, based on the movie about Little Orphan Annie.

Although much of Ehrlich's time was devoted to the corporate world of publishing, this executive life was not to her liking, and when her sister became ill in Vermont, Ehrlich took time off and went to care for her. She initially planned to be gone a matter of months; instead, she never returned to New York. She began writing more and then met a man who eventually became her husband. In 1990 Ehrlich returned to publishing as founding editor of Candlewick Press in Cambridge, Massachusetts, and for several years switched career focus from writing to editing. She stepped down from the position of vice president and editor-in-chief in 1996 to become editor-at-large, and since that time has concentrated once again on writing.

In 1985, while taking her first break from publishing, Ehrlich produced *Cinderella,* an adaptation for which she teamed up with a frequent collaborator, artist Susan Jeffers. In *Publishers Weekly* a reviewer commented that the pair's collaboration on *Cinderella* "surpasses them all," while a *Bulletin of the Center for Children's Books* critic noted that "Ehrlich's simplified adaptation . . . makes this edition particularly appropriate for reading aloud." Reviewing Ehrlich's version of the Grimm fairy tale *Rapunzel, Horn Book* contributor Carolyn K. Jenks noted that her "elegant, spare retelling" is "more distanced from the reader, creating a feeling of mysterious beauty." Ehrlich retells a Venetian fairy tale in *Pome and Peel,* in which Peel risks his life to save his brother Pome's bride from her father's curse. "Young readers will be entranced by this Venetian fairy tale, with its many classic ingredients," noted a *Publishers Weekly* critic of the book, while Betsy Hearne concluded in the *Bulletin of the Center for Children's Books* that the "total effect is sophisticated enough to appeal beyond the older picture book crowd to romantic fairy tale readers."

Ehrlich has also produced original picture books and young-adult novels, and her subjects for the former range from the daily lives of second-graders, to the loss of a pet to contemporary fairy tales. She teamed with illustrator Ori Sherman for *The Story of Hanukkah,* a "notable Hanukkah picture book that combines both cohesive storytelling and distinguished art," according to Betsy Hearne, writing in the *Bulletin of the Center for Children's Books.* A *Kirkus Reviews* critic commented of the book that the origin of the Festival of Lights is "retold in clear, well-cadenced, biblically formal language."

In *Kazam's Magic* Ehrlich introduces readers to a young magician whose magic tricks do not always turn out the way she intends. More tales about the youthful magician are served up in *Bravo, Kazam!,* another humorous easy reader, and an equally fanciful subject is featured in *Baby Dragon.* Brought to life in digitized multimedia

illustrations by Will Hillenbrand, *Baby Dragon* finds a young dragon getting into trouble when its mother is late in returning from an overnight trip. Instead of showing a youngster distraught over the absence of a parent, Ehrlich "emphasizes instead her protagonist's pint-sized determination," according to a *Publishers Weekly* contributor. In *School Library Journal* Mary Jean Smith described the book as a "lovely, reassuring tale" that inspire confidence in "young children . . . who have been sad and lonely in their parents' absence."

Another picture book, *The Girl Who Wanted to Dance,* features illustrations by Rebecca Walsh and introduces a young, motherless girl named Clara. While her father carries the burden of his sorrow over his missing wife, Clara turns to her grandmother, who cheers the girl with stories of her mother's love of dancing. Things in Clara's home become more somber after Grandmother dies, so the appearance of a troupe of traveling dancers lifts the girl's spirits. When she follows the performers on their journey to the next town, Clara is befriended by one of the women and learns that she has a skill for dancing herself. Reviewing the picture book, in which Ehrlich's surprising ending is captured in Rebecca Walsh's paintings, Jayne Damron noted in *School Library Journal* that *The Girl Who Wanted to Dance* "may

Ehrlich teams up with noted painter Wendell Minor to introduce young children to one of the first modern environmentalists in **Rachel: The Story of Rachel Carson.** (Illustration copyright © 2003 by Wendell Minor. Reproduced by permission of Houghton Mifflin Harcourt Publishing Company. This material may not be reproduced in any form or by any means without the prior written permission of the publisher.)

charm early elementary girls . . . patient enough to listen to the entire story." In *Kirkus Reviews* a writer was even more appreciative of the tale, noting that Ehrlich's "tender" story of "love, family and longing . . . is achingly exquisite," and a *Publishers Weekly* critic praised it as "both a haunting fairy tale and a parable for families separated by divorce or death."

Ehrlich has also collaborated with noted illustrator Wendell Minor on two picture-book biographies about notable Americans: environmentalist and biologist Rachel Carson and novelist Willa Cather. *Willa: The Story of Willa Cather* focuses on the life of the author of such western novels as *Oh Pioneers!* and *My Antonia,* while *Rachel: The Story of Rachel Carson* describes the work of the biologist whose book *Silent Spring* is credited with inspiring the environmental movement. Writing in *Booklist,* Hazel Rochman dubbed *Rachel* a "handsome picture book" in which "Ehrlich's lyrical prose grounds . . . big ideas in particulars that children can relate to," and a *Kirkus Reviews* writer concluded that "young readers will love the illustrations and enjoy the true story of a woman of passion and courage."

Ehrlich's rural Vermont life has inspired several of her stories, such as the picture books *Lucy's Winter Tale, Parents in the Pigpen, Pigs in the Tub,* and *Maggie and Silky and Joe.* With *Lucy's Winter Tale,* Ehrlich creates something of a modern fairy tale in her story of a farm girl named Lucy who performs with Ivan the juggler as he travels in search of Ivan's love, Martina. In the end, Lucy returns to her family, but will never forget the experience. "Ehrlich's poetic narrative puts her story in the special world of dream or allegory," noted a *Kirkus Reviews* commentator. Reviewing *Lucy's Winter Tale* in *School Library Journal,* Karen James referred to Ehrlich's "well-written text."

Parents in the Pigpen, Pigs in the Tub, described by a *Publishers Weekly* reviewer as "a barnyard switcheroo," tells of farm animals who tire of their routine lives and decide to move into the house. The family, in turn, takes up residence in the barn, but eventually things return to normal when both groups get tired of the new arrangement. "Ehrlich and [illustrator Steven] Kellogg . . . invest the naively accommodating family with a goofy cheerfulness that provides much of the book's humor," the *Publishers Weekly* writer added. Vanessa Elder, writing in *School Library Journal,* called *Parents in the Pigpen* "squeaky clean fun that's bound to get the children guffawing," and Maeve Visser Knoth wrote in *Horn Book* that the "rollicking tale combines some of Ehrlich's best storytelling with Kellogg's hilarious illustrations" to form "a delicious tall tale."

More somber in tone is *Maggie and Silky and Joe,* the story of a young farm boy who grows up with the family's cow dog, Maggie. When a stray puppy, Silky, comes to the farm, Maggie helps to train the younger dog. But Maggie grows old, and one day, taking refuge under the back porch during a thunder storm, she dies, and young

Joe must learn to deal with loss. A *Publishers Weekly* reviewer called *Maggie and Silky and Joe* a "tender story of the death of a beloved pet," noting that it manages to avoid sentimentality by "letting honest facts speak for themselves." In *Booklist* Rochman similarly asserted that "kids will feel Joe's sorrow, the physicality of his loss." Reviewing the same title in *School Library Journal,* Persson noted that Ehrlich "tells this 'boy loses dog' story with skilled restraint," and Persson concluded of *Maggie and Silky and Joe:* "All in all . . . this is a title that anyone who has ever loved and lost an animal will appreciate."

Although she has written several picture books, Ehrlich is perhaps better known for young-adult novels such as *Where It Stops, Nobody Knows.* The award-winning novel, which has remained popular since it was first published in 1988, was reissued in a new edition titled *Joyride.* Inspired by a girl who was a classmate of her son, Ehrlich's story focuses on Nina and Nina's mother, Joyce, who together move continually from place to place. There is a mystery surrounding these moves, for the teen can never let her friends know where she is going. Is it about the 16,000 dollars that Joyce has hidden or perhaps stolen? Is Joyce her mother's real name? Clue is laid upon clue and, according to a *Kirkus Reviews* critic, "the narrative is taut enough to hold attention until its believable, unsentimental conclusion." Zena Sutherland, reviewing the novel in *Bulletin of the Center for Children's Books,* called it "trenchant and touching." Awards committees also responded favorably to the book, and *Where It Stops, Nobody Knows* earned several honorary citations.

With *The Dark Card* Ehrlich broke new ground in subject matter for YA novels, exploring the life of a young girl in difficult circumstances. Trying to come to terms with her mother's death, seventeen-year-old Laura is lured into the glitzy world of Atlantic City's casinos. Dressing in her mother's clothes and jewelry, she assumes a new identity by night at the casinos, becoming involved with a slick gambler named Ari, who in one startling scene induces Laura to strip for him. Eventually Laura escapes from what has become a dangerous situation, although as Robert Strang noted in the *Bulletin of the Center for Children's Books,* her escape is "a relief rather than a victory." Strang added: "Laura's story is sad, but more significant, it's scary." A *Kirkus Reviews* critic commented that even "minor characters here are well drawn . . . while relationships are deftly portrayed," and concluded that the book presents teens with a "well-structured cautionary tale . . . that also thoughtfully explores the complicated feelings that can follow the loss of a flawed parent." A contributor for *Publishers Weekly* deemed *The Dark Card* "as alluring and emotionally taut" as *Where It Stops, Nobody Knows* and concluded that the author's "masterful control of language, ability to build suspense and keen psychological insights are sure to impress readers."

"Writing my two young-adult novels meant a great deal to me," Ehrlich commented in *St. James Guide to Young*

Adult Writers. "In them I wanted to tell truly gripping stories and to portray the pain and the searing discoveries of adolescence. This is a pivotal time in a human life and adults often flinch at remembering it. But I loved the intensity of recollection that came over me as I worked. The characters are made up and the stories of course are fiction, but I tried to tell the truth." In the same *St. James Guide* article, the contributing critic noted that in the characters of Nina and Laura, "Ehrlich presents portraits of adolescents on the edge of womanhood. Unlike characters in much other fiction . . . these young women strive for individuality against profoundly confused and confusing circumstances. . . . Female readers will recognize themselves similarly engaged. Ehrlich offers them confirmation and release."

In 1996 Ehrlich edited *When I Was Your Age,* a compilation—part fiction and part memoir—of stories of childhood from ten well-known writers for young people. Included in the collection is a tale by Laurence Yep and his discovery that his father really did love him for himself, and Mary Pope Osborne's discussion of how she kept a deflated rubber ball given to her by

Cover of **When I Was Your Age,** *a collection of coming-of-age stories is edited by Ehrlich and features a photograph by Christina Angarola.* (Candlewick Press, 2001. Cover photograph copyright © 2001 by Christina Angarola. Reproduced by permission of the photographer.)

her father before he went to the Korean War. Other writers featured are Susan Cooper, Avi, Nicholasa Mohr, Reeve Lindbergh, Walter Dean Myers, James Howe, Katherine Paterson, and Francisca Lia Block. Their stories, as well as Ehrlich's editing, earned praise from reviewers. Rochman noted that these ten stories "capture . . . childhood experiences" and further praised Ehrlich on her "fine introduction." Reviewing the collection in *Book Report,* Judith Beavers called it "superb," also noting that the underlying theme of all the tales "is that no matter the culture, no matter the era, growing up has never been easy." Nancy P. Reeder, writing in *School Library Journal,* called *When I Was Your Age* "a fascinating glimpse into a variety of times, places, plots, and people." "Fans of all ages will savor these perceptively chosen, affectingly disclosed episodes from the lives of favorite writers," concluded a reviewer for *Publishers Weekly.*

Ehrlich reprised *When I Was Your Age* with *When I Was Your Age, Volume Two,* which includes contributions from Norma Fox Mazer, Jane Yolen, Joseph Bruchac, Rita Williams-Garcia, Paul Fleischman, Howard Norman, E.L. Konigsburg, Michael J. Rosen, Kyoko Mori, and Karen Hesse. "While the settings, themes and characters of these memoirs are as eclectic as their creators' individual writing styles, all express a poetic understanding and insight," wrote a contributor to *Publishers Weekly* in a review of the work. "Ehrlich's second anthology of short childhood memoirs is as good as the first," proclaimed Rochman, the critic concluding in *Booklist* that *When I Was Your Age, Volume Two* "will be a great read aloud to get YA's started on writing their own personal stories that speak to all of us." Reviewing the same volume in *School Library Journal,* Katie O'Dell noted that "it is the immediacy of the emotional experiences that drive the stories and make this collection well worth reading aloud in the classroom and library."

"I have always been split between writing and editing," Ehrlich once commented to *SATA.* "Each feeds the other. When I'm writing myself, the editorial voice is always there, asking me what I'm doing and what I mean to do.

"For me as a writer, the trick is to banish that editorial voice in the first draft so that I can stretch out and explore my own mental impulses and get to know my characters. Later on though, in revision after revision, the editorial voice is invaluable. Every paragraph, sentence, and word in a story is important and should have meaning. What is shown about the characters, how is the plot advanced? Is the language as clear as possible in communicating the writer's intention?

"Oh, and one other thing about writing—it's awfully hard work. There's just no getting around that. You need to be willing to put in the time and to enjoy the process for itself."

Biographical and Critical Sources

BOOKS

St. James Guide to Young Adult Writers, 2nd edition, St. James Press (Detroit, MI), 1999.

Twentieth-Century Young Adult Writers, edited by Laura Standley Berger, St. James Press (Detroit, MI), 1994, pp. 198-200.

PERIODICALS

Booklist, July, 1994, Hazel Rochman, review of *Maggie and Silky and Joe,* p. 1954; April 15, 1996, Hazel Rochman, review of *When I Was Your Age: Original Stories about Growing Up,* p. 1437; April 15, 1999, Hazel Rochman, review of *When I Was Your Age, Volume Two: Original Stories about Growing Up,* p. 1530; April 15, 2002, Stephanie Zvirin, review of *Bravo Kazam!,* p. 1407; June 1, 2003, Hazel Rochman, review of *Rachel: The Story of Rachel Carson,* p. 1795.

Book Report, September-October, 1996, Judith Beavers, review of *When I Was Your Age,* p. 45.

Bulletin of the Center for Children's Books, October, 1985, review of *Cinderella,* p. 35; January, 1989, Zena Sutherland, review of *Where It Stops, Nobody Knows,* p. 120; December, 1989, Betsy Hearne, review of *The Story of Hanukkah,* p. 82; September, 1990, Betsy Hearne, review of *Pome and Peel,* p. 6; April, 1991, Robert Strang, review of *The Dark Card,* pp. 190-191.

Horn Book, November-December, 1989, Carolyn K. Jenks, review of *Rapunzel,* p. 779; January, 1994, Maeve Visser Knoth, review of *Parents in the Pigpen, Pigs in the Tub,* p. 62.

Kirkus Reviews, November 1, 1988, review of *Where It Stops, Nobody Knows,* p. 1603; July 15, 1989, review of *The Story of Hanukkah,* p. 1074; March 1, 1991, review of *The Dark Card,* p. 317; August 15, 1992, review of *Lucy's Winter Tale,* p. 1060; March 1, 2003, review of *Rachel: The Story of Rachel Carlson,* p. 382; July 15, 2008, review of *Baby Dragon;* January 1, 2009, review of *The Girl Who Wanted to Dance.*

Kliatt, July, 2002, Tricia Finch, review of *When I Was Your Age, Volume 2,* p. 33.

Publishers Weekly, September 27, 1985, review of *Cinderella,* p. 96; December 22, 1989, review of *Pome and Peel,* p. 56; February 22, 1991, review of *The Dark Card,* pp. 219-220; August 16, 1993, review of *Parents in the Pigpen, Pigs in the Tub,* p. 102; July 25, 1994, review of *Maggie and Silky and Joe,* p. 55; March 4, 1996, review of *When I Was Your Age,* p. 66; February 22, 1999, review of *When I Was Your Age, Volume Two,* p. 96; January 6, 2003, review of *Rachel,* p. 59; August 18, 2008, review of *Baby Dragon,* p. 61; January 26, 2009, review of *The Girl Who Wanted to Dance,* p. 119.

School Library Journal, October, 1987, Lauralyn Persson, review of *Leo, Zack, and Emmie Together Again,* pp. 110-111; September, 1992, Karen James, review of *Lucy's Winter Tale,* p. 202; October, 1993, Vanessa El-der, review of *Parents in the Pigpen, Pigs in the Tub,* p. 98; September, 1994, Lauralyn Persson, review of *Maggie and Silky and Joe,* p. 184; August, 1996, Nancy P. Reeder, review of *When I Was Your Age,* p. 152; July, 1999, Katie O'Dell, review of *When I Was Your Age, Volume Two,* p. 95; February, 2002, Anne Knickerbocker, review of *Kazam's Magic,* p. 100; May, 2003, Margaret Bush, review of *Rachel,* p. 136; September, 2008, Mary Jean Smith, review of *Baby Dragon,* p. 145; May, 2009, Jayne Damron, review of *The Girl Who Wanted to Dance,* p. 112.

Teen, February, 2002, Erin Zimring, review of *Joyride,* p. 107.

ONLINE

Harcourt Web site, http://www.harcourtbooks.com/ (June 1, 2010), interview with Ehrlich.*

* * *

FANTASKEY, Beth 1965-

Personal

Born 1965; married (husband a college professor); two children. *Education:* College degree; Pennsylvania State University, Ph.D. candidate (mass communication history). *Hobbies and other interests:* Running, travel, watching reality television.

Addresses

Home—Lewisburg, PA. *E-mail*—bethfantaskey@yahoo.com.

Career

Educator, journalist, and novelist. Former political speechwriter; freelance journalist. Susquehanna University, part-time English instructor.

Writings

Jessica's Guide to Dating on the Dark Side, Harcourt (New York, NY), 2009.

Jekel Loves Hyde, Harcourt (Boston, MA), 2010.

Sidelights

Leading something of a triple life, Ph.D. student and mother of two Beth Fantaskey spent the summer of 2006 writing her first novel, *Jessica's Guide to Dating on the Dark Side.* Tapping the popular interest in stories that mix romance with paranormal elements, such as Stephanie Meyer's *Twilight* and its sequels, Fantaskey also drew on her love of classic fiction by Jane Austen, the Brontës, and Herman Melville, among others.

Beth Fantaskey (Reproduced by permission.)

Fantaskey has enjoyed writing since childhood, and she worked as a speech writer and a freelance journalist before turning to fiction. In an interview with the *Lurv a la mode* Web log, she discussed the inspiration for her first novel. "My two daughters are adopted, and don't know anything about their biological parents," Fantaskey explained. "Sometimes I wonder, 'Who were their birth moms and dads?' Then one day I started wondering, 'What if their birth parents were really special somehow, or different?' Would that shock my children? Maybe even change who they are? That was how I came up with Jessica—a girl whose whole world is turned upside down by that kind of revelation, taken to the extreme."

Although many American girls raised on the Disney cartoons *Cinderella* and *Sleeping Beauty* would be thrilled to discover that they are a member of royalty, high-school senior Jessica Packwood finds that this fantasy has a dark side when she learns that her birth parents are members of Romanian vampire royalty in *Jessica's Guide to Dating on the Dark Side*. In addition, the teen has been promised in marriage to Lucius Vladescu, a handsome but arrogant vampire prince who has traveled to Jessica's Pennsylvania hometown and is now diligently courting her. Although Jessica wants to ignore her destiny and continue dating Jake, spurning marriage to Lucius—and her own transformation into a vampire—will rekindle a longstanding war between rival vampire clans. As Fantaskey's plot unfolds, Jessica and Lucius must grapple with their fates in what *School Library Journal* contributor Donna Rosenblum described as a "highly entertaining" story full of "action, drama, romance, as well as self-discovery." Within her vampire fantasy, "Fantaskey sustains a wholly believable contemporary teen world," noted Debbie Carton in

Booklist, the critic adding that Jessica's "wry sense of humor is delightful." Declaring that Fantaskey's novel ranks "ahead of the pack of *Twilight* wannabes," a *Publishers Weekly* critic concluded of *Jessica's Guide to Dating on the Dark Side* that "the romance sizzles, the plot develops ingeniously and suspense-fully, and the satire sings."

In *Jekel Loves Hyde,* Fantaskey revisions Robert Louis Stevenson's *The Strange Case of Dr. Jeykll and Mr. Hyde,* a well-known horror story in which a chemical formula unleashes a brutal doppelganger in the doctor who creates and drinks it. In the novel, shy Jill Jekel and handsome but troubled Tristen Hyde are high-school classmates. Although their paths have not previously crossed, when they are paired up in a chemistry project Jill decides to pursue a line of experimentation once followed by her murdered chemist father. As the suspense grows through the alternating narrative of the two teens, *Jekel Loves Hyde* readers are drawn in by Fantaskey's use of "compelling plot devices," according to *Booklist* critic Connie Fletcher. In *Publishers Weekly* a reviewer praised the "fiery" conclusion to *Jekel Loves*

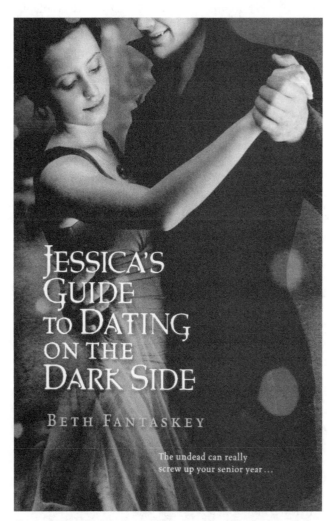

Cover of Fantaskey's supernatural romance **Jessica's Guide to Dating on the Dark Side,** *featuring artwork by Cliff Nielsen.* (Cover art © by Cliff Nielsen. Reprinted by permission of Houghton Mifflin Harcourt Publishing Company. All rights reserved.)

Hyde, noting that the story's "premise is creative, and there are plenty of twists to keep readers engaged."

Biographical and Critical Sources

PERIODICALS

Booklist, March 1, 2009, Debbie Carton, review of *Jessica's Guide to Dating on the Dark Side,* p. 38; April 15, 2010, Connie Fletcher, review of *Jekel Loves Hyde,* p. 42.

Bulletin of the Center for Children's Books, January, 2009, April Spisak, review of *Jessica's Guide to Dating on the Dark Side,* p. 196.

Journal of Adolescent and Adult Literacy, October, 2009, Kerri Mathew, review of *Jessica's Guide to Dating on the Dark Side,* p. 180.

Kirkus Reviews, January 1, 2009, review of *Jessica's Guide to Dating on the Dark Side.*

Publishers Weekly, January 5, 2009, review of *Jessica's Guide to Dating on the Dark Side,* p. 51; April 12, 2010, review of *Jekel Loves Hyde,* p. 53.

School Library Journal, March, 2009, Donna Rosenblum, review of *Jessica's Guide to Dating on the Dark Side,* p. 144.

Voice of Youth Advocates, June, 2009, Courtney Huse Wika, review of *Jessica's Guide to Dating on the Dark Side,* p. 149.

ONLINE

Beth Fantaskey Home Page, http://www.bethfantaskey.com (June 15, 2010).

Lurv a la mode Web log, http://lurvalamode.wordpress.com/ (January 13, 2009), interview with Fantaskey.

Wondrous Reads Web site, http://www.wondrousreads.com/ (April 21, 2009), interview with Fantaskey.

*   *   *

FITZMAURICE, Kathryn

Personal

Born in New York, NY; married Brian Fitzmaurice; children: Sam, Hugh. *Education:* Chapman University, M.Ed. (curriculum and instruction). *Hobbies and other interests:* Walking her dog.

Addresses

Home—Monarch Beach, CA.

Career

Writer. Former teacher of elementary grades; freelance writer, beginning 2004.

Member

Society of Children's Book Writers and Illustrators.

Awards, Honors

Booklist Top-Ten First Novels for Youth designation, 2009, and Southern California Independent Booksellers Association Book Award nomination, and Best Book designation, Bank Street College of Education, both 2010, all for *The Year the Swallows Came Early.*

Writings

The Year the Swallows Came Early, Bowen Press (New York, NY), 2009.

Sidelights

Kathryn Fitzmaurice was inspired to become a writer by her grandmother, science-fiction author Eleanor Robinson, who lived a somewhat unconventional life in New York City and did her work late at night, when her imagination was most unfettered. As a young teen, Fitzmaurice spent the summer with Robinson, learning the nuts and bolts of negotiating with an agent, as well as developing characters and story lines. Although Fitzmaurice eventually pursued a career in education, she realized that she had inherited the writing bug when she was given her grandmother's unfinished manuscripts at

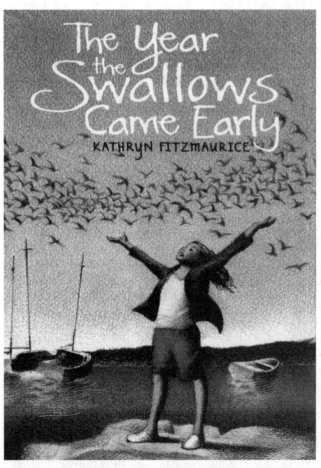

Cover of Kathryn Fitzmaurice's middle-grade coming-of-age novel **The Year the Swallows Came Early,** *featuring artwork by Raul Colón.* (Bowen Press, 2009. Jacket art © 2009 by Raul Colón. Used by permission of HarperCollins Children's Books, a division of HarperCollins Publishers.)

the older woman's death. When the younger woman began her own fiction-writing career years later, the main character of her first published novel bore her grandmother's name.

In Fitzmaurice's highly praised fiction debut, the middle-grade novel *The Year the Swallows Came Early*, eleven-year-old Eleanor "Groovy" Robinson has a dream: she wants to go to cooking school. Thanks to her grandmother's gift of money for college, she is confident that she will achieve her dream. Then her father is arrested, and Groovy learns that he has gambled away her inheritance. Crushed and feeling betrayed, the girl loses heart until she gains insight about the nature of love from both a good friend and a surprising source.

Writing that Fitzmaurice peoples her first novel with "three-dimensional characters whose imperfections make them believable and interesting," Nancy Menaldi-Scanlan added in her *School Library Journal* review that *The Year the Swallows Came Early* also benefits from a "well-structured plot" buoyed by "clear writing and authentic dialogue." A *Kirkus Reviews* writer also praised the novel, noting that the author's "daring, emotionally complex story" captures the complex emotional interactions young people often face in real life. In *Booklist* Ilene Cooper described *The Year the Swallows Came Early* as "a small, quiet, yet empowering story

with an underlying message of forgiveness," the critic adding that the coastal San Juan Capistrano setting creates an evocative backdrop to Fitzmaurice's tale.

Biographical and Critical Sources

PERIODICALS

Booklist, February 15, 2009, Ilene Cooper, review of *The Year the Swallows Came Early,* p. 81.
Kirkus Reviews, January 1, 2009, review of *The Year the Swallows Came Early.*
Publishers Weekly, January 12, 2009, review of *The Year the Swallows Came Early,* p. 47.
School Library Journal, February, 2009, Nancy Menaldi-Scanlan, review of *The Year the Swallows Came Early,* p. 98.

ONLINE

Kathryn Fitzmaurice Home Page, http://www.kathrynfitz maurice.com (May 31, 2010).
Orange County Register Online, http://www.ocregister. com/ (September 6, 2009), Peter Larsen, "OC Writer Gets Grandma's Gift of Inspiration."*

G-H

GLATT, Lisa 1963-

Personal

Born 1963; married David Hernandez (a poet and visual artist). *Education:* California State University, Long Beach, bachelor's degree; Sarah Lawrence College, M.F.A.

Addresses

Home—Long Beach, CA. *Office*—Department of English, California State University, Long Beach, 1250 Bellflower Blvd., Long Beach, CA 90840. *E-mail*—lisag412@yahoo.com; lglatt@csulb.edu.

Career

Educator and author. California State University, Long Beach, member of faculty beginning 1992; University of California, Los Angeles, lecturer, beginning 1992, professor of English, beginning 2006.

Awards, Honors

Mississippi Review Prize, 2002, for fiction; *Los Angeles Times* Book Prize for Best First Fiction shortlist, 2004, for *A Girl Becomes a Comma like That.*

Writings

FOR CHILDREN

(With Susan Greenberg) *Abigail Iris: The One and Only,* illustrated by Joy Allen, Walker Books for Young Readers (New York, NY), 2009.

(With Suzanne Greenberg) *Abigail Iris: The Pet Project,* illustrated by Joy Allen, Walker Books for Young Readers (New York, NY), 2010.

OTHER

Monsters and Other Lovers (poetry), Pearl Editions (Long Beach, CA), 1996.

Shelter (poetry), Pearl Editions (Long Beach, CA), 2000.

A Girl Becomes a Comma like That (novel), Simon & Schuster (New York, NY), 2004.

The Apple's Bruise (short stories), Simon & Schuster (New York, NY), 2005.

Contributor to publications, including *Columbia, Other Voices, Indiana Review,* and *Swink.*

Sidelights

Lisa Glatt began her writing career penning short fiction and poetry before moving on to novels and children's fiction. In a review of her story collection *The Apple's Bruise, Library Journal* critic Kellie Gillespie cited the writer's "readable style, . . . distinctive characters and coverage of universal themes," and a *Kirkus Reviews* writer maintained that Glatt "has a sharp eye for catching the incongruous detail that nicely derails her characters' tidy sense of themselves." Eventually, several of Glatt's stories merged into a longer text that became her first novel, *A Girl Becomes a Comma like That.* She has since turned to younger readers in the related books *Abigail Iris: The One and Only* and *Abigail Iris: The Pet Project.*

A Girl Becomes a Comma like That focuses on Rachel Spark, a poet and part-time college instructor whose mother is dying of breast cancer. Rachel has moved back home, and when her despair grows she brings a succession of random and somewhat questionable lovers to the apartment. Woven into Rachel's drama are the lives of three women who cross paths with her. A *Kirkus Reviews* contributor noted of *A Girl Becomes a Comma like That* that Glatt "has a good feel for how one's insecurities translate into risky behavior," and *New York Times Book Review* critic Lisa Zeidner called the novel "appealingly dark" even as she questioned whether its "patchwork construction" hinders readers' ability to keep the "characters straight." Noting the "vitality" of *A Girl Becomes a Comma like That,* Elizabeth Gold added in her *Washington Post* review that "Rachel, . . . far from being a comma, is a true—if prickly—heroine of her own story."

Joining fellow writer Suzanne Greenberg, Glatt turns to younger readers in her books about rambunctious third grader Abigail Iris. In *Abigail Iris: The One and Only* the eight year old sometimes feels that she is overshadowed by her three best friends, who come from more affluent, one-child families. When she joins Genevieve on a vacation to San Francisco, Abigail learns that there are things in her bustling, blended family that money cannot always buy. Illustrated with black-and-white drawings by Joy Allen, *Abigail Iris: The One and Only* was praised by a *Publishers Weekly* critic for its "spot-on . . . observations," while Lucinda Snyder wrote in *School Library Journal* that Glatt and Greenberg's "light, breezy" story is well matched by "drawings [that] . . . help convey the protagonist's charm" and also sustain the interest of reluctant readers. "With Allen's periodic homespun sketches and a breezy first-person text, this sweet slip of a story is recommended for those girls feeling the squeeze of a crowded and blended family," concluded a *Kirkus Reviews* writer.

Biographical and Critical Sources

PERIODICALS

Booklist, March 1, 2009, Carolyn Phelan, review of *Abigail Iris: The One and Only,* p. 43.
Kirkus Reviews, April 15, 2004, review of *A Girl Becomes a Comma like That,* p. 348; April 1, 2005, review of *The Apple's Bruise,* p. 373; February 1, 2009, review of *Abigail Iris: The One and Only.*
Library Journal, June 15, 2004, Bette-Lee Fox, review of *A Girl Becomes a Comma like That,* p. 58; May 15, 2005, Kellie Gillespie, review of *The Apple's Bruise,* p. 110.
New York Times Book Review, June 6, 2004, Lisa Zeidner, review of *A Girl Becomes a Comma like That,* p. 13.
O, June, 2004, review of *A Girl Becomes a Comma like That,* p. 148.
Publishers Weekly, April 5, 2004, review of *A Girl Becomes a Comma like That,* p. 34; April 11, 2005, review of *The Apple's Bruise,* p. 31; February 2, 2009, review of *Abigail Iris: The One and Only,* p. 49.
School Library Journal, March, 2009, Lucinda Snyder, review of *Abigail Iris: The One and Only,* p. 112.
Washington Post Book World, May 30, 2004, Elizabeth Gold, review of *A Girl Becomes a Comma like That,* p. T13.

ONLINE

California State University, Long Beach, Web site, http://www.csulb.edu/ (September, 2004), Richard Manly, "Glatt Garners Attention with First Novel"; (October 13, 2004) Ted Goslin, "English Professors Write as They Teach."
Lisa Glatt Home Page, http://www.lisaglatt.com (May 31, 2010).

Smallspiralnotebook.com, http://www.smallspiralnotebook.com/ (October 13, 2004), Felicia C. Sullivan, interview with Glatt.

*   *   *

GOODMAN, Emily

Personal

Born in Schenectady, NY. *Hobbies and other interests:* Plants, gardening, fantasy.

Addresses

Home—Brooklyn, NY.

Career

Horticulturalist, editor, and writer. Has worked as a zoo gardener.

Writings

Plant Secrets, illustrated by Phyllis Limbacher Tildes, Charlesbridge (Watertown, MA), 2008.

Contributor to periodicals.

Biographical and Critical Sources

PERIODICALS

Booklist, March 15, 2009, Carolyn Phelan, review of *Plant Secrets,* p. 63.
Bulletin of the Center for Children's Books, April 1, 2009, review of *Plant Secrets.*
Kirkus Reviews, January 1, 2009, review of *Plant Secrets.*
School Library Journal, March, 2009, Carol S. Surges, review of *Plant Secrets,* p. 134.

ONLINE

Charlesbridge Web site, http://www.charlesbridge.com/ (June 1, 2010), "Emily Goodman."*

*   *   *

HARTINGER, Brent 1964-

Personal

Born 1964, in WA; son of Harold (an attorney) and Mary Anne (a homemaker) Hartinger; partner of Michael Jensen (a writer). *Ethnicity:* "Caucasian." *Edu-*

Bret Hartinger (Photograph by Tim Cathersal. Reproduced by permission.)

cation: Gonzaga University, B.S., 1986. *Politics:* Democrat. *Hobbies and other interests:* Reading, playing computer games, traveling, attending movies and plays.

Addresses

Home—Tacoma, WA. *Agent*—Jennifer DeChiara Literary Agency, 254 Park Ave. S., Ste. 2L, New York, NY 10010. *E-mail*—brentsbrain@gmail.com.

Career

Novelist, playwright, and educator. Guest columnist, *News Tribune,* Tacoma, WA. Vermont College, Montpelier, writing instructor in M.F.A. Program in Creative Writing for Children and Young Adults. Also worked as a counselor in a group home for troubled adolescents. Oasis (support group for gay and lesbian young people), cofounder.

Member

Society of Children's Book Writers and Illustrators, Dramatists' Guild, Authors Supporting Intellectual Freedom (cofounder).

Awards, Honors

Audience Award, Dayton Playhouse Futurefest Festival of New Plays, and Festival of Emerging American Theatre Award runner-up, both for *The Starfish Scream;* Popular Paperback selection, American Library Association (ALA), and Books for the Teen Age selection, New York Public Library, both for *Geography Club;* Popular Paperback selection and Quick Pick for Reluctant Readers selection, both ALA, both for *The Last Chance Texaco;* Fort Lauderdale Film Festival Screenwriting-in-the-Sun Award; Judy Blume grant for best young-adult novel, Society of Children's Book Writers and Illustrators; Seattle Arts Commission Tacoma Artists Initiative grant and Development of a New Work grant; University of Southwestern Louisiana Young-Adult Fiction Prize; Lambda Book Award, Na-

tional Best Book Award, 2007, and Books for the Teen Age selection, New York Public Library, 2008, all for *Split Screen;* Gay & Lesbian Alliance against Defamation (GLAAD) Media Award, 2010, for Outstanding Digital Journalism Article.

Writings

Geography Club, HarperTempest (New York, NY), 2003.
The Last Chance Texaco, HarperTempest (New York, NY), 2004.
The Order of the Poison Oak (sequel to *Geography Club*), HarperTempest (New York, NY), 2005.
Grand & Humble, HarperTempest (New York, NY), 2006.
Dreamquest: Tales of Slumberia, Tor/Starscape (New York, NY), 2007.
Split Screen: Attack of the Soul-sucking Brain Zombies/ Bride of the Soul-sucking Brain Zombies (sequel to *Geography Club*), HarperTempest (New York, NY), 2007.
Project Sweet Life, HarperTeen (New York, NY), 2009.
Shadow Walkers, Flux (Minneapolis, MN), 2011.

Also author of plays, including *The Starfish Scream* (for young adults), produced at Dayton Playhouse Futurefest Festival of New Plays; a stage adaptation of *Geography Club,* produced in Seattle, WA; and a stage adaptation of *Grand & Humble.* Editor of *TheTorchOnline.com* (Web site devoted to fantasy). Contributor of numerous essays, articles, cartoons, and stories to periodicals, including *Omni, Boy's Life, Plays, Emmy, Seattle Weekly, Genre, San Francisco Bay Guardian, Noise,* and *Advocate.* Regular contributor to Afterelton.com (gay entertainment site). Contributor to anthologies, including *Rush Hour,* edited by Michael Cart, Random House, and *Young Warriors,* edited by Tamora Pierce and Josepha Sherman, Random House.

Sidelights

Brent Hartinger entered the vanguard of a sub-genre in young-adult literature in 2003 with the release of his first novel, *Geography Club.* That work, published to both critical and popular acclaim, deals with teenage homosexuality in a straightforward, honest, and sometimes amusing manner. Since the book debuted, Hartinger has gone on to write a number of sequels to *Geography Club,* and he has also branched out into fantasy, problem novels, and humorous adventures. "I like to write for all ages, but I particularly like writing for and about teenagers. I think it's because I identify so strongly with them," the author noted on his home page.

Despite his great success as a novelist and playwright, Hartinger never planned to become a writer. His artistic instincts were evident from an early age, however. Hartinger involved himself in a number of creative activities as a youngster, including editing and publishing his own newspaper, the "Weekly Worm," and he fre-

quently made movies, posters, and audio tapes with his two best friends. During that time, he noted on his home page, "I learned just how much fun it is to create—how satisfying it is to make something from nothing and to get swept up in the sheer joy of invention. Creating something you care about can be hard work, but because you care so much about it, it doesn't feel like work."

Hartinger's high-school experiences were another matter entirely. "It was even worse than I'd expected," he reported. "I wasn't popular, which didn't really bug me since I've never liked being the center of attention. But while all of my friends . . . were discovering girls, I was discovering I was gay. I went to Catholic schools, which made things much worse—a fact that I'm still pretty bitter about. I think it's absolutely criminal that gay kids are still forced to spend their adolescent years feeling as lonely, and as freakish, as I felt then." After graduating from college, Hartinger drifted for a time, trying his hand at acting (he had trouble remembering his lines) before deciding to write. When his first attempts at selling a novel failed, he turned to penning stage dramas, a number of which were produced to critical acclaim.

Cover of Hartinger's fiction debut, the teen novel Geography Club, *which addresses gay teen culture.* (HarperTempest, 2004. Cover art © 2003 by Howard Huang. Cover © 2004 by HarperCollins Publishers Inc. Used by permission of HarperCollins Children's Books, a division of HarperCollins Publishers.)

Although for over a decade Hartinger had been successfully writing articles, plays, and screenplays, it was not until he had racked up eight unpublished novels, thousands of query letters, and seventeen rejections of his then-current manuscript that *Geography Club* found a home at HarperCollins. In the work, Hartinger tells the story of high-school student Russel Middlebrook, who is convinced that he is the only homosexual person in his school. When Russel discovers differently, he and his new friends form the Geography Club, a secret support group. Unlike other publishers, HarperCollins decided to take a gamble on a book with possibly limited appeal, and the gamble paid off. As the author explained to *AfterElton.com* interviewer Michael Jensen, "The whole gay teen wave really broke in the mainstream media along with my book and with the books by Alex Sanchez. But I believe there's always been a market for these books—there have always been GLBT youth, right? It's that publishers didn't know about the market until they actually started publishing books for it."

Hartinger based his first-person novel on many of his own experiences growing up, and many of the characters were inspired by his friends and acquaintances. Explaining part of his motivation in writing the book to a contributor for the National Coalition against Censorship Web site, Hartinger remarked: "There is no greater underdog in the world than a gay or lesbian teenager. Depending on where they live, the whole world might be against: their families, their religion, their teachers, even their friends sometimes!" As he noted on his home page, *Geography Club* "gave me a chance to rewrite my teenage years but give it a little more of a happy ending." Despite the serious subject matter—acceptance—Hartinger wanted to employ a light touch, as he told Amanda Laughtland for the Tacoma *News Tribune.* "I wanted my book to be fun and funny—a fast read. Not broccoli, but dessert."

When it appeared in 2003, *Geography Club* attracted a readership among teens and adults alike. Several reviewers commented on the verisimilitude in *Geography Club,* among them *Horn Book* reviewer Roger Sutton, who ranked the work highly among books portraying gay characters and noted that Russel's "agonies of ostracism (and first love) are truly conveyed." A *Publishers Weekly* contributor also commented that the novel "does a fine job of presenting many of the complex realities of gay teen life." Writing in *School Library Journal,* Robert Gray praised Hartinger's characterizations, calling them "excellent" and predicting that teens of all sexual preferences will "find this novel intriguing." A *Kirkus Reviews* writer dubbed *Geography Club* "provocative, insightful, and . . . comforting."

Hoping to escape his image as the "gay kid," Russel takes a job at a summer camp for childhood burn survivors in *The Order of the Poison Oak,* a sequel to *Geography Club.* Along with friends Gunnar and Min, the teen heads to Camp Serenity, where he takes charge of a group of restless ten year olds. To bond with his

charges, Russel forms the Order of the Poison Oak, a secret group for outsiders of all types. Working past "his initial sense of discomfort around the burn survivors, with their visible scars and disabilities," as *Kliatt* reviewer Kathryn Kulpa noted, "Russel, with his less-obvious scars, gains an understanding of the common ground they occupy." He also finds himself involved in an awkward love triangle with Min and another counselor and comes to rely on the steadying influence of Otto, a burn survivor who now works at the camp. In her review for *Booklist,* Hazel Rochman praised Hartinger for spinning an "honest, tender, funny, first-person narrative that brings close what it's like to have a crush and hate a friend," while a *Kirkus Reviews* critic stated that in *The Order of the Poison Oak* Hartinger "creates a . . . touching and realistic portrait of gay teens."

Russel returns in the company of best friend Min in the flip-book addition to the series, *Split Screen: Attack of the Soul-sucking Brain Zombies/Bride of the Soul-sucking Brain Zombies.* Here the two protagonists take part in the filming of a zombie movie, and the same events are viewed from their very different perspectives. "You might say it's *Rashomon* for teens," Hartinger told *AfterElton.com* interviewer Jensen, "except the two books cover completely different events. It's not at all like reading the same book twice. That said, the two books definitely inform each other. You don't know the whole story until you read both books together." While serving as extras on the movie, which is being filmed in their hometown, Russel and Min still must navigate their private lives: Russel has to decide between two boyfriends, one long distance and one local, while Min learns to deal with her girlfriend's decision to keep her homosexuality private. Reviewing the work, *Lambda Book Report* contributor Bill Burleson called it an "enjoyable, compelling, and well-told story." Likewise, *School Library Journal* reviewer Kathleen E. Gruver thought that "there is a lot of humor in this book."

The Last Chance Texaco is based on Hartinger's experiences working as a counselor in a group home for troubled adolescents. The work concerns fifteen-year-old Lucy Pitt, a foster child whose parents were killed in a car accident when Lucy was seven years old. After being shuttled from one foster family to another, Lucy arrives at Kindle Home, an aging mansion known to its residents as "The Last Chance Texaco." Lucy knows that if she fails at Kindle Home, she will be sent to a high-security facility nicknamed Eat-Their-Young Island. Though Lucy is tested early and often by the other teen residents, she finds Kindle Home unlike any other place she has lived and is determined to stay. After a series of car fires in the neighborhood cast suspicion on the residents of the foster home, Lucy decides to investigate with the help of a new friend. "Hartinger clearly knows the culture, and Lucy speaks movingly (if occasionally too therapeutically) about her anger and grief," observed *Booklist* critic Rochman. Faith Brautigan, re-

viewing *The Last Chance Texaco* in *School Library Journal,* similarly noted of the work that "Hartinger excels at giving readers an insider's view of the subculture, with its myriad unspoken rules created by the kids, not the system."

Two seventeen-year-old boys from disparate backgrounds are haunted by strange premonitions in *Grand & Humble.* Told in alternating chapters, the work focuses on Harlan, a popular athlete whose father is a U.S. senator, and Manny, a sensitive theater geek whose own father must work hard to make ends meet. As both teens struggle to make sense of their terrifying nightmares, frequently containing visions connected to the intersection of Grand and Humble streets in their town, they begin to question their pasts and discover that a tragic event that occurred fourteen years earlier will forever link their fates. "Parallels and double meanings abound in this tricky, but satisfying, double narrative," noted a *Kirkus Reviews* critic, and Paula Rohrlick wrote in *Kliatt* that Hartinger's "taut and clever thriller . . . will appeal to mystery and suspense fans."

With *Dreamquest: Tales of Slumberia* Hartinger "deftly moves into the realm of fantasy," according to a *Publishers Weekly* reviewer. Hartinger also focuses on a

Cover of Hartinger's Dreamquest, *featuring eerie artwork by August N. Hall.* (Starscape/Tom Doherty Associates, 2007. Illustrated by August N. Hall. Reproduced by permission of the illustrator.)

younger protagonist in this outing, relating the story of eleven-year-old Julie whose dreams are troubled by the friction between her parents. One night she enters another reality while she sleeps, venturing into the land of Slumberia where she discovers her dreams are scripted. When one of the denizens of this land escapes from Slumberia, she causes havoc in Julie's waking life. The *Publishers Weekly* contributor further felt that this "winning pairing of a sincere message with hyperbolic humor should resonate with readers." Further praise for *Dreamquest* came from *School Library Journal* contributor Robyn Gioia, who noted that readers in search of "a fun but edgy book will enjoy stepping into this unusual world with its grim circumstances and adventure." As a *Kirkus Reviews* writer concluded, "Julie's entertaining and humorous quest leads to a satisfying conclusion."

Three teenage buddies devise an elaborate strategy to avoid working while on vacation in Hartinger's *Project Sweet Life*. Planning to spend their time swimming, bike riding, and spelunking, a trio of fifteen year olds, Dave, Victor, and Curtis, are shocked when their parents demand that they get summer jobs. Instead of scouring the want ads, however, they lie to their fathers, telling them they have found employment, and the teens then busy themselves with a number of schemes to earn as much money as they can with as little effort as possible. Their ill-advised plan only leads to chaos, though, resulting in "a hilarious story filled with mishaps, close calls, and outrageous adventures," according to Sarah K. Allen writing for *School Library Journal*. Reviewing the same work for *Booklist*, Lynn Rutan also found it "an amusing story with great teen appeal."

Becoming a writer involves being an avid reader, Hartinger maintained in a *Teenreads.com* interview with Carlie Webber, though he also noted that literary success depends on a number of factors. "Reading is actually good advice, and so is joining a critique group, for both writing and emotional support," he remarked. "But I think it's also important to learn everything you can about the BUSINESS of writing. Work at a library, bookstore, or publisher. Learn what people like to read, and why. Get to know the world of books, because no matter what you think of the business of publishing, it's the world you have to live in if you want to be a published writer."

Biographical and Critical Sources

PERIODICALS

Booklist, April 1, 2003, Hazel Rochman, review of *Geography Club*, p. 1387; January 1, 2004, Hazel Rochman, review of *The Last Chance Texaco*, p. 844; January 1, 2005, Hazel Rochman, review of *The Order of the Poison Oak*, p. 845; January 1, 2006, Hazel Rochman, review of *Grand & Humble*, pp. 83-84; October 1, 2008, Lynn Rutan, review of *Project Sweet Life*, p. 38.

Childhood Education, winter, 2004, Ann Pohl, review of *The Last Chance Texaco*, p. 107.
Horn Book, March-April, 2003, Roger Sutton, review of *Geography Club*, pp. 209-211.
Kirkus Reviews, December 15, 2002, review of *Geography Club*, p. 1850; March 1, 2004, review of *The Last Chance Texaco*, p. 223; January 15, 2005, review of *The Order of the Poison Oak*, p. 120; December 15, 2005, review of *Grand & Humble*, p. 1322; April 15, 2007, review of *Dreamquest: Tales of Slumberia*; January 1, 2009, review of *Project Sweet Life*.
Kliatt, March, 2004, Claire Rosser, review of *The Last Chance Texaco*, p. 11; January, 2006, Paula Rohrlick, review of *Grand & Humble*, p. 8; March, 2006, Kathryn Kulpa, review of *The Order of the Poison Oak*, p. 22.
Lambda Book Report, fall, 2008, Bill Burleson, interview with Hartinger and review of *Split Screen Split Screen: Attack of the Soul-sucking Brain Zombies/Bride of the Soul-sucking Brain Zombies*, both p. 38.
Public Libraries, July-August, 2006, "Geography of a Writer," p. 27.
Publishers Weekly, February 3, 2003, review of *Geography Club*, pp. 76-77; January 26, 2004, review of *The Last Chance Texaco*, p. 255; February 13, 2006, review of *Grand & Humble*, p. 90; May 21, 2007, review of *Dreamquest*, p. 55.
School Library Journal, February, 2003, Robert Gray, review of *Geography Club*, pp. 141-142; March, 2004, Faith Brautigan, review of *The Last Chance Texaco*, pp. 212-213; April, 2005, Hillias J. Martin, review of *The Order of the Poison Oak*, p. 134; February, 2006, Suzanne Gordon, review of *Grand & Humble*, p. 132; April, 2006, Brent Hartinger, Nancy Reeder, and Trev Jones, "Censorship or Information?," pp. 13-14; March, 2007, Kathleen E. Gruver, review of *Split Screen*, p. 210; February, 2008, Robyn Gioia, review of *Dreamquest*, p. 116; April, 2009, Sarah K. Allen, review of *Project Sweet Life*, p. 135.
Voice of Youth Advocates, February, 2006, Melissa Potter, review of *Grand & Humble*, pp. 485-486.

ONLINE

AfterElton.com, http://www.afterelton.com/ (February 5, 2007), Michael Jensen, "Attack of the Gay Teen Zombies."
Brent Hartinger Home Page, http://www.brenthartinger.com (June 1, 2010).
National Coalition against Censorship Web site, http://www.ncac.org/ (June 19, 2009), interview with Hartinger.
News Tribune Online (Tacoma, WA), http://www.Tribnet.com/ (March 2, 2003), Amanda Laughtland, "Gay Teen Novel Fills a Void."
Publishers Weekly Online, http://www.publishersweekly.com/ (March 21, 2003), Kevin Howell, "Gay YA Novel, *Geography Club*, Goes to the Head of the Class."
Teenreads.com, http://www.teenreads.com/ (April 12, 2005), Carlie Webber, interview with Hartinger.

HAZELAAR, Cor

Personal

Born in San Francisco, CA; married Matt Straub (a painter); children: Nola. *Education:* Pratt Institute, B.A. (illustration).

Addresses

Home—New York, NY. *E-mail*—info@corhazelaar.com.

Career

Illustrator, author, and print project specialist. Presenter at schools. *Exhibitions:* Work included in Society of Illustrator Original Art exhibition, 1995.

Awards, Honors

New York Times Best Illustrated Book designation, 1995, for *Dogs Everywhere.*

Writings

SELF-ILLUSTRATED

Dogs Everywhere, Knopf (New York, NY), 1995.
Zoo Dreams, Farrar, Straus & Giroux (New York, NY), 1997.

ILLUSTRATOR

Anne Shelby, *The Man Who Lived in a Hollow Tree,* Atheneum Books for Young Readers (New York, NY), 2009.

Sidelights

Cor Hazelaar moved to New York City to study illustration at Pratt Institute, and has worked in print production, primarily for magazines, since the early 1990s. This background has given her an awareness of design and an understanding of publishing technologies and processes that is unusual for an author/illustrator. Her works are characterized by thorough research, subtle color, and a unique, flat illustration style that enhances meaning in deceptively simple stories. Her first original self-illustrated book, *Dogs Everywhere,* was exhibited in the Society of Illustrators Original Art show in 1995 and awarded a Best Illustrated Book designation from the *New York Times.* In addition to creating a second book, *Zoo Dreams,* Hazelaar has also created the colorful collage-like illustrations for Anne Shelby's Appalachian-themed folk tale *The Man Who Lived in a Hollow Tree.*

The story of a tree-loving man who is given a second chance to enjoy the benefits of youth after he moves into a giant sycamore, *The Man Who Lived in a Hollow Tree* was praised by *Booklist* contributor Julie Cummins as "beautifully designed and charmingly told." In *Kirkus Reviews* a reviewer remarked in particular on Hazelaar's "pale, country-toned acrylics," which feature quilt motifs and "are the perfect folk touch" to pair with Shelby's tale.

Featuring Hazelaar's simple verse, *Dogs Everywhere* follows several frisky dogs on their daily walks, as they tug their owners along by leash, eager to arrive at the local park where they can run, fetch, and play with other dogs before going home to patiently wait for the next walk. In *Booklist* Ellen Mandel cited the book's combination of a "sparse text" and "sprightly illustrations," and a *Publishers Weekly* critic concluded that Hazelaar's "quaint and fanciful" images for *Dogs Everywhere,* featuring a "subtle and luminescent" grey-toned palette, make her "an artist to watch."

Inspired by Hazelaar's interest in city zoos, *Zoo Dreams* allows readers to enter a zoo at closing time, as the zoo keeper checks on each animal to be sure that all will be safe and comfortable during the night. Toucans perch on branches, while a polar bear curls up in a cozy ball, and a giraffe sleeps standing up. In *Publishers Weekly* a contributor wrote that Hazelaar's "tranquil, meditative" picture book features soft-toned illustrations that "convey a sense of quietude." Also recommending *Zoo Dreams* for bedtime reading, Maeve Visser Knoth added in *Horn Book* that the author's use of "simple shapes . . . beautifully convey the impression of dusk at the zoo."

Biographical and Critical Sources

PERIODICALS

Booklist, May 1, 1995, Ellen Mandel, review of *Dogs Everywhere,* p. 1580; June 1, 2009, Julie Cummins, review of *The Man Who Lived in a Hollow Tree,* p. 65.
Horn Book, March-April, 1997, Maeve Visser Knoth, review of *Zoo Dreams,* p. 192.
Kirkus Reviews, February 1, 2009, review of *The Man Who Lived in a Hollow Tree.*
Publishers Weekly, May 1, 1995, review of *Dogs Everywhere,* p. 57; January 27, 1997, review of *Zoo Dreams,* p. 105.

ONLINE

Cor Hazelaar Home Page, http://www.corhazelaar.com (May 31, 2010).

* * *

HENRY, Rohan

Personal

Born in Jamaica; married; children: one daughter.

Addresses

Home—Portland, ME.

Career

Educator and artist. Teacher at the elementary-grade level in ME.

Writings

SELF-ILLUSTRATED

The Perfect Gift, Stewart, Tabori & Chang (New York, NY), 2007.
Good Night, Baby Ruby, Abrams Books for Young Readers (New York, NY), 2009.

Sidelights

Jamaican-born artist Rohan Henry is an elementary-school teacher affiliated with the University of Maine's STRIVE-U program. In addition to his teaching, Henry has also created the picture books *The Perfect Gift* and *Good Night, Baby Ruby,* both of which pair warm-hearted stories with his evocative spot-tinted pen-and-ink illustrations.

In *The Perfect Gift* a bunny named Leo is determined to find a gift that captures his feelings for best friend Lucy, while the dilemma faced by a toddler who does not want her busy day to end is the focus of *Good Night, Baby Ruby.* In what a *Publishers Weekly* contributor described as a "simple . . . text that invites readers to in-

teract," Henry's story in *Good Night, Baby Ruby* describes parents' search for their bright-eyed daughter as the freshly bathed and pajama-clad Ruby scampers from one hiding place to another in order to avoid being tucked in for the night. Even the family cat joins in the search, which is captured in line drawings tinted with touches of blue, pink, red, and yellow. In *School Library Journal* Kathleen Fine predicted that *Good Night, Baby Ruby* "will resonate with young and old alike," and a *Kirkus Reviews* writer noted that the story's "wry language and amusing details" make Henry's picture book an "intriguing children's-book debut."

Biographical and Critical Sources

PERIODICALS

Kirkus Reviews, February 1, 2009, review of *Good Night, Baby Ruby.*
Publishers Weekly, January 26, 2009, review of *Good Night, Baby Ruby,* p. 118.
School Library Journal, March, 2009, Kathleen Finn, review of *Good Night, Baby Ruby,* p. 114.*

*   *   *

HOBAN, Julia

Personal

Daughter of Russell (an author) and Lillian (an illustrator and author) Hoban.

Addresses

Home—NY.

Career

Writer.

Writings

FOR CHILDREN

Amy Loves the Sun, illustrated by mother, Lillian Hoban, Harper & Row (New York, NY), 1988.
Amy Loves the Wind, illustrated by Lillian Hoban, Harper & Row (New York, NY), 1988.
Amy Loves the Rain, illustrated by Lillian Hoban, Harper & Row (New York, NY), 1989.
Amy Loves the Snow, illustrated by Lillian Hoban, Harper & Row (New York, NY), 1989.
Quick Chick, illustrated by Lillian Hoban, E.P. Dutton (New York, NY), 1989.
Buzby, illustrated by John Himmelman, Harper & Row (New York, NY), 1990.

Rohan Henry's naïf pen drawings capture the emotions in his picture-book story for **Good Night, Baby Ruby.** (Abrams Books for Young Readers, 2009. Illustration copyright © 2009 by Rohan Henry. Reproduced by permission.)

Buzby to the Rescue, illustrated by John Himmelman, HarperCollins (New York, NY), 1993.

NOVELS

Acting Normal, HarperCollins (New York, NY), 1998.
Willow, Dial (New York, NY), 2009, published as *Scarred,* Piatkus Books (London, England), 2010.

Adaptations

Willow was adapted as an audiobook read by Kim J. Ulrich, Random Audio, 2009.

Sidelights

Julia Hoban started her writing career working in collaboration with her mother, artist and children's-book author Lillian Hoban, creating picture-book texts for stories such as *Quick Chick* and *Amy Loves the Sun* and its sequels. Beginning in 1990, Hoban teamed with artist John Himmelman on the picture books *Buzby* and *Buzby to the Rescue,* but more recently she has turned her focus to older children, creating the dramatic young-adult novels *Acting Normal* and *Willow.*

Cover of Julia Hoban's dramatic teen novel Willow, *which finds a young woman haunted by a family tragedy.* (Dial Books, 2009. Cover photograph by istockphoto.com/Heidi Anglesey. Reproduced by permission of Dial Books, a division of Penguin Putnam Books for Young Readers.)

In *Acting Normal* Hoban deals with the serious issues of rape and sexual abuse in a story that finds eighteen-year-old child actress Stephanie in a therapist's office while trying to deal with an emotional breakdown. Unable to attend classes for over a year, the teen keeps in touch with Dahlia, a high-school friend who turns to Stephanie for comfort after she is assaulted by a truck driver. As readers follow Stephanie's interactions with her therapist, they learn—as she does—that her problems stem from a childhood trauma. Although *Booklist* contributor Hazel Rochman described *Acting Normal* as "more case history than novel," she added that Hoban's novel would be "a good [choice] . . . for group bibliotherapy." In addition to describing the life of a young actor, *Acting Normal* features "a relatively sensible narrator [that] readers can trust," according to a *Publishers Weekly* critic.

A tragic automobile accident that resulted in the death of a teen's parents is the focus of *Willow.* Even though she only had her learner's permit, Willow Randall was the designated driver during a family's dinner out, when she was behind the wheel during a tragic and fatal accident. Now the seventeen year old translates her feelings of guilt over the accident into self-destructive cutting. Although she lives with her older brother David and his wife, Willow is able to hide her cutting—and her pain—from him, thereby emotionally isolating herself from her only surviving family member. When new friend Guy learns Willow's secret, his effort to understand her contradictions "serves as a means for Willow to rediscover human connection," according to a *Publishers Weekly* critic. Praising Hoban's sensitive story in *School Library Journal,* Caryl Soriano wrote that *Willow* "takes readers on an intense journey that allows them to see a cutter's painful reality." A *Kirkus Reviews* writer highlighted Hoban's "sharp insight," recommending the novel as an "appropriately complex portrayal" of "a crucial subject."

Biographical and Critical Sources

PERIODICALS

Booklist, April 15, 1998, Hazel Rochman, review of *Acting Normal,* p. 1435.
Kirkus Reviews, February 1, 2009, review of *Willow.*
Publishers Weekly, May 4, 1998, review of *Acting Normal,* p. 214; April 20, 2009, review of *Willow,* p. 51.
School Library Journal, April, 2009, Caryl Soriano, review of *Willow,* p. 136.*

*   *   *

HORTON, Joan

Personal

Married; children: four. *Education:* Attended Hartford College for Women (now University of Hartford); University of Connecticut, B.A. and M.S.W.

Addresses

Home—Glastonbury, CT.

Career

Writer. Hartford Hospital, Hartford, CT, former medical technologist; former social worker.

Writings

Halloween Hoots and Howls, illustrated by JoAnn Adinolfi, Henry Holt (New York, NY), 1999.
I Brought My Rat for Show-and-tell, and Other Funny School Poems, illustrated by Melanie Siegel, Grosset & Dunlap (New York, NY), 2004.
Hippopotamus Stew, and Other Silly Animal Poems, illustrated by JoAnn Adinolfi, Henry Holt (New York, NY), 2006.
Math Attack!, illustrated by Kyrsten Brooker, Farrar, Straus & Giroux (New York, NY), 2009.

Sidelights

The author of *I Brought My Rat for Show-and-tell, and Other Funny School Poems, Math Attack!,* and *Hippopotamus Stew, and Other Silly Animal Poems,* among other books, Joan Horton spikes her children's tales with humor. A former medical technologist, Horton began writing for young people after her own four children were grown, and in her writing she taps her own love of the lighthearted rhyming childhood classics of Mother Goose. Reviewing the eighteen verses collected in *I Brought My Rat for Show-and-tell, and Other Funny School Poems, Booklist* critic Hazel Rochman cited Horton's ability to inspire young readers with her "joy with language."

Featuring colorful pastel-and-watercolor paintings by JoAnn Adinolfi, *Halloween Hoots and Howls* contains a collection of silly trick-or-treat verses that introduces a timid ghost, a witch with an out-of-control broomstick, and a very unscary Frankenstein, among others. Another collaboration with Adinolfi, *Hippopotamus Stew, and Other Silly Animal Poems,* introduces an equally quirky cast, although this time animals of all sorts— from jellyfish and whales to lizards and kangaroos— serve as Horton's subjects. "Pictures and words strike the same winsome, wacky tone" in *Halloween Hoots and Howls,* according to *Booklist* critic Susan Dove Lempke, the reviewer adding that Adinolfi's art interprets Horton's "poems to perfection." A *Publishers Weekly* critic wrote that Horton "zeroes in the kind of humor that will appeal to her target audience" in the twenty-one poems in *Hippopotamus Stew, and Other Silly Animal Poems,* while Rochman identified the author's "sly humor" as key to the book's appeal.

In *Math Attack!,* illustrated in colorful art by Canadian artist Kyrsten Brooker, Horton captures a girl's efforts to master the times tables, particularly the elusive solu-

Joan Horton shares her lighthearted humor with readers of **Halloween Hoots and Howls,** *a picture book featuring artwork by JoAnn Adinolfi.* (Illustration copyright © 1999 by JoAnn Adinolfi. Reprinted by permission of Henry Holt & Company, LLC.)

tion to seven multiplied by ten. Wrestling with the tangle of numbers multiplied by other numbers, the girl's overtaxed mind tosses out numerous numbers, filling her classroom, and even her town. In *Booklist* Carolyn Phelan praised the "well-crafted rhymed couplets" in *Math Attack!,* adding that the story's "quick pace" is captured in Brooker's "energetic" multimedia collage illustrations. Also praising the book in *School Library Journal,* Mary Hazelton commended Horton's verse, writing that her "rhyming text is well cadenced, with carefully chosen words that flow easily."

Biographical and Critical Sources

PERIODICALS

Booklist, September 1, 1999, Susan Dove Lempke, review of *Halloween Hoots and Howls,* p. 145; August, 2004, Hazel Rochman, review of *I Brought My Rat for Show-and-tell, and Other Funny School Poems,* p. 1938; February 1, 2006, Hazel Rochman, review of *Hippopotamus Stew, and Other Silly Animal Poems,* p. 52; January 1, 2009, Carolyn Phelan, review of *Math Attack!,* p. 92.
Kirkus Reviews, March 1, 2006, review of *Hippopotamus Stew, and Other Silly Animal Poems,* p. 231; February 1, 2009, review of *Math Attack!*

Publishers Weekly, September 27, 1999, review of *Halloween Hoots and Howls,* p. 47; March 20, 2006, review of *Hippopotamus Stew, and Other Silly Animal Poems,* p. 54; March 9, 2009, review of *Math Attack!,* p. 47.

School Library Journal, October, 2004, Anne Knickerbocker, review of *I Brought My Rat for Show-and-tell, and Other Funny School Poems,* p. 142; March, 2006, Grace Oliff, review of *Hippopotamus Stew, and Other Silly Animal Poems,* p. 209; March, 2009, Mary Hazelton, review of *Math Attack!,* p. 116.

ONLINE

Macmillan Web site, http://us.macmillan.com/ (June 15, 2010), "Joan Horton."*

* * *

HROMIC, Alma A.
See ALEXANDER, Alma

* * *

HUGHES, Carol 1955-

Personal

Born 1955, in Yorkshire, England; married; husband's name John (an animation artist); children: two daughters. *Education:* Attended Brighton College of Art, England.

Addresses

Home—Los Angeles, CA.

Career

Writer. Animation artist in London, England, including for Animation City (production company); writer, 1995—. Worked variously as a cleaner, office worker, T-shirt folder, receptionist, civil servant, and waitress.

Writings

Toots and the Upside-down House, illustrated by J. Garrett Sheldrew, Random House (New York, NY), 1996.
Jack Black and the Ship of Thieves, Bloomsbury (London, England), 1997, Random House (New York, NY), 2000.
Toots Upside Down Again, Bloomsbury (London, England), 1998, published as *Toots Underground,* Random House (New York, NY), 2001.
Toots Underwater, Bloomsbury (London, England), 1999.
Dirty Magic, Random House (New York, NY), 2006.
The Princess and the Unicorn, Random House (New York, NY), 2009.

Sidelights

Although Carol Hughes began her career as an artist, she now makes her living as the author of innovative works of fantasy, including *Jack Black and the Ship of Thieves* and *Dirty Magic.* Her books have won praise for their humorous approach to resolving interpersonal conflicts in families. "I have been a writer my whole life, but oddly enough I didn't realize it until I was grown up," Hughes noted in an essay on the Random House Web site. "Looking back I can see that I was always writing and making up stories."

Hughes grew up in Lancashire, England, where her parents were the proprietors of a small inn. As a young girl, she hoped to become a ballerina, but her height proved to be a detriment, and in her teens Hughes began to devote more time to artistic pursuits. She studied at the Brighton College of Art and began working as an animation artist in the pre-computer era, when it was necessary to painstakingly draw and color every frame by hand. Marrying a former colleague, Hughes moved with her husband John from England to the United States, where John accepted a job in San Francisco, California, and Carol, unable to secure a work permit, began writing to pass the time.

Five years later, Hughes's first book, *Toots and the Upside-down House,* was published. Toots is a lonely little girl, an only child whose mother died years before; Toots does not even remember her. Her father, immersed in his stamp collection, pays little attention to her. Mired in boredom one day, Toots decides to try standing on her head, and is surprised at how different the living room looks from this perspective. She is also astonished by the sight of a little fairy running across the ceiling and vanishing through a miniature door.

Soon Toots herself, shrunk by the little fairies, escapes into this miniature upside-down world, where she encounters fantastical talking plants and a host of other perverse-reverse phenomena, including frost that burns. She also discovers the evil house sprites, who are battling the good fairies for control of her house. By freezing the house's pipes, the evil ones hope to cause irreparable water damage to Toots's father's prized stamp collection. The scheming sprites try to win Toots to their side by promising to cast a spell that will gain her father's attention. Ultimately, Toots sides with the good pixies, whose job is to protect the house. She saves the stamp collection, and returns renewed to the real world. Hughes's "elaborate hierarchy of tiny, mythical creatures," noted a *Publishers Weekly* reviewer, offers "much to spark the imagination." Writing for *Booklist,* Helen Rosenberg praised *Toots and the Upside-down House* for its "Alice in Wonderland feel," and deemed it "a well-crafted, fast-paced fantasy."

In *Toots Upside Down Again,* which was published in the United States as *Toots Underground,* a flip on her garden swing places Toots once again in a magical upside-down world, where she is reunited with Cadet

Fairy Olive. The fairies enlist her to help combat a poisonous, ruinous weed that was dispatched by an evil waspgnat to blight the Fairy Squadron's Upside-Down Garden. "The waspgnat makes a thoroughly nasty adversary," a critic stated in *Kirkus Reviews,* and *Books for Keeps* reviewer Andrew Kidd appreciated an especially "amusing confrontation with two haughty maggots (who pronounce their name 'Maggo')." Comparing *Toots Upside Down Again* to the work of J.R.R. Tolkien, Kidd recommended Hughes's "exciting fantasy" to "fluent upper junior readers or lower junior listeners."

In *Toots Underwater* the young heroine must deal with a fairy crisis as well as her unresolved feelings toward her father's new girlfriend. "Hughes has created an intriguing upside-down world," Elaine Williams wrote in her review of the book for the *Times Educational Supplement.* "She has woven a wonderful flight of fancy out of Toots's attempts to resolve her raw feelings of frustration and jealousy."

Jack Black and the Ship of Thieves is another of Hughes's imaginative creations. *Carousel* critic Chris Stephenson cited the story's title alone as "a further display of the author's rich inventiveness, strong narrative drive, and sharp sense of fun." In this fast-paced fantasy story, title character Jack Black is experiencing a strained relationship with his honorable father, Captain Black. In contrast, he has nothing but admiration for his hero, a flying ace named Gadfly. When the captain allows Jack to go on the maiden voyage of the *Bellerophon,* the world's largest airship, along with Gadfly, Jack is ecstatic. On board, however, Jack inadvertently discovers that Gadfly is at the center of a plot to sabotage the craft. Before he can help, Jack falls out of the airship and into a mythical world full of sea monsters and pirates. Jack's father and his crew become stranded in the ice of the Polar Sea, but Jack, with the help of several new friends, comes to the rescue. Hughes' story "teems with memorable characters," wrote Stephenson, the critic adding that her "nonstop, breathless adventure" features "hair's-breadth escapes and more twists and turns than a bowl of spaghetti." *School Librarian* contributor Cherrie Warwick dubbed *Jack Black and the Ship of Thieves* "a superb book and impossible to put down."

Hughes presents a dark fantasy tale in *Dirty Magic,* a novel "that will have readers on the edge of their seats," according to *School Library Journal* reviewer Christi Voth. Frustrated with the antics his younger sister, Hannah, ten-year-old Joe lashes out at her, stating that he wishes she were dead. That night, Joe awakens to learn that Hannah has disappeared, and he is transported to a mysterious, war-ravaged world that is being torn apart by the rivalry between sister queens. There a "fetcher" named Katherine introduces Joe to Spider, an elderly blind man with magical abilities who can help the youngster locate his missing sister. "This dense but quick-paced fantasy offers suspense," Shelle Rosenfeld noted in *Booklist,* and a *Publishers Weekly* contributor

observed that the author "has a lucid imagination and paints a vivid, bleak and ruined world," then "wraps up her challenging story with a well-concealed twist." A critic in *Kirkus Reviews* praised Hughes's portrait of her main character, stating that "Joe's ignorance of the kingdoms at war is balanced by his knowledge of mechanics, sense of direction and self-reliance."

In *The Princess and the Unicorn,* a fairy attempts to prevent the destruction of her homeland. After Princess Eleanor spies a unicorn in Swinley Forest, she decides to take it back to Buckingham Palace, little realizing that both the creature and the forest will sicken and die if it leaves. Joyce, a fairy from the village of Swinley Hope, is assigned the task of returning the unicorn to its home, but her task is made more difficult by Eleanor's wicked governess, who has plans to sell the unicorn for her own profit. "Joyce and Eleanor are both plucky girls with imagination," a *Kirkus Reviews* contributor reported, and Carolyn Phelan maintained in *Booklist* that Joyce's "brave quest for the unicorn becomes the most satisfying part of the book."

Cover of Carol Hughes' elementary-grade fantasy The Princess and the Unicorn, *featuring artwork by Juliana Kolesova.* (Jacket art copyright © 2009 by Juliana Kolesova. Used by permission of Random House Children's Books, a division of Random House, Inc.)

Biographical and Critical Sources

PERIODICALS

Book, September, 2000, Kathleen Odean, review of *Jack Black and the Ship of Thieves,* p. 86.

Booklist, September 1, 1997, Helen Rosenberg, review of *Toots and the Upside-down House,* p. 125; October 15, 2000, Michael Cart, review of *Jack Black and the Ship of Thieves,* p. 438; October 1, 2006, Shelle Rosenfeld, review of *Dirty Magic,* p. 54; January 1, 2009, Carolyn Phelan, review of *The Princess and the Unicorn,* p. 84.

Books for Keeps, May, 1998, Andrew Kidd, review of *Toots Upside Down Again,* p. 25.

Carousel, spring, 1998, Chris Stephenson, "Carol Hughes," p. 29.

Horn Book, May, 1998, review of *Jack Black and the Ship of Thieves,* p. 569.

Kirkus Reviews, September 1, 2001, review of *Toots Underground,* p. 1291; October 15, 2006, review of *Dirty Magic,* p. 1072; January 1, 2009, review of *The Princess and the Unicorn.*

Publishers Weekly, May 19, 1997, review of *Toots and the Upside-down House,* p. 76; September 4, 2000, review of *Jack Black and the Ship of Thieves,* p. 108; December 18, 2006, review of *Dirty Magic,* p. 63.

School Librarian, November, 1997, Cherrie Warwick, review of *Jack Black and the Ship of Thieves,* p. 191.

School Library Journal, September, 2000, Starr E. Smith, review of *Jack Black and the Ship of Thieves,* p. 232; October, 2001, Elaine E. Knight, review of *Toots Underground,* p. 120; February, 2007, Christi Voth, review of *Dirty Magic,* p. 118; May, 2009, Cheri Dobbs, review of *The Princess and the Unicorn,* p. 110.

Times Educational Supplement, August 27, 1999, Elaine Williams, review of *Toots Underwater.*

ONLINE

Carol Hughes Home Page, http://www.udyllic.com (June 10, 2010).

Random House Web site, http://www.randomhouse.com/ (June 10, 2010), "Carol Hughes."*

J-K

JACOBS, Lee
   See STONE, Tanya Lee

*   *   *

JAVERNICK, Ellen 1938-

Personal

Born June 27, 1938, in Cleveland, OH; daughter of John (a physician) and Mary Janith (a lab technician) Work; married Frank Javernick (a teacher and coach), August 3, 1963; children: Mike, Becky, Andy, Matt, Lisa. *Education:* DePauw University, B.A., 1963; University of Northern Colorado, M.A. (early childhood education), 1989. *Hobbies and other interests:* Tennis, teaching swimming.

Addresses

Home—Loveland, CO.

Career

Author and educator. Elementary school teacher, beginning 1960, including Garfield School, Loveland, CO, beginning 1988; Loveland Preschool, Inc., director, 1976-88; freelance writer. Serves on local library board in Loveland, CO, and Catholic community services board for Larimer and Weld Counties, CO. Presenter at conferences.

Member

Society of Children's Book Writers and Illustrators (former president, Rocky Mountain chapter), Association for the Education of the Young Child.

Writings

Christmas Bulletin Boards, Walls, Windows, Doors, and More ("Bulletin Board" series), illustrated by Dan Grossmann, Shining Star (Goleta, CA), 1986.

Ellen Javernick (Reproduced by permission.)

Celebrate the Christian Family ("Celebrate" series), illustrated by Sarah Mohler, Shining Star (Goleta, CA), 1987.

Celebrate Me Made in God's Image ("Celebrate" series), Shining Star (Goleta, CA), 1988.

What If Everybody Did That?, illustrated by Richard Hackney, Children's Press (Danbury, CT), 1990, new edition, illustrated by Colleen Madden, Marshall Cavendish (New York, NY), 2010.

Where's Brooke? ("Rookie Reader" series), illustrated by Richard Hackney, Children's Press (Danbury, CT), 1992.

Double the Trouble ("Gifted and Talented Reader" series), illustrated by Diane O'Quinn Burke, Lowell House (Lowell, MA), 1994.

Time for Bed! ("Gifted and Talented Reader" series), illustrated by J.J. Smith-Moore, Lowell House (Lowell, MA), 1994.

Ms. Pollywog's Problem-solving Service ("Ready, Set, Read" series), illustrated by Meredith Johnson, Augsburg Fortress (Minneapolis, MN), 1995.

Patient Papas, Shortland (Australia), 1996.

Show and Tell, Scott, Foresman (Upper Saddle River, NJ), 1996.

God's House, illustrated by Virginia H. Richards and D. Thomas Halpin, Pauline Books & Media (Boston, MA), 1999.

The Birthday Pet, illustrated by Kevin O'Malley, Marshall Cavendish Children (New York, NY), 2009.

Contributor of articles and stories to numerous magazines and journals, including *Catholic Digest, Christian Home and School, Highlights for Children, Home Life, Hopscotch, Humpty Dumpty, Instructor, Jack and Jill, Junior Trails, Kidzone, Teaching PreK-12,* and *Young Children.*

Sidelights

During her career as an elementary school teacher in her home state of Colorado, as well as while raising her own five children, Ellen Javernick learned what books appeal to young children. In the mid-1980s she decided to put that knowledge to good use, beginning a second career writing original stories to entertain and encourage beginning readers. Featuring illustrations by a variety of artists, Javernick's stories include *Where's Brooke?, God's House, The Birthday Pet,* and *What If Everybody Did That?*

Featuring artwork by Kevin O'Malley, *The Birthday Pet* introduces Danny, a little boy who wants a pet box turtle and hopes that he will get one for his upcoming birthday. When the day comes, Danny is granted part of his wish: his mom, dad, brother, and sister each give him a pet. With the house now the home of a dog, cat, bird, and even a rat, there is still no turtle. Ultimately the boy and his family sort everything out, and each family member gets to keep the pet he or she selected while everyone pitches in to get Danny his turtle. In addition to praising Javernick's "simple yet clever" verses, Martha Simpson added in *School Library Journal* that O'Malley's "bright pencil and marker illustrations practically jump off the page." *The Birthday Pet* serves as a "humorous reminder that listening counts," according to a *Kirkus Reviews* writer, and Shelle Rosenfeld predicted in *School Library Journal* that children "will enjoy the [book's] simple, well-paced, rhyming text."

Javernick once told *SATA:* "When I was growing up in New Jersey the branch library down the street was my favorite place. I can remember it as clearly as my own

Javernick's picture book The Birthday Pet *follows a young animal-lover's quandary in illustrations by Kevin O'Malley.* (Marshall Cavendish Children, 2009. Illustration © 2009 by Kevin O'Malley. Reproduced by permission.)

bedroom. I can remember just where my favorite books were located on the shelves. I always dreamed that someday my books would be on library shelves and that other children would ride their bikes down to read them.

"When I grew up I had five children who kept me busy and supplied me with plenty of material to write about. Now I teach second grade and enjoy staying in touch with children. They're always saying, 'You ought to write about. . . .' My recent book, *Ms. Pollywog's Problem-Solving Service,* was written after I'd read my class *Mrs. Pigglewiggle,* and I asked them what problems they thought need solving."

Biographical and Critical Sources

PERIODICALS

Booklist, April 1, 2009, Shelle Rosenfeld, review of *The Birthday Pet,* p. 42.

Kirkus Reviews, February 1, 2009, review of *The Birthday Pet.*

School Library Journal, March, 2009, Martha Simpson, review of *The Birthday Pet,* p. 117.

ONLINE

Ellen Javernick Home Page, http://ellenjavernick.com (June 1, 2010).*

JONES, Marcia Thornton 1958-

Personal

Born July 15, 1958, in Joliet, IL; daughter of Robert Edwin (a federal government employee) and Thelma Helen (a homemaker) Thornton; married Stephen Walter Jones (a business manager), July 19, 1980. *Education:* University of Kentucky, A.B., 1980; Georgetown College, M.A., 1987. *Religion:* Roman Catholic. *Hobbies and other interests:* Beading crafts, hiking, reading good books, traveling.

Addresses

Home—Lexington, KY.

Career

Author and educator. St. Leo Elementary School, Versailles, KY, teacher, 1980-81; Sayre School, Lexington, KY, teacher, 1981-87; Office of the Auditor of Public Accounts, Frankfort, KY, principle administrative specialist, 1991; Fayette County Public Schools, Lexington, teacher, beginning 1991; currently full-time writer. University of Kentucky, community education instructor, 1990. Presenter at workshops.

Member

Society of Children's Book Writers and Illustrators, Lexington Writers Critique Group.

Awards, Honors

Sayre School Short Award for excellence in teaching, 1985; (with Debbie Dadey) Children's Choice selection, International Reading Association, and Children's Top 100 Books selection, National Education Association, both 1990, both for *Vampires Don't Wear Polka Dots;* (with Dady) Elba Award, 1996, for *Wizards Don't Need Computers;* (with Dady) Milner Award, 2002, for body of work; Maude Hart Lovelace Book Award, 2007, for *Champ.*

Writings

Godzilla Ate My Homework, illustrated by Robert Krogle, Scholastic (New York, NY), 1997.
Story Sparkers: A Creativity Guide for Children's Writers, Writer's Digest Books (Cincinnati, OH), 2000.
Champ, Scholastic (New York, NY), 2007.
Leprechaun on the Loose, illustrated by Cyd Moore, Scholastic (New York, NY), 2008.
The Tale of Jack Frost, illustrated by Priscilla Burris, Scholastic (New York, NY), 2008.
Ratfink, illustrated by C.B. Decker, Dutton Children's Books (New York, NY), 2010.

Contributing editor of *Kidstuff* magazine. Contributor to *Kicks* magazine.

"ADVENTURES OF THE BAILEY SCHOOL KIDS" SERIES; WITH DEBBIE DADEY

Vampires Don't Wear Polka Dots, illustrated by John Steven Gurney, Scholastic (New York, NY), 1990.
Werewolves Don't Go to Summer Camp, illustrated by John Steven Gurney, Scholastic (New York, NY), 1991.
Santa Claus Doesn't Mop Floors, illustrated by John Steven Gurney, Scholastic (New York, NY), 1991.
Leprechauns Don't Play Basketball, illustrated by John Steven Gurney, Scholastic (New York, NY), 1992.
Ghosts Don't Eat Potato Chips, illustrated by John Steven Gurney, Scholastic (New York, NY), 1992.
Frankenstein Doesn't Plant Petunias, illustrated by John Steven Gurney, Scholastic (New York, NY), 1993.
Aliens Don't Wear Braces, illustrated by John Steven Gurney, Scholastic (New York, NY), 1993.
Genies Don't Ride Bicycles, illustrated by John Steven Gurney, Scholastic (New York, NY), 1993.
Pirates Don't Wear Pink Sunglasses, illustrated by John Steven Gurney, Scholastic (New York, NY), 1993.
Witches Don't Do Back Flips, illustrated by John Steven Gurney, Scholastic (New York, NY), 1994.
Skeletons Don't Play Tubas, illustrated by John Steven Gurney, Scholastic (New York, NY), 1994.
Cupids Don't Flip Hamburgers, illustrated by John Steven Gurney, Scholastic (New York, NY), 1995.
Gremlins Don't Chew Bubble Gum, illustrated by John Steven Gurney, Scholastic (New York, NY), 1995.
Monsters Don't Scuba Dive, illustrated by John Steven Gurney, Scholastic (New York, NY), 1995.
Zombies Don't Play Soccer, illustrated by John Steven Gurney, Scholastic (New York, NY), 1995.
Dracula Doesn't Drink Lemonade, illustrated by John Steven Gurney, Scholastic (New York, NY), 1995.
Elves Don't Wear Hard Hats, illustrated by John Steven Gurney, Scholastic (New York, NY), 1995.
Martians Don't Take Temperatures, illustrated by John Steven Gurney, Scholastic (New York, NY), 1995.
Gargoyles Don't Drive Buses, illustrated by John Steven Gurney, Scholastic (New York, NY), 1996.
Wizards Don't Need Computers, illustrated by John Steven Gurney, Scholastic (New York, NY), 1996.
Mummies Don't Coach Softball, illustrated by John Steven Gurney, Scholastic (New York, NY), 1996.
Cyclops Doesn't Roller Skate, illustrated by John Steven Gurney, Scholastic (New York, NY), 1996.
Angels Don't Know Karate, illustrated by John Steven Gurney, Scholastic (New York, NY), 1996.
Dragons Don't Cook Pizza, illustrated by John Steven Gurney, Scholastic (New York, NY), 1997.
Bigfoot Doesn't Square Dance, illustrated by John Steven Gurney, Scholastic (New York, NY), 1997.
Mermaids Don't Run Track, illustrated by John Steven Gurney, Scholastic (New York, NY), 1997.
Bogeymen Don't Play Football, illustrated by John Steven Gurney, Scholastic (New York, NY), 1997.
Unicorns Don't Give Sleigh Rides, illustrated by John Steven Gurney, Scholastic (New York, NY), 1997.
Knights Don't Teach Piano, illustrated by John Steven Gurney, Scholastic (New York, NY), 1998.

Hercules Doesn't Pull Teeth, illustrated by John Steven Gurney, Scholastic (New York, NY), 1998.

Ghouls Don't Scoop Ice Cream, illustrated by John Steven Gurney, Scholastic (New York, NY), 1998.

Phantoms Don't Drive Sports Cars, illustrated by John Steven Gurney, Scholastic (New York, NY), 1998.

Giants Don't Go Snowboarding, illustrated by John Steven Gurney, Scholastic (New York, NY), 1998.

Frankenstein Doesn't Slam Hockey Pucks, illustrated by John Steven Gurney, Scholastic (New York, NY), 1998.

Trolls Don't Ride Roller Coasters, illustrated by John Steven Gurney, Scholastic (New York, NY), 1999.

Wolfmen Don't Hula Dance, illustrated by John Steven Gurney, Scholastic (New York, NY), 1999.

Goblins Don't Play Video Games, illustrated by John Steven Gurney, Scholastic (New York, NY), 1999.

Ninjas Don't Bake Pumpkin Pies, illustrated by John Steven Gurney, Scholastic (New York, NY), 1999.

Dracula Doesn't Rock and Roll, illustrated by John Steven Gurney, Scholastic (New York, NY), 1999.

Sea Monsters Don't Ride Motorcycles, illustrated by John Steven Gurney, Scholastic (New York, NY), 1999.

The Bride of Frankenstein Doesn't Bake Cookies, illustrated by John Steven Gurney, Scholastic (New York, NY), 2000.

Robots Don't Catch Chicken Pox, illustrated by John Steven Gurney, Scholastic (New York, NY), 2000.

Vikings Don't Wear Wrestling Belts, illustrated by John Steven Gurney, Scholastic (New York, NY), 2000.

Ghosts Don't Rope Wild Horses, illustrated by John Steven Gurney, Scholastic (New York, NY), 2000.

Wizards Don't Wear Graduation Gowns, illustrated by John Steven Gurney, Scholastic (New York, NY), 2000.

Sea Serpents Don't Juggle Water Balloons, illustrated by John Steven Gurney, Scholastic (New York, NY), 2000.

Frankenstein Doesn't Start Food Fights, illustrated by John Steven Gurney, Scholastic (New York, NY), 2003.

Dracula Doesn't Play Kickball, illustrated by John Steven Gurney, Scholastic (New York, NY), 2004.

Werewolves Don't Run for President, illustrated by John Steven Gurney, Scholastic (New York, NY), 2004.

The Abominable Snowman Doesn't Roast Marshmallows, illustrated by John Steven Gurney, Scholastic (New York, NY), 2005.

Dragons Don't Throw Snowballs, illustrated by John Steven Gurney, Scholastic (New York, NY), 2006.

"ADVENTURES OF THE BAILEY SCHOOL KIDS HOLIDAY SPECIAL" SERIES; WITH DEBBIE DADEY

Swamp Monsters Don't Chase Wild Turkeys, illustrated by John Steven Gurney, Scholastic (New York, NY), 2001.

Aliens Don't Carve Jack-O-Lanterns, illustrated by John Steven Gurney, Scholastic (New York, NY), 2001.

Mrs. Claus Doesn't Climb Telephone Poles, illustrated by John Steven Gurney, Scholastic (New York, NY), 2001.

Leprechauns Don't Play Fetch, illustrated by John Steven Gurney, Scholastic (New York, NY), 2002.

Ogres Don't Hunt Easter Eggs, illustrated by John Steven Gurney, Scholastic (New York, NY), 2002.

"BAILEY SCHOOL KIDS SUPER SPECIALS" SERIES; WITH DEBBIE DADEY

Mrs. Jeepers Is Missing, illustrated by John Steven Gurney, Scholastic (New York, NY), 1996.

Mrs. Jeepers' Batty Vacation, illustrated by John Steven Gurney, Scholastic (New York, NY), 1997.

Mrs. Jeepers' Secret Cave, illustrated by John Steven Gurney, Scholastic (New York, NY), 1998.

Mrs. Jeepers in Outer Space, illustrated by John Steven Gurney, Scholastic (New York, NY), 1999.

Mrs. Jeepers' Monster Class Trip, illustrated by John Steven Gurney, Scholastic (New York, NY), 2001.

Mrs. Jeepers on Vampire Island, illustrated by John Steven Gurney, Scholastic (New York, NY), 2001.

Mrs. Jeepers' Scariest Halloween Ever, illustrated by John Steven Gurney, Scholastic (New York, NY), 2005.

Mrs. Jeepers' Creepy Christmas, illustrated by John Steven Gurney, Scholastic (New York, NY), 2007.

"BAILEY SCHOOL KIDS JR. CHAPTER BOOKS" SERIES; WITH DEBBIE DADEY

Ghosts Do Splash in Puddles, illustrated by Joëlle Dreidemy, Scholastic (New York, NY), 2006.

Reindeer Do Wear Striped Underwear, illustrated by Joëlle Dreidemy, Scholastic (New York, NY), 2006.

Cupid Does Eat Chocolate-Covered Snails, illustrated by Joëlle Dreidemy, Scholastic (New York, NY), 2007.

Pirates Do Ride Scooters, illustrated by Joëlle Dreidemy, Scholastic (New York, NY), 2007.

Dragons Do Eat Homework, illustrated by Joëlle Dreidemy, Scholastic (New York, NY), 2007.

Wizards Do Roast Turkeys, illustrated by Joëlle Dreidemy, Scholastic (New York, NY), 2007.

Vampires Do Hunt Marshmallow Bunnies, illustrated by Joëlle Dreidemy, Scholastic (New York, NY), 2008.

"BAILEY CITY MONSTERS" SERIES; WITH DEBBIE DADEY

The Monsters Next Door, illustrated by John Steven Gurney, Scholastic (New York, NY), 1998.

Howling at the Hauntlys', illustrated by John Steven Gurney, Scholastic (New York, NY), 1998.

Vampire Trouble, illustrated by John Steven Gurney, Scholastic (New York, NY), 1998.

Kilmer's Pet Monster, illustrated by John Steven Gurney, Scholastic (New York, NY), 1999.

Double Trouble Monsters, illustrated by John Steven Gurney, Scholastic (New York, NY), 1999.

Spooky Spells, illustrated by John Steven Gurney, Scholastic (New York, NY), 1999.

Vampire Baby, illustrated by John Steven Gurney, Scholastic (New York, NY), 1999.

Snow Monster Mystery, illustrated by John Steven Gurney, Scholastic (New York, NY), 1999.

The Hauntlys' Hairy Surprise, illustrated by John Steven Gurney, Scholastic (New York, NY), 1999.

Happy Boo Day, illustrated by John Steven Gurney, Scholastic (New York, NY), 2000.

"TRIPLET TROUBLE" SERIES; WITH DEBBIE DADEY

Triplet Trouble and the Talent Show Mess, illustrated by John Speirs, Scholastic (New York, NY), 1995.

Triplet Trouble and the Runaway Reindeer, illustrated by John Speirs, Scholastic (New York, NY), 1995.

Triplet Trouble and the Red Heart Race, illustrated by John Speirs, Scholastic (New York, NY), 1996.

Triplet Trouble and the Field Day Disaster, illustrated by John Speirs, Scholastic (New York, NY), 1996.

Triplet Trouble and the Cookie Contest, illustrated by John Speirs, Scholastic (New York, NY), 1996.

Triplet Trouble and the Pizza Party, illustrated by John Speirs, Scholastic (New York, NY), 1996.

Triplet Trouble and the Bicycle Race, illustrated by John Speirs, Scholastic (New York, NY), 1997.

Triplet Trouble and the Class Trip, illustrated by John Speirs, Scholastic (New York, NY), 1997.

"BARKLEY'S SCHOOL FOR DOGS" SERIES; WITH DEBBIE DADEY

Playground Bully, illustrated by Amy Wummer, Volo (New York, NY), 2001.

Puppy Trouble, illustrated by Amy Wummer, Volo (New York, NY), 2001.

Top Dog, illustrated by Amy Wummer, Volo (New York, NY), 2001.

Ghost Dog, illustrated by Amy Wummer, Volo (New York, NY), 2001.

Snow Day, illustrated by Amy Wummer, Volo (New York, NY), 2001.

Sticks and Stones and Doggie Bones, illustrated by Amy Wummer, Volo (New York, NY), 2002.

Buried Treasure, illustrated by Amy Wummer, Volo (New York, NY), 2002.

Blue Ribbon Blues, illustrated by Amy Wummer, Volo (New York, NY), 2002.

Santa Dog, illustrated by Amy Wummer, Volo (New York, NY), 2002.

Tattle Tails, illustrated by Amy Wummer, Volo (New York, NY), 2002.

Puppy Love, illustrated by Amy Wummer, Volo (New York, NY), 2002.

Prize-winning Parade, illustrated by Amy Wummer, Volo (New York, NY), 2003.

"GHOSTVILLE" SERIES; WITH DEBBIE DADEY

Ghost Class, illustrated by Jeremy Tugeau, Scholastic (New York, NY), 2002.

Ghost Game, illustrated by Jeremy Tugeau, Scholastic (New York, NY), 2003.

New Ghoul in School, illustrated by Jeremy Tugeau, Scholastic (New York, NY), 2003.

Happy Haunting!, illustrated by Jeremy Tugeau, Scholastic (New York, NY), 2004.

Stage Fright, illustrated by Jeremy Tugeau, Scholastic (New York, NY), 2004.

Happy Boo-Day to You!, Scholastic (New York, NY), 2004.

Hide-and-Spook, Scholastic (New York, NY), 2004.

Ghosts Be Gone!, illustrated by Guy Francis, Scholastic (New York, NY), 2004.

Beware of the Blabbermouth!, illustrated by Guy Francis, Scholastic (New York, NY), 2004.

Class Trip to the Haunted House, illustrated by Guy Francis, Scholastic (New York, NY), 2005.

The Treasure Haunt, illustrated by Guy Francis, Scholastic (New York, NY), 2005.

Frights! Camera! Action!, illustrated by Guy Francis, Scholastic (New York, NY), 2005.

Guys and Ghouls, illustrated by Guy Francis, Scholastic (New York, NY), 2006.

Frighting like Cats and Dogs, illustrated by Guy Francis, Scholastic (New York, NY), 2006.

A Very Haunted Holiday, illustrated by Guy Francis, Scholastic (New York, NY), 2006.

Red, White, and Boo!, illustrated by Guy Francis, Scholastic (New York, NY), 2007.

No Haunting Zone!, illustrated by Guy Francis, Scholastic (New York, NY), 2007.

"KEYHOLDERS" SERIES; WITH DEBBIE DADEY

This Side of Magic, illustrated by Adam Stower, Starscape (New York, NY), 2009.

The Other Side of Magic, illustrated by Adam Stower, Starscape (New York, NY), 2009.

Inside the Magic, illustrated by Adam Stower, Starscape (New York, NY), 2009.

The Wrong Side of Magic, illustrated by Adam Stower, Starscape (New York, NY), 2009.

Sidelights

Marcia Thornton Jones is the author of dozens of books for young readers, including the works in the popular "Adventures of the Bailey School Kids" series, cowritten with Debbie Dadey. Jones and Dadey have earned plaudits for such lively tales as *Vampires Don't Wear Polka Dots, Skeletons Don't Play Tubas,* and *The Abominable Snowman Doesn't Roast Marshmallows,* all of which feature the humorous exploits of several classmates who investigate the strange goings-on in their hometown. "Our books are really silly with a touch of mystery and suspense," Jones told *Lexington Herald-Leader* Karla Ward.

Additionally, Jones, a former elementary school teacher, has written a number of solo titles, including the middle-grade novels *Godzilla Ate My Homework, Ratfink,* and *Champ* and the picture books *Leprechaun on the Loose* and *The Tale of Jack Frost.* "With every word I write, I have the potential to change a life," Jones remarked to Ward. "I'm still teaching, but my classroom has gotten very big."

Cover of Giants Don't Go Snowboarding, *an easy reader by Marcia Thornton Jones and Debbie Dadey that features artwork by John Steven Gurney.* (Illustration copyright © 1998 by Scholastic, Inc. Reproduced by permission of Scholastic, Inc.)

"There is magic in the written word," Jones once told *SATA*. "My most vivid childhood memories involve reading well-crafted stories that took me places I never imagined possible. Other children collected baseball cards and Barbie dolls. I collected paper and pencils. I wanted to create magic for myself, but no one ever taught me how to write—or even where to begin. So my efforts were limited, and even then I felt the isolated frustration writers feel when they're not sure if their work is good or not.

"During high school and college, my writing became formal as I completed theme after theme. No one taught me how to write themes either, but my grades indicated a knack for writing—or at least for fooling professors! After graduating with high distinction from the University of Kentucky, I dedicated myself to the teaching profession. My favorite thing about teaching was having the opportunity to read to my students. The stories I read were not necessarily classic literature. Instead, I shared books that made me laugh and cry and want to keep reading even after the story ended.

"I dreamed of having my name on books like these, but writing takes a great deal of self-confidence and discipline! Then I met Debbie. Debbie Dadey and I taught at

the same private school. Once, while working out in the weight room, we talked about our mutual dream of being published authors. We looked at each other and said, 'What's stopping us?' We started writing during our lunch period the next day, and continued to write every day for the next two years with little success.

"Then one day we had a really rough teaching experience. It seemed as if we were invisible because the students totally ignored us. 'What would it take to get their attention?' we asked. 'I suppose we'd have to grow eight feet, sprout horns and blow smoke before they'd pay attention?' The more we talked, the sillier we became. So we decided to write a story about it. *Vampires Don't Wear Polka Dots,* a story about a really rotten group of students who suspect their new teacher is a vampire, was written in three weeks."

The success of their first book encouraged Jones and Dadey to continue collaborating, work which was done largely during lunch in their school cafeteria. In *Frankenstein Doesn't Plant Petunias,* the children become convinced that a museum official is really a monster, and *Ghosts Don't Eat Potato Chips* concerns a youngster's attempt to discover if his aunt's house is haunted. The Bailey School students investigate the bizarre antics of an ophthalmologist in *Cyclops Doesn't Roller Skate,* and in *Wizards Don't Wear Graduation Gowns,* the youngsters question whether or not their new assistant principal possesses magical powers.

The popularity of the "Adventures of the Bailey School Kids" books prompted Jones and Dadey to branch out into companion series. The "Bailey City Monsters" series centers on a trio of children who believe that their new neighbors, the Hauntlys, are actually as spooky as their name implies, and the "Ghostville Elementary" books concern the ghouls who inhabit the basement classroom of Sleepy Hollow elementary school. Jones and Dadey's "Triplet Trouble" series features the escapades of the mischievous Tucker triplets, and the pair have also joined forces on the "Barkley's School for Dogs" and "Keyholders" series. Reviewing *This Side of Magic,* the first work in the "Keyholders" fantasy series, a *Publishers Weekly* critic stated that young readers "will be drawn to the likable, believable protagonists and the promise of more enticing magic and action" in future volumes.

Jones, who eventually left teaching to write full time, now collaborates with Dadey by phone, e-mail, and fax. They take turns writing chapters of their fast-selling books, employing what they refer to as the "hot potato" method of writing. Jones also keeps busy as a writing consultant, appearing at conferences and seminars across the country, and she has completed a number of solo titles, such as *Ratfink,* the story of a fifth-grader's special relationship with his increasingly forgetful grandfather. Logan's character is tested when his nemesis, Emily "the Snot" Scott, discovers an embarrassing photograph and uses it to blackmail him. "Hilarious and

heartbreaking, this novel adds depth and complexity to the usual triumph-over-the-bullies story," Hazel Rochman noted in her *Booklist* review of *Ratfink*.

"Writing is a big part of my life now," Jones once remarked to *SATA*. "It is full of emotion, dreams, and hopes. It challenges me to snip the threads of everyday life to weave something new and colorful. Most of all, writing is just plain old fun! That's the message I try to convey to writers at workshops and creative writing classes."

"Once upon a time, I read books that would take me to far away magical lands," Jones added. "Now I write them!"

Biographical and Critical Sources

PERIODICALS

Booklist, September 15, 1992, Sheilamae O'Hara, review of *Leprechauns Don't Play Basketball,* p. 148; June 1, 2009, Carolyn Phelan, review of *This Side of Magic,* p. 57; December 15, 2009, Hazel Rochman, review of *Ratfink,* p. 39.

Kirkus Reviews, April 29, 2009, review of *This Side of Magic.*

Lexington Herald-Leader (Lexington, KY), April 10, 2006, Karla Ward, "Literal Volumes of Work: Children's Author Finds Her Niche."

Publishers Weekly, May 4, 2009, review of *This Side of Magic,* p. 50.

ONLINE

Marcia Thornton Jones Home Page, http://www.marciatjones.com (June 10, 2010).

Scholastic Web site, http://www2.scholastic.com/ (June 10, 2010), "Marcia Thornton Jones."*

*   *   *

KATZ, Bobbi 1933-

Personal

Born May 2, 1933, in Newburgh, NY; daughter of George and Margaret Shapiro; married Harold D. Katz (an optometrist), July 15, 1956; children: Joshua, Lori. *Education:* Goucher College, B.A. (with honors), 1954; attended Hebrew University of Jerusalem. *Politics:* Democrat. *Religion:* Unitarian.

Addresses

Home—Port Ewen, NY. *E-mail*—bobbikatz@aol.com.

Career

Author, activist, and educator. Freelance writer and fashion editor in New York, NY, 1954-55; Department of Welfare, Newburgh, NY, social worker, 1956-59; Headstart, Newburgh, social worker, 1966-67. Greater Cornwall School District, creative writing consultant; conducts workshops at Poets House, New York, NY; judge for Jo-Anne Hirshfield Memorial Poetry Awards, 2010. *Arts in Action* radio program, host, 1969-71; Orange County SANE and Citizens for Peace, chairperson, 1960-61; Newburgh NAACP, education chairman, beginning 1964; also served as program director of an arts council and organizer of community service projects.

Member

Authors Guild, Phi Beta Kappa.

Awards, Honors

Notable Book designation, National Council of Teachers of English, 2001, for *A Rumpus of Rhymes.*

Writings

I'll Build My Friend a Mountain, Scholastic Book Services (New York, NY), 1972.

Jones and Dadey turn to fantasy in their first "Keyholders" novel, **This Side of Magic.** (Illustration copyright © 2009 by Adam Stower. Reproduced with permission of Palgrave Macmillan.)

Nothing but a Dog, illustrated by Esther Gilman, Feminist Press (New York, NY), 1972, illustrated by Jane Manning, Dutton (New York, NY), 2010.

Upside-Down and Inside-Out, Franklin Watts (New York, NY), 1973.

The Manifesto and Me—Meg, Franklin Watts (New York, NY), 1974.

1,001 Words, Franklin Watts (New York, NY), 1974.

Rod and Reel Trouble, Albert Whitman (Morton Grove, IL), 1974.

Snow Bunny, illustrated by Michael Norman, Albert Whitman (Morton Grove, IL), 1976.

Volleyball Jinx, illustrated by Michael Norman, Albert Whitman (Morton Grove, IL), 1977.

(Selector) *Bedtime Bear's Book of Bedtime Poems,* illustrated by Dora Leder, Random House (New York, NY), 1983.

Birthday Bear's Book of Birthday Poems, illustrated by Louise Walton and Deborah Borgo, Random House (New York, NY), 1983.

Month by Month: A Care Bear Book of Poems, illustrated by Bobbi Barto, Random House (New York, NY), 1984.

Play with the Care Bears, illustrated by Bobbi Bardo, Random House (New York, NY), 1985.

A Popple in Your Pocket and Other Funny Poems, illustrated by Joe Ewers, Random House (New York, NY), 1986.

Little Wrinkle's Surprise, illustrated by Guy Gilchrist, Happy House (New York, NY), 1987.

Peekaboo Animals, illustrated by Robin Kramer, Random House (New York, NY), 1989.

The Old Woman's Counting Book, illustrated by Pat Sustendal, Random House (New York, NY), 1989.

The Creepy, Crawly Book, illustrated by S.D. Schindler, Random House (New York, NY), 1989.

Poems for Small Friends, illustrated by Gyo Fujikawa, Random House (New York, NY), 1989.

The Care Bears and the Big Cleanup, illustrated by Richard Kolding, Random House (New York, NY), 1991.

Teenage Mutant Ninja Turtles: Don't Do Drugs: A Rap Song, illustrated by Isidre Mones, Random House (New York, NY), 1991.

Ghosts and Goose Bumps: Poems to Chill Your Bones, illustrated by Debra Kogan Ray, Random House (New York, NY), 1991.

Puddle Wonderful: Poems to Welcome Spring, illustrated by Mary Morgan, Random House (New York, NY), 1992.

A Family Hanukkah, illustrated by Caryl Herzfeld, Random House (New York, NY), 1992.

Meet Nelson Mandela, Random House (New York, NY), 1995.

The Story of Hanukkah, illustrated by Linda Dockey Graves, Random House (New York, NY), 1995.

Germs! Germs! Germs!, illustrated by Steve Björkman, Scholastic (New York, NY), 1996.

The Story of Passover, illustrated by Diane Paterson, Random House (New York, NY), 1996.

Could We Be Friends?: Poems for Pals, illustrated by Joung Un Kim, Mondo (Greenvale, NY), 1997.

Truck Talk: Rhymes on Wheels, Scholastic (New York, NY), 1997.

Lots of Lice, illustrated by Steve Björkman, Scholastic (New York, NY), 1998.

American History Poem, Scholastic (New York, NY), 1998.

Make Way for Tooth Decay, illustrated by Steve Björkman, Scholastic New York, NY), 1999.

We the People (poems), illustrated by Nina Crews, Greenwillow (New York, NY), 2000.

A Rumpus of Rhymes: A Book of Noisy Poems, illustrated by Susan Estelle Kwas, Dutton (New York, NY), 2001.

(Selector) *Pocket Poems,* illustrated by Marylin Hafner, Dutton (New York, NY), 2004.

Once around the Sun, illustrated by LeUyen Pham, Harcourt (Orlando, FL), 2006.

Trailblazers: Poems of Exploration, illustrated by Carin Berger, Greenwillow (New York, NY), 2007.

(Selector) *More Pocket Poems,* illustrated by Deborah Zemke, Dutton (New York, NY), 2009.

The Monsterologist: A Memoir in Rhyme, illustrated by Adam McCauley, Sterling Publishing (New York, NY), 2009.

Also author of educational materials for Scholastic Professional. Contributor of poetry to anthologies and magazines. Contributor to *Period Pieces: Stories for Girls,* HarperCollins (New York, NY), 2003.

Adaptations

A Family Hanukkah was adapted as an audiocassette, Random House, 1993.

Bobbi Katz's poetry collection **A Rumpus of Rhyme** *is brought to life in engaging primitive-style art by Susan Estelle Kwas.* (Illustration copyright © 2001 by Susan Estelle Kwas. Reproduced by permission of Dutton Children's Books, a division of Penguin Putnam Books for Young Readers.)

Sidelights

A prolific and popular writer for children, Bobbi Katz is best known for her verse collections, including *Pocket Poems, A Rumpus of Rhymes: A Book of Noisy Poems,* and *The Monsterologist: A Memoir in Rhyme.* "I love being a writer," Katz stated on the Balkin Buddies Web site, adding: "There's nothing better than finding just the right words to make a new connection between ideas or images."

In *Once around the Sun* Katz takes readers on a voyage through time from a child's perspective, following the changes that can be seen as the twelve months cycle through the calendar during the course of a single year. Praising LeUyen Pham's illustrations for the work as "brightly colored and full of energy," Hazel Rochman added in her *Booklist* review that *Once around the Sun* features a simple vocabulary that makes the collection "great for reading aloud." Katz's verses match Pham's art in their "visual and aural imagery as well as emotional intensity," noted Teresa Pfeifer in a *School Library Journal* review of the work, and a *Kirkus Reviews* contributor wrote that "Katz's dozen poetic paeans are accessible tumbles of imagery."

Inspired by Katz's research into diaries, letters, and other original written source material, *We the People: Poems* introduces sixty-five notable Americans through first-person poems that illuminate the people, places, and events that comprise the country's history. Similar in concept, *Trailblazers: Poems of Exploration* introduces readers to a host of explorers, from Vikings to Spanish conquistadors to American astronauts. The volume offers readers the opportunity "to consider not only the courage of these individuals, but also to broaden their horizons in terms of the definition of exploration," observed *School Library Journal* contributor Lee Bock. *Could We Be Friends?: Poems for Pals* contains twenty-four verses that, with humor and an occasional whiff of sadness, focus on the close bonds between friends, family members, and neighbors.

In *Pocket Poems* Katz collects over fifty favorite childhood verses designed for easy memorization. In addition to five of her own works, *Pocket Poems* includes verse by a wide variety of authors, from nineteenth-century poets Emily Dickinson and Lewis Carroll to modern-day rhymers Jack Prelutsky, Aileen Fisher, and William Cole. Decorated with watercolor-and-ink cartoons by Marylin Hafner, *Pocket Poems* was praised by Bock as a "child-friendly collection" that is perfectly sized to tuck into a pocket for use whenever the need for a short verse arises. In a companion volume, *More Pocket Poems,* Katz offers readers more than forty short verses, many of which celebrate the seasons of the year. Along with her original poems, Katz includes pieces by such celebrated writers as Eve Merriam, Emily Dickinson, Langston Hughes, Arnold Lobel, and Odgen Nash, along with a Navajo tribal chant and an excerpt from William Shakespeare's *Macbeth.* Sally R. Dow, writing

Marylin Hafner's engaging drawings team with Katz's compact verses for the aptly named Pocket Poems. (Illustration copyright © 2004 by Marylin Hafner. Reproduced by permission of Dutton Children's Books, a division of Penguin Putnam Books for Young Readers.)

in *School Library Journal,* praised "the joyous spirit of the poems," and *Booklist* reviewer Carolyn Phelan noted that the "attractive collection of light verse lends itself well to reading aloud."

Commenting on Katz's work in the *New York Times Book Review,* Marighy Dupuy wrote: "Not only are her poems engaging and lively, but she puts the words themselves front and center." The words that appear "front and center" in the twenty-eight verses assembled in *A Rumpus of Rhymes* are particularly delightful; as Lauren Peterson noted in *Booklist,* they offer young readers a chance "to be loud and silly" due to "an abundance of onomatopoeia." Noting that Katz's "rambunctious collection begs to be shared out loud," *School Library Journal* contributor Margaret C. Howell also praised the book's varied fonts, as well as the variety of rhythms that appear in the work.

The Monsterologist, a work more than ten years in the making, contains a variety of poems about werewolves, trolls, witches, vampires, and other mythological creatures. Presented as a series of letters, notes, and interviews from a scientist devoted to the study of monsters, the work is filled with "bursts of devilish humor and winking creepiness," according to *Booklist* reviewer Ian Chipman. First published in 1972, Katz's *Nothing but a Dog* was reissued in 2010 with new illustrations by Jane Manning. The work centers on a young girl who

Once around the Sun *pairs a year's worth of poems by Katz with Le Uyen Pham's colorful artwork.* (Illustration copyright © 2006 by LeUyen Pham. Reproduced by permission of Houghton Mifflin Harcourt Publishing Company. This material may not be reproduced in any form or by any means without the prior written permission of the publisher.)

longs for a furry, friendly pet to brighten her days. C.J. Connor, writing in *School Library Journal,* described *Nothing but a Dog* as "a nice, feel-good picture book."

Discussing the difference between writing poetry and prose, Katz once told *SATA:* "My poetry always comes from inside—from my deep need to express a feeling. The child in me writes picture books. My fiction is almost not mine. The characters emerge and seem to tell

their own stories. Even when writing within rigid boundaries that editors sometimes set, I find the characters become very real to me. I care what happens to them."

"I write only for children because I desperately want to return childhood to them," Katz added. "I hope to join those writers and artists who delight, sensitize, and give hope to children."

Biographical and Critical Sources

PERIODICALS

Booklist, September 1, 2001, Lauren Peterson, review of *A Rumpus of Rhymes: A Book of Noisy Poems,* p. 111; October, 1, 2001, Isabel Schon, review of *Germs! Germs! Germs!,* p. 328; February 1, 2004, Hazel Rochman, review of *Pocket Poems,* p. 978; April 15, 2006, Hazel Rochman, review of *Once around the Sun,* p. 49; January 1, 2009, Carolyn Phelan, review of *More Pocket Poems,* p. 88; September 15, 2009, Ian Chipman, review of *The Monsterologist: A Memoir In Rhyme,* p. 61.
Bulletin of the Center for Children's Books, July-August, 2006, Deborah Stevenson, review of *Once around the Sun,* p. 504.
Kirkus Reviews, July 1, 2001, review of *A Rumpus of Rhymes,* p. 942; February 15, 2004, review of *Pocket Poems,* p. 180; March 15, 2006, review of *Once around the Sun,* p. 293; February 1, 2009, review of *More Pocket Poems.*
New York Times Book Review, November 18, 2001, Marighy Dupuy, review of *A Book of Noisy Poems,* p. 37.
School Library Journal, November, 2001, Margaret C. Howell, review of *A Rumpus of Rhymes,* p. 146; February, 2004, Lee Bock, review of *Pocket Poems,* p. 132; April, 2006, Nina Lindsay, review of *We the People: Poems,* p. 57; May, 2006, Teresa Pfeifer, review of *Once around the Sun,* p. 114; July, 2007, Lee Bock, review of *Trailblazers: Poems of Exploration,* p. 117; February, 2009, Sally R. Dow, review of *More Pocket Poems,* p. 93; February, 2010, C.J. Connor, review of *Nothing but a Dog,* p. 88.

ONLINE

Balkin Buddies Web site, http://www.balkinbuddies.com/ (May 20, 2010), "Bobbi Katz."
Bobbi Katz Home Page, http://www.bobbikatz.com (May 20, 2010).
Seven Impossible Things before Breakfast Web log, http://blaine.org/sevenimpossiblethings/ (November 6, 2009), interview with Katz.*

*   *   *

KELLEY, Ann 1941-

Personal

Born December 17, 1941, in England; married; second husband named Robert; children: (first marriage) Nathan (deceased), Caroline.

Addresses

Home—St. Ives, Cornwall, England. *Agent*—Lindsey Fraser, lindsey.frasertiscali.co.uk. *E-mail*—Annkelley@ blue-earth.co.uk.

Career

Novelist, poet, and photographer. Teaches writing and poetry therapy privately and at workshops.

Awards, Honors

Branford Boase Award shortlist, 2005, for *The Burying Beatle;* Costa Children's Book Award, 2007, for *The Bower Bird;* several prizes for poetry; honorary teaching fellow, Peninsula College of Medicine and Dentistry.

Writings

"GUSSIE" YOUNG-ADULT NOVEL SERIES

The Burying Beatle, Luath Press (Edinburgh, Scotland), 2005.
The Bower Bird, Luath Press (Edinburgh, Scotland), 2007.
Inchworm, Luath Press (Edinburgh, Scotland), 2008.
A Snail's Broken Shell, Luath Press (Edinburgh, Scotland), 2010.

OTHER

Born and Bred (photography), Cornwall Books (Exeter, England), 1988.
The Poetry Remedy (poetry), Hypatia Trust & Patten Press (Newmill, England), 1999.
(And photographer) *Paper Whites* (poetry), 2001.
Sea Front (photography), 2005.
Because We Have Reached That Place (poetry), Oversteps Books (Salcombe, England), 2006.
Koh Tabu (young-adult novel), Oxford University Press (Oxford, England), 2010.
(With others) *The Light at St. Ives* (photography), Luath Press (Edinburgh, Scotland), 2010.

Also author of *Nine Lives: Cat Tales* (audio book).

Adaptations

The "Gussie" series was optioned for film by producer Anne Beresford and Artemisia Films.

Sidelights

Ann Kelley is an award-winning poet and novelist, as well as a photographer whose evocative images have been collected in the books *Born and Bred, Sea Front,* and *The Light at St. Ives.* Her writings for younger readers include the young-adult novels *The Burying Beatle, The Bower Bird,* and *Inchworm.*

Kelley's creativity as a visual artist and writer was sparked by a family tragedy, one that culminated in 1985 with the death of her twenty-four-year-old son Nathan. Born with a congenital heart condition called pulmonary atresia, Nathan was not expected to survive

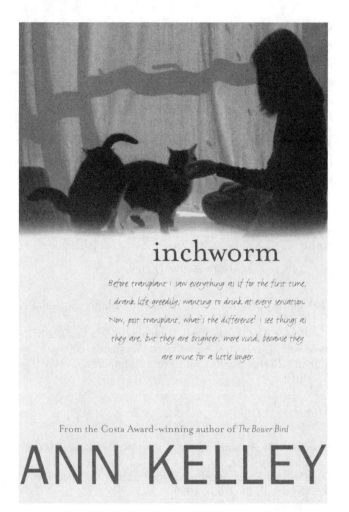

Cover of Ann Kelley's inspiring novel Inchworm, *which features Kelley's photography.* (Luath Press, 2008. Ann Kelley, illustrator. Reproduced by permission.)

long enough to learn to walk. Miraculously, the boy proved doctors wrong; in addition to walking, he demonstrated an amazing intellect and by age sixteen had made several discoveries in the area of marine biology. Nathan earned degrees at two English universities prior to his death at age twenty four.

Kelley coped with her grief over Nathan's death by writing poetry, and her work has been collected in books such as *The Poetry Remedy* and *Paper Whites,* the latter published in 2001. Her first novel, *The Burying Beetle,* honors Nathan's memory in its chronicle of twelve-year-old Gussie, who suffers from the same heart disease as did Kelley's son. In addition to sharing his Cornwall home, Gussie also shares Nathan's intellect and endless curiosity, and her desire to make the most of every moment of every day makes her an inspiring heroine.

Although Kelley did not intend to write a sequel to *The Burying Beetle,* many readers wrote to her with questions about Gussie, and these questions are answered in *The Bower Bird, Inchworm,* and *A Snail's Broken Shell.* In *The Bower Bird* Gussie awaits a heart and lung trans-

plant, and her thoughtful ruminations on life and death are balanced by day-to-day events involving family and her best friend Summer. The novel is composed as a diary, and Gussie's first-person narrative, "stuffed with plentiful . . . minutiae," captures the girl's "inventiveness and pluck," in the opinion of London *Observer* contributor Hermione Buckland-Ho.

In *Inchworm* readers reconnect with the optimistic Gussie while she is staying in London, near the hospital where she has received her new organs. Although spirits are lighter because Gussie's operation appears to have been a success, her parents' impending divorce saddens the girl, and she determines to try to bring the family back together—and also find a way to get a pet kitten—once her recovery is complete and she can return to Cornwall. "Brave yet vulnerable, mature and still naive, Gussie will win the hearts of readers," concluded Wendy Smith-D'Arezzo in *School Library Journal,* and a *Kirkus Reviews* critic called Kelley's heroine "a well-rounded character facing a trying situation with grace and verve."

Biographical and Critical Sources

PERIODICALS

Daily Telegraph (London, England), January 6, 2008, Olga Craig, "How Ann Kelley Gave Her Son the Happy Ending He Yearned For"; December 6, 2008, Kate Saunders, review of *Inchworm,* p. 24.
Kirkus Reviews, January 1, 2009, review of *Inchworm.*
Observer (London, England), January 27, 2008, Hermione Buckland-Ho, review of *The Bower Bird,* p. 27.
School Library Journal, April, 2009, Wendy Smith-D'Arezzo, review of *Inchworm,* p. 137.

ONLINE

Ann Kelley Home Page, http://www.annkelley.co.uk (May 31, 2010).*

* * *

KELLEY, Gary 1945-

Personal

Born 1945. *Education:* University of Northern Iowa, B.A. (art).

Addresses

Home—Cedar Falls, IA. *Agent*—Richard Solomon, 305 E. 50th St., New York, NY 10022.

Career

Artist, illustrator, educator, and muralist. Helman Associates, graphic designer and art director, beginning c. mid-1970s; freelance artist, beginning 1986. Ringling

School of Art, Sarasota, FL, member of faculty of Illustration Academy. Commissions include commemorative posters for 2002 Kentucky Derby. Lecturer at schools and other assemblies, including Smithsonian Institute, Society of Illustrators, San Francisco Academy of Art, Chicago Art Institute, Norman Rockwell Museum, Syracuse University, Rhode Island School of Design, and Ringling School of Art. *Exhibitions:* Works have been exhibited at numerous galleries and shows, including New York Art Directors shows, Bologna Book Fair, Society of Illustrators shows, Hearst Center for the Arts, and Gallagher-Bluedorn Performing Arts Center, Cedar Falls, IA. Mural installations include Barnes & Noble Bookstore, New York, NY, and McLeod Center Arena at University of Northern Idaho, Cedar Falls.

Awards, Honors

Society of Illustrators medal, 1981, and 26 other medals; Hamilton King Award, New York Society of Illustrators, 1992; Gold Louie Award for Best Illustration, 2002, for Kentucky Derby poster art; inducted into Society of Illustrators Hall of Fame, 2007; numerous other awards.

Writings

SELF-ILLUSTRATED

T Is for Toscana, Creative Editions (Mankato, MN), 2003.

ILLUSTRATOR

Mary Wollstonecraft Shelley, *Frankenstein,* adapted by Diana Stewart, Raintree (Milwaukee, WI), 1981.

Herman Melville, *Moby Dick,* adapted by Patricia Daniels, Raintree (Milwaukee, WI), 1982.

Joseph Heller, *Good as Gold* (limited edition), Franklin Library (Franklin Center, PA), 1982.

Ray Bradbury, *The Other Foot,* Creative Education (Mankato, MN), 1987.

Ray Bradbury, *The Veldt,* Creative Education (Mankato, MN), 1987.

Ray Bradbury, *The Fog Horn,* Creative Education (Mankato, MN), 1988.

Guy de Maupassant, *The Necklace,* Creative Education (Mankato, MN), 1992.

Washington Irving, *Rip Van Winkle,* Creative Education (Mankato, MN), 1993.

J. Patrick Lewis, *The Christmas of the Reddle Moon,* Dial Books (New York, NY), 1994.

Robert D. San Souci, *The Red Heels,* Dial Books (New York, NY), 1995.

Edgar Allan Poe, *Tales of Mystery and Imagination,* Creative Editions (Mankato, MN), 1996.

Bruce Coville, reteller, *William Shakespeare's Macbeth,* Dial Books (New York, NY), 1997.

J. Patrick Lewis, *Boshblobberbosh: Runcible Poems for Edward Lear,* Harcourt (San Diego, CA), 1998.

Maria Tallchief and Rosemary Wells, *Tallchief: America's Prima Ballerina,* Viking (New York, NY), 1999.

J. Patrick Lewis, *The Stolen Smile,* Creative Editions (Mankato, MN), 2004.

J. Patrick Lewis, *Black Cat Bone: The Life of Blues Legend Robert Johnson,* Creative Editions (Mankato, MN), 2006.

Aaron Frisch, *Dark Fiddler: The Life and Legend of Nicolo Paganini,* Creative Editions (Mankato, MN), 2008.

Doreen Rappaport, *Eleanor, Quiet No More,* Hyperion (New York, NY), 2009.

Doreen Rappaport, *Abe's Honest Words: The Life of Abraham Lincoln,* Hyperion (New York, NY), 2009.

Gary Kelley's illustration projects include creating artwork for a new edition of Guy de Maupassant's **The Necklace.** (Creative Editions, Inc., 1993. Illustration © 1992 by Gary Kelley. Reproduced by permission.)

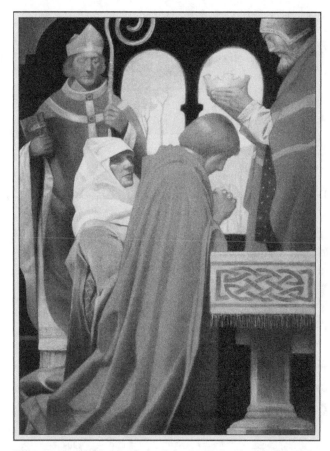

Kelley captures the drama of one of the world's best-known plays in his paintings for **William Shakespeare's Macbeth.** (Illustration copyright © 1997 by Gary Kelley. Reproduced by permission of Dial Books, a division of Penguin Putnam Books for Young Readers.)

Contributor of illustrations to periodicals, including *North American Review.*

Sidelights

Award-winning Iowa-based artist Gary Kelley is an illustrator, educator, and muralist. His artwork, which has appeared in such well-known periodicals as *Time* and the *New Yorker* and has been commissioned by the Kentucky Derby and the National Football League, also appears in dozens of books for children, including several modern-day classics. Winner of a record number of medals—twenty-seven—from the prestigious Society of Illustrators, Kelley was inducted into the society's Hall of Fame in 2007, joining the ranks of such artists as Maxfield Parrish, Norman Rockwell, and Howard Pyle.

After earning an art degree from the University of Northern Iowa, Kelley worked as a graphic designer and art director for several years, moving to book illustration in the mid-1970s. After becoming a freelance illustrator in 1986, he created illustrations for a series of fiction classics released by Midwest publishers Raintree and Creative Education before turning to picture books for younger children.

In 1994 Kelley teamed up with noted children's book author J. Patrick Lewis to produce *The Christmas of the*

Reddle Moon, a fanciful adaptation of an English folk tale and the first of several collaborations between the two men. Praised by a *Publishers Weekly* contributor, *The Christmas of the Reddle Moon* benefits from Kelley's pastel art, and his "snow-softened landscapes and shadowy interiors . . . create a setting worthy of the tale." In *Booklist* Hazel Rochman wrote that the "vivid poetic imagery" in Lewis's narrative is echoed by Kelley's "soft pastel illustrations."

Kelley's other collaborations with Lewis include *Black Cat Bone: The Life of Blues Legend Robert Johnson.* The book focuses on the life of the musician who, born in rural Mississippi, died tragically early at age twenty-seven, leaving behind a musical legacy that has made Johnson immortal among fans of the Delta Blues. In the nineteen poems that comprise his text, Lewis notes the legend that grew up to explain Johnson's talent: that the young guitarist sold his soul to the devil in exchange for his musical gift. "Kelley's . . . handsome compositions" feature "translucent and opaque washes, gestural brushstrokes, scratched line and a judicious use of glowing white," wrote a *Publishers Weekly* reviewer. Bill Ott concluded in *Booklist* that "Kelley's striking paintings, heavy with multiple shades of blue and brown, capture all the emotions that swirl around the Johnson myth." Citing the artist's "beautiful brooding illustrations," a *Kirkus Reviews* writer maintained that *Black Cat Bone* is "a stylish and artful work that will hold appeal for adults as well" as a younger audience.

In addition to his work with Lewis, Kelley has also seen his work paired with texts by Robert San Souci, Bruce Coville, Doreen Rappaport, and prima ballerina Maria Tallchief. Appraising *Tallchief: America's Prima Ballerina* in *Booklist,* Carolyn Phelan made a point of remarking on Kelley's pastel art. The illustrator "grasps forms with a cubist's awareness of the solidity of people and objects," Phelan asserted, calling Kelley's images "powerful and well executed." The book's "softly focused paintings underscore the lyrical tone" of Tallchief's life story, wrote a *Publishers Weekly* contributor, "enveloping the characters and settings in gauzy, dreamlike light."

In *Dark Fiddler: The Life and Legend of Nicolo Paganini* Aaron Frisch captures the mystery surrounding the life of the famous nineteenth-century Italian violinist, who legend has painted as a performer with fingers guided by the Devil himself. To capture the tantalizing story, which begins with Paganini's premature burial at age four and follows his stellar musical career, Kelley's "breathtaking, chalklike art that resembles the work of [nineteenth-century French painter Henri] Toulouse-Lautrec," according to *Booklist* reviewer Ilene Cooper. In *Eleanor, Quiet No More,* Rappaport's biography about First Lady Eleanor Roosevelt, "reclaims the legendary first lady's story for the younger set," according to a *Publishers Weekly* critic, and the "muted palette" featured in Kelley's "dramatic, strongly geometric compositions" creates "a striking visual counterpoint." Rap-

paport, who also collaborates with Kelley on the picture book *Abe's Honest Words: The Life of Abraham Lincoln,* "celebrates a noble, heroic, life in powerful, succinct prose," wrote Barbara Auerbach, the *School Library Journal* critic adding that the book's "evocative pictures tell the story of both [Roosevelt] . . . and her country."

Biographical and Critical Sources

PERIODICALS

Booklist, August, 1994, Hazel Rochman, review of *The Christmas of the Reddle Moon,* p. 2051; September, 1996, Stephanie Zvirin, review of *The Red Heels,* p. 131; November 1, 1997, Hazel Rochman, review of *William Shakespeare's Macbeth,* p. 464; November 1, 1999, Carolyn Phelan, review of *Tallchief: America's Prima Ballerina,* p. 526; January 1, 2007, Bill Ott, review of *Black Cat Bone,* p. 93; November 1, 2008, Ilene Cooper, review of *Dark Fiddler: The Life and Legend of Nicolo Paganini,* p. 54.

Horn Book, January, 2000, review of *Tallchief,* p. 103; March-April, 2009, Betty Carter, review of *Eleanor, Quiet No More,* p. 213.

Kirkus Reviews, September 1, 2006, review of *Black Cat Bone,* p. 906; December 15, 2008, review of *Dark Fiddler.*

Publishers Weekly, October 4, 1993, review of *Rip Van Winkle,* p. 80; September 19, 1994, review of *Christmas of the Reddle Moon,* p. 32; July 22, 1996, review of *The Red Heels,* p. 242; October 19, 1998, review of *Boshblobberbosh: Runcible Poems for Edward Lear,* p. 80; October 25, 1999, review of *Tallchief,* p. 80; November 3, 2003, review of *T Is for Toscana,* p. 76; August 28, 2006, review of *Black Cat Bone,* p. 53; February 16, 2009, review of *Eleanor, Quiet No More,* p. 127.

School Library Journal, January, 2005, Wendy Lukehart, review of *The Stolen Smile,* p. 132; December, 2006, Nina Lindsay, review of *Black Cat Bone,* p. 165; February, 2009, Joan Kindig, review of *Dark Fiddler,* p. 118.

ONLINE

Gary Kelley Home Page, http://garykelleyonline.com (June 1, 2010).

Illustration Academy Web site, http://www.illustration academy.com/ (October 27, 2007), "Gary Kelley."

Iowa Journal Online, http://www.iptv.org.iowajournal/ (June 17, 2007), interview with Kelley.*

*   *   *

KING, Amy
See KING, A.S.

*   *   *

KING, A.S. 1970-
(Amy King)

Personal

Born 1970, in Reading, PA; married; children. *Education:* College degree (photography).

Addresses

Home—PA. *E-mail*—asking@as-king.com.

Career

Author. Worked variously as a photographer, master printer, literacy teacher, contractor, and self-sufficient farmer. Presenter at schools.

Member

BackSpace Writers Group, ALAN.

Awards, Honors

Washington Square Fiction Contest runner-up; Glimmer Train Very Short Fiction Award runner-up; Best New American Voices nomination; American Library Association Best Books for Young Adults designation, Cybil Award finalist, and Indie Next List selection, all 2009, all for *The Dust of 100 Dogs.*

Writings

The Dust of 100 Dogs, Flux (Woodbury, MN), 2009.
Please Ignore Vera Dietz, Knopf (New York, NY), 2010.

Kelley's art gives a supernatural aura to Aaron Frisch's biography **Dark Fiddler: The Life and Legend of Nicolo Paganini.** (Creative Editions, 2008. Illustration copyright © 2008 Gary Kelley. Reproduced by permission.)

Contributor to periodicals, including Dublin *Sunday Tribune* and *Quality Women's Fiction.*

Sidelights

Although A.S. King was born and now lives in Pennsylvania, she lived in Ireland for over a decade and has enjoyed a peripatetic lifestyle. Trained as a photographer, King has raised rare poultry, contributed to literary magazines, and taught adult literacy while living off the land in Tipperary, Ireland. In Tipperary, she became interested in local history, notably the Cromwellian invasion, which was the starting point for her novel *The Dust of 100 Dogs.*

The Dust of 100 Dogs focuses on Emer Morrisey, a Cromwellian orphan turned teenaged pirate who meets a tragic end in Jamaica just after burying a lifetime's worth of riches that would have funded her retirement and allowed her to settle down to a quiet life with her lover. A curse condemning the dying Emer to the dust of one hundred dogs forces her to live out one hundred lives as a dog, after which she can return and complete her life as a human woman. Flash forward 300 years, to 1980s Pennsylvania, where Emer now finds herself sharing the body of American teenager Saffron Adams. Although Saffron has longed to escape her difficult family, the possessed teen is now haunted by memories of shipboard battles, violence, and a buried treasure in Jamaica that she is determined to retrieve. Although Mara Alpert noted in *School Library Journal* that King's novel "is not for the faint of heart" due to its focus on piratical and contemporary traumas, the critic added that *The Dust of 100 Dogs* will appeal to teens who prefer darker themes. In *Kirkus Reviews* a contributor asserted that the novel might be overly ambitious, but nonetheless dubbed King's debut "an undeniably original book."

Biographical and Critical Sources

PERIODICALS

Booklist, February 15, 2009, Ian Chipman, review of *The Dust of 100 Dogs,* p. 71.
Kirkus Reviews, January 1, 2009, review of *The Dust of 100 Dogs.*
Publishers Weekly, February 15, 2009, review of *The Dust of 100 Dogs,* p. 129.
School Library Journal, May, 2009, Mara Alpert, review of *The Dust of 100 Dogs,* p. 110.

ONLINE

A.S. King Home Page, http://www.as-king.com (June 15, 2010).
A.S. King Web site, http://www.as-king.info (June 15, 2010).
Cynsations Web log, http://cynthialeittichsmith.blogspot.com/ (March 12, 2009), Cynthia Leitich Smith, interview with King.

* * *

Cover of A.S. King's time-travel novel The Dust of 100 Dogs, *which mixes high-seas adventure with the problems of a modern American teen.* (Flux, 2009. Cover image © Digital Vision/PunchStock. Reproduced by permission.)

KLEVEN, Elisa 1958-
(Elisa Schneider)

Personal

Name pronounced "Clay-ven"; born October 14, 1958, in Los Angeles, CA; daughter of Stanley (a doctor) and Lorraine Art (an artist) Schneider; married Paul Kleven, July, 1984; children: Mia, Ben. *Education:* University of California, Berkeley, B.A., 1981, teaching credentials, 1983.

Addresses

Home—1028 Peralta Ave., Albany, CA 94706. *E-mail*—ekleven@aol.com.

Elisa Kleven (Photo courtesy of Elisa Kleven. Reproduced by permission.)

Career

Berkeley Hills Nursery School, Berkeley, CA, nursery school teacher, 1978-80; weaver and toy maker, 1980-84; Prospect School, El Cerrito, CA, fourth-grade and art teacher, 1984-86; writer and illustrator.

Member

Society of Children's Book Writers and Illustrators, Amnesty International, World Wildlife Fund, Humane Society of the United States, Phi Beta Kappa.

Awards, Honors

Parent's Choice award for illustration, and Notable Book designation, American Library Association, both for *Abuela; School Library Journal* Best Books designation, 1997, for *The Puddle Pail; New York Times* Best Illustrated Book of the Year Award, 2001, for *Sun Bread.*

Writings

SELF-ILLUSTRATED

(Under name Elisa Schneider) *The Merry-Go-Round Dog,* Knopf (New York, NY), 1988.
Ernst, Dutton (New York, NY), 1989.

The Lion and the Little Red Bird, Dutton (New York, NY), 1992.
The Paper Princess, Dutton (New York, NY), 1994.
Hooray, a Piñata!, Dutton (New York, NY), 1996.
The Puddle Pail, Dutton (New York, NY), 1997.
A Monster in the House, Dutton (New York, NY), 1998.
Sun Bread, Dutton (New York, NY), 2001.
The Dancing Deer and the Foolish Hunter, Dutton (New York, NY), 2002.
The Paper Princess Finds Her Way, Dutton (New York, NY), 2003.
The Paper Princess Flies Again: With Her Dog!, Tricycle (Berkeley, CA), 2005.
The Wishing Ball, Farrar, Straus & Giroux (New York, NY), 2006.
The Apple Doll, Farrar, Straus & Giroux (New York, NY), 2007.
A Carousel Tale, Tricycle Press (Berkeley, CA), 2009.
Welcome Home, Mouse, Tricycle Press (Berkeley, CA), 2010.

Author's works have been translated into Japanese, Korean, and Chinese.

ILLUSTRATOR

Isabel Wilner, *B Is for Bethlehem,* Dutton (New York, NY), 1990.
Arthur Dorros, *Abuela,* Dutton (New York, NY), 1991.
Tricia Brown, *The City by the Bay: A Magical Journey around San Francisco,* Chronicle (San Francisco, CA), 1993.
Karen Lotz, *Snow Song Whistling,* Dutton (New York, NY), 1993.
De Colores, and Other Latin-American Folk Songs for Children, edited and translated by Jose-Luis Orozco, Dutton (New York, NY), 1994.
Arthur Dorros, *The Island/La Isla,* Penguin (New York, NY), 1995.
Tony Johnston, *The Magic Maguey,* Harcourt (San Diego, CA), 1996.
Diez deditos/Ten Little Fingers, and Other Play Rhymes and Action Songs from Latin America, edited and translated by Jose-Luis Orozco, Dutton (New York, NY), 1997.
Julie Jaskol and Brian Lewis, *City of Angels: In and around Los Angeles,* Dutton (New York, NY), 1999.
Linda Glaser, *Our Big Home: An Earth Poem,* Millbrook Press (Brookfield, CT), 2000.
Fiestas: A Year of Latin-American Songs of Celebration, edited and translated by Jose-Luis Orozco, Dutton (New York, NY), 2002.
Tony Johnston, *The Whole Green World,* Farrar, Straus & Giroux (New York, NY), 2005.
Julia Durango, adaptor, *Angels Watching over Me,* Simon & Schuster (New York, NY), 2007.
Roseanne Thong, *Wish: Wishing Traditions around the World,* Chronicle Books (San Francisco, CA), 2008.

Thacher Hurd, *The Weaver,* Farrar, Straus & Giroux (New York, NY), 2009.

Contributor of illustrations to collections, including *In Every Tiny Grain of Sand: A Child's Book of Prayers and Praise,* Candlewick Press (Cambridge, MA), 2000.

Sidelights

A self-taught artist, Elisa Kleven is both an illustrator of children's books and the author/illustrator of engaging stories such as *The Paper Princess, The Wishing Tale,* and *The Apple Doll.* "I never attended art school, but learned a lot from my mother and grandmother,

A little girl creates a special day using her imagination in Kleven's self-illustrated picture book **The Paper Princess.** (Copyright © by Elisa Kleven, 1994. Reproduced by permission of Puffin Books, a division of Penguin Putnam Books for Young Readers.)

both of whom were artists," she explained to Elisabeth Sherwin for the *Printed Matter* Web site. Kleven's unique and colorful mixed-media illustrations have been lauded by reviewers, inspiring a *Publishers Weekly* critic to describe her work for Arthur Dorros's *The Island/La Isla,* as "a kaleidoscope of color and texture."

Kleven's illustrations often appearin multicultural titles, such as books dealing with Latin-American culture. In the anthology *De Colores, and Other Latin-American Folk Songs for Children* she highlights traditional songs with her colorful art, while her depiction of urban landmarks are a feature of Julie Jaskol and Brian Lewis's *City of Angels: In and around Los Angeles.* Reviewing the former, Maeve Visser Knoth commented in *Horn Book* on the book's "vibrant colors [and] richly detailed illustrations," while Ruth Ketchum noted in the same periodicals that Kleven's illustrations for *City of Angels* offer readers "an exuberant jumble of detail and pattern."

Other illustration projects include creating artwork for Linda Glaser's *Our Big Home: An Earth Poem,* Thatcher Hurd's *The Weaver,* and Julia Durango's *Angels Watching over Me,* the last an adaptation of an African-American spiritual. A *Publishers Weekly* critic praised Kleven's work for *Our Big Home* as "brilliant, busy art [that] gives [the book] its soul," while *Horn Book* reviewer Elena Abos asserted that her illustrations for the poetry collection *Diez deditos/Ten Little Fingers, and Other Play Rhymes and Action Songs from Latin America* "bubble over with vivid detail." For Durango's gentle story, Kleven uses ink, colored pencil, and water color to create what a *Kirkus Reviews* writer described as "aerial views of the earth [that are] globally teaming with life." A *Publishers Weekly* contributor asserted of the same book that "young ones will find both wonder and reassurance in her depiction of [animal] angels," while Judith Constantinides dubbed *Angels Watching over Me* "simply glorious" on the strength of Kleven's "breathtaking folk-style illustrations."

One of Kleven's self-illustrated titles, *Hooray, a Piñata!* introduces young Clara, who wants to celebrate her birthday with a piñata, but grows so attached to the toy-filled papier-maché dog that she does not want to break it. According to a *Publishers Weekly* reviewer, Kleven's "perky writing speaks confidently to the everyday emotional ups and downs in the lives of children." In *The Apple Doll* Lizzy would rather stay at home, where a shady apple tree grows outside her bedroom window, than brave her first day at school. She tries to bring a piece of home with her by making an apple doll she names Susanna. Unfortunately, her teacher does not allow toys at school, and things get worse when Susanna starts to shrivel. Fortunately, Lizzie and her mom find a way to preserve Susanna: they make her into a dried-apple doll! The "charm of this delightfully well-written picture book" is balanced by Kleven's illustrations, which range from "winsome vignettes" to double-page illustrations, noted Carolyn Phelan in *Booklist.* A *Pub-*

lishers Weekly critic recommended *The Apple Doll* for parents hoping "to conquer heading-to-school fears," and a *Kirkus Reviews* writer noted the book's pairing of "bright, textured, and bold" illustrations with a reassuring story that ends with instructions for readers wishing to make their own apple dolls.

Kleven tells other universal stories using animal characters. Her original folk tale *The Dancing Deer and the Foolish Hunter* is as much about staying in tune with the environment as it is about a magical deer. When a hunter takes the deer from her natural environment, she refuses to dance, because she needs the song of the birds. When the hunter gets her birds, the birds refuse to sing without the wind in the trees. The tale goes on until the hunter learns that things should stay where they belong and the deer teaches him to dance. "Kleven creates a mosaic effect by diminutive flashes of birds, fish, and leaves" in the backgrounds of her collages, wrote GraceAnne A. DeCandido of *Booklist. School Library Journal* critic Susan Helper noted that "Kleven's signature colorful collage illustrations sing with light and movement."

A blue crocodile named Ernst stars in *Ernst, The Puddle Pail, The Wishing Ball,* and *A Carousel Tale.* He celebrates his birthday in *Ernst,* tries to collect clouds and stars in *The Puddle Pail,* makes friends with a lonely kitten in *The Wishing Ball,* and becomes the caretaker of a treasured object in *A Carousel Tale.* Reviewing *The Puddle Pail* a *Publishers Weekly* critic concluded that Kleven's "slightly discursive style is ultimately suited to Ernst's dreamy personality."

In *The Wishing Ball,* Nellie the kitten and Ernst make a wish on a ball with a painted star on it, and by story's end the foundling kitten has found a cozy and secure home with a loving family. When his favorite merry-go-round closes for the winter months in *A Carousel Tale,* Ernst is entrusted with caring for a broken piece from one of the carousel animals: the wooden tail from his favorite brown dog. He treasures the tale and decorates it, then worries when it must be returned to the carousel keeper in the spring. Kleven's "characters for *The Wishing Ball* are charmingly expressive and her brushstrokes are lively and energetic," wrote a critic for *Kirkus Reviews. Booklist* contributor Ilene Cooper called the same book "immensely satisfying," adding that Kleven's "crowded, cozy pictures" place "a needy, determined, darling kitty right in the middle of it all." Reviewing *A Carousel Tale* for *Booklist,* Hazel Rochman wrote that Kleven's "colorfully detailed" images team with her engaging story to "celebrate the transforming power of art." In *Publishers Weekly* a reviewer concluded that the "warmth and individuality" in *A Carousel Tale* "captur[es] . . . the . . . sensory environment of the imaginative child."

In Kleven's *The Paper Princess* a paper doll blows away before a little girl can finish creating her. The princess's adventures continue in *The Paper Princess Finds Her Way,* in which the doll's creator grows too

Kleven's illustration projects include a multicultural story by Arthur Dorros titled **The Island/La Isla.** (Illustration copyright © 1995 by Elisa Kleven. Reproduced by permission of Puffin Books, a division of Penguin Putnam Books for Young Readers.)

old to play with her. The dog carries the princess outside to float away on the wind, and she travels with migrating butterflies to Mexico and a little girl named Lucy. "Kleven's story and art work in tandem to encourage entrance to the wide-open world of self-expression," a *Publishers Weekly* critic wrote of *The Paper Princess.* Calling the artwork "spectacular," *Booklist* reviewer Kathryn Broderick concluded that the book "is full of the spirit of creativity." "The sprightly mixed-media artwork . . . creates a breezy feeling for this heartening sequel," wrote Julie Cummins in *Booklist.*

Susan Scheps, writing for *School Library Journal,* deemed *The Paper Princess Finds Her Way* "as charming as the original." In her third appearance, *The Paper Princess Flies Again: With Her Dog!,* the paper girl and her paper dog fly off in search of a gift for Lucy's birthday. "Kleven's tale is a slight bit of whimsy that will appeal to imaginative young readers," wrote a *Kirkus Reviews* contributor of the book.

In *A Monster in the House* Kleven presents a story about an older sibling dealing with a new baby in the house.

The baby cries all the time, and the narrator describes the little "monster" in detail to a curious neighbor. The author/illustrator's text is accompanied by "luxuriantly detailed collages," according to John Peters in *Booklist.* A *Publishers Weekly* critic noted that Kleven's "playful descriptions and teasing tone depict realistic exchanges between two new friends." In *Sun Bread,* a baker and a dog decide to turn a cloudy day bright by baking a special bread to bring back the sun. The smells inspire the sun to push away the clouds and shine down on the world. Shelle Rosenfeld considered Kleven's illustrations for this "inventive" tale to be "enchanting, busy, [and] colorful." According to a *Publishers Weekly* contributor, Kleven's "buoyant rhyming text brims with shimmering imagery."

Kleven once told *SATA:* "A comment I hear often about my work is, 'It looks like you were having fun when you made this!' I never know exactly how to respond. I agonize a lot over my stories and my pictures: Is this a stupid idea? Is this a cluttered illustration?

"Yet once the flow and excitement of creation carries me safely beyond the internal critical voices, picture-book-making is indeed fun—so much fun I can't imagine not doing it. Creating the little make-believe world of a book—bringing characters to life, 'dressing' them, naming them, worrying over and loving them, giving them landscapes to roam in and skies to fly through—gives me the same deep joy and satisfaction that playing with beloved dolls and toys gave me in childhood.

"My advice to aspiring writers/illustrators of picture books would be to value and love your imaginations. Try not to forget that you're creating books for *children*—try to remember what you were thrilled and intrigued by, and what you loved, as a child. Don't be slick or gimmicky; while creating, try not to think about 'the market'—just the children."

Biographical and Critical Sources

PERIODICALS

Appleseeds, May, 2002, Patricia M. Newman, "Elisa Kleven: From Scraps to Magic," p. 24.

Booklist, October 15, 1993, Hazel Rochman, review of *Snow Song Whistling,* p. 453; July, 1994, Kathryn Broderick, review of *The Paper Princess,* p. 1955; December 15, 1994, Annie Ayres, review of *De Colores, and Other Latin-American Folk Songs for Children,* p. 750; November 1, 1995, Annie Ayres, review of *The Island/La Isla,* p. 476; July, 1996, Nancy McCray, review of *Abuela,* p. 1834; September 15, 1996, Stephanie Zvirin, review of *Hooray, a Piñata!,* p. 240; October 15, 1996, Annie Ayres, review of *The Magic Maguey,* p. 435; June 1, 1997, Stephanie Zvirin, review of *The Puddle Pail,* p. 1719; January 1, 1998, Karen Morgan, review of *Diez deditos/Ten Little Fingers, and Other Play Rhymes and Action Songs from Latin America,* p. 819; October 1, 1998, John Peters, review of *A Monster in the House,* p. 335; December 1, 1999, Michael Cart, review of *City of Angels: In and around Los Angeles,* p. 700; May 15, 2000, John Peters, review of *Our Big Home: An Earth Poem,* p. 1748; May 1, 2001, Shelle Rosenfeld, review of *Sun Bread,* p. 1691; February 15, 2002, GraceAnne A. DeCandido, review of *The Dancing Deer and the Foolish Hunter,* p. 1020; October 15, 2003, Julie Cummins, review of *The Paper Princess Finds Her Way,* p. 419; December 1, 2005, Julie Cummins, review of *The Paper Princess Flies Again: With Her Dog!,* p. 54; February 1, 2006, Ilene Cooper, review of *The Wishing Ball,* p. 55; August, 2007, Carolyn Phelan, review of *The Apple Doll,* p. 82; December 1, 2008, Carolyn Phelan, review of *Wish: Wishing Traditions around the World,* p. 54; February 15, 2009, Hazel Rochman, review of *A Carousel Tale,* p. 87.

Horn Book, January-February, 1995, Maeve Visser Knoth, review of *De Colores, and Other Latin-American Folk Songs for Children,* p. 66; May-June, 1995, Rudine Sims Bishop, review of *De Colores, and Other Latin-American Folk Songs for Children,* p. 316; March-April, 1996, Hanna B. Zeiger, review of *The Island/La Isla,* p. 230; March-April, 1998, Elena Abos, review of *Diez deditos/Ten Little Fingers, and Other Play Rhymes and Action Songs from Latin America,* p. 231; January, 2000, Ruth Ketchum, review of *City of Angels,* p. 99.

Kirkus Reviews, October 1, 2003, review of *The Paper Princess Finds Her Way,* p. 1225; September 15, 2005, review of *The Paper Princess Flies Again,* p. 1029; February 15, 2006, review of *The Wishing Doll,* p. 184; March 1, 2007, review of *Angels Watching over Me,* p. 221; August 1, 2007, review of *The Apple Doll;* October 15, 2008, review of *Wish;* February 1, 2009, review of *A Carousel Tale.*

Publishers Weekly, July 19, 1991, review of *Abuela,* p. 55; May 18, 1992, review of *The Lion and the Little Red Bird,* p. 68; October 4, 1993, review of *Snow Song Whistling,* p. 78; April 11, 1994, review of *The Paper Princess,* p. 64; October 9, 1995, review of *The Island/La Isla,* p. 84; September 16, 1996, review of *Hooray, a Piñata!,* p. 82; October 21, 1996, review of *The Magic Maguey,* p. 82; May 5, 1997, review of *The Puddle Pail,* p. 208; October 5, 1998, review of *A Monster in the House,* p. 89; August 23, 1999, review of *De Colores, and Other Latin-American Folk Songs for Children,* p. 61; November 1, 1999, review of *City of Angels,* p. 82; May 1, 2000, review of *Our Big Home,* p. 70; November 6, 2000, review of *Hooray, a Piñata!,* p. 93; May 21, 2001, review of *Sun Bread,* p. 106; May 14, 2007, review of *Angels Watching over Me,* p. 58; June 18, 2007, review of *The Apple Doll,* p. 53; November 3, 2008, review of *Wish,* p. 58; February 23, 2009, review of *A Carousel Tale,* p. 49.

School Library Journal, April, 2000, Rosie Peasley, review of *Our Big Home,* p. 104; June, 2001, Rosalyn Pierini, review of *Sun Bread,* p. 122; April, 2002, Su-

san Helper, review of *The Dancing Deer and the Foolish Hunter,* p. 113; October, 2003, Susan Scheps, review of *The Paper Princess Finds Her Way,* p. 128; December, 2005, Lisa S. Schindler, review of *The Paper Princess Flies Again,* p. 116; February, 2006, Rebecca Sheridan, review of *The Wishing Ball,* p. 104; May, 2007, Judith Constantinides, review of *Angels Watching over Me,* p. 91; March, 2009, Rachael Vilmar, review of *A Carousel Tale,* p. 119; April, 2009, Jayne Damron, review of *Wish,* p. 127.

ONLINE

Elisa Kleven Home Page, http://www.elisakleven.com (June 1, 2010).

Printed Matter Online, http://www.dcn.davis.ca.us/go/gizmo/ (May 2, 1999), Elisabeth Sherwin, "Davis Group Hears from Award-winning Writer, Her Editor."

Storyopolis Web site, http://www.storyopolis.com/ (September 28, 2006), "Elsa Kleven."*

L

LEE, Huy Voun 1969-

Personal

Name is pronounced "Wei-wen Lee"; born April 2, 1969, in Phnom Penh, Cambodia; immigrated to United States, 1975; naturalized citizen, 1983; daughter of Ming Ching and Sung Chen Lee; married Seiji Ikuta (a painter), November 9, 2000. *Education:* School of Visual Arts, B.F.A., 1992.

Addresses

Home—New York, NY. *Agent*—Lori Nowicki, Painted Words, 310 W. 97th St., Ste. 24, New York, NY 10025; loripainted-words.com. *E-mail*—hello@huyvounlee.com.

Career

Writer and illustrator. Authors Read Aloud, participant; former art teacher to senior citizens at Caring Community and Greenwich House, New York, NY; volunteer origami instructor at Museum of Natural History, New York, NY; gives readings of her works at public schools and other venues. *Exhibitions:* Works included in exhibitions at Steinbaum Krauss Gallery, Barnes & Noble at Astor Place, and Society of Illustrators, all New York, NY.

Writings

SELF-ILLUSTRATED CHILDREN'S BOOKS

At the Beach, Henry Holt (New York, NY), 1994.
In the Snow, Henry Holt (New York, NY), 1995.
In the Park, Henry Holt (New York, NY), 1998.
1, 2, 3, Go!, Henry Holt (New York, NY), 2000.
In the Leaves, Henry Holt (New York, NY), 2005.

ILLUSTRATOR

Chang and the Tiger (reader), McGraw-Hill (New York, NY), 1997.

James Preller, *Cardinal and Sunflower,* HarperCollins (New York, NY), 1998.
Ray Crennan, *Hiroko Makes the Team* (reader), McGraw-Hill (New York, NY), 1999.
April Pulley Sayre, *Honk, Honk, Goose!: Canada Geese Start a Family,* Henry Holt (New York, NY), 2009.
Paul DuBois Jacobs and Jennifer Swender, *Fire Drill,* Henry Holt (New York, NY), 2010.

Contributor of illustrations to *America,* Lee & Low, 1997.

OTHER

Contributor to periodicals, including *Cricket, Spider, Let's Find Out,* and *BLL Teacher Planning Guide.*

Sidelights

A native of Cambodia, Huy Voun Lee is a highly regarded illustrator of children's books, including *Honk, Honk, Goose!: Canada Geese Start a Family,* a work by April Pulley Sayre, and *Fire Drill,* a tale by Paul DuBois Jacobs and Jennifer Swender. Additionally, Lee has created a number of self-illustrated titles, such as *In the Leaves,* that feature her distinctive paper collages. "If my works can make someone smile," she noted on her home page, "then I think I succeeded my goal as an artist."

Lee made her literary debut in 1994 with *At the Beach,* a work she both wrote and illustrated. The tale concerns young Xiao Ming, a thoughtful boy who learns to write several Chinese characters while spending a day at the seashore with his mother. According to *Booklist* reviewer Julie Corsaro, Lee's "whimsical compositions have a strong sense of pattern, rhythm, and design." A reviewer in *Publishers Weekly* complimented the book's blend of story and art, calling *At the Beach* "a remarkably unified effort: everything works together to create a flawless picture book." *In the Snow,* a follow up, again features a day in the life of Xiao Ming and his mother, who use the scenic wonders in a wintry forest as a

learning opportunity. Lee's decorative cut-paper collages and colored borders "create a lively atmosphere for this memorable lesson in Chinese writing," noted Susan Dove Lempke in *Booklist*.

As Xiao Ming and his mother enjoy the beauties of nature on a spring day, the youngster learns a host of new Chinese characters in *In the Park*. Here Lee "uses an organic approach, exploring each word as mother and son come upon it in their travels," a contributor in *Publishers Weekly* stated. Set on a farm on an autumn day, *In the Leaves* again uses intricate collages and a spare text to introduce readers to the Mandarin Chinese alphabet. Lee "makes fine use of textured papers and pattern play in her collages," remarked *Booklist* critic Shelle Rosenfeld. Lee's self-illustrated counting book *1, 2, 3, Go!* "has all the festive ebullience of a Chinese New Year's dragon," wrote a *Publishers Weekly* reviewer. "With masterful simplicity," Each spread features a two-word phrase that pairs a number with a verb, accompanied by a cut-paper illustration and Chinese characters. "With masterful simplicity," Ellen Mandel stated in *Booklist*, "Lee leads readers to a preliminary appreciation of Chinese culture."

In *Honk, Honk, Goose!* Sayre looks at the mating rituals and nesting habits of the Canada Goose. "Lee's cut-paper collage illustrations fill the pages with color and movement," Farida S. Dowler observed in *School Library Journal*, and Abby Nolan, writing in *Booklist*, commented that the artwork is "simple yet expressive, and the tangible textures of nest and trees are set off by the expanses of solid-color sky and shoreline." Jacobs and Swender's *Fire Drill* a work told in verse, follows

a group of schoolchildren who practice evacuating the building after the alarm sounds in their classroom. "Appealing, cheerful illustrations in elemental shapes and colors and vibrant patterns portray the multicultural group," Rosenfeld noted in *Booklist*.

Lee once told *SATA*, "I cried a lot when I came to the United States from my war-torn country. In an effort to stop my persistent crying, my father recorded me and had me listen to myself over and over again. But every time the tape ended, I continued to cry. Then one day, he came home from Chinatown with a children's metal scissors and a glue stick, and I was hooked. I spent countless hours cutting and gluing.

"When I was seven my brother and I broke my parent's bedroom door mirror while playing Tarzan. I decided to decorate the whole door with colorful construction papers. It was my largest collage ever. Unfortunately, my mother did not enjoy my creation. By the time I was in third grade, I spent the weekends making tiny blank books and illustrating the covers. Today, I am lucky to make a career of illustrating interiors of children's books, as well as the covers."

Biographical and Critical Sources

PERIODICALS

Booklist, June 1, 1994, Julie Corsaro, review of *At the Beach,* p. 1832; October 15, 1995, Susan Dove Lempke, review of *In the Snow,* p. 412; June 1, 1998,

Cambodian-born artist Huy Voun Lee creates stylized artwork for April Pulley Sayre's picture book **Honk, Honk, Goose!** (Illustration copyright © 2009 by Huy Voun Lee. Reprinted by permission of Henry Holt and Company, LLC.)

Carolyn Phelan, review of *Cardinal and Sunflower,* p. 1781; July, 1998, Susan Dove Lempke, review of *In the Park,* p. 1886; February 1, 2001, Ellen Mandel, review of *1, 2, 3, Go!,* p. 1054; August, 2005, Shelle Rosenfeld, review of *In the Leaves,* p. 2035; March 1, 2009, Abby Nolan, review of *Honk, Honk, Goose!: Canada Geese Start a Family,* p. 45; April 15, 2010, Shelle Rosenfeld, review of *Fire Drill,* p. 50.

Horn Book, May-June, 2009, Danielle J. Ford, review of *Honk, Honk, Goose!,* p. 327.

Publishers Weekly, April 11, 1994, review of *At the Beach,* p. 64; September 4, 1995, review of *In the Snow,* p. 69; April 13, 1998, review of *In the Park,* p. 74; November 27, 2000, review of *1, 2, 3, Go!,* p. 76.

School Library Journal, July, 1994, John Philbrook, review of *At the Beach,* pp. 95-96; December, 1995, Susan Middleton, review of *In the Snow,* p. 84; May, 1998, Margaret A. Chang, review of *In the Park,* p. 119; June, 1998, Carolyn Jenks, review of *Cardinal and Sunflower,* p. 118; August, 2005, Rebecca Sheridan, review of *In the Leaves,* p. 99; April, 2009, Farida S. Dowler, review of *Honk, Honk, Goose!,* p. 126.

ONLINE

Huy Voun Lee Home Page, http://www.huyvounlee.com (May 20, 2010).

Painted Words Web site, http://www.painted-words.com/ (May 20, 2010), "Huy Voun Lee."

*   *   *

LEONHARD, Herb

Personal

Born in Munich, Germany; immigrated to United States at age three; married; wife's name Allyson; children: Laurent. *Education:* Pacific Northwest College of Art, B.F.A. (illustration), 1985.

Addresses

Home—WA. *E-mail*—herb@herbleonhard.com.

Career

Illustrator and graphic designer. McIntire Design Studio, Portland, OR, graphic designer and illustrator, 1984-86; freelance artist, beginning 1987; Circle Enterprises, Prosser, WA, general manager and art director, 1987-98; Sara Nelson Design, Ltd., Kennewick, WA, graphic designer and illustrator, beginning 1999.

Member

Graphic Artist's Guild, Society of Children's Book Writers and Illustrators.

Awards, Honors

Yakima Ad Federation Chinook Advertising Awards, Award of Merit, 2001, Award of Excellence and Best of Show nominee, both 2003, Judges' Choice and Gold Award, both 2007, and Gold Award, 2008; Spokane Regional Marcom Association Spark Awards, Award of Excellence, 2007, 2010, and Gold Award, 2008; Northwest Addy Award, 2007.

Writings

SELF-ILLUSTRATED

Sir Norman and the Dreaming Dragon, The Prancing Pony (Prosser, WA), 2008.

ILLUSTRATOR

Tori Amos, *Lyrics,* Music Sales Corporation/Omnibus (New York, NY), 2001.

Jan Walker, *An Inmate's Daughter,* Raven Pub. (Norris, MT), 2006.

Steve Richardson, *Billy's Mountain,* Impossible Dreams (Albuquerque, NM), 2007.

Janet Muirhead Hill, *Kyleah's Tree,* Raven Pub., Inc. (Norris, MT), 2008.

Joyce A. Stengel, *St. Patrick and the Three Brave Mice,* Pelican Pub. Co. (Gretna, LA), 2009.

David Davis, *A Southern Child's Garden of Verses,* Pelican Pub. Co. (Gretna, LA), 2010.

Jan Peck, *Way out West on My Little Pony,* Pelican Pub. (Gretna, LA), 2010.

Jane Sutcliffe, *Leonardo's Monster,* Pelican Pub. (Gretna, LA), 2010.

Also creator of coloring books.

Biographical and Critical Sources

PERIODICALS

Children's Bookwatch, April, 2007, review of *Billy's Mountain.*

Faierie, summer, 2008, review of *Sir Norman and the Dreaming Dragon.*

ForeWord, March-April, 2010, review of *Way out West on My Little Pony.*

Kirkus Reviews, February 1, 2009, review of *St. Patrick and the Three Brave Mice.*

Midwest Book Review, March, 2010, review of *Way out West on My Little Pony.*

ONLINE

Herb Leonhard Home Page, http://www.herbleonhard.com (June 15, 2010).

*   *   *

LEWIS, Kim 1951-

Personal

Born May 26, 1951, in Montreal, Quebec, Canada; married; husband's name Flea (a farm manager); children:

Sara, James. *Education:* Sir George Williams University, B.F.A. (with distinction), 1972; Hornsey College of Art, certificate, 1973. *Hobbies and other interests:* Hiking, gardening.

Addresses

Home—Hexham, Northumberland, England. *Office*—The Hearth, Main Rd., Horsley, Newcastle upon Tyne NE15 0NT, England.

Career

Author and artist. Camden Arts Centre, London, England, assistant to gallery administrator, 1973-75; Middlesex Polytechnic Fine Art Department, London, England, fine art printmaking technician, 1975-78; Charlotte Press Printmaking Workshop, Newcastle upon Tyne, England, resident lithographer, 1978-80; self-employed artist and printmaker, 1980—; author and illustrator of children's books, 1988—. *Exhibitions:* Group exhibitions include National Exhibition of Modern British Prints, London, England, 1975; Royal Academy Summer Show, London, 1976; Charlotte Press Printmaking Shows at Bondgate Gallery, Alnwick, England, Callerton Gallery, Ponteland, England, and Sallyport Gallery, Berwick upon Tweed, England, all 1978; Marsil Museum, Montreal, Quebec, Canada, 1978; Old School Arts Workshop, Middleham, England, 1979; and Northern Print Workshops, Laing Art Gallery, Newcastle, England, 1979. Solo exhibitions include Spectro Arts Workshop, Newcastle, 1978; Wallington Hall, Cambo, England, 1979; Stamfordham Galley, Stamfordham, England, 1984; Gossipgate Gaslight Gallery, Alston, England, 1985; Queen's Hall Arts Centre, Hexham, England, 1987; Gossipgate Garden Gallery, Carlisle, England, 1989; and "Over the Hills and Far Away: Tales from a Northumbrian Farm," touring England, 2003-05.

Awards, Honors

Board of Governors Medal for Creative Expression, 1971; A.E. Pinsky Medal, 1972; Birks Medal, 1972; Kate Greenaway Medal shortlist, British Library Association, 1990, for *The Shepherd Boy;* Sheffield Children's Book Award shortlist, 1996, for *My Friend Harry;* Parents' Choice Silver Honour, 1998, for *Emma's Lamb;* Children's Book Award shortlist, 1999, for *Just like Floss.*

Writings

SELF-ILLUSTRATED

The Shepherd Boy, Walker Books (London, England), 1990.
Emma's Lamb, Walker Books (London, England), 1991.
Floss, Walker Books (London, England), 1992.

First Snow, Walker Books (London, England), 1993.
The Last Train, Walker Books (London, England), 1994.
My Friend Harry, Walker Books (London, England), 1995.
One Summer Day, Candlewick Press (Cambridge, MA), 1996.
Friends, Candlewick Press (Cambridge, MA), 1997.
Just like Floss, Candlewick Press (Cambridge, MA), 1998.
Little Calf, Candlewick Press (Cambridge, MA), 2000.
Little Lamb, Candlewick Press (Cambridge, MA), 2000.
Little Puppy, Candlewick Press (Cambridge, MA), 2000.
Little Baa, Candlewick Press (Cambridge, MA), 2001.
Days on the Farm, Walker Books (London, England), 2001.
A Quilt for Baby, Walker Books (London, England), 2002, Candlewick Press (Cambridge, MA), 2003.
Goodnight, Harry, Walker Books (London, England), 2003, Candlewick Press (Cambridge, MA), 2004.
Here We Go, Harry, Candlewick Press (Cambridge, MA), 2005.
Hooray for Harry, Candlewick Press (Cambridge, MA), 2006.
A Puppy for Annie, Candlewick Press (Cambridge, MA), 2006.
Seymour and Henry, Candlewick Press (Cambridge, MA), 2009.

ILLUSTRATOR

Berlie Doherty, *Willa and Old Miss Annie,* Walker Books (London, England), 1994.
Sam McBratney, *I'm Not Your Friend,* HarperCollins (London, England), 2001, published as *I'll Always Be Your Friend,* HarperCollins (New York, NY), 2001.
(With Renée Graef) Janet Beeler Shaw, *Kirsten's Promise,* Pleasant Company Publications (Middleton, WI), 2003.

Also illustrator of several book covers for Bloodaxe Books.

Sidelights

British artist and writer Kim Lewis is the author of *Floss, Goodnight, Harry, Seymour and Henry,* and several other self-illustrated tales for young readers. Lewis's works often address pastoral themes, which arise from the day-to-day activities in her life on a working sheep farm. "She draws what she sees around her and provides us with an intimate portrait of farm life . . .," Jim McKenzie wrote in *Journey to the Hidden Kingdoms: A Guide to the Children's Books of Newcastle, North Tyneside, and Northumberland.* "The natural rhythms of the countryside: the routine of each day, the passing of the seasons, the birth of young animals and their growth to maturity, are all part of the cycle of stories that reflect different stages in the development of very young children."

Lewis is strongly influenced by the locale of her adopted country, England. Born in Canada, she moved to rural Northumberland after finishing her bachelor's degree. Enchanted by the landscape that was so similar to the

Kim Lewis pairs an entertaining, easy-to-read story with her detailed art in her rural-themed picture book **Just like Floss.** (Copyright © 1998 by Kim Lewis. Reproduced by permission of the publisher Candlewick Press, Inc., Cambridge, MA.)

area outside her native Montreal, she quickly fell in love with life in the English countryside. As Lewis once told *SATA:* "When I first came to Northumberland, it struck me as the part of England most like the countryside where I come from in Canada, so in that sense, I felt I had traveled a long way to 'come home.'

Lewis notes that the terrain and climate of Northumberland impacts her art and her writing. "Northern landscape, as well as hill farming life, can seem bleak to some, but it prevents sentimentality. The ideas in my books are influenced by this," she once remarked. "A border collie is used for work, not play; a winsome lamb belongs to a ewe, however much a child would like to keep it for herself; a shepherd's son has to learn to watch and wait before he can take his wished for place in the scheme of things; snow isn't just lovely and fluffy—it can blot out a familiar landscape, a favourite toy, and even the way home.

"I write about what I know and like to draw realistically from what I see, never trusting my imagination to come up with any material more amazing than what is

around. I like to include those quiet corners of a farm where machinery and tools rest, after work, in dark barns where rugged wool sacks are stacked and the wood is weathered to a hundred years' sort of soft grey. The cycle of farm work which follows the seasons, from lambing time to hay making and clipping, from calving to winter feeding, provides so much visual material that I never seem to tire of it. I have made lithographs and watercolours of these things, and now children's books."

The author's two children also became involved with the daily routines of working on a farm, and so it was a natural progression for Lewis to base the characters in her stories on her own children and their adventures, sometimes even naming her characters after them. "I wanted other farm children to recognise their own lives in the stories and city children to be able to 'walk into' the books as if visiting a hill farm for themselves," she explained. Lewis was inspired to write her first children's book, *The Shepherd Boy,* when her husband

landed a job as manager at a sheep farm in the North Tyne Valley. *The Shepherd Boy* tells of James's longing to be just like his father, who is a shepherd. By the end of the story, James receives a shepherd's crook and a sheepdog to raise as his own.

A sheepdog is also featured in *Floss,* in which the title character, a border collie, has to learn the difference between work and play. Floss returns in *Just like Floss,* in which two children have to decide which of the pups from Floss's litter they will keep. When the smallest pup, Sam, stands fast eyeball-to-eyeball with a big ewe, the children know immediately he is the one: a born sheepdog like his mother.

Two children are at the heart of *One Summer Day,* as well. Little Max loves tractors, and he always wants to follow when one goes by the window. When his friend Sara takes him for a walk, Max sees the tractor go by again, and now he feels both excited and satisfied. Hanna B. Zeiger, writing in *Horn Book,* praised the "gentle, sun-dappled illustrations" which "capture the unhurried pace of a small child's happy adventures," while a contributor for *Kirkus Reviews* called *One Summer Day* a "book with a drop of humor and a spoonful of wistfulness."

Another little boy, James, has a special relationship with a toy elephant in *My Friend Harry,* a picture book that shows "great finesse in portraying the relationship between a young child and his silent companion," according to *Booklist* critic Carolyn Phelan. The plush stuffed elephant takes on a life in his own in subsequent titles, including *Goodnight, Harry,* "a bedtime story that's as warm as it is irresistible," Liza Graybill noted in *School Library Journal.* The work centers on Harry's fruitless efforts to fall asleep one night, which include running in place and reading a book, until his friends, Lulu, a stuffed lamb, and Ted, a toy bear, devise a clever solution to his problem. "The velvety artwork has a dreamy quality," a *Kirkus Reviews* contributor noted, and Graybill also praised "the vivid, warm textures" of the stuffed toys.

In *Here We Go, Harry* the stuffed elephant spends an adventurous day playing with Lulu and Ted. After climbing a hill on a breezy day, the lamb and bear soar into the air, enjoying a brief thrill before landing softly in the grass. Harry, though, experiences some difficulty with his take-off and needs gentle encouragement from his pals to successfully take flight. *School Library Journal* reviewer Carolyn Janssen applauded the work, stating that "Lewis knows her audience and creates characters and situations with which youngsters will identify." The search for a missing blanket is the focus of *Hooray for Harry.* When Harry realizes that his favorite blanket has disappeared, Lulu and Ted help him retrace his steps, and along the way the three recount a host of shared activities from their busy day. "A nice sense of anticipation builds through the simple sequencing," Sally R. Dow wrote in *School Library Journal,* and a

critic in *Kirkus Reviews* maintained that the blend of "Lewis' pastoral illustrations with the winsomeness of the trio's activities epitomizes the nostalgic, idyllic innocence of childhood."

A real-life friendship is at the center of *Friends,* in which toddlers Sam and Alice get together on Sam's farm for a day of play. Hearing the clucking of a chicken as it lays an egg, they go to retrieve the egg, but on the way back to the house have a quarrel and break it. Everything works out fine, however, for when they hear the tell-tale clucking again, they get another egg and bring this one safely home. "You can almost smell the hay," wrote Miriam Lang Budin in *School Library Journal.* "Masterful."

Lewis sticks with rural themes in *Little Puppy, Little Calf,* and *Little Lamb.* These books all feature Katie's first gentle and magical moments with the newborn animals on her farm. She touches the newborn calf's nose, for example, and is licked on the face by the puppy. "What saves these books from sentimentality," noted *Booklist* critic Hazel Rochman, "are the facts about each animal" that Lewis integrates into her stories. Piper L. Nyman, reviewing the same three books in *School Library Journal,* commented on the "lush, rural landscapes" on the endpapers and the "gentle nature" of these tales.

In *Little Baa* Lewis presents a lamb dancing through the fields while its Ma nibbles grass nearby. Suddenly, when she looks up, Baa is gone. While the other baby lambs return to their mothers, Baa stays missing, and Ma wanders through the countryside in search of her baby. Floss, the border collie, helps out, finding the baby lamb and reuniting him with his mother, a reunion which *Booklist* critic Ilene Cooper found "quite touching." Cooper also called *Little Baa* "tender and lovely, a nice mix of animal behavior and human emotion," while Rachel Fox concluded in *School Library Journal* that young readers "will find its happy ending quite satisfying."

A mother expresses her love for her child in Lewis's *A Quilt for Baby.* As she readies a patchwork quilt for her infant, a woman tells the story behind the pictures stitched into the squares, each of which represent an aspect of the farm on which they live. "The rhythmic text flows along in a soothing way, making this a good, soporific story for bedtime," Phelan wrote in *Booklist.* In *A Puppy for Annie* Lewis describes the relationship between a girl and her energetic border collie, following the youngster's efforts to understand her dog's many moods. According to Linda Staskus in *School Library Journal,* "the realistic, soft pastel and colored-pencil art reflects the joys of owning and loving a puppy."

A pair of ducklings learns the value of following instructions in *Seymour and Henry.* When their mother decides that it is time to head home after a day of playing in the pond, duckling brothers Seymour and Henry

Lewis's illustrations capture the gentle nature of her original story for Seymour and Henry. (Copyright © 2009 by Kim Lewis. All rights reserved. Reproduced by permission of the publisher Candlewick Press, Inc., Cambridge, MA.)

run away and hide, preferring to explore their surroundings. When it starts to rain, however, the duo hastily returns to Mother's care. Lewis earned praise for her artwork, which portrays the ducklings as stuffed animals. "Done in pencil crayon and chalk pastel, the illustrations are soft-edged and sweet," wrote *School Library Journal* critic Amy Lilien-Harper, and a contributor in *Kirkus Reviews* noted that "the soft focus of Lewis's pencil crayon and chalk pastel illustrations should attract the very young."

"It is a great pleasure to write and draw about the small corners of country life for children, where the world is up close and new," Lewis concluded to *SATA.* "Drawing is my favourite thing, so I've always done it, regardless."

Biographical and Critical Sources

BOOKS

McKenzie, Jim, *Journey to the Hidden Kingdoms: A Guide to the Children's Books of Newcastle, North Tyneside, and Northumberland,* Powdene Publicity (Newcastle upon Tyne, England), 2004.

PERIODICALS

Booklist, October 15, 1995, Carolyn Phelan, review of *My Friend Harry,* p. 412; April 15, 1998, Hazel Rochman, review of *Friends,* p. 1450; January 1, 1999, Kathleen Squires, review of *Just like Floss,* p. 888; March 15, 2000, Hazel Rochman, review of *Little Puppy, Little Calf,* and *Little Lamb,* p. 1387; May 1, 2001, Ilene Cooper, review of *Little Baa,* p. 1691; April 15, 2003, Carolyn Phelan, review of *A Quilt for Baby,* p. 1479; June 1, 2006, Kathy Broderick, review of *Hooray for Harry,* p. 87; November 15, 2006, Stephanie Zvirin, review of *A Puppy for Annie,* p. 54.

Books for Keeps, January, 1996, review of *First Snow,* p. 6; November, 1996, review of *The Last Train,* p. 8.

Horn Book, July-August, 1996, Hanna B. Zeiger, review of *One Summer Day,* pp. 450-451; November-December, 1998, Marilyn Bousquin, review of *Just like Floss,* pp. 715-716.

Kirkus Reviews, June 15, 1996, review of *One Summer Day,* p. 901; November 1, 1998, review of *Just like Floss,* p. 1601; December 15, 2003, review of *Good Night, Harry,* p. 1452; March 15, 2006, review of *Hooray for Harry,* p. 294; January 1, 2009, review of *Seymour and Henry.*

Publishers Weekly, March 9, 1992, review of *Floss,* p. 55; February 2, 2009, review of *Seymour and Henry,* p. 48.

School Librarian, spring, 1998, Beverly Mathias, review of *Friend,* p. 19.

School Library Journal, July, 1991, Barbara Chatton, review of *Emma's Lamb,* p. 60; July, 1996, Christine A. Moesch, review of *One Summer Day,* p. 67; July, 1998, Miriam Lang Budin, review of *Friends,* p. 78; January, 1999, Kathy M. Newby, review of *Just like Floss,* p. 97; June, 2000, Piper L. Nyman, review of *Little Puppy, Little Calf,* and *Little Lamb,* p. 118; June, 2001, Rachel Fox, review of *Little Baa,* p. 124; November, 2003, Shelly B. Sutherland, review of *A Quilt for Baby,* p. 106; April, 2004, Liza Graybill, review of *Good Night, Harry,* p. 118; March, 2005, Carolyn Jansen, review of *Here We Go, Harry,* p. 175; April, 2006, Sally R. Dow, review of *Hooray for Harry,* p. 111; February, 2007, Linda Staskus, review of *A Puppy for Annie,* p. 90; May, 2009, Amy Lilien-Harper, review of *Seymour and Henry,* p. 82.

ONLINE

Kim Lewis Home Page, http://www.kimlewisbooks.co.uk (June 10, 2010).

Walker Books Web site, http://www.walker.co.uk/ (June 10, 2010), "Kim Lewis."*

*　　　*　　　*

LIESHOUT, Elle van
See van LIESHOUT, Elle

M

MacDONALD, Anne Louise 1955-

Personal

Born 1955, in Antigonish, Nova Scotia, Canada; married Frank MacDonald. *Education:* Attended university. *Hobbies and other interests:* Painting, photography, bonsai gardening.

Addresses

Home—Nova Scotia, Canada. *E-mail*—AnneLouise@ hugahorsefarm.com.

Career

Author and horsewoman. Worked variously as a veterinary assistant, dog groomer and trainer, commercial artist, and manager of a plant and animal care department. Hoof therapist and trimmer; teacher of natural horse and hoof care.

Writings

PICTURE BOOKS

Nanny-Mac's Cat, illustrated by Marie LaFrance, Ragweed (Charlottetown, Prince Edward Island, Canada), 1995.
The Memory Stone, illustrated by Joanne Ouellet, Ragweed (Charlottetown, Prince Edward Island, Canada), 1998.
The Dog Wizard, illustrated by Brenda Jones, Ragweed (Charlottetown, Prince Edward Island, Canada), 1999.

JUVENILE NOVELS

The Ghost Horse of Meadow Green, Pony (Danbury, CT), 2005.
Seeing Red, KCP Fiction (Toronto, Ontario, Canada), 2009.

Author's work has been translated into five languages.

OTHER

(And photographer) *My Natural Horses,* privately published, 2010.

Sidelights

Canadian author Anne Louise MacDonald began her writing career in the mid-1990s, after working with animals—particularly horses—for much of her life. Her first picture book, *Nanny-Mac's Cat,* took her a year to write, but others, such as *The Memory Stone* and *The Dog Wizard,* have come together more quickly. MacDonald's books for older readers include the middle-grade novels *The Ghost Horse of Meadow Green* and *Seeing Red.*

Growing up in Nova Scotia, Canada, as the third of seven children, MacDonald was a shy girl who gravitated to books and animals more than the children playing baseball and other games in her neighborhood. She got horse fever as a toddler, bicycled to every horse or pony living in the vicinity as soon as she was able, and started riding lessons at age twelve. MacDonald's first horse, a part-thoroughbred she named Highland Laird, came four years later. After she was forced to sell Laird, she spent seven years training and riding others' horses, but since 1990 MacDonald has had at least one horse as part of her family. Her first middle-grade novel, *The Ghost Horse of Meadow Green,* as well as her informational *My Natural Horses,* are an outgrowth of her passion for horses.

In *The Ghost Horse of Meadow Green* MacDonald creates a young protagonist named Kim, who shares her passion. When the sixth grader sees a majestic black horse in a field near her home, she is told that no horse is pastured there. Suspecting that the horse may have been a ghost, Kim begins to hear stories that confirm that suspicion. However, Ghost the horse soon proves to be real, and Kim hides him in a barn, helped by a new friend, Tim. While her family life grows increasingly difficult, Kim bonds with Ghost, until a visit from

Cover of Ann Louise MacDonald's coming-of-age novel Seeing Red, *which features elements of the supernatural as well as horses.* (Cover images © 2009 by Irene Luxbacher and Jupiterimages Corporation. Used by permission of Kids Can Press, Ltd., Toronto, Ontario, Canada.)

Gramma-Lou sheds light on some family history that lifts dark shadows from Kim's world. In *Quill & Quire* Nadine d'Etremont noted that *The Ghost Horse of Meadow Green* treats middle-grade "equine enthusiasts" to an "engaging first novel," while Ann Ketcheson wrote in *Canadian Review of Materials* that MacDonald's novel "is a coming-of-age tale where readers grow along with Kim as she learns self-esteem and assertiveness."

In *Seeing Red* readers meet fourteen-year-old Frankie Uccello, who seems to have a normal life except for his vivid dreams about flying. Although his father reassures him that flying dreams are normal, Frankie's dreams are special; they also hint at bad things that are about to happen. When he dreams that his friend Tim will take a bad fall off his horse, Frankie must decide whether to take his dreams seriously and risk being viewed as weird, like his mind-reading ninth-grade classmate Maura-Lee. A *Kirkus Reviews* writer wrote that in Mac-Donald's "evocative written" novel the author "deftly mixes" otherworldly elements into the life of an average teen, and Debbie Carton noted in *Booklist* that the rural-themed story features "likeable and realistic

teen[s]" and "warm, loving adult characters." Praising *Seeing Red*, Carol Schene commented in *School Library Journal* that MacDonald's tale features "a plot that interwines the everyday vicissitudes at school and home with some seemingly supernatural twists."

Biographical and Critical Sources

PERIODICALS

Booklist, March 1, 2009, Debbie Carton, review of *Seeing Red,* p. 44.
Canadian Review of Materials, May 13, 2005, Ann Ketcheson, review of *The Ghost Horse of Meadow Green;* March 20, 2009, Andrea Galbraith, review of *Seeing Red.*
Kirkus Reviews, February 1, 2009, review of *Seeing Red.*
Publishers Weekly, February 2, 2009, review of *Seeing Red,* p. 50.
Quill & Quire, January, 2005, Nadine d'Entremont, review of *The Ghost Horse of Meadow Green.*
Resource Links, October, 2005, Joan Marshall, review of *The Ghost Horse of Meadow Green,* p. 15.
School Library Journal, August, 2009, Carol Schene, review of *Seeing Red,* p. 108.

ONLINE

Anne Louise MacDonald Home Page, http://www.hugahorsefarm.com (June 15, 2010).

*   *   *

MACDONALD, Wendy
(Wendy M. Macdonald)

Personal

Born in Yarram, Victoria, Australia; married. *Education:* Melbourne University, medical degree. *Hobbies and other interests:* Australian history.

Addresses

Home—Melbourne, Victoria, Australia. *E-mail*—wendon@netspace.net.au.

Career

Writer.

Member

Australian Society of Authors, Australian Writer's Guild, Society of Children's Book Writers and Illustrators.

Awards, Honors

Eve Pownall Award for Information Books shortlist, Children's Book Council of Australia, 1996, for *The Voyage of the Endeavour;* Victorian Premier's Reading Challenge selections, for both *Training a Guide Dog* and *The Castaway Convict.*

Wendy Macdonald (Reproduced by permission.)

Writings

The Unseen Army Bacteria and Viruses, Reed International Books Australia (Port Melbourne, Victoria, Australia), 1992.

Mrs. Munday's Mailbag, Jacaranda Press (Milton, Queensland, Australia), 1992.

The Voyage of the Endeavour, illustrated by Julian Bruere, Cardigan Street Publishers (Carlton, Victoria, Australia), 1995.

Our Busy Bodies, Reed International Books Australia (Port Melbourne, Victoria, Australia), 1997.

The Food Journey, Reed International Books Australia (Port Melbourne, Victoria, Australia), 1997.

The Junkyard Dog, illustrated by Pat Reynolds, Thomson Nelson (Southbank, Victoria, Australia), 2000.

Glass, Reed International Books Australia (Port Melbourne, Victoria, Australia), 2000.

Training a Guide Dog, Heinemann (Port Melbourne, Victoria, Australia), 2001.

(As Wendy M. MacDonald) *Susie's Shoelaces,* illustrated by Lisa Coutts, Cambridge University Press (Cambridge, England), 2002.

The Man Who Measured the World, illustrated by Vasja Koman, Thomson Nelson (Southbank, Victoria, Australia), 2004.

The Castaway Convict, illustrated by Mark Wilson, University of Western Australia Press (Crawley, Western Australia, Australia), 2005.

Pharoah's Tomb, Omnibus Books (Malvern, South Australia, Australia), 2005.

Sabotage, Thomson Nelson (Southbank, Victoria, Australia), 2005.

The Captain's Diary, Rigby Harcourt (Port Melbourne, Victoria, Australia), 2007.

Galileo's Leaning Tower Experiment: A Science Adventure, illustrated by Paolo Rui, Charlesbridge (Watertown, MA), 2009.

"ZAPPER" READER SERIES

A *Great Big Zero,* Heinemann (Port Melbourne, Victoria, Australia), 1992.

The Body in the Bag, Heinemann (Port Melbourne, Victoria, Australia), 1992.

The Warning, Heinemann (Port Melbourne, Victoria, Australia), 1992.

The Stones and the Shakes, Heinemann (Port Melbourne, Victoria, Australia), 1993.

The Battle of the Bands, Heinemann (Port Melbourne, Victoria, Australia), 1993.

The Black Tattoo, illustrated by Trish Hill, Heinemann (Port Melbourne, Victoria, Australia), 1995.

Crocodile Creek, illustrated by Genevieve Rees, Heinemann (Port Melbourne, Victoria, Australia), 1995.

Off the Rails, illustrated by Genevieve Rees, Heinemann (Port Melbourne, Victoria, Australia), 1996.

First Flight, illustrated by Julian Bruere, Heinemann (Port Melbourne, Victoria, Australia), 1996.

Turkish Delight, Heinemann (Port Melbourne, Victoria, Australia), 1998.

I Wish I Had a Puppy, Heinemann (Port Melbourne, Victoria, Australia), 1998.

Freedom, illustrated by Warren Crossett, Heinemann (Port Melbourne, Victoria, Australia), 2000.

Lucy and the Lion, Heinemann (Port Melbourne, Victoria, Australia), 2001.

"AUSTRALIA'S CONVICTS" SERIES

Australia's Convicts, Macmillan Education Australia (South Yarra, Victoria, Australia), 1999.

Life at Sea, Macmillan Education Australia (South Yarra, Victoria, Australia), 1999.

Life in a New Land, Macmillan Education Australia (South Yarra, Victoria, Australia), 1999.

Transportation Ends, Macmillan Education Australia (South Yarra, Victoria, Australia), 1999.

Adaptations

Galileo's Leaning Tower Experiment was adapted as an audio book, Spoken Arts, 2009.

Sidelights

A native of Victoria, Australia, Wendy Macdonald is the author of more than thirty works of fiction and nonfiction for young readers, including books in the "Australia's Convicts" and "Zappers" series. Among her award-winning books is *The Voyage of the Endeavour,* which follows the travels of Captain James Cook.

In *Galileo's Leaning Tower Experiment: A Science Adventure,* Macdonald turns to historical fiction, depicting a well-known episode from the life of sixteenth-century Italian physicist, mathematician, and astronomer Galileo Galilei. While serving as a professor in the town of Pisa, Galileo spots a young boy named Massimo dropping a loaf of bread and a slab of cheese from a bridge onto his uncle's boat. Noting that the objects land at the same moment, thereby challenging Aristotle's teachings about bodies in motion, Galileo proposes a series of experiments, performed with Massimo's help, that culminate in a spectacular demonstration from atop the Leaning Tower of Pisa. "The story excels at teaching the concept involved," remarked Jeffrey A. French in *School Library Journal,* and *Booklist* critic Ian Chipman observed that Macdonald's work "should help young minds appreciate the value of questioning old ideas." According to a critic in *Kirkus Reviews, Galileo's Leaning Tower Experiment* offers readers "a glimpse of one of the most renowned experiments ever and a methodology for their future research too."

Biographical and Critical Sources

PERIODICALS

Booklist, February 15, 2009, Ian Chipman, review of *Galileo's Leaning Tower Experiment: A Science Adventure,* p. 77.
Kirkus Reviews, January 1, 2009, review of *Galileo's Leaning Tower Experiment.*
School Library Journal, June, 2009, Jeffrey A. French, review of *Galileo's Leaning Tower Experiment,* p. 110.

Italian artist Paolo Rui creates the artwork in Macdonald's historical picture book Galileo's Leaning Tower Experiment. (Charlesbridge, 2009. Illustration copyright © 2009 by Paolo Rui. Reproduced by permission.)

ONLINE

Wendy Macdonald Home Page, http://wendybooks.com.au (May 20, 2010).

*   *   *

MacDONALD, Wendy M.
See MacDONALD, Wendy

*   *   *

MANTHA, John 1960-

Personal

Born 1960, in Sault Ste. Marie, Ontario, Canada; married; wife's name Leanne; children: Lauren. *Education:* Ontario College of Art, B.F.A. (with honors).

Addresses

Home—Toronto, Ontario, Canada. *E-mail*—john.mantha@sympatico.ca.

Career

Artist and illustrator. Designer of coins for Royal Canadian Mint; freelance courtroom artist. *Exhibitions:* Works included in permanent collections at Ford Motor Company, Toronto Transit Commission, and Church of Our Lady of Good Counsel.

Awards, Honors

Children's Literature Roundtables of Canada Information Book Award, 2001, and Red Cedar Book Award selection, 2003, both for *The Kids Book of Canada's Railways* by Deborah Hodge; Hackmatack Award for Nonfiction nomination, 2006, for *The Kids Book of Canadian Exploration* by Ann-Maureen Owens and Jane Yealland; British Columbia Book Prize nomination, and Christie Harris Illustrated Children's Literature Prize, both c. 2006, both for *The Kids Book of Aboriginal Peoples in Canada* by Dianne Silvey; Red Cedar Information Book Award nomination, 2010, for both *The Siege* by Stephen Shapiro and *The Kids Book of Canada at War* by Elizabeth Macleod.

Illustrator

Pat Hancock, *The Kids Book of Canadian Prime Ministers,* Kids Can Press (Toronto, Ontario, Canada), 1998, revised edition, 2005.
Deborah Hodge, *The Kids Book of Canada's Railway and How the CPR Was Built,* Kids Can Press (Toronto, Ontario, Canada), 2000.
Maxine Trottier, *Storm at Batoche,* Stoddart Kids (New York, NY), 2000.
Eric Walters, *Hoop Crazy!,* Orca Book Pub. (Custer, WA), 2001.

John Mantha (Reproduced by permission.)

Eric Walters, *Long Shot,* Orca Book Pub. (Custer, WA), 2001.

Valerie Wyatt, *The Kids Book of Canadian Firsts,* Kids Can Press (Tonawanda, NY), 2001.

Carlotta Hacker, *The Kids Book of Canadian History,* Kids Can Press (Toronto, Ontario, Canada), 2002.

Eric Walters, *Road Trip,* Orca Book Publishers (Custer, WA), 2002.

Jennifer Glossop, *The Kids Book of World Religions,* Kids Can Press (Toronto, Ontario, Canada), 2003.

Elizabeth Macleod, *The Kids Book of Great Canadians,* Kids Can Press (Toronto, Ontario, Canada), 2004.

Ann-Maureen Owens and Jane Yealland, *The Kids Book of Canadian Exploration,* Kids Can Press (Toronto, Ontario, Canada), 2004.

Dianne Silvey, *The Kids Book of Aboriginal Peoples in Canada,* Kids Can Press (Toronto, Ontario, Canada), 2005.

Elizabeth Macleod, *The Kids Book of Great Canadian Women,* Kids Can Press (Toronto, Ontario, Canada), 2006.

Deborah Hodge, *The Kids Book of Canadian Immigration,* Kids Can Press (Toronto, Ontario, Canada), 2006.

Elizabeth Macleod, *The Kids Book of Canada at War,* Kids Can Press (Toronto, Ontario, Canada), 2007.

Stephen Shapiro, *The Siege: Under Attack in Renaissance Europe,* Annick Press (Toronto, Ontario, Canada), 2007.

Elizabeth Macleod, *Lucy Maud Montgomery,* Kids Can Press (Toronto, Ontario, Canada), 2008.

Mark Oakley, *The Seventh Expert: An Interactive Medieval Adventure,* Firefly Books (Richmond Hill, Ontario, Canada), 2008.

Elizabeth Macleod, *Samuel de Champlain,* Kids Can Press (Toronto, Ontario, Canada), 2008.

Diane Silvey, *Time of the Thunderbird,* Dundurn Press (Toronto, Ontario, Canada), 2008.

Elizabeth Macleod, *Marie Curie,* Kids Can Press (Toronto, Ontario, Canada), 2009.

Elizabeth Macleod, *Harry Houdini,* Kids Can Press (Toronto, Ontario, Canada), 2009.

Laura Scandiffio, *Crusades,* Annick Press (Toronto, Ontario, Canada), 2009.

Contributor to periodicals, including *Cottage Life* and *Bettery Homes & Gardens.*

Sidelights

Canadian artist John Mantha is an award-winning illustrator whose detailed paintings for the highly respected "Kids Book of. . ." series bring to life myriad aspects of Canadian history and culture. Reviewing series installment *The Kids Book of Aboriginal Peoples in Canada* for *Resource Links,* Adriane Pettit remarked on Dianne Silvey's "vibrantly illustrated" text, while Mantha's "realistic paintings" for Deborah Hodge's *The Kids Book of Canadian Immigration* "greatly enhance the text," according to *Resource Links* reviewer Victoria Pennell. *The Kids Book of Canada at War,* one of several books to team Mantha with writer Elizabeth Macleod, was cited by Pennell as "a very informative book" featuring artwork that is "rich in colorful and detail," and *Quill & Quire* critic Lian Goodall wrote that his "colour images provide a cheery visual touch" to Valerie Wyatt's *The Kids Book of Canadian Firsts.* Noting Mantha's reputation for depicting figures from history, Wyatt added that the artist's "illustrations . . . make readers feel they're meeting the famous person face to face."

Born in Sault Ste. Marie, Ontario, Mantha focused on painting during his high-school years and then enrolled at Ontario College of Art, where he earned a B.F.A. with honours. His medium of choice—oils and oil wash—allows him to create highly textured and realistically detailed images. In addition to book illustration, Mantha creates original works that he exhibits in galleries or creates on a commission basis. He has also worked, on occasion, as a court-room artist for Toronto's *Globe & Mail* newspaper and CTV News.

In addition to his work for the multi-volume "Kids Book of. . ." series, Mantha has illustrated several easy-reading biographies as well as stand-alone volumes. With a text by Macleod that profiles the famous French-born explorer, *Samuel de Champlain* contains "abundant pen-and-ink illustrations" by Mantha that "are finely rendered and enhance" Macleod's text, according to *School Library Journal* contributor Anne Chapman Callaghan. In similar fashion, his "softly rendered" paintings for *Marie Curie* capture the life of the Polish-born scientist with "enough detail to provide visual clues" to Macleod's easy-reading text, according to *Canadian Review of Materials* critic Rosemary Hollett.

Storm at Batoche, a novel by Maxine Trottier, focuses on the Riel Rebellion and the Battle of Batoche, an 1885 uprising against the northwest expansion of Canadian governance in which mixed-race politician Louis Riel led the prairie-dwelling Métis people against Canadian troops. Praised for introducing young readers to a controversial aspect of North-American history, this historical novel benefits from the artist's "wonderful colour illustrations," according to a *Resource Links* critic. Gail de Vos also praised Manthe's paintings in *Storm at Batoche,* describing them as "realistically. . . . rendered in a naive-type of illustrative style, [that is] slightly wooden but charming nonetheless."

Biographical and Critical Sources

PERIODICALS

Booklist, April 15, 2003, Ilene Cooper, review of *The Kids Book of World Religions,* p. 1467; May 1, 2009, Carolyn Phelan, review of *Marie Curie,* p. 62.

Canadian Review of Materials, October 5, 2001, Gail de Vos, review of *Storm at Batoche;* May 1, 2009, Rose-mary Hollett, review of *Marie Curie;* November 13, 2009, Gregory Bryan, review of *Harry Houdini.*

Globe & Mail (Toronto, Ontario, Canada), September 23, 2006, Susan Perren, review of *The Kids Book of Canadian Immigration,* p. D18.

Quill & Quire, September, 2000, Gwyneth Evans, review of *The Kids Book of Canada's Railway and How the CPR Was Built;* September, 2001, Lian Goodall, review of *The Kids Book of Canadian Firsts;* August, 2002, Laurie McNeill, review of *The Kids Book of Canadian History.*

Resource Links, February, 2001, review of *Storm at Batoche,* p. 9; December, 2002, Victoria Pennell, review of *The Kids Book of Canadian History,* p. 39; April, 2003, Linda Irvine, review of *The Kids Book of World Religions,* p. 24; April, 2004, Victoria Pennell, review of *The Kids Book of Great Canadians,* p. 31; October, 2005, Victoria Pennell, review of *The Kids Book of Canadian Prime Ministers,* p. 26; April, 2006, Adriane Pettit, review of *The Kids Book of Aboriginal Peoples,* p. 36; February, 2007, Victoria Pennell, review of *The Kids Book of Canadian Immigration,* p. 22; December, 2007, Karen Loch, review of *The Siege: Under Attack in Renaissance Europe,* p. 31.

School Library Journal, May, 2001, Susan Hepler, review of *Storm at Batoche,* p. 136; July, 2002, Kate Kohlbeck, review of *Long Shot,* p. 127; April, 2003, Nancy Call, review of *The Kids Book of World Religions,* p. 149; December, 2008, Anne Chapman Callaghan, review of *Samuel de Champlain,* p. 113; January, 2009, Kathleen Meulen, review of *The Seventh Expert: An Interactive Medieval Adventure,* p. 116.

ONLINE

John Mantha Home Page, http://www.johnmantha.com (May 31, 2010).

John Mantha Web log, http://johnmantha.blogspot.com (May 31, 2010).

　　　　*　　*　　*

McCORMACK, Caren McNelly

Personal
Born in TX; married; children: two daughters.

Addresses
Home—Los Altos, CA. *E-mail*—caren@carenmccormack.com.

Career
Writer for children.

Writings
The Fiesta Dress: A Quinceañera Tale, illustrated by Martha Avilés, Marshall Cavendish Children (Tarrytown, NY), 2009.

Mantha's illustration projects include creating the detailed art in **The Kids Book of Canadian Exploration** *by Ann-Maureen Owens and Jane Yealland.* (Illustration © 2004 by John Mantha. Used by permission of Kids Can Press Ltd., Toronto, Ontario, Canada.)

Caren McNelly McCormack (Photograph by Jon McCormack. Reproduced by permission.)

Contributor to periodicals, including *Highlights for Children.*

Biographical and Critical Sources

PERIODICALS

Bulletin of the Center for Children's Books, May, 2009, Hope Morrison, review of *The Fiesta Dress: A Quinceañera Tale,* p. 372.
Kirkus Reviews, February 1, 2009, review of *The Fiesta Dress.*
School Library Journal, March, 2009, Sandra Welzenbach, review of *The Fiesta Dress,* p. 122.

ONLINE

Caren McNelly McCormack Home Page, http://www.carenmccormack.com (June 15, 2010).*

* * *

McDOWELL, Marilyn Taylor

Personal

Married Peter McDowell; has children. *Education:* Katharine Gibbs School, degree; attended Institute of Children's Literature. *Hobbies and other interests:* Hiking, organic gardening.

Addresses

Home—North Chittendon, VT.

Career

Author. Formerly worked as an administrative assistant at an AZ dude ranch; former teacher; proprietor of children's book store. Volunteer librarian and storyteller; Presenter at schools. Volunteer at local food co-op.

Member

Society of Children's Book Writers and Illustrators, Authors Guild.

Awards, Honors

Tassy Walden New Voices Award, for picture-book text; Society of Children's Book Writers and Illustrators Letter of Merit, and *Booklist* Top Ten Historical Fiction for Youth designation, both 2009, both for *Carolina Harmony.*

Writings

Carolina Harmony, Delacorte Press (New York, NY), 2009.

Sidelights

Marilyn Taylor McDowell, the author of the middle-grade novel *Carolina Harmony,* grew up as part of a large farming family and learning the value of hard work and perseverance. She also gained a lifelong love of the natural world during her explorations of the woods, meadows, pastures, and ponds near her home. Libraries fueled her curiosity, and exploring her interests through books has become another lifelong habit. As McDowell asserted on her home page, "Reading is lifelong learning"; in the words of her mother, "If you can read, and read well, you can do anything."

Although McDowell graduated from a Boston business school and got her first job as an administrative assistant at a dude ranch in Tucson, Arizona, she eventually left work to start her own family. While her children were young, she decided to combine her interests in research with her love of the outdoors and her love of storytelling. Completing a writing course at the Institute of Children's Literature led to a picture-book text and then the manuscript that would become her first published novel, *Carolina Harmony.*

In *Carolina Harmony* readers meet Carolina, a ten-year-old orphan who lives in North Carolina's Blue Ridge Mountains with Auntie Shen. The time is 1964, and government meddling is slowly complicating Auntie Shen's off-the-grid life. Still, the strong, self-reliant woman manages to preserve a life free from outside interference until she suffers a stroke, leaving Carolina at the mercy of the state's foster system. Worried about her adopted aunt, and experiencing hardship as she is passed from family to family, Carolina finally finds a

new home at Harmony Farm, although her insecurities may cause her to lose it in what a *Kirkus Reviews* writer dubbed an "impressive debut" novel.

Carolina Harmony is enriched by McDowell's "nuanced narrative illuminat[ing] . . . the value and the potential pitfalls of both modern and mountain culture," the *Kirkus Reviews* critic added, and *School Library Journal* contributor Catherine Threadgill noted that "McDowell's prose reads easily and creates a wonderful sense of place." Recommending the novel for "thoughtful readers," Kathleen Isaacs asserted in *Booklist* that McDowell's affection for the Appalachian region comes through strongly, enriching her depictions of "the language, the environment, and the traditions of mountain culture" in *Carolina Harmony*.

Biographical and Critical Sources

PERIODICALS

Booklist, February 1, 2009, Kathleen Isaacs, review of *Carolina Harmony,* p. 40.

Cover of Marilyn Taylor McDowell's engaging middle-grade novel Carolina Harmony, *which is set in the Appalachian Mountains during the early twentieth century.* (Illustration copyright © 2009 by Delacorte Press, an imprint of Random House, Inc. Used by permission of Delacorte Press, an imprint of Random House Children's Books, a division of Random House, Inc.)

Kirkus Reviews, February 1, 2009, Marilyn Taylor McDowell, review of *Carolina Harmony.*
School Library Journal, August, 2009, Catherine Threadgill, review of *Carolina Harmony,* p. 109.

ONLINE

Marilyn Taylor McDowell Home Page, http://www.marilyntaylormcdowell.com (May 31, 2010).*

*   *   *

MICHALAK, Jamie 1973-

Personal

Born January 9, 1973, in Springfield, MA; daughter of John (a physical education teacher and football coach) and Judith (an executive assistant); married Kenneth White; children: Patrick, Finn. *Education:* University of Florida, B.A. (English), 1996; attended Rice University Publishing Program, 1996.

Addresses

Home—Barrington, RI. *Office*—Candlewick Press, 99 Dover St., Somerville, MA 02144. *E-mail*—jamiemichalak@yahoo.com.

Career

Author and editor of books for children. Dutton Children's Books, New York, NY, former editorial assistant; Little, Brown Children's Books, Boston, MA, managing editor, 1999-2001; Candlewick Press, Somerville, MA, editor, beginning 2001.

Member

Authors Guild, Authors League of America, Society of Children's Book Writers and Illustrators.

Awards, Honors

Best Book designation, *Kirkus Reviews,* and Best Book designation, Chicago Public Library, both 2009, both for *Joe and Sparky Get New Wheels.*

Writings

Larry and Rita, illustrated by Jill Newton, Candlewick Press (Cambridge, MA), 2007.
(Adaptor) *The Tale of Despereaux Movie Tie-in Junior Novelization* (based on the novel by Kate DiCamillo), Candlewick Press (Cambridge, MA), 2008.
Fairy Tea Party, illustrated by Kaori Watanabe, Tiger Tales, 2008.
Fairy Goodnight Kisses, illustrated by Kaori Watanabe, Tiger Tales, 2008.
Joe and Sparky Get New Wheels, illustrated by Frank Remkiewicz, Candlewick Press (Somerville, MA), 2009.

Jamie Michalak (Reproduced by permission.)

Joe and Sparky, Superstars!, illustrated by Frank Remkiewicz, Candlewick Press (Somerville, MA), 2011.

Sidelights

Jamie Michalak told *SATA:* "I was born in Springfield, Massachusetts, and grew up in the same neighborhood that Dr. Seuss once lived in. I've always been passionate about reading and writing. As a child, I'd write articles about my neighbors and the happenings on my street for my own newspaper, *The Biltmore Street News.*

"After graduating from the University of Florida with a B.A. in English, I attended the Rice University Publishing Program. Upon completion, I immediately moved to New York City to work in the publishing industry. I landed a position as an editorial assistant at Dutton Children's Books and fell in love with the world of children's book publishing. In 1999, I moved to Boston and became the managing editor of Little, Brown Children's Books. In 2001, I left to work as an editor at Candlewick Press.

"After the birth of my first son, I began editing from home and writing my own stories. My early reader *Joe and Sparky Get New Wheels,* illustrated by Frank Remkiewicz, was published in 2009. I created Joe and Sparky

during a visit from my sister, Julie, who was very ill at the time. She couldn't really do anything too physical, so we just wrote the story for our own entertainment. And once Frank came aboard as illustrator, I knew the story was in good hands. He has a great sense of humor, and his sensibility is perfect for the story. And Julie loved his work too.

"The follow up, *Joe and Sparky, Superstars!,* is about Sparky's search for his hidden talent. With lots of help from Joe, Sparky discovers that he has a rare gift for shadow puppetry.

"When not writing or editing, I can often be found playing with my two sons—marching in parades, walking planks, or singing badly in our band!"

Biographical and Critical Sources

PERIODICALS

Bulletin of the Center for Children's Books, April, 2009, Jeannette Hulick, review of *Joe and Sparky Get New Wheels,* p. 330.

Michalak's entertaining picture book **Joe and Sparky Get New Wheels** *features cartoon art by Frank Remkiewicz.* (Illustration copyright © 2009 by Frank Remkiewicz. Reproduced by permission of the publisher Candlewick Press, Inc., Cambridge, MA.)

Kirkus Reviews, December 15, 2008, review of *Fairy Goodnight Kisses;* February 1, 2009, review of *Joe and Sparky Get New Wheels.*

School Library Journal, April, 2009, Laura Scott, review of *Joe and Sparky Get New Wheels,* p. 112.

ONLINE

Jamie Michalak Home Page, http://www.jamiemichalak. com (June 1, 2010).

Jamie Michalak Web log, http://jamiemichalak.wordpress. com (June 1, 2010).

*　　*　　*

MITCHELL, Saundra 1974(?)-

Personal

Born c. 1974, in Indianapolis, IN; married; children: two. *Education:* Attended Vincennes University. *Hobbies and other interests:* Papermaking, ghost hunting, spending time with family.

Addresses

Home—Indianapolis, IN.

Career

Screenwriter, novelist, and producer. Dreaming Tree Films, Chicago, IL, writer until 2007; Fresh Films Emerging Screenwriters Program, head writer and executive producer of film series, beginning 2008. Formerly worked as a phone psychic, linguist, automobile salesperson, delivery driver, and layout waxer.

Awards, Honors

Pushcart Prize nomination, 2007 for short story "Ready to Wear"; ALAN Pick, and Cybils Award nomination, both 2009, and Society of Midland Authors Book Award for Children's Fiction, and Edgar Allan Poe Award nomination, Mystery Writers of America, both 2010, all for *Shadowed Summer;* screenplays honored at numerous national and international film festivals.

Writings

Shadowed Summer, Delacorte Press (New York, NY), 2009.

The Vespertime, Houghton Mifflin Harcourt (New York, NY), 2010.

Screenwriter for short films, including *Goodbye, Howard, Last Time We Met, No. 72, The Super Dupers, Book of Stories, On the Road,* and feature film *Revenge Ends,* 2008.

Contributor to periodicals, including *Common Ties, Edgar Literary Magazine, Parnassus, SmokeLong Quarterly, Summerset Review,* and *Vestal Review,* and in the anthology *Love and Sacrifice,* 2007.

Sidelights

A screenwriter and film producer based in Indiana, Saundra Mitchell made her novel debut with *Shadowed Summer.* Mitchell showed herself to be a versatile, experimental writer early on, and by high school she was spanning genres and producing everything from short stories and plays to comic books. She got her start in writing for film when her short story "Penance" was optioned for inclusion in a Canadian television series and Mitchell was hired to craft the screenplay. Since then, hundreds of films have been produced from her screenplays, and many have been screened before audiences at film festivals around the world. As head writer and producer for Fresh Films, she also teaches her craft to teenagers learning to create festival-quality short films.

Set in the small town of Ondine, Louisiana, *Shadowed Summer* spins a supernatural story surrounding the disappearance of seventeen-year-old Elijah Landry, who

Cover of Saundra Mitchell's young-adult mystery **Shadowed Summer,** *featuring artwork by Chad Michael Ward.* (Jacket illustration copyright © 2009 by Delacorte Press, a division of Random House, Inc. Used by permission of Delacorte Press, an imprint of Random House Children's Books, a division of Random House, Inc.)

had vanished from town decades before. This summer, fourteen year olds Iris Rhame and Collette plan to hone their amateur spellmaking skills and maybe even conjure up a spirit or two at the local cemetery. One night Iris spots Landry's ghost, and now she feels haunted by the dead boy. Researching the case, she is helped by Collette and Collette's tagalong boyfriend Ben Duvall. As Iris digs into the past, she begins to scratch the surface of secrets that others wish to keep hidden in a novel that *School Library Journal* contributor Caroline Tesauro recommended to "readers who like a supernatural twist to their coming-of-age stories." "Mitchell skillfully segues" between supernatural mystery and gothic romance, noted Connie Fletcher in *Booklist,* the critic praising *Shadowed Summer* as "highly atmospheric, with pulse-pounding suspense and an elegiac ending."

"I love writing films," Mitchell noted on her home page, discussing her varied career as a writer. "I love that filmmaking is so collaborative. But sometimes, it's nice to write something that's wholly yours. The characters say what you want to say, the way you want them to say it-the scene focuses on the vista you choose. I love working with actors and directors, but sometimes you want to keep all the toys to yourself!"

Biographical and Critical Sources

PERIODICALS

Booklist, February 15, 2009, Connie Fletcher, review of *Shadowed Summer,* p. 72.

Bulletin of the Center for Children's Books, February, 2009, Deborah Stevenson, review of *Shadowed Summer,* p. 249.

Kirkus Reviews, January 1, 2009, review of *Shadowed Summer.*

School Library Journal, April, 2009, Caroline Tesauro, review of *Shadowed Summer,* p. 140.

ONLINE

Saundra Mitchell Home Page, http://www.saundramitchell. com (May 31, 2010).*

*   *   *

MODESITT, Jeanne 1953-

Personal

Born August 2, 1953, in Long Beach, CA; daughter of George Edward (a physicist) and Lorraine Helen Modesitt; married Robin Thomas Spowart (a children's book illustrator), September 16, 1978. *Education:* University of California—Santa Cruz, B.A. (with honors), 1981; Oregon State University, M.A. (with honors), 1986. *Politics:* "Natural Law Party."

Jeanne Modesitt (Reproduced by permission.)

Addresses

Home—Kanab, UT.

Career

Writer. Volunteer at Best Friends Animal Sanctuary.

Member

Society of Children's Book Writers and Illustrators.

Writings

FOR CHILDREN; PICTURE BOOKS

Vegetable Soup, illustrated by Robin Spowart, Macmillan (New York, NY), 1988.

The Night Call, illustrated by Robin Spowart, Viking Kestrel (New York, NY), 1989.

The Story of Z, illustrated by Lonni Sue Johnson, Picture Book Studio (Saxonville, MA), 1990.

Sometimes I Feel like a Mouse: A Book about Feelings, illustrated by Robin Spowart, Scholastic (New York, NY), 1992.

(Compiler) *Songs of Chanukah,* illustrated by Robin Spowart, Little, Brown (Boston, MA), 1992.

Mama, If You Had a Wish, illustrated by Robin Spowart, Green Tiger Press (New York, NY), 1993.

Lunch with Milly, illustrated by Robin Spowart, Bridge-Water Books (Mahwah, NJ), 1995.

It's Hanukkah!, Holiday House (New York, NY), 1999.

Little Bunny's Easter Surprise, illustrated by Robin Spowart, Simon & Schuster (New York, NY), 1999.

One, Two, Three Valentine's Day: A Counting Book, illustrated by Robin Spowart, Boyds Mills Press (Honesdale, PA), 2002.

Little Bunny's Christmas Tree, illustrated by Robin Spowart, Simon & Schuster (New York, NY), 2002.

Mouse's Halloween Party, illustrated by Robin Spowart, Boyds Mills Press (Honesdale, PA), 2004.

Little Mouse's Happy Birthday, illustrated by Robin Spowart, Boyds Mills Press (Honesdale, PA), 2007.

Oh, What a Beautiful Day!: A Counting Book, illustrated by Robin Spowart, Boyds Mills Press (Honesdale, PA), 2009.

Contributor of short stories to children's periodicals, including *Spider* magazine.

Sidelights

Jeanne Modesitt is the author of more than a dozen picture books for young readers, including *Mama, If You Had a Wish* and *Oh, What a Beautiful Day!: A Counting Book.* Working primarily with her husband, illustrator Robin Spowart, Modesitt has earned recognition for her gentle, appealing narratives that often employ rhyming text. "I am married to one of my favorite children's book illustrators, Robin Spowart," she once playfully told *SATA.* "We like working together—maybe because we like each other (and each other's work) so much!"

The couple's first picture book, *Vegetable Soup,* which describes the successful efforts of two rabbits to make a meal with no carrots, earned the praise of a *Publishers Weekly* critic who called it "good company at anyone's table." *Night Call,* which tells how two stuffed animals help return a fallen star to the sky, was recommended by Carolyn Polese in *School Library Journal* as an "appealing bedtime story." In *The Story of Z* Modesitt describes the letter Z's attempts to form her own alphabet after becoming tired of always being last. This book received a good review from Ruth Semrau in *School Li-*

Modesitt's gentle story pairs with Robin Spowart's pastel-toned illustrations in the toddler-friendly **One, Two, Three Valentine's Day.** (Illustration copyright © 2002 by Robin Spowart. Reproduced by permission.)

brary Journal, who described the book as a story of "unparalleled zest" in which "every page zings with zip."

In Sometimes I Feel like a Mouse, different animals' facial expressions suggest a range of emotions, encouraging children to explore their own feelings. In Booklist Stephanie Zvirin recommended the work, calling it "a fine way to introduce difficult concepts to young children." Similarly, Modesitt's Mama, If You Had a Wish deals with children's feelings as a worried bunny is reassured by Mother bunny's words. A Publishers Weekly reviewer praised the book for achieving a "worthy purpose: promoting acceptance," and found its message "directly on target." A tale that complements Vegetable Soup, Lunch with Milly, tells the story of a child who invites an adult to lunch but forgets to make dessert. When Milly shows her hostess how they can get dessert together, the tale ends on a high note. In her School Library Journal review, Carolyn Noah punned that Modesitt's "readers will find Lunch with Milly to be a quietly satisfying snack."

A number of Modesitt's works involve humor because, as she told SATA, "I like writing funny stories most of all. That's because when I write them, I laugh, and I love to laugh. I also love to hear others laugh when they read my stories. Laughing is definitely one of my most favorite things in the world."

Among Modesitt and Spowart's holiday-themed books are It's Hanukkah!, One, Two, Three Valentine's Day: A Counting Book, and Little Bunny's Easter Surprise. The first picture book uses rhyming couplets to tell how a family of mice celebrates the holiday by lighting the menorah, eating latkes, and dancing Jewish dances. Little Bunny's Easter Surprise, which a Publishers Weekly reviewer called an "affectionate holiday tale," revolves around Little Bunny's efforts to amaze her parents by creating Easter baskets for each member of the family. Little Bunny's kindness is repaid by her younger brother, who prepares a surprise of his own. Carolyn Phelan, writing in Booklist, predicted that audiences will be pleased "to read a believable story in which children discover the rewards of giving pleasure to others." In a companion volume, Little Bunny's Christmas Tree, the protagonist joins her family in picking out the perfect tree to decorate. Linda Israelson, writing in School Library Journal, applauded Modesitt's "sweet, simple story," noting the potential of Little Bunny's Christmas Tree to become "a popular read-aloud or lap-sit choice."

One, Two, Three Valentine's Day, a work told in verse, follows a dapper mouse as it makes the rounds delivering holiday gifts to friends, including one little frog, three big badgers, and nine brown bunnies, until it arrives home to be greeted by its ten offspring. Modesitt's tale is a "charming celebration of a favorite holiday," stated Diane Foote in Booklist. The spookiest of holidays is the focus of Mouse's Halloween Party. When

Mouse reveals his plans for a big celebration, complete with costumes and cupcakes, friend Pig bursts into tears: she has decided to throw her own Halloween party and has invited the very same guests. Fortunately, Mouse devises a clever solution to the problem. According to Booklist contributor Ilene Cooper, Modesitt presents a dilemma "that children will easily relate to, and it will evoke empathy for both Pig and Mouse."

In Oh, What a Beautiful Day!, another verse narrative by Modesitt and Spowart, a young girl enjoys an imaginative outing during which she encounters increasing numbers of anthropomorphized creatures, from flipping ferrets to prancing pigs. "The rhymes will entice young ones to repeat the phrases," Booklist reviewer Julie Cummins maintained, and in School Library Journal Anne Beier called Oh, What a Beautiful Day! "a delightful addition to any counting-book collection."

Biographical and Critical Sources

PERIODICALS

Booklist, April 1, 1988, review of Vegetable Soup, p. 1352; November 1, 1989, review of The Night Call, p. 554; October 1, 1992, Stephanie Zvirin, review of Sometimes I Feel like a Mouse: A Book about Feelings, p. 337; February 1, 1999, Carolyn Phelan, review of

Modesitt and Spowart continue their creative collaboration in the upbeat counting book Oh, What a Beautiful Day. (Boyds Mills Press, 2009. Illustration © 2009 by Robin Spowart. Reproduced by permission.)

Little Bunny's Easter Surprise, p. 982; January 1, 2003, Diane Foote, review of *One, Two, Three Valentine's Day,* p. 908; September 15, 2003, GraceAnne A. DeCandido, review of *Little Bunny's Christmas Tree,* p. 247; August, 2004, Ilene Cooper, review of *Mouse's Halloween Party,* p. 1943; March 1, 2009, Julie Cummins, review of *Oh, What a Beautiful Day!: A Counting Book,* p. 53.

Horn Book, November-December, 1992, review of *Sometimes I Feel like a Mouse,* p. 712.

Kirkus Reviews, December 15, 1998, review of *Little Bunny's Easter Surprise,* p. 1801 November 15, 2002, review of *One, Two, Three Valentine's Day,* p. 1699; February 1, 2009, review of *Oh, What a Beautiful Day!*

Publishers Weekly, January 29, 1988, review of *Vegetable Soup,* 428; May 31, 1993, review of *Mama, If You Had a Wish,* p. 52; January 2, 1995, review of *Lunch with Milly,* p. 76; January 11, 1999, review of *Little Bunny's Easter Surprise,* p. 70; September 27, 1999, review of *It's Hanukkah!,* p. 52.

School Library Journal, January, 1990, Carolyn Polese, review of *The Night Call,* p. 86; January, 1991, Ruth Semrau, review of *The Story of Z,* p. 78; February, 1995, Carolyn Noah, review of *Lunch with Milly,* p. 229; October, 1999, review of *It's Hanukkah!,* p. 72; October, 2003, Linda Israelson, review of *Little Bunny's Christmas Tree,* p. 66; August, 2004, Linda Staskus, review of *Mouse's Halloween Party,* p. 90; May, 2007, Daisy Porter, review of *Little Mouse's Happy Birthday,* p. 104; June, 2009, Anne Beier, review of *Oh, What a Beautiful Day!,* p. 96.*

*   *   *

MOROZUMI, Atsuko 1955-

Personal

Born 1955, in Japan; immigrated to the United Kingdom; children: Vincent. *Education:* Royal College of Art, M.A.

Addresses

Home—Portsmouth, England.

Career

Writer and illustrator.

Awards, Honors

One Gorilla selected a *New York Times* Best Illustrated Children's Books of the Year, 1990.

Writings

SELF-ILLUSTRATED

And One Gorilla, Bodley Head (Oxford, England), 1990, published as *One Gorilla: A Counting Book,* Farrar, Straus (New York, NY), 1990.

Charlie's Picnic (lift-the-flap book), Random House of Canada (Toronto, Ontario, Canada), 1994, Mathew Price (Dallas, TX), 2010.

Charlie's Pets (lift-the-flap book), Random House of Canada (Toronto, Ontario, Canada), 1995, Mathew Price (Dallas, TX), 2010.

Charlie's Day (lift-the-flap book), Random House of Canada (Toronto, Ontario, Canada), 1995, Mathew Price (Dallas, TX), 2010.

The Lost Kitten (lift-the-flap book), Random House of Canada (Toronto, Ontario, Canada), 1995, Mathew Price (Dallas, TX), 2010.

My Friend Gorilla, Mathew Price (Sherborne, England), 1997, Farrar, Straus (New York, NY), 1998.

Mummy, Is That You?, Mathew Price (Sherborne, England), 2000, new edition published as *Mommy, Is That You?,* Mathew Price (Dallas, TX), 2008.

The Elves' First Christmas: The Untold Story of How the Elves First Met Santa, Mathew Price (Dallas, TX), 2010.

ILLUSTRATOR

Moe Price, *Why the Reindeer Were Chosen,* Pavilion Books (London, England), 1993, published as *The Reindeer Christmas,* Harcourt Brace (San Diego, CA), 1993.

Hans Christian Andersen, *The Wild Swans,* Hazar (London, England), 1997.

Mathew Price, *Join-in Stories for the Very Young,* Mathew Price (Sherborne, England), 1999.

Mathew Price, *Helping Daddy,* Knopf (New York, NY), 2000.

Mathew Price, *In the Park,* Knopf (New York, NY), 2000.

Mathew Price, *Playing,* Knopf (New York, NY), 2000.

Mathew Price, *Tell Me Another!: Read-aloud Stories for the Very Young,* Knopf (New York, NY), 2000.

Mathew Price, *Time for Bed,* Knopf (New York, NY), 2000.

Mathew Price, *Walt Disney's Dumbo,* Disney Press (New York, NY), 2000.

Mathew Price, *Let's Go Tommy,* Mathew Price (Sherborne, England), 2001.

Mathew Price, *Wake Up, Tommy,* Mathew Price (Sherborne, England), 2001.

Mathew Price, *Tommy and Baby Jo,* Mathew Price (Sherborne, England), 2001.

Mathew Price, *On the Farm,* Mathew Price (Sherborne, England), 2001.

Steve Augarde, *Rosie Goes to Playschool,* Mathew Price (Sherborne, England), 2003.

Mathew Price, *I Love Football,* Mathew Price (Sherborne, England), 2003.

Mathew Price, *Where Are You Going?,* Mathew Price (Sherborne, England), 2003.

Mathew Price, *Bedtime Stories for the Very Young,* Mathew Price (Sherborne, England), 2004.

Mathew Price, *In the Woods,* Mathew Price (Sherborne, England), 2005.

Mathew Price, *Our Pets,* Mathew Price (Sherborne, England), 2005.

Mathew Price, *Can I Play in the Mud?,* Mathew Price (Sherborne, England), 2005.

Mathew Price, *In the Jungle,* Mathew Price (Sherborne, England), 2005.

Mathew Price, *Animal Favourites,* Mathew Price (Sherborne, England), 2005.

Georgie Adams, *A House for Zebra and Other Stories,* Mathew Price (Sherborne, England), 2005.

Mathew Price, *Go Away Mr. Wolf!,* Mathew Price (Sherborne, England), 2007.

Mathew Price, *Our Pets,* Mathew Price (Sherborne, England), 2007.

Georgie Adams, *Animal Stories for Bedtime,* Mathew Price (Dallas, TX), 2009.

Mathew Price, *Can I Play Outside?,* Mathew Price (Dallas, TX), 2009.

Sidelights

British author and illustrator Atsuko Morozumi, a native of Japan, has created a number of well-received titles for children, including *One Gorilla: A Counting Book* and *The Elves' First Christmas: The Untold Story of How the Elves First Met Santa.* In *One Gorilla* readers follow the activities of a large primate and search for other animals among peaceful landscapes. In *School Library Journal* Lucinda Snyder Whitehurst offered a favorable assessment of the illustrations in *One Gorilla,* asserting that Morozumi's "illustrations, delicately drawn but vividly colored, have a misty quality to them

Cover of Atsuko Morozumi's colorful self-illustrated concept book **One Gorilla.** (Illustration copyright © 1990 by Atsuko Morozumi. Reproduced by permission of Sunburst Books, a division of Farrar, Straus & Giroux, LLC, and Mathew Price, Ltd.)

that adds to the air of fantasy" characterizing the story. The "pleasure never palls," lauded Susan Perren in a *Quill & Quire* review of the same book.

In *My Friend Gorilla,* a follow-up to *One Gorilla,* a gorilla stays with a human family during a spring and summer when the father, a zookeeper, brings it home after the local zoo shuts down. Eventually the zookeeper sends the gorilla back to its home in the jungle. Like Morozumi's debut, *My Friend Gorilla* elicited praise from reviewers. With its oversized watercolor illustrations, the book has "genuine child appeal," according to Beth Tegart, writing in *School Library Journal.* Although Tegart judged the plot to be somewhat "precious," she called the work as a whole a "delightful friendship" tale.

In her self-illustrated tale *Mommy Is That You?,* Morozumi follows the exploits of four ducklings who hatch from their eggs while in unfamiliar territory. "Morozumi's soft full-page illustrations perfectly match the soothing text," Donna Cardon maintained in *School Library Journal.* Morozumi tells the origin of Santa's helpers in *The Elves' First Christmas,* another self-illustrated work. Forced from their forest by woodcutters, the wee folk wander the globe seeking a new home. Drawn by a special light, the elves find themselves on a small farm that belongs to Santa Claus. He invites them to stay and helps them establish a village on the property; in return, the elves assist an exhausted Santa with preparations for the Christmas holiday. "The believable story reads like a traditional tale," a critic in *Kirkus Reviews* stated, and Eva Mitnick, writing in *School Library Journal,* commented that Morozumi's pictures "are warm and appealing."

Morozumi has also contributed the illustrations to several works by other authors. *Reindeer Christmas,* a story by Moe Price, tells the tale of how Santa Claus auditioned a variety of animals to pull his sleigh on Christmas Eve. In a review of the story for *Booklist,* Elizabeth Bush maintained that "Morozumi's large, delicately brushed paintings are filled with details that invite leisurely investigation," and "her interpretation, independent of the relatively spare text, develops the characters well." A *Publishers Weekly* critic highlighted the humor in Morozumi's art, asserting that "her scenes depicting the flying animals' mishaps portray just the right touch of humor without becoming slapstick."

As part of her work, Morozumi has enjoyed a successful relationship with children's author and publisher Mathew Price. In *Tell Me Another!: Read-aloud Stories for the Very Young,* Price offers gentle lessons in his playful tales. According to a *Publishers Weekly* reviewer, Morozumi's "paintings of appealing cuddly and downy creatures are consistently captivating," and *School Library Journal* critic Joy Fleishhacker similarly noted that the illustrations in *Tell Me Another!* "are colorful and appealing, showing fuzzy animals, interesting details, and bright backgrounds." *Animal Stories for*

Morozumi's illustration projects for other writers include creating artwork for Georgie Adams' **Animal Stories for Bedtime.** (Mathew Price, 2009. Illustration copyright © 2005 by Atsuko Morozumi. Reproduced by permission.)

Bedtime, a volume by Georgie Adams, contains a number of "seek-and-find" tales that encourage audience participation. "Large, uncluttered, brightly colored illustrations make the book visually appealing," Maryann H. Owen commented of Morozumi's contributions in *School Library Journal.*

Biographical and Critical Sources

PERIODICALS

Booklist, September 15, 1993, Elizabeth Bush, review of *The Reindeer Christmas,* pp. 159-160.

Kirkus Reviews, January 1, 1998, review of *My Friend Gorilla,* p. 60; April 1, 2009, review of *Animal Stories for Bedtime;* September 15, 2009, review of *The Elves' First Christmas: The Untold Story of How the Elves First Met Santa.*

Publishers Weekly, September 20, 1993, review of *The Reindeer Christmas,* p. 37; February 7, 2000, review of *Tell Me Another!: Read-Aloud Stories for the Very Young,* p. 84.

Quill & Quire, January, 1991, Susan Perren, review of *One Gorilla,* p. 23.

School Library Journal, January, 1991, Lucinda Snyder Whitehurst, review of *One Gorilla: A Counting Book,* p. 78; March, 1998, Beth Tegart, review of *My Friend Gorilla,* p. 185; August, 2000, Joy Fleishhacker, review of *Tell Me Another!,* p. 163; February, 2009, Donna Cardon, review of *Mommy Is That You?,* p. 80; May, 2009, Maryann H. Owen, review of *Animal Stories for Bedtime,* p. 69; October, 2009, Eva Mitnick, review of *The Elves' First Christmas,* p. 82.*

O-P

OS, Eric van
See VAN OS, Erik

*   *   *

OSTERWEIL, Adam 1972-

Personal
Born 1972, in Plainview, NY. *Education:* Cornell University, B.A. (classics); Stony Brook University, M.A. (liberal studies). *Hobbies and other interests:* Treasure hunting, video games, collecting comic books.

Addresses
Office—Springs School, 48 School St., East Hampton, NY 11937. *Agent*—Susan Schulman Literary Agency, 454 W. 44th St., New York, NY 10036; schulman@aol.com. *E-mail*—adam@adamosterweil.com.

Career
Educator and author. Springs Public School, East Hampton, NY, teacher of English.

Awards, Honors
Disney Adventures Book Award, and Best Children's Books of the Year designation, Bank Street College of Education, both 2002, both for *The Comic Book Kid.*

Writings

The Comic Book Kid, illustrated by Craig Smith, Front Street (Asheville, NC), 2001.
The Amulet of Komondor, illustrated by Peter Thorpe, Front Street (Asheville, NC), 2003.
The Lost Treasure of Talus Scree, illustrated by Peter Thorpe, Front Street (Asheville, NC), 2005.

The Baseball Card Kid (sequel to *The Comic Book Kid*), illustrated by Craig Smith, Front Street (Honesdale, PA), 2009.

Sidelights
Adam Osterweil, a middle-school English teacher in East Hampton, New York, is the author of a number of well-received adventure tales for preteens. In *The Comic Book Kid,* his debut title, Osterweil introduces Brian, a twelve-year-old comic-book collector who still regrets causing the accident that destroyed his father's prized possession: a copy of the very first issue of *Superman* that was worth more than 100,000 dollars. When Brian and his best friend, Paul, receive a new comic from the owner of their local store, they discover something strange: all of the panels in *TimeQuest* are blank. Then Paul accidentally activates a metal ring that spills from the comic's pages and the boys find themselves transported back in time to 75 million BC. Upon returning to their own era, Brian and Paul decide to travel to 1939—the year that the first *Superman* comic book was released—to purchase a new copy for Brian's dad. Their plan is complicated, however, by the ring's less-than-reliable technology. Osterweil's "lighthearted science-fiction story has plenty of quick action," remarked *School Library Journal* critic Elaine E. Knight, and in *Booklist* Ilene Cooper described *The Comic Book Kid* as "kid-appealingly gross."

The Baseball Card Kid, a sequel to *The Comic Book Kid,* continues the adventures of Brian and Paul. In this work, the boys hope to travel back in time so they can replace a rare and incredibly valuable baseball card that, legend has it, went down with the *Titanic.* After obtaining a newer and more powerful issue of the *TimeQuest* comic book, Brian and Paul journey to 1912 and inadvertently save the sinking ship, thus altering the course of history. To put things right, the boys must travel between the past and the future, battling vampires and mutant creatures during their treks along the space-time continuum. "The avalanche of zaniness nearly overwhelms the story," although Osterweil's

Adam Osterweil's boy-friendly chapter book The Baseball Card Kid *features illustrations by Craig Smith.* (Front Street, 2009. Illustration copyright © 2009 by Craig Smith. Reproduced by permission.)

"funny lines" pair well with Craig Smith's "manic illustrations," remarked *Booklist* critic Todd Morning. A contributor in *Kirkus Reviews* offered a more-positive assessment of the novel, stating that the author "laces his narrative with middle-grade-style yuks and injects frequent reviews of events into his breathlessly paced tale."

In *The Amulet of Komondor*, a fantasy-adventure tale, two middle-school students enter an exotic alternate world. Here Osterweil centers his story on Joe and Katie, who are huge fans of a popular trading-card game called DragonSteel. When the pair discovers a computer version of the game at a mysterious store, they are drawn into Komondor, a parallel universe, where they must locate the five pieces of a powerful dragon amulet before an evil emperor tracks them down first. According to a reviewer in *Publishers Weekly,* Osterweil "understands his topic, and he brings an appropriate level of energy to it." Saleena L. Davidson, writing in *School Library Journal,* commented of *The Amulet of Komondor* that the "fast-paced adventure is filled with action that is over the top and enjoyable."

The Lost Treasure of Talus Scree concerns Kiffin, a twelve year old who takes up against the forces of evil that enslave the adults on his world. With the help of Shelfy, his shape-shifting pet, and a set of magical rocks with almost limitless powers, Kiffin confronts the Overlord of Darkness and the Gremlin of Mischief. In *School Library Journal,* Steven Engelfried called *The Lost Treasure of Talus Scree* a "fast-paced, easy-to-follow adventure," adding that the novel may be suitable "for some reluctant readers, especially fans of graphic novels and video games."

"When I was little, I enjoyed reading comic books even before I could understand written words," Osterweil told *SATA.* "Old comic books were my springboard into reading, and even after I was a fluent reader I continued to enjoy them. One of my favorite comic authors is Carl Barks, who wrote and drew many famous adventure stories for Walt Disney involving Donald Duck and his extended family. I would guess that *The Comic Book Kid* and *The Baseball Card Kid* are influenced by Barks's sense of adventure, humor, and lighthearted tone."

Biographical and Critical Sources

PERIODICALS

Booklist, May 15, 2001, Ilene Cooper, review of *The Comic Book Kid,* p. 1753; November 15, 2003, Jennifer Mattson, review of *The Amulet of Komondor,* p. 610; March 15, 2009, Todd Morning, review of *The Baseball Card Kid,* p. 55.
Kirkus Reviews, September 15, 2003, review of *The Amulet of Komondor,* p. 1180; October 15, 2005, review of *The Lost Treasure of Talus Scree,* p. 1144; February 1, 2009, review of *The Baseball Card Kid.*
Publishers Weekly, October 27, 2003, review of *The Amulet of Komondor,* p. 69.
School Library Journal, August, 2001, Elaine E. Knight, review of *The Comic Book Kid,* p. 186; December, 2003, Saleena L. Davidson, review of *The Amulet of Komondor,* p. 158; January, 2006, Steven Engelfried, review of *The Lost Treasure of Talus Scree,* p. 141; June, 2009, Marilyn Taniguchi, review of *The Baseball Card Kid,* p. 134.

ONLINE

Adam Osterweil Home Page, http://www.adamosterweil. com (May 20, 2010).

*   *   *

POTTER, Katherine

Personal

Born in New York, NY; married; children: two daughters. *Education:* School of Visual Arts, B.F.A. (illustration).

Addresses

Home—Katonah, NY. *E-mail*—katherine@katherinepot ter.com.

Career

Illustrator and graphic designer. *Exhibitions:* Works included in Society of Illustrators Original Art exhibition, 1997.

Awards, Honors

Children's Choice designation, Children's Book Council, 1994, for *My Mother the Cat;* PEN West Children's Literature Award finalist, 1993, for *Spike.*

Writings

SELF-ILLUSTRATED

My Mother the Cat, Simon & Schuster Books for Young Readers (New York, NY), 1993.
Spike, Simon & Schuster Books for Young Readers (New York, NY), 1994.

ILLUSTRATOR

Montzalee Miller, *My Grandmother's Cookie Jar,* Price Stern Sloan (Los Angeles, CA), 1987.

Oscar Hammerstein II, *Rodgers and Hammerstein's In My Own Little Corner,* music by Richard Rodgers, Simon & Schuster Books for Young Readers (New York, NY), 1995.
Laurence Pringle, *Naming the Cat,* Walker & Co. (New York, NY), 1997.
Kathy Schulz, *Always Be Safe,* Children's Press (New York, NY), 2003.
Frances Park and Ginger Park, *The Have a Good Day Café,* Lee & Low Books (New York, NY), 2005.
Phillis Gershator, *Old House, New House,* Marshall Cavendish Children (Tarrytown, NY), 2009.

Contributor to periodicals.

Sidelights

Katherine Potter began illustrating children's books in the late 1980s, and she created her first original self-illustrated picture book, *My Mother the Cat,* in 1993. In addition to another original story, Potter has continued to work as an illustrator, and her images appear in books by authors such as Phillis Gershator, Frances and Ginger Park, and Laurence Pringle, where her colorful, nostalgic illustration style has drawn the praise of critics and readers alike.

In *Spike* Potter introduces readers to Jackson, a boy who is so quiet and well behaved that he is overlooked by everyone, even his own father. When Jackson scribbles a picture of a rambunctious child. Named Spike, the two-dimensional drawing magically comes to

Katherine Potter's nostalgic-themed illustrations capture the energy of Laurence Pringle's **Naming the Cat.** (Walker & Company, 1997. Illustration copyright © 1997 by Katherine Potter. Reproduced by permission.)

life and proceeds to create all manner of tumult in Jackson's placid life. Unseen but not unheard by the people around Jackson, Spike's smart-aleck comments cause adults to finally notice Jackson, albeit in a not-altogether-positive way. When Jackson erases Spike's mouth, the sketchy alter ego causes mischief with his arms, but when the boy contemplates erasing Spike altogether he realizes how much more fun life can be to those who are outspoken. Praising Potter's pastel-and-ink art, Mary M. Burns concluded in *Horn Book* that *Spike* reveals a "bold concept executed with finesse."

Potter teams up with Pringle, a writer well known for his nature-based nonfiction, to produce *Naming the Cat*. Based on Pringle's own pet-owning experiences, the story is one that many families can relate to: deciding upon just the right name for a new adopted kitten. When many suggestions have been considered and rejected, Dad suggests that the cat's own personality will eventually suggest the most appropriate name. After several near-tragedies are averted due to the curious kitten's quick reflexes, he earns the moniker Lucky. The "humorous sophistication" of Potter's art was noted by *Booklist* critic Kay Weisman, who predicted that *Naming the Cat* "will . . . be popular with cat lovers everywhere."

In her art for *The Have a Good Day Café,* a picture book by sisters Frances and Ginger Park, Potter brings to life the story of a boy's efforts to find a place for his Korean grandmother in the family food-cart business. Recommending the Parks' "intelligent, thoughtful tale" in her *School Library Journal* review, Elizabeth Bird also praised the "soft pastel illustrations" by Potter for "nicely complement[ing] this simple story," while a *Kirkus Reviews* writer noted that "delicate illustrations" enhance the "sensitive and inspiring portrait" of a close-knit immigrant family. *Old House, New House,* a book by Gershator, finds a little girl spending the summer at her family's cabin near a cranberry bog, where she enjoys being out of doors visiting the animals and making new friends. In the fall she must leave, but at the end of a long journey she finds herself at a new home full of new things to do. Potter's characteristic black-edged pastel drawings feature "elegiac images" of country living, and they combine with Gershator's text to produce "satisfying and simple . . . images," according to a *Kirkus Reviews* writer.

Biographical and Critical Sources

PERIODICALS

Booklist, September 1, 1993, Ilene Cooper, review of *My Mother the Cat,* p. 70; October 1, 1997, Kay Weisman, review of *Naming the Cat,* p. 338; September 1, 2005, Diane Foote, review of *The Have a Good Day Café,* p. 145.

Horn Book, July-August, 1994, Mary M. Burns, review of *Spike,* p. 443.

Potter captures the anxiety and excitement of a move to a new home in her artwork for Phillis Gershator's picture book Old House, New House. (Marshall Cavendish Children, 2009. Illustration copyright © 2009 by Katherine Potter. Reproduced by permission.)

Kirkus Reviews, September 1, 2005, review of *The Have a Good Day Café,* p. 980; February 1, 2009, review of *Old House, New House.*

Publishers Weekly, December 25, 1987, review of *My Grandmother's Cookie Jar,* p. 74; March 14, 1994, review of *Spike,* p. 72; June 16, 1997, review of *Naming the Cat,* p. 59; November 28, 2005, review of *The Have a Good Day Café,* p. 51.

School Library Journal, May, 1988, Karen K. Radtke, review of *My Grandmother's Cookie Jar,* p. 86; October, 1993, Jos. N. Holman, review of *My Mother the Cat,* p. 108; October, 1995, Kay McPherson, review of *Rodgers and Hammerstein's In My Own Little Corner,* p. 114; November, 1997, Caroline Ward, review of *Naming the Cat,* p. 97; August, 2005, Elizabeth Bird, review of *The Have a Good Day Café,* p. 104; March, 2009, Linda L. Walkins, review of *Old House, New House,* p. 112.

ONLINE

Katherine Potter Home Page, http://www.katherinepotter.com (May 31, 2010).

*   *   *

PROIMOS, James 1955-

Personal

Born 1955, in New York, NY; married; children: Annie. *Education:* Attended School of Visual Arts (New York, NY).

Addresses

Home—Baltimore, MD. *E-mail*—james@shinypear.com.

Career

Author illustrator, animator, director, and designer. Worked in advertising; copywriter and art director for twenty years in Denver, CO, New York, NY, Cleveland, OH, Los Angeles, CA, and Baltimore, MD; creator of promotional characters; *Generation O!* (animated television program), creator and designer, 2000-01; director of animated commercials. Patricia von Pleasantsquirrel Pictures (promotional agency), Los Angeles, CA, founder; Proimos Management (book packager), founder, 2007; Shiny Pear (creator of illustration, animation, and character designs), Baltimore, MD, co-founder with Carlson Bull, and director and producer.

Awards, Honors

Several advertising awards, including Clio awards, Addy awards, and One-Show awards; Cannes Lion award, for short film.

Writings

FOR CHILDREN; SELF-ILUSTRATED, EXCEPT AS NOTED

Joe's Wish, Harcourt Brace (San Diego, CA), 1998.
The Loudness of Sam, Harcourt Brace (San Diego, CA), 1999.
The Many Adventures of Johnny Mutton, Harcourt (San Diego, CA), 2001.
If I Were in Charge, the Rules Would Be Different (poetry), Scholastic (New York, NY), 2002.
Johnny Mutton, He's So Him!, Harcourt (San Diego, CA), 2003.
Cowboy Boy, Scholastic (New York, NY), 2003.
Mutton Soup: More Adventures of Johnny Mutton, Harcourt (Orlando, FL), 2004.
(With Tom Amico) *The Day the Dog Dressed like Dad,* Bloomsbury Children's Books (New York, NY), 2004.
(With Andy Rheingold) *When Guinea Pigs Fly!,* Scholastic (New York, NY), 2005.
(With Tom Amico) *Raisin and Grape,* illustrated by Andy Snair, Dial (New York, NY), 2006.
Patricia Von Pleasantsquirrel, Dial Books for Young Readers (New York, NY), 2009.
Paulie Pastrami Achieves World Peace, Little, Brown Books for Young Readers (New York, NY), 2009.
Todd's TV, Katherine Tegen Books (New York, NY), 2010.

Also author of scripts for film shorts and animated television series, many based on his books, including *Johnny Mutton,* TV Loonland; *Generation O!,* Kids' WB!; *The Switch-a-Roonies,* Scholastic Entertainment; *99 Sisters* and *Larry Parka, Polar Pig,* Nickelodeon; and *Boiled Peas and Carrot,* National Geographic Kids.

ILLUSTRATOR

Jacquelyn Reinach, *Little Raccoon, Here's Your Spoon!,* Random House (New York, NY), 2001.
Jacquelyn Reinach, *Little Owl, Here's Your Towel!,* Random House (New York, NY), 2001.
Jacquelyn Reinach, *Little Kangaroo, I Love You!,* Random House (New York, NY), 2001.
Jacquelyn Reinach, *Little Sheep, Time to Sleep!,* Random House (New York, NY), 2001.

Adaptations

The "Johnny Mutton" books and *The Loudness of Sam* were both adapted as animated television series.

Sidelights

Beginning his career as an advertising copywriter and art director, James Proimos discovered that his particular talent—creating amusingly drawn, boldly colored animated cartoon characters—is also a perfect match with the picture-book medium. Among the books he has written and illustrated for young children—including *The Loudness of Sam, Raisin and Grape,* and *The Many Adventures of Johnny Mutton*—are several char-

Cover of James Proimos's quirky cartoon story **Johnny Mutton, He's So Him!.** (Copyright © 2003. Reproduced by permission of Houghton Mifflin Harcourt Publishing Company. This material may not be reproduced in any form or by any means without the prior written permission of the publisher.)

acters that have made a similar leap between printed page and film, such as the woolly lamp Johnny Mutton. In addition to writing books, Proimos continues his dedicated efforts to populate the animated world via television cartoon programs such as *Generation O!*, *Larry Parka, Polar Pig,* and *The Switch-a-Roonies.*

Proimos began focusing on animated cartoons in the late 1990s, when he and a colleague worked together on an advertising campaign for the Taco Bell fast-food restaurant chain. The collaboration resulted in Nacho and Dog, an animated cat-and-dog duo that appeared in Taco Bell advertising for several years. From there, Proimos began devising more animated characters, among them a young rock singer named Molly O!, the star of *Generation O!,* on Kids' WB! beginning in 2000. A long list of other animated characters has followed from Proimos's fertile imagination and have found their way into books, television programming, and even commercials.

When *Generation O!* aired in 2000, Proimos was already a published author with two books to his credit: *Joe's Wish* and *The Loudness of Sam.* The first tells a quirky story about a grandfather and grandson who wish they could change places with one another, while *The Loudness of Sam* introduces an overindulged young boy who has never been taught that children should be seen and not heard. Praised as "refreshing" and "rambunctious" by a *Publishers Weekly* writer, the book features cartoon-style art with text balloons and high-energy colors.

Johnny Mutton, one of Proimos's most popular picture-book characters, makes his debut in *The Many Adventures of Johnny Mutton.* Johnny is a woolly lamb who is taken in by a motherly but rather nearsighted woman and raised like the woman's own son. Living among humans, the good-natured sheep fits right in, except for his unusual sense of humor. Describing Proimos's poofy protagonist as "both a loving son and an extroverted classroom cutup," a *Publishers Weekly* reviewer enjoyed the author's use of the comic-book format in recounting four amusing sagas in Mutton's life. In *Booklist,* Ilene Cooper also enjoyed the book, praising the "wild, rowdy art" and the "high ratio of laughs to pages." Johnny reappears in *Johnny Mutton, He's So Him!* and *Mutton Soup: More Adventures of Johnny Mutton,* each of which contains five stories. In *School Library Journal,* Nancy A. Gifford praised the "slapstick humor and amusing art" in *Johnny Mutton, He's So Him!,* while Carol Schene noted in the same periodical that *Mutton Soup* features stories that are "upbeat and nonchalantly wise." Noting that Proimos's "jokey premise . . . serves as a kind of eccentric metaphor for embracing individuality," Jennifer Mattson added in a *Booklist* review that *Mutton Soup* showcases Johnny's "irrepressible spirit" through its "zippy dialogue" and bright, cartoon drawings.

In *Patricia von Pleasantsquirrel* Proimos focuses on a young girl who decides to leave home and find a land in need of a princess. This way, she will be able to do

Proimos and colleague Tom Amico tell the story of an overreaching pet in the humorous **The Day the Dog Dressed like Dad.** (Bloomsbury Children's Books, 2004. Illustration copyright © 2004 by James Proimos. Reproduced by permission.)

all the things that are prohibited at home, such as eating dessert before dinner and living in luxurious surroundings that are protected by a moat. When she finds a land inhabited by hippos, Patricia rules happily until she tires of the hundreds of chores that come with the title of princess. Giving nods to picture-book greats such as Maurice Sendak, Shel Silverstein, and James Marshall, Proimos creates what *Horn Book* contributor Jennifer M. Brabander described as an "eccentric" story accompanied by "well-lined art." A *Publishers Weekly* contributor agreed, praised the "bold-lined" art in *Patricia von Pleasantsquirrel,* as well as "Patricia's postmodern sassiness," while a *Kirkus Reviews* writer predicted that Proimos's "tongue-in-cheek mini-epic will have [readers of all ages] . . . snickering."

A story mixing Proimos's "spare, droll text" with his humorous cartoon art, *Paulie Pastrami Achieves World Peace* finds a young boy learning to treat other as he likes to be treated, even when the "others" are non-human beings such as trees. His caring spreads ever further, and in an effort to inspire world peace, he delivers cupcakes to hometown businesses such as Furniture World and Toy World. Paulie finds the cupcakes equally effective on the playground, where he wins over a school bully in Proimos's upbeat tale. While a *Publishers Weekly* critic noted that *Paulie Pastrami Achieves World Peace* features a "blend of irony and parody" more likely to appeal to adults, a *Kirkus Re-*

Proimos takes on the role of both author and illustrator in his amusing save-the-planet story **Paulie Pastrami Achieves World Peace.** (Copyright © 2009 by James Proimos. Reproduced by permission of Little, Brown & Company. All rights reserved.)

views writer praised the book's titular hero as "a plucky . . . kid armed with a boatload of determination and a whole lot of heart."

While Proimos writes and illustrates most of his books, he sometimes works with collaborators. Fellow advertising copywriter Tom Amico contributed his creative talents to both *The Day the Dog Dressed like Dad* and *Raisin and Grape,* while animator Andy Snair contributed the artwork to the latter volume. *When Guinea Pigs Fly,* a story of a pair of guinea pigs that find themselves in a series of trying circumstances after being purchased by an irresponsible pet lover, was the result of a collaboration between Proimos and Andy Rheingold. *Raisin and Grape* is the story of a story-telling grandfather (a shriveled raisin) and grandson (a plump raisin) who spend the day together, while *The Day the Dog Dressed like Dad* finds the family pet donning hat and tie and taking care of father-type business after the human patriarch leaves home on a business trip. Dubbing *Raisin and Grape* "loving without being mushy," Hazel Rochman added in *Booklist* that the book "will be fun for sharing across generations."

For Proimos, seeing characters like Johnny Mutton and the little boy from *The Loudness of Sam* in print has been only the first step; from books, these quirky creations have gone on to win even more fans in animated form. The author/illustrator/animator "likes to start out in books because they have faster turnaround times," as Nancy Lees noted in *Kidscreen,* "and the publishing industry tends to give authors more creative control over the development of characters and stories." As Proimos explained to Lees, "Every other medium I've worked

in—even though the audience is the same—has a totally different set of rules of operation. With books, it's easier to just sort of do what I do."

Biographical and Critical Sources

PERIODICALS

Booklist, July, 1999, Ilene Cooper, review of *The Loudness of Sam,* p. 1953; June 1, 2001, Ilene Cooper, review of *The Many Adventures of Johnny Mutton,* p. 1872; May 15, 2002, Susan Dove Lempke, review of *If I Were in Charge the Rules Would Be Different,* p. 1596; September 1, 2003, Francisca Goldsmith, review of *Cowboy Boy,* p. 121; March 1, 2004, Jennifer Mattson, review of *Mutton Soup: More Adventures of Johnny Mutton,* p. 1198; May 1, 2006, Hazel Rochman, review of *Raisin and Grape,* p. 87; December 1, 2009, Shelle Rosenfeld, review of *Paulie Patrami Achieves World Peace,* p. 52.

Horn Book, September, 2001, review of *The Many Adventures of Johnny Mutton;* May-June, 2003, Peter D. Sieruta, review of *Johnny Mutton, He's So Him!,* p. 356; March-April, 2009, Jennifer M. Brabander, review of *Patricia von Pleasantsquirrel,* p. 185.

Kidscreen, January 1, 2005, Nancy Lees, "Hot Talent: Mixing It up at Creative Co-op Patricia von Pleasantsquirrel," p. 16.

Proimos teams up with Amico and artist Andy Snair to create the collaborative multigenerational story **Raisin and Grape.** (Illustration copyright © 2006 by Andy Snair. Reproduced by permission of Dial Books for Young Readers, a division of Penguin Putnam Books for Young Readers.)

Kirkus Reviews, January 1, 2002, review of *If I Were in Charge the Rules Would Be Different,* p. 49; March 1, 2003, review of *Johnny Mutton, He's So Him!,* p. 396; June 15, 2003, review of *Cowboy Boy,* p. 863; February 15, 2004, review of *Mutton Soup,* p. 184; August 15, 2004, review of *The Day the Dog Dressed like Dad,* p. 801; February 1, 2009, review of *Patricia von Pleasantsquirrel;* November 1, 2009, review of *Paulie Pastrami Achieves World Peace.*

Publishers Weekly, July 13, 1998, review of *Joe's Wish,* p. 77; March 1, 1999, review of *The Loudness of Sam,* p. 68; April 30, 2001, review of *The Many Adventures of Johnny Mutton,* p. 178; July 7, 2003, review of *Cowboy Boy,* p. 72; October 11, 2004, review of *The Day the Dog Dressed like Dad,* p. 79; November 30, 2009, review of *Paulie Pastrami Achieves World Peace,* p. 45.

School Library Journal, May, 2001, Maura Bresnahan, review of *The Many Adventures of Johnny Mutton,* p. 131; March, 2002, Lee Bock, review of *If I Were in Charge the Rules Would Be Different,* p. 219; August, 2003, Nancy A. Gifford, review of *Johnny Mutton, He's So Him!,* p. 140; November, 2003, John Sigwald, review of *Cowboy Boy,* p. 144; April, 2004, Carol Schene, review of *Mutton Soup,* p. 120; November, 2005, Karen T. Bilton, review of *When Guinea Pigs Fly!,* p. 104; March, 2006, Maryann H. Owen, review of *Raisin and Grape,* p. 174; November, 2005, Karen T. Bilton, review of *When Guinea Pigs Fly!,* p. 104; February, 2009, Lisa Egly Lehmuller, review of *Patricia von Pleasantsquirrel,* p. 84.

ONLINE

Chaos Kids Web site, http://chaoskids.com/ (June 10, 1010), "James Proimos."*

R

REMKIEWICZ, Frank 1939-

Personal
Born April 14, 1939, in Rockville, CT; son of Frank (a tool designer) and Clara Remkiewicz; married Sylvia Nissley (an art consultant); children: Sarah, Jessica, Madeleine. *Education:* Art Center College of Design, B.P.A. (with honors), 1965.

Addresses
Home—Sarasota, FL. *Agent*—Kendra Marcus, Book-Stop Literary Agency, 67 Meadow View Rd., Orinda, CA 94563; kendra@bookstopliterary.com. *E-mail*—info@remki.com.

Career
Illustrator and writer. Norcross Greeting Cards, New York, NY, staff illustrator, 1968-73; freelance author and illustrator, 1973—.

Awards, Honors
New York Times Ten Best of the Season citation, 1991, for *The Last Time I Saw Harris;* Children's Book of the Year designation, Bank Street College of education, 1992, for *I Hate Camping* by P.J. Peterson; Children's Choice Award, National Council for Reading, 1992; Oppenheim Toy Portfolio Gold Seal Award, 2009, for *Down by the Station* by Jennifer Riggs Vetter.

Writings

SELF-ILLUSTRATED

The Last Time I Saw Harris, Lothrop (Boston, MA), 1991.
Greedyanna, Lothrop (Boston, MA), 1992.
Final Exit for Cats: A Feline Suicide Guide, HarperCollins (New York, NY), 1992.
There's Only One Harris, Lothrop (Boston, MA), 1993.
The Bone Stranger, Lothrop (Boston, MA), 1994.
Fiona Wraps It Up, Lothrop (Boston, MA), 1995.
The Twelve Days of Christmas in Florida, Sterling (New York, NY), 2008.
Gus Gets Scared, Scholastic (New York, NY), 2010.
Gus Makes a Friend, Scholastic (New York, NY), 2010.

ILLUSTRATOR

Jean Fisher, editor, *Manuscript Writing,* Western Publishing, 1984.
Sarah Leslie, *The Saggy Baggy Elephant and the New Dance,* Golden Books (New York, NY), 1985.
Lada J. Kratky, *En chivo en la huerta,* Hampton-Brown (Carmel, CA), 1988.
Jean Langerman, *No Carrots for Harry!,* Parents Magazine Press (New York, NY), 1989.
Alma Flor Ada, *Una semilla nada mas,* Hampton-Brown (Carmel, CA), 1990.
Ellen Jackson, *Ants Can't Dance,* Macmillan (New York, NY), 1991.
P.J. Petersen, *I Hate Camping,* Dutton (New York, NY), 1991.
Patricia R. Giff, *I Love Saturday,* Puffin Books (New York, NY), 1991.
Nancy Lamb, *The Great Mosquito, Bull, and Coffin Caper,* Lothrop (Boston, MA), 1992.
Betsy Byars, *The Joy Boys,* Yearling (New York, NY), 1996.
Jonathan London, *Little Red Monkey,* Dutton (New York, NY), 1997.
Bill Maynard, *Incredible Ned,* Putnam (New York, NY), 1997.
Stuart J. Murphy, *Just Enough Carrots,* HarperCollins (New York, NY), 1997.
Mary Quattlebaum, *The Magic Squad and the Dog of Great Potential,* Delacorte (New York, NY), 1997.
Taylor Jordan, *Hiccup,* Golden Books (New York, NY), 1998.
Bill Maynard, *Quiet, Wyatt!,* Putnam (New York, NY), 1999.

Stuart J. Murphy, *Rabbit's Pajama Party,* HarperCollins (New York, NY), 1999.

David Martin, *Piggy and Dad,* Candlewick (Cambridge, MA), 2001.

Stuart J. Murphy, *Seaweed Soup,* HarperCollins (New York, NY), 2001.

J. Patrick Lewis, *Arithme-tickle: An Even Number of Odd Riddle-Rhymes,* Harcourt (San Diego, CA), 2002.

David Martin, *Piggy and Dad Play,* Candlewick (Cambridge, MA), 2002.

Stuart J. Murphy, *Less than Zero,* HarperCollins (New York, NY), 2003.

J. Patrick Lewis, *Scien-trickery: Riddles in Science,* Silver Whistle (San Diego, CA), 2004.

David Martin, *Piggy and Dad Go Fishing,* Candlewick Press (Cambridge, MA), 2005.

Jennifer Riggs Vetter, *Down by the Station,* Tricycle Press (Berkeley, CA), 2009.

Jamie Michalak, *Joe and Sparky Get New Wheels,* Candlewick Press (Somerville, MA), 2009.

Jamie Michalak, *Joe and Sparky, Superstars!,* Candlewick Press (Somerville, MA), 2010.

Illustrator of single-panel cartoons for various northern California newspapers.

Author's works have been translated into French, Japanese, Chinese, Korean, and Spanish.

ILLUSTRATOR; "HORRIBLE HARRY" SERIES BY SUZY KLINE

Horrible Harry in Room 2-B, Viking (New York, NY), 1988.

Horrible Harry and the Green Slime, Viking (New York, NY), 1989.

Horrible Harry and the Ant Invasion, Viking (New York, NY), 1989.

Horrible Harry's Secret, Viking (New York, NY), 1990.

Horrible Harry and the Christmas Surprise, Viking (New York, NY), 1991.

Horrible Harry and the Kickball Wedding, Viking (New York, NY), 1992.

Horrible Harry and the Dungeon, Viking (New York, NY), 1996.

Horrible Harry and the Purple People, Viking (New York, NY), 1997.

Horrible Harry and the Drop of Doom, Viking (New York, NY), 1998.

Horrible Harry Moves up to Third Grade, Viking (New York, NY), 1998.

Horrible Harry Goes to the Moon, Viking (New York, NY), 2000.

Horrible Harry at Halloween, Viking (New York, NY), 2000.

Horrible Harry Goes to Sea, Viking (New York, NY), 2001.

Horrible Harry and the Dragon War, Viking (New York, NY), 2002.

Horrible Harry and the Mud Gremlins, Viking (New York, NY), 2003.

Horrible Harry and the Holidaze, Viking (New York, NY), 2003

Horrible Harry and the Locked Closet, Viking (New York, NY), 2004.

Horrible Harry and the Goog, Viking (New York, NY), 2005.

Horrible Harry and the Triple Revenge, Viking (New York, NY), 2006.

Horrible Harry Cracks the Code, Viking (New York, NY), 2007.

Horrible Harry Bugs the Three Bears, Viking (New York, NY), 2008.

ILLUSTRATOR; "SONG LEE" SERIES BY SUZY KLINE

Song Lee in Room 2-B, Viking (New York, NY), 1993.

Song Lee and the Hamster Hunt, Viking (New York, NY), 1994.

Song Lee and the Leech Man, Viking (New York, NY), 1995.

Song Lee and the "I Hate You" Notes, Viking (New York, NY), 1999.

ILLUSTRATOR; "FROGGY" SERIES BY JONATHAN LONDON

Froggy Gets Dressed, Viking (New York, NY), 1992.

Let's Go Froggy, Viking (New York, NY), 1994.

Froggy Learns to Swim, Viking (New York, NY), 1995.

Froggy Goes to School, Viking (New York, NY), 1996.

Froggy's First Kiss, Viking (New York, NY), 1998.

Froggy Plays Soccer, Viking (New York, NY), 1999.

Froggy's Halloween, Viking (New York, NY), 1999.

Froggy Bakes a Cake, Viking (New York, NY), 2000.

Froggy Goes to Bed, Viking (New York, NY), 2000.

Froggy's Best Christmas, Viking (New York, NY), 2000.

Froggy Eats Out, Viking (New York, NY), 2001.

Froggy Takes a Bath, Viking (New York, NY), 2001.

Froggy Plays in the Band, Viking (New York, NY), 2002.

Froggy Goes to the Doctor, Viking (New York, NY), 2002.

Froggy's Baby Sister, Viking (New York, NY), 2003.

Froggy's Day with Dad, Viking (New York, NY), 2004.

Froggy's Sleepover, Viking (New York, NY), 2005.

Froggy Rides a Bike, Viking (New York, NY), 2006.

Froggy Plays T-ball, Viking (New York, NY), 2007.

Froggy Goes to Camp, Viking (New York, NY), 2008.

Froggy's Best Babysitter, Viking (New York, NY), 2009.

Froggy Goes to Hawai'i, Viking (New York, NY), 2010.

Adaptations

Several of the "Horrible Harry" and "Froggy" books have been adapted as sound recordings.

Sidelights

A former graphic artist, Frank Remkiewicz has provided the illustrations for more than seventy children's books, including works by such celebrated authors as Alma Flor Ada and Betsy Byars. He is perhaps best known as the illustrator for the popular "Horrible Harry" and "Song Lee" series, written by Suzy Kline, and the "Froggy" series, written by Jonathan London. Additionally, Remkiewicz's self-illustrated works, such as *The*

Bone Stranger and *Fiona Wraps It Up,* have met with a positive critical reception, his drawings described by a *Publishers Weekly* critic as "bold swatches of color crisply outlined."

Horrible Harry in Room 2-B, Remkiewicz's first collaboration with Kline, appeared in 1988 and introduces a mischievous grade-schooler named Harry. Narrated by Harry's friend Doug, the "Horrible Harry" series tells how Harry plays pranks and gets into trouble. As the series progresses, Harry develops a crush on classmate Song Lee—who has books in her own series—finds an arch-enemy in classmate Sidney, and progresses on with his classmates into the third grade. Whether facing a terrifying amusement park ride called the "Drop of Doom," solving mysteries of missing costume pieces at Halloween, or surviving being covered by leeches, Harry, Doug, Song Lee, and Sidney are always depicted in humorous cartoon illustrations. April Judge, reviewing *Song Lee and the Leech Man* for *Booklist,* commented that "Remkiewicz's cartoonlike black-ink sketches are well suited to the comic story" by Kline.

A contributor to *Kirkus Reviews* commented on the combination of "lively text and humorous drawings" in a review of Kline's entertaining *Horrible Harry Goes to Sea,* while Carolyn Phelan, reviewing the same title for *Booklist,* added that "Remkiewicz's cheerful ink drawings heighten the appeal." Another *Kirkus Reviews* critic, appraising *Horrible Harry and the Dragon War,* maintained that "Remkiewicz's signature illustrations add life" to the story. In *Horrible Harry Takes the Cake* the protagonist engages in a bit of chicanery while trying to get to the bottom of a mystery surrounding his teacher's new fiancée. Diane Eddington, writing in *School Library Journal,* observed of this book that Remkiewicz's "illustrations are clear and focused, and complement the story line and characters."

In 1992 Remkiewicz teamed up with London for *Froggy Gets Dressed,* the work that introduces readers to the misadventures of Froggy and his friends. Froggy seems to mess up all the time, but everything manages to turn out all right. When Froggy tries to play soccer in *Froggy Plays Soccer,* for instance, he gets knocked over by flying balls, misses important plays, and catches the ball with his hands. Even so, he manages to redeem himself by scoring a winning goal. In *Booklist,* Kay Weisman commented that "Remkiewicz's brightly colored artwork enhances London's humorous text."

Frank Remkiewicz's amusing "Froggy" character stars in several stories authored by Jonathan London, among them **Froggy** *Learns to Swim.* (Reproduced by permission of the author.)

In *Froggy Goes to Bed,* Froggy stalls as long as he can to stay awake just a little bit longer. He has managed to hide all the things he needs for bed—his pajamas, toothbrush, etc.—throughout the house, and can only go to sleep after a thorough search. Elizabeth O'Brien noted in *School Library Journal* that the "bold, funny cartoons vary" from small illustrations to full spreads, and Carolyn Phelan commented in her *Booklist* review that Remkiewicz's illustrations are "notable for their buoyancy of line and vibrancy of colors." In *Froggy Eats Out* Froggy goes to a nice restaurant with his parents only to make a mess of everything, even in front of his crush Frogilina. After the disaster at the restaurant, Froggy's parents try to make everything better by taking him out to the local "fast flies place." Gillian Engberg praised how the "bright, cartoonlike drawings" in *Froggy Eats Out* express Froggy's "irrepressible energy."

In *Froggy Plays in the Band* Froggy and all his friends—including Frogilina—join the marching band. This time it is Frogilina who causes catastrophe: when she misses a baton toss, it hits Froggy in the head and knocks him out right in front of the judges. A contributor to *Kirkus Reviews,* while noting that the book's plot seems somewhat forced, wrote that "Remkiewicz's illustrations keep the atmosphere as endearing as possible." Wanda Meyers-Hines predicted in *School Library Journal* that Froggy fans will be delighted by *Froggy Plays in the Band* and praised the book for its "vividly colorful and animated signature illustrations." In *Froggy Goes to the Doctor* Froggy is excited to have a day off from school, but loses his enthusiasm when he realizes seeing the doctor might mean getting a shot. A *Kirkus Reviews* contributor commented that London's story here is "energized by Remkiewicz's bustling watercolors."

In *Froggy's Day with Dad,* the energetic young amphibian heads to the park with his father, although a series of mishaps nearly ruins their special day. Remkiewicz's "simple, energetic illustrations match the pleasantly ordinary and sentimental tenor" of London's narrative, Holly T. Sneeringer remarked in *School Library Journal.* After a round of ghost stories, Froggy and friend Max find it difficult to stay in bed in *Froggy's Sleepover.* According to a *Kirkus Reviews* contributor, Remkiewicz's artwork for the book provides audiences with "a taste of both nighttime's spookiness and the beautiful sanctuary of home." In *Froggy Plays T-ball* the cheerful protagonist refuses to allow his misunderstanding of the game's rules to diminish his enthusiasm for the sport. "Remkiewicz's illustrations are easily recognizable, but vibrantly colored here with oranges and greens," Susan E. Murray reported in *School Library Journal.* In *Froggy Goes to Camp* the youngster's actions create chaos for school principal Mr. Mugwort, who also serves as the director of Camp Run-a-Muck. Writing in *School Library Journal,* Donna Cardon noted that "Remkiewcz's watercolor illustrations are humorous and action packed."

Horrible Harry Goes to Sea *is one of many humorous easy-reader collaborations between Remkiewicz and popular author Suzy Kline.* (Copyright © 2001 by Frank Remkiewicz. Reproduced by permission of Puffin Books, a division of Penguin Putnam Books for Young Readers.)

Remkiewicz teams up with Bill Maynard for two titles: *Incredible Ned* and *Quiet, Wyatt!* In the first story, Ned is a boy whose words manage to spring directly to life from his mouth. If he says "giraffe" in class, for instance, a real giraffe springs to life in front of his classroom. It is only through the help of an art teacher who teaches Ned to express himself through painting that Ned manages to free himself from his peculiar difficulties. Maynard and Remkiewicz's second book together, *Quiet, Wyatt!,* expresses Wyatt's frustration that everyone is always telling him to be quiet, whether they are older kids who do not have time to play with him, or adults who insist that he is too young to do the things he wants. Wyatt at first rebels, then becomes stubbornly quiet, but speaks in order to save a puppy whose life is in danger. A *Publishers Weekly* contributor commented on Remkiewicz's "cartoonishly cute characters" for *Quiet, Wyatt!,* and Hazel Rochman noted in *Booklist* that the "child-centered pictures show . . . the kid's view of what's important."

Remkiewicz has also joined forces with author David Martin for the read-aloud *Piggy and Dad Go Fishing.* In that tale, a youngster finds its difficult to bait his hook after a wiggling worm offers him a winning smile and later decides to treat his first catch with compassion. "Remkiewicz's summery watercolor-and-pencil cartoon illustrations clue listeners in to Piggy's emotions," Kitty Flynn stated in *Horn Book.* In *Down by the Station,* Jennifer Riggs Vetter offers an expanded version of the familiar childhood song about modes of transportation, presenting verses about sailboats, race cars, and rockets. "Remkiewicz uses candy-bright colors and a hint of goofy elasticity" in his illustrations for

In **Incredible Ned** *Remkiewicz contributes illustrations that give Bill Maynard's story a humorous spin.* (Illustration copyright © 1997 by Frank Remkiewicz. Reproduced by permission of Puffin Books, a division of Penguin Putnam Books for Young Readers.)

Vetter's text, according to *School Library Journal* reviewer Marge Loch-Wouters. An energetic giraffe mistakenly believes he has won a fancy sports car and convinces his pal, a quiet turtle, to take a spin around town in Jamie Michalak's *Joe and Sparky Get New Wheels.* "Remkiewicz's lively watercolor and Prismacolor pencil illustrations extend the action and jokes" in the amusing collaboration, remarked Laura Scott in *School Library Journal.*

Remkiewicz also has a number of educational titles to his credit, including Stuart J. Murphy's *Seaweed Soup.* In this work, Murphy introduces youngsters to the concepts of sets through the story of Turtle's well-attended lunch party. Remkiewicz's "bright watercolor cartoons . . . lend a deft and humorous touch to the proceedings," commented *School Library Journal* reviewer Judith Constantinides. In *Arithme-tickle: An Even Number of Odd Riddle-Rhymes,* a collection of math puzzles in verse by J. Patrick Lewis, the "bright, energetic watercolor-and-pencil illustrations amplify the humor in each challenge," Kathleen Whalin noted in *School Li-*

brary Journal. In Lewis's companion volume, *Scientrickery: Riddles in Science,* "Remkiewicz adds energetic art with zippy colors and accessible wit," according to *Booklist* critic Phelan.

Remkiewicz has also published several titles which he both writes and illustrates. *The Last Time I Saw Harris* tells the story of Edmund and his best friend, Harris the parrot. Harris can perform a number of unusual tricks, including identifying colors. When Edmund is about to teach Harris the color purple, a strong wind blows the parrot away, and Edmund and a chauffeur must set out to find him. According to *Booklist* contributor Ilene Cooper, "most of the humor com[es] . . . from the brightly colored, cartoon-style illustrations," while Martha V. Parravano concluded in *Horn Book* that in *The Last Time I Saw Harris* the "flat, spacious pictures . . . match the droll, understated—though utterly absurd—tale," resulting in "a delightful concoction." In *There's Only One Harris,* a companion volume, Edmund and his pet parrot put their fishing and violin-playing abilities skills to good use while hiking near a dangerous

waterfall. According to a *Publishers Weekly* contributor, Remkiewicz's "placid pictures and pacing combine for a deliberately low-velocity, deadpan wackiness."

Another original picture book, *Greedyanna* offers a plot that relies on a common situation taken to the extreme for comic effect. *Greedyanna* is about a demanding girl named Anna whose parents indulge her wishes because they believe that her behavior is only a passing phase. As recounted by her brother, Eddie, Anna eventually has her parents sleeping on the ground and eating lima beans during a family camping trip because she wants the tent to herself and she hates lima beans. Virginia E. Jeschelnig remarked in *School Library Journal* that "the watercolor cartoons nicely convey the humor of Eddie's predicament and carry the story for pre-readers. Anna's antics will surely amuse, and may even encourage an errant child to share."

In *The Bone Stranger* Remkiewicz creates a canine version of the Old West Lone Ranger hero. Boney, who runs a delicatessen, and his friend and employee Wolfgang, a recent immigrant to the Old West, may be regular citizens by day, but by night, Boney and Wolfgang fight the crime of thieving bands such as the Raccoon Brothers. Boney wears a mask, inviting the townsfolk rescued from the notorious raccoons to question the work of a masked dog. Nancy Vasilakis, writing in *Horn Book*, called *The Bone Stranger* "an absurdly funny takeoff on the Lone Ranger legend."

Remkiewicz's *Fiona Wraps It Up* features Fiona, a pink flamingo who speaks in rhyme. Fiona is about to lay an egg when she and her flock leave for their nesting grounds. However, when Fiona flies with her eyes closed after bragging that she can do it, she gets entirely lost and has to transport her egg to safety, avoiding such dangers as alligators and other hungry creatures. After meeting other rhyming characters, such as Rappin' Cap'n Otter, the flamingo makes her way to safety, and when her egg hatches, her baby also speaks in rhyme. "Remkiewicz's cartoons are neatly drawn," remarked a critic in *Publishers Weekly* in a review of *Fiona Wraps It Up.*

Remkiewicz once told *SATA:* "I was that kind of kid who was always reading or drawing. Since I was drawing well before I started school, I always considered art to have seniority over the likes of long division or medieval history. This attitude got me into difficulties more than once. My favorite subjects were horses, cartoons, wildlife, and contraptions that rolled, floated, tooted, or flew. My heroes of the day were illustrators like Bill Peet, Robert Lawson, and Kurt Weiss. They provided me with a screen-full of imagery that I'll never forget.

"Winter in kindergarten found us all painting Santa. Mine came out so well that I was to do it over again on a huge piece of brown paper that covered the chalkboard. Santa was bigger than me. I was excused from the regular stuff, given bigger brushes, more paint and

sure enough . . . here came Santa. Other teachers saw the mural-sized figure and 'borrowed' me to do the same for their classrooms. Flattered but embarrassed, I took heart since these gigs were getting me out of a lot of tedious activities like nap time, scissors, yarn, and flash cards. 'All I ever needed to know, I learned in kindergarten' may be true. Twenty years later I found myself on Madison Avenue at Norcross Greeting Cards . . . yes, drawing Santa Claus.

"I've always been drawn to the field of humor. Since I'm writing and illustrating my own stories now, I try to make them funny in an outrageous or off-the-wall way. During classroom presentations, again . . . I find myself by the chalkboard in front of the kids. Now we are seeking ways to write and draw those ideas that squeeze their way through the every day chores of our minds. It's a thrill to watch my own book being read by a group of children and I like it when they smile, but I love it when they laugh."

Biographical and Critical Sources

PERIODICALS

Booklist, December 1, 1990, Hazel Rochman, review of *Horrible Harry's Secret,* p. 751; November 15, 1991, Ilene Cooper, review of *The Last Time I Saw Harris,*

J. Patrick Lewis's amusing math-themed poetry collection **Arithme-Tickle** *is one of many books to benefit from Remkiewicz's cartoon art.*

p. 631; October 1, 1992, Hazel Rochman, review of *Horrible Harry and the Kickball Wedding,* p. 327; July, 1994, Hazel Rochman, review of *Song Lee and the Hamster Hunt,* p. 1948; October 1, 1995, April Judge, review of *Song Lee and the Leech Man,* p. 316; June 1, 1996, Hazel Rochman, review of *Froggy Goes to School,* p. 1735; August, 1996, Hazel Rochman, review of *Horrible Harry and the Dungeon,* p. 1900; February 1, 1997, Kay Weisman, review of *The Magic Squad and the Dog of Great Potential,* p. 942; October 1, 1997, Hazel Rochman, review of *Just Enough Carrots,* p. 336; December 1, 1997, Linda Perkins, review of *Little Red Monkey,* p. 642; February 15, 1998, Kay Weisman, review of *Horrible Harry and the Drop of Doom,* p. 1012; October 15, 1998, Lauren Peterson, review of *Horrible Harry Moves up to Third Grade,* p. 422; March 1, 1999, Kay Weisman, review of *Froggy Plays Soccer,* p. 1221; May 1, 1999, Hazel Rochman, review of *Song Lee and the "I Hate You" Notes,* p. 1594; June 1, 1999, Hazel Rochman, review of *Quiet, Wyatt!,* p. 1842; December 1, 1999, Marta Segal, review of *Rabbit's Pajama Party,* p. 708; March 15, 1999, Kay Weisman, review of *Hiccup,* p. 1337; September 1, 1999, Lauren Peterson, review of *Froggy's Halloween,* p. 149; March 1, 2000, Carolyn Phelan, review of *Froggy Goes to Bed,* p. 1250; September 15, 2000, Hazel Rochman, review of *Horrible Harry at Halloween,* p. 241; June 1, 2001, Gillian Engberg, review of *Froggy Eats Out,* p. 1892; September 1, 2001, Kathy Broderick, review of *Seaweed Soup,* p. 229; December 1, 2001, Carolyn Phelan, review of *Horrible Harry Goes to Sea,* p. 643; May 15, 2002, Diane Foote, review of *Arithme-Tickle: an Even Number of Odd Riddle-Rhymes,* p. 1595; June 1, 2002, Karen Hutt, review of *Horrible Harry and the Dragon War,* p. 1740; January 1, 2003, Catherine Andronik, review of *Froggy Goes to the Doctor,* p. 908; March 15, 2003, Hazel Rochman, review of *Horrible Harry and the Mud Gremlins,* p. 1327; September 1, 2003, Carolyn Phelan, review of *Horrible Harry and the Holidaze,* p. 134; February 15, 2004, Carolyn Phelan, review of *Scien-Trickery: Riddles in Science,* p. 1055; May 1, 2004, Stephanie Zvirin, review of *Horrible Harry and the Locked Closet,* p. 1499; April 1, 2005, Ilene Cooper, review of *Piggy and Dad Go Fishing,* p. 1369; April 15, 2005, Hazel Rochman, review of *Horrible Harry and the Goog,* p. 1456; February 1, 2006, Hazel Rochman, review of *Horrible Harry Takes the Cake,* p. 55; May 1, 2007, Carolyn Phelan, review of *Horrible Harry Cracks the Code,* p. 49; February 1, 2008, Carolyn Phelan, review of *Horrible Harry Bugs the Three Bears,* p. 40; April 1, 2009, Shauna Yusko, review of *Down by the Station,* p. 43.

Bulletin of the Center for Children's Books, May, 1989, Betsy Hearne, review of *Horrible Harry and the Green Slime,* p. 227.

Horn Book, September-October, 1991, Martha V. Parravano, review of *The Last Time I Saw Harris,* p. 588; May-June, 1994, Nancy Vasilakis, review of *The Bone Stranger,* p. 319; May-June, 1997, Elizabeth S. Watson, review of *The Magic Squad and the Dog of Great*

Potential, p. 327; July-August, 2005, Kitty Flynn, review of *Piggy and Dad Go Fishing,* p. 455.

Kirkus Reviews, July 15, 1994, review of *Song Lee and the Hamster Hunt,* p. 987; September 15, 2001, review of *Horrible Harry Goes to Sea,* p. 1360; December 1, 2001, review of *Froggy Plays in the Band,* p. 1686; April 15, 2002, review of *Horrible Harry and the Dragon War,* p. 572; August 1, 2002, review of *Froggy Goes to the Doctor,* p. 1135; February 1, 2003, review of *Horrible Harry and the Mud Gremlins,* p. 233; September 15, 2001, review of *Horrible Harry Goes to Sea,* p. 1360; December 1, 2001, review of *Froggy Plays in the Band,* p. 1686; April 15, 2002, review of *Horrible Harry and The Dragon War,* p. 572; August 1, 2002, review of *Froggy Goes to the Doctor,* p. 1135; March 15, 2002, review of *Arithme-Tickle,* p. 417; February 1, 2003, review of *Horrible Harry and the Mud Gremlins,* p. 233; March 15, 2004, review of *Scien-Trickery,* p. 273; January 1, 2005, review of *Froggy's Sleepover,* p. 54; May 1, 2005, review of *Piggy and Dad Go Fishing,* p. 542; February 1, 2009, review of *Joe and Sparky Get New Wheels;* April 1, 2009, review of *Down by the Station.*

Publishers Weekly, April 19, 1991, review of *Ants Can't Dance,* p. 66; October 18, 1991, review of *The Last Time I Saw Harris,* p. 61; March 16, 1992, review of *Greedyanna,* p. 79; August 3, 1992, review of *Froggy Gets Dressed,* p. 70; August 23, 1993, review of *There's Only One Harris,* p. 69; March 7, 1994, review of *Let's Go, Froggy!,* p. 68; May 23, 1994, review of *The Bone Stranger,* p. 87; March 20, 1995, review of *Fiona Raps It Up,* p. 61; August 11, 1997, review of *Incredible Ned,* p. 401; June 14, 1999, review of *Quiet, Wyatt!,* p. 69.

School Library Journal, November, 1991, Virginia E. Jeschelnig, review of *Greedyanna,* p. 107; September, 1993, Maggie McEwen, review of *Song Lee in Room 2B,* pp. 209-210; July, 1994, Jody McCoy, review of *The Bone Stranger,* p. 88; September, 1994, Christina Dorr, review of *Song Lee and the Hamster Hunt,* p. 187; March, 1995, John Peters, review of *Fiona Wraps It Up,* p. 186; September, 1997, Carrie A. Guarria, review of *Horrible Harry and the Purple People,* p. 184; November, 1997, Nina Lindsay, review of *Little Red Monkey,* p. 91; December, 1997, Pamela K. Bomboy, review of *Just Enough Carrots,* p. 113; March, 1998, Lauralyn Persson, review of *Froggy's First Kiss,* p. 182; August, 1998, Suzanne Hawley, review of *Horrible Harry and the Drop of Doom,* p. 142; September, 1998, Linda Binder, review of *Horrible Harry Moves up to Third Grade,* p. 175; June, 1999, Pat Leach, review of *Song Lee and the "I Hate You" Notes,* p. 99; September, 1999, Susan Lissim, review of *Rabbit's Pajama Party,* p. 198; February, 2000, Pat Leach, review of *Horrible Harry Goes to the Moon,* p. 96; June, 2000, Elizabeth O'Brien, review of *Froggy Goes to Bed,* p. 119; September, 2000, Janie Schomberg, review of *Horrible Harry at Halloween,* p. 202; October, 2000, review of *Froggy's Best Christmas,* p. 61; August, 2001, Kate McLean, review of *Froggy Eats Out,* p. 156; November, 2001, Ashley

Larsen, review of *Horrible Harry Goes to Sea,* p. 127; January, 2002, Judith Constantinides, review of *Seaweed Soup,* p. 122; April, 2002, Wanda Meyers-Hines, review of *Froggy Plays in the Band,* p. 116; August, 2002, Laurie von Mehren, review of *Horrible Harry and the Dragon War,* p. 159; October, 2003, Eva Mitnick, review of *Horrible Harry and the Holidaze,* p. 65; December, 2003, Andrea Tarr, review of *Froggy's Baby Sister,* p. 119; April, 2004, Corrina Austin, review of *Scien-Trickery,* p. 135; June, 2004, Holly T. Sneeringer, review of *Froggy's Day with Dad,* p. 114; November, 2004, Kristina Aaronson, review of *Horrible Harry and the Locked Closet,* p. 108; May, 2005, Barbara Auerbach, review of *Piggy and Dad Go Fishing,* p. 92; July, 2005, Lynda S. Poling, review of *Horrible Harry and the Goog,* p. 75; May, 2006, Diane Eddington, review of *Horrible Harry Takes the Cake,* p. 91; May, 2007, Susan E. Murray, review of *Froggy Plays T-ball,* p. 102; June, 2008, Donna Cardon, review of *Froggy Goes to Camp,* p. 108; April, 2009, Laura Scott, review of *Joe and Sparky Get New Wheels,* p. 112, and Marge Loch-Wouters, review of *Down by the Station,* p. 127.

ONLINE

Frank Remkiewicz Home Page, http://www.remkiewicz.com (May 20, 2010).

* * *

RICH, Naomi

Personal

Born in England. *Education:* Newnham College Cambridge, B.A. (English literature); Manchester University, PGCE. *Hobbies and other interests:* Nineteenth-century novels.

Addresses

Home—London, England.

Career

Educator and author. St. Paul's Girls' School, London, England, former teacher of English.

Awards, Honors

Faber-Waterstone's WOW Factor Award finalist,

Writings

Alis, Anderson Press (London, England), 2008, Viking (New York, NY), 2009.

Contributor to *Cambridge Quarterly.*

Sidelights

Naomi Rich never intended to write a full-length young-adult novel when she composed an exam question for her secondary-school English class. However, the descriptive paragraph the London teacher created to test student reading-comprehension skills tapped into her longstanding interest in England's Puritan movement, as well as her interest in dystopian fiction. After leaving her teaching post, Rich set about reworking this descriptive paragraph, expanding it into the well-received first novel *Alis.*

In *Alis* readers are transported to a fictional world that has much in common with late-nineteenth-century New England. Alis lives with her family in the small community of Freeborne, where a complex network of religious dictates and laws control much of daily life. When she is told by her parents that she will be wed to Freeborne's forty-year-old minister, the fourteen year old rebels. There is no one in Freeborne who will offer her a place to hide, so Alis flees to Two Rivers, a nearby community. Although the young woman finds a friend in a young man named Luke, her friendship ultimately forces him to flee when she falls afoul of the religious zealot Thomas. As the fates continue to turn against her, Alis decides to return to Freeborne, where her willingness to accept her fate are met with intolerance and an ultimate attempt to punish her with death.

Praising Rich for crafting a "rich plot," a *Publishers Weekly* critic noted that in *Alis* the young heroine's "desparate struggle to exercise free will in a theocracy will have audiences firmly gripped. A *Kirkus Reviews* writer cited the novel's "feminist themes" and praised Rich's "clean, unadorned style" and ability to create a "compelling, briskly paced tale," while also taking issue with the "deliberate ambiguity" of the story's historical setting. Noting that the novel is so full of "twists that readers won't anticipate the ending," Ilene Cooper concluded in *Booklist* that, while "such multi-layered stories" are unusual for first-time novelists, "Rich pulls it off" in *Alis.* In the *New York Times Book Review,* Jessica Bruder dubbed *Alis* a "fast-paced tale" that readers will find "hard to put down."

Discussing *Alis* in an interview for the *Vulpes Libris* Web log, Rich noted that her novel reflects her personal interest in "forms of society and worship that non-conformist varieties of Christianity have produced." She opted to set her novel in an ambiguous historical setting because "historical accuracy would have limited me to what has actually happened and I wanted to explore some pre-occupations of my own." "I suppose I want young female readers to absorb . . . the idea of female strength and courage," Rich explained to an interviewer in addressing the story's complex and even provocative themes. "I also want all readers to recognise that life is morally complex. I'd like young readers to see that religious belief can (though it does not always) lead even those who mean well to do terrible things."

Biographical and Critical Sources

PERIODICALS

Booklist, December 15, 2008, Ilene Cooper, review of *Alis,* p. 40.
Kirkus Reviews, January 1, 2009, review of *Alis.*
New York Times Book Review, June 14, 2009, Jessica Bruder, review of *Alis,* p. 13.
Publishers Weekly, December 22, 2009, review of *Alis,* p. 52.
School Library Journal, March, 2009, Joel Shoemaker, review of *Alis,* p. 152.

ONLINE

Vulpes Libres Web log, http://vulpeslibris.wordpress.com/ (January 4, 2008), interview with Rich.*

* * *

RITCHIE, Scot 1954-

Personal

Born September 12, 1954, in Vancouver, British Columbia, Canada; son of Ross Brian (an architect) and Geraldine (a writer) Ritchie. *Education:* University of British Columbia, B.F.A., 1974; studied in Athens, Greece. *Hobbies and other interests:* Travel, art.

Addresses

Home and office—Scot Ritchie Illustration and Design, Vancouver, British Columbia, Canada. *E-mail*—info@scotritchie.com.

Career

Author, illustrator, and graphic designer. R.O.D. Cards (greeting card company), Toronto, Ontario, Canada, owner, artist, and writer, 1978-89; freelance illustrator in Toronto and in Vancouver, British Columbia, Canada, 1989—. Scot Ritchie Illustration and Design, owner. *Exhibitions:* Works have been exhibited in National Gallery of Canada, Ottawa.

Awards, Honors

Alcuin Society Award for Excellence in Book Design, 1984; Parents' Guide to Children's Media Award, 2000, for *My Baby Brother and Me* by Jane Drake and Ann Love; Canadian Toy Testing Council Great Books for Children designation, 2001, for *Why?: The Best Ever Question and Answer Book about Nature, Science, and the World around You,* by Catherine Ripley; Amelia Frances Howard-Gibbon Illustrator's Award nomination, and Cybils Award shortlist for nonfiction picture books, both 2007, and "Give-Away Book of the Year" selection, Canadian Children's Book Center/Toronto

Dominion Bank, 2009, all for *Let's Go!* by Lizann Flatt; Norma Fleck Award for Canadian Nonfiction nomination, for *Follow That Map.*

Writings

SELF-ILLUSTRATED

Up, Up, and Away: A Round-the-World Puzzle Adventure, Little Hare Books (Surry Hills, New South Wales, Australia), 2005, Maple Tree Press (Toronto, Ontario, Canada), 2006.
Crazy Mazey Houses, Little Hare Books (Surry Hills, New South Wales, Australia), 2008.
Follow That Map!: A First Book of Mapping Skills, Kids Can Press (Tonawanda, NY), 2009.
Scot Ritchie's Ghouliest-Ever Puzzle Book, Little Hare Books (Surry Hills, New South Wales, Australia), 2010.

Also author/illustrator of puzzle and activity books published by Adams Media.

ILLUSTRATOR

Janet Munsil, *Dinner at Auntie Rose's,* Annick Press (Toronto, Ontario, Canada), 1984.
Gerrem Evans, *Brendan, Morgan, and the Best-Ever Cloud Machine,* Annick Press (Toronto, Ontario, Canada), 1985.
Kerry Westell, *Dinosaur Dreams,* Annick Press (Toronto, Ontario, Canada), 1989, revised, 1997.
Brenda Silsbe, *The Bears We Know,* Annick Press (Toronto, Ontario, Canada), 1989.
Laurie Wark, *Soccer,* Kids Can Press (Toronto, Ontario, Canada), 1994.
Laurie Wark, *Baseball,* Kids Can Press (Toronto, Ontario, Canada), 1994.
Laurie Wark, *Hockey,* Kids Can Press (Toronto, Ontario, Canada), 1994.
Catherine Ripley, *Why Is Soap So Slippery?, and Other Bathtime Questions,* Firefly (Toronto, Ontario, Canada), 1995.
Catherine Ripley, *Do Doors Open by Magic?, and Other Supermarket Questions,* Firefly (Toronto, Ontario, Canada), 1995.
Robert Heidbreder, *Eenie Meenie Manitoba: Playful Poems and Rollicking Rhymes,* Kids Can Press (Toronto, Ontario, Canada), 1996.
Catherine Ripley, *Why Do Stars Twinkle?, and Other Nighttime Questions,* Firefly (Toronto, Ontario, Canada), 1996.
Catherine Ripley, *Why Does Popcorn Pop?, and Other Kitchen Questions,* Firefly (Toronto, Ontario, Canada), 1997.
Catherine Ripley, *Why Is the Sky Blue?, and Other Outdoor Questions* Firefly (Toronto, Ontario, Canada), 1997.

Catherine Ripley, *Why Do Cows Moo?, and Other Farm Animal Questions,* Firefly (Toronto, Ontario, Canada), 1998.

Jane Drake and Ann Love, *My Mother and Me,* Kids Can Press (Toronto, Ontario, Canada), 2000.

Jane Drake and Ann Love, *My Father and Me,* Kids Can Press (Toronto, Ontario, Canada), 2000.

Jane Drake and Ann Love, *My Baby Brother and Me,* Kids Can Press (Toronto, Ontario, Canada), 2000.

Jane Drake and Ann Love, *My Baby Sister and Me,* Kids Can Press (Toronto, Ontario, Canada), 2000.

Jane Drake and Ann Love, *My Grandmother and Me,* Kids Can Press (Toronto, Ontario, Canada), 2000.

Jane Drake and Ann Love, *My Grandfather and Me,* Kids Can Press (Toronto, Ontario, Canada), 2000.

Catherine Ripley, *Why?: The Best Ever Question and Answer Book about Nature, Science, and the World around You,* Owl Books (Toronto, Ontario, Canada), 2001.

Jane Drake and Ann Love, *My New Home and Me: A Memory Scrapbook for Kids,* Kids Can Press (Toronto, Ontario, Canada), 2001.

Jane Drake and Ann Love, *My Family and Me,* Kids Can Press (Toronto, Ontario, Canada), 2002.

Jane Drake and Ann Love, *My Class and Me: Kindergarten,* Kids Can Press (Toronto, Ontario, Canada), 2003.

Jane Drake and Ann Love, *My Class and Me: First Grade,* Kids Can Press (Toronto, Ontario, Canada), 2003.

Jane Drake and Ann Love, *My Class and Me: Second Grade,* Kids Can Press (Toronto, Ontario, Canada), 2003.

Robert Heidbreder, *See Saw Saskatchewan: More Playful Poems from Coast to Coast,* Kids Can Press (Toronto, Ontario, Canada), 2003.

Lizann Flatt, *Let's Go!: The Story of Getting from There to Here,* Maple Tree (New York, NY), 2007.

Laura Mayne, *Great Teacher Projects,* Boston Mills Press (Erin, Ontario, Canada), 2009.

Tiffany Stone, Karine-Lynn Winters, and Lori Sherrit-Fleming, *Arhythmetic,* Gumboot Books (Vancouver, British Columbia, Canada), 2009.

Emily Smith Pearce, *Slowpoke,* Boyds Mills Press (Honesdale, PN), 2010.

Betty Borowski and Laura Mayne, *Meet the Teacher,* Boston Mills Press (Erin, Ontario, Canada), 2010.

Contributor to periodicals, including the *Chicago Tribune, Newsweek, New York Magazine, Readers Digest,* and *Wall St. Journal.*

Work featuring Ritchie's artwork has been translated into Arabic, Dutch, Finnish, French, Indonseian, Polish, Korean, and Braille.

Adaptations

Some of Ritchie's work has been adapted for videotape by the National Film Board of Canada.

Sidelights

Scot Ritchie is an artist based in western Canada who has created illustrations for picture books by numerous authors, including the prolific writing team of Jane

Scot Ritchie creates colorful illustrations that introduce an important skill in his picture book **Follow That Map!** (Kids Can Press, 2009. Used by permission of Kids Can Press, Ltd., Toronto, Ontario, Canada.)

Drake and Ann Love. In reviewing Ritchie's work for *Dinosaur Dreams,* a picture book by Kerry Westall, *Resource Links* contributor Anna Carino noted that the dino-stars of Westall's tale "are endearing as they assume human stances." Ritchie's two-page spreads for the book "celebrat[e] . . . the sense of playfulness and sheer joy associated with childhood," the critic added. His contributions to Robert Heidbreder's *See Saw Saskatchewan: More Playful Poems from Coast to Coast,* which appeals to a Canadian readership, were judged by *Resource Links* critic Connie Forst to be "humourous, joyful, colourful and funny and . . . add much to the poetry."

In addition to his work as an illustrator, Ritchie has also created the original self-illustrated picture books *Up, Up, and Away: A Round-the-World Puzzle Adventure, Crazy Mazey Houses, Scot Ritchie's Ghouliest-Ever Puzzle Book,* and *Follow That Map!: A First Book of Mapping Skills.* In addition to telling a story about Sally and her friends as they set out on a globe-spanning search to find family pets Max and Ollie, *Follow That Map!* mixes a "fanciful story" with useful "map-related information," according to *Booklist* contributor Carolyn Phelan. In *School Library Journal* Wendy Woodfill dubbed Ritchie's picture book a "clever introduction" to an important skill, adding that the author/illustrator includes a variety of maps—including topographical, weather, road, and even treasure maps—in which Sally's pets are hidden. "Bright, easy-to-follow illustrations do an excellent job of highlighting . . . major concepts," wrote *Quill & Quire* contributor Paul Challen, and in the Toronto *Globe & Mail* Susan Perren dubbed *Follow That Map!* a "funny . . . and useful book about maps and mapping."

As Ritchie told *SATA:* "I began illustrating at a very early age, although I guess it was called scribbling back then. In my early twenties, while still waiting on tables, I would do gallery shows around town, selling framed pieces. I was quite successful but realized very quickly that more money could be made by drawing something once, printing it up a thousand times, and then selling that. So a friend and I started R.O.D. Cards. At the time it was the largest all-Canadian greeting card company in Canada. We realized after about eleven years that competing with the giants of the business, like Hallmark, made it very difficult to be profitable. That's when I decided to try freelance work and was very fortunate to be taken on by a brand new agency in Toronto. We grew together over the next fourteen years learning from each other and eventually going our own ways.

"My main reason for doing what I do (aside from the financial rewards) is that I love drawing. I never forget how fortunate I am to be able to support myself doing that, although working freelance at home can be very trying. If I don't sit down at my desk, nobody is going to make me do it. And if there's an old *The Simpsons* rerun on television I had better be able to make up that viewing time later if I choose to watch it. After doing

this for over twenty years, I've developed a reliable habit of getting my day started at eight a.m. and writing down goals for the day. As I cross them off, I know I've accomplished something. As an entrepreneur, having some irons in the fire is almost as rewarding as receiving a check.

"I've been fortunate to have illustrated several children's books, and am now working on the seventh book for which I'm both author and illustrator. Recently a series of books I did was gathered into an anthology and sold around the world. I was very excited to see Korean, Polish, French, and Dutch translations.

"I've always felt that, if you just keep at it, you will rise to the top of your field. Of course, you have to have some level of quality in your work that makes it enjoyable to look at, but a big factor in any business is just the desire to keep at it when others fall by the wayside. Having worked in commercial illustration for fifteen years, I know how competitive it is. But through tough times I'm always sustained by being aware of what a huge reward it is."

Biographical and Critical Sources

PERIODICALS

Booklist, December 1, 1996, Hazel Rochman, review of *Why Do Stars Twinkle?, and Other Nighttime Questions,* p. 663; December 1, 1997, Hazel Rochman, review of *Why Does Popcorn Pop?, and Other Kitchen Questions,* p. 633; March 15, 2009, Carolyn Phelan, review of *Follow That Map!: A First Book of Mapping Skills,* p. 62.

Canadian Review of Materials, November 1, 1996, Jennifer Sullivan, review of *Why Do Stars Twinkle?, and Other Nighttime Questions;* November 9, 2007, Robert Groberman, review of *Let's Go!: The Story of Getting from There to Here.*

Globe & Mail (Toronto, Ontario, Canada), April 11, 2009, Susan Perren, review of *Follow That Map!,* p. F12.

Kirkus Reviews, February 1, 2009, review of *Follow That Map!*

Quill & Quire, November, 1996, Janet McNaughton, review of *Eenie Meenie Manitoba: Playful Poems and Rollicking Rhymes;* February, 1997, Hadley Dyer, review of *Why Is the Sky Blue?, and Other Outdoor Questions;* June, 1998, Etta Kaner, review of *Why Do Cows Moo?, and Other Farm Animal Questions;* January, 2003, Gwyneth Evans, review of *See Saw Saskatchewan: More Playful Poems from Coast to Coast;* March, 2009, Paul Challen, review of *Follow That Map!*

Resource Links, August, 1997, Karen Jollimore, review of *Why Is the Sky Blue?, and Other Outdoor Questions,* pp. 262-263; April, 2000, reviews of *My Father and Me,* p. 14, and *My Grandmother and Me,* and *My Grandfather and Me,* both p. 50; June, 2001, Joanne

de Groot, review of *My New Home and Me: A Memory Scrapbook for Kids,* p. 23; December, 2001, Elaine Rospad, review of *Why? The Best Ever Question and Answer Book about Nature, Science, and the World around You,* p. 29; June, 2002, Rosemary Anderson, review of *My Family and Me,* p. 20; April, 2003, Connie Forst, review of *See Saw Saskatchewan,* p. 3.

School Library Journal, December, 2001, Saleena L. Davidson, review of *Why?,* p. 128; August, 2008, Lizann Flat, review of *Let's Go!,* p. 110; October, 2009, Wendy Woodfill, review of *Follow That Map!,* p. 114.

ONLINE

Scot Ritchie Home Page, http://www.scotritchie.com (June 15, 2010).

*   *   *

RUI, Paolo 1962-

Personal

Born May 4, 1962, in Milan, Italy; married; wife's name Vicky, 1999; children: Leo. *Education:* Brera Academy of Fine Arts (Milan, Italy), degree (painting), 1985; attended Art Center College of Design, 1988-89.

Addresses

Home—Milan, Italy. *E-mail*—rui@sottomarino.org.

Career

Editorial and advertising illustrator. Freelance illustrator, beginning 1990; Studio Sottomarino, Milan, Italy, affiliated artist. Teacher of illustration at Arte e messaggio Art School, 1994-95, European Design Institute, beginning 2003. *Exhibitions:* Works included in exhibitions in Italy, Cuba, England, France, Greece, Hungary, Taiwan, and the United States, and at Bologna Children's Book Fair, 1999-2000.

Member

European Illustrators Forum (cofounder, 2004), Italian Illustrators Association (member, board of directors, 1992), Italian Illustrators Association (president, 2001-05), European Illustrators Forum (cofounder, 2004).

Awards, Honors

Mediastars Prize for billboard advertising, 1996; International Illustration Competition (Turin, Italy), prize, 2002; Italian Illustration Awards, 2006, 2007, 2008, 2009; Bimbi Volanti competition, special mention, 2008.

Illustrator

Brendan January, *Da Vinci: Renaissance Painter,* Mason Crest Publishers (Broomall, PA), 2003.

Richard Bowen, *Van Gogh: Modern Artist,* Mason Crest Publishers (Philadelphia, PA), 2003.

Jeanne Pettenati, *Galileo's Journal: 1609-1610,* Charlesbridge (Watertown, MA), 2006.

Wendy Macdonald, *Galileo's Leaning Tower Experiment: A Science Adventure,* Charlesbridge (Watertown, MA), 2009.

Biographical and Critical Sources

PERIODICALS

Booklist, August 1, 2006, Carolyn Phelan, review of *Galileo's Journal: 1609-1610,* p. 92; February 15, 2009, Ian Chipman, review of *Galileo's Leaning Tower Experiment: A Science Adventure,* p. 77.

Kirkus Reviews, January 1, 2009, review of *Galileo's Leaning Tower Experiment.*

School Library Journal, February, 2003, Toniann Scime, review of *Van Gogh: Modern Artist,* p. 152; September, 2006, Deanna Romriell, review of *Galileo's Journal,* p. 181; June, 2009, Jeffrey A. French, review of *Galileo's Leaning Tower Experiment,* p. 110.

ONLINE

Paolo Rui Home Page, http://www.paolorui.com (June 15, 2010).

Paolo Rui Web log, http://sirbumboom.blogspot.com (June 15, 2010).*

*   *   *

RUNYON, Brent 1976-

Personal

Born 1976; son of Don (a college administrator) and Linda (an elementary school teacher) Runyon; married Christina Egloff (a radio producer); children: three. *Education:* Attended Ithaca College.

Addresses

Home—Cape Cod, MA. *E-mail*—brent@burnjournals.com.

Career

Writer and radio producer. National Public Radio, contributor to program *This American Life;* reporter for *Falmouth Enterprise* (newspaper).

Awards, Honors

Georgia Peach Award for Young Readers nomination, 2005, for *The Burn Journals;* American Library Association/YALSA Best Books for Young Adults designation, 2010, for *Surface Tension.*

Writings

The Burn Journals (memoir), Alfred A. Knopf (New York, NY), 2004.
Maybe (novel), Alfred A. Knopf (New York, NY), 2006.
Surface Tension: A Novel in Four Summers, Alfred A. Knopf (New York, NY), 2009.

Sidelights

Brent Runyon's suicide attempt at age fourteen is the subject of his first book, *The Burn Journals.* As the title of the memoir suggests, Runyon attempted to end his life by donning a gasoline-soaked bathrobe and setting it on fire. Although the teen instantaneously changed his mind and jumped into a nearby shower, he still suffered severe burns over eighty-five percent of his body. Since writing his memoir, Runyon has continued to craft thoughtful fiction for adolescent readers, producing the well-received novels *Maybe* and *Surface Tension: A Novel in Four Summers.* All three books were written in collaboration with his wife, Christina Egloff.

Cover of Brent Runyon's dramatic coming-of-age memoir The Burn Journals. (Copyright © 2004 by Knopf Children. Used by permission of Alfred A. Knopf, an imprint of Random House Children's Books, a division of Random House, Inc.)

The Burn Journals chronicles Runyon's year of recovery as he underwent painful skin grafting, entered a rehabilitation center, and ultimately faced the terrifying prospect of returning to school. Although he had been depressed and made other less-drastic but noticeable attempts at suicide prior to the burning, he remains uncertain as to the reason why he decided to set himself on fire that particular day. When asked during an interview with Lynda Brill Comerford for *Publishers Weekly* what he hoped readers would gain from his harrowing memoir, Runyon replied: "Insight into the adolescent mind. What I truly wish could happen would be that this book could somehow travel back in time and land in the hands of me when I was thirteen years old. Then I would read the book and not set myself on fire."

A *Publishers Weekly* contributor called *The Burn Journals* "engrossing from first page to last" and went on to note that, "despite its dark subject matter, this powerful chronicle . . . expresses hope, celebrates life and provides an opportunity to slip inside the skin of a survivor with a unique perspective." Johanna Lewis, writing in *School Library Journal,* commented: "Depression, regret, and rebirth are the themes that tie the narrative, and the subtle tensions among the three are beautifully related, offering no neat resolution." In a review for *Horn Book,* Christine M. Heppermann noted of *The Burn Journals,* that "there's a lot of emotion beneath Runyon's narrative; when it does break through to the surface, it is all the more powerful for its simplicity and directness." *Booklist* contributor Jennifer Mattson stated that the memoir "can and should be ready by young adults, as much for its literary merit as for its authentic perspective on what it means to attempt suicide."

Runyon's novel *Maybe* focuses on a teenager dealing with the aftermath of his older brother's death. The protagonist finds himself in a new town and a new school when his family moves following the tragedy, and he must not only deal with his own overwhelming grief but also the usual sources of teenage anxiety. Miranda Doyle, writing for *School Library Journal,* described *Maybe* as "a superb exploration of sudden loss, romantic disappointment, and general adolescent angst." *Philadelphia Inquirer* contributor Katie Haegele maintained that the book's finest quality is its "accurate portrayal of a family's loss," adding that "Runyon tells us a story of survival without making it obvious that's what the book is about." A *Publishers Weekly* reviewer maintained that *Maybe* is "less intense but just as candid as" *The Burn Journals.* According to J.A. Kaszuba Locke in an online review for *Bookloons,* Runyon's novel's narrative "is moving and compelling, intense and intuitive—a read of interest to both teens and adults."

Luke, the narrator of *Surface Tension,* finds his impressions of life changing as he revisits his family's vacation home over a succession of four summers. At age thirteen Luke still reacts with boyish excitement to family hikes with his parents, but by age sixteen the teen views the changes in the local town with a more jaded

Runyon crafts a subtle story of a teen's coming of age in his young-adult novel Surface Tension. (Jacket photograph copyright © 2009 by Knopf Children. Used by permission of Alfred A. Knopf, an imprint of Random House Children's Books, a division of Random House, Inc.)

eye, understanding the shifts in the local economy but longing for the naivetée that he once had. Calling *Surface Tension* a "pensive summertime novel," Christine M. Heppermann added in *Horn Book* that "the book's strongest moments are the subtler ones" that reflect Luke's conflicts about growing older. Emily Chornomaz reviewed Runyon's novel in *School Library Journal,* describing the book as "a subtle and often humorous portrait how age influences one's outlook" and praising Luke as "delightfully honest." "With sensitivity and candor, Runyon reveals how life changes us all," concluded a *Kirkus Reviews* writer, adding that *Surface Tension* helps readers see "how these unavoidable changes can be full of both turmoil and wonder."

Discussing the transition from nonfiction to fiction with *Publishers Weekly* online interviewer Lynda Brill Comerford, Runyon noted that "fiction is like building a house from scratch. You know that there will be walls and doors, a kitchen and bath, but you're not sure where they'll be. Writing a memoir is more like restoring a house. Everything is already there. It's a present-tense remembering of the way things were. When I write a novel, I still make it as true and real as I can. There's the same kind of emotional truth there, but it doesn't hurt as badly to write it out. I have the freedom to take pieces of life and arrange them any way I want. I write about what life could have been like."

Biographical and Critical Sources

BOOKS

Runyon, Brent, *The Burn Journals,* Alfred A. Knopf (New York, NY), 2004.

PERIODICALS

Booklist, June 1, 2004, Jennifer Mattson, review of *The Burn Journals,* p. 1753; February 15, 2009, Ian Chipman, review of *Surface Tension: A Novel in Four Summers,* p. 76.
Horn Book, November-December, 2004, Christine M. Heppermann, review of *The Burn Journals,* p. 731; May-June, 2009, Christine M. Heppermann, review of *Surface Tension,* p. 307.
Kirkus Reviews, July 15, 2004, review of *The Burn Journals,* p. 693; February 1, 2009, review of *Surface Tension.*
People, December 6, 2004, Allison Adato and Tom Duffy, "The Third Degree."
Philadelphia Inquirer, November 29, 2006, Katie Haegele, review of *Maybe.*
Psychology Today, September-October, 2004, Willow Lawson, review of *The Burn Journals,* p. 28.
Publishers Weekly, October 11, 2004, review of *The Burn Journals,* p. 81; October 11, 2004, Lynda Brill Comerford, interview with Runyon, p. 81; October 30, 2006, review of *Maybe,* p. 64; February 23, 2009, review of *Surface Tension,* p. 51.
School Library Journal, November, 2004, Johanna Lewis, review of *The Burn Journals,* p. 172; November, 2006, Miranda Doyle, review of *Maybe,* p. 150; April, 2009, Emily Chornomaz, review of *Surface Tension,* p. 141.
Voice of Youth Advocates, August, 2009, Laura Woodruff, review of *Surface Tension,* p. 232.

ONLINE

Bookloons, http://www.bookloons.com/ (June 25, 2007), J.A. Kaszuba Locke, review of *Maybe.*
Burn Journals Web site, http://burnjournals.com/ (May 31, 2010).
Publishers Weekly Online, http://www.publishersweekly.com/ (March 26, 2009), Lynda Brill Comerford, interview with Runyon.
Random House Web site, http://www.randomhouse.com/ (February 25, 2005), "Brent Runyon."

S-V

SCHNEIDER, Elisa
    See KLEVEN, Elisa

*   *   *

SCHUBERT, Dieter

Personal

Born July 15, 1947, in Oschersleben, Germany; son of Erich (a locksmith) and Elfriede (a homemaker) Schubert; married Ingrid Gabrys (an illustrator), November 5, 1976; children: Hannah. *Education:* Münster Academy of Design, degree, 1975; attended Düsseldorf Academy of Art, 1975-76, University of Münster, 1975-77, and Gerrit Rietveld Academy (Amsterdam), 1977-80. *Hobbies and other interests:* Playing guitar, listening to good music.

Addresses

Home—Amsterdam, Netherlands.

Career

Author and illustrator. Tengelmann Wholesale Trade, Hamm, Germany, merchant, 1963-71; Academy of Restoration, Amsterdam, Netherlands, teacher, 1980—; author and illustrator, 1980—. Teacher of art expression workshop, Amsterdam, 1982—.

Awards, Honors

Golden Brush Award for Best Illustrated Picture Book of the Year (Netherlands), 1987, and Honour designation, International Board on Books for Young People, 1988, both for *Where's My Monkey?*

Writings

SELF-ILLUSTRATED

Ravenstreken, Lemniscaat (Rotterdam, Netherlands), 1982, published as *Jack in the Boat,* Kestrel (London, England), 1982.

Monkie, Lemniscaat (Rotterdam, Netherlands), 1986, translated as *Where's My Monkey?,* Dial (New York, NY), 1987.

SELF-ILLUSTRATED; WITH WIFE, INGRID SCHUBERT

Er ligt een krokodil onder mijn bed, Lemniscaat (Rotterdam, Netherlands), 1980, translated as *There's a Crocodile under My Bed,* McGraw-Hill (New York, NY), 1981, reprinted, Front Street/Lemniscaat (Asheville, NC), 2005.

Helemaal verkikkerd, Lemniscaat (Rotterdam, Netherlands), 1981, translated as *The Magic Bubble Trip,* Kane/Miller (New York, NY), 1985.

Kikj mij nou, NOT Verlag, 1982.

Ik kan niet slapen!, Lemniscaat (Rotterdam, Netherlands), 1983.

Platvoetje, Lemniscaat (Rotterdam, Netherlands), 1985, translated by Amy Gelman as *Little Bigfeet,* Carolrhoda (Minneapolis, MN), 1990.

Wie niet sterk is . . . , Lemniscaat (Rotterdam, Netherlands), 1989.

Santa Claus/Father Christmas, Lemniscaat (Rotterdam, Netherlands), 1989.

Die uitvinder, Stichting (Netherlands), 1989.

Woeste Willem, Lemniscaat (Rotterdam, Netherlands), 1993, translated as *Wild Will,* Carolrhoda (Minneapolis, MN), 1994.

Van mug tot oliphant, Lemniscaat (Rotterdam, Netherlands), 1995, translated and adapted by Leigh Sauerwein as *Amazing Animals,* Front Street (Asheville, NC), 1995.

Abracadabra, Lemniscaat (Rotterdam, Netherlands), 1997, Front Street (Asheville, NC), 1997.

(Retellers) *Een gat in mijn emmer,* Lemniscaat (Rotterdam, Netherlands), 1998, translated as *There's a Hole in My Bucket,* Front Street (Arden, NC), 1998.

Dat komt er nou van . . . , Lemniscaat (Rotterdam, Netherlands), 1999, translated as *Bear's Eggs,* Front Street (Asheville, NC), 1999.

Samen kunnen we alles, Lemniscaat (Rotterdam, Netherlands), 2000, translated as *Beaver's Lodge,* Front Street/Lemniscaat (Asheville, NC), 2001.

Er kan nog meer bij, Lemniscaat (Rotterdam, Netherlands), 2001, translated as *There's Always Room for One More,* Front Street/Lemniscaat (Asheville, NC), 2002.

Van kop tot start, Lemniscaat (Rotterdam, Netherlands), 2002.

Het grote boek van Beer en Egel, Lemniscaat (Rotterdam, Netherlands), 2003.

Gekke buren, Lemniscaat (Rotterdam, Netherlands), 2003, translated as *Hammer Soup,* Front Street/Lemniscaat (Asheville, NC), 2004.

Mijn held, Lemniscaat (Rotterdam, Netherlands), 2004, translated as *My Hero,* Front Street/Lemniscaat (Asheville, NC), 2004.

Het kleine boek van Beer en Egel, Lemniscaat (Rotterdam, Netherlands), 2005.

Platvoetje & Co., Lemniscaat (Rotterdam, Netherlands), 2005.

Doeboek: knutselen, puzzelen, tekenen, Lemniscaat (Rotterdam, Netherlands), 2005.

***Dieter and Ingrid Schubert create amusing self-illustrated stories such as* Abracadabra.** (Front Street Books, 1997. Copyright © 1996 by Lemniscaat b.v. Rotterdam. Reproduced by permission.)

Krokodil is jarig, Lemniscaat (Rotterdam, Netherlands), 2005.

Net mensen, Lemniscaat (Rotterdam, Netherlands), 2006, translated as *Like People,* Front Street/Lemniscaat (Honesdale, PA), 2008.

Engel, Lemniscaat (Rotterdam, Netherlands), 2007.

Ophelia, Lemniscaat (Rotterdam, Netherlands), 2008, Lemniscaat (Honesdale, PA), 2009.

Olifantensoep, Lemniscaat (Rotterdam, Netherlands), 2008, translated as *Elephant Soup,* Lemniscaat (Honesdale, PA), 2010.

Author's works have been published in translation.

TELEPLAYS; WITH INGRID SCHUBERT

Look at Me, Dutch School Television, 1982.

Who's Coming to My Little House?, Dutch School Television, 1982.

Father Christmas/Santa Claus, Dutch School Television, 1989.

Sidelights

German-born author and illustrator Dieter Schubert is known for his picture books for young children, especially his works done in collaboration with his wife, Ingrid Schubert, who is also an illustrator. Together, from their home in the Netherlands, the pair has produced a number of humorous and well-illustrated stories, several of which have been translated into English. Included among these works are *There's a Crocodile under My Bed, My Hero,* and *Ophelia,* as well as Schubert's solo efforts s *Jack in the Boat* and *Where's My Monkey?*

Schubert once told *SATA* how the couple's first book met with international success. "My wife Ingrid and I started to write and illustrate our own stories. In 1979 we contacted the publishing firm Lemniscaat who liked our first idea for a book. They made our first international contact at the Frankfurt Book Fair. In 1980 that first book, *There's a Crocodile under My Bed,* was translated into eleven languages and published in fourteen countries."

There's a Crocodile under My Bed, the couple's first published work, features a young girl named Peggy who discovers a crocodile in her room. Peggy's parents are on their way out for the evening and do not believe her. Left on their own, Peggy and the crocodile have a wonderful evening, and when Dad checks under her bed the next morning he does find a crocodile: one Peggy and her new reptile friend made from egg cartons the night before. A *Bulletin of the Center for Children's Books* critic called *There's a Crocodile under My Bed* a "pleasant . . . variant on a familiar theme." *School Library Journal* contributor Patricia Dooley noted that the "crayon art has character, liveliness and detail," and dubbed the book "a great debut for this author-illustrator team."

In *There's a Hole in My Bucket* the Schuberts retell a German folk song about a bear attempting to water the parched flowers growing outside his cave. After Bear

The Schuberts introduce an engaging menagerie of animal creatures in their picture books, such as the rotund star of **Ophelia.** (Lemniscaat, 2009. Copyright © 2008 by Ingrid and Dieter Schubert. Reproduced by permission.)

discovers that the bucket is damaged, his friend Hedgehog tries to help, but to no avail. Mother Nature eventually solves the problem herself, much to the animals' relief. "An appealing, decidedly inquisitive cast of woodland animals and insects peeks out from the Schuberts' softly shaded double-page illustrations," maintained a *Publishers Weekly* reviewer in discussing *There's a Hole in My Bucket. School Library Journal* contributor Carol Ann Wilson asserted: "Bear is an endearing fellow and children will delight in his challenges and good-natured acquiescence to fate."

Bear and Hedgehog make a return appearance in *Beaver's Lodge.* After their pal, Beaver, falls and hurts himself while building his lodge, the duo comes to his rescue, carrying Beaver to Bear's cave, tending to his injuries, and helping him fall asleep. When Beaver recovers, he gets quite a surprise: Bear and Hedgehog have finished constructing his lodge, though it lacks one vital feature. "The pictures manage to make the endearing characters seem both animal and human," Hazel Rochman commented in *Booklist,* and Be Astengo, writing in *School Library Journal,* similarly noted in *Booklist* that the Schuberts "capture the animals' expressions of hurt, excitement, and confusion perfectly."

In *There's Always Room for One More* Beaver invites Badger, Bear, Hedgehog, Mole, and Hare to join him for a ride on his boat, which is barely large enough to hold its owner. When his friends decline the offer, Bea-

ver crafts a makeshift raft that entices everyone to climb aboard, each new passenger testing the ability of Beaver's creation raft to stay afloat. "Appreciative onlookers will enjoy the stunning muted watercolor scenery," remarked Susan Weitz in *School Library Journal.*

In *Hammer Soup* the Schuberts offer their take on a pair of familiar tales: "Stone Soup" and "The Ant and the Grasshopper." The work centers on two vastly different neighbors: Kate, a tidy and industrious gardener, and Bruce, a genial but sloppy giant. When a winter storm destroys Bruce's ramshackle cabin, Kate invites him to share her home although she refuses to share her food. For his first meal, Bruce proposes an unlikely concoction: a soup made from water, salt, and a hammer. "Children will delight in the whimsical illustrations as well as in the humor of this book," *School Library Journal* critic Genevieve Gallagher stated. In the love story *My Hero,* a mouse must fulfill his promise to protect his girlfriend at all costs when the tree branch they sit upon breaks, leaving them vulnerable to a hungry cat. According to Julie Roach in *School Library Journal,* the Schuberts' watercolor pictures "manage to depict these rough and raw mice . . . in a funny and appealing way."

The Schuberts examine the various ways that animals—including elephants, owls, and tigers—care for their young, noting similarities between the behaviors of these creatures and the actions of humans in *Like People,* an informational work. "The prose is warm and soothing, but the art, packed with quasirealistic, playful animals, will have readers fully alert," commented a reviewer in *Publishers Weekly.* In the words of *School Library Journal* critic Maryann H. Owen, "this appealing title offers the valuable lesson that all living creatures have much in common." In *Ophelia,* the title character, a helpful hippopotamus, becomes concerned when she hears her neighbor, Kevin the alligator, groaning across the water. Convinced that Kevin has a tummy ache, Ophelia enlist the aid of Meerkat, who exaggerates the alligator's condition to Frog. As word spreads through the jungle, a host of animals join the rescue party, each convinced that Kevin needs immediate attention. "Delicate, full-bleed watercolors depict the characters with gentle humor," observed a contributor in *Kirkus Reviews.*

In addition to collaborating with wife Ingrid, Schubert also has produced a few books on his own, including the well-received picture book *Where's My Monkey?* In this wordless story, a boy loses his toy monkey while bicycle riding with his mother. The monkey is shuffled around by various animals, including rats, hedgehogs, and a large bird, before it finds a new home in a toy shop. When the boy spots the repaired monkey in the shop window, the two are quickly reunited. Betsy Hearne, writing in the *Bulletin of the Center for Children's Books,* noted that the book's "vivid, richly colored paintings . . . feature fine drafting and design," while *Horn Book* contributor Mary M. Burns appreciated the "appealing theme" and "carefully developed

conflict" in *Where's My Monkey?* Burns also noted that "few such productions could match this book for sheer charm . . . and [the] skill with which the pictures are sequenced."

Schubert once explained to *SATA* how he became interested in writing and illustrating books for children. "While in Germany and Holland I studied painting, drawing, and 'free' graphics. At the start of my studies I had been preoccupied with illustrating stories. During my study at the Gerrit Rietveld Academy, I was inspired by Piet Klaasse, a very famous illustrator in Holland, who at the time was a teacher there. I then started to spend more time on illustration.

"Although I started illustrating adult literature (Kafka), I soon began illustrating for children. I later preferred illustrating for very small children because I find them very fascinating in their thoughts and adventures. What is more, by making up stories and illustrating them one's own feelings from childhood come back again, and I take pleasure in that."

Biographical and Critical Sources

PERIODICALS

Booklist, May 15, 1998, Stephanie Zvirin, review of *There's a Hole in My Bucket,* p. 1628; October 1, 1999, John Peters and Gilbert Taylor, review of *Bear's Eggs,* p.

A fanciful original folk tale unfolds in the Schuberts' art for the picture book **Hammer Soup.** (Front Street/Lemniscaat, 2003. Copyright © 2003 by Ingrid and Dieter Schubert. Reproduced by permission.)

363; July, 2001, Hazel Rochman, review of *Beaver's Lodge,* p. 2020; March 15, 2009, Kay Weisman, review of *Ophelia,* p. 66.

Books for Keeps, March, 1988, Jill Bennett, review of *Little Big Feet,* p. 16.

Bulletin of the Center for Children's Books, July-August, 1981, Betsy Hearne, review of *Where's My Monkey?,* p. 218; June, 1987, review of *There's a Crocodile under My Bed,* p. 196.

Horn Book, July, 1987, Mary M. Burns, review of *Where's My Monkey?,* p. 456.

Kirkus Reviews, March 15, 2002, review of *There's Always Room for One More,* p. 426; April 15, 2004, review of *Hammer Soup,* p. 400; January 1, 2009, review of *Ophelia.*

Publishers Weekly, April 13, 1998, review of *There's a Hole in My Bucket,* p. 73; February 25, 2008, review of *Like People,* p. 77.

School Library Journal, August, 1981, Patricia Dooley, review of *There's a Crocodile under My Bed,* p. 60; July, 1998, Carol Ann Wilson, review of *There's a Hole in My Bucket,* p. 82; May, 2001, Be Astengo, review of *Beaver's Lodge,* p. 134; April, 2002, Susan Weitz, review of *There's Always Room for One More,* p. 122; September, 2004, Genevieve Gallagher, review of *Hammer Soup,* p. 179; October, 2005, Julie Roach, review of *My Hero,* p. 128; December, 2005, Linda M. Kenton, review of *There's a Crocodile under My Bed!,* p. 121; July, 2008, Maryann H. Owen, review of *Like People,* p. 92; March, 2009, Angela J. Reynolds, review of *Ophelia,* p. 127.

ONLINE

Boyds Mills Press Web site, http://www.boydsmillspress. com/ (June 10, 2010), "Dieter Schubert."*

*   *   *

SCHUBERT, Ingrid 1953-

Personal

Born March 29, 1953, in Essen, Germany; daughter of Oswald (a landlord) and Maria (a landlady) Gabrys; married Dieter Schubert (an illustrator), November 5, 1976; children: Hannah, two other daughters. *Education:* Münster Academy of Design, degree, 1976; attended Düsseldorf Academy of Art, 1976-77, University of Münster, 1976-77, and Gerrit Rietveld Academy (Amsterdam, Netherlands), 1977-80.

Addresses

Home—Amsterdam, Netherlands.

Career

Author, illustrator, and educator. Gabrys, Borken, Germany, merchant, 1968-70; worked as a potter in Stadtlohn, Germany, 1970-71; teacher in educational play-group for children, Münster, Germany, 1976-77; teacher at art expression workshop, Amsterdam, Netherlands, beginning 1981.

Writings

SELF-ILLUSTRATED; WITH HUSBAND, DIETER SCHUBERT

Er ligt een krokodil onder mijn bed, Lemniscaat (Rotterdam, Netherlands), 1980, translated as *There's a Crocodile under My Bed,* McGraw-Hill (New York, NY), 1981, reprinted, Front Street/Lemniscaat (Asheville, NC), 2005.

Helemaal verkikkerd, Lemniscaat (Rotterdam, Netherlands), 1981, translated as *The Magic Bubble Trip,* Kane/Miller (New York, NY), 1985.

Kikj mij nou, NOT Verlag, 1982.

Ik kan niet slapen!, Lemniscaat (Rotterdam, Netherlands), 1983.

Platvoetje, Lemniscaat (Rotterdam, Netherlands), 1985, translated by Amy Gelman as *Little Bigfeet,* Carolrhoda (Minneapolis, MN), 1990.

Wie niet sterk is . . . , Lemniscaat (Rotterdam, Netherlands), 1989.

Santa Claus/Father Christmas, Lemniscaat (Rotterdam, Netherlands), 1989.

Die uitvinder, Stichting (Netherlands), 1989.

Woeste Willem, Lemniscaat (Rotterdam, Netherlands), 1993, translated as *Wild Will,* Carolrhoda (Minneapolis, MN), 1994.

Van mug tot oliphant, Lemniscaat (Rotterdam, Netherlands), 1995, translated and adapted by Leigh Sauerwein as *Amazing Animals,* Front Street (Asheville, NC), 1995.

Abracadabra, Lemniscaat (Rotterdam, Netherlands), 1997, Front Street (Asheville, NC), 1997.

(Reteller, with Dieter Schubert) *Een gat in mijn emmer,* Lemniscaat (Rotterdam, Netherlands), 1998, translated as *There's a Hole in My Bucket,* Front Street (Arden, NC), 1998.

Dat komt er nou van . . . , Lemniscaat (Rotterdam, Netherlands), 1999, translated as *Bear's Eggs,* Front Street (Asheville, NC), 1999.

Samen kunnen we alles, Lemniscaat (Rotterdam, Netherlands), 2000, translated as *Beaver's Lodge,* Front Street/Lemniscaat (Asheville, NC), 2001.

Er kan nog meer bij, Lemniscaat (Rotterdam, Netherlands), 2001, translated as *There's Always Room for One More,* Front Street/Lemniscaat (Asheville, NC), 2002.

Van kop tot start, Lemniscaat (Rotterdam, Netherlands), 2002.

Het grote boek van Beer en Egel, Lemniscaat (Rotterdam, Netherlands), 2003.

Gekke buren, Lemniscaat (Rotterdam, Netherlands), 2003, translated as *Hammer Soup,* Front Street/Lemniscaat (Asheville, NC), 2004.

Mijn held, Lemniscaat (Rotterdam, Netherlands), 2004, translated as *My Hero,* Front Street/Lemniscaat (Asheville, NC), 2004.

Het kleine boek van Beer en Egel, Lemniscaat (Rotterdam, Netherlands), 2005.

Platvoetje & Co., Lemniscaat (Rotterdam, Netherlands), 2005.

Doeboek: knutselen, puzzelen, tekenen, Lemniscaat (Rotterdam, Netherlands), 2005.

Krokodil is jarig, Lemniscaat (Rotterdam, Netherlands), 2005.

Net mensen, Lemniscaat (Rotterdam, Netherlands), 2006, translated as *Like People,* Front Street/Lemniscaat (Honesdale, PA), 2008.

Engel, Lemniscaat (Rotterdam, Netherlands), 2007.

Ophelia, Lemniscaat (Rotterdam, Netherlands), 2008, Lemniscaat (Honesdale, PA), 2009.

Olifantensoep, Lemniscaat (Rotterdam, Netherlands), 2008, translated as *Elephant Soup,* Lemniscaat (Honesdale, PA), 2010.

Author's works have been published in translation.

TELEPLAYS; WITH DIETER SCHUBERT

Look at Me, Dutch School Television, 1982.

Who's Coming to My Little House?, Dutch School Television, 1982.

Father Christmas/Santa Claus, Dutch School Television, 1989.

Sidelights

Dutch author and illustrator Ingrid Schubert once told *SATA:* "In 1978, my teacher at Gerrit Rietveld Academy inspired and encouraged me to create children's books. My first commission was for illustrating a children's book by Roald Dahl. From that moment, my interest in children's literature grew. My husband, Dieter Schubert, also an illustrator, and I started to write and illustrate our own stories. In 1979, we contacted the publisher Lemniscaat, and they liked our first idea for a book. *There's a Crocodile under My Bed* was later translated into eleven languages and published in fourteen countries. We still enjoy working together making books for children."

For more information on Schubert, please see the entry on Dieter Schubert elsewhere in this volume.

Biographical and Critical Sources

PERIODICALS

Booklist, May 15, 1998, Stephanie Zvirin, review of *There's a Hole in My Bucket,* p. 1628; October 1, 1999, John Peters and Gilbert Taylor, review of *Bear's Eggs,* p. 363; July, 2001, Hazel Rochman, review of *Beaver's Lodge,* p. 2020; March 15, 2009, Kay Weisman, review of *Ophelia,* p. 66.

Books for Keeps, March, 1988, Jill Bennett, review of *Little Big Feet,* p. 16.

Bulletin of the Center for Children's Books, July-August, 1981, Betsy Hearne, review of *Where's My Monkey?,* p. 218; June, 1987, review of *There's a Crocodile under My Bed,* p. 196.

Horn Book, July, 1987, Mary M. Burns, review of *Where's My Monkey?,* p. 456.

Kirkus Reviews, March 15, 2002, review of *There's Always Room for One More,* p. 426; April 15, 2004, review of *Hammer Soup,* p. 400; January 1, 2009, review of *Ophelia.*

Ingrid Schubert joins her husband, Dieter Schubert, to create original picture books such as **There's a Hole in My Bucket.** (Front Street Books, 1998. Copyright © 1998 by Lemniscaat b.v. Rotterdam. Reproduced by permission.)

Publishers Weekly, April 13, 1998, review of *There's a Hole in My Bucket,* p. 73; February 25, 2008, review of *Like People,* p. 77.

School Library Journal, August, 1981, Patricia Dooley, review of *There's a Crocodile under My Bed,* p. 60; July, 1998, Carol Ann Wilson, review of *There's a Hole in My Bucket,* p. 82; May, 2001, Be Astengo, review of *Beaver's Lodge,* p. 134; April, 2002, Susan Weitz, review of *There's Always Room for One More,* p. 122; September, 2004, Genevieve Gallagher, review of *Hammer Soup,* p. 179; October, 2005, Julie Roach, review of *My Hero,* p. 128; December, 2005, Linda M. Kenton, review of *There's a Crocodile Under My Bed!,* p. 121; July, 2008, Maryann H. Owen, review of *Like People,* p. 92; March, 2009, Angela J. Reynolds, review of *Ophelia,* p. 127.

ONLINE

Boyds Mills Press Web site, http://www.boydsmillspress.com/ (June 10, 2010), "Ingrid Schubert."*

* * *

SIOMADES, Lorianne

Personal

Born in Harwinton, CT; children: one son, one daughter. *Education:* B.F.A. (graphic communications). *Hobbies and other interests:* Welding, mural painting.

Addresses

Home—CO. *E-mail*—lsiomades@comcast.net.

Career

Author, illustrator, and artist. Freelance designer; former creative director of an advertising agency. Designer of children's furniture. Presenter at schools. *Exhibitions:* Work exhibited in galleries.

Writings

SELF-ILLUSTRATED

A Place to Bloom, Boyds Mills Press (Honesdale, PA), 1997.

(Editor) *Look What You Can Make with Boxes,* photographs by Hank Schneider, Boyds Mills Press (Honesdale, PA), 1998.

My Box of Color, Boyds Mills Press (Honesdale, PA), 1998.

Kangaroo and Cricket, Boyds Mills Press (Honesdale, PA), 1999.

(Reteller) *The Itsy Bitsy Spider,* Boyds Mills Press (Honesdale, PA), 1999, board-book edition, 2001.

Lorianne Siomades (Reproduced by permission.)

(Reteller) *Three Little Kittens,* Boyds Mills Press (Honesdale, PA), 2000.

Cuckoo Can't Find You, Boyds Mills Press (Honesdale, PA), 2002.

Katy Did It!, Boyds Mills Press (Honesdale, PA), 2009.

ILLUSTRATOR

Kersten Hamilton, *This Is the Ocean,* Boyds Mills Press (Honesdale, PA), 2001.

Ann Purmell, *Where Wild Babies Sleep,* Boyds Mills Press (Honesdale, PA), 2003.

Sidelights

A collage artist whose brightly colored graphic images have been compared to those of well-known illustrator Eric Carle, Lorianne Siomades pairs her art with simple rhyming texts to create picture books designed to captivate toddlers. Beginning with *A Place to Bloom,* Siomades has adapted well-known stories such as *The Itsy Bitsy Spider* and *Three Little Kittens* in addition to creating original tales. In addition to her own books, she has also contributed her colorful collages to works by Kersten Hamilton and Ann Purmell. Praising the "handsome painted-paper collage scenes" the artist contributes to Purmell's *Where Wild Babies Sleep,* a *Kirkus Reviews* writer noted that Siomades' work is "more so-

phisticated" than that usually found in children's books. In *School Library Journal* Julie Roach noted that the colorful collages "appear to cast shadows, giving [them] a three-dimensional effect" that will encourage close observation.

Siomades gained a love of art and design while growing up in northwestern Connecticut, and she earned her college degree in graphic communications. A career in the advertising field followed, where she worked as a creative director for several years, but eventually Siomades left to focus on graphic design and sculpture. Her first book for children, *A Place to Bloom,* was published in 1997, and was followed by *My Box of Color* and *Kangaroo and Cricket.* A book of unusual animal comparisons, *Kangaroo and Cricket* features cut-paper collage overpainted with gouache and water color. Siomades gives her story's animal characters a "cartoonish look" by creating "simplified faces with round googly eyes," according to a *Publishers Weekly* critic.

Siomades revisits traditional rhymes in *The Itsy Bitsy Spider* and *Three Little Kittens,* both of which showcase her colorful mixed-media artwork. In the first story, a determined spider, outfitted with an umbrella and a flashlight, attempts the daunting climb up the waterspout. When the fateful downpour occurs, the spider is rescued by a butterfly and then sets out again, undaunted and better outfitted. In *Three Little Kittens* Siomades uses bright hues against a white background to convey the plight of the blue, pink, and orange kittens, adding a twist to the tale that involves missing pies and some clever, mitten-stealing mice. *The Itsy Bitsy Spider,* with its "color-splashed" images, was recommended by *Booklist* critic Julie Corsaro as "just right for toddler story times," while Sue Sherif noted in *School Library Journal* that *Three Little Kittens* "will rate high on the kid-appeal scale." In *Booklist,* Connie Fletcher dubbed *Three Little Kittens* an "effervescent" version of the

Siomades pairs her amusing art with an original story in the toddler friendly **Katy Did It!** (Boyds Mills Press, 2009. Illustration copyright © 2009 by Lorianne Siomades. All rights reserved. Reproduced by permission.)

well-known nursery song, adding that the artist "is adept at engaging very young children with the brightness of her illustrations."

Described by a *Kirkus Reviews* writer as a "splendid hidden-picture odyssey," *Cuckoo Can't Find You* treats young readers to a day with Cuckoo and other animal friends, as the group attempts to locate missing objects. Using texture, bold color, and complex designs, Siomades conceals the missing object for children to find in locations ranging from obvious to more challenging. Recommending the book to younger children, the *Kirkus Reviews* writer praised the artist's use of "luxurious" textures in her "cheerful" mixed-media art, dubbing *Cuckoo Can't Find You* "quite wonderful."

Another original tale, Siomades' *Katy Did It!,* finds an active little katydid happily hopping through her day, with her little brother Lou in tow. Although Katy ends up disrupting the little lives of a bee, a beetle, several aphids, and a spider, she eventually sets things to rights in a "bright, bouncy story [that] will be a favorite with youngsters," according to *School Library Journal* critic Mary Jean Smith. In *Kirkus Reviews* a writer noted Siomades' onomatopoeic text and remarked that "the repetitive text energizes this small tale" of insect adventure.

Siomades' illustration projects include the picture book **This Is the Ocean,** *featuring a text by Kersten Hamilton.* (Illustration copyright © 2001 by Lorianne Siomades. Reproduced by permission of Boyds Mills Press.)

Biographical and Critical Sources

PERIODICALS

Booklist, March 1, 1999, Julie Corsaro, review of *The Itsy Bitsy Spider,* p. 1223; February 15, 2000, Connie Fletcher, review of *Three Little Kittens,* p. 1122; April 15, 2001, Helen Rosenberg, review of *This Is the Ocean,* p. 1562.

Kirkus Reviews, March 15, 2002, review of *Cuckoo Can't Find You,* p. 427; September 1, 2003, review of *Where Wild Babies Sleep,* p. 1129; January 1, 2009, review of *Katy Did It!*

Publishers Weekly, August 16, 1999, review of *Kangaroo and Cricket,* p. 82.

School Library Journal, April, 2000, Sue Sherif, review of *Three Little Kittens* p. 114; June, 2001, Diane Olivo-Posner, review of *This Is the Ocean,* p. 136; June, 2002, Melinda Piehler, review of *Cuckoo Can't Find You,* p. 110; January, 2004, Julie Roach, review of *Where Wild Babies Sleep,* p. 104; March, 2009, Mary Jean Smith, review of *Katy Did It!,* p. 128.

ONLINE

Lorianne Siomades Home Page, http://www.loriannesiomades.com (June 15, 2010).

*   *   *

STONE, Tanya Lee 1965-
(Lee Jacobs)

Personal

Born 1965; married; children: two. *Education:* Oberlin College, B.A. (English); Southern Connecticut State University, M.A. (science education). *Hobbies and other interests:* Reading, writing, sushi, travel, singing, musical theater, playing piano, dancing.

Addresses

Home—VT. *Agent*—Rosemary Stimola, Stimola Literary Studio, 308 Chase Ct., Edgewater, NJ 07020.

Career

Author. Worked for eleven years as an editor for Holt, Rinehart & Winston, Macmillan, Grolier, and Blackbirch Press, New York, NY. Kindling Words (author's retreat), co-director; presenter at conferences.

Member

Society of Children's Book Writers and Illustrators, Authors Guild, National Council against Censorship, Assembly on Literature for Adolescents, PEN American Center, Authors Supporting Intellectual Freedom (AS IF!).

Tanya Lee Stone (Courtesy of Tanya Lee Stone.)

Awards, Honors

Sydney Taylor Award Notable Book designation, Association of Jewish Libraries, 2003, for *Ilan Ramon, Israel's First Astronaut;* Quick Picks for Reluctant Readers selection, American Library Association (ALA), International Reading Association Young Adult Choice designation, Texas Tayshas State Award listee, Kentucky Bluegrass Master Award listee, and Books for the Teen Age selection, New York Public Library, all 2006, all for *A Bad Boy Can Be Good for a Girl;* ALA Notable Book designation, CBC Notable Social Studies Book designation, Amelia Bloomer Award, and Comstock Award Honor Book designation (MN), all 2009, all for *Elizabeth Leads the Way;* Robert F. Sibert Medal, Orbis Pictus Honor Book designation, Flora Stieglitz Straus Award, Bank Street College of Education,, YALSA Excellence in Nonfiction finalist, ALA Notable Book designation, Jane Addams Award Honor Book designation, and *Boston Globe/Horn Book* Honor Book designation, all 2010, all for *Almost Astronauts.*

Writings

FICTION

A Bad Boy Can Be Good for a Girl (young-adult novel), Wendy Lamb (New York, NY), 2006.

Also author of a play based on _A Bad Boy Can Be Good for a Girl_. Contributor to periodicals, including _Voice of Youth Advocates, School Library Journal,_ and _New York Times._

PICTURE BOOKS

D Is for Dreidel: A Hanukkah Alphabet Book, illustrated by Dawn Apperley, Price Stern Sloan (New York, NY), 2002.

P Is for Passover: A Holiday Alphabet Book, illustrated by Margeaux Lucas, Price Stern Sloan (New York, NY), 2003.

M Is for Mistletoe: A Christmas Alphabet Book, illustrated by Claudine Gevry, Price Stern Sloan (New York, NY), 2003.

B Is for Bunny: A Springtime Alphabet Book, illustrated by Sue Ramá, Price Stern Sloan (New York, NY), 2006.

Elizabeth Leads the Way: Elizabeth Cady Stanton and the Right to Vote, illustrated by Rebecca Gibbon, Henry Holt (New York, NY), 2008.

Sandy's Circus: A Story about Alexander Calder, illustrated by Boris Kulikov, Viking (New York, NY), 2008.

T Is for Turkey: A True Thanksgiving Story, illustrated by Gerald Kelley, Price Stern Sloan (New York, NY), 2009.

H Is for Haunted House: A Halloween Alphabet Book, illustrated by Scott Burroughs, Price Stern Sloan (New York, NY), 2010.

A Is for America: A Patriotic Alphabet Book, illustrated by Gerald Kelley, Price Stern Sloan (New York, NY), 2010.

Who Says Women Can't Be Doctors?!: The Story of Elizabeth Blackwell, illustrated by Marjorie Priceman, Henry Holt (New York, NY), 2010.

NONFICTION

Medical Causes, Twenty-first Century Books (New York, NY), 1997.

Diana: Princess of the People, Millbrook Press (Brookfield, CT), 1999.

Rosie O'Donnell: America's Favorite Grown-up Kid, Millbrook Press (Brookfield, CT), 2000.

(With Edward Ricciuti and Jenny Tesar) _America's Top 100,_ Blackbirch Press (Woodbridge, CT), 2000.

Laura Welch Bush: First Lady, Millbrook Press (Brookfield, CT), 2001.

Oprah Winfrey: Success with an Open Heart, Millbrook Press (Brookfield, CT), 2001.

Ilan Ramon: Israel's First Astronaut, Millbrook Press (Brookfield, CT), 2003.

Abraham Lincoln, DK Publishing (New York, NY), 2005.

Amelia Earhart, DK Publishing (New York, NY), 2007.

Up Close: Ella Fitzgerald, Viking (New York, NY), 2008.

Almost Astronauts: Thirteen Women Who Dared to Dream, Candlewick Press (Somerville, MA), 2009.

Laura Ingalls Wilder, DK Publishing (New York, NY), 2009.

Courage Has No Color: The First African-American Paratroopers in WWII, Candlewick Press (Somerville, MA), 2011.

SERIES NONFICTION: "AMERICA'S TOP TEN"

America's Top Ten National Monuments, Blackbirch Press (Woodbridge, CT), 1998.

America's Top Ten Construction Wonders, Blackbirch Press (Woodbridge, CT), 1998.

SERIES NONFICTION: "MADE IN THE USA"

Teddy Bears: From Start to Finish, photographs by Gale Zucker, Blackbirch Press (Woodbridge, CT), 2000.

Snowboards: From Start to Finish, photographs by Gale Zucker, Blackbirch Press (Woodbridge, CT), 2000.

Toothpaste: From Start to Finish, photographs by Jill Brady, Blackbirch Press (Woodbridge, CT), 2001.

SERIES NONFICTION: "LIVING IN A WORLD OF. . ."

Living in a World of Blue: Where Survival Means Blending In, Blackbirch Press (Woodbridge, CT), 2001.

Living in a World of Brown: Where Survival Means Blending In, Blackbirch Press (Woodbridge, CT), 2001.

Living in a World of Green: Where Survival Means Blending In, Blackbirch Press (Woodbridge, CT), 2001.

Living in a World of White: Where Survival Means Blending In, Blackbirch Press (Woodbridge, CT), 2001.

SERIES NONFICTION: "MAKING OF AMERICA"

The Progressive Era and World War I, Raintree Steck-Vaughn (Austin, TX), 2001.

The Great Depression and World War II, Raintree Steck-Vaughn (Austin, TX), 2001.

SERIES NONFICTION: "BLASTOFF!"

Mars, Benchmark Books (New York, NY), 2002.

Saturn, Benchmark Books (New York, NY), 2003.

Venus, Benchmark Books (New York, NY), 2003.

Mercury, Benchmark Books (New York, NY), 2003.

SERIES NONFICTION: "WILD WILD WORLD"

Ants, Blackbirch Press (Detroit, MI), 2003.

Butterflies, Blackbirch Press (Detroit, MI), 2003.

Crocodilians, Blackbirch Press (Detroit, MI), 2003.

Dragonflies, Blackbirch Press (Detroit, MI), 2003.

Fireflies, Blackbirch Press (Detroit, MI), 2003.

Flamingoes, Blackbirch Press (Detroit, MI), 2003.

Grasshoppers, Blackbirch Press (Detroit, MI), 2003.

Hamsters, Blackbirch Press (Detroit, MI), 2003.

Kangaroos, Blackbirch Press (Detroit, MI), 2003.

Ladybugs, Blackbirch Press (Detroit, MI), 2003.

Lions, Blackbirch Press (Detroit, MI), 2003.

Lizards, Blackbirch Press (Detroit, MI), 2003.
Mantises, Blackbirch Press (Detroit, MI), 2003.
Mosquitoes, Blackbirch Press (Detroit, MI), 2003.
Sea Lions, Blackbirch Press (Detroit, MI), 2003.
Spiders, Blackbirch Press (Detroit, MI), 2003.
Turtles, Blackbirch Press (Detroit, MI), 2003.

SERIES NONFICTION: "WILD AMERICA"

Earthworm, Blackbirch Press (Detroit, MI), 2003.
Mouse, Blackbirch Press (Detroit, MI), 2003.

Also author of *Beaver, Crow, Rabbit, Deer, Raccoon, Turtle, Opossum, Skunk, Squirrel,* and *Toad.*

SERIES NONFICTION: "REGIONAL WILD AMERICA"

Unique Animals of the Pacific Coast, Blackbirch Press (Detroit, MI), 2005.
Unique Animals of the Northeast, Blackbirch Press (Detroit, MI), 2005.
Unique Animals of the Mountains and Prairies, Blackbirch Press (Detroit, MI), 2005.
Unique Animals of the Midwest, Blackbirch Press (Detroit, MI), 2005.
Unique Animals of the Islands, Blackbirch Press (Detroit, MI), 2005.
Unique Animals of the South, Blackbirch Press (Detroit, MI), 2005.
Unique Animals of Alaska, Blackbirch Press (Detroit, MI), 2005.
Unique Animals of the Southeast, Blackbirch Press (Detroit, MI), 2005.
Unique Animals of the Southwest, Blackbirch Press (Detroit, MI), 2005.
Unique Animals of Hawai'i, Blackbirch Press (Detroit, MI), 2005.

Sidelights

Tanya Lee Stone is the author of dozens of nonfiction books for young readers, including *Almost Astronauts: Thirteen Women Who Dared to Dream, Up Close: Ella Fitzgerald,* and *Amelia Earhart.* "I am passionate about nonfiction," Stone told *Suite 101* online interviewer Sue Reichard. "I just love coming across a little-known piece of history or an interesting topic in science and finding a way to get kids just as excited about it as I am." In addition to her nonfiction titles, Stone has also written illustrated biographies such as *Elizabeth Leads the Way: Elizabeth Cady Stanton and the Right to Vote* as well as alphabet books, and the young-adult novel *A Bad Boy Can Be Good for a Girl.*

Stone, whose father was also an author, developed an early interest in telling tales. "I've been writing stories since I was seven years old," she noted on the Random House Web site. "Some of them were even published—in the school newspaper." After graduating from Oberlin College with a degree in English, Stone moved

to New York City, where she spent eleven years in the publishing industry. "My editorial background has definitely been an advantage in terms of craft," she explained to Cynthia Leitich Smith on the *Cynsations* Web site. "I edited hundreds and hundreds of books before I wrote my first one for publication."

Since becoming an author, Stone has published dozens of titles about the natural world, and in her books for the "Living in a World of" series she examines animal camouflage. Ellen Heath, writing in *School Library Journal,* praised the "clever organization and . . . attractive, readable format" of the series titles. Stone's contributions to the "Regional Wild America" series, which focuses on animals from a variety of geographical regions, include *Unique Animals of the Mountains and Prairies* and *Unique Animals of Alaska.* Her "writing is clear," stated Kathy Piehl in a review of the series for *School Library Journal,* "and the well-designed pages feature photographs that reinforce the written information."

Stone has also written a number of well-received biographies, including *Oprah Winfrey: Success with an Open Heart*—dubbed "an upbeat title" by *Booklist* critic Gillian Engberg—and *Ilan Ramon: Israel's First Astronaut,* which *School Library Journal* contributor Jeffrey A. French deemed "an appealing and informative book." *Sandy's Circus: A Story about Alexander Calder* focuses on the twentieth-century French artist whose wire and metal sculptures include the famous miniature moveable circus named after him. Enhanced by illustra-

The life of modernist French sculptor Alexander Calder is the focus of Stone's picture book **Sandy's Circus,** *featuring artwork by Boris Kulikov.* (Illustration copyright © 2008 by Boris Kulikov. Reproduced by permission of Viking, a division of Penguin Putnam Books for Young Readers.)

tions by Boris Kulikov, *Sandy's Circus* "will ignite curiosity" in an artist whose creative process "seems as joyful and free-form as children's play," concluded Engberg.

Described by *Kliatt* contributor Claire Rosser as "one of the most honest treatments of teenage sexuality to be found in YA fiction," *A Bad Boy Can Be Good for a Girl* concerns three high-school students—Josie, Nicolette, and Aviva—who each fall for and are betrayed by the same manipulative senior, a young man who wants them only for sex. "I absolutely love reading and writing within this genre," the author remarked to Teri S. Lesesne in *Teacher Librarian*. "The urgency, passion, drama, and importance, all wrapped up in transitioning from being a kid to an adult, is the stuff of life. I love immersing myself in it."

"Stone's novel in verse, more poetic prose than poetry, packs a steamy, emotional wallop," in the opinion of *Booklist* contributor Cindy Dobrez, and *School Library Journal* reviewer Susan Oliver similarly noted of *A Bad Boy Can Be Good for a Girl* that "the free verse gives the stories a breathless, natural flow and changes tone with each narrator." In an interview with Brent Hartinger for the *AS IF!* Web site, Stone remarked that her focus in writing the novel was "in exploring the emotional ups and downs and realizations that go along with heading into that new and uncertain territory of intimate relationships." Her message to readers: "'Hey, this happens to all of us at one point or another—and pay attention, because this is how it happens, so if you can learn from these fictional girls' experiences, I hope it can help you avoid some pain and make you smarter about who you are and who you want to be.'"

Since writing her young-adult novel, Stone has increasingly focused on strong female characters and seeks to empower girls in books such as *Amelia Earhart, Up Close: Ella Fitzgerald,* and *Elizabeth Leads the Way.* Part of the "Up Close" series, Stone's biography of Fitzgerald details the personal and professional life of a shy, overweight girl with an amazing singing talent who became one of the greatest jazz singers ever. Praising the biography as "clearly written and well organized," John Peters added in *Booklist* that Stone "gives readers a great appreciation of a rare talent" in her book. In *Kirkus Reviews* a contributor cited the author's use of "extensive resources to set the record straight" regarding Fitzgerald's life, and went on to recommend *Up Close: Ella Fitzgerald* as "a remarkable look at race relations" in the United States over the course of the twentieth century.

Women who bravely take to the skies are Stone's focus in both *Amelia Earhart,* the biography of the first woman pilot to fly solo over the Atlantic Ocean, and her award-winning *Almost Astronauts: Thirteen Women Who Dared to Dream.* In *Almost Astronauts* readers meet thirteen women pilots who, in 1961 entered the astronaut training program and paved the way for fe-

Stone's nonfiction works include her biography of a noted American aviatrix, **Amelia Earhart.** (DK Publishing, 2007. Photograph copyright © by Corbis/Bettman. Reprinted by permission of DK Publishing, a member of Penguin Group (USA), Inc.)

male astronauts such as Sally Ride. Known as the Mercury 13, these well-qualified women entered the space program with high test scores and pilot experience, but were not allowed to train as astronauts due to political and social pressures. Stone parallels their efforts with the rise of the Women's Liberation Movement of the mid-twentieth century and the growth of interest in space exploration. The "chatty, immediate style" of Stone's narrative pairs with contemporary photographs to "make for a fast read," according to *Booklist* critic Hazel Rochman. A *Publishers Weekly* contributor praised the "gripping narrative" in Stone's story of perseverance, and a *Kirkus Reviews* writer concluded that the "passionately written account" in *Almost Astronauts* "introduces readers to a select group of courageous, independent women."

In *Elizabeth Leads the Way* Stone allows readers to return to the days before women could vote and describes the battle waged by American suffragist Elizabeth Cady Stanton. A participant of the Seneca Falls, New York, conference on women's rights that led to passage of the nineteenth amendment in August of 1920, Stanton dedi-

cated her life to advancing women's rights. Stone details the woman's story from childhood through old age in an easy-to-read text that *Booklist* critic Ilene Cooper deemed "a must for library shelves." Praising the book's "animated" tone, a *Publishers Weekly* critic added that *Elizabeth Leads the Way* is "energized" by illustrator Rebecca Gibbon's "vibrant folk-art" gouache-and-colored-pencil images. Stone's "energetic, lucid prose . . . focuses on Elizabeth's ideas and feelings rather than on specific events," noted Steven Engelfried in his *School Library Journal* review of *Elizabeth Leads the Way,* and her "well-conceived introduction is just right for a young audience."

Asked if she had any counsel for aspiring authors, Stone told Smith: "My advice is to make your nonfiction subject come to life for yourself as much as possible; make interesting connections, highlight unusual things kids may not know about a topic, and always keep in mind what is important to you, the writer, about your topic while you're writing. If you're passionate about the subject, I think that comes through in the writing." In thinking about what drives a writer's best work, whether it is nonfiction or fiction, Stone added: "It stems from an authentic desire to express both how we see the world as it is, and how we hope it can be."

Biographical and Critical Sources

PERIODICALS

Booklist, December 15, 2000, Ilene Cooper, review of *Rosie O'Donnell: America's Favorite Grown-up Kid,* p. 818; June 1, 2001, Gillian Engberg, review of *Oprah Winfrey: Success with an Open Heart,* p. 1876; September 15, 2001, Ilene Cooper, review of *Laura Welch Bush: First Lady,* p. 218; April 1, 2003, Carolyn Phelan, review of *Mercury,* p. 1395; December 1, 2003, Kay Weisman, review of *Ilan Ramon: Israel's First Astronaut,* p. 680; January 1, 2006, Cindy Dobrez, review of *A Bad Boy Can Be Good for a Girl,* p. 86; April 15, 2008, Ilene Cooper, review of *Elizabeth Leads the Way: Elizabeth Cady Stanton and the Right to Vote,* p. 46; June 1, 2008, Gillian Engberg, review of *Sandy's Circus: A Story about Alexander Calder,* p. 106; February 15, 2009, Hazel Rochman, review of *Almost Astronauts: Thirteen Women Who Dared to Dream,* p. 77.

Bulletin of the Center for Children's Books, April, 2006, Karen Coats, review of *A Bad Boy Can Be Good for a Girl,* p. 375.

Horn Book, January-February, 2006, Christine M. Hepperman, review of *A Bad Boy Can Be Good for a Girl,* p. 90; May-June, 2008, Betty Carter, review of *Elizabeth Leads the Way,* p. 342; September-October, 2008, Joanna Rudge Long, review of *Sandy's Circus,* p. 615; March-April, 2009, Danielle J. Ford, review of *Almost Astronauts,* p. 214.

Kirkus Reviews, January 1, 2006, review of *A Bad Boy Can Be Good for a Girl,* p. 45; April 15, 2008, review of *Elizabeth Leads the Way;* January 1, 2008, review of *Up Close: Ella Fitzgerald;* August 15, 2008, review of *Sandy's Circus;* January 1, 2009, review of *Almost Astronauts.*

Kliatt, January, 2006, Claire Rosser, review of *A Bad Boy Can Be Good for a Girl,* p. 12.

New York Times Book Review, July 12, 2009, review of *Almost Astronauts,* p. 13.

Publishers Weekly, February 24, 2003, review of *P Is for Passover,* p. 29; May 12, 2008, review of *Elizabeth Leads the Way,* p. 53; May 4, 2009, review of *Almost Astronauts,* p. 49; September 15, 2008, review of *Sandy's Circus,* p. 67; September 21, 2009, review of *T Is for Turkey: A Thanksgiving Story,* p. 56.

School Library Journal, January, 1998, Kathleen Isaacs, review of *Medical Causes,* p. 120, and Stephani Hutchinson, review of *America's Top-Ten National Monuments,* p. 132; February, 1998, Elden Younce, review of *America's Top-Ten Construction Wonders,* p. 122; August, 1999, Lisa Gangemi Kropp, review of *Diana: Princess of the People,* p. 180; December, 2000, Steve Clancy, review of *Snowboards: From Start to Finish,* p. 166; June, 2001, Lana Miles, review of *The Progressive Era and World War I,* p. 160; September, 2001, Debbie Feulner, review of *Laura Welch Bush,* p. 222; January, 2002, Ellen Heath, reviews of *Living in a World of Green: Where Survival Means Blending In* and *Living in a World of White: Where Survival Means Blending In,* p. 126; October, 2002, Mara Alpert, review of *D Is for Dreidel: A Hanukkah Alphabet Book,* p. 64; October, 2003, Susan Patron, review of *M Is for Mistletoe: A Christmas Alphabet Book,* p. 68; January, 2004, Jeffrey A. French, review of *Ilan Roman,* p. 160; March, 2005, Kathy Piehl, review of "Regional Wild America" series, p. 203; January, 2006, Susan Oliver, review of *A Bad Boy Can Be Good for a Girl,* p. 144; February, 2008, Carol Jones, review of *Ella Fitzgerald,* p. 139; May, 2008, Steven Engelfried, review of *Elizabeth Leads the Way,* p. 118; September, 2008, Barbara Elleman, review of *Sandy's Circus,* p. 169; March, 2009, John Peters, review of *Almost Astronauts,* p. 169.

Science Books & Films, May, 2003, reviews of *Mars,* p. 23, and *Venus,* p. 116; November-December, 2005, Robert Goode Patterson, review of "Regional Wild America" series, p. 271.

Teacher Librarian, February, 2006, Teri S. Lesesne, interview with Stone, p. 56.

Voice of Youth Advocates, April, 2006, Michele Winship, review of *A Bad Boy Can Be Good for a Girl,* p. 52.

ONLINE

Assembly on Literature for Adolescents Web site, http://ala-ya.org/ (August 27, 2007), *New Voices* interview with Stone.

Authors Supporting Intellectual Freedom! (AS IF!) Web site, http://asifnews.blogspot.com/ (June 7, 2007), Brent Hartinger, interview with Stone.

Cynsations Web site, http://cynthialeitichsmith.blogspot.com/ (February 14, 2006), Cynthia Leitich Smith, interview with Stone.

Random House Web site, http://www.randomhouse.com/ (July 20, 2007), "Tanya Lee Stone."

Suite101.com, http://www.suite101.com/ (May 1, 2004), Sue Reichard, "Tanya Lee Stone: Superb Children's Author."

Tanya Lee Stone Home Page, http://www.tanyastone.com (June 1, 2010).

Tanya Lee Stone Web log, http://tanyaleestone.livejournal. com (June 1, 2010).

* * *

STORMS, Patricia 1963-

Personal

Born March 28, 1963, in Winnipeg, Manitoba, Canada; married; husband's name Guy.

Addresses

Home—Toronto, Ontario, Canada. *E-mail*—gpstorms@ rogers.com.

Career

Author, illustrator, and editorial cartoonist. Worked in libraries for ten years; former desktop publisher and graphic designer; freelance artist and cartoonist, beginning c. 2002. Presenter and performer at schools, libraries, and festivals.

Member

Canadian Society of Children's Authors, Illustrators, and Performers, Society of Children's Book Writers and Illustrators, Canadian Children's Book Centre, National Cartoonists Society, Association of Canadian Editorial Cartoonists, Writer's Union of Canada.

Awards, Honors

Best Book for Kids and Teens designation, Canadian Children's Book Centre, 2008, for *13 Ghosts of Halloween* by Robin Muller; Cartoon of the Year Award, Ontario Community Newspapers Association Better Newspaper Awards, 2008.

Writings

SELF-ILLUSTRATED

You're My Guy Because . . . (cartoons), Red Rock Press (New York, NY), 2008.
The Pirate and the Penguin, Owlkids (Berkeley, CA), 2009.

LLUSTRATOR

Jack Booth, *Fifty Little Penguins,* Harcourt Canada, 2004.

Beth Crichley Charlton, *A Sticky Mess,* Scholastic Canada (Markham, Ontario, Canada), 2005.
R.J. Frampton, *Room 2B,* AEON Institute of Language Education, 2006.
Mary McHugh, *Good Granny/Bad Granny,* Chronicle Books (New York, NY), 2007.
Robin Muller, *13 Ghosts of Halloween,* Scholastic Canada (Toronto, Ontario, Canada), 2007.
Liam O'Donnell, *Democracy,* Capstone Press (Mankato, MN), 2008.
Barbara Todd, *Edward and the Eureka Lucky Wish Company,* Kids Can Press, 2009.
Diana R. Jenkins, *Saints of Note: The Comic Collection,* Pauline Books & Media (Boston, MA), 2009.

Contributor of illustrations to periodicals, including *Chickadee, Chronicle of Higher Education, City Bites, Dogs in Canada, First for Women, Funny Times, National Lampoon, National Post, Saturday Evening Post,* and *Woman's World.*

Author's works have been translated into French and Indonesian.

Sidelights

Canadian illustrator Patricia Storms has always enjoyed drawing funny pictures, so much so that cartooning was her part time job while she worked in libraries, as a

Patricia Storms' illustrations capture the hijinks in Robin Muller's picture book **13 Ghosts of Halloween.** (Kane Miller, 2009. Illustration copyright © 2007 by Patricia Storms. Reproduced by permission.)

desktop publisher, and as a graphic designer. In the early 2000s Storms decided to invest all her time in developing her artistic career, and she has since become an established illustrator and cartoonist. Her work, which has been published in magazines and newspapers in both Canada and the United States, sometimes in the form of editorial cartoons, has also made its way into several picture books by other writers.

Storms has also created an original, self-illustrated picture book, *The Pirate and the Penguin,* which *School Library Journal* contributor Meg Smith dubbed an "offbeat selection" that features "outlandish elements within the zany pages." In her humorous tale, a penguin hoping to escape the frigid weather of the South Pole and find adventure, jumps on a floating piece of ice and soon collides with a pirate ship. The pirate captain expresses envy for the penguin's uneventful life, and when the two switch places each finds what he has been looking for. Noting the appeal of Storms' "lowbrow take on [Mark Twain's novel] *The Prince and the Pauper,*" a *Kirkus Reviews* writer also praised the "wonderfully expressive faces" of the story's cartoon characters, while Gwyneth Evans noted that "Storms' cartooning background is evident in the liveliness she achieves with simple lines and few colours." "Visual humor abounds in this oddball tale," maintained a *Publishers Weekly* contributor in a review of *The Pirate and the Penguin.*

Biographical and Critical Sources

PERIODICALS

Canadian Review of Materials, December 21, 2007, Dave Jenkinson, review of *Good Granny/Bad Granny.*

Kirkus Reviews, August 15, 2009, review of *The Pirate and the Penguin.*

Publishers Weekly, October 12, 2009, review of *The Pirate and the Penguin,* p. 49.

Quill & Quire, June, 2009, Chelsea Donaldson, review of *Edward and the Eureka Lucky Wish Company;* November, 2009, Gwyneth Evans, review of *The Pirate and the Penguin.*

School Library Journal, August, 2009, Martha Simpson, review of *Edward and the Eureka Lucky Wish Company,* p. 86; November, 2009, Meg Smith, review of *The Pirate and the Penguin* p. 90.

ONLINE

Canadian Authors Web site, http://www.canadianauthors.net/ (May 31, 2010), "Patricia Storms."

Patricia Storms Home Page, http://stormsillustration.com (May 31, 2010).

Patricia Storms Web log, http://storms.typepad.com (May 31, 2010).

SUSSMAN, Michael 1953-
(Michael B. Sussman)

Personal

Born 1953; married; children: Oliver. *Education:* Hampshire College, B.A. (music composition and performance), 1980; Hahnemann University, Psy.D. (clinical psychology), 1987. Menninger Foundation, postdoctoral fellow.

Addresses

Home—MA. *E-mail*—crudmuzzler@aol.com.

Career

Psychologist and author. Stoney Brook Counseling Center, Cambridge, MA, staff psychologist, 1990-92; in private practice, Charlestown, MA, 1992-98; Harvard University, Cambridge, clinical instructor in psychology, 1992-97; freelance writer, 2005—.

Writings

FOR CHILDREN

Otto Grows Down, illustrated by Scott Magoon, Sterling Pub. Co. (New York, NY), 2009.

OTHER

(As Michael B. Sussman) *A Curious Calling: Unconscious Motivations for Practicing Psychotherapy,* Jason Aronson (Northvale, NJ), 1992, reprinted, 2007.

(Editor, as Michael B. Sussman) *A Perilous Calling: The Hazards of Psychotherapy Practice,* Wiley (New York, NY), 1995.

Sidelights

Michael Sussman began writing in middle school, where an interest in music focused his efforts on song lyrics and performance. Following this interest, he earned a degree in music before changing direction and undertaking the training needed to become a clinical psychologist. Although Sussman continues to focus on his profession as both a teacher and a writer, the birth of his son Oliver prompted him to channel his writing in yet another area, and the picture book *Otto Grows Down* is the result.

Inspired by a joke created by five-year-old Oliver, *Otto Grows Down* focuses on a little boy who learns that ill-conceived birthday wishes often have unfortunate consequences. When six-year-old Otto blows out the candles on his birthday cake while wishing that his new sister Anna had never been born, time turns around and the boy begins to grow younger at an alarming rate. When Otto watches his parents pack up the baby and leave to return her to the hospital, he is not too alarmed, but soon he begins to un-paint pictures, take baths that

Michael Sussman's humorous time-bending story for **Otto Grows Down** *is brought to life in Scott Magoon's cartoon art.* (Sterling, 2009. Illustration copyright © 2009 by Scott Magoon. Reproduced by permission.)

wash the dirt on rather than off, and grow younger and younger until diapers and baby food loom in his future. Praising *Otto Grows Down*, a *Kirkus Reviews* writer maintained that the "deadpan drollery" of Scott Magoon's illustrations reflect "the quirkiness of Sussman's premise," and in *Booklist* Ilene Cooper agreed that the book's "eye-catching art" captures the fun of the sibling-rivalry saga. In *School Library Journal* contributor Trish Sabini noted the "humor and poignancy" in the mix of story and art, the critic calling *Otto Grows Down* "a refreshing take" on a perennial childhood "rite of passage."

Biographical and Critical Sources

PERIODICALS

Booklist, April 15, 2009, Ilene Cooper, review of *Otto Grows Down,* p. 47.
Kirkus Reviews, February 1, 2009, Michael Sussman, review of *Otto Grows Down.*
School Library Journal, April, 2009, Trish Sabini, review of *Otto Grows Down,* p. 117.

ONLINE

Michael Sussman Home Page, http://www.ottogrowsdown. com (May 31, 2010).

*   *   *

SUSSMAN, Michael B.
See SUSSMAN, Michael

*   *   *

van LIESHOUT, Elle 1963-

Personal

Born July 21, 1963, in Odiliapeel, Netherlands; married Eric van Os (a writer); children: Anna, Lot (son). *Education:* Trained as a teacher.

Addresses

Home—Tilberg, Netherlands. *E-mail*—info@eric vanosenellevanlieshout.nl.

Career

Author of books for children.

Awards, Honors

(With Eric van Os) Kinderboekwinkelprijs, 2008, for *Klapzoen.*

Writings

FOR CHILDREN; WITH HUSBAND, ERIC VAN OS

Een klap voor de grap, Zwijsen, 1992.

Jop is op de juf, Zwijsen, 1994.

Je bent zomaar geen engeltje, Zwijsen, 1995.

Er loopt een liedje door de lucht, Zwijsen, 1995.

O mijn lieve, lieve lien, Zwijsen, 1999.

Vang dat kind even op, Zwijsen, 2000.

Lekker weer, beer!, illustrated by Paula Gerritsen, Kimio, 2001.

Ik was zo'n steentje in jouw schoen, DiVer/Zirkoon, 2001.

Iiieeek, een luis!, illustrated by Paula Gerritsen, Gottmer (Haarlem, Netherlands), 2001.

Wie o wie?, Gottmer (Haarlem, Netherlands), 2001.

Dansen in het maanlich, Gottmer (Haarlem, Netherlands), 2002.

Wee wee wee punt muis punt en el, Maretak, 2002.

De man die in sprookjes geloofde, DiVers/Zirkoon, 2002.

Fijn feestje, illustrated by Paula Gerritsen, Lemniscaat (Rotterdam, Netherlands), 2002, translated as *A Nice Party,* Front Street/Lemniscaat (Asheville, NC), 2002.

Een koning van niks, illustrated by Paula Gerritsen, Lemniscaat (Rotterdam, Netherlands), 2004, translated as *The Nothing King,* Front Street/Lemniscatt (Asheville, NC), 2004.

De wens, illustrated by Paula Gerritsen, Lemniscaat (Rotterdam, Netherlands), 2006, translated as *The Wish,* Front Street/Lemniscaat (Honesdale, PA), 2006.

Het grote prentenboekenliedjesboek, Lemniscaat (Rotterdam, Netherlands), 2006.

Julia en Ot, en een cavia alstublieft, illustrated by Harmen van Straaten, Lemniscaat (Rotterdam, Netherlands), 2006.

Dames en heren: Julia en Ot!, illustrated by Harmen van Straaten, Lemniscaat (Rotterdam, Netherlands), 2006.

Bergen zand met hoedjes op, illustrated by Paula Gerritsen, Zwijsen, 2007.

Mejuffrouw Muis en haar heerlijke huis, illustrated by Marije Tolman, Lemniscaat (Rotterdam, Netherlands), 2007.

Mejuffrouw Muis naar de Costa del Sol, illustrated by Marije Tolman, Lemniscaat (Rotterdam, Netherlands), 2007.

Mejuffrouw Muis in het ziekenhuis, illustrated by Marije Tolman, Lemniscaat (Rotterdam, Netherlands), 2007.

Koe en daarmee Koe, illustrated by Piet Grobler, Lemniscaat (Rotterdam, Netherlands), 2008.

Mejuffrouw Muis doet aan de lijn, illustrated by Marije Tolman, Lemniscaat (Rotterdam, Netherlands), 2008.

Schatje en Scheetje, illustrated by Mies van Hout, Lemniscaat (Rotterdam, Netherlands), 2008, translated as *Lovey and Dovey,* Front Street/Lemniscaat (Honesdale, PA), 2009.

O, o, Octopus!, illustrated by Mies van Hout, Lemniscaat (Rotterdam, Netherlands), 2009.

Mejuffrouw Muis krijgt muisjes, illustrated by Marije Tolman, Lemniscaat (Rotterdam, Netherlands), 2009.

De kleine kerst koning, illustrated by Marjolijn Krijger, Gottmer (Haarlem, Netherlands), 2010.

Also author of beginning readers.

Author's works have been translated into several languages, including French, Italian, Japanese, Korean, and Spanish.

Sidelights

Working in collaboration with her husband, Eric van Os, Elle van Lieshout is popular in her native Netherlands for her many books for young children. Os and van Lieshout were both educated as teachers, and their stories, songs, and poetry reflect their understanding of the likes and needs of young children and beginning readers. Teaming up with illustrators such as Paula Gerritsen, Piet Grobler, and Mies Van Lieshout among others, the couple's gentle stories often feature animal

Elle van Lieshout and Eric van Os join illustrator Paula Gerritsen to create the award-winning picture book **The Wish.** (Front Street/Lemniscaat, 2006. Paula Gerritsen, illustrator. Reproduced by permission.)

characters. English-language readers have been able to enjoy their work in translation in the books *A Nice Party, The Nothing King, The Wish,* and *Lovey and Dovey.*

Van Lieshout was the youngest of eight siblings and was raised on a farm near Odiliapeel, Netherlands. After college, she married fellow teacher van Os, and the authors now make their home in the city of Tilburg, where they write books and raise their two children.

In *A Nice Party* van Lieshout and van Os tell the story of Gus, a bear who is not looking forward to his upcoming birthday because of the noisy but good-hearted relatives who will gather to give him a party. Friend Boris thinks up the perfect gift for Gus—a fishing-trip getaway—and the partygoers celebrate the bear's special day without realizing that the birthday bear is not there. Children will "be charmed by the goofy protagonists" in *A Nice Party,* noted a *Kirkus Reviews* critic, and in *School Library Journal* Melinda Piehler praised Gerritsen's "softly textured illustrations" in a book that "has a certain liberating appeal." Bears also star in *The Nothing King,* in which King Bear abandons his royal home for a cozy apartment and eventually convinces his queen to do likewise. The authors' "delightful" story will likely inspire "a lively [storyhour] discussion of the true necessities for a happy life," predicted Rachel G. Payne in her *School Library Journal* review of *The Nothing King.*

Human characters are the focus of both *The Wish* and *Lovey and Dovey,* two stories by van Lieshout and van Os that capture the joy of simple things. In *The Wish* a woman named Lila lives an isolated existence with her cat, growing her own food on her small homestead near the sea. When winter comes Lila's pantry shelves grow empty, but when she spots a wishing star the modest woman wishes for a modest gift: enough flour to survive until spring. *Lovey and Dovey* finds two lovers are imprisoned in a dungeon for stealing a pair of blue socks. When Lovey states her wish for a glimpse of the outside world, Dovey manages to capture the sun, the moon, and other natural beauties to brighten Lovey's cell. In *Publishers Weekly* a contributor dubbed *Lovey and Dovey* "quirky, playful and altogether inviting," and Carolyn Phelan wrote in *Booklist* that the love-affirming picture book makes "a rewarding choice for reading aloud."

Biographical and Critical Sources

PERIODICALS

Booklist, December 15, 2004, Hazel Rochman, review of *The Nothing King,* p. 747; January 1, 2007, Carolyn Phelan, review of *The Wish,* p. 118.

Kirkus Reviews, April 15, 2003, review of *A Nice Party,* p. 612; November 15, 2004, review of *The Nothing King,* p. 1094; January 1, 2009, review of *Lovey and Dovey.*

Publishers Weekly, January 10, 2005, review of *The Nothing King,* p. 54; January 8, 2007, review of *The Wish,* p. 50; January 19, 2009, review of *Lovey and Dovey,* p. 59.

School Library Journal, August, 2003, Melinda Piehler, review of *A Nice Party,* p. 145; January, 2005, Rachel G. Payne, review of *The Nothing King,* p. 98; March, 2007, Linda L. Walkins, review of *The Wish,* p. 188; April, 2009, Marianne Saccardi, review of *Lovey and Dovey,* p. 118.

ONLINE

Boyds Mills Press Web site, http://www.boydsmillspress.com/ (May 31, 2010), "Eric van Os."

Elle van Lieshout and Eric van Os Home Page, http://www.erikvanosenellevanlieshout.nl (May 31, 2010).*

*   *   *

van OS, Erik 1963-

Personal

Born December 8, 1963, in Berkel-Enshot, Netherlands; married Elle van Lieshout (an author); children: Anna, Lot. *Education:* Trained as a teacher. *Hobbies and other interests:* Music.

Addresses

Home—Tilberg, Netherlands. *E-mail*—info@eric vanosenellevanlieshout.nl.

Career

Author of books for children.

Awards, Honors

(With Elle van Lieshout) Kinderboekwinkelprijs, 2008, for *Klapzoen.*

Writings

FOR CHILDREN; WITH WIFE, ELLE VAN LIESHOUT

Een klap voor de grap, Zwijsen, 1992.

Jop is op de juf, Zwijsen, 1994.

Je bent zomaar geen engeltje, Zwijsen, 1995.

Er loopt een liedje door de lucht, Zwijsen, 1995.

O mijn lieve, lieve lien, Zwijsen, 1999.

Vang dat kind even op, Zwijsen, 2000.

Lekker weer, beer!, illustrated by Paula Gerritsen, Kimio, 2001.

Ik was zo'n steentje in jouw schoen, DiVer/Zirkoon, 2001.

Iiieeek, een luis!, illustrated by Paula Gerritsen, Gottmer (Haarlem, Netherlands), 2001.

Wie o wie?, Gottmer (Haarlem, Netherlands), 2001.

Dansen in het maanlich, Gottmer (Haarlem, Netherlands), 2002.

Wee wee wee punt muis punt en el, Maretak, 2002.

De man die in sprookjes geloofde, DiVers/Zirkoon, 2002.

Fijn feestje, illustrated by Paula Gerritsen, Lemniscaat (Rotterdam, Netherlands), 2002, translated as *A Nice Party,* Front Street/Lemniscaat (Asheville, NC), 2002.

Een koning van niks, illustrated by Paula Gerritsen, Lemniscaat (Rotterdam, Netherlands), 2004, translated as *The Nothing King,* Front Street/Lemniscatt (Asheville, NC), 2004.

De wens, illustrated by Paula Gerritsen, Lemniscaat (Rotterdam, Netherlands), 2006, translated as *The Wish,* Front Street/Lemniscaat (Honesdale, PA), 2006.

Het grote prentenboekenliedjesboek, Lemniscaat (Rotterdam, Netherlands), 2006.

Julia en Ot, en een cavia alstublieft, illustrated by Harmen van Straaten, Lemniscaat (Rotterdam, Netherlands), 2006.

Dames en heren: Julia en Ot!, illustrated by Harmen van Straaten, Lemniscaat (Rotterdam, Netherlands), 2006.

Bergen zand met hoedjes op, illustrated by Paula Gerritsen, Zwijsen, 2007.

Mejuffrouw Muis en haar heerlijke huis, illustrated by Marije Tolman, Lemniscaat (Rotterdam, Netherlands), 2007.

Mejuffrouw Muis naar de Costa del Sol, illustrated by Marije Tolman, Lemniscaat (Rotterdam, Netherlands), 2007.

Mejuffrouw Muis in het ziekenhuis, illustrated by Marije Tolman, Lemniscaat (Rotterdam, Netherlands), 2007.

Koe en daarmee Koe, illustrated by Piet Grobler, Lemniscaat (Rotterdam, Netherlands), 2008.

Mejuffrouw Muis doet aan de lijn, illustrated by Marije Tolman, Lemniscaat (Rotterdam, Netherlands), 2008.

Schatje en Scheetje, illustrated by Mies van Hout, Lemniscaat (Rotterdam, Netherlands), 2008, translated as *Lovey and Dovey,* Front Street/Lemniscaat (Honesdale, PA), 2009.

O, o, Octopus!, illustrated by Mies van Hout, Lemniscaat (Rotterdam, Netherlands), 2009.

Mejuffrouw Muis krijgt muisjes, illustrated by Marije Tolman, Lemniscaat (Rotterdam, Netherlands), 2009.

De kleine kerst koning, illustrated by Marjolijn Krijger, Gottmer (Haarlem, Netherlands), 2010.

Also author of beginning readers.

Author's works have been translated into several languages, including French, Italian, Japanese, Korean, and Spanish.

Sidelights

For SIDELIGHTS, see entry on Elle van Lieshout, elsewhere in this volume.

Biographical and Critical Sources

PERIODICALS

Booklist, December 15, 2004, Hazel Rochman, review of *The Nothing King,* p. 747; January 1, 2007, Carolyn Phelan, review of *The Wish,* p. 118.

Kirkus Reviews, April 15, 2003, review of *A Nice Party,* p. 612; November 15, 2004, review of *The Nothing King,* p. 1094; January 1, 2009, review of *Lovey and Dovey.*

Publishers Weekly, January 10, 2005, review of *The Nothing King,* p. 54; January 8, 2007, review of *The Wish,* p. 50; January 19, 2009, review of *Lovey and Dovey,* p. 59.

School Library Journal, August, 2003, Melinda Piehler, review of *A Nice Party,* p. 145; January, 2005, Rachel G. Payne, review of *The Nothing King,* p. 98; March, 2007, Linda L. Walkins, review of *The Wish,* p. 188; April, 2009, Marianne Saccardi, review of *Lovey and Dovey,* p. 118.

ONLINE

Boyds Mills Press Web site, http://www.boydsmillspress.com/ (May 31, 2010), "Eric van Os."

Elle van Lieshout and Eric van Os Home Page, http://www.erikvanosenellevanlieshout.nl (May 31, 2010).*

W-Z

WALSH, Rebecca

Personal

Female. *Education:* Rhode Island School of Design, degree (illustration), 2000.

Addresses

Home—Cambridge, MA. *Agent*—Jane Feder, 305 E. 24th St., New York, NY 10010.

Career

Illustrator, beginning 2000.

Illustrator

Robert D. San Souci, *The Well at the End of the World,* Chronicle Books (San Francisco, CA), 2004.
Nancy C. Wood, *How the Tiny People Grew Tall: An Original Creation Tale,* Candlewick Press (Cambridge, MA), 2005.
Amy Ehrlich, *The Girl Who Wanted to Dance,* Candlewick Press (Somerville, MA), 2009.

Sidelights

A graduate of the prestigious Rhode Island School of Design, Rebecca Walsh has become respected in the field of children's publishing through her contributions to books by Robert D. San Souci, Nancy C. Wood, and Amy Ehrlich. Her first illustration project, San Souci's *The Well at the End of the World,* retells a British folk story about a royal princess whose homely looks belie a commonsensical wisdom. When her father falls ill, Princess Rosamond searches for the healing well that promises a cure, and her kindness to those she meets along the way is rewarded handsomely. However, when Rosamond's jealous stepsister Zenobia attempts to walk the same path, neither her intentions nor her attitude matches those of her well-meaning sister, with predictable fairy-tale results. Praising Walsh's detailed and "richly hued" acrylic-and-water color paintings for the book, Kathleen Simonetta added in *School Library Journal* that they "expand the narrative by imparting a fairy-tale setting and show lots of action and expression." Dubbing the story "delightful," a *Kirkus Reviews* writer credited Walsh's "colorful paintings" for injecting "energy, humor, and a sense of courage" into San Souci's inspired retelling, while in *Publishers Weekly* a contributor asserted that the "talented" artist's "distinctive style combines royal splendor with ordinary homespun details."

Rebecca Walsh introduces her distinctive style of illustration to readers of Robert D. San Souci's **The Well at the End of the World.** (Copyright © 2004 by Rebecca Walsh. Used with permission of Chronicle Books LLC, San Francisco. Visit ChronicleBooks.com.)

Walsh received substantial praise for the illustrations she contributed to Amy Ehrlich's **The Girl Who Wanted to Dance.** (Illustration copyright © 2009 by Rebecca Walsh. Reproduced by permission of the publisher Candlewick Press, Inc., Cambridge, MA.)

Walsh has made good on the promise of her picture-book debut in her more-recent illustration work. Wood's *How the Tiny People Grew Tall: An Original Creation Tale* finds a race of small and timid people growing in stature as they bravely climb to Earth's surface and learn important lessons, and here Walsh's "lively" illustrations actually "buoy" the story's somber text, according to a *Kirkus Reviews* critic. In *The Girl Who Wanted to Dance,* a story by Ehrlich, Walsh contributes what a *Publishers Weekly* critic described as "lush paintings of an idealized old world" within which young Clara learns of the fate of her mother and the source of her passion for music and dancing. The artist's "gentle period paintings" in *The Girl Who Wanted to Dance* "set a cozy and inviting tone," wrote Jayne Damron in *School Library Journal,* and a *Kirkus Reviews* contributor deemed Ehrlich and Walsh's picture-book collaboration "achingly exquisite."

Biographical and Critical Sources

PERIODICALS

Booklist, October 1, 2004, Jennifer Mattson, review of *The Well at the End of the World,* p. 336; November 15, 2005, Hazel Rochman, review of *How the Tiny People Grew Tall: An Original Creation Tale,* p. 54.

Kirkus Reviews, September 15, 2004, review of *The Well at the End of the World,* p. 920; November 1, 2005, review of *How the Tiny People Grew Tall,* p. 1189; January 1, 2009, review of *The Girl Who Want to Dance.*

Publishers Weekly, November 15, 2004, review of *The Well at the End of the World,* p. 59; January 26, 2009, review of *The Girl Who Wanted to Dance,* p. 119.

School Library Journal, November, 2004, Kathleen Simonetta, review of *The Well at the End of the World,* p. 117; January, 2006, Suzanne Myers Harold, review of *How the Tiny People Grew Tall,* p. 115; March, 2009, Jayne Damron, review of *The Girl Who Wanted to Dance,* p. 112.

ONLINE

Jane Feder Web site, http://www.janefeder.com/ (June 15, 2010), "Rebecca Walsh."*

* * *

WEAVER, Will 1950-
(William Weller Weaver)

Personal

Born January 19, 1950, in Park Rapids, MN; son of Harold Howard (a farmer) and Arlys A. Weaver; married Rosalie Mary Nonnemacher (a teacher), March 2, 1975; children: Caitlin Rose, Owen Harte. *Education:* Attended Saint Cloud State University, 1968-69; University of Minnesota, B.A., 1972; Stanford University, M.A., 1979. *Politics:* "Progressive." *Hobbies and other interests:* Mountain hiking, hunting and fishing, studying short story form, rock and roll.

Addresses

Home—Bemidji, MN. *Agent*—Catherine Balkin, Balkin Buddies Associates, 209 Lincoln Pl., Ste. 2C, Brooklyn, NY 11217. *E-mail*—wweaver@paulbunyan.net.

Career

Writer and educator. Farmer, Park Rapids, MN, 1977-81; Bemidji State University, Bemidji, MN, part-time writing instructor, 1979-81, associate professor, 1981-90, professor of English, 1990-2006.

Awards, Honors

Minnesota State Arts Board fellowship for fiction, 1979, 1983; "Grandfather, Heart of the Fields" named among Top Ten Stories of 1984, PEN/Library of Congress; "Dispersal" named among Top Ten Stories of 1985, PEN/Library of Congress; Bush Foundation fiction fellow, 1987-88; Friends of American Writers Award, 1989; Minnesota Book Award for Fiction, 1989; Pick of the Lists selection, American Booksellers Association,

1993, and Best Books for Young Adults designation, American Library Association (ALA), 1994, both for *Striking Out;* Best Books for Young Adults designation, ALA, and Distinguished Book Award, International Reading Association, both 1996, and Best Books for Teens listee in Texas and Iowa, all for *Farm Team;* South Carolina Best Books designation, Texas Lone Star listee, and Minnesota Book Award finalist, 1999, all for *Hard Ball;* Minnesota Book Award for young adult fiction, 2007, for *Defect.*

Writings

YOUNG-ADULT NOVELS

Striking Out, HarperCollins (New York, NY), 1993.
Farm Team, HarperCollins (New York, NY), 1995.
Hard Ball, HarperCollins (New York, NY), 1998.
Memory Boy, HarperCollins (New York, NY), 2001.
Claws, HarperCollins (New York, NY), 2003.
Full Service, Farrar, Straus (New York, NY), 2005.
Defect, Farrar, Straus (New York, NY), 2007.
Saturday Night Dirt, Farrar, Straus (New York, NY), 2008.

OTHER

Red Earth, White Earth (adult novel), Simon & Schuster (New York, NY), 1986, Borealis Books (St. Paul, MN), 2006.
A Gravestone Made of Wheat (short stories), Simon & Schuster (New York, NY), 1989.
Barns of Minnesota, photographs by Doug Ohman, Minnesota Historical Society Press (St. Paul, MN), 2005.
Sweet Land: New and Selected Stories, Borealis Books (St. Paul, MN), 2006.

Contributor to periodicals, including *Loonfeather, Prairie Schooner, Hartford Courant, San Francisco Chronicle, Kansas City Star, Chicago Tribune, Minneapolis Tribune, Newsday, Minnesota Conservation Volunteer, Northern Literary Quarterly, Milkweed Chronicles, Library Journal, Chapel Hill Advocate,* and *Minnesota Monthly.* Stories anthologized in *Ultimate Sports,* edited by Donald Gallo, Delacorte (New York, NY), 1995; *No Easy Answers,* edited by Gallo, Delacorte, 1997; and *Time Capsule,* edited by Gallo, Delacorte, 1999.

Adaptations

Red Earth, White Earth was adapted as a television film, Columbia Broadcasting System (CBS-TV), 1989; *Sweet Land* was a film adaptation of the short story "A Gravestone Made of Wheat."

Sidelights

Will Weaver writes novels for both adult and young-adult readers that are grounded in the author's home in the upper Midwest. His novels for older readers have

earned Weaver praise as "a writer of uncommon natural talent," from Frank Levering in the *Los Angeles Times Book Review,* and his work for teen readers has been equally lauded.

Weaver turned to young-adult fiction after publishing a highly successful adult novel and story collection, and he penned a trio of books built around the central character of Billy Baggs. These books contain the same nuance of detail and depth of characterization as his adult fiction. Billy is a farm boy for whom baseball becomes a release, a passion, a metaphor for life's potentials.

Weaver was raised on a dairy farm near Park Rapids, Minnesota, where his family farmed 150 acres. One of three children, he attended the local country school. His parents, of Scandinavian descent, were devout in their Christian beliefs and had little use for modern things such as television. "Farm life could be hard, but it had its advantages," Weaver later recalled of his childhood. "There was so much independence on the farm. Sure there was work every day of the year, but there was also the kind of freedom for a young kid there that you could not find in town. You could drive at a young age and go fishing and hunting." Without the interruption of television, there was plenty of time for the imagination and for getting outside and doing things. Books came in the form of *Readers Digest* condensed books, which inspired Weaver's early interest in reading.

During his high-school years Weaver attended an urban school in Park Rapids, where he felt the disadvantages of his less-sophisticated, country education. A steady "B" student, he enjoyed being out in nature more than sitting behind a desk. However, one of his English teachers took an interest in Weaver, encouraging his writing and appreciation of literature. "This altered my direction," Weaver recalled. "Here was a teacher showing interest in my abilities and it gave me great confidence."

Weaver took classes at Saint Cloud State University, then earned his B.A. at the University of Minnesota. After graduation, he moved to California's San Francisco Bay Area, where he began writing. "I was lonely for the Midwest and started to write about it. The early sketches led to short stories." Soon he was joined in California by his girlfriend from his college days, and the two were married. On the strength of a couple of short stories, Weaver was admitted to Stanford's prestigious writing program, where once again he felt the consummate outsider. "Here I was, this rube from the Midwest, with a few pages of short stories in my notebooks while other students had stories published in major magazines or were sons or daughters of famous writers. It was a somewhat traumatic experience at first, but then later I discovered the value of the experience." Weaver and his wife also began careers in California's Silicon Valley. Starting as a technical writer, Weaver soon became manager of a high-tech company, but eventually the couple decided to return to the Midwest.

At first settling in Minneapolis-St. Paul, the couple soon migrated farther north. Weaver took over the running of his father's dairy farm for two years, but found that farm life was not for him. During this time he also taught at nearby Bemidji State University, and he ultimately parlayed teaching into a full-time job. Now writing more seriously, he began fashioning his short stories into a much larger work, the novel *Red Earth, White Earth.*

Weaver spent two years on his first novel, a tale of the return of a prodigal son to the Minnesota of his youth. Like Weaver, this fictional protagonist also returns from Silicon Valley, and once back in the Midwest must confront unrest between Native Americans and local farmers. *Red Earth, White Earth* earned critical praise and became a television movie three years after its publication. Suddenly Weaver was a literary figure, a "Midwestern voice," and his short-story collection *A Gravestone Made of Wheat* also impressed critics. With these two works he resolved the overall theme of his writing: "I began to see that I wanted to capture with my writing some of the small-farm texture that is so rapidly disappearing. I want to record that in a texture of aesthetic realism."

While struggling through a second adult novel and work as a tenured college professor, Weaver discovered a new audience for his writing while listening to his children, who were then in middle school. "They were full of stories from school and about their friends, and there I was hiding out in my study, struggling with my novel. . . . I was reminded of my own youth. I suddenly thought that I would write books my kids might enjoy reading." Coupling this new focus with his son's newfound interest in baseball, Weaver produced his next book, *Striking Out,* a tale of a thirteen-year-old farm boy who uses baseball to transcend his feelings of being an outsider.

Taking place in 1970, *Striking Out* focuses on Billy Baggs, a teen trying to come to terms with the gruesome death of his older brother five years earlier. Billy still feels responsible for the accidental death, and the austere life of do's and don'ts imposed by his stern father, Abner, makes the teen's life that much more difficult. Abner, a victim of childhood polio, expects the worst from life and often gets it. Billy's mother, on the other hand, is still hopeful about life; with her savings she buys a typewriter and teaches herself the skills needed to get a job at a local medical clinic. Billy fears he is destined for the same life his father has come to hate: a life spent on the farm. However, when he becomes involved with a youth baseball league and shows talent, Billy is aided by the team's supportive coach in convincing Abner to let him play ball. Ultimately, the task now falls to Billy to overcome his feelings of not belonging and deal with the jealousy of some teammates in order to prove to himself that his life can be what he chooses to make it.

"If this plot suggests a throwback to the . . . sports-oriented series from the 1940s and '50s," noted a *Publishers Weekly* reviewer of *Striking Out,* "the subplots, involving teenage sex and the mother's decision to take an office job in town, are clearly the stuff of contemporary YA fiction." This same reviewer concluded that a "wealth of lovingly recounted details evokes the difficult daily life on a small dairy farm, while flashes of humor serve as relief." Dolores J. Sarafinski commented in the *Voice of Youth Advocates* that "Weaver prevents the plot from becoming too cloying by the realistic representation of life on the farm and Billy's sexual interest in a young neighbor. . . . Weaver writes well and students ten years old and up will enjoy Billy's struggle, the baseball experience, and the vivid description of life on the farm." Betsy Hearne, writing in the *Bulletin of the Center for Children's Books,* pointed out the "clearly focussed plot" and the "fine-tuned psychological and physical pacing" in *Striking Out,* predicting that the novel will "hold junior high school and high school readers." Mary Harris Veeder declared in Chicago's *Tribune Books* that Weaver's name should be added to the list of the "few talented authors for this age group who manage to catch the significance of sports as the language in which much growing up expresses itself." Veeder concluded that "many boys stop reading for fun in middle school; [*Striking Out*] . . . is good enough to change that."

Weaver continues the saga of Billy Baggs in *Farm Team* and *Hard Ball,* which follow Billy's progress at ages fourteen and fifteen respectively. In the former novel, the action picks up where it left off in *Striking Out,* with Billy's father taking revenge on a used-car salesman who sold his wife a clunker. After running amok in the used-car lot with a tractor, Abner is carted off to jail, leaving Billy to spend the summer working the farm with no time for pitching fast balls. Billy's mom comes to the rescue, helping to set up a playing field on their property and initiating Friday night games for some relaxation. Billy leads a makeshift group of country kids on the farm team, and they ultimately defeat the pompous town kids in a game ending on a fly ball hit by Billy's rival, King Kenwood, and caught by Billy's dog.

While some reviewers found *Farm Team* less substantive than *Striking Out, School Library Journal* critic Todd Morning dubbed the novel "a successful sequel," and wrote that the final game is "wonderfully evoked." Morning concluded that "most readers will come away from *Farm Team* looking forward to the next installment in the life of Billy Baggs." A reviewer for *Publishers Weekly* commented that "Weaver combines wickedly sharp wit with a love of baseball and intimate knowledge of farm life to yield an emotionally satisfying tale" with a "good old-fashioned ending."

Hard Ball continues the competition between Billy and King Kenwood, but in this story the two must learn to deal with each other as well as the expectations of their respective fathers. King is from the better side of town, a child of privilege. The boys compete on the baseball field as well as for the heart of Suzy, a romantic rivalry that adds piquancy to their feud. It does not help that their fathers are as much at odds with one another as the sons are. As a result of a physical fight between Billy and King, the coach suggests that the boys spend a week together, splitting the time between each household. In the process, King gains a grudging admiration for the harsh farm life Billy endures and also begins to see how difficult Billy's father can be. Billy, in turn, learns that a "softer" life does not necessarily mean an easier one.

Claire Rosser, reviewing *Hard Ball* in *Kliatt,* noted that "there's a welcome earthiness here, in the language and in the farm situations, which add humor and realism." Rosser concluded that "Weaver gets this world exactly right, with the haves and have nots living separate lives, even in sparsely populated Minnesota farmland." Mary McCarthy commented in the *Voice of Youth Advocates* that "Billy is an engaging, realistic character who leaves the reader rooting for more" and termed *Hard Ball* "an excellent read for a hot summer night, baseball fan or not." A *Kirkus Reviews* critic dubbed the book an "offbeat, exciting narrative," while a contributor to the *Bulletin of the Center for Children's Books* concluded that "Weaver will have readers in the palm of his glove."

Memory Boy is a change of pace from Weaver's "Billy Baggs" novels. While also taking place in Minnesota, this is a Minnesota of a near future, shortly after a massive volcano on the order of Krakatoa has dumped huge amounts of ash on the region and polluted the air with toxic volcanic emissions. Chaos has erupted along with the volcano, and now rioters, looters, and other desperate people roam the region, searching for a safe place to stay. Sixteen-year-old Miles Newell realizes that the wilderness is the safest place to be. He jury-rigs a homemade vehicle powered by bicycle and sailboat parts to transport his parents and younger sister to a small cabin he knows is located in the state's northern forest. Dealing with a host of obstacles on their journey, the Newells reach the cabin only to find that it has been taken over by squatters, forcing the quick-witted teen to come up with a new plan.

Earning the author comparisons to books by noted author Gary Paulsen, *Memory Boy* was immediately embraced by readers and critics alike. Praising Weaver's survival tale, a *Publishers Weekly* reviewer noted that the author "plants enough familiar details so that readers can relate—including . . . McDonald's restaurants" where "meals cost ten times as much" and spins an exciting tale wherein "danger lurks around every corner." "The post-apocalyptic future has never been so close or real as in this short, engrossing read," noted Debbie Carton in *Booklist,* while *School Library Journal* contributor Beth Wright praised courageous Miles as "a likeable, skateboarding wiseacre, bright and good with his hands," who, "like many a son," is "always secretly hoping for his father's approval."

In *Claws* the life of Jed Berg, another sixteen-year-old Minnesota teen, is also disrupted, but by far-less-cataclysmic means. Jed has enjoyed a comfortable life, with a stable family life and a good report card, but all his assumptions about his world change when he receives an e-mailed photograph of his father in the arms of a strange woman. The e-mailer, the woman's daughter, is contacting Jed because she is trying to put an end to the affair; in fact, she threatens to make the affair public if Jed does not find a way to convince his father to end it.

While some reviewers noted that the repercussions stemming from Jed's sudden knowledge tend to overwhelm the second part of *Claws* with melodrama as the family's life is turned upside down and everything falls apart, *Booklist* contributor Ilene Cooper noted that "Jed's first-person narrative catches the normality and sweetness of his life," and his predicament illustrates the fragile nature of family life. Weaver's "wonderful use of language ably reflects the teen's turmoil" in *Claws*, wrote *School Library Journal* contributor Betsy Fraser, the critic citing Jed's inability to control the "anger and hurt over his father's behavior" and the physical outbursts that result in a school detention. Also praising Weaver's character study, Fraser deemed *Claws* "a good choice for fans of more serious fiction."

Full Service takes place in a small town in Minnesota where, over the summer of 1965, Paul works at a Shell gas station and gains a measure of maturity. The product of a religious family and a sheltered upbringing, Paul encounters all manner of new things when he starts his job, ranging from adultery to drag racing, petty theft, and a retired Chicago mobster who might very well be a murderer. Paul even finds himself dealing with the personal temptations of sex, much to his surprise and dismay. His parents, while aware of the sins and evils of the world, maintain their piety and adhere to their own principles, beliefs that are not always what Paul agrees with or even understands. Ultimately, the teen is forced to decide what parts of his upbringing he agrees with, and just where his own moral center lies.

Appraising *Full Service*, a contributor for *Kirkus Reviews* pointed out that "it's unusual to see individual conscience modeled without preachiness, and without endorsing any particular beliefs." Joel Shoemaker, writing for *School Library Journal*, commented that "teens will likely relate to details such as Paul's secretly listening to the radio under the blankets at night and his razor-sharp observations of his loving father." Roger Sutton, in a review for *Horn Book*, found that in *Full Service* "Weaver evokes the rural setting with much exactness, no nostalgia, and involving immediacy."

In *Saturday Night Dirt*, Weaver recounts the experiences of a group of teens and adults alike in a small Minnesota town where the local dirt-track raceway, Headwaters Speedway, is the primary attraction on a hot summer night. Ace driver Trace thinks that his mechanic may be doing something to his car in an attempt to sabotage the race for him. Beau Kim, with no money for a proper race car, has put his together himself, culled from spare parts from numerous junkers. There are other drivers, including both a teenage girl and a Native American, and the track itself is managed by a young girl named Melody who relies on volunteers to keep things going and prays that it will not rain until the day's races are over. Weaver rotates the story's point of view from chapter to chapter, allowing readers to get inside the heads of the various characters and their different roles. Paula Rohrlick, in a review for *Kliatt*, suggested that *Saturday Night Dirt* "holds lots of appeal for motorheads and race fans as well as reluctant readers." Jeffrey A. French, writing for *School Library Journal*, commented that Weaver's story "presents a fascinating look at small-time racing where the love of it gives the glitz of NASCAR its roots."

Of his writing process, Weaver once explained: "I generally work without an outline; I only like to know a chapter or two ahead—like writing only as far as I can see by headlights. But the trouble is, sometimes you take the wrong turn with this method. You have to be flexible; you need to be able to start all over again, to throw away what does not work." Much of Weaver's writing is confined to the summer months when he is free of his teaching obligations. "I work about half a day," he noted. "I get between three and ten pages a day and I do my writing in a study off the garage."

Weaver remains a firm believer in revision. "I always tell aspiring writers that they must be ready to revise," he explained. "Only Mozart got it right the first time. Some of my short stories have been through twenty revisions; my novels through six to ten rewrites. I am very concerned with quality. If there is anything that will cement a writer's reputation, it's the sense that each book is as good as or better than the last one. That's a real goal of mine."

Biographical and Critical Sources

PERIODICALS

Booklist, February 1, 2001, Debbie Carton, review of *Memory Boy*, p. 1046; April 15, 2003, Ilene Cooper, review of *Claws*, p. 1463.

Bulletin of the Center for Children's Books, February, 1994, Betsy Hearne, review of *Striking Out*, p. 204; May, 1998, review of *Hard Ball*, p. 343.

Horn Book, November 1, 2005, Roger Sutton, review of *Full Service*.

Kirkus Reviews, December 1, 1997, review of *Hard Ball*, p. 1781; February 1, 2003, review of *Claws*, p. 242; September 15, 2005, review of *Full Service*, p. 1036; March 15, 2008, review of *Saturday Night Dirt*.

Kliatt, July, 1998, Claire Rosser, review of *Hard Ball*, p. 9; March, 2003, Paula Rohrlick, review of *Claws*, p. 17; July, 2003, Barbara Jo McKee, review of *Memory*

Boy, p. 35; March, 2004, Paula Rohrlick, review of *Claws,* p. 24; March 1, 2008, Paula Rohrlick, review of *Saturday Night Dirt,* p. 22.

Los Angeles Times Book Review, October 19, 1986, Frank Levering, review of *Red Earth, White Earth,* p. 9.

New York Times Book Review, March 12, 1989, Andy Solomon, review of *A Gravestone Made of Wheat,* p. 22.

Publishers Weekly, August 30, 1993, review of *Striking Out,* p. 97; June 26, 1995, review of *Farm Team,* p. 108; January 22, 2001, review of *Memory Boy,* p. 325; January 13, 2003, review of *Claws,* p. 61.

School Library Journal, July, 1995, Todd Morning, review of *Farm Team,* p. 96; June, 2001, Beth Wright, review of *Memory Boy,* p. 159; March, 2003, Betsy Fraser, review of *Claws,* p. 242.

Tribune Books (Chicago, IL), June 19, 1994, Mary Harris Veeder, review of *Striking Out,* p. 6.

Voice of Youth Advocates, December, 1993, Dolores J. Sarafinski, review of *Striking Out,* p. 304; June, 1998, Mary McCarthy, review of *Hard Ball,* p. 126.

ONLINE

Will Weaver Home Page, http://www.willweaverbooks. com (July 10, 2010).*

*   *   *

WEAVER, William Weller
See WEAVER, Will

*   *   *

WEBER, Lisa K.

Personal
Female. *Education:* Parsons School of Design, B.F.A. (illustration), 2000.

Addresses
Home—Brooklyn, NY. *E-mail*—lisa@creatureco.com.

Career
Artist and illustrator. *Exhibitions:* Work included in exhibitions in New York, NY, and Philadelphia, PA.

Illustrator
Lauren Baratz-Logsted, with Greg and Jackie Logsted, *Annie's Adventures,* Houghton Mifflin Harcourt (Boston, MA), 2008.

Lauren Baratz-Logsted, with Greg and Jackie Logsted, *Durinda's Dangers,* Houghton Mifflin Harcourt (Boston, MA), 2008.

Lauren Baratz-Logsted, with Greg and Jackie Logsted, *Georgia's Greatness,* Houghton Mifflin Harcourt (Boston, MA), 2009.

Lauren Baratz-Logsted, with Greg and Jackie Logsted, *Jackie's Jokes,* Houghton Mifflin Harcourt (Boston, MA), 2009.

Sean Tulien, *Pecos Bill, Colossal Cowboy* (graphic novel), Stone Arch Books (Minneapolis, MN), 2010.

Also illustrator for volumes in "Graphic Classics" graphic-novel series, including *Gothic Classics,* 2007. Contributor to periodicals, including *Rosebud 25* and *Cricket.*

Biographical and Critical Sources

PERIODICALS

Publishers Weekly, May 7, 2007, review of *Gothic Classics,* p. 48.

ONLINE

Graphic Classics Web site, http://www.graphicclassics. com/ (May 31, 2010), "Lisa K. Weber."

Lisa K. Weber Home Page, http://www.creatureco.com (June 15, 2010).*

*   *   *

WEINGARTEN, Lynn

Personal
Born in Chappaqua, NY.

Addresses
Home—New York, NY. *E-mail*—lynn@lynnweingarten. com.

Career
Writer. Alloy Entertainment, New York, NY, former book editor.

Writings

Wherever Nina Lies (novel), Scholastic/Point (New York, NY), 2009.

Sidelights
In her well-received debut novel, *Wherever Nina Lies,* Lynn Weingarten blends elements of mystery and romance, telling the story of a teenager who embarks on a cross-country trek to find her older sister, an artistic nonconformist who disappeared two years earlier. Weingarten remarked in an interview on the *Point* Web site

that the idea for the work came to her during a discussion with some editors at Scholastic, after she decided to leave her job at a media company and write full time. "In particular they were looking to do a YA book that would include drawings that would play a pivotal role in the story," Weingarten recalled. "I said I would love to and then tried to come up with a plot that would be a natural fit for the format."

Wherever Nina Lies centers on Ellie Wrigley, a sensitive sixteen year old whose life has been turned upside down since her beloved older sister, Nina, went missing. When Ellie finds one of Nina's drawings at a local thrift shop, accompanied by a phone number, she becomes determined to investigate. Aided by Sean, a recent acquaintance who also lost a sibling some years earlier, Ellie heads west, following a series of clues that lead to a startling revelation.

Wherever Nina Lies earned solid reviews. "Weingarten offers a fully dimensional story," Frances Bradburn wrote in *Booklist,* and a critic in *Kirkus Reviews* noted that "quirky characters, misplaced trust and the very questionable kindness of a stranger guarantee a riveting

Cover of Lynn Weingarten's young-adult novel **Wherever Nina Lies,** *which chronicles the adventures of a questioning teen.* (Cover photo copyright © 2008 by Michael Frost. Reproduced by permission of Scholastic, Inc.)

read." Although a *Publishers Weekly* contributor found some elements of the plot to be improbable, the critic concluded of *Wherever Nina Lies* that "Weingarten's fast-paced, chatty style will keep readers tuned in."

Biographical and Critical Sources

PERIODICALS

Booklist, February 15, 2009, review of *Wherever Nina Lies,* p. 76.
Kirkus Reviews, January 1, 2009, review of *Wherever Nina Lies.*
Publishers Weekly, December 15, 2008, review of *Wherever Nina Lies,* p. 55.
School Library Journal, August, 2009, Jennifer Barnes, review of *Wherever Nina Lies,* p. 116.

ONLINE

Lynn Weingarten Home Page, http://www.lynnweingarten.com (May 20, 2010).
Point Web site, http://www.thisispoint.com/ (May 20, 2010), interview with Weingarten.*

*   *   *

WEISSMAN, Elissa Brent

Personal

Born in NY; married; husband's name Grant. *Education:* Johns Hopkins University, B.A. (writing seminars), 2005; Roehampton University, M.A. (children's literature).

Addresses

Home—Baltimore, MD. *E-mail*—elissa@ebweissman.com.

Career

Author and educator. Instructor in writing for children at University of Baltimore and Towson University; presenter at writing workshops.

Writings

Standing for Socks, Atheneum Books for Young Readers (New York, NY), 2009.
The Trouble with Mark Hopper, Dutton Children's Books (New York, NY), 2009.
Nerd Camp, Atheneum Books for Young Readers (New York, NY), 2011.

Elissa Brent Weissman (Photograph by Michael Olliver. Reproduced by permission.)

Sidelights

Elissa Brent Weissman mined the story ideas she conceived in junior high school to create her first novel, *Standing for Socks.* Determined to become a writer as a young girl growing up on Long Island, New York, Weissman pursued a degree in creative writing at Johns Hopkins University, and she completed the novel during her senior year. Geared for middle-grade readers, *Standing for Socks* was accepted for publication and released only months before Weismman's second novel, *The Trouble with Mark Hopper.*

In *Standing for Socks* readers meet Fara Ross, an eleven year old who hopes to make a difference by becoming president of her sixth-grade student council. Although Fara's dreams seemed far off in fifth grade, everything changed the day she accidentally puts on two mismatched socks. Her wardrobe foible is interpreted as a stand for nonconformity, and as a sixth grader she is now considered something of a local celebrity whose trademark mismatched socks inspire others to take creative risks. Fame proves frustrating, however, because people associate the serious-minded Fara with footwear rather than with the bigger issues she is passionate about. Things get worse when this fame threatens to eclipse Fara's election win and also damage her relationship with friends.

Calling Fara's narrative "appealing" and "lively," Shelle Rosenfeld added in *Booklist* that *Standing for Socks* is an "enjoyable" story in which "diverse characters and thought-provoking ideas . . . will engage young people." Noting Weissman's injection of "whimsy" and her indulgence in wordplay about socks, *School Library Journal* reviewer Amelia Jenkins added that the au-

thor's "writing is clear," while readers of *Standing for Socks* will enjoy "kids' voices [that] are realistically silly."

A common name causes problems in *The Trouble with Mark Hopper,* Weissman's second novel for middle-grade readers. After a family move to the town of Greenburgh, Maryland, sixth grader Mark Geoffrey Hopper arrives at his new middle school to find that another student is also named Mark Hopper. The other Mark Hopper is a straight-A know-it-all with a reputation for being unkind; because both boys look somewhat alike, the new Mark Hopper is mistaken for the other boy and people do not get to know him for who he is: an shy but easy-going preteen with average intelligence and a talent for art. When Mark and Mark are teamed up in a study group, their personalities come into conflict, but ultimately they both learn a lesson about "integrity" and "what it means to be a true friend," as Maria D. LaRocco noted in her *School Library Journal* review. In *Horn Book* Susan Dove Lempke praised Weissman's ability to capture "realistic school interactions" in her novel, adding that "a very funny supporting character" injects *The Trouble with Mark Hopper* with "a lot of kid appeal."

Biographical and Critical Sources

PERIODICALS

Booklist, March 15, 2009, Shelle Rosenfeld, review of *Standing for Socks,* p. 62.
Horn Book, November-December, 2009, Susan Dove Lempke, review of *The Trouble with Mark Hopper,* p. 689.
Kirkus Reviews, February 1, 2009, review of *Standing for Socks*; June 1, 2009, review of *The Trouble with Mark Hopper.*
Publishers Weekly, July 13, 2009, review of *The Trouble with Mark Hopper,* p. 59.
School Library Journal, April, 2009, Amelia Jenkins, review of *Standing for Socks,* p. 144; August, 2009, Maria D. LaRocco, review of *The Trouble with Mark Hopper,* p. 116.

ONLINE

Children's Literature Booking Service Web site, http://www.childrenslit.com/ (June 1, 2010), "Elissa Brent Weissman."
Elissa Brent Weissman Home Page, http://www.ebweissman.com (June 1, 2010).
Merrick Life Online, http://www.merricklife.com/ (January 8, 2010), "Merrick Native's Book Signing."

*   *   *

ZUCKERMAN, Amy

Personal

Partner of Lew Rudolph; children: Julia.

Addresses

Home—Amherst, MA.

Career

Journalist, photojournalist, and author. A-Z International (international market research firm), Amherst, MA, founder; Hidden Tech (business group), founder, 2002. Co-founder of Technology Communications Group and Global Knowledge Productions. Tourist consultant to organizations, including Mid-Atlantic Center for the Arts; member of Creative Economy Initiative.

Awards, Honors

President's Award, American National Standards Institute, 2001; named U.S. Small Business Administration Home-based Business Champion for Massachusetts/New England, 2005.

Writings

FOR CHILDREN

(With James Daly) *2030: A Day in the Life of Tomorrow's Kids,* illustrated by John Manders, Dutton Children's Books (New York, NY), 2009.

OTHER

Surrogate Parenting, Pharos, 1988.
ISO 9000 Made Easy: A Cost-saving Guide to Documentation and Registration, AMACOM (New York, NY), 1995.
(With David Biederman) *Importing and Exporting: A Complete Guide to International Trading,* Warren, Gorham & Lamont (New York, NY), 1995.
International Standards Desk Reference: Your Passport to World Markets, ISO 9000, CE Mark, QS-9000, SSM, ISO 14000, Q 9000, American, European, and Global Standards Systems, AMACOM (New York, NY), 1997.
(With David Biederman) *Exporting and Importing: Negotiating Global Markets,* AMACOM (New York, NY), 1998.
Tech Trending, Capstone Press (Minneapolis, MN), 2001.

Author of other business publications, including *Hidden Tech and the Valley: At the Cutting Edge of the Global Interest Economy.* Contributor to periodicals, including *Atlanta Constitution, Business 2.0, Journal of Commerce, Kirkus Reviews, New York Times Book Review,* Worcester, MA, *Sunday Telegram,* and *World Trade.*

Sidelights

An award-winning journalist, Amy Zuckerman is best known for her technical writing, which appears in periodicals as well as in books such as *Tech Trending.* While observing the way technology—everything from personal computers to mobile devices such as Mp3 players, cell phones, and I-Pods—have shaped the world of her daughter, Julia, Zuckerman was eventually inspired to write about the human environment and society that this growth in technology will create in the future.

Working in collaboration with fellow journalist James Daly and illustrator John Manders, Zuckerman's *2030: A Day in the Life of Tomorrow's Kids* looks forward to the near future, helping young readers understand the real-world possibilities suggested by current advances in science and technology. From buildings constructed by giant snap-together plastic blocks to skateboards that hover above the ground and wristwatches that constantly transmit health data to doctors, *2030* will be a boon to "any librarian who's been stumped by a child's request for a book about . . . 'the real future,'" according to *Booklist* contributor Carolyn Phelan. In *School Library Journal* Steven Engelfried cited the coauthors' "breezy narrative," noting that the future world Daly and Zuckerman taps into current concerns: they foresee vegetarian diets consisting of genetically engineered vegetables, solar and wind power, massive recycling, and other eco-friendly advances. In a *Futurist* review of *2030* a contributor predicted that, while "school will still be in session, . . . most kids will be excited to go."

Biographical and Critical Sources

PERIODICALS

Booklist, January 1, 2009, Carolyn Phelan, review of *2030: A Day in the Life of Tomorrow's Kids,* p. 86.
Futurist, January-February, 2010, review of *2030,* p. 57.
Kirkus Reviews, February 1, 2009, review of *2030.*
School Library Journal, March, 2009, Steven Engelfried, review of *2030,* p. 139.

ONLINE

A-Z International Web site, http://www.a-zinternational.com/ (June 15, 2010), "Amy Zuckerman."
2030 Web log, http://www.2030book.com/ (May 31, 2010), "Amy Zuckerman."*

Illustrations Index

(In the following index, the number of the *volume* in which an illustrator's work appears is given *before* the colon, and the *page number* on which it appears is given *after* the colon. For example, a drawing by Adams, Adrienne appears in Volume 2 on page 6, another drawing by her appears in Volume 3 on page 80, another drawing in Volume 8 on page 1, and so on and so on. . . .)

YABC

Index references to *YABC* refer to listings appearing in the two-volume *Yesterday's Authors of Books for Children,* also published by Gale, Cengage Learning. *YABC* covers prominent authors and illustrators who died prior to 1960.

A

Aas, Ulf *5:* 174
Abbe, S. van
  See van Abbe, S.
Abel, Raymond *6:* 122; *7:* 195; *12:* 3; *21:* 86; *25:* 119
Abelliera, Aldo *71:* 120
Abolafia, Yossi *60:* 2; *93:* 163; *152:* 202
Abrahams, Hilary *26:* 205; *29:* 24, 25; *53:* 61
Abrams, Kathie *36:* 170
Abrams, Lester *49:* 26
Abulafia, Yossi *154:* 67; *177:* 3
Accardo, Anthony *191:* 3, 8
Accornero, Franco *184:* 8
Accorsi, William *11:* 198
Acs, Laszlo *14:* 156; *42:* 22
Acuna, Ed *198:* 79
Adams, Adrienne *2:* 6; *3:* 80; *8:* 1; *15:* 107; *16:* 180; *20:* 65; *22:* 134, 135; *33:* 75; *36:* 103, 112; *39:* 74; *86:* 54; *90:* 2, 3
Adams, Connie J. *129:* 68
Adams, John Wolcott *17:* 162
Adams, Lynn *96:* 44
Adams, Norman *55:* 82
Adams, Pam *112:* 1, 2
Adams, Sarah *98:* 126; *164:* 180
Adams, Steve *209:* 64
Adamson, George *30:* 23, 24; *69:* 64
Addams, Charles *55:* 5
Addison, Kenneth *192:* 173
Addy, Sean *180:* 8
Ade, Rene *76:* 198; *195:* 162
Adinolfi, JoAnn *115:* 42; *176:* 2; *217:* 79
Adkins, Alta *22:* 250
Adkins, Jan *8:* 3; *69:* 4; *144:* 2, 3, 4; *210:* 11, 17, 18, 19
Adler, Kelynn *195:* 47
Adler, Peggy *22:* 6; *29:* 31
Adler, Ruth *29:* 29
Adlerman, Daniel *163:* 2
Adragna, Robert *47:* 145
Agard, Nadema *18:* 1
Agee, Jon *116:* 8, 9, 10; *157:* 4; *196:* 3, 4, 5, 6, 7, 8
Agre, Patricia *47:* 195
Aguirre, Alfredo *152:* 218
Ahjar, Brian *207:* 126
Ahl, Anna Maria *32:* 24
Ahlberg, Allan *68:* 6, 7, 9; *165:* 5; *214:* 9

Ahlberg, Janet *68:* 6, 7, 9; *214:* 9
Aicher-Scholl, Inge *63:* 127
Aichinger, Helga *4:* 5, 45
Aitken, Amy *31:* 34
Akaba, Suekichi *46:* 23; *53:* 127
Akasaka, Miyoshi *YABC 2:* 261
Akib, Jamel *181:* 13; *182:* 99
Akino, Fuku *6:* 144
Alain *40:* 41
Alajalov *2:* 226
Albert, Chris *200:* 64
Alborough, Jez *86:* 1, 2, 3; *149:* 3
Albrecht, Jan *37:* 176
Albright, Donn *1:* 91
Alcala, Alfredo *91:* 128
Alcantará, Felipe Ugalde *171:* 186
Alcorn, John *3:* 159; *7:* 165; *31:* 22; *44:* 127; *46:* 23, 170
Alcorn, Stephen *110:* 4; *125:* 106; *128:* 172; *150:* 97; *160:* 188; *165:* 48; *201:* 113; *203:* 39; *207:* 3
Alcott, May *100:* 3
Alda, Arlene *44:* 24; *158:* 2
Alden, Albert *11:* 103
Aldridge, Andy *27:* 131
Aldridge, George *105:* 125
Aldridge, Sheila *192:* 4
Alejandro, Cliff *176:* 75
Alex, Ben *45:* 25, 26
Alexander, Ellen *91:* 3
Alexander, Lloyd *49:* 34
Alexander, Martha *3:* 206; *11:* 103; *13:* 109; *25:* 100; *36:* 131; *70:* 6, 7; *136:* 3, 4, 5; *169:* 120
Alexander, Paul *85:* 57; *90:* 9
Alexeieff, Alexander *14:* 6; *26:* 199
Alfano, Wayne *80:* 69
Aliki
  See Brandenberg, Aliki
Allamand, Pascale *12:* 9
Allan, Judith *38:* 166
Alland, Alexandra *16:* 255
Allen, Gertrude *9:* 6
Allen, Graham *31:* 145
Allen, Jonathan *131:* 3, 4; *177:* 8, 9, 10
Allen, Joy *168:* 185; *217:* 6, 7
Allen, Pamela *50:* 25, 26, 27, 28; *81:* 9, 10; *123:* 4, 5
Allen, Raul *207:* 94
Allen, Rowena *47:* 75

Allen, Thomas B. *81:* 101; *82:* 248; *89:* 37; *104:* 9
Allen, Tom *85:* 176
Allender, David *73:* 223
Alley, R.W. *80:* 183; *95:* 187; *156:* 100, 153; *169:* 4, 5; *179:* 17
Allison, Linda *43:* 27
Allon, Jeffrey *119:* 174
Allport, Mike *71:* 55
Almquist, Don *11:* 8; *12:* 128; *17:* 46; *22:* 110
Aloise, Frank *5:* 38; *10:* 133; *30:* 92
Alsenas, Linas *186:* 2
Alter, Ann *206:* 4, 5
Althea
  See Braithwaite, Althea
Altschuler, Franz *11:* 185; *23:* 141; *40:* 48; *45:* 29; *57:* 181
Alvin, John *117:* 5
Ambrus, Victor G. *1:* 6, 7, 194; *3:* 69; *5:* 15; *6:* 44; *7:* 36; *8:* 210; *12:* 227; *14:* 213; *15:* 213; *22:* 209; *24:* 36; *28:* 179; *30:* 178; *32:* 44, 46; *38:* 143; *41:* 25, 26, 27, 28, 29, 30, 31, 32; *42:* 87; *44:* 190; *55:* 172; *62:* 30, 144, 145, 148; *86:* 99, 100, 101; *87:* 66, 137; *89:* 162; *134:* 160
Ames, Lee J. *3:* 12; *9:* 130; *10:* 69; *17:* 214; *22:* 124; *151:* 13
Amini, Mehrdokht *211:* 119
Amon, Aline *9:* 9
Amoss, Berthe *5:* 5
Amstutz, André *152:* 102; *214:* 11, 16
Amundsen, Dick *7:* 77
Amundsen, Richard E. *5:* 10; *24:* 122
Ancona, George *12:* 11; *55:* 144; *145:* 7; *208:* 13
Anderson, Alasdair *18:* 122
Andersen, Bethanne *116:* 167; *162:* 189; *175:* 17; *191:* 4, 5
Anderson, Bob *139:* 16
Anderson, Brad *33:* 28
Anderson, Brian *211:* 8
Anderson, C.W. *11:* 10
Anderson, Carl *7:* 4
Anderson, Catherine Corley *72:* 2
Anderson, Cecil *127:* 152
Anderson, David Lee *118:* 176
Anderson, Derek *169:* 9; *174:* 180
Anderson, Doug *40:* 111
Anderson, Erica *23:* 65
Anderson, Laurie *12:* 153, 155
Anderson, Lena *99:* 26

Anderson, Peggy Perry *179:* 2
Anderson, Sara *173:* 3
Anderson, Scoular *138:* 13; *201:* 6
Anderson, Susan *90:* 12
Anderson, Tara *188:* 132; *211:* 115
Anderson, Wayne *23:* 119; *41:* 239; *56:* 7; *62:* 26; *147:* 6; *202:* 4, 5
Andreasen, Daniel *86:* 157; *87:* 104; *103:* 201, 202; *159:* 75; *167:* 106, 107; *168:* 184; *180:* 247; *186:* 9; *212:* 101
Andrew, Ian *111:* 37; *116:* 12; *166:* 2
Andrew, John *22:* 4
Andrews, Benny *14:* 251; *31:* 24; *57:* 6, 7; *183:* 8
Andrews, Vaughn *166:* 28
Anelay, Henry *57:* 173
Angel, Marie *47:* 22
Angelo, Valenti *14:* 8; *18:* 100; *20:* 232; *32:* 70
Anglund, Joan Walsh *2:* 7, 250, 251; *37:* 198, 199, 200
Anholt, Catherine *74:* 8; *131:* 7; *141:* 5
Anholt, Laurence *141:* 4
Anno, Mitsumasa *5:* 7; *38:* 25, 26, 27, 28, 29, 30, 31, 32; *77:* 3, 4; *157:* 10, 11
Antal, Andrew *1:* 124; *30:* 145
Antram, David *152:* 133
Apostolou, Christy Hale
See Hale, Christy
Apple, Margot *33:* 25; *35:* 206; *46:* 81; *53:* 8; *61:* 109; *64:* 21, 22, 24, 25, 27; *71:* 176; *77:* 53; *82:* 245; *92:* 39; *94:* 180; *96:* 107; *152:* 4, 5; *162:* 192, 194; *173:* 44; *214:* 21, 22, 23, 24
Appleyard, Dev *2:* 192
Aragones, Sergio *48:* 23, 24, 25, 26, 27
Araneus *40:* 29
Arbo, Cris *103:* 4
Archambault, Matt *85:* 173; *138:* 19, 20; *143:* 33; *145:* 144; *179:* 103; *187:* 7
Archer, Janet *16:* 69; *178:* 156
Ardizzone, Edward *1:* 11, 12; *2:* 105; *3:* 258; *4:* 78; *7:* 79; *10:* 100; *15:* 232; *20:* 69,178; *23:* 223; *24:* 125; *28:* 25, 26, 27, 28, 29, 30, 31,33, 34, 35, 36, 37; *31:* 192, 193; *34:* 215, 217; *60:* 173; *64:* 145; *87:* 176; *YABC 2:* 25
Arena, Jill *176:* 49
Arenella, Roy *14:* 9
Argemi, David *197:* 2
Argent, Kerry *103:* 56; *138:* 17; *158:* 134
Arihara, Shino *201:* 98
Arisman, Marshall *162:* 50
Armer, Austin *13:* 3
Armer, Laura Adams *13:* 3
Armer, Sidney *13:* 3
Armitage, David *47:* 23; *99:* 5; *155:* 4
Armitage, Eileen *4:* 16
Armstrong, George *10:* 6; *21:* 72
Armstrong, Shelagh *102:* 114
Armstrong-Ellis, Carey *185:* 196
Arno, Enrico *1:* 217; *2:* 22, 210; *4:* 9; *5:* 43; *6:* 52; *29:* 217, 219; *33:* 152; *35:* 99; *43:* 31, 32, 33; *45:* 212, 213, 214; *72:* 72; *74:* 166; *100:* 169
Arnold, Alli *187:* 40, 41
Arnold, Caroline *174:* 5
Arnold, Emily *76:* 7, 9, 10
Arnold, Katya *115:* 11; *168:* 2, 3
Arnold, Tedd *116:* 14; *133:* 152; *160:* 5; *208:* 24, 25, 26, 176
Arnosky, Jim *22:* 20; *70:* 9, 10, 11; *118:* 3, 5; *160:* 8, 10; *189:* 5, 7, 8, 9, 10; *217:* 11, 12, 13, 14
Arnsteen, Katy Keck *105:* 97; *116:* 145
Arsenault, Isabelle *207:* 7
Arrowood, Clinton *12:* 193; *19:* 11; *65:* 210
Artell, Mike *89:* 8
Arting, Fred J. *41:* 63
Artzybasheff, Boris *13:* 143; *14:* 15; *40:* 152, 155
Aruego, Ariane *6:* 4

Aruego, José *4:* 140; *6:* 4; *7:* 64; *33:* 195; *35:* 208; *68:* 16, 17; *75:* 46; *93:* 91, 92; *94:* 197; *109:* 65, 67; *125:* 2, 3, 4, 5; *127:* 188; *143:* 25; *178:* 17, 19, 74; *188:* 166; *202:* 164
Arzoumanian, Alik *177:* 12; *194:* 115
Asare, Meshack *86:* 9; *139:* 19
Ascensios, Natalie *105:* 139
Asch, Frank *5:* 9; *66:* 2, 4, 6, 7, 9, 10; *102:* 18, 19,21; *154:* 12
Ashby, Gail *11:* 135
Ashby, Gil *146:* 4
Ashby, Gwynneth *44:* 26
Ashley, C.W. *19:* 197
Ashmead, Hal *8:* 70
Ashton, Tim *211:* 204
Aska, Warabe *56:* 10
Assel, Steven *44:* 153; *77:* 22, 97
Astrop, John *32:* 56
Atene, Ann *12:* 18
Atherton, Lisa *38:* 198
Atkinson, Allen *60:* 5
Atkinson, J. Priestman *17:* 275
Atkinson, Janet *86:* 147; *103:* 138
Atkinson, Mike *127:* 74
Atkinson, Wayne *40:* 46
Attard, Karl *196:* 22, 23
Attebery, Charles *38:* 170
Atwell, Debby *150:* 6
Atwood, Ann *7:* 9
Aubrey, Meg Kelleher *77:* 159
Auch, Herm *173:* 7, 8
Auch, Mary Jane *173:* 7
Augarde, Steve *25:* 22; *159:* 7; *210:* 43, 44
Austerman, Miriam *23:* 107
Austin, Margot *11:* 16
Austin, Robert *3:* 44
Austin, Virginia *81:* 205; *127:* 221
Auth, Tony *51:* 5; *192:* 18
Avendano, Dolores *158:* 74
Avedon, Richard *57:* 140
Averill, Esther *1:* 17; *28:* 39, 40, 41
Axeman, Lois *2:* 32; *11:* 84; *13:* 165; *22:* 8; *23:* 49; *61:* 116; *101:* 124
Axtel, David *155:* 110
Ayer, Jacqueline *13:* 7
Ayer, Margaret *15:* 12; *50:* 120
Ayers, Alan *91:* 58; *107:* 169
Ayliffe, Alex *95:* 164
Ayto, Russell *111:* 5; *112:* 54; *206:* 7, 8; *213:* 56
Azarian, Mary *112:* 9, 10; *114:* 129; *117:* 171; *137:* 163; *171:* 4, 5; *181:* 161; *188:* 128

B

B.T.B.
See Blackwell, Basil T.
Baasansuren, Bolormaa *216:* 40
Babbitt, Bradford *33:* 158
Babbitt, Natalie *6:* 6; *8:* 220; *68:* 20; *70:* 242, 243; *194:* 8, 9
Baca, Maria *104:* 5
Bacchus, Andy *94:* 87
Bacha, Andy *109:* 169
Bachelet, Gilles *196:* 18
Bachem, Paul *48:* 180; *67:* 65; *144:* 206
Back, Adam *63:* 125
Back, George *31:* 161
Backes, Nick *190:* 72
Backhouse, Colin *78:* 142
Bacon, Bruce *4:* 74
Bacon, Paul *7:* 155; *8:* 121; *31:* 55; *50:* 42; *56:* 175; *62:* 82, 84
Bacon, Peggy *2:* 11, 228; *46:* 44
Baek, Matthew J. *169:* 95; *202:* 8
Baer, Julie *161:* 2
Baicker-McKee, Carol *177:* 15; *180:* 215
Bailey, Peter *58:* 174; *87:* 221; *194:* 12
Bailey, Sheila *155:* 11

Baker, Alan *22:* 22; *61:* 134; *93:* 11, 12; *146:* 6, 7, 10
Baker, Charlotte *2:* 12
Baker, Garin *89:* 65
Baker, Jeannie *23:* 4; *88:* 18, 19, 20
Baker, Jim *22:* 24
Baker, Joe *82:* 188; *111:* 55; *124:* 70; *197:* 73
Baker, Keith *179:* 6, 7
Baker, Leslie *112:* 214; *132:* 103, 246; *180:* 74, 246
Baldacci, Rudy *184:* 9
Baldridge, Cyrus LeRoy *19:* 69; *44:* 50
Baldus, Jackie *216:* 81
Baldus, Zachary *152:* 231; *187:* 60
Balet, Jan *11:* 22
Balian, Lorna *9:* 16; *91:* 16
Balit, Christina *102:* 24; *159:* 9; *162:* 118, 119; *212:* 2, 3
Ballantyne, R.M. *24:* 34
Ballis, George *14:* 199
Balouch, Kristen *176:* 11
Baltzer, Hans *40:* 30
Banbery, Fred *58:* 15
Bancroft, Bronwyn *216:* 42
Banfill, A. Scott *98:* 7; *112:* 59
Bang, Molly *24:* 37, 38; *69:* 8, 9, 10; *111:* 7,9, 10, 11; *140:* 11; *158:* 37, 38, 39; *195:* 3; *215:* 11, 12, 13, 14
Banik, Yvette Santiago *21:* 136
Banks, Erin Bennett *211:* 12
Banner, Angela
See Maddison, Angela Mary
Bannerman, Helen *19:* 13, 14
Banning, Greg *202:* 98
Bannon, Laura *6:* 10; *23:* 8
Bantock, Nick *74:* 229; *95:* 6
Banyai, Istvan *185:* 209; *193:* 14, 16; *209:* 155
Baptist, Michael *37:* 208
Baracca, Sal *135:* 206
Baranaski, Marcin *182:* 113
Barasch, Lynne *126:* 16; *186:* 15
Barbarin, Lucien C., Jr. *89:* 88
Barbour, Karen *96:* 5; *74:* 209; *170:* 16
Bare, Arnold Edwin *16:* 31
Bare, Colleen Stanley *32:* 33
Barger, Jan *147:* 11
Bargery, Geoffrey *14:* 258
Barkat, Jonathan *149:* 177; *164:* 254; *181:* 106; *184:* 186; *196:* 11; *198:* 148
Barker, Carol *31:* 27
Barker, Cicely Mary *49:* 50, 51
Barkley, James *4:* 13; *6:* 11; *13:* 112
Barks, Carl *37:* 27, 28, 29, 30, 31, 32, 33, 34
Barling, Joy *62:* 148
Barling, Tom *9:* 23
Barlow, Gillian *62:* 20
Barlow, Perry *35:* 28
Barlowe, Dot *30:* 223
Barlowe, Wayne *37:* 72; *84:* 43; *105:* 5
Barnard, Bryn *88:* 53; *13:* 55; *169:* 13; *193:* 194
Barneda, David *206:* 11
Barner, Bob *29:* 37; *128:* 33; *136:* 19, 20; *177:* 27
Barnes, Hiram P. *20:* 28
Barnes, Tim *137:* 28
Barnes-Murphy, Rowan *88:* 22
Barnett, Charles II *175:* 150
Barnett, Ivan *70:* 14
Barnett, Moneta *16:* 89; *19:* 142; *31:* 102; *33:* 30, 31, 32; *41:* 153; *61:* 94, 97
Barney, Maginel Wright *39:* 32, 33, 34; *YABC 2:* 306
Barnum, Jay Hyde *11:* 224; *20:* 5; *37:* 189, 190
Baron, Alan *80:* 3; *89:* 123
Barr, George *60:* 74; *69:* 64
Barragán, Paula S. *134:* 116; *186:* 158; *216:* 43, 44, 197
Barrall, Tim *115:* 152
Barraud, Martin *189:* 38

Barrauds *33:* 114
Barrer-Russell, Gertrude *9:* 65; *27:* 31
Barret, Robert *85:* 134
Barrett, Angela *40:* 136, 137; *62:* 74; *75:* 10;
    76: 142; *144:* 137; *145:* 14
Barrett, Jennifer *58:* 149
Barrett, John E. *43:* 119
Barrett, Moneta *74:* 10
Barrett, Peter *55:* 169; *86:* 111
Barrett, Robert *62:* 145; *77:* 146; *82:* 35
Barrett, Ron *14:* 24; *26:* 35
Barron, John N. *3:* 261; *5:* 101; *14:* 220
Barrow, Ann *13:* 27
Barrows, Walter *14:* 268
Barry, Ethelred B. *37:* 79; *YABC 1:* 229
Barry, James *14:* 25
Barry, Katharina *2:* 159; *4:* 22
Barry, Robert E. *6:* 12
Barry, Scott *32:* 35
Barshaw, Ruth McNally *203:* 9
Bartenbach, Jean *40:* 31
Barth, Ernest Kurt *2:* 172; *3:* 160; *8:* 26; *10:*
    31
Bartholomew, Caty *208:* 153
Bartholomew, Marie *200:* 66
Bartlett, Alison *101:* 88; *165:* 93; *209:* 51
Barton, Byron *8:* 207; *9:* 18; *23:* 66; *80:* 181;
    90: 18, 19, 20, 21; *126:* 29, 30
Barton, Harriett *30:* 71
Barton, Jill *129:* 108; *135:* 120; *145:* 185, 189;
    184: 177
Bartram, Robert *10:* 42
Bartsch, Jochen *8:* 105; *39:* 38
Bascove, Barbara *45:* 73
Base, Graeme *101:* 15, 16, 17, 18; *162:* 8, 10,
    12
Baseman, Gary *174:* 12
Bash, Barbara *132:* 9
Baskin, Leonard *30:* 42, 43, 46, 47; *49:* 125,
    126, 128, 129,133; *173:* 120
Bass, Saul *49:* 192
Bassett, Jeni *40:* 99; *64:* 30
Basso, Bill *99:* 139; *189:* 134
Batchelor, Joy *29:* 41, 47, 48
Bate, Norman *5:* 16
Bates, Amy June *188:* 170; *189:* 27, 28
Bates, Leo *24:* 35
Batet, Carmen *39:* 134
Batherman, Muriel *31:* 79; *45:* 185
Battaglia, Aurelius *50:* 44
Batten, John D. *25:* 161, 162
Batten, Mary *162:* 14, 15
Battles, Asa *32:* 94, 95
Bauer, Carla *193:* 6
Bauer, Jutta *150:* 32
Bauernschmidt, Marjorie *15:* 15
Baum, Allyn *20:* 10
Baum, Willi *4:* 24, 25; *7:* 173
Bauman, Leslie *61:* 121
Baumann, Jill *34:* 170
Baumhauer, Hans *11:* 218; *15:* 163, 165, 167
Baxter, Glen *57:* 100
Baxter, Leon *59:* 102
Baxter, Robert *87:* 129
Bayer, Herbert *181:* 16
Bayley, Dorothy *37:* 195
Bayley, Nicola *40:* 104; *41:* 34, 35; *69:* 15;
    129: 33, 34, 35
Baylin, Mark *158:* 233
Baynes, Pauline *2:* 244; *3:* 149; *13:* 133,
    135,137, 141; *19:* 18, 19, 20; *32:* 208, 213,
    214; *36:* 105, 108; *59:* 12, 13, 14, 16, 17,
    18, 20; *100:* 158, 159, 243; *133:* 3, 4
Beach, Lou *150:* 150; *207:* 117, 118
Beame, Rona *12:* 40
Bean, Jonathan *196:* 102
Bear's Heart *73:* 215
Beard, Dan *22:* 31, 32
Beard, J.H. *YABC 1:* 158
Bearden, Romare *9:* 7; *22:* 35
Beardshaw, Rosalind *169:* 22; *190:* 22

Beardsley, Aubrey *17:* 14; *23:* 181; *59:* 130,
    131
Bearman, Jane *29:* 38
Beaton, Cecil *24:* 208
Beaton, Clare *125:* 28; *208:* 67
Beauce, J.A. *18:* 103
Beaujard, Sophie *81:* 54
Beccia, Carlyn *189:* 29
Bechtold, Lisze *208:* 29
Beck, Charles *11:* 169; *51:* 173
Beck, Ian *138:* 27; *182:* 150; *190:* 25
Beck, Melinda *203:* 112
Beck, Ruth *11:* 11
Becker, Harriet *12:* 211
Beckerman, Jonathan *208:* 194
Beckett, Sheilah *25:* 5; *33:* 37, 38
Beckhoff, Harry *1:* 78; *5:* 163
Beckhorn, Susan Williams *189:* 32
Beckman, Kaj *45:* 38, 39, 40, 41
Beckman, Per *45:* 42, 43
Beddows, Eric *72:* 70
Bedford, F.D. *20:* 118, 122; *33:* 170; *41:* 220,
    221,230, 233
Bee, Joyce *19:* 62
Bee, William *188:* 6
Beeby, Betty *25:* 36
Beech, Carol *9:* 149
Beech, Mark *192:* 122
Beek *25:* 51, 55, 59
Beeke, Tiphanie *177:* 127; *204:* 140; *212:* 178
Beekman, Doug *125:* 146, 148
Beerbohm, Max *24:* 208
Beeson, Bob *108:* 57
Begin, Mary Jane *82:* 13; *206:* 13
Beha, Philippe *172:* 85
Behr, Joyce *15:* 15; *21:* 132; *23:* 161
Behrens, Hans *5:* 97
Beier, Ellen *135:* 170; *139:* 47; *183:* 164
Beinicke, Steve *69:* 18
Beisner, Monika *46:* 128, 131; *112:* 127
Belden, Charles J. *12:* 182
Belina, Renate *39:* 132
Bell, Corydon *3:* 20
Bell, Graham *54:* 48
Bell, Julia *151:* 214
Bell, Julie *159:* 172; *165:* 18
Bell, Thomas P. *76:* 182
Bellamy, Glen *127:* 15
Beltran, Alberto *43:* 37
Bemelmans, Ludwig *15:* 19, 21; *100:* 27
Ben-Ami, Doron *75:* 96; *84:* 107; *108:* 132;
    110: 63; *159:* 157; *197:* 142
Bendall-Brunello, John *150:* 4; *157:* 163; *185:*
    3, 4; *203:* 5
Benda, Wladyslaw T. *15:* 256; *30:* 76, 77; *44:*
    182
Bender, Robert *77:* 162; *79:* 13; *160:* 23
Bendick, Jeanne *2:* 24; *68:* 27, 28
Benioff, Carol *121:* 42; *175:* 23
Benner, Cheryl *80:* 11
Bennett, Charles H. *64:* 6
Bennett, Erin Susanne *165:* 216
Bennett, F.I. *YABC 1:* 134
Bennett, James *146:* 240
Bennett, Jill *26:* 61; *41:* 38, 39; *45:* 54
Bennett, Rainey *15:* 26; *23:* 53
Bennett, Richard *15:* 45; *21:* 11, 12, 13; *25:*
    175
Bennett, Susan *5:* 55
Benny, Mike *142:* 78; *203:* 13, 14; *207:* 85
Benoit, Elise *77:* 74
Benson, Linda *60:* 130; *62:* 91; *75:* 101; *79:*
    156; *134:* 129
Benson, Patrick *68:* 162; *147:* 17, 18, 19, 20
Bentley, Carolyn *46:* 153
Bentley, James *149:* 30
Bentley, Roy *30:* 162
Benton, Jim *172:* 22
Benton, Thomas Hart *2:* 99
Berelson, Howard *5:* 20; *16:* 58; *31:* 50

Berenstain, Jan *12:* 47; *64:* 33, 34, 36, 37, 38,
    40, 42, 44; *135:* 25, 28, 31, 35
Berenstain, Stan *12:* 47; *64:* 33, 34, 36, 37, 38,
    40, 42, 44; *135:* 25, 28, 31, 35
Berenzy, Alix *65:* 13; *73:* 6; *78:* 115
Berg, Joan *1:* 115; *3:* 156; *6:* 26, 58
Berg, Ron *36:* 48, 49; *48:* 37, 38; *67:* 72
Bergen, David *115:* 44; *207:* 34
Berger, Barbara *77:* 14
Berger, Carin *185:* 6
Berger, William M. *14:* 143; *YABC 1:* 204
Bergherr, Mary *74:* 170; *151:* 123
Bergin, Mark *114:* 8, 9; *143:* 95; *160:* 26, 27
Bergstreser, Douglas *69:* 76
Bergum, Constance R. *121:* 14, 15; *208:* 31,
    32, 33; *209:* 176
Bering, Claus *13:* 14
Berkeley, Jon *139:* 218
Berkowitz, Jeanette *3:* 249
Berman, Paul *66:* 14
Berman, Rachel *217:* 26
Bernal, Richard *154:* 176
Bernadette
    See Watts, Bernadette
Bernard, Gary *216:* 71
Bernardin, James *112:* 24; *167:* 94
Bernasconi, Pablo *183:* 10, 11
Bernath, Stefen *32:* 76
Berner, Rotraut Susanne *214:* 32
Bernhard, Durga *80:* 13
Bernstein, Michel J. *51:* 71
Bernstein, Ted *38:* 183; *50:* 131
Bernstein, Zena *23:* 46
Berridge, Celia *86:* 63
Berrill, Jacquelyn *12:* 50
Berry, Erick
    See Best, Allena
Berry, Holly *205:* 116; *210:* 49, 50
Berry, William D. *14:* 29; *19:* 48
Berry, William A. *6:* 219
Berson, Harold *2:* 17, 18; *4:* 28, 29, 220; *9:*
    10; *12:* 19; *17:* 45; *18:* 193; *22:* 85; *34:* 172;
    44: 120; *46:* 42; *80:* 240
Bertholf, Bret *187:* 9; *189:* 32, 33
Berton, Patsy *99:* 16
Bertschmann, Harry *16:* 1
Besco, Don *70:* 99
Beskow, Elsa *20:* 13, 14, 15
Bess, Clayton *63:* 94
Best, Allena *2:* 26; *34:* 76
Betera, Carol *74:* 68
Bethell, Thomas N. *61:* 169
Bethers, Ray *6:* 22
Betteridge, Deirdre *214:* 34
Bettina
    See Ehrlich, Bettina
Betts, Ethel Franklin *17:* 161, 164, 165; *YABC
    2:* 47
Betz, Rudolf *59:* 161
Bewick, Thomas *16:* 40, 41, 43, 44, 45, 47;
    54: 150; *YABC 1:* 107
Beyer, Paul J. III *74:* 24
Bezencon, Jacqueline *48:* 40
Biamonte, Daniel *40:* 90
Bianchi, John *91:* 19
Bianco, Pamela *15:* 31; *28:* 44, 45, 46
Bible, Charles *13:* 15
Bice, Clare *22:* 40
Biedrzycki, David *186:* 170
Bierman, Don *57:* 184
Biggers, John *2:* 123
Biggs, Brian *192:* 38; *196:* 15; *207:* 170
Bikadoroff, Roxanna *201:* 74
Bileck, Marvin *3:* 102; *40:* 36, 37
Bilibin, Ivan *61:* 8, 9, 12, 13, 14, 15, 151, 152,
    154, 162
Billington, Patrick *98:* 71
Billout, Guy *144:* 38, 39
Bimen, Levent *5:* 179
Binch, Caroline *81:* 18; *140:* 15, 16; *144:* 115;
    211: 82

Binder, Hannes *169:* 163
Bing, Christopher *126:* 34
Binger, Bill *121:* 46
Binks, Robert *25:* 150
Binzen, Bill *24:* 47
Birch, Reginald *15:* 150; *19:* 33, 34, 35, 36; *37:* 196,197; *44:* 182; *46:* 176; *YABC 1:* 84; *2:* 34, 39
Birchall, Mark *123:* 188
Bird, Esther Brock *1:* 36; *25:* 66
Birdsong, Keith *167:* 85
Birkett, Georgie *204:* 121
Birkett, Rachel *78:* 206
Birling, Paul *109:* 30
Birmingham, Christian *132:* 243; *143:* 114; *209:* 58
Birmingham, Lloyd P. *12:* 51; *83:* 13
Biro, Val *1:* 26; *41:* 42; *60:* 178; *67:* 23, 24; *84:* 242, 243
Bischoff, Ilse *44:* 51
Bishop, Don *199:* 133
Bishop, Gavin *97:* 17, 18; *144:* 42, 44; *216:* 52, 55, 56, 57
Bishop, Kathleen Wong *115:* 67
Bishop, Rich *56:* 43
Bite, I. *60:* 14
Bittinger, Ned *93:* 117; *205:* 115
Bjorklund, Lorence *3:* 188, 252; *7:* 100; *9:* 113; *10:* 66; *19:* 178; *33:* 122, 123; *35:* 36, 37, 38, 39,41, 42, 43; *36:* 185; *38:* 93; *47:* 106; *66:* 194; *YABC 1:* 242
Bjorkman, Steve *91:* 199; *160:* 110; *198:* 18
Blabey, Aaron *214:* 35
Black Sheep *164:* 100
Blackburn, Loren H. *63:* 10
Blackall, Sophie *194:* 140; *209:* 157
Blackford, John *137:* 105; *180:* 36
Blackwell, Basil T. *YABC 1:* 68, 69
Blackwood, Freya *199:* 9
Blackwood, Gary L. *118:* 17
Blades, Ann *16:* 52; *37:* 213; *50:* 41; *69:* 21; *99:* 215
Blair, Jay *45:* 46; *46:* 155
Blaisdell, Elinore *1:* 121; *3:* 134; *35:* 63
Blake, Anne Catharine *189:* 71
Blake, Francis *198:* 4
Blake, Quentin *3:* 170; *10:* 48; *13:* 38; *21:* 180; *26:* 60; *28:* 228; *30:* 29, 31; *40:* 108; *45:* 219; *46:* 165, 168; *48:* 196; *52:* 10, 11, 12,13, 14, 15, 16, 17; *73:* 41, 43; *78:* 84, 86; *80:* 250, 251; *84:* 210, 211, 212; *87:* 177; *96:* 24, 26, 28; *124:* 79; *125:* 32, 34; *181:* 139; *211:* 26, 27
Blake, Robert J. *37:* 90; *53:* 67; *54:* 23; *160:* 28, 29
Blake, William *30:* 54, 56, 57, 58, 59, 60
Blanchard, N. Taylor *82:* 140
Blass, Jacqueline *8:* 215
Blazek, Scott R. *91:* 71
Bleck, Cathie *118:* 116
Bleck, Linda *204:* 124
Blegvad, Erik *2:* 59; *3:* 98; *5:* 117; *7:* 131; *11:* 149; *14:* 34, 35; *18:* 237; *32:* 219; *60:* 106; *66:* 16, 17, 18, 19; *70:* 233; *76:* 18; *82:* 106; *87:* 45; *100:* 188; *129:* 125; *132:* 17, 18, 19, 20; *176:* 14; *200:* 100; *YABC 1:* 201
Blessen, Karen *93:* 126
Bliss, Corinne Demas *37:* 38
Bliss, Harry *196:* 27, 28, 29
Blitt, Barry *179:* 199; *187:* 13
Bloch, Lucienne *10:* 12
Blondon, Herve *129:* 48; *183:* 22
Bloom, Lloyd *35:* 180; *36:* 149; *47:* 99; *62:* 117; *68:* 231; *72:* 136; *75:* 185; *83:* 99; *108:* 19
Bloom, Suzanne *172:* 23, 24
Blossom, Dave *34:* 29
Blumenschein, E.L. *YABC 1:* 113, 115
Blumer, Patt *29:* 214
Blundell, Kim *29:* 36

Bluthenthal, Diana Cain *93:* 32; *104:* 106; *177:* 26
Blythe, Benjamin *128:* 7
Blythe, Gary *112:* 52; *181:* 166; *182:* 64; *185:* 7; *186:* 116, 117
Boake, Kathy *176:* 185
Board, Perry *171:* 99
Boardman, Gwenn *12:* 60
Boatwright, Phil *211:* 195
Bober, Richard *125:* 145; *132:* 40
Bobri *30:* 138; *47:* 27
Bock, Vera *1:* 187; *21:* 41
Bock, William Sauts *8:* 7; *14:* 37; *16:* 120; *21:* 141; *36:* 177; *62:* 203
Bodecker, N(iels) M(ogens) *8:* 13; *14:* 2; *17:* 55, 56, 57; *73:* 22, 23, 24
Boehm, Linda *40:* 31
Bogacki, Tomek *138:* 31, 32; *144:* 123; *202:* 13
Bogan, Paulette *197:* 152; *201:* 17
Bogdan, Florentina *107:* 43
Bohdal, Susi *22:* 44; *101:* 20
Bohlen, Nina *58:* 13
Boies, Alex *96:* 53
Bok, Chip *205:* 16
Bolam, Emily *101:* 216; *159:* 12; *205:* 59
Bolian, Polly *3:* 270; *4:* 30; *13:* 77; *29:* 197
Bolle, Frank *87:* 100; *208:* 101
Bollen, Roger *79:* 186; *83:* 16
Bolling, Vickey *114:* 44
Bollinger, Peter *101:* 7; *128:* 198; *172:* 26
Bolognese, Don *2:* 147, 231; *4:* 176; *7:* 146; *17:* 43; *23:* 192; *24:* 50; *34:* 108; *36:* 133; *71:* 24, 25; *103:* 131; *129:* 39, 40
Bolster, Rob *186:* 169
Bolton, A.T. *57:* 158
Bond, Arnold *18:* 116
Bond, Barbara Higgins *21:* 102
Bond, Bruce *52:* 97
Bond, Felicia *38:* 197; *49:* 55, 56; *89:* 170; *90:* 171; *126:* 37
Bond, Higgins *177:* 22, 23; *209:* 175
Bonn, Pat *43:* 40
Bonner, Hannah *197:* 13, 14
Bonners, Susan *41:* 40; *85:* 36; *94:* 99, 100; *151:* 105, 106
Bono, Mary *184:* 73
Bonsall, Crosby *23:* 6
Boon, Debbie *103:* 6; *144:* 188
Boon, Emilie *86:* 23, 24
Boone, Debbie *165:* 77
Boore, Sara *60:* 73
Bootman, Colin *155:* 13; *159:* 35; *174:* 192
Booth, Franklin *YABC 2:* 76
Booth, George *191:* 13
Booth, Graham *32:* 193; *37:* 41, 42
Borda, Juliette *102:* 188
Bordier, Georgette *16:* 54
Boren, Tinka *27:* 128
Borges, Jose Francisco *119:* 62
Borja, Robert *22:* 48
Born, Adolf *49:* 63
Bornstein, Ruth *14:* 44; *88:* 45, 46; *107:* 30
Borten, Helen *3:* 54; *5:* 24
Bosin, Blackbear *69:* 104
Bossom, Naomi *35:* 48
Bostock, Mike *83:* 221; *114:* 14; *188:* 205
Boston, Peter *19:* 42
Bosustow, Stephen *34:* 202
Boszko, Ron *75:* 47
Bottner, Barbara *14:* 46
Boucher, Joelle *41:* 138
Boulat, Pierre *44:* 40
Boulet, Susan Seddon *50:* 47
Bouma, Paddy *118:* 25; *128:* 16
Bour, Daniele *66:* 145
Bourke-White, Margaret *15:* 286, 287; *57:* 102
Boutavant, Marc *200:* 136
Boutet de Monvel, M. *30:* 61, 62, 63, 65
Bowen, Betsy *105:* 222
Bowen, Richard *42:* 134

Bowen, Ruth *31:* 188
Bower, Ron *29:* 33
Bowers, David *95:* 38; *115:* 20; *127:* 169, 170; *165:* 57; *207:* 11
Bowers, Tim *185:* 35; *201:* 41
Bowman, Claire *174:* 177
Bowman, Eric *151:* 23
Bowman, Leslie *85:* 203; *105:* 108; *116:* 76; *128:* 234; *182:* 24, 25
Bowman, Peter *146:* 214, 215; *150:* 115
Bowser, Carolyn Ewing *22:* 253
Boxall, Ed *178:* 28
Boyd, Aaron *158:* 242
Boyd, Patti *45:* 31
Boyle, Eleanor Vere *28:* 50, 51
Boynton, Sandra *57:* 13, 14, 15; *107:* 36, 37; *152:* 12, 13, 14
Bozzo, Frank *4:* 154
Brabbs, Derry *55:* 170
Brace, Eric *132:* 193, 194; *152:* 71; *184:* 195; *197:* 6; *201:* 54
Brackers de Hugo, Pierre *115:* 21
Bradford, June *158:* 138
Bradford, Ron *7:* 157
Bradley, David P. *69:* 105
Bradley, Richard D. *26:* 182
Bradley, William *5:* 164
Brady, Irene *4:* 31; *42:* 37; *68:* 191
Bragg, Michael *32:* 78; *46:* 31
Bragg, Ruth Gembicki *77:* 18
Brainerd, John W. *65:* 19
Braithwaite, Althea *23:* 12, 13; *119:* 16
Brak, Syd *146:* 187
Bralds, Braldt *90:* 28; *91:* 151
Bram, Elizabeth *30:* 67
Bramley, Peter *4:* 3
Brandenberg, Aliki *2:* 36, 37; *24:* 222; *35:* 49, 50, 51,52, 53, 54, 56, 57; *75:* 15, 17; *92:* 205; *113:* 18, 19, 20; *157:* 28; *156:* 111
Brandenburg, Alexa *75:* 19
Brandenburg, Jim *47:* 58; *150:* 212
Brandi, Lillian *31:* 158
Brandon, Brumsic, Jr. *9:* 25
Brannen, Sarah S. *202:* 15; *216:* 199
Bransom, Paul *17:* 121; *43:* 44
Braren, Loretta Trezzo *87:* 193
Brassard, France *186:* 22
Braun, Wendy *80:* 17, 18; *213:* 14
Brautigam, Don *115:* 175, 176
Brazell, Derek *75:* 105; *79:* 9
Breathed, Berkeley *86:* 27, 28, 29; *161:* 13, 14
Breckenreid, Julia *192:* 209
Breen, Steve *186:* 23
Brennan, Steve *83:* 230; *101:* 184
Brenner, Fred *22:* 85; *36:* 34; *42:* 34
Brett, Bernard *22:* 54
Brett, Harold M. *26:* 98, 99, 100
Brett, Jan *30:* 135; *42:* 39; *71:* 31, 32; *130:* 23, 24, 25, 26, 27; *171:* 15, 16
Brewer, Paul *106:* 115; *145:* 202
Brewer, Sally King *33:* 44
Brewster, Patience *40:* 68; *45:* 22, 183; *51:* 20; *66:* 144; *89:* 4; *97:* 30, 31; *212:* 99
Brick, John *10:* 15
Brickman, Robin D. *131:* 88; *142:* 150; *155:* 18; *178:* 109; *184:* 32
Bridge, David R. *45:* 28
Bridgman, L.J. *37:* 77
Bridwell, Norman *4:* 37; *138:* 36, 37, 40
Brierley, Louise *91:* 22; *96:* 165; *183:* 51
Briggs, Harry *172:* 187
Briggs, Raymond *10:* 168; *23:* 20, 21; *66:* 29, 31, 32; *131:* 28, 29; *184:* 15, 16
Brigham, Grace A. *37:* 148
Bright, Robert *24:* 55
Brighton, Catherine *107:* 39; *206:* 23
Brinckloe, Julie *13:* 18; *24:* 79, 115; *29:* 35; *63:* 140; *81:* 131
Brion *47:* 116
Brisley, Joyce L. *22:* 57
Brisson, James F. *110:* 60

Brittingham, Geoffrey 88: 37
Brix-Henker, Silke 81: 194
Broadway, Hannah 208: 104
Brock, Charles E. 15: 97; 19: 247, 249; 23: 224, 225; 36: 88; 42: 41, 42, 43, 44, 45; 100: 189; YABC 1: 194, 196, 203
Brock, Emma 7: 21
Brock, Henry Matthew 15: 81; 16: 141; 19: 71; 34: 115; 40: 164; 42: 47, 48, 49; 49: 66
Brocksopp, Arthur 57: 157
Broda, Ron 136: 180; 174: 123
Brodkin, Gwen 34: 135
Brodovitch, Alexi 52: 22
Bromhall, Winifred 5: 11; 26: 38
Bromley, Lizzy 159: 179
Bronson, Linda 150: 210; 174: 133; 203: 16, 17
Brooke, L. Leslie 16: 181, 182, 183, 186; 17: 15, 16, 17; 18: 194
Brooker, Christopher 15: 251
Brooker, Kyrsten 111: 94; 140: 28; 162: 111; 175: 108; 186: 42, 225; 199: 12; 201: 30
Brooks, Erik 166: 52; 182: 30
Brooks, Karen Stormer 186: 110
Brooks, Maya Itzna 92: 153
Brooks, Ron 94: 15; 197: 188; 212: 6, 7, 8, 9
Brooks, S.G. 178: 127
Broomfield, Maurice 40: 141
Brotman, Adolph E. 5: 21
Brown, Buck 45: 48
Brown, Calef 179: 18; 210: 206; 217: 30, 31
Brown, Christopher 62: 124, 125, 127, 128
Brown, Craig McFarland 73: 28; 84: 65
Brown, Dan 61: 167; 115: 183, 184; 116: 28, 29; 193: 190; 200: 21, 23
Brown, David 7: 47; 48: 52
Brown, Denise 11: 213
Brown, Don 172: 29
Brown, Elbrite 195: 39; 198: 5
Brown, Ford Madox 48: 74
Brown, Hunter 191: 111, 112
Brown, Judith Gwyn 1: 45; 7: 5; 8: 167; 9: 182, 190; 20: 16, 17, 18; 23: 142; 29: 117; 33: 97; 36: 23, 26; 43: 184; 48: 201, 223; 49: 69; 86: 227; 110: 188; 153: 7
Brown, Kathryn 98: 26
Brown, Lisa 187: 175
Brown, Laurie Krasny 99: 30
Brown, Marc (Tolon) 10: 17, 197; 14: 263; 51: 18; 53: 11, 12, 13, 15, 16, 17; 75: 58; 80: 24, 25, 26; 82: 261; 99: 29; 145: 22, 23, 25, 27; 162: 198
Brown, Marcia 7: 30; 25: 203; 47: 31, 32, 33, 34, 35,36, 37, 38, 39, 40, 42, 43, 44; YABC 1: 27
Brown, Margery W. 5: 32, 33; 10: 3
Brown, Martin 101: 43
Brown, Mary Barrett 97: 74
Brown, Palmer 36: 40
Brown, Paul 25: 26; 26: 107
Brown, Richard 61: 18; 67: 30
Brown, Rick 78: 71; 150: 154
Brown, Robert S. 85: 33
Brown, Rod 157: 142
Brown, Ruth 55: 165; 86: 112, 113; 105: 16, 17, 18; 171: 178
Brown, Trevor 99: 160; 139: 247; 189: 206
Browne, Anthony 45: 50, 51, 52; 61: 21, 22, 23, 24, 25; 105: 21, 22, 23, 25
Browne, Dik 8: 212; 67: 32, 33, 35, 37, 39
Browne, Gordon 16: 97; 64: 114, 116, 117, 119, 121
Browne, Hablot K. 15: 65, 80; 21: 14, 15, 16, 17, 18, 19,20; 24: 25
Browne, Jane 165: 222
Browning, Coleen 4: 132
Browning, Mary Eleanor 24: 84
Bruce, Robert 23: 23
Brude, Dick 48: 215
Bruel, Nick 166: 41; 205: 17, 18
Brule, Al 3: 135

Brumbeau, Jeff 157: 29
Bruna, Dick 43: 48, 49, 50; 76: 27, 28
Brundage, Frances 19: 244
Brunhoff, Jean de 24: 57, 58
Brunhoff, Laurent de 24: 60; 71: 35, 36, 37
Brunkus, Denise 84: 50; 123: 117; 178: 209; 193: 99; 204: 10, 11, 12; 209: 202
Brunson, Bob 43: 135
Bryan, Ashley 31: 44; 72: 27, 28, 29; 107: 92; 116: 192; 132: 24; 178: 33, 34, 35; 208: 83
Bryant, Laura J. 176: 36; 183: 168; 214: 141
Bryant, Michael 93: 74
Brychta, Alex 21: 21
Bryer, Diana 107: 121
Bryson, Bernarda 3: 88, 146; 39: 26; 44: 185; 131: 40
Buba, Joy 12: 83; 30: 226; 44: 56
Buchanan, George 166: 198
Buchanan, Lilian 13: 16
Buchanan, Rachel 171: 71
Bucholtz-Ross, Linda 44: 137
Buchs, Thomas 40: 38
Buck, Margaret Waring 3: 30
Buckhardt, Marc 172: 59
Buckley, Mike 166: 180
Budwine, Greg 175: 172
Buehner, Mark 104: 12, 15; 105: 160; 119: 98; 157: 188; 159: 39, 40, 43; 192: 111
Buehr, Walter 3: 31
Buff, Conrad 19: 52, 53, 54
Buff, Mary 19: 52, 53
Bull, Charles Livingston 18: 207; 88: 175, 176
Bullen, Anne 3: 166, 167
Buller, Jon 205: 21
Bullock, Kathleen 77: 24
Bumgarner-Kirby, Claudia 77: 194
Burbank, Addison 37: 43
Burchard, Peter Duncan 3: 197; 5: 35; 6: 158, 218; 143: 17
Burckhardt, Marc 94: 48; 110: 89; 196: 41; 199: 116
Burger, Carl 3: 33; 45: 160, 162
Burgeson, Marjorie 19: 31
Burgess, Anne 76: 252
Burgess, Gelett 32: 39, 42
Burgess, Mark 157: 31
Burke, Jim 179: 19; 185: 63
Burke, Phillip 95: 117
Burkert, Nancy Ekholm 18: 186; 22: 140; 24: 62, 63,64, 65; 26: 53; 29: 60, 61; 46: 171; YABC 1: 46
Burkhardt, Bruce 142: 86
Burkhardt, Melissa A. 142: 86
Burleson, Joe 104: 35; 172: 139
Burn, Doris 6: 172
Burn, Jeffrey 89: 125; 152: 132
Burn, Ted
    See Burn, Thomas E.
Burn, Thomas E. 151: 41
Burnard, Damon 115: 23
Burnett, Lindy 210: 59
Burnett, Virgil 44: 42
Burningham, John 9: 68; 16: 60, 61; 59: 28, 29, 30,31, 32, 33, 35; 111: 18, 19, 21; 160: 37
Burns, Howard M. 12: 173
Burns, Jim 47: 70; 86: 32; 91: 197; 123: 16
Burns, M.F. 26: 69
Burns, Raymond 9: 29
Burns, Robert 24: 106
Burr, Dan 65: 28; 108: 134; 164: 203; 182: 68
Burr, Dane 12: 2
Burra, Edward YABC 2: 68
Burrell, Galen 56: 76
Burri, Rene 41: 143; 54: 166
Burridge, Marge Opitz 14: 42
Burris, Burmah 4: 81
Burroughs, John Coleman 41: 64
Burroughs, Studley O. 41: 65
Burton, Marilee Robin 46: 33

Burton, Virginia Lee 2: 43; 44: 49, 51; 100: 46, 47; YABC 1: 24; 147: 56
Busoni, Rafaello 1: 186; 3: 224; 6: 126; 14: 5; 16: 62, 63
Butchkes, Sidney 50: 58
Butler, Geoff 94: 20
Butler, Ralph 116: 212
Butterfield, Ned 1: 153; 27: 128; 79: 63
Butterworth, Ian 184: 48, 49
Butterworth, Nick 106: 43, 44; 149: 34
Buxton, John 123: 12
Buzelli, Christopher 105: 149
Buzonas, Gail 29: 88
Buzzell, Russ W. 12: 177
Byard, Carole 39: 44; 57: 18, 19, 20; 60: 60; 61: 93, 96; 69: 210; 78: 246; 79: 227
Byars, Betsy 46: 35
Byfield, Barbara Ninde 8: 18
Byfield, Graham 32: 29
Bynum, Janie 176: 50
Byrd, Robert 13: 218; 33: 46; 158: 70; 212: 100
Byrd, Samuel 123: 104

C

Cabat, Erni 74: 38
Cabban, Vanessa 138: 73; 176: 39; 185: 65
Cabrera, Jane 103: 24; 152: 27; 182: 33, 34
Caceres, Ana Palmero 198: 106
Caddy, Alice 6: 41
Cady, Harrison 17: 21, 23; 19: 57, 58
Caffrey, Aileen 72: 223; 141: 154
Cairns, Julia 177: 37
Caldecott, Randolph 16: 98, 103; 17: 32, 33, 36, 38, 39; 26: 90; 100: 49, 50; YABC 2: 172
Calder, Alexander 18: 168
Calderón, Gloria 179: 5
Calderon, W. Frank 25: 160
Caldwell, Ben 105: 75; 149: 60; 195: 61
Caldwell, Clyde 98: 100; 116: 39; 208: 145
Caldwell, Doreen 23: 77; 71: 41
Caldwell, John 46: 225
Call, Greg 126: 135; 165: 49; 182: 105, 163; 197: 18, 19; 200: 159; 209: 166; 212: 161
Callahan, Kevin 22: 42
Callahan, Philip S. 25: 77
Callan, Jamie 59: 37
Calvin, James 61: 92
Camburn-Bracalente, Carol A. 118: 22
Cameron, Chad 190: 144
Cameron, Julia Margaret 19: 203
Cameron, Scott 99: 18
Camm, Martin 140: 208, 209, 210
Campbell, Ann 11: 43; 123: 182; 183: 68
Campbell, Bill 89: 39
Campbell, Ken 126: 143; 205: 162
Campbell, Robert 55: 120
Campbell, Rod 51: 27; 98: 34
Campbell, Walter M. YABC 2: 158
Camps, Luis 28: 120, 121; 66: 35
Canga, C.B. 187: 165
Caniglia, Jeremy 201: 89
Cann, Helen 124: 50; 141: 78; 170: 138; 179: 22, 23
Cannell, Jon 196: 43
Cannon, Janell 78: 25; 128: 40
Canright, David 36: 162
Cantone, AnnaLaura 182: 146; 196: 80
Canty, Thomas 85: 161; 92: 47; 113: 192; 134: 60; 185: 117
Canyon, Christopher 150: 44; 151: 112
Caparo, Antonio Javier 204: 128
Caporale, Wende 70: 42
Capp, Al 61: 28, 30, 31, 40, 41, 43, 44
Cappon, Manuela 154: 64
Caras, Peter 36: 64
Caraway, Caren 57: 22

Caraway, James *3:* 200, 201
Carbe, Nino *29:* 183
Cares, Linda *67:* 176
Carigiet, Alois *24:* 67
Carle, Eric *4:* 42; *11:* 121; *12:* 29; *65:* 32,33,
34, 36; *73:* 63, 65; *163:* 55, 56
Carling, Amelia Lau *164:* 46
Carlino, Angela *168:* 43; *188:* 20
Carlson, Nancy L. *41:* 116; *56:* 25; *90:* 45;
144: 48, 50; *213:* 24, 25, 26
Carlluccio, Maria *175:* 129
Carmi, Giora *79:* 35; *149:* 40; *208:* 126
Carpenter, Nancy *76:* 128; *86:* 173; *89:* 171;
131: 186; *134:* 8; *138:* 215; *153:* 204; *159:*
93; *165:* 232; *211:* 134; *216:* 113
Carr, Archie *37:* 225
Carrick, Donald *5:* 194; *39:* 97; *49:* 70; *53:*
156; *63:* 15, 16, 17, 18, 19, 21; *80:* 131; *86:*
151; *118:* 24
Carrick, Malcolm *28:* 59, 60
Carrick, Paul *118:* 26; *194:* 28
Carrick, Valery *21:* 47
Carrier, Lark *71:* 43
Carroll, Jim *88:* 211; *140:* 177; *153:* 99; *195:*
75
Carroll, Lewis
See Dodgson, Charles L.
Carroll, Michael *72:* 5
Carroll, Pamela *84:* 68; *128:* 214; *199:* 130
Carroll, Ruth *7:* 41; *10:* 68
Carter, Abby *81:* 32; *97:* 121; *102:* 61; *163:*
139; *164:* 125; *184:* 22, 23; *191:* 85
Carter, Barbara *47:* 167, 169
Carter, David A. *114:* 24, 25; *170:* 42, 43
Carter, Don *124:* 54; *184:* 100; *192:* 43, 44, 45
Carter, Harry *22:* 179
Carter, Helene *15:* 38; *22:* 202, 203; *YABC 2:*
220, 221
Carter, Penny *173:* 91
Cartlidge, Michelle *49:* 65; *96:* 50, 51
Cartwright, Reg *63:* 61, 62; *78:* 26; *143:* 4
Cartwright, Shannon *176:* 81
Carty, Leo *4:* 196; *7:* 163; *58:* 131
Cary *4:* 133; *9:* 32; *20:* 2; *21:* 143
Cary, Page *12:* 41
Casale, Paul *71:* 63; *109:* 122; *136:* 28
Case, Chris *209:* 23
Case, Sandra E. *16:* 2
Caseley, Judith *87:* 36; *159:* 47, 48, 49
Casilla, Robert *78:* 7; *167:* 124; *211:* 41; *212:*
165
Casino, Steve *85:* 193
Cassel, Lili
See Wronker, Lili Cassel
Cassel-Wronker, Lili
See Wronker, Lili Cassel
Cassels, Jean *8:* 50; *150:* 119; *173:* 37; *186:*
182
Cassen, Melody *140:* 51
Cassity, Don *104:* 24
Cassler, Carl *75:* 137, 138; *82:* 162
Casson, Hugh *65:* 38, 40, 42, 43
Castellon, Federico *48:* 45, 46, 47, 48
Castle, Jane *4:* 80
Castro, Antonio *84:* 71
Casu, Danny "casroc" *201:* 10
Catalano, Dominic *94:* 79; *163:* 60, 61; *162:*
54
Catalanotto, Peter *63:* 170; *70:* 23; *71:* 182;
72: 96; *74:* 114; *76:* 194, 195; *77:* 7; *79:*
157; *80:* 28, 67; *83:* 157; *85:* 27; *108:* 11;
113: 30, 31, 33, 34, 36; *114:* 27, 28, 29; *117:*
53; *124:* 168; *159:* 54, 55; *195:* 19, 20, 21,
22, 24, 174; *200:* 156; *207:* 103; *209:* 184
Catania, Tom *68:* 82
Cather, Carolyn *3:* 83; *15:* 203; *34:* 216
Catlin, George *214:* 172
Catrow, David *117:* 179; *152:* 31, 33; *173:* 24;
206: 29
Cauley, Lorinda Bryan *44:* 135; *46:* 49
Cayard, Bruce *38:* 67

Cazet, Denys *52:* 27; *99:* 39, 40; *163:* 65, 66;
191: 25, 27, 28
Ceccoli, Nicoletta *181:* 39; *188:* 99; *199:* 118;
209: 6
Cecil, Randy *127:* 132, 133; *187:* 16, 17; *191:*
168; *209:* 5
Cellini, Joseph *2:* 73; *3:* 35; *16:* 116; *47:* 103
Cepeda, Joe *90:* 62; *109:* 91; *134:* 172; *159:*
57, 58, 164; *197:* 157; *203:* 69, 95; *215:* 38,
39, 40
Chabrian, Debbi *45:* 55
Chabrian, Deborah *51:* 182; *53:* 124; *63:* 107;
75: 84; *79:* 85; *82:* 247; *89:* 93; *101:* 197;
212: 13
Chagnon, Mary *37:* 158
Chalmers, Mary *3:* 145; *13:* 148; *33:* 125; *66:*
214
Chamberlain, Christopher *45:* 57
Chamberlain, Margaret *46:* 51; *106:* 89; *188:*
193; *212:* 16, 17
Chamberlain, Nigel *78:* 140
Chambers, C.E. *17:* 230
Chambers, Dave *12:* 151
Chambers, Jill *134:* 110
Chambers, Mary *4:* 188
Chambliss, Maxie *42:* 186; *56:* 159; *93:* 163,
164; *103:* 178; *186:* 33, 34; *196:* 39
Champlin, Dale *136:* 124
Chan, Harvey *96:* 236; *99:* 153; *143:* 218;
179: 144; *211:* 219
Chan, Peter *207:* 21
Chandler, David P. *28:* 62
Chaney, Howard *139:* 27
Chang, Warren *101:* 209
Chapel, Jody *68:* 20
Chapman, C.H. *13:* 83, 85, 87
Chapman, Frederick T. *6:* 27; *44:* 28
Chapman, Gaye *203:* 133
Chapman, Gaynor *32:* 52, 53
Chapman, Jane *145:* 186; *150:* 56; *166:* 220;
174: 202; *176:* 43, 44; *179:* 131; *202:* 189;
212: 20, 21, 22; *216:* 123, 225
Chapman, Lynne *175:* 31; *197:* 25; *208:* 44
Chappell, Warren *3:* 172; *21:* 56; *27:* 125
Charles, Donald *30:* 154, 155
Charlip, Remy *4:* 48; *34:* 138; *68:* 53, 54; *119:*
29, 30; *210:* 63, 64
Charlot, Jean *1:* 137, 138; *8:* 23; *14:* 31; *48:*
151; *56:* 21
Charlot, Martin *64:* 72
Charlton, Michael *34:* 50; *37:* 39
Charmatz, Bill *7:* 45
Chartier, Normand *9:* 36; *52:* 49; *66:* 40; *74:*
220; *145:* 169; *168:* 91; *177:* 108
Chase, Lynwood M. *14:* 4
Chast, Roz *97:* 39, 40; *212:* 25
Chastain, Madye Lee *4:* 50
Chateron, Ann *152:* 19
Chatterton, Martin *68:* 102; *152:* 19
Chau, Tungwai *140:* 35
Chauncy, Francis *24:* 158
Chayka, Doug *145:* 97; *177:* 150; *196:* 46;
212: 58
Chee, Cheng-Khee *79:* 42; *81:* 224; *180:* 245
Chen, Chih-sien *90:* 226
Chen, Tony *6:* 45; *19:* 131; *29:* 126; *34:* 160
Chen, Yong *183:* 34
Cheney, T.A. *11:* 47
Cheng, Andrea *205:* 28
Cheng, Judith *36:* 45; *51:* 16
Chermayeff, Ivan *47:* 53
Cherry, David *93:* 40
Cherry, Lynne *34:* 52; *65:* 184; *87:* 111; *99:*
46, 47
Chesak, Lina *135:* 118
Chess, Victoria *12:* 6; *33:* 42, 48, 49; *40:* 194;
41: 145; *69:* 80; *72:* 100; *92:* 33, 34; *104:*
167
Chessare, Michele *41:* 50; *56:* 48; *69:* 145
Chesterton, G.K. *27:* 43, 44, 45, 47
Chestnutt, David *47:* 217

Chesworth, Michael *75:* 24, 152; *88:* 136; *94:*
25; *98:* 155; *160:* 42; *207:* 23, 24, 25; *214:*
145
Chetham, Celia *134:* 34
Chetwin, Grace *86:* 40
Cheung, Irving *158:* 96
Chevalier, Christa *35:* 66
Chew, Ruth *7:* 46; *132:* 147
Chewning, Randy *92:* 206
Chichester Clark, Emma *72:* 121; *77:* 212; *78:*
209; *87:* 143; *117:* 37, 39, 40; *144:* 138;
156: 24, 25; *209:* 26
Chifflart *47:* 113, 127
Child, Lauren *119:* 32; *183:* 30, 31
Chin, Alex *28:* 54
Chitwood, Susan Tanner *163:* 16
Cho, Shinta *8:* 126
Chodos-Irvine, Margaret *52:* 102, 103, 107;
152: 44
Choi, Yangsook *171:* 134; *173:* 135; *178:* 38,
39, 40
Chollat, Emilie *170:* 203
Chollick, Jay *25:* 175
Choma, Christina *99:* 169
Chomey, Steve *188:* 53
Chorao, Kay *7:* 200, 201; *8:* 25; *11:* 234; *33:*
187; *35:* 239; *69:* 35; *70:* 235; *123:* 174;
193: 179; *215:* 43, 44, 45, 46
Chow, Frances J. Soo Ping *206:* 36
Chowdhury, Subrata *62:* 130; *162:* 22, 23
Christelow, Eileen *38:* 44; *83:* 198, 199; *90:*
57, 58; *184:* 26
Christensen, Bonnie *93:* 100; *153:* 67; *213:* 29,
30
Christensen, Gardell Dano *1:* 57
Christensen, James C. *140:* 226
Christiana, David *90:* 64; *135:* 13; *171:* 7;
195: 26, 27
Christiansen, Per *40:* 24
Christie, R. Gregory *116:* 107; *127:* 20, 21;
162: 179; *164:* 114; *165:* 137; *174:* 157;
179: 172; *185:* 17, 18, 19; *200:* 2; *204:* 85;
215: 207
Christy, Howard Chandler *17:* 163, 164, 165,
168, 169; *19:* 186, 187; *21:* 22, 23, 24, 25
Christy, Jana *194:* 21
Chronister, Robert *23:* 138; *63:* 27; *69:* 167
Church, Caroline Jayne *179:* 27
Church, Frederick *YABC 1:* 155
Chute, Marchette *1:* 59
Chwast, Jacqueline *1:* 63; *2:* 275; *6:* 46, 47;
11: 125; *12:* 202; *14:* 235
Chwast, Seymour *3:* 128, 129; *18:* 43; *27:*
152; *92:* 79; *96:* 56, 57, 58; *146:* 32, 33;
197: 99
Cieslawksi, Steve *101:* 142; *127:* 116; *158:*
169, 171; *190:* 174; *212:* 85
Cinelli, Lisa *146:* 253
Cirlin, Edgard *2:* 168
Clairin, Georges *53:* 109
Clapp, John *105:* 66; *109:* 58; *126:* 7; *129:*
148; *130:* 165; *195:* 48
Clark, Brenda *119:* 85; *153:* 55
Clark, David *77:* 164; *134:* 144, 145; *216:* 66,
67
Clark, Emma Chichester
See Chichester Clark, Emma
Clark, Victoria *35:* 159
Clarke, Greg *169:* 134; *215:* 47, 115
Clarke, Gus *72:* 226; *134:* 31
Clarke, Harry *23:* 172, 173
Clarke, Peter *75:* 102
Claverie, Jean *38:* 46; *88:* 29
Clavis, Philippe Goossens *182:* 167
Clay, Wil *203:* 29
Clayton, Elaine *159:* 60; *209:* 32
Clayton, Robert *9:* 181
Cleary, Brian P. *186:* 37
Cleaver, Elizabeth *8:* 204; *23:* 36
Cleland, T.M. *26:* 92
Clemens, Peter *61:* 125

Clement, Charles *20:* 38
Clement, Gary *186:* 79; *191:* 32
Clement, Janet *182:* 50
Clement, Nathan *200:* 30
Clement, Rod *97:* 42
Clement, Stephen *88:* 3
Clementson, John *84:* 213
Clemesha, David *192:* 49, 50
Clevin, Jorgen *7:* 50
Clifford, Judy *34:* 163; *45:* 198
Clokey, Art *59:* 44
Clouse, Dennis *187:* 158
Clouse, James *84:* 15
Clouse, Nancy L. *78:* 31; *114:* 90
Clover, Peter *152:* 45
Cneut, Carll *156:* 166; *165:* 67; *197:* 26
Coalson, Glo *9:* 72, 85; *25:* 155; *26:* 42; *35:* 212; *53:* 31; *56:* 154; *94:* 37, 38, 193
Cober, Alan E. *17:* 158; *32:* 77; *49:* 127
Cober-Gentry, Leslie *92:* 111
Cocca-Leffler, Maryann *80:* 46; *136:* 60; *139:* 193; *194:* 31, 33, 34
Cochran, Bobbye *11:* 52
CoConis, Ted *4:* 41; *46:* 41; *51:* 104
Cocozza, Chris *87:* 18; *110:* 173; *111:* 149
Cockroft, Jason *152:* 20
Coerr, Eleanor *1:* 64; *67:* 52
Coes, Peter *35:* 172
Cogancherry, Helen *52:* 143; *69:* 131; *77:* 93; *78:* 220; *109:* 204; *110:* 129; *203:* 92
Coggins, Jack *2:* 69
Cohen, Alix *7:* 53
Cohen, Miriam *155:* 23, 24
Cohen, Nancy R. *165:* 35
Cohen, Santiago *164:* 26; *215:* 52, 199
Cohen, Sheldon *105:* 33, 34; *166:* 46, 47
Cohen, Vincent O. *19:* 243
Cohen, Vivien *11:* 112
Coker, Paul *51:* 172
Colbert, Anthony *15:* 41; *20:* 193
Colby, C.B. *3:* 47
Cole, Babette *58:* 172; *96:* 63, 64; *155:* 29
Cole, Brock *68:* 223; *72:* 36, 37, 38, 192; *127:* 23; *136:* 64, 65; *197:*
Cole, Gwen *87:* 185
Cole, Henry *178:* 120; *181:* 42, 43; *189:* 60; *213:* 35, 36
Cole, Herbert *28:* 104
Cole, Michael *59:* 46
Cole, Olivia H.H. *1:* 134; *3:* 223; *9:* 111; *38:* 104
Cole, Rachael *209:* 39
Colin, Paul *102:* 59; *123:* 118; *126:* 152; *192:* 129
Colley, Jacqui *202:* 20
Collicott, Sharleen *98:* 39; *143:* 29, 30
Collier, Bryan *126:* 54; *151:* 166; *174:* 16, 17, 18; *204:* 18, 19; *208:* 84; *211:* 143
Collier, David *13:* 127
Collier, John *27:* 179; *208:* 154
Collier, Steven *50:* 52
Collier-Morales, Roberta *168:* 61
Collins, Heather *66:* 84; *67:* 68; *81:* 40; *98:* 192, 193; *129:* 95, 96, 98
Collins, Matt *167:* 90
Collins, Ross *140:* 23, 24; *200:* 36, 37; *209:* 54
Colman, Audrey *146:* 161
Colón, Raul *108:* 112; *113:* 5; *117:* 167; *134:* 112; *146:* 23; *159:* 92; *166:* 73; *180:* 107; *186:* 156; *190:* 6; *193:* 24, 205; *202:* 21, 22, 23; *217:* 68
Colonna, Bernard *21:* 50; *28:* 103; *34:* 140; *43:* 180; *78:* 150
Comport, Sally Wern *117:* 169; *169:* 104; *190:* 42; *207:* 50
Conahan, Carolyn *215:* 17
Conde, J.M. *100:* 120
Condon, Grattan *54:* 85 Condon, Ken *161:* 44; *195:* 28, 29
Cone, Ferne Geller *39:* 49

Cone, J. Morton *39:* 49
Conklin, Paul *43:* 62
Connelly, Gwen *212:* 30
Connelly, James *198:* 12
Connolly, Howard *67:* 88
Connolly, Jerome P. *4:* 128; *28:* 52
Connolly, Peter *47:* 60
Conoly, Walle *110:* 224
Conover, Chris *31:* 52; *40:* 184; *41:* 51; *44:* 79; *213:* 39
Constantin, Pascale *207:* 159
Contreras, Gerry *72:* 9
Converse, James *38:* 70
Conway *62:* 62
Conway, Michael *69:* 12; *81:* 3; *92:* 108
Cook, Ande *188:* 135
Cook, G.R. *29:* 165
Cook, Joel *108:* 160
Cookburn, W.V. *29:* 204
Cooke, Donald E. *2:* 77
Cooke, Tom *52:* 118
Coomaraswamy, A.K. *50:* 100
Coombs, Charles *43:* 65
Coombs, Deborah *139:* 175
Coombs, Patricia *2:* 82; *3:* 52; *22:* 119; *51:* 32, 33, 34, 35, 36, 37, 38, 39, 40, 42, 43
Cooney, Barbara *6:* 16, 17, 50; *12:* 42; *13:* 92; *15:* 145; *16:* 74, 111; *18:* 189; *23:* 38, 89, 93; *32:* 138; *38:* 105; *59:* 48, 49, 51, 52, 53; *74:* 222; *81:* 100; *91:* 25; *96:* 71, 72, 74; *100:* 149; *YABC2:* 10
Cooper, Elisha *157:* 38, 39
Cooper, Floyd *79:* 95; *81:* 45; *84:* 82; *85:* 74; *91:* 118; *96:* 77, 78; *103:* 149; *144:* 54; *145:* 151; *159:* 198; *176:* 133, 134; *187:* 26, 27, 28, 29; *188:* 22; *199:* 175
Cooper, Heather *50:* 39
Cooper, Helen *102:* 42, 43, 44
Cooper, Mario *24:* 107
Cooper, Marjorie *7:* 112
Cope, Jane *61:* 201; *108* 52
Copeland, Mark *180:* 12
Copelman, Evelyn *8:* 61; *18:* 25
Copley, Heather *30:* 86; *45:* 57
Corace, Jen *208:* 48
Corbett, Grahame *30:* 114; *43:* 67
Corbino, John *19:* 248
Corcos, Lucille *2:* 223; *10:* 27; *34:* 66
Cordell, Matthew *197:* 93; *199:* 20, 21
Corey, Robert *9:* 34
Corlass, Heather *10:* 7
Cornell, James *27:* 60
Cornell, Jeff *11:* 58
Cornell, Laura *94:* 179; *95:* 25
Corr, Christopher *204:* 98
Corral, Ridrigs *212:* 87
Corrigan, Barbara *8:* 37
Corrigan, Patrick *145:* 149
Corwin, Judith Hoffman *10:* 28
Corwin, Oliver *191:* 119
Cory, Fanny Y. *20:* 113; *48:* 29
Cosentino, Ralph *169:* 32
Cosgrove, Margaret *3:* 100; *47:* 63; *82:* 133
Costabel, Eva Deutsch *45:* 66, 67
Costanza, John *58:* 7, 8, 9
Costello, Chris *86:* 78
Costello, David F. *23:* 55
Côté, Geneviéve *184:* 37, 39; *210:* 256; *211:* 151
Cote, Nancy *126:* 139; *156:* 101; *174:* 101; *182:* 53, 54, 55
Cottenden, Jeff *190:* 45
Couch, Greg *94:* 124; *110:* 13; *162:* 31; *168:* 149; *199:* 22; *216:* 144
Councell, Ruth Tietjen *79:* 29
Courtney, Cathy *58:* 69, 144; *59:* 15; *61:* 20, 87
Courtney, R. *35:* 110
Counihan, Claire *133:* 106
Cousineau, Normand *89:* 180; *112:* 76
Cousins, Lucy *172:* 53, 54; *205:* 34, 35

Couture, Christin *41:* 209
Covarrubias, Miguel *35:* 118, 119, 123, 124, 125
Coville, Katherine *32:* 57; *36:* 167; *92:* 38
Covington, Neverne *113:* 87
Cowdrey, Richard *169:* 170; *178:* 205; *204:* 22, 23; *215:* 31
Cowell, Cressida *140:* 39
Cowell, Lucinda *77:* 54
Cowles, Rose *203:* 164, 167
Cox *43:* 93
Cox, Charles *8:* 20
Cox, David *56:* 37; *90:* 63; *119:* 38
Cox, Palmer *24:* 76, 77
Cox, Steve *140:* 96
Coxe, Molly *69:* 44
Coxon, Michele *158:* 80
Crabb, Gordon *70:* 39
Crabtree, Judith *98:* 42
Craft, Kinuko *22:* 182; *36:* 220; *53:* 122, 123, 148,149; *74:* 12; *81:* 129; *86:* 31; *89:* 139; *127:* 27, 28, 29; *132:* 142; *139:* 38
Craig, Daniel *177:* 67; *180:* 11; *185:* 203; *211:* 212
Craig, David *136:* 198; *205:* 37
Craig, Helen *49:* 76; *62:* 70, 71, 72; *69:* 141; *94:* 42, 43, 44; *112:* 53; *135:* 101, 102; *213:* 45, 46, 47, 55, 81, 82
Crane, Alan H. *1:* 217
Crane, H.M. *13:* 111
Crane, Jack *43:* 183
Crane, Jordan *174:* 21
Crane, Walter *18:* 46, 47, 48, 49, 53, 54, 56, 57, 59, 60, 61; *22:* 128; *24:* 210, 217; *100:* 70, 71
Cravath, Lynne W. *98:* 45; *182:* 58, 59; *216:* 48
Crawford, Allen *212:* 181
Crawford, Denise *137:* 213
Crawford, Will *43:* 77
Credle, Ellis *1:* 69
Czekaj, Jef *217:* 44
Crespi, Francesca *87:* 90
Cressy, Michael *124:* 55; *203:* 132
Crews, Donald *32:* 59, 60; *76:* 42, 43, 44
Crews, Nina *97:* 49
Crichlow, Ernest *74:* 88; *83:* 203
Crilley, Mark *210:* 71
Croft, James *150:* 57
Crofut, Bob *80:* 87; *81:* 47
Crofut, Susan *23:* 61
Croll, Carolyn *80:* 137; *102:* 52
Cross, Peter *56:* 78; *63:* 60, 65
Crowe, Elizabeth *88:* 144
Crowell, Pers *3:* 125
Cruikshank, George *15:* 76, 83; *22:* 74, 75, 76, 77, 78, 79,80, 81, 82, 84, 137; *24:* 22, 23
Crump, Fred H. *11:* 62
Cruz, Ray *6:* 55; *70:* 234; *123:* 173; *172:* 192
Csatari, Joe *44:* 82; *55:* 152; *63:* 25, 28; *102:* 58
Cuetara, Mittie *158:* 85
Cuffari, Richard *4:* 75; *5:* 98; *6:* 56; *7:* 13,84, 153; *8:* 148, 155; *9:* 89; *11:* 19; *12:* 55, 96,114; *15:* 51, 202; *18:* 5; *20:* 139; *21:* 197; *22:* 14, 192; *23:* 15, 106; *25:* 97; *27:* 133; *28:* 196; *29:* 54; *30:* 85; *31:* 35; *36:* 101; *38:* 171; *42:* 97; *44:* 92, 192; *45:* 212, 213; *46:* 36, 198; *50:* 164; *54:* 80, 136, 137, 145; *56:* 17; *63:* 66; *66:* 49, 50; *70:* 41; *71:* 132; *77:* 157; *78:* 58, 149; *79:* 120; *85:* 2, 152
Cugat, Xavier *19:* 120
Cumings, Art *35:* 160
Cummings, Chris *29:* 167
Cummings, Michael *159:* 142
Cummings, Pat *42:* 61; *61:* 99; *69:* 205; *71:* 57,58; *78:* 24, 25; *93:* 75; *107:* 49, 50; *164:* 259; *203:* 45, 46
Cummings, Richard *24:* 119
Cunette, Lou *20:* 93; *22:* 125

Cunningham, Aline *25:* 180
Cunningham, David *11:* 13
Cunningham, Imogene *16:* 122, 127
Cunningham, Kelley *176:* 159
Cupples, Pat *107:* 12; *126:* 109; *182:* 13; *198:* 68; *217:* 21, 22
Curlee, Lynn *98:* 48; *141:* 39; *190:* 48
Currey, Anna *190:* 145; *202:* 130, 132
Curry, John Steuart *2:* 5; *19:* 84; *34:* 36; *144:* 126
Curry, Tom *127:* 131; *185:* 25, 26
Curtis, Bruce *23:* 96; *30:* 88; *36:* 22
Curtis, Neil *167:* 30
Curtis, Stacy *205:* 38
Cusack, Margaret *58:* 49, 50, 51
Cushman, Doug *65:* 57; *101:* 39, 40; *133:* 179; *157:* 45; *186:* 157; *210:* 76, 77
Cutting, Ann *196:* 194
Cyrus, Kurt *132:* 39; *179:* 36, 37
Czechowski, Alicia *95:* 21; *171:* 37
Czernecki, Stefan *117:* 173

D

Dabcovich, Lydia *25:* 105; *40:* 114; *99:* 75, 76
Dacey, Bob *82:* 175; *152:* 65
d'Achille, Gino *127:* 175, 176
Dailey, Don *78:* 197
Dain, Martin J. *35:* 75
Dale, Penny *127:* 224; *151:* 57; *160:* 89; *197:* 75
Dale, Rae *72:* 197
Daley, Joann *50:* 22
Dalton, Anne *40:* 62; *63:* 119
Daly, Deborah M. *74:* 213
Daly, Jim *103:* 60; *150:* 48
Daly, Jude *138:* 118, 119; *213:* 41
Daly, Nicholas *37:* 53; *76:* 48, 49
Daly, Niki *107:* 15; *114:* 38, 39, 40; *164:* 86; *192:* 53; *198:* 26, 27
Daly, Paul *97:* 205
Dalziel, Brothers *33:* 113
D'Amato, Alex *9:* 48; *20:* 25
D'Amato, Janet *9:* 48; *20:* 25; *26:* 118
D'Amico, Steve *170:* 52
Danalis, Johnny *167:* 27
D'Andrea, Domenick *183:* 108
Daniel, Alan *23:* 59; *29:* 110; *76:* 50, 53, 55, 56; *153:* 76 *115:* 74; *134:* 70
Daniel, Lea *76:* 53, 55; *153:* 76
Daniel, Lewis C. *20:* 216
Daniels, Beau *73:* 4
Daniels, Steve *22:* 16
Daniels, Stewart *56:* 12
Dann, Bonnie *31:* 83
Dann, Penny *82:* 128
Danska, Herbert *24:* 219
Danyell, Alice *20:* 27
Dardik, Helen *208:* 200
Darley, F.O.C. *16:* 145; *19:* 79, 86, 88, 185; *21:* 28,36; *35:* 76, 77, 78, 79, 80, 81; *YABC 2:* 175
Darling, Lois *3:* 59; *23:* 30, 31
Darling, Louis *1:* 40, 41; *2:* 63; *3:* 59; *23:* 30,31; *43:* 54, 57, 59; *121:* 53
Darnell, K.L. *210:* 247
Darrow, David R. *84:* 101
Darrow, Whitney, Jr. *13:* 25; *38:* 220, 221
Darwin, Beatrice *43:* 54
Darwin, Len *24:* 82
Dastolfo, Frank *33:* 179
Dauber, Liz *1:* 22; *3:* 266; *30:* 49
Daugherty, James *3:* 66; *8:* 178; *13:* 27, 28, 161; *18:* 101; *19:* 72; *29:* 108; *32:* 156; *42:* 84; *YABC 1:* 256; *2:* 174
d'Aulaire, Edgar Parin *5:* 51; *66:* 53
d'Aulaire, Ingri Parin *5:* 51; *66:* 53
Davalos, Felipe *99:* 197; *159:* 66; *174:* 163

Davenier, Christine *125:* 88; *127:* 32; *128:* 152; *179:* 39, 40; *216:* 84, 85, 86, 87
Davick, Linda *151:* 124; *208:* 187
David, Jacques-Louis *193:* 22
David, Jonathan *19:* 37
Davidson, Kevin *28:* 154
Davidson, Raymond *32:* 61
Davie, Helen K. *77:* 48, 49
Davies, Andy Robert *205:* 169
Davies, Lottie *214:* 69
Davis, Allen *20:* 11; *22:* 45; *27:* 222; *29:* 157; *41:* 99; *47:* 99; *50:* 84; *52:* 105
Davis, Bette J. *15:* 53; *23:* 95
Davis, Dimitris *45:* 95
Davis, Eleanor *209:* 33
Davis, Hendon *151:* 122
Davis, Jack E. *145:* 139; *175:* 84, 85; *208:* 102; *210:* 81, 82; *213:* 151
Davis, Jim *32:* 63, 64
Davis, Katie *152:* 52, 53, 54; *208:* 52
Davis, Lambert *110:* 23, 24; *176:* 58
Davis, Marguerite *31:* 38; *34:* 69, 70; *100:* 34; *YABC 1:* 126, 230
Davis, Nelle *69:* 191
Davis, Paul *78:* 214
Davis, Rich *206:* 38
Davis, Stuart *211:* 69
Davis, Yvonne LeBrun *94:* 144
Davisson, Virginia H. *44:* 178
DaVolls, Andy *85:* 53
Dawson, Diane *24:* 127; *42:* 126; *52:* 130; *68:* 104
Dawson, Janine *215:* 198
Dawson, Willow *208:* 54; *216:* 119
Day, Alexandra *67:* 59; *97:* 54; *166:* 65; *169:* 40; *197:* 50, 51, 52, 54
Day, Larry *169:* 88; *185:* 59
Day, Rob *94:* 110; *127:* 24; *197:* 32
Dean, Bob *19:* 211
Dean, David *192:* 55
de Angeli, Marguerite *1:* 77; *27:* 62, 65, 66, 67, 69, 70, 72; *100:* 75, 76; *YABC 1:* 166
DeArmond, Dale *70:* 47
Deas, Michael *27:* 219, 221; *30:* 156; *67:* 134; *72:* 24; *75:* 155; *84:* 206; *88:* 124
Deas, Rich *191:* 87; *193:* 10; *212:* 79
deBarros, Jim *196:* 60
Debon, Nicolas *151:* 60; *177:* 46
de Bosschere, Jean *19:* 252; *21:* 4; *186:* 44, 45
De Bruyn, M(onica) G. *13:* 30, 31
Decker, C.B. *172:* 120; *215:* 94
De Cuir, John F. *1:* 28, 29
Deeter, Catherine *74:* 110; *103:* 150; *137:* 50
Degen, Bruce *40:* 227, 229; *57:* 28, 29; *56:* 156; *75:* 229; *76:* 19; *81:* 36, 37; *92:* 26; *93:* 199; *97:* 56, 58, 59; *124:* 40; *147:* 39, 40, 41; *168:* 23; *205:* 45, 46
De Grazia *14:* 59; *39:* 56, 57
DeGrazio, George *88:* 40
deGroat, Diane *9:* 39; *18:* 7; *23:* 123; *28:* 200, 201; *31:* 58, 59; *34:* 151; *41:* 152; *43:* 88; *46:* 40, 200; *49:* 163; *50:* 89; *52:* 30, 34; *54:* 43; *63:* 5; *70:* 136; *71:* 99; *73:* 117,156; *77:* 34; *85:* 48; *86:* 201; *87:* 142; *90:* 72, 73, 143; *95:* 182; *111:* 123; *118:* 160; *126:* 8; *130:* 130; *138:* 93, 94; *169:* 46, 47
de Groot, Lee *6:* 21
Deines, Brian *110:* 139
DeJohn, Marie *89:* 78
Dekhteryov, B. *61:* 158
de Kiefte, Kees *94:* 107
Delacre, Lulu *36:* 66; *156:* 35; *202:* 10, 53; *209:* 36
Delaney, A. *21:* 78
Delaney, Michael *180:* 16
Delaney, Molly *80:* 43
Delaney, Ned *28:* 68; *56:* 80; *102:* 11
DeLapine, Jim *79:* 21
De La Roche Saint Andre, Anne *75:* 37
de Larrea, Victoria *6:* 119, 204; *29:* 103; *72:* 203; *87:* 199

DeLeon, Melanie *210:* 43
Delessert, Étienne *7:* 140; *46:* 61, 62, 63, 65, 67, 68; *130:* 38, 39, 40, 41, 42; *179:* 46, 47, 48, 49; *YABC 2:* 209
Delezenne, Christine *186:* 126
Del Negro, Janice *196:* 161
Delon, Melanie *216:* 30
DeLorenzo, Christopher *154:* 149
Delulio, John *15:* 54
DeLuna, Tony *88:* 95
Demarest, Chris L. *45:* 68, 69, 70; *73:* 172, 173, 176; *78:* 106; *82:* 48, 49; *89:* 212; *92:* 86; *128:* 57, 58; *175:* 46, 48
De Mejo, Oscar *40:* 67
De Muth, Roger *205:* 184
Demi *11:* 135; *15:* 245; *66:* 129, 130; *89:* 216; *102:* 66, 67, 68; *210:* 86, 87, 89
Denetsosie, Hoke *13:* 126; *82:* 34
Denise, Christopher *147:* 43, 44; *176:* 101; *193:* 35, 36, 37; *201:* 37
Dennis, Morgan *18:* 68, 69; *64:* 89
Dennis, Wesley *2:* 87; *3:* 111; *11:* 132; *18:* 71, 72, 73, 74; *22:* 9; *24:* 196, 200; *46:* 178; *69:* 94, 96; *129:* 62
Denos, Julia *202:* 26
Denslow, W.W. *16:* 84, 85, 86, 87; *18:* 19, 20, 24; *29:* 211; *100:* 21
Denton, Kady MacDonald *110:* 82; *130:* 70; *181:* 54, 55, 56; *192:* 75
Denton, Terry *72:* 163; *174:* 26; *186:* 52; *196:* 83, 84
DePalma, Mary Newell *132:* 114; *139:* 75; *185:* 30, 31; *186:* 121; *213:* 62
dePaola, Tomie *8:* 95; *9:* 93; *11:* 69; *25:* 103; *28:* 157; *29:* 80; *39:* 52, 53; *40:* 226; *46:* 187; *59:* 61, 62, 63, 64, 65, 66, 67, 68, 69, 71, 72, 74; *62:* 19; *108:* 63, 67, 68, 70; *155:* 62, 64, 66; *180:* 105; *200:* 47, 48, 49, 50
Deraney, Michael J. *77:* 35; *78:* 148
deRosa, Dee *70:* 48; *71:* 210; *91:* 78
Dervaux, Isabelle *111:* 117
DeSaix, Deborah Durland *180:* 15; *188:* 24
De Saulles, Tony *119:* 39
de Seve, Peter *146:* 261; *207:* 78
Deshaprabhu, Meera Dayal *86:* 192
Desimini, Lisa *86:* 68; *94:* 47; *96:* 7; *104:* 107; *125:* 194; *131:* 180; *172:* 56; *216:* 89, 90
de St. Menin, Charles *70:* 17
Detmold, Edward J. *22:* 104, 105, 106, 107; *35:* 120; *64:* 5; *YABC 2:* 203
Detrich, Susan *20:* 133
Deutermann, Diana *77:* 175
DeVelasco, Joseph E. *21:* 51
de Veyrac, Robert *YABC 2:* 19
DeVille, Edward A. *4:* 235
de Visser, John *55:* 119
Devito, Bert *12:* 164
Devlin, Harry *11:* 74; *74:* 63, 65; *136:* 77, 78
Dewan, Ted *108:* 73; *157:* 55; *165:* 129
Dewar, Nick *133:* 122
Dewdney, Anna *184:* 43, 44
Dewey, Ariane *7:* 64; *33:* 195; *35:* 208; *68:* 16,17; *75:* 46; *93:* 91; *94:* 197; *109:* 65, 66, 67; *125:* 2, 3, 4, 5; *127:* 188; *143:* 25; *178:* 17, 19, 74; *188:* 166; *202:* 164
Dewey, Jennifer (Owings) *58:* 54; *64:* 214; *65:* 207; *88:* 169; *103:* 45
Dewey, Kenneth *39:* 62; *51:* 23; *56:* 163
de Zanger, Arie *30:* 40
Diakité, Baba Wagué *174:* 28
Diamond, Donna *21:* 200; *23:* 63; *26:* 142; *35:* 83, 84, 85, 86, 87, 88, 89; *38:* 78; *40:* 147; *44:* 152; *50:* 144; *53:* 126; *69:* 46, 47, 48, 201; *71:* 133; *123:* 19
Dias, Ron *71:* 67
Diaz, David *80:* 213; *96:* 83, 84; *108:* 228; *110:* 29; *149:* 106; *150:* 63; *179:* 160; *184:* 95, 97; *189:* 51, 52, 53
Dibley, Glin *138:* 83; *141:* 128; *211:* 162

DiCesare, Joe _70:_ 38; _71:_ 63, 106; _79:_ 214; _93:_ 147; _116:_ 217; _143:_ 111; _166:_ 57
Dick, John Henry _8:_ 181
Dickens, Frank _34:_ 131
Dickey, Robert L. _15:_ 279
Dickson, Mora _84:_ 21
Didier, Sam _166:_ 114
Dietz, James _128:_ 223; _193:_ 136
di Fate, Vincent _37:_ 70; _90:_ 11; _93:_ 60; _109:_ 219, 220
Di Fiori, Lawrence _10:_ 51; _12:_ 190; _27:_ 97; _40:_ 219; _93:_ 57; _130:_ 45
Digby, Desmond _97:_ 180
Dignan, James _196:_ 143
Di Grazia, Thomas _32:_ 66; _35:_ 241
Dillard, Annie _10:_ 32
Dillard, Sarah _136:_ 186; _217:_ 53
Dillon, Corinne B. _1:_ 139
Dillon, Diane _4:_ 104, 167; _6:_ 23; _13:_ 29; _15:_ 99; _26:_ 148; _27:_ 136, 201; _51:_ 29, 48, 51, 52, 53, 54,55, 56, 57, 58, 59, 60, 61, 62; _54:_ 155; _56:_ 69; _58:_ 127,128; _61:_ 95; _62:_ 27; _64:_ 46; _68:_ 3; _69:_ 209; _74:_ 89; _79:_ 92; _86:_ 89; _92:_ 28, 177; _93:_ 7, 210; _94:_ 239, 240; _97:_ 167; _106:_ 58, 59,61, 64; _107:_ 3; _139:_ 246; _167:_ 77; _189:_ 202; _191:_ 191; _194:_ 45, 46, 48, 49
Dillon, Leo _4:_ 104, 167; _6:_ 23; _13:_ 29; _15:_ 99; _26:_ 148; _27:_ 136, 201; _51:_ 29, 48, 51, 52, 53, 54,55, 56, 57, 58, 59, 60, 61, 62; _54:_ 155; _56:_ 69; _58:_ 127,128; _61:_ 95; _62:_ 27; _64:_ 46; _68:_ 3; _69:_ 209; _74:_ 89; _79:_ 92; _86:_ 89; _92:_ 28, 177; _93:_ 7, 210; _94:_ 239, 240; _97:_ 167; _106:_ 58, 59,61, 64; _107:_ 3; _139:_ 246; _167:_ 77; _189:_ 202; _191:_ 191; _194:_ 45, 46, 48, 49
Dillon, Sharon Saseen _59:_ 179, 188
DiMaccio, Gerald _121:_ 80
DiMaggio, Joe _36:_ 22
DiMassi, Gina _169:_ 17
Dinan, Carol _25:_ 169; _59:_ 75
Dines, Glen _7:_ 66, 67
Dinesen, Thomas _44:_ 37
Dinh, Pham Viet _167:_ 184
Dinnerstein, Harvey _42:_ 63, 64, 65, 66, 67, 68; _50:_ 146
Dinsdale, Mary _10:_ 65; _11:_ 171
Dinyer, Eric _86:_ 148; _109:_ 163; _110:_ 239; _124:_ 11; _150:_ 69; _170:_ 4; _171:_ 30
Dion, Nathalie _170:_ 124; _213:_ 52
DiRocco, Carl _181:_ 23
DiSalvo-Ryan, DyAnne _59:_ 77; _62:_ 185; _117:_ 46; _144:_ 64; _150:_ 153; _186:_ 162
Disney, Walt _28:_ 71, 72, 73, 76, 77, 78, 79, 80, 81, 87, 88, 89,90, 91, 94
DiTerlizzi, Tony _105:_ 7; _147:_ 22; _154:_ 31, 32, 33; _214:_ 74
Divito, Anna _83:_ 159
Dixon, Don _74:_ 17; _109:_ 196
Dixon, Larry _127:_ 125
Dixon, Maynard _20:_ 165
Doares, Robert G. _20:_ 39
Dob, Bob _205:_ 14
Dobias, Frank _22:_ 162
Dobrin, Arnold _4:_ 68
Dobson, Steven Gaston _102:_ 103
Dockray, Tracy _139:_ 77
Docktor, Irv _43:_ 70
Dodd, Ed _4:_ 69
Dodd, Emma _203:_ 57
Dodd, Julie _74:_ 73
Dodd, Lynley _35:_ 92; _86:_ 71; _132:_ 45, 46, 47
Dodge, Bill _96:_ 36; _118:_ 7, 8, 9; _133:_ 135
Dodgson, Charles L. _20:_ 148; _33:_ 146; _YABC 2:_ 98
Dodson, Bert _9:_ 138; _14:_ 195; _42:_ 55; _54:_ 8; _60:_ 49; _101:_ 125
Dodson, Liz Brenner _105:_ 117; _111:_ 15
Dohanos, Stevan _16:_ 10
Dolce, J. Ellen _74:_ 147; _75:_ 41
Dolch, Marguerite P. _50:_ 64

Dolesch, Susanne _34:_ 49
Dollar, Diane _57:_ 32
Dolobowsky, Mena _81:_ 54
Dolson, Hildegarde _5:_ 57
Domanska, Janina _6:_ 66, 67; _YABC 1:_ 166
Domi _134:_ 113
Dominguez, El _53:_ 94
Domjan, Joseph _25:_ 93
Domm, Jeffrey C. _84:_ 69; _135:_ 70
Donahey, William _68:_ 209
Donahue, Dorothy _76:_ 170
Donahue, Vic _2:_ 93; _3:_ 190; _9:_ 44
Donald, Elizabeth _4:_ 18
Donalty, Alison _149:_ 195, 196, 197
Donato _85:_ 59; _149:_ 204; _191:_ 19
Donato, Michael A. _200:_ 143
Doner, Kim _208:_ 57
Doney, Todd L.W. _87:_ 12; _93:_ 112; _98:_ 135; _101:_ 57; _104:_ 40; _118:_ 163; _135:_ 162, 163; _151:_ 18
Donna, Natalie _9:_ 52
Donohue, Dorothy _95:_ 2; _132:_ 30; _176:_ 54, 55; _178:_ 77, 78, 79
Dooling, Michael _82:_ 19; _105:_ 55; _106:_ 224; _125:_ 135; _171:_ 46; _172:_ 12; _176:_ 120; _197:_ 89
Doran, Ben-Ami _128:_ 189
Doran, Colleen _211:_ 48
Dore, Gustave _18:_ 169, 172, 175; _19:_ 93, 94, 95, 96, 97, 98,99, 100, 101, 102, 103, 104, 105; _23:_ 188; _25:_ 197, 199
Doremus, Robert _6:_ 62; _13:_ 90; _30:_ 95, 96, 97; _38:_ 97
Dorfman, Ronald _11:_ 128
Doriau _86:_ 59; _91:_ 152
Dorman, Brandon _197:_ 35; _204:_ 6; _210:_ 104; _212:_ 95; _216:_ 156
Dormer, Frank W. _200:_ 55
Dorros, Arthur _78:_ 42, 43; _91:_ 28
Doruyter, Karel _165:_ 105
dos Santos, Joyce Audy _57:_ 187, 189
Doty, Roy _28:_ 98; _31:_ 32; _32:_ 224; _46:_ 157; _82:_ 71; _142:_ 7
Doucet, Bob _132:_ 238; _169:_ 159
Dougherty, Charles _16:_ 204; _18:_ 74
Doughty, Rebecca _177:_ 174
Doughty, Thomas _118:_ 31; _140:_ 60
Douglas, Aaron _31:_ 103
Douglas, Carole Nelson _73:_ 48
Douglas, Goray _13:_ 151
Dow, Brian _150:_ 92
Dowd, Jason _132:_ 51, 52; _164:_ 244
Dowd, Vic _3:_ 244; _10:_ 97
Dowden, Anne Ophelia _7:_ 70, 71; _13:_ 120
Dowdy, Mrs. Regera _29:_ 100
Downard, Barry _202:_ 32
Downes, Belinda _180:_ 29
Downing, Julie _60:_ 140; _81:_ 50; _86:_ 200; _99:_ 129
Doyle, Janet _56:_ 31
Doyle, Richard _21:_ 31, 32, 33; _23:_ 231; _24:_ 177; _31:_ 87
Draper, Angie _43:_ 84
Drath, Bill _26:_ 34
Drawson, Blair _17:_ 53; _126:_ 65
Dray, Matt _177:_ 47
Drescher, Henrik _105:_ 60, 62, 63; _172:_ 72
Drescher, Joan _30:_ 100, 101; _35:_ 245; _52:_ 168; _137:_ 52
Dressell, Peggy _186:_ 41
Drew, Janet _201:_ 177
Drew, Patricia _15:_ 100
Dronzek, Laura _199:_ 28, 29; _207:_ 69
Drummond, Allan _209:_ 41
Drummond, V.H. _6:_ 70
Drury, Christian Potter _105:_ 97; _186:_ 224
Dubanevich, Arlene _56:_ 44
Dubin, Jill _205:_ 56; _217:_ 25
Dubois, Claude K. _196:_ 2
Dubois, Gerard _182:_ 9
DuBurke, Randy _187:_ 89

Ducak, Danilo _99:_ 130; _108:_ 214
Duchesne, Janet _6:_ 162; _79:_ 8
Duda, Jana _102:_ 155; _209:_ 134
Dudash, C. Michael _32:_ 122; _77:_ 134; _82:_ 149; _212:_ 93, 94
Duer, Douglas _34:_ 177
Duewell, Kristina _195:_ 76
Duffy, Daniel Mark _76:_ 37; _101:_ 196; _108:_ 147, 148
Duffy, Joseph _38:_ 203
Duffy, Pat _28:_ 153
Dugan, Karen _181:_ 26; _202:_ 35
Dugin, Andrej _77:_ 60
Dugina, Olga _77:_ 60
Duke, Chris _8:_ 195; _139:_ 164
Duke, Kate _87:_ 186; _90:_ 78, 79, 80, 81; _192:_ 21, 59, 60, 61, 63
Duke, Marion _165:_ 87
Dulac, Edmund _19:_ 108, 109, 110, 111, 112, 113, 114, 115, 117; _23:_ 187; _25:_ 152; _YABC 1:_ 37; _2:_ 147
Dulac, Jean _13:_ 64
Dumas, Philippe _52:_ 36, 37, 38, 39, 40, 41, 42, 43, 45; _119:_ 40, 41, 42
Dunaway, Nancy _108:_ 161
Dunbar, James _76:_ 63
Dunbar, Polly _181:_ 60, 61; _211:_ 51, 52, 53; _212:_ 42
Duncan, Beverly _72:_ 92
Duncan, John _116:_ 94
Dunn, H.T. _62:_ 196
Dunn, Harvey _34:_ 78, 79, 80, 81
Dunn, Iris _5:_ 175
Dunn, Phoebe _5:_ 175
Dunne, Jeanette _72:_ 57, 173, 222
Dunnick, Regan _176:_ 51; _178:_ 83, 84
Dunnington, Tom _3:_ 36; _18:_ 281; _25:_ 61; _31:_ 159; _35:_ 168; _48:_ 195; _79:_ 144; _82:_ 230
Dunn-Ramsey, Marcy _117:_ 131
Dunrea, Olivier _59:_ 81; _118:_ 53, 54; _124:_ 43
Duntze, Dorothee _88:_ 28; _160:_ 76
Dupasquier, Philippe _86:_ 75; _104:_ 76; _151:_ 63
duPont, Lindsay Harper _207:_ 39
DuQuette, Keith _90:_ 83; _155:_ 73, 74
Durand, Delphine _200:_ 56
Durham, Sarah _192:_ 248
Durney, Ryan _208:_ 122
Duroussy, Nathalie _146:_ 150
Durrell, Julie _82:_ 62; _94:_ 62
Dutz _6:_ 59
Duvoisin, Roger _2:_ 95; _6:_ 76, 77; _7:_ 197; _28:_ 125; _30:_ 101, 102, 103, 104, 105, 107; _47:_ 205; _84:_ 254
Dyer, Dale _141:_ 71
Dyer, Jane _75:_ 219; _129:_ 28; _147:_ 49, 50, 51; _168:_ 121; _190:_ 4; _191:_ 57, 59, 60; _203:_ 4
Dyer, Sarah _212:_ 40
Dypold, Pat _15:_ 37

E

E.V.B.
See Boyle, Eleanor Vere (Gordon)
Eachus, Jennifer _29:_ 74; _82:_ 201; _164:_ 153
Eadie, Bob _63:_ 36
Eagle, Bruce _95:_ 119
Eagle, Ellen _82:_ 121; _89:_ 3
Eagle, Jeremy _141:_ 71
Eagle, Michael _11:_ 86; _20:_ 9; _23:_ 18; _27:_ 122; _28:_ 57; _34:_ 201; _44:_ 189; _73:_ 9; _78:_ 235; _85:_ 43
Earl-Bridges, Michele _159:_ 128
Earle, Edwin _56:_ 27
Earle, Olive L. _7:_ 75
Earle, Vana _27:_ 99
Earley, Lori _132:_ 2; _186:_ 4; _195:_ 8
Early, Margaret _72:_ 59
East, Stella _131:_ 223
Eastman, P.D. _33:_ 57

Easton, Reginald *29:* 181
Eaton, Tom *4:* 62; *6:* 64; *22:* 99; *24:* 124
Ebbeler, Jeffrey *193:* 62; *206:* 45
Ebel, Alex *11:* 89
Eberbach, Andrea *192:* 115
Ebert, Len *9:* 191; *44:* 47
Echevarria, Abe *37:* 69
Echo Hawk, Bunky *187:* 192
Eckersley, Maureen *48:* 62
Eckert, Horst *72:* 62
Ede, Janina *33:* 59
Edens, Cooper *49:* 81, 82, 83, 84, 85; *112:* 58
Edens, John *109:* 115
Edgar, Sarah E. *41:* 97
Edgerton, Perky *195:* 144
Edliq, Emily S. *131:* 107
Edrien *11:* 53
Edwards, Freya *45:* 102
Edwards, George Wharton *31:* 155
Edwards, Gunvor *2:* 71; *25:* 47; *32:* 71; *54:* 106
Edwards, Jeanne *29:* 257
Edwards, Linda Strauss *21:* 134; *39:* 123; *49:* 88, 89
Edwards, Michelle *152:* 62, 63
Edwards, Wallace *170:* 55
Egan, Tim *155:* 76, 77, 78
Egge, David *102:* 71
Eggenhofer, Nicholas *2:* 81
Eggleton, Bob *74:* 40; *81:* 190, 191; *105:* 6; *121:* 183; *149:* 203; *166:* 215
Egielski, Richard *11:* 90; *16:* 208; *33:* 236; *38:* 35; *49:* 91, 92, 93, 95, 212, 213, 214, 216; *79:* 122; *106:* 67, 68, 69; *134:* 135; *144:* 244; *163:* 82, 84; *207:* 125
Ehlert, Lois *35:* 97; *69:* 51; *112:* 7; *113:* 208; *128:* 63, 64, 65; *172:* 77, 79, 80
Ehrlich, Bettina *1:* 83
Eitan, Ora *160:* 165
Eichenberg, Fritz *1:* 79; *9:* 54; *19:* 248; *23:* 170; *24:* 200; *26:* 208; *50:* 67, 68, 69, 70, 71, 72, 73, 74, 75, 77, 79, 80, 81; *60:* 165; *100:* 137; *YABC 1:* 104, 105; *2:* 213
Einsel, Naiad *10:* 35; *29:* 136
Einsel, Walter *10:* 37
Einzig, Susan *3:* 77; *43:* 78; *67:* 155; *129:* 154
Eisner, Will *165:* 82, 83
Eitzen, Allan *9:* 56; *12:* 212; *14:* 226; *21:* 194; *38:* 162; *76:* 218
Eldridge, H. *54:* 109
Eldridge, Harold *43:* 83
Elgaard, Greta *19:* 241
Elgin, Kathleen *9:* 188; *39:* 69
Ellacott, S.E. *19:* 118
Elliot, David *192:* 26; *208:* 62, 63
Elliott, Mark *93:* 69; *105:* 108; *107:* 123; *140:* 53; *165:* 189; *173:* 67; *195:* 95; *203:* 67; *210:* 99
Elliott, Sarah M. *14:* 58
Ellis, Carson *216:* 210
Ellis, Dianne *130:* 208
Ellis, Jan Davey *88:* 50; *115:* 80
Ellis, Richard *130:* 47, 48
Ellison, Chris *196:* 66; *199:* 131; *207:* 193
Ellison, Pauline *55:* 21
Ellwand, David *213:* 60
Elmer, Richard *78:* 5
Elmore, Larry *90:* 8
Elschner, Géraldine *183:* 38
Elwell, Peter *195:* 150
Elwell, Tristan *110:* 39; *121:* 182; *127:* 46; *137:* 144; *141:* 173; *151:* 236; *158:* 264; *167:* 119, 120, 121; *169:* 20; *190:* 12; *202:* 16
Elzbieta *88:* 80, 81
Ember, Kathi *214:* 147
Emberley, Ed *8:* 53; *70:* 53, 54; *146:* 65, 69, 70
Emberley, Michael *34:* 83; *80:* 72; *119:* 47, 48; *147:* 100; *158:* 115; *189:* 62, 64; *203:* 87, 89

Emerling, Dorothy *104:* 27
Emery, Leslie *49:* 187
Emmett, Bruce *49:* 147; *80:* 175; *101:* 206
Emry-Perrott, Jennifer *61:* 57
Emshwiller, Ed *174:* 45
Endle, Kate *191:* 167; *207:* 41
Engel, Diana *70:* 57
Engle, Mort *38:* 64
Englebert, Victor *8:* 54
English, Mark *101:* 207
Enik, Ted *142:* 39
Enos, Randall *20:* 183
Enright, Maginel Wright *19:* 240, 243; *39:* 31, 35, 36
Enrique, Romeo *34:* 135
Ensor, Barbara *180:* 30
Epstein, Stephen *50:* 142, 148
Erdogan, Buket *174:* 179
Erdrich, Louise *141:* 62
Erhard, Walter *1:* 152
Erickson, Jim *196:* 190
Erickson, Phoebe *11:* 83; *59:* 85
Erikson, Mel *31:* 69
Eriksson, Eva *63:* 88, 90, 92, 93; *203:* 99; *207:* 44
Ering, Timothy Basil *131:* 100; *176:* 63, 64; *202:* 29; *204:* 8
Erlbruch, Wolf *181:* 66
Ernst, Lisa Campbell *47:* 147; *95:* 47; *154:* 46, 47, 48; *154:* 88; *212:* 45
Esco, Jo *61:* 103
Escourido, Joseph *4:* 81
Escrivá, Viví *119:* 51; *181:* 36
Essakalli, Julie Klear *200:* 58
Este, Kirk *33:* 111
Estep, David *73:* 57
Estes, Eleanor *91:* 66
Estoril, Jean *32:* 27
Estrada, Pau *74:* 76
Estrada, Ric *5:* 52, 146; *13:* 174
Etchemendy, Teje *38:* 68
Etheredges, the *73:* 12
Etienne, Kirk-Albert *145:* 184
Ets, Marie Hall *2:* 102
Ettlinger, Doris *171:* 98; *186:* 106; *197:* 126; *214:* 125
Eulalie *YABC 2:* 315
Evangelista, Theresa M. *213:* 67
Evans, Greg *73:* 54, 55, 56; *143:* 40, 41
Evans, Katherine *5:* 64
Evans, Leslie *144:* 227; *207:* 57; *214:* 88
Evans, Shane W. *159:* 142; *160:* 190; *168:* 39; *188:* 88; *189:* 66, 67, 68
Everitt, Betsy *151:* 110
Ewart, Claire *76:* 69; *145:* 59, 60
Ewing, Carolyn *66:* 143; *79:* 52
Ewing, Juliana Horatia *16:* 92
Eyolfson, Norman *98:* 154

F

Fabian, Limbert *136:* 114
Facklam, Paul *132:* 62
Falconer, Ian *125:* 66; *179:* 59
Falconer, Pearl *34:* 23
Falkenstern, Lisa *70:* 34; *76:* 133; *78:* 171; *127:* 16; *191:* 151
Falls, C.B. *1:* 19; *38:* 71, 72, 73, 74
Falter, John *40:* 169, 170
Falwell, Cathryn *118:* 77; *137:* 185; *196:* 71, 72
Fancher, Lou *138:* 219; *141:* 64; *144:* 199; *177:* 51; *214:* 95
Fanelli, Sara *89:* 63; *126:* 69
Faria, Rosana *150:* 143
Faricy, Patrick *185:* 182; *212:* 61
Farooqi, Musharraf Ali *207:* 46
Farmer, Andrew *49:* 102
Farmer, Peter *24:* 108; *38:* 75

Farnsworth, Bill *93:* 189; *116:* 147; *124:* 8; *135:* 52; *146:* 242, 243, 244; *182:* 176; *186:* 31, 83, 84, 85; *191:* 197
Farquharson, Alexander *46:* 75
Farrell, David *40:* 135
Farrell, Russell *196:* 38
Farris, David *74:* 42
Fasolino, Teresa *118:* 145
Fatigati, Evelyn *24:* 112
Fatus, Sophie *182:* 74; *190:* 218
Faul-Jansen, Regina *22:* 117
Faulkner, Jack *6:* 169
Faulkner, Matt *161:* 174; *167:* 75
Fava, Rita *2:* 29
Fax, Elton C. *1:* 101; *4:* 2; *12:* 77; *25:* 107
Fay *43:* 93
Fearnley, Jan *153:* 82, 83; *205:* 63, 64, 65
Fearrington, Ann *146:* 80
Federspiel, Marian *33:* 51
Fedorov, Nickolai Ivanovich *110:* 102
Feelings, Tom *5:* 22; *8:* 56; *12:* 153; *16:* 105; *30:* 196; *49:* 37; *61:* 101; *69:* 56, 57; *93:* 74; *105:* 88
Fehr, Terrence *21:* 87
Feiffer, Jules *3:* 91; *8:* 58; *61:* 66, 67, 70, 74, 76,77, 78; *111:* 47, 48, 49, 50; *132:* 122; *157:* 62; *201:* 48, 49, 50
Feigeles, Neil *41:* 242
Feldman, Elyse *86:* 7
Feller, Gene *33:* 130
Fellows, Muriel H. *10:* 42
Felstead, Cathie *116:* 85
Felts, Shirley *33:* 71; *48:* 59
Fennell, Tracy *171:* 69
Fennelli, Maureen *38:* 181
Fenton, Carroll Lane *5:* 66; *21:* 39
Fenton, Mildred Adams *5:* 66; *21:* 39
Ferguson, Peter *177:* 30, 31; *181:* 154; *197:* 4; *199:* 40; *215:* 104
Ferguson, Walter W. *34:* 86
Fernandes, Eugenie *77:* 67; *205:* 68
Fernandes, Stanislaw *70:* 28
Fernandez, Fernando *77:* 57
Fernandez, Laura *77:* 153; *101:* 117; *131:* 222; *170:* 119; *175:* 182
Ferrari, Alex *188:* 121
Ferrington, Susan *172:* 22
Fetz, Ingrid *11:* 67; *12:* 52; *16:* 205; *17:* 59; *29:* 105; *30:* 108, 109; *32:* 149; *43:* 142; *56:* 29; *60:* 34; *85:* 48; *87:* 146
Fiammenghi, Gioia *9:* 66; *11:* 44; *12:* 206; *13:* 57, 59; *52:* 126, 129; *66:* 64; *85:* 83; *91:* 161; *166:* 169
Fiedler, Joseph Daniel *96:* 42; *113:* 173; *129:* 164; *146:* 17; *159:* 68; *162:* 104
Field, Rachel *15:* 113
Fielding, David *70:* 124
Fieser, Stephen *152:* 36
Fine, Howard *145:* 159; *159:* 64; *165:* 134; *174:* 129; *181:* 68
Fine, Peter K. *43:* 210
Finger, Helen *42:* 81
Fink, Sam *18:* 119
Finlay, Winifred *23:* 72
Finney, Pat *79:* 215
Fiore, Peter *99:* 196; *125:* 139; *144:* 225; *160:* 169; *180:* 72; *212:* 103
Fiorentino, Al *3:* 240
Firehammer, Karla *174:* 202
Firmin, Charlotte *29:* 75; *48:* 70
Firmin, Peter *58:* 63, 64, 65, 67, 68, 70, 71
Firth, Barbara *81:* 208; *127:* 218; *179:* 62
Fischel, Lillian *40:* 204
Fischer, Hans *25:* 202
Fischer, Scott M. *207:* 37; *217:* 29
Fischer-Nagel, Andreas *56:* 50
Fischer-Nagel, Heiderose *56:* 50
Fisher, Carolyn *154:* 50
Fisher, Chris *79:* 62; *158:* 248; *188:* 195
Fisher, Cynthia *117:* 45; *137:* 118; *195:* 40
Fisher, Jeffrey *142:* 80

Fisher, Leonard Everett *3:* 6; *4:* 72, 86; *6:* 197; *9:* 59; *16:* 151, 153; *23:* 44; *27:* 134; *29:* 26; *34:* 87, 89, 90, 91, 93, 94, 95, 96; *40:* 206; *50:* 150; *60:* 158; *73:* 68, 70, 71, 72, 73; *176:* 71, 72, 73; *208:* 131; *YABC 2:* 169
Fisher, Lois *20:* 62; *21:* 7
Fisher, Valorie *177:* 55; *214:* 92
Fisk, Nicholas *25:* 112
Fitschen, Marilyn *2:* 20, 21; *20:* 48
Fitz-Maurice, Jeff *175:* 2
Fitzgerald, F.A. *15:* 116; *25:* 86, 87
Fitzgerald, Joanne *157:* 153, 154; *198:* 34, 35
Fitzgerald, Royce *205:* 5
Fitzhugh, Louise *1:* 94; *9:* 163; *45:* 75, 78
Fitzhugh, Susie *11:* 117
Fitzpatrick, Jim *109:* 130
Fitzpatrick, Marie-Louise *125:* 69, 70; *189:* 72, 73
Fitzsimmons, Arthur *14:* 128
Fix, Philippe *26:* 102
Flack, Marjorie *21:* 67; *100:* 93; *YABC 2:* 122
Flagg, James Montgomery *17:* 227
Flavin, Teresa *132:* 115; *186:* 119
Flax, Zeona *2:* 245
Fleetwood, Tony *171:* 51
Fleishman, Seymour *14:* 232; *24:* 87
Fleming, Denise *71:* 179; *81:* 58; *126:* 71, 72, 73; *173:* 52, 53
Fleming, Guy *18:* 41
Flesher, Vivienne *85:* 55
Fletcher, Claire *80:* 106; *157:* 159
Flint, Russ *74:* 80
Floate, Helen *111:* 163
Floca, Brian *155:* 88, 89; *190:* 10, 66, 67
Floethe, Richard *3:* 131; *4:* 90
Floherty, John J., Jr. *5:* 68
Flook, Helen *160:* 81
Flora, James *1:* 96; *30:* 111, 112
Florczak, Robert *166:* 51
Florian, Douglas *19:* 122; *83:* 64, 65; *125:* 71, 72, 74, 76; *128:* 130; *177:* 58, 60
Flory, Jane *22:* 111
Flower, Renee *125:* 109
Floyd, Gareth *1:* 74; *17:* 245; *48:* 63; *62:* 35,36, 37, 39, 40, 41; *74:* 245; *79:* 56
Fluchere, Henri A. *40:* 79
Flynn, Alice *183:* 2
Flynn, Barbara *7:* 31; *9:* 70
Fogarty, Thomas *15:* 89
Foley, Greg *190:* 69
Folger, Joseph *9:* 100
Folkard, Charles *22:* 132; *29:* 128, 257, 258
Foott, Jeff *42:* 202
Forberg, Ati *12:* 71, 205; *14:* 1; *22:* 113; *26:* 22; *48:* 64, 65
Ford, George *24:* 120; *31:* 70, 177; *58:* 126; *81:* 103; *107:* 91; *136:* 100; *194:* 47; *208:* 81
Ford, Gilbert *199:* 10
Ford, H.J. *16:* 185, 186
Ford, Jason *174:* 119
Ford, Pamela Baldwin *27:* 104
Fordham, John *168:* 160, 161
Foreman, Michael *2:* 110, 111; *67:* 99; *73:* 78, 79, 80,81, 82; *93:* 146; *135:* 55, 56, 57; *184:* 58, 59; *216:* 100, 101, 102, 103
Forrester, Victoria *40:* 83
Forsey, Chris *140:* 210
Fortnum, Peggy *6:* 29; *20:* 179; *24:* 211; *26:* 76, 77, 78; *39:* 78; *58:* 19, 21, 23, 27; *YABC 1:* 148
Fortune, Eric *191:* 52
Foster, Brad W. *34:* 99
Foster, Genevieve *2:* 112
Foster, Gerald L. *7:* 78; *198:* 40
Foster, Jon *146:* 18; *198:* 7
Foster, Laura Louise *6:* 79
Foster, Marian Curtis *23:* 74; *40:* 42
Foster, Sally *58:* 73, 74
Foucher, Adele *47:* 118

Foust, Mitch *168:* 50
Fowler, Jim *184:* 190
Fowler, Mel *36:* 127
Fowler, Richard *87:* 219
Fowles, Shelley *165:* 127; *205:* 72
Fox, Charles Phillip *12:* 84
Fox, Christyan *188:* 36
Fox, Jim *6:* 187
Fox, Nathan *208:* 64
Fox-Davies, Sarah *76:* 150; *182:* 63; *199:* 42, 43
Frace, Charles *15:* 118
Frailey, Joy *72:* 108
Frame, Paul *2:* 45, 145; *9:* 153; *10:* 124; *21:* 71; *23:* 62; *24:* 123; *27:* 106; *31:* 48; *32:* 159; *34:* 195; *38:* 136; *42:* 55; *44:* 139; *60:* 39, 40, 41, 42, 43, 44, 46; *73:* 183
Frampton, David *85:* 72; *102:* 33; *139:* 182; *152:* 37; *189:* 171
Francis, Guy *198:* 164
Francois, Andre *25:* 117
Francoise
   See Seignobosc, Francoise
Frank, Lola Edick *2:* 199
Frank, Mary *4:* 54; *34:* 100
Franke, Phil *45:* 91
Frankel, Alona *66:* 70
Frankel, Julie *40:* 84, 85, 202
Frankenberg, Robert *22:* 116; *30:* 50; *38:* 92, 94, 95; *68:* 111
Frankfeldt, Gwen *84:* 223; *110:* 92
Frankland, David *169:* 137; *182:* 164; *201:* 159
Franklin, Ashton *165:* 144
Franklin, John *24:* 22
Franson, Leanne R. *111:* 57, 58; *151:* 7
Frascino, Edward *9:* 133; *29:* 229; *33:* 190; *48:* 80, 81, 82, 83, 84, 85, 86
Frasconi, Antonio *6:* 80; *27:* 208; *53:* 41, 43, 45, 47,48; *68:* 145; *73:* 226; *131:* 68
Fraser, Betty *2:* 212; *6:* 185; *8:* 103; *31:* 72,73; *43:* 136; *111:* 76
Fraser, Eric *38:* 78; *41:* 149, 151
Fraser, F.A. *22:* 234
Fraser, James *171:* 68
Fraser, Mary Ann *137:* 63; *214:* 98
Frasier, Debra *69:* 60; *112:* 67; *182:* 81, 82, 83
Fraustino, Lisa Rowe *146:* 87
Frazee, Marla *72:* 98; *105:* 79, 80; *151:* 67, 68; *164:* 165; *171:* 190, 191; *187:* 53, 54,55, 56, 143
Frazetta, Frank *41:* 72; *58:* 77, 78, 79, 80, 81, 82, 83
Frazier, Craig *177:* 63
Freas, John *25:* 207
Fredrickson, Mark *103:* 33
Freeland, Michael J. *118:* 115
Freeman, Don *2:* 15; *13:* 249; *17:* 62, 63, 65, 67, 68; *18:* 243; *20:* 195; *23:* 213, 217; *32:* 155; *55:* 129
Freeman, Irving *67:* 150
Freeman, Laura *144:* 111; *200:* 62, 63
Freeman, Pietri *140:* 223
Freeman, Tom *167:* 118
Freeman, Tor *164:* 93
Fregosi, Claudia *24:* 117
Fremaux, Charlotte Murray *138:* 29; *141:* 95
French, Fiona *6:* 82, 83; *75:* 61; *109:* 170; *132:* 79, 80, 81, 82
French, Martin *163:* 4
French, S. Terrell *216:* 106
Frendak, Rodney *126:* 97, 98
Freschet, Gina *175:* 73
Freynet, Gilbert *72:* 221
Fried, Janice *202:* 121
Frieden, Sarajo *213:* 119
Friedman, Judith *43:* 197; *131:* 221
Friedman, Marvin *19:* 59; *42:* 86
Frinta, Dagmar *36:* 42
Frith, Michael K. *15:* 138; *18:* 120
Fritz, Ronald *46:* 73; *82:* 124

Fromm, Lilo *29:* 85; *40:* 197
Frost, A.B. *17:* 6, 7; *19:* 123, 124, 125, 126, 127, 128, 129,130; *100:* 119; *YABC 1:* 156, 157, 160; *2:* 107
Frost, Helen *183:* 51
Frost, Kristi *118:* 113
Frost, Michael *151:* 209; *209:* 44; *212:* 70
Froud, Brian *150:* 82, 83
Froud, Wendy *151:* 237
Fry, Guy *2:* 224
Fry, Rosalie *3:* 72; *YABC 2:* 180, 181
Fry, Rosalind *21:* 153, 168
Fryer, Elmer *34:* 115
Fuchs, Bernie *110:* 10; *162:* 46
Fuchs, Erich *6:* 84
Fuchshuber, Annegert *43:* 96
Fufuka, Mahiri *32:* 146
Fuge, Charles *144:* 91, 93
Fujikawa, Gyo *39:* 75, 76; *76:* 72, 73, 74
Fulford, Deborah *23:* 159
Fuller, Margaret *25:* 189
Fulweiler, John *93:* 99
Funai, Mamoru *38:* 105
Funfhausen, Christian *196:* 30
Funk, Tom *7:* 17, 99
Furchgott, Terry *29:* 86
Furness, William Henry, Jr. *94:* 18
Furukawa, Mel *25:* 42
Fusari, Erika *164:* 227

G

Gaadt, David *78:* 212; *121:* 166; *201:* 171
Gaadt, George *71:* 9
Gaber, Susan *99:* 33; *115:* 57, 58; *164:* 195; *169:* 61, 62, 63; *185:* 50, 51; *188:* 124
Gaberell, J. *19:* 236
Gable, Brian *195:* 68, 69
Gabler, Mirko *99:* 71; *195:* 32
Gabor, Tim *216:* 61
Gackenbach, Dick *19:* 168; *41:* 81; *48:* 89, 90, 91, 92,93, 94; *54:* 105; *79:* 75, 76, 77
Gad, Victor *87:* 161
Gaetano, Nicholas *23:* 209
Gaffney-Kessell, Walter *94:* 219; *174:* 188
Gag, Flavia *17:* 49, 52
Gag, Wanda *100:* 101, 102; *YABC 1:* 135, 137, 138, 141, 143
Gagnon, Cecile *11:* 77; *58:* 87
Gaillard, Jason *200:* 69; *204:* 74
Gal, Laszlo *14:* 127; *52:* 54, 55, 56; *65:* 142; *68:* 150; *81:* 185; *96:* 104, 105
Galazinski, Tom *55:* 13
Galbraith, Ben *200:* 70
Galdone, Paul *1:* 156, 181, 206; *2:* 40, 241; *3:* 42,144; *4:* 141; *10:* 109, 158; *11:* 21; *12:* 118, 210; *14:* 12; *16:* 36, 37; *17:* 70, 71, 72, 73, 74; *18:* 111, 230; *19:* 183; *21:* 154; *22:* 150, 245; *33:* 126; *39:* 136, 137; *42:* 57; *51:* 169; *55:* 110; *66:* 80, 82, 139; *72:* 73; *100:* 84
Gale, Cathy *140:* 22; *143:* 52; *213:* 166
Gall, Chris *176:* 79, 80
Gallagher, Jack *187:* 100
Gallagher, S. Saelig *105:* 154; *198:* 91
Gallagher, Sears *20:* 112Gallagher-Cole, Mernie *206:* 56
Galloway, Ewing *51:* 154
Galouchka, Annouchka Gravel *95:* 55; *182:* 40
Galster, Robert *1:* 66
Galsworthy, Gay John *35:* 232
Galvez, Daniel *125:* 182
Gamble, Kim *112:* 64, 65; *124:* 77; *183:* 40, 42, 43, 56, 57; *187:* 170

Gammell, Stephen *7:* 48; *13:* 149; *29:* 82; *33:* 209; *41:* 88; *50:* 185, 186, 187; *53:* 51, 52, 53, 54, 55, 56,57, 58; *54:* 24, 25; *56:* 147, 148, 150; *57:* 27, 66; *81:* 62, 63; *87:* 88; *89:* 10; *106:* 223; *126:* 2; *128:* 71, 73, 74, 77; *154:* 34; *211:* 210

Gamper, Ruth *84:* 198

Gampert, John *58:* 94

Ganly, Helen *56:* 56

Gannett, Ruth Chrisman *3:* 74; *18:* 254; *33:* 77, 78

Gannon, Ned *205:* 6

Gantschev, Ivan *45:* 32

Garafano, Marie *73:* 33

Garbot, Dave *131:* 106

Garbutt, Bernard *23:* 68

Garcia *37:* 71

Garcia, Manuel *74:* 145

Garcia-Franco, Rebecca *173:* 46

Gardiner, Lindsey *178:* 128; *186:* 137

Gardner, Earle *45:* 167

Gardner, Joan *40:* 87

Gardner, Joel *40:* 87, 92

Gardner, John *40:* 87

Gardner, Lucy *40:* 87

Gardner, Richard
    See Cummings, Richard

Gardner, Sally *171:* 177; *177:* 66, 68

Gargiulo, Frank *84:* 158

Garland, Michael *36:* 29; *38:* 83; *44:* 168; *48:* 78, 221, 222; *49:* 161; *60:* 139; *71:* 6, 11; *72:* 229; *74:* 142; *89:* 187; *93:* 183; *104:* 110; *131:* 55; *139:* 209; *168:* 56; *208:* 72, 73, 75

Garland, Peggy *60:* 139

Garland, Sarah *62:* 45; *135:* 67, 68; *171:* 118

Garn, Aimee *75:* 47

Garner, Joan *128:* 170

Garneray, Ambroise Louis *59:* 140

Garnett, Eve *3:* 75

Garnett, Gary *39:* 184

Garns, Allen *80:* 125; *84:* 39; *165:* 231; *209:* 44

Garófoli, Viviana *186:* 123

Garraty, Gail *4:* 142; *52:* 106

Garrett, Agnes *46:* 110; *47:* 157

Garrett, Edmund H. *20:* 29

Garrett, Tom *107:* 194; *215:* 179

Garrick, Jacqueline *67:* 42, 43; *77:* 94

Garrison, Barbara *19:* 133; *104:* 146; *109:* 87

Garro, Mark *108:* 131; *128:* 210

Garvey, Robert *98:* 222

Garza, Carmen Lomas *80:* 211; *182:* 86

Garza, Xavier *184:* 64

Gates, Frieda *26:* 80

Gaughan, Jack *26:* 79; *43:* 185

Gaver, Becky *20:* 61

Gavril, David *211:* 196

Gawing, Toby *72:* 52

Gay, Marie-Louise *68:* 76, 77, 78; *102:* 136; *126:* 76, 78, 81, 83; *127:* 55, 56; *179:* 70, 72, 73, 74

Gay, Zhenya *19:* 135, 136

Gaydos, Tim *62:* 201

Gazsi, Ed *80:* 48

Gazso, Gabriel *73:* 85

Geary, Clifford N. *1:* 122; *9:* 104; *51:* 74

Geary, Rick *142:* 44, 46

Gee, Frank *33:* 26

Geehan, Wayne *157:* 181

Geer, Charles *1:* 91; *3:* 179; *4:* 201; *6:* 168; *7:* 96; *9:* 58; *10:* 72; *12:* 127; *39:* 156,157, 158, 159, 160; *42:* 88, 89, 90, 91; *55:* 111, 116

Geerinck, Manuel *173:* 128

Gehm, Charlie *36:* 65; *57:* 117; *62:* 60, 138

Geis, Alissa Imre *189:* 77

Geisel, Theodor Seuss *1:* 104, 105, 106; *28:* 108, 109, 110,111, 112, 113; *75:* 67, 68, 69, 70, 71; *89:* 127, 128; *100:* 106, 107, 108

Geisert, Arthur *92:* 67, 68; *133:* 72, 73, 74; *165:* 97, 98; *171:* 64, 65

Geldart, William *15:* 121; *21:* 202

Genia *4:* 84

Gentry, Cyrille R. *12:* 66

Genzo, John Paul *136:* 74

George, Jean *2:* 113

George, Lindsay Barrett *95:* 57; *155:* 97, 98

Geraghty, Paul *130:* 60, 61

Gerard, Jean Ignace *45:* 80

Gerard, Rolf *27:* 147, 150

Gerber, Mark *61:* 105

Gerber, Mary Jane *112:* 124; *171:* 56

Gerber, Stephanie *71:* 195

Gerdstein, Mordecai *169:* 105

Gergely, Tibor *54:* 15, 16

Geritz, Franz *17:* 135

Gerlach, Geff *42:* 58

Gerrard, Roy *47:* 78; *90:* 96, 97, 98, 99

Gerritsen, Paula *177:* 69; *217:* 166

Gershinowitz, George *36:* 27

Gerstein, Mordicai *31:* 117; *47:* 80, 81, 82, 83, 84, 85, 86; *51:* 173; *69:* 134; *107:* 122; *142:* 49, 52; *165:* 209; *176:* 119; *178:* 95, 97, 99; *215:* 173

Gervase *12:* 27

Geter, Tyrone *146:* 249; *150:* 86

Getz, Arthur *32:* 148

Gévry, Claudine *188:* 47

Gewirtz, Bina *61:* 81

Giancola, Donato *95:* 146; *164:* 226

Gibala-Broxholm, Scott *205:* 76

Gibbons, Gail *23:* 78; *72:* 77, 78, 79; *82:* 182; *104:* 65; *160:* 99, 100; *201:* 59, 60, 62

Gibbs, Tony *40:* 95

Gibran, Kahlil *32:* 116

Gibson, Barbara Leonard *205:* 77; *212:* 151

Gider, Iskender *81:* 193

Giebfried, Rosemary *170:* 135

Giesen, Rosemary *34:* 192, 193

Giffard, Hannah *83:* 70

Giguere, George *20:* 111

Gilbert, John *19:* 184; *54:* 115; *YABC 2:* 287

Gilbert, W.S. *36:* 83, 85, 96

Gilbert, Yvonne *116:* 70; *128:* 84; *149:* 119; *185:* 69; *192:* 25; *195:* 81

Gilchrist, Jan Spivey *72:* 82, 83, 84, 85, 87; *77:* 90; *105:* 89, 91; *130:* 63, 64; *155:* 105, 107; *182:* 67

Giles, Will *41:* 218

Gili, Phillida *70:* 73

Gill, Margery *4:* 57; *7:* 7; *22:* 122; *25:* 166; *26:* 146, 147

Gillen, Denver *28:* 216

Gillette, Henry J. *23:* 237

Gilliam, Stan *39:* 64, 81

Gillies, Chuck *62:* 31

Gilliland, Jillian *87:* 58

Gillman, Alec *98:* 105

Gilman, Esther *15:* 124

Gilman, Phoebe *104:* 70, 71

Gilpin, Stephen *213:* 68

Ginsberg, Sari *111:* 184

Ginsburg, Max *62:* 59; *68:* 194 Girard, Roge *161:* 30

Girouard, Patrick *155:* 100

Giovanopoulos, Paul *7:* 104; *60:* 36

Giovine, Sergio *79:* 12; *93:* 118; *139:* 118; *205:* 114

Gist, E.M. *206:* 60

Githens, Elizabeth M. *5:* 47

Gladden, Scott *99:* 108; *103:* 160; *193:* 46, 47

Gladstone, Gary *12:* 89; *13:* 190

Gladstone, Lise *15:* 273

Glanzman, Louis S. *2:* 177; *3:* 182; *36:* 97, 98; *38:* 120, 122; *52:* 141, 144; *71:* 191; *91:* 54, 56

Glaser, Byron *154:* 59, 60

Glaser, Milton *3:* 5; *5:* 156; *11:* 107; *30:* 26; *36:* 112; *54:* 141; *151:* 70

Glass, Andrew *36:* 38; *44:* 133; *48:* 205; *65:* 3; *68:* 43, 45; *90:* 104, 105; *150:* 89

Glass, Marvin *9:* 174

Glasser, Judy *41:* 156; *56:* 140; *69:* 79; *72:* 101

Glattauer, Ned *5:* 84; *13:* 224; *14:* 26

Glauber, Uta *17:* 76

Gleeson, J.M. *YABC 2:* 207

Glegg, Creina *36:* 100

Glienke, Amelie *63:* 150

Gliewe, Unada *3:* 78, 79; *21:* 73; *30:* 220

Gliori, Debi *72:* 91; *138:* 82; *162:* 37; *189:* 79, 81, 82

Glovach, Linda *7:* 105

Gobbato, Imero *3:* 180, 181; *6:* 213; *7:* 58; *9:* 150; *18:* 39; *21:* 167; *39:* 82, 83; *41:* 137, 251; *59:* 177

Goble, Paul *25:* 121; *26:* 86; *33:* 65; *69:* 68, 69; *131:* 79, 80

Goble, Warwick *46:* 78, 79; *194:* 143

Godal, Eric *36:* 93

Godkin, Celia *145:* 84, 86

Godfrey, Michael *17:* 279

Godon, Ingrid *166:* 163; *186:* 99

Goede, Irene *208:* 87

Goembel, Ponder *42:* 124

Goffe, Toni *61:* 83, 84, 85; *89:* 11; *90:* 124; *178:* 118

Goffstein, M.B. *8:* 71; *70:* 75, 76, 77

Golbin, Andre *15:* 125

Gold, Robert *166:* 151, 152

Goldfeder, Cheryl *11:* 191

Goldfinger, Jennifer P. *185:* 71

Goldsborough, June *5:* 154, 155; *8:* 92, *14:* 226; *19:* 139; *54:* 165

Goldsmith, Robert *110:* 77

Goldstein, Barry *198:* 147

Goldstein, Leslie *5:* 8; *6:* 60; *10:* 106

Goldstein, Nathan *1:* 175; *2:* 79; *11:* 41, 232; *16:* 55

Goldstrom, Robert *98:* 36; *145:* 51, 52

Golembe, Carla *79:* 80, 81; *136:* 91; *144:* 113; *193:* 53

Golin, Carlo *74:* 112

Gomez, Elena *188:* 122; *191:* 72

Gomez, Elizabeth *127:* 70; *133:* 76

Gomi, Taro *64:* 102; *103:* 74, 76

Gon, Adriano *101:* 112

Gonsalves, Ron *178:* 213; *212:* 196

Gonzalez, Maya Christina *104:* 3; *136:* 92; *215:* 4, 5

Gonzalez, Yolanda *212:* 65

Good, Karen Hillard *212:* 143; *214:* 103

Goodall, John S. *4:* 92, 93; *10:* 132; *66:* 92, 93; *YABC 1:* 198

Goode, Diane *15:* 126; *50:* 183; *52:* 114, 115; *76:* 195; *84:* 94; *99:* 141; *114:* 76, 77, 78; *170:* 99, 101

Goodelman, Aaron *40:* 203

Goodenow, Earle *40:* 97

Goodfellow, Peter *62:* 95; *94:* 202

Goodman, Joan Elizabeth *50:* 86

Goodman, Vivienne *82:* 251; *146:* 181, 182

Goodnow, Patti *117:* 33

Goodwin, Harold *13:* 74

Goodwin, Philip R. *18:* 206

Goor, Nancy *39:* 85, 86

Goor, Ron *39:* 85, 86

Goossens, Philippe *195:* 71

Gorbachev, Valeri *89:* 96; *112:* 97; *143:* 63, 64; *184:* 66, 67, 68, 101

Gordon, David *216:* 159

Gordon, Gwen *12:* 151

Gordon, Margaret *4:* 147; *5:* 48, 49; *9:* 79

Gordon, Mike *101:* 62, 63, 64

Gordon, Russell *136:* 204; *137:* 214

Gordon, Walter *138:* 9

Gore, Leonid *89:* 51; *94:* 74; *136:* 8; *158:* 117; *166:* 136; *168:* 36; *170:* 107; *181:* 94; *185:* 73

Gorecka-Egan, Erica *18:* 35

Gorey, Edward *1:* 60, 61; *13:* 169; *18:* 192; *20:* 201; *29:* 90, 91, 92, 93, 94, 95, 96, 97, 98, 99, 100; *30:* 129; *32:* 90; *34:* 200, *65:* 48; *68:* 24, 25; *69:* 79; *70:* 80, 82, 83, 84; *85:* 136; *127:* 62
Gorsline, Douglas *1:* 98; *6:* 13; *11:* 113; *13:* 104; *15:* 14; *28:* 117, 118; *YABC 1:* 15
Gorton, Julia *108:* 94; *178:* 81, 82
Gosfield, Josh *118:* 165, 166; *149:* 67
Gosner, Kenneth *5:* 135
Gosney, Joy *167:* 142
Gotlieb, Jules *6:* 127
Goto, Scott *115:* 86; *136:* 69; *203:* 77, 78
Gott, Barry *197:* 95; *212:* 102
Gottlieb, Dale *67:* 162; *107:* 16; *149:* 6
Goudey, Ray *97:* 86
Gough, Alan *91:* 57
Gough, Philip *23:* 47; *45:* 90
Gould, Chester *49:* 112, 113, 114, 116, 117, 118
Gould, Jason *151:* 232
Gourbault, Martine *177:* 159
Govern, Elaine R. *26:* 94
Gower, Teri *102:* 184
Gowing, Toby *60:* 25; *63:* 33; *78:* 70, 252; *83:* 228; *86:* 187; *93:* 145; *108:* 133; *110:* 217; *184:* 125
Grabianski *20:* 144
Grabianski, Janusz *39:* 92, 93, 94, 95
Graboff, Abner *35:* 103, 104
Graef, Renée *61:* 188; *72:* 207; *204:* 45; *210:* 249
Grafe, Max *156:* 173; *178:* 237; *192:* 240; *198:* 51
Graham, A.B. *11:* 61
Graham, Bob *101:* 66, 67, 68; *151:* 74, 75; *187:* 65, 67, 68, 70
Graham, Georgia *188:* 3; *190:* 75
Graham, L. *7:* 108
Graham, Margaret Bloy *11:* 120; *18:* 305, 307
Graham, Mark *88:* 208; *159:* 153; *182:* 3
Grahame-Johnstone, Janet *13:* 61
Grahame-Johnstone, Anne *13:* 61
Grainger, Sam *42:* 95
Gralley, Jean *166:* 86
Gramatky, Hardie *1:* 107; *30:* 116, 119, 120, 122, 123
Gran, Julie *168:* 118
Granahan, Julie *84:* 84
GrandPré, Mary *84:* 131; *109:* 199; *118:* 76; *180:* 65; *184:* 70, 71, 180; *192:* 87; *215:* 24
Grandström, Brita *176:* 139
Grandville, J.J. *45:* 81, 82, 83, 84, 85, 86, 87, 88; *47:* 125; *64:* 10
Granger, Paul *39:* 153
Granström, Brita *162:* 35; *167:* 46
Grant, (Alice) Leigh *10:* 52; *15:* 131; *20:* 20; *26:* 119; *48:* 202
Grant, Gordon *17:* 230, 234; *25:* 123, 124, 125, 126; *52:* 69; *YABC 1:* 164
Grant, Melvyn *159:* 186, 187; *170:* 48, 49; *213:* 168, 169
Grant, Michelle *210:* 95
Grant, Renee *77:* 40
Grant, Shirley *109:* 45
Graves, Elizabeth *45:* 101
Graves, Keith *167:* 89; *191:* 74; *216:* 34
Gray, Harold *33:* 87, 88
Gray, Les *82:* 76; *83:* 232
Gray, Reginald *6:* 69
Greco, Tony *184:* 6
Greder, Armin *76:* 235
Green, Ann Canevari *62:* 48
Green, Eileen *6:* 97
Green, Elizabeth Shippen *139:* 109
Green, Jonathan *86:* 135; *105:* 109
Green, Ken *111:* 68
Green, Michael *32:* 216
Green, Robina *87:* 138
Green, Jonathan *157:* 105
Greene, Jeffrey *117:* 93

Greenaway, Kate *17:* 275; *24:* 180; *26:* 107; *41:* 222, 232; *100:* 115, 116; *YABC 1:* 88, 89; *2:* 131, 133, 136,138, 139, 141
Greenberg, Melanie Hope *72:* 93; *80:* 125; *101:* 174; *133:* 180; *186:* 189; *214:* 105
Greenseid, Diane *178:* 106, 107
Greenstein, Elaine *150:* 100
Greenwald, Sheila *1:* 34; *3:* 99; *8:* 72
Greger, Carol *76:* 86
Gregorian, Joyce Ballou *30:* 125
Gregory, Emilian *177:* 146; *187:* 10
Gregory, Fran *130:* 4; *140:* 93
Gregory, Frank M. *29:* 107
Greiffenhagen, Maurice *16:* 137; *27:* 57; *YABC 2:* 288
Greiner, Robert *6:* 86
Gretter, J. Clemens *31:* 134
Gretz, Susanna *7:* 114
Gretzer, John *1:* 54; *3:* 26; *4:* 162; *7:* 125; *16:* 247; *18:* 117; *28:* 66; *30:* 85, 211; *33:* 235; *56:* 16
Grey, Mini *166:* 90; *192:* 71
Grey Owl *24:* 41
Gri *25:* 90
Grieder, Walter *9:* 84
Griesbach/Martucci *59:* 3
Grifalconi, Ann *2:* 126; *3:* 248; *11:* 18; *13:* 182; *46:* 38; *50:* 145; *66:* 99, 100, 101, 104, 106; *69:* 38; *70:* 64; *87:* 128; *90:* 53; *93:* 49; *128:* 48; *133:* 79, 81; *210:* 111
Griffin, Gillett Good *26:* 96
Griffin, James *30:* 166
Griffin, John Howard *59:* 186
Griffin, Rachel *131:* 23
Griffith, Gershom *94:* 214
Griffiths, Dave *29:* 76
Griffiths, Dean *168:* 180; *169:* 182
Grimly, Gris *186:* 102; *192:* 112; *197:* 86
Grimsdell, Jeremy *83:* 75
Grimwood, Brian *82:* 89
Gringhuis, Dirk *6:* 98; *9:* 196
Gripe, Harald *2:* 127; *74:* 98
Grisha *3:* 71
Grobler, Piet *201:* 100
Grohmann, Susan *84:* 97
Gropper, William *27:* 93; *37:* 193
Gros *60:* 199
Grose, Helen Mason *YABC 1:* 260; *2:* 150
Grossman, Nancy *24:* 130; *29:* 101
Grossman, Robert *11:* 124; *46:* 39
Groth, John *15:* 79; *21:* 53, 54; *83:* 230
Grover, Lorie Ann *168:* 59
Grubb, Lisa *160:* 116
Grue, Lisa *187:* 193
Gruelle, Johnny *35:* 107
Gschwind, William *11:* 72
Guarnaccia, Steven *201:* 170, 173
Guay-Mitchell, Rebecca *110:* 95, 96; *135:* 240; *180:* 76; *181:* 71, 73; *216:* 77
Guback, Georgia *88:* 102
Gudeon, Karla *212:* 67
Guerguerion, Claudine *105:* 73
Guevara, Susan *97:* 87; *167:* 49; *194:* 54
Guggenheim, Hans *2:* 10; *3:* 37; *8:* 136
Guhathaakurta, Ajanta *183:* 199
Guida, Lisa Chauncy *172:* 188
Guilbeau, Honore *22:* 69
Guillette, Joseph *137:* 37
Guisewite, Cathy *57:* 52, 53, 54, 56, 57
Gukova, Julia *95:* 104; *154:* 103; *168:* 195
Gundersheimer, Karen *35:* 240; *82:* 100
Gunderson, Nick *57:* 120
Gunnella *192:* 144
Gurney, James *76:* 97; *86:* 32
Gurney, John Steven *75:* 39, 82; *110:* 175; *143:* 67, 68; *169:* 172; *217:* 50, 88
Gusman, Annie *38:* 62
Gustafson, Scott *34:* 111; *43:* 40
Gustavson, Adam *104:* 10; *171:* 183; *176:* 87; *197:* 94; *204:* 35
Guthridge, Bettina *108:* 79; *186:* 92

Guthrie, R. Dale *64:* 143
Guthrie, Robin *20:* 122
Gutierrez, Akemi *172:* 87; *205:* 135
Gutierrez, Alan *136:* 31, 32
Gutierrez, Rudy *97:* 162; *203:* 79; *216:* 158
Gutmann, Bessie Pease *73:* 93, 94
Gwynne, Fred *41:* 94, 95
Gyberg, Bo-Erik *38:* 131

H

Haas, Irene *17:* 77; *87:* 46; *96:* 117
Hack, Konrad *51:* 127
Hader, Berta H. *16:* 126
Hader, Elmer S. *16:* 126
Haeffele, Deborah *76:* 99
Haemer, Alan *62:* 109
Hafner, Marylin *22:* 196, 216; *24:* 44; *30:* 51; *35:* 95; *51:* 25, 160, 164; *86:* 16; *105:* 196; *121:* 93, 94; *149:* 208, 209; *179:* 82, 83, 84, 115; *190:* 200; *201:* 29; *217:* 91
Hagerty, Sean *62:* 181
Hague, Michael *32:* 128; *48:* 98, 99, 100, 101, 103, 105,106, 107, 108, 109, 110; *49:* 121; *51:* 105; *64:* 14, 15; *79:* 134; *80:* 91, 92; *83:* 135; *100:* 241; *102:* 29; *129:* 101, 103, 104; *185:* 80, 81, 82; *215:* 89
Hair, Jonathan *115:* 135
Halas, John *29:* 41, 47, 48
Haldane, Roger *13:* 76; *14:* 202
Hale, Bruce *203:* 83
Hale, Christy *79:* 124; *84:* 200; *114:* 201; *128:* 2, 3; *146:* 203; *158:* 243; *167:* 99; *179:* 87
Hale, Irina *26:* 97
Hale, James Graham *88:* 207
Hale, Kathleen *17:* 79; *66:* 114, 116, 118
Hale, Nathan *210:* 115, 116; *214:* 179
Haley, Amanda *205:* 82, 83
Haley, Gail E. *43:* 102, 103, 104, 105; *78:* 65, 67; *136:* 106, 107
Hall, Amanda *96:* 110
Hall, August N. *217:* 74
Hall, Chuck *30:* 189
Hall, Douglas *15:* 184; *43:* 106, 107; *86:* 100; *87:* 82; *129:* 72
Hall, H. Tom *1:* 227; *30:* 210
Hall, Melanie *116:* 48, 49; *169:* 77, 78
Hall, Sydney P. *31:* 89
Hall, Tim *164:* 196; *202:* 41
Hall, Vicki *20:* 24
Hallinan, P.K. *39:* 98
Hallman, Tom *98:* 166
Hally, Greg *101:* 200; *151:* 224
Halperin, Wendy Anderson *96:* 151; *125:* 96, 97, 98, 99; *139:* 22; *140:* 84; *200:* 77, 78; *210:* 157; *215:* 65
Halpern, Joan *10:* 25
Halpern, Shari *174:* 172
Halsey, Megan *96:* 172; *114:* 185; *180:* 8; *185:* 85
Halstead, Virginia *125:* 105
Halverson, Janet *49:* 38, 42, 44
Hallensleben, Georg *134:* 5, 6; *172:* 17
Hamanaka, Sheila *71:* 100
Hamann, Brad *78:* 151
Hamann, Sigune *104:* 115
Hamberger, John *6:* 8; *8:* 32; *14:* 79; *34:* 136; *88:* 78
Hamil, Tom *14:* 80; *43:* 163
Hamilton, Bill and Associates *26:* 215
Hamilton, Helen S. *2:* 238
Hamilton, J. *19:* 83, 85, 87
Hamilton, Laurie *116:* 210
Hamilton, Todd Cameron *84:* 15
Hamlin, Janet *97:* 136; *124:* 90; *137:* 157; *182:* 117
Hamlin, Louise *71:* 135
Hammill, Matt *206:* 65
Hammond, Chris *21:* 37

Hammond, Elizabeth *5:* 36, 203
Hampshire, Michael *5:* 187; *7:* 110, 111; *48:* 150; *51:* 129
Hampson, Denman *10:* 155; *15:* 130
Hampton, Blake *41:* 244
Handford, Martin *64:* 105, 106, 107, 109
Handforth, Thomas *42:* 100, 101, 102, 103, 104, 105, 107
Handville, Robert *1:* 89; *38:* 76; *45:* 108, 109
Hane, Roger *17:* 239; *44:* 54
Haney, Elizabeth Mathieu *34:* 84
Hanke, Ted *71:* 10
Hankinson, Phil *181:* 164
Hanley, Catherine *8:* 161
Hann, Jacquie *19:* 144
Hanna, Cheryl *91:* 133
Hanna, Wayne A. *67:* 145
Hannon, Mark *38:* 37
Hanrahan, Kelly-Anne *203:* 142
Hansen, Gaby *159:* 11; *186:* 25
Hansen, Mia *149:* 76
Hanson, Joan *8:* 76; *11:* 139
Hanson, Peter E. *52:* 47; *54:* 99, 100; *73:* 21; *84:* 79; *116:* 144
Hansson, Gunilla *64:* 111, 112
Hardcastle, Nick *121:* 82; *175:* 185
Hardy, David A. *9:* 96; *119:* 74
Hardy, Paul *YABC 2:* 245 *Haring, Keith 145:* 65
Harlan, Jerry *3:* 96
Harlin, Greg *89:* 194; *103:* 82; *118:* 161; *121:* 167; *182:* 76; *201:* 172; *215:* 76
Harman, Dominic *206:* 48
Harness, Cheryl *106:* 80; *131:* 87; *178:* 111; *200:* 39
Harnischfeger, *18:* 121
Harper, Arthur *YABC 2:* 121
Harper, Betty *126:* 90
Harper, Jamie *174:* 71; *214:* 212
Harper, Piers *79:* 27; *105:* 102; *161:* 67
Harrington, Glenn *82:* 18; *94:* 66, 68; *185:* 118
Harrington, Jack *83:* 162
Harrington, Richard *5:* 81
Harris, Andrew N. *191:* 78
Harris, Jim *127:* 130; *183:* 4
Harris, John *83:* 25
Harris, Nick *86:* 177
Harris, Susan Yard *42:* 121
Harrison, Florence *20:* 150, 152
Harrison, Harry *4:* 103
Harrison, Jack *28:* 149
Harrison, Mark *105:* 157; *165:* 190
Harrison, Ted *56:* 73
Harsh, Fred *72:* 107
Harston, Jerry *105:* 143
Hart, Lewis *98:* 115
Hart, Thomas *181:* 165
Hart, William *13:* 72
Hartland, Jessie *171:* 80, 81; *186:* 165
Hartung, Susan Kathleen *150:* 107, 108; *173:* 106; *175:* 106; *192:* 78; *211:* 19
Hartelius, Margaret *10:* 24
Hartshorn, Ruth *5:* 115; *11:* 129
Harvey, Amanda *145:* 44
Harvey, Bob *48:* 219
Harvey, Gerry *7:* 180
Harvey, Lisa *97:* 21
Harvey, Paul *88:* 74
Harvey, Roland *71:* 88; *123:* 63; *179:* 94
Haskamp, Steve *195:* 36
Hassall, Joan *43:* 108, 109
Hassell, Hilton *YABC 1:* 187
Hassett, John *162:* 59
Hasselriis, Else *18:* 87; *YABC 1:* 96
Hastings, Glenn *89:* 183
Hastings, Ian *62:* 67
Hauman, Doris *2:* 184; *29:* 58, 59; *32:* 85, 86, 87
Hauman, George *2:* 184; *29:* 58, 59; *32:* 85, 86, 87

Hausherr, Rosmarie *15:* 29
Hawkes, Kevin *78:* 72; *104:* 198; *105:* 197; *112:* 109; *126:* 87; *144:* 88; *149:* 210; *150:* 110, 135; *156:* 94; *164:* 35; *186:* 18; *190:* 197; *198:* 152; *201:* 70, 71, 72
Hawkins, Jacqui *112:* 86; *162:* 64
Hawkinson, John *4:* 109; *7:* 83; *21:* 64
Hawkinson, Lucy *21:* 64
Hawthorne, Mike *140:* 228
Haxton, Elaine *28:* 131
Haydock, Robert *4:* 95
Hayes, Geoffrey *26:* 111; *44:* 133; *91:* 85; *207:* 63
Hayes, Karel *207:* 65
Haynes, Max *72:* 107
Hays, Michael *73:* 207; *83:* 93; *139:* 197; *146:* 202, 250; *202:* 47
Haywood, Carolyn *1:* 112; *29:* 104
Heale, Jonathan *104:* 117
Healy, Daty *12:* 143
Healy, Deborah *58:* 181, 182; *101:* 111
Heap, Sue *102:* 207; *150:* 113, 114; *187:* 84, 85, 87
Hearn, Diane Dawson *79:* 99; *113:* 13; *209:* 71, 72; *211:* 106
Hearon, Dorothy *34:* 69
Heaslip, William *57:* 24, 25
Hechtkopf, H. *11:* 110
Heck, Ed *173:* 81
Hector, Julian *205:* 85
Hedderwick, Mairi *30:* 127; *32:* 47; *36:* 104, 77; *86:* *145:* 91, 93, 95
Heffernan, Phil *146:* 197; *195:* 172
Hefter, Richard *28:* 170; *31:* 81, 82; *33:* 183
Hehenberger, Shelly *126:* 91
Heigh, James *22:* 98
Heighway, Richard *25:* 160; *64:* 4
Heighway-Bury, Robin *159:* 89
Heine, Helme *67:* 86; *135:* 91, 92
Heinly, John *45:* 113
Hellard, Susan *81:* 21; *204:* 82; *209:* 92
Hellebrand, Nancy *26:* 57
Heller, Linda *46:* 86
Heller, Ruth M. *66:* 125; *77:* 30, 32
Hellmuth, Jim *38:* 164
Helms, Georgeann *33:* 62
Helquist, Brett *142:* 203; *146:* 133, 134; *156:* 10; *173:* 25; *180:* 106; *187:* 90, 91; *193:* 12
Helweg, Hans *41:* 118; *50:* 93; *58:* 22, 26
Hemingway, Edward *212:* 71
Hemphill, Helen *179:* 95
Henba, Bobbie *90:* 195
Henderling, Lisa *214:* 65
Henderson, Dave *73:* 76; *75:* 191, 192, 193, 194; *82:* 4
Henderson, D.F. *216:* 77
Henderson, Douglas *103:* 68
Henderson, Kathy *55:* 32; *155:* 118
Henderson, Keith *35:* 122
Henderson, Meryl *127:* 58, 60; *169:* 81
Hendrix, John *187:* 133; *208:* 106, 107, 108; *216:* 115
Hendry, Linda *80:* 104; *83:* 83; *164:* 216
Hengeveld, Dennis *142:* 86
Henkes, Kevin *43:* 111; *108:* 106, 107, 108
Henneberger, Robert *1:* 42; *2:* 237; *25:* 83
Henriquez, Celeste *103:* 137
Henriquez, Elsa *82:* 260
Henriquez, Emile F. *89:* 88; *211:* 56
Henry, Everett *29:* 191
Henry, Matthew *117:* 58
Henry, Paul *93:* 121; *194:* 125
Henry, Rohan *217:* 77
Henry, Thomas *5:* 102
Hensel *27:* 119
Henshaw, Jacqui *141:* 127
Henstra, Friso *8:* 80; *36:* 70; *40:* 222; *41:* 250; *73:* 100, 101
Henterly, Jamichael *93:* 4

Heo, Yumi *89:* 85, 86; *94:* 89, 90; *146:* 40, 137, 138; *163:* 227; *201:* 192
Hepple, Norman *28:* 198
Herbert, Helen *57:* 70
Herbert, Jennifer *189:* 47
Herbert, Wally *23:* 101
Herbster, Mary Lee *9:* 33
Herder, Edwin *182:* 104
Herge
See Remi, Georges
Hermansen, Pal *133:* 113
Hermanson, Dennis *10:* 55
Hermes, Gertrude *54:* 161
Herr, Margo *57:* 191
Herr, Susan *83:* 163
Herriman, George *140:* 74, 75, 76, 77, 78
Herriman, Lisa *87:* 190
Herring, Michael *121:* 76; *182:* 103
Herrington, Roger *3:* 161
Herscovici, C. *165:* 240
Hescox, Richard *85:* 86; *90:* 30; *139:* 35
Heslop, Mike *38:* 60; *40:* 130
Hess, Lydia J. *85:* 17
Hess, Mark *111:* 146; *113:* 207
Hess, Paul *134:* 47; *166:* 133; *193:* 13
Hess, Richard *42:* 31
Hester, Ronnie *37:* 85
Heuser, Olga J. *121:* 116
Heusser, Sibylle *168:* 195
Heustis, Louise L. *20:* 28
Hewgill, Jodi *201:* 90
Hewitson, Jennifer *74:* 119; *124:* 167
Hewitt, Kathryn *80:* 126; *149:* 105; *184:* 93; *196:* 36
Hewitt, Margaret *84:* 112
Heyduck-Huth, Hilde *8:* 82
Heyer, Carol *74:* 122; *130:* 72, 73; *192:* 35; *203:* 78
Heyer, Hermann *20:* 114, 115
Heyer, Marilee *102:* 108
Heyman, Ken *8:* 33; *34:* 113
Heyne, Ulrike *146:* 151
Heywood, Karen *48:* 114
Hickling, P.B. *40:* 165
Hickman, Stephen *85:* 58; *136:* 33; *171:* 128
Hierstein, Judith *56:* 40; *162:* 168; *212:* 72
Higashi, Sandra *154:* 59, 60
Higginbottom, J. Winslow *8:* 170; *29:* 105, 106
Higgins, Chester *101:* 79
Higham, David *50:* 104
Hilb, Nora *176:* 8
Hild, Anja *215:* 194
Hildebrandt, Greg *8:* 191; *55:* 35, 36, 38, 39, 40, 42, 46; *172:* 110
Hildebrandt, Tim *8:* 191; *55:* 44, 45, 46
Hilder, Rowland *19:* 207
Hill, Eric *66:* 127, 128; *133:* 91
Hill, Gregory *35:* 190
Hill, Pat *49:* 120
Hillenbrand, Will *84:* 115; *92:* 76, 80; *93:* 131; *104:* 168; *128:* 137; *145:* 187; *146:* 184; *147:* 105, 106, 107; *152:* 59; *184:* 179; *195:* 34, 180; *196:* 125; *210:* 122, 123, 124; *217:* 62
Hilliard, Richard *183:* 74
Hillier, Matthew *45:* 205
Hillman, Priscilla *48:* 115
Hills, Tad *113:* 4; *137:* 147; *173:* 83; *208:* 199
Himler, Ronald *6:* 114; *7:* 162; *8:* 17, 84, 125; *14:* 76; *19:* 145; *26:* 160; *31:* 43; *38:* 116; *41:* 44, 79; *43:* 52; *45:* 120; *46:* 43; *54:* 44, 83; *58:* 180; *59:* 38; *68:* 146; *69:* 231; *70:* 98; *71:* 177, 178; *77:* 219; *79:* 212; *83:* 62; *89:* 5; *91:* 160; *92:* 91, 92, 93; *94:* 93; *95:* 69, 174, 194; *99:* 99, 112; *113:* 92; *118:* 114; *137:* 73, 74, 77, 167; *163:* 99; *165:* 138; *178:* 9, 220; *183:* 77, 79, 80, 81; *184:* 80, 83; *215:* 151
Himmelman, John *47:* 109; *65:* 87; *94:* 96, 97; *159:* 85

Hinds, Bill *37:* 127, 130
Hines, Anna Grossnickle *51:* 90; *74:* 124; *95:* 78, 79,80, 81
Hines, Bob *135:* 149, 150
Hirao, Amiko *203:* 98
Hiroko *99:* 61
Hiroshige *25:* 71
Hirsh, Marilyn *7:* 126
Hiscock, Bruce *137:* 80, 81; *204:* 51, 53
Hissey, Jane *103:* 90; *130:* 81
Hitch, Jeff *99:* 206; *128:* 86
Hitz, Demi *11:* 135; *15:* 245; *66:* 129, 130; *152:* 94, 95
Hnizdovsky, Jacques *32:* 96; *76:* 187
Ho, Kwoncjan *15:* 132
Hoban, Lillian *1:* 114; *22:* 157; *26:* 72; *29:* 53; *40:* 105, 107, 195; *41:* 80; *69:* 107, 108; *71:* 98; *77:* 168; *106:* 50; *113:* 86; *136:* 118
Hoban, Tana *22:* 159; *104:* 82, 83, 85
Hobbie, Jocelyn *190:* 78; *196:* 92
Hobbie, Nathaniel *196:* 92
Hobbs, Leigh *166:* 95
Hoberman, Norman *5:* 82
Hobson, Sally *77:* 185
Hockerman, Dennis *39:* 22; *56:* 23
Hodgell, P.C. *42:* 114
Hodges, C. Walter *2:* 139; *11:* 15; *12:* 25; *23:* 34; *25:* 96; *38:* 165; *44:* 197; *45:* 95; *100:* 57; *YABC 2:* 62, 63
Hodges, David *9:* 98
Hodgetts, Victoria *43:* 132
Hofbauer, Imre *2:* 162
Hoff, Syd *9:* 107; *10:* 128; *33:* 94; *72:* 115,116, 117, 118; *138:* 114, 115
Hoffman, Rosekrans *15:* 133; *50:* 219; *63:* 97
Hoffman, Sanford *38:* 208; *76:* 174; *88:* 160, 161; *151:* 156
Hoffmann, Felix *9:* 109
Hoffnung, Gerard *66:* 76, 77
Hofsinde, Robert *21:* 70
Hogan, Inez *2:* 141
Hogan, Jamie *192:* 94; *198:* 177
Hogarth, Burne *41:* 58; *63:* 46, 48, 49, 50, 52, 53, 54, 55,56
Hogarth, Paul *41:* 102, 103, 104; *YABC 1:* 16
Hogarth, William *42:* 33
Hogenbyl, Jan *1:* 35
Hogner, Nils *4:* 122; *25:* 144
Hogrogian, Nonny *3:* 221; *4:* 106, 107; *5:* 166; *7:* 129; *15:* 2; *16:* 176; *20:* 154; *22:* 146; *25:* 217; *27:* 206; *74:* 127, 128, 129, 149, 152; *127:* 99; *YABC 2:* 84, 94
Hokanson, Lars *93:* 111; *172:* 137; *212:* 88
Hokusai *25:* 71
Hol, Colby *126:* 96
Holberg, Richard *2:* 51
Holbrook, Kathy *107:* 114
Holdcroft, Tina *38:* 109
Holden, Caroline *55:* 159
Holder, Heidi *36:* 99; *64:* 9
Holder, Jim *204:* 163
Holder, Jimmy *151:* 224
Holderness, Grizelda *215:* 107
Hole, Stian *204:* 55
Holiday, Henry *YABC 2:* 107
Holl, F. *36:* 91
Holland, Brad *45:* 59, 159
Holland, Gay W. *128:* 105
Holland, Janice *18:* 118
Holland, Marion *6:* 116
Holland, Richard *216:* 109, 124
Holldobler, Turid *26:* 120
Holliday, Keaf *144:* 236
Holling, Holling C. *15:* 136, 137
Hollinger, Deanne *12:* 116
Holm, Sharon Lane *114:* 84; *115:* 52
Holmes, B. *3:* 82
Holmes, Bea *7:* 74; *24:* 156; *31:* 93
Holmes, Dave *54:* 22
Holmes, Lesley *135:* 96
Holmgren, George Ellen *45:* 112

Holmlund, Heather D. *150:* 140
Holt, Norma *44:* 106
Holt, Pater *151:* 188
Holtan, Gene *32:* 192
Holub, Joan *149:* 72
Holyfield, John *149:* 231
Holz, Loretta *17:* 81
Hom, Nancy *79:* 195
Homar, Lorenzo *6:* 2
Homer, Winslow *128:* 8; *YABC 2:* 87
Honey, Elizabeth *112:* 95, 96; *137:* 93, 94
Honeywood, Varnette P. *110:* 68, 70
Hong, Lily Toy *76:* 104
Honigman, Marian *3:* 2
Honore, Paul *42:* 77, 79, 81, 82
Hood, Alun *69:* 145, 218; *72:* 41; *80:* 226; *87:* 4; *95:* 139
Hood, Susan *12:* 43
Hook, Christian *104:* 103
Hook, Frances *26:* 188; *27:* 127
Hook, Jeff *14:* 137; *103:* 105
Hook, Richard *26:* 188
Hooks *63:* 30
Hooper, Hadley *177:* 145
Hoover, Carol A. *21:* 77
Hoover, Russell *12:* 95; *17:* 2; *34:* 156
Hope, James *141:* 116
Hopkins, Chris *99:* 127
Hopkinson, Leigh *202:* 70
Hopman, Philip *178:* 184
Hoppe, Paul *209:* 85
Hoppin, Augustus *34:* 66
Horacek, Judy *211:* 86
Horacek, Petr *163:* 117; *214:* 113
Horder, Margaret *2:* 108; *73:* 75
Horen, Michael *45:* 121
Horne, Daniel *73:* 106; *91:* 153; *109:* 127; *110:* 232; *164:* 176
Horne, Richard *111:* 80
Horowitz, Dave *204:* 58
Horse, Harry *128:* 195; *169:* 86
Horton, Anthony *211:* 98
Horvat, Laurel *12:* 201
Horvath, David *192:* 95
Horvath, Ferdinand Kusati *24:* 176
Horvath, Maria *57:* 171
Horwitz, Richard *57:* 174
Hotchkiss, De Wolfe *20:* 49
Hough, Charlotte *9:* 112; *13:* 98; *17:* 83; *24:* 195
Houlihan, Ray *11:* 214
House, Caroline *183:* 121
Housman, Laurence *25:* 146, 147
Houston, James *13:* 107; *74:* 132, 134, 135
Hovland, Gary *88:* 172; *171:* 148
Hoyt, Eleanor *158:* 231
How, W.E. *20:* 47
Howard, Alan *16:* 80; *34:* 58; *45:* 114
Howard, Arthur *165:* 111, 112; *190:* 5
Howard, J.N. *15:* 234
Howard, John *33:* 179
Howard, Kim *116:* 71
Howard, Paul *142:* 126, 129; *144:* 187
Howard, Rob *40:* 161
Howarth, Daniel *170:* 34
Howe, John *79:* 101; *80:* 150; *115:* 47; *176:* 106; *207:* 32, 35
Howe, Phillip *79:* 117; *175:* 115
Howe, Stephen *1:* 232
Howell, Karen *119:* 123
Howell, Pat *15:* 139
Howell, Troy *23:* 24; *31:* 61; *36:* 158; *37:* 184; *41:* 76, 235; *48:* 112; *56:* 13; *57:* 3; *59:* 174; *63:* 5; *74:* 46; *89:* 188; *90:* 231; *95:* 97; *98:* 130; *99:* 189; *153:* 156, 157, 158; *176:* 104; *199:* 96, 98
Howes, Charles *22:* 17
Hoyt, Ard *145:* 141; *190:* 82; *207:* 148
Hranilovich, Barbara *127:* 51
Hu, Ying-Hwa *116:* 107; *152:* 236; *173:* 171
Huang, Benrei *137:* 55

Huang, Zhong-Yang *117:* 30, 32; *213:* 18
Hubbard, Woodleigh Marx *98:* 67; *115:* 79; *160:* 138; *214:* 120
Hubley, Faith *48:* 120, 121, 125, 130, 131, 132, 134
Hubley, John *48:* 125, 130, 131, 132, 134
Hudak, Michal *143:* 74
Hudnut, Robin *14:* 62
Huerta, Catherine *76:* 178; *77:* 44, 45; *90:* 182; *210:* 202
Huffaker, Sandy *10:* 56
Huffman, Joan *13:* 33
Huffman, Tom *13:* 180; *17:* 212; *21:* 116; *24:* 132; *33:* 154; *38:* 59; *42:* 147
Hughes, Arthur *20:* 148, 149, 150; *33:* 114, 148, 149
Hughes, Darren *95:* 44
Hughes, David *36:* 197
Hughes, Shirley *1:* 20, 21; *7:* 3; *12:* 217; *16:* 163; *29:* 154; *63:* 118; *70:* 102, 103, 104; *73:* 169; *88:* 70; *110:* 118, 119; *159:* 103
Hugo, Victor *47:* 112
Huliska-Beith, Laura *204:* 108
Hull, Cathy *78:* 29
Hull, Richard *95:* 120; *123:* 175; *172:* 195
Hulsmann, Eva *16:* 166
Hume, Lachie *189:* 93
Hummel, Berta *43:* 137, 138, 139
Hummel, Lisl *29:* 109; *YABC 2:* 333, 334
Humphrey, Henry *16:* 167
Humphreys, Graham *25:* 168
Humphries, Tudor *76:* 66; *80:* 4; *124:* 4, 5
Huneck, Stephen *183:* 88, 89
Hunt, James *2:* 143
Hunt, Jonathan *84:* 120
Hunt, Paul *119:* 104; *129:* 135; *139:* 160; *173:* 112
Hunt, Robert *110:* 206, 235; *147:* 136, 137; *170:* 3; *211:* 76
Hunt, Scott *190:* 143
Hunter, Anne *133:* 190; *178:* 150
Huntington, Amy *180:* 99
Hurd, Clement *2:* 148, 149; *64:* 127, 128, 129, 131, 133, 134,135, 136; *100:* 37, 38
Hurd, Peter *24:* 30, 31,; *YABC 2:* 56
Hurd, Thacher *46:* 88, 89; *94:* 114, 115, 116; *123:* 81, 82, 84
Hurlimann, Ruth *32:* 99
Hurst, Carol Otis *185:* 92
Hurst, Philip *196:* 79
Hurst, Tracey *192:* 238
Hussar, Michael *114:* 113; *117:* 159
Hustler, Tom *6:* 105
Hutchins, Laurence *55:* 22
Hutchins, Pat *15:* 142; *70:* 106, 107, 108; *178:* 131, 132
Hutchinson, Sascha *95:* 211
Hutchinson, William M. *6:* 3, 138; *46:* 70
Hutchison, Paula *23:* 10
Hutton, Clarke *YABC 2:* 335
Hutton, Kathryn *35:* 155; *89:* 91
Hutton, Warwick *20:* 91
Huyette, Marcia *29:* 188
Hyatt, John *54:* 7
Hyatt, Mitch *178:* 162
Hyde, Maureen *82:* 17; *121:* 145, 146
Hyman, David *117:* 64
Hyman, Miles *210:* 132
Hyman, Trina Schart *1:* 204; *2:* 194; *5:* 153; *6:* 106; *7:* 138, 145; *8:* 22; *10:* 196; *13:* 96; *14:* 114; *15:* 204; *16:* 234; *20:* 82; *22:* 133; *24:* 151; *25:* 79, 82; *26:* 82; *29:* 83; *31:* 37, 39; *34:* 104; *38:* 84, 100, 128; *41:* 49; *43:* 146; *46:* 91, 92, 93, 95, 96, 97, 98, 99, 100, 101, 102, 103, 104, 105,108, 109, 111, 197; *48:* 60, 61; *52:* 32; *60:* 168; *66:* 38; *67:* 214; *72:* 74; *75:* 92; *79:* 57; *82:* 95, 238; *89:* 46; *95:* 91, 92, 93; *100:* 33, 199; *132:* 12; *147:* 33, 35, 36; *167:* 58, 60; *177:* 189, 190; *211:* 188

I

Ibarra, Rosa *147:* 91
Ibatoulline, Bagram *156:* 48; *174:* 33, 82; *202:* 30; *211:* 213
Ichikawa, Satomi *29:* 152; *41:* 52; *47:* 133, 134,135, 136; *78:* 93, 94; *80:* 81; *146:* 143, 145, 146; *208:* 117, 118, 119
Ide, Jacqueline *YABC 1:* 39
Ilsley, Velma *3:* 1; *7:* 55; *12:* 109; *37:* 62; *38:* 184
Imai, Ayano *190:* 85, 86
in den Bosch, Nicole *150:* 204
Inga *1:* 142
Ingman, Bruce *134:* 50; *182:* 91, 92; *214:* 10
Ingpen, Robert *109:* 103, 104; *132:* 138; *137:* 177; *166:* 103; *181:* 140
Ingraham, Erick *21:* 177; *84:* 256; *103:* 66
Inkpen, Mick *99:* 104, 105; *106:* 44
Innerst, Stacy *149:* 104
Innocenti, Roberto *21:* 123; *96:* 122; *159:* 111, 197; *199:* 176
Inoue, Yosuke *24:* 118
Iofin, Michael *97:* 157
Iosa, Ann *63:* 189
Ipcar, Dahlov *1:* 124, 125; *49:* 137, 138, 139, 140, 141, 142,143, 144, 145; *147:* 122, 124, 126
Irvin, Fred *13:* 166; *15:* 143, 144; *27:* 175
Irving, Jay *45:* 72
Irving, Laurence *27:* 50
Isaac, Joanne *21:* 76
Isaacs, Gary *170:* 188
Isadora, Rachel *43:* 159, 160; *54:* 31; *79:* 106, 107,108; *121:* 100, 102; *165:* 116, 117; *204:* 61, 63, 64
Ishmael, Woodi *24:* 111; *31:* 99
Ives, Ruth *15:* 257
Iwai, Melissa *149:* 233; *183:* 92; *199:* 115
Iwamura, Kazuo *213:* 87

J

Jabar, Cynthia *101:* 201; *210:* 134, 135
Jackness, Andrew *94:* 237
Jackson, Julian *91:* 104, 106
Jackson, Michael *43:* 42
Jackson, Shelley *79:* 71; *99:* 109; *187:* 82
Jacob, Murv *89:* 30
Jacobi, Kathy *62:* 118
Jacobs, Barbara *9:* 136
Jacobs, Lou, Jr. *9:* 136; *15:* 128
Jacobsen, Laura *176:* 98; *177:* 85, 86
Jacobson, Rick *131:* 222; *170:* 119
Jacobus, Tim *79:* 140; *109:* 126; *129:* 180
Jacques, Robin *1:* 70; *2:* 1; *8:* 46; *9:* 20; *15:* 187; *19:* 253; *32:* 102, 103, 104; *43:* 184; *73:* 135; *YABC 1:* 42
Jaeggi, Yoshiko *186:* 184
Jaffee, Al *66:* 131, 132
Jago *216:* 122
Jagr, Miloslav *13:* 197
Jahn-Clough, Lisa *88:* 114; *152:* 104; *193:* 70, 71
Jahnke, Robert *84:* 24
Jainschigg, Nicholas *80:* 64; *91:* 138; *95:* 63; *99:* 25; *108:* 50; *171:* 41
Jakesavic, Nenad *85:* 102
Jakobsen, Kathy *116:* 83
Jakubowski, Charles *14:* 192
Jambor, Louis *YABC 1:* 11
James, Ann *73:* 50; *82:* 113; *158:* 61; *183:* 44
James, Brian *140:* 91
James, Curtis E. *182:* 93
James, Derek *35:* 187; *44:* 91; *61:* 133; *74:* 2; *80:* 57; *86:* 88; *130:* 30; *179:* 29
James, Gilbert *YABC 1:* 43

James, Gordon C. *195:* 89
James, Harold *2:* 151; *3:* 62; *8:* 79; *29:* 113; *51:* 195; *74:* 90
James, Kennon *126:* 211
James, Robin *50:* 106; *53:* 32, 34, 35
James, Simon *202:* 73, 74
James, Will *19:* 150, 152, 153, 155, 163
Janosch
    See Eckert, Horst
Janovitch, Marilyn *68:* 168
Janovitz, Marilyn *87:* 187; *130:* 198; *194:* 91
Jansons, Inese *48:* 117
Jansson, Alexander *216:* 59
Jansson, Tove *3:* 90; *41:* 106, 108, 109, 110, 111, 113, 114
Jaques, Faith *7:* 11, 132, 133; *21:* 83, 84; *69:* 114,116; *73:* 170
Jaques, Frances Lee *29:* 224
Jarrett, Clare *201:* 77
Jauss, Anne Marie *1:* 139; *3:* 34; *10:* 57, 119; *11:* 205; *23:* 194
Jay, Alison *158:* 97, 98; *183:* 126, 127; *196:* 95, 96, 97, 98; *200:* 72, 73, 74; *212:* 39
Jeffers, Oliver *175:* 111; *213:* 89
Jeffers, Susan *17:* 86, 87; *25:* 164, 165; *26:* 112; *50:* 132, 134, 135; *70:* 111, 112, 113; *137:* 107, 108, 109, 110, 111; *202:* 77, 78
Jefferson, Louise E. *4:* 160
Jenkin-Pearce, Susie *78:* 16
Jenkins, Debra Reid *85:* 202; *114:* 89; *173:* 134
Jenkins, Jean *98:* 79, 102
Jenkins, Leonard *157:* 169; *167:* 128; *189:* 96, 97; *190:* 89
Jenkins, Patrick *72:* 126
Jenkins, Steve *124:* 177; *154:* 90, 91, 92, 93; *185:* 194; *188:* 81, 82, 83, 84, 85, 86
Jenks, Aleta *73:* 117; *124:* 225
Jenkyns, Chris *51:* 97
Jensen, Bruce *95:* 39
Jensinius, Kirsten *56:* 58
Jeram, Anita *89:* 135; *102:* 122, 123; *129:* 112; *154:* 96, 97, 98; *164:* 154; *203:* 123, 124
Jernigan, E. Wesley *85:* 92
Jerome, Karen A. *72:* 194
Jeruchim, Simon *6:* 173; *15:* 250
Jeschke, Susan *20:* 89; *39:* 161; *41:* 84; *42:* 120
Jessel, Camilla *29:* 115
Jessell, Tim *159:* 3; *177:* 87; *181:* 95; *205:* 4; *213:* 74
Jeyaveeran, Ruth *182:* 100
Jiang, Cheng An *109:* 108
Jiang, Wei *109:* 108
Jimenez, Maria *77:* 158; *93:* 127
Jobling, Curtis *138:* 74
Jocelyn, Marthe *118:* 83; *137:* 219; *163:* 119, 120; *198:* 62
Joerns, Consuelo *38:* 36; *44:* 94
John, Diana *12:* 209
John, Helen *1:* 215; *28:* 204
Johns, Elizabeth *127:* 33
Johns, Jasper *61:* 172
Johns, Jeanne *24:* 114
Johnson, Adrian *143:* 50
Johnson, Bruce *9:* 47
Johnson, Cathy *92:* 136
Johnson, Crockett
    See Leisk, David
Johnson, D. William *23:* 104
Johnson, D.B. *183:* 98, 139
Johnson, David *175:* 18; *191:* 91
Johnson, Gillian *119:* 175; *164:* 217; *215:* 99
Johnson, Harper *1:* 27; *2:* 33; *18:* 302; *19:* 61; *31:* 181; *44:* 46, 50, 95
Johnson, Ingrid *37:* 118
Johnson, James Ralph *1:* 23, 127
Johnson, James David *12:* 195
Johnson, Jane *48:* 136

Johnson, Joel Peter *98:* 18; *128:* 111; *201:* 13; *213:* 189
Johnson, John E. *34:* 133
Johnson, Kevin *72:* 44
Johnson, Kevin Eugene *109:* 215
Johnson, Larry *47:* 56; *123:* 107; *159:* 203
Johnson, Layne *187:* 94; *209:* 63
Johnson, Margaret S. *35:* 131
Johnson, Meredith Merrell *71:* 181; *83:* 158; *89:* 103; *104:* 88
Johnson, Milton *1:* 67; *2:* 71; *26:* 45; *31:* 107; *60:* 112; *68:* 96
Johnson, Pamela *16:* 174; *52:* 145; *62:* 140; *73:* 116; *85:* 64
Johnson, Paul Brett *83:* 95; *132:* 119
Johnson, Stephen T. *80:* 15; *131:* 35; *141:* 96, 145; *164:* 187; *175:* 32; *189:* 99, 100; *208:* 43
Johnson, Steve *138:* 219; *141:* 64; *144:* 199; *177:* 51; *214:* 95
Johnson, William R. *38:* 91
Johnson-Petrov, Arden *115:* 206
Johnston, David McCall *50:* 131, 133
Johnston, Lynne *118:* 85, 87, 89; *216:* 127, 128, 131
Johnstone, Anne *8:* 120; *36:* 89
Johnstone, Janet Grahame *8:* 120; *36:* 89
Jonas, Ann *50:* 107, 108, 109; *135:* 113
Jones, Bob *71:* 5; *77:* 199
Jones, Carol *5:* 131; *72:* 185, 186; *153:* 111, 112
Jones, Chuck *53:* 70, 71
Jones, Curtis *211:* 144
Jones, Davy *89:* 176
Jones, Douglas B. *185:* 192; *202:* 82
Jones, Elizabeth Orton *18:* 124, 126, 128, 129
Jones, Harold *14:* 88; *52:* 50
Jones, Holly *127:* 3
Jones, Jeff *41:* 64
Jones, Laurian *25:* 24, 27
Jones, Margaret *74:* 57
Jones, Noah Z. *182:* 37; *203:* 159
Jones, Randy *131:* 104
Jones, Richard *127:* 222
Jones, Robert *25:* 67
Jones, Wilfred *35:* 115; *YABC 1:* 163
Jordan, Charles *89:* 58
Jordan, Jess *158:* 136; *203:* 111
Jordan, Martin George *84:* 127
Jordan, Richard *84:* 36
Jorgenson, Andrea *91:* 111
Jorisch, Stéphane *153:* 56, 193; *177:* 29; *178:* 138, 139; *187:* 23; *211:* 182
Joseph, James *53:* 88
Joudrey, Ken *64:* 145; *78:* 6
Joyce, William *72:* 131, 132, 133, 134; *73:* 227; *145:* 37
Joyner, Jerry *34:* 138
Joyner, Loraine M. *209:* 17
Joysmith, Brenda *210:* 237
Juan, Ana *175:* 38; *179:* 111, 112; *213:* 9
Jucker, Sita *5:* 93
Judge, Lita *192:* 99
Judkis, Jim *37:* 38
Juhasz, Victor *31:* 67
Jullian, Philippe *24:* 206; *25:* 203
Jung, Tom *91:* 217
Junge, Alexandra *183:* 37
Junge, Walter *67:* 150
Jupo, Frank *7:* 148, 149
Jurisch, Stephane *154:* 105
Justice, Martin *34:* 72

K

Kabatova-Taborska, Zdenka *107:* 153
Kachik, John *165:* 230
Kaczman, James *156:* 98
Kadair, Deborah Ousley *184:* 45, 89

Kahl, David *74:* 95; *97:* 35; *109:* 174; *110:* 213; *198:* 15
Kahl, M.P. *37:* 83
Kahl, Virginia *48:* 138
Kakimoo, Kozo *11:* 148
Kalett, Jim *48:* 159, 160, 161
Kalin, Victor *39:* 186
Kalis, Jennifer *207:* 82
Kalman, Maira *96:* 131, 132; *137:* 115
Kalmenoff, Matthew *22:* 191
Kalow, Gisela *32:* 105
Kamen, Gloria *1:* 41; *9:* 119; *10:* 178; *35:* 157; *78:* 236; *98:* 82
Kaminsky, Jef *102:* 153
Kandell, Alice *35:* 133
Kane, Henry B. *14:* 90; *18:* 219, 220
Kane, Robert *18:* 131
Kanfer, Larry *66:* 141
Kangas, Juli *200:* 88
Kappes, Alfred *28:* 104
Karalus, Bob *41:* 157
Karas, G. Brian *80:* 60; *99:* 179; *115:* 41; *118:* 50; *136:* 168; *145:* 166; *149:* 245; *159:* 65; *171:* 192; *178:* 142, 143; *202:* 38; *209:* 142
Karasz, Ilonka *128:* 163
Karlin, Eugene *10:* 63; *20:* 131
Karlin, Nurit *63:* 78; *103:* 110
Karpinski, Tony *134:* 160
Kasamatsu, Shiro *139:* 155
Kasparavicius, Kestutis *139:* 210
Kassian, Olena *64:* 94
Kastner, Jill *79:* 135; *117:* 84, 85
Kasuya, Masahiro *41:* 206, 207; *51:* 100
Kasza, Keiko *191:* 99, 100, 101, 102, 103
Katona, Robert *21:* 85; *24:* 126
Katz, Avi *199:* 55
Katz, Karen *158:* 123
Kauffer, E. McKnight *33:* 103; *35:* 127; *63:* 67
Kaufman, Angelika *15:* 156
Kaufman, Joe *33:* 119
Kaufman, John *13:* 158
Kaufman, Stuart *62:* 64; *68:* 226; *137:* 44
Kaufmann, John *1:* 174; *4:* 159; *8:* 43, 1; *10:* 102; *18:* 133, 134; *22:* 251
Kaye, Graham *1:* 9; *67:* 7, 8
Kaye, M.M. *62:* 95
Kazalovski, Nata *40:* 205
Keane, Bil *4:* 135
Kearney, David *72:* 47; *121:* 83
Keating, Pamel T. *77:* 37
Keats, Ezra Jack *3:* 18, 105, 257; *14:* 101, 102; *33:* 129; *57:* 79, 80, 82, 83, 84, 87
Keegan, Charles *166:* 211
Keegan, Marcia *9:* 122; *32:* 93
Keeler, Patricia A. *81:* 56; *183:* 102, 103
Keely, Jack *119:* 95
Keely, John *26:* 104; *48:* 214
Keen, Eliot *25:* 213
Keep, Richard C. *170:* 122
Keeping, Charles *9:* 124, 185; *15:* 28, 134; *18:* 115; *44:* 194, 196; *47:* 25; *52:* 3; *54:* 156; *69:* 123, 124; *74:* 56; *155:* 9
Keeter, Susan *168:* 46; *183:* 192
Keith, Eros *4:* 98; *5:* 138; *31:* 29; *43:* 220; *52:* 91, 92, 93, 94; *56:* 64, 66; *60:* 37; *79:* 93
Keleinikov, Andrei *65:* 101, 102
Kelen, Emery *13:* 115
Keller, A.J. *62:* 198
Keller, Arthur I. *26:* 106
Keller, Dick *36:* 123, 125
Keller, Holly *45:* 79; *76:* 118, 119, 120, 121; *108:* 137, 138, 140; *157:* 117, 118, 119; *216:* 136
Keller, Katie *79:* 222; *93:* 108
Keller, Laurie *196:* 105, 106
Keller, Ronald *45:* 208
Kelley, Gary *183:* 105; *216:* 78; *217:* 95, 96, 97
Kelley, Marty *211:* 91

Kelley, True *41:* 114, 115; *42:* 137; *75:* 35; *92:* 104, 105; *124:* 62; *130:* 100, 101; *179:* 120, 121, 122; *192:* 251
Kellogg, Steven *8:* 96; *11:* 207; *14:* 130; *20:* ; *201:* 38 58; *29:* 140, 141; *30:* 35; *41:* 141; *57:* 89, 90, 92,93, 94, 96; *59:* 182; *73:* 141; *77:* 129; *130:* 105, 106; *177:* 94, 95, 96, 97; *199:* 57; *217:* 61; *YABC 1:* 65, 73
Kelly, Billy *158:* 143
Kelly, Geoff *97:* 196; *112:* 25
Kelly, Irene *147:* 134; *210:* 144, 145
Kelly, John *194:* 186
Kelly, Joseph *174:* 94
Kelly, Kathleen M. *71:* 109
Kelly, Laura *89:* 217
Kelly, True *163:* 87
Kelly, Walt *18:* 136, 137, 138, 139, 140, 141, 144, 145, 146, 148, 149
Kemble, E.W. *34:* 75; *44:* 178; *YABC 2:* 54, 59
Kemly, Kathleen *209:* 165
Kemp-Welsh, Lucy *24:* 197; *100:* 214
Kendall, Jane *150:* 105; *186:* 109
Kendall, Peter *152:* 85
Kendrick, Dennis *79:* 213
Kennaway, Adrienne *60:* 55, 56; *171:* 88, 89
Kennedy, Anne *212:* 34
Kennedy, Doug *189:* 104
Kennedy, Paul Edward *6:* 190; *8:* 132; *33:* 120
Kennedy, Richard *3:* 93; *12:* 179; *44:* 193; *100:* 15; *YABC 1:* 57
Kent, Jack *24:* 136; *37:* 37; *40:* 81; *84:* 89; *86:* 150; *88:* 77
Kent, Rockwell *5:* 166; *6:* 129; *20:* 225, 226, 227,229; *59:* 144
Kenyon, Tony *81:* 201; *127:* 74
Kepes, Juliet *13:* 119
Kerins, Anthony *76:* 84
Kerr, Judity *24:* 137
Kerr, Phyllis Forbes *72:* 141
Kessler, Leonard *1:* 108; *7:* 139; *14:* 107, 227; *22:* 101; *44:* 96; *67:* 79; *82:* 123
Kest, Kristin *168:* 99; *173:* 23
Kesteven, Peter *35:* 189
Ketcham, Hank *28:* 140, 141, 142
Kettelkamp, Larry *2:* 164
Key, Alexander *8:* 99
Khalsa, Dayal Kaur *62:* 99
Kiakshuk *8:* 59
Kid, Tom *207:* 54
Kidd, Chip *94:* 23
Kidd, Richard *152:* 110
Kidd, Tom *64:* 199; *81:* 189; *185:* 173
Kiddell-Monroe, Joan *19:* 201; *55:* 59, 60; *87:* 174; *121:* 112
Kidder, Harvey *9:* 105; *80:* 41
Kidwell, Carl *43:* 145
Kieffer, Christa *41:* 89
Kiesler, Kate *110:* 105; *136:* 142
Kiff, Ken *40:* 45
Kilbride, Robert *37:* 100
Kilby, Don *141:* 144
Kim, David *201:* 79; *202:* 97
Kim, Glenn *99:* 82
Kimball, Anton *78:* 114; *119:* 105
Kimball, Yeffe *23:* 116; *37:* 88
Kimber, Murray *171:* 91
Kimmel, Warren *176:* 112
Kincade, Orin *34:* 116
Kindersley, Barnabas *96:* 110
Kindred, Wendy *7:* 151
King, Colin *53:* 3
King, Robin *10:* 164, 165
King, Stephen Michael *141:* 31; *197:* 191
King, Tara Calahan *139:* 172
King, Tony *39:* 121
Kingman, Dong *16:* 287; *44:* 100, 102, 104
Kingsley, Charles *YABC 2:* 182
Kingston, Julie *147:* 14
Kingston, Maxine Hong *53:* 92
Kinney, Jeff *187:* 97

Kipling, John Lockwood *YABC 2:* 198
Kipling, Rudyard *YABC 2:* 196
Kipniss, Robert *29:* 59
Kirchherr, Astrid *55:* 23
Kirchhoff, Art *28:* 136
Kirk, Daniel *153:* 115, 116, 117; *173:* 101; *196:* 113, 114, 115, 116
Kirk, David *117:* 88, 89; *161:* 97, 98
Kirk, Ruth *5:* 96
Kirk, Steve *170:* 37
Kirk, Tim *32:* 209, 211; *72:* 89; *83:* 49
Kirmse, Marguerite *15:* 283; *18:* 153
Kirsch, Vincent X. *124:* 207
Kirschner, Ruth *22:* 154
Kirwan, Wednesday *198:* 73
Kish, Ely *73:* 119; *79:* 2
Kitamura, Satoshi *62:* 102; *98:* 91; *101:* 147; *138:* 2; *143:* 83, 85, 86; *201:* 83
Kiss, Andrew *168:* 115
Kitchel, JoAnn E. *133:* 32
Kitchen, Bert *70:* 126; *193:* 49
Kittelsen, Theodor *62:* 14
Kiuchi, Tatsuro *114:* 71
Kiwak, Barbara *172:* 135
Klahr, Susan *176:* 196
Klapholz, Mel *13:* 35
Klee, Jutte *209:* 136
Klein, Bill *89:* 105
Klein, Robert *55:* 77
Klein, Suzanna *63:* 104
Kleinman, Zalman *28:* 143
Kleven, Elisa *173:* 96, 97; *217:* 100, 102
Kline, Michael *127:* 66
Klise, M. Sarah *180:* 117, 118; *181:* 97
Knabel, Lonnie *73:* 103; *75:* 187, 228; *194:* 216
Kneen, Maggie *140:* 139
Knight, Ann *34:* 143
Knight, Christopher *13:* 125
Knight, Hilary *1:* 233; *3:* 21; *15:* 92, 158, 159; *16:* 258, 259, 260; *18:* 235; *19:* 169; *35:* 242; *46:* 167; *52:* 116; *69:* 126, 127; *132:* 129; *YABC 1:* 168, 169, 172
Knorr, Laura *200:* 91
Knorr, Peter *126:* 92, 93
Knotts, Howard *20:* 4; *25:* 170; *36:* 163
Knutson, Barbara *112:* 134; *202:* 108
Knutson, Kimberley *115:* 90
Kobayashi, Ann *39:* 58
Kochalka, James *196:* 120, 121, 122
Kocsis, J.C.
See Paul, James
Kodman, Stanislawa *201:* 85
Koehler, Hanne Lore *176:* 203
Koehn, Ilse *34:* 198; *79:* 123
Koelsch, Michael *99:* 182; *107:* 164; *109:* 239; *138:* 142; *150:* 94; *176:* 105; *187:* 63; *198:* 63
Koering, Ursula *3:* 28; *4:* 14; *44:* 5; *64:* 140,141; *85:* 46
Koerner, Henry
See Koerner, W.H.D.
Koerner, W.H.D. *14:* 216; *21:* 88, 89, 90, 91; *23:* 211
Koetsch, Mike *166:* 68
Koffler, Camilla *36:* 113
Kogan, Deborah Ray *161:* 101, 102
Koide, Yasuko *50:* 114
Kolado, Karen *102:* 228
Kolesova, Juliana *217:* 81
Komoda, Kiyo *9:* 128; *13:* 214
Kompaneyets, Marc *169:* 92
Konashevich, Vladimir *61:* 160
Konashevicha, V. *YABC 1:* 26
Konigsburg, E.L. *4:* 138; *48:* 141, 142, 144, 145; *94:* 129, 130; *126:* 129, 130, 131; *194:* 95, 98
Kono, Erin Eitter *177:* 99
Kooiker, Leonie *48:* 148
Koonook, Simon *65:* 157

Koontz, Robin Michal *136:* 155
Koopmans, Loek *101:* 121
Kopelke, Lisa *154:* 107
Kopper, Lisa *72:* 152, 153; *105:* 135, 136
Korach, Mimi *1:* 128, 129; *2:* 52; *4:* 39; *5:* 159; *9:* 129; *10:* 21; *24:* 69
Koren, Edward *5:* 100; *65:* 65, 67
Kosaka, Fumi *164:* 130
Koscielniak, Bruce *99:* 122; *153:* 120, 121, 122
Koshkin, Alexander *92:* 180
Kossin, Sandy *10:* 71; *23:* 105
Kostin, Andrej *26:* 204
Kosturko, Bob *164:* 56
Kotzky, Brian *68:* 184
Kovacevic, Zivojin *13:* 247
Kovalski, Maryann *58:* 120; *84:* 88; *97:* 124, 125, 126; *158:* 3; *186:* 80
Kozjan, Drazen *209:* 99
Krahn, Fernando *2:* 257; *34:* 206; *49:* 152
Kramer, Anthony *33:* 81
Kramer, David *96:* 162; *109:* 132; *150:* 220
Kramer, Frank *6:* 121
Krantz, Kathy *35:* 83
Kratter, Paul *139:* 65
Kraus, Robert *13:* 217; *65:* 113; *93:* 93, 94
Krause, Jon *176:* 62
Krauss, Trisha *174:* 10
Kredel, Fritz *6:* 35; *17:* 93, 94, 95, 96; *22:* 147; *24:* 175; *29:* 130; *35:* 77; *YABC 2:* 166, 300
Kreloff, Eliot *189:* 107, 108; *205:* 182
Krementz, Jill *17:* 98; *49:* 41
Krenina, Katya *117:* 106; *125:* 133; *176:* 117
Kresin, Robert *23:* 19
Krieger, Salem *54:* 164
Kriegler, Lyn *73:* 29
Krinitz, Esther Nisenthal *193:* 196
Krommes, Beth *128:* 141; *149:* 136; *181:* 100, 101; *184:* 105; *188:* 125; *208:* 135; *209:* 185
Krone, Mike *101:* 71
Kronheimer, Ann *135:* 119
Krosoczka, Jarrett J. *155:* 142; *200:* 93, 94
Kruck, Gerald *88:* 181
Krudop, Walter Lyon *199:* 19
Krupinski, Loretta *67:* 104; *102:* 131; *161:* 105, 106
Krupp, Robin Rector *53:* 96, 98
Krush, Beth *1:* 51, 85; *2:* 233; *4:* 115; *9:* 61; *10:* 191; *11:* 196; *18:* 164, 165; *32:* 72; *37:* 203; *43:* 57; *60:* 102, 103, 107, 108, 109
Krush, Joe *2:* 233; *4:* 115; *9:* 61; *10:* 191; *11:* 196; *18:* 164, 165; *32:* 72, 91; *37:* 203; *43:* 57; *60:* 102, 103, 107, 108, 109
Krych, Duane *91:* 43
Krykorka, Vladyana *96:* 147; *143:* 90, 91; *168:* 14
Kubick, Dana *165:* 91; *212:* 104, 105, 212
Kubinyi, Laszlo *4:* 116; *6:* 113; *16:* 118; *17:* 100; *28:* 227; *30:* 172; *49:* 24, 28; *54:* 23; *167:* 149
Kubricht, Mary *73:* 118
Kucharik, Elena *139:* 31
Kuchera, Kathleen *84:* 5
Kuhn, Bob *17:* 91; *35:* 235
Kulikov, Boris *163:* 185; *185:* 23; *205:* 99, 100; *217:* 160
Kulka, Joe *188:* 110
Kukalis, Romas *90:* 27; *139:* 37
Kuklin, Susan *63:* 82, 83, 84
Kunhardt, Dorothy *53:* 101
Kunhardt, Edith *67:* 105, 106
Kunstler, Mort *10:* 73; *32:* 143
Kurchevsky, V. *34:* 61
Kurczok, Belinda *121:* 118
Kurelek, William *8:* 107
Kuriloff, Ron *13:* 19
Kurisu, Jane *160:* 120
Kuskin, Karla *2:* 170; *68:* 115, 116; *111:* 116
Kutzer, Ernst *19:* 249
Kuzma, Steve *57:* 8; *62:* 93

Kuznetsova, Berta *74:* 45
Kvasnosky, Laura McGee *93:* 103; *142:* 83; *182:* 108
Kwas, Susan Estelle *179:* 116; *217:* 90
Kyong, Yunmee *165:* 139

L

LaBlanc, Andre *24:* 146
Laboccetta, Mario *27:* 120
LaBrose, Darcie *157:* 134
Labrosse, Darcia *58:* 88; *108:* 77; *178:* 89
LaCava, Vince *95:* 118
Laceky, Adam *32:* 121
Lacis, Astra *85:* 117
Lacome, Julie *174:* 96, 97
La Croix *YABC 2:* 4
Ladd, London *206:* 50
Ladwig, Tim *98:* 212; *117:* 76; *215:* 32
La Farge, Margaret *47:* 141
LaFave, Kim *64:* 177; *72:* 39; *97:* 146; *99:* 172; *106:* 123; *149:* 126; *196:* 128, 129
Lafontaine, Roger *167:* 158
Lafrance, Marie *197:* 109
Lagarrigue, Jerome *136:* 102; *187:* 81
Laimgruber, Monika *11:* 153
Laio, Jimmy *213:* 57
Laite, Gordon *1:* 130, 131; *8:* 209; *31:* 113; *40:* 63; *46:* 117
Laliberté, Louise-Andrée *169:* 98
LaMarche, Jim *46:* 204; *61:* 56; *94:* 69; *114:* 22; *129:* 163; *162:* 78, 80
Lamb, Jim *10:* 117
Lambase, Barbara *101:* 185; *150:* 221; *166:* 234
Lambert, J.K. *38:* 129; *39:* 24
Lambert, Sally Anne *133:* 191
Lambert, Saul *23:* 112; *33:* 107; *54:* 136
Lambert, Stephen *109:* 33; *174:* 99
Lambo, Don *6:* 156; *35:* 115; *36:* 146
Lamontagne, Jacques *166:* 227
Lamut, Sonja *57:* 193
Lamut, Sonya *85:* 102
Landa, Peter *11:* 95; *13:* 177; *53:* 119
Landau, Jacob *38:* 111
Landis, Joan *104:* 23; *203:* 32
Landon, Lucinda *79:* 31
Landshoff, Ursula *13:* 124
Landström, Lena *146:* 165, 166
Landström, Olof *146:* 166, 168; *170:* 22
Lane, Daniel *112:* 60
Lane, John R. *8:* 145
Lane, John *15:* 176, 177; *30:* 146
Lane, Nancy *166:* 74
Lang, G.D. *48:* 56
Lang, Gary *73:* 75
Lang, Jerry *18:* 295
Langdo, Bryan *186:* 187; *191:* 113, 114, 115
Lange, Dorothea *50:* 141
Langley, Jonathan *162:* 128
Langner, Nola *8:* 110; *42:* 36
Lanino, Deborah *105:* 148
Lantz, Paul *1:* 82, 102; *27:* 88; *34:* 102; *45:* 123
Larkin, Bob *84:* 225
Laroche, Giles *126:* 140; *146:* 81
LaRochelle, David *171:* 97
Larrecq, John *44:* 108; *68:* 56
Larsen, Suzanne *1:* 13
Larson, Gary *57:* 121, 122, 123, 124, 125, 126, 127
Larsson, Carl *35:* 144, 145, 146, 147, 148, 149, 150, 152, 153, 154
Larsson, Karl *19:* 177
Lartitegui, Ana G. *105:* 167
LaRue, Jenna *167:* 20
La Rue, Michael D. *13:* 215
Lasker, Joe *7:* 186, 187; *14:* 55; *38:* 115; *39:* 47; *83:* 113, 114, 115

Latham, Barbara *16:* 188, 189; *43:* 71
Lathrop, Dorothy *14:* 117, 118, 119; *15:* 109; *16:* 78, 79, 81; *32:* 201, 203; *33:* 112; *YABC 2:* 301
Lattimore, Eleanor Frances *7:* 156
Lauden, Claire *16:* 173
Lauden, George, Jr. *16:* 173
Laune, Paul *2:* 235; *34:* 31
Laure, Jason *49:* 53; *50:* 122
Lauter, Richard *63:* 29; *67:* 111; *77:* 198
Lavallee, Barbara *74:* 157; *92:* 154; *96:* 126; *145:* 193; *166:* 125, 126; *186:* 155; *192:* 172
Lave, Fitz Hugh *59:* 139
Lavis, Stephen *43:* 143; *87:* 137, 164, 165
Layton, Neal *152:* 120, 121; *182:* 65; *187:* 103, 105, 106
Law, Jenny *201:* 31
Lawrason, June *168:* 30
Lawrence, John *25:* 131; *30:* 141; *44:* 198, 200; *214:* 7
Lawrence, Stephen *20:* 195
Lawson, Carol *6:* 38; *42:* 93, 131; *174:* 56; *189:* 89; *209:* 59
Lawson, George *17:* 280
Lawson, Robert *5:* 26; *6:* 94; *13:* 39; *16:* 11; *20:* 100, 102, 103; *54:* 3; *66:* 12; *100:* 144, 145; *YABC 2:* 222, 224, 225, 227, 228, 229, 230, 231, 232, 233, 234, 235, 237, 238, 239, 240, 241
Layfield, Kathie *60:* 194
Lazare, Jerry *44:* 109; *74:* 28
Lazarevich, Mila *17:* 118
Lazarus, Claire *103:* 30
Lazarus, Keo Felker *21:* 94
Lazzaro, Victor *11:* 126
Lea, Bob *166:* 208; *203:* 108
Lea, Tom *43:* 72, 74
Leacroft, Richard *6:* 140
Leaf, Munro *20:* 99
Leake, Donald *70:* 41
Leander, Patricia *23:* 27
Lear, Edward *18:* 183, 184, 185
Lear, Rebecca *149:* 46
Lebenson, Richard *6:* 209; *7:* 76; *23:* 145; *44:* 191; *87:* 153
Le Cain, Errol *6:* 141; *9:* 3; *22:* 142; *25:* 198; *28:* 173; *68:* 128, 129; *86:* 49
Lechon, Daniel *113:* 211
Leder, Dora *129:* 172
Ledger, Bill *181:* 58
Leduc, Bernard *102:* 36
Lee, Alan *62:* 25, 28
Lee, Bryce *99:* 60; *101:* 195; *196:* 53
Lee, Chinlun *181:* 138; *182:* 112
Lee, Declan *191:* 20
Lee, Dom *83:* 118, 120; *93:* 123; *121:* 121, 126; *146:* 174, 175, 206, 207; *174:* 204
Lee, Doris *13:* 246; *32:* 183; *44:* 111
Lee, Hector Viveros *115:* 96
Lee, Ho Baek *200:* 160
Lee, Huy Voun *217:* 106
Lee, Jeanne M. *158:* 56
Lee, Jared *93:* 200; *157:* 229; *215:* 113, 191, 192, 193
Lee, Jody *81:* 121; *82:* 225; *91:* 155; *100:* 182
Lee, Jody A. *127:* 124, 126, 127
See also Lee, Jody
Lee, Manning de V. *2:* 200; *17:* 12; *27:* 87; *37:* 102, 103, 104; *YABC 2:* 304
Lee, Margaret *213:* 179
Lee, Marie G. *138:* 157
Lee, Paul *97:* 100; *105:* 72, 209; *109:* 177; *128:* 113; *202:* 45
Lee, Robert J. *3:* 97; *67:* 124
Lee, Victor *96:* 228; *105:* 182; *140:* 196; *208:* 191
Lee, Virginia *208:* 139, 140
Leech, Dorothy *98:* 76
Leech, John *15:* 59
Leedy, Loreen *84:* 142; *128:* 144, 145, 146; *175:* 125, 126, 127

Leeman, Michael *44:* 157
Leeming, Catherine *87:* 39
Lees, Harry *6:* 112
LeFever, Bill *88:* 220, 221
Legenisel *47:* 111
Legrand, Edy *18:* 89, 93
Lehman, Barbara *73:* 123; *170:* 130
Lehrman, Rosalie *2:* 180
Leichman, Seymour *5:* 107
Leick, Bonnie *205:* 104
Leighton, Clare *25:* 130; *33:* 168; *37:* 105, 106, 108,109
Leisk, David *1:* 140, 141; *11:* 54; *30:* 137, 142, 143,144
Leister, Brian *89:* 45; *106:* 37; *114:* 67; *149:* 236
Leloir, Maurice *18:* 77, 80, 83, 99
Lemaître, Pascal *144:* 175; *176:* 130; *189:* 135
Lemieux, Michele *100:* 148; *139:* 153
Lemke, Horst *14:* 98; *38:* 117, 118, 119
Lemke, R.W. *42:* 162
Lemon, David Gwynne *9:* 1
LeMoult, Adolph *82:* 116
Lenn, Michael *136:* 89
Lennon, John *114:* 100
Lennox, Elsie *95:* 163; *143:* 160
Lenski, Lois *1:* 144; *26:* 135, 137, 139, 141; *100:* 153, 154
Lent, Blair *1:* 116, 117; *2:* 174; *3:* 206, 207; *7:* 168, 169; *34:* 62; *68:* 217; *133:* 101; *183:* 60
Leonard, David *212:* 149
Leonard, Richard *91:* 128
Leonard, Tom *207:* 95
Leone, Leonard *49:* 190
Lerner, Carol *86:* 140, 141, 142
Lerner, Judith *116:* 138
Lerner, Sharon *11:* 157; *22:* 56
Leroux-Hugon, Helene *132:* 139
Leslie, Cecil *19:* 244
Lessac, Frané *80:* 182, 207; *96:* 182; *202:* 58; *209:* 104
Lessing, Erich *167:* 52; *173:* 60
Lester, Alison *50:* 124; *90:* 147, 148; *129:* 130
Lester, Mike *208:* 50
Lethcoe, Jason *191:* 116, 117
Le Tord, Bijou *49:* 156; *95:* 112
Leutz, Emanuel *165:* 27
Levai, Blaise *39:* 130
Levert, Mireille *211:* 101
Levin, Ted *12:* 148
Levine, David *43:* 147, 149, 150, 151, 152; *64:* 11
Levine, Joe *71:* 88
Levine, Marge *81:* 127
Levinson, David *178:* 232
Levit, Herschel *24:* 223
Levstek, Ljuba *131:* 192; *134:* 216; *149:* 65; *168:* 180
Levy, Jessica Ann *19:* 225; *39:* 191
Levy, Lina *117:* 126
Lewin, Betsy *32:* 114; *48:* 177; *90:* 151; *91:* 125; *92:* 85; *115:* 105; *169:* 110, 111; *178:* 47; *186:* 188; *194:* 201
Lewin, Ted *4:* 77; *8:* 168; *20:* 110; *21:* 99,100; *27:* 110; *28:* 96, 97; *31:* 49; *45:* 55; *48:* 223; *60:* 20, 119, 120; *62:* 139; *66:* 108; *71:* 12; *72:* 21; *74:* 226; *76:* 139, 140; *77:* 82; *79:* 87; *85:* 49, 177; *86:* 55; *88:* 182; *93:* 28, 29; *94:* 34, 182, 194; *99:* 156; *104:* 8; *115:* 123; *118:* 74; *119:* 114, 116; *131:* 54; *145:* 99; *165:* 151; *177:* 75; *178:* 42; *190:* 30; *192:* 86; *195:* 101, 102; *203:* 52
Lewis, Allen *15:* 112
Lewis, E.B. *88:* 143; *93:* 109; *119:* 79; *124:* 113; *128:* 49; *151:* 167; *168:* 110; *173:* 121; *174:* 66; *176:* 7; *184:* 150; *185:* 191; *211:* 108, 109, 110, 111
Lewis, H.B. *170:* 124
Lewis, J. Patrick *162:* 83
Lewis, Jan *81:* 22

Lewis, Kim *136:* 165; *217:* 109, 111
Lewis, Richard W. *52:* 25
Lewis, Robin Baird *98:* 193
Leydon, Rita Floden *21:* 101
Li, Xiojun *187:* 172
Liao, Jimmy *202:* 100
Lichtenheld, Tom *152:* 125, 126
Lieblich, Irene *22:* 173; *27:* 209, 214
Lieder, Rick *108:* 197; *199:* 58, 59, 60
Lies, Brian *92:* 40; *141:* 101; *150:* 138; *190:* 97, 98, 99,
Liese, Charles *4:* 222
Life, Kay *79:* 49
Lifton, Robert Jay *66:* 154
Lightburn, Ron *86:* 153; *91:* 122
Lightfoot, Norman R. *45:* 47
Lignell, Lois *37:* 114
Lill, Debra *121:* 70
Lilly, Charles *8:* 73; *20:* 127; *48:* 53; *72:* 9,16; *77:* 98; *102:* 94
Lilly, Ken *37:* 224
Lim, John *43:* 153
Limona, Mercedes *51:* 183
Lin, Grace *143:* 217; *162:* 86, 87; *174:* 185
Lincoln, Patricia Henderson *27:* 27; *78:* 127
Lindahn, Ron *84:* 17
Lindahn, Val *84:* 17
Lindberg, Howard *10:* 123; *16:* 190
Lindberg, Jeffrey *64:* 77; *77:* 71; *79:* 54; *80:* 149; *174:* 109; *179:* 52
Linden, Seymour *18:* 200, 201, *43:* 140
Lindenbaum, Pija *144:* 143; *183:* 113
Linder, Richard *27:* 119
Lindman, Maj *43:* 154
Lindsay, Norman *67:* 114
Lindsay, Vachel *40:* 118
Lindstrom, Jack *145:* 118
Line, Les *27:* 143
Linell
  See Smith, Linell
Lionni, Leo *8:* 115; *72:* 159, 160, 161
Lipinsky, Lino *2:* 156; *22:* 175
Lippincott, Gary A. *70:* 35; *119:* 118
Lippman, Peter *8:* 31; *31:* 119, 120, 160
Lisi, Victoria *89:* 145
Lisker, Emily *169:* 114
Lisker, Sonia O. *16:* 274; *31:* 31; *44:* 113, 114
Lisowski, Gabriel *47:* 144; *49:* 157
Lissim, Simon *17:* 138
Little, Ed *89:* 145; *151:* 53
Little, Harold *16:* 72
Little, Mary E. *28:* 146
Littlewood, Karen *165:* 126; *211:* 112
Litty, Julie *111:* 63
Litzinger, Rosanne *151:* 101; *176:* 118; *196:* 133, 134, 135; *208:* 129; *209:* 147
Liu, Lesley *143:* 72
Lively, Lorna *19:* 216
Livingston, Susan *95:* 22
Liwska, Renata *164:* 113; *199:* 25, 69
Ljungkvist, Laura *180:* 120
Llerena, Carlos Antonio *19:* 181
Lloyd, Errol *11:* 39; *22:* 178
Lloyd, Megan *77:* 118; *80:* 113; *97:* 75; *117:* 94, 95; *189:* 121, 122; *208:* 128; *211:* 72
Lloyd, Sam *183:* 116, 117
Lo, Beth *165:* 154
Lo, Koon-chiu *7:* 134
Loates, Glen *63:* 76
Lobel, Anita *6:* 87; *9:* 141; *18:* 248; *55:* 85,86, 87, 88, 93, 104; *60:* 67; *78:* 263; *82:* 110; *96:* 157, 159; *101:* 84; *132:* 35; *162:* 93, 94
Lobel, Arnold *1:* 188, 189; *5:* 12; *6:* 147; *7:* 167, 209; *18:* 190, 191; *25:* 39, 43; *27:* 40; *29:* 174; *52:* 127; *55:* 89, 91, 94, 95, 97, 98, 99, 100, 101, 102,103, 105, 106; *60:* 18, 31; *66:* 181, 183; *75:* 57; *82:* 246; *136:* 146
Lobel, Gillian *190:* 21
Locker, Thomas *109:* 134
Lodge, Bernard *107:* 125, 126; *153:* 93
Loeb, Jeph *153:* 177

Lodge, Jo *112:* 119
Loefgren, Ulf *3:* 108
Loescher, Ann *20:* 108
Loescher, Gil *20:* 108
Loew, David *93:* 184; *171:* 120; *211:* 187
Lofting, Hugh *15:* 182, 183; *100:* 161, 162
Lofts, Pamela *60:* 188
Loh, George *38:* 88
Lomberg, Jon *58:* 160
Lonette, Reisie *11:* 211; *12:* 168; *13:* 56; *36:* 122; *43:* 155
Long, Ethan *168:* 146; *178:* 12; *182:* 120, 121; *196:* 124
Long, Laurel *162:* 135; *190:* 11; *203:* 113, 114
Long, Loren *99:* 176; *172:* 65; *182:* 78; *188:* 114, 115
Long, Melinda *152:* 128
Long, Miles *115:* 174
Long, Sally *42:* 184
Long, Sylvia *74:* 168; *132:* 63; *179:* 134
Longoni, Eduardo *73:* 85
Longtemps, Ken *17:* 123; *29:* 221; *69:* 82
Looser, Heinz *YABC 2:* 208
Lopez, Loretta *190:* 100
López, Rafael *197:* 160; *198:* 85
Lopshire, Robert *6:* 149; *21:* 117; *34:* 166; *73:* 13
Lord, John Vernon *21:* 104; *23:* 25; *51:* 22
Lorenz, Albert *40:* 146; *115:* 127
Loretta, Sister Mary *33:* 73
Lorraine, Walter H. *3:* 110; *4:* 123; *16:* 192; *103:* 119
Los, Marek *146:* 22; *193:* 23
Loss, Joan *11:* 163
Louderback, Walt *YABC 1:* 164
Loughridge, Stuart *214:* 131
Louis, Catherine *212:* 186
Lousada, Sandra *40:* 138
Louth, Jack *149:* 252; *151:* 191, 192
Love, Judy *173:* 43; *196:* 40
Lovelock, Brian *214:* 132, 197
Low, Joseph *14:* 124, 125; *18:* 68; *19:* 194; *31:* 166; *80:* 239
Low, William *62:* 175; *80:* 147; *112:* 194; *150:* 202; *169:* 175; *177:* 110; *192:* 27
Lowe, Vicky *177:* 130
Lowenheim, Alfred *13:* 65, 66
Lowenstein, Sallie *116:* 90, 91
Lowitz, Anson *17:* 124; *18:* 215
Lowrey, Jo *8:* 133
Lubach, Vanessa *142:* 152
Lubell, Winifred *1:* 207; *3:* 15; *6:* 151
Lubin, Leonard B. *19:* 224; *36:* 79, 80; *45:* 128, 129,131, 132, 133, 134, 135, 136, 137, 139, 140, 141; *70:* 95; *YABC2:* 96
Lucas, David *208:* 148
Lucht, Irmgard *82:* 145
Ludwig, Helen *33:* 144, 145
Luebs, Robin *212:* 109
Lufkin, Raymond *38:* 138; *44:* 48
Luhrs, Henry *7:* 123; *11:* 120
Lujan, Tonita *82:* 33
Lupo, Dom *4:* 204
Lustig, Loretta *30:* 186; *46:* 134, 135, 136, 137
Lutes, Jason *210:* 163
Luthardt, Kevin *172:* 125, 126; *217:* 2
Luxbacher, Irene *153:* 145
Luzak, Dennis *52:* 121; *99:* 142
Lydbury, Jane *82:* 98
Lydecker, Laura *21:* 113; *42:* 53
Lynch, Charles *16:* 33
Lynch, Marietta *29:* 137; *30:* 171
Lynch, P.J. *126:* 228; *129:* 110; *132:* 247; *183:* 64; *207:* 184; *213:* 100, 101, 102
Lyne, Alison Davis *188:* 118, 198
Lyon, Carol *102:* 26
Lyon, Elinor *6:* 154
Lyon, Fred *14:* 16
Lyon, Lea *212:* 110
Lyon, Tammie *175:* 170

Lyons, Oren *8:* 193
Lyster, Michael *26:* 41

M

Maas, Dorothy *6:* 175
Maas, Julie *47:* 61
Macaulay, David *46:* 139, 140, 141, 142, 143, 144, 145, 147, 149, 150; *72:* 167, 168, 169; *137:* 129, 130, 131, 132
MacCarthy, Patricia *69:* 141
Macdonald, Alister *21:* 55
Macdonald, Roberta *19:* 237; *52:* 164
MacDonald, Norman *13:* 99
MacDonald, Ross *201:* 103
MacDonald, Suse *54:* 41; *109* 138; *130:* 156; *193:* 106, 107, 109, 110
Mace, Varian *49:* 159
MacEachern, Stephen *206:* 2
Macguire, Robert Reid *18:* 67
Machetanz, Fredrick *34:* 147, 148
MacInnes, Ian *35:* 59
MacIntyre, Elisabeth *17:* 127, 128
Mack, Jeff *161:* 128; *194:* 119, 120
Mack, Stan *17:* 129; *96:* 33
Mackay, Donald *17:* 60
MacKaye, Arvia *32:* 119
Mackenzie, Robert *204:* 78
Mackenzie, Stuart *73:* 213
MacKenzie, Garry *33:* 159
Mackie, Clare *87:* 134
Mackinlay, Miguel *27:* 22
MacKinstry, Elizabeth *15:* 110; *42:* 139, 140, 141, 142, 143,144, 145
MacLeod, Lee *91:* 167
Maclise, Daniel *YABC 2:* 257
Macnaughton, Tina *182:* 145
MacRae, Tom *181:* 112
Madden, Don *3:* 112, 113; *4:* 33, 108, 155; *7:* 193; *78:* 12; *YABC 2:* 211
Maddison, Angela Mary *10:* 83
Madsen, Jim *146:* 259; *152:* 237; *184:* 106; *197:* 21; *202:* 103, 104
Maestro, Giulio *8:* 124; *12:* 17; *13:* 108; *25:* 182; *54:* 147; *59:* 114, 115, 116, 117, 118, 121, 123, 124, 125,126, 127; *68:* 37, 38; *106:* 129, 130, 131, 136, 137, 138
Maffia, Daniel *60:* 200
Maggio, Viqui *58:* 136, 181; *74:* 150; *75:* 90; *85:* 159; *90:* 158; *109:* 184; *193:* 113
Magnus, Erica *77:* 123
Magnuson, Diana *28:* 102; *34:* 190; *41:* 175
Magoon, Scott *181:* 104; *217:* 165
Magovern, Peg *103:* 123
Maguire, Sheila *41:* 100
Magurn, Susan *91:* 30
Mahony, Will *37:* 120
Mahony, Will *85:* 116
Mahood, Kenneth *24:* 141
Mahurin, Matt *164:* 225; *175:* 95; *189:* 37; *196:* 14; *209:* 163
Maik, Henri *9:* 102
Maione, Heather *106:* 5; *178:* 8; *189:* 126, 127; *193:* 58
Maisto, Carol *29:* 87
Maitland, Antony *1:* 100, 176; *8:* 41; *17:* 246; *24:* 46; *25:* 177, 178; *32:* 74; *60:* 65, 195; *67:* 156; *87:* 131; *101:* 110
Majewski, Dawn W. *169:* 95
Mak, Kam *72:* 25; *75:* 43; *87:* 186; *97:* 24; *102:* 154; *149:* 195; *186:* 28; *209:* 132
Makie, Pam *37:* 117
Maktima, Joe *116:* 191
Maland, Nick *99:* 77
Male, Alan *132:* 64
Malone, James Hiram *84:* 161
Malone, Nola Langner *82:* 239
Malone, Peter *191:* 121, 122, 123
Malsberg, Edward *51:* 175

Malvern, Corinne *2:* 13; *34:* 148, 149
Manchess, Gregory *165:* 241; *203:* 119
Mancusi, Stephen *63:* 198, 199
Mandelbaum, Ira *31:* 115
Manders, John *138:* 152, 155; *188:* 171; *190:* 92; *199:* 5; *217:* 52
Manet, Edouard *23:* 170
Mangiat, Jeff *173:* 127
Mangurian, David *14:* 133
Manham, Allan *42:* 109; *77:* 180; *80:* 227
Manley, Matt *103:* 167; *117:* 98; *172:* 49; *212:* 207
Manna, Giovanni *178:* 44
Manniche, Lise *31:* 121
Manning, Jane *96:* 203
Manning, Jo *63:* 154
Manning, Lawrence *191:* 153
Manning, Maurie J. *211:* 116
Manning, Mick *176:* 139
Manning, Samuel F. *5:* 75
Mantel, Richard *57:* 73; *63:* 106; *82:* 255
Mantha, John *205:* 164; *217:* 117
Maraja *15:* 86; *YABC 1:* 28; *2:* 115
Marcellino, Fred *20:* 125; *34:* 222; *53:* 125; *58:* 205; *61:* 64, 121, 122; *68:* 154, 156, 157, 158, 159; *72:* 25; *86:* 184; *98:* 181; *118:* 129, 130, 131; *149:* 218; *194:* 7
Marchesi, Stephen *34:* 140; *46:* 72; *50:* 147; *66:* 239; *70:* 33; *73:* 18, 114, 163; *77:* 47, 76,147; *78:* 79; *80:* 30; *81:* 6; *89:* 66; *93:* 21,130; *94:* 94; *97:* 66; *98:* 96; *114:* 115, 116
Marchiori, Carlos *14:* 60
Marciano, John Bemelmans *118:* 133; *167:* 110, 111, 112
Marcus, Barry David *139:* 248; *145:* 18
Maren, Julie *199:* 73
Margules, Gabriele *21:* 120
Mariana
    See Foster, Marian Curtis
Mariano, Michael *52:* 108
Marino, Dorothy *6:* 37; *14:* 135
Mario, Heide Stetson *101:* 202
Maris, Ron *71:* 123
Maritz, Nicolaas *85:* 123
Mark, Mona *65:* 105; *68:* 205; *116:* 213
Markham, R.L. *17:* 240
Marklew, Gilly *211:* 118
Marks, Alan *104:* 104; *109:* 182; *164:* 92; *185:* 134; *187:* 120, 121, 122
Marks, Cara *54:* 9
Marks, Colin *203:* 129
Marokvia, Artur *31:* 122
Marquez, Susan *108:* 121
Marrella, Maria Pia *62:* 116
Marriott, Pat *30:* 30; *34:* 39; *35:* 164, 165, 166; *44:* 170; *48:* 186, 187, 188, 189, 191, 192, 193; *91:* 92
Mars, W.T. *1:* 161; *3:* 115; *4:* 208, 225; *5:* 92, 105, 186; *8:* 214; *9:* 12; *13:* 121; *27:* 151; *31:* 180; *38:* 102; *48:* 66; *62:* 164, 165; *64:* 62; *68:* 229; *79:* 55
Marschall, Ken *85:* 29
Marsh, Christine *3:* 164
Marsh, James *73:* 137
Marsh, Reginald *17:* 5; *19:* 89; *22:* 90, 96
Marshall, Anthony D. *18:* 216
Marshall, Felicia *170:* 190
Marshall, James *6:* 160; *40:* 221; *42:* 24, 25, 29; *51:* 111, 112, 113, 114, 115, 116, 117, 118, 119, 120, 121; *64:* 13; *75:* 126, 127, 128, 129; *102:* 10, 12; *216:* 26, 28
Marshall, Janet *97:* 154
Marstall, Bob *55:* 145; *84:* 153, 170; *104:* 145; *154:* 166, 167, 168
Martchenko, Michael *50:* 129, 153, 155, 156, 157; *83:* 144,145; *154:* 137, 138, 139
Marten, Ruth *129:* 52
Martin, Brad *199:* 186
Martin, Charles E. *70:* 144
Martin, Courtney A. *214:* 28

Martin, David Stone *24:* 232; *62:* 4
Martin, Fletcher *18:* 213; *23:* 151
Martin, Rene *7:* 144; *42:* 148, 149, 150
Martin, Richard E. *51:* 157; *131:* 203
Martin, Ron *32:* 81
Martin, Stefan *8:* 68; *32:* 124, 126; *56:* 33
Martin, Whitney *166:* 137
Martinez, Ed *58:* 192; *72:* 231; *77:* 33; *80:* 214; *167:* 123
Martinez, John *6:* 113; *118:* 13; *139:* 143
Martinez, Sergio *158:* 190
Martini, Angela *183:* 161
Martiniere, Stephan *171:* 130
Marton, Jirina *95:* 127, 128; *144:* 145
Martorell, Antonio *84:* 6; *97:* 161
Martucci, Griesbach *52:* 106
Marvin, Frederic *83:* 86
Marx, Robert F. *24:* 143
Marzollo, Jean *190:* 127
Masefield, Judith *19:* 208, 209
Masheris, Robert *78:* 51
Masiello, Ralph *186:* 171; *214:* 134
Mason, George F. *14:* 139
Mason, Robert *84:* 96
Masse, Josée *208:* 45; *217:* 19
Massey, Barbara *68:* 142
Massie, Diane Redfield *16:* 194
Massie, Kim *31:* 43
Massini, Sarah *213:* 79
Mataya, David *121:* 66
Mathers, Petra *119:* 135; *163:* 104; *176:* 143, 144; *187:* 142; *196:* 101
Mathewuse, James *51:* 143
Mathieu, Joseph *14:* 33; *39:* 206; *43:* 167; *56:* 180; *79:* 126; *94:* 147; *185:* 140
Matje, Martin *169:* 177, 178; *172:* 180
Matsubara, Naoko *12:* 121
Matsuda, Shizu *13:* 167
Matsuoka, Mei *192:* 135; *214:* 84
Matte, L'Enc *22:* 183
Mattelson, Marvin *36:* 50, 51
Matheson, Jenny *180:* 132
Matthews, Elizabeth *194:* 128
Matthews, F. Leslie *4:* 216
Matthews, Tina *190:* 130
Mattingly, David *71:* 76, 77; *82:* 64; *91:* 216, 217; *109:* 25
Matulay, Laszlo *5:* 18; *43:* 168
Matus, Greta *12:* 142
Maughan, Bill *181:* 31; *211:* 211
Mauldin, Bill *27:* 23
Mauterer, Erin Marie *119:* 5
Mawicke, Tran *9:* 137; *15:* 191; *47:* 100
Mawson, Matt *74:* 115
Max, Peter *45:* 146, 147, 148, 149, 150
Maxie, Betty *40:* 135
Maxwell, John Alan *1:* 148
May, Steve *204:* 30
Mayan, Earl *7:* 193
Mayer, Bill *200:* 138
Mayer, Danuta *117:* 103
Mayer, Marianna *32:* 132
Mayer, Mercer *11:* 192; *16:* 195, 196; *20:* 55, 57; *32:* 129, 130, 132, 133, 134; *41:* 144, 248, 252; *58:* 186; *73:* 140, 142, 143; *137:* 137, 138
Mayforth, Hal *166:* 77
Mayhew, James *85:* 121; *138:* 187; *149:* 140; *204:* 81
Mayhew, Richard *3:* 106
Mayo, Gretchen Will *38:* 81; *84:* 166
Mays, Victor *5:* 127; *8:* 45, 153; *14:* 245; *23:* 50; *34:* 155; *40:* 79; *45:* 158; *54:* 91; *66:* 240
Mazal, Chanan *49:* 104
Maze, Deborah *71:* 83
Mazellan, Ron *75:* 97, 98; *210:* 169
Mazetti, Alan *112:* 72
Mazille, Capucine *96:* 168
Mazza, Adriana Saviozzi *19:* 215
Mazzella, Mary Jo *82:* 165

Mazzetti, Alan *45:* 210
McAfee, Steve *135:* 146; *167:* 176; *191:* 84; *210:* 117
McAlinden, Paul *112:* 128
McBride, Angus *28:* 49; *103:* 40
McBride, Will *30:* 110
McCaffery, Janet *38:* 145
McCall, Bruce *209:* 119
McCallum, Graham *78:* 78
McCallum, Stephen *141:* 143; *156:* 5; *166:* 228
McCann, Gerald *3:* 50; *4:* 94; *7:* 54; *41:* 121
McCarthy, Dan *174:* 74
McCarthy, Linda *177:* 128
McCarthy, Meghan *168:* 134; *199:* 74
McCauley, Adam *157:* 36; *184:* 199; *193:* 100; *209:* 122
McCay, Winsor *41:* 124, 126, 128, 129, 130, 131; *134:* 77, 79
McClary, Nelson *1:* 111
McClements, George *196:* 146
McClennan, Connie *210:* 181
McClintock, Barbara *57:* 135; *95:* 130; *146:* 190; *213:* 3, 5, 107, 108
McClintock, Theodore *14:* 141
McCloskey, Robert *1:* 184, 185; *2:* 186, 187; *17:* 209; *39:* 139, 140, 141, 142, 143, 146, 147, 148; *85:* 150, 151; *100:* 172, 173, 174
McClung, Robert *2:* 189; *68:* 166, 167
McClure, Gillian *31:* 132; *150:* 53
McConnel, Jerry *31:* 75, 187
McConnell, Mary *102:* 49
McCord, Kathleen Garry *78:* 236
McCormack, John *66:* 193
McCormick, A.D. *35:* 119
McCormick, Dell J. *19:* 216
McCoy, Glenn *212:* 132
McCrady, Lady *16:* 198; *39:* 127
McCrea, James *3:* 122; *33:* 216
McCrea, Ruth *3:* 122; *27:* 102; *33:* 216
McCue, Lisa *65:* 148, 149; *77:* 54; *80:* 132; *175:* 33; *177:* 133, 135; *212:* 136, 137, 138
McCully, Emily Arnold *2:* 89; *4:* 120, 121, 146, 197; *5:* 2, 129; *7:* 191; *11:* 122; *15:* 210; *33:* 23; *35:* 244; *37:* 122; *39:* 88; *40:* 103; *50:* 30,31, 32, 33, 34, 35, 36, 37; *52:* 89, 90; *57:* 6; *62:* 3; *70:* 195; *86:* 82; *96:* 192; *97:* 93; *110:* 143,144; *117:* 47; *167:* 96; *210:* 175, 176
McCurdy, Michael *13:* 153; *24:* 85; *81:* 160; *82:* 157, 158; *86:* 125; *97:* 92; *117:* 178; *132:* 6; *147:* 159, 160
McCusker, Paul *99:* 19
McDaniel, Jerry *132:* 135
McDaniel, Preston *160:* 206; *170:* 139
McDermott, Beverly Brodsky *11:* 180
McDermott, Gerald *16:* 201; *74:* 174, 175; *163:* 150, 151
McDermott, Mike *96:* 187
McDonald, Jill *13:* 155; *26:* 128
McDonald, Mercedes *169:* 118
McDonald, Ralph J. *5:* 123, 195
McDonnell, Flora *146:* 199, 200
McDonnell, Patrick *179:* 153, 154
McDonough, Don *10:* 163
McElligott, Matt *196:* 147
McElmurry, Jill *137:* 148; *163:* 141; *202:* 186
McElrath-Eslick, Lori *129:* 145; *142:* 21; *173:* 123; *202:* 194; *204:* 88, 89
McEntee, Dorothy *37:* 124
McEwan, Keith *88:* 116; *165:* 122, 123
McEwen, Katharine *169:* 34
McFall, Christie *12:* 144
McFeely, Daniel *160:* 213
McGaw, Laurie *109:* 243; *143:* 216; *211:* 218
McGee, Barbara *6:* 165
McGee, Marni *163:* 153
McGillvray, Kim *158:* 171; *165:* 213; *186:* 183; *190:* 175
McGinley-Nally, Sharon *131:* 19
McGinnis, Robert *110:* 113; *177:* 80

McGovern, Tara *98:* 171
McGraw, Sheila *83:* 146
McGregor, Barbara *200:* 155
McGregor, Malcolm *23:* 27
McGrory, Anik *193:* 120
McGuire, Robert *204:* 57; *209:* 86
McGuirk, Leslie *152:* 159
McHale, John *138:* 190
McHenry, E.B. *193:* 122
McHugh, Tom *23:* 64
McIntosh, Jon *42:* 56
McKay, Donald *2:* 118; *32:* 157; *45:* 151, 152
McKean, Dave *150:* 71; *174:* 156; *197:* 83, 118
McKeating, Eileen *44:* 58
McKee, David *10:* 48; *21:* 9; *70:* 154, 155; *107:* 139, 140, 141; *134:* 218; *158:* 148, 149, 150, 151
McKee, Diana *109:* 185
McKelvey, Patrick *164:* 141
McKendry, Joe *170:* 136
McKeveny, Tom *164:* 60; *173:* 79
McKie, Roy *7:* 44
McKie, Todd *205:* 181
McKillip, Kathy *30:* 153
McKinney, Ena *26:* 39
McKinnon, James *136:* 75
McKowen, Scott *172:* 63; *202:* 49
McLachlan, Edward *5:* 89
McLaren, Chesley *53:* 53; *213:* 112
McLaren, Kirsty *123:* 99; *124:* 226
Mclean, Andrew *113:* 117, 118, 120, 121; *172:* 130, 131
Mclean, Janet *172:* 130
McLean, Meg *94:* 196
McLean, Sammis *32:* 197
McLean, Wilson *90:* 29; *113:* 195
McLoughlin, John C. *47:* 149
McLoughlin, Wayne *102:* 230; *134:* 178; *216:* 196
McMahon, Robert *36:* 155; *69:* 169
McManus, Shawn *85:* 71
McMenemy, Sarah *156:* 139 ; *211:* 93
McMillan, Bruce *22:* 184
McMullan, James *40:* 33; *67:* 172; *87:* 142; *99:* 63, 64; *189:* 133; *196:* 51
McMullen, Nigel *146:* 177
McNeely, Tom *162:* 55
McNaught, Harry *12:* 80; *32:* 136
McNaughton, Colin *39:* 149; *40:* 108; *92:* 144, 145, 146; *134:* 104, 106; *211:* 122, 123, 124
McNicholas, Maureen *38:* 148
McNicholas, Shelagh *173:* 61; *191:* 125, 126
McPhail, David *14:* 105; *23:* 135; *37:* 217, 218, 220,221; *47:* 151, 152, 153, 154, 155, 156, 158, 159, 160, 162, 163, 164; *71:* 211; *81:* 139, 140, 142; *86:* 123; *132:* 150; *140:* 129, 131, 132; *183:* 134, 135, 137; *189:* 132
McPhee, Richard B. *41:* 133
McPheeters, Neal *78:* 132; *86:* 90; *99:* 162; *111:* 141; *142:* 162
McQuade, Jacqueline *124:* 223
McQueen, Lucinda *28:* 149; *41:* 249; *46:* 206; *53:* 103
McQuillan, Mary *153:* 97; *200:* 140
McVay, Tracy *11:* 68
McVicker, Charles *39:* 150
Mead, Ben Carlton *43:* 75
Meade, Holly *90:* 102; *94:* 101; *149:* 8; *151:* 107
Mecray, John *33:* 62
Meddaugh, Susan *20:* 42; *29:* 143; *41:* 241; *77:* 50; *84:* 173, 174, 175, 176, 177, 178; *125:* 160, 161, 162; *176:* 148, 149, 150, 151
Meehan, Dennis B. *56:* 144
Meents, Len W. *73:* 147, 150
Meers, Tony *99:* 113
Meisel, Paul *98:* 137; *124:* 18; *162:* 180; *179:* 16; *181:* 62; *194:* 154
Melanson, Luc *149:* 229; *198:* 97, 98
Melendez, Francisco *72:* 180

Melling, David *202:* 199
Melnychuk, Monika *153:* 65
Melo, Esperança *196:* 90
Melo, John *16:* 285; *58:* 203
Meloni, Maria Teresa *98:* 62
Meltzer, Ericka
    See O'Rourke, Ericka
Menasco, Milton *43:* 85
Menchin, Scott *188:* 129
Mendelson, Steven T. *86:* 154
Mendelssohn, Felix *19:* 170
Mendola, Christopher *88:* 223
Meng, Heinz *13:* 158
Merian, Maria Sibylla *140:* 88
Mero, Lee *34:* 68
Merrell, David *205:* 3
Merrill, Frank T. *16:* 147; *19:* 71; *YABC 1:* 226, 229,273
Merriman, Rachel *98:* 108; *114:* 122; *149:* 142
Merveille, David *200:* 142
Meryman, Hope *27:* 41
Meryweather, Jack *10:* 179
Meseldzija, Petar *168:* 97
Meserve, Jessica *184:* 137; *211:* 127
Messick, Dale *64:* 150, 151, 152
Meth, Harold *24:* 203
Meyer, Herbert *19:* 189
Meyer, Renate *6:* 170
Meyers, Bob *11:* 136
Meyers, Nancy *172:* 124
Meynell, Louis *37:* 76
Micale, Albert *2:* 65; *22:* 185
Miccuci, Charles *82:* 163; *144:* 150
Micich, Paul *164:* 163
Middleton, Jeffrey *177:* 173
Middleton, Joshua *208:* 146
Middleton-Sandford, Betty *2:* 125
Mieke, Anne *45:* 74
Mighell, Patricia *43:* 134
Miglio, Paige *101:* 203; *151:* 223; *201:* 118, 119; *204:* 162
Mikec, Larry *204:* 125
Mikolaycak, Charles *9:* 144; *12:* 101; *13:* 212; *21:* 121; *22:* 168; *30:* 187; *34:* 103, 150; *37:* 183; *43:* 179; *44:* 90; *46:* 115, 118, 119; *49:* 25; *78:* 121, 122, 205, 207; *81:* 4
Milelli, Pascal *129:* 66; *135:* 153; *187:* 45
Miles, Elizabeth *117:* 77
Miles, Jennifer *17:* 278
Milgrim, David *158:* 157; *187:* 125, 126, 128
Milhous, Katherine *15:* 193; *17:* 51
Millais, John E. *22:* 230, 231
Millard, C.E. *28:* 186
Millard, Kerry *105:* 124; *204:* 93, 94
Miller, Don *15:* 195; *16:* 71; *20:* 106; *31:* 178
Miller, Edna *29:* 148
Miller, Edward *115:* 64; *183:* 140, 141
Miller, Frank J. *25:* 94
Miller, Grambs *18:* 38; *23:* 16
Miller, Ian *99:* 128
Miller, Jane *15:* 196
Miller, Marcia *13:* 233
Miller, Marilyn *1:* 87; *31:* 69; *33:* 157
Miller, Mitchell *28:* 183; *34:* 207
Miller, Phil *175:* 150
Miller, Shane *5:* 140
Miller, Virginia *81:* 206
Millman, Isaac *172:* 18
Mills, Elaine *72:* 181
Mills, Judith Christine *130:* 168, 169
Mills, Lauren *92:* 170
Mills, Yaroslava Surmach *35:* 169, 170; *46:* 114
Millsap, Darrel *51:* 102
Milone, Karen *89:* 169
Milord, Susan *147:* 163, 164; *200:* 144
Milton, Debbie *162:* 161
Mims, Ashley *170:* 51
Miner, Julia *98:* 69

Minor, Wendell *39:* 188; *52:* 87; *56:* 171; *58:* 116; *62:* 56; *66:* 109; *74:* 93; *78:* 129; *94:* 67; *117:* 12, 13; *124:* 84, 86; *136:* 121; *164:* 168, 169; *170:* 71; *199:* 79, 80, 81, 82; *217:* 63
Minter, Daniel *176:* 154; *179:* 177
Mirocha, Paul *81:* 133; *192:* 148; *194:* 36
Misako Rocks! *192:* 149, 150
Mitchell, Judith *109:* 117
Mitchell, Mark *91:* 208
Mitchell, Tracy *190:* 15
Mitgutsch, Ali *76:* 161
Mitsuhashi, Yoko *45:* 153
Miyake, Yoshi *38:* 141
Mizumura, Kazue *10:* 143; *18:* 223; *36:* 159
Mochi, Ugo *8:* 122; *38:* 150
Mock, Paul *55:* 83; *123:* 32
Modarressi, Mitra *90:* 236; *126:* 168; *173:* 165, 166; *200:* 147, 148
Modell, Frank *39:* 152
Mogenson, Jan *74:* 183
Mohn, Susan *89:* 224
Mohr, Mark *133:* 201
Mohr, Nicholasa *8:* 139; *113:* 127
Molan, Christine *60:* 177; *84:* 183
Moldon, Peter L. *49:* 168
Molk, Laurel *92:* 150
Mollica, Gene *197:* 11
Momaday, N. Scott *48:* 159
Mombourquette, Paul *112:* 91; *126:* 142
Monk, Julie *165:* 231; *191:* 96
Monks, Lydia *189:* 136, 137
Monroy, Manuel *199:* 192
Montgomery, Lucy *150:* 126
Montgomery, Michael G. *208:* 159
Montgomery-Higham, Amanda *169:* 131
Monteiel, David *201:* 95
Montiel, David *69:* 106; *84:* 145
Montijo, Rhode *193:* 164
Montresor, Beni *2:* 91; *3:* 138; *38:* 152, 153, 154,155, 156, 157, 158, 159, 160; *68:* 63
Montserrat, Pep *128:* 135; *181:* 119; *184:* 53
Moon, Carl *25:* 183, 184, 185
Moon, Eliza *14:* 40
Moon, Ivan *22:* 39; *38:* 140
Moore, Adrienne *67:* 147
Moore, Agnes Kay Randall *43:* 187
Moore, Cyd *117:* 107, 108; *159:* 137, 138; *186:* 148, 149, 151; *203:* 15; *214:* 138, 139
Moore, Gustav *127:* 181, 182; *170:* 162, 163
Moore, Jackie *128:* 79
Moore, Janet *63:* 153
Moore, Margie *176:* 156
Moore, Mary *29:* 160
Moore, Patrick *184:* 121
Moore, Yvette *101:* 11, 12; *154:* 141
Mora, Giovanni *179:* 127; *184:* 11
Mora, Raul Mina *20:* 41
Moraes, Odilon *102:* 144
Morales, Yuyi *154:* 144
Moran, Rosslyn *111:* 26
Moran, Tom *60:* 100
Mordan, C.B. *193:* 115
Mordvinoff, Nicolas *15:* 179
Moreno, René King *169:* 59; *190:* 133, 209; *212:* 52
Morgan, Barbara *169:* 116
Morgan, Jacqui *58:* 57
Morgan, Mary *114:* 133, 134, 135; *123:* 11; *213:* 115, 116, 117
Morgan, Tom *42:* 157
Morgan, Pierr *173:* 148
Morgenstern, Michael *158:* 7, 57; *171:* 103; *174:* 60
Morice, Dave *93:* 142
Morin, Paul *73:* 132; *79:* 130; *88:* 140; *137:* 143
Moriuchi, Mique *177:* 203
Morning, Tuesday *205:* 25
Morozumi, Atsuko *110:* 155; *217:* 126, 127

Morrill, Leslie *18:* 218; *29:* 177; *33:* 84; *38:* 147; *42:* 127; *44:* 93; *48:* 164, 165, 167, 168, 169, 170,171; *49:* 162; *63:* 136, 180; *70:* 72; *71:* 70, 91,92; *72:* 228; *80:* 163, 164, 165; *90:* 121; *121:* 88; *178:* 117
Morrill, Rowena A. *84:* 16; *98:* 163
Morris *47:* 91
Morris, Frank *55:* 133; *60:* 28; *76:* 2
Morris, Harry O. *119:* 138
Morris, Jackie *128:* 194; *144:* 119; *151:* 146; *202:* 126, 127; *204:* 83; *211:* 80; *214:* 163
Morris, Jennifer E. *179:* 157
Morris, Oradel Nolen *128:* 180
Morris, Tony *62:* 146; *70:* 97
Morrison, Bill *42:* 116; *66:* 170; *69:* 40
Morrison, Gordon *87:* 150; *113:* 93; *128:* 181, 182; *183:* 144, 145, 146
Morrison, Frank *169:* 162; *205:* 156
Morrison, Taylor *159:* 144, 145; *187:* 131
Morrow, Gray *2:* 64; *5:* 200; *10:* 103, 114; *14:* 175
Morse, Scott *200:* 149, 150
Morton, Lee Jack *32:* 140
Morton, Marian *3:* 185
Mosberg, Hilary *117:* 195; *118:* 164; *149:* 55
Moser, Barry *56:* 68, 117, 118, 119, 120, 121, 122, 123, 124; *59:* 141; *60:* 160; *79:* 91, 147, 149, 151, 152; *82:* 81; *90:* 118; *91:* 35; *95:* 210; *97:* 91, 93; *102:* 152; *126:* 4; *128:* 175; *133:* 141; *138:* 167, 171, 174; *153:* 205; *174:* 130; *185:* 152, 154; *195:* 163; *204:* 115; *209:* 201
Moser, Cara *90:* 118; *138:* 167
Moses, Grandma *18:* 228
Moses, Will *178:* 170, 171
Moskof, Martin Stephen *27:* 152
Mosley, Francis *57:* 144
Moss, Donald *11:* 184
Moss, Geoffrey *32:* 198
Moss, Marissa *71:* 130; *104:* 127; *163:* 156; *216:* 164, 165, 166
Most, Bernard *48:* 173; *91:* 142, 143; *134:* 120
Mowll, Joshua *188:* 133
Mowry, Carmen *50:* 62
Moxley, Sheila *96:* 174; *169:* 26; *206:* 16
Moyers, William *21:* 65
Moyler, Alan *36:* 142
Mozley, Charles *9:* 87; *20:* 176, 192, 193; *22:* 228; *25:* 205; *33:* 150; *43:* 170, 171, 172, 173, 174; *YABC2:* 89
Mueller, Hans Alexander *26:* 64; *27:* 52, 53
Mugnaini, Joseph *11:* 35; *27:* 52, 53; *35:* 62
Mujica, Rick *72:* 67; *88:* 95; *111:* 53; *180:* 185; *197:* 70
Mullen, Douglas *180:* 178
Muller, Robin *86:* 161
Muller, Steven *32:* 167
Muller, Jorg *35:* 215; *67:* 138, 139
Mulock, Julie *163:* 112
Mullins, Edward S. *10:* 101
Mullins, Patricia *51:* 68
Multer, Scott *80:* 108
Munari, Bruno *15:* 200
Munch, Edvard *140:* 143
Munowitz, Ken *14:* 148; *72:* 178, 179
Muñoz, Claudio *208:* 161
Munoz, William *42:* 160
Munro, Roxie *58:* 134; *136:* 177; *137:* 218; *184:* 133, 134
Munsinger, Lynn *33:* 161; *46:* 126; *71:* 92; *82:* 80; *89:* 218; *92:* 125; *94:* 157, 158, 159, 160; *98:* 196; *103:* 198; *142:* 143; *145:* 133, 134, 136; *153:* 203; *176:* 162; *177:* 140, 141, 142; *189:* 113, 114, 116, 117; *201:* 42
Munson, Russell *13:* 9
Munster, Sebastian *166:* 107
Munzar, Barbara *149:* 75
Murdocca, Salvatore *73:* 212; *98:* 132; *111:* 168; *157:* 228; *164:* 257
Murphy, Bill *5:* 138; *130:* 170
Murphy, Jill *37:* 142; *70:* 166; *142:* 132, 134

Murphy, Kelly *130:* 212; *143:* 119; *176:* 158; *190:* 135
Murphy, Liz *210:* 183; *212:* 157
Murphy, Mary *196:* 158
Murphy, Tom *192:* 40
Murr, Karl *20:* 62
Murray, Joe *175:* 37
Murray, Ossie *43:* 176
Mussino, Attilio *29:* 131; *100:* 164
Mutchler, Dwight *1:* 25
Myers, Bernice *9:* 147; *36:* 75; *81:* 146, 147, 148
Muth, Jon J. *165:* 169; *167:* 109; *190:* 227; *193:* 59
Myers, Christopher *183:* 150; *193:* 139
Myers, Duane O. *99:* 145
Myers, Tim *147:* 168
Myers, V.G. *142:* 41
Myers, Lou *11:* 2

N

Nachreiner, Tom *29:* 182
Nacht, Merle *65:* 49
Nadler, Ellis *88:* 91
Nagle, Shane *180:* 223
Nagy, Ian *195:* 64
Najaka, Marlies *62:* 101
Nakai, Michael *30:* 217; *54:* 29
Nakata, Hiroe *157:* 156; *162:* 30; *205:* 124, 125
Nakatani, Chiyoko *12:* 124
Narahashi, Keiko *77:* 188; *82:* 213; *115:* 142, 143, 144
Nascimbene, Yan *133:* 128; *173:* 132, 133
Nash, Lesa *87:* 135
Nash, Linell *46:* 175
Nash, Scott *130:* 36; *188:* 196
Naso, John *33:* 183
Nason, Thomas W. *14:* 68
Nasser, Muriel *48:* 74
Nast, Thomas *21:* 29; *28:* 23; *51:* 132, 133, 134, 135,136, 137, 138, 139, 141
Nasta, Vincent *78:* 185
Natale, Vincent *76:* 3; *78:* 125; *112:* 47; *166:* 81; *174:* 189; *185:* 212; *197:* 59
Natchev, Alexi *96:* 177
Nathan, Charlott *125:* 151
Nathan, Cheryl *150:* 104; *186:* 112
Natti, Susanna *20:* 146; *32:* 141, 142; *35:* 178; *37:* 143; *71:* 49; *93:* 98; *125:* 166, 168; *126:* 228; *151:* 6; *178:* 8; *188:* 106
Navarra, Celeste Scala *8:* 142
Naylor, Penelope *10:* 104
Nazz, James *72:* 8
Nebel, M. *45:* 154
Neebe, William *7:* 93
Needham, Dave *196:* 85
Needler, Jerry *12:* 93
Neel, Alice *31:* 23
Neely, Beth *119:* 184
Neely, Keith R. *46:* 124
Neff, Leland *78:* 74
Negri, Rocco *3:* 213; *5:* 67; *6:* 91, 108; *12:* 159
Negrin, Fabian *174:* 125; *175:* 15
Neidigh, Sherry *128:* 53; *204:* 101, 102, 103
Neilan, Eujin Kim *180:* 241; *200:* 151, 152
Neill, John R. *18:* 8, 10, 11, 21, 30; *100:* 22
Neilsen, Cliff *158:* 131; *177:* 112, 121; *209:* 8; *215:* 150
Neilsen, Terese *116:* 74
Nelson, Craig *62:* 151; *153:* *183:* 86
Nelson, Gail White *68:* 140
Nelson, Jennifer *129:* 152; *199:* 132
Nelson, Kadir *151:* 185; *154:* 146, 147; *157:* 189, 222; *181:* 122, 124; *197:* 155; *213:* 122, 123, 124
Nelson, S.D. *131:* 34; *181:* 126, 127

Ness, Evaline *1:* 164, 165; *2:* 39; *3:* 8; *10:* 147; *12:* 53; *26:* 150, 151, 152, 153; *49:* 30, 31, 32; *56:* 30; *60:* 113
Neubecker, Robert *170:* 143; *214:* 157
Neville, Vera *2:* 182
Nevins, Daniel *191:* 173
Nevwirth, Allan *79:* 168
Newberry, Clare Turlay *1:* 170
Newbold, Greg *108:* 125; *145:* 199; *151:* 23; *193:* 178; *197:* 10; *199:* 92, 93
Newfeld, Frank *14:* 121; *26:* 154
Newman, Andy *149:* 61; *195:* 63
Newman, Ann *43:* 90
Newman, Barbara Johansen *191:* 137, 138
Newsham, Ian *143:* 162
Newsom, Carol *40:* 159; *44:* 60; *47:* 189; *65:* 29; *70:* 192; *80:* 36; *85:* 137, 138; *92:* 167; *191:* 82
Newsom, Tom *49:* 149; *71:* 13, 62; *75:* 156; *91:* 113
Newton, Jill *83:* 105; *200:* 154
Ng, Michael *29:* 171
Ng, Simon *167:* 7
Nguyen, Vincent *189:* 49
Nicholson, William *15:* 33, 34; *16:* 48
Nickens, Bessie *104:* 153
Nicklaus, Carol *45:* 194; *62:* 132, 133
Nickle, John *181:* 128
Nickless, Will *16:* 139
Nicholas, Corasue *154:* 20
Nicolas *17:* 130, 132, 133; *YABC 2:* 215
Niebrugge, Jane *6:* 118
Nielsen, Cliff *95:* 207, 208; *105:* 58; *114:* 112; *124:* 12; *125:* 91, 92; *132:* 224; *135:* 187; *136:* 40; *137:* 168; *145:* 54; *149:* 28; *158:* 129; *165:* 64, 158; *168:* 169; *170:* 6; *175:* 114, 116; *187:* 75, 76; *194:* 107; *197:* 172; *201:* 14; *208:* 192; *211:* 186; *216:* 215; *217:* 67
Nielsen, Jon *6:* 100; *24:* 202
Nielsen, Kay *15:* 7; *16:* 211, 212, 213, 215, 217; *22:* 143; *YABC 1:* 32, 33
Niemann, Christoph *191:* 141
Niland, Deborah *25:* 191; *27:* 156; *135:* 50; *172:* 143
Niland, Kilmeny *25:* 191; *75:* 143
Nino, Alex *59:* 145
Ninon *1:* 5; *38:* 101, 103, 108
Nissen, Rie *44:* 35
Nithael, Mark *158:* 237
Nivola, Claire A. *78:* 126; *140:* 147; *208:* 164
Nixon, K. *14:* 152
Nobati, Eugenia *194:* 118
Noble, Louise *61:* 170
Noble, Marty *97:* 168; *125:* 171
Noble, Trinka Hakes *39:* 162; *84:* 157
Noda, Takayo *168:* 143
Noguchi, Yoshie *30:* 99
Nolan, Dennis *42:* 163; *67:* 163; *78:* 189; *82:* 225; *83:* 26; *92:* 169, 170; *103:* 166; *111:* 35; *112:* 213; *127:* 171; *166:* 161; *194:* 218
Noll, Sally *82:* 171
Nolte, Larry *121:* 63, 65
Nones, Eric Jon *61:* 111; *76:* 38; *77:* 177
Noonan, Daniel *100:* 224
Noonan, Julia *4:* 163; *7:* 207; *25:* 151; *91:* 29; *95:* 149
Norcia, Ernie *108:* 155; *140:* 47
Nordenskjold, Birgitta *2:* 208
Noreika, Robert *173:* 20; *217:* 24
Norling, Beth *149:* 153, 154; *209:* 77
Norman, Elaine *77:* 72, 176; *94:* 35; *136:* 63; *178:* 42
Norman, Mary *36:* 138, 147
Norman, Michael *12:* 117; *27:* 168
Northway, Jennifer *85:* 96
Nostlinger, Christiana *162:* 131
Novak, Linda *166:* 205
Novak, Matt *104:* 132, 133; *165:* 173, 174; *204:* 104, 106

Novelli, Luca *61:* 137
Novgorodoff, Danica *215:* 133
Nugent, Cynthia *106:* 189; *205:* 126, 127; *209:* 180
Numeroff, Laura Joffe *28:* 161; *30:* 177
Nurse, Chris *164:* 91
Nussbaumer, Paul *16:* 219; *39:* 117
Nutt, Ken *72:* 69; *97:* 170
Nyce, Helene *19:* 219
Nygren, Tord *30:* 148; *127:* 164

O

Oakley, Graham *8:* 112; *30:* 164, 165; *84:* 188,189, 190, 191, 192
Oakley, Thornton *YABC 2:* 189
Oberheide, Heide *118:* 37
Obligado, Lilian *2:* 28, 66, 67; *6:* 30; *14:* 179; *15:* 103; *25:* 84; *61:* 138, 139, 140, 141, 143
Oblinski, Rafael *190:* 139
Obrant, Susan *11:* 186
O'Brien, Anne Sibley *53:* 116, 117; *155:* 115; *213:* 127
O'Brien, John *41:* 253; *72:* 12; *89:* 59, 60; *98:* 16; *161:* 185; *169:* 16; *180:* 196
O'Brien, Patrick *193:* 142, 143, 144
O'Brien, Teresa *87:* 89
O'Brien, Tim *93:* 25; *136:* 94; *164:* 57; *169:* 57; *173:* 55; *175:* 86; *184:* 192; *191:* 134; *193:* 137; *210:* 159
O'Clair, Dennis *127:* 25
O'Connor, George *183:* 153
Odell, Carole *35:* 47
Odem, Mel *99:* 164; *167:* 84, 87
O'Donohue, Thomas *40:* 89
Oechsli, Kelly *5:* 144, 145; *7:* 115; *8:* 83, 183; *13:* 117; *20:* 94; *81:* 199
Ofer, Avi *208:* 143
Offen, Hilda *42:* 207
Ogden, Bill *42:* 59; *47:* 55
Ogg, Oscar *33:* 34
Ogle, Nancy Gray *163:* 144
Ohi, Ruth *90:* 175, 177; *131:* 63; *135:* 106; *175:* 107; *179:* 55
Ohlsson, Ib *4:* 152; *7:* 57; *10:* 20; *11:* 90; *19:* 217; *41:* 246; *82:* 106; *92:* 213
Ohtomo, Yasuo *37:* 146; *39:* 212, 213
O'Keefe, Jennifer *136:* 184
O'Kelley, Mattie Lou *36:* 150
Olbinski, Rafal *149:* 27; *158:* 77; *203:* 36
O'Leary, Chris *208:* 166
Oleynikov, Igor *202:* 134
Oliver, Isaac *171:* 182
Oliver, Jenni *23:* 121; *35:* 112
Oliver, Narelle *152:* 192; *197:* 129, 130
Oller, Erika *128:* 186; *134:* 126
Olschewski, Alfred *7:* 172
Olsen, Ib Spang *6:* 178, 179; *81:* 164
Olson, Alan *77:* 229
Olson-Brown, Ellen *183:* 154
Olugebefola, Ademola *15:* 205
O'Malley, Kevin *94:* 180; *106:* 8; *113:* 108; *136:* 70; *157:* 193; *191:* 146; *203:* 78; *217:* 84
O'Neil, Dan IV *7:* 176
O'Neill, Catharine *72:* 113; *84:* 78; *134:* 153
O'Neill, Jean *22:* 146
O'Neill, Martin *187:* 39; *203:* 118
O'Neill, Michael J. *54:* 172
O'Neill, Rose *48:* 30, 31
O'Neill, Steve *21:* 118
Ono, Chiyo *7:* 97
Orbaan, Albert *2:* 31; *5:* 65, 171; *9:* 8; *14:* 241; *20:* 109
Orbach, Ruth *21:* 112
Orback, Craig *197:* 132
Orfe, Joan *20:* 81
Org, Ed *119:* 93
Ormai, Stella *72:* 129

Ormerod, Jan *55:* 124; *70:* 170, 171; *90:* 39; *132:* 172, 173, 174; *147:* 98
Ormsby, Virginia H. *11:* 187
O'Rourke, Ericka *108:* 216; *117:* 194; *111:* 142; *119:* 194; *137:* 152; *150:* 134; *167:* 64; *172:* 164; *188:* 163; *191:* 172; *201:* 15; *203:* 75; *209:* 130
O'Rourke, Ericka Meltzer
See O'Rourke, Ericka
Orozco, Jose Clemente *9:* 177
Orr, Forrest W. *23:* 9
Orr, N. *19:* 70
Ortiz, Vilma *88:* 158
Osborn, Kathy *152:* 232; *199:* 101, 102; *206:* 67
Osborn, Robert *65:* 49
Osborne, Billie Jean *35:* 209
Osmond, Edward *10:* 111
O'Sullivan, Tom *3:* 176; *4:* 55; *78:* 195
Otani, June *124:* 42; *156:* 53
Otis, Rebecca *185:* 92
Ottley, Matt *147:* 221; *171:* 133
Otto, Svend *22:* 130, 141; *67:* 188, 189
Oudry, J.B. *18:* 167
Oughton, Taylor *5:* 23; *104:* 136
Overeng, Johannes *44:* 36
Overlie, George *11:* 156
Owens, Carl *2:* 35; *23:* 521
Owens, Gail *10:* 170; *12:* 157; *19:* 16; *22:* 70; *25:* 81; *28:* 203, 205; *32:* 221, 222; *36:* 132; *46:* 40; *47:* 57; *54:* 66, 67, 68, 69, 70, 71, 72, 73; *71:* 100; *73:* 64; *77:* 157; *80:* 32; *82:* 3; *99:* 226
Owens, Mary Beth *113:* 202, 203; *191:* 148, 149
Owens, Nubia *84:* 74
Oxenbury, Helen *3:* 150, 151; *24:* 81; *68:* 174, 175,176; *81:* 209; *84:* 213, 245; *129:* 56; *149:* 159; *184:* 181
Oz, Robin *88:* 167; *185:* 181

P

Padgett, Jim *12:* 165
Page, Gail *205:* 128
Page, Homer *14:* 145
Page, Mark *162:* 70
Paget, Sidney *24:* 90, 91, 93, 95, 97
Paget, Walter *64:* 122
Paillot, Jim *173:* 89
Pajouhesh, Noushin *160:* 121
Pak *12:* 76
Pak, Yu Cha *86:* 174
Paladino, Lance *134:* 30
Palazzo, Tony *3:* 152, 153
Palecek, Josef *56:* 136; *89:* 158
Palen, Debbie *135:* 88; *195:* 148, 149
Palencar, John Jude *84:* 12, 45; *85:* 87; *92:* 187; *99:* 128; *110:* 204; *150:* 122; *171:* 86; *207:* 36
Palin, Nicki *81:* 201; *89:* 161
Palladini, David *4:* 113; *40:* 176, 177, 178, 179, 181,224, 225; *50:* 138; *78:* 186
Pallarito, Don *43:* 36
Palmer, Carol *158:* 230; *195:* 187
Palmer, Heidi *15:* 207; *29:* 102
Palmer, Jan *42:* 153; *82:* 161
Palmer, Judd *153:* 160, 161
Palmer, Juliette *6:* 89; *15:* 208
Palmer, Kate Salley *104:* 143; *154:* 169
Palmer, Lemuel *17:* 25, 29
Palmisciano, Diane *110:* 62; *162:* 26; *202:* 138, 139
Palmquist, Eric *38:* 133
Pamintuan, Macky *214:* 160
Panesis, Nicholas *3:* 127
Panter, Gary *182:* 191
Panton, Doug *52:* 99
Paparone, Pamela *129:* 174

Papas, William *11:* 223; *50:* 160
Papin, Joseph *26:* 113
Papish, Robin Lloyd *10:* 80
Papp, Robert *198:* 41; *205:* 130
Paradis, Susan *40:* 216
Paraquin, Charles H. *18:* 166
Pardo DeLange, Alex *179:* 128; *211:* 135, 136
Paris, Peter *31:* 127
Park, Nick *113:* 143
Park, Seho *39:* 110
Park, W.B. *22:* 189
Parker, Ant *82:* 87, 88; *104:* 121
Parker, Lewis *2:* 179
Parker, Nancy Winslow *10:* 113; *22:* 164; *28:* 47, 144; *52:* 7; *69:* 153; *91:* 171, 174; *132:* 175
Parker, Robert *4:* 161; *5:* 74; *9:* 136; *29:* 39
Parker, Robert Andrew *11:* 81; *29:* 186; *39:* 165; *40:* 25; *41:* 78; *42:* 123; *43:* 144; *48:* 182; *54:* 140; *74:* 141; *91:* 24; *111:* 115; *151:* 201; *154:* 156; *200:* 163, 164; *211:* 67
Parker-Rees, Guy *149:* 145; *193:* 149, 150
Parkin, Trevor *140:* 151
Parkins, David *114:* 123; *146:* 176; *176:* 168; *192:* 107
Parkinson, Kathy *71:* 143; *144:* 234
Parkinson, Keith *70:* 66
Parks, Gordon, Jr. *33:* 228
Parnall, Peter *5:* 137; *16:* 221; *24:* 70; *40:* 78; *51:* 130; *69:* 17, 155; *136:* 22, 23, 24
Parnall, Virginia *40:* 78
Paros, Jennifer *210:* 197
Parow, Lorraine *158:* 127
Parr, Todd *134:* 139, 140; *179:* 163, 164, 165
Parrish, Anne *27:* 159, 160
Parrish, Dillwyn *27:* 159
Parrish, Maxfield *14:* 160, 161, 164, 165; *16:* 109; *18:* 12, 13; *YABC 1:* 149, 152, 267; *2:* 146, 149
Parry, David *26:* 156
Parry, Marian *13:* 176; *19:* 179
Parsons, Garry *197:* 135
Partch, Virgil *45:* 163, 165
Pascal, David *14:* 174
Paschkis, Julie *177:* 153, 154
Pasquier, J.A. *16:* 91
Pastel, Elyse *201:* 123
Pasternak, Robert *119:* 53
Paterson, Diane *13:* 116; *39:* 163; *59:* 164, 165, 166,167; *72:* 51, 53; *129:* 175; *177:* 156, 157
Paterson, Helen *16:* 93
Patkau, Karen *112:* 123
Paton, Jane *15:* 271; *35:* 176
Patricelli, Leslie *207:* 129
Patrick, John *139:* 190
Patrick, Pamela *90:* 160; *93:* 211; *105:* 12
Patrick, Tom *190:* 103
Patterson, Geoffrey *54:* 75
Patterson, Robert *25:* 118
Patti, Joyce *187:* 145, 146
Patz, Nancy *111:* 40; *154:* 161; *214:* 80
Paul, James *4:* 130; *23:* 161
Paul, Korky *102:* 85
Paull, Grace *24:* 157; *87:* 127
Paulsen, Ruth Wright *79:* 160, 164; *189:* 146
Pavlov, Elena *80:* 49
Payne, Adam S. *135:* 166
Payne, C.F. *145:* 138, 140; *179:* 168
Payne, Joan Balfour *1:* 118
Payne, Tom *170:* 27
Payson, Dale *7:* 34; *9:* 151; *20:* 140; *37:* 22
Payzant, Charles *21:* 147
Peacock, Ralph *64:* 118
Peake, Mervyn *22:* 136, 149; *23:* 162, 163, 164; *YABC2:* 307
Pearson, Larry *38:* 225
Pearson, Tracey Campbell *64:* 163, 164, 167, 168, 169; *118:* 51; *156:* 169, 171, 172; *163:* 140

Peat, Fern B. *16:* 115
Peck, Anne Merriman *18:* 241; *24:* 155
Peck, Beth *66:* 242; *79:* 166; *80:* 136; *91:* 34; *95:* 9; *101:* 77; *164:* 197; *190:* 170
Peddicord, Jane Ann *199:* 106
Pedersen, Janet *193:* 152; *217:* 57
Pedersen, Judy *66:* 217; *121:* 36; *172:* 67
Pedersen, Vilhelm *YABC 1:* 40
Pederson, Sharleen *12:* 92
Pedlar, Elaine *161:* 45
Peek, Merle *39:* 168
Peet, Bill *2:* 203; *41:* 159, 160, 161, 162, 163; *78:* 158, 159, 160, 161
Peguero, Adrian *116:* 133
Peguero, Gerard *116:* 133
Pels, Winslow Pinney *55:* 126
Peltier, Leslie C. *13:* 178
Peltzer, Marc *202:* 92
Penberthy, Mark *171:* 78
Pendle, Alexy *7:* 159; *13:* 34; *29:* 161; *33:* 215; *86:* 62
Pendola, Joanne *76:* 203; *81:* 125; *105:* 181; *178:* 152, 153
Pene du Bois, William *4:* 70; *10:* 122; *26:* 61; *27:* 145, 211; *35:* 243; *41:* 216; *68:* 180, 181; *73:* 45
Penfound, David *102:* 185
Pennington, Eunice *27:* 162
Peppe, Mark *28:* 142
Peppe, Rodney *4:* 164, 165; *74:* 187, 188, 189
Pepper, Hubert *64:* 143
Percy, Graham *63:* 2
Pericoli, Matteo *178:* 177
Perini, Ben *173:* 77
Perkins, David *60:* 68
Perkins, Lucy Fitch *72:* 199
Perkins, Lynne Rae *172:* 146; *212:* 153
Perl, Susan *2:* 98; *4:* 231; *5:* 44, 45, 118; *6:* 199; *8:* 137; *12:* 88; *22:* 193; *34:* 54, 55; *52:* 128; *YABC 1:* 176
Perrone, Donna *72:* 166
Perry, Marie Fritz *165:* 180
Perry, Patricia *29:* 137; *30:* 171
Perry, Roger *27:* 163
Perske, Martha *46:* 83; *51:* 108, 147
Persson, Stina *175:* 166
Pesek, Ludek *15:* 237
Petach, Heidi *149:* 166; *200:* 207
Peters, David *72:* 205; *182:* 116
Petersen, Jeff *181:* 95
Petersham, Maud *17:* 108, 147, 148, 149, 150, 151, 152, 153
Petersham, Miska *17:* 108, 147, 148, 149, 150, 151, 152, 153
Peterson, Eric *109:* 125
Peterson, Nisse *27:* 27
Peterson, R.F. *7:* 101
Peterson, Russell *7:* 130
Petie, Haris *2:* 3; *10:* 41, 118; *11:* 227; *12:* 70
Petricic, Dusan *153:* 75, 76, 77; *170:* 12; *172:* 13; *176:* 170; *179:* 56
Petrides, Heidrun *19:* 223
Petrone, Valeria *159:* 160; *171:* 92; *186:* 173; *204:* 49; *216:* 208
Petrosino, Tamara *177:* 40; *193:* 154, 155
Petruccio, Steven James *67:* 159; *127:* 5
Pettingill, Ondre *64:* 181; *70:* 64
Peyo *40:* 56, 57
Peyton, K.M. *15:* 212
Pfeifer, Herman *15:* 262
Pfister, Marcus *83:* 165, 166, 167; *146:* 152; *150:* 160; *207:* 132, 134, 135, 136
Pfloog, Jan *124:* 60
Pham, LeUyen *160:* 48; *175:* 154, 156; *179:* 149; *201:* 124, 125, 126, 127; *204:* 28; *208:* 206; *217:* 92
Phelan, Matt *182:* 160; *184:* 222; *215:* 140, 141
Phillips, Craig *70:* 151; *207:* 74
Phillips, Douglas *1:* 19
Phillips, F.D. *6:* 202

Phillips, Louise *133:* 67
Phillips, Matt *184:* 173
Phillips, Thomas *30:* 55
Philpot, Glyn *54:* 46
Phiz
    See Browne, Hablot K.
Piatti, Celestino *16:* 223
Pica, Steve *115:* 181
Picarella, Joseph *13:* 147
Picart, Gabriel *121:* 165; *201:* 169
Pichon, Liz *174:* 139
Pickard, Charles *12:* 38; *18:* 203; *36:* 152
Picken, George A. *23:* 150
Pickens, David *22:* 156
Pickering, Jimmy *195:* 152; *197:* 163
Pienkowski, Jan *6:* 183; *30:* 32; *58:* 140, 141, 142,143, 146, 147; *73:* 3; *87:* 156, 157; *131:* 189
Pieper, Christiane *200:* 168
Pignataro, Anna *163:* 220 *Pileggi, Steve 145:* 122
Pilkey, Dav *68:* 186; *115:* 164, 166; *166:* 173, 174, 175
Pimlott, John *10:* 205
Pincus, Harriet *4:* 186; *8:* 179; *22:* 148; *27:* 164, 165; *66:* 202
Pini, Wendy *89:* 166
Pinkett, Neil *60:* 8
Pinkney, Brian *81:* 184, 185; *94:* 107; *113:* 146, 147; *117:* 121, 166; *132:* 145; *158:* 108, 191; *160:* 189; *200:* 8
Pinkney, Jerry *8:* 218; *10:* 40; *15:* 276; *20:* 66; *24:* 121; *33:* 109; *36:* 222; *38:* 200; *41:* 165, 166, 167, 168, 169, 170, 171, 173, 174; *44:* 198; *48:* 51; *53:* 20; *56:* 61, 68; *58:* 184; *60:* 59; *61:* 91; *71:* 146, 148, 149; *72:* 17; *73:* 149; *74:* 159,192; *75:* 45; *80:* 206; *81:* 44; *85:* 144; *95:* 50; *107:* 158, 159, 160; *108:* 164; *112:* 114, 115; *133:* 58; *195:* 140
Pinkwater, Daniel Manus *8:* 156; *46:* 180, 181, 182, 185, 188, 189, 190; *151:* 161 *76:* 178, 179, 180; *210:* 203
Pinkwater, Manus
    See Pinkwater, Daniel Manus
Pinkwater, Jill *114:* 160, 161; *158:* 179; *188:* 143, 145, 146
Pinto, Ralph *10:* 131; *45:* 93
Pinto, Sara *200:* 165
Pinon, Mark *74:* 22
Piven, Hanoch *173:* 142
Pistolesi *73:* 211
Pitcairn, Ansel *188:* 10
Pittman, Helena Clare *71:* 151
Pitz, Henry C. *4:* 168; *19:* 165; *35:* 128; *42:* 80; *YABC 2:* 95, 176
Pitzenberger, Lawrence J. *26:* 94
Pitzer, Susanna *181:* 131
Plant, Andrew *214:* 166
Player, Stephen *82:* 190
Plecas, Jennifer *84:* 201; *106:* 124; *149:* 168; *205:* 180
Ploog, Mike *180:* 19
Plowden, David *52:* 135, 136
Plume, Ilse *170:* 149
Plummer, William *32:* 31
Podevin, Jean François *184:* 185
Podwal, Mark *56:* 170, 173; *101:* 154, 155, 157; *149:* 176; *160:* 194
Pogany, Willy *15:* 46, 49; *19:* 222, 256; *25:* 214; *44:* 142, 143, 144, 145, 146, 147, 148
Pohrt, Tom *67:* 116; *104:* 80; *152:* 199; *195:* 154; *199:* 85
Poirson, V.A. *26:* 89
Polacco, Patricia *74:* 195, 196, 197, 198; *123:* 121, 122, 123; *180:* 189, 190, 191, 193, 194; *212:* 168, 170, 171
Polgreen, John *21:* 44
Polhemus, Coleman *210:* 209
Politi, Leo *1:* 178; *4:* 53; *21:* 48; *47:* 173,174, 176, 178, 179, 180, 181
Pollema-Cahill, Phyllis *123:* 126

Pollen, Samson *64:* 80
Polonsky, Arthur *34:* 168
Polseno, Jo *1:* 53; *3:* 117; *5:* 114; *17:* 154; *20:* 87; *32:* 49; *41:* 245
Pomaska, Anna *117:* 148
Pons, Bernadette *184:* 100
Ponter, James *5:* 204
Poole, Colin *111:* 27
Poortvliet, Rien *6:* 212; *65:* 165, 166, 167
Pope, Kevin *183:* 158
Popp, Wendy *72:* 122; *158:* 68
Poppel, Hans *71:* 154, 155
Porfirio, Guy *76:* 134
Portal, Colette *6:* 186; *11:* 203
Porter, George *7:* 181
Porter, Janice Lee *136:* 175; *164:* 37
Porter, John *113:* 47
Porter, Pat Grant *84:* 112; *125:* 101
Porter, Sue *146:* 246, 247; *213:* 139, 140, 141
Porter, Walter *124:* 175
Posada, Mia *187:* 151
Posen, Michael *175:* 82
Posthuma, Sieb *150:* 163
Postier, Jim *202:* 140; *204:* 25
Postma, Lidia *79:* 17
Potter, Beatrix *100:* 194, 195; *132:* 179, 180, 181, 182; *YABC 1:* 208, 209, 210, 212, 213
Potter, Giselle *117:* 123; *143:* 44; *144:* 170, 197; *149:* 7; *150:* 165; *187:* 152, 153; *190:* 198; *196:* 152; *200:* 12
Potter, Katherine *104:* 147; *171:* 135; *173:* 136; *217:* 130, 131
Potter, Miriam Clark *3:* 162
Poulin, Stephane *98:* 140, 141
Poullis, Nick *146:* 210
Powell, Constance Buffington *174:* 141
Powell, Gary *151:* 208
Powell, Ivan *67:* 219
Power, Margaret *105:* 122
Powers, Daniel *161:* 173
Powers, Richard M. *1:* 230; *3:* 218; *7:* 194; *26:* 186
Powledge, Fred *37:* 154
Powzyk, Joyce *74:* 214
Poydar, Nancy *96:* 149; *190:* 180, 181, 182
Pracher, Richard *91:* 166
Prachaticka, Marketa *126:* 126
Prange, Beckie *181:* 169
Prap, Lila *177:* 165
Prater, John *103:* 142, 143, 144; *149:* 172
Pratt, Charles *23:* 29
Pratt, Christine Joy *214:* 167
Pratt, George *116:* 208; *212:* 37
Pratt, Pierre *150:* 73; *166:* 183; *168:* 172; *201:* 27; *208:* 171, 172, 173
Prebenna, David *73:* 174
Preiss-Glasser, Robin *123:* 176; *152* 40; *172:* 194
Press, Jenny *116:* 95
Preston, Mark *152:* 162
Pretro, Korinna *91:* 126
Prevost, Mikela *209:* 111
Price, Christine *2:* 247; *3:* 163, 253; *8:* 166
Price, Cynthia *118:* 156
Price, Edward *33:* 34
Price, Garrett *1:* 76; *2:* 42
Price, Hattie Longstreet *17:* 13
Price, Nick *216:* 173
Price, Norman *YABC 1:* 129
Price, Willard *48:* 184
Priceman, Marjorie *81:* 171; *136:* 169; *156:* 200; *168:* 153, 154; *188:* 45
Priestley, Alice *168:* 33
Priestley, Chris *198:* 144
Primavera, Elise *26:* 95; *58:* 151; *73:* 37; *80:* 79; *86:* 156; *105:* 161; *213:* 157
Primrose, Jean *36:* 109
Prince, Alison *86:* 188, 189
Prince, Leonora E. *7:* 170
Pritchett, Shelley *116:* 148
Prittie, Edwin J. *YABC 1:* 120

Proimos, James *176:* 4; *217:* 132, 133, 134
Proimos, John *173:* 144
Prosmitsky, Jenya *132:* 33
Provensen, Alice *37:* 204, 215, 222; *70:* 176, 177, 178, 180, 71:* 213; *147:* 184; *191:* 190
Provensen, Martin *37:* 204, 215, 222; *70:* 176, 177, 178, 180; *71:* 213; *191:* 190
Pucci, Albert John *44:* 154
Pudlo *8:* 59
Puggaard, Ulla *196:* 25
Pullen, Zachary *211:* 161
Pulver, Harry, Jr. *159:* 159
Pulver, Robin *160:* 4
Punchatz, Don *99:* 57
Purdy, Susan *8:* 162
Pursell, Weimer *55:* 18
Purtscher, Alfons *97:* 6
Puskas, James *5:* 141
Pyk, Jan *7:* 26; *38:* 123
Pyle, Chuck *99:* 149; *191:* 83
Pyle, Howard *16:* 225, 226, 227, 228, 230, 231, 232, 235; *24:* 27; *34:* 124, 125, 127, 128; *59:* 132; *100:* 198

Q

Quackenbush, Robert *4:* 190; *6:* 166; *7:* 175, 178; *9:* 86; *11:* 65, 221; *41:* 154; *43:* 157; *70:* 185, 186; *71:* 137; *85:* 47; *92:* 148; *133:* 154, 164, 169
Qualls, Sean *177:* 167, 168; *193:* 43
Quennell, Marjorie (Courtney) *29:* 163, 164
Quidor, John *19:* 82
Quirk, John *62:* 170
Quirk, Thomas *12:* 81

R

Rackham, Arthur *15:* 32, 78, 214-227; *17:* 105, 115; *18:* 233; *19:* 254; *20:* 151; *22:* 129, 131, 132, 133; *23:* 175; *24:* 161, 181; *26:* 91; *32:* 118; *64:* 18; *100:* 9, 16, 203, 204; *YABC 1:* 25, 45, 55, 147; *2:* 103, 142, 173, 210
Racz, Michael *56:* 134
Raczka, Bob *191:* 155, 156
Radcliffe, Andrew *82:* 215
Rader, Laura *101:* 219; *197:* 147; *203:* 53
Radunsky, Vladimir *177:* 170; *192:* 30
Radzinski, Kandy *212:* 174
Rafilson, Sidney *11:* 172
Raglin, Tim *125:* 24
Raible, Alton *1:* 202, 203; *28:* 193; *35:* 181; *110:* 207
Raine, Patricia *82:* 74; *88:* 154
Ramá, Sue *173:* 45; *185:* 186; *190:* 184
Ramhorst, John *117:* 11
Ramirez, Gladys *177:* 19
Ramirez, Jose *207:* 27
Ramsey, James *16:* 41
Ramsey, Marcy Dunn *82:* 11; *180:* 186
Ramus, Michael *51:* 171
Rand, Paul *6:* 188
Rand, Ted *67:* 9, 10, 121, 123; *74:* 190; *84:* 170; *103:* 170; *112:* 6; *114:* 73; *139:* 168; *143:* 194; *156:* 154; *161:* 9, 10; *200:* 38; *204:* 7
Randazzo, Tony *81:* 98
Randell, William *55:* 54
Rane, Walter *93:* 144; *143:* 109; *184:* 126
Rankin, Joan *163:* 40; *212:* 176
Rankin, Laura *176:* 173, 174; *179:* 150
Ransome, Arthur *22:* 201

Ransome, James E. *74:* 137; *75:* 80; *84:* 181; *94:* 108; *117:* 115; *123:* 128, 129, 130; *158:* 101, 102; *159:* 205; *178:* 188, 189, 190; *216:* 114
Rantz, Don *119:* 184
Rao, Anthony *28:* 126
Raphael, Elaine *23:* 192; *71:* 24, 25
Rappaport, Eva *6:* 190
Raschka, Chris *80:* 187, 189, 190; *97:* 211; *115:* 210; *117:* 151, 152, 153, 154; *143:* 195; *145:* 153; *166:* 190, 191; *170:* 114; *207:* 140, 143, 144, 145; *208:* 82
Rash, Andy *158:* 178; *162:* 172; *210:* 204
Raskin, Ellen *2:* 208, 209; *4:* 142; *13:* 183; *22:* 68; *29:* 139; *36:* 134; *38:* 173, 174, 175, 176, 177, 178,179, 180, 181; *60:* 163; *86:* 81
Rathmann, Peggy *93:* 32; *94:* 168; *157:* 212, 214
Ratkus, Tony *77:* 133
Ratzkin, Lawrence *40:* 143
Rau, Margaret *9:* 157
Raverat, Gwen *YABC 1:* 152
Ravid, Joyce *61:* 73
Ravielli, Anthony *1:* 198; *3:* 168; *11:* 143
Ravilious, Robin *77:* 169
Rawlins, Donna *72:* 198; *73:* 15, 129
Rawlins, Janet *76:* 79
Rawlings, Steve *143:* 139; *151:* 54; *208:* 150
Rawlinson, Debbie *75:* 132
Ray, Deborah Kogan *8:* 164; *29:* 238; *50:* 112, 113; *62:* 119; *78:* 191; *203:* 149, 150, 151
Ray, Jane *96:* 166; *97:* 104; *152:* 208; *190:* 221; *196:* 165
Ray, Ralph *2:* 239; *5:* 73
Rayann, Omar *162:* 205; *186:* 29, 30
Rayevsky, Robert *64:* 17; *70:* 173; *80:* 204; *117:* 79; *190:* 187, 188
Raymond, Larry *31:* 108; *97:* 109
Rayner, Hugh *151:* 170
Rayner, Mary *22:* 207; *47:* 140; *72:* 191; *87:* 171, 172; *192:* 104
Rayner, Shoo
    See Rayner, Hugh
Raynes, John *71:* 19
Raynor, Dorka *28:* 168
Raynor, Paul *24:* 73
Rayyan, Omar *110:* 222; *112:* 17; *125:* 131
Razzi, James *10:* 127
Read, Alexander D. *20:* 45
Reader, Dennis *71:* 157
Reasoner, Charles *53:* 33, 36, 37
Rebenschied, Shane *203:* 76; *215:* 124
Reczuch, Karen *115:* 132; *145:* 131
Redlich, Ben *163:* 221; *198:* 193
Reddy, Mike *203:* 67
Reed, Joseph *116:* 139
Reed, Lynn Rowe *115:* 173; *171:* 146; *208:* 177; *215:* 144, 145
Reed, Mike *211:* 147; *215:* 131
Reed, Tom *34:* 171
Reeder, Colin *74:* 202; *77:* 113
Rees, Mary *134:* 219
Reese, Bob *60:* 135
Reeve, Philip *171:* 50
Reeves, Eira B. *130:* 173, 174; *141:* 151
Reeves, Rick *181:* 179
Reeves, Rosie *202:* 200
Regan, Dana *117:* 116
Regan, Laura *103:* 198; *153:* 206
Reichert, Renée *169:* 127
Reid, Barbara *82:* 178; *92:* 17; *93:* 169, 170
Reid, Stephen *19:* 213; *22:* 89
Reim, Melanie *104:* 151; *150:* 98
Reinert, Kirk *89:* 138; *195:* 129
Reinertson, Barbara *44:* 150; *62:* 103
Reiniger, Lotte *40:* 185
Reisberg, Mira *119:* 2
Reisch, Jesse *158:* 130
Reiser, Lynn *81:* 175; *138:* 184; *180:* 200
Reiss, John J. *23:* 193
Relf, Douglas *3:* 63

Relyea, C.M. *16:* 29; *31:* 153
Remi, Georges *13:* 184
Remington, Frederic *19:* 188; *41:* 178, 179, 180, 181, 183,184, 185, 186, 187, 188; *62:* 197
Remkiewicz, Frank *67:* 102; *77:* 171; *80:* 130; *113:* 107; *152:* 116; *152:* 211, 212; *157:* 148; *217:* 120, 138, 139, 140, 141
Rendon, Maria *116:* 141; 192; *134:* 152
Renfro, Ed *79:* 176
Renier, Aaron *202:* 141; *207:* 119
Renlie, Frank *11:* 200
Reschofsky, Jean *7:* 118
Rethi *60:* 181
Rethi, Lili *2:* 153; *36:* 156
Reusswig, William *3:* 267
Revell, Cindy *195:* 93
Rex, Adam *156:* 172; *169:* 91; *186:* 178, 179; *215:* 103
Rex, Michael *157:* 147; *191:* 159, 160
Rey, H.A. *1:* 182; *26:* 163, 164, 166, 167, 169; *69:* 172, 173, 174, 175; *86:* 195, 196, 197; *100:* 211; *YABC 2:* 17
Rey, Luis V. *201:* 162
Reynolds, Adrian *192:* 159, 160
Reynolds, Doris *5:* 71; *31:* 77
Reynolds, Peter H. *142:* 12; *179:* 175, 176; *202:* 113, 114
Rhead, Louis *31:* 91; *100:* 228
Rhodes, Andrew *38:* 204; *50:* 163; *54:* 76; *61:* 123, 124; *87:* 200
Ribbons, Ian *3:* 10; *37:* 161; *40:* 76
Ricci, Regolo *93:* 22; *164:* 148
Rice, Elizabeth *2:* 53, 214
Rice, Eve *34:* 174, 175; *91:* 172
Rice, James *22:* 210; *93:* 173
Rich, Anna *212:* 180
Rich, Martha *195:* 16
Richards, Chuck *170:* 154
Richards, George *40:* 116, 119, 121; *44:* 179
Richards, Henry *YABC 1:* 228, 231
Richardson, Ernest *2:* 144
Richardson, Frederick *18:* 27, 31
Richardson, John *110:* 88
Richman, Hilda *26:* 132
Richmond, George *24:* 179
Riddell, Chris *114:* 170, 195; *166:* 179; *199:* 164, 166, 167
Riddle, Tohby *74:* 204; *151:* 179
Riding, Peter *63:* 195
Rieniets, Judy King *14:* 28
Riger, Bob *2:* 166
Riggio, Anita *73:* 191; *85:* 63; *137:* 184; *172:* 165
Riley, Jon *74:* 70
Riley, Kenneth *22:* 230
Riley, Terry *203:* 100
Riley-Webb, Charlotte *153:* 143
Rinaldi, Angelo *165:* 60, 69
Ringgold, Faith *71:* 162; *114:* 173, 174, 176; *187:* 160, 161, 163
Ringi, Kjell *12:* 171
Rios, Tere
    See Versace, Marie
Rioux, Jo *215:* 110
Ripper, Charles L. *3:* 175
Ripplinger, Henry *117:* 31
Ritchie, Scot *217:* 145
Ritchie, William *74:* 183
Ritter, John *175:* 14
Ritz, Karen *41:* 117; *72:* 239; *87:* 125; *102:* 7; *106:* 6
Rivas, Victor *209:* 193
Rivers, Ruth *178:* 193
Rivkin, Jay *15:* 230
Rivoche, Paul *45:* 125
Roach, Marilynne *9:* 158
Robbin, Jodi *44:* 156, 159
Robbins, Frank *42:* 167
Robbins, Ken *147:* 191, 192
Robbins, Ruth *52:* 102

Roberts, Cliff *4:* 126
Roberts, David *154:* 4, 6; *191:* 162; *196:* 184; *197:* 105; *210:* 257
Roberts, Doreen *4:* 230; *28:* 105
Roberts, Jim *22:* 166; *23:* 69; *31:* 110
Roberts, Tony *109:* 195, 214
Roberts, W. *22:* 2, 3
Robertson, M.P. *197:* 153
Robins, Arthur *137:* 172; *151:* 225; *204:* 161
Robinson, Aminah Brenda Lynn *86:* 205; *103:* 55; *159:* 175
Robinson, Charles [1870-1937] *17:* 157, 171, 172, 173, 175, 176; *24:* 207; *25:* 204; *YABC 2:* 308, 309, 310, 331
Robinson, Charles *3:* 53; *5:* 14; *6:* 193; *7:* 150; *7:* 183; *8:* 38; *9:* 81; *13:* 188; *14:* 248, 249; *23:* 149; *26:* 115; *27:* 48; *28:* 191; *32:* 28; *35:* 210; *36:* 37; *48:* 96; *52:* 33; *53:* 157; *56:* 15; *62:* 142; *77:* 41; *111:* 148
Robinson, Jerry *3:* 262
Robinson, Joan G. *7:* 184
Robinson, Lolly *90:* 227
Robinson, T.H. *17:* 179, 181, 182, 183; *29:* 254
Robinson, W. Heath *17:* 185, 187, 189, 191, 193, 195, 197, 199, 202; *23:* 167; *25:* 194; *29:* 150; *YABC 1:* 44; *2:* 183
Rocco, John *187:* 4; *188:* 151; *208:* 180, 181, 182; *213:* 94
Roche, Christine *41:* 98
Roche, Denis *99:* 184; *180:* 32; *196:* 168
Roche, P.K. *57:* 151, 152
Rocker, Fermin *7:* 34; *13:* 21; *31:* 40; *40:* 190,191
Rocklen, Margot *101:* 181
Rockwell, Anne *5:* 147; *33:* 171, 173; *71:* 166, 167,168; *114:* 183, 184; *194:* 152, 155
Rockwell, Gail *7:* 186
Rockwell, Harlow *33:* 171, 173, 175
Rockwell, Lizzy *114:* 182; *162:* 182; *185:* 189
Rockwell, Norman *23:* 39, 196, 197, 199, 200, 203, 204, 207; *41:* 140, 143; *123:* 47; *YABC 2:* 60
Rockwood, Richard *119:* 75
Rodanas, Kristina *156:* 183, 184
Rodegast, Roland *43:* 100
Rodgers, Frank *69:* 177
Rodriguez, Albert G. *182:* 50
Rodriguez, Christina *184:* 12
Rodriguez, Edel *204:* 86
Rodriguez, Joel *16:* 65
Rodriguez, Robert *145:* 145; *212:* 33
Rodriguez-Howard, Pauline *177:* 18
Roe, Monika *210:* 94
Roeckelein, Katrina *134:* 223
Roennfeldt, Robert *66:* 243
Roever, J.M. *4:* 119; *26:* 170
Roffey, Maureen *33:* 142, 176, 177
Rogasky, Barbara *46:* 90
Rogé *173:* 160
Rogers, Carol *2:* 262; *6:* 164; *26:* 129
Rogers, Chris M. *150:* 59; *196:* 61
Rogers, Forest *87:* 160; *101:* 76
Rogers, Frances *10:* 130
Rogers, Gregory *104:* 76; *126:* 57; *171:* 26
Rogers, Jacqueline *78:* 249; *80:* 34; *86:* 54 *103:* 70; *115:* 72; *129:* 173; *131:* 57, 225; *143:* 211; *153:* 100; *193:* 186; *203:* 51; *213:* 144, 145, 146; *214:* 142
Rogers, Sherry *191:* 66
Rogers, Walter S. *31:* 135, 138; *67:* 65, 168; *100:* 81
Rogers, William A. *15:* 151, 153, 154; *33:* 35
Rogoff, Barbara *95:* 20
Rohmann, Eric *103:* 152; *198:* 151
Rojankovsky, Feodor *6:* 134, 136; *10:* 183; *21:* 128,129, 130; *25:* 110; *28:* 42; *68:* 120
Rolfsen, Alf *62:* 15
Rolston, Steve *209:* 154
Romain, Trevor *134:* 157
Roman, Barbara J. *103:* 171

Romas *114:* 111; *165:* 63
Romano, Robert *64:* 68
Romero, Alejandro *187:* 185
Roos, Maryn *168:* 198
Root, Barry *80:* 212; *90:* 196; *146:* 78; *156:* 165; *159:* 161; *182:* 18, 172
Root, Kimberly Bulcken *86:* 72; *98:* 21; *108:* 111; *127:* 114; *159:* 162; *176:* 134; *192:* 163
Roper, Bob *65:* 153
Roraback, Robin *111:* 156
Rorer, Abigail *43:* 222; *85:* 155
Rosales, Melodye *80:* 35
Rosamilia, Patricia *36:* 120
Rose, Carl *5:* 62
Rose, David S. *29:* 109; *70:* 120
Rose, Gerald *68:* 200, 201; *86:* 48
Rose, Ted *93:* 178
Rosen, Elizabeth *205:* 137
Rosenbaum, Jonathan *50:* 46
Rosenberg, Amye *74:* 207, 208
Rosenberry, Vera *87:* 22, 26; *144:* 212, 213; *158:* 120
Rosenblum, Richard *11:* 202; *18:* 18
Rosenstiehl, Agnès *203:* 153
Rosier, Lydia *16:* 236; *20:* 104; *21:* 109; *22:* 125; *30:* 151, 158; *42:* 128; *45:* 214; *77:* 227, 228
Rosing, Jens *85:* 142
Ross
    See Thomson, Ross
Ross, Christine *83:* 172, 173
Ross, Clare Romano *3:* 123; *21:* 45; *48:* 199
Ross, Dave *32:* 152; *57:* 108
Ross, Graham *199:* 4
Ross, Herbert *37:* 78
Ross, John *3:* 123; *21:* 45
Ross, Johnny *32:* 190
Ross, Larry *47:* 168; *60:* 62
Ross, Ruth *109:* 233
Ross, Tony *17:* 204; *56:* 132; *65:* 176, 177, 179; *90:* 123; *123:* 186, 187, 190; *130:* 188, 190, 191, 192; *132:* 242; *174:* 159; *176:* 181, 182, 183; *202:* 198
Rossetti, Dante Gabriel *20:* 151, 153
Rostant, Larry *180:* 221; *194:* 108; *195:* 96; *197:* 12; *207:* 53; *210:* 189
Roth, Arnold *4:* 238; *21:* 133
Roth, Julie Jersild *180:* 206
Roth, Marci *135:* 223
Roth, R.G. *184:* 50
Roth, Rob *105:* 98; *146:* 41
Roth, Robert *176:* 159
Roth, Roger *61:* 128; *190:* 192
Roth, Ruby *216:* 185
Roth, Stephanie *136:* 171, 172
Roth, Susan L. *80:* 38; *93:* 78; *134:* 165, 166; *181:* 145, 146
Rothenberg, Joani Keller *162:* 190, 191
Rothman, Michael *139:* 62; *184:* 34 *Rotman, Jeffrey L. *145:* 30
Rotondo, Pat *32:* 158
Roughsey, Dick *35:* 186
Rouille, M. *11:* 96
Rounds, Glen *8:* 173; *9:* 171; *12:* 56; *32:* 194; *40:* 230; *51:* 161, 162, 166; *56:* 149; *70:* 198, 199; *YABC 1:* 1, 2, 3; *112:* 163
Roundtree, Katherine *114:* 88; *168:* 102
Rovetch, Lissa *201:* 164
Rowan, Evadne *52:* 51
Rowe, Eric *111:* 161
Rowe, Gavin *27:* 144; *72:* 47; *88:* 201
Rowe, John *132:* 70, 71; *180:* 126
Rowell, Kenneth *40:* 72
Rowen, Amy *52:* 143
Rowena *116:* 101
Rowland, Andrew *164:* 136
Rowland, Jada *83:* 73
Rowles, Daphne *58:* 24
Roy, Jeroo *27:* 229; *36:* 110
Royo *118:* 32; *144:* 105, 106, 108; *165:* 19; *166:* 166

Rubel, Nicole *18:* 255; *20:* 59; *81:* 66, 67; *95:* 169, 170; *119:* 60; *135:* 177, 179, 180; *169:* 68; *181:* 150
Rubel, Reina *33:* 217
Rud, Borghild *6:* 15
Ruddell, Gary *110:* 238; *116:* 207
Rudolph, Norman Guthrie *17:* 13
Rue, Leonard Lee III *37:* 164
Rueda, Claudia *183:* 170, 171
Ruelle, Karen Gray *126:* 193
Ruff, Donna *50:* 173; *72:* 203; *78:* 49; *80:* 120,121; *93:* 162; *164:* 121
Ruffins, Reynold *10:* 134, 135; *41:* 191, 192, 193, 194, 195, 196; *125:* 187, 188, 189; *162:* 197
Ruhlin, Roger *34:* 44
Rui, Paolo *217:* 115
Ruiz, Art *95:* 154; *110:* 91
Rumford, James *193:* 167
Runnerstroem, Bengt Arne *75:* 161
Ruse, Margaret *24:* 155
Rush, Ken *98:* 74
Rush, Peter *42:* 75
Russell, Charles M. *167:* 171
Russell, E.B. *18:* 177, 182
Russell, Jim *53:* 134
Russell, P. Craig *80:* 196; *146:* 102; *162:* 186
Russo, Marisabina *84:* 51; *106:* 164; *151:* 183; *188:* 153, 154, 155, 156
Russo, Susan *30:* 182; *36:* 144
Russon, Mary *87:* 145
Ruth, Greg *183:* 125
Ruth, Rod *9:* 161
Rutherford, Alexa *110:* 108
Rutherford, Jenny *78:* 5
Rutherford, Meg *25:* 174; *34:* 178, 179; *69:* 73; *72:* 31
Rutland, Jonathan *31:* 126
Ruurs, Margriet *147:* 195
Ruzzier, Sergio *159:* 176, 177; *163:* 184; *210:* 214, 216
Ryan, Amy *188:* 50
Ryan, Will *86:* 134
Ryden, Hope *8:* 176
Rylant, Cynthia *112:* 170, 172
Rymer, Alta M. *34:* 181
Ryniak, Christopher *178:* 11
Rystedt, Rex *49:* 80

S

Saaf, Chuck *49:* 179
Saaf, Donald *101:* 220; *124:* 180
Sabaka, Donna R. *21:* 172
Sabin, Robert *45:* 35; *60:* 30; *99:* 161
Sabuda, Robert *170:* 166, 167, 168
Sacker, Amy *16:* 100
Saelig, S.M. *129:* 73; *173:* 59
Saffioti, Lino *36:* 176; *48:* 60
Saflund, Birgitta *94:* 2
Sagsoorian, Paul *12:* 183; *22:* 154; *33:* 106; *87:* 152
Sahara, Tony *168:* 106; *177:* 181; *178:* 228; *186:* 132; *207:* 89
Sahlberg, Myron *57:* 165
Saidens, Amy *145:* 162; *191:* 131; *210:* 129
Saint Exupery, Antoine de *20:* 157
Saint James, Synthia *152:* 220; *188:* 90; *200:* 7
Sakai, Komako *213:* 148
Saldutti, Denise *39:* 186; *57:* 178
Sale, Morton *YABC 2:* 31
Sale, Tim *153:* 177
Salerno, Steven *150:* 79; *176:* 188; *202:* 39; *216:* 190
Salter, George *72:* 128, 130
Saltzberg, Barney *135:* 184, 185; *194:* 160
Saltzman, David *86:* 209
Salwowski, Mark *71:* 54

Salzman, Yuri *86:* 12
Sambourne, Linley *YABC 2:* 181
Sampson, Katherine *9:* 197
Samson, Anne S. *2:* 216
San Souci, Daniel *40:* 200; *96:* 199, 200; *113:* 171; *157:* 149; *170:* 69; *192:* 167, 168
Sancha, Sheila *38:* 185
Sanchez, Enrique O. *155:* 84
Sand, George X. *45:* 182
Sandberg, Lasse *15:* 239, 241
Sanders, Beryl *39:* 173
Sanderson, Ruth *21:* 126; *24:* 53; *28:* 63; *33:* 67; *41:* 48, 198, 199, 200, 201, 202, 203; *43:* 79; *46:* 36,44; *47:* 102; *49:* 58; *62:* 121, 122; *85:* 3; *109:* 207, 208, 209, 210; *172:* 157, 158
Sandia *119:* 74
Sandin, Joan *4:* 36; *6:* 194; *7:* 177; *12:* 145,185; *20:* 43; *21:* 74; *26:* 144; *27:* 142; *28:* 224, 225; *38:* 86; *41:* 46; *42:* 35; *59:* 6; *80:* 136; *94:* 188; *140:* 116; *153:* 179, 180; *197:* 168
Sandland, Reg *39:* 215
Sandoz, Edouard *26:* 45, 47
Sanford, John *66:* 96, 97
Sanger, Amy Wilson *205:* 140
Sankey, Tom *72:* 103
Sano, Kazuhiko *153:* 208; *195:* 171; *203:* 21
Santat, Dan *188:* 160
Santiago, Wilfred *210:* 48
Santore, Charles *54:* 139; *200:* 171, 172
Santoro, Christopher *74:* 215
Santos, Jesse J. *99:* 24
Sapieha, Christine *1:* 180
Saport, Linda *123:* 137, 138; *215:* 29
Sara
  See De La Roche Saint Andre, Anne
Sarcone-Roach, Julia *215:* 158
Sardinha, Rick *175:* 151
Sarg, Tony *YABC 2:* 236
Sargent, Claudia *64:* 181
Sargent, Robert *2:* 217
Saris *1:* 33
Sarony *YABC 2:* 170
Saroff, Phyllis V. *202:* 160
Sasaki, Goro *170:* 46
Sasaki, Ellen Joy *216:* 49
Sasek, Miroslav *16:* 239, 240, 241, 242
Sassman, David *9:* 79
Satty *29:* 203, 205
Sauber, Robert *40:* 183; *76:* 256; *78:* 154; *87:* 92
Saunders, Dave *85:* 163, 164, 165
Savadier, Elivia *84:* 50; *145:* 45; *164:* 206
Savage, Naomi *56:* 172
Savage, Steele *10:* 203; *20:* 77; *35:* 28
Savage, Stephen *174:* 182
Savio *76:* 4
Savitt, Sam *8:* 66, 182; *15:* 278; *20:* 96; *24:* 192; *28:* 98
Sawyer, Kem Knapp *84:* 228, 229
Say, Allen *28:* 178; *69:* 182, 183, 232; *110:* 194, 195,196; *161:* 154, 155
Sayles, Elizabeth *82:* 93; *105:* 155; *109:* 116; *180:* 64
Scabrini, Janet *13:* 191; *44:* 128
Scanlan, Peter *83:* 27; *153:* 165; *187:* 149
Scanlon, Paul *83:* 87
Scannell, Reece *105:* 105
Scarry, Huck *35:* 204, 205
Scarry, Richard *2:* 220, 221; *18:* 20; *35:* 193, 194, 195,196, 197, 198, 199, 200, 201, 202; *75:* 165, 167, 168
Schachner, Judith Byron *88:* 180; *92:* 163; *93:* 102; *142:* 82; *178:* 199, 200; *190:* 140
Schade, Susan *205:* 21
Schaeffer, Mead *18:* 81, 94; *21:* 137, 138, 139; *47:* 128
Schaffer, Amanda *90:* 206
Schanzer, Rosalyn *138:* 192, 193
Scharl, Josef *20:* 132; *22:* 128

Scheel, Lita *11:* 230
Scheffler, Axel *180:* 23, 24
Scheib, Ida *29:* 28
Schermer, Judith *30:* 184
Schick, Eleanor *82:* 210, 211; *144:* 222
Schick, Joel *16:* 160; *17:* 167; *22:* 12; *27:* 176; *31:* 147, 148; *36:* 23; *38:* 64; *45:* 116, 117; *52:* 5, 85; *104:* 159
Schields, Gretchen *75:* 171, 203
Schindelman, Joseph *1:* 74; *4:* 101; *12:* 49; *26:* 51; *40:* 146; *56:* 158; *73:* 40
Schindler, Edith *7:* 22
Schindler, S.D. *38:* 107; *46:* 196; *74:* 162; *75:* 172, 173; *99:* 133; *112:* 177; *118:* 185, 186; *121:* 71; *136:* 159; *143:* 45; *149:* 120; *156:* 30; *169:* 135; *171:* 161, 162, 163; *172:* 9; *186:* 163; *194:* 109; *195:* 35; *198:* 170, 171, 172
Schlesinger, Bret *7:* 77
Schmid, Eleanore *12:* 188; *126:* 196, 197
Schmiderer, Dorothy *19:* 224
Schmidt, Bill *73:* 34; *76:* 220, 222, 224
Schmidt, Elizabeth *15:* 242
Schmidt, George Paul *132:* 122
Schmidt, Karen Lee *54:* 12; *71:* 174; *92:* 56; *94:* 190, 191; *127:* 103
Schmidt, Lynette *76:* 205
Schmitz, Tamara *207:* 147
Schneider, Christine M. *171:* 165
Schneider, Howie *181:* 159
Schneider, Rex *29:* 64; *44:* 171
Schnurr, Edward *170:* 62
Schoberle, Cecile *80:* 200; *92:* 134
Schoenherr, Ian *32:* 83; *173:* 41
Schoenherr, John *1:* 146, 147, 173; *3:* 39, 139; *17:* 75; *29:* 72; *32:* 83; *37:* 168, 169, 170; *43:* 164, 165; *45:* 160, 162; *51:* 127; *66:* 196, 197, 198; *68:* 83; *72:* 240; *75:* 225; *88:* 176
Scholder, Fritz *69:* 103
Schomburg, Alex *13:* 23
Schongut, Emanuel *4:* 102; *15:* 186; *47:* 218, 219; *52:* 147, 148, 149, 150; *185:* 27
Schoonover, Frank *17:* 107; *19:* 81, 190, 233; *22:* 88,129; *24:* 189; *31:* 88; *41:* 69; *YABC 2:* 282, 316
Schories, Pat *164:* 210
Schottland, Miriam *22:* 172
Schramm, Ulrik *2:* 16; *14:* 112
Schreiber, Elizabeth Anne *13:* 193
Schreiber, Ralph W. *13:* 193
Schreiter, Rick *14:* 97; *23:* 171; *41:* 247; *49:* 131
Schroades, John *214:* 129
Schroeder, Binette *56:* 128, 129
Schroeder, E. Peter *12:* 112
Schroeder, Ted *11:* 160; *15:* 189; *30:* 91; *34:* 43
Schrotter, Gustav *22:* 212; *30:* 225
Schubert, Dieter *101:* 167, 168; *217:* 151, 152, 153, 155
Schubert, Ingrid *217:* 151, 152, 153, 155
Schubert-Gabrys, Ingrid *101:* 167, 168
Schucker, James *31:* 163
Schuett, Stacey *72:* 137; *208:* 204
Schulder, Lili *146:* 29
Schulke, Debra *57:* 167
Schulke, Flip *57:* 167
Schulz, Barbara *167:* 24
Schulz, Charles M. *10:* 137, 138, 139, 140, 141, 142; *118:* 192, 193, 194, 196, 199
Schutzer, Dena *109:* 32
Schwark, Mary Beth *51:* 155; *72:* 175
Schwartz, Amy *47:* 191; *82:* 100; *83:* 178, 179, 180,181; *129:* 107; *131:* 197, 198; *189:* 166, 168
Schwartz, Carol *124:* 41; *130:* 199
Schwartz, Charles *8:* 184
Schwartz, Daniel *46:* 37
Schwartz, Joanie *124:* 170
Schwartzberg, Joan *3:* 208

Schwarz, Viviane *204:* 132
Schweitzer, Iris *2:* 137; *6:* 207
Schweninger, Ann *29:* 172; *82:* 246; *159:* 202; *168:* 166; *211:* 193
Schwinger, Laurence *84:* 44; *91:* 61
Scofield, Penrod *61:* 107; *62:* 160
Scott, Anita Walker *7:* 38
Scott, Art *39:* 41
Scott, Frances Gruse *38:* 43
Scott, Julian *34:* 126
Scott, Roszel *33:* 238
Scott, Sally *87:* 27
Scott, Steve *166:* 230, 231; *171:* 93
Scott, Trudy *27:* 172
Scotton, Rob *214:* 183
Scrace, Carolyn *143:* 95, 96
Scrambly, Crab *198:* 196
Scribner, Joanne *14:* 236; *29:* 78; *33:* 185; *34:* 208; *78:* 75; *164:* 237; *203:* 73
Scrofani, Joseph *31:* 65; *74:* 225
Scroggs, Kirk *187:* 169
Seaman, Mary Lott *34:* 64
Searle, Ronald *24:* 98; *42:* 172, 173, 174, 176, 177, 179; *66:* 73, 74; *70:* 205, 206, 207
Searle, Townley *36:* 85
Sebree, Charles *18:* 65
Sedacca, Joseph M. *11:* 25; *22:* 36
Seder, Jason *108:* 102
Seeger, Laura Vaccaro *172:* 162
Seegmiller, Don *174:* 57
Seely, David *164:* 173
Seeley, Laura L. *97:* 105
Segal, John *178:* 202
Segar, E.C. *61:* 179, 181
Segur, Adrienne *27:* 121
Seibold, J. Otto *83:* 188, 190, 191; *149:* 212, 214, 215, 216; *196:* 177, 179; *215:* 204
Seignobosc, Francoise *21:* 145, 146
Sejima, Yoshimasa *8:* 187
Selig, Sylvie *13:* 199
Seltzer, Isadore *6:* 18; *133:* 59
Seltzer, Meyer *17:* 214
Selven, Maniam *144:* 133
Selway, Martina *169:* 157
Selznick, Brian *79:* 192; *104:* 25; *117:* 175; *126:* 156; *134:* 171; *158:* 76, 78; *169:* 70; *171:* 172, 173; *191:* 106; *192:* 130; *197:* 158; *203:* 35; *205:* 92; *210:* 219, 220, 221, 222
Sempe, Jean-Jacques *47:* 92; *YABC 2:* 109
Sendak, Maurice *1:* 135, 190; *3:* 204; *7:* 142; *15:* 199; *17:* 210; *27:* 181, 182, 183, 185, 186, 187, 189,190, 191, 192, 193, 194, 195, 197, 198, 199, 203; *28:* 181, 182; *32:* 108; *33:* 148, 149; *35:* 238; *44:* 180, 181; *45:* 97, 99; *46:* 174; *73:* 225; *91:* 10, 11 *YABC1:* 167; *113:* 163, 165, 167, 168; *118:* 153; *127:* 161
Senders, Marci *180:* 79
Sengler, Johanna *18:* 256
Senn, Steve *60:* 145
Seredy, Kate *1:* 192; *14:* 20, 21; *17:* 210
Sergeant, John *6:* 74
Serra, Sebastía *212:* 215
Servello, Joe *10:* 144; *24:* 139; *40:* 91; *70:* 130, 131; *146:* 159
Seton, Ernest Thompson *18:* 260-269, 271
Seuss, Dr.
  See Geisel, Theodor
Severin, John Powers *7:* 62
Sewall, Marcia *15:* 8; *22:* 170; *37:* 171, 172, 173; *39:* 73; *45:* 209; *62:* 117; *69:* 185, 186; *71:* 212; *90:* 232; *96:* 127; *102:* 101; *107:* 129; *119:* 176, 177, 178, 180
Seward, James *70:* 35
Seward, Prudence *16:* 243
Sewell, Helen *3:* 186; *15:* 308; *33:* 102; *38:* 189, 190, 191, 192
Seymour, Stephen *54:* 21
Sfar, Joann *182:* 183
Shachat, Andrew *82:* 179

Shadbolt, Robert *203:* 68
Shahn, Ben *39:* 178; *46:* 193
Shalansky, Len *38:* 167
Shanks, Anne Zane *10:* 149
Shannon, David *57:* 137; *107:* 184; *112:* 216; *135:* 12; *152:* 223, 224, 225; *158:* 192; *212:* 159, 160, 163
Sharkey, Niamh *213:* 152
Sharp, Paul *52:* 60
Sharp, William *6:* 131; *19:* 241; *20:* 112; *25:* 141
Sharratt, Nick *102:* 207, 208; *104:* 163; *153:* 198; *175:* 176; *192:* 208; *199:* 141, 142, 143, 184, 187, 188
Shaw, Barclay *74:* 14, 16; *118:* 138
Shaw, Charles *21:* 135; *38:* 187; *47:* 124; *126:* 219
Shaw, Charles G. *13:* 200
Shaw-Smith, Emma *144:* 117
Shea, Edmund *56:* 19
Shearer, Ted *43:* 193, 194, 195, 196
Sheban, Chris *182:* 185; *190:* 102, 104; *202:* 28; *204:* 112, 114; *209:* 150; *210:* 107
Shecter, Ben *16:* 244; *25:* 109; *33:* 188, 191; *41:* 77
Shed, Greg *74:* 94; *84:* 204; *129:* 149, *167:* 91; *179:* 192
Sheeban, Chris *144:* 190; *158:* 163
Shefcik, James *48:* 221, 222; *60:* 141
Shefelman, Karl *58:* 168
Shefelman, Tom *204:* 137
Shefts, Joelle *48:* 210
Shein, Bob *139:* 189
Sheinkin, Stephen *204:* 139
Shekerjian, Haig *16:* 245
Shekerjian, Regina *16:* 245; *25:* 73
Sheldon, David *184:* 174; *185:* 204; *211:* 189
Shelley, John *186:* 223
Shemie, Bonnie *96:* 207
Shenton, Edward *45:* 187, 188, 189; *YABC 1:* 218, 219, 221
Shepard, Ernest H. *3:* 193; *4:* 74; *16:* 101; *17:* 109; *25:* 148; *33:* 152, 199, 200, 201, 202, 203, 204, 205, 206,207; *46:* 194; *98:* 114; *100:* 111, 178, 179, 217, 219, 220,221; *YABC 1:* 148, 153, 174, 176, 180, 181
Shepard, Mary *4:* 210; *22:* 205; *30:* 132, 133; *54:* 150, 152, 153, 157, 158; *59:* 108, 109, 111; *100:* 246
Shepherd, Amanda *198:* 14
Shepherd, Irana *171:* 112
Sheppard, Kate *195:* 176
Shepperson, Rob *96:* 153; *177:* 163; *178:* 204; *197:* 34; *205:* 108
Sheridan, Brian *196:* 193
Sherman, Theresa *27:* 167
Sherwan, Earl *3:* 196
Shields, Charles *10:* 150; *36:* 63
Shields, Leonard *13:* 83, 85, 87
Shiffman, Lena *139:* 167; *168:* 136
Shigley, Neil K. *66:* 219
Shillabeer, Mary *35:* 74
Shilston, Arthur *49:* 61; *62:* 58
Shimin, Symeon *1:* 93; *2:* 128, 129; *3:* 202; *7:* 85; *11:* 177; *12:* 139; *13:* 202, 203; *27:* 138; *28:* 65; *35:* 129; *36:* 130; *48:* 151; *49:* 59; *56:* 63, 65, 153
Shimizu, Yuko *215:* 197
Shine, Andrea *104:* 165; *128:* 34
Shinn, Everett *16:* 148; *18:* 229; *21:* 149, 150, 151; *24:* 218
Shinn, Florence Scovel *63:* 133, 135
Shore, Robert *27:* 54; *39:* 192, 193; *YABC 2:* 200
Shortall, Leonard *4:* 144; *8:* 196; *10:* 166; *19:* 227, 228, 229, 230; *25:* 78; *28:* 66, 167; *33:* 127; *52:* 125; *73:* 12, 212
Shortt, T.M. *27:* 36
Shpitalnik, Vladimir *83:* 194
Shropshire, Sandy *170:* 191
Shtainments, Leon *32:* 161

Shulevitz, Uri *3:* 198, 199; *17:* 85; *22:* 204; *27:* 212; *28:* 184; *50:* 190, 191, 192, 193, 194, 195, 196,197, 198, 199, 201; *106:* 181, 182, 183; *165:* 203, 205; *166:* 138
Shulman, Dee *180:* 140
Shupe, Bobbi *139:* 80, 81
Shute, A.B. *67:* 196
Shute, Linda *46:* 59; *74:* 118
Siberell, Anne *29:* 193
Sibley, Don *1:* 39; *12:* 196; *31:* 47
Sibthorp, Fletcher *94:* 111, 112
Sidjakov, Nicolas *18:* 274
Siebel, Fritz *3:* 120; *17:* 145
Siebold, J. Otto *158:* 227
Siegel, Hal *74:* 246
Sieger, Ted *189:* 172
Siegl, Helen *12:* 166; *23:* 216; *34:* 185, 186
Silin-Palmer, Pamela *184:* 102
Sill, John *140:* 194; *141:* 157
Sills, Joyce *5:* 199
Silva, Simon *108:* 122
Silver, Maggie *85:* 210
Silveria, Gordon *96:* 44
Silverstein, Alvin *8:* 189
Silverstein, Shel *33:* 211; *92:* 209, 210
Silverstein, Virginia *8:* 189
Silvey, Joe *135:* 203
Simard, Remy *95:* 156
Simmons, Elly *110:* 2; *127:* 69; *134:* 181
Simon, Eric M. *7:* 82
Simon, Hilda *28:* 189
Simon, Howard *2:* 175; *5:* 132; *19:* 199; *32:* 163, 164, 165
Simont, Marc *2:* 119; *4:* 213; *9:* 168; *13:* 238,240; *14:* 262; *16:* 179; *18:* 221; *26:* 210; *33:* 189, 194; *44:* 132; *58:* 122; *68:* 117; *73:* 204, 205, 206; *74:* 221; *126:* 199, 200; *133:* 195; *164:* 128
Sims, Agnes *54:* 152
Sims, Blanche *44:* 116; *57:* 129; *75:* 179, 180; *77:* 92; *104:* 192; *152:* 117; *156:* 160; *160:* 70; *168:* 174, 175; *198:* 17
Singer, Edith G. *2:* 30
Singer, Gloria *34:* 56; *36:* 43
Singer, Julia *28:* 190
Singh, Jen *178:* 146
Sinquette, Jaclyn *215:* 83
Simont, Marc *163:* 40
Siracusa, Catherine *68:* 135; *82:* 218
Sís, Peter *67:* 179, 181, 183, 184, 185; *96:* 96, 98; *106:* 193, 194, 195; *149:* 224, 226; *180:* 177; *192:* 180, 182
Sivard, Robert *26:* 124
Sivertson, Liz *116:* 84
Skardinski, Stanley *23:* 144; *32:* 84; *66:* 122; *84:* 108
Slack, Michael *185:* 108; *189:* 173, 174
Slackman, Charles B. *12:* 201
Slade, Christian *193:* 187; *204:* 134
Slade, Paul *61:* 170
Slark, Albert *99:* 212; *205:* 161
Slater, Rod *25:* 167
Slavin, Bill *182:* 14, 15; *196:* 90; *199:* 148, 149, 150; *217:* 20
Sloan, Joseph *16:* 68
Sloane, Eric *21:* 3; *52:* 153, 154, 155, 156, 157, 158, 160
Sloat, Teri *164:* 231
Slobodkin, Louis *1:* 200; *3:* 232; *5:* 168; *13:* 251; *15:* 13, 88; *26:* 173, 174, 175, 176, 178, 179; *60:* 180
Slobodkina, Esphyr *1:* 201
Slonim, David *166:* 167, 168
Small, David *50:* 204, 205; *79:* 44; *95:* 189, 190, 191; *126:* 203, 204; *136:* 119; *143:* 201, 202, 203; *144:* 246; *150:* 5; *161:* 176; *183:* 181, 182, 183, 184; *200:* 211; *212:* 86; *216:* 202, 203, 204
Small, W. *33:* 113

Smalley, Janet *1:* 154
Smath, Jerry *198:* 179, 180
Smedley, William T. *34:* 129
Smee, David *14:* 78; *62:* 30
Smee, Nicola *167:* 156
Smith, A.G., Jr. *35:* 182
Smith, Ali *204:* 68
Smith, Alvin *1:* 31, 229; *13:* 187; *27:* 216; *28:* 226; *48:* 149; *49:* 60
Smith, Andy *188:* 20; *207:* 151
Smith, Anne *194:* 147
Smith, Anne Warren *41:* 212
Smith, Barry *75:* 183
Smith, Brian *200:* 183
Smith, Carl *36:* 41
Smith, Cat Bowman *146:* 39; *164:* 219; *201:* 55, 184
Smith, Craig *97:* 197; *172:* 175; *206:* 40; *215:* 19; *217:* 129
Smith, Donald A. *178:* 7
Smith, Doris Susan *41:* 139
Smith, Douglas *189:* 159; *213:* 170
Smith, Duane *171:* 152; *208:* 97
Smith, E. Boyd *19:* 70; *22:* 89; *26:* 63; *YABC 1:* 4, 5, 240, 248, 249
Smith, Edward J. *4:* 224
Smith, Elwood H. *157:* 231; *181:* 79; *203:* 160, 161, 162
Smith, Eunice Young *5:* 170
Smith, Gary *113:* 216
Smith, George *102:* 169
Smith, Howard *19:* 196
Smith, J. Gerard *95:* 42
Smith, Jacqueline Bardner *27:* 108; *39:* 197
Smith, Jay J. *61:* 119
Smith, Jeff *93:* 191
Smith, Jessie Willcox *15:* 91; *16:* 95; *18:* 231; *19:* 57, 242; *21:* 29, 156, 157, 158, 159, 160, 161; *34:* 65; *100:* 223; *YABC 1:* 6; *2:* 180, 185, 191, 311, 325
Smith, Jos. A. *52:* 131; *72:* 120; *74:* 151; *84:* 147, 148; *85:* 146; *87:* 96; *94:* 219; *96:* 97; *104:* 33; *108:* 126, 127, 128; *111:* 140; *136:* 145; *181:* 173; *200:* 213; *201:* 94
Smith, Kenneth R. *47:* 182
Smith, Keri *216:* 60
Smith, Kevin Warren *89:* 112
Smith, Kristin *209:* 197
Smith, L.H. *35:* 174
Smith, Lane *76:* 211, 213; *88:* 115; *105:* 202, 203,204, 205; *131:* 207; *160:* 217, 221; *179:* 183, 184, 185, 186; *199:* 122, 123, 124, 126
Smith, Lee *29:* 32
Smith, Linell Nash *2:* 195
Smith, Maggie Kaufman *13:* 205; *35:* 191; *110:* 158; *178:* 226; *190:* 204; *209:* 145
Smith, Mavis *101:* 219
Smith, Moishe *33:* 155
Smith, Philip *44:* 134; *46:* 203
Smith, Ralph Crosby *2:* 267; *49:* 203
Smith, Robert D. *5:* 63
Smith, Sally J. *84:* 55
Smith, Susan Carlton *12:* 208
Smith, Terry *12:* 106; *33:* 158
Smith, Virginia *3:* 157; *33:* 72
Smith, William A. *1:* 36; *10:* 154; *25:* 65
Smith-Moore, J.J. *98:* 147
Smolinski, Dick *84:* 217
Smoljan, Joe *112:* 201
Smollin, Mike *39:* 203
Smyth, Iain *105:* 207
Smyth, M. Jane *12:* 15
Smythe, Fiona *151:* 213
Smythe, Theresa *141:* 37
Snair, Andy *176:* 4
Sneed, Brad *125:* 25; *191:* 175, 176; *211:* 194
Snyder, Andrew A. *30:* 212
Snyder, Jerome *13:* 207; *30:* 173
Snyder, Joel *28:* 163
So, Meilo *162:* 201; *208:* 188

Soentpiet, Chris K. *97:* 208; *110:* 33; *159:* 184; *161:* 10; *163:* 130
Sofia *1:* 62; *5:* 90; *32:* 166; *86:* 43
Sofilas, Mark *93:* 157
Sogabe, Aki *207:* 153
Sohn, Jiho *182:* 78
Sokol, Bill *37:* 178; *49:* 23
Sokolov, Kirill *34:* 188
Solbert, Ronni *1:* 159; *2:* 232; *5:* 121; *6:* 34; *17:* 249
Solomon, Michael *174:* 115
Solonevich, George *15:* 246; *17:* 47
Soma, Liana *81:* 118
Soman, David *90:* 122; *102:* 126; *140:* 120; *93:* 188; *43, 89; *200:* 180, 181
Sommer, Robert *12:* 211
Song, Jae *203:* 27
Soo, Kean *201:* 185
Sorel, Edward *4:* 61; *36:* 82; *65:* 191, 193; *126:* 214
Sorensen, Henri *196:* 58
Sorensen, Henrik *62:* 16
Sorensen, Svend Otto *22:* 130, 141; *67:* 188, 189
Sorra, Kristin *155:* 80
Sosa, Hernan *198:* 66
Sostre, Maria *187:* 36
Sotomayor, Antonio *11:* 215
Souhami, Jessica *112:* 128; *176:* 193
Sousa, Natalie C. *209:* 89
Souza, Diana *71:* 139
Sovak, Jan *115:* 190
Sowards, Ben *215:* 62
Soyer, Moses *20:* 177
Spaenkuch, August *16:* 28
Spafford, Suzy *160:* 228
Spain, Valerie *105:* 76
Spain, Sunday Sahara *133:* 204
Spalenka, Greg *149:* 69; *151:* 228; *184:* 195; *191:* 21; *196:* 12; *198:* 181, 182, 201; *208:* 92
Spanfeller, James *1:* 72, 149; *2:* 183; *19:* 230, 231,232; *22:* 66; *36:* 160, 161; *40:* 75; *52:* 166; *76:* 37
Spangler, Brie *212:* 188
Sparks, Mary Walker *15:* 247
Spears, Rick *182:* 187
Speidel, Sandra *78:* 233; *94:* 178; *134:* 180; *210:* 67
Speirs, John *67:* 178
Spence, Geraldine *21:* 163; *47:* 196
Spence, Jim *38:* 89; *50:* 102
Spencer, Laurie *113:* 12
Spencer, Mark *57:* 170
Spengler, Kenneth J. *146:* 256
Sperling, Andrea *133:* 182
Spiegel, Beth *184:* 203
Spiegel, Doris *29:* 111
Spiegelman, Art *109:* 227
Spier, Jo *10:* 30
Spier, Peter *3:* 155; *4:* 200; *7:* 61; *11:* 78; *38:* 106; *54:* 120, 121, 122, 123, 124, 125, 126, 127, 128, 129, 130,131, 132, 133, 134
Spilka, Arnold *5:* 120; *6:* 204; *8:* 131
Spirin, Gennady *95:* 196, 197; *113:* 172; *128:* 9; *129:* 49; *134:* 210; *153:* 9; *204:* 143, 144, 145
Spiro, Ruth *208:* 197
Spivak, I. Howard *8:* 10; *13:* 172
Spohn, David *72:* 233
Spohn, Kate *87:* 195; *147:* 201, 202
Spollen, Christopher J. *12:* 214
Spooner, Malcolm *40:* 142
Spowart, Robin *82:* 228; *92:* 149; *133:* 131; *176:* 163; *177:* 183, 184; *217:* 123, 124
Sprague, Kevin *150:* 60; *196:* 62
Spranger, Nina *201:* 199
Sprattler, Rob *12:* 176
Spring, Bob *5:* 60
Spring, Ira *5:* 60
Springer, Harriet *31:* 92

Spudvilas, Anne *110:* 74; *197:* 192; *199:* 154
Spurll, Barbara *78:* 199; *88:* 141, 142; *99:* 215
Spurrier, Steven *28:* 198
Spuvilas, Anne *85:* 114
Spy
See Ward, Leslie
Squires, Stuart *127:* 74
St. Aubin, Bruno *179:* 54
St. John, J. Allen *41:* 62
Staake, Bob *209:* 168, 169
Stabin, Victor *101:* 131; *164:* 158
Stadler, John *62:* 33; *204:* 149
Stadnyk, Greg *212:* 55
Staffan, Alvin E. *11:* 56; *12:* 187
Stahl, Ben *5:* 181; *12:* 91; *49:* 122; *71:* 128; *87:* 206; *112:* 107
Stair, Gobin *35:* 214
Stallwood, Karen *73:* 126
Stamaty, Mark Alan *12:* 215
Stammen, JoEllen McAllister *113:* 14
Stampnick, Ken *51:* 142
Stanbridge, Joanne *150:* 91
Stanley, Diane *3:* 45; *37:* 180; *80:* 217, 219
Stanley, Sanna *145:* 228
Starcke, Helmut *86:* 217
Stark, Ken *197:* 102
Starr, Branka *73:* 25
Stasiak, Krystyna *49:* 181; *64:* 194
Staub, Leslie *103:* 54
Staunton, Ted *112:* 192
Stawicki, Matt *164:* 250
Stead, L. *55:* 51, 56
Steadman, Broeck *97:* 185, 186; *99:* 56; *121:* 48; *208:* 190
Steadman, Henry *211:* 130
Steadman, Ralph *32:* 180; *123:* 143, 145
Stearn, Nick *183:* 26
Steckler, June *90:* 178
Steele, Robert Gantt *169:* 174
Steichen, Edward *30:* 79
Steig, William *18:* 275, 276; *70:* 215, 216, 217, 218; *111:* 173, 174, 175, 176, 177
Stein, David Ezra *211:* 168
Stein, Harve *1:* 109
Steinberg, Saul *47:* 193
Steinel, William *23:* 146
Steiner, Charlotte *45:* 196
Steiner, Joan *110:* 219; *199:* 160, 161
Steirnagel, Michael *80:* 56
Stemp, Eric *60:* 184
Stephens, Alice Barber *66:* 208, 209
Stephens, Charles H. *YABC 2:* 279
Stephens, Pam *198:* 69
Stephens, Pat *126:* 110; *128:* 101
Stephens, William M. *21:* 165
Steptoe, Javaka *151:* 203, 204; *190:* 169; *213:* 163, 164
Steptoe, John *8:* 197; *57:* 9; *63:* 158, 159, 160, 161,163, 164, 165, 166, 167; *96:* 4; *105:* 87
Stern, Simon *15:* 249, 250; *17:* 58; *34:* 192, 193
Sterret, Jane *53:* 27
Stetsios, Debbie *165:* 108, 109
Steven, Kat *158:* 237
Stevens, David *62:* 44
Stevens, Helen *189:* 31; *207:* 83
Stevens, Janet *40:* 126; *57:* 10, 11; *80:* 112; *90:* 221, 222; *109:* 156; *130:* 34; *166:* 202; *176:* 53, 116; *193:* 199, 200, 202; *208:* 127; *212:* 182
Stevens, Mary *11:* 193; *13:* 129; *43:* 95
Stevenson, Harvey *66:* 143; *80:* 201, 221; *153:* 60; *191:* 166
Stevenson, James *42:* 182, 183; *51:* 163; *66:* 184; *71:* 185, 187, 188; *78:* 262; *87:* 97; *113:* 182, 183,184, 185; *161:* 182, 183
Stevenson, Sucie *92:* 27; *104:* 194, 195; *112:* 168; *160:* 202; *194:* 172, 173; *195:* 166
Stewart, April Blair *75:* 210
Stewart, Arvis *33:* 98; *36:* 69; *60:* 118; *75:* 91; *127:* 4

Stewart, Charles 2: 205
Stewart, Joel 151: 205; 211: 170, 171
Stieg, William 172: 58
Stiles, Fran 26: 85; 78: 56; 82: 150
Stillman, Susan 44: 130; 76: 83
Stimpson, Tom 49: 171
Stimson, James 208: 46
Stinemetz, Morgan 40: 151
Stinson, Paul 110: 86
Stirnweis, Shannon 10: 164
Stites, Joe 86: 96
Stobbs, William 1: 48, 49; 3: 68; 6: 20; 17: 117, 217; 24: 150; 29: 250; 60: 179; 87: 204, 205,206
Stock, Catherine 37: 55; 65: 198; 72: 7; 99: 225; 114: 197, 198, 199; 126: 3; 145: 161; 161: 82; 173: 149; 208: 210; 214: 192,194
Stockman, Jack 113: 24
Stoeke, Janet Morgan 90: 225; 136: 196; 202: 182, 183
Stoerrle, Tom 55: 147
Stolp, Jaap 49: 98
Stolp, Todd 89: 195
Stone, David L. 87: 154
Stone, David 9: 173
Stone, David K. 4: 38; 6: 124; 9: 180; 43: 182; 60: 70
Stone, Helen V. 6: 209
Stone, Helen 44: 121, 122, 126
Stone, Kazuko G. 134: 43
Stone, Kyle M. 202: 185
Stone, Phoebe 86: 212; 134: 213; 162: 188; 205: 145
Stone, Steve 166: 213; 208: 185
Stone, Tony 150: 34, 35
Storms, Patricia 217: 163
Storrings, Michael 191: 108; 216: 217
Stoud, Virginia A. 89: 31
Stover, Jill 82: 234
Stower, Adam 217: 89
Strachan, Bruce 205: 146
Stratton, Helen 33: 151
Stratton-Porter, Gene 15: 254, 259, 263, 264, 268, 269
Straub, Matt 192: 176
Straub, Phillip 197: 22
Streano, Vince 20: 173
Street, Janet Travell 84: 235
Streeter, Clive 121: 2
Strickland, Shadra 209: 179
Stringer, Lauren 129: 187; 154: 172, 173; 161: 127; 183: 187, 188
Strodl, Daniel 47: 95
Strogart, Alexander 63: 139
Stromoski, Rick 111: 179; 124: 161, 190
Strong, Joseph D., Jr. YABC 2: 330
Stroyer, Poul 13: 221
Strugnell, Ann 27: 38
Struzan, Drew 117: 6
Stubbs, William 73: 196
Stubis, Talivaldis 5: 182, 183; 10: 45; 11: 9; 18: 304; 20: 127
Stubley, Trevor 14: 43; 22: 219; 23: 37; 28: 61; 87: 26
Stuck, Marion 104: 44
Stuecklen, Karl W. 8: 34, 65; 23: 103
Stull, Betty 11: 46
Stutzman, Mark 119: 99
Stutzmann, Laura 73: 185
Suarez, Maribel 162: 208; 200: 202
Suave, Gordon 209: 66
Suba, Susanne 4: 202, 203; 14: 261; 23: 134; 29: 222; 32: 30
Sue, Majella Lue 209: 182; 212: 146
Sueling, Barbara 98: 185
Sueling, Gwenn 98: 186
Sugarman, Tracy 3: 76; 8: 199; 37: 181, 182
Sugimoto, Yugo 170: 144
Sugita, Yutaka 36: 180, 181
Suh, John 80: 157
Sullivan, Dorothy 89: 113

Sullivan, Edmund J. 31: 86
Sullivan, James F. 19: 280; 20: 192
Sully, Tom 104: 199, 200; 182: 77
Sumichrast, Jozef 14: 253; 29: 168, 213
Sumiko 46: 57
Summers, Leo 1: 177; 2: 273; 13: 22
Summers, Mark 118: 144
Summers, Mike 190: 176
Sutton, Judith 94: 164
Svarez, Juan 56: 113
Svendsen, Mark 181: 176
Svolinsky, Karel 17: 104
Swain, Carol 172: 182
Swain, Su Zan Noguchi 21: 170
Swan, Susan 22: 220, 221; 37: 66; 60: 146; 145: 205; 181: 168
Swann, Susan 86: 55
Swanson, Karl 79: 65; 89: 186
Swarner, Kristina 203: 62; 215: 184
Swayne, Sam 53: 143, 145
Swayne, Zoa 53: 143, 145
Swearingen, Greg 152: 56; 165: 135; 173: 2
Sweat, Lynn 25: 206; 57: 176; 73: 184; 168: 178
Sweet, Darrell K. 60: 9; 69: 86; 74: 15; 75: 215; 76: 130, 131; 81: 96, 122; 82: 253; 83: 11; 84: 14; 85: 37; 89: 140; 90: 6; 91: 137,139; 95: 160, 161; 126: 25; 185: 175; 195: 132
Sweet, Darrell K. 1: 163; 4: 136; 164: 175
Sweet, Melissa 71: 94; 72: 172; 111: 82; 139: 53, 58; 141: 88; 142: 231; 155: 121; 159: 121, 122; 172: 185; 188: 127; 209: 81; 211: 174, 175
Sweet, Ozzie 31: 149, 151, 152
Sweetland, Robert 12: 194
Swiatkowska, Gabi 132: 43; 175: 139; 180: 218; 183: 176
Swope, Martha 43: 160; 56: 86, 87, 89
Sylvada, Peter 154: 174
Sylvester, Natalie G. 22: 222
Szafran, Gene 24: 144
Szasz, Susanne 13: 55, 226; 14: 48
Szekeres, Cyndy 2: 218; 5: 185; 8: 85; 11: 166; 14: 19; 16: 57, 159; 26: 49, 214; 34: 205; 60: 150, 151, 152, 153, 154; 73: 224; 74: 218; 131: 213, 215
Szpura, Beata 81: 68; 119: 65; 168: 201

T

Taback, Simms 40: 207; 52: 120; 57: 34; 80: 241; 104: 202, 203; 170: 176, 177; 205: 183
Taber, Patricia 75: 124
Tabor, Nancy Maria Grande 89: 210; 161: 188
Taddei, Richard 112: 13, 14
Tadgell, Nicole 150: 77; 161: 20; 177: 186; 209: 16
Tadiello, Ed 133: 200
Tafuri, Nancy 39: 210; 75: 199, 200; 92: 75; 130: 215, 216, 217
Tailfeathers, Gerald 86: 85
Tait, Douglas 12: 220; 74: 105, 106
Takabayashi, Mari 113: 112; 130: 22; 156: 169
Takahashi, Hideko 136: 160; 187: 6; 209: 152, 187
Takakjian, Portia 15: 274
Takashima, Shizuye 13: 228
Talarczyk, June 4: 173
Talbott, Hudson 84: 240; 163: 100; 212: 191, 192, 193
Tallarico, Tony 116: 197
Tallon, Robert 2: 228; 43: 200, 201, 202, 203, 204, 205,206, 207, 209
Tamaki, Jillian 201: 188
Tamas, Szecsko 29: 135
Tamburine, Jean 12: 222
Tanaka, Yoko 215: 187
Tancredi, Sharon 215: 127

Tandy, H.R. 13: 69
Tandy, Russell H. 65: 9; 100: 30, 131
Tang, Charles 81: 202; 90: 192
Tang, Susan 80: 174; 108: 158
Tang, You-shan 63: 100
Tankersley, Paul 69: 206; 133: 219
Tannenbaum, Robert 48: 181
Tanner, Jane 87: 13; 97: 37
Tanner, Tim 72: 192; 84: 35
Tanobe, Miyuki 23: 221
Tarabay, Sharif 110: 149; 113: 123; 169: 83
Tarkington, Booth 17: 224, 225
Tarlow, Phyllis 61: 198
Tate, Don 159: 141, 191; 183: 69; 186: 120
Tauss, Herbert 95: 179
Tauss, Marc 117: 160; 126: 155; 178: 221; 197: 7
Tavares, Matt 159: 192, 193; 198: 188, 189, 190; 199: 86
Taylor, Ann 41: 226
Taylor, Dahl 129: 157
Taylor, Geoff 93: 156; 197: 173, 175; 204: 151, 152
Taylor, Isaac 41: 228
Taylor, Mike 143: 99, 100
Teague, Mark 83: 6; 139: 241; 170: 180, 181; 205: 150, 151
Teale, Edwin Way 7: 196
Teason, James 1: 14
Teckentrup, Britta 200: 191, 192
Teeple, Lyn 33: 147
Tee-Van, Helen Damrosch 10: 176; 11: 182
Teicher, Dick 50: 211
Teichman, Mary 77: 220; 124: 208; 127: 22; 197: 33
Temertey, Ludmilla 96: 232; 104: 43, 45; 109: 244
Tempest, Margaret 3: 237, 238; 88: 200
Temple, Frances 85: 185, 186, 187
Temple, Herbert 45: 201
Templeton, Owen 11: 77
ten Cate, Marijke 183: 193
Tenggren, Gustaf 18: 277, 278, 279; 19: 15; 28: 86; YABC2: 145
Tennent, Julie 81: 105
Tenneson, Joyce 153: 166
Tenney, Gordon 24: 204
Tenniel, John 74: 234, 235; 100: 89; YABC 2: 99; 153: 63
Tepper, Matt 116: 80
Terkel, Ari 103: 162
Terry, Michael 180: 209
Terry, Will 131: 73; 205: 155
Teskey, Donald 71: 51
Tessler, Manya 200: 193
Thacher, Mary M. 30: 72
Thackeray, William Makepeace 23: 224, 228
Thamer, Katie 42: 187
Tharlet, Eve 146: 149
Thelwell, Norman 14: 201
Theobalds, Prue 40: 23
Theurer, Marilyn Churchill 39: 195
Thiesing, Lisa 89: 134; 95: 202; 156: 190; 159: 195
Thiewes, Sam 133: 114
Thistlethwaite, Miles 12: 224
Thollander, Earl 11: 47; 18: 112; 22: 224
Thomas, Allan 22: 13
Thomas, Art 48: 217
Thomas, Eric 28: 49
Thomas, Harold 20: 98
Thomas, Jacqui 125: 95
Thomas, Jan 197: 180
Thomas, Mark 42: 136
Thomas, Martin 14: 255
Thomas, Middy 177: 114
Thompson, Arthur 34: 107
Thompson, Carol 85: 189; 95: 75; 102: 86; 147: 166; 189: 179, 180, 181; 190: 84; 207: 18
Thompson, Colin 95: 204

Thompson, Ellen *51:* 88, 151; *60:* 33; *67:* 42; *77:* 148; *78:* 75, 219; *79:* 122, 170; *84:* 219; *85:* 97; *87:* 37; *88:* 192, 194; *89:* 80; *93:* 37; *98:* 59; *132:* 14

Thompson, George W. *22:* 18; *28:* 150; *33:* 135

Thompson, John *58:* 201; *102:* 226; *124:* 154; *128:* 228; *129:* 157; *150:* 49; *185:* 160; *191:* 192

Thompson, Julie *44:* 158

Thompson, Katherine *132:* 146

Thompson, K. Dyble *84:* 6

Thompson, Miles *152:* 77

Thompson, Sharon *74:* 113; *158:* 60; *165:* 87

Thomson, Arline K. *3:* 264

Thomson, Bill *186:* 160

Thomson, Hugh *26:* 88

Thomson, Ross *36:* 179

Thorkelson, Gregg *95:* 183, 184; *98:* 58; *165:* 30, 31

Thorn, Lori *189:* 119

Thornberg, Dan *104:* 125

Thornburgh, Rebecca McKillip *143:* 37

Thorne, Diana *25:* 212

Thornhill, Jan *77:* 213

Thorpe, Peter *58:* 109

Thorvall, Kerstin *13:* 235

Threadgall, Colin *77:* 215

Thurber, James *13:* 239, 242, 243, 245, 248, 249

Thurman, Mark *63:* 173; *168:* 116

Tibbles, Jean-Paul *115:* 200

Tibbles, Paul *45:* 23

Tibo, Gilles *67:* 207; *107:* 199, 201

Tichenor, Tom *14:* 207

Tichnor, Richard *90:* 218

Tiegreen, Alan *36:* 143; *43:* 55, 56, 58; *77:* 200; *94:* 216, 217; *121:* 54, 59

Tierney, Tom *113:* 198, 200, 201

Tildes, Phyllis Limbacher *210:* 240

Tilley, Debbie *102:* 134; *133:* 226; *137:* 101; *159:* 96; *190:* 211, 212; *213:* 51

Tillman, Nancy *211:* 129, 178

Tilney, F.C. *22:* 231

Timbs, Gloria *36:* 90

Timmins, Harry *2:* 171

Timmons, Bonnie *194:* 189

Tinkelman, Murray *12:* 225; *35:* 44

Titherington, Jeanne *39:* 90; *58:* 138; *75:* 79; *135:* 161

Tjader, Ella *209:* 14

Tobin, Nancy *145:* 197

Toddy, Irving *172:* 144

Tokunbo, Dimitrea *181:* 183; *187:* 182, 183

Tolbert, Jeff *128:* 69

Toledo, Francisco *197:* 182; *198:* 199

Toledo, Natalia *197:* 182

Tolford, Joshua *1:* 221

Tolkien, J.R.R. *2:* 243; *32:* 215

Tolman, Marije *195:* 43

Tolmie, Ken *15:* 292

Tomei, Lorna *47:* 168, 171

Tomes, Jacqueline *2:* 117; *12:* 139

Tomes, Margot *2:* 120, 121; *16:* 207; *18:* 250; *20:* 7; *25:* 62; *27:* 78, 79; *29:* 81, 199; *33:* 82; *36:* 186, 187, 188, 189, 190; *46:* 129; *56:* 71; *58:* 183; *70:* 228; *75:* 73, 75; *80:* 80; *83:* 97; *90:* 205

Tommaso, Rich *200:* 198

Toner, Raymond John *10:* 179

Tong, Gary *66:* 215

Tongier, Stephen *82:* 32

Tooke, Susan *173:* 162

Toothill, Harry *6:* 54; *7:* 49; *25:* 219; *42:* 192

Toothill, Ilse *6:* 54

Topolski, Feliks *44:* 48

Torbert, Floyd James *22:* 226

Torgersen, Don *55:* 157

Torline, Kevin *169:* 171

Tormey, Bertram M. *75:* 3, 4

Torrecilla, Pablo *176:* 207

Torres, Leyla *156:* 199, 201

Torrey, Helen *87:* 41

Torrey, Marjorie *34:* 105

Torrey, Richard *189:* 182; *205:* 24

Toschik, Larry *6:* 102

Totten, Bob *13:* 93

Toy, Julie *128:* 112

Trachok, Cathy *131:* 16

Tracy, Libba *82:* 24

Trago, Keith *158:* 253

Trail, Lee *55:* 157

Trang, To Ngoc *167:* 180

Trang, Winson *89:* 151

Trapani, Iza *116:* 202; *214:* 203

Travers, Bob *49:* 100; *63:* 145

Treatner, Meryl *95:* 180

Tremain, Ruthven *17:* 238

Tremain, Ruthven *17:* 238

Tresilian, Stuart *25:* 53; *40:* 212

Trez, Alain *17:* 236

Trezzo, Loretta *86:* 45

Trier, Walter *14:* 96

Trimby, Elisa *47:* 199

Trinkle, Sally *53:* 158

Triplett, Gina *182:* 193; *188:* 100; *198:* 38

Tripp, F.J. *24:* 167

Tripp, Wallace *2:* 48; *7:* 28; *8:* 94; *10:* 54,76; *11:* 92; *31:* 170, 171; *34:* 203; *42:* 57; *60:* 157; *73:* 182

Trivas, Irene *53:* 4; *54:* 168; *82:* 46, 101

Trnka, Jiri *22:* 151; *43:* 212, 213, 214, 215; *YABC 1:* 30, 31

Trondheim, Lewis *182:* 183

Troughton, Joanna *37:* 186; *48:* 72

Troyer, Johannes *3:* 16; *7:* 18

Trudeau, G.B. *35:* 220, 221, 222; *48:* 119, 123, 126, 127,128, 129, 133; *168:* 189

Trueman, Matthew *165:* 208; *183:* 191

Truesdell, Sue *55:* 142; *108:* 219, 220; *212:* 202

Tryon, Leslie *84:* 7; *139:* 214; *143:* 10; *181:* 10

Tseng, Jean *72:* 195; *94:* 102; *119:* 126; *151:* 106; *173:* 138, 139; *200:* 158

Tseng, Mou-sien *72:* 195; *94:* 102; *119:* 126; *151:* 106; *173:* 138, 139; *200:* 158

Tsinajinie, Andy *2:* 62

Tsinganos, Jim *180:* 142

Tsugami, Kyuzo *18:* 198, 199

Tucker, Ezra *156:* 31

Tuckwell, Jennifer *17:* 205

Tudor, Bethany *7:* 103

Tudor, Tasha *18:* 227; *20:* 185, 186, 187; *36:* 111; *69:* 196, 198; *100:* 44; *YABC 2:* 46, 314; *160:* 234

Tuerk, Hanne *71:* 201

Tugeau, Jeremy *199:* 170; *203:* 96

Tulloch, Maurice *24:* 79

Tunis, Edwin *1:* 218, 219; *28:* 209, 210, 211, 212

Tunnicliffe, C.F. *62:* 176; *177; 178, 179;* 181

Turkle, Brinton *1:* 211, 213; *2:* 249; *3:* 226; *11:* 3; *16:* 209; *20:* 22; *50:* 23; *67:* 50; *68:* 65; *79:* 205, 206, 207; *128:* 47; *YABC 1:* 79

Turnbull, Christopher J. *143:* 99, 100

Turner, Gwenda *59:* 195

Turner, Helen *203:* 154

Turska, Krystyna *12:* 103; *31:* 173, 174, 175; *56:* 32,34; *100:* 66

Tusa, Tricia *72:* 242; *111:* 180, 181; *157:* 165; *164:* 186; *189:* 40; *201:* 9; *207:* 163, 164

Tusan, Stan *6:* 58; *22:* 236, 237

Tworkov, Jack *47:* 207

Tyers, Jenny *89:* 220

Tylden-Wright, Jenny *114:* 119

Tyrol, Adelaide Murphy *103:* 27

Tyrrell, Frances *107:* 204

Tzimoulis, Paul *12:* 104

U

Uchida, Yoshiko *1:* 220

Uderzo *47:* 88

Udovic, David *189:* 185; *195:* 201

Ueno, Noriko *59:* 155

Ugliano, Natascia *196:* 186

Ulm, Robert *17:* 238

Ulrich, George *73:* 15; *75:* 136, 139; *99:* 150

Ulriksen, Mark *101:* 58; *182:* 43; *210:* 243

Unada *84:* 67

See Gliewe, Unada

Underhill, Liz *53:* 159

Underwood, Beck *192:* 36

Underwood, Clarence *40:* 166

Unger, Jim *67:* 208

Ungerer, Tomi *5:* 188; *9:* 40; *18:* 188; *29:* 175; *33:* 221, 222, 223, 225; *71:* 48; *106:* 209, 210, 211, 212

Unwin, Nora S. *3:* 65, 234, 235; *4:* 237; *44:* 173, 174; *YABC 1:* 59; *2:* 301

Upitis, Alvis *145:* 179

Urban, Helle *149:* 243

Urbanovic, Jackie *86:* 86; *189:* 186, 187

U'ren, Andrea *213:* 177

Uris, Jill *49:* 188, 197

Ursell, Martin *50:* 51

Utpatel, Frank *18:* 114

Utz, Lois *5:* 190

V

Vagin, Vladimir *66:* 10; *142:* 215

Vaillancourt, Francois *107:* 199

Vainio, Pirkko *123:* 157, 158

Valério, Geraldo *180:* 225; *194:* 116

Vallejo, Boris *62:* 130; *72:* 212; *91:* 38; *93:* 61

Van Abbe, S. *16:* 142; *18:* 282; *31:* 90; *YABC 2:* 157, 161

Van Allsburg, Chris *37:* 205, 206; *53:* 161, 162, 163, 165,166, 167, 168, 169, 170, 171; *105:* 215, 216, 217, 218; *156:* 176, 177, 178

Vance, James *65:* 28

Van Der Linde, Henry *99:* 17

van der Meer, Ron *98:* 204, 205

van der Meer, Atie *98:* 204, 205

Vandivert, William *21:* 175

Van Dongen, H.R. *81:* 97

Van Dusen, Chris W. *173:* 169

Vane, Mitch *210:* 160

Van Everen, Jay *13:* 160; *YABC 1:* 121

Van Fleet, John *165:* 12, 13

Van Frankenhuyzen, Gijsbert *145:* 230; *149:* 164; *184:* 151; *210:* 248

van Genechten, Guido *165:* 226

van Haeringen, Annemarie *193:* 206

Van Horn, William *43:* 218

van Hout, Mies *195:* 191; *207:* 58

van Kampen, Vlasta *194:* 217

van Lawick, Hugo *62:* 76, 79

Van Lieshout, Maria *201:* 196

Van Loon, Hendrik Willem *18:* 285, 289, 291

Van Munching, Paul *83:* 85

van Ommen, Sylvia *186:* 192

Van Patter, Bruce *183:* 195

Van Rynbach, Iris *102:* 192

Van Sciver, Ruth *37:* 162

VanSeveren, Joe *63:* 182

Van Stockum, Hilda *5:* 193

Van Vleet, John *213:* 180

Van Wassenhove, Sue *202:* 193

Van Wely, Babs *16:* 50; *79:* 16

Van Wright, Cornelius *72:* 18; *102:* 208; *116:* 107; *152:* 236; *173:* 170, 171; *199:* 185

Van Zyle, Jon *103:* 125; *160:* 181, 182; *176:* 199, 200

Vardzigulyants, Ruben *90:* 54

Varga, Judy *29:* 196
Vargo, Kurt *79:* 224
Varley, Susan *61:* 199; *63:* 176, 177; *101:* 148; *134:* 220
Varon, Sara *195:* 208
Vasconcellos, Daniel *80:* 42
Vasiliu, Mircea *2:* 166, 253; *9:* 166; *13:* 58; *68:* 42
Vaughn, Frank *34:* 157
Vavra, Robert *8:* 206
Vawter, Will *17:* 163
Vayas, Diana *71:* 61
Vazquez, Carlos *125:* 184
Veeder, Larry *18:* 4
Velasquez, Eric *45:* 217; *61:* 45; *63:* 110, 111; *88:* 162; *90:* 34, 144; *94:* 213; *107:* 147; *132:* 192; *138:* 213; *159:* 126; *181:* 184; *184:* 96; *191:* 16; *192:* 234; *208:* 37; *214:* 81
Velasquez, Jose A. *63:* 73
Velez, Walter *71:* 75; *91:* 154; *121:* 181; *168:* 49; *207:* 52
Velthuijs, Max *110:* 228, 229
Vendrell, Carme Sole *42:* 205
Venezia, Mike *54:* 17
Venti, Anthony Bacon *124:* 103; *126:* 26
Venturo, Piero *61:* 194, 195
Ver Beck, Frank *18:* 16, 17
Verkaaik, Ben *110:* 209
Verling, John *71:* 27
Verney, John *14:* 225; *75:* 8
Vernon, Ursula *204:* 157
Verrier, Suzanne *5:* 20; *23:* 212
Versace, Marie *2:* 255
Verstraete, Randy *108:* 193
Vess, Charles *215:* 201
Vestal, H.B. *9:* 134; *11:* 101; *27:* 25; *34:* 158
Vestergaard, Hope *190:* 203
Vicatan *59:* 146
Vickrey, Robert *45:* 59, 64
Victor, Joan Berg *30:* 193
Vieceli, Emma *210:* 245
Viereck, Ellen *3:* 242; *14:* 229
Vigna, Judith *15:* 293; *102:* 194, 195, 196, 197
Vila, Laura *207:* 172
Vilato, Gaspar E. *5:* 41
Villiard, Paul *51:* 178
Vimnera, A. *23:* 154
Vincent, Eric *34:* 98
Vincent, Felix *41:* 237
Vincent, Gabrielle *121:* 175
Vip *45:* 164
Viskupic, Gary *83:* 48
Vitale, Stefano *109:* 71, 107; *114:* 219, 220; *123:* 106; *138:* 232; *180:* 228, 229; *212:* 38
Vivas, Julie *51:* 67, 69; *96:* 225; *197:* 190; *199:* 71
Voake, Charlotte *114:* 221, 222; *180:* 232
Vo-Dinh, Mai *16:* 272; *60:* 191
Vogel, Ilse-Margret *14:* 230
Voigt, Erna *35:* 228
Vojnar, Kamil *95:* 31; *114:* 4; *115:* 62; *121:* 90; *124:* 72; *130:* 31; *141:* 81; *146:* 196; *150:* 123; *158:* 5, 6; *158:* 154; *171:* 119, 188; *179:* 15; *180:* 112; *203:* 74
Vojtech, Anna *42:* 190; *108:* 222, 223; *150:* 203; *174:* 173
von Buhler, Cynthia *149:* 237; *162:* 177; *177:* 205; *180:* 77; *185:* 214, 215, 216
von Roehl, Angela *126:* 191
von Schmidt, Eric *8:* 62; *50:* 209, 210
von Schmidt, Harold *30:* 80
Vosburgh, Leonard *1:* 161; *7:* 32; *15:* 295, 296; *23:* 110; *30:* 214; *43:* 181
Voss, Tom *127:* 104
Voter, Thomas W. *19:* 3, 9
Vroman, Tom *10:* 29
Vulliamy, Clara *72:* 65

W

Waber, Bernard *47:* 209, 210, 211, 212, 213, 214; *95:* 215, 216, 217; *156:* 203, 205, 206, 207
Wachenje, Benjamin *194:* 170
Wack, Jeff *95:* 140; *110:* 90
Wagner, John *8:* 200; *52:* 104
Wagner, Ken *2:* 59
Wagner, Michael *211:* 159
Waide, Jan *29:* 225; *36:* 139
Wainwright, Jerry *14:* 85
Waites, Joan C. *171:* 2
Wakeen, Sandra *47:* 97
Wakiyama, Hanako *171:* 96; *192:* 236; *200:* 16
Waldherr, Kris *81:* 186
Waldman, Bruce *15:* 297; *43:* 178
Waldman, Neil *35:* 141; *50:* 163; *51:* 180; *54:* 78; *77:* 112; *79:* 162; *82:* 174; *84:* 5, 56, 106; *94:* 232, 233, 234; *96:* 41; *111:* 139; *113:* 9; *118:* 30; *142:* 220, 223; *203:* 173, 174
Waldrep, Richard *111:* 147; *198:* 202
Walker, Brian *144:* 128
Walker, Charles *1:* 46; *4:* 59; *5:* 177; *11:* 115; *19:* 45; *34:* 74; *62:* 168; *72:* 218
Walker, Dugald Stewart *15:* 47; *32:* 202; *33:* 112
Walker, Gil *8:* 49; *23:* 132; *34:* 42
Walker, Jeff *55:* 154; *123:* 116
Walker, Jim *10:* 94
Walker, Mort *8:* 213
Walker, Norman *41:* 37; *45:* 58
Walker, Stephen *12:* 229; *21:* 174
Wallace, Beverly Dobrin *19:* 259
Wallace, Cly *87:* 93
Wallace, Ian *53:* 176, 177; *56:* 165, 166; *58:* 4; *98:* 4; *101:* 191; *112:* 124; *141:* 197, 198, 199, 200; *151:* 212
Wallace, John *105:* 228
Wallace, Nancy Elizabeth *141:* 204; *186:* 195, 197, 199
Wallenta, Adam *123:* 180
Waller, S.E. *24:* 36
Wallner, Alexandra *15:* 120; *156:* 183
Wallner, John C. *9:* 77; *10:* 188; *11:* 28; *14:* 209; *31:* 56, 118; *37:* 64; *51:* 186, 187, 188, 189, 190, 191,192, 193, 194, 195; *52:* 96; *53:* 23, 26; *71:* 99; *73:* 158; *89:* 215; *141:* 9
Wallner, John *162:* 17
Wallower, Lucille *11:* 226
Walotsky, Ron *93:* 87
Walsh, Ellen Stoll *99:* 209; *147:* 219; *194:* 194, 195, 196
Walsh, Rebecca *158:* 193; *217:* 169, 170
Walsh, Vivian *149:* 215; *158:* 227
Walters, Anita *205:* 163
Walters, Audrey *18:* 294
Walther, Tom *31:* 179
Walton, Garry *69:* 149
Walton, Tony *11:* 164; *24:* 209; *153:* 8; *177:* 73
Waltrip, Lela *9:* 195
Waltrip, Mildred *3:* 209; *37:* 211
Waltrip, Rufus *9:* 195
Wan *12:* 76
Wan, Shelly *212:* 131
Wang, Shaoli *216:* 220
Wang, Suling *191:* 183; *213:* 194
Warburton, Sarah *154:* 187
Wappers, G. *121:* 40
Ward, Chad Michael *217:* 121
Ward, Fred *52:* 19
Ward, Helen *72:* 244; *144:* 240, 242
Ward, John *42:* 191; *96:* 54; *97:* 110; *123:* 105; *124:* 71; *173:* 66
Ward, Keith *2:* 107; *132:* 69
Ward, Leslie *34:* 126; *36:* 87

Ward, Lynd *1:* 99, 132, 133, 150; *2:* 108, 158, 196, 259; *18:* 86; *27:* 56; *29:* 79, 187, 253, 255; *36:* 199,200, 201, 202, 203, 204, 205, 206, 207, 209; *43:* 34; *56:* 28; *60:* 116; *100:* 65
Ward, Peter *37:* 116
Waring, Geoff *172:* 84
Warhola, James *92:* 5; *115:* 85, 87; *118:* 174, 175, 177; *176:* 84; *187:* 189, 190
Warner, Ben *159:* 171
Warner, Peter *14:* 87
Warner, Sally *214:* 210
Warnes, Tim *175:* 159; *202:* 188; *216:* 224
Warnick, Elsa *113:* 223
Warren, Betsy *2:* 101
Warren, Jim *85:* 81
Warren, Marion Cray *14:* 215
Warshaw, Jerry *30:* 197, 198; *42:* 165
Wasden, Kevin *102:* 162
Washington, Nevin *20:* 123
Washington, Phyllis *20:* 123
Wasserman, Amy L. *92:* 110; *209:* 95
Waterman, Stan *11:* 76
Watkins-Pitchford, D.J. *6:* 215, 217
Watling, James *67:* 210; *78:* 112; *101:* 81; *117:* 189, 190; *127:* 119, 120
Watson, Aldren A. *2:* 267; *5:* 94; *13:* 71; *19:* 253; *32:* 220; *42:* 193, 194, 195, 196, 197, 198, 199, 200, 201; *YABC 2:* 202
Watson, G. *83:* 162
Watson, Gary *19:* 147; *36:* 68; *41:* 122; *47:* 139
Watson, J.D. *22:* 86
Watson, Jesse Joshua *197:* 124; *199:* 181; *202:* 136
Watson, Karen *11:* 26
Watson, Mary *117:* 193
Watson, Richard Jesse *62:* 188, 189; *211:* 201
Watson, Wendy *5:* 197; *13:* 101; *33:* 116; *46:* 163; *64:* 12; *74:* 242, 243; *91:* 21; *142:* 228; *215:* 79
Watt, Mélanie *136:* 206; *193:* 211
Wattenberg, Jane *174:* 200; *185:* 46; *187:* 108
Watterson, Bill *66:* 223, 225, 226
Watts, Bernadette *4:* 227; *103:* 182, 183
Watts, James *59:* 197; *74:* 145; *86:* 124
Watts, John *37:* 149
Watts, Leslie Elizabeth *150:* 207; *165:* 106; *209:* 67
Watts, Stan *116:* 205
Weatherby, Mark Alan *77:* 141
Webb, Jennifer *110:* 79
Webb, Lanny *142:* 175
Webb, Sophie *135:* 214
Webber, Helen *3:* 141
Webber, Irma E. *14:* 238
Weber, Erik *56:* 19, 20
Weber, Florence *40:* 153
Weber, Jill *127:* 227, 228; *189:* 163; *208:* 157; *209:* 190, 191; *216:* 46
Weber, Roland *61:* 204
Weber, Sam *190:* 227
Weber, William J. *14:* 239
Webster, Jean *17:* 241
Weeks, Sarah *162:* 39
Wegman, William *78:* 243
Wegner, Fritz *14:* 250; *20:* 189; *44:* 165; *86:* 62
Weidenear, Reynold H. *21:* 122
Weigel, Jeff *170:* 193
Weihs, Erika *4:* 21; *15:* 299; *72:* 201; *107:* 207, 208
Weil, Lisl *7:* 203; *10:* 58; *21:* 95; *22:* 188,217; *33:* 193
Weiman, Jon *50:* 162, 165; *52:* 103; *54:* 78, 79, 81; *78:* 80; *82:* 107; *93:* 82; *97:* 69; *105:* 179; *193:* 65
Weiner, Greg *215:* 21
Weiner, Sandra *14:* 240
Weiner, Scott *55:* 27
Weinhaus, Karen Ann *53:* 90; *71:* 50; *86:* 124

Weinman, Brad *197:* 20
Weinstock, Robert *204:* 165, 166
Weisgard, Leonard *1:* 65; *2:* 191, 197, 204, 264, 265; *5:* 108; *21:* 42; *30:* 200, 201, 203, 204; *41:* 47; *44:* 125; *53:* 25; *85:* 196, 198, 200, 201; *100:* 139,207; *YABC 2:* 13
Weisman, David *173:* 47
Weiss, Ellen *44:* 202
Weiss, Emil *1:* 168; *7:* 60
Weiss, Harvey *1:* 145, 223; *27:* 224, 227; *68:* 214; *76:* 245, 246, 247
Weiss, Nicki *33:* 229
Weissman, Bari *49:* 72; *90:* 125; *139:* 142
Weitzman, David L. *172:* 199
Welch, Sheila Kelly *130:* 221
Welkes, Allen *68:* 218
Wellington, Monica *99:* 223; *157:* 259, 260, 261
Welliver, Norma *76:* 94
Wellner, Fred *127:* 53
Wells, Frances *1:* 183
Wells, H.G. *20:* 194, 200
Wells, Haru *53:* 120, 121
Wells, Robert E. *184:* 208
Wells, Rosemary *6:* 49; *18:* 297; *60:* 32; *66:* 203; *69:* 215, 216; *114:* 227; *118:* 149, 150; *156:* 188, 189, 190, 191; *207:* 180, 181, 182, 183
Wells, Rufus III *56:* 111, 113
Wells, Susan *22:* 43
Wendelin, Rudolph *23:* 234
Wengenroth, Stow *37:* 47
Weninger, Brigitte *189:* 192, 194
Werenskiold, Erik *15:* 6; *62:* 17
Werner, Honi *24:* 110; *33:* 41; *88:* 122
Werth, Kurt *7:* 122; *14:* 157; *20:* 214; *39:* 128
Wesson,
West, Harry A. *124:* 38
Westcott, Nadine Bernard *68:* 46; *84:* 49; *86:* 133; *106:* 199; *111:* 78; *113:* 111; *130:* 224; *139:* 54; *158:* 256; *194:* 199
Westerberg, Christine *29:* 226
Westerduin, Anne *105:* 229
Westerman, Johanna *162:* 206
Weston, Martha *29:* 116; *30:* 213; *33:* 85, 100; *53:* 181, 182, 183, 184; *77:* 95; *80:* 152; *119:* 196,197, 198, 199; *127:* 189; *133:* 196; *209:* 199
Wetherbee, Margaret *5:* 3
Wexler, Jerome *49:* 73; *150:* 129
Whalley, Peter *50:* 49
Whatley, Bruce *186:* 93, 95; *207:* 127; *213:* 183, 184
Wheatley, Arabelle *11:* 231; *16:* 276
Wheeler, Cindy *49:* 205
Wheeler, Dora *44:* 179
Wheelright, Rowland *15:* 81; *YABC 2:* 286
Whelan, Michael *56:* 108; *70:* 27, 29, 67, 68, 148; *74:* 18; *84:* 14; *91:* 195, 196; *95:* 147; *98:* 150, 151; *106:* 157; *113:* 218, 220; *116:* 99, 100
Whelan, Patrick *135:* 145
Whistler, Rex *16:* 75; *30:* 207, 208
White, Beth *216:* 139
White, Craig *110:* 130; *119:* 193; *130:* 33; *179:* 31
White, David Omar *5:* 56; *18:* 6
White, Joan *83:* 225
White, Martin *51:* 197; *85:* 127
Whitear *32:* 26
Whitehead, Beck *86:* 171
Whitehead, S.B. *154:* 132
Whithorne, H.S. *7:* 49
Whitman, Candace *208:* 208
Whitney, George Gillett *3:* 24
Whitney, Jean *99:* 53
Whitson, Paul *102:* 161
Whittam, Geoffrey *30:* 191
Whyte, Mary *96:* 127
Wiberg, Harald *38:* 127; *93:* 215
Wick, Walter *77:* 128

Wickstrom, Sylvie *106:* 87; *169:* 180; *214:* 110
Wickstrom, Thor *200:* 205
Widener, Terry *105:* 230; *106:* 7; *163:* 23; *200:* 17; *209:* 195
Wiese, Kurt *3:* 255; *4:* 206; *14:* 17; *17:* 18, 19; *19:* 47; *24:* 152; *25:* 212; *32:* 184; *36:* 211,213, 214, 215, 216, 217, 218; *45:* 161; *100:* 92
Wiesner, David *33:* 47; *51:* 106; *57:* 67; *58:* 55; *64:* 78, 79, 81; *69:* 233; *72:* 247, 248, 249, 251,252, 253, 254; *83:* 134; *104:* 31; *117:* 197, 199, 200, 202; *139:* 223, 224; *151:* 51; *181:* 189, 190
Wiesner, William *4:* 100; *5:* 200, 201; *14:* 262
Wiggins, George *6:* 133
Wijngaard, Juan *111:* 36; *114:* 124
Wikkelsoe, Otto *45:* 25, 26
Wikland, Ilon *5:* 113; *8:* 150; *38:* 124, 125, 130; *127:* 162
Wikler, Madeline *114:* 233
Wilbur, C. Keith, M.D. *27:* 228
Wilburn, Kathy *53:* 102; *68:* 234
Wilcox, Cathy *105:* 123
Wilcox, J.A.J. *34:* 122
Wilcox, Lydia *207:* 187
Wilcox, R. Turner *36:* 219
Wild, Jocelyn *46:* 220, 221, 222; *80:* 117
Wilde, George *7:* 139
Wildsmith, Brian *16:* 281, 282; *18:* 170, 171; *66:* 25; *69:* 224, 225, 227; *77:* 103; *83:* 218; *124:* 214,217, 219
Wildsmith, Mike *140:* 229
Wilhelm, Hans *58:* 189, 191; *73:* 157; *77:* 127; *135:* 229, 230, 233, 234; *196:* 209
Wilkin, Eloise *36:* 173; *49:* 208, 209, 210
Wilkinson, Barry *50:* 213
Wilkinson, Gerald *3:* 40
Wilkon, Jozef *31:* 183, 184; *71:* 206, 207, 209; *133:* 222
Wilks, Mike *34:* 24; *44:* 203
Willems, Mo *154:* 245, 246, 247; *180:* 236, 237, 239
Willey, Bee *103:* 129; *139:* 159; *173:* 115
Willhoite, Michael A. *71:* 214
William, Maria *168:* 51
Williams, Berkeley, Jr. *64:* 75
Williams, Ferelith Eccles *22:* 238
Williams, Garth *1:* 197; *2:* 49, 270; *4:* 205; *15:* 198, 302, 304, 307; *16:* 34; *18:* 283, 298, 299, 300, 301; *29:* 177, 178, 179, 232, 233, 241, 242, 243, 244, 245, 248; *40:* 106; *66:* 229, 230, 231, 233, 234; *71:* 192; *73:* 218, 219, 220; *78:* 261; *100:* 251, 252, 255; *136:* 117; *YABC 2:* 15, 16, 19
Williams, J. Scott *48:* 28
Williams, Jennifer *102:* 201
Williams, Jenny *60:* 202; *81:* 21; *88:* 71
Williams, Kent *180:* 18
Williams, Kit *44:* 206, 207, 208, 209, 211, 212
Williams, Marcia *97:* 214; *159:* 208, 209
Williams, Maureen *12:* 238
Williams, Patrick *14:* 218
Williams, Richard *44:* 204, 206; *72:* 229; *74:* 133; *78:* 155, 237; *91:* 178; *110:* 212; *136:* 201, 202, 203; *152:* 115
Williams, Sam *124:* 222; *153:* 11; *177:* 201, 202; *180:* 34; *212:* 49
Williams, Sophy *135:* 236
Williams, Vera B. *53:* 186, 187, 188, 189; *102:* 201, 202, 203; *210:* 65
Williamson, Alex *177:* 180; *205:* 50
Williamson, Mel *60:* 9
Willingham, Fred *104:* 206; *154:* 157
Willis, Adam *181:* 75; *209:* 11
Willmore, J.T. *54:* 113, 114
Wilsdorf, Anne *180:* 122; *189:* 124; *191:* 195
Wilson, Anne *160:* 114
Wilson, Charles Banks *17:* 92; *43:* 73
Wilson, Connie *113:* 179
Wilson, Dagmar *10:* 47

Wilson, Dawn *67:* 161; *81:* 120; *113:* 158
Wilson, Edward A. *6:* 24; *16:* 149; *20:* 220, 221; *22:* 87; *26:* 67; *38:* 212, 214, 215, 216, 217
Wilson, Forrest *27:* 231
Wilson, Gahan *35:* 234; *41:* 136
Wilson, George *76:* 87
Wilson, Helen Miranda *140:* 61
Wilson, Jack *17:* 139
Wilson, Janet *77:* 154; *96:* 114; *99:* 219, 220; *153:* 64 *106:* 122; *130:* 210; *145:* 178; *173:* 64
Wilson, John *22:* 240
Wilson, Maurice *46:* 224
Wilson, Patten *35:* 61
Wilson, Peggy *15:* 4; *84:* 20
Wilson, Phil *181:* 29
Wilson, Rowland B. *30:* 170
Wilson, Sarah *50:* 215
Wilson, Tom *33:* 232
Wilson, W.N. *22:* 26
Wilson-Max, Ken *170:* 196; *180:* 181
Wilton, Nicholas *103:* 52; *183:* 111
Wilwerding, Walter J. *9:* 202
Wimmer, Mike *63:* 6; *70:* 121; *75:* 186; *76:* 21,22, 23; *91:* 114; *97:* 45, 68; *98:* 28; *107:* 130; *146:* 21; *149:* 47; *173:* 126; *193:* 21, 25; *194:* 204, 205
Winborn, Marsha *78:* 34; *99:* 70; *192:* 20
Winch, John *165:* 233
Winchester, Linda *13:* 231
Wind, Betty *28:* 158
Windham, Kathryn Tucker *14:* 260
Windham, Sophie *184:* 212
Winfield, Alison *115:* 78; *214:* 121
Winfield, Wayne *72:* 23
Wing, Gary *64:* 147
Wing, Ron *50:* 85
Wingerter, Linda S. *132:* 199; *174:* 181; *200:* 196
Winick, Judd *124:* 227, 228, 229
Winn-Lederer, Ilene *202:* 91
Winnick, Karen B. *211:* 207
Winslow, Will *21:* 124
Winstead, Rosie *180:* 243
Winsten, Melanie Willa *41:* 41
Winter, Jeanette *151:* 240, 241, 242; *184:* 215, 217, 218, 219
Winter, Milo *15:* 97; *19:* 221; *21:* 181, 203, 204, 205; *64:* 19; *YABC 2:* 144
Winter, Paula *48:* 227
Winter, Susan *163:* 177; *182:* 201
Winters, Greg *70:* 117
Winters, Nina *62:* 194
Wise, Louis *13:* 68
Wiseman, Ann *31:* 187
Wiseman, B. *4:* 233
Wishnefsky, Phillip *3:* 14
Wiskur, Darrell *5:* 72; *10:* 50; *18:* 246
Wisniewski, David *95:* 220, 221
Wisniewski, Robert *95:* 10; *119:* 192
Witschonke, Alan *153:* 149, 150
Witt, Dick *80:* 244
Wittmann, Patrick *162:* 204
Wittman, Sally *30:* 219
Wittner, Dale *99:* 43
Wittwer, Hala *158:* 267; *195:* 80
Woehr, Lois *12:* 5
Wohlberg, Meg *12:* 100; *14:* 197; *41:* 255
Wohnoutka, Mike *137:* 68; *190:* 199; *195:* 218; *205:* 132
Wojtowycz, David *167:* 168
Woldin, Beth Weiner *34:* 211
Wolf, Elizabeth *133:* 151; *208:* 175
Wolf, J. *16:* 91
Wolf, Janet *78:* 254
Wolf, Linda *33:* 163
Wolfe, Corey *72:* 213
Wolfe, Frances *216:* 227
Wolfe, Gillian *199:* 193

Wolff, Ashley *50:* 217; *81:* 216; *156:* 216, 217; *170:* 57; *174:* 174; *184:* 72; *203:* 181, 182, 183, 184
Wolff, Glenn *178:* 230
Wolff, Jason *213:* 186
Wolfsgruber, Linda *166:* 61
Wondriska, William *6:* 220
Wong, Janet S. *98:* 225; *152:* 43
Wong, Nicole *174:* 13; *214:* 216; *215:* 25
Wonsetler, John C. *5:* 168
Wood, Audrey *50:* 221, 222, 223; *81:* 219, 221; *198:* 206
Wood, Don *50:* 220, 225, 226, 228, 229; *81:* 218, 220; *139:* 239, 240
Wood, Grant *19:* 198
Wood, Heather *133:* 108
Wood, Ivor *58:* 17
Wood, Jakki *211:* 209
Wood, Muriel *36:* 119; *77:* 167; *171:* 55; *187:* 46
Wood, Myron *6:* 220
Wood, Owen *18:* 187; *64:* 202, 204, 205, 206, 208, 210
Wood, Rob *193:* 48
Wood, Ruth *8:* 11
Woodbridge, Curtis *133:* 138; *204:* 113
Wooding, Sharon L. *66:* 237
Woodruff, Liza *132:* 239; *182:* 46, 204
Woodruff, Thomas *171:* 73
Woods, John, Jr. *109:* 142
Woodson, Jack *10:* 201
Woodson, Jacqueline *94:* 242
Woodward, Alice *26:* 89; *36:* 81
Wool, David *26:* 27
Woolley, Janet *112:* 75
Woolman, Steven *106:* 47; *163:* 73
Wooten, Vernon *23:* 70; *51:* 170
Worboys, Evelyn *1:* 166, 167
Word, Reagan *103:* 232
Wormell, Christopher *154:* 251; *202:* 206
Worth, Jo *34:* 143
Worth, Wendy *4:* 133
Wosmek, Frances *29:* 251
Wrenn, Charles L. *38:* 96; *YABC 1:* 20, 21
Wright, Barbara Mullarney *98:* 161
Wright, Cliff *168:* 203
Wright, Dare *21:* 206
Wright-Frierson, Virginia *58:* 194; *110:* 246
Wright, George *YABC 1:* 268
Wright, Joseph *30:* 160
Wronker, Lili Cassel *3:* 247; *10:* 204; *21:* 10
Wu, Donald *200:* 18
Wummer, Amy *154:* 181; *168:* 150; *176:* 85; *201:* 202, 203
Wyant, Alexander Helwig *110:* 19
Wyatt, David *97:* 9; *101:* 44; *114:* 194; *140:* 20; *167:* 13; *188:* 48
Wyatt, Stanley *46:* 210
Wyeth, Andrew *13:* 40; *YABC 1:* 133, 134
Wyeth, Jamie *41:* 257
Wyeth, N.C. *13:* 41; *17:* 252, 253, 254, 255, 256, 257, 258, 259, 264, 265, 266, 267, 268; *18:* 181; *19:* 80, 191, 200; *21:* 57, 183; *22:* 91; *23:* 152; *24:* 28, 99; *35:* 61; *41:* 65; *100:* 206; *YABC1:* 133, 223; *2:* 53, 75, 171, 187, 317
Wyman, Cherie R. *91:* 42

Wynne, Patricia J. *210:* 260

X

Xuan, YongSheng *119:* 202, 207, 208; *140:* 36; *187:* 21

Y

Yaccarino, Dan *141:* 208, 209; *147:* 171; *192:* 244, 245; *207:* 168
Yakovetic, Joe *59:* 202; *75:* 85
Yalowitz, Paul *93:* 33; *211:* 92
Yamaguchi, Marianne *85:* 118
Yamasaki, James *167:* 93
Yang, Belle *170:* 198
Yang, Jay *1:* 8; *12:* 239
Yap, Weda *6:* 176
Yaroslava
    See Mills, Yaroslava Surmach
Yashima, Taro *14:* 84
Yates, John *74:* 249, 250
Yates, Kelly *208:* 214
Yayo *178:* 88
Yeatts, Tabatha *215:* 210
Yee, Cora *166:* 233
Yee, Wong Herbert *115:* 216, 217; *172:* 204, 205; *194:* 59
Yelchin, Eugene *204:* 4
Yeo, Brad *135:* 121; *192:* 106
Yerxa, Leo *181:* 195
Yezerski, Thomas F. *162:* 29
Ylla
    See Koffler, Camilla
Yohn, F.C. *23:* 128; *YABC 1:* 269
Yoo, Taeeun *191:* 198
Yorinks, Adrienne *144:* 248; *200:* 214
Yorke, David *80:* 178
Yoshida, Toshi *77:* 231
Yoshikawa, Sachiko *168:* 104; *177:* 28; *181:* 196, 197
Youll, Paul *91:* 218
Youll, Stephen *92:* 227; *118:* 136, 137; *164:* 248; *202:* 92
Young, Amy L. *185:* 218; *190:* 46
Young, Cybéle *167:* 9
Young, Ed *7:* 205; *10:* 206; *40:* 124; *63:* 142; *74:* 250, 251, 252, 253; *75:* 227; *81:* 159; *83:* 98; *94:* 154; *115:* 160; *137:* 162; *YABC 2:* 242; *173:* 174, 175, 176; *205:* 29; *212:* 82
Young, Mary O'Keefe *77:* 95; *80:* 247; *134:* 214; *140:* 213; *211:* 223, 225
Young, Noela *8:* 221; *89:* 231; *97:* 195
Young, Paul *190:* 222
Young, Selina *153:* 12; *201:* 204, 205
Yum, Hyewon *211:* 228
Yun, Cheng Mung *60:* 143

Z

Zacharow, Christopher *88:* 98
Zacks, Lewis *10:* 161
Zadig *50:* 58

Zaffo, George *42:* 208
Zagwyn, Deborah Turney *138:* 227
Zahares, Wade *193:* 219
Zaid, Barry *50:* 127; *51:* 201
Zaidenberg, Arthur *34:* 218, 219, 220
Zalben, Jane Breskin *7:* 211; *79:* 230, 231, 233; *170:* 202
Zallinger, Jean *4:* 192; *8:* 8, 129; *14:* 273; *68:* 36; *80:* 254; *115:* 219, 220, 222
Zallinger, Rudolph F. *3:* 245
Zakrajsek, Molly *177:* 146
Zappa, Ahmet *180:* 250
Zebot, George *83:* 214
Zecca, Katherine *207:* 195
Zeck, Gerry *40:* 232
Zeff, Joe *181:* 98
Zeifert, Harriet *154:* 265, 267
Zeiring, Bob *42:* 130
Zeldich, Arieh *49:* 124; *62:* 120
Zeldis, Malcah *86:* 239; *94:* 198; *146:* 265, 266
Zelinsky, Paul O. *14:* 269; *43:* 56; *49:* 218-223; *53:* 111; *68:* 195; *102:* 219, 222, 221, 222; *154:* 255, 256, 257; *171:* 141; *185:* 96
Zelvin, Diana *72:* 190; *76:* 101; *93:* 207
Zemach, Kaethe *149:* 250
Zemach, Margot *3:* 270; *8:* 201; *21:* 210, 211; *27:* 204, 205, 210; *28:* 185; *49:* 22, 183, 224; *53:* 151; *56:* 146; *70:* 245, 246; *92:* 74
Zeman, Ludmila *153* 212
Zemsky, Jessica *10:* 62
Zepelinsky, Paul *35:* 93
Zerbetz, Evon *127:* 34; *158:* 109
Zezejl, Daniel *197:* 74
Zhang, Ange *101:* 190; *172:* 41
Zhang, Son Nang *163:* 113; *170:* 206
Ziegler, Jack *84:* 134
Zimdars, Berta *129:* 155
Zimet, Jay *147:* 94; *152:* 74; *196:* 75
Zimic, Tricia *72:* 95
Zimmer, Dirk *38:* 195; *49:* 71; *56:* 151; *65:* 214; *84:* 159; *89:* 26; *147:* 224
Zimmer, Tracie Vaughn *169:* 183
Zimmerman, Andrea *192:* 49, 50
Zimmermann, H. Werner *101:* 223; *112:* 197
Zimnik, Reiner *36:* 224
Zingone, Robin *180:* 134
Zinkeisen, Anna *13:* 106
Zinn, David *97:* 97
Zoellick, Scott *33:* 231
Zollars, Jaime *190:* 190
Zonia, Dhimitri *20:* 234, 235
Zorn, Peter A., Jr. *142:* 157
Zudeck, Darryl *58:* 129; *63:* 98; *80:* 52
Zug, Mark *88:* 131; *204:* 169
Zulewski, Tim *164:* 95
Zuma *99:* 36
Zvorykin, Boris *61:* 155
Zweifel, Francis *14:* 274; *28:* 187
Zwerger, Lisbeth *54:* 176, 178; *66:* 246, 247, 248; *130:* 230, 231, 232, 233; *181:* 92; *194:* 224, 225, 226
Zwinger, Herman H. *46:* 227
Zwolak, Paul *67:* 69, 71, 73, 74

Author Index

The following index gives the number of the volume in which an author's biographical sketch, Autobiography Feature, Brief Entry, or Obituary appears.

This index includes references to all entries in the following series, which are also published by The Gale Group.

YABC—*Yesterday's Authors of Books for Children: Facts and Pictures about Authors and Illustrators of Books for Young People from Early Times to 1960*

CLR—*Children's Literature Review: Excerpts from Reviews, Criticism, and Commentary on Books for Children*

SAAS—*Something about the Author Autobiography Series*

A

Aardema, Verna 1911-2000 .... *107*
  Obituary *119*
  Earlier sketches in SATA *:4, 68*
  See also CLR *17*
  See also SAAS *8*
Aaron, Chester 1923- *216*
  Autobiography Feature *216*
  Earlier sketches in SATA *9, 74*
  See also SAAS *12*
Aaseng, Nate
  See Aaseng, Nathan
Aaseng, Nathan 1953- *172*
  Brief entry *38*
  Earlier sketches in SATA *51, 88*
  See also CLR *54*
  See also SAAS *12*
Abadzis, Nick 1965- *193*
Abalos, Rafael 1956-
  See Abalos, Rafael
Abalos, Rafael 1956- *197*
Abbas, Jailan 1952- *91*
Abbey, Lynn
  See Abbey, Marilyn Lorraine
Abbey, Marilyn Lorraine 1948- *156*
Abbott, Alice
  See Borland, Kathryn Kilby
  and Speicher, Helen Ross S(mith)
Abbott, Jacob 1803-1879 .... *22*
Abbott, Manager Henry
  See Stratemeyer, Edward L.
Abbott, R(obert) Tucker 1919-1995 .... *61*
  Obituary *87*
Abbott, Sarah
  See Zolotow, Charlotte
Abbott, Tony 1952- *205*
  Earlier sketch in SATA *159*
Abdelsayed, Cindy 1962- *123*
Abdul, Raoul 1929- *12*
Abeele, Veronique van den *196*
Abel, Raymond 1911- *12*
Abell, Kathleen 1938- *9*
Abelove, Joan *110*
Abels, Harriette S(heffer) 1926- *50*
Abercrombie, Barbara 1939- *182*
  Earlier sketch in SATA *16*
Abercrombie, Barbara Mattes
  See Abercrombie, Barbara

Abercrombie, Lynn
  See Sorrells, Walter
Abernethy, Robert G(ordon) 1927- *5*
Abisch, Roslyn Kroop 1927- *9*
Abisch, Roz
  See Abisch, Roslyn Kroop
Ablow, Gail 1962- *198*
Abodaher, David J. (Naiph) 1919- *17*
Abolafia, Yossi 1944-
  See Abulafia, Yossi
Abouzeid, Chris *175*
Abrahall, Clare Hoskyns
  See Hoskyns-Abrahall, Clare (Constance Drury)
Abrahams, Hilary (Ruth) 1938- *29*
Abrahams, Peter 1947- *194*
Abrahams, Robert David 1905-1998 .... *4*
Abramovitz, Anita (Zeltner Brooks) 1914- *5*
Abrams, Joy 1941- *16*
Abrams, Lawrence F. *58*
  Brief entry *47*
Abrashkin, Raymond 1911-1960 .... *50*
Abulafia, Yossi 1944- *177*
  Brief entry *46*
  Earlier sketch in SATA *60*
Acampora, Paul *175*
Accardo, Anthony *191*
Acer, David *206*
Achebe, Albert Chinualumogu
  See Achebe, Chinua
Achebe, Chinua 1930- *40*
  Brief entry *38*
  Earlier sketch in SATA *38*
  See also CLR *20*
Ackerman, Diane 1948- *102*
Ackerman, Eugene (Francis) 1888-1974 ...... *10*
Ackerman, Karen 1951- *126*
Ackerman, Susan Yoder 1945- *92*
Ackison, Wendy Wassink 1956- *103*
Ackley, Peggy Jo 1955- *58*
Ackroyd, Peter 1949- *153*
Acorn, John (Harrison) 1958- *79*
Acredolo, Linda (Potter) 1947- *159*
Acs, Laszlo (Bela) 1931- *42*
  Brief entry *32*
Acuff, Selma Boyd 1924- *45*
Ada, Alma Flor 1938- *181*
  Earlier sketches in SATA *43, 84, 143*
  See also CLR *62*

Adair, Gilbert 1944- *98*
Adair, Ian 1942- *53*
Adair, Margaret Weeks (?)-1971 .... *10*
Adam, Cornel
  See Lengyel, Cornel Adam
Adam, Mark
  See Alexander, Marc
Adam, Robert 1948- *93*
Adams, Adrienne 1906- *90*
  Earlier sketch in SATA *8*
  See also CLR *73*
Adams, Andy 1859-1935
  See YABC *1*
Adams, Barbara Johnston 1943- *60*
Adams, Bruin
  See Ellis, Edward S.
Adams, Captain Bruin
  See Ellis, Edward S.
Adams, Captain J. F. C.
  See Ellis, Edward S.
Adams, Dale
  See Quinn, Elisabeth
Adams, Daniel
  See Nicole, Christopher (Robin)
Adams, Debra
  See Speregen, Devra Newberger
Adams, Diane 1960- *217*
Adams, Douglas 1952-2001 .... *116*
  Obituary *128*
Adams, Douglas Noel
  See Adams, Douglas
Adams, Edith
  See Shine, Deborah
Adams, Florence 1932- *61*
Adams, Georgie 1945- *216*
Adams, Harriet S(tratemeyer) 1892(?)-1982 .. *1*
  Obituary *29*
Adams, Harrison
  See Rathborne, St. George (Henry)
  and Stratemeyer, Edward L.
Adams, Hazard 1926- *6*
Adams, Hazard Simeon
  See Adams, Hazard
Adams, John Anthony 1944- *67*
Adams, Laurie 1941- *33*
Adams, Lowell
  See Joseph, James (Herz)
Adams, Nicholas
  See Pine, Nicholas

Adams, Nicholas
   See Smith, Sherwood
Adams, Nicholas
   See Doyle, Debra
   and Macdonald, James D.
Adams, Pam 1919- *112*
Adams, Pamela
   See Adams, Pam
Adams, Richard 1920- *69*
   Earlier sketch in SATA *7*
   See also CLR *121*
Adams, Richard George
   See Adams, Richard
Adams, Ruth Joyce *14*
Adams, Tricia
   See Kite, Pat
Adams, William Taylor 1822-1897 .... *28*
Adam Smith, Janet (Buchanan) 1905-1999 .. *63*
Adamson, Gareth 1925-1982(?) *46*
   Obituary *30*
Adamson, George 1906-1989
   Obituary *63*
Adamson, George (Worsley) 1913-2005 ...... *30*
Adamson, Graham
   See Groom, Arthur William
Adamson, Joy(-Friederike Victoria)
   1910-1980 .... *11*
   Obituary *22*
Adamson, Wendy Writson 1942- *22*
Addasi, Maha 1968- *205*
Addison, Kenneth 1949(?)-2005 .... *187*
Addison, Kenneth L.
   See Addison, Kenneth
Addona, Angelo F. 1925- *14*
Addy, Sharon Hart 1943- *192*
   Earlier sketch in SATA *108*
Addy, Ted
   See Winterbotham, R(ussell) R(obert)
Adelberg, Doris
   See Orgel, Doris
Adelson, Leone 1908- *11*
Adinolfi, JoAnn *176*
Adkins, Jan 1944- *210*
   Autobiography Feature *210*
   Earlier sketches in SATA *8, 69, 144*
   See also CLR *77*
   See also SAAS *19*
Adler, C. S. 1932- *126*
   Earlier sketches in SATA *26, 63, 102*
   See also CLR *78*
   See also SAAS *15*
Adler, Carole Schwerdtfeger
   See Adler, C. S.
Adler, David A. 1947- *178*
   Earlier sketches in SATA *14, 70, 106, 151*
   See also CLR *108*
Adler, Irene
   See Penzler, Otto
   and Storr, Catherine (Cole)
Adler, Irving 1913- *29*
   Autobiography Feature *164*
   Earlier sketch in SATA *1*
   See also CLR *27*
   See also SAAS *15*
Adler, Larry 1939- *36*
Adler, Peggy *22*
Adler, Ruth 1915-1968 .... *1*
Adlerman, Daniel (Ezra) 1963- *163*
   Earlier sketch in SATA *96*
Adlerman, Kim
   See Adlerman, Kimberly M(arie)
Adlerman, Kimberly M(arie) 1964- *163*
   Earlier sketch in SATA *96*
Adoff, Arnold 1935- *96*
   Earlier sketches in SATA *5, 57*
   See also CLR *7*
   See also SAAS *15*
Adoff, Jaime *163*
Adoff, Jaime Levi
   See Adoff, Jaime

Adorjan, Carol (Madden) 1934- *71*
   Earlier sketch in SATA *10*
Adrian, Frances
   See Polland, Madeleine A(ngela Cahill)
Adrian, Mary
   See Jorgensen, Mary Venn
Adshead, Gladys L(ucy) 1896-1985 .... *3*
Aesop 620(?)B.C.-560(?)B.C. *64*
   See also CLR *14*
Aesop, Abraham
   See Newbery, John
Affabee, Eric
   See Stine, R.L.
Agapida, Fray Antonio
   See Irving, Washington
Agard, John 1949- *138*
Agard, Nadema 1948- *18*
Agarwal, Deepa 1947- *141*
Agee, Jon 1960- *196*
   Earlier sketches in SATA *116, 157*
Agell, Charlotte 1959- *214*
   Earlier sketches in SATA *99, 150*
Agent Orange
   See Moseley, James W(illett)
Aghill, Gordon
   See Garrett, Randall
   and Silverberg, Robert
Agle, Nan Hayden 1905- *3*
   See also SAAS *10*
Agnew, Edith J(osephine) 1897-1988 .... *11*
Agonito, Joseph *177*
Agonito, Rosemary 1937- *177*
Aguilar, David *214*
Aguilar, David A.
   See Aguilar, David
Ahern, Margaret McCrohan 1921- *10*
Ahl, Anna Maria 1926- *32*
Ahlberg, Allan 1938- *214*
   Brief entry *35*
   Earlier sketches in SATA *68, 120, 165*
   See also CLR *18*
Ahlberg, Janet 1944-1994 .... *120*
   Brief entry *32*
   Obituary *83*
   Earlier sketch in SATA *68*
   See also CLR *18*
Aho, Julia Kay
   See Kay, Julia
Aichinger, Helga 1937- *4*
Aiken, Clarissa (M.) Lorenz 1899-1992 .... *12*
   Obituary *109*
Aiken, Conrad 1889-1973 .... *30*
   Earlier sketch in SATA *3*
Aiken, Conrad Potter
   See Aiken, Conrad
Aiken, Joan (Delano) 1924-2004 .... *73*
   Autobiography Feature *109*
   Obituary *152*
   Earlier sketches in SATA *2, 30*
   See also CLR *90*
   See also SAAS *1*
Aillaud, Cindy Lou 1955- *184*
Ainsley, Alix
   See Steiner, Barbara A(nnette)
Ainsworth, Catherine Harris 1910- *56*
Ainsworth, Norma 1911-1987 .... *9*
Ainsworth, Ruth (Gallard) 1908- *73*
   Earlier sketch in SATA *7*
Ainsworth, William Harrison 1805-1882 ..... *24*
Aistrop, Jack 1916- *14*
Aitken, Amy 1952- *54*
   Brief entry *40*
Aitken, Dorothy 1916- *10*
Aitmatov, Chingiz 1928-2008 .... *56*
Aitmatov, Chingiz Torekulovich
   See Aitmatov, Chingiz
Akaba, Suekichi 1910- *46*
Akers, Floyd
   See Baum, L. Frank
Akib, Jamel *181*
Aks, Patricia 1926-1994 .... *68*

Alagoa, Ebiegberi Joe 1933- *108*
Alain
   See Brustlein, Daniel
Alajalov, Constantin 1900-1987
   Obituary *53*
Alalou, Ali *203*
Alalou, Elizabeth *203*
Alan, David
   See Horsfield, Alan
Alan, Robert
   See Silverstein, Robert Alan
Alarcon, Francisco X. 1954- *215*
   Earlier sketch in SATA *104*
Alarcon, Francisco Xavier
   See Alarcon, Francisco X.
Alarcon, Karen Beaumont
   See Beaumont, Karen
Albert, Burton 1936- *22*
Albert, Louise 1928- *157*
Albert, Michael 1966- *202*
Albert, Richard E. 1909-1999 .... *82*
Albert, Susan Wittig 1940- *107*
Alberts, Frances Jacobs 1907-1989 .... *14*
Albertson, Susan
   See Wojciechowski, Susan
Albion, Lee Smith *29*
Alborough, Jez 1959- *149*
   Earlier sketch in SATA *86*
Albrecht, Lillie (Vanderveer H.)
   1894-1985 .... *12*
Albyn, Carole Lisa 1955- *83*
Alchemy, Jack
   See Gershator, David
Alcock, Gudrun 1908- *56*
   Brief entry *33*
Alcock, Vivien (Dolores) 1924-2003 .... *76*
   Brief entry *38*
   Obituary *148*
   Earlier sketch in SATA *45*
   See also CLR *26*
Alcorn, John 1935- *31*
   Brief entry *30*
Alcorn, Stephen 1958- *207*
   Earlier sketch in SATA *110*
Alcott, Louisa May 1832-1888 .... *100*
   See also YABC *1*
   See also CLR *109*
Alda, Arlene 1933- *205*
   Brief entry *36*
   Earlier sketches in SATA *44, 106, 158*
   See also CLR *93*
Alden, Isabella (Macdonald) 1841-1930 ..... *115*
   See also YABC *2*
Alden, Sue
   See Francis, Dorothy
Alderman, Clifford Lindsey 1902-1988 .... *3*
Alderson, Sue Ann 1940- *59*
   Brief entry *48*
Alding, Peter
   See Jeffries, Roderic
Aldis, Dorothy (Keeley) 1896-1966 .... *2*
Aldiss, Brian W. 1925- *34*
Aldiss, Brian Wilson
   See Aldiss, Brian W.
Aldon, Adair
   See Meigs, Cornelia Lynde
Aldous, Allan (Charles) 1911- *27*
Aldrich, Ann
   See Meaker, Marijane
Aldrich, Bess Streeter 1881-1954
   See CLR *70*
Aldrich, Thomas (Bailey) 1836-1907 .... *114*
   Earlier sketch in SATA *17*
Aldridge, (Harold Edward) James 1918- *87*
Aldridge, Josephine Haskell *14*
Aldridge, Sheila 1974- *192*
Aleas, Richard
   See Appelt, Kathi
Alegria, Malin 1974(?)- *190*
Alegria, Ricardo E(nrique) 1921- *6*
Aleksin, Anatolii Georgievich 1924- *36*

Alenov, Lydia 1948- *61*
Alex, Ben (a pseudonym) 1946- *45*
Alex, Marlee (a pseudonym) 1948- *45*
Alexander, Alma 1963- *217*
Alexander, Anna B(arbara Cooke) 1913- *1*
Alexander, Anne
  See Alexander, Anna B(arbara Cooke)
Alexander, Ellen 1938- *91*
Alexander, Frances (Laura) 1888-1979 .... *4*
Alexander, Janet 1907-1994 .... *97*
  Earlier sketch in SATA *1*
Alexander, Jocelyn Anne Arundel 1930- *22*
Alexander, Linda 1935- *2*
Alexander, Lloyd 1924-2007 .... *135*
  Obituary *182*
  Earlier sketches in SATA *3, 49, 81, 129*
  See also CLR *48*
  See also SAAS *19*
Alexander, Lloyd Chudley
  See Alexander, Lloyd
Alexander, Marc 1929- *117*
Alexander, Martha 1920- *136*
  Earlier sketches in SATA *11, 70*
Alexander, Rae Pace
  See Alexander, Raymond Pace
Alexander, Raymond Pace 1898-1974 .... *22*
Alexander, Robert *200*
Alexander, Rod
  See Pellowski, Michael (Joseph)
Alexander, Sally Hobart 1943- *84*
Alexander, Sue 1933-2008 .... *136*
  Obituary *195*
  Earlier sketches in SATA *12, 89*
  See also SAAS *15*
Alexander, Vincent Arthur 1925-1980
  Obituary *23*
Alexeieff, Alexandre A. 1901-1979 .... *14*
Alger, Horatio, Jr.
  See Stratemeyer, Edward L.
Alger, Horatio, Jr. 1832-1899 .... *16*
  See also CLR *87*
Alger, Leclaire (Gowans) 1898-1969 .... *15*
Aliki
  See Brandenberg, Aliki
Alkema, Chester Jay 1932- *12*
Al-Khalili, Jim 1962- *124*
Alkiviades, Alkis 1953- *105*
Alkouatli, Claire *186*
Allaby, John Michael
  See Allaby, Michael
Allaby, Michael 1933- *167*
Allamand, Pascale 1942- *12*
Allan, Mabel Esther 1915-1998 .... *75*
  Earlier sketches in SATA *5, 32*
  See also CLR *43*
  See also SAAS *11*
Allan, Nicholas 1956- *123*
  Earlier sketch in SATA *79*
Allan-Meyer, Kathleen 1918- *51*
  Brief entry *46*
Allard, Harry *216*
  See Allard, Harry G(rover), Jr.
Allard, Harry G.
  See Allard, Harry
Allard, Harry G(rover), Jr. 1928- *102*
  Earlier sketch in SATA *42*
  See also CLR *85*
  See Allard, Harry
Allee, Marjorie Hill 1890-1945 .... *17*
Allen, Adam
  See Epstein, Beryl
  and Epstein, Samuel
Allen, Alex B.
  See Heide, Florence Parry
Allen, Allyn
  See Eberle, Irmengarde
Allen, Betsy
  See Harrison, Elizabeth (Allen) Cavanna
Allen, Bob 1961- *76*
Allen, Gertrude E(lizabeth) 1888-1984 .... *9*

Allen, Grace
  See Hogarth, Grace (Weston Allen)
Allen, Jeffrey (Yale) 1948- *42*
Allen, John
  See Perry, Ritchie (John Allen)
Allen, Jonathan 1957- *177*
  Earlier sketch in SATA *131*
Allen, Jonathan Dean
  See Allen, Jonathan
Allen, Joy 1948- *217*
Allen, Judy (Christina) 1941- *124*
  Earlier sketch in SATA *80*
Allen, Kenneth S. 1913-1981 .... *56*
Allen, Leroy 1912- *11*
Allen, Linda 1925- *33*
Allen, Marjorie 1931- *22*
Allen, Maury 1932- *26*
Allen, Merritt Parmelee 1892-1954 .... *22*
Allen, Nancy Kelly 1949- *171*
  Earlier sketch in SATA *127*
Allen, Nina (Stroemgren) 1935- *22*
Allen, Pamela (Kay) 1934- *123*
  Earlier sketches in SATA *50, 81*
  See also CLR *44*
Allen, Raul *205*
Allen, Rodney F. 1938-1999 .... *27*
Allen, Roger MacBride 1957- *105*
Allen, Ruth
  See Peterson, Esther (Allen)
Allen, Samuel W(ashington) 1917- *9*
Allen, T. D.
  See Allen, Terril Diener
Allen, Terril Diener 1908- *35*
Allen, Terry D.
  See Allen, Terril Diener
Allen, Thomas B. 1929- *193*
  Earlier sketches in SATA *45, 140*
Allen, Thomas Benton
  See Allen, Thomas B.
Allen, Tom
  See Allen, Thomas B.
Allende, Isabel 1942- *163*
  See also CLR *99*
Allerton, Mary
  See Govan, (Mary) Christine Noble
Alley, Robert W.
  See Alley, R.W.
Alley, R.W. *211*
  Earlier sketch in SATA *169*
Alley, Zoe B. *214*
Alleyn, Ellen
  See Rossetti, Christina
Allington, Richard L(loyd) 1947- *39*
  Brief entry *35*
Allison, Amy 1956- *138*
Allison, Bob *14*
Allison, Diane Worfolk *78*
Allison, Jennifer *173*
Allison, Linda 1948- *43*
Allison, Margaret
  See Klam, Cheryl
Allman, Barbara 1950- *137*
Allmendinger, David F(rederick), Jr. 1938- . *35*
Allred, Alexandra Powe 1965- *144*
Allred, Gordon T(hatcher) 1930- *10*
Allsop, Kenneth 1920-1973 .... *17*
Allsopp, Sophie *188*
Alma, Ann 1946- *201*
Almedingen, E. M.
  See Almedingen, Martha Edith von
Almedingen, Martha Edith von 1898-1971 .... *3*
Almon, Russell
  See Clevenger, William R.
  and Downing, David A(lmon)
Almond, David 1951- *158*
  Earlier sketch in SATA *114*
  See also CLR *85*
Almond, Linda Stevens 1881(?)-1987
  Obituary *50*
Almquist, Don 1929- *11*
Alonzo, Sandra *199*

Alphin, Elaine Marie 1955- *139*
  Autobiography Feature *139*
  Earlier sketches in SATA *80, 130*
Alsenas, Linas 1979- *186*
Alsop, Mary O'Hara 1885-1980 .... *34*
  Obituary *24*
  Earlier sketch in SATA *2*
Alter, Anna 1974- *206*
  Earlier sketch in SATA *135*
Alter, Judith 1938- *101*
  Earlier sketch in SATA *52*
Alter, Judith MacBain
  See Alter, Judith
Alter, Judy
  See Alter, Judith
Alter, Robert Edmond 1925-1965 .... *9*
Alter, Stephen 1956- *187*
Althea
  See Braithwaite, Althea
Altman, Linda Jacobs 1943- *21*
Altman, Suzanne
  See Orgel, Doris
  and Schecter, Ellen
Alton, Steve *169*
Altschuler, Franz 1923- *45*
Altsheler, Joseph A(lexander) 1862-1919
  See YABC *1*
Alvarez, John
  See del Rey, Lester
Alvarez, Joseph A. 1930- *18*
Alvarez, Julia 1950- *129*
al-Windawi, Thura
  See Windawi, Thura al-
Alyer, Philip A.
  See Stratemeyer, Edward L.
Amado, Elisa *193*
Amann, Janet 1951- *79*
Amato, Carol A. 1942- *92*
Amato, Mary 1961- *178*
  Earlier sketch in SATA *140*
Ambrose, Stephen E. 1936-2002 .... *138*
  Earlier sketch in SATA *40*
Ambrose, Stephen Edward
  See Ambrose, Stephen E.
Ambrus, Gyozo Laszlo 1935- *1*
  See also SAAS *4*
Ambrus, Victor G.
  See Ambrus, Gyozo Laszlo
Amend, Bill 1962- *147*
Amerman, Lockhart 1911-1969 .... *3*
Ames, Evelyn 1908-1990 .... *13*
  Obituary *64*
Ames, Gerald 1906-1993 .... *11*
  Obituary *74*
Ames, Lee J(udah) 1921- *151*
  Earlier sketch in SATA *3*
Ames, Mildred 1919-1994 .... *85*
  Earlier sketches in SATA *22, 81*
Amico, Tom 1960(?)- *176*
Amit, Ofra 1966- *205*
Ammon, Richard 1942- *124*
Amon, Aline 1928- *9*
Amory, Jay
  See Lovegrove, James
Amoss, Berthe 1925- *112*
  Earlier sketch in SATA *5*
Amstutz, Andre 1925- *214*
Anastasio, Dina 1941- *94*
  Brief entry *30*
  Earlier sketch in SATA *37*
Anaya, Rudolfo 1937-
  See CLR *129*
Anaya, Rudolfo A.
  See Anaya, Rudolfo
Anaya, Rudolpho Alfonso
  See Anaya, Rudolfo
Anckarsvard, Karin Inez Maria 1915-1969 .... *6*
Ancona, George 1929- *208*
  Autobiography Feature *208*
  Earlier sketches in SATA *12, 85, 145, 192*
  See also SAAS *18*

Anders, C. J.
  See Bennett, Cherie
Anders, Isabel 1946- *101*
Anders, Lou *176*
Andersdatter, Karla M(argaret) 1938- *34*
Andersen, Bethanne 1954- *191*
Andersen, Hans Christian 1805-1875 .... *100*
  See also YABC *1*
  See also CLR *113*
Andersen, Ted
  See Boyd, Waldo T.
Andersen, Yvonne 1932- *27*
Anderson, Bernice G(oudy) 1894-1997 .... *33*
Anderson, Bob 1944- *139*
  Earlier sketch in SATA *136*
Anderson, Brad 1924- *33*
  Brief entry *31*
Anderson, Bradley Jay
  See Anderson, Brad
Anderson, Brian 1974- *211*
Anderson, C. C.
  See Anderson, Catherine Corley
Anderson, C(larence) W(illiam) 1891-1971 . *11*
Anderson, Carolyn Dunn
  See Dunn, Carolyn
Anderson, Catherine C.
  See Anderson, Catherine Corley
Anderson, Catherine Corley 1909-2001 .... *72*
Anderson, Clifford
  See Gardner, Richard (M.)
Anderson, Daryl Shon 1963- *93*
Anderson, Dave
  See Anderson, David
Anderson, David 1929- *60*
Anderson, Derek 1969- *169*
Anderson, Eloise Adell 1927- *9*
Anderson, George
  See Groom, Arthur William
Anderson, Grace Fox 1932- *43*
Anderson, J(ohn) R(ichard) L(ane)
  1911-1981 .... *15*
  Obituary *27*
Anderson, Jodi Lynn *182*
Anderson, John David *197*
Anderson, John L. 1905- *2*
Anderson, Joy 1928- *1*
Anderson, Kevin J. 1962- *117*
  Earlier sketch in SATA *74*
Anderson, Kevin James
  See Anderson, Kevin J.
Anderson, Kirsty 1978- *108*
Anderson, K.J.
  See Moesta, Rebecca
Anderson, Laurie Halse 1961- *186*
  Earlier sketches in SATA *95, 132*
  See also CLR *138*
Anderson, LaVere Francis Shoenfelt
  1907-1998 .... *27*
Anderson, Leone Castell 1923- *53*
  Brief entry *49*
Anderson, Lisa G. 1963- *108*
Anderson, Lonzo
  See Anderson, John L.
Anderson, Lucia (Lewis) 1922- *10*
Anderson, Madelyn Klein 1926-2005 .... *28*
Anderson, Margaret J(ean) 1931- *27*
  See also SAAS *8*
Anderson, Marilyn D. 1943- *144*
Anderson, Mary 1939- *82*
  Earlier sketch in SATA *7*
  See also SAAS *23*
Anderson, Matthew Tobin
  See Anderson, M.T.
Anderson, Mona 1910-2004 .... *40*
Anderson, Mrs. Melvin
  See Anderson, Catherine Corley
Anderson, M.T. 1968- *182*
  Earlier sketches in SATA *97, 146*
Anderson, Norman Dean 1928- *22*
Anderson, Peggy Perry 1953- *179*
  Earlier sketch in SATA *84*

Anderson, Poul 1926-2001 .... *90*
  Autobiography Feature *106*
  Brief entry *39*
  See also CLR *58*
Anderson, Poul William
  See Anderson, Poul
Anderson, Rachel 1943- *86*
  Earlier sketch in SATA *34*
  See also SAAS *18*
Anderson, Rebecca J.
  See Anderson, R.J.
Anderson, Rebecca M.
  See Moesta, Rebecca
Anderson, Rebecca Moesta
  See Moesta, Rebecca
Anderson, Richard
  See Anderson, J(ohn) R(ichard) L(ane)
Anderson, R.J. 1970(?)- *216*
Anderson, Sara *173*
Anderson, Scoular *201*
Anderson, (Tom) Scoular *138*
Anderson, Susan 1952- *90*
Anderson, Thomas Scoular
  See Anderson, Scoular
Anderson, W. B.
  See Schultz, James Willard
Anderson, Wayne 1946- *202*
  Earlier sketches in SATA *56, 147*
Andersson, Kenneth 1970- *200*
Andre, Evelyn M. 1924- *27*
Andre, Evelyn Marie
  See Andre, Evelyn M.
Andreasen, Dan *186*
Andreassen, Karl
  See Boyd, Waldo T.
Andreassi, K. Robert
  See DeCandido, Keith R.A.
Andree, Louise
  See Coury, Louise Andree
Andrew, Ian 1962- *166*
  Earlier sketch in SATA *116*
Andrew, Ian Peter
  See Andrew, Ian
Andrew, Prudence (Hastings) 1924- *87*
Andrews, Benny 1930-2006 .... *31*
  Obituary *178*
Andrews, Eleanor Lattimore
  See Lattimore, Eleanor Frances
Andrews, Elton V.
  See Pohl, Frederik
Andrews, F(rank) Emerson 1902-1978 .... *22*
Andrews, J(ames) S(ydney) 1934- *4*
Andrews, Jan 1942- *167*
  Brief entry *49*
  Earlier sketches in SATA *58, 98*
Andrews, Julie 1935- *153*
  Earlier sketch in SATA *7*
  See also CLR *85*
Andrews, Laura
  See Coury, Louise Andree
Andrews, Roy Chapman 1884-1960 .... *19*
Andrews, Tamra 1959- *129*
Andrews, V(irginia) C(leo) 1924(?)-1986
  Obituary *50*
Andrews, Wendy
  See Sharmat, Marjorie Weinman
Andrews, William G. 1930- *74*
Andrews, William George
  See Andrews, William G.
Andrezel, Pierre
  See Blixen, Karen
Andriani, Renee
  See Williams-Andriani, Renee
Andriola, Alfred J. 1912-1983
  Obituary *34*
Andrist, Ralph K. 1914-2004 .... *45*
Andronik, Catherine M. *189*
Andryszewski, Tricia 1956- *148*
  Earlier sketch in SATA *88*
Anelli, Melissa 1979- *215*
Angel, Ann 1952- *192*

Angel, Carl *178*
Angel, Marie 1923- *47*
Angeles, Peter A. 1931- *40*
Angeletti, Roberta 1964- *124*
Angeli, Marguerite (Lofft) de
  See de Angeli, Marguerite (Lofft)
Angell, Judie 1937- *78*
  Earlier sketch in SATA *22*
  See also CLR *33*
Angell, Madeline 1919- *18*
Angelo, Valenti 1897- *14*
Angelou, Maya 1928- *136*
  Earlier sketch in SATA *49*
  See also CLR *53*
Angier, Bradford -1997 .... *12*
Angle, Kimberly Greene *203*
Angle, Paul M(cClelland) 1900-1975
  Obituary *20*
Anglund, Joan Walsh 1926- *2*
  See also CLR *94*
Ango, Fan D.
  See Longyear, Barry B(rookes)
Angrist, Stanley W(olff) 1933- *4*
Anholt, Catherine 1958- *131*
  Earlier sketch in SATA *74*
Anholt, Laurence 1959- *141*
  Earlier sketch in SATA *74*
Anita
  See Daniel, Anita
Anmar, Frank
  See Nolan, William F.
Annett, Cora
  See Scott, Cora Annett (Pipitone)
Annie-Jo
  See Blanchard, Patricia
  and Suhr, Joanne
Annixter, Jane
  See Sturtzel, Jane Levington
Annixter, Paul
  See Sturtzel, Howard A(llison)
Anno, Mitsumasa 1926- *157*
  Earlier sketches in SATA *5, 38, 77*
  See also CLR *122*
Anrooy, Francine Van
  See Van Anrooy, Francine
Ansary, Mir Tamim 1948- *140*
Anstey, Caroline 1958- *81*
Antell, Will D. 1935- *31*
Anthony, Barbara
  See Barber, Antonia
Anthony, C. L.
  See Smith, Dorothy Gladys
Anthony, Edward 1895-1971 .... *21*
Anthony, John
  See Beckett, Ronald Brymer
  and Ciardi, John (Anthony)
  and Sabini, John Anthony
Anthony, Joseph Patrick 1964- *103*
Anthony, Patricia 1947- *109*
Anthony, Piers 1934- *129*
  Autobiography Feature *129*
  Earlier sketch in SATA *84*
  See also CLR *118*
  See also SAAS *22*
Anthony, Susan C(arol) 1953- *87*
Anticaglia, Elizabeth 1939- *12*
Antieau, Kim *214*
Antilles, Kem
  See Moesta, Rebecca
Antle, Nancy 1955- *102*
Antolini, Margaret Fishback 1904-1985
  Obituary *45*
Anton, Michael J(ames) 1940- *12*
Antonacci, Robert J(oseph) 1916- *45*
  Brief entry *37*
Anvil, Christopher 1925-2009 .... *102*
Anzaldua, Gloria (Evanjelina) 1942-2004
  Obituary *154*
Aoki, Hisako 1942- *45*
Apfel, Necia H(alpern) 1930- *51*
  Brief entry *41*

Aphrodite, J.
  See Livingston, Carole
Apikuni
  See Schultz, James Willard
Apostolina, M. 184
Apostolina, Michael
  See Apostolina, M.
Apostolou, Christine Hale 1955- 179
  Earlier sketches in SATA 82, 128
Appel, Allen (R.) 1945- 115
Appel, Benjamin 1907-1977 39
  Obituary 21
Appel, Martin 1948- 45
Appel, Martin Eliot
  See Appel, Martin
Appel, Marty
  See Appel, Martin
Appelbaum, Diana Muir Karter 1953- 132
Appelt, Kathi 1954- 190
  Earlier sketches in SATA 83, 129
Apperley, Dawn 1969- 135
Appiah, Peggy 1921-2006 84
  Earlier sketch in SATA 15
  See also SAAS 19
Apple, Margot 214
  Brief entry 42
  Earlier sketches in SATA 64, 152
Applebaum, Stan 1922- 45
Applegate, K.A.
  See Applegate, Katherine
Applegate, Katherine 1956- 196
  Earlier sketches in SATA 109, 162
  See also CLR 90
Applegate, Katherine Alice
  See Applegate, Katherine
Appleton, Victor
  See Barrett, Neal, Jr.
  and Doyle, Debra
  and Macdonald, James D.
  and Stratemeyer, Edward L.
  and Vardeman, Robert E.
Appleton, Victor II
  See Goulart, Ron
Appollo 1969- 214
Appollodorus, Olivier
  See Apple, Margot
Apsler, Alfred 1907-1982 10
Aragones, Sergio 1937- 48
  Brief entry 39
Araujo, Frank P. 1937- 86
Arbo, Cris 1950- 103
Arbuckle, Dorothy Fry 1910-1982
  Obituary 33
Arbuthnot, May Hill 1884-1969 2
Archambault, John 163
  Earlier sketches in SATA 67, 112
Archbold, Rick 1950- 97
Archer, Colleen Rutherford 1949- 164
Archer, Frank
  See O'Connor, Richard
Archer, Jules 1915- 85
  Earlier sketch in SATA 4
  See also SAAS 5
Archer, Lily 1981- 193
Archer, Marion Fuller 1917- 11
Archer, Nathan
  See Watt-Evans, Lawrence
Archer, Peggy 1947- 199
Archibald, Joe
  See Archibald, Joseph S(topford)
Archibald, Joseph S(topford) 1898-1986 3
  Obituary 47
Ard, William
  See Jakes, John
Ardagh, Philip 1961- 154
Ardai, Charles 1969- 85
Arden, Barbi
  See Stoutenburg, Adrien (Pearl)
Arden, William
  See Lynds, Dennis

Ardizzone, Edward (Jeffrey Irving)
  1900-1979 28
  Obituary 21
  Earlier sketch in SATA 1
  See also CLR 3
Ardley, Neil 1937- 121
  Earlier sketch in SATA 43
Ardley, Neil Richard
  See Ardley, Neil
Arehart-Treichel, Joan 1942- 22
Arena, Felice 1968- 151
Arenella, Roy 1939- 14
Argent, Kerry 1960- 138
Arguelles, Francisco Xavier
  See Stork, Francisco X.
Argueta, Jorge 179
Arihara, Shino 1973- 201
Arkin, Alan 1934- 59
  Brief entry 32
Arkin, Alan Wolf
  See Arkin, Alan
Arksey, Neil 158
Arlen, Leslie
  See Nicole, Christopher (Robin)
Arley, Robert
  See Jackson, Mike
Armer, Alberta (Roller) 1904-1986 9
Armer, Laura Adams 1874-1963 13
Armistead, John 1941- 130
Armitage, David 1943- 155
  Brief entry 38
  Earlier sketch in SATA 99
Armitage, Frank
  See Carpenter, John
Armitage, Ronda (Jacqueline) 1943- 155
  Brief entry 38
  Earlier sketches in SATA 47, 99
Armour, Richard (Willard) 1906-1989 14
  Obituary 61
Armstrong, Alan 1939- 172
Armstrong, Alan W.
  See Armstrong, Alan
Armstrong, George D. 1927- 10
Armstrong, Gerry (Breen) 1929- 10
Armstrong, Jeannette (C.) 1948- 102
Armstrong, Jennifer 1961- 165
  Autobiography Feature 120
  Earlier sketches in SATA 77, 111
  See also CLR 66
  See also SAAS 24
Armstrong, Louise 43
  Brief entry 33
Armstrong, Martin Donisthorpe
  1882-1974 115
Armstrong, Matthew 1975- 188
Armstrong, Matthew S.
  See Armstrong, Matthew
Armstrong, Ralph Richard
  See Armstrong, Richard
Armstrong, Richard 1903-1986 11
Armstrong, William H(oward) 1914-1999 4
  Obituary 111
  See also CLR 117
  See also SAAS 7
Armstrong-Ellis, Carey (Fraser) 1956- 145
Arndt, Ursula (Martha H.) 56
  Brief entry 39
Arneson, D(on) J(on) 1935- 37
Arnett, Caroline
  See Cole, Lois Dwight
Arnett, Jack
  See Goulart, Ron
Arnette, Robert
  See Silverberg, Robert
Arno, Enrico 1913-1981 43
  Obituary 28
Arnold, Ann 1953(?)- 207

Arnold, Caroline 1944- 174
  Brief entry 34
  Earlier sketches in SATA 36, 85, 131
  See also CLR 61
  See also SAAS 23
Arnold, Elizabeth 1944- 164
Arnold, Elliott 1912-1980 5
  Obituary 22
Arnold, Emily 1939- 134
  Autobiography Feature 134
  Earlier sketches in SATA 5, 50, 76, 110
  See also CLR 46
  See also SAAS 7
  See McCully, Emily Arnold
Arnold, Gillian Clare
  See Cross, Gillian
Arnold, Katya 1947- 168
  Earlier sketches in SATA 82, 115
Arnold, Louise 175
Arnold, Louise Claire
  See Arnold, Louise
Arnold, Marsha Diane 1948- 147
  Earlier sketch in SATA 93
Arnold, Nick 1961- 113
Arnold, Oren 1900-1980 4
Arnold, Susan (Riser) 1951- 58
Arnold, Tedd 1949- 208
  Earlier sketches in SATA 69, 116, 160
Arnoldy, Julie
  See Bischoff, Julia Bristol
Arnosky, James Edward 1946- 189
  Earlier sketches in SATA 70, 118
  See also CLR 93
  See Arnosky, Jim
Arnosky, Jim 217
  See Arnosky, James Edward
Arnott, Kathleen 1914- 20
Arnov, Boris, Jr. 1926- 12
Arnow, Harriette (Louisa) Simpson
  1908-1986 42
  Obituary 47
Arnsteen, Katy Keck 1934- 68
Arnstein, Helene S(olomon) 1915- 12
Arntson, Herbert E(dward) 1911-1982 12
Aroner, Miriam 82
Aronin, Ben 1904-1980
  Obituary 25
Aronson, Marc 1950- 189
  Autobiography Feature 189
  Earlier sketches in SATA 126, 175
Aronson, Marc Henry
  See Aronson, Marc
Aronson, Sarah 196
Aronson, Virginia 1954- 122
Arora, Shirley (Lease) 1930- 2
Arrasmith, Patrick 176
Arrick, Fran
  See Angell, Judie
Arrigan, Mary 1943- 142
Arrington, Aileen 183
Arrington, Stephen L. 1948- 97
Arrington, Stephen Lee
  See Arrington, Stephen L.
Arrley, Richmond
  See Delany, Samuel R., Jr.
Arrowood, (McKendrick Lee) Clinton
  1939- 19
Arrowsmith, Pat 1930- 59
Arsenault, Isabelle 1978- 207
Artell, Mike 1948- 183
  Earlier sketches in SATA 89, 134
Arthur, Robert (Andrew) 1909-1969
  See Arthur, Robert, (Jr.)
Arthur, Robert, (Jr.) 1909-1969 118
Arthur, Ruth M(abel) 1905-1979 26
  Earlier sketch in SATA 7
Artis, Vicki Kimmel 1945- 12
Artzybasheff, Boris (Miklailovich)
  1899-1965 14
Aruego, Ariane
  See Dewey, Ariane

Aruego, Jose 1932- *178*
  Earlier sketches in SATA *6, 68, 125*
  See also CLR 5
Aruego, Jose Espiritu
  See Aruego, Jose
Arundel, Honor (Morfydd) 1919-1973 .... *4*
  Obituary *24*
  See also CLR 35
Arundel, Jocelyn
  See Alexander, Jocelyn Anne Arundel
Arvey, Michael 1948- *79*
Arzoumanian, Alik *177*
Asare, Meshack (Yaw) 1945- *139*
  Earlier sketch in SATA *86*
Asaro, Catherine 1955- *165*
  Earlier sketch in SATA *101*
Asaro, Catherine Ann 1955-
  See Asaro, Catherine
Asay, Donna Day 1945- *127*
Asbjornsen, Peter Christen 1812-1885 .... *15*
  See also CLR *104*
Asch, Frank 1946- *154*
  Earlier sketches in SATA *5, 66, 102*
Ash, Jutta 1942- *38*
Ashabranner, Brent 1921- *166*
  Earlier sketches in SATA *1, 67, 130*
  See also CLR 28
  See also SAAS 14
Ashabranner, Brent Kenneth
  See Ashabranner, Brent
Ashbless, William
  See Blaylock, James P.
  and Powers, Tim
Ashby, Gil 1958- *146*
Ashby, Gwynneth 1922- *44*
Ashby, Ruth *170*
Ashby, Yvonne 1955- *121*
Ashe, Arthur (Robert, Jr.) 1943-1993 .... *65*
  Obituary *87*
Ashe, Geoffrey (Thomas) 1923- *17*
  Autobiography Feature *125*
Ashe, Mary Ann
  See Lewis, Mary
Asher, Bridget
  See Baggott, Julianna
Asher, Sandra Fenichel
  See Asher, Sandy
Asher, Sandy 1942- *71*
  Autobiography Feature *158*
  Brief entry *34*
  Earlier sketch in SATA *36*
  See also SAAS 13
Asheron, Sara
  See Moore, Lilian
Ashey, Bella
  See Breinburg, Petronella
Ashford, Daisy
  See Ashford, Margaret Mary
Ashford, Jeffrey
  See Jeffries, Roderic
Ashford, Margaret Mary 1881-1972 .... *10*
Ashland, Monk 1972- *207*
Ashley, Bernard (John) 1935- *155*
  Brief entry *39*
  Earlier sketches in SATA *47, 79*
  See also CLR 4
Ashley, Elizabeth
  See Salmon, Annie Elizabeth
Ashley, Ray
  See Abrashkin, Raymond
Ashman, Linda 1960- *203*
  Earlier sketch in SATA *150*
Ashton, Lorayne
  See Gottfried, Theodore Mark
Ashton, Warren T.
  See Adams, William Taylor
Asimov, Isaac 1920-1992 .... *74*
  Earlier sketches in SATA *1, 26*
  See also CLR 79
Asinof, Eliot 1919-2008 .... *6*

Asinof, Eliot Tager
  See Asinof, Eliot
Aska, Warabe
  See Masuda, Takeshi
Asprin, Robert 1946-2008 .... *92*
Asprin, Robert L.
  See Asprin, Robert
Asprin, Robert Lynn
  See Asprin, Robert
Asquith, Cynthia Mary Evelyn (Charteris)
  1887-1960 .... *107*
Asquith, Ros *153*
Astley, Juliet
  See Lofts, Norah (Robinson)
Aston, Dianna Hutts 1964- *176*
Aston, James
  See White, T(erence) H(anbury)
Ata, Te 1895-1995 .... *119*
Atene, Ann
  See Atene, (Rita) Anna
Atene, (Rita) Anna 1922- *12*
Atheling, William, Jr.
  See Blish, James
Atkins, Catherine *160*
Atkins, Jeannine 1953- *172*
  Earlier sketch in SATA *113*
Atkinson, Allen G. 1953(?)-1987 .... *60*
  Brief entry *46*
  Obituary *55*
Atkinson, Elizabeth *215*
Atkinson, M. E.
  See Frankau, Mary Evelyn Atkinson
Atkinson, Margaret Fleming *14*
Atteberry, Kevan J. *186*
Attema, Martha 1949- *156*
  Earlier sketch in SATA *94*
Atticus
  See Davies, Hunter
  and Fleming, Ian
  and Pawle, Gerald Strachan
  and Wilson, (Thomas) Woodrow
Atwater, Florence (Hasseltine Carroll)
  1896-1979 .... *66*
  Earlier sketch in SATA *16*
  See also CLR 19
Atwater, Montgomery Meigs 1904-1976 ...... *15*
Atwater, Richard (Tupper) 1892-1948 .... *66*
  Brief entry *27*
  Earlier sketch in SATA *54*
  See also CLR 19
Atwater-Rhodes, Amelia 1984- *170*
  Earlier sketch in SATA *124*
Atwell, Debby 1953- *150*
  Earlier sketch in SATA *87*
Atwood, Ann (Margaret) 1913-1992 .... *7*
Atwood, Margaret 1939- *170*
  Earlier sketch in SATA *50*
Atwood, Margaret Eleanor
  See Atwood, Margaret
Aubrey, Meg Kelleher 1963- *83*
Aubry, Claude B. 1914-1984 .... *29*
  Obituary *40*
Auch, Herm *173*
Auch, Mary Jane *173*
  Earlier sketch in SATA *138*
Auch, M.J.
  See Auch, Mary Jane
Auclair, Joan 1960- *68*
Auel, Jean 1936- *91*
Auel, Jean M.
  See Auel, Jean
Auel, Jean Marie
  See Auel, Jean
Auer, Martin 1951- *77*
Augarde, Steve 1950- *210*
  Earlier sketches in SATA *25, 159*
Augarde, Steven Andre
  See Augarde, Steve
Augelli, John P(at) 1921- *46*
Augustine, Mildred
  See Benson, Mildred

Ault, Phil
  See Ault, Phillip H(alliday)
Ault, Phillip H(alliday) 1914- *23*
Ault, Rosalie Sain 1942- *38*
Ault, Roz
  See Ault, Rosalie Sain
Aung, (Maung) Htin 1909- *21*
Auntie Deb
  See Coury, Louise Andree
Auntie Louise
  See Coury, Louise Andree
Aunt Weedy
  See Alcott, Louisa May
Auseon, Andrew 1976- *217*
  Earlier sketch in SATA *166*
Austen, Carrie
  See Bennett, Cherie
Austin, Carrie
  See Seuling, Barbara
Austin, Elizabeth S. 1907-1977 .... *5*
Austin, Harry
  See McInerny, Ralph
Austin, Margot 1909(?)-1990 .... *11*
  Obituary *66*
Austin, Michael *178*
Austin, Oliver L(uther), Jr. 1903-1988 .... *7*
  Obituary *59*
Austin, Patricia 1950- *137*
Austin, R. G.
  See Gelman, Rita Golden
  and Lamb, Nancy
Austin, Virginia 1951- *152*
  Earlier sketch in SATA *80*
Auteur, Hillary
  See Gottfried, Theodore Mark
Auth, Tony
  See Auth, William Anthony, Jr.
Auth, William Anthony, Jr. 1942- *192*
Autry, Gloria Diener
  See Allen, Terril Diener
Auvil, Peggy A 1954- *122*
Auvil, Peggy Appleby
  See Auvil, Peggy A
Aveni, Anthony F. 1938- *181*
Aveni, Anthony Francis
  See Aveni, Anthony F.
Averbeck, Jim 1963- *201*
Averill, Esther (Holden) 1902-1992 .... *28*
  Obituary *72*
  Earlier sketch in SATA *1*
Avery, A. A.
  See Montgomery, Rutherford George
Avery, Al
  See Montgomery, Rutherford George
Avery, Gillian 1926- *137*
  Autobiography Feature *137*
  Earlier sketches in SATA *7, 75*
  See also SAAS 6
Avery, Gillian Elise
  See Avery, Gillian
Avery, Kay 1908- *5*
Avery, Lorraine
  See Older, Effin
  and Older, Jules
Avery, Lynn
  See Cole, Lois Dwight
Avi 1937- *190*
  Earlier sketches in SATA *14, 71, 108, 156*
  See also CLR 68
Avishai, Susan 1949- *82*
Avril, Francois 1961- *191*
Avril, Lynne
  See Cravath, Lynne W.
Awdry, Christopher Vere 1940- *67*
Awdry, Wilbert Vere 1911-1997 .... *94*
  See also CLR 23
Axelrod, Amy *131*
Axelsen, Stephen 1953- *165*
Axton, David
  See Koontz, Dean
Ayars, James S(terling) 1898-1986 .... *4*

Aye, A. K.
  See Edwards, Hazel (Eileen)
Ayer, Eleanor H. 1947-1998 .... *121*
  Earlier sketch in SATA *78*
Ayer, Jacqueline 1930- *13*
Ayer, Margaret (?)-1981 .... *15*
Aylesworth, Jim 1943- *213*
  Earlier sketches in SATA *38, 89, 139*
  See also CLR *89*
Aylesworth, Thomas G(ibbons) 1927-1995 .. *88*
  Earlier sketch in SATA *4*
  See also CLR *6*
  See also SAAS *17*
Ayliffe, Alex *190*
Aylward, Marcus
  See Alexander, Marc
Aymar, Brandt 1911- *22*
Ayme, Marcel (Andre) 1902-1967 .... *91*
  See also CLR *25*
Ayres, Becky
  See Hickox, Rebecca (Ayres)
Ayres, Katherine 1947- *187*
Ayres, Pam 1947- *90*
Ayres, Patricia Miller 1923-1985
  Obituary *46*
Aytmatov, Chingiz
  See Aitmatov, Chingiz
Ayto, Russell 1960- *206*
  Earlier sketches in SATA *111, 166*
Azaid
  See Zaidenberg, Arthur
Azar, Penny 1952- *121*
Azarian, Mary 1940- *171*
  Earlier sketch in SATA *112*
Azore, Barbara 1934- *188*

B

Baasansuren, Bolormaa 1982- *216*
Baastad, Babbis Friis
  See Friis-Baastad, Babbis Ellinor
Bab
  See Gilbert, W(illiam) S(chwenck)
Babbis, Eleanor
  See Friis-Baastad, Babbis Ellinor
Babbitt, Lucy Cullyford 1960- *85*
Babbitt, Natalie 1932- *194*
  Earlier sketches in SATA *6, 68, 106*
  See also CLR *141*
  See also SAAS *5*
Babbitt, Natalie Zane Moore
  See Babbitt, Natalie
Babcock, Chris 1963- *83*
Babcock, Dennis 1948- *22*
Babcock, Dennis Arthur
  See Babcock, Dennis
Baber, Carolyn Stonnell 1936- *96*
Baboni, Elena *198*
Baca, Ana 1967- *191*
Baca, Maria 1951- *104*
Bach, Alice (Hendricks) 1942- *93*
  Brief entry *27*
  Earlier sketch in SATA *30*
Bach, Bellamy
  See Windling, Terri
Bach, Mary 1960- *125*
Bach, Richard 1936- *13*
Bach, Richard David
  See Bach, Richard
Bache, Ellyn 1942- *124*
Bachel, Beverly K. 1957- *142*
Bachelet, Gilles 1952- *196*
Bachman, Fred 1949- *12*
Bachman, Richard
  See King, Stephen
Bachrach, Deborah *80*
Backus, James Gilmore 1913-1989
  Obituary *63*

Backus, Jim
  See Backus, James Gilmore
Bacmeister, Rhoda W(arner) 1893-1991 .... *11*
Bacon, Betty
  See Bacon, Elizabeth
Bacon, Elizabeth 1914-2001 .... *3*
  Obituary *131*
Bacon, Joan Chase
  See Bowden, Joan Chase
Bacon, Josephine Dodge (Daskam)
  1876-1961 .... *48*
Bacon, Margaret Frances
  See Bacon, Peggy
Bacon, Margaret Hope 1921- *6*
Bacon, Martha Sherman 1917-1981 .... *18*
  Obituary *27*
  See also CLR *3*
Bacon, Melvin 1950- *93*
Bacon, Melvin L.
  See Bacon, Melvin
Bacon, Peggy 1895-1987 .... *50*
Bacon, R(onald) L(eonard) 1924- *84*
  Earlier sketch in SATA *26*
Baddiel, Ivor 1963- *210*
Baden, Robert 1936- *70*
Baden-Powell, Robert (Stephenson Smyth)
  1857-1941 .... *16*
Badt, Karin L(uisa) 1963- *91*
Bae, Hyun-Joo *186*
Baehr, Kingsley M. 1937- *89*
Baehr, Patricia 1952- *65*
Baehr, Patricia Goehner
  See Baehr, Patricia
Baek, Matthew J. 1971- *202*
Baer, Jill
  See Gilbert, (Agnes) Joan (Sewell)
Baer, Judy 1951- *71*
Baer, Julie 1960- *161*
Baer-Block, Roxanna *172*
Baerg, Harry J(ohn) 1909-1996 .... *12*
Baeten, Lieve 1954- *83*
Bagert, Brod 1947- *191*
  Earlier sketch in SATA *80*
Baggette, Susan K. 1942- *126*
Baggott, Julianna 1969- *197*
Bagnold, Enid 1889-1981 .... *25*
  Earlier sketch in SATA *1*
Baguley, Elizabeth 1959- *199*
Bahlke, Valerie Worth -1994
  See Worth, Valerie
Bahous, Sally 1939- *86*
Bahr, Mary (Madelyn) 1946- *95*
Bahr, Robert 1940- *38*
Bahti, Tom 1926-1972 .... *57*
  Brief entry *31*
Bai, Durga *211*
Baicker-McKee, Carol 1958- *177*
Bailey, Alice Cooper 1890-1978 .... *12*
Bailey, Anne 1958- *71*
Bailey, Bernadine (Freeman) 1901-1995 ...... *14*
Bailey, Carolyn Sherwin 1875-1961 .... *14*
Bailey, Debbie 1954- *123*
Bailey, Donna (Veronica Anne) 1938- *68*
Bailey, Jane H(orton) 1916- *12*
Bailey, John (Robert) 1940- *52*
Bailey, Len *193*
Bailey, Linda 1948- *217*
  Earlier sketches in SATA *107, 182*
Bailey, Maralyn Collins (Harrison) 1941- *12*
Bailey, Matilda
  See Radford, Ruby L(orraine)
Bailey, Maurice Charles 1932- *12*
Bailey, Pearl (Mae) 1918-1990 .... *81*
Bailey, Peter 1946- *194*
Bailey, Ralph Edgar 1893-1982 .... *11*
Bailey, Sheila (Lucas) 1960- *155*
Baillie, Allan 1943- *151*
  Earlier sketch in SATA *87*
  See also CLR *49*
  See also SAAS *21*

Baillie, Allan Stuart
  See Baillie, Allan
Baines, John (David) 1943- *71*
Bains, Larry
  See Sabin, Louis
Baird, Alison 1963- *138*
Baird, Bil 1904-1987 .... *30*
  Obituary *52*
Baird, Thomas (P.) 1923-1990 .... *45*
  Brief entry *39*
  Obituary *64*
Baird, William Britton
  See Baird, Bil
Baity, Elizabeth Chesley 1907-1989 .... *1*
Baiul, Oksana 1977- *108*
Bajoria, Paul 1964- *187*
Bakeless, John (Edwin) 1894-1978 .... *9*
Bakeless, Katherine Little 1895-1992 .... *9*
Baker, Alan 1951- *146*
  Earlier sketches in SATA *22, 93*
Baker, Augusta 1911-1998 .... *3*
Baker, Barbara 1947- *192*
Baker, Betty Lou 1928-1987 .... *73*
  Obituary *54*
  Earlier sketch in SATA *5*
Baker, Carin Greenberg 1959- *79*
Baker, Charlotte 1910- *2*
Baker, Christina
  See Kline, Christina Baker
Baker, Christopher W. 1952- *144*
Baker, Deirdre 1955- *195*
Baker, E.D. *190*
Baker, (Mary) Elizabeth (Gillette) 1923- *7*
Baker, Gayle Cunningham 1950- *39*
Baker, James W. 1924- *65*
  Earlier sketch in SATA *22*
Baker, James W. 1926- *122*
Baker, Janice E(dla) 1941- *22*
Baker, Jeanette *178*
Baker, Jeannie 1950- *156*
  Earlier sketches in SATA *23, 88*
  See also CLR *28*
Baker, Jeffrey J(ohn) W(heeler) 1931- *5*
Baker, Jim
  See Baker, James W.
Baker, Keith 1953- *179*
Baker, Ken 1962- *133*
Baker, Laura Nelson 1911- *3*
Baker, Margaret 1890-1965 .... *4*
Baker, Margaret J(oyce) 1918- *12*
  See also SAAS *8*
Baker, Mary Gladys Steel 1892-1974 .... *12*
Baker, (Robert) Michael (Graham) 1938- *4*
Baker, Nina (Brown) 1888-1957 .... *15*
Baker, Pamela J. 1947- *66*
Baker, Rachel 1904-1978 .... *2*
  Obituary *26*
Baker, Roberta *206*
Baker, Rosalie F. 1945- *166*
Baker, Samm Sinclair 1909-1997 .... *12*
  Obituary *96*
Baker, Sharon Reiss 1962- *207*
Baker, Susan (Catherine) 1942-1991 .... *29*
Balaam
  See Lamb, G(eoffrey) F(rederick)
Balan, Bruce 1959- *113*
Balcavage, Dynise 1965- *137*
Balch, Glenn 1902-1989 .... *3*
  Obituary *83*
  See also SAAS *11*
Baldacci, David 1960- *184*
Baldacci, David G.
  See Baldacci, David
  and Baldacci, David
Balderose, Nancy Ward 1952- *93*
Balderson, Margaret 1935- *151*
Baldini, Michelle *205*
Baldry, Cherith 1947- *167*
  Earlier sketch in SATA *72*
Balducci, Carolyn 1946- *5*

Balducci, Carolyn Feleppa
See Balducci, Carolyn
Baldwin, Alex
See Griffin, W.E.B.
Baldwin, Anne Norris 1938- 5
Baldwin, Clara 11
Baldwin, Gordo
See Baldwin, Gordon C(ortis)
Baldwin, Gordon C(ortis) 1908-1983 12
Baldwin, James 1841-1925 24
Baldwin, James 1924-1987 9
Obituary 54
Baldwin, Louis 1919- 110
Baldwin, Margaret
See Weis, Margaret
Baldwin, Stan(ley C.) 1929- 62
Brief entry 28
Bales, Carol Ann 1940- 57
Brief entry 29
Balet, Jan (Bernard) 1913- 11
Balgassi, Haemi 1971- 131
Balian, Lorna 1929- 91
Earlier sketch in SATA 9
Balit, Christina 1961- 212
Earlier sketches in SATA *102, 159*
Ball, Duncan 1941- 73
Ball, Zachary
See Janas, Frankie-Lee
and Masters, Kelly R(ay)
Ballantine, Lesley Frost
See Frost, Lesley
Ballantyne, R(obert) M(ichael) 1825-1894 ... 24
See also CLR 137
Ballard, James G.
See Ballard, J.G.
Ballard, James Graham
See Ballard, J.G.
Ballard, Jane
See Gorman, Carol
Ballard, J.G. 1930-2009 93
Obituary 203
Ballard, Jim G.
See Ballard, J.G.
Ballard, John 1945- 110
Ballard, Lowell C(lyne) 1904-1986 12
Obituary 49
Ballard, (Charles) Martin 1929- 1
Ballard, Mignon F. 1934- 64
Brief entry 49
Ballard, Mignon Franklin
See Ballard, Mignon F.
Ballard, Robert D(uane) 1942- 85
See also CLR 60
Ballard, Robin 1965- 126
Balliett, Blue 1955- 156
Ballinger, Bryan 1968- 161
Ballouhey, Pierre 1944- 90
Balogh, Penelope 1916-1975 1
Obituary 34
Balouch, Kristen 176
Balow, Tom 1931- 12
Baltazzi, Evan S(erge) 1921- 90
Balterman, Marcia Ridlon 1942- 22
Baltimore, J.
See Catherall, Arthur
Baltzer, Hans (Adolf) 1900- 40
Balzano, Jeanne (Koppel) 1912- 7
Bambara, Toni Cade 1939-1995 112
Bamfylde, Walter
See Bevan, Tom
Bamman, Henry A. 1918- 12
Banat, D. R.
See Bradbury, Ray
Bancroft, Bronwyn 1958- 216
Bancroft, Griffing 1907-1999 6
Bancroft, Laura
See Baum, L. Frank
Bandel, Betty 1912- 47
Baner, Skulda Vanadis 1897-1964 10
Banerjee, Anjali 174
Banfill, A. Scott 1956- 98

Bang, Betsy 1912- 48
Brief entry 37
Bang, Garrett
See Bang, Molly
Bang, Molly 1943- 215
Earlier sketches in SATA *24, 69, 111, 158*
See also CLR 8
Bang, Molly Garrett
See Bang, Molly
Bang-Campbell, Monika 1975(?)- 195
Earlier sketch in SATA *140*
Banjo, The
See Paterson, A(ndrew) B(arton)
Banke, Cecile de
See de Banke, Cecile
Banks, Erin Bennett 1978- 211
Banks, Kate 1960- 200
Earlier sketches in SATA *134, 172*
Banks, Laura Stockton Voorhees 1908(?)-1980
Obituary 23
Banks, Lynne Reid
See Reid Banks, Lynne
Banks, Merry 197
Banks, Michael A. 1951- 101
Banks, Paul 1952- 174
Banks, Sara (Jeanne Gordon Harrell) 26
See Harrell, Sara (Jeanne) Gordon
Bannatyne-Cugnet, Elizabeth Jo-Anne
See Bannatyne-Cugnet, Jo
Bannatyne-Cugnet, Jo 1951- 101
Banner, Angela
See Maddison, Angela Mary
Bannerman, Helen (Brodie Cowan Watson)
1862(?)-1946 19
See also CLR 144
Banning, Evelyn I. 1903-1993 36
Bannon, Laura (?)-1963 6
Bannor, Brett 1959- 143
Banta, Susan 181
Bantock, Nick 1950(?)- 95
Banyai, Istvan 193
Barakat, Ibtisam 1963- 186
Barasch, Lynne 1939- 186
Earlier sketches in SATA *74, 126*
Barbalet, Margaret 1949- 77
Barbary, James
See Baumann, Amy Beeching
and Beeching, Jack
Barbash, Shepard 1957- 84
Barbe, Walter Burke 1926- 45
Barber, Antonia 1932- 163
Earlier sketch in SATA *29*
Barber, Atiim Kiambu
See Barber, Tiki
Barber, Lynda
See Graham-Barber, Lynda
Barber, Lynda Graham
See Graham-Barber, Lynda
Barber, Richard (William) 1941- 35
Barber, Ronde 1975- 182
Barber, Tiki 1975- 182
Barbera, Joe 1911-2006 51
Obituary 179
Barbera, Joseph
See Barbera, Joe
Barbera, Joseph Roland
See Barbera, Joe
Barberis, Juan C(arlos) 1920- 61
Barbour, Karen 1956- 170
Earlier sketches in SATA *63, 121*
Barbour, Ralph Henry 1870-1944 16
Barclay, Bill
See Moorcock, Michael
Barclay, Isabel
See Dobell, I(sabel) M(arian) B(arclay)
Barclay, William Ewert
See Moorcock, Michael
Barclay, William Ewert
See Moorcock, Michael
Bardhan-Quallen, Sudipta 1977- 214
Earlier sketch in SATA *168*

Bardoe, Cheryl 181
Bare, Arnold Edwin 1920- 16
Bare, Colleen Stanley 32
Bar-el, Dan 199
Barenholtz, Bernard 1914-1989
Obituary 64
Bargar, Gary W. 1947-1985 63
Barger, Jan 1948- 147
Barish, Matthew 1907-2000 12
Barkan, Joanne 127
Earlier sketch in SATA *77*
Barker, Albert W. 1900- 8
Barker, Carol (Minturn) 1938- 31
Barker, Cicely Mary 1895-1973 49
Brief entry 39
See also CLR 88
Barker, Melvern 1907-1989 11
Barker, S. Omar 1894-1985 10
Barker, Squire Omar
See Barker, S. Omar
Barker, Will 1913-1983 8
Barkin, Carol 1944- 52
Earlier sketch in SATA *42*
Barklem, Jill 1951- 96
See also CLR 31
Barkley, Brad 178
Barkley, James Edward 1941- 6
Barks, Carl 1901-2000 37
Barley, Janet Crane 1934- 95
Barlow, Steve 1952- 211
Barnaby, Ralph S(tanton) 1893-1986 9
Barnard, A. M.
See Alcott, Louisa May
Barnard, Bryn 1956- 169
Earlier sketch in SATA *115*
Barne, Kitty
See Barne, Marion Catherine
Barne, Marion Catherine 1883-1957 97
Barneda, David 206
Barner, Bob 1947- 136
Earlier sketch in SATA *29*
Barnes, Dawn 1957- 175
Barnes, Derrick 191
Barnes, Derrick D.
See Barnes, Derrick
Barnes, (Frank) Eric Wollencott 1907-1962 . 22
Barnes, Joyce Annette 1958- 85
Barnes, Laura T. 1958- 119
Barnes, Loutricia
See Barnes-Svarney, Patricia L(ou)
Barnes, Malcolm 1909(?)-1984
Obituary 41
Barnes, Michael 1934- 55
Barnes-Murphy, Frances 1951- 88
Barnes-Murphy, Rowan 1952- 88
Barnes-Svarney, Patricia L(ou) 1953- 67
Barnet, Nancy 1954- 84
Barnett, Ivan 1947- 70
Barnett, Lincoln (Kinnear) 1909-1979 36
Barnett, Moneta 1922-1976 33
Barnett, Naomi 1927- 40
Barney, Maginel Wright 1881(?)-1966 39
Brief entry 32
Barnhart, Clarence L(ewis) 1900-1993 48
Obituary 78
Barnouw, Adriaan Jacob 1877-1968
Obituary 27
Barnouw, Victor 1915-1989 43
Brief entry 28
Barnstone, Willis 1927- 20
Barnum, Jay Hyde 1888(?)-1962 20
Barnum, P. T., Jr.
See Stratemeyer, Edward L.
Barnum, Richard 67
Earlier sketch in SATA *1*
Barnum, Theodore
See Stratemeyer, Edward L.
Barnwell, Ysaye M. 1946- 200
Baron, Kathy 1954- 90
Baron, Virginia Olsen 1931- 46
Brief entry 28

Barr, Donald 1921-2004 20
    Obituary 152
Barr, George 1907-1992 2
Barr, Jene 1922-1985 16
    Obituary 42
Barr, Nevada 1952- 126
    Earlier sketch in SATA 115
Barragan, Paula 1963- 216
Barrer, Gertrude
    See Barrer-Russell, Gertrude
Barrer-Russell, Gertrude 1921- 27
Barrett, Angela (Jane) 1955- 145
    Earlier sketch in SATA 75
Barrett, Ethel 87
    Brief entry 44
Barrett, Joyce Durham 1943- 138
Barrett, Judi 204
    See Barrett, Judith
Barrett, Judith 1941- 26
    See also CLR 98
    See Barrett, Judi
Barrett, Robert T(heodore) 1949- 92
Barrett, Ron 1937- 14
Barrett, Susan (Mary) 1938- 113
Barrett, Tracy 1955- 207
    Earlier sketches in SATA 84, 115, 156
Barrett, William E(dmund) 1900-1986
    Obituary 49
Barretta, Gene 214
    Earlier sketch in SATA 176
Barretton, Grandall
    See Garrett, Randall
Barrie, Baronet
    See Barrie, J. M.
Barrie, J. M. 1860-1937 100
    See also YABC 1
    See also CLR 124
Barrie, James Matthew
    See Barrie, J. M.
Barringer, William 1940-1996 153
Barrington, Michael
    See Moorcock, Michael
Barris, George 1925- 47
Barrol, Grady
    See Bograd, Larry
Barron, Rex 1951- 84
Barron, T.A. 1952- 192
    Earlier sketches in SATA 83, 126
    See also CLR 86
Barron, Thomas Archibald
    See Barron, T.A.
Barron, Tom
    See Barron, T.A.
Barrow, Lloyd H. 1942- 73
Barrows, Annie 1962- 180
Barry, Dan 1958- 177
Barry, Dana (Marie Malloy) 1949- 139
Barry, James P(otvin) 1918- 14
Barry, Katharina Watjen 1936- 4
Barry, Robert 1931- 6
Barry, Robert Everett
    See Barry, Robert
Barry, Scott 1952- 32
Barry, Sheila Anne -2003 91
Barshaw, Ruth McNally 203
Bartell, Susan S. 175
Bartenbach, Jean 1918- 40
Barth, Edna 1914-1980 7
    Obituary 24
Barth, Kelly L. 1964- 152
Barthelme, Donald 1931-1989 7
    Obituary 62
Barth-Grozinger, Inge 1950- 185
Bartholomew, Barbara 1941- 86
    Brief entry 42
Bartholomew, Jean
    See Beatty, Patricia (Robbins)
Bartlett, Alison 153
Bartlett, Philip A. 1
Bartlett, Robert Merrill 1899-1995 12

Bartoletti, Susan Campbell 1958- 173
    Earlier sketches in SATA 88, 129, 135
Barton, Byron 1930- 126
    Earlier sketches in SATA 9, 90
Barton, Jill(ian) 1940- 75
Barton, May Hollis 67
    Earlier sketch in SATA 1
Barton, Pat
    See Arrowsmith, Pat
Bartos-Hoeppner, Barbara 1923- 5
Bartram, Simon 156
Bartsch, Jochen 1906- 39
Baruch, Dorothy W(alter) 1899-1962 21
Barunga, Albert 1912(?)-1977 120
Baryshnikov, Mikhail 1948- 192
Bas, Rutger
    See Rutgers van der Loeff-Basenau, An(na)
    Maria Margaretha
Base, Graeme 1958- 162
    Earlier sketches in SATA 67, 101
    See also CLR 22
Base, Graeme Rowland
    See Base, Graeme
Baseman, Gary 1960- 174
Bash, Barbara 1948- 132
Bashevis, Isaac
    See Singer, Isaac Bashevis
Bashevis, Yitskhok
    See Singer, Isaac Bashevis
Bashista, Adrienne Ehlert 203
Basile, Gloria Vitanza 1929- 180
Baskin, Leonard 1922-2000 120
    Brief entry 27
    Earlier sketch in SATA 30
Baskin, Nora Raleigh 1961- 189
    Earlier sketch in SATA 129
Bason, Lillian 1913- 20
Bass, L. G.
    See Geringer, Laura
Bassett, Jeni 1959- 64
    Brief entry 43
Bassett, John Keith
    See Keating, Lawrence A.
Bassett, Lisa 1958- 61
Bassil, Andrea
    See Nilsen, Anna
Bastyra, Judy 108
Basye, Dale E. 205
Bataille, Marion 1963- 209
Bat-Ami, Miriam 1950- 150
    Autobiography Feature 150
    Earlier sketches in SATA 82, 122
Bate, Lucy 1939-1993 18
Bate, Norman (Arthur) 1916- 5
Bateman, Colin 1962- 172
Bateman, Donna M. 190
Bateman, Teresa 1957- 216
    Earlier sketches in SATA 112, 168
Bates, Amy June 189
Bates, Barbara S(nedeker) 1919- 12
Bates, Betty
    See Bates, Elizabeth
Bates, Dianne 1948- 147
Bates, Elizabeth 1921- 19
Bates, Ivan 175
Bates, Katharine Lee 1859-1929 113
Bates, Martine
    See Leavitt, Martine
Bateson, Catherine 1960- 197
    Earlier sketch in SATA 157
Batey, Tom 1946- 52
    Brief entry 41
Bath, Kevin P.
    See Bath, K.P.
Bath, K.P. 1959- 171
Batherman, Muriel
    See Sheldon, Muriel
Batson, Larry 1930- 35
Batt, Tanya Robyn 1970- 131
Battaglia, Aurelius 1910- 50
    Brief entry 33

Batten, H(arry) Mortimer 1888-1958 25
Batten, Mary 1937- 162
    Earlier sketches in SATA 5, 102
Batterberry, Ariane Ruskin 1935- 13
Batterberry, Michael Carver 1932-2010 32
Battle-Lavert, Gwendolyn 1951- 155
    Earlier sketches in SATA 85, 131
Battles, (Roxy) Edith 1921- 7
Baudouy, Michel-Aime 1909- 7
Bauer, A.C.E. 201
Bauer, Caroline Feller 1935- 98
    Brief entry 46
    Earlier sketch in SATA 52
    See also SAAS 24
Bauer, Fred 1934- 36
Bauer, Helen 1900-1988 2
Bauer, Joan 1951- 160
    Earlier sketch in SATA 117
Bauer, Jutta 1955- 150
Bauer, Marion Dane 1938- 192
    Autobiography Feature 144
    Earlier sketches in SATA 20, 69, 113, 144
    See also SAAS 9
Bauer, Michael Gerard 1955(?)- 167
Bauer, Steven 1948- 125
Bauerschmidt, Marjorie 1926- 15
Baughman, Dorothy 1940- 61
Baum, Allyn Z(elton) 1924-1997 98
    Earlier sketch in SATA 20
Baum, L. Frank
    See Thompson, Ruth Plumly
Baum, L. Frank 1856-1919 100
    Earlier sketch in SATA 18
    See also CLR 107
Baum, Louis 1948- 182
    Brief entry 52
    Earlier sketch in SATA 64
Baum, Louis F.
    See Baum, L. Frank
Baum, Lyman Frank
    See Baum, L. Frank
Baum, Maxie 188
Baum, Willi 1931- 4
Baumann, Amy Beeching 1922- 10
Baumann, Amy Brown Beeching
    See Baumann, Amy Beeching
Baumann, Hans 1914- 2
    See also CLR 35
Baumann, Kurt 1935- 21
Baumgartner, Barbara 1939- 86
Baurys, Flo 1938- 122
Baurys, Florence
    See Baurys, Flo
Bausum, Ann 173
Bawden, Nina 1925- 132
    Earlier sketches in SATA 4, 72
    See also CLR 51
    See also SAAS 16
Bawden, Nina Mary Mabey
    See Bawden, Nina
Baxter, Valerie
    See Meynell, Laurence Walter
Bay, Jeanette Graham 1928- 88
Bayer, Harold
    See Gregg, Andrew K.
Bayer, Jane E. (?)-1985
    Obituary 44
Bayley, Nicola 1949- 129
    Earlier sketches in SATA 41, 69
Baylor, Byrd 1924- 136
    Earlier sketches in SATA 16, 69
    See also CLR 3
Baynes, Pauline 1922-2008 133
    Obituary 196
    Earlier sketches in SATA 19, 59
Baynes, Pauline Diana
    See Baynes, Pauline
Bayoc, Cbabi 186
Bayrock, Fiona 215
BB
    See Watkins-Pitchford, Denys James

Beach, Charles
  See Reid, (Thomas) Mayne
Beach, Charles Amory *1*
Beach, Edward L. 1918-2002 .... *12*
  Obituary *140*
Beach, Edward Latimer
  See Beach, Edward L.
Beach, Lisa 1957- *111*
Beach, Lynn
  See Lance, Kathryn
Beach, Stewart T(aft) 1899-1979 .... *23*
Beachcroft, Nina 1931- *18*
Beagle, Peter S. 1939- *130*
  Earlier sketch in SATA *60*
Beagle, Peter Soyer
  See Beagle, Peter S.
Beaglehole, Helen 1946- *117*
Beake, Lesley 1949- *209*
Beale, Fleur *107*
Bealer, Alex W(inkler III) 1921-1980 .... *8*
  Obituary *22*
Beales, Valerie 1915- *74*
Beals, Carleton 1893-1979 .... *12*
Beals, Frank Lee 1881-1972
  Obituary *26*
Beam, Matt 1970- *187*
Beame, Rona 1934- *12*
Beamer, Charles 1942- *43*
Beamer, George Charles, Jr.
  See Beamer, Charles
Bean, Jonathan 1979- *194*
Bean, Normal
  See Burroughs, Edgar Rice
Beaney, Jan
  See Udall, Jan Beaney
Beaney, Jane
  See Udall, Jan Beaney
Bear, Carolyn
  See Rayban, Chloe
Bear, Greg 1951- *105*
  Earlier sketch in SATA *65*
Bear, Gregory Dale
  See Bear, Greg
Bearanger, Marie
  See Messier, Claire
Beard, Charles A(ustin) 1874-1948 .... *18*
Beard, Dan(iel Carter) 1850-1941 .... *22*
Beard, Darleen Bailey 1961- *96*
Bearden, Romare (Howard) 1914(?)-1988 ... *22*
  Obituary *56*
Beardmore, Cedric
  See Beardmore, George
Beardmore, George 1908-1979 .... *20*
Beardshaw, Rosalind 1969- *190*
Beardsley, Martyn R. 1957- *150*
Bearman, Jane (Ruth) 1917- *29*
Beaton, Clare 1947- *125*
Beatty, Elizabeth
  See Holloway, Teresa (Bragunier)
Beatty, Hetty Burlingame 1907-1971 .... *5*
Beatty, Jerome, Jr. 1918- *5*
Beatty, John (Louis) 1922-1975 .... *6*
  Obituary *25*
Beatty, Patricia (Robbins) 1922-1991 .... *73*
  Obituary *68*
  Earlier sketches in SATA *1, 30*
  See also SAAS *4*
Beaty, Andrea *186*
Beaty, Mary (T.) 1947- *146*
Beaudoin, Sean *210*
Beaumont, Karen 1954- *204*
Beccia, Carlyn *189*
Bechard, Margaret 1953- *164*
  Earlier sketch in SATA *85*
Bechtel, Louise Seaman 1894-1985 .... *4*
  Obituary *43*
Bechtold, Lisze *208*
Beck, Barbara L. 1927- *12*
Beck, Ian 1947- *190*
  Earlier sketch in SATA *138*
  See Beck, Ian Archibald

Beck, Peggy 1949- *171*
Beck, Scott *197*
Becker, Beril 1901-1999 .... *11*
Becker, Bonny *184*
Becker, Deborah Zimmett 1955- *138*
Becker, Helaine 1961- *142*
Becker, John (Leonard) 1901- *12*
Becker, John E(mil) 1942- *148*
Becker, Joyce 1936- *39*
Becker, May Lamberton 1873-1958 .... *33*
Becker, Neesa 1951- *123*
Becker, Shari *174*
Beckerman, Chad W. *198*
Beckett, Sheilah 1913- *33*
Beckhorn, Susan Williams 1953- *189*
Beckles Willson, Robina 1930- *27*
Beckman, Delores 1914-1994 .... *51*
Beckman, Gunnel 1910- *6*
  See also CLR *25*
  See also SAAS *9*
Beckman, Kaj
  See Beckman, Karin
Beckman, Karin 1913- *45*
Beckman, Per (Frithiof) 1913- *45*
Bedard, Michael 1949- *154*
  Earlier sketch in SATA *93*
  See also CLR *35*
Beddor, Frank *194*
Beddows, Eric
  See Nutt, Ken
Bedford, A. N.
  See Watson, Jane Werner
Bedford, Annie North
  See Watson, Jane Werner
Bedford, David *159*
Bedoukian, Kerop 1907-1981 .... *53*
Bee, Jay
  See Brainerd, John W(hiting)
Bee, William *188*
Beebe, B. F.
  See Johnson, B. F.
Beebe, (Charles) William 1877-1962 .... *19*
Beeby, Betty 1923- *25*
Beech, Mark 1971- *191*
Beech, Webb
  See Griffin, W.E.B.
Beecham, Jahnna *161*
Beechcroft, William
  See Hallstead, William F(inn III)
Beeching, Jack 1922- *14*
Beeke, Tiphanie *163*
Beeler, Janet
  See Shaw, Janet
Beeler, Nelson F(rederick) 1910-1978 .... *13*
Beere, Peter 1951- *97*
Beers, Dorothy Sands 1917- *9*
Beers, Lorna 1897-1989 .... *14*
Beers, V(ictor) Gilbert 1928- *130*
  Earlier sketch in SATA *9*
Beeton, Max
  See Redding, Robert Hull
Begay, Shonto 1954- *137*
Begaye, Lisa Shook
  See Beach, Lisa
Begin, Mary Jane 1963- *82*
Begin-Callanan, Mary Jane
  See Begin, Mary Jane
Begley, Kathleen A. 1948- *21*
Begley, Kathleen Anne
  See Begley, Kathleen A.
Beha, Philippe *211*
Behan, Leslie
  See Gottfried, Theodore Mark
Behler, Deborah A. 1947- *145*
Behler, John L. 1943-2006 .... *145*
  Obituary *173*
Behler, John Luther
  See Behler, John L.
Behn, Harry 1898-1973 .... *2*
  Obituary *34*
Behnke, Frances L. *8*

Behr, Joyce 1929- *15*
Behrens, June York 1925- *19*
Behrman, Carol H(elen) 1925- *144*
  Earlier sketch in SATA *14*
Beifuss, John, (Jr.) 1959- *92*
Beil, Karen Magnuson 1950- *124*
Beiler, Edna 1923- *61*
Beinicke, Steve 1956- *69*
Beirne, Barbara 1933- *71*
Beiser, Arthur 1931- *22*
Beiser, Germaine 1931- *11*
Belair, Richard L. 1934- *45*
Belaney, Archibald Stansfeld 1888-1938 ...... *24*
  See also CLR *32*
Belasen, Amy 1983- *213*
Belbin, David 1958- *164*
  Earlier sketch in SATA *106*
Belden, Wilanne Schneider 1925- *56*
Belfrage, Sally 1936-1994 .... *65*
  Obituary *79*
Belknap, B. H.
  See Ellis, Edward S.
Belknap, Boynton
  See Ellis, Edward S.
Belknap, Boynton M.D.
  See Ellis, Edward S.
Bell, Anthea 1936- *148*
  Earlier sketch in SATA *88*
Bell, Cathleen Davitt 1971- *203*
Bell, Cece *202*
Bell, Clare (Louise) 1952- *99*
Bell, Corydon Whitten 1894-1980 .... *3*
Bell, David Owen 1949- *99*
Bell, Emerson
  See Stratemeyer, Edward L.
Bell, Emily Mary
  See Cason, Mabel Earp
Bell, Frank
  See Benson, Mildred
Bell, Gertrude (Wood) 1911-1987 .... *12*
Bell, Gina
  See Balzano, Jeanne (Koppel)
Bell, Hilari 1958- *197*
  Earlier sketch in SATA *151*
Bell, Jadrien
  See Golden, Christie
Bell, Janet
  See Clymer, Eleanor
Bell, Janet Cheatham 1937- *127*
Bell, Krista 1950- *215*
  Earlier sketch in SATA *126*
Bell, Krista Anne Blakeney
  See Bell, Krista
Bell, Margaret E(lizabeth) 1898-1990 .... *2*
Bell, Mary Reeves 1946- *88*
Bell, Norman (Edward) 1899- *11*
Bell, Raymond Martin 1907-1999 .... *13*
Bell, Siobhan *177*
Bell, Thelma Harrington 1896-1985 .... *3*
Bell, William 1945- *90*
  See also CLR *91*
Bellairs, John (Anthony) 1938-1991 .... *160*
  Obituary *66*
  Earlier sketches in SATA *2, 68*
  See also CLR *37*
Beller, Susan Provost 1949- *128*
  Earlier sketch in SATA *84*
  See also CLR *106*
Bellingham, Brenda 1931- *99*
  Brief entry *51*
Bello, Rosario de
  See De Bello, Rosario
Belloc, Hilaire 1870-1953 .... *112*
  See also YABC *1*
  See also CLR *102*
Belloc, Joseph Hilaire Pierre Sebastien Rene
  Swanton
  See Belloc, Hilaire
Belloc, Joseph Peter Rene Hilaire
  See Belloc, Hilaire

Belloc, Joseph Pierre Hilaire
See Belloc, Hilaire
Belloli, Andrea P. A. 1947- 86
Bell-Rehwoldt, Sheri 1962- 199
Bellville, Cheryl Walsh 1944- 54
Brief entry 49
Bell-Zano, Gina
See Balzano, Jeanne (Koppel)
Belpre, Pura 1899-1982 16
Obituary 30
Belting, Natalia Maree 1915-1997 6
Belton, John Raynor 1931- 22
Belton, Sandra 1939- 186
Earlier sketches in SATA 85, 134
Belton, Sandra Yvonne
See Belton, Sandra
Beltran, Alberto 1923- 43
Beltran-Hernandez, Irene 1945- 74
Belvedere, Lee
See Grayland, Valerie (Merle Spanner)
Bemelmans, Ludwig 1898-1962 100
Earlier sketch in SATA 15
See also CLR 93
Benander, Carl D. 1941- 74
Benary, Margot
See Benary-Isbert, Margot
Benary-Isbert, Margot 1889-1979 2
Obituary 21
See also CLR 12
Benasutti, Marion 1908-1992 6
Benatar, Raquel 1955- 167
Benchley, Nathaniel (Goddard) 1915-1981 .. 25
Obituary 28
Earlier sketch in SATA 3
Benchley, Peter 1940-2006 164
Earlier sketches in SATA 3, 89
Benchley, Peter Bradford
See Benchley, Peter
Bendall-Brunello, John 185
Bender, Edna 1941- 92
Bender, Esther 1942- 88
Bender, Lucy Ellen 1942- 22
Bender, Robert 1962- 160
Earlier sketch in SATA 79
Bendick, Jeanne 1919- 135
Earlier sketches in SATA 2, 68
See also CLR 5
See also SAAS 4
Bendick, Robert L(ouis) 1917- 11
Benedetto, William R. 1928- 180
Benedetto, William Ralph
See Benedetto, William R.
Benedict, Andrew
See Arthur, Robert, (Jr.)
Benedict, Dorothy Potter 1889-1979 11
Obituary 23
Benedict, Lois Trimble 1902-1967 12
Benedict, Rex 1920-1995 8
Benedict, Stewart H(urd) 1924- 26
Beneduce, Ann Keay 128
Benet, Laura 1884-1979 3
Obituary 23
Benet, Stephen Vincent 1898-1943
See YABC 1
Benet, Sula 1906-1982 21
Obituary 33
Ben-Ezer, Ehud 1936- 122
Benezra, Barbara (Beardsley) 1921- 10
Benham, Leslie 1922- 48
Benham, Lois (Dakin) 1924- 48
Benham, Mary Lile 1914-1991 55
Benjamin, E. M. J.
See Bache, Ellyn
Benjamin, Floella 1949- 206
Benjamin, Nora
See Kubie, Nora Gottheil Benjamin
Benjamin, Saragail Katzman 1953- 86
Benner, Cheryl 1962- 80
Benner, Judith Ann 1942- 94
Bennett, Alice
See Ziner, Florence

Bennett, Cherie 1960- 158
Earlier sketch in SATA 97
Bennett, Dorothea
See Young, Dorothea Bennett
Bennett, Erin Susanne
See Banks, Erin Bennett
Bennett, Holly 1957- 181
Bennett, James (W.) 1942- 153
Autobiography Feature 153
Earlier sketches in SATA 93, 148
Bennett, Jay 1912- 87
Brief entry 27
Earlier sketch in SATA 41
See also SAAS 4
Bennett, Jill (Crawford) 1934- 41
Bennett, John 1865-1956
See YABC 1
Bennett, Penelope (Agnes) 1938- 94
Bennett, Rachel
See Hill, Margaret (Ohler)
Bennett, Rainey 1907-1998 15
Obituary 111
Bennett, Richard 1899- 21
Bennett, Russell H(oradley) 1896- 25
Bennett, Veronica 1953- 178
Bennett, William (John) 1943- 102
Benning, Elizabeth
See Rice, Bebe Faas
Benny, Mike 1964- 203
Benson, Elizabeth P(olk) 1924- 65
Benson, Kathleen 1947- 183
Earlier sketches in SATA 62, 111
Benson, Linda M(aria) 1959- 84
Benson, Mildred 1905-2002 100
Obituary 135
Earlier sketches in SATA 1, 65, 67
Benson, Mildred Augustine Wirt
See Benson, Mildred
Benson, Mildred Wirt
See Benson, Mildred
Benson, Millie
See Benson, Mildred
Benson, Patrick 1956- 147
Benson, Sally 1900-1972 35
Obituary 27
Earlier sketch in SATA 1
Bentley, Judith (McBride) 1945- 89
Earlier sketch in SATA 40
Bentley, Karen
See Taschek, Karen
Bentley, Nancy (L.) 1946- 78
Bentley, Nicolas Clerihew 1907-1978
Obituary 24
Bentley, Phyllis Eleanor 1894-1977 6
Obituary 25
Bentley, Roy 1947- 46
Bentley, William (George) 1916- 84
Benton, Jim 1963- 172
ben Uzair, Salem
See Horne, Richard Henry Hengist
Ben-Zvi, Rebeccca Tova
See O'Connell, Rebecca
Bercaw, Edna Coe 1961- 124
Berck, Judith 1960- 75
Berelson, Howard 1940- 5
Berends, Polly Berrien 1939- 50
Brief entry 38
Berenstain, Jan 1923- 135
Earlier sketches in SATA 12, 64, 129
See also CLR 150
See also SAAS 20
Berenstain, Janice
See Berenstain, Jan
Berenstain, Michael 1951- 45
Berenstain, Mike
See Berenstain, Michael
Berenstain, Stan 1923-2005 135
Obituary 169
Earlier sketches in SATA 12, 64, 129
See also CLR 150
See also SAAS 20

Berenstain, Stanley
See Berenstain, Stan
Berenzy, Alix 1957- 168
Earlier sketch in SATA 65
Beresford, Elisabeth 1928- 141
Earlier sketches in SATA 25, 86
See also SAAS 20
Berg, Adriane G(ilda) 1948- 152
Berg, Dave
See Berg, David
Berg, David 1920-2002 27
Obituary 137
Berg, Elizabeth 1948- 104
Berg, Jean Horton 1913-1995 6
Berg, Joan
See Victor, Joan Berg
Berg, Ron 1952- 48
Bergaust, Erik 1925-1978 20
Bergel, Colin J. 1963- 137
Bergen, Joyce 1949- 95
Berger, Barbara (Helen) 1945- 77
Berger, Carin 185
Berger, Gilda 1935- 88
Brief entry 42
Berger, Josef 1903-1971 36
Berger, Lou 1950- 213
Berger, Melvin H. 1927- 158
Autobiography Feature 124
Earlier sketches in SATA 5, 88
See also CLR 32
See also SAAS 2
Berger, Phil 1942-2001 62
Berger, Samantha (Allison) 1969- 140
Berger, Terry 1933- 8
Bergey, Alyce 1934- 45
Bergey, Alyce Mae
See Bergey, Alyce
Bergin, Mark 1961- 160
Earlier sketch in SATA 114
Berglin, Ruth Marie 1970- 181
Bergman, Donna 1934- 73
Bergman, Mara 1956- 196
Bergman, Tamar 1939- 95
Bergren, Lisa T.
See Bergren, Lisa Tawn
Bergren, Lisa Tawn 200
Bergsma, Jody Lynn 163
Bergstein, Rita M. 211
Bergum, Constance R. 1952- 208
Earlier sketch in SATA 121
Berk, Ari 208
Berkebile, Fred D(onovan) 1900-1978
Obituary 26
Berkeley, Jon 1962- 204
Berkes, Marianne 217
Earlier sketch in SATA 173
Berkey, Barry Robert 1935- 24
Berkowitz, Freda Pastor 1908-1994 12
Berkus, Clara Widess 1909- 78
Berlan, Kathryn Hook 1946- 78
Berlfein, Judy Reiss 1958- 79
Berlin, Eric 1968- 195
Berliner, Don 1930- 33
Berliner, Franz 1930- 13
Berlitz, Charles (L. Frambach) 1914-2003 32
Obituary 151
Berman, Linda 1948- 38
Berman, Paul (Lawrence) 1949- 66
Berman, Rachel 1946- 217
Berna, Paul 1910-1994 15
Obituary 78
See also CLR 19
Bernadette
See Watts, (Anna) Bernadette
Bernard, Bruce 1928-2000 78
Obituary 124
Bernard, George I. 1949- 39
Bernard, Jacqueline (de Sieyes) 1921-1983 ... 8
Obituary 45
Bernard, Patricia 1942- 181
Earlier sketch in SATA 106

Bernard, Trish
  See Bernard, Patricia
Bernardin, James (B.) 1966- 112
Bernardo, Anilu 184
Bernards, Neal 1963- 71
Bernasconi, Pablo 1973- 183
Bernays, Anne 1930- 32
Berner, Rotraut Susanne 1948- 214
Bernhard, Durga T. 1961- 80
Bernhard, Emery 1950- 80
Bernheimer, Kate 201
Bernier-Grand, Carmen T. 1947- 202
Bernstein, Daryl (Evan) 1976- 81
Bernstein, Joanne E(ckstein) 1943- 15
Bernstein, Jonathan 217
Bernstein, Margery 1933- 114
Bernstein, Nina 1949- 180
Bernstein, Theodore M(enline) 1904-1979 ... 12
  Obituary 27
Berrien, Edith Heal
  See Heal, Edith
Berrill, Jacquelyn (Batsel) 1905- 12
Berrington, John
  See Brownjohn, Alan
Berry, B. J.
  See Berry, Barbara J.
Berry, Barbara J. 1937- 7
Berry, Erick
  See Best, (Evangel) Allena Champlin
Berry, Holly 1957- 210
Berry, James 1924- 110
  Earlier sketch in SATA 67
  See also CLR 143
Berry, Jane Cobb 1915(?)-1979
  Obituary 22
Berry, Joy 1944- 58
  Brief entry 46
Berry, Joy Wilt
  See Berry, Joy
Berry, Lynne 190
Berry, William D(avid) 1926- 14
Bersani, Shennen 1961- 164
Berson, Harold 1926- 4
Bertagna, Julie 1962- 151
Bertholf, Bret 189
Bertin, Charles-Francois
  See Berlitz, Charles (L. Frambach)
Bertolet, Paul
  See McLaughlin, Frank
Berton, Pierre (Francis de Marigny)
  1920-2004 99
  Obituary 158
Bertrand, Cecile 1953- 76
Bertrand, Diane Gonzales 1956- 177
  Earlier sketch in SATA 106
Bertrand, Lynne 1963- 164
  Earlier sketch in SATA 81
Beskow, Elsa (Maartman) 1874-1953 20
  See also CLR 17
Bess, Clayton
  See Locke, Robert
Besson, Luc 1959- 199
Best, (Evangel) Allena Champlin 1892-1974 . 2
  Obituary 25
Best, Cari 1951- 200
  Earlier sketches in SATA 107, 149
Best, (Oswald) Herbert 1894-1980 2
Bestall, A(lfred) E(dmeades) 1892-1986 97
  Obituary 48
Betancourt, Jeanne 1941- 148
  Brief entry 43
  Earlier sketches in SATA 55, 96
Beth, Mary
  See Miller, Mary Beth
Bethancourt, T. Ernesto
  See Paisley, Tom
Bethel, Dell 1929- 52
Bethell, Jean (Frankenberry) 1922- 8
Bethers, Ray 1902-1973 6
Bethke, Bruce Raymond 1955- 114

Bethlen, T.D.
  See Silverberg, Robert
Bethune, J. G.
  See Ellis, Edward S.
Bethune, J. H.
  See Ellis, Edward S.
Betteridge, Anne
  See Potter, Margaret
Betteridge, Deirdre 214
Bettina
  See Ehrlich, Bettina Bauer
Bettmann, Otto Ludwig 1903-1998 46
Bettoli, Delana 187
Betts, James
  See Haynes, Betsy
Betz, Eva Kelly 1897-1968 10
Bevan, Tom 1868-1930(?)
  See YABC 2
Bevis, Mary 1939- 202
Bewick, Thomas 1753-1828 16
Beyer, Audrey White 1916- 9
Beyer, Paul J. III 1950- 74
Beynon, John
  See Harris, John (Wyndham Parkes Lucas)
  Beynon
Bezencon, Jacqueline (Buxcel) 1924- 48
Bhatia, Jamunadevi 1919- 48
Bhatia, June
  See Bhatia, Jamunadevi
Bial, Morrison David 1917- 62
Bial, Raymond 1948- 165
  Earlier sketches in SATA 76, 116
Biala
  See Brustlein, Janice Tworkov
Biale, Rachel 1952- 99
Bialk, Elisa
  See Krautter, Elisa (Bialk)
Bianchi, John 1947- 91
Bianchi, Robert S(teven) 1943- 92
Bianco, Margery
  See Bianco, Margery Williams
Bianco, Margery Williams 1881-1944 15
  See also CLR 146
Bianco, Pamela 1906- 28
Bibby, Violet 1908-1996 24
Bible, Charles 1937- 13
Bibo, Bobette
  See Gugliotta, Bobette
Bice, Clare 1909-1976 22
Bickerstaff, Isaac
  See Swift, Jonathan
Bidner, Jenni 1963- 193
Biegel, Paul 1925- 79
  Earlier sketch in SATA 16
  See also CLR 27
  See also SAAS 18
Biemiller, Carl L(udwig), Jr. 1912-1979 40
  Obituary 21
Bienenfeld, Florence L(ucille) 1929- 39
Bierhorst, John (William) 1936- 149
  Autobiography Feature 149
  Earlier sketches in SATA 6, 91
  See also SAAS 10
Biggar, Joan R. 1936- 120
Biggar, Joan Rawlins
  See Biggar, Joan R.
Biggle, Lloyd, Jr. 1923-2002 65
Biggs, Brian 1968- 192
Bilal, Abdel W(ahab) 1970- 92
Bilbrough, Norman 1941- 111
Bildner, Phil 173
Bileck, Marvin 1920- 40
Bilibin, Ivan (Iakolevich) 1876-1942 61
Bill, Alfred Hoyt 1879-1964 44
Billam, Rosemary 1952- 61
Billings, Charlene W(interer) 1941- 41
Billingsley, Franny 1954- 132
Billington, Elizabeth T(hain) 50
  Brief entry 43

Billout, Guy (Rene) 1941- 144
  Earlier sketch in SATA 10
  See also CLR 33
Bilson, Geoffrey 1938-1987 99
Binch, Caroline (Lesley) 1947- 140
  Earlier sketch in SATA 81
Bing, Christopher (H.) 126
Bingham, Caroline 1962- 158
Bingham, Jane M. 1941- 163
Bingham, Jane Marie
  See Bingham, Jane M.
Bingham, Janet 1959- 200
Bingham, Kelly 1967- 207
Bingham, Sam 1944- 96
Bingham, Samuel A.
  See Bingham, Sam
Bingley, Margaret (Jane Kirby) 1947- 72
Binkley, Anne
  See Rand, Ann (Binkley)
Binzen, Bill
  See Binzen, William
Binzen, William 24
Birch, David (W.) 1913-1996 89
Birch, Reginald B(athurst) 1856-1943 19
Birchman, David 1949- 72
Birchmore, Daniel A. 1951- 92
Bird, Carmel 1940- 124
Bird, E(lzy) J(ay) 1911- 58
Birdsall, Jeanne 1952(?)- 170
Birdseye, Tom 1951- 148
  Earlier sketches in SATA 66, 98
Birenbaum, Barbara 1941- 65
Birmingham, Lloyd P(aul) 1924- 83
  Earlier sketch in SATA 12
Birmingham, Ruth
  See Sorrells, Walter
Birney, Betty G. 1947- 169
  Earlier sketch in SATA 98
Biro, B.
  See Biro, B. S.
Biro, B. S. 1921- 1
  See also CLR 28
  See also SAAS 13
Biro, Val
  See Biro, B. S.
Bischoff, Julia Bristol 1899-1970 12
Bishop, Bonnie 1943- 37
Bishop, Claire Huchet 1899(?)-1993 14
  Obituary 74
  See also CLR 80
Bishop, Courtney
  See Ruemmler, John D(avid)
Bishop, Curtis (Kent) 1912-1967 6
Bishop, Elizabeth 1911-1979
  Obituary 24
Bishop, Gavin 1946- 216
  Earlier sketches in SATA 97, 144
Bishop, Kathleen Wong 1954- 120
Bishop, Kathy
  See Bishop, Kathleen Wong
Bishop, Nic 1955- 161
  Earlier sketch in SATA 107
Bisset, Donald 1910-1995 86
  Earlier sketch in SATA 7
Bisson, Terry 1942- 99
Bisson, Terry Ballantine
  See Bisson, Terry
Bitter, Gary G(len) 1940- 22
Bixby, William (Courtney) 1920-1986 6
  Obituary 47
Bjoerk, Christina 1938- 99
  Earlier sketch in SATA 67
  See also CLR 22
Bjork, Christina
  See Bjoerk, Christina
Bjorklund, Lorence F. 1913-1978 35
  Brief entry 32
Bjorkman, Steve 163
Blabey, Aaron 1975(?)- 214
Black, Algernon David 1900-1993 12
  Obituary 76

Black, Holly 1971- 210
  Earlier sketch in SATA 147
Black, Irma Simonton 1906-1972 2
  Obituary 25
Black, Kat 217
Black, Katherine
  See Black, Kat
Black, Mansell
  See Trevor, Elleston
Black, MaryAnn
  See Easley, MaryAnn
Black, Susan Adams 1953- 40
Blackall, Bernie 1956- 126
Blackall, Sophie 182
Blackburn, Claire
  See Altman, Linda Jacobs
Blackburn, John(ny) Brewton 1952- 15
Blackburn, Joyce Knight 1920- 29
Blacker, Terence 1948- 194
Blacker, Tina
  See Louise, Tina
Blackett, Veronica Heath 1927- 12
Blackie, Jean Cutler 1943- 79
Blacklin, Malcolm
  See Chambers, Aidan
Blacklock, Dyan 1951- 112
Blackman, Malorie 1962- 196
  Earlier sketches in SATA 83, 128
Blackton, Peter
  See Wilson, Lionel
Blackwood, Alan 1932- 70
Blackwood, Freya 199
Blackwood, Gary
  See Blackwood, Gary L.
Blackwood, Gary L. 1945- 169
  Earlier sketches in SATA 72, 118
Blade, Alexander
  See Garrett, Randall
  and Hamilton, Edmond
  and Silverberg, Robert
Blades, Ann (Sager) 1947- 69
  Earlier sketch in SATA 16
  See also CLR 15
Bladow, Suzanne Wilson 1937- 14
Blaine, Chris
  See Gardner, Craig Shaw
Blaine, John
  See Goodwin, Harold L(eland)
Blaine, Marge
  See Blaine, Margery Kay
Blaine, Margery Kay 1937- 11
Blair, Alison
  See Lerangis, Peter
Blair, Anne Denton 1914-1993 46
Blair, David Nelson 1954- 80
Blair, Eric
  See Orwell, George
Blair, Jay 1953- 45
Blair, Lucile
  See Yeakley, Marjory Hall
Blair, Margaret Whitman 1951- 124
Blair, Mary 1911-1978 195
Blair, Pauline Hunter
  See Clarke, Pauline
Blair, Ruth Van Ness 1912-1999 12
Blair, Shannon
  See Kaye, Marilyn
Blair, Walter 1900-1992 12
  Obituary 72
Blaisdell, Bob
  See Blaisdell, Robert
Blaisdell, Robert 1959- 105
Blake, Bronwyn 1940- 149
Blake, Francis 198
Blake, Jon 1954- 171
  Earlier sketch in SATA 78
Blake, Olive
  See Supraner, Robyn
Blake, Quentin 1932- 211
  Earlier sketches in SATA 9, 52, 96, 125
  See also CLR 31

Blake, Robert 1949- 42
Blake, Robert J. 160
Blake, Walker E.
  See Griffin, W.E.B.
Blake, William 1757-1827 30
  See also CLR 52
Blakely, Gloria 1950- 139
Blakely, Roger K. 1922- 82
Blakeney, Jay D.
  See Chester, Deborah
Blakey, Nancy 1955- 94
Blanc, Esther S. 1913-1997 66
Blanc, Mel 1908-1989
  Obituary 64
Blanchard, Patricia 125
Blanchet, M(uriel) Wylie 1891-1961 106
Blanco, Richard L(idio) 1926- 63
Bland, E.
  See Nesbit, E.
Bland, Edith Nesbit
  See Nesbit, E.
Bland, Fabian
  See Nesbit, E.
Blane, Gertrude
  See Blumenthal, Gertrude
Blank, Clarissa Mabel 1915-1965 62
Blankenship, LeeAnn 1944- 181
Blassingame, Wyatt Rainey 1909-1985 34
  Obituary 41
  Earlier sketch in SATA 1
Blatchford, Claire H. 1944- 94
Blauer, Ettagale 1940- 49
Bleck, Linda 207
Bledsoe, Glen L. 1951- 108
Bledsoe, Glen Leonard
  See Bledsoe, Glen L.
Bledsoe, Karen E. 1962- 167
  Earlier sketch in SATA 108
Bledsoe, Karen Elizabeth
  See Bledsoe, Karen E.
Bledsoe, Lucy Jane 1957- 162
  Earlier sketch in SATA 97
Bleeker, Sonia
  See Zim, Sonia Bleeker
Blegen, Daniel M. 1950- 92
Blegvad, Erik 1923- 132
  Earlier sketches in SATA 14, 66
Blegvad, Lenore 1926- 176
  Earlier sketches in SATA 14, 66
Bley, Anette 1967- 188
Blish, James 1921-1975 66
Blish, James Benjamin
  See Blish, James
Blishen, Edward (William) 1920-1996 66
  Obituary 93
  Earlier sketch in SATA 8
Bliss, Corinne Demas 1947- 131
  Earlier sketch in SATA 37
  See Demas, Corinne
Bliss, Frederick
  See Card, Orson Scott
Bliss, Gillian
  See Paton Walsh, Jill
Bliss, Harry 1964- 196
  Earlier sketch in SATA 156
Bliss, Reginald
  See Wells, H. G.
Bliss, Ronald G(ene) 1942- 12
Blitt, Barry 187
Bliven, Bruce, Jr. 1916-2002 2
Blixen, Karen 1885-1962 44
Blizzard, Gladys S. (?)-1992 79
Blobaum, Cindy 1966- 123
Bloch, Lucienne 1909-1999 10
Bloch, Marie Halun 1910-1998 6
  See also SAAS 9
Bloch, Robert (Albert) 1917-1994 12
  Obituary 82
Bloch, Serge 1956- 213
Blochman, Lawrence G(oldtree)
  1900-1975 22

Block, Francesca Lia 1962- 213
  Earlier sketches in SATA 80, 116, 158
  See also CLR 116
  See also SAAS 21
Block, Irvin 1917- 12
Blomgren, Jennifer (Alice) 1954- 136
Blonder, Terry Joyce
  See Golson, Terry
Blood, Charles Lewis 1929- 28
Bloom, Barbara Lee 1943- 146
Bloom, Freddy 1914-2000 37
  Obituary 121
Bloom, Lloyd 1947- 108
  Brief entry 43
Bloom, Suzanne 1950- 172
Bloomfield, Michaela 1966- 70
Bloor, Edward 1950- 201
  Earlier sketches in SATA 98, 155
Bloor, Edward William
  See Bloor, Edward
Blos, Joan W. 1928- 153
  Autobiography Feature 153
  Brief entry 27
  Earlier sketches in SATA 33, 69, 109
  See also CLR 18
  See also SAAS 11
Blos, Joan Winsor
  See Blos, Joan W.
Blough, Glenn O(rlando) 1907-1995 1
Blue, Rose 1931- 166
  Autobiography Feature 117
  Earlier sketches in SATA 5, 91, 93
  See also SAAS 24
Blue, Zachary
  See Stine, R.L.
Bluemle, Elizabeth 209
Bluggage, Oranthy
  See Alcott, Louisa May
Blumberg, Leda 1956- 59
Blumberg, Rhoda 1917- 123
  Earlier sketches in SATA 35, 70
  See also CLR 21
Blume, Judy 1938- 195
  Earlier sketches in SATA 2, 31, 79, 142
  See also CLR 69
Blume, Judy Sussman
  See Blume, Judy
Blume, Lesley M.M. 1975- 180
Blumenthal, Deborah 204
  Earlier sketch in SATA 161
Blumenthal, Gertrude 1907-1971
  Obituary 27
Blumenthal, Shirley 1943- 46
Blutig, Eduard
  See Gorey, Edward (St. John)
Bly, Janet 1945- 43
Bly, Janet Chester
  See Bly, Janet
Bly, Stephen A(rthur) 1944- 116
  Earlier sketch in SATA 43
Blyler, Allison Lee 1966- 74
Blythe, Gary 1959- 185
Blyton, Carey 1932-2002 9
  Obituary 138
Blyton, Enid 1897-1968 25
  See also CLR 31
Blyton, Enid Mary
  See Blyton, Enid
Bo, Ben
  See Richardson, V.A.
Boardman, Fon Wyman, Jr. 1911-2000 6
Boardman, Gwenn R.
  See Petersen, Gwenn Boardman
Boase, Wendy 1944-1999 28
  Obituary 110
Boatner, Mark Mayo III 1921- 29
Bobbe, Dorothie de Bear 1905-1975 1
  Obituary 25
Bober, Natalie S. 1930- 134
  Earlier sketch in SATA 87
  See also SAAS 23

Bobette, Bibo
  See Gugliotta, Bobette
Bobri, Vladimir V. 1898-1986 .... *47*
  Brief entry *32*
Bobritsky, Vladimir
  See Bobri, Vladimir V.
Bochak, Grayce 1956- *76*
Bock, Hal
  See Bock, Harold I.
Bock, Harold I. 1939- *10*
Bock, William Sauts Netamux'we 1939- *14*
Bodanis, David *179*
Bode, Janet 1943-1999 .... *96*
  Obituary *118*
  Earlier sketch in SATA *60*
Bode, N.E.
  See Baggott, Julianna
Bodecker, N(iels) M(ogens) 1922-1988 .... *73*
  Obituary *54*
  Earlier sketch in SATA *8*
Bodeen, S. A. 1965- *158*
  Earlier sketch in SATA *114*
Boden, Hilda
  See Bodenham, Hilda Morris
Bodenham, Hilda Morris 1901- *13*
Bodett, Thomas Edward 1955- *70*
Bodett, Tom
  See Bodett, Thomas Edward
Bodie, Idella F(allaw) 1925- *89*
  Earlier sketch in SATA *12*
Bodker, Cecil
  See Bodker, Cecil
Bodker, Cecil 1927- *133*
  Earlier sketch in SATA *14*
  See also CLR *23*
Bodsworth, (Charles) Fred(erick) 1918- *27*
Boeckman, Charles 1920- *12*
Boegehold, Betty (Doyle) 1913-1985
  Obituary *42*
Boelts, Maribeth 1964- *200*
  Earlier sketches in SATA *78, 163*
Boerst, William J. 1939- *170*
  Earlier sketch in SATA *121*
Boesch, Mark J(oseph) 1917- *12*
Boesen, Victor 1908- *16*
Bogacki, Tomek 1950- *214*
  Earlier sketch in SATA *138*
Bogaerts, Gert 1965- *80*
Bogan, Paulette 1960- *201*
  Earlier sketch in SATA *129*
Bogart, Jo Ellen 1945- *92*
  See also CLR *59*
Boggs, Ralph Steele 1901-1994 .... *7*
Bograd, Larry 1953- *89*
  Earlier sketch in SATA *33*
  See also SAAS *21*
Bogue, Gary 1938- *195*
Bogue, Gary L.
  See Bogue, Gary
Bohdal, Susi 1951- *101*
  Earlier sketch in SATA *22*
Bohlen, Nina 1931- *58*
Bohlmeijer, Arno 1956- *94*
Bohner, Charles (Henry) 1927- *62*
Bohnhoff, Maya Kaathryn 1954- *88*
Boiger, Alexandra *178*
Boissard, Janine 1932- *59*
Bojunga, Lygia
  See Nunes, Lygia Bojunga
Bojunga-Nunes, Lygia
  See Nunes, Lygia Bojunga
Bok, Arthur
  See Bok, Chip
Bok, Chip 1952- *205*
Bolam, Emily 1969- *206*
Boland, Janice *98*
Bolden, Tonya 1959- *188*
  Earlier sketches in SATA *79, 138*
Bolden, Tonya Wilyce
  See Bolden, Tonya

Boles, Paul Darcy 1916-1984 .... *9*
  Obituary *38*
Bolian, Polly 1925- *4*
Bollen, Roger 1941(?)- *83*
  Brief entry *29*
Bolliger, Max 1929- *7*
Bollinger, Max 1929- *167*
Bollinger, Peter *172*
Bolognese, Don(ald Alan) 1934- *129*
  Earlier sketches in SATA *24, 71*
Bolognese, Elaine 1933- *23*
Bolotin, Norman (Phillip) 1951- *93*
Bolton, Carole 1926- *6*
Bolton, Elizabeth
  See St. John, Nicole
Bolton, Evelyn
  See Bunting, Eve
Bonar, Veronica
  See Bailey, Donna (Veronica Anne)
Bond, B. J.
  See Heneghan, James
Bond, Bruce 1939- *61*
Bond, Felicia 1954- *126*
  Earlier sketch in SATA *49*
Bond, Gladys Baker 1912- *14*
Bond, Higgins 1951- *177*
  Earlier sketch in SATA *83*
Bond, J. Harvey
  See Winterbotham, R(ussell) R(obert)
Bond, (Thomas) Michael 1926- *157*
  Earlier sketches in SATA *6, 58*
  See also CLR *95*
  See also SAAS *3*
Bond, Nancy 1945- *159*
  Autobiography Feature *159*
  Earlier sketches in SATA *22, 82*
  See also CLR *11*
  See also SAAS *13*
Bond, Nancy Barbara
  See Bond, Nancy
Bond, Rebecca 1972- *214*
  Earlier sketch in SATA *130*
Bond, Ruskin 1934- *87*
  Earlier sketch in SATA *14*
Bondie, J. D.
  See Cunningham, Chet
Bondoux, Anne-Laure 1971- *175*
Bone, Ian 1956- *158*
  Earlier sketch in SATA *117*
Bonehill, Captain Ralph
  See Stratemeyer, Edward L.
Bonestell, Chesley 1888-1986
  Obituary *48*
Bonham, Barbara Thomas 1926- *7*
Bonham, Frank 1914-1989 .... *49*
  Obituary *62*
  Earlier sketch in SATA *1*
  See also SAAS *3*
Boniface, William 1963- *182*
  Earlier sketch in SATA *102*
Bonino, Louise
  See Williams, Louise Bonino
Bonk, John J. *189*
Bonn, Pat
  See Bonn, Patricia Carolyn
Bonn, Patricia Carolyn 1948- *43*
Bonner, Hannah *197*
Bonner, Mary Graham 1890-1974 .... *19*
Bonner, Mike 1951- *121*
Bonners, Susan 1947- *85*
  Brief entry *48*
Bonnet-Rampersaud, Louise *173*
Bonning, Tony 1948- *169*
Bonsall, Crosby Barbara (Newell)
  1921-1995 .... *23*
  Obituary *84*
Bonsall, Joseph S. 1948- *119*
Bonsignore, Joan 1959- *140*

Bontemps, Arna 1902-1973 .... *44*
  Obituary *24*
  Earlier sketch in SATA *2*
  See also CLR *6*
Bontemps, Arnaud Wendell
  See Bontemps, Arna
Bonzon, Paul-Jacques 1908-1978 .... *22*
Boock, Paula 1964- *134*
Booher, Dianna Daniels 1948- *33*
Book, Rick 1949- *119*
Book, Rita
  See Holub, Joan
Bookman, Charlotte
  See Zolotow, Charlotte
Boon, Debbie 1960- *103*
Boon, Emilie (Laetitia) 1958- *86*
Boone, Charles Eugene
  See Boone, Pat
Boone, Pat 1934- *7*
Booraem, Ellen *211*
Boorman, Linda 1940- *46*
Boorman, Linda Kay
  See Boorman, Linda
Boorstin, Daniel J(oseph) 1914-2004 .... *52*
Boos, Ben 1971- *206*
Booth, Coe *187*
Booth, Ernest Sheldon 1915-1984 .... *43*
Booth, George 1926- *191*
Booth, Graham (Charles) 1935- *37*
Bootman, Colin *159*
Borden, Louise 1949- *190*
  Autobiography Feature *141*
  Earlier sketches in SATA *68, 104, 141*
Bordier, Georgette 1924- *16*
Borgman, James
  See Borgman, Jim
Borgman, James Mark
  See Borgman, Jim
Borgman, Jim 1954- *122*
Borgo, Lacy Finn 1972- *194*
Boring, Mel 1939- *168*
  Earlier sketch in SATA *35*
Borja, Corinne 1929- *22*
Borja, Robert 1923- *22*
Borland, Hal
  See Borland, Harold Glen
Borland, Harold Glen 1900-1978 .... *5*
  Obituary *24*
Borland, Kathryn Kilby 1916- *16*
Borlenghi, Patricia 1951- *79*
Born, Adolf 1930- *49*
Bornstein, Ruth Lercher
  See Bornstein-Lercher, Ruth
Bornstein-Lercher, Ruth 1927- *88*
  Autobiography Feature *107*
  Earlier sketch in SATA *14*
Borski, Lucia Merecka *18*
Borten, Helen Jacobson 1930- *5*
Bortolotti, Dan 1969- *157*
Borton, Elizabeth
  See Trevino, Elizabeth B(orton) de
Borton, Lady 1942- *98*
Borton de Trevino, Elizabeth
  See Trevino, Elizabeth B(orton) de
Bortstein, Larry 1942-2010 .... *16*
Bortz, Alfred B(enjamin) 1944- *139*
  Earlier sketch in SATA *74*
Bortz, Fred
  See Bortz, Alfred B(enjamin)
Bosch, Pseudonymous *199*
Bosco, Jack
  See Holliday, Joseph
Boshell, Gordon 1908-1991 .... *15*
Boshinski, Blanche 1922- *10*
Bosman, Paul 1929- *107*
Bosse, Malcolm (Joseph, Jr.) 1926-2002 .... *136*
  Earlier sketch in SATA *35*
Bosserman, (Charles) Phillip 1931- *84*
Bossom, Naomi 1933- *35*
Bostock, Mike 1962- *114*

Boston, L(ucy) M(aria Wood) 1892-1990 .... *19*
   Obituary *64*
   See also CLR *3*
Bostrom, Kathleen (Susan) Long 1954- *139*
Bostrom, Kathy
   See Bostrom, Kathleen (Susan) Long
Boswell, Addie *208*
Boswell, Addie Kay
   See Boswell, Addie
Bosworth, J. Allan 1925- *19*
Bothwell, Jean (?)-1977 .... *2*
Botkin, B(enjamin) A(lbert) 1901-1975 .... *40*
Botsford, Ward 1927-2004 .... *66*
Botting, Douglas (Scott) 1934- *43*
Bottner, Barbara 1943- *170*
   Autobiography Feature *121*
   Earlier sketches in SATA *14, 93*
   See also SAAS *26*
Bottone, Frank G., Jr. 1969- *141*
Bouchard, David 1952- *213*
   Earlier sketch in SATA *117*
Boucher, (Clarence) Carter 1954- *129*
Boudelang, Bob
   See Pell, Ed(ward)
Boughton, Richard 1954- *75*
Boulet, Susan Seddon 1941- *50*
Boulle, Pierre (Francois Marie-Louis)
   1912-1994 .... *22*
   Obituary *78*
Boulton, Jane 1921- *91*
Bouma, Paddy 1947- *128*
Bour, Daniele 1939- *62*
Bourbonniere, Sylvie 1966- *182*
Bourdon, David 1934-1998 .... *46*
Bourgeois, Paulette 1951- *153*
Bourne, Lesley
   See Marshall, Evelyn
Bourne, Miriam Anne 1931-1989 .... *16*
   Obituary *63*
Boutavant, Marc 1970- *200*
Boutet de Monvel, (Louis) M(aurice)
   1850(?)-1913 .... *30*
   See also CLR *32*
Bouwman, Heather M.
   See Bouwman, H.M.
Bouwman, H.M. *209*
Bova, Ben 1932- *133*
   Earlier sketches in SATA *6, 68*
   See also CLR *96*
Bova, Benjamin William
   See Bova, Ben
Bovaird, Anne E(lizabeth) 1960- *90*
Bow, Patricia 1946- *168*
Bowden, Joan Chase 1925- *51*
   Brief entry *38*
Bowe, Julie 1962- *194*
Bowen, Alexandria Russell *97*
Bowen, Andy Russell
   See Bowen, Alexandria Russell
Bowen, Anne 1952- *202*
   Earlier sketch in SATA *170*
Bowen, Betty Morgan
   See West, Betty
Bowen, Catherine (Shober) Drinker
   1897-1973 .... *7*
Bowen, David
   See Bowen, Joshua David
Bowen, Fred 1953- *136*
Bowen, Joshua David 1930- *22*
Bowen, Rhys
   See Quin-Harkin, Janet
Bowen, Robert Sydney 1900-1977 .... *52*
   Obituary *21*
Bowermaster, Jon 1954- *135*
   Earlier sketch in SATA *77*
Bowers, Terrell L. 1945- *101*
Bowers, Terry
   See Bowers, Terrell L.
Bowers, Tim *185*

Bowie, C. W.
   See Old, Wendie C(orbin)
   and Wirths, Claudine (Turner) G(ibson)
Bowie, Jim
   See Norwood, Victor G(eorge) C(harles)
   and Stratemeyer, Edward L.
Bowkett, Stephen 1953- *67*
Bowler, Jan Brett
   See Brett, Jan
Bowler, Tim 1953- *209*
   Earlier sketch in SATA *149*
Bowman, Catherine
   See Smith, Cat Bowman
Bowman, Crystal 1951- *105*
Bowman, James Cloyd 1880-1961 .... *23*
Bowman, John S(tewart) 1931- *16*
Bowman, Kathleen (Gill) 1942- *52*
   Brief entry *40*
Bowman, Leslie
   See Bowman, Leslie W.
Bowman, Leslie W. *182*
Bowsher, Melodie *195*
Boxall, Ed *178*
Boyce, Frank Cottrell *182*
Boyce, George A(rthur) 1898- *19*
Boyd, Candy Dawson 1946- *72*
   See also CLR *50*
Boyd, Pauline
   See Schock, Pauline
Boyd, Selma
   See Acuff, Selma Boyd
Boyd, Waldo T. 1918- *18*
Boyden, Linda 1948- *143*
Boyer, Allen B. 1963- *153*
Boyer, Robert E(rnst) 1929- *22*
Boyes, Vivien 1952- *106*
Boyes, Vivien Elizabeth
   See Boyes, Vivien
Boyle, Ann (Peters) 1916- *10*
Boyle, Eleanor Vere (Gordon) 1825-1916 .... *28*
Boyle, Robert H. 1928- *65*
Boylston, Helen Dore 1895-1984 .... *23*
   Obituary *39*
Boyne, John 1971- *181*
Boynton, Sandra (Keith) 1953- *152*
   Brief entry *38*
   Earlier sketches in SATA *57, 107*
   See also CLR *105*
Boz
   See Dickens, Charles
Braasch, Gary *201*
Bracken, Charles
   See Pellowski, Michael (Joseph)
Brackers de Hugo, Pierre 1960- *115*
Brackett, Dolli Tingle 1911-1993 .... *137*
Brackett, Virginia 1950- *166*
   Earlier sketch in SATA *121*
Brackett, Virginia Roberts Meredith
   See Brackett, Virginia
Bradbury, Bianca (Ryley) 1908-1982 .... *56*
   Earlier sketch in SATA *3*
Bradbury, Edward P.
   See Moorcock, Michael
Bradbury, Ray 1920- *123*
   Earlier sketches in SATA *11, 64*
Bradbury, Ray Douglas
   See Bradbury, Ray
Bradby, Marie *161*
Bradfield, Carl 1942- *91*
Bradford, Ann (Liddell) 1917- *56*
   Brief entry *38*
Bradford, Barbara Taylor 1933- *66*
Bradford, Chris 1974- *215*
Bradford, Karleen 1936- *96*
   Earlier sketch in SATA *48*
Bradford, Lois J(ean) 1936- *36*
Bradford, Richard (Roark) 1932-2002 .... *59*
   Obituary *135*
Bradley, Duane
   See Sanborn, Duane
Bradley, Kimberly Brubaker 1967- *179*

Bradley, Marion Zimmer 1930-1999 .... *139*
   Obituary *116*
   Earlier sketch in SATA *90*
Bradley, Timothy J. *193*
Bradley, Virginia 1912- *23*
Bradley, Will
   See Strickland, Brad
Bradman, Tony 1954- *152*
   Earlier sketch in SATA *81*
Bradshaw, Gillian (Joan) 1949- *118*
Bradshaw, Gillian 1956- *127*
Bradshaw, Gillian Marucha
   See Bradshaw, Gillian
Bradstreet, T. J.
   See Thesman, Jean
Brady, Esther Wood 1905-1987 .... *31*
   Obituary *53*
Brady, Irene 1943- *4*
Brady, Kimberly S. 1953- *101*
Brady, Kimberley Smith
   See Brady, Kimberley S.
Brady, Lillian 1902- *28*
Bragdon, Elspeth MacDuffie 1897-1980 .... *6*
Bragdon, Lillian Jacot *24*
Brager, Bruce L. 1949- *146*
Bragg, Mabel Caroline 1870-1945 .... *24*
Bragg, Michael 1948- *46*
Bragg, Ruth Gembicki 1943- *77*
Brahm, Sumishta 1954- *58*
Brailsford, Frances
   See Wosmek, Frances
Brainerd, John W(hiting) 1918- *65*
Braithwaite, Althea 1940- *23*
   Autobiography Feature *119*
   See also SAAS *24*
Bram, Elizabeth 1948- *30*
Brancato, Robin F. 1936- *97*
   See also CLR *32*
   See also SAAS *9*
Brancato, Robin Fidler
   See Brancato, Robin F.
Branch, Muriel Miller 1943- *152*
   Earlier sketch in SATA *94*
Brand, Christianna
   See Lewis, Mary
Brand, Rebecca
   See Charnas, Suzy McKee
Brande, Robin *194*
Brandel, Marc 1919- *71*
Brandenberg, Alexa (Demetria) 1966- *97*
Brandenberg, Aliki 1929- *157*
   Earlier sketches in SATA *2, 35, 75, 113*
   See also CLR *71*
Brandenberg, Franz 1932- *75*
   Earlier sketches in SATA *8, 35*
Brandenburg, Jim 1945- *87*
Brandhorst, Carl T(heodore) 1898-1988 .... *23*
Brandis, Marianne 1938- *149*
   Earlier sketches in SATA *59, 96*
Brandon, Brumsic, Jr. 1927- *9*
Brandon, Curt
   See Bishop, Curtis (Kent)
Brandreth, Gyles 1948- *28*
Brandreth, Gyles Daubeney
   See Brandreth, Gyles
Brandt, Catharine 1905-1997 .... *40*
Brandt, Keith
   See Sabin, Louis
Brandt, Sue R(eading) 1916- *59*
Branfield, John (Charles) 1931- *11*
Branley, Henrietta 1946-1999 .... *106*
Branley, Franklyn M(ansfield) 1915-2002 .. *136*
   Earlier sketches in SATA *4, 68*
   See also CLR *13*
   See also SAAS *16*
Brannen, Sarah S. *202*
Branscum, Robbie (Tilley) 1937-1997 .... *72*
   Obituary *96*
   Earlier sketch in SATA *23*
   See also SAAS *17*
Bransom, (John) Paul 1885-1979 .... *43*

Brashares, Ann 1967- *188*
  Earlier sketch in SATA *145*
  See also CLR *113*
Brassard, France 1963- *186*
Braswell, E.J.
  See Lynn, Tracy
Braswell, Elizabeth J.
  See Lynn, Tracy
Braswell, Liz
  See Lynn, Tracy
Bratton, Helen 1899-1986 .... *4*
Bratun, Katy 1950- *160*
  Earlier sketch in SATA *83*
Braude, Michael 1936- *23*
Braun, Lilian Jackson 1916(?)- *109*
Brautigan, Richard 1935-1984 .... *56*
Brautigan, Richard Gary
  See Brautigan, Richard
Bray, Libba *203*
  Earlier sketch in SATA *159*
Bray, Martha E.
  See Bray, Libba
Braymer, Marjorie Elizabeth 1911-1988 .... *6*
Breathed, Berke 1957- *161*
  Earlier sketch in SATA *86*
Breathed, Berkeley
  See Breathed, Berke
Breathed, Guy Berkeley
  See Breathed, Berke
Brecht, Edith 1895-1975 .... *6*
  Obituary *25*
Breck, Vivian
  See Breckenfeld, Vivian Gurney
Breckenfeld, Vivian Gurney 1895-1992 .... *1*
Breda, Tjalmar
  See DeJong, David C(ornel)
Bredeson, Carmen 1944- *163*
  Earlier sketch in SATA *98*
Breen, M.E. *216*
Breen, Molly
  See Breen, M.E.
Breen, Steve 1970- *186*
Breinburg, Petronella 1927- *11*
  See also CLR *31*
Breisky, William J(ohn) 1928- *22*
Brenaman, Miriam *172*
Brennan, Caitlin
  See Tarr, Judith
Brennan, Gale (Patrick) 1927- *64*
  Brief entry *53*
Brennan, Herbie 1940- *214*
  Autobiography Feature *214*
  Earlier sketches in SATA *140, 183*
Brennan, James Herbert
  See Brennan, Herbie
Brennan, Jan
  See Brennan, Herbie
Brennan, J.H.
  See Brennan, Herbie
Brennan, Joseph Lomas 1903-2000 .... *6*
Brennan, Linda Crotta 1952- *130*
Brennan, Tim
  See Conroy, John Wesley
Brennan-Nelson, Denise *203*
Brenner, Anita 1905-1974 .... *56*
Brenner, Barbara (Johnes) 1925- *124*
  Earlier sketches in SATA *4, 42, 76*
  See also SAAS *14*
Brenner, Fred 1920- *36*
  Brief entry *34*
Brent, Hope 1935(?)-1984
  Obituary *39*
Brent, Stuart 1912-2010 .... *14*
Breskin, Jane
  See Zalben, Jane Breskin
Breslin, Theresa *128*
  Autobiography Feature *128*
  Earlier sketch in SATA *70*
Breslow, Maurice 1935- *72*
Breslow, Maurice A
  See Breslow, Maurice

Breslow, Susan 1951- *69*
Brett, Bernard 1925- *22*
Brett, Grace N(eff) 1900-1975 .... *23*
Brett, Jan 1949- *171*
  Earlier sketches in SATA *42, 71, 130*
  See also CLR *27*
Brett, Jan Churchill
  See Brett, Jan
Brett Bowler, Jan
  See Brett, Jan
Brewer, Heather 1973- *196*
Brewer, James D. 1951- *108*
Brewer, Sally King 1947- *33*
Brewster, Benjamin
  See Folsom, Franklin (Brewster)
Brewster, Hugh 1950- *191*
  Earlier sketch in SATA *95*
Brewster, Patience 1952- *97*
Brewton, John E(dmund) 1898-1982 .... *5*
Brian, Janeen (Paulette) 1948- *141*
Briant, Ed *180*
Brick, John 1922-1973 .... *10*
Brickman, Robin D. 1954- *155*
Bride, Nadja
  See Nobisso, Josephine
Bridgers, Sue Ellen 1942- *90*
  Autobiography Feature *109*
  Earlier sketch in SATA *22*
  See also CLR *18*
  See also SAAS *1*
Bridges, Laurie
  See Bruck, Lorraine
Bridges, Ruby (Nell) 1954- *131*
Bridges, William (Andrew) 1901-1984 .... *5*
Bridwell, Norman (Ray) 1928- *138*
  Earlier sketches in SATA *4, 68*
  See also CLR *96*
Brier, Howard M(axwell) 1903-1969 .... *8*
Brierley, (Louise) 1958- *59*
Briggs, Katharine Mary 1898-1980 .... *101*
  Obituary *25*
Briggs, Peter 1921-1975 .... *39*
  Obituary *31*
Briggs, Raymond 1934- *184*
  Earlier sketches in SATA *23, 66, 131*
  See also CLR *10*
Briggs, Raymond Redvers
  See Briggs, Raymond
Bright, Paul 1949- *182*
Bright, Robert Sr.) 1902-1988 .... *63*
  Obituary *60*
  Earlier sketch in SATA *24*
Bright, Robert Douglas
  See Bright, Robert Sr.)
Bright, Sarah
  See Shine, Deborah
Brightfield, Richard 1927- *65*
  Brief entry *53*
Brightfield, Rick
  See Brightfield, Richard
Brighton, Catherine 1943- *206*
  Earlier sketches in SATA *65, 107*
Brignall, Richard 1977(?)- *213*
Brill, Marlene Targ 1945- *124*
  Earlier sketch in SATA *77*
Brimberg, Stanlee 1947- *9*
Brimner, Larry Dane 1949- *170*
  Autobiography Feature *112*
  Earlier sketch in SATA *79*
Brin, David 1950- *65*
Brin, Ruth Firestone 1921- *22*
Brinckloe, Julie 1950- *13*
Brinckloe, Julie Lorraine
  See Brinckloe, Julie
Brindel, June (Rachuy) 1919- *7*
Brindle, Max
  See Fleischman, Sid
Brindze, Ruth 1903-1984 .... *23*

Brink, Carol Ryrie 1895-1981 .... *100*
  Obituary *27*
  Earlier sketches in SATA *1, 31*
  See also CLR *149*
Brinsmead, H. F(ay)
  See Brinsmead, H(esba) F(ay)
Brinsmead, H. F.
  See Brinsmead, H(esba) F(ay)
Brinsmead, H(esba) F(ay) 1922- *78*
  Earlier sketch in SATA *18*
  See also CLR *47*
  See also SAAS *5*
Briquebec, John
  See Rowland-Entwistle, (Arthur) Theodore
  (Henry)
Brisbane, Henry R.
  See Ellis, Edward S.
Brisco, P. A.
  See Matthews, Patricia
Brisco, Patty
  See Matthews, Patricia
  and Matthews, Clayton (Hartley)
Briscoe, Jill (Pauline) 1935- *56*
  Brief entry *47*
Brisley, Joyce Lankester 1896-1978 .... *22*
  Obituary *84*
Brissenden, Connie
  See Brissenden, Constance
Brissenden, Constance 1947- *150*
Brisson, Pat 1951- *177*
  Autobiography Feature *133*
  Earlier sketches in SATA *67, 128, 133*
Britt, Albert 1874-1969
  Obituary *28*
Britt, Dell 1934- *1*
Brittain, Bill
  See Brittain, William
Brittain, C. Dale 1948- *82*
Brittain, William 1930- *76*
  Earlier sketch in SATA *36*
  See also SAAS *7*
Brittingham, Geoffrey (Hugh) 1959- *76*
Brittney, L. *209*
Britton, Kate
  See Stegeman, Janet Allais
Britton, Louisa
  See McGuire, Leslie (Sarah)
Britton, Rick 1952- *82*
Bro, Margueritte (Harmon) 1894-1977 .... *19*
  Obituary *27*
Broach, Elise 1963- *173*
Broadhead, Helen Cross 1913- *25*
Broadway, Hannah *208*
Brochmann, Elizabeth 1938- *41*
Brock, Betty (Carter) 1923-2003 .... *4*
  Obituary *150*
Brock, C(harles) E(dmund) 1870-1938 .... *42*
  Brief entry *32*
Brock, Delia
  See Ephron, Delia
Brock, Emma L(illian) 1886-1974 .... *8*
Brock, H(enry) M(atthew) 1875-1960 .... *42*
Brockett, Eleanor Hall 1913-1967 .... *10*
Brockman, C(hristian) Frank 1902-1985 ...... *26*
Brockmeier, Kevin 1972- *176*
Broda, Ron 1954- *209*
Broderick, Dorothy M. 1929- *5*
Brodeur, Ruth Wallace
  See Wallace-Brodeur, Ruth
Brodie, Sally
  See Cavin, Ruth (Brodie)
Brodsky, Beverly
  See McDermott, Beverly Brodsky
Brody, Wendy
  See Staub, Wendy Corsi
Broekel, Rainer Lothar
  See Broekel, Ray
Broekel, Ray 1923- *38*
Broekstra, Lorette 1964- *189*
  Earlier sketch in SATA *124*

Brogden, Sherryl
   See Jordan, Sherryl
Broger, Achim
   See Broger, Achim
Broger, Achim 1944- 31
Broida, Marian 154
Brokamp, Marilyn 1920- 10
Broman, Fred
   See Moseley, James W(illett)
Bromhall, Winifred 26
Brommer, Gerald F(rederick) 1927- 28
Brondfield, Jerome 1913-1998 22
Brondfield, Jerry
   See Brondfield, Jerome
Bronner, Stephen Eric 1949- 101
Bronowski, Jacob 1908-1974 55
Bronson, Alice
   See Watkins, Dawn L.
Bronson, Linda 203
Bronson, Lynn
   See Lampman, Evelyn Sibley
Bronson, Wilfrid Swancourt 1894-1985
   Obituary 43
Brook, Judith (Penelope) 1926- 59
   Brief entry 51
Brook, Judy
   See Brook, Judith (Penelope)
Brooke, L(eonard) Leslie 1862-1940 17
   See also CLR 20
Brooke, William J. 1946- 139
Brooke-Haven, P.
   See Wodehouse, P. G.
Brooker, Kyrsten 199
Brookins, Dana 1931- 28
Brooks, Anita
   See Abramovitz, Anita (Zeltner Brooks)
Brooks, Bill 1939- 59
Brooks, Bruce 1950- 112
   Brief entry 53
   Earlier sketch in SATA 72
   See also CLR 25
Brooks, Caryl 1924- 84
Brooks, Charlotte K(endrick) 1918-1998 24
   Obituary 112
Brooks, Erik 1972- 182
   Earlier sketch in SATA 152
Brooks, George
   See Baum, L. Frank
Brooks, Gwendolyn 1917-2000 6
   Obituary 123
   See also CLR 27
Brooks, Gwendolyn Elizabeth
   See Brooks, Gwendolyn
Brooks, Jerome 1931- 23
Brooks, Kevin 1959- 197
   Earlier sketch in SATA 150
Brooks, Kevin M.
   See Brooks, Kevin
Brooks, Laurie 209
Brooks, Lester 1924- 7
Brooks, Martha 1944- 134
   Autobiography Feature 134
   Earlier sketches in SATA 68, 121
Brooks, Maurice (Graham) 1900- 45
Brooks, Polly Schoyer 1912- 12
Brooks, Ron 1948- 212
   Brief entry 33
   Earlier sketch in SATA 94
Brooks, Ronald George
   See Brooks, Ron
Brooks, Terry 1944- 60
Brooks, Walter R(ollin) 1886-1958 17
Brooks-Hill, Helen (Mason) 1908-1994 59
Broome, Errol 1937- 158
   Earlier sketch in SATA 105
Brophy, Nannette 1963- 73
Brosnan, James Patrick 1929- 14
Brosnan, Jim
   See Brosnan, James Patrick
Brostoff, Anita 1931- 132

Brothers Grimm
   See Grimm, Jacob Ludwig Karl
   and Grimm, Wilhelm Karl
Brothers Hildebrandt, The
   See Hildebrandt, Greg
   and Hildebrandt, Tim
Broun, Emily
   See Sterne, Emma Gelders
Brouwer, S. W.
   See Brouwer, Sigmund (W.)
Brouwer, Sigmund (W.) 1959- 109
Brow, Thea 1934- 60
Brower, Millicent 8
Brower, Pauline 1929- 22
Browin, Frances Williams 1898-1986 5
Brown, Alexis
   See Baumann, Amy Beeching
Brown, Anne Ensign 1937- 61
Brown, Beverly Swerdlow 97
Brown, Bill
   See Brown, William L(ouis)
Brown, Billye Walker
   See Cutchen, Billye Walker
Brown, Bob
   See Brown, Robert Joseph
Brown, Buck 1936- 45
Brown, Calef 217
   Earlier sketch in SATA 179
Brown, Cassie 1919-1986 55
Brown, Charlotte Lewis 181
Brown, Conrad 1922- 31
Brown, Craig McFarland 1947- 73
Brown, David
   See Brown, David A(lan)
   and Myller, Rolf
Brown, Dee 1908-2002 110
   Obituary 141
   Earlier sketch in SATA 5
Brown, Dee Alexander
   See Brown, Dee
Brown, Don 1949- 200
   Earlier sketch in SATA 172
Brown, Drew T. III 1955- 83
Brown, Drollene P. 1939- 53
Brown, Elbrite 198
Brown, Eleanor Frances 1908-1987 3
Brown, Elizabeth Ferguson 1937- 153
Brown, Elizabeth M(yers) 1915- 43
Brown, Fern G. 1918- 34
Brown, (Robert) Fletch 1923- 42
Brown, Fornan 1901-1996 71
   Obituary 88
Brown, George Earl 1883-1964 11
Brown, George Mackay 1921-1996 35
Brown, Irene Bennett 1932- 3
Brown, Irving
   See Adams, William Taylor
Brown, Ivor (John Carnegie) 1891-1974 5
   Obituary 26
Brown, Jane Clark 1930- 81
Brown, Janet Mitsui 87
Brown, Jo 1964- 170
Brown, Joanne 1933- 147
Brown, Joe David 1915-1976 44
Brown, Joseph E(dward) 1929- 59
   Brief entry 51
Brown, Judith Gwyn 1933- 20
Brown, Kathryn 1955- 168
   Earlier sketch in SATA 98
Brown, Kathy
   See Brown, Kathryn
Brown, Ken (James) 129
Brown, Kevin 1960- 101
Brown, Laurene Krasny 1945- 99
   Earlier sketch in SATA 54
Brown, Laurie Krasny
   See Brown, Laurene Krasny
Brown, Lloyd Arnold 1907-1966 36
Brown, Mahlon A.
   See Ellis, Edward S.

Brown, Marc (Tolon) 1946- 145
   Earlier sketches in SATA 10, 53, 80
   See also CLR 29
Brown, Marcia (Joan) 1918- 47
   Earlier sketch in SATA 7
   See also CLR 12
Brown, Margaret Wise 1910-1952 100
   See also YABC 2
   See also CLR 107
Brown, Margery (Wheeler) 78
   Earlier sketch in SATA 5
Brown, Marion Marsh 1908-2001 6
Brown, Myra Berry 1918- 6
Brown, Palmer 1919- 36
Brown, Pamela (Beatrice) 1924-1989 5
   Obituary 61
Brown, Peter 1979- 178
Brown, Rachel W.N. 1947- 203
Brown, Reeve Lindbergh
   See Lindbergh, Reeve
Brown, Richard E. 1946- 61
Brown, Robert Joseph 1907-1989 14
Brown, Roderick (Langmere) Haig-
   See Haig-Brown, Roderick (Langmere)
Brown, Rosalie
   See Moore, Rosalie (Gertrude)
Brown, Roswell
   See Webb, Jean Francis (III)
Brown, Roy (Frederick) 1921-1982 51
   Obituary 39
Brown, Ruth 1941- 170
   Earlier sketch in SATA 105
Brown, Scott 1971- 134
Brown, Sue Ellen 1954- 81
Brown, Tricia 1954- 114
Brown, Vinson 1912-1991 19
Brown, Walter R(eed) 1929- 19
Brown, Will
   See Ainsworth, William Harrison
Brown, William L(ouis) 1910-1964 5
Browne, Anthony 1946- 163
   Brief entry 44
   Earlier sketches in SATA 45, 61, 105
   See also CLR 19
Browne, Anthony Edward Tudor
   See Browne, Anthony
Browne, Dik
   See Browne, Richard Arthur Allen
Browne, Hablot Knight 1815-1882 21
Browne, Matthew
   See Rands, William Brighty
Browne, Nicki M.
   See Browne, N.M.
Browne, Nicky Matthews
   See Browne, N.M.
Browne, N.M. 1960- 167
Browne, Richard Arthur Allen 1917-1989 ... 67
   Brief entry 38
Browne, Vee F. 1956- 214
   Earlier sketch in SATA 90
Browning, Robert 1812-1889
   See YABC 1
   See also CLR 97
Brownjohn, Alan 1931- 6
Brownlee, Walter 1930- 62
Brownlie, Betty 1946- 159
Brownlow, Kevin 1938- 65
Brownlow, Mike 183
Brownridge, William R(oy) 1932- 94
Broyles, Anne 1953- 201
Bruce, Dorita Fairlie 1885-1970
   Obituary 27
Bruce, (William) Harry 1934- 77
Bruce, Mary 1927- 1
Bruchac, Joseph III
   See Bruchac, Joseph
Bruchac, Joseph 1942- 176
   Autobiography Feature 176
   Earlier sketches in SATA 42, 89, 131
   See also CLR 46

Bruchac, Margaret M.
See Bruchac, Marge
Bruchac, Marge 181
Bruck, Lorraine 1921- 55
Brief entry 46
Bruel, Nick 205
Earlier sketch in SATA 166
Bruel, Robert O. 1929-2002 189
Bruemmer, Fred 1929- 47
Brugman, Alyssa (F.) 1974- 152
Brumbeau, Jeff 1955- 157
Bruna, Dick 1927- 76
Brief entry 30
Earlier sketch in SATA 43
See also CLR 7
Brunhoff, Jean de 1899-1937 24
See also CLR 116
Brunhoff, Laurent de 1925- 150
Earlier sketches in SATA 24, 71
See also CLR 116
Brunkus, Denise 204
Brunskill, Elizabeth Ann Flatt
See Flatt, Lizann
Brush, Karen A(lexandra) 1960- 85
Brussel-Smith, Bernard 1914- 58
Brust, Steven 1955- 121
Earlier sketch in SATA 86
Brust, Steven K. Zoltan
See Brust, Steven
Brustlein, Daniel 1904- 40
Brustlein, Janice Tworkov -2000 40
Obituary 126
Brutschy, Jennifer 1960- 84
Bryan, Ashley 1923- 178
Earlier sketches in SATA 31, 72, 132
See also CLR 66
Bryan, Ashley F.
See Bryan, Ashley
Bryan, Dorothy M. 1896(?)-1984
Obituary 39
Bryan, Jennifer 190
Bryan, Sean 192
Bryant, Bernice (Morgan) 1908-1976 11
Bryant, Jen 1960- 175
Earlier sketch in SATA 94
Bryant, Jennifer
See Bryant, Jen
Bryant, Jennifer Fisher
See Bryant, Jen
Bryant, Laura J. 176
Brychta, Alex 1956- 21
Brynie, Faith H. 1946- 113
Brynie, Faith Hickman
See Brynie, Faith H.
Bryson, Bernarda 1903-2004 9
Buba, Joy Flinsch 1904- 44
Buchan, Bryan 1945- 36
Buchan, John 1875-1940
See YABC 2
Buchan, Stuart 1942-1987
Obituary 54
Buchanan, Debby 1952- 82
Buchanan, Deborah Leevonne
See Buchanan, Debby
Buchanan, Jane 1956- 160
Buchanan, Paul 1959- 116
Buchanan, Sue 1939- 139
Buchheimer, Naomi Barnett
See Barnett, Naomi
Buchignani, Walter 1965- 84
Buchmann, Stephen L. 194
Buchwald, Art 1925-2007 10
Buchwald, Arthur
See Buchwald, Art
Buchwald, Emilie 1935- 7
Buck, Gisela 1941- 101
Buck, Lewis 1925- 18
Buck, Margaret Waring 1905-1997 3
Buck, Nola
See Godwin, Laura

Buck, Pearl S. 1892-1973 25
Earlier sketch in SATA 1
Buck, Pearl Sydenstricker
See Buck, Pearl S.
Buck, Siegfried 1941- 101
Buckalew, Clare B.
See Dunkle, Clare B.
Buckeridge, Anthony (Malcolm)
1912-2004 85
Earlier sketch in SATA 6
Buckholtz, Eileen (Garber) 1949- 54
Brief entry 47
Buckingham, Royce 1966- 210
Buckingham, Royce Scott
See Buckingham, Royce
Buckler, Ernest 1908-1984 47
Buckless, Andrea K. 1968- 117
Buckley, Helen E(lizabeth) 1918- 90
Earlier sketch in SATA 2
Buckley, James, Jr. 1963- 166
Earlier sketch in SATA 114
Buckley, Michael 177
Buckley, Susan 184
Buckley, Susan Washburn
See Buckley, Susan
Buckley-Archer, Linda 185
Buckmaster, Henrietta
See Stephens, Henrietta Henkle
Bucks, Brad
See Holub, Joan
Budd, E. S.
See Sirimarco, Elizabeth
Budd, Lillian (Peterson) 1897-1989 7
Budhos, Marina 173
Buehler, Stephanie Jona 1956- 83
Buehner, Caralyn (M.) 1963- 159
Earlier sketch in SATA 104
Buehner, Mark 1959- 159
Earlier sketch in SATA 104
Buehr, Walter Franklin 1897-1971 3
Buell, Ellen Lewis
See Cash, Ellen Lewis Buell
Buell, Janet 1952- 185
Earlier sketch in SATA 106
Buergel, Paul-Hermann H. 1949- 83
Buettner, Dan 1960- 95
Buff, Conrad 1886-1975 19
Buff, Mary (E. Marsh) 1890-1970 19
Buffett, Jimmy 1946- 110
Earlier sketch in SATA 76
Buffie, Margaret 1945- 161
Earlier sketches in SATA 71, 107
See also CLR 39
Bugbee, Emma 1888(?)-1981
Obituary 29
Bugni, Alice 1951- 122
Buhhos, Marina Tamar
See Budhos, Marina
Bujold, Lois McMaster 1949- 136
Bulfinch, Thomas 1796-1867 35
Bulion, Leslie 1958- 209
Earlier sketch in SATA 161
Bull, Angela (Mary) 1936- 45
Bull, Emma 1954- 190
Autobiography Feature 103
Earlier sketch in SATA 99
Bull, Norman John 1916- 41
Bull, Peter (Cecil) 1912-1984
Obituary 39
Bull, Schuyler M. 1974- 138
Bulla, Clyde R. 1914-2007 139
Obituary 182
Earlier sketches in SATA 2, 41, 91
See also SAAS 6
Bullard, Lisa 1961- 142
Buller, Jon 205
Bullock, Kathleen (Mary) 1946- 77
Bullock, Robert (D.) 1947- 92
Bulpin, (Barbara) Vicki 92
Bulwer-Lytton, Edward 1803-1873 23

Bulwer-Lytton, Edward George Earle Lytton
See Bulwer-Lytton, Edward
Bumstead, Kathleen Mary 1918-1987 53
Bundles, A'Lelia Perry 1952- 76
Bunge, Daniela 1973- 207
Bunin, Catherine 1967- 30
Bunin, Sherry 1925- 30
Bunkers, Suzanne L. 1950- 136
Bunting, A.E.
See Bunting, Eve
Bunting, Anne Evelyn
See Bunting, Eve
Bunting, Eve 1928- 196
Earlier sketches in SATA 18, 64, 110, 158
See also CLR 82
Bunting, Glenn (Davison) 1957- 22
Bunyan, John 1628-1688
See CLR 124
Bupp, Walter
See Garrett, Randall
Burack, Sylvia K. 1916-2003 35
Obituary 143
Burbank, Addison (Buswell) 1895-1961 37
Burch, Joann J(ohansen) 75
Burch, Robert J(oseph) 1925- 74
Earlier sketch in SATA 1
See also CLR 63
Burchard, Peter Duncan 1921- 143
Earlier sketches in SATA 5, 74
See also SAAS 13
Burchard, S. H.
See Burchard, Sue
Burchard, Sue 1937- 22
Burchardt, Nellie 1921- 7
Burckhardt, Marc 1962- 196
Burdett, Lois 117
Burdick, Eugene (Leonard) 1918-1965 22
Burford, Eleanor
See Hibbert, Eleanor Alice Burford
Burg, Ann E. 1954- 217
Burg, Shana 1968- 204
Burgan, Michael 1960- 167
Earlier sketch in SATA 118
Burger, Carl 1888-1967 9
Burgess, Ann Marie
See Gerson, Noel Bertram
Burgess, Barbara Hood 1926- 69
Burgess, Em
See Burgess, Mary Wyche
Burgess, (Frank) Gelett 1866-1951 32
Brief entry 30
Burgess, Mark 157
Burgess, Mary Wyche 1916- 18
Burgess, Melvin 1954- 198
Earlier sketches in SATA 96, 146
Burgess, Michael
See Gerson, Noel Bertram
Burgess, Robert F(orrest) 1927- 4
Burgess, Starling
See Tudor, Tasha
Burgess, Thornton Waldo 1874-1965 17
Burgess, Trevor
See Trevor, Elleston
Burgwyn, Mebane Holoman 1914-1992 7
Burke, David 1927- 46
Burke, Diana G.
See Gallagher, Diana G.
Burke, Diana Gallagher
See Gallagher, Diana G.
Burke, Dianne O'Quinn 1940- 89
Burke, Janine 1952- 139
Burke, Jim 1973- 179
Burke, John
See O'Connor, Richard
Burke, Katie 1953- 168
Burke, Patrick 1958- 114
Burke, Ralph
See Garrett, Randall
and Silverberg, Robert
Burkert, Nancy Ekholm 1933- 24
See also SAAS 14

Burkett, D. Brent *194*
Burke-Weiner, Kimberly 1962- *95*
Burks, Brian 1955- *95*
Burland, Brian (Berkeley) 1931- *34*
Burland, C. A.
   See Burland, Cottie (Arthur)
Burland, Cottie (Arthur) 1905-1983 .... *5*
Burleigh, Robert 1936- *193*
   Earlier sketches in SATA *55, 98, 146*
Burlingame, (William) Roger 1889-1967 .... *2*
Burman, Alice Caddy 1896(?)-1977
   Obituary *24*
Burman, Ben Lucien 1896-1984 .... *6*
   Obituary *40*
Burn, Doris 1923- *1*
Burn, Ted
   See Burn, Thomas E.
Burn, Thomas E. 1940- *150*
Burnard, Damon 1963- *115*
Burnett, Constance Buel 1893-1975 .... *36*
Burnett, Frances Eliza Hodgson
   See Burnett, Frances Hodgson
Burnett, Frances Hodgson 1849-1924 .... *100*
   See also YABC *2*
   See also CLR *122*
Burnett, Lindy *210*
Burnett Bossi, Lisa *193*
Burney, Anton
   See Hopkins, (Hector) Kenneth
Burnford, Sheila (Philip Cochrane Every)
   1918-1984 .... *3*
   Obituary *38*
   See also CLR *2*
Burnham, Gretchen
   See Sprague, Gretchen
Burnham, Nicole 1970- *161*
Burnham, Niki
   See Burnham, Nicole
Burnham, Sophy 1936- *65*
Burningham, John 1936- *160*
   Earlier sketches in SATA *16, 59, 111*
   See also CLR *9*
Burningham, Robin Yoko
   See Racoma, Robin Yoko
Burningham, Sarah O'Leary *216*
Burns, Diane L. 1950- *81*
   See also SAAS *24*
Burns, Eloise Wilkin
   See Wilkin, Eloise
Burns, Florence M. 1905-1988 .... *61*
Burns, Khephra 1950- *92*
Burns, Loree Griffin *193*
Burns, Marilyn 1941- *96*
   Brief entry *33*
Burns, Olive Ann 1924-1990 .... *65*
Burns, Paul C. *5*
Burns, Ray
   See Burns, Raymond (Howard)
Burns, Raymond (Howard) 1924- *9*
Burns, Theresa 1961- *84*
Burns, William A. 1909-1999 .... *5*
Burr, Dan 1951- *65*
Burr, Lonnie 1943- *47*
Burrell, Roy E(ric) C(harles) 1923- *72*
Burroughs, Edgar Rice 1875-1950 .... *41*
Burroughs, Jean Mitchell 1908- *28*
Burroughs, Polly 1925- *2*
Burroway, Janet (Gay) 1936- *23*
Burstein, Chaya M(alamud) 1923- *64*
Burstein, Fred 1950- *83*
Burstein, John 1949- *54*
   Brief entry *40*
Burstein, Stanley M.
   See Burstein, Stanley Mayer
Burstein, Stanley Mayer 1941- *175*
Bursztynski, Sue 1953- *114*
Burt, Jesse Clifton 1921-1976 .... *46*
   Obituary *20*
Burt, Olive Woolley 1894-1981 .... *4*
Burtinshaw, Julie *185*
Burton, Gennett 1945- *95*

Burton, Hester (Wood-Hill) 1913-2000 .... *74*
   Earlier sketch in SATA *7*
   See also CLR *1*
   See also SAAS *8*
Burton, Leslie
   See McGuire, Leslie (Sarah)
Burton, Marilee Robin 1950- *82*
   Earlier sketch in SATA *46*
Burton, Maurice 1898-1992 .... *23*
Burton, Rebecca 1970- *183*
Burton, Robert (Wellesley) 1941- *22*
Burton, Virginia Lee 1909-1968 .... *100*
   Earlier sketch in SATA *2*
   See also CLR *11*
Burton, William H(enry) 1890-1964 .... *11*
Busby, Ailie *192*
Busby, Cylin 1970- *118*
Busby, Edith (A. Lake) (?)-1964
   Obituary *29*
Busby, John 1942- *209*
Buscaglia, (Felice) Leo(nardo) 1924-1998 ... *65*
Buscaglia, Leo F.
   See Buscaglia, (Felice) Leo(nardo)
Busch, Phyllis S. 1909- *30*
Bush, Anne Kelleher
   See Kelleher, Anne
Bush, Catherine 1961- *128*
Bush, Jenna 1981- *208*
Bush, Laura 1946- *208*
Bushmiller, Ernest Paul 1905-1982 .... *31*
Bushmiller, Ernie
   See Bushmiller, Ernest Paul
Bushnell, Jack 1952- *86*
Busoni, Rafaello 1900-1962 .... *16*
Buss, Helen M.
   See Clarke, Margaret
Busse, Sarah Martin *194*
Busselle, Rebecca 1941- *80*
Bustard, Anne 1951- *173*
Butcher, Kristin 1951- *140*
Butenko, Bohdan 1931- *90*
Butler, Beverly Kathleen 1932- *7*
Butler, Bill
   See Butler, William Vivian
   and Butler, Ernest Alton
   and Butler, William Huxford
Butler, Charles 1963- *175*
   Earlier sketch in SATA *121*
Butler, Charles Cadman
   See Butler, Charles
Butler, Dori Hillestad 1965- *207*
   Earlier sketch in SATA *164*
Butler, Dorothy 1925- *73*
Butler, Geoff 1945- *94*
Butler, M. Christina 1934- *170*
   Earlier sketch in SATA *72*
Butler, Octavia 1947-2006 .... *84*
   See also CLR *65*
Butler, Octavia E.
   See Butler, Octavia
Butler, Octavia Estelle
   See Butler, Octavia
Butler, Vivian
   See Butler, William Vivian
Butler, William
   See Butler, William Vivian
Butler, William Vivian 1927-1987 .... *79*
Butters, Dorothy Gilman
   See Gilman, Dorothy
Butterworth, Emma Macalik 1928- *43*
Butterworth, Nick 1946- *149*
   Earlier sketch in SATA *106*
Butterworth, Oliver 1915-1990 .... *1*
   Obituary *66*
Butterworth, W.E.
   See Griffin, W.E.B.
Butterworth, William E.
   See Griffin, W.E.B.
Butterworth, William Edmund III
   See Griffin, W.E.B.
Butts, Ed 1951- *177*

Butts, Edward P.
   See Butts, Ed
Butts, Ellen R. 1942- *93*
Butts, Ellen Rubinstein
   See Butts, Ellen R.
Butzer, C. M. 1974- *212*
Buxton, Ralph
   See Silverstein, Alvin
   and Silverstein, Virginia B.
Buzzeo, Toni 1951- *215*
   Earlier sketch in SATA *135*
Byalick, Marcia 1947- *141*
   Earlier sketch in SATA *97*
Byard, Carole (Marie) 1941- *57*
Byars, Betsy 1928- *163*
   Autobiography Feature *108*
   Earlier sketches in SATA *4, 46, 80*
   See also CLR *72*
   See also SAAS *1*
Byars, Betsy Cromer
   See Byars, Betsy
Byfield, Barbara Ninde 1930- *8*
Byman, Jeremy 1944- *129*
Bynum, Janie *133*
Byrd, Elizabeth 1912-1989 .... *34*
Byrd, Nicole
   See Zach, Cheryl (Byrd)
Byrd, Robert (John) 1942- *158*
   Earlier sketches in SATA *33, 112*
Byrd, Tim 1964- *216*
Byrne, Mary Gregg 1951- *162*

C

C. 3. 3.
   See Wilde, Oscar
C. E. M.
   See Mastrangelo, Charles E(lmer)
Cabaniss, J(ames) Allen 1911-1997 .... *5*
Cabat, Erni 1914- *74*
Cabban, Vanessa 1971- *176*
Cable, Mary 1920- *9*
Cabot, Meg 1967- *217*
   Earlier sketches in SATA *127, 175*
   See also CLR *85*
Cabot, Meggin
   See Cabot, Meg
Cabot, Meggin Patricia
   See Cabot, Meg
Cabot, Patricia
   See Cabot, Meg
Cabral, O. M.
   See Cabral, Olga
Cabral, Olga 1909- *46*
Cabrera, Cozbi A. 1963- *177*
Cabrera, Jane 1968- *182*
   Earlier sketches in SATA *103, 152*
Cabrera, Marcela 1966- *90*
Caddy, Alice
   See Burman, Alice Caddy
Cade, Toni
   See Bambara, Toni Cade
Cadmus and Harmonia
   See Buchan, John
Cadnum, Michael 1949- *165*
   Earlier sketches in SATA *87, 121*
   See also CLR *78*
Caduto, Michael J. 1955- *103*
Cadwallader, Sharon 1936- *7*
Cady, (Walter) Harrison 1877(?)-1970 .... *19*
Caffey, Donna (J.) 1954- *110*
Cagle, Malcolm W(infield) 1918- *32*
Cahn, Rhoda 1922- *37*
Cahn, William 1912-1976 .... *37*
Cain, Arthur H(omer) 1913-1981 .... *3*
Cain, Christopher
   See Fleming, Thomas
Cain, Sheridan 1952- *186*

Caine, Geoffrey
  See Walker, Robert W.
Caines, Jeannette (Franklin) 1938- *78*
  Brief entry *43*
  See also CLR 24
Cairns, Trevor 1922- *14*
Calabro, Marian 1954- *79*
Caldecott, Moyra 1927- *22*
Caldecott, Randolph (J.) 1846-1886 .... *100*
  Earlier sketch in SATA *17*
  See also CLR 110
Calder, Charlotte 1952- *125*
Calder, David 1932-1997 .... *105*
Calder, Lyn
  See Calmenson, Stephanie
Calder, Marie D(onais) 1948- *96*
Calderone-Stewart, Lisa
  See Calderone-Stewart, Lisa-Marie
Calderone-Stewart, Lisa-Marie 1958- *123*
Caldwell, Doreen (Mary) 1942- *71*
Caldwell, John C(ope) 1913-1984 .... *7*
Caletti, Deb 1963- *171*
Calhoun, B. B. 1961- *98*
Calhoun, Chad
  See Barrett, Neal, Jr.
  and Cunningham, Chet
  and Goulart, Ron
Calhoun, Dia 1959- *183*
  Earlier sketch in SATA *129*
Calhoun, Mary
  See Wilkins, Mary Huiskamp
Calhoun, T.B.
  See Bisson, Terry
Cali, Davide 1972- *190*
Calif, Ruth 1922- *67*
Calkins, Franklin
  See Stratemeyer, Edward L.
Call, Greg *197*
Call, Hughie Florence 1890-1969 .... *1*
Callahan, Dorothy M. 1934- *39*
  Brief entry *35*
Callahan, Dorothy Monahan
  See Callahan, Dorothy M.
Callahan, Philip Serna 1923- *25*
Callan, Jamie 1954- *59*
Callan, Jim 1951- *181*
Callaway, Bernice (Anne) 1923- *48*
Callaway, Kathy 1943- *36*
Callen, Larry
  See Callen, Lawrence Willard, Jr.
Callen, Lawrence Willard, Jr. 1927- *19*
Calley, Karin 1965- *92*
Calmenson, Stephanie 1952- *211*
  Brief entry *37*
  Earlier sketches in SATA *51, 84, 139*
Calonita, Jen *216*
Calvert, Elinor H.
  See Lasell, Elinor H.
Calvert, John
  See Leaf, (Wilbur) Munro
Calvert, Pam 1966- *205*
Calvert, Patricia 1931- *132*
  Earlier sketches in SATA *45, 69*
  See also SAAS 17
Camburn, Carol A.
  See Camburn-Bracalente, Carol A.
Camburn-Bracalente, Carol A. 1962- *118*
Cameron, Ann 1943- *129*
  Earlier sketches in SATA *27, 89*
  See also SAAS 20
Cameron, Edna M. 1905-1999 .... *3*
Cameron, Eleanor (Frances) 1912-1996 .... *25*
  Obituary *93*
  Earlier sketch in SATA *1*
  See also CLR 72
  See also SAAS 10
Cameron, Elizabeth
  See Nowell, Elizabeth Cameron
Cameron, Elizabeth Jane 1910-1976 .... *32*
  Obituary *30*

Cameron, Ian
  See Payne, Donald Gordon
Cameron, M(alcolm) G(ordon) Graham
  See Graham-Cameron, M(alcolm) G(ordon)
Cameron, M. Graham
  See Graham-Cameron, M(alcolm) G(ordon)
Cameron, Mike Graham
  See Graham-Cameron, M(alcolm) G(ordon)
Cameron, Polly 1928- *2*
Cameron, Scott 1962- *84*
Camp, Charles L. 1893-1975
  Obituary *31*
Camp, Lindsay 1957- *133*
Camp, Madeleine L'Engle
  See L'Engle, Madeleine
Camp, Walter (Chauncey) 1859-1925
  See YABC *1*
Campbell, (Elizabeth) Andrea 1963- *50*
Campbell, Ann R. 1925- *11*
Campbell, Bill 1960- *89*
Campbell, Bruce
  See Epstein, Samuel
Campbell, Camilla 1905-1992 .... *26*
Campbell, Carole R. 1939- *125*
Campbell, Hope 1925- *20*
Campbell, Hugh 1930- *90*
Campbell, Jane
  See Edwards, Jane Campbell
Campbell, Julie
  See Tatham, Julie Campbell
Campbell, Patricia J(ean) 1930- *45*
Campbell, Patty
  See Campbell, Patricia J(ean)
Campbell, Peter A. 1948- *99*
Campbell, R. W.
  See Campbell, Rosemae Wells
Campbell, Robin
  See Strachan, Ian
Campbell, Rod 1945- *98*
  Brief entry *44*
  Earlier sketch in SATA *51*
Campbell, Rosemae Wells 1909- *1*
Campbell, Sarah C. 1966- *207*
Camper, Cathy 1956- *170*
Campion, Nardi Reeder 1917-2007 .... *22*
Campling, Elizabeth 1948- *53*
Campoy, F. Isabel 1946- *181*
  Earlier sketch in SATA *143*
Camps, Luis 1928- *66*
Canales, Viola 1957- *141*
Candell, Victor 1903-1977
  Obituary *24*
Canfield, Dorothea F.
  See Fisher, Dorothy (Frances) Canfield
Canfield, Dorothea Frances
  See Fisher, Dorothy (Frances) Canfield
Canfield, Dorothy
  See Fisher, Dorothy (Frances) Canfield
Canfield, Jack 1944- *164*
Canfield, Jane White 1897-1984 .... *32*
  Obituary *38*
Canfield, Muriel 1935- *94*
Canga, C.B. 1976- *216*
Canga, Chris
  See Canga, C.B.
Caniff, Milton 1907-1988
  Obituary *58*
Caniff, Milton Arthur Paul
  See Caniff, Milton
Cann, Helen 1969- *179*
  Earlier sketch in SATA *124*
Cann, Kate 1954- *152*
  Earlier sketch in SATA *103*
Cannan, Joanna
  See Pullein-Thompson, Joanna Maxwell
Cannell, Jon *196*
Cannell, Jonathan C.
  See Cannell, Jon
Cannon, A.E. *202*
  Earlier sketches in SATA *93, 163*

Cannon, Ann Edwards
  See Cannon, A.E.
Cannon, Bettie (Waddell) 1922- *59*
Cannon, Curt
  See Hunter, Evan
Cannon, Eileen E(mily) 1948- *119*
Cannon, Frank
  See Mayhar, Ardath
Cannon, Janell 1957- *128*
  Earlier sketch in SATA *78*
  See also CLR 120
Cannon, Marian G. 1923- *85*
Cannon, Taffy
  See Cannon, Eileen E(mily)
Cantone, AnnaLaura *182*
Cantrell, Julie 1973- *217*
Canusi, Jose
  See Barker, S. Omar
Canyon, Christopher 1966- *150*
  Earlier sketch in SATA *104*
Caparo, Antonio
  See Caparo, Antonio Javier
Caparo, Antonio Javier *205*
Capek, Michael 1947- *142*
  Earlier sketch in SATA *96*
Capes, Bernard (Edward Joseph)
  1854-1918 .... *116*
Caple, Kathy *193*
Caple, Laurie 1958- *201*
Caplin, Alfred Gerald 1909-1979 .... *61*
  Obituary *21*
Caponigro, John Paul 1965- *84*
Capote, Truman 1924-1984 .... *91*
Capp, Al
  See Caplin, Alfred Gerald
Cappel, Constance 1936- *22*
Cappetta, Cynthia 1949- *125*
Cappo, Nan Willard 1955- *143*
Capps, Benjamin (Franklin) 1922- *9*
Cappy Dick
  See Cleveland, George
Captain Kangaroo
  See Keeshan, Robert J.
Captain Wheeler
  See Ellis, Edward S.
Captain Young of Yale
  See Stratemeyer, Edward L.
Capucilli, Alyssa Satin 1957- *203*
  Earlier sketches in SATA *115, 163*
Capucine
  See Mazille, Capucine
Caraher, Kim(berley Elizabeth) 1961- *105*
Caraker, Mary 1929- *74*
Caras, Roger A(ndrew) 1928-2001 .... *12*
  Obituary *127*
Caravantes, Peggy 1935- *140*
Caraway, Caren 1939- *57*
Carbone, Elisa 1954- *173*
  Earlier sketches in SATA *81, 137*
Carbone, Elisa Lynn
  See Carbone, Elisa
Carbonnier, Jeanne 1894-1974 .... *3*
  Obituary *34*
Card, Orson Scott 1951- *127*
  Earlier sketch in SATA *83*
  See also CLR 116
Care, Felicity
  See Coury, Louise Andree
Carew, Jan 1925- *51*
  Brief entry *40*
Carew, Jan Rynveld
  See Carew, Jan
Carey, Bonnie
  See Marshall, Bonnie C.
Carey, Charles W., Jr. 1951- *170*
Carey, Ernestine Gilbreth 1908-2006 .... *2*
  Obituary *177*
Carey, Janet Lee 1954(?)- *185*
Carey, Lisa *110*
Carey, M. V.
  See Carey, Mary V(irginia)

Carey, Mary V(irginia) 1925-1994 .... *44*
  Brief entry *39*
Carey, Peter 1943- *94*
Carey, Peter Philip
  See Carey, Peter
Carey, Valerie Scho 1949- *60*
Carheden, Goorel Kristina
  See Naaslund, Goorel Kristina
Carigiet, Alois 1902-1985 .... *24*
  Obituary *47*
  See also CLR *38*
Carini, Edward 1923- *9*
Carkeet, David 1946- *75*
Carle, Eric 1929- *163*
  Earlier sketches in SATA *4, 65, 120*
  See also CLR *72*
  See also SAAS *6*
Carleton, Captain L. C.
  See Ellis, Edward S.
Carleton, Captain Latham C.
  See Ellis, Edward S.
Carleton, Latham C.
  See Ellis, Edward S.
Carley, V(an Ness) Royal 1906-1976
  Obituary *20*
Carling, Amelia Lau 1949- *164*
  Earlier sketch in SATA *119*
Carlisle, Carolyn
  See Hawes, Louise
Carlisle, Clark
  See Holding, James (Clark Carlisle, Jr.)
Carlisle, Olga Andreyev 1930- *35*
Carlock, Miriam
  See Eyerly, Jeannette
Carls, Claudia 1978- *198*
Carlsen, G(eorge) Robert 1917- *30*
Carlsen, Ruth C(hristoffer) 1918- *2*
Carlson, Bernice Wells 1910- *8*
Carlson, Christopher C. *202*
Carlson, Dale (Bick) 1935- *1*
Carlson, Daniel (Bick) 1960- *27*
Carlson, Kirsten 1968- *192*
Carlson, Kirsten M.
  See Carlson, Kirsten
Carlson, Laurie 1952- *173*
  Earlier sketch in SATA *101*
Carlson, Laurie Winn
  See Carlson, Laurie
Carlson, Melody 1956- *171*
  Earlier sketch in SATA *113*
Carlson, Nancy 1953- *213*
  Brief entry *45*
  Earlier sketches in SATA *56, 90, 144*
Carlson, Nancy L.
  See Carlson, Nancy
Carlson, Natalie Savage 1906-1997 .... *68*
  Earlier sketch in SATA *2*
  See also SAAS *4*
Carlson, Susan Johnston 1953- *88*
Carlson, Vada F. 1897- *16*
Carlstrom, Nancy White 1948- *215*
  Brief entry *48*
  Earlier sketches in SATA *53, 92, 156*
Carlton, Keith
  See Robertson, Keith (Carlton)
Carlton, Susan 1960- *195*
Carlyon, Richard *55*
Carman, Patrick 1966- *197*
  Earlier sketch in SATA *161*
Carmer, Carl (Lamson) 1893-1976 .... *37*
  Obituary *30*
Carmer, Elizabeth Black 1904- *24*
Carmi, Giora 1944- *149*
  Earlier sketch in SATA *79*
Carmichael, Carrie
  See Carmichael, Harriet
Carmichael, Harriet *40*
Carmody, Isobelle 1958- *191*
  Earlier sketch in SATA *161*
Carmody, Isobelle Jane
  See Carmody, Isobelle

Carney, Elizabeth 1981- *199*
Carney, Jeff 1962- *196*
Carney, Mary Lou 1949- *170*
Carol, Bill J.
  See Knott, William C(ecil, Jr.)
Caron, Romi
  See Caron-Kyselkova', Romana
Caron-Kyselkova', Romana 1967- *94*
Caroselli, Remus F(rancis) 1916- *36*
Carpelan, Bo 1926- *8*
Carpelan, Bo Gustaf Bertelsson
  See Carpelan, Bo
Carpenter, (John) Allan 1917- *81*
  Earlier sketch in SATA *3*
Carpenter, Angelica Shirley 1945- *153*
  Earlier sketch in SATA *71*
Carpenter, Frances 1890-1972 .... *3*
  Obituary *27*
Carpenter, John 1948- *58*
Carpenter, John Howard
  See Carpenter, John
Carpenter, Johnny
  See Carpenter, John
Carpenter, Nancy *215*
Carpenter, Nancy Sippel
  See Carpenter, Nancy
Carpenter, Patricia (Healy Evans) 1920- *11*
Carr, Glyn
  See Styles, (Frank) Showell
Carr, Harriett H(elen) 1899-1977 .... *3*
Carr, Jan 1953- *132*
  Earlier sketch in SATA *89*
Carr, M. J.
  See Carr, Jan
Carr, Mary Jane 1899-1988 .... *2*
  Obituary *55*
Carr, Philippa
  See Hibbert, Eleanor Alice Burford
Carr, Roger Vaughan 1937- *95*
Carrel, Annette Felder 1929- *90*
Carrick, Carol (Hatfield) 1935- *118*
  Earlier sketches in SATA *7, 63*
  See also SAAS *18*
Carrick, Donald (F.) 1929-1989 .... *63*
  Earlier sketch in SATA *7*
Carrick, Malcolm 1945- *28*
Carrick, Paul 1972- *194*
Carrier, Lark 1947- *71*
  Brief entry *50*
Carrier, Roch 1937- *166*
  Earlier sketch in SATA *105*
Carrighar, Sally 1898-1985 .... *24*
Carrillo, Patricia S.
  See Carrillo, P.S.
Carrillo, P.S. *209*
Carrington, G. A.
  See Cunningham, Chet
Carrington, Marsha Gray 1954- *168*
  Earlier sketch in SATA *111*
Carris, Joan 1938- *182*
  Brief entry *42*
  Earlier sketch in SATA *44*
Carris, Joan Davenport
  See Carris, Joan
Carroll, Curt
  See Bishop, Curtis (Kent)
Carroll, Elizabeth
  See Barkin, Carol
  and James, Elizabeth
Carroll, Jaye
  See Carroll, Michael
Carroll, Jenny
  See Cabot, Meg
Carroll, (Archer) Latrobe 1894-1996 .... *7*
Carroll, Laura
  See Parr, Lucy
Carroll, Lewis 1832-1898 .... *100*
  See also YABC *2*
  See also CLR *108*
Carroll, Michael 1966- *203*

Carroll, Raymond 1924- *86*
  Brief entry *47*
Carruth, Hayden 1921-2008 .... *47*
  Obituary *197*
Carryl, Charles E. 1841-1920 .... *114*
Carryl, Charles Edward
  See Carryl, Charles E.
Carse, Robert 1902-1971 .... *5*
Carson, J(ohn) Franklin 1920-1981 .... *1*
  Obituary *107*
Carson, Mary Kay 1964- *200*
  Earlier sketch in SATA *150*
Carson, Rachel 1907-1964 .... *23*
Carson, Rachel Louise
  See Carson, Rachel
Carson, Rosalind
  See Chittenden, Margaret
Carson, S. M.
  See Gorsline, (Sally) Marie
Carson, William C. 1928- *154*
Carter, Abby *184*
Carter, Alden R 1947- *137*
  Earlier sketch in SATA *67*
  See also CLR *22*
  See also SAAS *18*
Carter, Alden Richardson
  See Carter, Alden R
Carter, Andy 1948- *134*
Carter, Angela 1940-1992 .... *66*
  Obituary *70*
Carter, Angela Olive
  See Carter, Angela
Carter, Anne Laurel 1953- *209*
  Earlier sketch in SATA *135*
Carter, Asa Earl
  See Carter, Forrest
Carter, Avis Murton
  See Allen, Kenneth S.
Carter, Bruce
  See Hough, Richard (Alexander)
Carter, Carol S(hadis) 1948- *124*
Carter, David A. 1957- *170*
  Earlier sketch in SATA *114*
Carter, Don 1958- *192*
  Earlier sketch in SATA *124*
Carter, Dorothy Sharp 1921- *8*
Carter, Forrest 1927(?)-1979 .... *32*
Carter, Helene 1887-1960 .... *15*
Carter, (William) Hodding, Jr. 1907-1972 ...... *2*
  Obituary *27*
Carter, James Earl, Jr.
  See Carter, Jimmy
Carter, Jimmy 1924- *79*
Carter, Katharine J(ones) 1905-1984 .... *2*
Carter, Lin(wood Vrooman) 1930-1988 ...... *91*
Carter, Mike 1936- *138*
Carter, Nick
  See Avallone, Michael (Angelo, Jr.)
  and Ballard, (Willis) Todhunter
  and Crider, Bill
  and Cassiday, Bruce (Bingham)
  and Chastain, Thomas
  and Dey, Frederic (Merrill) Van Rensselaer
  and Garside, Jack
  and Hayes, Ralph E(ugene)
  and Henderson, M(arilyn) R(uth)
  and Lynds, Dennis
  and Lynds, Gayle (Hallenbeck)
  and Randisi, Robert J.
  and Rasof, Henry
  and Stratemeyer, Edward L.
  and Smith, Martin Cruz
  and Swain, Dwight V(reeland)
  and Vardeman, Robert E.
  and Wallmann, Jeffrey M(iner)
  and White, Lionel
Carter, Peter 1929- *57*
Carter, Phyllis Ann
  See Eberle, Irmengarde
Carter, Samuel (Thomson) III 1904-1988 .... *37*
  Obituary *60*

Carter, William E. 1926-1983 .... *1*
 Obituary 35
Cartlidge, Michelle 1950- 96
 Brief entry 37
 Earlier sketch in SATA 49
Cartner, William Carruthers 1910- *11*
Cartwright, Ann 1940- 78
Cartwright, Reg(inald Ainsley) 1938- 64
Cartwright, Sally 1923- 9
Carusone, Al 1949- 89
Carvell, Marlene 172
Carver, John
 See Gardner, Richard (M.)
Carwell, L'Ann
 See McKissack, Patricia C.
Cary
 See Cary, Louis F(avreau)
Cary, Barbara Knapp 1912(?)-1975
 Obituary 31
Cary, Kate 1967(?)- *174*
Cary, Louis F(avreau) 1915- 9
Caryl, Jean
 See Kaplan, Jean Caryl Korn
Casanova, Mary 1957- *186*
 Earlier sketches in SATA 94, 136
Cascone, A.G.
 See Cascone, Annette
 and Cascone, Gina
Cascone, Annette 1960- 103
Cascone, Gina 1955- 103
Case, Chris 1976- 209
Case, Marshal T(aylor) 1941- 9
Case, Michael
 See Howard, Robert West
Caseley, Judith 1951- 159
 Brief entry 53
 Earlier sketch in SATA 87
Casewit, Curtis W(erner) 1922-2002 4
Casey, Barbara (Louise) 1944- 147
 Earlier sketch in SATA 79
Casey, Brigid 1950- 9
Casey, Tina 1959- 141
Cash, Ellen Lewis Buell 1905-1989
 Obituary 64
Cash, Megan Montague 160
Cashore, Kristin 1976(?)- 206
Casilla, Robert 1959- 211
 Earlier sketches in SATA 75, 146
Cason, Mabel Earp 1892-1965 10
Cass, Joan E(velyn) *1*
Cass-Beggs, Barbara 1904- 62
Cassedy, Patrice (Rinaldo) 1953- 149
Cassedy, Sylvia 1930-1989 77
 Obituary 61
 Earlier sketch in SATA 27
 See also CLR 26
Cassel, Lili
 See Wronker, Lili Cassel
Cassels, Jean 173
Cassidy, Anne 1952- 166
Cassidy, Anne Josephine
 See Cassidy, Anne
Cassidy, Cathy 1962- 183
Casson, Hugh Maxwell 1910-1999 65
 Obituary 115
Cassutt, Michael 1954- 78
Cassutt, Michael Joseph
 See Cassutt, Michael
Castaldi, Elicia 194
Castaldo, Nancy Fusco 1962- 151
 Earlier sketch in SATA 93
Castaneda, Omar S. 1954- 71
Castell, Megan
 See Williams, Jeanne
Castellanos, Jane Mollie Robinson
 1913-2001 9
Castellon, Federico 1914-1971 48
Castellucci, Cecil 1969- 176
Castillo, Edmund L. 1924-2005 .... *1*
 Obituary 167
Castillo, Lauren 195

Castle, Lee
 See Ogan, George F.
 and Ogan, Margaret E. (Nettles)
Castle, Paul
 See Howard, Vernon (Linwood)
Castle, Robert
 See Hamilton, Edmond
Castrovilla, Selene 1966- 186
Caswell, Brian 1954- 171
 Earlier sketch in SATA 97
Caswell, Helen (Rayburn) 1923- 12
Catalano, Dominic 1956- 163
 Earlier sketch in SATA 76
Catalano, Grace (A.) 1961- 99
Catalanotto, Peter 1959- 195
 Autobiography Feature 113
 Earlier sketches in SATA 70, 114, 159
 See also CLR 68
 See also SAAS 25
Catanese, P. W. 1961- 179
Cate, Annette LeBlanc 196
Cate, Dick
 See Cate, Richard Edward Nelson
Cate, Richard Edward Nelson 1932- 28
Cather, Willa 1873-1947 30
 See also CLR 98
Catherall, Arthur 1906-1980 74
 Earlier sketches in SATA 3, 4
Cathon, Laura E(lizabeth) 1908-1991 27
Catlett, Elizabeth 1919(?)- 82
Catlin, Wynelle 1930- 13
Catlow, Nikalas
 See Catlow, Niki
Catlow, Niki 1975- 193
Cato, Heather 105
Cato, Sheila 114
Catran, Ken 1944- 190
Catrow, David 206
 See Catrow, David J. III
Catrow, David J. III 152
 See Catrow, David
Catt, Louis
 See French, Vivian
Cattell, James 1954- 123
Catton, (Charles) Bruce 1899-1978 2
 Obituary 24
Catz, Max
 See Glaser, Milton
Caudell, Marian 1930- 52
Caudill, Rebecca 1899-1985 .... *1*
 Obituary 44
Cauley, Lorinda Bryan 1951- 46
 Brief entry 43
Caulfield, Peggy F. 1926-1987
 Obituary 53
Cauman, Samuel 1910-1971 48
Causley, Charles (Stanley) 1917-2003 66
 Obituary 149
 Earlier sketch in SATA 3
 See also CLR 30
Cavallaro, Ann (Abelson) 1918- 62
Cavallo, Diana 1931- 7
Cavanagh, Helen (Carol) 1939- 98
 Brief entry 37
 Earlier sketch in SATA 48
Cavanah, Frances 1899-1982 31
 Earlier sketch in SATA *1*
Cavanna, Betty
 See Harrison, Elizabeth (Allen) Cavanna
Cavanna, Elizabeth
 See Harrison, Elizabeth (Allen) Cavanna
Cave, Kathryn 1948- 123
 Earlier sketch in SATA 76
Cavendish, Peter
 See Horler, Sydney
Cavin, Ruth (Brodie) 1918- 38
Cavoukian, Raffi 1948- 68
Cawley, Winifred 1915- 13
Cazeau, Charles J(ay) 1931- 65

Cazet, Denys 1938- 191
 Brief entry 41
 Earlier sketches in SATA 52, 99, 163
Cazzola, Gus 1934- 73
Cebulash, Mel 1937- 91
 Earlier sketch in SATA 10
Ceccoli, Nicoletta 181
Cecil, Randy 1968- 187
Cecka, Melanie 199
Ceder, Georgiana Dorcas -1985 10
Celenza, Anna Harwell 133
Celestino, Martha Laing
 See Laing, Martha
Cepeda, Joe 215
 Earlier sketch in SATA 159
Cerf, Bennett (Alfred) 1898-1971 7
Cerf, Christopher (Bennett) 1941- 2
Cermak, Martin
 See Duchacek, Ivo D(uka)
Cerullo, Mary M. 1949- 145
 Earlier sketch in SATA 86
Cervon, Jacqueline
 See Moussard, Jacqueline
Cetin, Frank Stanley 1921- 2
Chabon, Michael 1963- 145
Chabrian, Deborah
 See Chabrian, Deborah L.
Chabrian, Deborah L. 212
Chaconas, D.J.
 See Chaconas, Dori
Chaconas, Dori 1938- 208
 Earlier sketches in SATA 145, 175
Chaconas, Doris J.
 See Chaconas, Dori
Chadwick, Lester 67
 Earlier sketch in SATA *1*
Chaffee, Allen 3
Chaffin, Lillie D(orton) 1925- 4
Chaikin, Miriam 1924- 152
 Earlier sketches in SATA 24, 102
Chall, Marsha Wilson 150
Challand, Helen J(ean) 1921- 64
Challans, Mary
 See Renault, Mary
Chalmers, Mary (Eileen) 1927- 6
 See also SAAS 14
Chamberlain, Barbara A.
 See Azore, Barbara
Chamberlain, Margaret 1954- 212
 Earlier sketch in SATA 46
Chamberlin, Kate 1945- 105
Chamberlin, Mary 1960- 177
Chamberlin, Rich 177
Chamberlin, Richard
 See Chamberlin, Rich
Chambers, Aidan 1934- 171
 Earlier sketches in SATA 1, 69, 108
 See also CLR 151
 See also SAAS 12
Chambers, Bradford 1922-1984
 Obituary 39
Chambers, Catherine E.
 See St. John, Nicole
Chambers, John W. 1933- 57
 Brief entry 46
Chambers, Kate
 See St. John, Nicole
Chambers, Margaret Ada Eastwood 1911- 2
Chambers, Peggy
 See Chambers, Margaret Ada Eastwood
Chambers, Robert W(illiam) 1865-1933 107
Chambliss, Maxie 186
Chan, Gillian 1954- 147
 Earlier sketch in SATA 102
Chan, Peter 1980(?)- 207
Chance, James T.
 See Carpenter, John
Chance, John T.
 See Carpenter, John
Chance, Stephen
 See Turner, Philip (William)

Chandler, Caroline A(ugusta) 1906-1979 22
  Obituary 24
Chandler, David P. 1933- 28
Chandler, David Porter
  See Chandler, David P.
Chandler, Edna Walker 1908-1982 11
  Obituary 31
Chandler, Jennifer
  See Westwood, Jennifer
Chandler, Karen 1959- 122
Chandler, Linda S(mith) 1929- 39
Chandler, Pauline 175
Chandler, Robert 1953- 40
Chandler, Ruth Forbes 1894-1978 2
  Obituary 26
Chandonnet, Ann F. 1943- 92
Chaney, Jill 1932- 87
Chang, Chih-Wei 1966- 111
Chang, Cindy 1968- 90
Chang, Margaret 1941- 71
Chang, Margaret Scrogin
  See Chang, Margaret
Chang, Raymond 1939- 142
  Earlier sketches in SATA *71, 142 PEN*
Chanin, Michael 1952- 84
Channel, A. R.
  See Catherall, Arthur
Chapian, Marie 1938- 29
Chapin, Alene Olsen Dalton 1915(?)-1986
  Obituary 47
Chapin, Tom 1945- 83
Chapman, Allen 67
  Earlier sketch in SATA *1*
Chapman, Cheryl O(rth) 1948- 80
Chapman, (Constance) Elizabeth (Mann)
  1919- 10
Chapman, Gaye 1970- 200
Chapman, Gaye Coralie
  See Chapman, Gaye
Chapman, Gaynor 1935- 32
Chapman, Gillian 1955- 120
Chapman, Jane 1970- 212
  Earlier sketches in SATA *122, 176*
Chapman, Jean 104
  Earlier sketch in SATA *34*
  See also CLR *65*
Chapman, John Stanton Higham 1891-1972
  Obituary 27
Chapman, Lee
  See Bradley, Marion Zimmer
Chapman, Lynne 1960- 197
Chapman, Lynne F(erguson) 1963- 150
  Earlier sketch in SATA *94*
Chapman, Maristan
  See Chapman, John Stanton Higham
Chapman, Vera (Ivy May) 1898-1996 33
Chapman, Walker
  See Silverberg, Robert
Chappell, Audrey 1954- 72
Chappell, Crissa-Jean 198
Chappell, Warren 1904-1991 68
  Obituary 67
  Earlier sketch in SATA *6*
  See also SAAS *10*
Chapra, Mimi 182
Charbonneau, Eileen 1951- 118
  Earlier sketch in SATA *84*
Charbonnet, Gabrielle 1961- 81
Chardiet, Bernice 1927(?)- 27
Chardiet, Bernice Kroll
  See Chardiet, Bernice
Charest, Emily MacLachlan 198
Charles, Donald
  See Meighan, Donald Charles
Charles, Louis
  See Stratemeyer, Edward L.
Charles, Nicholas
  See Kuskin, Karla
Charles, Nicholas J.
  See Kuskin, Karla
Charles, Norma 153

Charles, Veronika Martenova 182
Charlip, Remy 1929- 119
  Earlier sketches in SATA *4, 68*
  See also CLR *8*
Charlot, Jean 1898-1979 8
  Obituary 31
Charlot, Martin 1944- 64
Charlot, Martin Day
  See Charlot, Martin
Charlton, Michael (Alan) 1923- 34
Charlton-Trujillo, e.E. 189
Charmatz, Bill 1925-2005 7
Charnas, Suzy McKee 1939- 110
  Earlier sketch in SATA *61*
Charosh, Mannis 1906- 5
Chartier, Normand L. 1945- 66
Chase, Alice
  See McHargue, Georgess
Chase, Alyssa 1965- 92
Chase, Andra 1942- 91
Chase, Emily
  See Aks, Patricia
  and Garwood, Julie
  and Sachs, Judith
  and White, Carol
Chase, Mary (Coyle) 1907-1981 17
  Obituary 29
Chase, Mary Ellen 1887-1973 10
Chase, Paula 214
Chase, Richard 1904-1988 64
  Obituary 56
Chase, Samantha
  See Glick, Ruth (Burtnick)
Chast, Roz 1954- 212
  Earlier sketch in SATA *97*
Chastain, Madye Lee 1908-1989 4
Chataway, Carol 1955- 140
Chatterjee, Debjani 1952- 83
Chauncy, Nan(cen Beryl Masterman)
  1900-1970 6
  See also CLR *6*
Chaundler, Christine 1887-1972 1
  Obituary 25
Chayka, Doug 196
Chbosky, Stephen 1972- 164
Cheaney, Janie B.
  See Cheaney, J.B.
Cheaney, J.B. 1950- 188
Chee, Cheng-Khee 1934- 79
Cheese, Chloe 1952- 118
Chekhonte, Antosha
  See Chekhov, Anton
Chekhov, Anton 1860-1904 90
Chekhov, Anton Pavlovich
  See Chekhov, Anton
Chelushkin, Kirill 1968- 186
Chen, Anthony 1929- 6
Chen, Chih-Yuan 1975- 216
  Earlier sketch in SATA *155*
Chen, Ju-Hong 1941- 78
Chen, Pauline 1966- 202
Chen, Sara
  See Odgers, Sally Farrell
Chen, Tony
  See Chen, Anthony
Chen, Yong 1963- 183
Chen, Yuan-tsung 1932- 65
Chen, Zhiyuan
  See Chen, Chih-Yuan
Chenault, Nell
  See Smith, Linell Nash
Chen Chih-Yuan
  See Chen, Chih-Yuan
Chenery, Janet (Dai) 1923- 25
Cheney, Cora 1916-1999 3
  Obituary 110
Cheney, Glenn (Alan) 1951- 99
Cheney, Lynne V. 1941- 152
Cheney, Lynne Vincent
  See Cheney, Lynne V.

Cheney, Ted
  See Cheney, Theodore Albert
Cheney, Theodore A. Rees
  See Cheney, Theodore Albert
Cheney, Theodore Albert 1928- 11
Cheng, Andrea 1957- 205
  Earlier sketches in SATA *128, 172*
Cheng, Christopher 1959- 173
  Earlier sketch in SATA *106*
Cheng, Judith 1955- 36
Cheng, Shan
  See Jiang, Cheng An
Cheripko, Jan 1951- 155
  Earlier sketch in SATA *83*
Chermayeff, Ivan 1932- 47
Chernenko, Dan
  See Chernenko, Dan
Chernoff, Dorothy A.
  See Ernst, (Lyman) John
Chernoff, Goldie Taub 1909- 10
Cherry, Carolyn Janice
  See Cherryh, C.J.
Cherry, Lynne 1952- 99
  Earlier sketch in SATA *34*
Cherryh, C.J. 1942- 172
  Earlier sketch in SATA *93*
Cherryholmes, Anne
  See Price, Olive
Cheshire, Simon 172
Chesler, Bernice 1932-2002 59
Chess, Victoria (Dickerson) 1939- 92
  Earlier sketch in SATA *33*
Chessa, Francesca 191
Chester, Deborah 1957- 85
Chester, Kate
  See Guccione, Leslie Davis
Chesterton, G. K. 1874-1936 27
Chesterton, Gilbert Keith
  See Chesterton, G. K.
Chesworth, Michael 207
  Earlier sketch in SATA *160*
Chetin, Helen 1922- 6
Chetwin, Grace 86
  Brief entry 50
Chevalier, Christa 1937- 35
Chevalier, Tracy 1962- 128
Chew, Ruth 1920-2010 7
Chichester Clark, Emma 1955- 209
  Earlier sketches in SATA *117, 156, 69*
Chidsey, Donald Barr 1902-1981 3
  Obituary 27
Chiefari, Janet D. 1942- 58
Chien, Catia 193
Chien-min, Lin
  See Rumford, James
Child, L. Maria
  See Child, Lydia Maria
Child, Lauren 1965- 183
  Earlier sketches in SATA *119, 160*
Child, Lincoln 1957- 113
Child, Lincoln B.
  See Child, Lincoln
Child, Lydia Maria 1802-1880 67
Child, Mrs.
  See Child, Lydia Maria
Child, Philip 1898-1978 47
Children's Shepherd, The
  See Westphal, Arnold Carl
Childress, Alice 1920-1994 81
  Earlier sketches in SATA *7, 48*
  See also CLR *14*
Childs, H(alla) Fay (Cochrane) 1890-1971 1
  Obituary 25
Chilton, Charles (Frederick William)
  1917- 102
Chima, Cinda Williams 192
Chimaera
  See Farjeon, Eleanor
Chin, Richard (M.) 1946- 52
Chinery, Michael 1938- 26
Chin-Lee, Cynthia 1958- 102

Chin-Lee D., Cynthia
  See Chin-Lee, Cynthia
Chippendale, Lisa A. 158
Chipperfield, Joseph Eugene 1912-1980(?) .. 87
  Earlier sketch in SATA 2
Chisholm, P. F.
  See Finney, Patricia
Chislett, Gail (Elaine) 1948- 58
Chittenden, Elizabeth F. 1903-1999 9
Chittenden, Margaret 1935- 28
Chittum, Ida 1918- 7
Chitwood, Suzanne Tanner 1958- 160
Chmielarz, Sharon Lee 1940- 72
Choate, Judith (Newkirk) 1940- 30
Chocolate, Debbi 1954- 96
Chocolate, Deborah M. Newton
  See Chocolate, Debbi
Chodos-Irvine, Margaret 211
  Earlier sketch in SATA 152
Choi, Sook Nyul 1937- 73
  Autobiography Feature 126
  See also CLR 53
Choi, Yangsook 178
Choldenko, Gennifer 1957- 182
  Earlier sketch in SATA 135
Chorao, Kay 1936- 215
Chorao, (Ann Mc)Kay (Sproat) 1936- 162
  Earlier sketches in SATA 8, 69
Choron, Sandra (Zena Samelson) 1950- ... 146
Choung, Eun-hee 199
Chown, Marcus 1959- 137
Choyce, Lesley 1951- 165
  Earlier sketch in SATA 94
Choyce, Lesley Willis
  See Choyce, Lesley
Chrisman, Arthur Bowie 1889-1953 124
  See also YABC 1
Christelow, Eileen 1943- 184
  Autobiography Feature 120
  Brief entry 35
  Earlier sketches in SATA 38, 90
Christensen, Bonnie 1951- 213
  Earlier sketches in SATA 110, 157
Christensen, Gardell Dano 1907-1991 1
Christensen, Laurie
  See Steding, Laurie
Christesen, Barbara 1940- 40
Christgau, Alice Erickson 1902-1977 13
Christian, Mary Blount 1933- 9
Christiana, David 195
Christie, Agatha 1890-1976 36
Christie, Agatha Mary Clarissa
  See Christie, Agatha
Christie, Ann Philippa
  See Pearce, Philippa
Christie, Gregory
  See Christie, R. Gregory
Christie, Philippa
  See Pearce, Philippa
Christie, R. Gregory 1971- 185
  Earlier sketch in SATA 127
Christopher, John
  See Youd, Samuel
Christopher, Louise
  See Hale, Arlene
Christopher, Matt(hew Frederick)
  1917-1997 80
  Obituary 99
  Earlier sketches in SATA 2, 47
  See also CLR 119
  See also SAAS 9
Christopher, Milbourne 1914(?)-1984 46
Christy, Howard Chandler 1873-1952 21
Chrustowski, Rick 176
Chrystie, Frances N(icholson) 1904-1986 ... 60
Chu, Daniel 1933- 11
Chukovsky, Kornei (Ivanovich) 1882-1969 . 34
  Earlier sketch in SATA 5
Church, Caroline Jayne 179
Church, Richard 1893-1972 3
Churchill, E(lmer) Richard 1937- 11

Churchill, Elizabeth
  See Hough, Richard (Alexander)
Chute, B(eatrice) J(oy) 1913-1987 2
  Obituary 53
Chute, Marchette (Gaylord) 1909-1994 1
Chwast, Jacqueline 1932- 6
Chwast, Seymour 1931- 146
  Earlier sketches in SATA 18, 96
Ciardi, John (Anthony) 1916-1986 65
  Obituary 46
  Earlier sketch in SATA 1
  See also CLR 19
  See also SAAS 26
Ciccone, Madonna Louise Veronica
  See Madonna
Ciddor, Anna 1957- 213
Ciment, James D. 1958- 140
Cirrone, Dorian 182
Cisneros, Sandra 1954-
  See CLR 123
Citra, Becky 1954- 137
Citrin, Michael 1965(?)- 183
Claflin, Willy 1944- 208
Clair, Andree 19
Clampett, Bob 1914(?)-1985 44
  Obituary 38
Clampett, Robert
  See Clampett, Bob
Clapp, John 1968- 109
Clapp, Patricia 1912- 74
  Earlier sketch in SATA 4
  See also SAAS 4
Clare, Ellen
  See Sinclair, Olga
Clare, Helen
  See Clarke, Pauline
Claremont, Chris 1950- 87
Claremont, Christopher Simon
  See Claremont, Chris
Clark, Ann Nolan 1896-1995 82
  Obituary 87
  Earlier sketch in SATA 4
  See also CLR 16
  See also SAAS 16
Clark, Champ 1923-2002 47
Clark, Christopher (Anthony) Stuart
  See Stuart-Clark, Christopher (Anthony)
Clark, Clara Gillow 1951- 154
  Earlier sketch in SATA 84
Clark, David 216
  See Hardcastle, Michael
Clark, David Allen
  See Ernst, (Lyman) John
Clark, Emma Chichester
  See Chichester Clark, Emma
Clark, Frank J(ames) 1922- 18
Clark, Garel
  See Garelick, May
Clark, Halsey
  See Deming, Richard
Clark, Joan
  See Benson, Mildred
Clark, Joan 1934- 182
  Earlier sketches in SATA 59, 96
Clark, Leonard 1905-1981 30
  Obituary 29
Clark, M. R.
  See Clark, Mavis Thorpe
Clark, Margaret (D.) 1943- 126
Clark, Margaret Goff 1913- 82
  Earlier sketch in SATA 8
Clark, Mary Higgins 1929- 46
Clark, Mavis Thorpe 1909-1999 74
  Earlier sketch in SATA 8
  See also CLR 30
  See also SAAS 5
Clark, Merle
  See Gessner, Lynne
Clark, Patricia Denise 1921- 117
Clark, Patricia Finrow 1929- 11
Clark, Ronald Harry 1904-1999 193

Clark, Ronald William 1916-1987 2
  Obituary 52
Clark, Sherryl 1956- 149
Clark, Van D(eusen) 1909-1974 2
Clark, Virginia
  See Gray, Patricia (Clark)
Clark, Walter Van Tilburg 1909-1971 8
Clarke, Arthur
  See Clarke, Arthur C.
Clarke, Arthur C. 1917-2008 115
  Obituary 191
  Earlier sketches in SATA 13, 70
  See also CLR 119
Clarke, Arthur Charles
  See Clarke, Arthur C.
Clarke, Clorinda 1917- 7
Clarke, Elizabeth L. 1934- 103
Clarke, Greg 1959- 215
Clarke, Gus 1948- 134
Clarke, J.
  See Clarke, Judith
Clarke, James Hall
  See Rowland-Entwistle, (Arthur) Theodore
  (Henry)
Clarke, Joan B. 1921- 42
  Brief entry 27
Clarke, John
  See Laklan, Carli
  and Sontup, Dan(iel)
Clarke, Judith 1943- 164
  Earlier sketches in SATA 75, 110
  See also CLR 61
Clarke, Julia 1950- 138
Clarke, Kenneth 1957- 107
Clarke, Lea
  See Rowland-Entwistle, (Arthur) Theodore
  (Henry)
Clarke, Margaret 1941-
  See CLR 99
Clarke, Mary Stetson 1911-1994 5
Clarke, Michael
  See Newlon, (Frank) Clarke
Clarke, Pauline 1921- 131
  Earlier sketch in SATA 3
  See also CLR 28
Clarkson, E(dith) Margaret 1915- 37
Clarkson, Ewan 1929- 9
Claudia, Susan
  See Goulart, Ron
  and Johnston, William
Claverie, Jean 1946- 38
Clay, Patrice 1947- 47
Clay, Wil 203
Clayman, Deborah Paula
  See Da Costa, Deborah
Claypool, Jane
  See Miner, Jane Claypool
Clayton, Elaine 1961- 209
  Earlier sketches in SATA 94, 159
Clayton, Lawrence (Otto, Jr.) 1945- 75
Clayton, Sandra 1951- 110
Cle, Troy 202
Clea, Super
  See Hantman, Clea
Cleary, Beverly 1916- 121
  Earlier sketches in SATA 2, 43, 79
  See also CLR 72
  See also SAAS 20
Cleary, Beverly Atlee Bunn
  See Cleary, Beverly
Cleary, Brian P. 1959- 186
  Earlier sketches in SATA 93, 132
Cleaver, Bill
  See Cleaver, William J.
Cleaver, Carole 1934- 6
Cleaver, Elizabeth (Ann Mrazik)
  1939-1985 23
  Obituary 43
  See also CLR 13
Cleaver, Hylton Reginald 1891-1961 49

Cleaver, Vera 1919-1993 76
    Earlier sketch in SATA 22
    See also CLR 6
Cleaver, Vera Allen
    See Cleaver, Vera
Cleaver, William J. 1920-1981 22
    Obituary 27
    See also CLR 6
Cleishbotham, Jebediah
    See Scott, Sir Walter
Cleland, Mabel
    See Widdemer, Mabel Cleland
Clem, Margaret H(ollingsworth) 1923- 90
Clemens, James
    See Rollins, James
Clemens, Samuel
    See Twain, Mark
Clemens, Samuel Langhorne
    See Twain, Mark
Clemens, Virginia Phelps 1941- 35
Clement, Gary 191
Clement, Janet 182
Clement, Nathan 1966- 200
Clement, Priscilla Ferguson 1942- 171
Clement, Rod 97
Clement-Moore, Rosemary 188
Clements, Andrew 1949- 203
    Earlier sketches in SATA 104, 158
Clements, Bruce 1931- 178
    Earlier sketches in SATA 27, 94
Clemesha, David 192
Clemons, Elizabeth
    See Nowell, Elizabeth Cameron
Clerk, N. W.
    See Lewis, C. S.
Cleveland, Bob
    See Cleveland, George
Cleveland, George 1903(?)-1985
    Obituary 43
Cleveland-Peck, Patricia 80
Cleven, Cathrine
    See Cleven, Kathryn Seward
Cleven, Kathryn Seward 2
Clevenger, William R. 1954- 84
Clevenger, William Russell
    See Clevenger, William R.
Clevin, Joergen 1920- 7
Clevin, Jorgen
    See Clevin, Joergen
Clewes, Dorothy (Mary) 1907-2003 86
    Obituary 138
    Earlier sketch in SATA 1
Clifford, David
    See Rosenberg, Eth Clifford
Clifford, Eth
    See Rosenberg, Eth Clifford
Clifford, Harold B(urton) 1893-1988 10
Clifford, Margaret Cort 1929- 1
Clifford, Martin
    See Hamilton, Charles (Harold St. John)
Clifford, Mary Louise Beneway 1926- 23
Clifford, Peggy
    See Clifford, Margaret Cort
Clifford, Rachel Mark
    See Lewis, Brenda Ralph
Clifton, Lucille 1936-2010 128
    Earlier sketches in SATA 20, 69
    See also CLR 5
Clifton, Thelma Lucille
    See Clifton, Lucille
Climo, Shirley 1928- 166
    Autobiography Feature 110
    Brief entry 35
    Earlier sketches in SATA 39, 77
    See also CLR 69
Cline-Ransome, Lesa 201
Clinton, Catherine 1952- 203
Clinton, Cathryn 1957- 136
Clinton, Dirk
    See Silverberg, Robert

Clinton, Jon
    See Prince, J(ack) H(arvey)
Clippinger, Carol 193
Clish, (Lee) Marian 1946- 43
Clive, Clifford
    See Hamilton, Charles (Harold St. John)
Clokey, Art 1921- 59
Cloudsley-Thompson, J(ohn) L(eonard)
    1921- 19
Clouse, Nancy L. 1938- 78
Clover, Peter 1952- 215
    Earlier sketch in SATA 152
Clutha, Janet Paterson Frame
    See Frame, Janet
Clymer, Eleanor 1906-2001 85
    Obituary 126
    Earlier sketch in SATA 9
    See also SAAS 17
Clyne, Patricia (Edwards) 31
Cneut, Carll 1969- 197
Coalson, Glo 1946- 94
    Earlier sketch in SATA 26
Coates, Anna 1958- 73
Coates, Belle 1896-1986 2
Coates, Ruth Allison 1915- 11
Coats, Alice M(argaret) 1905-1976 11
Coatsworth, Elizabeth (Jane) 1893-1986 100
    Obituary 49
    Earlier sketches in SATA 2, 56
    See also CLR 2
Cobalt, Martin
    See Mayne, William
Cobb, Jane
    See Berry, Jane Cobb
Cobb, Mary 1931- 88
Cobb, Vicki 1938- 136
    Autobiography Feature 136
    Earlier sketches in SATA 8, 69, 131
    See also CLR 2
    See also SAAS 6
Cobbett, Richard
    See Pluckrose, Henry (Arthur)
Cober, Alan E(dwin) 1935-1998 7
    Obituary 101
Cobham, Sir Alan
    See Hamilton, Charles (Harold St. John)
Coburn, Jake 1978- 155
Cocagnac, Augustin Maurice(-Jean) 1924- 7
Cocca-Leffler, Maryann 1958- 194
    Earlier sketches in SATA 80, 136
Cochran, Bill 187
Cochran, Bobbye A. 1949- 11
Cochran, Thomas 1955- 198
Cochrane, Hamilton E.
    See Cochrane, Mick
Cochrane, Mick 1956- 215
Cockcroft, Jason 217
Cockett, Mary 3
Cocks, Peter 204
Cocovini, Abby 202
Coddell, Esme Raji
    See Codell, Esme Raji
Codell, Esme Raji 1968- 160
Cody, C. S.
    See Waller, Leslie
Cody, Jess
    See Cunningham, Chet
Coe, Anne (E.) 1949- 95
Coe, Douglas
    See Epstein, Beryl
    and Epstein, Samuel
Coe, Lloyd 1899(?)-1976
    Obituary 30
Coen, Rena Neumann 1925- 20
Coerr, Eleanor (Beatrice) 1922- 67
    Earlier sketch in SATA 1
Cofer, Judith Ortiz 1952- 164
    Earlier sketch in SATA 110
Coffelt, Nancy 1961- 189
Coffey, Brian
    See Koontz, Dean

Coffin, Geoffrey
    See Mason, F(rancis) van Wyck
Coffin, M. T.
    See Stanley, George Edward
Coffman, Ramon Peyton 1896-1989 4
Cogan, Karen 1954- 125
Coggins, Jack (Banham) 1911-2006 2
Cohen, Barbara 1932-1992 77
    Obituary 74
    Earlier sketch in SATA 10
    See also SAAS 7
Cohen, Daniel (E.) 1936- 70
    Earlier sketch in SATA 8
    See also CLR 43
    See also SAAS 4
Cohen, Deborah Bodin 1968- 180
Cohen, Jan Barger
    See Barger, Jan
Cohen, Jene Barr
    See Barr, Jene
Cohen, Joan Lebold 1932- 4
Cohen, Judith Love 1933- 78
Cohen, Miriam 1926-1955 155
    Earlier sketches in SATA 29, 106
    See also SAAS 11
Cohen, Nora 75
Cohen, Paul 1945- 58
Cohen, Paul S.
    See Cohen, Paul
Cohen, Peter Zachary 1931- 150
    Earlier sketch in SATA 4
Cohen, Robert Carl 1930- 8
Cohen, Santiago 1954- 215
Cohen, Sholom 1951- 94
Cohn, Angelo 1914-1997 19
Cohn, Diana 194
Cohn, Rachel 1968- 161
Coit, Margaret Louise 1922-2003 2
    Obituary 142
Colasanti, Susane 1973- 214
Colato Lainez, Rene 1970- 176
Colbert, Anthony 1934-2007 15
Colbert, Nancy A. 1936- 139
Colby, C(arroll) B(urleigh) 1904-1977 35
    Earlier sketch in SATA 3
Colby, Jean Poindexter 1909-1993 23
Cole, Annette
    See Steiner, Barbara A(nnette)
Cole, Babette 1949- 155
    Earlier sketches in SATA 61, 96
Cole, Betsy 1940- 83
Cole, Brock 1938- 200
    Earlier sketches in SATA 72, 136
    See also CLR 18
Cole, Davis
    See Elting, Mary
Cole, Hannah 1954- 74
Cole, Henry 1955- 213
    Earlier sketch in SATA 181
Cole, Jack -1974
    See Stewart, John
Cole, Jackson
    See Curry, Thomas Albert
    and Germano, Peter B.
    and Heckelmann, Charles N(ewman)
    and Newton, D(wight) B(ennett)
    and Schisgall, Oscar
Cole, Jennifer
    See Zach, Cheryl (Byrd)
Cole, Joanna 1944- 168
    Brief entry 37
    Earlier sketches in SATA 49, 81, 120
    See also CLR 40
Cole, Lois Dwight 1903-1979 10
    Obituary 26
Cole, Michael 1947- 59
Cole, Samantha
    See Cole, Stephen
Cole, Sheila 1939- 171
    Earlier sketches in SATA 24, 95

Cole, Sheila R.
See Cole, Sheila
Cole, Sheila Rotenberg
See Cole, Sheila
Cole, Stephen 1971- 161
Cole, William (Rossa) 1919-2000 71
Earlier sketch in SATA 9
See also SAAS 9
Coleman, Andrew
See Pine, Nicholas
Coleman, Clare
See Bell, Clare (Louise)
and Easton, M(alcolm) Coleman
Coleman, Janet Wyman 184
Coleman, Loren 1947- 164
Coleman, Loren Elwood, Jr.
See Coleman, Loren
Coleman, Mary Ann 1928- 83
Coleman, Michael
See Jones, Allan Frewin
Coleman, Michael 1946- 199
Autobiography Feature 133
Earlier sketches in SATA 108, 133
Coleman, Rowan 187
Coleman, William L(eRoy) 1938- 49
Brief entry 34
Coleman, Wim 1926- 212
Coles, Robert (Martin) 1929- 23
Colfer, Eoin 1965- 197
Earlier sketch in SATA 148
See also CLR 112
Colin, Ann
See Ure, Jean
Collard, Sneed B. III 1959- 184
Earlier sketches in SATA 84, 139
Colledge, Anne 1939- 142
Colley, Jacqui 1965- 202
Collicott, Sharleen 1937- 143
Earlier sketch in SATA 98
Collier, Bryan 204
Earlier sketches in SATA 126, 174
Collier, Christopher 1930- 70
Earlier sketch in SATA 16
See also CLR 126
Collier, Ethel 1903-1999 22
Collier, James Lincoln 1928- 166
Earlier sketches in SATA 8, 70
See also CLR 126
See also SAAS 21
Collier, Jane
See Collier, Zena
Collier, Kristi 182
Collier, Steven 1942- 61
Collier, Zena 1926- 23
Collings, Gillian 1939- 102
Collington, Peter 1948- 99
Earlier sketch in SATA 59
Collins, Ace 1953- 82
Collins, Andrew J.
See Collins, Ace
Collins, B.R. 1981- 214
Collins, David R(aymond) 1940-2001 121
Earlier sketch in SATA 7
Collins, Heather 1946- 81
Collins, Hunt
See Hunter, Evan
Collins, Michael
See Lynds, Dennis
Collins, Michael 1930- 58
Collins, Pat Lowery 1932- 217
Earlier sketches in SATA 31, 151
Collins, Paul 1954- 126
Collins, Ross 1972- 200
Collins, Ruth Philpott 1890-1975
Obituary 30
Collins, Suzanne 180
Collins, Yvonne 194
Collinson, A. S.
See Collinson, Alan S.
Collinson, Alan S. 1934- 80
Collinson, Roger (Alfred) 1936- 133

Collison, Linda 1953- 185
Collodi, Carlo 1826-1890 100
Earlier sketch in SATA 29
See also CLR 120
Colloms, Brenda 1919- 40
Colman, Hila 1909-2008 53
Earlier sketch in SATA 1
See also SAAS 14
Colman, Morris 1899(?)-1981
Obituary 25
Colman, Penny (Morgan) 1944- 160
Autobiography Feature 160
Earlier sketches in SATA 77, 114
Colman, Warren (David) 1944- 67
Colombo, John Robert 1936- 50
Colon, Raul 156
Colon, Raul 1952- 202
Colonius, Lillian 1911-1992 3
Colorado, Antonio J.
See Colorado (Capella), Antonio J(ulio)
Colorado (Capella), Antonio J(ulio)
1903-1994 23
Obituary 79
Colquhoun, Glenn 1964- 165
Colston, Fifi E. 1960- 150
Colt, Martin
See Epstein, Beryl
and Epstein, Samuel
Colum, Padraic 1881-1972 15
See also CLR 36
Columbus, Chris 1959- 97
Columbus, Christopher
See Columbus, Chris
Columella
See Moore, Clement Clarke
Colver, Anne 1908- 7
Colvin, James
See Moorcock, Michael
Colwell, Eileen (Hilda) 1904-2002 2
Colwyn, Stewart
See Pepper, Frank S.
Coman, Carolyn 1951- 197
Earlier sketch in SATA 127
Combs, Lisa M.
See McCourt, Lisa
Combs, Robert
See Murray, John
Comfort, Jane Levington
See Sturtzel, Jane Levington
Comfort, Mildred Houghton 1886-1976 3
Comins, Ethel M(ae) 11
Comins, Jeremy 1933- 28
Commager, Henry Steele 1902-1998 23
Obituary 102
Comora, Madeleine 190
Compere, Mickie
See Davidson, Margaret
Compestine, Ying Chang 1963- 187
Earlier sketch in SATA 140
Comport, Sally Wern 190
Compton, Patricia A. 1936- 75
Comte, The Great
See Hawkesworth, Eric
Comus
See Ballantyne, R(obert) M(ichael)
Comyns, Nance
See Comyns-Toohey, Nantz
Comyns-Toohey, Nantz 1956- 86
Conahan, Carolyn
See Conahan, Carolyn Digby
Conahan, Carolyn Digby 1961- 216
Conan Doyle, Arthur
See Doyle, Sir Arthur Conan
Condie, Ally 204
Condie, Allyson B.
See Condie, Ally
Condit, Martha Olson 1913- 28
Condon, Bill 1949- 142
Condon, Judith 83
Condon, Ken 195
Condy, Roy 1942- 96

Cone, Ferne Geller 1921- 39
Cone, Molly (Lamken) 1918- 151
Autobiography Feature 151
Earlier sketches in SATA 1, 28, 115
See also SAAS 11
Cone, Patrick 1954- 89
Coney, Michael G. 1932-2005 61
Obituary 170
Coney, Michael Greatrex
See Coney, Michael G.
Coney, Mike
See Coney, Michael G.
Conford, Ellen 1942- 162
Earlier sketches in SATA 6, 68, 110
See also CLR 71
Conger, Lesley
See Suttles, Shirley (Smith)
Conklin, Gladys Plemon 1903- 2
Conklin, Paul S. 1929(?)-2003 43
Brief entry 33
Obituary 147
Conkling, Hilda 1910-1986 23
Conlan, Kathleen Elizabeth 1950- 145
Conlan, Kathy
See Conlan, Kathleen Elizabeth
Conley, Robyn 1963- 125
Conley-Weaver, Robyn
See Conley, Robyn
Conlon-McKenna, Marita 1956- 71
Conly, Jane Leslie 1948- 164
Earlier sketches in SATA 80, 112
Conly, Robert Leslie 1918(?)-1973 23
See also CLR 2
Connell, Kirk
See Chapman, John Stanton Higham
Connell, Tom 206
Connelly, Gwen 1952- 212
Connelly, Marc(us Cook) 1890-1980
Obituary 25
Connolly, Jerome P(atrick) 1931- 8
Connolly, Pat 1943- 74
Connolly, Peter 1935- 105
Earlier sketch in SATA 47
Conover, Chris 1950- 213
Earlier sketch in SATA 31
Conquest, Owen
See Hamilton, Charles (Harold St. John)
Conrad, Joseph 1857-1924 27
Conrad, Pam 1947-1996 133
Brief entry 49
Obituary 90
Earlier sketches in SATA 52, 80
See also CLR 18
See also SAAS 19
Conroy, Jack
See Conroy, John Wesley
Conroy, John Wesley 1899-1990 19
Obituary 65
Conroy, Robert
See Goldston, Robert (Conroy)
Constable, Kate 1966- 172
Constant, Alberta Wilson 1908-1981 22
Obituary 28
Constantin, Pascale 185
Conway, Celeste 210
Conway, David 1970- 213
Conway, Diana C. 1943- 91
Conway, Diana Cohen
See Conway, Diana C.
Conway, Gordon
See Hamilton, Charles (Harold St. John)
Cook, Ande 192
Cook, Bernadine 1924- 11
Cook, Fred J(ames) 1911-2003 2
Obituary 145
Cook, Glen 1944- 171
Earlier sketch in SATA 108
Cook, Glen Charles
See Cook, Glen
Cook, Hugh 1956- 85

Cook, Hugh, Walter Gilbert
See Cook, Hugh
Cook, Jean Thor 1930- 94
Cook, Joel 1934- 79
Cook, Joseph Jay 1924- 8
Cook, Lisa Broadie 157
Cook, Lyn
See Waddell, Evelyn Margaret
Cook, Roy
See Silverberg, Robert
Cook, Sally 207
Cook, Trish 175
Cooke, Ann
See Cole, Joanna
Cooke, Arthur
See Lowndes, Robert A(ugustine) W(ard)
Cooke, Barbara
See Alexander, Anna B(arbara Cooke)
Cooke, David Coxe 1917- 2
Cooke, Donald Ewin 1916-1985 2
Obituary 45
Cooke, Frank E. 1920- 87
Cooke, Jean (Isobel Esther) 1929- 74
Cooke, John Estes
See Baum, L. Frank
Cooke, Trish 1962- 129
Cookson, Catherine (McMullen) 1906-1998 .. 9
Obituary 116
Cooley, Beth 210
Cooley, Elizabeth
See Cooley, Beth
Cooley, Regina Francoise 1940- 177
Coolidge, Olivia E(nsor) 1908- 26
Earlier sketch in SATA *1*
Cooling, Wendy 169
Earlier sketch in SATA *111*
Coombs, Charles I(ra) 1914-1994 43
Earlier sketch in SATA *3*
See also SAAS *15*
Coombs, Chick
See Coombs, Charles I(ra)
Coombs, Jonathan 204
Coombs, Kate 190
Coombs, Patricia 1926- 51
Earlier sketch in SATA *3*
See also SAAS *22*
Cooney, Barbara 1917-2000 96
Obituary 123
Earlier sketches in SATA *6, 59*
See also CLR *23*
Cooney, Caroline B. 1947- 179
Brief entry 41
Earlier sketches in SATA *48, 80, 113, 130*
Cooney, Doug 181
Cooney, Nancy Evans 1932- 42
Coontz, Otto 1946- 33
Cooper, Ann (Catharine) 1939- 104
Cooper, Dutch
See Kuyper, Sjoerd
Cooper, Elisha 1971- 157
Earlier sketch in SATA *99*
Cooper, Elizabeth Keyser -1992 47
Cooper, Floyd 187
Earlier sketches in SATA *96, 144*
See also CLR *60*
Cooper, Gordon 1932- 23
Cooper, Helen 1963- 169
Earlier sketch in SATA *102*
Cooper, Henry S. F., Jr. 1933- 65
Cooper, Henry Spotswood Fenimore, Jr.
See Cooper, Henry S. F., Jr.
Cooper, Ilene 1948- 145
Earlier sketches in SATA *66, 97*
Cooper, James Fenimore 1789-1851 19
See also CLR *105*
Cooper, John R. 1
Cooper, Kay 1941- 11
Cooper, Lee Pelham 1926- 5
Cooper, Lester (Irving) 1919-1985 32
Obituary 43

Cooper, Lettice (Ulpha) 1897-1994 35
Obituary 82
Cooper, Louise 1952-2009 152
Cooper, M.E.
See Davis, Maggie S.
Cooper, M.E.
See Lerangis, Peter
Cooper, Melrose
See Kroll, Virginia L.
Cooper, Michael L. 1950- 181
Earlier sketches in SATA *79, 117*
Cooper, Patrick 1949- 134
Cooper, Susan 1935- 151
Earlier sketches in SATA *4, 64, 104*
See also CLR *67*
See also SAAS *6*
Cooper, Susan Mary
See Cooper, Susan
Cope, Jane U(rsula) 1949- 108
Copeland, Helen 1920- 4
Copeland, Mark 1956- 180
Copeland, Paul W. 23
Coplans, Peta 1951- 84
Copley (Diana) Heather Pickering 1918- 45
Coppard, A(lfred) E(dgar) 1878-1957
See YABC *1*
Copper, Melinda 1952- 172
Copper, Melinda McConnaughey
See Copper, Melinda
Corace, Jen 208
Coralie
See Anderson, Catherine Corley
Corbett, Grahame 43
Brief entry 36
Corbett, Scott 1913- 42
Earlier sketch in SATA *2*
See also CLR *1*
See also SAAS *2*
Corbett, Sue 174
Corbett, W(illiam) J(esse) 1938- 102
Brief entry 44
Earlier sketch in SATA *50*
See also CLR *19*
Corbin, Sabra Lee
See Malvern, Gladys
Corbin, William
See McGraw, William Corbin
Corbman, Marjorie 1987- 179
Corby, Dan
See Catherall, Arthur
Corcoran, Barbara (Asenath) 1911-2003 77
Autobiography Feature 125
Earlier sketch in SATA *3*
See also CLR *50*
See also SAAS *20*
Corcos, Lucille 1908-1973 10
Cordell, Alexander
See Graber, Alexander
Cordell, Matthew 1975- 199
Corder, Zizou
See Young, Louisa
Corella, Joseph
See Odgers, Sally Farrell
Coren, Alan 1938-2007 32
Obituary 187
Corey, Dorothy 23
Corey, Shana 1974- 133
Corfe, Thomas Howell 1928- 27
Corfe, Tom
See Corfe, Thomas Howell
Corfield, Robin Bell 1952- 74
Corlett, William 1938-2005 46
Brief entry 39
Cormack, M(argaret) Grant 1913- 11
Cormack, Maribelle B. 1902-1984 39
Cormier, Robert 1925-2000 83
Obituary 122
Earlier sketches in SATA *10, 45*
See also CLR *55*
Cormier, Robert Edmund
See Cormier, Robert

Cornelius, Carol 1942- 40
Cornelius, Kay 1933- 157
Cornell, J.
See Cornell, Jeffrey
Cornell, James (Clayton, Jr.) 1938- 27
Cornell, Jean Gay 1920- 23
Cornell, Jeffrey 1945- 11
Cornell, Laura 189
Cornish, D.M. 1972- 185
Cornish, Sam(uel James) 1935- 23
Cornwall, Nellie
See Sloggett, Nellie
Cornwell, Autumn 195
Corr, Christopher 1955- 189
Correy, Lee
See Stine, G(eorge) Harry
Corrick, James A. 1945- 76
Corrigan, (Helen) Adeline 1909- 23
Corrigan, Barbara 1922- 8
Corrigan, Eireann 1977- 163
Corrin, Sara 1918- 86
Brief entry 48
Corrin, Stephen 86
Brief entry 48
Corsi, Wendy
See Staub, Wendy Corsi
Cort, M. C.
See Clifford, Margaret Cort
Cort, Margaret
See Clifford, Margaret Cort
Corwin, Judith H(offman) 1946- 10
Corwin, Oliver
See Corwin, Oliver J.
Corwin, Oliver J. 206
Cory, Rowena
See Lindquist, Rowena Cory
Cosby, Bill 1937- 110
Earlier sketch in SATA *66*
Cosby, William Henry, Jr.
See Cosby, Bill
and Cosby, Bill
Cosentino, Ralph 169
Cosgrave, John O'Hara II 1908-1968
Obituary 21
Cosgrove, Margaret (Leota) 1926- 47
Cosgrove, Stephen E(dward) 1945- 53
Brief entry 40
Coskey, Evelyn 1932- 7
Cosner, Shaaron 1940- 43
Cossi, Olga 1921- 216
Earlier sketches in SATA *67, 102*
Costabel, Eva Deutsch 1924- 45
Costabel-Deutsch, Eva
See Costabel, Eva Deutsch
Coste, Marion 1938- 183
Costello, David 174
Costello, David F(rancis) 1904-1990 23
Cte, Genevieve 1964- 184
Cote, Nancy 1952- 182
Cott, Jonathan 1942- 23
Cottam, Clarence 1899-1974 25
Cotten, Cynthia 188
Cottin, Menena 1950- 213
Cottle, Joan 1960- 135
Cottler, Joseph 1899-1996 22
Cottonwood, Joe 1947- 92
Cottrell, Leonard 1913-1974 24
Cottringer, Anne 1952- 150
Earlier sketch in SATA *97*
Couch, Greg 199
Coulman, Valerie 1969- 161
Couloumbis, Audrey 173
Counsel, June 1926- 70
Countryman, The
See Whitlock, Ralph
Courlander, Harold 1908-1996 6
Obituary 88
Coursen, Valerie 1965(?)- 102
Courtis, Stuart Appleton 1874-1969
Obituary 29

Courtland, Tyler
  See Stevens, Serita
Courtney, Dayle
  See Goldsmith, Howard
Coury, Louise Andree 1895(?)-1983
  Obituary 34
Cousins, Linda 1946- 90
Cousins, Lucy 1964- 205
  Earlier sketch in SATA 172
Cousins, Margaret 1905-1996 2
  Obituary 92
Cousteau, Jacques 1910-1997 98
  Earlier sketch in SATA 38
Cousteau, Jacques-Yves
  See Cousteau, Jacques
Couture, Christin 1951- 73
Couvillon, Jacques 195
Covert, Ralph 1968- 197
Coville, Bruce 1950- 216
  Autobiography Feature 155
  Earlier sketches in SATA 32, 77, 118, 155
Covington, Dennis 109
Covington, Linda
  See Windsor, Linda
Cowan, Catherine 121
Cowan, Rebecca M.
  See Moesta, Rebecca
Cowan, Rebecca Moesta
  See Moesta, Rebecca
Coward, Fiona 1963- 178
Cowdrey, Richard 1959- 204
Cowell, Cressida 1966- 140
Cowen, Eve
  See Werner, Herma
Cowen, Ida 1898-1993 64
Cowie, Leonard W(allace) 1919- 4
Cowles, Kathleen
  See Krull, Kathleen
Cowley, Cassia Joy
  See Cowley, Joy
Cowley, Joy 1936- 164
  Autobiography Feature 118
  Earlier sketches in SATA 4, 90
  See also CLR 55
  See also SAAS 26
Cowley, Marjorie 1925- 111
Cox, (Christopher) Barry 1931- 62
Cox, Clinton 1934- 108
  Earlier sketch in SATA 74
Cox, David 1933- 56
Cox, David Dundas
  See Cox, David
Cox, Donald William 1921- 23
Cox, Jack
  See Cox, John Roberts
Cox, John Roberts 1915-1981 9
Cox, Judy 1954- 198
  Earlier sketches in SATA 117, 160
Cox, Marion Monroe 1898-1983
  Obituary 34
Cox, Palmer 1840-1924 24
  See also CLR 24
Cox, Vic 1942- 88
Cox, Vicki 1945- 158
Cox, Victoria 1945- 44
Cox, Wallace 1924-1973 25
Cox, Wally
  See Cox, Wallace
Cox, William R(obert) 1901-1988 46
  Brief entry 31
  Obituary 57
Coxe, Molly 1959- 101
  Earlier sketch in SATA 69
Coxon, Michele 1950- 158
  Earlier sketch in SATA 76
Coy, Harold 1902-1986 3
Coy, John 1958- 171
  Earlier sketch in SATA 120
Craats, Rennay 1973- 131
Crabtree, Judith 1928- 98
  Earlier sketch in SATA 63

Crabtree, Julie 1970- 214
Cracker, Edward E.B.
  See Odgers, Sally Farrell
Craft, Elizabeth 1971(?)- 204
Craft, K. Y.
  See Craft, Kinuko Y.
Craft, Kinuko Y. 1940- 127
  Earlier sketch in SATA 65
Craft, Kinuko Yamabe
  See Craft, Kinuko Y.
Craft, Ruth 1935- 87
  Brief entry 31
Craig, A. A.
  See Anderson, Poul
Craig, Alisa
  See MacLeod, Charlotte (Matilda)
Craig, David
  See James, Bill
Craig, Helen 1934- 213
  Earlier sketches in SATA 46, 49, 94
Craig, Joe 1979- 198
Craig, Joe Alexander
  See Craig, Joe
Craig, John Eland
  See Chipperfield, Joseph Eugene
Craig, John Ernest 1921- 23
Craig, Kit
  See Reed, Kit
Craig, M. F.
  See Craig, Mary (Francis) Shura
Craig, M. Jean 17
Craig, M. S.
  See Craig, Mary (Francis) Shura
Craig, Margaret (Maze) 1911-1964 9
Craig, Mary
  See Craig, Mary (Francis) Shura
Craig, Mary Shura
  See Craig, Mary (Francis) Shura
Craig, Mary (Francis) Shura 1923-1991 86
  Obituary 65
  Earlier sketch in SATA 6
  See also SAAS 7
Craig, Ruth 1922- 95
Craik, Mrs.
  See Craik, Dinah Maria (Mulock)
Craik, Dinah Maria (Mulock) 1826-1887 34
Crandall, Court 1965- 175
Crandell, Rachel 1943- 152
Crane, Barbara (Joyce) 1934- 31
Crane, Caroline 1930- 11
Crane, Jordan 1973- 174
Crane, M. A.
  See Wartski, Maureen (Ann Crane)
Crane, Royston Campbell 1901-1977
  Obituary 22
Crane, Stephen 1871-1900
  See YABC 2
  See also CLR 132
Crane, Stephen Townley
  See Crane, Stephen
Crane, Walter 1845-1915 100
  Earlier sketch in SATA 18
  See also CLR 56
Crane, William D(wight) 1892-1976 1
Cranfield, Ingrid 1945- 74
Cranshaw, Stanley
  See Fisher, Dorothy (Frances) Canfield
Crary, Elizabeth (Ann) 1942- 99
  Brief entry 43
Crary, Margaret (Coleman) 1906-1986 9
Craste, Marc 201
Cravath, Lynne Avril
  See Cravath, Lynne W.
Cravath, Lynne W. 1951- 182
  Earlier sketches in SATA 98, 148
Craven, Thomas 1889-1969 22
Crawford, Charles P. 1945- 28
Crawford, Deborah 1922- 6
Crawford, John E(dmund) 1904-1971 3
Crawford, K(aren) Michael 1959- 155

Crawford, Mel 1925- 44
  Brief entry 33
Crawford, Phyllis 1899- 3
Crawley, Dave 177
Cray, Roberta
  See Emerson, Ru
Crayder, Dorothy 7
Crayder, Teresa
  See Colman, Hila
Crayon, Geoffrey
  See Irving, Washington
Craz, Albert G. 1926- 24
Crebbin, June 1938- 169
  Earlier sketch in SATA 80
Crecy, Jeanne
  See Williams, Jeanne
Credle, Ellis 1902-1998 1
Creech, Sharon 1945- 172
  Earlier sketches in SATA 94, 139
  See also CLR 89
Creeden, Sharon 1938- 91
Creel, Ann Howard 1953- 187
Creighton, (Mary) Helen 1899-1989
  Obituary 64
Creighton, Jill 1949- 96
Crenson, Victoria 1952- 159
  Earlier sketch in SATA 88
Cresp, Gael 1954- 119
Crespo, George 1962- 82
Cresswell, Helen 1934-2005 79
  Obituary 168
  Earlier sketches in SATA 1, 48
  See also CLR 18
  See also SAAS 20
Cressy, Michael 1955- 124
Cressy, Mike
  See Cressy, Michael
Cretan, Gladys (Yessayan) 1921- 2
Cretzmeyer, Stacy (Megan) 1959- 124
Crew, Gary 1947- 163
  Earlier sketches in SATA 75, 110
  See also CLR 42
Crew, Helen (Cecilia) Coale 1866-1941
  See YABC 2
Crew, Linda (Jean) 1951- 137
  Earlier sketch in SATA 71
Crews, Donald 1938- 76
  Brief entry 30
  Earlier sketch in SATA 32
  See also CLR 7
Crews, Nina 1963- 158
  Earlier sketch in SATA 97
Crichton, John Michael
  See Crichton, Michael
Crichton, Michael 1942-2008 88
  Obituary 199
  Earlier sketch in SATA 9
Crider, Allen Billy
  See Crider, Bill
Crider, Bill 1941- 99
Crilley, Mark 1966- 210
  Autobiography Feature 148
  Earlier sketches in SATA 120, 148
Crimi, Carolyn 1959- 176
Cripps, Enid Margaret
  See Appiah, Peggy
Crisler, Curtis L. 188
Crisman, Ruth 1914- 73
Crisp, Marta Marie
  See Crisp, Marty
Crisp, Marty 1947- 128
Crispin, A(nn) C(arol) 1950- 86
Crist, James J. 1961- 168
Cristall, Barbara 79
Crist-Evans, Craig 1954- 153
Crocker, Carter 193
Crocker, Nancy 1956- 185
Crofford, Emily (Ardell) 1927- 61
Crofut, William E. III 1934- 23
Croggon, Alison 1962- 194

Croll, Carolyn 1945- *102*
    Brief entry *52*
    Earlier sketch in SATA *56*
Croman, Dorothy Young
    See Rosenberg, Dorothy
Cromie, Alice Hamilton 1914-2000 .... *24*
Cromie, William J(oseph) 1930- *4*
Crompton, Anne Eliot 1930- *73*
    Earlier sketch in SATA *23*
Crompton, Richmal
    See Lamburn, Richmal Crompton
Cronbach, Abraham 1882-1965 .... *11*
Crone, Ruth 1919-2003 .... *4*
Cronin, A(rchibald) J(oseph) 1896-1981 ...... *47*
    Obituary *25*
Cronin, Doreen (A.) *125*
Cronin, Doreen 1966(?)- *178*
    See also CLR *136*
Cronin, Doreen A.
    See Cronin, Doreen
Crook, Beverly Courtney *38*
    Brief entry *35*
Crook, Connie Brummel 1930- *168*
    Earlier sketch in SATA *98*
Crook, Constance
    See Crook, Connie Brummel
Crosby, Alexander L. 1906-1980 .... *2*
    Obituary *23*
Crosby, Harry C.
    See Anvil, Christopher
Crosby, Margaret
    See Rathmann, Peggy
Crosher, G. R. *14*
Cross, Gilbert B. 1939- *60*
    Brief entry *51*
Cross, Gillian 1945- *178*
    Autobiography Feature *178*
    Earlier sketches in SATA *38, 71, 110, 165*
    See also CLR *28*
Cross, Gillian Clare
    See Cross, Gillian
Cross, Helen Reeder
    See Broadhead, Helen Cross
Cross, Peter 1951- *95*
Cross, Sarah *216*
Cross, Shauna 1976(?)- *196*
Cross, Tom 1954- *146*
Cross, Verda 1914- *75*
Cross, Wilbur Lucius III 1918- *2*
Crossland, Caroline 1964- *83*
Crossley-Holland, Kevin 1941- *165*
    Earlier sketches in SATA *5, 74, 120*
    See also CLR *84*
    See also SAAS *20*
Crossley-Holland, Kevin John William
    See Crossley-Holland, Kevin
Crouch, Karen Hillard
    See Good, Karen Hillard
Crouch, Marcus 1913-1996 .... *4*
Crout, George C(lement) 1917- *11*
Crow, Donna Fletcher 1941- *40*
Crow, Francis Luther
    See Luther, Frank
Crow, Kristyn *208*
Crowe, Andrew *111*
Crowe, Carole 1943- *204*
Crowe, Chris *206*
Crowe, Ellie *203*
Crowe, John
    See Lynds, Dennis
Crowe, (Bettina) Peter Lum 1911- *6*
Crowell, Grace Noll 1877-1969 .... *34*
Crowell, Pers 1910-1990 .... *2*
Crowell, Robert Leland 1909-2001 .... *63*
Crowfield, Christopher
    See Stowe, Harriet Beecher
Crowley, Arthur 1945- *38*
Crowley, Arthur McBlair
    See Crowley, Arthur
Crowley, John 1942- *140*
    Earlier sketch in SATA *65*

Crowley, Suzanne 1963- *196*
Crowley, Suzanne Carlisle
    See Crowley, Suzanne
Crownfield, Gertrude 1867-1945
    See YABC *1*
Crowther, James Gerald 1899-1983 .... *14*
Crowther, Robert 1948- *163*
Cruikshank, George 1792-1878 .... *22*
    See also CLR *63*
Cruise, Robin 1951- *179*
Crum, Shutta *192*
    Earlier sketch in SATA *134*
Crummel, Susan Stevens 1949- *176*
    Earlier sketch in SATA *130*
Crump, Fred H., Jr. 1931- *76*
    Earlier sketch in SATA *11*
Crump, J(ames) Irving 1887-1979 .... *57*
    Obituary *21*
Crump, William D(rake) 1949- *138*
Crunden, Reginald
    See Cleaver, Hylton Reginald
Crunk, T.
    See Crunk, Tony
Crunk, Tony 1956- *130*
Crutcher, Chris 1946- *196*
    Earlier sketches in SATA *52, 99, 153*
    See also CLR *28*
Crutcher, Christopher C.
    See Crutcher, Chris
Cruz, Ray(mond) 1933- *6*
Cruz Martinez, Alejandro (?)-1987 .... *74*
Crystal, Billy 1947- *154*
Crystal, William
    See Crystal, Billy
Ctvrtek, Vaclav 1911-1976
    Obituary *27*
Cuetara, Mittie 1957- *158*
    Earlier sketch in SATA *106*
Cuffari, Richard 1925-1978 .... *66*
    Obituary *25*
    Earlier sketch in SATA *6*
Cuffe-Perez, Mary 1946- *199*
Cullen, Countee 1903-1946 .... *18*
Cullen, Lynn *190*
Culliford, Pierre 1928-1992 .... *40*
    Obituary *74*
Cullinan, Bernice E(llinger) 1926- *135*
Culp, Louanna McNary 1901-1965 .... *2*
Culper, Felix
    See McCaughrean, Geraldine
Cumbaa, Stephen 1947- *72*
Cumming, Peter 1951- *168*
Cumming, Primrose Amy 1915- *24*
Cumming, Robert 1945- *65*
Cummings, Betty Sue 1918- *15*
    See also SAAS *9*
Cummings, John Michael 1963(?)- *216*
Cummings, Mary 1951- *185*
Cummings, Parke 1902-1987 .... *2*
    Obituary *53*
Cummings, Pat 1950- *203*
    Earlier sketches in SATA *42, 71, 107*
    See also CLR *48*
    See also SAAS *13*
Cummings, Phil 1957- *123*
    Earlier sketch in SATA *74*
Cummings, Priscilla 1951- *170*
    Earlier sketch in SATA *129*
Cummings, Richard
    See Gardner, Richard (M.)
Cummins, Julie *200*
Cummins, Maria Susanna 1827-1866
    See YABC *1*
Cumpliano, Ina *207*
Cuneo, Mary Louise -2001 .... *85*
Cunliffe, John Arthur 1933- *86*
    Earlier sketch in SATA *11*
Cunliffe, Marcus (Falkner) 1922-1990 .... *37*
    Obituary *66*
Cunnane, Kelly *175*

Cunningham, Bob
    See May, Julian
Cunningham, Captain Frank
    See Glick, Carl (Cannon)
Cunningham, Cathy
    See Cunningham, Chet
Cunningham, Chet 1928- *23*
Cunningham, Dale S(peers) 1932- *11*
Cunningham, Dru *91*
Cunningham, E. V.
    See Fast, Howard
Cunningham, Julia (Woolfolk) 1916- *132*
    Earlier sketches in SATA *1, 26*
    See also SAAS *2*
Cunningham, Lawrence J. 1943- *125*
Cunningham, Virginia
    See Holmgren, Virginia C(unningham)
Curiae, Amicus
    See Fuller, Edmund (Maybank)
Curie, Eve 1904-2007 .... *1*
    Obituary *188*
Curlee, Lynn 1947- *190*
    Earlier sketches in SATA *98, 141*
Curley, Daniel 1918-1988 .... *23*
    Obituary *61*
Curley, Marianne 1959- *175*
    Earlier sketch in SATA *131*
Currey, Anna *194*
Currie, Robin 1948- *120*
Currie, Stephen 1960- *132*
    Earlier sketch in SATA *82*
Curry, Ann (Gabrielle) 1934- *72*
Curry, Jane L(ouise) 1932- *138*
    Autobiography Feature *138*
    Earlier sketches in SATA *1, 52, 90*
    See also CLR *31*
    See also SAAS *6*
Curry, Peggy Simson 1911-1987 .... *8*
    Obituary *50*
Curry, Tom *185*
Curtis, Bruce (Richard) 1944- *30*
Curtis, Chara M(ahar) 1950- *78*
Curtis, Christopher Paul 1953- *187*
    Earlier sketches in SATA *93, 140*
    See also CLR *68*
Curtis, Gavin 1965- *107*
Curtis, Jamie Lee 1958- *144*
    Earlier sketch in SATA *95*
    See also CLR *88*
Curtis, Jennifer Keats *185*
Curtis, Marci *160*
Curtis, Munzee
    See Caseley, Judith
Curtis, Neil 1950-2006 .... *202*
Curtis, Patricia 1921- *101*
    Earlier sketch in SATA *23*
Curtis, Peter
    See Lofts, Norah (Robinson)
Curtis, Philip (Delacourt) 1920- *62*
Curtis, Richard 1937- *29*
Curtis, Richard Alan
    See Curtis, Richard
Curtis, Richard Hale
    See Deming, Richard
    and Levinson, Leonard
    and Rothweiler, Paul Roger
Curtis, Stacy *205*
Curtis, Wade
    See Pournelle, Jerry (Eugene)
Curtiss, A(rlene) B. 1934- *90*
Cusack, Margaret 1945- *58*
Cushman, Doug 1953- *210*
    Earlier sketches in SATA *65, 101, 157*
Cushman, Jerome *2*
Cushman, Karen 1941- *147*
    Earlier sketch in SATA *89*
    See also CLR *55*
Cusick, Richie Tankersley 1952- *140*
    Earlier sketch in SATA *67*
Cutbill, Andy 1972- *201*
Cutchen, Billye Walker 1930- *15*

Cutchins, Judy 1947- 59
Cutler, Daniel S. 1951- 78
Cutler, Daniel Solomon
  See Cutler, Daniel S.
Cutler, Ebbitt 1923- 9
Cutler, Ivor 1923-2006 24
  Obituary 174
Cutler, Jane 1936- 162
  Earlier sketches in SATA 75, 118
Cutler, May Ebbitt
  See Cutler, Ebbitt
Cutler, Samuel
  See Folsom, Franklin (Brewster)
Cutlip, Kimbra L(eigh-Ann) 1964- 128
Cutrate, Joe
  See Spiegelman, Art
Cutt, W(illiam) Towrie 1898-1981 16
  Obituary 85
Cuyler, Margery 1948- 195
  Earlier sketches in SATA 39, 99, 156
Cuyler, Margery Stuyvesant
  See Cuyler, Margery
Cuyler, Stephen
  See Bates, Barbara S(nedeker)
Cyrus, Kurt 1954- 179
  Earlier sketch in SATA 132
Czajkowski, James
  See Rollins, James
Czekaj, Jef 1969- 217
Czernecki, Stefan 1946- 178

                            D

Dabba Smith, Frank 174
Dabcovich, Lydia 99
  Brief entry 47
  Earlier sketch in SATA 58
Dace, Dolores B(oelens) 1929- 89
Da Costa, Deborah 193
Daddo, Andrew 1967- 198
Dadey, Debbie 1959- 217
  Earlier sketches in SATA 73, 136
Dahl, Borghild (Margarethe) 1890-1984 7
  Obituary 37
Dahl, Roald 1916-1990 73
  Obituary 65
  Earlier sketches in SATA 1, 26
  See also CLR 111
Dahlberg, Maurine F. 1951- 171
Dahlstedt, Marden (Stewart) 1921-1983 8
  Obituary 110
Dahme, Joanne 206
Dain, Martin J. 1924-2000 35
Dakos, Kalli 1950- 115
  Earlier sketch in SATA 80
Dale, Anna 1971- 170
Dale, Gary
  See Reece, Colleen L.
Dale, George E.
  See Asimov, Isaac
Dale, Jack
  See Holliday, Joseph
Dale, Kim 1957- 123
Dale, Margaret J(essy) Miller 1911- 39
Dale, Mitzi
  See Hemstock, Gillian
Dale, Norman
  See Denny, Norman (George)
Dale, Penny 1954- 151
  Earlier sketch in SATA 70
Daley, Michael J. 170
Dalgliesh, Alice 1893-1979 17
  Obituary 21
  See also CLR 62
Dalkey, Kara 1953- 132
Dalkey, Kara Mia
  See Dalkey, Kara
Dallas, Ruth 1919- 86

Dalmas, John
  See Jones, John R(obert)
Dalton, Alene
  See Chapin, Alene Olsen Dalton
Dalton, Annie 1948- 140
  Earlier sketch in SATA 40
Dalton, Kit
  See Cunningham, Chet
Dalton, Pamela
  See Johnson, Pamela
Dalton, Sean
  See Chester, Deborah
Dalton, Sheila 1949- 108
D'Aluisio, Faith 1957- 205
Daly, James 1962- 217
Daly, Jim
  See Stratemeyer, Edward L.
Daly, Jude 1951- 177
Daly, Kathleen N(orah) 124
  Brief entry 37
Daly, Maureen 1921-2006 129
  Obituary 176
  Earlier sketch in SATA 2
  See also CLR 96
  See also SAAS 1
Daly, Nicholas 1946- 164
  Earlier sketches in SATA 37, 76, 114
  See also CLR 41
  See also SAAS 21
  See Daly, Niki
Daly, Niki 198
  See Daly, Nicholas
D'Amato, Alex 1919- 20
D'Amato, Janet (Potter) 1925- 9
Damerow, Gail 1944- 83
Damerow, Gail Jane
  See Damerow, Gail
D'Amico, Carmela 170
D'Amico, Steve 170
Damrell, Liz 1956- 77
Damrosch, Helen
  See Tee-Van, Helen Damrosch
Dana, Barbara 1940- 22
Dana, Richard Henry, Jr. 1815-1882 26
Danachair, Caoimhin O
  See Danaher, Kevin
Danaher, Kevin 1913-2002 22
Danakas, John 1963- 94
Dandi
  See Mackall, Dandi Daley
D'Andrea, Kate
  See Steiner, Barbara A(nnette)
Dangerfield, Balfour
  See McCloskey, (John) Robert
Daniel, Alan 1939- 76
  Brief entry 53
Daniel, Anita 1893(?)-1978 23
  Obituary 24
Daniel, Anne
  See Steiner, Barbara A(nnette)
Daniel, Becky 1947- 56
Daniel, Claire 1949- 164
Daniel, Colin
  See Windsor, Patricia
Daniel, Hawthorne 1890- 8
Daniel, (Donna) Lee 1944- 76
Daniel, Rebecca
  See Daniel, Becky
Daniels, Guy 1919-1989 11
  Obituary 62
Daniels, Lucy
  See Oldfield, Jenny
Daniels, Max
  See Gellis, Roberta
Daniels, Olga
  See Sinclair, Olga
Daniels, Patricia 1955- 93
Daniels, Zoe
  See Laux, Constance
Dank, Gloria Rand 1955- 56
  Brief entry 46

Dank, Leonard D(ewey) 1929- 44
Dank, Milton 1920- 31
Dann, Max 1955- 62
Danneberg, Julie 1958- 173
Dantz, William R.
  See Philbrick, Rodman
Danziger, Dianne 213
Danziger, Paula 1944-2004 149
  Brief entry 30
  Obituary 155
  Earlier sketches in SATA 36, 63, 102
  See also CLR 20
Darby, Gene Kegley
  See Darby, Jean (Kegley)
Darby, J. N.
  See Govan, (Mary) Christine Noble
Darby, Jean (Kegley) 1921- 68
Darby, Patricia (Paulsen) 14
Darby, Ray(mond) 1912-1982 7
d'Arcy, Willard
  See Cox, William R(obert)
Dare, Geena
  See McNicoll, Sylvia (Marilyn)
Darian, Shea 1959- 97
Daringer, Helen Fern 1892-1986 1
Darke, Marjorie 1929- 87
  Earlier sketch in SATA 16
Darley, F(elix) O(ctavius) C(arr)
  1822-1888 35
Darling, David J. 1953- 60
  Brief entry 44
Darling, Kathy
  See Darling, Mary Kathleen
Darling, Lois (MacIntyre) 1917-1989 3
  Obituary 64
Darling, Louis, (Jr.) 1916-1970 3
  Obituary 23
Darling, Mary Kathleen 1943- 124
  Earlier sketches in SATA 9, 79
Darling, Sandra Louise Woodward
  See Day, Alexandra
Darnell, K(athryn) L(ynne) 1955- 150
Darroll, Sally
  See Odgers, Sally Farrell
Darrow, Sharon 181
Darrow, Whitney, (Jr.) 1909-1999 13
  Obituary 115
Darwin, Len
  See Darwin, Leonard
Darwin, Leonard 1916- 24
Dasent, Sir George Webbe 1817-1896 62
  Brief entry 29
Dash, Joan 1925- 142
Daskam, Josephine Dodge
  See Bacon, Josephine Dodge (Daskam)
D'ath, Justin 1953- 174
  Earlier sketch in SATA 106
Dauer, Rosamond 1934- 23
Daugherty, Charles Michael 1914- 16
Daugherty, James (Henry) 1889-1974 13
  See also CLR 78
Daugherty, Richard D(eo) 1922- 35
Daugherty, Sonia Medwedeff (?)-1971
  Obituary 27
d'Aulaire, Edgar Parin 1898-1986 66
  Obituary 47
  Earlier sketch in SATA 5
  See also CLR 21
d'Aulaire, Ingri 1904-1980 66
  Obituary 24
  Earlier sketch in SATA 5
  See also CLR 21
d'Aulaire, Ingri Mortenson Parin
  See d'Aulaire, Ingri
Dave, Dave
  See Berg, David
Daveluy, Paule Cloutier 1919- 11
Davenier, Christine 1961- 216
  Earlier sketches in SATA 127, 179
Davenport, John 1960- 156
Daves, Michael 1938- 40

David, A. R.
  See David, A(nn) Rosalie
David, A(nn) Rosalie 1946- 103
David, Jonathan
  See Ames, Lee J(udah)
David, Lawrence 1963- 165
  Earlier sketch in SATA *111*
David, Peter 1956- 72
David, Peter Allen
  See David, Peter
David, Rosalie
  See David, A(nn) Rosalie
Davidson, Alice Joyce 1932- 54
  Brief entry 45
Davidson, Basil 1914-2010 13
Davidson, (Marie) Diane 1924- 91
Davidson, Hugh
  See Hamilton, Edmond
Davidson, Jessica 1915-1986 5
Davidson, Judith 1953- 40
Davidson, Lionel 1922-2009 87
Davidson, Margaret 1936- 5
Davidson, Marion
  See Garis, Howard R.
Davidson, Mary R. 1885-1973 9
Davidson, Mary S. 1940- 61
Davidson, Mickie
  See Davidson, Margaret
Davidson, Nicole
  See Jensen, Kathryn
Davidson, R.
  See Davidson, Raymond
Davidson, Raymond 1926- 32
Davidson, Rosalie 1921- 23
Davie, Helen K(ay) 1952- 148
  Earlier sketch in SATA *77*
Davies, Andrew (Wynford) 1936- 27
Davies, Andy Robert 200
Davies, Bettilu D(onna) 1942- 33
Davies, Hunter 1936- 55
  Brief entry 45
Davies, Jacqueline 1962- 186
  Earlier sketch in SATA *155*
Davies, Joan 1934- 50
  Brief entry 47
Davies, Nicola 1958- 182
  Earlier sketches in SATA *99, 150*
Davies, Peter J(oseph) 1937- 52
Davies, Sumiko 1942- 46
Davis, (A.) Aubrey 1949- 153
Davis, Barbara Steincrohn
  See Davis, Maggie S.
Davis, Bette J. 1923- 15
Davis, Burke 1913- 4
Davis, Christopher 1928- 6
Davis, D(elbert) Dwight 1908-1965 33
Davis, Daniel S(heldon) 1936- 12
Davis, David R. 1948- 106
Davis, Donald 1944- 169
  Earlier sketch in SATA *93*
Davis, Donald D.
  See Davis, Donald
Davis, Eleanor 1983(?)- 209
Davis, Emma
  See Davis, Maggie S.
Davis, Gibbs 1953- 102
  Brief entry 41
  Earlier sketch in SATA *46*
Davis, Grania 1943- 88
  Brief entry 50
Davis, H(arold) L(enoir) 1896-1960 114
Davis, Hubert J(ackson) 1904-1997 31
Davis, Jack E. 210
Davis, Jacky 204
Davis, James Robert 1945- 32
Davis, Jenny 1953- 74
Davis, Jim
  See Davis, James Robert
Davis, Julia 1900(?)-1993 6
  Obituary 75
Davis, Karen (Elizabeth) 1944- 109

Davis, Katie 1959(?)- 208
  Earlier sketch in SATA *152*
Davis, Lambert 176
Davis, Leslie
  See Guccione, Leslie Davis
Davis, Louise Littleton 1921- 25
Davis, Maggie S. 1943- 57
Davis, Marguerite 1889- 34
Davis, Mary L(ee) 1935- 9
Davis, Mary Octavia 1901-1976 6
Davis, Nelle 1958- 73
Davis, Ossie 1917-2005 81
  See also CLR *56*
Davis, Paxton 1925-1994 16
Davis, Rich 1958- 206
Davis, Robert 1881-1949
  See YABC *1*
Davis, Robin W(orks) 1962- 87
Davis, Russell Gerard 1922- 3
Davis, Tanita S. 212
Davis, Tim(othy N.) 1957- 94
Davis, Verne Theodore 1889-1973 6
Davis, Yvonne 1927- 115
Davol, Marguerite W. 1928- 146
  Earlier sketch in SATA *82*
DaVolls, Andy (P.) 1967- 85
DaVolls, Linda 1966- 85
Davys, Sarah
  See Manning, Rosemary
Dawes, Claiborne 1935- 111
Dawson, Arthur L. 207
Dawson, Elmer A. 67
  Earlier sketch in SATA *1*
Dawson, Imogen (Zoe) 1948- 126
  Earlier sketch in SATA *90*
Dawson, Janine 1957- 196
Dawson, Mary 1919- 11
Dawson, Willow 1975- 208
Day, A(rthur) Grove 1904-1994 59
Day, Alexandra 1941- 197
  Autobiography Feature 197
  Earlier sketches in SATA *67, 97, 169*
  See also CLR *22*
  See also SAAS *19*
Day, Beth (Feagles) 1924- 33
Day, Donna
  See Asay, Donna Day
Day, Edward C. 1932- 72
Day, Jon 1936(?)- 79
Day, Karen 187
Day, Larry 1956- 181
Day, Nancy 1953- 140
Day, Nancy Raines 1951- 148
  Earlier sketch in SATA *93*
Day, Shirley 1962- 94
Day, Thomas 1748-1789
  See YABC *1*
Day, Trevor 1955- 124
Dazey, Agnes J(ohnston) 2
Dazey, Frank M. 2
Deacon, Alexis 1978- 139
Deacon, Eileen
  See Geipel, Eileen
Deacon, Richard
  See McCormick, (George) Donald (King)
Deadman, Ronald 1919-1988(?)
  Obituary 56
Deak, Erzsi 1959- 152
Dean, Anabel 1915- 12
Dean, Carolee 1962- 148
Dean, Claire 1976- 215
Dean, David 1976- 192
Dean, Karen Strickler 1923- 49
Dean, Ruth (Brigham) 1947- 145
Dean, Zoey
  See Bennett, Cherie
de Angeli, Marguerite (Lofft) 1889-1987 ... 100
  Obituary 51
  Earlier sketches in SATA *1, 27*
  See also CLR *1*
Deans, Karen 195

Deans, Sis Boulos 1955- 136
  Earlier sketch in SATA *78*
DeArmand, Frances Ullmann 1904(?)-1984 . 10
  Obituary 38
DeArmond, Dale 1914- 70
DeArmond, Dale Burlison
  See DeArmond, Dale
Deary, Terry 1946- 171
  Brief entry 41
  Earlier sketches in SATA *51, 101*
Deaver, Julie Reece 1953- 68
de Banke, Cecile 1889-1965 11
De Bello, Rosario 1923- 89
Debon, Nicolas 186
  Earlier sketch in SATA *151*
de Bono, Edward 1933- 66
de Brissac, Malcolm
  See Dickinson, Peter
de Brunhoff, Jean
  See Brunhoff, Jean de
De Brunhoff, Laurent
  See Brunhoff, Laurent de
De Bruyn, Monica G. 1952- 13
De Bruyn, Monica Jean Grembowicz
  See De Bruyn, Monica G.
DeBry, Roger K. 1942- 91
de Camp, Catherine Crook 1907-2000 83
  Earlier sketch in SATA *12*
de Camp, L. Sprague 1907-2000 83
  Earlier sketch in SATA *9*
de Camp, Lyon Sprague
  See de Camp, L. Sprague
DeCandido, Keith R.A. 112
Dechausay, Sonia E. 94
Decker, C.B. 172
Decker, Cynthia B.
  See Decker, C.B.
Decker, Duane 1910-1964 5
Decker, Timothy 1974- 197
DeClements, Barthe 1920- 131
  Earlier sketches in SATA *35, 71*
  See also CLR *23*
DeClements, Barthe Faith
  See DeClements, Barthe
de Clercq Zubli, Rita la Fontaine 1929- 199
de Conte, Sieur Louis
  See Twain, Mark
Dedman, Stephen 108
Dee, Catherine 1964- 138
Dee, Ruby
  See Wallace, Ruby Ann
Deedy, Carmen Agra 1960- 196
Deedy, John 1923- 24
Deegan, Paul Joseph 1937- 48
  Brief entry 38
Deem, James M. 1950- 191
  Autobiography Feature 191
  Earlier sketches in SATA *75, 134*
Deem, James Morgan
  See Deem, James M.
Deeter, Catherine 1947- 137
DeFelice, Cynthia 1951- 165
  Earlier sketches in SATA *79, 121*
DeFelice, Cynthia C.
  See DeFelice, Cynthia
Defoe, Daniel 1660(?)-1731 22
  See also CLR *61*
DeFord, Deborah H. 123
deFrance, Anthony
  See DiFranco, Anthony (Mario)
Degen, Bruce 1945- 205
  Brief entry 47
  Earlier sketches in SATA *57, 97, 147*
DeGering, Etta (Belle) Fowler 1898-1996 7
De Goldi, Kate 1959- 123
De Goldi, Kathleen Domenica
  See De Goldi, Kate
de Goursac, Olivier 1959- 184
De Grazia, Ettore 1909-1982 39
De Grazia, Ted
  See De Grazia, Ettore

deGroat, Diane 1947- 169
   Earlier sketches in SATA 31, 90
deGros, J. H.
   See Villiard, Paul
de Grummond, Lena Young 62
   Earlier sketch in SATA 6
de Hamel, Joan Littledale 1924- 86
De Haven, Tom 1949- 72
de Hugo, Pierre
   See Brackers de Hugo, Pierre
Deiss, Joseph Jay 1915- 12
de Jenkins, Lyll Becerra 1925-1997 102
DeJong, David C(ornel) 1905-1967 10
de Jong, Dola
   See de Jong, Dorothea Rosalie
de Jong, Dorothea Rosalie 1911-2003 7
   Obituary 149
DeJong, Meindert 1906-1991 2
   Obituary 68
   See also CLR 73
DeJonge, Joanne E. 1943- 56
Deka, Connie
   See Laux, Constance
de Kay, Ormonde (Jr.) 1923-1998 7
   Obituary 106
DeKeyser, Stacy 1959- 214
de Kiriline, Louise
   See Lawrence, Louise de Kiriline
Dekker, Carl
   See Laffin, John (Alfred Charles)
   and Lynds, Dennis
deKruif, Paul (Henry) 1890-1971 50
   Earlier sketch in SATA 5
Delacre, Lulu 1957- 209
   Earlier sketches in SATA 36, 156
DeLaCroix, Alice 1940- 195
   Earlier sketch in SATA 75
de la Cruz, Melissa 1971- 179
De la Garza, Phyllis 1942- 169
De Lage, Ida 1918- 11
de la Mare, Walter (John) 1873-1956 16
   See also CLR 148
Delaney, Harry 1932- 3
Delaney, Joseph 1945- 172
Delaney, M.C.
   See Delaney, Michael
Delaney, Michael 1955- 180
   Earlier sketch in SATA 96
Delaney, Michael Clark
   See Delaney, Michael
Delaney, Ned 1951- 28
Delaney, Thomas Nicholas III
   See Delaney, Ned
DeLange, Alex Pardo
   See Pardo DeLange, Alex
Delano, Hugh 1933- 20
Delano, Marfe Ferguson 215
Delany, Samuel R., Jr. 1942- 92
Delany, Samuel Ray
   See Delany, Samuel R., Jr.
de la Pena, Matt 205
De La Ramee, Marie Louise 1839-1908 20
de la Roche, Mazo 1879-1961 64
De La Roche Saint Andre, Anne 1950- 75
Delaune, (Jewel) Lynn (de Grummond) 7
DeLaurentis, Louise Budde 1920- 12
del Barco, Lucy Salamanca 1900(?)-1989
   Obituary 64
Delderfield, Eric R(aymond) 1909-1995 14
Delderfield, Ronald Frederick 1912-1972 20
DeLeeuw, Adele (Louise) 1899-1988 30
   Obituary 56
   Earlier sketch in SATA 1
De Leon, Nephtali 1945- 97
Delessert, Etienne 1941- 179
   Brief entry 27
   Earlier sketches in SATA 46, 130
   See also CLR 81
Delgado, James P. 1958- 122
de Lint, Charles 1951- 207
   Earlier sketches in SATA 115, 157

de Lint, Charles Henri Diederick Hofsmit
   See de Lint, Charles
Delmar, Roy
   See Wexler, Jerome (LeRoy)
Del Negro, Janice M. 197
Deloria, Vine, Jr. 1933-2005 21
   Obituary 171
Deloria, Vine Victor, Jr.
   See Deloria, Vine, Jr.
del Rey, Lester 1915-1993 22
   Obituary 76
Delrio, Martin
   See Doyle, Debra
   and Macdonald, James D.
Delton, Judy 1931-2001 77
   Obituary 130
   Earlier sketch in SATA 14
   See also SAAS 9
Delulio, John 1938- 15
Delving, Michael
   See Williams, Jay
de Marcken, Gail 186
Demarest, Chris L. 1951- 175
   Brief entry 44
   Earlier sketches in SATA 45, 82, 128
Demarest, Christopher Lynn
   See Demarest, Chris L.
Demarest, Doug
   See Barker, Will
De Mari, Silvana 1953- 193
Demas, Corinne 203
   See Bliss, Corinne Demas
Demas, Vida 1927- 9
Dematons, Charlotte 1957- 203
DeMatteis, J.M. 1953- 180
DeMatteis, John Marc
   See DeMatteis, J.M.
De Mejo, Oscar 1911-1992 40
Demers, Dominique 1956- 177
de Messieres, Nicole 1930- 39
Demi 1942- 210
   Earlier sketches in SATA 11, 66, 102, 152
   See also CLR 58
Demijohn, Thom
   See Disch, Thomas M.
   and Sladek, John
Deming, Richard 1915-1983 24
Deming, Sarah 191
de Monfreid, Dorothee 1973- 189
Demuth, Patricia Brennan 1948- 84
   Brief entry 51
Dendinger, Roger E. 1952- 158
Denenberg, Barry 1940- 175
Dengler, Marianna (Herron) 1935- 103
Dengler, Sandy 1939- 54
   Brief entry 40
Denim, Sue
   See Pilkey, Dav
Denise, Anika 210
Denise, Christopher 1968- 193
   Earlier sketch in SATA 147
Denman, K.L. 1957- 186
Denmark, Harrison
   See Zelazny, Roger
Dennard, Deborah 1953- 136
   Earlier sketch in SATA 78
Denney, Diana 1910-2000 25
   Obituary 120
Dennis, Morgan 1891(?)-1960 18
Dennis, Wesley 1903-1966 18
Denniston, Elinore 1900-1978
   Obituary 24
Denny, Norman (George) 1901-1982 43
Denos, Julia 202
Denslow, Sharon Phillips 1947- 142
   Earlier sketch in SATA 68
Denslow, W(illiam) W(allace) 1856-1915 16
   See also CLR 15
Dent, Grace 1973- 187

Denton, Kady MacDonald 181
   Earlier sketches in SATA 66, 110
   See also CLR 71
Denton, Terry 1950- 186
Denver, Walt
   See Redding, Robert Hull
   and Sherman, Jory (Tecumseh)
Denzel, Justin F(rancis) 1917-1999 46
   Brief entry 38
Denzer, Ann Wiseman
   See Wiseman, Ann (Sayre)
DePalma, Mary Newell 1961- 185
   Earlier sketch in SATA 139
De Palma, Toni 199
dePaola, Thomas Anthony 1934- 155
   Earlier sketches in SATA 11, 59, 108
   See also CLR 81
   See also SAAS 15
   See dePaola, Tomie
dePaola, Tomie 200
   See dePaola, Thomas Anthony
deParrie, Paul 1949- 74
DePauw, Linda Grant 1940- 24
DeRan, David 1946- 76
Derby, Ken 1956- 181
Derby, Kenneth R.
   See Derby, Ken
Derby, Pat 1942- 172
Derby, Sally 1934- 189
   Earlier sketches in SATA 89, 132
de Regniers, Beatrice Schenk (Freedman)
   1914-2000 68
   Obituary 123
   Earlier sketch in SATA 2
   See also SAAS 6
Dereske, Jo 1947- 72
Deriso, Christine Hurley 1961- 210
Derleth, August (William) 1909-1971 5
Derman, Martha (Winn) 74
Derman, Sarah Audrey 1915- 11
DeRoberts, Lyndon
   See Silverstein, Robert Alan
de Roo, Anne Louise 1931-1997 84
   Earlier sketch in SATA 25
   See also CLR 63
deRosa, Dee 70
Derrick, Lionel
   See Cunningham, Chet
Derrickson, Jim 1959- 141
Derry Down Derry
   See Lear, Edward
Dervaux, Isabelle 1961- 106
Derwent, Lavinia 14
Desai, Anita 1937- 126
   Earlier sketch in SATA 63
DeSaix, Deborah Durland 188
De Saulles, Tony 1958- 119
Desbarats, Peter 1933- 39
de Selincourt, Aubrey 1894-1962 14
de Seve, Randall 198
Deshpande, Chris 1950- 69
Desimini, Lisa 1964- 216
   Earlier sketches in SATA 86, 148
Desjarlais, John 1953- 71
Desjarlais, John J.
   See Desjarlais, John
Desmoinaux, Christel 1967- 149
   Earlier sketch in SATA 103
Desmond, Adrian 1947- 51
Desmond, Adrian J.
   See Desmond, Adrian
Desmond, Adrian John
   See Desmond, Adrian
Desmond, Alice Curtis 1897-1990 8
Desnoettes, Caroline 183
DeSpain, Pleasant 1943- 87
Desputeaux, Helene 1959- 95
Dessen, Sarah 1970- 172
   Earlier sketch in SATA 120
Detine, Padre
   See Olsen, Ib Spang

de Trevino, Elizabeth B.
  See Trevino, Elizabeth B(orton) de
de Trevino, Elizabeth Borton
  See Trevino, Elizabeth B(orton) de
Detwiler, Susan Dill 1956- 58
Deuker, Carl 1950- 196
  Earlier sketches in SATA *82, 150*
Deutsch, Babette 1895-1982 1
  Obituary 33
Deutsch, Eva Costabel
  See Costabel, Eva Deutsch
Deutsch, Helen 1906-1992 76
Deutsch, Kurt
  See Singer, Kurt D.
De Valera, Sinead 1879(?)-1975
  Obituary 30
Devaney, John 1926-1994 12
de Varennes, Monique 1947- 168
de Varona, Frank J. 1943- 83
Devereux, Frederick L(eonard), Jr.
  1914-1993 9
Devi, Nila
  See Woody, Regina Jones
deVinck, Christopher 1951- 85
DeVita, James 195
DeVito, Cara 1956- 80
Devlin, Dorothy Wende
  See Devlin, Wende
Devlin, Harry 1918-2001 136
  Earlier sketches in SATA *11, 74*
Devlin, Wende 1918-2002 74
  Earlier sketch in SATA *11*
Devon, Paddie 1953- 92
Devons, Sonia 1974- 72
Devorah-Leah 111
de Vos, Gail 1949- 122
DeVries, Douglas 1933- 122
De Waard, E(lliott) John 1935- 7
Dewan, Ted 1961- 157
  Earlier sketch in SATA *108*
Dewdney, Anna 184
Dewdney, Selwyn (Hanington) 1909-1979 ... 64
DeWeese, Gene
  See DeWeese, Thomas Eugene
DeWeese, Jean
  See DeWeese, Thomas Eugene
DeWeese, Thomas Eugene 1934- 46
  Brief entry 45
Dewey, Ariane 1937- 178
  Earlier sketches in SATA *7, 109*
Dewey, Jennifer (Owings) 1941- 103
  Brief entry 48
  Earlier sketch in SATA *58*
Dewey, Kenneth Francis 1940- 39
Dewin, Howie
  See Howie, Betsy
De Wire, Elinor 1953- 180
deWit, Dorothy (May Knowles) 1916-1980 . 39
  Obituary 28
Dexter, Alison 1966- 125
Dexter, John
  See Bradley, Marion Zimmer
Deyneka, Anita 1943- 24
Deyrup, Astrith Johnson 1923- 24
Dezern, Chad 201
Dhami, Narinder 1958- 152
Dhondy, Farrukh 1944- 152
  Earlier sketch in SATA *65*
  See also CLR *41*
Diakite, Baba Wague 1961- 174
Diakite, Penda 1993(?)- 174
Diamond, Arthur 1957- 76
Diamond, Donna 1950- 69
  Brief entry 30
  Earlier sketch in SATA *35*
Diamond, Petra
  See Sachs, Judith
Diamond, Rebecca
  See Sachs, Judith
Dias, Earl Joseph 1916- 41
Dias, Ron 1937- 71

Diaz, David 1959(?)- 189
  Earlier sketches in SATA *96, 150*
  See also CLR *65*
Dibley, Glin 188
DiCamillo, Kate 1964- 202
  Earlier sketches in SATA *121, 163*
  See also CLR *117*
Di Certo, J(oseph) J(ohn) 1933- 60
DiCianni, Ron 1952- 107
Dick, Trella Lamson 1889-1974 9
Dickens, Charles 1812-1870 15
  See also CLR *95*
Dickens, Charles John Huffam
  See Dickens, Charles
Dickens, Frank
  See Huline-Dickens, Frank William
Dickens, Monica (Enid) 1915-1992 4
  Obituary 74
Dickerson, Roy Ernest 1886-1965
  Obituary 26
Dickinson, Emily 1830-1886 29
Dickinson, Emily Elizabeth
  See Dickinson, Emily
Dickinson, Mary 1949- 48
  Brief entry 41
Dickinson, Mary-Anne
  See Rodda, Emily
Dickinson, Peter 1927- 150
  Earlier sketches in SATA *5, 62, 95*
  See also CLR *125*
Dickinson, Peter Malcolm de Brissac
  See Dickinson, Peter
Dickinson, Susan 1931- 8
Dickinson, Terence 1943- 102
Dickinson, W(illiam) Croft 1897-1963 13
Dickson, Gordon R. 1923-2001 77
Dickson, Gordon Rupert
  See Dickson, Gordon R.
Dickson, Helen
  See Reynolds, Helen Mary Greenwood Camp-
bell
Dickson, Naida 1916- 8
Diehn, Gwen 1943- 80
Dierssen, Andreas 1962- 190
Diesen, Deborah 1967- 200
Dieterich, Michele M. 1962- 78
Dietz, David H(enry) 1897-1984 10
  Obituary 41
Dietz, Lew 1907-1997 11
  Obituary 95
Diffily, Deborah 159
Di Fiori, Larry
  See Di Fiori, Lawrence
Di Fiori, Lawrence 1934- 130
DiFranco, Anthony (Mario) 1945- 42
Digby, Anne 1935- 72
Digges, Jeremiah
  See Berger, Josef
Digman, Kristina 1959- 176
D'Ignazio, Fred 1949- 39
  Brief entry 35
D'Ignazio, Frederick
  See D'Ignazio, Fred
Di Grazia, Thomas (?)-1983 32
Dijkstra, Lida 1961- 195
Dikty, Julian May
  See May, Julian
Dillard, Annie 1945- 140
  Earlier sketch in SATA *10*
Dillard, Kristine 1964- 113
Dillard, Polly Hargis 1916- 24
Dillard, Sarah 1961- 217
Diller, Harriett 1953- 78
Dillon, Anna
  See Scott, Michael
Dillon, Barbara 1927- 44
  Brief entry 39
Dillon, Diane 1933- 194
  Earlier sketches in SATA *15, 51, 106*
  See also CLR *44*

Dillon, Diane Claire
  See Dillon, Diane
Dillon, Eilis 1920-1994 74
  Autobiography Feature 105
  Obituary 83
  Earlier sketch in SATA *2*
  See also CLR *26*
Dillon, Jana (a pseudonym) 1952- 117
Dillon, Leo 1933- 194
  Earlier sketches in SATA *15, 51, 106*
  See also CLR *44*
Dillon, Sharon Saseen
  See Saseen, Sharon (Dillon)
Dils, Tracey E. 1958- 83
Dilson, Jesse 1914-1988 24
Dinan, Carolyn 59
  Brief entry 47
Dines, Carol 1956- 175
Dines, (Harry) Glen 1925-1996 7
Dinesen, Isak
  See Blixen, Karen
Dinessi, Alex
  See Schembri, Jim
Dinneen, Betty 1929- 61
Dinnerstein, Harvey 1928- 42
Dinsdale, Tim(othy Kay) 1924-1987 11
Dion, Nathalie 1964- 213
Dionne, Erin 1975- 217
Diop, Birago (Ismael) 1906-1989
  Obituary 64
Diouf, Sylviane A. 168
Diouf, Sylviane Anna
  See Diouf, Sylviane A.
DiPucchio, Kelly 204
  Earlier sketch in SATA *159*
Dirk
  See Gringhuis, Richard H.
Dirks, Wilhelmina 1916- 59
Dirks, Willy
  See Dirks, Wilhelmina
Dirtmeister
  See Tomecek, Steve
DiSalvo, DyAnne 1960- 144
  Earlier sketch in SATA *59*
DiSalvo-Ryan, DyAnne
  See DiSalvo, DyAnne
Disch, Thomas M. 1940-2008 92
  Obituary 195
  See also CLR *18*
  See also SAAS *15*
Disch, Thomas Michael
  See Disch, Thomas M.
Disch, Tom
  See Disch, Thomas M.
Disher, Garry 1949- 125
  Earlier sketch in SATA *81*
Disney, Walt(er Elias) 1901-1966 28
  Brief entry 27
Ditchfield, Christin 1973- 189
DiTerlizzi, Tony 1969- 214
  Earlier sketch in SATA *154*
DiTerlooney, Tiny
  See DiTerlizzi, Tony
Divakaruni, Chitra Banerjee 1956- 160
Di Valentin, Maria (Amelia) Messuri
  1911-1985 7
Divine, Arthur Durham 1904-1987
  Obituary 52
Divine, David
  See Divine, Arthur Durham
Dixon, Ann 1954- 212
  Earlier sketches in SATA *77, 127*
Dixon, Ann Renee
  See Dixon, Ann
Dixon, Dougal 1947- 190
  Earlier sketches in SATA *45, 127*

Dixon, Franklin W.
  See Barrett, Neal, Jr.
  and Goulart, Ron
  and Lantz, Francess L(in)
  and Lerangis, Peter
  and McFarlane, Leslie
  and Stanley, George Edward
  and Stratemeyer, Edward L.
Dixon, Jeanne 1936- 31
Dixon, Paige
  See Corcoran, Barbara (Asenath)
Dixon, Peter L(ee) 1931- 6
Dixon, Rachel 1952- 74
Djoleto, (Solomon Alexander) Amu 1929- ... 80
d'lacey, Chris 1949- 165
Doak, Annie
  See Dillard, Annie
Doane, Pelagie 1906-1966 7
Dob, Bob 207
Dobell, I(sabel) M(arian) B(arclay)
  1909-1998 11
Dobie, J(ames) Frank 1888-1964 43
Dobkin, Alexander 1908-1975
  Obituary 30
Dobler, Lavinia G. 1910- 6
Dobrin, Arnold 1928- 4
Dobson, Jill 1969- 140
Dobson, Julia 1941- 48
Dobson, Mary 1954- 117
DoCampo, Valeria 1976- 217
Docherty, James
  See Docherty, Jimmy
Docherty, Jimmy 1976- 204
Dockery, Wallene T. 1941- 27
Dockray, Tracy 1962- 139
Dockrey, Karen 1955- 103
Doctor, Bernard
  See Doctor, Bernard Aquina
Doctor, Bernard Aquina 1950- 81
Doctor X
  See Nourse, Alan E(dward)
Dodd, Ed(ward Benton) 1902-1991 4
  Obituary 68
Dodd, Emma 1969- 203
Dodd, Lynley (Stuart) 1941- 132
  Earlier sketches in SATA 35, 86
  See also CLR 62
Dodd, Marty 1921- 142
Dodd, Quentin 1972- 137
Dodds, Bill 1952- 78
Dodds, Dayle Ann 1952- 201
  Earlier sketches in SATA 75, 150
Doder, Josh 1968- 187
Dodge, Bertha S(anford) 1902-1995 8
Dodge, Fremont
  See Grimes, Lee
Dodge, Gil
  See Hano, Arnold
Dodge, Mary (Elizabeth) Mapes
  1831(?)-1905 100
  Earlier sketch in SATA 21
  See also CLR 62
Dodgson, Charles Lutwidge
  See Carroll, Lewis
Dodson, Kenneth MacKenzie 1907-1999 11
Dodson, Susan 1941- 50
  Brief entry 40
Doerrfeld, Cori 1964- 214
Dogar, Sharon 1962- 211
Dogyear, Drew
  See Gorey, Edward (St. John)
Doherty, Berlie 1943- 111
  Earlier sketch in SATA 72
  See also CLR 21
  See also SAAS 16
Doherty, Charles Hugh 1913- 6
Doherty, Craig A. 1951- 169
  Earlier sketch in SATA 83
Doherty, Katherine M(ann) 1951- 83
Doherty, Kieran 1945- 164
Dokas, Dara 1968- 216

Dokey, Cameron 1956- 97
Dolan, Edward F(rancis), Jr. 1924- 94
  Brief entry 31
  Earlier sketch in SATA 45
Dolan, Ellen M(eara) 1929-1998 88
Dolan, Sean J. 1958- 74
Dolce, J. Ellen 1948- 75
Dolch, Edward William 1889-1961 50
Dolch, Marguerite Pierce 1891-1978 50
Dollar, Diane (Hills) 1933- 57
Dolson, Hildegarde
  See Lockridge, Hildegarde (Dolson)
Domanska, Janina 1913(?)-1995 68
  Obituary 84
  Earlier sketch in SATA 6
  See also CLR 40
  See also SAAS 18
Dominguez, Angel 1953- 76
Domino, John
  See Averill, Esther (Holden)
Domjan, Joseph (Spiri) 1907-1992 25
Domm, Jeffrey C. 1958- 84
Donahue, Dorothy 178
Donald, Rhonda Lucas 1962- 147
Donalds, Gordon
  See Shirreffs, Gordon D(onald)
Donaldson, Bryna
  See Stevens, Bryna
Donaldson, Gordon 1913-1993 64
  Obituary 76
Donaldson, Joan 1953- 78
Donaldson, Julia 1948- 180
  Earlier sketches in SATA 82, 132
Donaldson, Stephen R. 1947- 121
Donaldson, Stephen Reeder
  See Donaldson, Stephen R.
Doner, Kim 1955- 208
  Earlier sketch in SATA 91
Doney, Todd L. W. 1959- 104
Dong-Sung, Kim 1970- 195
Dong-Sung Kim
  See Dong-Sung, Kim
Donkin, Nance (Clare) 1915- 95
Donna, Natalie 1934-1979 9
Donnelly, Elfie 1950-
  See CLR 104
Donnelly, Jennifer 1963- 154
Donnelly, Matt 1972- 148
Donnio, Sylviane 188
Donofrio, Beverly 1950- 209
Donoghue, Emma 1969- 101
Donohue, Moira Rose 1954- 201
Donoughue, Carol 1935- 139
Donovan, Frank (Robert) 1906-1975
  Obituary 30
Donovan, Gail 1962- 217
Donovan, John 1928-1992 72
  Brief entry 29
  See also CLR 3
Donovan, Mary Lee 1961- 86
Donovan, William
  See Berkebile, Fred D(onovan)
Donze, Mary Terese 1911- 89
Doob, Leonard W(illiam) 1909-2000 8
Dooley, Norah 1953- 74
Dooling, Michael 1958- 105
Dor, Ana
  See Ceder, Georgiana Dorcas
Doran, Colleen 1963- 211
Dore, (Louis Christophe Paul) Gustave
  1832-1883 19
Doremus, Robert 1913- 30
Doren, Marion (Walker) 1928- 57
Dorenkamp, Michelle 1957- 89
Dorflinger, Carolyn 1953- 91
Dorfman, Joaquin 1979- 180
Dorfman, Joaquin Emiliano
  See Dorfman, Joaquin
Dorian, Edith M(cEwen) 1900-1983 5
Dorian, Harry
  See Hamilton, Charles (Harold St. John)

Dorian, Marguerite 7
Dorin, Patrick C(arberry) 1939- 59
  Brief entry 52
Dorman, Brandon 194
Dorman, Michael 1932- 7
Dorman, N. B. 1927- 39
Dormer, Frank W. 200
Dorris, Michael 1945-1997 75
  Obituary 94
  See also CLR 58
Dorris, Michael A.
  See Dorris, Michael
Dorris, Michael Anthony
  See Dorris, Michael
Dorritt, Susan
  See Schlein, Miriam
Dorros, Alex 1991- 194
Dorros, Arthur 1950- 168
  Earlier sketches in SATA 78, 122
  See also CLR 42
  See also SAAS 20
Dorros, Arthur M.
  See Dorros, Arthur
Dorson, Richard M(ercer) 1916-1981 30
Doss, Helen (Grigsby) 1918- 20
Doss, Margot Patterson 6
dos Santos, Joyce Audy 1949- 57
  Brief entry 42
Dothers, Anne
  See Chess, Victoria (Dickerson)
Dotlich, Rebecca Kai 1951- 182
Dottig
  See Grider, Dorothy
Dotts, Maryann J. 1933- 35
Doty, Jean Slaughter 1929- 28
Doty, Roy 1922- 28
Doubtfire, Dianne (Abrams) 1918- 29
Doucet, Sharon Arms 1951- 144
  Autobiography Feature 144
  Earlier sketch in SATA 125
Dougherty, Charles 1922- 18
Dougherty, Terri (L.) 1964- 146
Doughty, Rebecca 1955- 174
Douglas, Blaise 1960- 101
Douglas, Carole Nelson 1944- 73
Douglas, Garry
  See Kilworth, Garry
Douglas, James McM.
  See Griffin, W.E.B.
Douglas, Kathryn
  See Ewing, Kathryn
Douglas, Leonard
  See Bradbury, Ray
Douglas, Lola
  See Zeises, Lara M.
Douglas, Marjory Stoneman 1890-1998 10
Douglas, Michael
  See Bright, Robert Sr.)
Douglas, Michael
  See Crichton, Michael
Douglas, Shirley Stewart
  See Tepper, Sheri S.
Douglass, Barbara 1930- 40
Douglass, Frederick 1817(?)-1895 29
Douglass, Keith
  See Cunningham, Chet
Douty, Esther M(orris) 1909-1978 8
  Obituary 23
Dow, Emily R. 1904-1987 10
Dow, Vicki
  See McVey, Vicki
Dowd, John David 1945- 78
Dowd, Siobhan 1960-2007 204
Dowdell, Dorothy (Florence) Karns 1910- ... 12
Dowden, Anne Ophelia Todd 1907-2007 7
  Obituary 180
  See also SAAS 10
Dowdey, Landon Gerald 1923- 11
Dowdy, Mrs. Regera
  See Gorey, Edward (St. John)

Dowell, Frances O'Roark 1964- 205
  Earlier sketch in SATA *157*
Dower, Laura 1967- 185
Dowling, Terry 1947- 101
Downard, Barry 1956- 202
Downer, Ann 1960- 155
Downer, Marion 1892(?)-1971 25
Downes, Belinda 1962- 180
Downey, Fairfax D(avis) 1893-1990 3
  Obituary 66
Downey, Lisa 214
Downey, Lynn 1961- 185
Downham, Jenny 1964- 192
Downie, John 1931- 87
Downie, Mary Alice 1934- 171
  Earlier sketches in SATA *13, 87*
Downie, Mary Alice Dawe
  See Downie, Mary Alice
Downing, David A(lmon) 1958- 84
Downing, Johnette 184
Downing, Julie 1956- 148
  Earlier sketch in SATA *81*
Downing, Paula E. 1951- 80
Downing, Warwick
  See Downing, Wick
Downing, Wick 1931- 138
Dowswell, Paul 1957- 184
Doyle, A. Conan
  See Doyle, Sir Arthur Conan
Doyle, Sir Arthur Conan 1859-1930 24
  See also CLR *106*
Doyle, Brian 1935- 156
  Earlier sketches in SATA *67, 104*
  See also CLR *22*
  See also SAAS *16*
Doyle, Charlotte 1937- 178
  Earlier sketch in SATA *94*
Doyle, Charlotte Lackner
  See Doyle, Charlotte
Doyle, Conan
  See Doyle, Sir Arthur Conan
Doyle, Debra 1952- 165
  Earlier sketch in SATA *105*
Doyle, Donovan
  See Boegehold, Betty (Doyle)
Doyle, John
  See Graves, Robert
Doyle, Malachy 1954- 165
  Earlier sketch in SATA *120*
  See also CLR *83*
Doyle, Richard 1824-1883 21
Doyle, Sir A. Conan
  See Doyle, Sir Arthur Conan
Dr. A
  See Asimov, Isaac
  and Silverstein, Alvin
  and Silverstein, Virginia B.
Dr. Alphabet
  See Morice, Dave
Dr. Fred
  See Bortz, Alfred B(enjamin)
Dr. Laura
  See Schlessinger, Laura (Catherine)
Dr. Seuss 1904-1991 100
  Obituary 67
  Earlier sketches in SATA *1, 28, 75*
  See also CLR *100*
Dr. Zed
  See Penrose, Gordon
Drabble, Margaret 1939- 48
Drackett, Phil(ip Arthur) 1922- 53
Draco, F.
  See Davis, Julia
Dracup, Angela 1943- 74
Dragisic, Patricia 116
Dragonwagon, Crescent 1952- 186
  Autobiography Feature 186
  Earlier sketches in SATA *11, 41, 75, 133*
  See also SAAS *14*
Drake, David 1945- 85

Drake, David Allen
  See Drake, David
Drake, Frank
  See Hamilton, Charles (Harold St. John)
Drake, Jane 1954- 82
Drake, Salamanda
  See Barlow, Steve
Drakeford, Dale B 1952- 113
Drakeford, Dale Benjamin
  See Drakeford, Dale B
Draper, Hastings
  See Jeffries, Roderic
Draper, Sharon
  See Draper, Sharon M.
Draper, Sharon M. 1948- 195
  Autobiography Feature 146
  Earlier sketches in SATA *98, 146*
  See also CLR *57*
Draper, Sharon Mills
  See Draper, Sharon M.
Drapier, M. B.
  See Swift, Jonathan
Drawson, Blair 1943- 126
  Earlier sketch in SATA *17*
Dray, Matt 1967- 177
Dray, Matthew Frederick
  See Dray, Matt
Dresang, Eliza (Carolyn Timberlake) 1941- . 19
Drescher, Henrik 1955- 172
  Earlier sketches in SATA *67, 105*
  See also CLR *20*
Drescher, Joan E(lizabeth) 1939- 137
  Earlier sketch in SATA *30*
Dressen-McQueen, Stacey 191
Dreves, Veronica R. 1927-1986
  Obituary 50
Drew, Patricia 1938- 15
Drew, Patricia Mary
  See Drew, Patricia
Drewery, Mary 1918- 6
Drewery, Melanie 1970- 165
Drewry, Henry N(athaniel) 1924- 138
Dreyer, Ellen 177
Drial, J. E.
  See Laird, Jean E(louise)
Drimmer, Frederick 1916-2000 60
  Obituary 124
Driskill, J. Lawrence 1920- 90
Driskill, Larry
  See Driskill, J. Lawrence
Driving Hawk, Virginia
  See Sneve, Virginia Driving Hawk
Dron, Laura
  See Matthews, L. S.
Dronzek, Laura 199
Drucker, Malka 1945- 214
  Brief entry 29
  Earlier sketches in SATA *39, 111*
Drucker, Olga Levy 1927- 79
Druitt, Tobias
  See Purkiss, Diane
Drummond, Allan 1957- 209
Drummond, V(iolet) H(ilda) 1911-2000 6
Drummond, Walter
  See Silverberg, Robert
Drury, Clare Marie
  See Hoskyns-Abrahall, Clare (Constance
  Drury)
Drury, Roger W(olcott) 1914-1996 15
Druse, Eleanor
  See King, Stephen
Dryden, Pamela
  See St. John, Nicole
D.T., Hughes
  See Hughes, Dean
Duane, Diane (Elizabeth) 1952- 145
  Brief entry 46
  Earlier sketches in SATA *58, 95*
Dubanevich, Arlene 1950- 56
Dubelaar, Thea 1947- 60
Dubin, Jill 205

du Blane, Daphne
  See Groom, Arthur William
Duble, Kathleen Benner 1958- 164
Dubois, Claude K. 1960- 196
DuBois, Rochelle Holt 1946- 41
Du Bois, Shirley Graham 1907(?)-1977 24
  See Graham, Shirley
Du Bois, W. E. B. 1868-1963 42
Du Bois, William Edward Burghardt
  See Du Bois, W. E. B.
du Bois, William Pene
  See Pene du Bois, William (Sherman)
Duboise, Novella 1911-1999 88
Dubosarsky, Ursula 1961- 193
  Earlier sketches in SATA *107, 147*
DuBose, LaRocque (Russ) 1926- 2
Dubrovin, Vivian 1931- 139
  Earlier sketch in SATA *65*
DuBurke, Randy 172
Ducey, Jean Sparks 1915- 93
Duchacek, Ivo D(uka) 1913-1988
  Obituary 55
Du Chaillu, Paul (Belloni) 1835(?)-1903 26
Ducharme, Dede Fox
  See Ducharme, Lilian Fox
Ducharme, Lilian Fox 1950- 122
Ducornet, Erica 1943- 7
Ducornet, Rikki
  See Ducornet, Erica
Duden, Jane 1947- 136
Duder, Tessa 1940- 117
  Earlier sketch in SATA *80*
  See also CLR *43*
  See also SAAS *23*
Dudley, Helen
  See Hope Simpson, Jacynth
Dudley, Martha Ward 1909(?)-1985
  Obituary 45
Dudley, Nancy
  See Cole, Lois Dwight
Dudley, Robert
  See Baldwin, James
Dudley, Ruth H(ubbell) 1905-2001 11
Dudley-Smith, T.
  See Trevor, Elleston
Due, Linnea A. 1948- 64
Dueck, Adele 1955- 97
Dueland, Joy V(ivian) 27
Duerr, Gisela 1968- 89
Duey, Kathleen 1950- 199
  Earlier sketch in SATA *132*
Dufault, Joseph Ernest Nephtali
  See James, Will(iam Roderick)
Duff, Annis (James) 1904(?)-1986
  Obituary 49
Duff, Maggie
  See Duff, Margaret K(app)
Duff, Margaret K(app) 1916-2003 37
  Obituary 144
Duffey, Betsy (Byars) 1953- 131
  Earlier sketch in SATA *80*
Duffie, Charles 1960- 144
Duffield, Katy S. 1961- 147
Duffy, Carol Ann 1955- 165
  Earlier sketch in SATA *95*
Duffy Stone, Heather 217
Dugan, Jack
  See Griffin, W.E.B.
Dugan, John Kevin
  See Griffin, W.E.B.
Dugan, Karen 202
Dugan, Karen M.
  See Dugan, Karen
Dugan, Michael (Gray) 1947- 15
Duggan, Alfred Leo 1903-1964 25
Duggan, Maurice 1922-1974 40
  Obituary 30
Duggan, Maurice Noel
  See Duggan, Maurice
Dugger, Elizabeth L.
  See Kanell, Beth

Duggleby, John 1952- 94
Dugin, Andrej 1955- 77
Dugina, Olga 1964- 77
du Jardin, Rosamond Neal 1902-1963 2
Duka, Ivo
　See Duchacek, Ivo D(uka)
Duke, Kate 1956- 192
　Earlier sketches in SATA *90, 148*
　See also CLR *51*
Duke, Will
　See Gault, William Campbell
Dulac, Edmund 1882-1953 19
Dumas, Alexandre (pere) 1802-1870 18
　See also CLR *134*
Dumas, Jacqueline 1946- 55
Dumas, Philippe 1940- 119
　Earlier sketch in SATA *52*
du Maurier, Daphne 1907-1989 27
　Obituary 60
Dumbleton, Mike 1948- 206
　Earlier sketches in SATA *73, 124*
Dunbar, Fiona 1961- 167
Dunbar, Joyce 1944- 213
　Earlier sketches in SATA *76, 112, 162*
Dunbar, Paul Laurence 1872-1906 34
Dunbar, Polly 1980(?)- 211
　Earlier sketch in SATA *181*
Dunbar, Robert E(verett) 1926- 32
Duncan, Alexandra
　See Moore, Ishbel (Lindsay)
Duncan, Alice Faye 1967- 168
　Earlier sketch in SATA *95*
Duncan, Gregory
　See McClintock, Marshall
Duncan, Jane
　See Cameron, Elizabeth Jane
Duncan, Julia K.
　See Benson, Mildred
Duncan, Lois 1934- 141
　Autobiography Feature 141
　Earlier sketches in SATA *1, 36, 75, 133*
　See also CLR *129*
　See also SAAS *2*
Duncan, Norman 1871-1916
　See YABC *1*
Duncan, Terence
　See Nolan, William F.
Duncombe, Frances (Riker) 1900-1994 25
　Obituary 82
Dungy, Anthony
　See Dungy, Tony
Dungy, Tony 1955- 206
Dunham, Montrew 1919- 162
Dunham, Montrew Goetz
　See Dunham, Montrew
Dunkle, Clare B. 1964- 155
Dunlap, Julie 1958- 84
Dunleavy, Deborah 1951- 133
Dunlop, Agnes M. R. (?)-1982 87
Dunlop, Eileen (Rhona) 1938- 76
　Earlier sketch in SATA *24*
　See also SAAS *12*
Dunmore, Helen 1952- 201
Dunn, Anne M. 1940- 107
Dunn, Carolyn 1965- 208
Dunn, Harvey T(homas) 1884-1952 34
Dunn, Herb
　See Gutman, Dan
Dunn, John M. (III) 1949- 93
Dunn, Judy
　See Spangenberg, Judith Dunn
Dunn, Mary Lois 1930- 6
Dunnahoo, Terry Janson 1927- 7
Dunne, Jeanette 1952- 72
Dunne, Kathleen 1933- 126
Dunne, Marie
　See Clark, Ann Nolan
Dunne, Mary Collins 1914- 11
Dunne, Mary Jo
　See Dunne, Mary Collins

Dunnett, Kaitlyn
　See Emerson, Kathy Lynn
Dunnett, Margaret (Rosalind) 1909-1977 42
Dunnick, Regan 178
Dunrea, Olivier 1953- 160
　Brief entry 46
　Earlier sketches in SATA *59, 118*
Dunrea, Olivier Jean-Paul Dominique
　See Dunrea, Olivier
Dunton, Dorothy 1912- 92
Dupasquier, Philippe 1955- 151
　Earlier sketch in SATA *86*
duPont, Lindsay 207
duPont, Lindsay Harper
　See duPont, Lindsay
DuPrau, Jeanne 1944- 215
　Earlier sketch in SATA *144*
Dupuy, T(revor) N(evitt) 1916-1995 4
　Obituary 86
DuQuette, Keith 1960- 155
　Earlier sketch in SATA *90*
Duran, Gloria 1924- 171
Duran, Gloria Bradley
　See Duran, Gloria
Duranceau, Suzanne 1952- 162
Durand, Delphine 1971- 200
Durand, Hallie 1964(?)- 216
Durango, Julia 1967- 215
　Earlier sketch in SATA *173*
Durant, Alan 1958- 214
　Earlier sketches in SATA *121, 165*
Durant, John 1902- 27
Durbin, William 1951- 174
　Earlier sketch in SATA *143*
Durell, Ann 1930- 66
Durkee, Sarah 173
Durney, Ryan 205
Durrant, Lynda 1954- 212
　Earlier sketches in SATA *96, 148*
Durrant, Sabine 210
Durrell, Gerald (Malcolm) 1925-1995 8
　Obituary 84
Durrell, Julie 1955- 94
Durrett, Deanne 1940- 144
　Earlier sketch in SATA *92*
Durst, Sarah Beth 1974- 203
Du Soe, Robert C. 1892-1958
　See YABC *2*
Dussling, Jennifer 1970- 143
　Earlier sketch in SATA *96*
DuTemple, Lesley A. 1952- 113
Dutton, Sandra 191
Dutz
　See Davis, Mary Octavia
Duval, Katherine
　See James, Elizabeth
Duval, Kathy 1946- 181
Duvall, Aimee
　See Thurlo, Aimee
　and Thurlo, David
Duvall, Evelyn Millis 1906- 9
Duvall, Jill D. 1932- 102
Duvall, Jill Donovan
　See Duvall, Jill D.
Duvoisin, Roger (Antoine) 1904-1980 30
　Obituary 23
　Earlier sketch in SATA *2*
　See also CLR *23*
Dwiggins, Don(ald J.) 1913-1988 4
　Obituary 60
Dwight, Allan
　See Cole, Lois Dwight
Dwyer, Deanna
　See Koontz, Dean
Dwyer, K.R.
　See Koontz, Dean
Dyck, Peter J. 1914- 75
Dyer, James (Frederick) 1934- 37
Dyer, Jane 191
　Earlier sketch in SATA *147*
Dyer, Sarah 1978- 212

Dyer, Sarah L.
　See Dyer, Sarah
Dyess, John (Foster) 1939- 76
Dygard, Thomas J. 1931-1996 97
　Obituary 92
　Earlier sketch in SATA *24*
　See also SAAS *15*
Dyke, John 1935- 35

E

E. V. L.
　See Lucas, E(dward) V(errall)
Eagar, Frances (Elisabeth Stuart)
　1940-1978 11
　Obituary 55
Eager, Edward (McMaken) 1911-1964 17
　See also CLR *43*
Eager, George 1921- 56
Eager, George B.
　See Eager, George
Eagle, Ellen 1953- 61
Eagle, Kin
　See Adlerman, Daniel (Ezra)
　and Adlerman, Kimberly M(arie)
Eagle, Mike 1942- 11
Earle, Olive L(ydia) 1888-1982 7
Earle, William
　See Johns, W(illiam) E(arle)
Earls, Nick 1963- 156
　Earlier sketch in SATA *95*
Early, Jack
　See Scoppettone, Sandra
Early, Jon
　See Johns, W(illiam) E(arle)
Early, Margaret 1951- 72
Earnshaw, Brian 1929- 17
Earnshaw, Micky 1939- 88
Earnshaw, Spencer Wright
　See Earnshaw, Micky
Easley, MaryAnn 94
Eason, Alethea 1957- 197
Eastman, Charles A(lexander) 1858-1939
　See YABC *1*
Eastman, P(hilip) D(ey) 1909-1986 33
　Obituary 46
Easton, Kelly 1960- 192
　Earlier sketch in SATA *141*
Eastwick, Ivy (Ethel) O(live) 3
Eaton, Anne T(haxter) 1881-1971 32
Eaton, Anthony 1971- 167
Eaton, George L.
　See Verral, Charles Spain
Eaton, Janet
　See Givens, Janet E(aton)
Eaton, Jeanette 1886-1968 24
Eaton, Maxwell III 1981- 199
Eaton, Tom 1940- 22
Ebbeler, Jeff
　See Ebbeler, Jeffrey
Ebbeler, Jeffrey 1974- 206
Ebel, Alex 1927- 11
Eber, Dorothy (Margaret) Harley 1930- 27
Eberhart, Sheri S.
　See Tepper, Sheri S.
Eberle, Irmengarde 1898-1979 2
　Obituary 23
Eble, Diane 1956- 74
Eboch, Chris 113
Eccles Williams, Ferelith 1920- 22
Echeverria-Bis, Olivia 217
Echeverria Gyorkos, Charmaine 216
Echlin, Kim 1955- 166
Eckblad, Edith Berven 1923- 23
Ecke, Wolfgang 1927-1983
　Obituary 37

Author Index

Eckert, Allan W. 1931- *91*
  Brief entry *27*
  Earlier sketch in SATA *29*
  See also SAAS *21*
Eckert, Horst 1931- *72*
  Earlier sketch in SATA *8*
  See also CLR *26*
Ecklar, Julia (Marie) 1964- *112*
Eddings, David 1931-2009 .... *91*
Eddings, David Carroll
  See Eddings, David
Ede, Janina 1937- *33*
Edell, Celeste *12*
Edelman, Lily (Judith) 1915-1981 .... *22*
Edelson, Edward 1932- *51*
Edens, Cooper 1945- *166*
  Earlier sketches in SATA *49, 112*
Edens, (Bishop) David 1926- *39*
Edey, Maitland A(rmstrong) 1910-1992 .... *25*
  Obituary *71*
Edgerton, Perky *196*
Edgeworth, Maria 1768-1849 .... *21*
  See also CLR *153*
Edgson, Alison *211*
Edgy, Wardore
  See Gorey, Edward (St. John)
Edison, Theodore
  See Stratemeyer, Edward L.
Edler, Tim(othy) 1948- *56*
Edmiston, Jim 1948- *80*
Edmonds, I(vy) G(ordon) 1917- *8*
Edmonds, Walter D(umaux) 1903-1998 .... *27*
  Obituary *99*
  Earlier sketch in SATA *1*
  See also SAAS *4*
Edmund, Sean
  See Pringle, Laurence
Edsall, Marian (Stickney) 1920- *8*
Edwards, Al
  See Nourse, Alan E(dward)
Edwards, Anne 1927- *35*
Edwards, Audrey 1947- *52*
  Brief entry *31*
Edwards, Becky (Jane) 1966- *125*
Edwards, Bertram
  See Edwards, Herbert Charles
Edwards, Bronwen Elizabeth
  See Rose, Wendy
Edwards, Cecile Pepin 1916- *25*
Edwards, David 1962- *198*
Edwards, Dorothy 1914-1982 .... *88*
  Obituary *31*
  Earlier sketch in SATA *4*
Edwards, F. E.
  See Nolan, William F.
Edwards, Frank B. 1952- *93*
Edwards, Gunvor *32*
Edwards, Harvey 1929- *5*
Edwards, Hazel (Eileen) 1945- *135*
Edwards, Herbert Charles 1912- *12*
Edwards, Jane Campbell 1932- *10*
Edwards, Julia
  See Stratemeyer, Edward L.
Edwards, Julie
  See Andrews, Julie
Edwards, Julie Andrews
  See Andrews, Julie
Edwards, June
  See Bhatia, Jamunadevi
Edwards, Linda Strauss 1948- *49*
  Brief entry *42*
Edwards, Margaret (Alexander) 1902-1988
  Obituary *56*
Edwards, Michelle 1955- *152*
  Earlier sketch in SATA *70*
Edwards, Monica le Doux Newton
  1912-1998 .... *12*
Edwards, Olwen
  See Gater, Dilys
Edwards, Page (Lawrence, Jr.) 1941-1999 ... *59*
Edwards, Pamela Duncan *189*

Edwards, R. T.
  See Goulart, Ron
Edwards, Sally (Cary) 1929- *7*
Edwards, Samuel
  See Gerson, Noel Bertram
Edwards, Wallace 1957(?)- *170*
Eeckhout, Emmanuelle 1976- *208*
Egan, E. W. 1922- *35*
Egan, Edward Welstead
  See Egan, E. W.
Egan, Kerry *175*
Egan, Lorraine Hopping 1960- *134*
  Earlier sketch in SATA *91*
Egan, Tim 1957- *191*
  Earlier sketches in SATA *89, 155*
Egermeier, Elsie E(milie) 1890-1986 .... *65*
Eggenberger, David 1918- *6*
Eggleston, Edward 1837-1902 .... *27*
Egielski, Richard 1952- *163*
  Earlier sketches in SATA *11, 49, 106*
Egypt, Ophelia Settle 1903-1984 .... *16*
  Obituary *38*
Ehlert, Lois 1934- *172*
  Earlier sketches in SATA *35, 69, 128*
  See also CLR *28*
Ehlert, Lois Jane
  See Ehlert, Lois
Ehling, Katalin Olah 1941- *93*
Ehrenfreund, Norbert 1921- *86*
Ehrenhaft, Daniel 1970- *185*
Ehrenhaft, Daniel Parker
  See Ehrenhaft, Daniel
Ehrhardt, Karen 1963- *184*
Ehrlich, Amy 1942- *217*
  Earlier sketches in SATA *25, 65, 96, 132*
Ehrlich, Bettina Bauer 1903-1985 .... *1*
Ehrlich, Fred *205*
Ehrlich, Fred M.D.
  See Ehrlich, Fred
Ehrlich, H. M.
  See Ziefert, Harriet
Eichenberg, Fritz 1901-1990 .... *50*
  Earlier sketch in SATA *9*
Eichler, Margrit 1942- *35*
Eichner, James A. 1927- *4*
Eidson, Thomas 1944- *112*
Eifert, Virginia (Louise) S(nider) 1911-1966 . *2*
Eige, (Elizabeth) Lillian 1915- *65*
Eiken, J. Melia 1967- *125*
Einhorn, Edward 1970- *204*
Einsel, Naiad *10*
Einsel, Walter 1926- *10*
Einzig, Susan 1922- *43*
Eiseman, Alberta 1925- *15*
Eisenberg, Azriel (Louis) 1903-1985 .... *12*
Eisenberg, Lisa 1949- *155*
  Brief entry *50*
  Earlier sketch in SATA *57*
Eisenberg, Phyllis Rose 1924- *41*
Eisner, Vivienne
  See Margolis, Vivienne
Eisner, Will 1917-2005 .... *165*
  Earlier sketch in SATA *31*
Eisner, William Erwin
  See Eisner, Will
Eitzen, Allan 1928- *9*
Eitzen, Ruth (Carper) 1924- *9*
Ekwensi, C. O. D.
  See Ekwensi, Cyprian
Ekwensi, Cyprian 1921-2007 .... *66*
Ekwensi, Cyprian Odiatu Duaka
  See Ekwensi, Cyprian
Elam, Richard M(ace, Jr.) 1920- *9*
Elborn, Andrew
  See Clements, Andrew
  and Clements, Andrew
Elboz, Stephen 1956- *152*
Eldin, Peter 1939- *154*
Eldon, Kathy 1946- *107*
Eldridge, Marion *199*
Elfman, Blossom 1925- *8*

Elgin, Kathleen 1923- *39*
Elia
  See Lamb, Charles
Eliot, A. D.
  See Jewett, Sarah Orne
Eliot, Alice
  See Jewett, Sarah Orne
Eliot, Anne
  See Cole, Lois Dwight
Eliot, Dan
  See Silverberg, Robert
Elish, Dan 1960- *204*
  Earlier sketches in SATA *68, 129*
Elisha, Ron 1951- *104*
Elisofon, Eliot 1911-1973
  Obituary *21*
Elkeles, Simone 1970- *187*
Elkin, Benjamin 1911-1995 .... *3*
Elkins, Dov Peretz 1937- *5*
Ellacott, S(amuel) E(rnest) 1911- *19*
Elleman, Barbara 1934- *147*
Ellen, Jaye
  See Nixon, Joan Lowery
Eller, Scott
  See Holinger, William (Jacques)
  and Shepard, Jim
Ellery, Amanda *216*
Ellestad, Myrvin
  See Ellestad, Myrvin H.
Ellestad, Myrvin H. 1921- *120*
Elliot, Bruce
  See Field, Edward
Elliot, David 1952- *208*
  Earlier sketch in SATA *122*
Elliott, Bruce
  See Field, Edward
Elliott, David 1947- *201*
  Earlier sketch in SATA *163*
Elliott, Don
  See Silverberg, Robert
Elliott, Elizabeth Shippen Green
  See Green, Elizabeth Shippen
Elliott, Janice 1931-1995 .... *119*
Elliott, Joey
  See Houk, Randy
Elliott, Laura Malone 1957- *197*
Elliott, L.M.
  See Elliott, Laura Malone
Elliott, Louise *111*
Elliott, Mark 1949- *210*
Elliott, Odette 1939- *75*
Elliott, Patricia 1946- *176*
Elliott, Sarah M(cCarn) 1930- *14*
Elliott, (Robert) Scott 1970- *153*
Elliott, William
  See Bradbury, Ray
Elliott, Zetta *206*
Ellis, (Mary) Amabel (Nassau Strachey)
  Williams
  See Williams-Ellis, (Mary) Amabel (Nassau
  Strachey)
Ellis, Ann Dee *210*
Ellis, Anyon
  See Rowland-Entwistle, (Arthur) Theodore
  (Henry)
Ellis, Carson 1975- *190*
Ellis, Carson Friedman
  See Ellis, Carson
Ellis, Deborah 1960- *187*
  Earlier sketch in SATA *129*
Ellis, E. S.
  See Ellis, Edward S.
Ellis, Edward S. 1840-1916
  See YABC *1*
Ellis, Edward Sylvester
  See Ellis, Edward S.
Ellis, Ella Thorp 1928- *127*
  Earlier sketch in SATA *7*
  See also SAAS *9*
Ellis, Harry Bearse 1921-2004 .... *9*

Ellis, Herbert
  See Wilson, Lionel
Ellis, Mel(vin Richard) 1912-1984 7
  Obituary 39
Ellis, Richard 1938- 130
Ellis, Sarah 1952- 179
  Earlier sketches in SATA *68, 131*
  See also CLR *42*
Ellison, Chris 196
Ellison, Elizabeth Stow 1970- 209
Ellison, Emily 114
Ellison, Lucile Watkins 1907(?)-1979 50
  Obituary 22
Ellison, Virginia H(owell) 1910- 4
Ellsberg, Edward 1891-1983 7
Ellsworth, Loretta 1954- 199
Ellsworth, Mary Ellen (Tressel) 1940- 146
Ellwand, David 1965(?)- 213
Elmer, Robert 1958- 154
  Earlier sketch in SATA *99*
Elmore, (Carolyn) Patricia 1933- 38
  Brief entry 35
El-Moslimany, Ann P(axton) 1937- 90
Elschner, Geraldine 1954- 183
Elspeth
  See Bragdon, Elspeth MacDuffie
Elster, Jean Alicia 1953- 150
Elting, Mary 1906- 88
  Earlier sketch in SATA *2*
  See also SAAS *20*
Elvgren, Jennifer Riesmeyer 179
Elwart, Joan Potter 1927- 2
Elwood, Ann 1931- 55
  Brief entry 52
Elwood, Roger 1943-2007 58
Ely, Lesley 212
Elya, Susan Middleton 1955- 202
  Earlier sketches in SATA *106, 159*
Elzbieta 88
Ember, Kathi 190
Emberley, Barbara A. 1932- 146
  Earlier sketches in SATA *8, 70*
  See also CLR *5*
Emberley, Barbara Anne
  See Emberley, Barbara A.
Emberley, Ed 1931- 146
  Earlier sketches in SATA *8, 70*
  See also CLR *81*
Emberley, Edward Randolph
  See Emberley, Ed
Emberley, Michael 1960- 189
  Earlier sketches in SATA *34, 80, 119*
Embry, Margaret Jacob 1919-1975 5
Emecheta, Buchi 1944- 66
Emecheta, Florence Onye Buchi
  See Emecheta, Buchi
Emerson, Alice B.
  See Benson, Mildred
Emerson, Kathy Lynn 1947- 63
Emerson, Kevin 209
Emerson, Ru 1944- 107
  Earlier sketch in SATA *70*
Emerson, Sally 1952- 111
Emerson, William K(eith) 1925- 25
Emert, Phyllis R. 1947- 93
Emert, Phyllis Raybin
  See Emert, Phyllis R.
Emery, Anne (McGuigan) 1907- 33
  Earlier sketch in SATA *1*
Emmens, Carol Ann 1944- 39
Emmett, Jonathan 1965- 188
  Earlier sketch in SATA *138*
Emmons, Della (Florence) Gould 1890-1983
  Obituary 39
Emory, Jerry 1957- 96
Emrich, Duncan (Black Macdonald)
  1908-1970(?) 11
Emshwiller, Carol 1921- 174
  Autobiography Feature 174
Emshwiller, Carol Fries
  See Emshwiller, Carol

Emslie, M. L.
  See Simpson, Myrtle L(illias)
Ende, Michael (Andreas Helmuth)
  1929-1995 130
  Brief entry 42
  Obituary 86
  Earlier sketch in SATA *61*
  See also CLR *138*
Enderle, Dotti 1954- 203
  Earlier sketch in SATA *145*
Enderle, Judith (Ann) Ross 1941- 89
  Autobiography Feature 114
  Earlier sketch in SATA *38*
  See also SAAS *26*
Endle, Kate 207
Enell, Trinka (Gochenour) 1951- 79
Enfield, Carrie
  See Smith, Susan Vernon
Engdahl, Sylvia Louise 1933- 4
  Autobiography Feature 122
  See also CLR *2*
  See also SAAS *5*
Engel, Diana 1947- 70
Engelbreit, Mary 1952- 169
Engelhart, Margaret S. 1924- 59
Engelmann, Kim (V.) 1959- 87
England, George Allan 1877-1936 102
Englart, Mindi Rose 1965- 146
Engle, Eloise
  See Paananen, Eloise (Katherine)
Engle, Margarita 1951- 193
Englebert, Victor 1933- 8
English, James W(ilson) 1915- 37
English, Karen 202
Engstrom, Elizabeth 1951- 110
Enright, D(ennis) J(oseph) 1920-2002 25
  Obituary 140
Enright, Dominique 194
Enright, Elizabeth (Wright) 1909-1968 9
  See also CLR *4*
Ensor, Barbara 180
Ensor, Robert (T.) 1922- 93
Enthoven, Sam 1974- 187
Entwistle, (Arthur) Theodore (Henry) Rowland
  See Rowland-Entwistle, (Arthur) Theodore
  (Henry)
Enys, Sarah L.
  See Sloggett, Nellie
Epanya, Christian A(rthur Kingue) 1956- 91
Ephraim, Shelly S(chonebaum) 1952- 97
Ephron, Delia 1944- 197
  Brief entry 50
  Earlier sketch in SATA *65*
Epler, Doris M. 1928- 73
Epp, Margaret A(gnes) 1913- 20
Eppenstein, Louise (Kohn) 1892-1987
  Obituary 54
Epple, Anne Orth 1927- 20
Epstein, Anne Merrick 1931- 20
Epstein, Beryl 1910- 31
  Earlier sketch in SATA *1*
  See also CLR *26*
  See also SAAS *17*
Epstein, Beryl M. Williams
  See Epstein, Beryl
Epstein, Perle S(herry) 1938- 27
Epstein, Rachel S. 1941- 102
Epstein, Samuel 1909-2000 31
  Earlier sketch in SATA *1*
  See also CLR *26*
  See also SAAS *17*
Erdman, Loula Grace 1905(?)-1976 1
Erdoes, Richard 1912- 33
  Brief entry 28
Erdogan, Buket 187
Erdrich, Karen Louise
  See Erdrich, Louise
Erdrich, Louise 1954- 141
  Earlier sketch in SATA *94*
Erickson, Betty J. 1923- 97

Erickson, Betty Jean
  See Erickson, Betty J.
Erickson, John R. 1943- 136
  Earlier sketch in SATA *70*
Erickson, Jon 1948- 141
Erickson, Phoebe 59
Erickson, Russell E(verett) 1932- 27
Erickson, Sabra Rollins 1912-1995 35
Erickson, Walter
  See Fast, Howard
Ericson, Walter
  See Fast, Howard
Ericsson, Jennifer A. 170
Erikson, Mel 1937- 31
Eriksson, Eva 1949- 207
Ering, Timothy Basil 176
Erlanger, Baba
  See Trahey, Jane
Erlbach, Arlene 1948- 160
  Earlier sketches in SATA *78, 115*
Erlbruch, Wolf 1948- 181
Erlich, Lillian (Feldman) 1910-1983 10
Erlings, Fridrik 1962- 196
Erlingsson, Fri****rik
  See Erlings, Fridrik
Ermatinger, James W. 1959- 170
Ernest, William
  See Berkebile, Fred D(onovan)
Ernst, (Lyman) John 1940- 39
Ernst, Kathleen
  See Ernst, Kathleen A.
Ernst, Kathleen A. 1959- 162
Ernst, Kathryn (Fitzgerald) 1942- 25
Ernst, Lisa Campbell 1957- 212
  Brief entry 44
  Earlier sketches in SATA *55, 95, 154*
Erskine, Kathryn 193
Ervin, Janet Halliday 1923- 4
Erwin, Will
  See Eisner, Will
Esbaum, Jill 213
  Earlier sketch in SATA *174*
Esbensen, Barbara J(uster) 1925-1996 97
  Brief entry 53
  Earlier sketch in SATA *62*
Eschbacher, Roger 160
Eschmeyer, R. E. 1898-1989 29
Escriva, Vivi 182
Eseki, Bruno
  See Mphahlele, Es'kia
Esekie, Bruno
  See Mphahlele, Es'kia
Eshmeyer, Reinhart Ernst
  See Eschmeyer, R. E.
Eskridge, Ann E. 1949- 84
Espeland, Pamela (Lee) 1951- 128
  Brief entry 38
  Earlier sketch in SATA *52*
Espinosa, Laura 203
Espinosa, Leo 203
Espriella, Don Manuel Alvarez
  See Southey, Robert
Espy, Willard R(ichardson) 1910-1999 38
  Obituary 113
Essakalli, Julie Klear 200
Essrig, Harry 1912- 66
Estep, Irene Compton 5
Esterl, Arnica 1933- 77
Estes, Eleanor (Ruth) 1906-1988 91
  Obituary 56
  Earlier sketch in SATA *7*
  See also CLR *70*
Estoril, Jean
  See Allan, Mabel Esther
Estrada, Pau 1961- 200
  Earlier sketch in SATA *74*
Etchemendy, Nancy 1952- 166
  Earlier sketch in SATA *38*
Etchemendy, Nancy Elise Howell
  See Etchemendy, Nancy
Etchison, Birdie L(ee) 1937- 38

Etchison, Craig 1945- *133*
Etherington, Frank 1945- *58*
Eton, Robert
  See Meynell, Laurence Walter
Ets, Marie Hall 1893-1984 .... *2*
  See also CLR *33*
Ettlinger, Doris 1950- *173*
Eunson, (John) Dale 1904-2002 .... *5*
  Obituary *132*
Evan, Frances Y. 1951- *167*
Evanoff, Vlad 1916- *59*
Evans, Cambria 1981- *178*
Evans, Douglas 1953- *144*
  Earlier sketch in SATA *93*
Evans, Eva (Knox) 1905-1998 .... *27*
Evans, Freddi Williams 1957- *211*
  Earlier sketch in SATA *134*
Evans, Greg 1947- *143*
  Earlier sketch in SATA *73*
Evans, Hubert Reginald 1892-1986 .... *118*
  Obituary *48*
Evans, Katherine (Floyd) 1901-1964 .... *5*
Evans, Larry
  See Evans, Laurence Chubb
Evans, Laurence Chubb 1939- *88*
Evans, Lawrence Watt
  See Watt-Evans, Lawrence
Evans, Leslie 1953- *214*
Evans, Lezlie *180*
Evans, Mari 1923- *10*
Evans, Mark *19*
Evans, Nancy 1950- *65*
Evans, Nate *201*
Evans, Patricia Healy
  See Carpenter, Patricia (Healy Evans)
Evans, (Alice) Pearl 1927- *83*
Evans, Shane W. *189*
Evans, Shirlee 1931- *58*
Evans, Tabor
  See Cameron, Lou
  and Knott, William C(ecil, Jr.)
  and Wallmann, Jeffrey M(iner)
  and Whittington, Harry (Benjamin)
Evarts, Esther
  See Benson, Sally
Evarts, Hal G., (Jr.) 1915-1989 .... *6*
Everett, Gail
  See Hale, Arlene
Evernden, Margery 1916- *5*
Eversole, Robyn 1971- *74*
Eversole, Robyn H.
  See Eversole, Robyn
Eversole, Robyn Harbert
  See Eversole, Robyn
Evslin, Bernard 1922-1993 .... *83*
  Brief entry *28*
  Obituary *77*
  Earlier sketch in SATA *45*
Ewart, Claire 1958- *145*
  Earlier sketch in SATA *76*
Ewart, Franzeska G. 1950- *205*
Ewen, David 1907-1985 .... *4*
  Obituary *47*
Ewing, Juliana (Horatia Gatty) 1841-1885 ... *16*
  See also CLR *78*
Ewing, Kathryn 1921- *20*
Eyerly, Jeannette 1908-2008 .... *86*
  Obituary *196*
  Earlier sketch in SATA *4*
  See also SAAS *10*
Eyerly, Jeannette Hyde
  See Eyerly, Jeannette
Eyre, Dorothy
  See McGuire, Leslie (Sarah)
Eyre, Frank 1910-1988
  Obituary *62*
Eyre, Katherine Wigmore 1901-1970 .... *26*
Ezzell, Marilyn 1937- *42*
  Brief entry *38*

F

Fabe, Maxene 1943- *15*
Faber, Doris (Greenberg) 1924- *78*
  Earlier sketch in SATA *3*
Faber, Harold 1919-2010 .... *5*
Fabre, Jean Henri (Casimir) 1823-1915 ...... *22*
Fabry, Glenn 1961- *205*
Facklam, Margaret
  See Thomas, Peggy
Facklam, Margery (Metz) 1927- *132*
  Earlier sketches in SATA *20, 85*
Fadden, David Kanietakeron *196*
Fadiman, Clifton (Paul) 1904-1999 .... *11*
  Obituary *115*
Fagan, Cary 1957- *186*
Fahs, Sophia Blanche Lyon 1876-1978 ...... *102*
Failing, Barbara Larmon *182*
Fain, Sarah 1971- *204*
Fair, David 1952- *96*
Fair, Sylvia 1933- *13*
Fairfax-Lucy, Brian (Fulke Cameron-Ramsay)
  1898-1974 .... *6*
  Obituary *26*
Fairfield, Flora
  See Alcott, Louisa May
Fairlie, Gerard 1899-1983
  Obituary *34*
Fairman, Joan A(lexandra) 1935- *10*
Faithfull, Gail 1936- *8*
Falcone, L(ucy) M. 1951- *155*
Falconer, Ian 1959- *179*
  Earlier sketch in SATA *125*
  See also CLR *146*
Falconer, James
  See Kirkup, James
Falconer, Lee N.
  See May, Julian
Falkner, Brian 1962- *206*
Falkner, Leonard 1900-1977 .... *12*
Fall, Andrew
  See Arthur, Robert, (Jr.)
Fall, Thomas
  See Snow, Donald Clifford
Faller, Regis 1968- *187*
Falls, C(harles) B(uckles) 1874-1960 .... *38*
  Brief entry *27*
Falstein, Louis 1909-1995 .... *37*
Falwell, Cathryn 1952- *196*
Fancher, Lou 1960- *177*
Fanelli, Sara 1969- *126*
  Earlier sketch in SATA *89*
Fanning, Leonard M(ulliken) 1888-1967 ...... *5*
Fantaskey, Beth 1965- *217*
Faralla, Dana 1909- *9*
Faralla, Dorothy W.
  See Faralla, Dana
Farb, Peter 1929-1980 .... *12*
  Obituary *22*
Farber, Norma 1909-1984 .... *75*
  Obituary *38*
  Earlier sketch in SATA *25*
Fardell, John 1967- *195*
Fardell, John William
  See Fardell, John
Faria, Rosana *213*
Farish, Terry 1947- *146*
  Earlier sketch in SATA *82*
Farjeon, (Eve) Annabel 1919-2004 .... *11*
  Obituary *153*
Farjeon, Eleanor 1881-1965 .... *2*
  See also CLR *34*
Farley, Carol (J.) 1936- *137*
  Earlier sketch in SATA *4*
Farley, Terri *165*
Farley, Walter (Lorimer) 1915-1989 .... *132*
  Earlier sketches in SATA *2, 43*
Farlow, James O(rville, Jr.) 1951- *75*
Farmer, Jacqueline *210*
Farmer, Nancy 1941- *161*
  Earlier sketches in SATA *79, 117*

Farmer, Patti 1948- *79*
Farmer, Penelope (Jane) 1939- *105*
  Brief entry *39*
  Earlier sketch in SATA *40*
  See also CLR *8*
  See also SAAS *22*
Farmer, Peter 1950- *38*
Farmer, Philip Jose
  See Farmer, Philip Jose
Farmer, Philip Jose 1918-2009 .... *93*
  Obituary *201*
Farmer, Philipe Jos
  See Farmer, Philip Jose
Farnham, Burt
  See Clifford, Harold B(urton)
Farnsworth, Bill 1958- *186*
  Earlier sketches in SATA *84, 135*
Farooqi, Musharraf Ali 1968- *207*
Farquhar, Margaret C(utting) 1905-1988 ...... *13*
Farquharson, Alexander 1944- *46*
Farquharson, Martha
  See Finley, Martha
Farr, Diana *82*
  Earlier sketch in SATA *3*
Farr, Finis (King) 1904-1982 .... *10*
Farr, Richard 1960- *209*
Farrar, Jill
  See Morris, Jill
Farrar, Susan Clement 1917- *33*
Farrell, Ben
  See Cebulash, Mel
Farrell, John 1951- *204*
Farrell, Patrick
  See Odgers, Sally Farrell
Farrell, Sally
  See Odgers, Sally Farrell
Farrer, Vashti *167*
Farrington, Benjamin 1891-1974
  Obituary *20*
Farrington, S(elwyn) Kip, Jr. 1904-1983 ...... *20*
Farris, Christine King 1927- *206*
Farshtey, Greg(ory T.) 1965- *148*
Farthing, Alison 1936- *45*
  Brief entry *36*
Farthing-Knight, Catherine 1933- *92*
Fassler, Joan (Grace) 1931- *11*
Fast, Howard 1914-2003 .... *7*
  Autobiography Feature *107*
Fast, Howard Melvin
  See Fast, Howard
Fasulo, Michael 1963- *83*
Fatchen, Max 1920- *84*
  Earlier sketch in SATA *20*
  See also SAAS *20*
Fate, Marilyn
  See Collins, Paul
Father Goose
  See Ghigna, Charles
Fatigati, Evelyn 1948- *24*
Fatigati, Frances Evelyn
  See Fatigati, Evelyn
Fatio, Louise 1904-1993 .... *6*
Fatus, Sophie 1957- *182*
Faulhaber, Martha 1926- *7*
Faulkner, Anne Irvin 1906- *23*
Faulkner, Frank
  See Ellis, Edward S.
Faulkner, Nancy
  See Faulkner, Anne Irvin
Faulknor, Cliff(ord Vernon) 1913- *86*
Favole, Robert J(ames) 1950- *125*
Fax, Elton Clay 1909-1993 .... *25*
Faxon, Lavinia
  See Russ, Lavinia (Faxon)
Feagles, Anita M.
  See Feagles, Anita MacRae
Feagles, Anita MacRae 1927- *9*
Feagles, Elizabeth
  See Day, Beth (Feagles)
Feague, Mildred H. 1915- *14*

Fearnley, Jan 1965- 205
  Earlier sketch in SATA 153
Fearrington, Ann (Peyton) 1945- 146
Fecher, Constance
  See Heaven, Constance (Christina)
Feder, Chris Welles 1938- 81
Feder, Harriet K. 1928- 73
Feder, Paula (Kurzband) 1935- 26
Federici, Debbie 1965- 175
Federici, Debbie Tanner
  See Federici, Debbie
Feelings, Muriel 1938- 16
  See also CLR 5
  See also SAAS 8
Feelings, Muriel Lavita Grey
  See Feelings, Muriel
Feelings, Thomas 1933-2003 69
  Obituary 148
  Earlier sketch in SATA 8
  See also CLR 58
  See also SAAS 19
Feelings, Tom
  See Feelings, Thomas
Fehler, Gene 1940- 201
  Earlier sketch in SATA 74
Fehrenbach, T(heodore) R(eed, Jr.) 1925- 33
Feiffer, Jules 1929- 201
  Earlier sketches in SATA 8, 61, 111, 157
Feiffer, Jules Ralph
  See Feiffer, Jules
Feiffer, Kate 1964- 206
  Earlier sketch in SATA 170
Feig, Barbara Krane 1937- 34
Feikema, Feike
  See Manfred, Frederick (Feikema)
Feil, Hila 1942- 12
Feilen, John
  See May, Julian
Feinberg, Barbara Jane 1938- 123
  Earlier sketch in SATA 58
Feinberg, Barbara Silberdick
  See Feinberg, Barbara Jane
Feinstein, John 1956- 195
  Earlier sketch in SATA 163
Feldman, Anne (Rodgers) 1939- 19
Feldman, Elane 79
Feldman, Jody 200
Felin, M. Sindy 194
Felix
  See Vincent, Felix
Fell, Derek 1939- 167
Fell, Derek John
  See Fell, Derek
Fellowes, Julian 1950- 198
Fellows, Muriel H. 10
Fellows, Stan 1957- 177
Fellows, Stanley
  See Fellows, Stan
Felsen, Henry Gregor 1916-1995 1
  See also SAAS 2
Felstead, Cathie 1954- 192
Feltenstein, Arlene 1934- 119
Feltenstine, Arlene H.
  See Feltenstein, Arlene
Felton, Harold William 1902-1991 1
Felton, Ronald Oliver 1909- 3
Felts, Shirley 1934- 33
Felts, Susannah 1973- 214
Fenderson, Lewis H., Jr. 1907-1983 47
  Obituary 37
Fenner, Carol (Elizabeth) 1929-2002 89
  Obituary 132
  Earlier sketch in SATA 7
  See also SAAS 24
Fenner, Phyllis R(eid) 1899-1982 1
  Obituary 29
Fensham, Elizabeth 169
Fenten, Barbara D(oris) 1935- 26
Fenten, D(onald) X. 1932- 4
Fenton, Carroll Lane 1900-1969 5

Fenton, Edward 1917-1995 7
  Obituary 89
Fenton, Joe 213
Fenton, Mildred Adams 1899-1995 21
Fenwick, Patti
  See Grider, Dorothy
Feravolo, Rocco Vincent 1922- 10
Ferber, Brenda A. 1967- 184
Ferber, Edna 1887-1968 7
Fergus, Charles 114
Ferguson, Alane 1957- 182
  Earlier sketch in SATA 85
Ferguson, Bob
  See Ferguson, Robert Bruce
Ferguson, Cecil 1931- 45
Ferguson, Peter 1968- 199
Ferguson, Robert Bruce 1927-2001 13
Ferguson, Sarah 1959- 180
  Earlier sketches in SATA 66, 110
Ferguson, Sarah Margaret
  See Ferguson, Sarah
Ferguson, Walter (W.) 1930- 34
Fergusson, Erna 1888-1964 5
Fermi, Laura 1907-1977 6
  Obituary 28
Fern, Eugene A. 1919-1987 10
  Obituary 54
Fern, Tracey E. 202
Fernandes, Eugenie 1943- 205
  Earlier sketches in SATA 77, 139
Fernandez, Laura 1960- 171
Ferraiolo, Jack D. 208
Ferrari, Maria 123
Ferreiro, Carmen 1958- 158
Ferrell, Nancy Warren 1932- 70
Ferri, Giuliano 1965- 197
Ferrier, Lucy
  See Penzler, Otto
Ferris, Helen Josephine 1890-1969 21
Ferris, James Cody
  See McFarlane, Leslie
Ferris, Jean 1939- 202
  Brief entry 50
  Earlier sketches in SATA 56, 105, 149
Ferris, Jeri Chase 1937- 84
Ferry, Charles 1927- 92
  Earlier sketch in SATA 43
  See also CLR 34
  See also SAAS 20
Fetz, Ingrid 1915- 30
Feydy, Anne Lindbergh
  See Sapieyevski, Anne Lindbergh
Fiammenghi, Gioia 1929- 66
  Earlier sketch in SATA 9
Fiarotta, Noel
  See Ficarotta, Noel
Fiarotta, Phyllis
  See Ficarotta, Phyllis
Ficarotta, Noel 1944- 15
Ficarotta, Phyllis 1942- 15
Fichter, George S. 1922-1993 7
Ficocelli, Elizabeth 189
Fidler, Kathleen (Annie) 1899-1980 87
  Obituary 45
  Earlier sketch in SATA 3
Fiedler, Jean(nette Feldman) 4
Fiedler, Joseph Daniel 159
Fiedler, Lisa 185
Field, Dorothy 1944- 97
Field, Edward 1924- 109
  Earlier sketch in SATA 8
Field, Elinor Whitney 1889-1980
  Obituary 28
Field, Eugene 1850-1895 16
Field, Gans T.
  See Wellman, Manly Wade
Field, James 1959- 113
Field, Peter
  See Drago, Harry Sinclair
  and Dresser, Davis
  and Mann, E(dward) B(everly)

Field, Rachel (Lyman) 1894-1942 15
  See also CLR 21
Fielding, Kate
  See Oldfield, Jenny
Fields, Bryan W. 1958(?)- 188
Fields, Lisa 1984(?)- 216
Fields, Terri 1948- 191
Fields, T.S.
  See Fields, Terri
Fienberg, Anna 1956- 183
  Earlier sketch in SATA 112
Fiery, Ann
  See Barrows, Annie
Fife, Dale (Odile Hollerbach) 1901- 18
Fighter Pilot, A
  See Johnston, H(ugh) A(nthony) S(tephen)
Figler, Jeanie 1949- 123
Figley, Marty Rhodes 1948- 158
  Earlier sketch in SATA 88
Figueredo, D(anilo) H. 1951- 155
Figueroa, Pablo 1938- 9
Fijan, Carol 1918- 12
Filderman, Diane E(lizabeth) 1959- 87
Files, Meg 1946- 107
Fillmore, Parker H(oysted) 1878-1944
  See YABC 1
Filstrup, Chris
  See Filstrup, E(dward) Christian
Filstrup, E(dward) Christian 1942- 43
Filstrup, Janie
  See Merrill, Jane
Finchler, Judy 1943- 93
Finder, Martin
  See Salzmann, Siegmund
Findlay, Jamieson 1958- 169
Findon, Joanne 1957- 161
Fine, Anne 1947- 197
  Earlier sketches in SATA 29, 72, 111, 160
  See also CLR 25
  See also SAAS 15
Fine, Edith Hope 169
Fine, Howard 1961- 181
Fine, Jane
  See Ziefert, Harriet
Finger, Charles J(oseph) 1869(?)-1941 42
Fink, William B(ertrand) 1916- 22
Finke, Blythe Foote 1922- 26
Finkel, George (Irvine) 1909-1975 8
Finkelstein, Norman H. 1941- 137
  Earlier sketch in SATA 73
Finkelstein, Norman Henry
  See Finkelstein, Norman H.
Finlay, Alice Sullivan 1946- 82
Finlay, Winifred Lindsay Crawford
  (McKissack) 1910-1989 23
Finlayson, Ann 1925- 8
Finley, Martha 1828-1909 43
  See also CLR 148
Finley, Mary Peace 1942- 83
Finn, Mary 208
Finney, Jack 1911-1995 109
Finney, Patricia 1958- 163
Finney, Shan 1944- 65
Finney, Walter Braden
  See Finney, Jack
Firer, Ben Zion
  See Firer, Benzion
Firer, Benzion 1914- 64
Fireside, Bryna J. 1932- 73
Firmin, Charlotte 1954- 29
Firmin, Peter 1928- 58
  Earlier sketch in SATA 15
Firth, Barbara 179
Fischbach, Julius 1894-1988 10
Fischer, John
  See Fluke, Joanne
Fischer, R.J.
  See Fluke, Joanne
Fischer, Scott M. 1971- 195
Fischer-Nagel, Andreas 1951- 56
Fischer-Nagel, Heiderose 1956- 56

Fischler, Shirley (Walton) 66
Fischler, Stan(ley I.) 66
  Brief entry 36
Fischtrom, Harvey 1933-1974 3
Fishback, Margaret
  See Antolini, Margaret Fishback
Fishbone, Greg R. 195
Fisher, Aileen (Lucia) 1906-2002 73
  Obituary 143
  Earlier sketches in SATA 1, 25
  See also CLR 49
Fisher, Barbara 1940- 44
  Brief entry 34
Fisher, Carolyn 1968- 154
Fisher, Catherine 1957- 155
Fisher, Chris 1958- 80
Fisher, Clavin C(argill) 1912- 24
Fisher, Cynthia 195
Fisher, Dorothy (Frances) Canfield 1879-1958
  See YABC 1
  See also CLR 71
Fisher, Gary L. 1949- 86
Fisher, John 1909-1996 15
Fisher, John Oswald Hamilton
  See Fisher, John
Fisher, Laura Harrison 1934- 5
Fisher, Leonard Everett 1924- 176
  Autobiography Feature 122
  Earlier sketches in SATA 4, 34, 73, 120
  See also CLR 18
  See also SAAS 1
Fisher, Lois I. 1948- 38
  Brief entry 35
Fisher, Margery (Turner) 1913-1992 20
  Obituary 74
Fisher, Marshall Jon 1963- 113
Fisher, Nikki
  See Strachan, Ian
Fisher, Robert (Tempest) 1943- 47
Fisher, Suzanne
  See Staples, Suzanne Fisher
Fisher, Valorie 214
  Earlier sketch in SATA 177
Fishman, Cathy Goldberg 1951- 106
Fisk, Nicholas
  See Higginbottom, David
Fisk, Pauline 1948- 160
  Earlier sketch in SATA 66
Fiske, Tarleton
  See Bloch, Robert (Albert)
Fisscher, Catharina G. M. 1958- 142
Fisscher, Tiny
  See Fisscher, Catharina G. M.
Fitch, Clarke
  See Sinclair, Upton
Fitch, John IV
  See Cormier, Robert
Fitch, Sheree 1956- 178
  Earlier sketch in SATA 108
Fitschen, Dale 1937- 20
Fitzalan, Roger
  See Trevor, Elleston
Fitzgerald, Captain Hugh
  See Baum, L. Frank
FitzGerald, Cathleen 1932-1987
  Obituary 50
Fitzgerald, Dawn 175
Fitzgerald, Edward Earl 1919-2001 20
Fitzgerald, F(rancis) A(nthony) 1940- 15
Fitzgerald, Joanne 1956- 198
Fitzgerald, John D(ennis) 1907(?)-1988 20
  Obituary 56
  See also CLR 1
Fitzgerald, Merni Ingrassia 1955- 53
Fitzgibbon, Terry 1948- 121
Fitzhardinge, Joan Margaret 1912- 73
  Earlier sketch in SATA 2
  See also CLR 5
  See also SAAS 3

Fitzhugh, Louise (Perkins) 1928-1974 45
  Obituary 24
  Earlier sketch in SATA 1
  See also CLR 72
Fitzhugh, Percy Keese 1876-1950 65
Fitzmaurice, Kathryn 217
Fitzpatrick, Marie-Louise 1962- 189
  Earlier sketch in SATA 125
FitzRalph, Matthew
  See McInerny, Ralph
Fitz-Randolph, Jane (Currens) 1915- 51
Fitzsimons, Cecilia 1952- 97
Fitzsimons, Cecilia A.L.
  See Fitzsimons, Cecilia
Flack, Marjorie 1897-1958 100
  See also YABC 2
  See also CLR 28
Flack, Naomi John White -1999 40
  Brief entry 35
Flake, Sharon G. 166
Flanagan, John 1944- 180
Flanagan, John Anthony
  See Flanagan, John
Flannery, Kate
  See De Goldi, Kate
Flatt, Lizann 1966- 88
Fleagle, Gail S(hatto) 1940- 117
Fleetwood, Jenni 1947- 80
Fleischer, Jane
  See Oppenheim, Joanne
Fleischhauer-Hardt, Helga 1936- 30
Fleischman, Albert Sidney
  See Fleischman, Sid
Fleischman, John 1948- 145
Fleischman, Paul 1952- 156
  Brief entry 32
  Earlier sketches in SATA 39, 72, 110
  See also CLR 66
  See also SAAS 20
Fleischman, Sid 1920-2010 185
  Earlier sketches in SATA 8, 59, 96, 148
  See also CLR 15
Fleischner, Jennifer 1956- 188
  Earlier sketch in SATA 93
Fleisher, Paul 1948- 132
  Earlier sketch in SATA 81
Fleisher, Robbin 1951-1977 52
  Brief entry 49
Fleishman, Seymour 1918- 66
  Brief entry 32
Fleming, A. A.
  See Arthur, Robert, (Jr.)
Fleming, Alice Mulcahey 1928- 9
Fleming, Candace 1962- 190
  Earlier sketches in SATA 94, 143
Fleming, Denise 1950- 173
  Earlier sketches in SATA 81, 126
Fleming, Elizabeth P. 1888-1985
  Obituary 48
Fleming, Ian 1908-1964 9
Fleming, Ian Lancaster
  See Fleming, Ian
Fleming, Ronald Lee 1941- 56
Fleming, Sally
  See Walker, Sally M(acArt)
Fleming, Stuart
  See Knight, Damon (Francis)
Fleming, Susan 1932- 32
Fleming, Thomas 1927- 8
Fleming, Thomas James
  See Fleming, Thomas
Fleming, Virginia (Edwards) 1923- 84
Flesch, Y.
  See Flesch, Yolande
Flesch, Yolande 1950- 55
Flesch, Yolande Catarina
  See Flesch, Yolande
Fletcher, Charlie May Hogue 1897-1977 3
Fletcher, Colin 1922-2007 28
Fletcher, Dirk
  See Cunningham, Chet

Fletcher, George U.
  See Pratt, (Murray) Fletcher
Fletcher, Helen Jill 1910- 13
Fletcher, Ralph 1953- 195
  Earlier sketches in SATA 105, 149
  See also CLR 104
Fletcher, Ralph J.
  See Fletcher, Ralph
Fletcher, Richard E. 1917(?)-1983
  Obituary 34
Fletcher, Rick
  See Fletcher, Richard E.
Fletcher, Susan 1951- 181
  Earlier sketches in SATA 70, 110
Fletcher, Susan Clemens
  See Fletcher, Susan
Fleur, Paul
  See Pohl, Frederik
Flexner, James Thomas 1908-2003 9
Flinn, Alex 1966- 198
  Earlier sketch in SATA 159
Flint, Helen 1952- 102
Flint, Russ 1944- 74
Flitner, David, Jr. 1949- 7
Flitner, David Perkins
  See Flitner, David, Jr.
Floca, Brian 190
  Earlier sketch in SATA 155
Floethe, Louise Lee 1913-1988 4
Floethe, Richard 1901-1998 4
Floherty, John Joseph 1882-1964 25
Flood, Bo
  See Flood, Nancy Bo
Flood, Nancy Bo 1945- 130
Flood, Pansie Hart 1964- 140
Flood, William 1942- 129
Flooglebuckle, Al
  See Spiegelman, Art
Flora, James (Royer) 1914-1998 30
  Obituary 103
  Earlier sketch in SATA 1
  See also SAAS 6
Flores-Galbis, Enrique 1952- 186
Florian, Douglas 1950- 177
  Earlier sketches in SATA 19, 83, 125
Flory, Jane Trescott 1917- 22
Flournoy, Valerie 1952- 95
Flournoy, Valerie Rose
  See Flournoy, Valerie
Flowerdew, Phyllis -1994 33
Flowers, Pam 1946- 136
Flowers, Sarah 1952- 98
Floyd, Gareth 1940- 62
  Brief entry 31
Fluchere, Henri 1914-1991 40
Fluke, Joanne 1943- 88
Flutsztejn-Gruda, Ilona 1930- 170
Flynn, Barbara 1928- 9
Flynn, Jackson
  See Bensen, Donald R.
  and Shirreffs, Gordon D(onald)
Flynn, Nicholas
  See Odgers, Sally Farrell
Flynn, Pat 1968- 214
Flynn, Patrick
  See Flynn, Pat
Flynn, Rachel 1953- 171
  Earlier sketch in SATA 109
Flynn, Warren (G.) 1950- 154
Fodor, R. V. 1944- 25
Fodor, Ronald Victor
  See Fodor, R. V.
Fogelin, Adrian 1951- 175
  Earlier sketch in SATA 129
Foley, (Anna) Bernice Williams 1902-1987 . 28
Foley, Greg E. 1969- 190
Foley, June 1944- 44
Foley, (Mary) Louise Munro 1933- 106
  Brief entry 40
  Earlier sketch in SATA 54

Foley, Rae
See Denniston, Elinore
Folke, Will
See Bloch, Robert (Albert)
Follett, Helen Thomas 1884(?)-1970
Obituary 27
Folsom, Franklin (Brewster) 1907-1995 5
Obituary 88
Folsom, Michael (Brewster) 1938-1990 40
Obituary 88
Fontenot, Mary Alice 1910-2003 91
Obituary 209
Earlier sketch in SATA 34
Fontes, Justine 172
Fontes, Ron 1952- 183
Foon, Dennis 1951- 119
Fooner, Michael 22
Foote, Timothy (Gilson) 1926- 52
Forberg, Ati
See Forberg, Beate Gropius
Forberg, Beate Gropius 1925- 22
Forbes, Anna 1954- 101
Forbes, Bryan 1926- 37
Forbes, Cabot L.
See Hoyt, Edwin P(almer), Jr.
Forbes, Esther 1891-1967 100
Earlier sketch in SATA 2
See also CLR 147
Forbes, Graham B. 1
Forbes, Kathryn
See McLean, Kathryn (Anderson)
Forbes, Robert
See Arthur, Robert, (Jr.)
Ford, Albert Lee
See Stratemeyer, Edward L.
Ford, Barbara 56
Brief entry 34
Ford, Bernette 212
Ford, Bernette G.
See Ford, Bernette
Ford, B.G.
See Ford, Bernette
Ford, Brian J(ohn) 1939- 49
Ford, Carolyn 1938- 98
Ford, Carolyn Mott
See Ford, Carolyn
Ford, Christine 1953- 176
Ford, David
See Baldacci, David
and Baldacci, David
Ford, David B.
See Baldacci, David
Ford, David Baldacci
See Baldacci, David
Ford, Elbur
See Hibbert, Eleanor Alice Burford
Ford, Ellen 1949- 89
Ford, George (Jr.) 31
Ford, Hilary
See Youd, Samuel
Ford, Hildegarde
See Morrison, Velma Ford
Ford, Jerome W. 1949- 78
Ford, Jerry
See Ford, Jerome W.
Ford, Juwanda G(ertrude) 1967- 102
Ford, Marcia
See Radford, Ruby L(orraine)
Ford, Nancy K(effer) 1906-1961
Obituary 29
Ford, Peter 1936- 59
Ford, S. M.
See Uhlig, Susan
Forde, Catherine 1961- 170
Foreman, Mark 199
Foreman, Michael 1938- 216
Earlier sketches in SATA 2, 73, 129, 135, 184
See also CLR 32
See also SAAS 21
Foreman, Wilmoth 1939- 153

Forest, Antonia 1915-2003 29
Obituary 149
Forest, Dial
See Gault, William Campbell
Forest, Heather 1948- 185
Earlier sketch in SATA 120
Forester, C. S. 1899-1966 13
Forester, Cecil Scott
See Forester, C. S.
Forester, Victoria 214
Forman, Brenda 1936- 4
Forman, James
See Forman, James D.
Forman, James D. 1932-2009 70
Earlier sketch in SATA 8
Forman, James Douglas
See Forman, James D.
Forman, Mark L.
See Forman, M.L.
Forman, M.L. 1964- 215
Forman, Ruth 1970- 186
Forrest, Elizabeth
See Salsitz, Rhondi Vilott
Forrest, Mary
See Pausacker, Jenny
Forrest, Sybil
See Markun, Patricia Maloney
Forrestal, Elaine 1941- 165
Earlier sketch in SATA 117
Forrester, Frank H. 1919(?)-1986
Obituary 52
Forrester, Helen
See Bhatia, Jamunadevi
Forrester, Jade
See Pausacker, Jenny
Forrester, Marian
See Schachtel, Roger
Forrester, Sandra 1949- 166
Earlier sketch in SATA 90
Forrester, Victoria 1940- 40
Brief entry 35
Forsee, (Frances) Aylesa -1986 1
Forsey, Chris 1950- 59
Forshay-Lunsford, Cin 1965- 60
Forster, E. M. 1879-1970 57
Forster, Edward Morgan
See Forster, E. M.
Forsyth, Kate 1966- 154
Fort, Paul
See Stockton, Francis Richard
Forte, Maurizio 1961- 110
Fortey, Richard 1946- 109
Fortey, Richard A.
See Fortey, Richard
Fortey, Richard Alan
See Fortey, Richard
Forth, Melissa D(eal) 96
Fortnum, Peggy
See Nuttall-Smith, Margaret Emily Noel
Fortune, Eric 182
Forward, Robert L(ull) 1932-2002 82
Foster, Alan Dean 1946- 70
Foster, Brad W. 1955- 34
Foster, Doris Van Liew 1899-1993 10
Foster, E(lizabeth) C(onnell) 1902- 9
Foster, Elizabeth 1902- 12
Foster, Elizabeth 1905-1963 10
Foster, F. Blanche 1919- 11
Foster, G(eorge) Allen 1907-1969 26
Foster, Genevieve (Stump) 1893-1979 2
Obituary 23
See also CLR 7
Foster, Gerald L. 198
Foster, Hal
See Foster, Harold
Foster, Harold 1892-1982 31
Foster, Jeanne
See Williams, Jeanne
Foster, John
See Foster, John L(ouis)
and Furcolo, Foster

Foster, John (Thomas) 1925- 8
Foster, John L(ouis) 1941- 102
Foster, Juliana 196
Foster, Laura Louise (James) 1918- 6
Foster, Leila Merrell 1929- 73
Foster, Lynne 1937- 74
Foster, Margaret Lesser 1899(?)-1979
Obituary 21
Foster, Marian Curtis 1909-1978 23
Foster, Mark 1961- 197
Foster, Sally 58
Fotheringham, Edwin 201
Foulds, E. V.
See Foulds, Elfrida Vipont
Foulds, Elfrida Vipont 1902-1992 52
Fountas, Angela Jane 180
Fourie, Corlia 1944- 91
Fourth Brother, The
See Aung, (Maung) Htin
Fowke, Edith (Margaret) 1913-1996 14
Fowles, John 1926-2005 22
Obituary 171
Fowles, John Robert
See Fowles, John
Fowles, Shelley 1956- 205
Fox, Aileen 1907-2005 58
Obituary 170
Fox, Aileen Mary
See Fox, Aileen
Fox, Annie 1950- 175
Fox, Charles Philip 1913-2003 12
Obituary 150
Fox, Christyan 188
Fox, Diane 188
Fox, Eleanor
See St. John, Wylly Folk
Fox, Fontaine Talbot, Jr. 1884-1964
Obituary 23
Fox, Fred 1903(?)-1981
Obituary 27
Fox, Freeman
See Hamilton, Charles (Harold St. John)
Fox, Geoffrey 1941- 73
Fox, Grace
See Anderson, Grace Fox
Fox, Helen 1962- 181
Fox, Larry 30
Fox, Lorraine 1922-1976 27
Earlier sketch in SATA 11
Fox, Louisa
See Kroll, Virginia L.
Fox, Mary Virginia 1919- 152
Brief entry 39
Earlier sketches in SATA 44, 88
Fox, Mem 211
See Fox, Merrion Frances
Fox, Merrion Frances 1946- 155
Earlier sketches in SATA 51, 103
See also CLR 80
See Fox, Mem
Fox, Michael W(ilson) 1937- 15
Fox, Norma Diane
See Mazer, Norma Fox
Fox, Paula 1923- 167
Earlier sketches in SATA 17, 60, 120
See also CLR 96
Fox, Robert J. 1927- 33
Fox, Robert Joseph
See Fox, Robert J.
Fox-Davies, Sarah 1956- 199
Foyt, Victoria .... 187.
Fradin, Dennis
See Fradin, Dennis Brindell
Fradin, Dennis Brindell 1945- 185
Earlier sketches in SATA 29, 90, 135
Fradin, Judith Bloom 1945- 185
Earlier sketches in SATA 90, 152
Frailey, Paige (Menefee) 1965- 82
Frame, Janet 1924-2004 119

Frame, Paul 1913-1994 60
  Brief entry 33
  Obituary 83
Frances, Miss
  See Horwich, Frances R(appaport)
Franchere, Ruth 18
Francis, Charles
  See Holme, Bryan
Francis, Dee
  See Haas, Dorothy F.
Francis, Dorothy 1926- 127
  Earlier sketch in SATA *10*
Francis, Dorothy B.
  See Francis, Dorothy
Francis, Dorothy Brenner
  See Francis, Dorothy
Francis, Jaye
  See Pausacker, Jenny
Francis, Pamela (Mary) 1926- *11*
Franck, Eddie
  See Cooke, Frank E.
Franco, Betsy 188
  Earlier sketch in SATA *150*
Franco, Eloise (Bauder) 1910- 62
Franco, Johan (Henri Gustave) 1908-1988 ... 62
Franco, Marjorie 38
Francois, Andre 1915-2005 25
Francoise
  See Seignobosc, Francoise
Frank, Anne 1929-1945 87
  Brief entry 42
  See also CLR *101*
Frank, Annelies Marie
  See Frank, Anne
Frank, Daniel B. 1956- 55
Frank, Emily R.
  See Frank, E.R.
Frank, E.R. 1967- 157
Frank, Helene
  See Vautier, Ghislaine
Frank, Hillary 1976- 148
Frank, John 199
Frank, Josette 1893-1989 10
  Obituary 63
Frank, Lucy 1947- 166
  Earlier sketch in SATA *94*
Frank, Mary 1933- 34
Frank, R., Jr.
  See Ross, Frank (Xavier), Jr.
Frankau, Mary Evelyn Atkinson 1899-1974 .. 4
Frankel, Alona 1937- 66
Frankel, Bernice 9
Frankel, Edward 1910- 44
Frankel, Ellen 1951- 78
Frankel, Julie 1947- 40
  Brief entry 34
Frankenberg, Robert 1911- 22
Frankland, David 207
Franklin, Cheryl J. 1955- 70
Franklin, Harold 1926- 13
Franklin, Kristine L. 1958- 124
  Earlier sketch in SATA *80*
Franklin, Lance
  See Lantz, Francess L(in)
Franklin, Madeleine
  See L'Engle, Madeleine
Franklin, Madeleine L'Engle
  See L'Engle, Madeleine
Franklin, Madeleine L'Engle Camp
  See L'Engle, Madeleine
Franklin, Max
  See Deming, Richard
Franklin, Steve
  See Stevens, Franklin
Franson, Leanne R. 1963- 111
Franson, Scott E. 1966- 192
Franzen, Nils-Olof 1916- 10
Frascino, Edward 48
  Brief entry 33
  See also SAAS *9*

Frasconi, Antonio 1919- 131
  Earlier sketches in SATA *6, 53*
  See also SAAS *11*
Fraser, Betty
  See Fraser, Elizabeth Marr
Fraser, Elizabeth Marr 1928- 31
Fraser, Eric (George) 1902-1983 38
Fraser, Mary Ann 1959- 214
  Earlier sketches in SATA *76, 137*
  See also SAAS *23*
Fraser, Wynnette (McFaddin) 1925- 90
Frasier, Debra 1953- 182
  Earlier sketches in SATA *69, 112*
Fraustino, Lisa Rowe 1961- 146
  Autobiography Feature 146
  Earlier sketch in SATA *84*
Frazee, Marla 1958- 187
  Earlier sketches in SATA *105, 151*
Frazetta, Frank 1928-2010 58
Frazier, Craig 1955- 177
Frazier, Neta (Osborn) Lohnes 1890-1990 7
Frazier, Sundee T. 1968- 198
Frazier, Sundee Tucker
  See Frazier, Sundee T.
Frederic, Mike
  See Cox, William R(obert)
Frederick, Heather Vogel 207
Fredericks, Anthony D. 1947- 113
Freed, Alvyn M. 1913-1993 22
Freedman, Benedict 1919- 27
Freedman, Claire 185
Freedman, Deborah 1960- 191
Freedman, Jeff 1953- 90
Freedman, Nancy 1920- 27
Freedman, Russell 1929- 175
  Earlier sketches in SATA *16, 71, 123*
  See also CLR *71*
Freedman, Russell Bruce
  See Freedman, Russell
Freeman, Barbara C. 1906-1999 28
Freeman, Barbara Constance
  See Freeman, Barbara C.
Freeman, Bill
  See Freeman, William Bradford
Freeman, Don 1908-1978 17
  See also CLR *90*
Freeman, Ira Maximilian 1905-1987 21
Freeman, Kimberley
  See Wilkins, Kim
Freeman, Laura 200
Freeman, Lucy (Greenbaum) 1916-2004 24
Freeman, Mae 1907-1985 25
Freeman, Mae Blacker
  See Freeman, Mae
Freeman, Marcia S. 1937- 102
Freeman, Marcia Sheehan
  See Freeman, Marcia S.
Freeman, Martha 1956- 201
  Earlier sketches in SATA *101, 152*
Freeman, Nancy 1932- 61
Freeman, Peter J.
  See Calvert, Patricia
Freeman, Sarah (Caroline) 1940- 66
Freeman, Tor 1977- 164
Freeman, VicToria
  See Freeman, Tor
Freeman, William Bradford 1938- 58
  Brief entry 48
Fregosi, Claudia (Anne Marie) 1946- 24
Freitas, Donna 1972- 205
French, Allen 1870-1946
  See YABC *1*
French, Dorothy Kayser 1926- 5
French, Fiona 1944- 132
  Earlier sketches in SATA *6, 75*
  See also CLR *37*
  See also SAAS *21*

French, Jackie 186
  Autobiography Feature 139
  Earlier sketches in SATA *108, 139*
  See French, Jackie Anne
    and French, Jacqueline Anne
French, Kathryn
  See Mosesson, Gloria R(ubin)
French, Martin 176
French, Michael 1944- 49
  Brief entry 38
French, Paul
  See Asimov, Isaac
French, S. Terrell 216
French, Simon 1957- 147
  Earlier sketch in SATA *86*
French, Vivian 209
  Earlier sketch in SATA *165*
Frenette, Liza 126
Freschet, Gina 1960- 175
  Earlier sketch in SATA *139*
Frewer, Glyn (M.) 1931- *11*
Frey, Darcy 98
Freymann, Saxton 1958(?)- 178
Freymann-Weyr, (Rhoda) Garret (Michaela)
  1965- 145
Frick, C. H.
  See Irwin, Constance (H.) Frick
Frick, Constance
  See Irwin, Constance (H.) Frick
Fricke, Aaron 1962- 89
Fridell, Ron 1943- 124
Fried, Janice 197
Friedlander, Joanne K(ohn) 1930- 9
Friedman, Aimee 1979- 189
Friedman, D. Dina 1957- 180
Friedman, Debra 1955- 150
Friedman, Estelle (Ehrenwald) 1920- 7
Friedman, Frieda 1905- 43
Friedman, Ina R(osen) 1926- 136
  Brief entry 41
  Earlier sketch in SATA *49*
Friedman, Jerrold David
  See Gerrold, David
Friedman, Judi 1935- 59
Friedman, Laurie 1964- 179
  Earlier sketch in SATA *138*
Friedman, Marvin 1930- 42
  Brief entry 33
Friedman, Robin 1968- 162
Friedmann, Stan 1953- 80
Friedrich, Otto (Alva) 1929-1995 33
Friedrich, Priscilla 1927- 39
Friend, Catherine 1957(?)- 194
Friend, David Michael 1975- 195
Friend, Natasha 1972- 184
Friendlich, Dick
  See Friendlich, Richard J.
Friendlich, Richard J. 1909- *11*
Friermood, Elisabeth Hamilton 1903-1992 5
Friesen, Bernice (Sarah Anne) 1966- 105
Friesen, Gayle 1960- 200
  Earlier sketch in SATA *109*
Friesen, Jonathan 1967(?)- 206
Friesner, Esther 1951- 207
  Earlier sketches in SATA *71, 168*
Friesner, Esther M.
  See Friesner, Esther
Friis-Baastad, Babbis Ellinor 1921-1970 7
Frimmer, Steven 1928- 31
Frischmuth, Barbara 1941- 114
Friskey, Margaret (Richards) 1901-1995 5
Fritts, Mary Bahr
  See Bahr, Mary (Madelyn)
Fritz, Jean (Guttery) 1915- 163
  Autobiography Feature 122
  Earlier sketches in SATA *1, 29, 72, 119*
  See also CLR *96*
  See also SAAS *2*
Froehlich, Margaret W(alden) 1930- 56
Frois, Jeanne 1953- 73
Froissart, Jean 1338(?)-1410(?) 28

Froman, Elizabeth Hull 1920-1975 .... *10*
Froman, Robert (Winslow) 1917- *8*
Fromm, Lilo 1928- *29*
Frommer, Harvey 1937- *41*
Frost, A(rthur) B(urdett) 1851-1928 .... *19*
Frost, Elizabeth
    See Frost-Knappman, Elizabeth
Frost, Erica
    See Supraner, Robyn
Frost, Helen 1949- *194*
    Autobiography Feature *194*
    Earlier sketches in SATA *157, 183*
Frost, Helen Marie
    See Frost, Helen
Frost, Lesley 1899-1983 .... *14*
    Obituary *34*
Frost, Robert 1874-1963 .... *14*
    See also CLR *67*
Frost, Robert Lee
    See Frost, Robert
Frost, Shelley 1960- *138*
Frost-Knappman, Elizabeth 1943- *179*
Froud, Brian 1947- *150*
Fry, Annette R(iley) *89*
Fry, Christopher 1907-2005 .... *66*
Fry, Edward Bernard 1925- *35*
Fry, Rosalie Kingsmill 1911-1992 .... *3*
    See also SAAS *11*
Fry, Virginia Lynn 1952- *95*
Frye, Sally
    See Moore, Elaine
Fuchs, Bernie 1932- *162*
    Earlier sketch in SATA *95*
Fuchs, Erich 1916- *6*
Fuchshuber, Annegert 1940- *43*
Fuerst, Jeffrey B. 1956- *143*
Fuertes, Gloria 1918-1998 .... *115*
Fuge, Charles 1966- *144*
    Earlier sketch in SATA *74*
Fujikawa, Gyo 1908-1998 .... *76*
    Brief entry *30*
    Obituary *110*
    Earlier sketch in SATA *39*
    See also CLR *25*
    See also SAAS *16*
Fujita, Tamao 1905-1999 .... *7*
Fujiwara, Kim 1957- *81*
Fujiwara, Michiko 1946- *15*
Fuka, Vladimir 1926-1977
    Obituary *27*
Fulcher, Jennifer
    See Westwood, Jennifer
Fuller, Catherine Leuthold 1916- *9*
Fuller, Edmund (Maybank) 1914- *21*
Fuller, Iola
    See McCoy, Iola Fuller
Fuller, John G(rant, Jr.) 1913-1990 .... *65*
Fuller, Kathleen
    See Gottfried, Theodore Mark
Fuller, Lois Hamilton 1915- *11*
Fuller, Margaret 1810-1850 .... *25*
Fuller, Maud
    See Petersham, Maud
Fuller, Roy (Broadbent) 1912-1991 .... *87*
Fuller, Sarah Margaret
    See Fuller, Margaret
Fults, John Lee 1932- *33*
Funk, Thompson 1911- *7*
Funk, Tom
    See Funk, Thompson
Funke, Cornelia 1958- *209*
    Earlier sketches in SATA *154, 174*
    See also CLR *145*
Funke, Cornelia Caroline
    See Funke, Cornelia
Funke, Lewis 1912-1992 .... *11*
Fuqua, Jonathon Scott 1966- *141*
Furbee, Mary R.
    See Furbee, Mary Rodd
Furbee, Mary Rodd 1954- *138*
Furchgott, Terry 1948- *29*

Furlong, Monica (Mavis) 1930-2003 .... *86*
    Obituary *142*
Furlonger, Patricia
    See Wrightson, Patricia
Furman, Gertrude Lerner Kerman 1909- *21*
Furniss, Tim 1948- *49*
Furrow, Robert 1985- *172*
Furukawa, Toshi 1924- *24*
Fusillo, Archimede 1962- *137*
Futcher, Jane P. 1947- *76*
Futehali, Zahida
    See Whitaker, Zai
Fyleman, Rose (Amy) 1877-1957 .... *21*
Fyson, Jenny Grace
    See Fyson, J.G.
Fyson, J.G. 1904-1998 .... *42*

G

Gaan, Margaret 1914- *65*
Gaber, Susan 1956- *169*
    Earlier sketch in SATA *115*
Gaberman, Judie Angell
    See Angell, Judie
Gabhart, Ann
    See Gabhart, Ann H.
Gabhart, Ann H. 1947- *75*
Gable, Brian 1949- *195*
Gabler, Mirko 1951- *77*
Gabriel, Adriana
    See Rojany, Lisa
Gabrys, Ingrid Schubert
    See Schubert-Gabrys, Ingrid
Gackenbach, Dick 1927- *79*
    Brief entry *30*
    Earlier sketch in SATA *48*
Gadd, Jeremy 1949- *116*
Gaddis, Vincent H. 1913-1997 .... *35*
Gadler, Steve J. 1905-1985 .... *36*
Gaeddert, Lou Ann (Bigge) 1931- *103*
    Earlier sketch in SATA *20*
Gaeddert, Louann
    See Gaeddert, Lou Ann (Bigge)
Gaer, Joseph 1897-1969 .... *118*
Gaer, Yossef
    See Gaer, Joseph
Gaetz, Dayle Campbell 1947- *138*
Gaffney, Timothy R. 1951- *170*
    Earlier sketch in SATA *69*
Gaffron, Norma 1931- *97*
Gaffron, Norma Bondeson
    See Gaffron, Norma
Gag, Flavia 1907-1979
    Obituary *24*
Gag, Wanda (Hazel) 1893-1946 .... *100*
    See also YABC *1*
    See also CLR *150*
Gage, Brian *162*
Gage, Wilson
    See Steele, Mary Q(uintard Govan)
Gagliano, Eugene M. 1946- *150*
Gagliardo, Ruth Garver 1895(?)-1980
    Obituary *22*
Gagnon, Cecile 1936- *58*
Gaillard, Jason 1965- *200*
Gaiman, Neil 1960- *197*
    Earlier sketches in SATA *85, 146*
    See also CLR *109*
Gaiman, Neil Richard
    See Gaiman, Neil
Gainer, Cindy 1962- *74*
Gaines, Ernest J. 1933- *86*
    See also CLR *62*
Gaines, Ernest James
    See Gaines, Ernest J.
Gaither, Gloria 1942- *127*

Gal, Laszlo 1933- *96*
    Brief entry *32*
    Earlier sketch in SATA *52*
    See also CLR *61*
Galbraith, Ben 1980- *200*
Galbraith, Kathryn O(sebold) 1945- *85*
Galdone, Paul 1907(?)-1986 .... *66*
    Obituary *49*
    Earlier sketch in SATA *17*
    See also CLR *16*
Galindo, Claudia 1979- *203*
Galinsky, Ellen 1942- *23*
Gall, Chris 1961- *176*
Gallagher, Diana G. 1946- *153*
Gallagher, Lurlene Nora
    See McDaniel, Lurlene
Gallagher-Cole, Mernie 1958- *206*
Gallant, Roy A(rthur) 1924- *110*
    Earlier sketches in SATA *4, 68*
    See also CLR *30*
Gallardo, Evelyn 1948- *78*
Gallaz, Christophe 1948- *162*
    See also CLR *126*
Gallego Garcia, Laura 1977- *173*
Gallico, Paul 1897-1976 .... *13*
Gallico, Paul William
    See Gallico, Paul
Gallo, Donald R. 1938- *112*
    Autobiography Feature *104*
Gallo, Donald Robert
    See Gallo, Donald R.
Galloway, Owateka (S.) 1981- *121*
Galloway, Priscilla 1930- *112*
    Earlier sketch in SATA *66*
Gallup, Joan 1957- *128*
Galouchko, Annouchka Gravel 1960- *95*
Galt, Thomas Franklin, Jr. 1908-1989 .... *5*
Galt, Tom
    See Galt, Thomas Franklin, Jr.
Galvin, Matthew R. 1950- *93*
Galvin, Matthew Reppert
    See Galvin, Matthew R.
Gamble, Kim 1952- *183*
    Earlier sketches in SATA *81, 124*
Gambrell, Jamey *82*
Gamerman, Martha 1941- *15*
Gammell, Stephen 1943- *128*
    Earlier sketches in SATA *53, 81*
    See also CLR *83*
Ganly, Helen (Mary) 1940- *56*
Gannett, Ruth Chrisman (Arens)
    1896-1979 .... *33*
Gannett, Ruth Stiles 1923- *3*
Gannij, Joan *208*
Gannij, Joan Levine
    See Gannij, Joan
Gannon, Ned 1974- *205*
Gannon, Robert Haines 1931- *8*
Gano, Lila 1949- *76*
Gans, Roma 1894-1996 .... *45*
    Obituary *93*
Gant, Matthew
    See Hano, Arnold
Gantner, Susan (Verble) 1939- *63*
Gantos, Jack 1951- *169*
    Earlier sketches in SATA *20, 81, 119*
    See also CLR *85*
Gantos, John Bryan, Jr.
    See Gantos, Jack
Ganz, Yaffa 1938- *61*
    Brief entry *52*
Garafano, Marie 1942- *84*
Garant, Andre J. 1968- *123*
Garbe, Ruth Moore
    See Moore, Ruth (Ellen)
Garber, Esther
    See Lee, Tanith
Garcia, Cristina 1958- *208*
Garcia, Emma 1969- *198*
Garcia, Yolanda P. 1952- *113*

Garcia, Yolanda Pacheco
    See Garcia, Yolanda P.
Gard, Janice
    See Latham, Jean Lee
Gard, Joyce
    See Reeves, Joyce
Gard, Robert Edward 1910-1992 18
    Obituary 74
Gard, (Sanford) Wayne 1899-1986
    Obituary 49
Gardam, Jane 1928- 130
    Brief entry 28
    Earlier sketches in SATA 39, 76
    See also CLR 12
    See also SAAS 9
Gardam, Jane Mary
    See Gardam, Jane
Gardella, Tricia 1944- 96
Garden, Nancy 1938- 147
    Autobiography Feature 147
    Earlier sketches in SATA 12, 77, 114
    See also CLR 51
    See also SAAS 8
Gardiner, John Reynolds 1944-2006 64
    Obituary 174
Gardiner, Lindsey 1971- 144
Gardner, Craig Shaw 1949- 99
Gardner, Dic
    See Gardner, Richard (M.)
Gardner, Graham 159
Gardner, Hugh 1910-1986
    Obituary 49
Gardner, Jane Mylum 1946- 83
Gardner, Jeanne LeMonnier 1925- 5
Gardner, John, Jr. 1933-1982 40
    Obituary 31
Gardner, John Champlin, Jr.
    See Gardner, John, Jr.
Gardner, John E(dward) 1917- 192
Gardner, Lyn 192
Gardner, Martin 1914-2010 142
    Earlier sketch in SATA 16
Gardner, Miriam
    See Bradley, Marion Zimmer
Gardner, Richard (M.) 1931- 24
Gardner, Richard A(lan) 1931-2003 13
    Obituary 144
Gardner, Sally 177
Gardner, Sandra 1940- 70
Gardner, Scot 1968- 143
Gardner, Sheldon 1934- 33
Gardner, Ted
    See Gardner, Theodore Roosevelt II
Gardner, Theodore Roosevelt
    See Gardner, Theodore Roosevelt II
Gardner, Theodore Roosevelt II 1934- 84
Garelick, May 1910-1989 19
Garfield, James B. 1881-1984 6
    Obituary 38
Garfield, Leon 1921-1996 76
    Obituary 90
    Earlier sketches in SATA 1, 32
    See also CLR 21
Garfinkle, Debra L.
    See Garfinkle, D.L.
Garfinkle, D.L. 187
Garis, Howard R. 1873-1962 13
Garis, Howard Roger
    See Garis, Howard R.
Garland, Mark 1953- 79
Garland, Mark A.
    See Garland, Mark
Garland, Michael 1952- 208
    Earlier sketch in SATA 168
Garland, Sarah 1944- 135
    Earlier sketch in SATA 62
Garland, Sherry 1948- 145
    Autobiography Feature 145
    Earlier sketches in SATA 73, 114

Garner, Alan 1934- 69
    Autobiography Feature 108
    Earlier sketch in SATA 18
    See also CLR 130
Garner, David 1958- 78
Garner, Eleanor Ramrath 1930- 122
Garner, James Finn 1960(?)- 92
Garnet, A. H.
    See Slote, Alfred
Garnett, Eve C. R. 1900-1991 3
    Obituary 70
Garofoli, Viviana 1970- 186
Garou, Louis P.
    See Bowkett, Stephen
Garraty, John A. 1920-2007 23
    Obituary 189
Garraty, John Arthur
    See Garraty, John A.
Garren, Devorah-Leah
    See Devorah-Leah
Garret, Maxwell R. 1917- 39
Garretson, Victoria Diane
    See Cox, Victoria
Garrett, Helen 1895- 21
Garrett, Randall 1927-1987 180
Garrett, Richard 1920- 82
Garrigue, Sheila 1931- 21
Garrison, Barbara 1931- 163
    Earlier sketch in SATA 19
Garrison, Frederick
    See Sinclair, Upton
Garrison, Mary 1952- 146
Garrison, Peter
    See Gardner, Craig Shaw
Garrison, Webb B(lack) 1919-2000 25
Garrity, Jennifer Johnson 1961- 124
Garrity, Linda K. 1947- 128
Garsee, Jeannine 199
Garst, Doris Shannon 1894-1981 1
Garst, Shannon
    See Garst, Doris Shannon
Garth, Will
    See Hamilton, Edmond
    and Kuttner, Henry
Garthwaite, Marion H(ook) 1893-1981 7
Garton, Malinda D(ean) (?)-1976
    Obituary 26
Garvie, Maureen 1944- 175
Garvie, Maureen McCallum
    See Garvie, Maureen
Garza, Carmen Lomas 1948- 182
Garza, Xavier 184
Gascoigne, Bamber 1935- 62
Gaskins, Pearl Fuyo 1957- 134
Gasperini, Jim 1952- 54
    Brief entry 49
Gater, Dilys 1944- 41
Gates, Doris 1901-1987 34
    Obituary 54
    Earlier sketch in SATA 1
    See also SAAS 1
Gates, Frieda 1933- 26
Gates, Susan 1950- 153
Gates, Viola R. 1931- 101
Gathorne-Hardy, Jonathan G. 1933- 124
    Earlier sketch in SATA 26
Gatti, Anne 1952- 103
Gatty, Juliana Horatia
    See Ewing, Juliana (Horatia Gatty)
Gauch, Patricia Lee 1934- 80
    Earlier sketch in SATA 26
    See also CLR 56
    See also SAAS 21
Gaudasinska, Elzbieta 1943- 190
Gaul, Randy 1959- 63
Gault, Clare 1925- 36
Gault, Frank 1926-1982 36
    Brief entry 30
Gault, William Campbell 1910-1995 8
Gauthier, Gail 1953- 203
    Earlier sketches in SATA 118, 160

Gaver, Becky
    See Gaver, Rebecca
Gaver, Rebecca 1952- 20
Gavin, Jamila 1941- 125
    Earlier sketch in SATA 96
Gay, Amelia
    See Hogarth, Grace (Weston Allen)
Gay, Francis
    See Gee, H(erbert) L(eslie)
Gay, Kathlyn 1930- 144
    Earlier sketch in SATA 9
Gay, Marie-Louise 1952- 179
    Earlier sketches in SATA 68, 126
    See also CLR 27
    See also SAAS 21
Gay, Michel 1947- 162
Gay, Zhenya 1906-1978 19
Gaze, Gillian
    See Barklem, Jill
Gear, Kathleen M. O'Neal
    See Gear, Kathleen O'Neal
Gear, Kathleen O'Neal 1954- 166
    Earlier sketch in SATA 71
Gear, W. Michael 1955- 166
    Earlier sketch in SATA 71
Geary, Rick 1946- 142
Geason, Susan 1946- 122
Gedalof, Robin
    See McGrath, Robin
Gedge, Pauline (Alice) 1945- 101
Gee, H(erbert) L(eslie) 1901-1977
    Obituary 26
Gee, Maurice 1931- 101
    Earlier sketch in SATA 46
    See also CLR 56
Gee, Maurice Gough
    See Gee, Maurice
Geehan, Wayne (E.) 1947- 107
Geer, Charles 1922- 42
    Brief entry 32
Geeslin, Campbell 1925- 163
    Earlier sketch in SATA 107
Gehman, Mary W. 1923- 86
Gehr, Mary 1910(?)-1997 32
    Obituary 99
Geipel, Eileen 1932- 30
Geis, Alissa Imre 1976- 189
Geis, Darlene Stern 1918(?)-1999 7
    Obituary 111
Geisel, Helen 1898-1967 26
Geisel, Theodor Seuss
    See Dr. Seuss
Geisert, Arthur 1941- 171
    Brief entry 52
    Earlier sketches in SATA 56, 92, 133
    See also CLR 87
    See also SAAS 23
Geisert, Arthur Frederick
    See Geisert, Arthur
Geisert, Bonnie 1942- 165
    Earlier sketch in SATA 92
Geist, Ken 191
Gelber, Lisa 210
Geldart, William 1936- 15
Gelinas, Paul J. 1904-1996 10
Gellis, Roberta 1927- 128
Gellis, Roberta Leah Jacobs
    See Gellis, Roberta
Gellman, Marc 112
Gelman, Amy 1961- 72
Gelman, Jan 1963- 58
Gelman, Rita Golden 1937- 131
    Brief entry 51
    Earlier sketch in SATA 84
Gelman, Steve 1934- 3
Gemming, Elizabeth 1932- 11
Gendel, Evelyn W. 1916(?)-1977
    Obituary 27
Gennaro, Joseph F., Jr. 1924- 53
Gennaro, Joseph Francis, Jr.
    See Gennaro, Joseph F., Jr.

Gentieu, Penny 204
Gentile, Petrina 1969- 91
Gentle, Mary 1956- 48
Gentleman, David (William) 1930- 7
Gentry, Marita 215
Geoghegan, Adrienne 1962- 143
George, Barbara
  See Katz, Bobbi
George, Emily
  See Katz, Bobbi
George, Gail
  See Katz, Bobbi
George, Jean
  See George, Jean Craighead
George, Jean C.
  See George, Jean Craighead
George, Jean Craighead 1919- 170
  Earlier sketches in SATA *2, 68, 124*
  See also CLR *136*
George, Jessica Day 1976- 210
George, John L(othar) 1916- 2
George, Kristine O'Connell 1954- 156
  Earlier sketch in SATA *110*
George, Lindsay Barrett 1952- 206
  Earlier sketches in SATA *95, 155*
George, S. C. 1898- 11
George, Sally
  See Orr, Wendy
George, Sidney Charles
  See George, S. C.
George, Twig C. 1950- 114
George, W(illiam) Lloyd 1900(?)-1975
  Obituary 30
Georgiou, Constantine 1927- 7
Georgiou, Theo
  See Odgers, Sally Farrell
Geraghty, Paul 1959- 130
Gerard, Jean Ignace Isidore 1803-1847 45
Geras, Adele 1944- 180
  Autobiography Feature 180
  Earlier sketches in SATA *23, 87, 129, 173*
  See also SAAS *21*
Geras, Adele Daphne Weston
  See Geras, Adele
Gerber, Carole 1947- 207
Gerber, Linda 213
Gerber, Merrill Joan 1938- 170
  Autobiography Feature 170
  Earlier sketches in SATA *64, 127*
Gerber, Perren 1933- 104
Gerberg, Mort 1931- 64
Gergely, Tibor 1900-1978 54
  Obituary 20
Geringer, Laura 1948- 164
  Earlier sketches in SATA *29, 94*
Gerler, William R(obert) 1917-1996 47
Gerrard, Jean 1933- 51
Gerrard, Roy 1935-1997 90
  Brief entry 45
  Obituary 99
  Earlier sketch in SATA *47*
  See also CLR *23*
Gerritsen, Paula 1956- 177
Gerrold, David 1944- 144
  Earlier sketch in SATA *66*
Gershator, David 1937- 180
Gershator, Phillis 1942- 188
  Earlier sketches in SATA *90, 158*
Gershon, Dann 1955- 187
Gershon, Gina 1962- 187
Gerson, Corinne 1927- 37
Gerson, Mary-Joan 136
  Earlier sketch in SATA *79*
Gerson, Noel Bertram 1914-1988 22
  Obituary 60
Gerstein, Mordicai 1935- 178
  Brief entry 36
  Earlier sketches in SATA *47, 81, 142*
  See also CLR *102*
Gertridge, Allison 1967- 132
Gervais, Bernadette 1959- 80

Gervay, Susanne 183
Gesner, Clark 1938-2002 40
  Obituary 143
Gessner, Lynne 1919- 16
Geter, Tyrone 150
Getz, David 1957- 91
Getzinger, Donna 1968- 128
Geus, Mireille 1964- 207
Gevirtz, Eliezer 1950- 49
Gevry, Claudine 188
Gewe, Raddory
  See Gorey, Edward (St. John)
Ghan, Linda (R.) 1947- 77
Ghent, Natale 1962- 148
Gherman, Beverly 1934- 123
  Earlier sketch in SATA *68*
Ghigna, Charles 1946- 153
  Earlier sketch in SATA *108*
Giacobbe, Beppe 1953- 174
Giambastiani, Kurt R. A. 1958- 141
Giannini, Enzo 1946- 68
Gibala-Broxholm, Scott 1959(?)- 205
Gibbons, Alan 1953- 198
  Earlier sketch in SATA *124*
Gibbons, Faye 1938- 103
  Earlier sketch in SATA *65*
Gibbons, Gail 1944- 201
  Earlier sketches in SATA *23, 72, 104, 160*
  See also CLR *8*
  See also SAAS *12*
Gibbons, Gail Gretchen
  See Gibbons, Gail
Gibbons, Kaye 1960- 117
Gibbs, Adrea 1960- 126
Gibbs, Alonzo (Lawrence) 1915-1992 5
Gibbs, (Cecilia) May 1877-1969
  Obituary 27
Gibbs, Tony
  See Gibbs, Wolcott, Jr.
Gibbs, Wolcott, Jr. 1935- 40
Giblin, James Cross 1933- 197
  Earlier sketches in SATA *33, 75, 122*
  See also CLR *29*
  See also SAAS *12*
Gibson, Andrew (William) 1949- 72
Gibson, Barbara L. 205
Gibson, Barbara Leonard
  See Gibson, Barbara L.
Gibson, Betty 1911- 75
Gibson, Jo
  See Fluke, Joanne
Gibson, Josephine
  See Hine, Sesyle Joslin
  and Hine, Al(fred Blakelee)
Gibson, Sarah P. 1962- 211
Gibson, William 1914-2008 66
  Obituary 199
Gibson, William Ford
  See Gibson, William
Gidal, Nachum
  See Gidal, Tim Nachum
Gidal, Sonia (Epstein) 1922- 2
Gidal, Tim Nachum 1909-1996 2
Gidalewitsch, Nachum
  See Gidal, Tim Nachum
Gideon, Melanie 1963- 175
Giegling, John A(llan) 1935- 17
Gifaldi, David 1950- 209
  Earlier sketch in SATA *76*
Giff, Patricia Reilly 1935- 203
  Earlier sketches in SATA *33, 70, 121, 160*
Giffard, Hannah 1962- 83
Gifford, Clive 1966- 198
Gifford, Griselda 1931- 171
  Earlier sketch in SATA *42*
Gifford, Kerri 1961- 91
Gifford, Peggy 1952- 191
Gilbert, Ann
  See Taylor, Ann
Gilbert, Anne Yvonne 1951- 185
Gilbert, Barbara Snow 1954- 97

Gilbert, Catherine
  See Murdock, Catherine Gilbert
Gilbert, Frances
  See Collings, Gillian
Gilbert, Harriett 1948- 30
Gilbert, (Agnes) Joan (Sewell) 1931- 10
Gilbert, John (Raphael) 1926- 36
Gilbert, Nan
  See Gilbertson, Mildred Geiger
Gilbert, Roby Goodale 1966- 90
Gilbert, Ruth Gallard Ainsworth
  See Ainsworth, Ruth (Gallard)
Gilbert, Sara (Dulaney) 1943- 82
  Earlier sketch in SATA *11*
Gilbert, Sheri L. 157
Gilbert, Suzie 1956- 97
Gilbert, W(illiam) S(chwenck) 1836-1911 ... 36
Gilbert, Yvonne
  See Gilbert, Anne Yvonne
Gilbertson, Mildred Geiger 1908-1988 2
Gilbreath, Alice 1921- 12
Gilbreth, Frank B., Jr. 1911-2001 2
Gilbreth, Frank Bunker
  See Gilbreth, Frank B., Jr.
Gilchrist, Jan Spivey 1949- 130
  Earlier sketch in SATA *72*
Gilden, Mel 1947- 97
Giles, Gail 196
  Earlier sketch in SATA *152*
Gilfond, Henry 2
Gilge, Jeanette 1924- 22
Gili, Phillida 1944- 70
Gill, Derek (Lewis Theodore) 1919-1997 9
Gill, Margery Jean 1925- 22
Gill, Shelley 176
Gill, Stephen 1932- 63
Gillespie, Carol Ann 1951- 158
Gillett, Mary (Bledsoe) 7
Gillette, Henry Sampson 1915- 14
Gillette, J. Lynett 1946- 103
Gillette, Jan Lynett
  See Gillette, J. Lynett
Gilley, Jeremy 1969- 174
Gillham, Bill
  See Gillham, W(illiam) E(dwin) C(harles)
Gillham, W(illiam) E(dwin) C(harles)
  1936- 42
Gilliam, Stan 1946- 39
  Brief entry 35
Gilliland, Alexis A. 1931- 72
Gilliland, Alexis Arnaldus
  See Gilliland, Alexis A.
Gilliland, (Cleburne) Hap 1918- 92
Gilliland, Judith Heide 180
Gillmor, Don 1954- 127
Gilman, Dorothy 1923- 5
Gilman, Esther 1925- 15
Gilman, Laura Anne 178
Gilman, Phoebe 1940-2002 104
  Obituary 141
  Earlier sketch in SATA *58*
Gilmore, Iris 1900-1982 22
Gilmore, Kate 1931- 87
Gilmore, Mary (Jean Cameron) 1865-1962 . 49
Gilmore, Rachna 1953- 209
Gilmore, Susan 1954- 59
Gilpin, Stephen 213
  Earlier sketch in SATA *177*
Gilroy, Beryl (Agatha) 1924- 80
Gilson, Barbara
  See Gilson, Charles James Louis
Gilson, Charles James Louis 1878-1943
  See YABC *2*
Gilson, Jamie 1933- 176
  Brief entry 34
  Earlier sketches in SATA *37, 91*
Gimpel, Carolyn
  See Hart, Carolyn
Ginsburg, Mirra 1909-2000 92
  Earlier sketch in SATA *6*
  See also CLR *45*

Giovanni, Nikki 1943- 208
  Earlier sketches in SATA *24, 107*
  See also CLR 73
Giovanni, Yolanda Cornelia
  See Giovanni, Nikki
Giovanni, Yolande Cornelia
  See Giovanni, Nikki
Giovanni, Yolande Cornelia, Jr.
  See Giovanni, Nikki
Giovanopoulos, Paul (Arthur) 1939- 7
Gipson, Billie
  See Letts, Billie
Gipson, Fred(erick Benjamin) 1908-1973 2
  Obituary 24
Girard, Linda (Walvoord) 1942- 41
Giraudon, David 1975- 215
Girion, Barbara 1937- 78
  Earlier sketch in SATA *26*
  See also SAAS 14
Girl, Nerdy
  See Castellucci, Cecil
Girouard, Patrick 1957- 155
Girzone, Joseph F. 1930- 76
Girzone, Joseph Francis
  See Girzone, Joseph F.
Gise, Joanne
  See Mattern, Joanne
Gist, E.M. 206
Gittings, Jo (Grenville) Manton 1919- 3
Gittings, Robert (William Victor) 1911-1992 . 6
  Obituary 70
Givens, Janet E(aton) 1932- 60
Givner, Joan 1936- 171
Givner, Joan Mary
  See Givner, Joan
Gladstone, Eve
  See Werner, Herma
Gladstone, Gary 1935- 12
Gladstone, M(yron) J. 1923- 37
Glanville, Brian (Lester) 1931- 42
Glanzman, Louis S. 1922- 36
Glaser, Byron 1954- 154
Glaser, Dianne E(lizabeth) 1937- 50
  Brief entry 31
Glaser, Isabel Joshlin 1929- 94
Glaser, Milton 1929- 151
  Earlier sketch in SATA *11*
Glaser, Shirley 151
Glaspell, Susan 1882(?)-1948
  See YABC 2
Glass, Andrew 1949- 150
  Brief entry 46
  Earlier sketch in SATA *90*
Glass, Linzi 175
Glass, Linzi Alex
  See Glass, Linzi
Glasscock, Amnesia
  See Steinbeck, John
Glassman, Bruce 1961- 76
Glatt, Lisa 1963- 217
Glauber, Uta (Heil) 1936- 17
Glazer, Thomas (Zachariah) 1914-2003 9
Glazer, Tom
  See Glazer, Thomas (Zachariah)
Gleasner, Diana (Cottle) 1936- 29
Gleason, Judith 1929- 24
Gleason, Katherine (A.) 1960- 104
Gleeson, Libby 1950- 142
  Autobiography Feature 142
  Earlier sketches in SATA *82, 118*
Gleiter, Jan 1947- 111
Gleitzman, Morris 1953- 156
  Earlier sketch in SATA *88*
  See also CLR 88
Glen, Maggie 1944- 88
Glendinning, Richard 1917-1988 24
Glendinning, Sally
  See Glendinning, Sara W(ilson)
Glendinning, Sara W(ilson) 1913-1993 24
Glenn, John W. 195

Glenn, Mel 1943- 93
  Brief entry 45
  Earlier sketch in SATA *51*
  See also CLR 51
Glenn, Patricia Brown 1953- 86
Glenn, Sharlee 159
Glenn, Sharlee Mullins
  See Glenn, Sharlee
Glennon, Karen M. 1946- 85
Gles, Margaret Breitmaier 1940- 22
Glick, Carl (Cannon) 1890-1971 14
Glick, Ruth (Burtnick) 1942- 125
Glick, Virginia Kirkus 1893-1980
  Obituary 23
Gliewe, Unada (Grace) 1927- 3
Glimmerveen, Ulco 1958- 85
Glines, Carroll V(ane), Jr. 1920- 19
Gliori, Debi 1959- 189
  Earlier sketches in SATA *72, 138*
Globe, Leah Ain 1900- 41
Glori Ann
  See Blakely, Gloria
Glovach, Linda 1947- 105
  Earlier sketch in SATA *7*
Glover, Denis (James Matthews) 1912-1980 . 7
Glubok, Shirley (Astor) 146
  Autobiography Feature 146
  Earlier sketches in SATA *6, 68*
  See also CLR *1*
  See also SAAS 7
Gluck, Felix 1923-1981
  Obituary 25
Glyman, Caroline A. 1967- 103
Glynne-Jones, William 1907-1977 11
Gobbato, Imero 1923- 39
Gobbletree, Richard
  See Quackenbush, Robert M(ead)
Goble, Dorothy 26
Goble, Paul 1933- 131
  Earlier sketches in SATA *25, 69*
  See also CLR 21
Goble, Warwick (?)-1943 46
Godden, (Margaret) Rumer 1907-1998 36
  Obituary 109
  Earlier sketch in SATA *3*
  See also CLR 20
  See also SAAS 12
Gode, Alexander
  See Gode von Aesch, Alexander (Gottfried
  Friedrich)
Gode von Aesch, Alexander (Gottfried
  Friedrich) 1906-1970 14
Godfrey, Jane
  See Bowden, Joan Chase
Godfrey, Martyn
  See Godfrey, Martyn N.
  and Godfrey, Martyn N.
Godfrey, Martyn N. 1949-2000 95
  See also CLR 57
Godfrey, William
  See Youd, Samuel
Godkin, Celia 1948- 145
  Earlier sketch in SATA *66*
Godkin, Celia Marilyn
  See Godkin, Celia
Godon, Ingrid 1958- 186
Godwin, Laura 1956- 179
Godwin, Sam
  See Pirotta, Saviour
Godwin, Sarah Massini
  See Massini, Sarah
Goede, Irene 1966- 208
Goedecke, Christopher (John) 1951- 81
Goekler, Susan
  See Wooley, Susan Frelick
Goembel, Ponder 204
Goertzen, Glenda 172
Goettel, Elinor 1930- 12
Goetz, Delia 1898-1996 22
  Obituary 91
Goffe, Toni 1936- 61

Goffstein, Brooke
  See Goffstein, Marilyn Brooke
Goffstein, M. B.
  See Goffstein, Marilyn Brooke
Goffstein, Marilyn Brooke 1940- 70
  Earlier sketch in SATA *8*
  See also CLR 3
Goforth, Ellen
  See Francis, Dorothy
Gogol, Sara 1948-2004 80
Goh, Chan Hon 1969- 145
Going, Kelly L.
  See Going, K.L.
Going, Kelly Louise
  See Going, K.L.
Going, K.L. 199
  Earlier sketch in SATA *156*
Golann, Cecil Paige 1921-1995 11
Golbin, Andree 1923- 15
Gold, Alison Leslie 1945- 104
Gold, August 1955- 215
Gold, Bernice 150
Gold, Phyllis
  See Goldberg, Phyllis
Gold, Robert S(tanley) 1924- 63
Gold, Sharlya 9
Gold, Susan
  See Gold, Susan Dudley
Gold, Susan Dudley 1949- 147
Goldberg, Grace 1956- 78
Goldberg, Herbert S. 1926- 25
Goldberg, Jacob 1943- 94
Goldberg, Jake
  See Goldberg, Jacob
Goldberg, Myla 1972(?)- 210
Goldberg, Phyllis 1941- 21
Goldberg, Stan J. 1939- 26
Goldberg, Susan 1948- 71
Goldberg, Whoopi 1955- 119
Goldberger, Judith M. 1948- 80
Goldblatt, Stacey 1969(?)- 191
Golden, Christie 1963- 167
  Earlier sketch in SATA *116*
Goldentyer, Debra 1960- 84
Goldfeder, Cheryl
  See Pahz, Cheryl Suzanne
Goldfeder, James
  See Pahz, James Alon
Goldfeder, Jim
  See Pahz, James Alon
Goldfinger, Jennifer P. 1963- 185
Goldfrank, Helen Colodny 1912- 6
Goldin, Augusta 1906-1999 13
Goldin, Barbara Diamond 1946- 129
  Autobiography Feature 129
  Earlier sketch in SATA *92*
  See also SAAS 26
Goldin, David 1963- 101
Golding, Julia 1969- 188
Golding, Theresa Martin 1960- 150
Golding, William 1911-1993
  See CLR *130*
Golding, William Gerald
  See Golding, William
Goldman, Alex J. 1917- 65
Goldman, E. M. 1943- 103
Goldman, Eleanor Maureen
  See Goldman, E. M.
Goldman, Elizabeth 1949- 90
Goldman, Judy 1955- 212
Goldman, Steven 1964- 207
Goldring, Ann 1937- 149
Goldsborough, June 1923- 19
Goldschmidt, Judy 202
Goldsmith, Connie 1945- 147
Goldsmith, Howard 1943- 108
  Earlier sketch in SATA *24*
Goldsmith, John Herman Thorburn 1903-1987
  Obituary 52
Goldsmith, Oliver 1730(?)-1774 26
Goldsmith, Ruth M. 1919- 62

Goldstein, Nathan 1927- 47
Goldstein, Philip 1910-1997 23
Goldston, Robert (Conroy) 1927- 6
Goldstone, Bruce 183
Goldstone, Lawrence A.
   See Treat, Lawrence
Goldszmit, Henryk 1878-1942 65
   See also CLR 152
Golembe, Carla 1951- 79
Golenbock, Peter 1946- 99
Goll, Reinhold W(eimar) 1897-1993 26
Gollub, Matthew 1960- 134
   Earlier sketch in SATA 83
Golson, Terry 213
Golson, Terry Blonder
   See Golson, Terry
Gomes, Filomena 1965- 183
Gomez, Elena 191
Gomez, Elizabeth 133
Gomez-Freer, Elizabeth
   See Gomez, Elizabeth
Gomi, Taro 1945- 103
   Earlier sketch in SATA 64
   See also CLR 57
Gondosch, Linda 1944- 58
Gonsalves, Rob 1959- 209
Gonyea, Mark 194
Gonzalez, Catherine Troxell 1917-2000 87
Gonzalez, Christina
   See Gonzalez, Maya Christina
Gonzalez, Gloria 1940- 23
Gonzalez, Julie 1958- 174
Gonzalez, Julie Sehers
   See Gonzalez, Julie
Gonzalez, Lucia M. 1957- 202
Gonzalez, Maya
   See Gonzalez, Maya Christina
Gonzalez, Maya Christina 1964- 175
   Earlier sketch in SATA 115
Gonzalez, Rigoberto 1970- 147
Goobie, Beth 1959- 128
Good, Alice 1950- 73
Good, Clare
   See Romano, Clare
Good, Karen Hillard 214
Goodall, Daphne Machin
   See Machin Goodall, Daphne (Edith)
Goodall, Jane 1934- 111
Goodall, John S(trickland) 1908-1996 66
   Obituary 91
   Earlier sketch in SATA 4
   See also CLR 25
Goodbody, Slim
   See Burstein, John
Goode, Diane 1949- 170
   Earlier sketches in SATA 15, 84, 114
Goode, Diane Capuozzo
   See Goode, Diane
Goode, Stephen Ray 1943- 55
   Brief entry 40
Goodenow, Earle 1913- 40
Goodhart, Pippa 1958- 196
   Earlier sketch in SATA 153
Goodhue, Thomas W. 1949- 143
Goodin, Sallie (Brown) 1953- 74
Goodman, Alison 1966- 111
Goodman, Deborah Lerme 1956- 50
   Brief entry 49
Goodman, Elaine 1930- 9
Goodman, Emily 217
Goodman, Joan Elizabeth 1950- 162
   Earlier sketches in SATA 50, 94
Goodman, Susan E. 1952- 181
Goodman, Walter 1927-2002 9
Goodman Koz, Paula 211
Goodrich, Samuel Griswold 1793-1860 23
Goodsell, Jane Neuberger 1921(?)-1988
   Obituary 56
Goodweather, Hartley
   See King, Thomas

GoodWeather, Hartley
   See King, Thomas
Goodwin, Hal
   See Goodwin, Harold L(eland)
Goodwin, Harold L(eland) 1914-1990 51
   Obituary 65
   Earlier sketch in SATA 13
Goodwin, William 1943- 117
Goor, Nancy (Ruth Miller) 1944- 39
   Brief entry 34
Goor, Ron(ald Stephen) 1940- 39
   Brief entry 34
Goossen, Agnes
   See Epp, Margaret A(gnes)
Goossens, Philippe 1963- 195
Gootman, Marilyn E. 1944- 179
Gopnik, Adam 1956- 171
Gorbachev, Valeri 1944- 184
   Autobiography Feature 143
   Earlier sketches in SATA 98, 143
Gordion, Mark
   See Turtledove, Harry
Gordon, Ad
   See Hano, Arnold
Gordon, Amy 1949- 197
   Earlier sketches in SATA 115, 156
Gordon, Bernard Ludwig 1931-2010 27
Gordon, Colonel H. R.
   See Ellis, Edward S.
Gordon, David
   See Garrett, Randall
Gordon, Donald
   See Payne, Donald Gordon
Gordon, Dorothy 1893-1970 20
Gordon, Esther S(aranga) 1935- 10
Gordon, Frederick 1
Gordon, Gaelyn 1939-1997
   See CLR 75
Gordon, Garrett
   See Garrett, Randall
Gordon, Gary
   See Edmonds, I(vy) G(ordon)
Gordon, Hal
   See Goodwin, Harold L(eland)
Gordon, Jeffie Ross
   See Enderle, Judith (Ann) Ross
   and Gordon, Stephanie Jacob
Gordon, John
   See Gesner, Clark
Gordon, John (William) 1925- 84
Gordon, Lew
   See Baldwin, Gordon C(ortis)
Gordon, Margaret (Anna) 1939- 9
Gordon, Mike 1948- 101
Gordon, Mildred 1912-1979
   Obituary 24
Gordon, Selma
   See Lanes, Selma Gordon
Gordon, Sheila 1927- 88
   See also CLR 27
Gordon, Shirley 1921- 48
   Brief entry 41
Gordon, Sol 1923- 11
Gordon, Stephanie Jacob 1940- 89
   Autobiography Feature 114
   Earlier sketch in SATA 64
   See also SAAS 26
Gordon, Stewart
   See Shirreffs, Gordon D(onald)
Gordons, The
   See Gordon, Mildred
   and Gordon, Gordon
Gore, Leonid 185
Gorelick, Molly C(hernow) 1920-2003 9
   Obituary 153
Gorey, Edward (St. John) 1925-2000 70
   Brief entry 27
   Obituary 118
   Earlier sketch in SATA 29
   See also CLR 36
Gorham, Charles Orson 1868-1936 36

Gorham, Michael
   See Folsom, Franklin (Brewster)
Gorman, Carol 187
   Earlier sketch in SATA 150
Gorman, Jacqueline Laks 1955- 148
Gorman, Mike 206
Gormley, Beatrice 1942- 202
   Brief entry 35
   Earlier sketches in SATA 39, 127
Gorog, Judith (Katharine Allen) 1938- 75
   Earlier sketch in SATA 39
Gorrell, Gena K. 1946- 170
Gorsline, Douglas (Warner) 1913-1985 11
   Obituary 43
Gorsline, (Sally) Marie 1928- 28
Gorsline, S. M.
   See Gorsline, (Sally) Marie
Gorton, Kaitlyn
   See Emerson, Kathy Lynn
Gorton, Kathy Lynn
   See Emerson, Kathy Lynn
Goryan, Sirak
   See Saroyan, William
Goschke, Julia 1973- 208
Goscinny, Rene 1926-1977 47
   Brief entry 39
   See also CLR 37
Goss, Clay(ton E.) 1946- 82
Goss, Gary 1947- 124
Goss, Mini 1963- 186
Goto, Scott 203
Gott, Barry 197
Gottesman, S. D.
   See Kornbluth, C(yril) M.
   and Lowndes, Robert A(ugustine) W(ard)
   and Pohl, Frederik
Gottfried, Ted
   See Gottfried, Theodore Mark
Gottfried, Theodore Mark 1928- 150
   Earlier sketch in SATA 85
Gottlieb, Gerald 1923- 7
Gottlieb, William P. 1917-2006 24
Gottlieb, William Paul
   See Gottlieb, William P.
Goudey, Alice E(dwards) 1898-1993 20
Goudge, Eileen 1950- 88
Goudge, Elizabeth (de Beauchamp)
   1900-1984 2
   Obituary 38
   See also CLR 94
Gough, Catherine
   See Mulgan, Catherine
Gough, Philip 1908-1986 45
Gough, Sue 1940- 106
Goulart, Ron 1933- 67
   Earlier sketch in SATA 1
Goulart, Ronald Joseph
   See Goulart, Ron
Gould, Alberta 1945- 96
Gould, Chester 1900-1985 49
   Obituary 43
Gould, Jean R(osalind) 1909-1993 11
   Obituary 77
Gould, Lilian 6
Gould, Marilyn 1928- 76
   Earlier sketch in SATA 15
Gould, Robert 154
Gould, Steven 1955- 95
Gould, Steven Charles
   See Gould, Steven
Gourley, Catherine 1950- 190
   Earlier sketch in SATA 95
Gourse, Leslie 1939-2004 89
Govan, (Mary) Christine Noble 1898-1985 9
Gove, Doris 1944- 72
Govenar, Alan 1952- 189
Govenar, Alan Bruce
   See Govenar, Alan
Govern, Elaine 1939- 26
Gowen, L. Kris 1968- 156

Graaf, Peter
  See Youd, Samuel
Graber, Alexander 1914-1997 98
  Earlier sketch in SATA 7
Graber, George Alexander
  See Graber, Alexander
Graber, Janet 1942- 170
Graber, Richard (Fredrick) 1927- 26
Grabianski, Janusz 1928-1976 39
  Obituary 30
Graboff, Abner 1919-1986 35
Grace, Fran(ces Jane) 45
Grace, N.B.
  See Harper, Suzanne
Grace, Theresa
  See Mattern, Joanne
Gracza, Margaret Young 1928- 56
Graduate of Oxford, A
  See Ruskin, John
Grady, Denise 1952- 189
Graeber, Charlotte Towner 106
  Brief entry 44
  Earlier sketch in SATA 56
Graef, Renee 1956- 204
Graeme, Roderic
  See Jeffries, Roderic
Graf, Michael
  See Graf, Mike
Graf, Mike 1960- 164
Grafe, Max 198
Graff, Lisa 1981- 188
Graff, Polly Anne Colver
  See Colver, Anne
Graff, (S.) Stewart 1908- 9
Graham, Ada 1931- 11
Graham, Alastair 1945- 74
Graham, Arthur Kennon
  See Harrison, David L.
Graham, Bob 1942- 187
  Earlier sketches in SATA 63, 101, 151
  See also CLR 31
Graham, Brenda Knight 1942- 32
Graham, Charlotte
  See Bowden, Joan Chase
Graham, Eleanor 1896-1984 18
  Obituary 38
Graham, Ennis
  See Molesworth, Mary Louisa
Graham, Frank, Jr. 1925- 11
Graham, Georgia 1959- 190
Graham, Ian 1953- 112
Graham, John 1926-2007 11
Graham, Kennon
  See Harrison, David L.
Graham, Larry
  See Graham, Lawrence
Graham, Lawrence 1962- 63
Graham, Lawrence Otis
  See Graham, Lawrence
Graham, Linda
  See Graham-Barber, Lynda
Graham, Lorenz (Bell) 1902-1989 74
  Obituary 63
  Earlier sketch in SATA 2
  See also CLR 10
  See also SAAS 5
Graham, Margaret Bloy 1920- 11
Graham, Robin Lee 1949- 7
Graham, Shirley 1896(?)-1977
  See Du Bois, Shirley Graham
Graham-Barber, Lynda 1944- 159
  Earlier sketch in SATA 42
Graham-Cameron, M.
  See Graham-Cameron, M(alcolm) G(ordon)
Graham-Cameron, M(alcolm) G(ordon)
  1931- 53
  Brief entry 45
Graham-Cameron, Mike
  See Graham-Cameron, M(alcolm) G(ordon)

Grahame, Kenneth 1859-1932 100
  See also YABC 1
  See also CLR 135
Gralley, Jean 166
Gramatky, Hardie 1907-1979 30
  Obituary 23
  Earlier sketch in SATA 1
  See also CLR 22
Grambling, Lois G. 1927- 206
  Earlier sketches in SATA 71, 148
Grambo, Rebecca L(ynn) 1963- 109
Grammer, June Amos 1927- 58
Grand, Samuel 1912-1988 42
Grandits, John 1949- 192
GrandPre, Mary 1954- 184
Grandville, J. J.
  See Gerard, Jean Ignace Isidore
Grandville, Jean Ignace Isidore Gerard
  See Gerard, Jean Ignace Isidore
Granfield, Linda 1950- 160
  Earlier sketch in SATA 96
Grange, Peter
  See Nicole, Christopher (Robin)
Granger, Margaret Jane 1925(?)-1977
  Obituary 27
Granger, Michele 1949- 88
Granger, Peggy
  See Granger, Margaret Jane
Granowsky, Alvin 1936- 101
Granstaff, Bill 1925- 10
Granstrom, Brita 1969- 167
  Earlier sketch in SATA 111
Grant, Bruce 1893-1977 5
  Obituary 25
Grant, Cynthia D. 1950- 147
  Earlier sketches in SATA 33, 77
Grant, Eva 1907-1996 7
Grant, Evva H. 1913-1977
  Obituary 27
Grant, Gordon 1875-1962 25
Grant, Gwen(doline Ellen) 1940- 47
Grant, Judyann Ackerman 211
Grant, Katie M.
  See Grant, K.M.
Grant, K.M. 175
Grant, (Alice) Leigh 1947- 10
Grant, Matthew G.
  See May, Julian
Grant, Maxwell
  See Gibson, Walter B(rown)
  and Lynds, Dennis
Grant, Melvyn 183
Grant, Myrna (Lois) 1934- 21
Grant, Neil 1938- 154
  Earlier sketch in SATA 14
Grant, Nicholas
  See Nicole, Christopher (Robin)
Grant, Richard 1948- 80
Grant, Skeeter
  See Spiegelman, Art
Grater, Michael 1923- 57
Gratz, Alan 1972- 212
Gravel, Fern
  See Hall, James Norman
Gravelle, Karen 1942- 166
  Earlier sketch in SATA 78
Graves, Charles Parlin 1911-1972 4
Graves, Keith 191
  Earlier sketch in SATA 156
Graves, Robert 1895-1985 45
Graves, Robert von Ranke
  See Graves, Robert
Graves, Valerie
  See Bradley, Marion Zimmer
Gravett, Emily 1972(?)- 189
Gray, Betsy
  See Poole, Gray Johnson
Gray, Caroline
  See Nicole, Christopher (Robin)
Gray, Claudia 213
Gray, Dianne E. 183

Gray, Elizabeth Janet
  See Vining, Elizabeth Gray
Gray, Genevieve S(tuck) 1920-1995 4
Gray, Harold (Lincoln) 1894-1968 33
  Brief entry 32
Gray, Jenny
  See Gray, Genevieve S(tuck)
Gray, John Lee
  See Jakes, John
Gray, Judith A. 1949- 93
Gray, Judith Anne
  See Gray, Judith A.
Gray, Keith 151
Gray, Kes 1960- 153
Gray, Les 1929- 82
Gray, Libba Moore 1937- 83
Gray, Luli 1945- 149
  Earlier sketch in SATA 90
Gray, Marian
  See Pierce, Edith Gray
Gray, Nicholas Stuart 1922-1981 4
  Obituary 27
Gray, Nigel 1941- 104
  Earlier sketch in SATA 33
Gray, (Lucy) Noel (Clervaux) 1898-1983 47
Gray, Patricia (Clark) 7
Gray, Patsey
  See Gray, Patricia (Clark)
Gray, Rita 184
Graydon, Shari 1958- 158
Grayland, V. Merle
  See Grayland, Valerie (Merle Spanner)
Grayland, Valerie (Merle Spanner) 7
Grayson, Devin (Kalile) 1970- 119
Grayson, Kristine
  See Rusch, Kristine Kathryn
Grayson, Paul 1946- 79
Graystone, Lynn
  See Brennan, Joseph Lomas
Great Comte, The
  See Hawkesworth, Eric
Greaves, Margaret 1914-1995 87
  Earlier sketch in SATA 7
Greaves, Nick 1955- 77
Gree, Alain 1936- 28
Green, Adam
  See Weisgard, Leonard (Joseph)
Green, Anne Canevari 1943- 62
Green, Brian
  See Card, Orson Scott
Green, Cliff(ord) 1934- 126
Green, Connie Jordan 1938- 80
Green, D.
  See Casewit, Curtis W(erner)
Green, Elizabeth Shippen 1871-1954 139
Green, Hannah
  See Greenberg, Joanne (Goldenberg)
Green, Jane 1937- 9
Green, Jessica 211
Green, John 1977(?)- 170
Green, Mary Moore 1906- 11
Green, Morton 1937- 8
Green, Norma B(erger) 1925- 11
Green, Phyllis 1932- 20
Green, Roger (Gilbert) Lancelyn 1918-1987 . 2
  Obituary 53
Green, (James Le)Roy 1948- 89
Green, Sheila Ellen 1934- 148
  Earlier sketches in SATA 8, 87
Green, Timothy 1953- 91
Greenaway, Kate 1846-1901 100
  See also YABC 2
  See also CLR 111
Greenbank, Anthony Hunt 1933- 39
Greenberg, David 1954- 171
Greenberg, David T.
  See Greenberg, David
Greenberg, Harvey R. 1935- 5
Greenberg, Jan 1942- 211
  Earlier sketches in SATA 61, 125
Greenberg, Joanne (Goldenberg) 1932- 25

Greenberg, Melanie Hope 1954- *214*
  Earlier sketch in SATA *72*
Greenberg, Polly 1932- *52*
  Brief entry *43*
Greenblat, Rodney Alan 1960- *106*
Greenburg, Dan 1936- *175*
  Earlier sketch in SATA *102*
Greene, Bette 1934- *161*
  Earlier sketches in SATA *8, 102*
  See also CLR *140*
  See also SAAS *16*
Greene, Carla 1916- *67*
  Earlier sketch in SATA *1*
Greene, Carol *102*
  Brief entry *44*
  Earlier sketch in SATA *66*
Greene, Constance C(larke) 1924- *72*
  Earlier sketch in SATA *11*
  See also CLR *62*
  See also SAAS *11*
Greene, Edgar
  See Papademetriou, Lisa
Greene, Ellin 1927- *23*
Greene, Graham 1904-1991 .... *20*
Greene, Graham Henry
  See Greene, Graham
Greene, Jacqueline Dembar 1946- *212*
  Earlier sketches in SATA *76, 131*
Greene, Laura Offenhartz 1935- *38*
Greene, Meg
  See Malvasi, Meg Greene
Greene, Michele 1962- *178*
Greene, Michele Dominguez
  See Greene, Michele
Greene, Rhonda Gowler 1955- *160*
  Earlier sketch in SATA *101*
Greene, Stephanie 1950- *173*
  Earlier sketch in SATA *127*
Greene, Wade 1933- *11*
Greene, Yvonne
  See Flesch, Yolande
Greenfeld, Howard (Scheinman) 1928- *140*
  Earlier sketch in SATA *19*
Greenfeld, John(ua Joseph) 1928- *62*
Greenfield, Eloise 1929- *155*
  Earlier sketches in SATA *19, 61, 105*
  See also CLR *38*
  See also SAAS *16*
Greenhaus, Thelma Nurenberg 1903-1984
  Obituary *45*
Greenhut, Josh
  See Mercer, Sienna
Greening, Hamilton
  See Hamilton, Charles (Harold St. John)
Greenlaw, M. Jean 1941- *107*
Greenleaf, Barbara Kaye 1942- *6*
Greenleaf, Peter 1910-1997 .... *33*
Greenlee, Sharon 1935- *77*
Greeno, Gayle 1949- *81*
Greenseid, Diane 1948- *178*
  Earlier sketch in SATA *93*
Greenspun, Adele Aron 1938- *142*
  Earlier sketch in SATA *76*
Greenstein, Elaine 1959- *150*
  Earlier sketch in SATA *82*
Greenwald, Sheila
  See Green, Sheila Ellen
Greenwood, Barbara 1940- *129*
  Earlier sketch in SATA *90*
Greenwood, Mark 1958- *202*
Greenwood, Pamela D. 1944- *115*
Greer, Richard
  See Garrett, Randall
  and Silverberg, Robert
Gregg, Andrew K. 1929- *81*
Gregg, Charles T(hornton) 1927- *65*
Gregg, Walter H(arold) 1919- *20*
Gregor, Arthur 1923- *36*
Gregor, Lee
  See Pohl, Frederik
Gregori, Leon 1919- *15*

Gregorian, Joyce Ballou 1946-1991 .... *30*
  Obituary *83*
Gregorich, Barbara 1943- *184*
  Earlier sketch in SATA *66*
Gregorowski, Christopher 1940- *30*
Gregory, Diana (Jean) 1933- *49*
  Brief entry *42*
Gregory, Harry
  See Gottfried, Theodore Mark
Gregory, Jean
  See Ure, Jean
Gregory, Kristiana 1951- *212*
  Earlier sketches in SATA *74, 136*
Gregory, Nan 1944- *192*
  Earlier sketch in SATA *148*
Gregory, Philippa 1954- *122*
Gregory, Stephen
  See Penzler, Otto
Gregory, Valiska 1940- *82*
Greif, Jean-Jacques 1944- *195*
Greisman, Joan Ruth 1937- *31*
Grendon, Stephen
  See Derleth, August (William)
Grenville, Pelham
  See Wodehouse, P. G.
Gretz, Susanna 1937- *7*
Gretzer, John *18*
Grewdead, Roy
  See Gorey, Edward (St. John)
Grey, Carol
  See Lowndes, Robert A(ugustine) W(ard)
Grey, Christopher *191*
Grey, Christopher Peter
  See Grey, Christopher
Grey, Jerry 1926- *11*
Grey, Mini *205*
  Earlier sketch in SATA *166*
Greybeard the Pirate
  See Macintosh, Brownie
Grey Owl
  See Belaney, Archibald Stansfeld
Gri
  See Denney, Diana
Gribbin, John 1946- *159*
Gribbin, John R.
  See Gribbin, John
Grice, Frederick 1910-1983 .... *6*
Grider, Dorothy 1915- *31*
Gridley, Marion E(leanor) 1906-1974 .... *35*
  Obituary *26*
Grieco-Tiso, Pina 1954- *108*
Grieder, Walter 1924- *9*
Griego, Tony A. 1955- *77*
Griese, Arnold A(lfred) 1921- *9*
Griessman, Annette 1962- *170*
  Earlier sketch in SATA *116*
Grieve, James 1934- *146*
Grifalconi, Ann 1929- *210*
  Earlier sketches in SATA *2, 66, 133*
  See also CLR *35*
  See also SAAS *16*
Griffin, Adele 1970- *195*
  Earlier sketches in SATA *105, 153*
Griffin, Elizabeth May 1985- *89*
Griffin, Gillett Good 1928- *26*
Griffin, Judith Berry *34*
Griffin, Kitty 1951- *137*
Griffin, Peni R. 1961- *193*
  Earlier sketches in SATA *67, 99*
Griffin, Steven A. 1953- *89*
Griffin, Steven Arthur
  See Griffin, Steven A.
Griffin, W.E.B. 1929- *5*
Griffith, Connie 1946- *89*
Griffith, Gershom 1960- *85*
Griffith, Helen V. 1934- *87*
  Autobiography Feature *107*
  Earlier sketch in SATA *39*
Griffith, Helen Virginia
  See Griffith, Helen V.

Griffith, Jeannette
  See Eyerly, Jeannette
Griffith, Saul 1974- *200*
Griffiths, Andy 1961- *196*
  Earlier sketch in SATA *152*
Griffiths, G(ordon) D(ouglas) 1910-1973
  Obituary *20*
Griffiths, Helen 1939- *86*
  Earlier sketch in SATA *5*
  See also CLR *75*
  See also SAAS *5*
Grigson, Jane (McIntire) 1928-1990 .... *63*
Grimes, Lee 1920- *68*
Grimes, Nikki 1950- *174*
  Earlier sketches in SATA *93, 136*
  See also CLR *42*
Grimly, Gris *186*
Grimm, Jacob Ludwig Karl 1785-1863 .... *22*
  See also CLR *112*
Grimm, Wilhelm Karl 1786-1859 .... *22*
  See also CLR *112*
Grimm, William C(arey) 1907-1992 .... *14*
Grimm and Grim
  See Grimm, Jacob Ludwig Karl
  and Grimm, Wilhelm Karl
Grimm Brothers
  See Grimm, Jacob Ludwig Karl
  and Grimm, Wilhelm Karl
Grimsdell, Jeremy 1942- *83*
Grimshaw, Nigel (Gilroy) 1925- *23*
Grimsley, Gordon
  See Groom, Arthur William
Grindley, Jane Sally
  See Grindley, Sally
Grindley, Sally 1953- *148*
Gringhuis, Dirk
  See Gringhuis, Richard H.
Gringhuis, Richard H. 1918-1974 .... *6*
  Obituary *25*
Grinnell, David
  See Wollheim, Donald A(llen)
Grinnell, George Bird 1849-1938 .... *16*
Grinspoon, David
  See Grinspoon, David H.
Grinspoon, David H. 1959- *156*
Grinspoon, David Harry
  See Grinspoon, David H.
Gripe, Maria 1923- *74*
  Earlier sketch in SATA *2*
  See also CLR *5*
Gripe, Maria Kristina
  See Gripe, Maria
Grobler, Piet 1959- *201*
Groch, Judith (Goldstein) 1929- *25*
Grode, Redway
  See Gorey, Edward (St. John)
Groener, Carl
  See Lowndes, Robert A(ugustine) W(ard)
Groening, Matt 1954- *116*
  Earlier sketch in SATA *81*
Grohmann, Susan 1948- *84*
Grohskopf, Bernice *7*
Grol, Lini R(icharda) 1913- *9*
Grollman, Earl A. 1925- *22*
Groom, Arthur William 1898-1964 .... *10*
Grooms, Duffy 1964- *169*
Gross, Alan 1947- *54*
  Brief entry *43*
Gross, Ernie 1913- *67*
Gross, Philip 1952- *164*
  Earlier sketch in SATA *84*
Gross, Philip John
  See Gross, Philip
Gross, Ruth Belov 1929- *33*
Gross, Sarah Chokla 1906-1976 .... *9*
  Obituary *26*
Grosser, Morton 1931- *74*
Grosser, Vicky 1958- *83*
Grossman, Bill 1948- *126*
  Earlier sketch in SATA *72*
Grossman, Nancy 1940- *29*

Grossman, Patricia 1951- 73
Grossman, Robert 1940- 11
Grote, JoAnn A. 1951- 113
Groten, Dallas 1951- 64
Groth, John (August) 1908-1988 21
    Obituary 56
Groth-Fleming, Candace
    See Fleming, Candace
Grove, Vicki 1948- 151
    Autobiography Feature 151
    Earlier sketch in SATA *122*
Grover, Lorie Ann 1964- 168
Grover, Wayne 1934- 69
Groves, Georgina
    See Symons, (Dorothy) Geraldine
Groves, Maketa 1950- 107
Groves, Seli 77
Grubb, Lisa 160
Gruber, Michael 1940- 173
Gruber, Terry (deRoy) 1953- 66
Gruelle, John 1880-1938 35
    Brief entry 32
    See also CLR *34*
Gruelle, Johnny
    See Gruelle, John
Gruenberg, Sidonie Matsner 1881-1974 2
    Obituary 27
Gruhzit-Hoyt, Olga (Margaret) 1922- 127
    Earlier sketch in SATA *16*
Grummer, Arnold E(dward) 1923- 49
Grunewalt, Pine
    See Kunhardt, Edith
Grunwell, Jeanne Marie 1971- 147
Grupper, Jonathan 137
Gryski, Camilla 1948- 72
Guarino, Dagmar
    See Guarino, Deborah
Guarino, Deborah 1954- 68
Guay, Georgette (Marie Jeanne) 1952- 54
Guay, Rebecca 209
Guay-Mitchell, Rebecca
    See Guay, Rebecca
Guback, Georgia 88
Guccione, Leslie Davis 1946- 111
    Earlier sketch in SATA *72*
Guck, Dorothy 1913-2002 27
Gudeon, Karla 212
Guerny, Gene
    See Gurney, Gene
Guest, Elissa Haden 1953- 125
Guest, Jacqueline 1952- 135
Guevara, Susan 167
    Earlier sketch in SATA *97*
Gugler, Laurel Dee 95
Gugliotta, Bobette 1918-1994 7
Guianan, Eve 1965- 102
Guiberson, Brenda Z. 1946- 211
    Earlier sketches in SATA *71, 124*
Guibert, Emmanuel 1964- 181
Guile, Melanie 1949- 152
    Earlier sketch in SATA *104*
Guillaume, Jeanette G. Flierl 1899-1990 8
Guillot, Rene 1900-1969 7
    See also CLR *22*
Guisewite, Cathy 1950- 57
Guisewite, Cathy Lee
    See Guisewite, Cathy
Gulbis, Stephen 1959- 142
Gulley, Judie 1942- 58
Gump, P. Q.
    See Card, Orson Scott
Gundrey, Elizabeth 1924- 23
Gunn, James E. 1923- 35
Gunn, James Edwin
    See Gunn, James E.
Gunn, Robin Jones 1955- 84
Gunnella 1956- 197
Gunning, Monica Olwen 1930- 161
Gunston, Bill
    See Gunston, William Tudor
Gunston, William Tudor 1927- 9

Gunterman, Bertha Lisette 1886(?)-1975
    Obituary 27
Gunther, John 1901-1970
Guravich, Dan 1918- 74
Gurko, Leo 1914- 9
Gurko, Miriam 1910(?)-1988 9
    Obituary 58
Gurney, Gene 1924- 65
Gurney, James 1958- 120
    Earlier sketch in SATA *76*
Gurney, John Steven 1962- 143
    Earlier sketch in SATA *75*
Gustafson, Sarah R.
    See Riedman, Sarah R(egal)
Gustafson, Scott 1956- 34
Gustavson, Adam 1974- 214
    Earlier sketch in SATA *176*
Guthrie, A(lfred) B(ertram), Jr. 1901-1991 .. 62
    Obituary 67
Guthrie, Anne 1890-1979 28
Guthrie, Donna W. 1946- 105
    Earlier sketch in SATA *63*
Gutierrez, Akemi 172
Gutierrez, Rudy 203
Gutman, Bill 128
    Brief entry 43
    Earlier sketch in SATA *67*
Gutman, Dan 1955- 188
    Earlier sketches in SATA *77, 139*
Gutman, Naham 1899(?)-1981
    Obituary 25
Gutmann, Bessie Pease 1876-1960 73
Guy, Geoffrey 1942- 153
Guy, Ginger Foglesong 1954- 171
Guy, Rosa 1925- 122
    Earlier sketches in SATA *14, 62*
    See also CLR *137*
Guy, Rosa Cuthbert
    See Guy, Rosa
Guy, Susan 1948- 149
Guymer, (Wilhelmina) Mary 1909- 50
Guzman, Lila 1952- 168
Guzman, Rick 1957- 168
Gwaltney, Doris 1932- 181
Gwynne, Fred(erick Hubbard) 1926-1993 41
    Brief entry 27
    Obituary 75
Gwynne, Oscar A.
    See Ellis, Edward S.
Gwynne, Oswald A.
    See Ellis, Edward S.
Gyorkos, Charmaine Echeverria
    See Echeverria Gyorkos, Charmaine

H

Haab, Sherri 1964- 169
    Earlier sketch in SATA *91*
Haar, Jaap ter
    See ter Haar, Jaap
Haarsma, P.J. 183
Haas, Carolyn Buhai 1926- 43
Haas, Dan 1957- 105
Haas, Dorothy F. 46
    Brief entry 43
    See also SAAS *17*
Haas, Irene 1929- 96
    Earlier sketch in SATA *17*
Haas, James E. 1943- 40
Haas, James Edward
    See Haas, James E.
Haas, Jessie 1959- 215
Haas, (Katherine) Jessie 1959- 135
    Autobiography Feature 135
    Earlier sketch in SATA *98*
Haas, Merle S. 1896(?)-1985
    Obituary 41
Habenstreit, Barbara 1937- 5
Haber, Karen 1955- 78

Haber, Louis 1910-1988 12
Hacker, Randi 1951- 185
Hacker, Randi Dawn
    See Hacker, Randi
Hackett, John Winthrop 1910-1997 65
Hacks, Peter 1928-2003
    Obituary 151
Haddix, Margaret Peterson 1964- 187
    Earlier sketches in SATA *94, 125*
Haddon, Mark 1962- 155
Hader, Berta (Hoerner) 1891(?)-1976 16
Hader, Elmer (Stanley) 1889-1973 16
Hadithi, Mwenye
    See Hobson, Bruce
Hadley, Franklin
    See Winterbotham, R(ussell) R(obert)
Hadley, Lee 1934-1995 89
    Brief entry 38
    Obituary 86
    Earlier sketch in SATA *47*
    See also CLR *40*
    See also SAAS *14*
Haeffele, Deborah 1954- 76
Haenel, Wolfram 1956- 89
    See also CLR *64*
Hafner, Marylin 1925- 179
    Earlier sketches in SATA *7, 121*
Haft, Erin
    See Ehrenhaft, Daniel
Hager, Alan 1940- 176
Hager, Alice Rogers 1894-1969
    Obituary 26
Hager, Betty 1923- 89
Hager, Jenna Bush
    See Bush, Jenna
Hager, Sarah 171
Hager, Thomas 1953- 119
Hager, Tom
    See Hager, Thomas
Hagerup, Klaus 1946- 186
Haggard, H(enry) Rider 1856-1925 16
Haggerty, James J(oseph) 1920- 5
Hagon, Priscilla
    See Allan, Mabel Esther
Hague, Kathleen 1949- 49
    Brief entry 45
Hague, Michael 1948- .... • 185
    Brief entry 32
    Earlier sketches in SATA *48, 80, 129*
Hague, Michael R.
    See Hague, Michael
Hague, Susan Kathleen
    See Hague, Kathleen
Hahn, Emily 1905-1997 3
    Obituary 96
Hahn, Hannelore 8
Hahn, James (Sage) 1947- 9
Hahn, Lynn 1949- 9
Hahn, Mary Downing 1937- 208
    Autobiography Feature 157
    Brief entry 44
    Earlier sketches in SATA *50, 81, 138, 157*
    See also SAAS *12*
Hahn, Michael T. 1953- 92
Hahn, Mona Lynn
    See Hahn, Lynn
Haig-Brown, Roderick (Langmere)
    1908-1976 12
    See also CLR *31*
Haight, Anne Lyon 1895-1977
    Obituary 30
Haight, Rip
    See Carpenter, John
Haight, Sandy 1949- 79
Haij, Vera
    See Jansson, Tove (Marika)
Haines, Gail Kay 1943- 11
Haines, Margaret Ann Beck
    See Beck, Peggy
Haining, Peter 1940-2007 14
    Obituary 188

Haining, Peter Alexander
See Haining, Peter
Hains, Harriet
See Watson, Carol
Hajdusiewicz, Babs Bell *163*
Hakim, Joy 1931- *173*
Earlier sketch in SATA *83*
Halacy, D. S., Jr. 1919-2002 .... *36*
See also SAAS *8*
Halacy, Dan
See Halacy, D. S., Jr.
Halam, Ann
See Jones, Gwyneth A.
Haldane, Roger John 1945- *13*
Hale, Arlene 1924-1982 .... *49*
Hale, Bruce 1957- *203*
Earlier sketch in SATA *123*
Hale, Christy
See Apostolou, Christine Hale
Hale, Edward Everett 1822-1909 .... *16*
Hale, Glenn
See Walker, Robert W.
Hale, Helen
See Mulcahy, Lucille Burnett
Hale, Irina 1932- *26*
Hale, Kathleen 1898-2000 .... *66*
Obituary *121*
Earlier sketch in SATA *17*
Hale, Linda (Howe) 1929- *6*
Hale, Lucretia P.
See Hale, Lucretia Peabody
Hale, Lucretia Peabody 1820-1900 .... *26*
See also CLR *105*
Hale, Marian *194*
Hale, Nancy 1908-1988 .... *31*
Obituary *57*
Hale, Nathan 1976- *210*
Hale, Shannon *200*
Earlier sketch in SATA *158*
Haley, Amanda *205*
Haley, Gail E(inhart) 1939- *161*
Autobiography Feature *161*
Brief entry *28*
Earlier sketches in SATA *43, 78, 136*
See also CLR *21*
See also SAAS *13*
Haley, Neale *52*
Halfmann, Janet 1944- *208*
Hall, Adam
See Trevor, Elleston
Hall, Adele 1910- *7*
Hall, Anna Gertrude 1882-1967 .... *8*
Hall, August *207*
Hall, Barbara 1961- *68*
Hall, Becky 1950- *186*
Hall, Beverly B. 1918- *95*
Hall, Borden
See Yates, Raymond F(rancis)
Hall, Brian P(atrick) 1935- *31*
Hall, Cameron
See del Rey, Lester
Hall, Caryl
See Hansen, Caryl (Hall)
Hall, Donald 1928- *97*
Earlier sketch in SATA *23*
Hall, Donald Andrew, Jr.
See Hall, Donald
Hall, Douglas 1931- *43*
Hall, Elizabeth 1929- *77*
Hall, Elvajean 1910-1984 .... *6*
Hall, Francie 1940- *166*
Hall, James Norman 1887-1951 .... *21*
Hall, Jesse
See Boesen, Victor
Hall, Katy
See McMullan, Kate
Hall, Kirsten Marie 1974- *67*
Hall, Lynn 1937- *79*
Earlier sketches in SATA *2, 47*
See also SAAS *4*
Hall, Malcolm 1945- *7*

Hall, Marcellus *203*
Hall, Marjory
See Yeakley, Marjory Hall
Hall, Melanie W. 1949- *169*
Earlier sketches in SATA *78, 116*
Hall, Patricia 1940- *136*
Hall, Rosalys Haskell 1914- *7*
Hall, Willis 1929-2005 .... *66*
Hallard, Peter
See Catherall, Arthur
Hallas, Richard
See Knight, Eric
Hall-Clarke, James
See Rowland-Entwistle, (Arthur) Theodore
(Henry)
Hallensleben, Georg 1958- *173*
Haller, Dorcas Woodbury 1946- *46*
Hallett, Mark 1947- *83*
Halliburton, Richard 1900-1939(?) *81*
Halliburton, Warren J. 1924- *19*
Halliday, Brett
See Dresser, Davis
and Johnson, (Walter) Ryerson
and Terrall, Robert
Halliday, William R(oss) 1926- *52*
Hallin, Emily Watson 1916-1995 .... *6*
Hallinan, P. K. 1944- *39*
Brief entry *37*
Hallinan, Patrick Kenneth
See Hallinan, P. K.
Hallman, Ruth 1929- *43*
Brief entry *28*
Hallowell, Tommy
See Hill, Thomas
Hall-Quest, (Edna) Olga W(ilbourne)
1899-1986 .... *11*
Obituary *47*
Halls, Kelly Milner 1957- *131*
Hallstead, William F(inn III) 1924- *11*
Hallward, Michael 1889-1982 .... *12*
Halperin, Michael *156*
Halperin, Wendy Anderson 1952- *200*
Earlier sketches in SATA *80, 125*
Halpern, Julie 1975- *198*
Halpin, Brendan 1968- *193*
Halpin, Marlene 1927- *88*
Halse, Laurie Beth
See Anderson, Laurie Halse
Halsell, Grace (Eleanor) 1923-2000 .... *13*
Halsey, Megan *185*
Halsted, Anna Roosevelt 1906-1975
Obituary *30*
Halter, Jon C(harles) 1941- *22*
Halverson, Deborah *202*
Halvorson, Marilyn 1948- *123*
Hamalian, Leo 1920- *41*
Hamberger, John 1934- *14*
Hamblin, Dora Jane 1920- *36*
Hambly, Barbara 1951- *108*
Hambly, Barbara Joan
See Hambly, Barbara
Hamer, Martyn
See Eldin, Peter
Hamerstrom, Frances 1907-1998 .... *24*
Hamil, Thomas Arthur 1928- *14*
Hamill, Ethel
See Webb, Jean Francis (III)
Hamilton, (John) Alan 1943- *66*
Hamilton, Alice
See Cromie, Alice Hamilton
Hamilton, Anita 1919- *92*
Hamilton, Buzz
See Hemming, Roy G.
Hamilton, Carol (Jean Barber) 1935- *94*
Hamilton, Charles (Harold St. John)
1876-1961 .... *13*
Hamilton, Charles 1913-1996 .... *65*
Obituary *93*
Hamilton, Clive
See Lewis, C. S.

Hamilton, Dorothy (Drumm) 1906-1983 ...... *12*
Obituary *35*
Hamilton, Edith 1867-1963 .... *20*
Hamilton, Edmond 1904-1977 .... *118*
Hamilton, (Muriel) Elizabeth (Mollie)
1906- *23*
Hamilton, Emma Walton 1962- *177*
Hamilton, Franklin
See Silverberg, Robert
Hamilton, Gail
See Corcoran, Barbara (Asenath)
and Dodge, Mary Abigail
Hamilton, Kersten 1958- *204*
Earlier sketch in SATA *134*
Hamilton, K.R.
See Hamilton, Kersten
Hamilton, Martha 1953- *183*
Earlier sketch in SATA *123*
Hamilton, Mary (E.) 1927- *55*
Hamilton, Mollie
See Kaye, M.M.
Hamilton, Morse 1943-1998 .... *101*
Earlier sketch in SATA *35*
Hamilton, Peter F. 1960- *109*
Hamilton, Priscilla
See Gellis, Roberta
Hamilton, Ralph
See Stratemeyer, Edward L.
Hamilton, Virginia 1936-2002 .... *123*
Obituary *132*
Earlier sketches in SATA *4, 56, 79*
See also CLR *127*
Hamilton, Virginia Esther
See Hamilton, Virginia
Hamilton-Paterson, James 1941- *82*
Hamlet, Ova
See Lupoff, Richard A(llen)
Hamley, D. C.
See Hamley, Dennis
Hamley, Dennis 1935- *69*
Earlier sketch in SATA *39*
See also CLR *47*
See also SAAS *22*
Hamley, Dennis C.
See Hamley, Dennis
Hamlin, Peter J. 1970- *84*
Hamm, Diane Johnston 1949- *78*
Hammer, Charles 1934- *58*
Hammer, Richard 1928- *6*
Hammerman, Gay M(orenus) 1926- *9*
Hammill, Matt 1982- *206*
Hammond, Andrew 1970- *181*
Hammond, Ralph
See Hammond Innes, Ralph
Hammond, Winifred G(raham) 1899-1992 ... *29*
Obituary *107*
Hammond Innes, Ralph 1913-1998 .... *116*
Hammontree, Marie (Gertrude) 1913- *13*
Hample, Zack 1977- *161*
Hampshire, Joyce Gregorian
See Gregorian, Joyce Ballou
Hampshire, Susan 1942- *98*
Hampson, (Richard) Denman 1929- *15*
Hampson, Frank 1918(?)-1985
Obituary *46*
Hampton, Wilborn 1940- *196*
Earlier sketch in SATA *156*
Hamre, Leif 1914- *5*
Hamsa, Bobbie 1944- *52*
Brief entry *38*
Han, Jenny 1981- *175*
Han, Lu
See Stickler, Soma Han
Han, Soma
See Stickler, Soma Han
Han, Suzanne Crowder 1953- *89*
Hancock, Mary A. 1923- *31*
Hancock, Sibyl 1940- *9*
Hand, Elizabeth 1957- *167*
Earlier sketch in SATA *118*

Handford, Martin (John) 1956- *64*
See also CLR 22
Handforth, Thomas (Schofield) 1897-1948 .. *42*
Handler, Daniel
See Snicket, Lemony
Handville, Robert (Tompkins) 1924- *45*
Hane, Roger 1940-1974
Obituary *20*
Hanel, Wolfram
See Haenel, Wolfram
Haney, Lynn 1941- *23*
Hanff, Helene 1916-1997 .... *97*
Earlier sketch in SATA *11*
Hanft, Josh 1956- *197*
Hanft, Joshua E.
See Hanft, Josh
Hanley, Boniface Francis 1924- *65*
Hanlon, Emily 1945- *15*
Hann, Jacquie 1951- *19*
Hann, Judith 1942- *77*
Hanna, Bill
See Hanna, William (Denby)
Hanna, Cheryl 1951- *84*
Hanna, Dan *200*
Hanna, Jack (Bushnell) 1947- *74*
Hanna, Nell(ie L.) 1908- *55*
Hanna, Paul R(obert) 1902-1988 .... *9*
Hanna, William (Denby) 1910-2001 .... *51*
Obituary *126*
Hannam, Charles 1925- *50*
Hannan, Peter 1954- *187*
Hannigan, Katherine *170*
Hannon, Ezra
See Hunter, Evan
Hann-Syme, Marguerite *127*
Hano, Arnold 1922- *12*
Hano, Renee Roth
See Roth-Hano, Renee
Hanover, Terri
See Huff, Tanya
Hansen, Ann Larkin 1958- *96*
Hansen, Brooks 1965- *104*
Hansen, Caryl (Hall) 1929- *39*
Hansen, Ian V. 1929- *113*
Hansen, Jennifer 1972- *156*
Hansen, Joyce 1942- *172*
Autobiography Feature *172*
Brief entry *39*
Earlier sketches in SATA *46, 101*
See also CLR *21*
See also SAAS *15*
Hansen, Joyce Viola
See Hansen, Joyce
Hansen, Mark Victor *112*
Hansen, Ron 1947- *56*
Hansen, Ronald Thomas
See Hansen, Ron
Hanser, Richard (Frederick) 1909-1981 .... *13*
Hanson, Joan 1938- *8*
Hanson, Joseph E. 1894(?)-1971
Obituary *27*
Hanson, Mary Elizabeth *188*
Hanson, Warren 1949- *155*
Hansson, Gunilla 1939- *64*
Hantman, Clea *200*
Harald, Eric
See Boesen, Victor
Harazin, S. A. *210*
Harcourt, Ellen Knowles 1890(?)-1984
Obituary *36*
Hard, Charlotte (Ann) 1969- *98*
Hardcastle, Michael 1933- *47*
Brief entry *38*
See Clark, David
Harding, Lee 1937- *32*
Brief entry *31*
Hardinge, Frances 1973- *210*
Hardt, Helga Fleischhauer
See Fleischhauer-Hardt, Helga
Hardwick, Richard Holmes, Jr. 1923- *12*

Hardy, Alice Dale *67*
Earlier sketch in SATA *1*
Hardy, David A(ndrews) 1936- *9*
Hardy, Jon 1958- *53*
Hardy, LeAnne 1951- *154*
Hardy, Stuart
See Schisgall, Oscar
Hare, Norma Q(uarles) 1924- *46*
Brief entry *41*
Harel, Nira 1936- *154*
Harford, Henry
See Hudson, W(illiam) H(enry)
Hargrave, Leonie
See Disch, Thomas M.
Hargreaves, (Charles) Roger 1935-1988
Obituary *56*
Hargrove, James 1947- *57*
Brief entry *50*
Hargrove, Jim
See Hargrove, James
Harik, Elsa
See Marston, Elsa
Harik, Elsa M.
See Marston, Elsa
Harik, Elsa Marston
See Marston, Elsa
Hariton, Anca I. 1955- *79*
Hark, Mildred
See McQueen, Mildred Hark
Harkaway, Hal
See Stratemeyer, Edward L.
Harkins, Philip 1912-1997 .... *6*
Obituary *129*
Harlan, Elizabeth 1945- *41*
Brief entry *35*
Harlan, Glen
See Cebulash, Mel
Harlan, Judith 1949- *135*
Earlier sketch in SATA *74*
See also CLR *81*
Harland, Richard 1947- *152*
Harlee, J. V.
See Leese, Jennifer L.B.
Harler, Ann
See Van Steenwyk, Elizabeth (Ann)
Harley, Avis *183*
Harley, Bill 1954- *208*
Earlier sketch in SATA *87*
Harlow, Joan Hiatt 1932- *157*
Harman, Fred 1902(?)-1982
Obituary *30*
Harman, Hugh 1903-1982
Obituary *33*
Harmelink, Barbara (Mary) *9*
Harmer, Mabel 1894-1992 .... *45*
Harmon, Dan
See Harmon, Daniel E(lton)
Harmon, Daniel E(lton) 1949- *157*
Harmon, Margaret 1906- *20*
Harmon, Michael 1969- *189*
Harmon, Michael B.
See Harmon, Michael
Harmon, William (Ruth) 1938- *65*
Harnan, Terry 1920- *12*
Harness, Cheryl 1951- *178*
Earlier sketch in SATA *131*
Harnett, Cynthia (Mary) 1893-1981 .... *5*
Obituary *32*
Harper, Anita 1943- *41*
Harper, Betty 1946- *126*
Harper, Charise
See Harper, Charise Mericle
Harper, Charise Mericle *179*
Harper, Elaine
See Hallin, Emily Watson
Harper, Ellen
See Noble, Marty
Harper, Jamie *174*
Harper, Jessica 1949- *148*
Harper, Jo 1932- *169*
Earlier sketch in SATA *97*

Harper, Lee *201*
Harper, Mary Wood
See Dixon, Jeanne
Harper, Piers 1966- *161*
Earlier sketch in SATA *105*
Harper, Suzanne *194*
Harper, Wilhelmina 1884-1973 .... *4*
Obituary *26*
Harrah, Madge 1931- *154*
Harrah, Michael 1940- *41*
Harrah, Monique
See Harrah, Madge
Harrar, George E. 1949- *124*
Harrell, Beatrice Orcutt 1943- *93*
Harrell, Janice 1945- *70*
Harries, Joan 1922- *39*
Harrill, Ronald 1950- *90*
Harrington, Denis J(ames) 1932- *88*
Harrington, Evelyn Davis 1911- *5*
Harrington, Janice N. 1956- *187*
Harrington, Lyn
See Harrington, Evelyn Davis
Harris, Alan 1944- *71*
Harris, Aurand 1915-1996 .... *37*
Obituary *91*
Harris, Bob
See Harris, Robert J.
Harris, Carol Flynn 1933- *135*
Harris, Catherine
See Ainsworth, Catherine Harris
Harris, Christie
See Harris, Christie (Lucy) Irwin
Harris, Christie (Lucy) Irwin 1907-2002 ...... *74*
Autobiography Feature *116*
Earlier sketch in SATA *6*
See also CLR *47*
See also SAAS *10*
Harris, Christine 1955- *105*
Harris, Colver
See Colver, Anne
Harris, David 1942- *118*
Harris, David William
See Harris, David
Harris, Dorothy Joan 1931- *153*
Earlier sketch in SATA *13*
Harris, Geraldine 1951- *54*
Harris, Geraldine Rachel
See Harris, Geraldine
Harris, Jacqueline L. 1929- *62*
Harris, Janet 1932-1979 .... *4*
Obituary *23*
Harris, Jesse
See Standiford, Natalie
Harris, Joan 1946- *146*
Harris, Joe 1928- *201*
Harris, Joel Chandler 1848-1908 .... *100*
See also YABC *1*
See also CLR *128*
Harris, John (Wyndham Parkes Lucas) Beynon
1903-1969 .... *118*
Harris, Johnson
See Harris, John (Wyndham Parkes Lucas)
Beynon
Harris, Jonathan 1921-1997 .... *52*
Harris, Larry Vincent 1939- *59*
Harris, Lavinia
See St. John, Nicole
Harris, Leon A., Jr. 1926-2000 .... *4*
Harris, Lois V. *199*
Harris, Lorle K(empe) 1912-2001 .... *22*
Harris, Marilyn
See Springer, Marilyn Harris
Harris, Mark Jonathan 1941- *84*
Earlier sketch in SATA *32*
Harris, Mary K(athleen) 1905-1966 .... *119*
Harris, Robert J. 1955- *195*
Harris, Robie H. 1940- *203*
Brief entry *53*
Earlier sketches in SATA *90, 147*
Harris, Robin
See Shine, Deborah

Harris, Rosemary (Jeanne) 82
    Earlier sketch in SATA 4
    See also CLR 30
    See also SAAS 7
Harris, Ruth Elwin 1935- 164
Harris, Sherwood 1932-2009 25
Harris, Steven Michael 1957- 55
Harris, Trudy 1949- 191
    Earlier sketch in SATA 128
Harris-Filderman, Diane
    See Filderman, Diane E(lizabeth)
Harrison, C(hester) William 1913-1994 35
Harrison, Carol
    See Harrison, Carol Thompson
Harrison, Carol Thompson 113
Harrison, David L. 1937- 186
    Earlier sketches in SATA 26, 92, 150
Harrison, Deloris 1938- 9
Harrison, Edward Hardy 1926- 56
Harrison, Elizabeth (Allen) Cavanna
    1909-2001 30
    Earlier sketch in SATA 1
    See also SAAS 4
Harrison, Harry 1925- 4
Harrison, Harry Max
    See Harrison, Harry
Harrison, Mette Ivie 1970- 202
    Earlier sketch in SATA 149
Harrison, Michael 1939- 106
Harrison, Molly (Hodgett) 1909-2002 41
Harrison, Sarah 1946- 63
Harrison, Ted
    See Harrison, Edward Hardy
Harsh, Fred (T.) 1925- 72
Harshaw, Ruth H(etzel) 1890-1968 27
Harshman, Marc 1950- 109
    Earlier sketch in SATA 71
Hart, Alexandra 1939- 14
Hart, Alison
    See Leonhardt, Alice
Hart, Bruce 1938-2006 57
    Brief entry 39
Hart, Carole 1943- 57
    Brief entry 39
Hart, Carolyn 1936- 74
Hart, Carolyn G.
    See Hart, Carolyn
Hart, Carolyn Gimpel
    See Hart, Carolyn
Hart, Jan Siegel 1940- 79
Hart, Joyce 1954- 148
Hart, Karen 185
Hart, Lenore 171
Hart, Philip S. 1944- 180
Hart, Virginia 1949- 83
Harte, Bret 1836(?)-1902 26
Harte, Francis Brett
    See Harte, Bret
Harter, Debbie 1963- 107
Hartfield, Claire 1957- 147
Hartinger, Brent 1964- 217
    Earlier sketches in SATA 145, 174
Hartland, Jessie 171
Hartley, Ellen (Raphael) 1915-1980 23
Hartley, Fred Allan III 1953- 41
Hartley, William B(rown) 1913-1980 23
Hartling, Peter
    See Hartling, Peter
Hartling, Peter 1933- 66
    See also CLR 29
Hartman, Cassie 202
Hartman, Dan 1955- 202
Hartman, Evert 1937- 38
    Brief entry 35
Hartman, Jane E. 1928- 47
Hartman, Jane Evangeline
    See Hartman, Jane E.
Hartman, Louis F(rancis) 1901-1970 22
Hartman, Rachel 174
Hartman, Victoria 1942- 91

Hartnett, Sonya 1968- 176
    Earlier sketches in SATA 93, 130
Hartshorn, Ruth M. 1928- 11
Hartung, Susan Kathleen 192
    Earlier sketch in SATA 150
Hartwig, Manfred 1950- 81
Harvey, Brett 1936- 61
Harvey, Edith 1908(?)-1972
    Obituary 27
Harvey, Gill 189
Harvey, Karen D. 1935- 88
Harvey, Roland 1945- 179
    Earlier sketches in SATA 71, 123
Harvey-Fitzhenry, Alyxandra 1974- 189
Harwick, B. L.
    See Keller, Beverly L(ou)
Harwin, Brian
    See Henderson, LeGrand
Harwood, Pearl Augusta (Bragdon)
    1903-1998 9
Haseley, Dennis 1950- 157
    Brief entry 44
    Earlier sketches in SATA 57, 105
Hashmi, Kerri 1955- 108
Haskell, Arnold L(ionel) 1903-1981(?) 6
Haskins, James
    See Haskins, James S.
Haskins, James S. 1941-2005 132
    Autobiography Feature 132
    Earlier sketches in SATA 9, 69, 105
    See also CLR 39
    See also SAAS 4
Haskins, Jim
    See Haskins, James S.
Hasler, Eveline 1933- 181
Hasler, Joan 1931- 28
Hass, Robert 1941- 94
Hassall, Joan 1906-1988 43
    Obituary 56
Hassett, Ann 1958- 162
Hassett, John 162
Hassler, Jon 1933-2008 19
    Obituary 191
Hassler, Jon Francis
    See Hassler, Jon
Hastings, Beverly
    See Barkin, Carol
    and James, Elizabeth
Hastings, Graham
    See Jeffries, Roderic
Hastings, Ian 1912- 62
Hastings, Victor
    See Disch, Thomas M.
Haszard, Patricia Moyes 1923-2000 63
Hatch, Lynda S. 1950- 90
Hathaway, Barbara 164
Hathorn, Elizabeth
    See Hathorn, Elizabeth Helen
Hathorn, Elizabeth Helen 1943- 156
    Autobiography Feature 156
    Earlier sketches in SATA 74, 120
Hathorn, Libby 1943-
    See Hathorn, Elizabeth Helen
Hatkoff, Craig 1954- 192
Hatlo, Jimmy 1898-1963
    Obituary 23
Hatton, Caroline 1957- 205
Hauff, Wilhelm 1802-1827
    See CLR 155
Haugaard, Erik Christian 1923- 68
    Earlier sketch in SATA 4
    See also CLR 11
    See also SAAS 12
Haugaard, Kay 117
Haugen, Hayley Mitchell 1968- 172
Haugen, Tormod 1945- 66
Hauman, Doris 1898-1984 32
Hauman, George 1890-1961 32
Hauptly, Denis J. 1945- 57
Hauptly, Denis James
    See Hauptly, Denis J.

Hauser, Jill Frankel 1950- 127
Hauser, Margaret L(ouise) 1909- 10
Hausherr, Rosmarie 1943- 86
Hausman, Gerald 1945- 180
    Earlier sketches in SATA 13, 90, 132
    See also CLR 89
Hausman, Gerry
    See Hausman, Gerald
Hauth, Katherine B. 1940- 99
Hautman, Pete 1952- 173
    Earlier sketches in SATA 82, 128
Hautman, Peter Murray
    See Hautman, Pete
Hautzig, Deborah 1956- 106
    Earlier sketch in SATA 31
Hautzig, Esther Rudomin 1930-2009 148
    Earlier sketches in SATA 4, 68
    See also CLR 22
    See also SAAS 15
Havel, Geoff 1955- 152
Havel, Jennifer
    See Havill, Juanita
Havelin, Kate 1961- 143
Haven, Paul 1971(?)- 213
Havighurst, Walter (Edwin) 1901-1994 1
    Obituary 79
Haviland, Virginia 1911-1988 6
    Obituary 54
Havill, Juanita 1949- 155
    Earlier sketch in SATA 74
Hawes, Judy 1913- 4
Hawes, Louise 1943- 180
    Earlier sketch in SATA 60
Hawke, Rosanne 1953- 165
    Earlier sketch in SATA 124
Hawke, Rosanne Joy
    See Hawke, Rosanne
Hawkes, Kevin 1959- 201
    Earlier sketches in SATA 78, 150
Hawkes, Nigel 1943- 119
Hawkesworth, Eric 1921- 13
Hawking, Lucy 1969- 197
Hawkins, Arthur 1903-1985 19
Hawkins, Colin 1945- 162
    Earlier sketch in SATA 112
Hawkins, Jacqui 162
    Earlier sketch in SATA 112
Hawkins, Jimmy 1941- 188
Hawkins, Laura 1951- 74
Hawkins, (Helena Ann) Quail 1905-2002 6
    Obituary 141
Hawkinson, John (Samuel) 1912-1994 4
Hawkinson, Lucy (Ozone) 1924-1971 21
Hawks, Robert 1961- 85
Hawley, Mabel C. 67
    Earlier sketch in SATA 1
Haworth, Danette 207
Haworth-Attard, Barbara 1953- 215
Hawthorne, Captain R. M.
    See Ellis, Edward S.
Hawthorne, Nathaniel 1804-1864
    See YABC 2
    See also CLR 103
Hay, Jeff T. 154
Hay, John 1915- 13
Hay, Samantha 213
Hay, Timothy
    See Brown, Margaret Wise
Hayashi, Leslie Ann 1954- 115
Hayashi, Nancy 1939- 186
    Earlier sketch in SATA 80
Haycak, Cara 1961- 180
Haycock, Kate 1962- 77
Haycraft, Howard 1905-1991 6
    Obituary 70
Haycraft, Molly Costain 1911- 6
Hayden, Gwendolen Lampshire 1904- 35
Hayden,
    See Hayden, Robert Earl
Hayden, Robert C(arter), Jr. 1937- 47
    Brief entry 28

Hayden, Robert E.
  See Hayden, Robert Earl
Hayden, Robert Earl 1913-1980 .... *19*
  Obituary *26*
Hayden, Torey L. 1951- *163*
  Earlier sketch in SATA *65*
Hayden, Torey Lynn
  See Hayden, Torey L.
Hayes, Carlton J(oseph) H(untley)
  1882-1964 .... *11*
Hayes, Daniel 1952- *109*
  Earlier sketch in SATA *73*
Hayes, Geoffrey 1947- *207*
  Earlier sketches in SATA *26, 91*
Hayes, Joe 1945- *131*
  Earlier sketch in SATA *88*
Hayes, John F. 1904-1980 .... *11*
Hayes, Karel 1949- *207*
Hayes, Rosemary *158*
Hayes, Sarah 1945- *208*
Hayes, Sheila 1937- *51*
  Brief entry *50*
Hayes, Will *7*
Hayes, William D(imitt) 1913-1976 .... *8*
Haynes, Betsy 1937- *94*
  Brief entry *37*
  Earlier sketch in SATA *48*
  See also CLR *90*
Haynes, David 1955- *97*
Haynes, Linda
  See Swinford, Betty (June Wells)
Haynes, Mary 1938- *65*
Haynes, Max 1956- *72*
Hays, Anna Jane *214*
Hays, H(offmann) R(eynolds) 1904-1980 .... *26*
Hays, Thomas Anthony 1957- *84*
Hays, Tony
  See Hays, Thomas Anthony
Hays, Wilma Pitchford 1909- *28*
  Earlier sketch in SATA *1*
  See also CLR *59*
  See also SAAS *3*
Hayward, Linda 1943- *185*
  Brief entry *39*
  Earlier sketch in SATA *101*
Haywood, Carolyn 1898-1990 .... *75*
  Obituary *64*
  Earlier sketches in SATA *1, 29*
  See also CLR *22*
Hazelaar, Cor *217*
Hazell, Rebecca (Eileen) 1947- *141*
Hazen, Barbara Shook 1930- *178*
  Earlier sketches in SATA *27, 90*
Hazen, Lynn E. *202*
Head, Gay
  See Hauser, Margaret L(ouise)
Head, Tom 1978- *167*
Headley, Elizabeth
  See Harrison, Elizabeth (Allen) Cavanna
Headley, Justina Chen 1968- *176*
Headstrom, (Birger) Richard 1902-1985 .... *8*
Heady, Eleanor B(utler) 1917-1979 .... *8*
Heagy, William D. 1964- *76*
Heal, Edith 1903-1995 .... *7*
Heal, Gillian 1934- *89*
Heale, Jay (Jeremy Peter Wingfield) 1937- .. *84*
Healey, Brooks
  See Albert, Burton
Healey, Larry 1927- *44*
  Brief entry *42*
Heap, Sue 1954- *187*
  Earlier sketch in SATA *150*
Heaps, Willard A(llison) 1908-1987 .... *26*
Hearn, Diane Dawson 1952- *209*
  Earlier sketch in SATA *79*
Hearn, Emily
  See Valleau, Emily
Hearn, Julie 1958- *212*
  Earlier sketch in SATA *152*
Hearn, Lian
  See Rubinstein, Gillian

Hearn, Sneed
  See Gregg, Andrew K.
Hearne, Betsy 1942- *146*
  Earlier sketches in SATA *38, 95*
Heath, Charles D(ickinson) 1941- *46*
Heath, Veronica
  See Blackett, Veronica Heath
Heaven, Constance (Christina) 1911- *7*
Hebert-Collins, Sheila 1948- *111*
Hecht, George J(oseph) 1895-1980
  Obituary *22*
Hecht, Henri Joseph 1922- *9*
Hechtkopf, Henryk 1910- *17*
Heck, Bessie (Mildred) Holland 1911-1995 . *26*
Heck, Ed 1963- *173*
Heckert, Connie K(aye Delp) 1948- *82*
Hector, Julian *205*
Hedderwick, Mairi 1939- *145*
  Earlier sketches in SATA *30, 77*
Hedges, Sid(ney) G(eorge) 1897-1974 .... *28*
Hedrick, Irene Hope 1920- *175*
Heelan, Jamee Riggio 1965- *146*
Heerboth, Sharon
  See Leon, Sharon
Heffernan, John 1949- *168*
  Earlier sketch in SATA *121*
Heffron, Dorris 1944- *68*
Hefter, Richard 1942- *31*
Hegamin, Tonya C. 1975- *209*
Hegarty, Reginald Beaton 1906-1973 .... *10*
Hehenberger, Shelly 1968- *126*
Heidbreder, Robert 1947- *196*
  Earlier sketch in SATA *130*
Heidbreder, Robert K.
  See Heidbreder, Robert
Heide, Florence Parry 1919- *192*
  Earlier sketches in SATA *32, 69, 118*
  See also CLR *60*
  See also SAAS *6*
Heiderstadt, Dorothy 1907-2001 .... *6*
Heidi Louise
  See Erdrich, Louise
Heidler, David S(tephen) 1955- *132*
Heidler, Jeanne T. 1956- *132*
Heilbroner, Joan Knapp 1922- *63*
Heilbrun, Lois Hussey 1922(?)-1987
  Obituary *54*
Heiligman, Deborah 1958- *193*
  Earlier sketches in SATA *90, 144*
Heilman, Joan Rattner *50*
Heimann, Rolf 1940- *164*
  Earlier sketch in SATA *120*
Hein, Lucille Eleanor 1915-1994 .... *20*
Heine, Helme 1941- *135*
  Earlier sketch in SATA *67*
  See also CLR *18*
Heinlein, Robert A. 1907-1988 .... *69*
  Obituary *56*
  Earlier sketch in SATA *9*
  See also CLR *75*
Heinlein, Robert Anson
  See Heinlein, Robert A.
Heins, Ethel L(eah) 1918-1997 .... *101*
Heins, Paul 1909- *13*
Heintze, Carl 1922- *26*
Heinz, Bill
  See Heinz, W. C.
Heinz, Brian J. 1946- *181*
  Earlier sketch in SATA *95*
Heinz, Brian James
  See Heinz, Brian J.
Heinz, W. C. 1915-2008 .... *26*
Heinz, Wilfred Charles
  See Heinz, W. C.
Heinzen, Mildred
  See Masters, Mildred
Heisel, Sharon E(laine) 1941- *125*
  Earlier sketch in SATA *84*
Heitzmann, William Ray 1948- *73*
Heitzmann, Wm. Ray
  See Heitzmann, William Ray

Helakoski, Leslie *178*
Helberg, Shirley Adelaide Holden 1919- ... *138*
Helfer, Andrew *187*
Helfer, Ralph 1937- *177*
Helfman, Elizabeth S(eaver) 1911-2001 .... *3*
Helfman, Harry Carmozin 1910-1995 .... *3*
Helgerson, Joseph 1950- *181*
Hellard, Susan *182*
Hellberg, Hans-Eric 1927- *38*
Heller, Linda 1944- *46*
  Brief entry *40*
Heller, Mike
  See Hano, Arnold
Heller, Ruth M. 1924- *112*
  Earlier sketch in SATA *66*
Hellman, Hal
  See Hellman, Harold
Hellman, Harold 1927- *4*
Helman, Andrea (Jean) 1946- *160*
  Earlier sketch in SATA *107*
Helmer, Diana Star 1962- *86*
Helmer, Marilyn *160*
  Earlier sketch in SATA *112*
Helps, Racey 1913-1971 .... *2*
  Obituary *25*
Helquist, Brett *187*
  Earlier sketch in SATA *146*
Helweg, Hans H. 1917- *50*
  Brief entry *33*
Helyar, Jane Penelope Josephine 1933- *5*
  Autobiography Feature *138*
  See also SAAS *2*
Hemingway, Edward 1969(?)- *212*
Hemmant, Lynette 1938- *69*
Hemming, Roy G. 1928-1995 .... *11*
  Obituary *86*
Hemphill, Helen 1955- *179*
Hemphill, Kris (Harrison) 1963- *118*
Hemphill, Martha Locke 1904-1973 .... *37*
Hemphill, Stephanie *190*
Hemstock, Gillian 1956- *173*
Henba, Bobbie 1926- *87*
Henbest, Nigel 1951- *55*
  Brief entry *52*
Henderley, Brooks *1*
Henderson, Aileen Kilgore 1921- *178*
Henderson, Aileen Mary
  See Fox, Aileen
Henderson, Gordon 1950- *53*
Henderson, Kathy 1949- *155*
  Brief entry *53*
  Earlier sketches in SATA *55, 95*
Henderson, Lauren 1966- *201*
Henderson, LeGrand 1901-1965 .... *9*
Henderson, Nancy Wallace 1916- *22*
Henderson, Zenna (Chlarson) 1917-1983 .... *5*
Hendrickson, Walter Brookfield, Jr. 1936- *9*
Hendrix, John 1976- *208*
Hendry, Diana 1941- *213*
  Earlier sketches in SATA *68, 106*
Hendry, Frances Mary 1941- *171*
  Earlier sketch in SATA *110*
Hendry, Linda (Gail) 1961- *83*
Heneghan, James 1930- *160*
  Earlier sketches in SATA *53, 97*
Henkes, Kevin 1960- *207*
  Earlier sketches in SATA *43, 76, 108, 154*
  See also CLR *108*
Henn, Astrid *214*
Hennessy, Barbara G.
  See Hennessy, B.G.
Hennessy, Barbara Gulbrandsen
  See Hennessy, B.G.
Hennessy, B.G. 1951- *175*
Henney, Carolee Wells 1928- *102*
Henriod, Lorraine 1925- *26*
Henriquez, Emile F. 1937- *170*
  Earlier sketch in SATA *89*
Henry, April 1959- *174*
Henry, Ernest 1948- *107*
Henry, Joanne Landers 1927- *6*

Henry, Maeve 1960- 75
Henry, Marguerite 1902-1997 100
    Obituary 99
    See also CLR 4
    See also SAAS 7
Henry, Marie H. 1935- 65
Henry, Marilyn 1939- 117
Henry, Marion
    See del Rey, Lester
Henry, O. 1862-1910
    See YABC 2
Henry, Oliver
    See Henry, O.
Henry, Rohan 217
Henry, T. E.
    See Rowland-Entwistle, (Arthur) Theodore
    (Henry)
Henschel, Elizabeth Georgie 56
Henson, Heather 206
Henson, James Maury
    See Henson, Jim
Henson, Jim 1936-1990 43
    Obituary 65
Henstra, Friso 1928- 73
    Earlier sketch in SATA 8
    See also SAAS 14
Hentoff, Nat(han Irving) 1925- 133
    Brief entry 27
    Earlier sketches in SATA 42, 69
    See also CLR 52
Henty, G(eorge) A(lfred) 1832-1902 64
    See also CLR 76
Heo, Yumi 1964- 206
    Earlier sketches in SATA 94, 146
Hepler, Heather 177
Herald, Kathleen
    See Peyton, Kathleen Wendy
Herb, Angela M. 1970- 92
Herbert, Cecil
    See Hamilton, Charles (Harold St. John)
Herbert, Don 1917-2007 2
    Obituary 184
Herbert, Donald Jeffrey
    See Herbert, Don
Herbert, Frank 1920-1986 37
    Obituary 47
    Earlier sketch in SATA 9
Herbert, Frank Patrick
    See Herbert, Frank
Herbert, Helen (Jean) 1947- 57
Herbert, Janis 1956- 139
Herbert, Wally 1934-2007 23
Herbert, Walter William
    See Herbert, Wally
Herbst, Judith 1947- 74
Herda, D.J. 1948- 80
Herge
    See Remi, Georges
Heritage, Martin
    See Horler, Sydney
Herkimer, L(awrence) R(ussell) 1925(?)- 42
Herlihy, Dirlie Anne 1935- 73
Herlong, Madaline
    See Herlong, M.H.
Herlong, M.H. 211
Herman, Charlotte 1937- 203
    Earlier sketches in SATA 20, 99
Hermanson, Dennis (Everett) 1947- 10
Hermes, Jules 1962- 92
Hermes, Patricia 1936- 191
    Earlier sketches in SATA 31, 78, 141
Hermes, Patricia Mary
    See Hermes, Patricia
Hernandez, Natalie Nelson 1929- 123
Herndon, Ernest 91
Herold, Ann Bixby 1937- 72
Herrera, Juan Felipe 1948- 127
Herrick, Steven 1958- 209
    Earlier sketches in SATA 103, 156
Herriman, George (Joseph) 1880-1944 140

Herriot, James 1916-1995 135
    Brief entry 44
    Earlier sketch in SATA 86
    See also CLR 80
Herrmanns, Ralph 1933- 11
Herrold, Tracey
    See Dils, Tracey E.
Herron, Carolivia 1947- 203
Herron, Edward A(lbert) 1912- 4
Herschler, Mildred Barger 130
Hersey, John 1914-1993 25
    Obituary 76
Hersey, John Richard
    See Hersey, John
Hershberger, Priscilla (Gorman) 1951- 81
Hershenhorn, Esther 1945- 151
Hershey, Kathleen M. 1934- 80
Hershey, Mary 173
Hersom, Kathleen 1911- 73
Hertz, Grete Janus 1915- 23
Herzig, Alison Cragin 1935- 87
Herzog, Brad 1968- 131
Heslewood, Juliet 1951- 82
Hess, Lilo 1916- 4
Hess, Paul 1961- 134
Hesse, Hermann 1877-1962 50
Hesse, Karen 1952- 215
    Autobiography Feature 113
    Earlier sketches in SATA 74, 103, 158
    See also CLR 141
    See also SAAS 25
Hest, Amy 1950- 193
    Earlier sketches in SATA 55, 82, 129
Heuer, Karsten 1968(?)- 202
Heuer, Kenneth John 1927- 44
Heuman, William 1912-1971 21
Heuston, Kimberley 1960- 167
Heuston, Kimberley Burton
    See Heuston, Kimberley
Hewes, Agnes Danforth 1874-1963 35
Hewett, Anita 1918-1989 13
Hewett, Joan 1930- 140
    Earlier sketch in SATA 81
Hewett, Richard 1929- 81
Hewitson, Jennifer 1961- 97
Hewitt, Margaret 1961- 84
Hewitt, Sally 1949- 127
Hext, Harrington
    See Phillpotts, Eden
Hey, Nigel S(tewart) 1936- 20
Heyduck-Huth, Hilde 1929- 8
Heyer, Carol 1950- 130
    Earlier sketch in SATA 74
Heyer, Marilee 1942- 102
    Earlier sketch in SATA 64
Heyerdahl, Thor 1914-2002 52
    Earlier sketch in SATA 2
Heyes, (Nancy) Eileen 1956- 150
    Earlier sketch in SATA 80
Heyliger, William 1884-1955
    See YABC 1
Heyman, Ken(neth Louis) 1930- 114
    Earlier sketch in SATA 34
Heyward, (Edwin) DuBose 1885-1940 21
Heywood, Karen 1946- 48
Hezlep, William (Earl) 1936- 88
Hiaasen, Carl 1953- 208
Hibbert, Arthur Raymond
    See Hibbert, Christopher
Hibbert, Christopher 1924-2008 4
    Obituary 201
Hibbert, Eleanor Alice Burford 1906-1993 2
    Obituary 74
Hickman, Estella (Lee) 1942- 111
Hickman, Janet 1940- 127
    Earlier sketch in SATA 12
Hickman, Martha Whitmore 1925- 26
Hickman, Pamela 1958- 186
    Earlier sketch in SATA 128
Hickock, Will
    See Harrison, C(hester) William

Hickok, Lorena A. 1893-1968 20
Hickox, Rebecca (Ayres) 116
Hicks, Barbara Jean 1953- 165
Hicks, Betty 191
Hicks, Clifford B. 1920- 50
Hicks, Eleanor B.
    See Coerr, Eleanor (Beatrice)
Hicks, Harvey
    See Stratemeyer, Edward L.
Hicks, Peter 1952- 111
Hicyilmaz, Gaye 1947- 157
    Earlier sketch in SATA 77
Hieatt, Constance B(artlett) 1928- 4
Hiebert, Ray Eldon 1932- 13
Hierstein, Judith 212
Hierstein, Judy
    See Hierstein, Judith
Higdon, Hal 1931- 4
Higginbottom, David 1923- 87
    Earlier sketch in SATA 25
Higginbottom, J(effrey) Winslow 1945- 29
Higgins, Joanna 1945- 125
Higgins, Simon (Richard) 1958- 105
Higginsen, Vy 79
High, Linda Oatman 1958- 188
    Autobiography Feature 188
    Earlier sketches in SATA 94, 145
High, Philip E. 1914- 119
High, Philip Empson
    See High, Philip E.
Higham, David 1949- 50
Higham, David Michael
    See Higham, David
Higham, Jon Atlas
    See Higham, Jonathan Huw
Higham, Jonathan Huw 1960- 59
Highet, Helen
    See MacInnes, Helen (Clark)
Hightman, Jason 1971(?)- 189
Hightman, J.P.
    See Hightman, Jason
Hightower, Florence Cole 1916-1981 4
    Obituary 27
Highwater, Jamake (Mamake)
    1942(?)-2001 69
    Brief entry 30
    Earlier sketch in SATA 32
    See also CLR 17
Hilb, Nora 1953- 178
Hildebrandt, Greg 1939- 172
    Brief entry 33
    Earlier sketch in SATA 55
Hildebrandt, Tim 1939-2006 55
    Brief entry 33
Hildebrandt, Timothy
    See Hildebrandt, Tim
Hildebrandts, The
    See Hildebrandt, Greg
    and Hildebrandt, Tim
Hilder, Rowland 1905-1993 36
    Obituary 77
Hildick, E. W.
    See Hildick, Wallace
Hildick, Wallace 1925-2001 68
    Earlier sketch in SATA 2
    See also SAAS 6
Hilgartner, Beth 1957- 58
Hill, Alexis
    See Craig, Mary (Francis) Shura
    and Glick, Ruth (Burtnick)
Hill, Anthony R. 1942- 164
    Earlier sketch in SATA 91
Hill, Anthony Robert
    See Hill, Anthony R.
Hill, David 1942- 152
    Earlier sketch in SATA 103
Hill, Donna (Marie) 1921- 124
    Earlier sketch in SATA 24
Hill, Douglas 1935-2007 78
    Earlier sketch in SATA 39

Hill, Douglas Arthur
    See Hill, Douglas
Hill, Elizabeth Starr 1925- *143*
    Earlier sketch in SATA *24*
Hill, Eric 1927- *133*
    Brief entry *53*
    Earlier sketch in SATA *66*
    See also CLR *13*
Hill, Gordon
    See Eldin, Peter
Hill, Grace Brooks *67*
    Earlier sketch in SATA *1*
Hill, Grace Livingston 1865-1947
    See YABC *2*
Hill, Helen M(orey) 1915- *27*
Hill, John
    See Koontz, Dean
Hill, Johnson
    See Kunhardt, Edith
Hill, Judy I. R.
    See Roberts, Judy I.
Hill, Kathleen Louise 1917- *4*
Hill, Kay
    See Hill, Kathleen Louise
Hill, Kirkpatrick 1938- *188*
    Earlier sketches in SATA *72, 126*
Hill, Laban
    See Hill, Laban Carrick
Hill, Laban Carrick *170*
Hill, Lee Sullivan 1958- *96*
Hill, Lorna 1902-1991 .... *12*
Hill, Margaret (Ohler) 1915- *36*
Hill, Meg
    See Hill, Margaret (Ohler)
Hill, Meredith
    See Craig, Mary (Francis) Shura
Hill, Monica
    See Watson, Jane Werner
Hill, Pamela Smith 1954- *112*
Hill, Ralph Nading 1917-1987 .... *65*
Hill, Robert W(hite) 1919-1982 .... *12*
    Obituary *31*
Hill, Ruth A.
    See Viguers, Ruth Hill
Hill, Ruth Livingston
    See Munce, Ruth Hill
Hill, Stuart 1958- *186*
Hill, Susan 1942- *183*
Hill, Susan Elizabeth
    See Hill, Susan
Hill, Susanna Leonard 1965- *193*
Hill, Thomas 1960- *82*
Hillcourt, William 1900-1992 .... *27*
Hillenbrand, Will 1960- *210*
    Earlier sketches in SATA *84, 147*
Hiller, Ilo (Ann) 1938- *59*
Hillerman, Anthony Grove
    See Hillerman, Tony
Hillerman, Tony 1925-2008 .... *6*
    Obituary *198*
Hillert, Margaret 1920- *91*
    Earlier sketch in SATA *8*
Hilliard, Richard *183*
Hillman, Ben 1957- *202*
Hillman, Elizabeth 1942- *75*
Hillman, John 1952- *120*
Hillman, Martin
    See Hill, Douglas
Hillman, Priscilla 1940- *48*
    Brief entry *39*
Hillman, Shane *200*
Hills, C.A.R. 1955- *39*
Hills, Charles Albert Reis
    See Hills, C.A.R.
Hills, Tad *173*
Hilton, Irene Pothus -1979 .... *7*
Hilton, James 1900-1954 .... *34*
Hilton, Margaret Lynette 1946- *105*
    Earlier sketch in SATA *68*
    See also CLR *25*
    See also SAAS *21*

Hilton, Nette
    See Hilton, Margaret Lynette
Hilton, Ralph 1907-1982 .... *8*
Hilton, Suzanne 1922- *4*
Hilton-Bruce, Anne
    See Hilton, Margaret Lynette
Him, George 1937-1982
    Obituary *30*
Himelblau, Linda -2005 .... *179*
Himelstein, Shmuel 1940- *83*
Himler, Ann 1946- *8*
Himler, Ronald 1937- *183*
    Earlier sketches in SATA *6, 92, 137*
Himler, Ronald Norbert
    See Himler, Ronald
Himmelman, John C(arl) 1959- *159*
    Earlier sketches in SATA *47, 94*
Hinckley, Helen
    See Jones, Helen Hinckley
Hind, Dolores (Ellen) 1931- *53*
    Brief entry *49*
Hindin, Nathan
    See Bloch, Robert (Albert)
Hindley, Judy 1940- *179*
    Earlier sketch in SATA *120*
Hinds, P. Mignon *98*
Hinds, Patricia Mignon
    See Hinds, P. Mignon
Hine, Sesyle Joslin 1929- *2*
Hines, Anna Grossnickle 1946- *209*
    Brief entry *45*
    Earlier sketches in SATA *51, 95, 141*
    See also SAAS *16*
Hines, Gary (Roger) 1944- *136*
    Earlier sketch in SATA *74*
Hinman, Bonnie 1950- *216*
Hinojosa, Maria (de Lourdes) 1961- *88*
Hinton, Nigel 1941- *166*
Hinton, S. E. 1950- *160*
    Earlier sketches in SATA *19, 58, 115*
    See also CLR *23*
Hinton, Sam 1917-2009 .... *43*
Hinton, Susan Eloise
    See Hinton, S. E.
Hintz, Martin 1945- *128*
    Brief entry *39*
    Earlier sketch in SATA *47*
Hintz, Stephen V. 1975- *129*
Hippopotamus, Eugene H.
    See Kraus, (Herman) Robert
Hirano, Cathy 1957- *68*
Hirao, Amiko *203*
Hirsch, Karen 1941- *61*
Hirsch, Odo *157*
    Earlier sketch in SATA *111*
Hirsch, Phil 1926- *35*
Hirsch, S. Carl 1913-1990 .... *2*
    See also SAAS *7*
Hirschfelder, Arlene B. 1943- *138*
    Earlier sketch in SATA *80*
Hirschi, Ron 1948- *192*
    Earlier sketches in SATA *56, 95*
Hirschmann, Linda (Ann) 1941- *40*
Hirsh, Marilyn 1944-1988 .... *7*
    Obituary *58*
Hirshberg, Al(bert Simon) 1909-1973 .... *38*
Hiscock, Bruce 1940- *204*
    Earlier sketches in SATA *57, 137*
Hiser, Constance 1950- *71*
Hiser, Iona Seibert -1998 .... *4*
Hislop, Julia Rose Catherine 1962- *74*
Hissey, Jane 1952- *130*
    Autobiography Feature *130*
    Earlier sketches in SATA *58, 103*
Hissey, Jane Elizabeth
    See Hissey, Jane
Hitchcock, Alfred (Joseph) 1899-1980 .... *27*
    Obituary *24*
Hite, Sid 1954- *175*
    Earlier sketches in SATA *75, 136*
Hitte, Kathryn 1919- *16*

Hitz, Demi
    See Demi
Hitzeroth, Deborah L. 1961- *78*
Hnizdovsky, Jacques 1915- *32*
Ho, Louise *185*
Ho, Minfong 1951- *151*
    Earlier sketches in SATA *15, 94*
    See also CLR *28*
Hoagland, Edward (Morley) 1932- *51*
Hoare, Robert J(ohn) 1921-1975 .... *38*
Hoban, Julia *217*
Hoban, Lillian 1925-1998 .... *69*
    Obituary *104*
    Earlier sketch in SATA *22*
    See also CLR *67*
Hoban, Russell 1925- *136*
    Earlier sketches in SATA *1, 40, 78*
    See also CLR *139*
Hoban, Russell Conwell
    See Hoban, Russell
Hoban, Tana 1917(?)-2006 .... *104*
    Obituary *173*
    Earlier sketches in SATA *22, 70*
    See also CLR *76*
    See also SAAS *12*
Hobart, Lois (Elaine) *7*
Hobbie, Holly 1944- *178*
    See also CLR *88*
Hobbie, Jocelyn *190*
Hobbie, Nathaniel *196*
Hobbs, Leigh 1953- *166*
Hobbs, Valerie 1941- *193*
    Autobiography Feature *145*
    Earlier sketches in SATA *93, 145*
    See also CLR *148*
Hobbs, Will 1947- *177*
    Autobiography Feature *127*
    Earlier sketches in SATA *72, 110*
    See also CLR *59*
Hobbs, William Carl
    See Hobbs, Will
Hoberman, Mary Ann 1930- *158*
    Earlier sketches in SATA *5, 72, 111*
    See also CLR *22*
    See also SAAS *18*
Hobson, Bruce 1950- *62*
Hobson, Burton (Harold) 1933- *28*
Hobson, Laura Z(ametkin) 1900-1986 .... *52*
Hobson, Sally 1967- *172*
    Earlier sketch in SATA *84*
Hoce, Charley E. *174*
Hochman, David *202*
Hochschild, Arlie Russell 1940- *11*
Hockaby, Stephen
    See Mitchell, Gladys (Maude Winifred)
Hockenberry, Hope
    See Newell, Hope Hockenberry
Hodge, Deborah 1954- *163*
    Earlier sketch in SATA *122*
Hodge, P. W.
    See Hodge, Paul W(illiam)
Hodge, Paul W(illiam) 1934- *12*
Hodgell, P(atricia) C(hristine) 1951- *42*
Hodges, C. Walter 1909-2004 .... *2*
    Obituary *158*
Hodges, Carl G. 1902-1964 .... *10*
Hodges, Cyril Walter
    See Hodges, C. Walter
Hodges, Elizabeth Jamison *1*
Hodges, Margaret 1911-2005 .... *167*
    Obituary *172*
    Earlier sketches in SATA *1, 33, 75, 117*
    See also SAAS *9*
Hodges, Margaret Moore
    See Hodges, Margaret
Hodgetts, Blake Christopher 1967- *43*
Hodgkins, Fran 1964- *199*
Hodgkinson, Leigh 1975- *202*
Hodgman, Ann 1956- *198*
Hodgson, Harriet (W.) 1935- *84*
Hoehne, Marcia 1951- *89*

Hoellwarth, Cathryn Clinton
    See Clinton, Cathryn
Hoestlandt, Jo 1948- 94
Hoestlandt, Jocelyne
    See Hoestlandt, Jo
Hoexter, Corinne K. 1927- 6
Hoeye, Michael 1947- 136
Hoff, Carol 1900-1979 11
Hoff, Mary (King) 1956- 157
    Earlier sketch in SATA 74
Hoff, Syd(ney) 1912-2004 138
    Obituary 154
    Earlier sketches in SATA 9, 72
    See also CLR 83
    See also SAAS 4
Hoffman, Edwin D. 49
Hoffman, Elizabeth P(arkinson) 1921-2003
    Obituary 153
Hoffman, Mary 1945- 211
    Earlier sketches in SATA 59, 97, 144
    See also SAAS 24
Hoffman, Mat 1972- 150
Hoffman, Nina Kiriki 1955- 160
Hoffman, Phyllis M. 1944- 4
Hoffman, Phyllis Miriam
    See Hoffman, Phyllis M.
Hoffman, Rosekrans 1926- 15
Hoffmann, E(rnst) T(heodor) A(madeus)
    1776-1822 27
    See also CLR 133
Hoffmann, Felix 1911-1975 9
Hoffmann, Heinrich 1809-1894
    See CLR 122
Hoffmann, Margaret Jones 1910- 48
Hoffmann, Peggy
    See Hoffmann, Margaret Jones
Hofher, Catherine Baxley 1954- 130
Hofher, Cathy
    See Hofher, Catherine Baxley
Hofmeyr, Dianne (Louise) 138
Hofsepian, Sylvia A. 1932- 74
Hofsinde, Robert 1902-1973 21
Hogan, Bernice Harris 1929- 12
Hogan, Inez 1895-1973 2
Hogan, James P. 1941-2010 81
Hogan, James Patrick
    See Hogan, James P.
Hogan, Jamie 192
Hogan, Linda 1947- 132
Hogan, Mary 1957- 210
Hogarth, Burne 1911-1996 89
    Earlier sketch in SATA 63
Hogarth, Grace (Weston Allen) 1905-1995 .. 91
Hogarth, Jr.
    See Kent, Rockwell
Hogarth, (Arthur) Paul 1917-2001 41
Hogg, Garry 1902-1976 2
Hogg, Gary 1957- 172
    Earlier sketch in SATA 105
Hogner, Dorothy Childs 4
Hogner, Nils 1893-1970 25
Hogrogian, Nonny 1932- 74
    Autobiography Feature 127
    Earlier sketch in SATA 7
    See also CLR 95
    See also SAAS 1
Hoh, Diane 1937- 102
    Brief entry 48
    Earlier sketch in SATA 52
Hoke, Helen
    See Watts, Helen L. Hoke
Hoke, Helen L.
    See Watts, Helen L. Hoke
Hoke, John 1925- 7
Hoke, John Lindsay
    See Hoke, John
Hokenson, Terry 1948- 193
Hol, Coby 1943- 126
Holabird, Katharine 1948- 213
    Earlier sketches in SATA 62, 135
Holaday, Bobbie 1922- 153

Holbeach, Henry
    See Rands, William Brighty
Holberg, Ruth L(angland) 1889-1984 1
Holbrook, Kathy 1963- 107
Holbrook, Peter
    See Glick, Carl (Cannon)
Holbrook, Sabra
    See Erickson, Sabra Rollins
Holbrook, Sara 131
Holbrook, Stewart Hall 1893-1964 2
Holcomb, Jerry (Leona) Kimble 1927- 113
Holcomb, Nan
    See McPhee, Norma H.
Holden, Elizabeth Rhoda
    See Lawrence, Louise
Holding, James (Clark Carlisle, Jr.)
    1907-1997 3
Hole, Stian 1969- 204
Holeman, Linda 1949- 136
    Autobiography Feature 136
    Earlier sketch in SATA 102
Holinger, William (Jacques) 1944- 90
Holisher, Desider 1901-1972 6
Holl, Adelaide Hinkle 1910- 8
Holl, Kristi
    See Holl, Kristi D.
Holl, Kristi D. 1951- 51
Holl, Kristi Diane
    See Holl, Kristi D.
Holland, Gay W. 1941- 128
Holland, Isabelle (Christian) 1920-2002 70
    Autobiography Feature 103
    Obituary 132
    Earlier sketch in SATA 8
    See also CLR 57
Holland, Janice 1913-1962 18
Holland, John L(ewis) 1919- 20
Holland, Joyce
    See Morice, Dave
Holland, Julia 1954- 106
Holland, Lynda (H.) 1959- 77
Holland, Lys
    See Gater, Dilys
Holland, Marion 1908-1989 6
    Obituary 61
Holland, Richard 1976- 216
Hollander, John 1929- 13
Hollander, Nicole 1940(?)- 101
Hollander, Paul
    See Silverberg, Robert
Hollander, Phyllis 1928- 39
Hollander, Zander 1923- 63
Holldobler, Turid 1939- 26
Holliday, Joe
    See Holliday, Joseph
Holliday, Joseph 1910- 11
Holling, Holling C(lancy) 1900-1973 15
    Obituary 26
    See also CLR 50
Hollingsworth, Alvin C(arl) 1930- 39
Hollingsworth, Mary 1947- 166
    Earlier sketch in SATA 91
Holloway, Teresa (Bragunier) 1906- 26
Hollyer, Belinda 204
Holm, (Else) Anne (Lise) 1922-1998 1
    See also CLR 75
    See also SAAS 7
Holm, Jennifer L. 1968(?)- 183
    Earlier sketches in SATA 120, 163
Holm, Matthew 1974- 174
Holm, Sharon Lane 1955- 114
    Earlier sketch in SATA 78
Holman, Felice 1919- 82
    Earlier sketch in SATA 7
    See also SAAS 17
Holm and Hamel
    See Holm, Jennifer L.
Holmberg, Bo R. 1945- 203
Holme, Bryan 1913-1990 26
    Obituary 66

Holmes, Barbara Ware 1945- 127
    Earlier sketch in SATA 65
Holmes, Elizabeth 1957- 191
Holmes, Elizabeth Ann
    See Holmes, Elizabeth
Holmes, John
    See Souster, (Holmes) Raymond
Holmes, Marjorie (Rose) 1910-2002 43
Holmes, Martha 1961- 72
Holmes, Mary Tavener 1954- 199
Holmes, Mary Z(astrow) 1943- 80
Holmes, Oliver Wendell 1809-1894 34
Holmes, Peggy 1898- 60
Holmes, Raymond
    See Souster, (Holmes) Raymond
Holmes, Rick
    See Hardwick, Richard Holmes, Jr.
Holmes, Sara Lewis 186
Holmgren, Helen Jean 1930- 45
Holmgren, Sister George Ellen
    See Holmgren, Helen Jean
Holmgren, Virginia C(unningham) 1909- 26
Holmquist, Eve 1921- 11
Holt, Kimberly Willis 1960- 179
    Earlier sketch in SATA 122
Holt, Margaret 1937- 4
Holt, Margaret Van Vechten (Saunders)
    1899-1963 32
Holt, Michael (Paul) 1929- 13
Holt, Rackham
    See Holt, Margaret Van Vechten (Saunders)
Holt, Rochelle L.
    See DuBois, Rochelle Holt
Holt, Stephen
    See Thompson, Harlan
Holt, Victoria
    See Hibbert, Eleanor Alice Burford
Holtei, Christa 1953- 214
Holton, Leonard
    See Wibberley, Leonard
Holtz, Thomas R., Jr. 1965- 203
Holtze, Sally Holmes 1952- 64
Holtzman, Jerome 1926-2008 57
    Obituary 194
Holub, Joan 1956- 149
    Earlier sketch in SATA 99
Holub, Josef 1926- 175
Holubitsky, Katherine 1955- 165
    Earlier sketch in SATA 121
Holyer, Erna Maria 1925- 22
Holyer, Ernie
    See Holyer, Erna Maria
Holz, Loretta 1943- 17
Holz, Loretta Marie
    See Holz, Loretta
Homel, David 1952- 97
Homze, Alma C. 1932- 17
Honey, Elizabeth 1947- 137
    Autobiography Feature 137
    Earlier sketch in SATA 112
Honeycutt, Natalie 1945- 97
Hong, Lily Toy 1958- 76
Hong, Maxine Ting Ting
    See Kingston, Maxine Hong
Honig, Donald 1931- 18
Honig, Donald Martin
    See Honig, Donald
Honness, Elizabeth H. 1904- 2
Hoobler, Dorothy 1941- 161
    Earlier sketches in SATA 28, 109
Hoobler, Thomas 161
    Earlier sketches in SATA 28, 109
Hood, Joseph F. 1925- 4
Hood, Robert E. 1926- 21
Hood, Sarah
    See Killough, (Karen) Lee
Hook, Brendan 1963- 105
Hook, Frances 1912-1983 27
Hook, Geoffrey R(aynor) 1928- 103
Hook, Jeff
    See Hook, Geoffrey R(aynor)

Hook, Martha 1936- 27
Hooker, Richard
  See Heinz, W. C.
Hooker, Ruth 1920-1998 21
hooks, bell 1952(?)- 170
  Earlier sketch in SATA *115*
Hooks, William H(arris) 1921- 94
  Earlier sketch in SATA *16*
Hoon, Patricia Easterly 1954- 90
Hooper, Byrd
  See St. Clair, Byrd Hooper
Hooper, Mary 1948- 205
  Earlier sketch in SATA *160*
Hooper, Maureen Brett 1927- 76
Hooper, Meredith 1939- 159
  Earlier sketches in SATA *28, 101*
Hooper, Meredith Jean
  See Hooper, Meredith
Hooper, Patricia 1941- 95
Hoopes, Lyn Littlefield 1953- 49
  Brief entry 44
Hoopes, Ned E(dward) 1932- 21
Hoopes, Roy 1922-2009 11
Hoose, Phillip 1947- 215
  Earlier sketch in SATA *137*
Hoover, H(elen) M(ary) 1935- 132
  Brief entry 33
  Earlier sketches in SATA *44, 83*
  See also SAAS *8*
Hoover, Helen (Drusilla Blackburn)
  1910-1984 12
  Obituary 39
Hope, Christopher 1944- 62
Hope, Christopher David Tully
  See Hope, Christopher
Hope, Laura Lee
  See Goulart, Ron
  and Stanley, George Edward
Hope Simpson, Jacynth 1930- 12
Hopf, Alice (Martha) L(ightner) 1904-1988 ... 5
  Obituary 55
Hopkins, A. T.
  See Turngren, Annette
Hopkins, C. M.
  See Hopkins, Cathy
Hopkins, Cathy 1953- 165
Hopkins, Cathy M.
  See Hopkins, Cathy
Hopkins, Clark 1895-1976
  Obituary 34
Hopkins, Ellen 1955- 128
  See Hopkins, Ellen L.
Hopkins, Ellen L.
  See Hopkins, Ellen
Hopkins, Jackie
  See Hopkins, Jackie Mims
Hopkins, Jackie Mims 1952- 178
  Earlier sketch in SATA *92*
Hopkins, Joseph G(erard) E(dward) 1909- ... 11
Hopkins, (Hector) Kenneth 1914-1988
  Obituary 58
Hopkins, Lee Bennett 1938- 215
  Earlier sketches in SATA *3, 68, 125, 168*
  See also CLR *44*
  See also SAAS *4*
Hopkins, Lyman
  See Folsom, Franklin (Brewster)
Hopkins, Marjorie 1911-1999 9
Hopkins, Mary R(ice) 1956- 97
Hopkinson, Amanda 1948- 84
Hopkinson, Deborah 1952- 216
  Autobiography Feature 180
  Earlier sketches in SATA *76, 108, 159, 180*
  See also CLR *118*
Hopman, Philip 1961- 177
Hoppe, Joanne 1932- 42
Hoppe, Matthias 1952- 76
Hoppe, Paul 209
Hopper, Nancy J. 1937- 38
  Brief entry 35

Hopping, Lorraine Jean
  See Egan, Lorraine Hopping
Horacek, Judy 1961- 211
Horaek, Petr 214
  Earlier sketch in SATA *163*
Horenstein, Henry 1947- 108
Horgan, Paul (George Vincent O'Shaughnessy)
  1903-1995 13
  Obituary 84
Horlak, E.E.
  See Tepper, Sheri S.
Horler, Sydney 1888-1954 102
Horn, Sandra Ann 1944- 154
Hornblow, Arthur, Jr. 1893-1976 15
Hornblow, Leonora 1920-2005 18
  Obituary 171
Hornblow, Leonora Schinasi
  See Hornblow, Leonora
Horne, Constance 1927- 149
Horne, Richard 1960-2007 169
  Obituary 180
  Earlier sketch in SATA *111*
Horne, Richard Henry Hengist
  1802(?)-1884 29
Horner, Althea (Jane) 1926- 36
Horner, Dave 1934- 12
Horner, Jack 1946- 106
Horner, John R.
  See Horner, Jack
Horner, John Robert
  See Horner, Jack
Hornik, Laurie Miller 159
Horniman, Joanne 1951- 167
  Earlier sketch in SATA *98*
Hornos, Axel 1907-1994 20
Hornstein, Reuben Aaron 1912- 64
Horowitz, Anthony 1955- 195
  Earlier sketch in SATA *137*
Horowitz, Dave 1970- 204
  Earlier sketch in SATA *172*
Horowitz, Ruth 1957- 136
Horrocks, Anita 1958- 169
Horse, Harry
  See Horne, Richard
Horsfield, Alan 1939- 153
Hort, Lenny 179
Horton, James O. 1943- 173
Horton, James Oliver
  See Horton, James O.
Horton, Joan 217
Horton, Madelyn (Stacey) 1962- 77
Horvath, Betty 1927- 4
Horvath, David 1972(?)- 192
Horvath, Polly 1957- 194
  Earlier sketches in SATA *85, 140*
  See also CLR *90*
Horwich, Frances R(appaport) 1908-2001 11
  Obituary 130
Horwitz, Elinor Lander 45
  Brief entry 33
Horwood, William 1944- 85
Hosford, Dorothy (Grant) 1900-1952 22
Hosford, Jessie 1892-1990 5
Hoshi, Shin'ichi 1926- 101
Hoshino, Felicia 1968- 189
Hoskyns-Abrahall, Clare (Constance
  Drury) 13
Hosler, Danamarie 1978- 184
Hossack, Sylvia 1939- 83
Hossack, Sylvie Adams
  See Hossack, Sylvia
Hosseini, Khaled 1965- 156
Hossell, Karen Price
  See Price, Karen
Hosta, Dar 192
Hostetler, Marian 1932- 91
Houck, Carter 1924- 22
Hough, Charlotte 1924-2008 9
  Obituary 202
Hough, Helen Charlotte
  See Hough, Charlotte

Hough, Judy Taylor 1932- 63
  Brief entry 51
  Earlier sketch in SATA *56*
Hough, Richard (Alexander) 1922-1999 17
Houghton, Eric 1930- 7
Houk, Randy 1944- 97
Houlehen, Robert J. 1918- 18
Houlton, Peggy Mann 1925(?)-1990 6
Household, Geoffrey (Edward West)
  1900-1988 14
  Obituary 59
Housman, Laurence 1865-1959 25
Houston, Dick 1943- 74
Houston, Gloria 138
  Autobiography Feature 138
  Earlier sketch in SATA *81*
Houston, James A(rchibald) 1921-2005 74
  Obituary 163
  Earlier sketch in SATA *13*
  See also CLR *3*
  See also SAAS *17*
Houston, James D. 1933-2009 78
  Obituary 203
Houston, James Dudley
  See Houston, James D.
Houston, James Dudley
  See Houston, James D.
Houston, Jeanne Toyo Wakatsuki
  See Houston, Jeanne Wakatsuki
Houston, Jeanne Wakatsuki 1934- 168
  Autobiography Feature 168
  Earlier sketch in SATA *78*
Houston, Juanita C. 1921- 129
Houton, Kathleen
  See Kilgore, Kathleen
Houts, Amy F. 164
Hovey, Kate 158
Howard, Alan 1922- 45
Howard, Alyssa
  See Buckholtz, Eileen (Garber)
  and Glick, Ruth (Burtnick)
  and Titchener, Louise
Howard, Arthur 1948- 212
  Earlier sketch in SATA *165*
Howard, Arthur Charles
  See Howard, Arthur
Howard, Elizabeth Fitzgerald 1927- 119
  Earlier sketch in SATA *74*
Howard, Ellen 1943- 184
  Earlier sketches in SATA *67, 99*
Howard, Jane R(uble) 1924- 87
Howard, Norman Barry 1949- 90
Howard, P. M.
  See Howard, Pauline Rodriguez
Howard, Paul 1967- 190
  Earlier sketch in SATA *118*
Howard, Pauline Rodriguez 1951- 124
Howard, Prosper
  See Hamilton, Charles (Harold St. John)
Howard, Robert West 1908-1988 5
Howard, Todd 1964- 135
Howard, Tristan
  See Currie, Stephen
Howard, Vernon (Linwood) 1918-1992 40
  Obituary 73
Howard, Warren F.
  See Pohl, Frederik
Howarth, Daniel 188
Howarth, David (Armine) 1912-1991 6
  Obituary 68
Howarth, Lesley 1952- 94
Howe, Deborah 1946-1978 29
Howe, James 1946- 161
  Earlier sketches in SATA *29, 71, 111*
  See also CLR *9*
Howe, John F. 1957- 79
Howe, Norma 1930- 126
Howe, Peter 1942- 214
Howell, Pat 1947- 15
Howell, S.
  See Styles, (Frank) Showell

Howell, Simmone 1971- *214*
Howell, Virginia
  See Ellison, Virginia H(owell)
Howes, Barbara 1914-1996 .... *5*
Howie, Betsy 1962- *215*
Howie, Diana 1945- *122*
Howie, Diana Melson
  See Howie, Diana
Howker, Janni 1957- *72*
  Brief entry *46*
  See also CLR *14*
  See also SAAS *13*
Howland, Ethan 1963- *131*
Hoy, Linda 1946- *65*
Hoy, Nina
  See Roth, Arthur J(oseph)
Hoyle, Geoffrey 1942- *18*
Hoyt, Ard *190*
Hoyt, Edwin P(almer), Jr. 1923- *28*
Hoyt, Erich 1950- *140*
  Earlier sketch in SATA *65*
Hoyt, Olga
  See Gruhzit-Hoyt, Olga (Margaret)
Hrdlitschka, Shelley 1956- *167*
  Earlier sketch in SATA *111*
Hrdlitschka, Shelley Joanne
  See Hrdlitschka, Shelley
Hromic, Alma A.
  See Alexander, Alma
Htin Aung, U.
  See Aung, (Maung) Htin
Hu, Ying-Hwa *173*
Huang, Benrei 1959- *86*
Hubalek, Linda K. 1954- *111*
Hubbard, Crystal *209*
Hubbard, Margaret Ann
  See Priley, Margaret (Ann) Hubbard
Hubbard, Michelle Calabro 1953- *122*
Hubbard, Patricia 1945- *124*
Hubbard, Woodleigh Marx *160*
  Earlier sketch in SATA *98*
Hubbell, Patricia 1928- *186*
  Earlier sketches in SATA *8, 132*
Hubery, Julia *195*
Hubley, Faith Elliot 1924-2001 .... *48*
  Obituary *133*
Hubley, John 1914-1977 .... *48*
  Obituary *24*
Huck, Charlotte S. 1922- *136*
  Earlier sketch in SATA *82*
Hudak, Michal 1956- *143*
Hudson, Cheryl Willis 1948- *160*
  Earlier sketch in SATA *81*
Hudson, Jan 1954-1990 .... *77*
  See also CLR *40*
Hudson, Jeffery
  See Crichton, Michael
Hudson, Jeffrey
  See Crichton, Michael
Hudson, (Margaret) Kirsty 1947- *32*
Hudson, Margaret
  See Shuter, Jane (Margaret)
Hudson, W(illiam) H(enry) 1841-1922 .... *35*
Hudson, Wade 1946- *162*
  Earlier sketch in SATA *74*
Huelsmann, Eva 1928- *16*
Huerlimann, Bettina 1909-1983 .... *39*
  Obituary *34*
Huerlimann, Ruth 1939- *32*
  Brief entry *31*
Huff, Barbara A. 1929- *67*
Huff, Tanya 1957- *171*
  Earlier sketch in SATA *85*
Huff, Tanya Sue
  See Huff, Tanya
Huff, T.S.
  See Huff, Tanya
Huff, Vivian 1948- *59*
Huffaker, Sandy 1943- *10*
Huffman, Tom *24*
Huggins, Nathan Irvin 1927-1989 .... *63*

Huggins, Peter 1951- *178*
Hughes, Carol 1955- *217*
  Earlier sketch in SATA *108*
Hughes, Dean 1943- *139*
  Earlier sketches in SATA *33, 77*
  See also CLR *76*
Hughes, Eden
  See Griffin, W.E.B.
Hughes, Edward James
  See Hughes, Ted
Hughes, James Langston
  See Hughes, Langston
Hughes, Langston 1902-1967 .... *33*
  Earlier sketch in SATA *4*
  See also CLR *17*
Hughes, Libby *71*
Hughes, Matilda
  See MacLeod, Charlotte (Matilda)
Hughes, Monica 1925-2003 .... *162*
  Earlier sketches in SATA *15, 70, 119*
  See also CLR *60*
  See also SAAS *11*
Hughes, Monica Ince
  See Hughes, Monica
Hughes, Pat *197*
Hughes, Richard (Arthur Warren)
  1900-1976 .... *8*
  Obituary *25*
Hughes, Sara
  See Saunders, Susan
Hughes, Shirley 1927- *159*
  Earlier sketches in SATA *16, 70, 110*
  See also CLR *15*
Hughes, Susan 1960- *216*
Hughes, Ted 1930-1998 .... *49*
  Brief entry *27*
  Obituary *107*
  See also CLR *131*
Hughes, Thomas 1822-1896 .... *31*
Hughes, Virginia
  See Campbell, Hope
Hughes, Walter (Llewellyn) 1910-1993 .... *26*
Hughey, Roberta 1942- *61*
Hugo, Pierre Brackers de
  See Brackers de Hugo, Pierre
Hugo, Victor 1802-1885 .... *47*
Hugo, Victor Marie
  See Hugo, Victor
Huline-Dickens, Frank William 1931- *34*
Huling, Jan *172*
Huliska-Beith, Laura *175*
Hull, Eleanor (Means) 1913- *21*
Hull, Eric Traviss
  See Harnan, Terry
Hull, H. Braxton
  See Jacobs, Helen Hull
Hull, Jesse Redding
  See Hull, Jessie Redding
Hull, Jessie Redding 1932- *51*
Hull, Katharine 1921-1977 .... *23*
Hull, Lise (E.) 1954- *148*
Hull, Maureen 1949- *142*
Hulme, Joy N. 1922- *161*
  Earlier sketches in SATA *74, 112*
Hults, Dorothy Niebrugge 1898-2000 .... *6*
Humble, Richard 1945- *60*
Hume, Lachie *189*
Hume, Lotta Carswell *7*
Hume, Ruth Fox 1922-1980 .... *26*
  Obituary *22*
Hume, Stephen Eaton 1947- *136*
Hummel, Berta 1909-1946 .... *43*
Hummel, Sister Maria Innocentia
  See Hummel, Berta
Hummon, Marcus 1960- *213*
Humphrey, Carol Sue 1956- *167*
Humphrey, Henry (III) 1930- *16*
Humphrey, Kate
  See Forsyth, Kate
Humphrey, Sandra McLeod 1936- *95*
Humphreys, Martha 1943- *71*

Humphreys, Susan L.
  See Lowell, Susan
Hundal, Nancy 1957- *128*
Huneck, Stephen 1949- *183*
  Earlier sketch in SATA *129*
Hungerford, Hesba Fay
  See Brinsmead, H(esba) F(ay)
Hungerford, Pixie
  See Brinsmead, H(esba) F(ay)
Hunkin, Tim 1950- *53*
Hunkin, Timothy Mark Trelawney
  See Hunkin, Tim
Hunt, Angela Elwell 1957- *159*
  Earlier sketch in SATA *75*
Hunt, Bernice 1920- *4*
Hunt, Charlotte Dumaresq
  See Demi
Hunt, Francesca
  See Holland, Isabelle (Christian)
Hunt, Irene 1907-2001 .... *91*
  Earlier sketch in SATA *2*
  See also CLR *1*
Hunt, Janie Louise 1963- *102*
Hunt, Jonathan 1966- *84*
Hunt, Joyce 1927- *31*
Hunt, Linda 1940- *39*
Hunt, Lisa B(ehnke) 1967- *84*
Hunt, Mabel Leigh 1892-1971 .... *1*
  Obituary *26*
Hunt, Morton M(agill) 1920- *22*
Hunt, Nigel
  See Greenbank, Anthony Hunt
Hunt, Peter (Leonard) 1945- *76*
Hunter, Anne B. 1966- *118*
Hunter, Bernice Thurman 1922-2002 .... *85*
  Brief entry *45*
Hunter, Bobbi Dooley 1945- *89*
Hunter, Captain Marcy
  See Ellis, Edward S.
Hunter, Chris
  See Fluke, Joanne
Hunter, Clingham M.D.
  See Adams, William Taylor
Hunter, Edith Fisher 1919- *31*
Hunter, Erin
  See Cary, Kate
Hunter, Evan 1926-2005 .... *25*
  Obituary *167*
Hunter, George E.
  See Ellis, Edward S.
Hunter, Hilda 1921- *7*
Hunter, Jana
  See Hunter, Jana Novotny
Hunter, Jana Novotny *190*
Hunter, Jim 1939- *65*
Hunter, Kristin
  See Lattany, Kristin Hunter
Hunter, Leigh
  See Etchison, Birdie L(ee)
Hunter, Lieutenant Ned
  See Ellis, Edward S.
Hunter, Mel 1927-2004 .... *39*
Hunter, Mollie 1922- *139*
  Autobiography Feature *139*
  Earlier sketches in SATA *2, 54, 106*
  See also CLR *25*
  See also SAAS *7*
Hunter, Ned
  See Ellis, Edward S.
Hunter, Norman (George Lorimer)
  1899-1995 .... *84*
  Earlier sketch in SATA *26*
Hunter, Ryan Ann
  See Greenwood, Pamela D.
  and Macalaster, Elizabeth G.
Hunter, Sara Hoagland 1954- *98*
Hunter Blair, Pauline
  See Clarke, Pauline
Huntington, Amy 1956- *180*
  Earlier sketch in SATA *138*
Huntington, Geoffrey *145*

Huntington, Harriet E(lizabeth) 1909- *1*
Huntsberry, William E(mery) 1916- *5*
Hurd, Clement (G.) 1908-1988 .... *64*
    Obituary *54*
    Earlier sketch in SATA *2*
    See also CLR *49*
Hurd, Edith Thacher 1910-1997 .... *64*
    Obituary *95*
    Earlier sketch in SATA *2*
    See also CLR *49*
    See also SAAS *13*
Hurd, (John) Thacher 1949- *94*
    Autobiography Feature *123*
    Brief entry *45*
    Earlier sketch in SATA *46*
Hurley, Jo
    See Dower, Laura
Hurley, Tonya *207*
Hurlimann, Bettina
    See Huerlimann, Bettina
Hurlimann, Ruth
    See Huerlimann, Ruth
Hurmence, Belinda 1921- *77*
    See also CLR *25*
    See also SAAS *20*
Hurst, Carol Otis 1933-2007 .... *185*
    Earlier sketch in SATA *130*
Hurt-Newton, Tania 1968- *84*
Hurwin, Davida Wills 1950- *180*
Hurwitz, Johanna 1937- *175*
    Earlier sketches in SATA *20, 71, 113*
    See also SAAS *18*
Hurwood, Bernhardt J. 1926-1987 .... *12*
    Obituary *50*
Husain, Shahrukh 1950- *108*
Huser, Glen 1943- *151*
Hutchens, Paul 1902-1977 .... *31*
Hutchins, Carleen M.
    See Hutchins, Carleen Maley
Hutchins, Carleen Maley 1911-2009 .... *9*
    Obituary *206*
Hutchins, Hazel J. 1952- *175*
    Brief entry *51*
    Earlier sketches in SATA *81, 135*
    See also SAAS *24*
Hutchins, Pat 1942- *178*
    Earlier sketches in SATA *15, 70, 111*
    See also CLR *20*
    See also SAAS *16*
Hutchins, Ross Elliott 1906- *4*
Hutchison, Linda 1942- *152*
Huthmacher, J. Joseph 1929- *5*
Hutto, Nelson (Allen) 1904-1985 .... *20*
Hutton, Kathryn 1915- *89*
Hutton, Sam
    See Jones, Allan Frewin
Hutton, Warwick 1939-1994 .... *20*
    Obituary *83*
    See also SAAS *17*
Huxley, Aldous 1894-1963 .... *63*
    See also CLR *151*
Huxley, Aldous Leonard
    See Huxley, Aldous
Huxley, Elspeth (Josceline Grant)
    1907-1997 .... *62*
    Obituary *95*
Hyde, Catherine R.
    See Hyde, Catherine Ryan
Hyde, Catherine Ryan 1955- *141*
Hyde, Dayton O(gden) *9*
Hyde, Hawk
    See Hyde, Dayton O(gden)
Hyde, Jeannette
    See Eyerly, Jeannette
Hyde, Margaret O. 1917- *139*
    Earlier sketches in SATA *1, 42, 76*
    See also CLR *23*
    See also SAAS *8*
Hyde, Margaret Oldroyd
    See Hyde, Margaret O.

Hyde, Shelley
    See Reed, Kit
Hyde, Wayne Frederick 1922- *7*
Hylander, Clarence J(ohn) 1897-1964 .... *7*
Hyman, Miles 1962- *210*
Hyman, Paula Chase
    See Chase, Paula
Hyman, Robin 1931- *12*
Hyman, Robin Phiilip
    See Hyman, Robin
Hyman, Trina Schart 1939-2004 .... *95*
    Obituary *158*
    Earlier sketches in SATA *7, 46*
    See also CLR *50*
Hymes, Lucia M(anley) 1907-1998 .... *7*
Hyndman, Jane Andrews Lee 1912-1978 ..... *46*
    Obituary *23*
    Earlier sketch in SATA *1*
Hyndman, Robert Utley 1906-1973 .... *18*
Hynes, Pat *98*

I

Iannone, Jeanne
    See Balzano, Jeanne (Koppel)
Ibatoulline, Bagram 1965(?)- *174*
Ibbitson, John Perrie 1955- *102*
Ibbotson, Eva 1925- *156*
    Earlier sketches in SATA *13, 103*
Ibbotson, M. C(hristine) 1930- *5*
Icenoggle, Jodi 1967- *168*
Icenoggle, Jodi O.
    See Icenoggle, Jodi
Ichikawa, Satomi 1949- *208*
    Brief entry *36*
    Earlier sketches in SATA *47, 78, 146*
    See also CLR *62*
Iggulden, Hal 1972- *196*
Ignoffo, Matthew 1945- *92*
Igus, Toyomi 1953- *112*
    Earlier sketch in SATA *76*
Ihimaera, Witi (Tame) 1944- *148*
Ikeda, Daisaku 1928- *77*
Ilowite, Sheldon A. 1931- *27*
Ilsey, Dent
    See Chapman, John Stanton Higham
Ilsley, Dent
    See Chapman, John Stanton Higham
Ilsley, Velma (Elizabeth) 1918- *12*
Imai, Ayano 1980- *190*
Imai, Miko 1963- *90*
Imershein, Betsy 1953- *62*
Immel, Mary Blair 1930- *28*
Immell, Myra H. 1941- *92*
Impey, Rose 1947- *152*
    Earlier sketch in SATA *69*
Ingelow, Jean 1820-1897 .... *33*
Ingermanson, Randall 1958- *134*
Ingermanson, Randy
    See Ingermanson, Randall
Ingersoll, Norman 1928- *79*
Ingham, Colonel Frederic
    See Hale, Edward Everett
Ingman, Bruce 1963- *182*
    Earlier sketch in SATA *134*
Ingman, Nicholas 1948- *52*
Ingold, Jeanette *128*
Ingpen, Robert 1936- *166*
    Earlier sketch in SATA *109*
Ingpen, Robert Roger
    See Ingpen, Robert
Ingraham, Erick 1950- *145*
Ingraham, Leonard W(illiam) 1913-2003 .... *4*
Ingram, Scott 1948- *167*
    Earlier sketch in SATA *92*
Ingram, W. Scott
    See Ingram, Scott
Ingrams, Doreen 1906-1997 .... *97*
    Earlier sketch in SATA *20*

Ingrid, Charles
    See Salsitz, Rhondi Vilott
Ingves, Gunilla 1939- *101*
Ingves, Gunilla Anna Maria Folkesdotter
    See Ingves, Gunilla
Inkpen, Mick 1952- *154*
    Earlier sketch in SATA *99*
Innes, (Ralph) Hammond
    See Hammond Innes, Ralph
Innes, Ralph Hammond
    See Hammond Innes, Ralph
Innocenti, Roberto 1940- *159*
    Earlier sketch in SATA *96*
    See also CLR *126*
Innocenti and Gallaz
    See Gallaz, Christophe
    and Innocenti, Roberto
Inns, Chris *212*
Inyart, Gene
    See Namovicz, Gene Inyart
Ionesco, Eugene 1909-1994 .... *7*
    Obituary *79*
Ipcar, Dahlov (Zorach) 1917- *147*
    Autobiography Feature *147*
    Earlier sketches in SATA *1, 49*
    See also SAAS *8*
Ireland, Karin *151*
    Earlier sketch in SATA *101*
Ironside, Jetske 1940- *60*
Irvin, Fred 1914- *15*
Irvine, Georgeanne 1955- *72*
Irvine, Joan 1951- *80*
Irving, Alexander
    See Hume, Ruth Fox
Irving, Robert
    See Adler, Irving
Irving, Washington 1783-1859
    See YABC *2*
    See also CLR *97*
Irwin, Ann(abelle Bowen) 1915-1998 .... *89*
    Brief entry *38*
    Obituary *106*
    Earlier sketch in SATA *44*
    See also CLR *40*
    See also SAAS *14*
Irwin, Constance (H.) Frick 1913-1995 .... *6*
Irwin, Hadley
    See Hadley, Lee
    and Irwin, Ann(abelle Bowen)
Irwin, Keith Gordon 1885-1964 .... *11*
Isaac, Joanne 1934- *21*
Isaacs, Anne 1949- *185*
    Earlier sketch in SATA *90*
Isaacs, Jacob
    See Kranzler, George G(ershon)
Isaacson, Philip M(arshal) 1924- *87*
Isadora, Rachel 1953(?)- *204*
    Brief entry *32*
    Earlier sketches in SATA *54, 79, 121, 165*
    See also CLR *7*
Isbell, Rebecca T(emple) 1942- *125*
Isham, Charlotte H(ickock) 1912- *21*
Ishida, Jui *176*
Ish-Kishor, Judith 1892-1972 .... *11*
Ish-Kishor, Sulamith 1896-1977 .... *17*
Ishmael, Woodi 1914-1995 .... *31*
    Obituary *109*
Isle, Sue 1963- *105*
Israel, Elaine 1945- *12*
Israel, Marion Louise 1882-1973
    Obituary *26*
Iterson, S(iny) R(ose) Van
    See Van Iterson, S(iny) R(ose)
Ivanko, John D. 1966- *111*
Ivanko, John Duane
    See Ivanko, John D.
Iversen, Jeremy 1980(?)- *174*
Iversen, Jeremy Watt
    See Iversen, Jeremy
Iverson, Carol (L.) 1941- *145*
Iverson, Diane 1950- *122*

Iverson, Eric G.
 See Turtledove, Harry
Ivery, Martha M. 1948- *124*
Ives, David 1951- *173*
Ives, Morgan
 See Bradley, Marion Zimmer
Ives, Penny 1956- *215*
Iwai, Melissa *183*
Iwamatsu, Jun Atsushi 1908-1994 .... *81*
 Earlier sketch in SATA *14*
 See also CLR *4*
Iwamura, Kazuo 1939- *213*
Iwasaki (Matsumoto), Chihiro 1918-1974
 See CLR *18*

J

Jabar, Cynthia *210*
Jablonski, Carla *184*
Jac, Lee
 See Morton, Lee Jack, Jr.
Jacka, Martin 1943- *72*
Jackson, Alison 1953- *160*
 Earlier sketches in SATA *73, 108*
Jackson, Anne 1896(?)-1984
 Obituary *37*
Jackson, Barry
 See Jackson, Barry E.
Jackson, Barry E. *200*
Jackson, C(aary) Paul 1902-1991 .... *6*
Jackson, Caary
 See Jackson, C(aary) Paul
Jackson, Charlotte E. (Cobden) 1903(?)-1989
 Obituary *62*
Jackson, Dave
 See Jackson, J. David
Jackson, Donna M. 1959- *206*
Jackson, Ellen 1943- *214*
 Earlier sketches in SATA *75, 115, 167*
 See Jackson, Ellen B.
Jackson, Ellen B. *214*
 See Jackson, Ellen
Jackson, Garnet Nelson 1944- *87*
Jackson, Geoffrey (Holt Seymour) 1915-1987
 Obituary *53*
Jackson, Gina
 See Fluke, Joanne
Jackson, Guida M. 1930- *71*
Jackson, J. David 1944- *91*
Jackson, Jacqueline 1928- *65*
Jackson, Jacqueline Dougan
 See Jackson, Jacqueline
Jackson, Jesse 1908-1983 .... *29*
 Obituary *48*
 Earlier sketch in SATA *2*
 See also CLR *28*
Jackson, Marjorie 1928- *127*
Jackson, Melanie 1956- *141*
Jackson, Mike 1946- *91*
Jackson, Neta J. 1944- *91*
Jackson, O. B.
 See Jackson, C(aary) Paul
Jackson, Rob 1961- *176*
Jackson, Robert B(lake) 1926- *8*
Jackson, Robert Bradley
 See Jackson, Rob
Jackson, Sally
 See Kellogg, Jean (Defrees)
Jackson, Shirley 1919-1965 .... *2*
Jackson, Woody 1948- *92*
Jackson Issa, Kai *205*
Jacob, Helen Pierce 1927- *21*
Jacobin
 See Bisson, Terry
Jacobs, Deborah Lynn *187*
Jacobs, Flora Gill 1918-2006 .... *5*
 Obituary *178*

Jacobs, Francine 1935- *150*
 Brief entry *42*
 Earlier sketch in SATA *43*
Jacobs, Frank 1929- *30*
Jacobs, Helen Hull 1908-1997 .... *12*
Jacobs, Joseph 1854-1916 .... *25*
Jacobs, Judy 1952- *69*
Jacobs, Laurie A. 1956- *89*
Jacobs, Leah
 See Gellis, Roberta
Jacobs, Lee
 See Stone, Tanya Lee
Jacobs, Leland Blair 1907-1992 .... *20*
 Obituary *71*
Jacobs, Linda
 See Altman, Linda Jacobs
Jacobs, Lou(is), Jr. 1921- *2*
Jacobs, Shannon K. 1947- *77*
Jacobs, Susan
 See Quinn, Susan
Jacobs, William Jay 1933- *89*
 Earlier sketch in SATA *28*
Jacobsen, Laura *177*
Jacobson, Daniel 1923- *12*
Jacobson, Jennifer
 See Jacobson, Jennifer Richard
Jacobson, Jennifer Richard 1958- *170*
Jacobson, Morris K(arl) 1906- *21*
Jacobson, Rick *170*
Jacopetti, Alexandra
 See Hart, Alexandra
Jacques, Brian 1939- *176*
 Earlier sketches in SATA *62, 95, 138*
 See also CLR *21*
Jacques, Robin 1920-1995 .... *32*
 Brief entry *30*
 Obituary *86*
 See also SAAS *5*
Jaekel, Susan M. 1948- *89*
Jaffe, Michele *179*
Jaffe, Michele Sharon
 See Jaffe, Michele
Jaffee, Al(lan) 1921- *66*
 Earlier sketch in SATA *37*
Jagendorf, Moritz (Adolf) 1888-1981 .... *2*
 Obituary *24*
Jago 1979- *216*
Jahn, Joseph Michael
 See Jahn, Michael
Jahn, Michael 1943- *28*
Jahn, Mike
 See Jahn, Michael
Jahn-Clough, Lisa 1967- *193*
 Earlier sketches in SATA *88, 152*
Jahsmann, Allan Hart 1916- *28*
Jakes, John 1932- *62*
Jakes, John William
 See Jakes, John
James, Andrew
 See Kirkup, James
James, Ann 1952- *168*
 Earlier sketches in SATA *82, 117*
James, Betsy *183*
James, Bill 1929- *205*
James, B.J.
 See James, Brian
James, Brian 1976- *212*
 Earlier sketch in SATA *140*
James, Bronte
 See Nash, Renea Denise
James, Captain Lew
 See Stratemeyer, Edward L.
James, Charlie 1961- *185*
James, Curtis E. *182*
James, Dynely
 See Mayne, William
James, Edwin
 See Gunn, James E.
James, Elizabeth 1942- *97*
 Earlier sketches in SATA *39, 45, 52*

James, Emily
 See Standiford, Natalie
James, Gordon C. 1973- *195*
James, Harry Clebourne 1896-1978 .... *11*
James, J. Alison 1962- *146*
 Earlier sketch in SATA *83*
James, Josephine
 See Sterne, Emma Gelders
James, Mary
 See Meaker, Marijane
James, Matt *201*
James, Philip
 See del Rey, Lester
 and Moorcock, Michael
James, Robin 1953- *50*
James, Robin Irene
 See James, Robin
James, Simon *202*
 See Kunen, James Simon
James, T. F.
 See Fleming, Thomas
James, Tegan
 See Odgers, Sally Farrell
James, Will(iam Roderick) 1892-1942 .... *19*
Jameson, W. C. 1942- *93*
Jamieson, Ian R.
 See Goulart, Ron
Jamiolkowski, Raymond M. 1953- *81*
Jane, Mary Childs 1909- *6*
Jane, Pamela *158*
Janeczko, Paul B(ryan) 1945- *155*
 Earlier sketches in SATA *53, 98*
 See also CLR *47*
 See also SAAS *18*
Janes, Edward C. 1908-1984 .... *25*
Janes, Edward Clarence
 See Janes, Edward C.
Janes, J(oseph) Robert 1935- *148*
 Brief entry *50*
 Earlier sketch in SATA *101*
Janeway, Elizabeth (Hall) 1913-2005 .... *19*
Janger, Kathleen N. 1940- *66*
Jango-Cohen, Judith 1955- *208*
Janice
 See Brustlein, Janice Tworkov
Janisch, Heinz 1960- *181*
Janosch
 See Eckert, Horst
Janover, Caroline (Davis) 1943- *141*
 Earlier sketch in SATA *89*
Janovitz, Marilyn *194*
Jansen, Jared
 See Cebulash, Mel
Janson, Dora Jane (Heineberg) 1916- *31*
Janson, H(orst) W(oldemar) 1913-1982 .... *9*
Jansson, Tove (Marika) 1914-2001 .... *41*
 Earlier sketch in SATA *3*
 See also CLR *125*
Janus, Grete
 See Hertz, Grete Janus
Jaques, Faith 1923-1997 .... *97*
 Earlier sketches in SATA *21, 69*
Jaquith, Priscilla 1908- *51*
Jaramillo, Mari-Luci 1928- *139*
Jarman, Julia 1946- *198*
 Earlier sketch in SATA *133*
Jarman, Rosemary Hawley 1935- *7*
Jarrell, Mary Von Schrader 1914- *35*
Jarrell, Randall 1914-1965 .... *7*
 See also CLR *111*
Jarrett, Clare 1952- *201*
Jarrett, Roxanne
 See Werner, Herma
Jarrow, Gail 1952- *185*
 Earlier sketch in SATA *84*
Jarvis, E.K.
 See Ellison, Harlan
 and Silverberg, Robert
Jarvis, Robin 1963- *181*
Jaskol, Julie 1958- *127*

Jasner, W. K.
    See Watson, Jane Werner
Jassem, Kate
    See Oppenheim, Joanne
Jauss, Anne Marie 1902(?)-1991 .... *10*
    Obituary *69*
Javernick, Ellen 1938- *217*
    Earlier sketch in SATA *89*
Javins, Marie 1966- *212*
Jay, Alison *196*
Jayne, Lieutenant R. H.
    See Ellis, Edward S.
Jaynes, Clare
    See Mayer, Jane Rothschild
Jeake, Samuel, Jr.
    See Aiken, Conrad
Jean-Bart, Leslie 1954- *121*
Jeapes, Ben 1965- *174*
Jecan, Gavriel 1962- *200*
Jefferds, Vincent H(arris) 1916- *59*
    Brief entry *49*
Jefferies, (John) Richard 1848-1887 .... *16*
Jeffers, Dawn *189*
Jeffers, Oliver 1977- *213*
    Earlier sketch in SATA *175*
Jeffers, Susan 1942- *202*
    Earlier sketches in SATA *17, 70, 129, 137*
    See also CLR *30*
Jefferson, Sarah
    See Farjeon, (Eve) Annabel
Jeffries, Roderic 1926- *4*
Jeffries, Roderic Graeme
    See Jeffries, Roderic
Jenkin-Pearce, Susie 1943- *80*
Jenkins, A. M. 1961- *174*
Jenkins, Amanda McRaney
    See Jenkins, A. M.
Jenkins, Debra Reid
    See Reid Jenkins, Debra
Jenkins, Emily 1967- *174*
    Earlier sketch in SATA *144*
Jenkins, Jean *98*
Jenkins, Jerry B. 1949- *149*
Jenkins, Jerry Bruce
    See Jenkins, Jerry B.
Jenkins, Leonard *189*
Jenkins, Marie M(agdalen) 1909- *7*
Jenkins, Martin 1959- *216*
Jenkins, M.D.
    See Jenkins, Martin
Jenkins, Patrick 1955- *72*
Jenkins, Steve 1952- *188*
    Earlier sketch in SATA *154*
Jenkins, William A(twell) 1922-1998 .... *9*
Jenkyns, Chris 1924- *51*
Jennewein, James *215*
Jennewein, Jim
    See Jennewein, James
Jennings, Christopher S. 1971(?)- *201*
Jennings, Coleman A(lonzo) 1933- *64*
Jennings, C.S.
    See Jennings, Christopher S.
Jennings, Dana Andrew 1957- *93*
Jennings, Elizabeth (Joan) 1926-2001 .... *66*
Jennings, Gary 1928-1999 .... *9*
    Obituary *117*
Jennings, Gary Gayne
    See Jennings, Gary
Jennings, Linda 1937- *211*
Jennings, Linda M.
    See Jennings, Linda
Jennings, Patrick 1962- *205*
    Earlier sketches in SATA *96, 160*
Jennings, Paul 1943- *165*
    Earlier sketch in SATA *88*
    See also CLR *40*
Jennings, Richard W. 1945- *185*
    Earlier sketch in SATA *136*
Jennings, Robert
    See Hamilton, Charles (Harold St. John)

Jennings, S. M.
    See Meyer, Jerome Sydney
Jennings, Sharon 1954- *95*
Jennings, Sharon Elizabeth
    See Jennings, Sharon
Jennison, C. S.
    See Starbird, Kaye
Jennison, Keith Warren 1911-1995 .... *14*
Jensen, Kathryn 1949- *81*
Jensen, Kristine Mary 1961- *78*
Jensen, Niels 1927- *25*
Jensen, Vickie (Dee) 1946- *81*
Jensen, Virginia Allen 1927- *8*
Jenson-Elliott, Cynthia L(ouise) 1962- *143*
Jeram, Anita 1965- *154*
    Earlier sketches in SATA *71, 102*
Jerman, Jerry 1949- *89*
Jernigan, E. Wesley 1940- *85*
Jernigan, Gisela (Evelyn) 1948- *85*
Jeschke, Susan 1942- *42*
    Brief entry *27*
Jessel, Camilla (Ruth) 1937- *143*
    Earlier sketch in SATA *29*
Jessell, Tim *177*
Jessey, Cornelia
    See Sussman, Cornelia Silver
Jewel
    See Kilcher, Jewel
Jewell, Nancy 1940- *109*
    Brief entry *41*
Jewett, Eleanore Myers 1890-1967 .... *5*
Jewett, Sarah Orne 1849-1909 .... *15*
Jewett, Theodora Sarah Orne
    See Jewett, Sarah Orne
Jezard, Alison 1919- *57*
    Brief entry *34*
Jiang, Cheng An 1943- *109*
Jiang, Ji-li 1954- *101*
Jiang, Zheng An
    See Jiang, Cheng An
Jiler, John 1946- *42*
    Brief entry *35*
Jimenez, Francisco 1943- *108*
Jinks, Catherine 1963- *207*
    Earlier sketches in SATA *94, 155*
Jobb, Jamie 1945- *29*
Jobling, Curtis *131*
Jocelyn, Ann Henning 1948- *92*
Jocelyn, Marthe 1956- *198*
    Earlier sketches in SATA *118, 163*
Joerns, Consuelo *44*
    Brief entry *33*
Joey D
    See Macaulay, Teresa
Johansen, Krista V.
    See Johansen, K.V.
Johansen, K.V 1968- *186*
Johansen, K.V. 1968- *186*
    Earlier sketch in SATA *129*
Johansson, Philip *163*
John, Antony 1972- *206*
John, Joyce *59*
Johns, Avery
    See Cousins, Margaret
Johns, Elizabeth 1943- *88*
Johns, Janetta
    See Quin-Harkin, Janet
Johns, Linda 1945- *173*
Johns, W(illiam) E(arle) 1893-1968 .... *55*
Johns, Captain W. E.
    See Johns, W(illiam) E(arle)
Johnson, A.
    See Johnson, Annabell
Johnson, A. E.
    See Johnson, Annabell
    and Johnson, Edgar (Raymond)
Johnson, Angela 1961- *188*
    Earlier sketches in SATA *69, 102, 150*
    See also CLR *33*
Johnson, Annabel
    See Johnson, Annabell

Johnson, Annabell 1921- *72*
    Earlier sketch in SATA *2*
Johnson, Art 1946- *123*
Johnson, B. F. 1920- *1*
Johnson, Benjamin F., of Boone
    See Riley, James Whitcomb
Johnson, Bettye 1858-1919
    See Rogers, Bettye
Johnson, Caryn
    See Goldberg, Whoopi
Johnson, Caryn E.
    See Goldberg, Whoopi
Johnson, Caryn Elaine
    See Goldberg, Whoopi
Johnson, Charles R. 1925- *11*
Johnson, Charlotte Buel
    See von Wodtke, Charlotte Buel Johnson
Johnson, Chuck
    See Johnson, Charles R.
Johnson, Crockett
    See Leisk, David (Johnson)
Johnson, D(ana) William 1945- *23*
Johnson, Daniel Shahid 1954- *73*
Johnson, David
    See Johnson, David A.
Johnson, David A. 1951- *191*
Johnson, D.B. 1944- *183*
    Earlier sketch in SATA *146*
Johnson, Dianne 1960- *130*
Johnson, Dinah
    See Johnson, Dianne
Johnson, Dolores 1949- *69*
Johnson, Donald B.
    See Johnson, D.B.
Johnson, Dorothy M(arie) 1905-1984 .... *6*
    Obituary *40*
Johnson, E(ugene) Harper *44*
Johnson, Edgar (Raymond) 1912-1990 .... *72*
    Earlier sketch in SATA *2*
Johnson, Eleanor Murdock 1892-1987
    Obituary *54*
Johnson, Elizabeth 1911-1984 .... *7*
    Obituary *39*
Johnson, Eric W(arner) 1918-1994 ....
    Obituary *82*
    Earlier sketch in SATA *8*
Johnson, Evelyne 1922- *20*
Johnson, Fred 19(?)-1982 .... *63*
Johnson, Gaylord 1884-1972 .... *7*
Johnson, Gerald White 1890-1980 .... *19*
    Obituary *28*
Johnson, Gillian 1963- *215*
Johnson, Harper
    See Johnson, E(ugene) Harper
Johnson, Harriett 1908-1987
    Obituary *53*
Johnson, James Ralph 1922- *1*
Johnson, James Weldon 1871-1938 .... *31*
    See also CLR *32*
Johnson, Jane 1951- *48*
Johnson, Joan J. 1942- *59*
Johnson, John E(mil) 1929- *34*
Johnson, Johnny 1901-1995
    See Johnson, (Walter) Ryerson
Johnson, Kathleen Jeffrie 1950- *186*
Johnson, La Verne B(ravo) 1925- *13*
Johnson, Layne *187*
Johnson, Lee Kaiser 1962- *78*
Johnson, Lissa H(alls) 1955- *65*
Johnson, Lois Smith 1894-1993 .... *6*
Johnson, Lois Walfrid 1936- *130*
    Earlier sketches in SATA *22, 91*
Johnson, Margaret S(weet) 1893-1964 .... *35*
Johnson, Marguerite Annie
    See Angelou, Maya
Johnson, Mary Frances K. 1929(?)-1979
    Obituary *27*
Johnson, Maud Battle 1918(?)-1985
    Obituary *46*
Johnson, Maureen 1973- *200*
Johnson, Meredith Merrell 1952- *104*

Johnson, Milton 1932- *31*
Johnson, Neil 1954- *135*
  Earlier sketch in SATA *73*
Johnson, Pamela 1949- *71*
Johnson, Patricia Polin 1956- *84*
Johnson, Paul Brett 1947- *132*
  Earlier sketch in SATA *83*
Johnson, Rebecca L. 1956- *147*
  Earlier sketch in SATA *67*
Johnson, Rick L. 1954- *79*
Johnson, (Walter) Ryerson 1901-1995 .... *10*
  Obituary *106*
Johnson, Scott 1952- *119*
  Earlier sketch in SATA *76*
Johnson, Sherrie 1948- *87*
Johnson, Shirley K(ing) 1927- *10*
Johnson, Siddie Joe 1905-1977
  Obituary *20*
Johnson, Spencer 1938- *145*
  Brief entry *38*
Johnson, Stacie
  See Myers, Walter Dean
Johnson, Stephen T. 1964- *189*
  Earlier sketches in SATA *84, 141*
Johnson, Steve 1960- *177*
Johnson, Sue Kaiser 1963- *78*
Johnson, Sylvia A. *166*
  Brief entry *52*
  Earlier sketch in SATA *104*
Johnson, William R. *38*
Johnson, William Weber 1909-1992 .... *7*
Johnson-Feelings, Dianne
  See Johnson, Dianne
Johnston, Agnes Christine
  See Dazey, Agnes J(ohnston)
Johnston, Annie Fellows 1863-1931 .... *37*
Johnston, Dorothy Grunbock 1915-1979 ...... *54*
Johnston, Ginny 1946- *60*
Johnston, H(ugh) A(nthony) S(tephen)
  1913-1967 .... *14*
Johnston, Janet 1944- *71*
Johnston, Jeffry W. *188*
Johnston, Johanna 1914(?)-1982 .... *12*
  Obituary *33*
Johnston, Julie 1941- *110*
  Autobiography Feature *128*
  Earlier sketch in SATA *78*
  See also CLR *41*
  See also SAAS *24*
Johnston, Lynn 1947- *216*
  Earlier sketch in SATA *118*
Johnston, Lynn Beverley
  See Johnston, Lynn
Johnston, Mark *194*
Johnston, Norma
  See St. John, Nicole
Johnston, Portia
  See Takakjian, Portia
Johnston, Susan Taylor 1942- *180*
  Earlier sketches in SATA *8, 83, 128*
Johnston, Tim(othy Patrick) 1962- *146*
Johnston, Tony
  See Johnston, Susan Taylor
Joinson, Carla *160*
Jolin, Paula *186*
Jonas, Ann 1932- *135*
  Brief entry *42*
  Earlier sketch in SATA *50*
  See also CLR *74*
Jonell, Lynne 1956- *196*
  Earlier sketch in SATA *109*
Jones, Adrienne 1915-2000 .... *82*
  Earlier sketch in SATA *7*
  See also SAAS *10*
Jones, Allan Frewin 1954- *204*
Jones, Annabel
  See Lewis, Mary
Jones, Betty Millsaps 1940- *54*
Jones, Carol 1942- *153*
  Earlier sketch in SATA *79*
Jones, Carrie 1971- *191*

Jones, Charles M.
  See Jones, Chuck
Jones, Charlotte Foltz 1945- *122*
  Earlier sketch in SATA *77*
Jones, Chuck 1912-2002 .... *53*
  Obituary *133*
Jones, Constance *112*
Jones, Constance A.
  See Jones, Constance
Jones, David 1956- *202*
Jones, Diana Wynne 1934- *160*
  Earlier sketches in SATA *9, 70, 108*
  See also CLR *120*
  See also SAAS *7*
Jones, Douglas B. *202*
Jones, Douglas C(lyde) 1924-1998 .... *52*
Jones, Elizabeth McDavid *155*
Jones, Elizabeth Orton 1910-2005 .... *18*
  Obituary *164*
Jones, Evan 1915-1996 .... *3*
Jones, Frewin
  See Jones, Allan Frewin
Jones, Geraldine
  See McCaughrean, Geraldine
Jones, Gillingham
  See Hamilton, Charles (Harold St. John)
Jones, Gwyneth A. 1952- *159*
Jones, Gwyneth Ann
  See Jones, Gwyneth A.
Jones, Harold 1904-1992 .... *14*
  Obituary *72*
Jones, Helen Hinckley 1903-1991 .... *26*
Jones, Helen L(ouise) 1903-1973
  Obituary *22*
Jones, Hettie 1934- *42*
  Brief entry *27*
Jones, Hortense P. 1918- *9*
Jones, J. Sydney 1948- *101*
Jones, Jasmine
  See Papademetriou, Lisa
Jones, Jennifer (Berry) 1947- *90*
Jones, Jessie Mae Orton 1887(?)-1983
  Obituary *37*
Jones, John R(obert) 1926- *76*
Jones, Jon Sydney
  See Jones, J. Sydney
Jones, Judith
  See James, Bill
Jones, Kimberly K. 1957- *187*
Jones, Marcia Thornton 1958- *217*
  Earlier sketches in SATA *73, 115*
Jones, Martha T(annery) 1931- *130*
Jones, Mary Alice 1898(?)-1980 .... *6*
Jones, McClure *34*
Jones, Noah Z. *182*
Jones, Patrick 1961- *210*
  Earlier sketch in SATA *136*
Jones, Penelope 1938- *31*
Jones, Rebecca C(astaldi) 1947- *99*
  Earlier sketch in SATA *33*
Jones, Robin D(orothy) 1959- *80*
Jones, Sanford W.
  See Thorn, John
Jones, Sylvie *185*
Jones, Sylvie Michelle
  See Jones, Sylvie
Jones, Terence Graham Parry 1942- *127*
  Brief entry *51*
  Earlier sketch in SATA *67*
Jones, Terry
  See Jones, Terence Graham Parry
Jones, Tim Wynne
  See Wynne-Jones, Tim
Jones, Traci L. *186*
Jones, V. M. 1958- *147*
Jones, Veda Boyd 1948- *119*
Jones, Victoria Mary
  See Jones, V. M.
Jones, Volcano
  See Mitchell, Adrian

Jones, Weyman (B.) 1928- *4*
  See also SAAS *11*
Jones, William Glynne
  See Glynne-Jones, William
Jonk, Clarence 1906-1987 .... *10*
Jonsberg, Barry 1951- *168*
Joos, Francoise 1956- *78*
Joos, Frederic 1953- *78*
Joosse, Barbara M. 1949- *164*
  Earlier sketches in SATA *52, 96*
Joosse, Barbara Monnot
  See Joosse, Barbara M.
Jordan, Alexis Hill
  See Glick, Ruth (Burtnick)
  and Titchener, Louise
Jordan, Anne Devereaux 1943- *80*
Jordan, Chris
  See Philbrick, Rodman
Jordan, Deloris *191*
Jordan, Don
  See Howard, Vernon (Linwood)
Jordan, Hope Dahle 1905-1995 .... *15*
Jordan, Jael (Michal) 1949- *30*
Jordan, June 1936-2002 .... *136*
  Earlier sketch in SATA *4*
  See also CLR *10*
Jordan, June Meyer
  See Jordan, June
Jordan, Lee
  See Scholefield, Alan
Jordan, Martin George 1944- *84*
Jordan, Robert 1948-2007 .... *95*
Jordan, Robert K.
  See Jordan, Robert
Jordan, Rosa 1939- *191*
Jordan, Roslyn M. *189*
Jordan, Sherryl 1949- *122*
  Earlier sketch in SATA *71*
  See also SAAS *23*
Jordan, Shirley 1930- *154*
Jordan, Tanis 1946- *84*
Jorgensen, Ivar
  See Ellison, Harlan
  and Garrett, Randall
Jorgensen, Mary Venn -1995 .... *36*
Jorgensen, Norman 1954- *157*
Jorgenson, Ivar
  See Silverberg, Robert
Jorisch, Stephane *178*
Joseph, Anne
  See Coates, Anna
Joseph, James (Herz) 1924- *53*
Joseph, Joan 1939- *34*
Joseph, Joseph M(aron) 1903-1979 .... *22*
Joseph, Patrick
  See O'Malley, Kevin
Josephs, Rebecca
  See Talbot, Toby
Josephson, Judith Pinkerton 1943- *198*
Josh
  See Twain, Mark
Joshua, Peter
  See Stone, Peter
Joslin, Mary 1953- *176*
Joslin, Sesyle
  See Hine, Sesyle Joslin
Joubert, Beverly 1957- *204*
Joubert, Dereck *204*
Journet, Mireille
  See Marokvia, Mireille
Joyce, Bill
  See Joyce, William
Joyce, J(ames) Avery 1902-1987 .... *11*
  Obituary *50*
Joyce, Peter 1937- *127*
Joyce, William 1957- *118*
  Brief entry *46*
  Earlier sketch in SATA *72*
  See also CLR *26*
Joyner, Jerry 1938- *34*
Juan, Ana 1961- *179*

Jubb, Sophie *210*
Jubert, Herve *185*
Juby, Susan 1969- *202*
  Earlier sketch in SATA *156*
Jucker, Sita 1921- *5*
Judah, Aaron 1923- *118*
Judd, Cyril
  See Kornbluth, C(yril) M.
  and Merril, Judith
  and Pohl, Frederik
Judd, Denis (O'Nan) 1938- *33*
Judd, Frances K.
  See Benson, Mildred
Jude, Conny *81*
Judge, Lita *192*
Judson, Clara Ingram 1879-1960 .... *38*
  Brief entry *27*
Judy, Stephen
  See Tchudi, Stephen N.
Judy, Stephen N.
  See Tchudi, Stephen N.
Juhasz, Victor 1954- *177*
Jukes, Mavis 1947- *111*
  Brief entry *43*
  Earlier sketch in SATA *72*
  See also SAAS *12*
Jules, Jacqueline 1956- *183*
  Earlier sketch in SATA *148*
Julesberg, Elizabeth Rider Montgomery
  1902-1985 .... *34*
  Obituary *41*
  Earlier sketch in SATA *3*
Julian, Jane
  See Wiseman, David
Jumpp, Hugo
  See MacPeek, Walter G.
Jungman, Ann *165*
Jupo, Frank J. 1904-1981 .... *7*
Jurmain, Suzanne 1945- *169*
  Earlier sketch in SATA *72*
Jurmain, Suzanne Tripp
  See Jurmain, Suzanne
Juster, Norton 1929- *132*
  Earlier sketch in SATA *3*
  See also CLR *112*
Justus, May 1898-1989 .... *1*
  Obituary *106*
Juvenilia
  See Taylor, Ann

K

Kaaberbol, Lene
  See Kaaberbol, Lene
Kaaberbol, Lene 1960- *159*
Kabdebo, Tamas
  See Kabdebo, Thomas
Kabdebo, Thomas 1934- *10*
Kabibble, Osh
  See Jobb, Jamie
Kacer, Kathy 1954- *184*
  Earlier sketch in SATA *142*
Kaczman, James *156*
Kadair, Deborah Ousley *184*
Kadesch, Robert R(udstone) 1922- *31*
Kadohata, Cynthia 1956(?)- *180*
  Earlier sketch in SATA *155*
  See also CLR *121*
Kadohata, Cynthia L.
  See Kadohata, Cynthia
Kaempfert, Wade
  See del Rey, Lester
Kaestner, Erich 1899-1974 .... *14*
  See also CLR *153*
Kahl, Jonathan (D.) 1959- *77*
Kahl, M(arvin) P(hilip) 1934- *37*
Kahl, Virginia (Caroline) 1919-2004 .... *48*
  Brief entry *38*
  Obituary *158*

Kahn, Joan 1914-1994 .... *48*
  Obituary *82*
Kahn, Katherine Janus 1942- *167*
  Earlier sketch in SATA *90*
Kahn, Peggy
  See Katz, Bobbi
Kahn, Roger 1927- *37*
Kahukiwa, Robyn 1940- *134*
Kains, Josephine
  See Goulart, Ron
Kaizuki, Kiyonori 1950- *72*
Kajikawa, Kimiko *212*
Kakimoto, Kozo 1915- *11*
Kalashnikoff, Nicholas 1888-1961 .... *16*
Kalb, Jonah 1926- *23*
Kalbacken, Joan 1925- *96*
Kalechofsky, Roberta 1931- *92*
Kaler, James Otis 1848-1912 .... *15*
Kalis, Jennifer *207*
Kalish, Claire M. 1947- *92*
Kallen, Stuart A. 1955- *126*
  Earlier sketch in SATA *86*
Kallen, Stuart Arnold
  See Kallen, Stuart A.
Kallevig, Christine Petrell 1955- *164*
Kalman, Bobbie 1947- *63*
Kalman, Maira 1949- *137*
  Earlier sketch in SATA *96*
  See also CLR *32*
Kalnay, Francis 1899-1992 .... *7*
Kaloustian, Rosanne 1955- *93*
Kalow, Gisela 1946- *32*
Kalstein, Dave *175*
Kamara, Mariatu *214*
Kamen, Gloria 1923- *98*
  Earlier sketch in SATA *9*
Kamerman, Sylvia E.
  See Burack, Sylvia K.
Kamm, Josephine (Hart) 1905-1989 .... *24*
Kammerman, Sylvia K.
  See Burack, Sylvia K.
Kandel, Michael 1941- *93*
Kandell, Alice S. 1938- *35*
Kane, Bob 1916-1998 .... *120*
Kane, Henry Bugbee 1902-1971 .... *14*
Kane, L. A.
  See Mannetti, Lisa
Kane, Robert W. 1910- *18*
Kane, Wilson
  See Bloch, Robert (Albert)
Kanefield, Teri 1960- *135*
Kanell, Beth *215*
Kaner, Etta 1947- *198*
  Earlier sketch in SATA *126*
Kanetzke, Howard W(illiam) 1932- *38*
Kangas, Juli 1958- *200*
Kann, Elizabeth *180*
Kann, Victoria *180*
Kanninen, Barbara *196*
Kanninen, Barbara J.
  See Kanninen, Barbara
Kanoza, Muriel Canfield
  See Canfield, Muriel
Kantner, Seth 1965- *179*
Kanzawa, Toshiko
  See Furukawa, Toshi
Kanzler, John 1963- *188*
Kaplan, Andrew 1960- *78*
Kaplan, Anne Bernays
  See Bernays, Anne
Kaplan, Bess 1927- *22*
Kaplan, Boche 1926- *24*
Kaplan, Elizabeth 1956- *83*
Kaplan, Elizabeth A.
  See Kaplan, Elizabeth
Kaplan, Irma 1900- *10*
Kaplan, Jean Caryl Korn 1926- *10*
Kaplow, Robert 1954- *70*
Karageorge, Michael
  See Anderson, Poul
Karas, G. Brian 1957- *178*

Karas, George Brian
  See Karas, G. Brian
Karasz, Ilonka 1896-1981
  Obituary *29*
Karen, Ruth 1922-1987 .... *9*
  Obituary *54*
Kark, Nina Mary
  See Bawden, Nina
Karl, Herb 1938- *73*
Karl, Jean E(dna) 1927-2000 .... *122*
  Earlier sketch in SATA *34*
  See also SAAS *10*
Karlin, Bernie 1927- *68*
Karlin, Eugene 1918- *10*
Karlin, Nurit *103*
  Earlier sketch in SATA *63*
Karnes, Frances A. 1937- *110*
Karp, Naomi J. 1926- *16*
Karpinski, J. Rick
  See Karpinski, John Eric
Karpinski, John Eric 1952- *81*
Karpinski, Rick
  See Karpinski, John Eric
Karr, Kathleen 1946- *212*
  Earlier sketches in SATA *82, 127*
Karr, Phyllis Ann 1944- *119*
Karwoski, Gail 1949- *127*
Karwoski, Gail Langer
  See Karwoski, Gail
Kashiwagi, Isami 1925- *10*
Kaslik, Ibi
  See Kaslik, Ibolya Emma
Kaslik, Ibolya Emma 1973- *185*
Kassem, Lou 1931- *62*
  Brief entry *51*
Kastel, Warren
  See Silverberg, Robert
Kastner, Erich
  See Kaestner, Erich
Kastner, Jill (Marie) 1964- *117*
  Earlier sketch in SATA *70*
Kasuya, Masahiro 1937- *51*
Kasza, Keiko 1951- *191*
  Earlier sketch in SATA *124*
Kataphusin
  See Ruskin, John
Katchen, Carole 1944- *9*
Katcher, Brian 1975- *203*
Kathryn
  See Searle, Kathryn Adrienne
Kato, Aya 1982- *202*
Katona, Robert 1949- *21*
Katsarakis, Joan Harries
  See Harries, Joan
Katz, Alan *185*
Katz, Avi 1949- *199*
Katz, Avner 1939- *103*
Katz, Bobbi 1933- *217*
  Earlier sketches in SATA *12, 179*
Katz, Fred(eric Phillip) 1938- *6*
Katz, Jane B(resler) 1934- *33*
Katz, Karen 1947- *195*
  Earlier sketch in SATA *158*
Katz, Marjorie P.
  See Weiser, Marjorie P(hillis) K(atz)
Katz, Susan 1945- *156*
Katz, Welwyn Wilton 1948- *96*
  Autobiography Feature *118*
  Earlier sketch in SATA *62*
  See also CLR *45*
Katz, William 1940- *98*
Katz, William Loren 1927- *13*
Kaufman, Bel *57*
Kaufman, Jeff 1955- *84*
Kaufman, Joe 1911-2001 .... *33*
Kaufman, Joseph
  See Kaufman, Joe
Kaufman, Mervyn D. 1932- *4*
Kaufmann, Angelika 1935- *15*
Kaufmann, John 1931- *18*
Kaula, Edna Mason 1906-1987 .... *13*

Kaur Khalsa, Dayal
  See Khalsa, Dayal Kaur
Kavaler, Lucy 1930- 23
Kavanagh, Jack 1920- 85
Kavanagh, P(atrick) J(oseph Gregory)
  1931- 122
Kavanaugh, Ian
  See Webb, Jean Francis (III)
Kay, Alan N. 1965- 144
Kay, Elizabeth 1949- 165
Kay, Guy Gavriel 1954- 167
  Earlier sketch in SATA *121*
Kay, Helen
  See Goldfrank, Helen Colodny
Kay, Jackie 1961- 165
  Earlier sketch in SATA *97*
Kay, Jacqueline Margaret
  See Kay, Jackie
Kay, Julia 205
Kay, Mara 13
Kay, Verla 1946- 210
  Earlier sketch in SATA *120*
Kaye, Danny 1913-1987
  Obituary 50
Kaye, Geraldine (Hughesdon) 1925- 85
  Earlier sketch in SATA *10*
Kaye, Judy
  See Baer, Judy
Kaye, Marilyn 1949- 110
  Earlier sketch in SATA *56*
Kaye, Mary Margaret
  See Kaye, M.M.
Kaye, M.M. 1908-2004 62
  Obituary 152
Kaye, Mollie
  See Kaye, M.M.
Kaye, Peggy 1948- 143
Keach, James P. 1950- 125
Keams, Geri 1951- 117
Keane, Bil 1922- 4
Keane, Dave 1965- 216
Keaney, Brian 1954- 188
  Earlier sketch in SATA *106*
Kearney, Meg 1964- 178
Kearny, Jillian
  See Goulart, Ron
Keating, Bern
  See Keating, Leo Bernard
Keating, Frank 1944- 143
Keating, Lawrence A. 1903-1966 23
Keating, Leo Bernard 1915- 10
Keats, Emma 1899(?)-1979(?) 68
Keats, Ezra Jack 1916-1983 57
  Obituary 34
  Earlier sketch in SATA *14*
  See also CLR *35*
Keefer, Catherine
  See Ogan, George F.
  and Ogan, Margaret E. (Nettles)
Keefer, Janice Kulyk
  See Kulyk Keefer, Janice
Keegan, Marcia 1943- 104
  Earlier sketch in SATA *9*
Keehn, Sally M. 1947- 165
  Earlier sketch in SATA *87*
Keel, Frank
  See Keeler, Ronald F(ranklin)
Keeler, Patricia 183
Keeler, Patricia A.
  See Keeler, Patricia
Keeler, Ronald F(ranklin) 1913-1983 47
Keely, Jack 1951- 119
Keen, Martin L. 1913-1992 4
Keenan, Sheila 1953- 95
Keene, Ann T. 1940- 86
Keene, Ann Todd
  See Keene, Ann T.

Keene, Carolyn
  See Benson, Mildred
  and Goulart, Ron
  and Lerangis, Peter
  and McFarlane, Leslie
  and Stanley, George Edward
  and Stratemeyer, Edward L.
Keens-Douglas, Richardo 1953- 154
  Earlier sketch in SATA *95*
Keep, Linda Lowery
  See Lowery, Linda
Keep, Richard 1949- 170
Keep, Richard Cleminson
  See Keep, Richard
Keeping, Charles (William James)
  1924-1988 69
  Obituary 56
  Earlier sketch in SATA *9*
  See also CLR *34*
Keeshan, Robert J. 1927-2004 32
  Obituary 151
Kehlenbeck, Angela 1959- 186
Kehret, Peg 1936- 212
  Autobiography Feature 149
  Earlier sketches in SATA *73, 108, 149*
Keillor, Garrison 1942- 58
Keillor, Gary Edward
  See Keillor, Garrison
Keir, Christine
  See Pullein-Thompson, Christine
Keister, Douglas 1948- 88
Keith, Doug 1952- 81
Keith, Eros 1942- 52
Keith, Hal 1934- 36
Keith, Harold (Verne) 1903-1998 74
  Earlier sketch in SATA *2*
Keith, Robert
  See Applebaum, Stan
Keleinikov, Andrei 1924- 65
Kelemen, Julie 1959- 78
Kelen, Emery 1896-1978 13
  Obituary 26
Kelleam, Joseph E(veridge) 1913-1975 31
Kelleher, Anne 1959- 97
Kelleher, Annette 1950- 122
Kelleher, Daria Valerian 1955- 79
Kelleher, Victor (Michael Kitchener)
  1939- 129
  Brief entry 52
  Earlier sketch in SATA *75*
  See also CLR *36*
Keller, Beverly L(ou) 91
  Earlier sketch in SATA *13*
Keller, Charles 1942- 82
  Earlier sketch in SATA *8*
Keller, Debra 1958- 94
Keller, Dick 1923- 36
Keller, Emily 96
Keller, Gail Faithfull
  See Faithfull, Gail
Keller, Holly 1942- 216
  Brief entry 42
  Earlier sketches in SATA *76, 108, 157*
  See also CLR *45*
Keller, Irene (Barron) 1927-2002 36
  Obituary 139
Keller, Laurie 1961(?)- 196
Kelley, Ann 1941- 217
Kelley, Ellen A. 185
Kelley, Ellen Chavez
  See Kelley, Ellen A.
Kelley, Gary 1945- 217
  Earlier sketch in SATA *183*
Kelley, Leo P(atrick) 1928- 32
  Brief entry 31
Kelley, Marty 1971- 211
Kelley, Patrick (G.) 1963- 129
Kelley, Patte 1947- 93
Kelley, True 1946- 179

Kelley, True (Adelaide) 1946- 130
  Brief entry 39
  Earlier sketches in SATA *41, 92*
Kelley, True Adelaide
  See Kelley, True
Kellin, Sally Moffet 1932- 9
Kelling, Furn L. 1914-2000 37
Kellogg, Gene
  See Kellogg, Jean (Defrees)
Kellogg, Jean (Defrees) 1916-1978 10
Kellogg, Steven 1941- 177
  Earlier sketches in SATA *8, 57, 130*
  See also CLR *6*
Kellogg, Steven Castle
  See Kellogg, Steven
Kellow, Kathleen
  See Hibbert, Eleanor Alice Burford
Kelly, C. M. O.
  See Gibbs, (Cecilia) May
Kelly, Clint 1950- 140
Kelly, Eric P(hilbrook) 1884-1960
  See YABC *1*
Kelly, Fiona
  See Coleman, Michael
  and Hendry, Frances Mary
  and Jones, Allan Frewin
  and Oldfield, Jenny
  and Welford, Sue
Kelly, Irene 1957- 210
  Earlier sketch in SATA *147*
Kelly, Jacqueline 216
Kelly, Jeff
  See Kelly, Jeffrey
Kelly, Jeffrey 1946- 65
Kelly, Joanne (W.) 1934- 87
Kelly, Kate 1958- 91
Kelly, Kathleen M. 1964- 71
Kelly, Katy 1955- 215
  Earlier sketch in SATA *169*
Kelly, Lauren
  See Oates, Joyce Carol
Kelly, Laurene 1954- 123
Kelly, Martha Rose 1914-1983 37
Kelly, Marty
  See Kelly, Martha Rose
Kelly, Mij 166
Kelly, Ralph
  See Geis, Darlene Stern
Kelly, Regina Z(immerman) 1898-1986 5
Kelly, Rosalie (Ruth) 43
Kelly, Tom 1961- 191
Kelly, Walt(er Crawford) 1913-1973 18
Kelsey, Alice Geer 1896-1982 1
Kelsey, Elin 1961- 159
Kelsey, Marybeth 216
Kemly, Kathleen 1958- 197
Kemnitz, Thomas Milton, Jr. 1984- 152
Kemnitz, Tom, Jr.
  See Kemnitz, Thomas Milton, Jr.
Kemp, Gene 1926- 75
  Earlier sketch in SATA *25*
  See also CLR *29*
Kempner, Mary Jean 1913-1969 10
Kempter, Christa 1945- 187
Kempton, Jean Welch 1914- 10
Kenah, Katharine 1949- 182
Kenda, Margaret 1942- 71
Kendall, Carol (Seeger) 1917- 74
  Earlier sketch in SATA *11*
  See also SAAS *7*
Kendall, Gideon 1966- 215
Kendall, Katherine
  See Applegate, Katherine
Kendall, Lace
  See Stoutenburg, Adrien (Pearl)
Kendall, Martha E. 87
Kendall, Russ 1957- 83
Kenealy, James P. 1927- 52
  Brief entry 29
Kenealy, Jim
  See Kenealy, James P.

Kennaway, Adrienne 1945- *171*
   Earlier sketch in SATA *60*
Kennedy, Anne 1955- *198*
Kennedy, Anne Vittur
   See Kennedy, Anne
Kennedy, Brendan 1970- *57*
Kennedy, Dana Forrest 1917- *74*
Kennedy, Dorothy M(intzlaff) 1931- *53*
Kennedy, Doug 1963- *189*
   Earlier sketch in SATA *122*
Kennedy, Frances 1937- *192*
Kennedy, James *214*
   See Monahan, James
Kennedy, John F. 1917-1963 .... *11*
Kennedy, John Fitzgerald
   See Kennedy, John F.
Kennedy, Joseph Charles 1929- *130*
   Autobiography Feature *130*
   Earlier sketches in SATA *14, 86*
   See also CLR *27*
   See also SAAS *22*
   See Kennedy, X. J.
Kennedy, Kim *189*
Kennedy, Marlane 1962- *210*
Kennedy, Pamela (J.) 1946- *87*
Kennedy, Paul E(dward) 1929- *113*
   Earlier sketch in SATA *33*
Kennedy, Richard (Pitt) 1910-1989
   Obituary *60*
Kennedy, (Jerome) Richard 1932- *22*
Kennedy, Robert 1938- *63*
Kennedy, T.A. 1953- *42*
   Brief entry *35*
Kennedy, Teresa
   See Kennedy, T.A.
Kennedy, Teresa A.
   See Kennedy, T.A.
Kennedy, William 1928- *57*
Kennedy, William Joseph
   See Kennedy, William
Kennedy, X. J.
   See CLR *27*
   See also SAAS *22*
   See Kennedy, Joseph Charles
Kennell, Ruth Epperson 1893-1977 .... *6*
   Obituary *25*
Kennemore, Tim 1957- *133*
Kennen, Ally *190*
Kennett, David 1959- *206*
   Earlier sketch in SATA *121*
Kennison, Ruth *202*
Kenny, Ellsworth Newcomb 1909-1971
   Obituary *26*
Kenny, Herbert Andrew 1912-2002 .... *13*
Kenny, Jude
   See Daly, Jude
Kenny, Kathryn
   See Bowden, Joan Chase
   and Krull, Kathleen
   and Sanderlin, Owenita (Harrah)
   and Stack, Nicolete Meredith
Kenny, Kevin
   See Krull, Kathleen
Kensinger, George
   See Fichter, George S.
Kensington, Kathryn Wesley
   See Rusch, Kristine Kathryn
Kent, Alexander
   See Reeman, Douglas Edward
Kent, David
   See Lambert, David
Kent, Deborah Ann 1948- *155*
   Brief entry *41*
   Earlier sketches in SATA *47, 104*
Kent, Jack
   See Kent, John Wellington
Kent, John Wellington 1920-1985 .... *24*
   Obituary *45*
Kent, Lisa 1942- *90*
Kent, Mallory
   See Lowndes, Robert A(ugustine) W(ard)

Kent, Margaret 1894- *2*
Kent, Rockwell 1882-1971 .... *6*
Kent, Rose *188*
Kent, Sherman 1903-1986 .... *20*
   Obituary *47*
Kenward, Jean 1920- *42*
Kenworthy, Leonard S. 1912-1991 .... *6*
Kenyon, Karen (Smith) 1938- *145*
Kenyon, Kate
   See Adorjan, Carol (Madden)
   and Ransom, Candice F.
Kenyon, Ley 1913-1990 .... *6*
Keown, Elizabeth *78*
Kepes, Juliet A(ppleby) 1919-1999 .... *13*
Kephart, Beth 1960- *196*
Kerby, Mona 1951- *202*
   Earlier sketch in SATA *75*
Kerigan, Florence 1896-1984 .... *12*
Kerley, Barbara 1960- *191*
   Earlier sketch in SATA *138*
Kerman, Gertrude
   See Furman, Gertrude Lerner Kerman
Kerns, Thelma 1929- *116*
Kerr, Anne Louise
   See Mackey, Weezie Kerr
Kerr, Bob 1951- *120*
Kerr, Jessica 1901-1991 .... *13*
Kerr, (Anne-)Judith 1923-1970 .... *24*
Kerr, M. E.
   See Meaker, Marijane
Kerr, P.B.
   See Kerr, Philip
Kerr, Philip 1956- *168*
Kerr, Phyllis Forbes 1942- *72*
Kerr, Tom 1950- *77*
Kerrin, Jessica Scott *174*
Kerry, Frances
   See Kerigan, Florence
Kerry, Lois
   See Duncan, Lois
Kershen, (L.) Michael 1982- *82*
Kerven, Rosalind 1954- *83*
Ker Wilson, Barbara 1929- *121*
   Earlier sketches in SATA *20, 70*
   See also SAAS *18*
Keselman, Gabriela 1953- *128*
Kesey, Ken 1935-2001 .... *66*
   Obituary *131*
Kesey, Ken Elton
   See Kesey, Ken
Kesler, Jay 1935- *65*
Kessel, Joyce Karen 1937- *41*
Kessler, Cristina *190*
Kessler, Ethel 1922- *44*
   Brief entry *37*
Kessler, Leonard P. 1921- *14*
Kessler, Liz 1966- *206*
Kest, Kristin 1967- *168*
   Earlier sketch in SATA *118*
Kesteven, G. R.
   See Crosher, G. R.
Ketcham, Hank
   See Ketcham, Henry King
Ketcham, Henry King 1920-2001 .... *28*
   Brief entry *27*
   Obituary *128*
Ketcham, Sallie 1963- *124*
Ketchum, Liza 1946- *132*
   Earlier sketch in SATA *78*
Ketner, Mary Grace 1946- *75*
Kettelkamp, Larry (Dale) 1933- *2*
   See also SAAS *3*
Ketteman, Helen 1945- *167*
   Earlier sketches in SATA *73, 115*
Kettle, Peter
   See Glover, Denis (James Matthews)
Kevles, Bettyann Holtzmann 1938- *23*
Key, Alexander (Hill) 1904-1979 .... *8*
   Obituary *23*
Key, Samuel M.
   See de Lint, Charles

Key, Watt 1970- *189*
Keyes, Daniel 1927- *37*
Keyes, Diane *207*
Keyes, Fenton 1915-1999 .... *34*
Keyes, Greg 1963- *116*
Keyes, J. Gregory
   See Keyes, Greg
Keyser, Marcia 1933- *42*
Keyser, Sarah
   See McGuire, Leslie (Sarah)
Khalid, Mohamed Nor
   See Lat
Khalsa, Dayal Kaur 1943-1989 .... *62*
   See also CLR *30*
Khan, Hena *214*
Khan, Rukhsana 1962- *165*
   Earlier sketch in SATA *118*
Khanshendel, Chiron
   See Rose, Wendy
Kheirabadi, Masoud 1951- *158*
Khemir, Sabiha *87*
Kherdian, David 1931- *74*
   Autobiography Feature *125*
   Earlier sketch in SATA *16*
   See also CLR *24*
Khing, T.T. 1933- *192*
Kibbe, Pat (Hosley) *60*
Kidd, Diana 1933-2000 .... *150*
Kidd, Richard 1952-2008 .... *152*
   Obituary *194*
Kidd, Ronald 1948- *173*
   Earlier sketches in SATA *42, 92*
Kiddell, John 1922- *3*
Kiddell-Monroe, Joan 1908-1972 .... *55*
Kidwell, Carl 1910- *43*
Kiefer, Irene 1926- *21*
Kiefer, Kathleen Balmes 1957- *142*
Kiepper, Shirley Morgan 1933- *10*
Kierstead, Vera M.
   See Kierstead-Farber, Vera M.
Kierstead-Farber, Vera M. 1913- *121*
Kierstead-Farber, Vera May
   See Kierstead-Farber, Vera M.
Kiesel, Stanley 1925- *35*
Kiesler, Kate (A.) 1971- *152*
   Earlier sketch in SATA *90*
Kihn, Greg 1952- *110*
Kikukawa, Cecily H(arder) 1919- *44*
   Brief entry *35*
Kilcher, Jewel 1974- *109*
Kile, Joan 1940- *78*
Kilgore, Kathleen 1946- *42*
Kilian, Crawford 1941- *35*
Killdeer, John
   See Mayhar, Ardath
Killien, Christi 1956- *73*
Killilea, Marie (Lyons) 1913-1991 .... *2*
Killingback, Julia 1944- *63*
Killough, (Karen) Lee 1942- *64*
Kilpatrick, Don *206*
Kilreon, Beth
   See Walker, Barbara (Jeanne) K(erlin)
Kilworth, Garry 1941- *216*
   Earlier sketch in SATA *94*
Kilworth, Garry D.
   See Kilworth, Garry
Kilworth, Garry Douglas
   See Kilworth, Garry
Kim, David 1977- *201*
Kim, Helen 1899-1970 .... *98*
Kim, Joung Un 1970- *205*
Kimball, Gayle 1943- *90*
Kimball, Violet T(ew) 1932- *126*
Kimball, Yeffe 1914-1978 .... *37*
Kimber, Murray 1964- *171*
Kimble, Warren *176*
Kimbrough, Emily 1899-1989 .... *2*
   Obituary *59*
Kimeldorf, Martin 1948- *121*
Kimeldorf, Martin R.
   See Kimeldorf, Martin

Kimenye, Barbara 1940(?)- *121*
Kimmel, Elizabeth Cody *209*
  Earlier sketch in SATA *170*
Kimmel, Eric A. 1946- *208*
  Earlier sketches in SATA *13, 80, 125, 176*
Kimmel, Margaret Mary 1938- *43*
  Brief entry *33*
Kimmelman, Burt 1947- *180*
Kimmelman, Leslie 1958- *211*
  Earlier sketches in SATA *85, 156*
Kincaid, Jamaica 1949-
  See CLR *63*
Kincher, Jonni 1949- *79*
Kindl, Patrice 1951- *128*
  Earlier sketch in SATA *82*
  See also CLR *132*
Kindred, Wendy (Good) 1937- *7*
Kinerk, Robert *199*
Kines, Pat Decker 1937- *12*
King, Adam
  See Hoare, Robert J(ohn)
King, Alison
  See Martini, Teri
King, (Maria) Anna 1964- *72*
King, A.S. 1970- *217*
King, Billie Jean 1943- *12*
King, Christine
  See Farris, Christine King
King, Christopher (L.) 1945- *84*
King, (David) Clive 1924- *144*
  Earlier sketch in SATA *28*
King, Colin 1943- *76*
King, Cynthia 1925- *7*
King, Daniel (John) 1963- *130*
King, Daren 1972- *197*
King, Elizabeth 1953- *83*
King, Frank O. 1883-1969
  Obituary *22*
King, Frank R. 1904-1999 .... *127*
King, Jane
  See Currie, Stephen
King, Jeanette (Margaret) 1959- *105*
King, Larry L. 1929- *66*
King, Laurie R. 1952- *88*
King, Marian 1900(?)-1986 .... *23*
  Obituary *47*
King, Martin Luther, Jr. 1929-1968 .... *14*
King, Mary Ellen 1958- *93*
King, Paul
  See Drackett, Phil(ip Arthur)
King, Paula
  See Downing, Paula E.
King, Stephen 1947- *161*
  Earlier sketches in SATA *9, 55*
  See also CLR *124*
King, Stephen Edwin
  See King, Stephen
King, Stephen Michael *157*
King, Steve
  See King, Stephen
King, Thomas 1943- *96*
King, Thomas Hunt
  See King, Thomas
King, Tony 1947- *39*
King, Willie Christine
  See Farris, Christine King
Kingfisher, Rupert *209*
Kingman, Dong (Moy Shu) 1911-2000 .... *44*
Kingman, Lee
  See Natti, Lee
Kingsland, Leslie William 1912- *13*
Kingsley, Charles 1819-1875
  See YABC *2*
  See also CLR *77*
Kingsley, Emily Perl 1940- *33*
Kingsley, Kaza *193*
King-Smith, Dick 1922- *192*
  Brief entry *38*
  Earlier sketches in SATA *47, 80, 135*
  See also CLR *40*
Kingston, Maxine Hong 1940- *53*

Kingston, Maxine Ting Ting Hong
  See Kingston, Maxine Hong
Kinney, C. Cle(land) 1915- *6*
Kinney, Harrison 1921- *13*
Kinney, Jean Stout 1912- *12*
Kinney, Jeff 1971- *187*
Kinsey, Elizabeth
  See Clymer, Eleanor
Kinsey, Helen 1948- *82*
Kinsey-Warnock, Natalie 1956- *167*
  Earlier sketches in SATA *71, 116*
Kinzel, Dorothy 1950- *57*
Kinzel, Dottie
  See Kinzel, Dorothy
Kipling, Joseph Rudyard
  See Kipling, Rudyard
Kipling, Rudyard 1865-1936 .... *100*
  See also YABC *2*
  See also CLR *65*
Kippax, Frank
  See Needle, Jan
Kirby, David 1944- *78*
Kirby, David K.
  See Kirby, David
Kirby, David Kirk
  See Kirby, David
Kirby, Margaret
  See Bingley, Margaret (Jane Kirby)
Kirby, Susan E. 1949- *62*
Kirk, Connie Ann 1957- *167*
Kirk, Daniel 1952- *196*
  Earlier sketches in SATA *107, 153*
Kirk, David 1955- *161*
  Earlier sketch in SATA *117*
Kirk, Heather 1949- *166*
Kirk, Ruth (Kratz) 1925- *5*
Kirkham, Dinah
  See Card, Orson Scott
Kirkland, Will
  See Hale, Arlene
Kirkpatrick, Katherine (Anne) 1964- *113*
Kirkup, James 1918-2009 .... *12*
Kirkus, Virginia
  See Glick, Virginia Kirkus
Kirkwood, Kathryn
  See Fluke, Joanne
Kirsch, Vincent X. *211*
Kirshenbaum, Binnie *79*
Kirshner, David S. 1958- *123*
Kirtland, G. B.
  See Hine, Sesyle Joslin
  and Hine, Al(fred Blakelee)
Kirwan, Wednesday *198*
Kish, Eleanor M(ary) 1924- *73*
Kish, Ely
  See Kish, Eleanor M(ary)
Kishida, Eriko 1929- *12*
Kisinger, Grace Gelvin (Maze) 1913-1965 .. *10*
Kissel, Richard *209*
Kissin, Eva H. 1923- *10*
Kissinger, Rosemary K.
  See Updyke, Rosemary K.
Kistler, John M. 1967- *160*
Kitamura, Satoshi 1956- *201*
  Earlier sketches in SATA *62, 98, 143*
  See also CLR *60*
Kitchen, Bert
  See Kitchen, Herbert Thomas
Kitchen, Herbert Thomas 1940- *70*
Kite, L. Patricia
  See Kite, Pat
Kite, Pat 1940- *78*
Kitt, Tamara
  See de Regniers, Beatrice Schenk (Freedman)
Kittinger, Jo S(usenbach) 1955- *148*
  Earlier sketch in SATA *96*
Kituomba
  See Odaga, Asenath (Bole)
Kitzinger, Sheila 1929- *57*
Kiwak, Barbara 1966- *103*

Kjelgaard, James Arthur 1910-1959 .... *17*
  See also CLR *81*
  See Kjelgaard, Jim
Kjelgaard, Jim
  See Kjelgaard, James Arthur
Kjelle, Marylou Morano 1954- *146*
Klages, Ellen 1954- *196*
Klagsbrun, Francine (Lifton) *36*
Klaits, Barrie 1944- *52*
Klam, Cheryl *191*
Klaperman, Gilbert 1921- *33*
Klaperman, Libby Mindlin 1921-1982 .... *33*
  Obituary *31*
Klass, David 1960- *207*
  Earlier sketches in SATA *88, 142*
Klass, Morton 1927-2001 .... *11*
Klass, Sheila Solomon 1927- *99*
  Autobiography Feature *126*
  Earlier sketch in SATA *45*
  See also SAAS *26*
Klause, Annette Curtis 1953- *175*
  Earlier sketch in SATA *79*
  See also CLR *104*
Klaveness, Jan O'Donnell 1939- *86*
Kleberger, Ilse 1921- *5*
Kleeberg, Irene (Flitner) Cumming 1932- *65*
Klein, Aaron E. 1930-1998 .... *45*
  Brief entry *28*
Klein, Bill 1945- *89*
Klein, David 1919-2001 .... *59*
Klein, Frederick C. 1938- *154*
Klein, Gerda Weissmann 1924- *44*
Klein, H(erbert) Arthur *8*
Klein, James 1932- *115*
Klein, Leonore (Glotzer) 1916- *6*
Klein, Lisa 1958- *211*
Klein, Lisa M.
  See Klein, Lisa
Klein, Mina C(ooper) 1906-1979 .... *8*
Klein, Norma 1938-1989 .... *57*
  Earlier sketch in SATA *7*
  See also CLR *19*
  See also SAAS *1*
Klein, Rachel S. 1953- *105*
Klein, Robin 1936- *164*
  Brief entry *45*
  Earlier sketches in SATA *55, 80*
  See also CLR *21*
Klemin, Diana *65*
Klemm, Barry 1945- *104*
Klemm, Edward G., Jr. 1910-2001 .... *30*
Klemm, Roberta K(ohnhorst) 1884-1975 ..... *30*
Kleven, Elisa 1958- *217*
  Earlier sketches in SATA *76, 173*
  See also CLR *85*
Klevin, Jill Ross 1935- *39*
  Brief entry *38*
Kliban, B(ernard) 1935-1990 .... *35*
  Obituary *66*
Klier, Kimberly Wagner *208*
Klimo, Kate *214*
Klimowicz, Barbara 1927- *10*
Kline, Christina Baker 1964- *101*
Kline, James
  See Klein, James
Kline, Jim
  See Kline, Jim
Kline, Lisa Williams 1954- *143*
Kline, Suzy 1943- *193*
  Autobiography Feature *193*
  Brief entry *48*
  Earlier sketches in SATA *67, 99, 152*
Kliros, Thea 1935- *106*
Klise, Kate *181*
Klise, M. Sarah 1961- *180*
  Earlier sketch in SATA *128*
Klots, Alexander Barrett 1903-1989
  Obituary *62*
Klug, Ron(ald) 1939- *31*
Knaak, Richard A. 1961- *166*
  Earlier sketch in SATA *86*

Knaak, Richard Allen
See Knaak, Richard A.
Knapman, Timothy 200
Knapp, Edward
See Kunhardt, Edith
Knapp, Ron 1952- 34
Knebel, Fletcher 1911-1993 36
Obituary 75
Kneeland, Linda Clarke 1947- 94
Knickerbocker, Diedrich
See Irving, Washington
Knifesmith
See Cutler, Ivor
Knigge, Robert (R.) 1921(?)-1987 50
Knight, Anne (Katherine) 1946- 34
Knight, Brenda 112
Knight, Christopher G. 1943- 96
Knight, Damon (Francis) 1922-2002 9
Obituary 139
Knight, David C(arpenter) 1925-1984 14
See also CLR 38
Knight, Eric 1897-1943 18
Knight, Eric Mowbray
See Knight, Eric
Knight, Francis Edgar 1905- 14
Knight, Frank
See Knight, Francis Edgar
Knight, Hilary 1926- 132
Earlier sketches in SATA 15, 69
Knight, Joan
See Knight, Joan (MacPhail)
Knight, Joan (MacPhail) 159
Earlier sketch in SATA 82
Knight, Kathryn Lasky
See Lasky, Kathryn
Knight, Mallory T.
See Hurwood, Bernhardt J.
Knight, Ruth Adams 1898-1974
Obituary 20
Knight, Theodore O. 1946- 77
Knobloch, Dorothea 1951- 88
Knoepfle, John (Ignatius) 1923- 66
Knorr, Laura 1971- 200
Knott, Bill
See Knott, William C(ecil, Jr.)
Knott, William C(ecil, Jr.) 1927- 3
Knotts, Howard (Clayton, Jr.) 1922- 25
Knowles, Anne 1933- 37
Knowles, Jo 1970- 197
Knowles, Johanna Beth
See Knowles, Jo
Knowles, John 1926-2001 89
Obituary 134
Earlier sketch in SATA 8
See also CLR 98
Knox, Calvin M.
See Silverberg, Robert
Knox, (Mary) Eleanor Jessie 1909-2000 59
Earlier sketch in SATA 30
Knox, Elizabeth 1959- 176
Knox, Elizabeth Fiona
See Knox, Elizabeth
Knox, James
See Brittain, William
Knox, Jolyne 1937- 76
Knudsen, James 1950- 42
Knudsen, Michelle 1974- 171
Knudson, Mike 1965- 209
Knudson, R. R.
See Knudson, Rozanne
Knudson, Richard L(ewis) 1930- 34
Knudson, Rozanne 1932-2008 79
Earlier sketch in SATA 7
See also SAAS 18
Knutson, Barbara 1959-2005 166
Knutson, Kimberley 115
Knye, Cassandra
See Disch, Thomas M.
Kobayashi, Masako Matsuno 1935- 6
Kober, Shahar 1979- 213
Koch, Dorothy Clarke 1924- 6

Koch, Kenneth 1925-2002 65
Koch, Kenneth Jay
See Koch, Kenneth
Koch, Phyllis (Mae) McCallum 1911- 10
Kochalka, James 1967- 196
Kocsis, J. C.
See Paul, James
Koda-Callan, Elizabeth 1944- 140
Earlier sketch in SATA 67
Kodman, Stanislawa 201
Koehler, Phoebe 1955- 85
Koehler-Pentacoff, Elizabeth 1957- 160
Earlier sketch in SATA 96
Koehn, Ilse
See Van Zwienen, Ilse Charlotte Koehn
Koeller, Carol 192
Koenig, Viviane 1950- 80
Koering, Ursula 1921-1976 64
Koerner, W(illiam) H(enry) D(avid)
1878-1938 21
Koertge, Ron 1940- 209
Earlier sketches in SATA 53, 92, 131
Koestler-Grack, Rachel A. 1973- 156
Koff, Richard Myram 1926- 62
Koffinke, Carol 1949- 82
Kogan, Deborah
See Kogan Ray, Deborah
Kogan Ray, Deborah 1940- 203
Earlier sketches in SATA 8, 50, 161
Kogawa, Joy 1935- 99
Kogawa, Joy Nozomi
See Kogawa, Joy
Kogler, Jennie
See Kogler, Jennifer Anne
Kogler, Jennifer Anne 1982(?)- 174
Kohara, Kazuno 207
Kohl, Herbert 1937- 47
Kohl, Herbert R.
See Kohl, Herbert
Kohl, MaryAnn F(aubion) 1947- 144
Earlier sketch in SATA 74
Kohler, Julilly H(ouse) 1908-1976
Obituary 20
Kohn, Bernice
See Hunt, Bernice
Kohn, Rita (T.) 1933- 89
Kohner, Frederick 1905-1986 10
Obituary 48
Koide, Tan 1938-1986 50
Koike, Kay 1940- 72
Koja, Kathe 1960- 199
Earlier sketch in SATA 155
Koja, Stephan 198
Kolar, Bob 1960(?)- 206
Kolb, Larry J. 1953- 175
Kolba, St. Tamara 22
Kolibalova, Marketa
See Kolibalova, Marketa
Kolibalova, Marketa 1953- 126
Koller, Jackie French 1948- 157
Earlier sketches in SATA 72, 109
See also CLR 68
Kolodny, Nancy J. 1946- 76
Kolosov, Jacqueline 1967- 199
Komaiko, Leah 1954- 164
Earlier sketch in SATA 97
Komisar, Lucy 1942- 9
Komoda, Beverly 1939- 25
Komoda, Kiyo 1937- 9
Kompaneyets, Marc 1974- 169
Komroff, Manuel 1890-1974 2
Obituary 20
Konigsberg, Bill 1970- 207
Konigsburg, E.L. 1930- 194
Earlier sketches in SATA 4, 48, 94, 126
See also CLR 81
Konigsburg, Elaine Lobl
See Konigsburg, E.L.
Koning, Hans 1921-2007 5
Obituary 182

Koningsberger, Hans
See Koning, Hans
Konkle, Janet Everest 1917- 12
Kono, Erin Eitter 1973- 177
Konzak, Burt 1946- 151
Koob, Theodora (J. Foth) 1918- 23
Kooiker, Leonie
See Kooyker-Romijn, Johanna Maria
Koons, James
See Pernu, Dennis
Koontz, Dean 1945- 165
Earlier sketch in SATA 92
Koontz, Dean R.
See Koontz, Dean
Koontz, Dean Ray
See Koontz, Dean
Koontz, Robin Michal 1954- 136
Earlier sketch in SATA 70
Kooyker, Leonie
See Kooyker-Romijn, Johanna Maria
Kooyker-Romijn, Johanna Maria 1927- 48
Kooyker-Romyn, Johanna Maria
See Kooyker-Romijn, Johanna Maria
Kopelke, Lisa 1963- 154
Kopper, Lisa (Esther) 1950- 105
Brief entry 51
Koppes, Steven N. 1957- 169
Koppes, Steven Nelson
See Koppes, Steven N.
Korach, Mimi 1922- 9
Koralek, Jenny 1934- 215
Earlier sketches in SATA 71, 140
Korczak, Janusz
See Goldszmit, Henryk
Koren, Edward (Benjamin) 1935- 148
Earlier sketch in SATA 5
Koren, Edward 1935- 206
Korinets, Iurii Iosifovich
See Korinetz, Yuri (Iosifovich)
Korinetz, Yuri (Iosifovich) 1923- 9
See also CLR 4
Korman, Bernice 1937- 78
Korman, Gordon 1963- 167
Brief entry 41
Earlier sketches in SATA 49, 81, 119
See also CLR 25
Korman, Gordon Richard
See Korman, Gordon
Korman, Justine 1958- 70
Kornblatt, Marc 1954- 147
Earlier sketch in SATA 84
Kornprobst, Jacques 1937- 177
Korte, Gene J. 1950- 74
Korthues, Barbara 1971- 203
Korty, Carol 1937- 15
Koscielniak, Bruce 1947- 153
Earlier sketches in SATA 67, 99
Koshin, Alexander (A.) 1952- 86
Kositsky, Lynne 1947- 158
Koskenmaki, Rosalie
See Maggio, Rosalie
Koss, Amy Goldman 1954- 158
Earlier sketch in SATA 115
Kossin, Sandy (Sanford) 1926- 10
Kossman, Nina 1959- 84
Kostecki-Shaw, Jenny Sue 203
Kostick, Conor 1964- 186
Kotzwinkle, William 1938- 146
Earlier sketches in SATA 24, 70
See also CLR 6
Kouhi, Elizabeth 1917- 54
Brief entry 49
Kouts, Anne 1945- 8
Koutsky, Jan Dale 1955- 146
Kovacs, Deborah 1954- 132
Earlier sketch in SATA 79
Kovalski, Maryann 1951- 175
Earlier sketches in SATA 58, 97
See also CLR 34
See also SAAS 21

Kowalski, Kathiann M. 1955- *151*
  Earlier sketch in SATA *96*
Koz, Paula G.
  See Goodman Koz, Paula
Kozjan, Drazen *209*
Kraft, Betsy Harvey 1937- *157*
Kraft, Erik P. *193*
Krahn, Fernando 1935- *49*
  Brief entry *31*
  See also CLR *3*
Krakauer, Hoong Yee Lee 1955- *86*
Krakauer, Jon 1954- *108*
Kramer, George
  See Heuman, William
Kramer, Nora 1896(?)-1984 .... *26*
  Obituary *39*
Kramer, Remi (Thomas) 1935- *90*
Krantz, Hazel (Newman) *12*
Kranzler, George G(ershon) 1916- *28*
Kranzler, Gershon
  See Kranzler, George G(ershon)
Krasilovsky, Phyllis 1926- *38*
  Earlier sketch in SATA *1*
  See also CLR *83*
  See also SAAS *5*
Krasne, Betty
  See Levine, Betty K(rasne)
Krasner, Steven 1953- *154*
Krasno, Rena 1923- *104*
Kratman, Tom *175*
Kraus, Joanna Halpert 1937- *87*
Kraus, (Herman) Robert 1925-2001 .... *93*
  Obituary *130*
  Earlier sketches in SATA *4, 65*
  See also SAAS *11*
Krauss, Ruth (Ida) 1911-1993 .... *30*
  Obituary *75*
  Earlier sketch in SATA *1*
  See also CLR *42*
Krautter, Elisa (Bialk) 1912(?)-1990 .... *1*
  Obituary *65*
Krautwurst, Terry 1946- *79*
Kray, Robert Clement 1930- *82*
Krech, Bob 1956- *185*
Krech, Robert
  See Krech, Bob
Kredel, Fritz 1900-1973 .... *17*
Kreikemeier, Gregory Scott 1965- *85*
Kreloff, Elliot *189*
Krementz, Jill 1940- *134*
  Earlier sketches in SATA *17, 71*
  See also CLR *5*
  See also SAAS *8*
Kremer, Marcie
  See Sorenson, Margo
Krenina, Katya 1968- *101*
Krensky, Stephen 1953- *188*
  Brief entry *41*
  Earlier sketches in SATA *47, 93, 136*
Krensky, Stephen Alan
  See Krensky, Stephen
Kresh, Paul 1919-1997 .... *61*
  Obituary *94*
Kress, Nancy 1948- *147*
  Autobiography Feature *147*
  Earlier sketch in SATA *85*
Kricher, John C. 1944- *113*
Krieger, Melanie *96*
Krinitz, Esther Nisenthal 1927-2001 .... *194*
Kripke, Dorothy Karp *30*
Krisher, Trudy 1946- *160*
  Earlier sketch in SATA *86*
Krisher, Trudy B.
  See Krisher, Trudy
Krishnaswami, Uma 1956- *182*
  Earlier sketch in SATA *144*
Kristiansen, Teddy 1964- *210*
Kristiansen, Teddy H.
  See Kristiansen, Teddy
Kristof, Jane 1932- *8*
Kroeber, Theodora (Kracaw) 1897-1979 .... *1*

Kroeger, Mary Kay 1950- *92*
Krohn, Katherine E(lizabeth) 1961- *125*
  Earlier sketch in SATA *84*
Kroll, Francis Lynde 1904-1973 .... *10*
Kroll, Steven 1941- *212*
  Autobiography Feature *135*
  Earlier sketches in SATA *19, 66, 125, 135*
  See also SAAS *7*
Kroll, Virginia L. 1948- *168*
  Earlier sketches in SATA *76, 114*
Kroll, Virginia Louisa
  See Kroll, Virginia L.
Kromhout, Rindert 1958- *189*
Krommes, Beth 1956- *208*
  Earlier sketch in SATA *128, 181*
Kronenwetter, Michael 1943- *62*
Kroniuk, Lisa
  See Berton, Pierre (Francis de Marigny)
Kropp, Paul 1948- *38*
  Brief entry *34*
  See also CLR *96*
Kropp, Paul Stephan
  See Kropp, Paul
Krosoczka, Jarrett J. 1977- *200*
  Earlier sketch in SATA *155*
Krovatin, Christopher 1985- *171*
Krudop, Walter
  See Krudop, Walter Lyon
Krudop, Walter Lyon 1966- *210*
Kruess, James
  See Kruss, James
Kruglik, Gerald *187*
Krull, Kathleen 1952- *184*
  Autobiography Feature *106*
  Brief entry *39*
  Earlier sketches in SATA *52, 80, 149*
  See also CLR *44*
Krumgold, Joseph (Quincy) 1908-1980 .... *48*
  Obituary *23*
  Earlier sketch in SATA *1*
Krupinski, Loretta 1940- *161*
  Earlier sketches in SATA *67, 102*
Krupnick, Karen 1947- *89*
Krupp, E(dwin) C(harles) 1944- *123*
  Earlier sketch in SATA *53*
Krupp, Robin Rector 1946- *53*
Krush, Beth 1918- *18*
Krush, Joe 1918-
  See Krush, Joseph P.
Krush, Joseph P. 1918- *18*
Kruss, James 1926-1997 .... *8*
  See also CLR *9*
Kruusval, Catarina 1951- *201*
Krykorka, Vladyana 1945- *96*
Krystoforski, Andrej 1943- *196*
Kubick, Dana *212*
Kubie, Eleanor Gottheil
  See Kubie, Nora Gottheil Benjamin
Kubie, Nora Benjamin
  See Kubie, Nora Gottheil Benjamin
Kubie, Nora Gottheil Benjamin 1899-1988 . *39*
  Obituary *59*
Kubinyi, Laszlo 1937- *94*
  Earlier sketch in SATA *17*
Kudlinski, Kathleen V. 1950- *213*
  Earlier sketch in SATA *150*
Kuehnert, Stephanie 1979- *205*
Kuenstler, Morton 1927- *10*
Kuh, Charlotte 1892(?)-1985
  Obituary *43*
Kuharski, Janice 1947- *128*
Kuhn, Dwight *199*
Kuijer, Guus 1942- *179*
Kujoth, Jean Spealman 1935-1975
  Obituary *30*
Kuklin, Susan 1941- *163*
  Earlier sketches in SATA *63, 95*
  See also CLR *51*
Kulikov, Boris 1966- *205*
  Earlier sketch in SATA *170*
Kulka, Joe *188*

Kulling, Monica 1952- *89*
Kullman, Harry 1919-1982 .... *35*
Kulyk Keefer, Janice 1952- *132*
Kumin, Maxine 1925- *12*
Kumin, Maxine Winokur
  See Kumin, Maxine
Kunhardt, Dorothy (Meserve) 1901-1979 .... *53*
  Obituary *22*
Kunhardt, Edith 1937- *67*
Kunjufu, Jawanza 1953- *73*
Kunstler, Morton
  See Kuenstler, Morton
Kuntz, J(ohn) L. 1947- *91*
Kuntz, Jerry 1956- *133*
Kupferberg, Herbert 1918-2001 .... *19*
Kuratomi, Chizuko 1939- *12*
  See also CLR *32*
Kurczok, Belinda 1978- *121*
Kurelek, William 1927-1977 .... *8*
  Obituary *27*
  See also CLR *2*
Kurian, George 1928- *65*
Kurjian, Judi(th M.) 1944- *127*
Kurland, Gerald 1942- *13*
Kurland, Michael 1938- *118*
  Earlier sketch in SATA *48*
Kurland, Michael Joseph
  See Kurland, Michael
Kuroi, Ken 1947- *120*
Kurokawa, Mitsuhiro 1954- *88*
Kurten, Bjorn (Olof) 1924-1988 .... *64*
Kurtz, Jane 1952- *139*
  Earlier sketch in SATA *91*
  See also CLR *123*
Kurtz, Katherine 1944- *182*
  Earlier sketches in SATA *76, 126*
Kurtz, Katherine Irene
  See Kurtz, Katherine
Kurz, Rudolf 1952- *95*
Kushner, Donn (J.) 1927- *52*
  See also CLR *55*
Kushner, Ellen 1955- *202*
  Earlier sketch in SATA *98*
Kushner, Ellen Ruth
  See Kushner, Ellen
Kushner, Jill Menkes 1951- *62*
Kushner, Lawrence 1943- *169*
  Earlier sketch in SATA *83*
Kushner, Tony 1956- *160*
Kuskin, Karla 1932-2009 .... *164*
  Obituary *206*
  Earlier sketches in SATA *2, 68, 111*
  See also CLR *4*
  See also SAAS *3*
Kuskin, Karla Seidman
  See Kuskin, Karla
Kusugak, Michael 1948- *143*
Kusugak, Michael Arvaarluk
  See Kusugak, Michael
Kutner, Merrily 1948- *196*
Kuttner, Paul 1922- *18*
Kuyper, Sjoerd 1952- *177*
Kuzma, Kay 1941- *39*
Kvale, Velma R(uth) 1898-1979 .... *8*
Kvasnosky, Laura McGee 1951- *182*
  Earlier sketches in SATA *93, 142*
Kwasney, Michelle D. 1960- *162*
Kyle, Benjamin
  See Gottfried, Theodore Mark
Kyle, Elisabeth
  See Dunlop, Agnes M. R.
Kyte, Kathy S. 1946- *50*
  Brief entry *44*

Author Index

L

L., Barry
  See Longyear, Barry B(rookes)
L., Tommy
  See Lorkowski, Thomas V(incent)
Labatt, Mary 1944- 215
Labouisse, Eve Curie
  See Curie, Eve
Labouisse, Eve Denise
  See Curie, Eve
Lace, William W. 1942- 126
Lacey, Joshua
  See Doder, Josh
Lachner, Dorothea
  See Knobloch, Dorothea
Lachtman, Ofelia Dumas 1919- 179
Lackey, Mercedes R. 1950- 127
  Earlier sketch in SATA 81
Lackey, Mercedes Ritchie
  See Lackey, Mercedes R.
Lacoe, Addie 78
Lacombe, Benjamin 1982- 198
Lacome, Julie 1961- 174
  Earlier sketch in SATA 80
Lacy, Leslie Alexander 1937- 6
Ladd, Cheryl (Jean) 1951- 113
Ladd, London 1972(?)- 206
Ladd, Louise 1943- 97
Ladd, Veronica
  See Miner, Jane Claypool
Laden, Nina 1962- 148
  Earlier sketch in SATA 85
Lader, Lawrence 1919-2006 6
  Obituary 178
LaDoux, Rita C. 1951- 74
Lady, A
  See Taylor, Ann
Lady Mears
  See Tempest, Margaret Mary
Lady of Quality, A
  See Bagnold, Enid
La Farge, Oliver 1901-1963 19
La Farge, Oliver Hazard Perry
  See La Farge, Oliver
La Farge, Phyllis 14
LaFave, Kim 196
LaFaye, A. 1970- 156
  Earlier sketch in SATA 105
LaFaye, Alexandria R.T.
  See LaFaye, A.
LaFevers, R.L. 191
LaFevers, Robin L.
  See LaFevers, R.L.
Laffin, John (Alfred Charles) 1922- 31
LaFontaine, Bruce 1948- 176
  Earlier sketch in SATA 114
La Fontaine, Jean de 1621-1695 18
Lafrance, Marie 1955- 197
Lager, Claude
  See Lapp, Christiane (Germain)
Lager, Marilyn 1939- 52
Lagercrantz, Rose (Elsa) 1947- 39
Lagerloef, Selma
  See Lagerlof, Selma
Lagerlof, Selma 1858-1940 15
  See also CLR 7
Laguna, Sofie 1968- 158
LaHaye, Tim 1926- 149
LaHaye, Timothy F.
  See LaHaye, Tim
Laidlaw, Rob 205
Laiken, Deirdre S(usan) 1948- 48
  Brief entry 40
Laimgruber, Monika 1946- 11
Lain, Anna
  See Lamb, Nancy
Laing, Alexander (Kinnan) 1903-1976 117
Laing, Martha 1951- 39

Laird, Christa 1944- 108
  Autobiography Feature 120
  See also SAAS 26
Laird, Elizabeth (Mary Risk) 1943- 159
  Earlier sketches in SATA 77, 114
  See also CLR 65
Laird, Jean E(louise) 1930- 38
Laite, Gordon 1925- 31
Lake, Harriet
  See Taylor, Paula (Wright)
Lakeman, Victoria
  See Forester, Victoria
Lakin, Patricia 1944- 190
Laklan, Carli 1907-1988 5
Laliberte, Louise-Andree 1958- 169
Lalicki, Barbara 61
Lalicki, Tom 1949- 186
Lally, Soinbhe 1945- 119
LaMarche, Jim 162
Lamb, Albert 187
Lamb, Beatrice Pitney 1904-1997 21
Lamb, Charles 1775-1834 17
Lamb, Elizabeth Searle 1917- 31
Lamb, G(eoffrey) F(rederick) 10
Lamb, Harold (Albert) 1892-1962 53
Lamb, Lynton (Harold) 1907-1977 10
Lamb, Mary Ann 1764-1847 17
Lamb, Nancy 1939- 80
Lamb, Robert (Boyden) 1941- 13
Lamba, Marie 195
Lambert, David 1932- 84
  Brief entry 49
Lambert, David Compton
  See Lambert, David
Lambert, Janet 1895(?)-1973 25
Lambert, Martha L. 113
Lambert, Saul 1928- 23
Lambert, Stephen 174
Lamburn, Richmal Crompton 1890-1969 5
Lamensdorf, Len 1930- 120
Lamensdorf, Leonard
  See Lamensdorf, Len
Laminack, Lester L. 1956- 163
  Earlier sketch in SATA 120
Lammle, Leslie 1965- 213
Lamont, Priscilla 200
Lamorisse, Albert (Emmanuel) 1922-1970 ... 23
Lampert, Emily 1951- 52
  Brief entry 49
Lamplugh, Lois 1921- 17
Lampman, Evelyn Sibley 1907-1980 87
  Obituary 23
  Earlier sketch in SATA 4
Lamprey, Louise 1869-1951
  See YABC 2
Lampton, Chris
  See Lampton, Christopher F.
Lampton, Christopher
  See Lampton, Christopher F.
Lampton, Christopher F. 67
  Brief entry 47
Lamstein, Sarah 1943- 174
  Earlier sketch in SATA 126
Lamstein, Sarah Marwil
  See Lamstein, Sarah
Lanagan, Margo 1960- 201
  Earlier sketch in SATA 163
Lancaster, Bruce 1896-1963 9
Lancaster, Matthew 1973(?)-1983
  Obituary 45
Lance, Kathryn 1943- 76
Land, Barbara (Neblett) 1923- 16
Land, Jane
  See Borland, Kathryn Kilby
  and Speicher, Helen Ross S(mith)
Land, Myrick (Ebben) 1922-1998 15
Land, Ross
  See Borland, Kathryn Kilby
  and Speicher, Helen Ross S(mith)
Landau, Elaine 1948- 141
  Earlier sketches in SATA 10, 94

Landau, Jacob 1917- 38
Landeck, Beatrice 1904-1978 15
Landin, Les 1923- 2
Landis, J(ames) D(avid) 1942- 60
  Brief entry 52
Landis, James D.
  See Landis, J(ames) D(avid)
Landis, Jill Marie 1948- 101
Landman, Tanya 207
Landmann, Bimba 1968- 176
Landon, Dena 1978(?)- 168
Landon, Lucinda 1950- 56
  Brief entry 51
Landon, Margaret (Dorothea Mortenson)
  1903-1993 50
Landowne, Youme 1970- 211
Landry, Leo 202
Landshoff, Ursula 1908-1989 13
Landstrom, Lena 1943- 206
  Earlier sketch in SATA 146
Landstrom, Olof 1943- 146
Landy, Derek 1974- 210
Lane, Alison Hoffman 215
Lane, Carolyn 1926-1993 10
Lane, Connie
  See Laux, Constance
Lane, Dakota 1959- 166
  Earlier sketch in SATA 105
Lane, Jerry
  See Martin, Patricia Miles
Lane, John (Richard) 1932- 15
Lane, Leena 199
Lane, Margaret 1907-1994 65
  Brief entry 38
  Obituary 79
Lane, Rose Wilder 1887-1968 29
  Brief entry 28
Lanes, Selma Gordon 1929- 3
Lanfredi, Judy 1964- 83
Lang, Andrew 1844-1912 16
  See also CLR 101
Lang, Aubrey 169
Lang, Lang 1982- 208
Lang, Paul 1948- 83
Lang, Susan S. 1950- 68
Lang, T.T.
  See Taylor, Theodore
Langart, Darrell T.
  See Garrett, Randall
Langdo, Bryan 1973- 191
  Earlier sketch in SATA 138
Lange, John
  See Crichton, Michael
Lange, Karen E. 190
Lange, Suzanne 1945- 5
Langley, Andrew 1949- 166
  Earlier sketch in SATA 104
Langley, Charles P(itman) III 1949- 103
Langley, Jonathan 1952- 122
Langley, Noel 1911-1980
  Obituary 25
Langley, Wanda 173
Langner, Nola
  See Malone, Nola Langner
Langone, John (Michael) 1929- 46
  Brief entry 38
Langreuter, Jutta 1944- 122
Langrish, Katherine 177
Langsen, Richard C. 1953- 95
Langstaff, John 1920-2005 68
  Obituary 172
  Earlier sketch in SATA 6
  See also CLR 3
Langstaff, John Meredith
  See Langstaff, John
Langstaff, Launcelot
  See Irving, Washington
Langston, Laura 1958- 186

Langton, Jane 1922- 200
   Autobiography Feature 140
   Earlier sketches in SATA 3, 68, 129, 140
   See also CLR 33
   See also SAAS 5
Lanier, Sidney 1842-1881 18
Lanier, Sterling E. 1927-2007 109
Lanier, Sterling Edmund
   See Lanier, Sterling E.
Lanino, Deborah 1964- 123
Lankford, Mary D. 1932- 112
   Earlier sketch in SATA 77
Lannin, Joanne 1951- 121
Lannin, Joanne A.
   See Lannin, Joanne
Lansdale, Joe R. 1951- 116
Lansdale, Joe Richard
   See Lansdale, Joe R.
Lansing, Alfred 1921-1975 35
Lansing, Karen E. 1954- 71
Lansky, Vicki 1942- 177
Lanthier, Jennifer 1964- 204
Lantier-Sampon, Patricia 1952- 92
Lantz, Fran
   See Lantz, Francess L(in)
Lantz, Francess L(in) 1952-2004 153
   Autobiography Feature 153
   Obituary 159
   Earlier sketches in SATA 63, 109
Lantz, Paul 1908- 45
Lantz, Walter 1900-1994 37
   Obituary 79
Lanza, Barbara 1945- 101
Lapp, Christiane (Germain) 1948- 74
Lappin, Peter 1911-1999 32
Larbalestier, Justine 178
Lardy, Philippe 1963- 168
LaReau, Jenna 181
LaReau, Kara 181
Larios, Julie 1949- 178
Larios, Julie Hofstrand
   See Larios, Julie
Larkin, Amy
   See Burns, Olive Ann
Larkin, Maia
   See Wojciechowska, Maia (Teresa)
Larkspur, Penelope
   See Wyatt, Valerie
Laroche, Giles 1956- 126
   Earlier sketch in SATA 71
LaRochelle, David 1960- 171
   Earlier sketch in SATA 115
Larom, Henry V. 1903(?)-1975
   Obituary 30
LaRose, Linda 125
Larrabee, Lisa 1947- 84
Larrecq, John M(aurice) 1926-1980 44
   Obituary 25
Larrick (Crosby), Nancy 1910-2004 4
Larsen, Anita 1942- 78
Larsen, Egon 1904- 14
Larsen, Rebecca 1944- 54
Larson, Eve
   See St. John, Wylly Folk
Larson, Gary 1950- 57
Larson, Hope 1982- 205
Larson, Ingrid D(ana) 1965- 92
Larson, Jean Russell 1930- 121
Larson, Kirby 1954- 181
   Earlier sketch in SATA 96
Larson, Norita D(ittberner) 1944- 29
Larson, William H. 1938- 10
Larsson, Carl (Olof) 1853-1919 35
LaSalle, Charles A.
   See Ellis, Edward S.
LaSalle, Charles E.
   See Ellis, Edward S.
Lasell, Elinor H. 1929- 19
Lasell, Fen H.
   See Lasell, Elinor H.

Lasenby, Jack 1931- 172
   Earlier sketches in SATA 65, 103
Laser, Michael 1954- 117
Lash, Joseph P. 1909-1987 43
Lasher, Faith B. 1921- 12
Lasker, David 1950- 38
Lasker, Joe
   See Lasker, Joseph Leon
Lasker, Joseph Leon 1919- 83
   Earlier sketch in SATA 9
   See also SAAS 17
Laski, Marghanita 1915-1988 55
Laskin, Pamela L. 1954- 75
Lasky, Kathryn 1944- 210
   Earlier sketches in SATA 13, 69, 112, 157
   See also CLR 140
Lasky Knight, Kathryn
   See Lasky, Kathryn
Lass, Bonnie 131
Lassalle, C. E.
   See Ellis, Edward S.
Lassiter, Mary
   See Hoffman, Mary
Lassiter, Rhiannon 1977- 157
Lat 1951- 196
Latham, Barbara 1896- 16
Latham, Frank B(rown) 1910-2000 6
Latham, Jean Lee 1902-1995 68
   Earlier sketch in SATA 2
   See also CLR 50
Latham, Mavis
   See Clark, Mavis Thorpe
Latham, Philip
   See Richardson, Robert S(hirley)
Lathrop, Dorothy P(ulis) 1891-1980 14
   Obituary 24
Lathrop, Francis
   See Leiber, Fritz (Reuter, Jr.)
Latimer, Jim 1943- 80
Latta, Rich
   See Latta, Richard
Latta, Richard 1946- 113
Latta, Sara L. 1960- 174
Lattany, Kristin
   See Lattany, Kristin Hunter
Lattany, Kristin (Eggleston) Hunter 1931- . 154
   Autobiography Feature 154
   Earlier sketch in SATA 132
Lattany, Kristin Hunter 1931-2008 132
   Earlier sketch in SATA 12
   See also CLR 3
   See also SAAS 10
Lattimore, Eleanor Frances 1904-1986 7
   Obituary 48
Lattin, Ann
   See Cole, Lois Dwight
Lauber, Patricia (Grace) 1924- 138
   Earlier sketches in SATA 1, 33, 75
   See also CLR 16
Laugesen, Malene 207
Laugesen, Malene Reynolds
   See Laugesen, Malene
Laugesen, Mary E(akin) 1906-1995 5
Laughbaum, Steve 1945- 12
Laughlin, Florence Young 1910-2001 3
Laughlin, Rosemary 1941- 123
Launder, Sally 206
Laure, Ettagale
   See Blauer, Ettagale
Laure, Jason 1940- 50
   Brief entry 44
Laurence, Ester Hauser 1935- 7
Laurence, Jean Margaret Wemyss
   See Laurence, Margaret
Laurence, Margaret 1926-1987
   Obituary 50
Laurie, Rona 1916- 55
Laurin, Anne
   See McLaurin, Anne
Lauritzen, Jonreed 1902-1979 13

Lauscher, Hermann
   See Hesse, Hermann
Lauture, Denize 1946- 86
Laux, Connie
   See Laux, Constance
Laux, Constance 1952- 97
Laux, Dorothy 1920- 49
Lavallee, Barbara 1941- 166
   Earlier sketch in SATA 74
Lavender, David (Sievert) 1910-2003 97
   Obituary 145
   Earlier sketch in SATA 64
Lavender, William D. 1921- 143
Laverne, Christine 175
Lavert, Gwendolyn Battle 1951-
   See Battle-Lavert, Gwendolyn
Laverty, Donald
   See Blish, James
   and Knight, Damon (Francis)
Lavigne, Louis-Dominique 107
Lavine, David 1928- 31
Lavine, Sigmund Arnold 1908-1986 82
   Earlier sketch in SATA 3
   See also CLR 35
Lavond, Paul Dennis
   See Kornbluth, C(yril) M.
   and Lowndes, Robert A(ugustine) W(ard)
   and Pohl, Frederik
Lawford, Paula Jane 1960- 57
   Brief entry 53
Lawhead, Stephen R. 1950- 109
Lawhead, Steve
   See Lawhead, Stephen R.
Lawlor, Laurie 1953- 137
   Earlier sketch in SATA 80
Lawlor, William
   See Lawlor, William T.
Lawlor, William T. 1951- 183
Lawrence, Ann (Margaret) 1942-1987 41
   Obituary 54
Lawrence, Caroline 1954- 203
Lawrence, Iain 1955- 183
   Earlier sketch in SATA 135
Lawrence, J. T.
   See Rowland-Entwistle, (Arthur) Theodore (Henry)
Lawrence, Jerome 1915-2004 65
Lawrence, John 1933- 30
Lawrence, Josephine 1890(?)-1978
   Obituary 24
Lawrence, Louise 1943- 119
   Earlier sketches in SATA 38, 78
Lawrence, Louise de Kiriline 1894-1992 13
Lawrence, Lynn
   See Garland, Sherry
Lawrence, Margery H. 1889-1969 120
Lawrence, Michael 1943- 132
Lawrence, Mildred Elwood 1907-1997 3
Lawrence, R(onald) D(ouglas) 1921- 55
Lawrinson, Julia 1969- 141
Lawson, Amy
   See Gordon, Amy
Lawson, Carol (Antell) 1946- 42
Lawson, Don(ald Elmer) 1917-1990 9
Lawson, Joan 1906- 55
Lawson, Julie 1947- 126
   Earlier sketch in SATA 79
   See also CLR 89
Lawson, Marion Tubbs 1896-1994 22
Lawson, Robert 1892-1957 100
   See also YABC 2
   See also CLR 73
Lawton, Clive A. 1951- 145
Laxdal, Vivienne 1962- 112
Laybourn, Emma 193
Laycock, George (Edwin) 1921- 5
Layne, Laura
   See Knott, William C(ecil, Jr.)
Layne, Steven L. 171
Layson, Annelex Hofstra 1938(?)- 211

Layton, Neal 1971- 187
  Earlier sketch in SATA *152*
Layton, Neal Andrew
  See Layton, Neal
Lazare, Gerald John 1927- 44
Lazare, Jerry
  See Lazare, Gerald John
Lazarevich, Mila 1942- 17
Lazarus, Keo Felker 1913-1993 21
  Obituary 129
Lea, Alec 1907- 19
Lea, Bob 1952- 203
Lea, Joan
  See Neufeld, John (Arthur)
Leach, Maria 1892-1977 39
  Brief entry 28
Leacock, Elspeth 1946- 131
Leacroft, Helen (Mabel Beal) 1919- 6
Leacroft, Richard (Vallance Becher) 1914- 6
Leaf, Margaret P. 1909(?)-1988
  Obituary 55
Leaf, (Wilbur) Munro 1905-1976 20
  See also CLR *25*
Leaf, VaDonna Jean 1929- 26
Leah, Devorah
  See Devorah-Leah
Leakey, Richard E(rskine Frere) 1944- 42
Leal, Ann Haywood 216
Leander, Ed
  See Richelson, Geraldine
Lear, Edward 1812-1888 100
  Earlier sketch in SATA *18*
  See also CLR *75*
Lears, Laurie 1955- 127
Leasor, James 1923-2007 54
Leasor, Thomas James
  See Leasor, James
Leavitt, Jerome E(dward) 1916- 23
Leavitt, Martine 1953- 170
LeBar, Mary E(velyn) 1910-1982 35
LeBlanc, Annette M. 1965- 68
LeBlanc, L(ee) 1913- 54
LeBox, Annette 1943- 145
Lebrun, Claude 1929- 66
Le Cain, Errol (John) 1941-1989 68
  Obituary 60
  Earlier sketch in SATA *6*
Lechner, Jack 201
Lechner, John 1966- 200
Lecourt, Nancy (Hoyt) 1951- 73
Ledbetter, Suzann 1953- 119
Leder, Jane Mersky 1945- 61
  Brief entry 51
Lederer, Muriel 1929- 48
Lederer, William J. 1912-2009 62
Lederer, William Julius
  See Lederer, William J.
Lee, Amanda
  See Baggett, Nancy
  and Buckholtz, Eileen (Garber)
  and Glick, Ruth (Burtnick)
Lee, Benjamin 1921- 27
Lee, Betsy 1949- 37
Lee, Carol
  See Fletcher, Helen Jill
Lee, Carol Ann 1969- 185
Lee, Chinlun 182
Lee, Cora
  See Anderson, Catherine Corley
Lee, Dennis (Beynon) 1939- 102
  Earlier sketch in SATA *14*
  See also CLR *3*
Lee, Dom 1959- 146
  Autobiography Feature 121
  Earlier sketch in SATA *83*
  See also SAAS *26*
Lee, Doris Emrick 1905-1983 44
  Obituary 35
Lee, Edward
  See Lee, J. Edward
Lee, Elizabeth Rogers 1940- 90

Lee, Harper 1926- 11
Lee, Hector Viveros 1962- 115
Lee, Howard N.
  See Goulart, Ron
Lee, Huy Voun 1969- 217
  Earlier sketch in SATA *129*
Lee, Insu 213
Lee, J. Edward 1953- 130
Lee, Jared 1943- 215
Lee, Jared D.
  See Lee, Jared
Lee, Jeanne M. 1943- 138
Lee, John R(obert) 1923-1976 27
Lee, Jordan
  See Scholefield, Alan
Lee, Joseph Edward
  See Lee, J. Edward
Lee, Julian
  See Latham, Jean Lee
Lee, Linda
  See Eyerly, Jeannette
Lee, Liz
  See Lee, Elizabeth Rogers
Lee, Lucy
  See Talbot, Charlene Joy
Lee, Lyn 1953- 128
Lee, Manning de Villeneuve 1894-1980 37
  Obituary 22
Lee, Marian
  See Clish, (Lee) Marian
Lee, Marie G. 1964- 178
  Earlier sketches in SATA *81, 130*
Lee, Marie Myung-Ok
  See Lee, Marie G.
Lee, Mary Price 1934- 82
  Earlier sketch in SATA *8*
Lee, Mildred
  See Scudder, Mildred Lee
Lee, Nelle Harper
  See Lee, Harper
Lee, Richard S. 1927- 82
Lee, Robert C. 1931- 20
Lee, Robert Edwin 1918-1994 65
  Obituary 82
Lee, Robert J. 1921- 10
Lee, Roy
  See Hopkins, Clark
Lee, Sally 1943- 67
Lee, Suzy 193
Lee, Tammie
  See Townsend, Thomas L.
Lee, Tanith 1947- 185
  Earlier sketches in SATA *8, 88, 134*
Lee, Virginia 1976- 208
Leech, Ben
  See Bowkett, Stephen
Leeds, Contance 188
Leedy, Loreen 1959- 175
  Brief entry 50
  Earlier sketches in SATA *54, 84, 128*
Leedy, Loreen Janelle
  See Leedy, Loreen
Lee-Hostetler, Jeri 1940- 63
Leekley, Thomas B(riggs) 1910-2001 23
Leeming, Jo Ann
  See Leeming, Joseph
Leeming, Joseph 1897-1968 26
Leemis, Ralph B. 1954- 72
Leese, Jennifer L.B. 1970- 163
Leeson, Muriel 1920- 54
Leeson, R. A.
  See Leeson, Robert (Arthur)
Leeson, Robert (Arthur) 1928- 76
  Earlier sketch in SATA *42*
Lee Tae-Jun 1904-1956(?) 194
Lee-Tai, Amy 1964- 189
Leffland, Ella 1931- 65
Leffler, Silke 197
Lefler, Irene (Whitney) 1917- 12
LeFrak, Karen 182

Le Gallienne, Eva 1899-1991 9
  Obituary 68
Legg, Gerald 1947- 143
Legg, Sarah Martha Ross Bruggeman (?)-1982
  Obituary 40
LeGrand
  See Henderson, LeGrand
Le Guin, Ursula K. 1929- 194
  Earlier sketches in SATA *4, 52, 99, 149*
  See also CLR *91*
Le Guin, Ursula Kroeber
  See Le Guin, Ursula K.
Legum, Colin 1919-2003 10
Lehman, Barbara 1963- 170
  Earlier sketch in SATA *115*
Lehman, Bob 91
Lehman, Elaine 91
Lehmann, Debra Lynn
  See Vanasse, Deb
Lehn, Cornelia 1920- 46
Lehne, Judith Logan 1947- 93
Lehr, Delores 1920- 10
Lehr, Norma 1930- 71
Leiber, Fritz (Reuter, Jr.) 1910-1992 45
  Obituary 73
Leibold, Jay 1957- 57
  Brief entry 52
Leichman, Seymour 1933- 5
Leick, Bonnie 205
Leigh, Nila K. 1981- 81
Leigh, Tom 1947- 46
Leigh-Pemberton, John 1911-1997 35
Leighton, Clare (Veronica Hope)
  1899-1989 37
Leighton, Margaret (Carver) 1896-1987 1
  Obituary 52
Leijten, Aileen 216
Leiner, Al(an) 1938- 83
Leiner, Katherine 1949- 93
Leipold, L. Edmond 1902-1983 16
Leisk, David (Johnson) 1906-1975 30
  Obituary 26
  Earlier sketch in SATA *1*
  See also CLR *98*
Leister, Mary 1917- 29
Leitch, Patricia 1933- 98
  Earlier sketch in SATA *11*
Leitner, Isabella 1924- 86
Lekich, John 202
Leland, Bob 1956- 92
Leland, Robert E.
  See Leland, Bob
Lematre, Pascal 1967- 176
Lember, Barbara Hirsch 1941- 92
LeMieux, A.C. 1954- 125
  Earlier sketch in SATA *90*
LeMieux, Anne
  See LeMieux, A.C.
LeMieux, Anne Connelly
  See LeMieux, A.C.
Lemieux, Michele 1955- 139
Lemke, Horst 1922- 38
Lemna, Don 1936- 216
Lenain, Thierry 1959- 201
Lenanton, Carola Mary Anima Oman
  See Oman, Carola (Mary Anima)
Lenard, Alexander 1910-1972
  Obituary 21
Lendroth, Susan 207
L'Engle, Madeleine 1918-2007 128
  Obituary 186
  Earlier sketches in SATA *1, 27, 75*
  See also CLR *57*
  See also SAAS *15*
L'Engle, Madeleine Camp Franklin
  See L'Engle, Madeleine
Lengyel, Cornel Adam 1915- 27
Lengyel, Emil 1895-1985 3
  Obituary 42
Lennon, John 1940-1980 114

Lennon, John Ono
  See Lennon, John
Leno, Jay 1950- *154*
LeNoir, Janice 1941- *89*
Lens, Sidney 1912-1986 .... *13*
  Obituary *48*
Lenski, Lois 1893-1974 .... *100*
  Earlier sketches in SATA *1, 26*
  See also CLR 26
Lent, Blair 1930-2009 .... *133*
  Obituary *200*
  Earlier sketch in SATA *2*
Lent, Henry Bolles 1901-1973 .... *17*
Lent, John 1948- *108*
Leodhas, Sorche Nic
  See Alger, Leclaire (Gowans)
Leokum, Arkady 1916(?)- *45*
Leon, Carol Boyd *212*
Leon, Sharon 1959- *79*
Leonard, Alison 1944- *70*
Leonard, Anna
  See Gilman, Laura Anne
Leonard, Constance (Brink) 1923- *42*
  Brief entry *40*
Leonard, Dutch
  See Leonard, Elmore
Leonard, Elmore 1925- *163*
Leonard, Elmore John, Jr.
  See Leonard, Elmore
Leonard, Jonathan N(orton) 1903-1975 .... *36*
Leonard, Laura 1923- *75*
Leonard, Tom 1955- *207*
Leonetti, Mike 1958- *202*
Leong, Gor Yun
  See Ellison, Virginia H(owell)
Leonhard, Herb *217*
Leonhardt, Alice 1950- *152*
Lerangis, Peter 1955- *171*
  Earlier sketch in SATA *72*
Lerman, Josh *215*
Lerner, Aaron 1920-2007 .... *35*
  Obituary *179*
Lerner, Aaron Bunsen
  See Lerner, Aaron
Lerner, Carol 1927- *86*
  Earlier sketch in SATA *33*
  See also CLR 34
  See also SAAS 12
Lerner, Gerda 1920- *65*
Lerner, Harriet 1944- *101*
Lerner, Marguerite Rush 1924-1987 .... *11*
  Obituary *51*
Lerner, Sharon (Ruth) 1938-1982 .... *11*
  Obituary *29*
Leroe, Ellen W(hitney) 1949- *99*
  Brief entry *51*
  Earlier sketch in SATA *61*
Leroux, Gaston 1868-1927 .... *65*
Leroux-Hugon, Helene 1955- *132*
LeRoy, Gen *52*
  Brief entry *36*
Lerrigo, Marion Olive 1898-1968
  Obituary *29*
LeShan, Eda J(oan) 1922-2002 .... *21*
  See also CLR 6
LeSieg, Theo.
  See Dr. Seuss
Lesinski, Jeanne M. 1960- *120*
Leslie, Robert Franklin 1911-1990 .... *7*
Leslie, Roger 1961- *168*
Leslie, Roger James
  See Leslie, Roger
Leslie, Sarah
  See McGuire, Leslie (Sarah)
LeSourd, Catherine
  See Marshall, (Sarah) Catherine (Wood)
Lessac, Frane
  See Lessac, Frane
Lessac, Frane 1954- *209*
  Earlier sketches in SATA *61, 148*

Lessem, Dino Don
  See Lessem, Don
Lessem, Don 1951- *182*
  Earlier sketches in SATA *97, 155*
Lesser, Margaret 1899(?)-1979
  Obituary *22*
Lesser, Rika 1953- *53*
Lester, Alison 1952- *129*
  Earlier sketches in SATA *50, 90*
Lester, Helen 1936- *189*
  Earlier sketches in SATA *46, 92, 145*
Lester, Julius 1939- *157*
  Earlier sketches in SATA *12, 74, 112*
  See also CLR 143
Lester, Julius Bernard
  See Lester, Julius
Lester, Mike 1955- *206*
  Earlier sketch in SATA *131*
Le Sueur, Meridel 1900-1996 .... *6*
Leszczynski, Diana *211*
Lethcoe, Jason *191*
Le Tord, Bijou 1945- *95*
  Earlier sketch in SATA *49*
Letts, Billie 1938- *121*
Letts, Elizabeth
  See Alalou, Elizabeth
Leuck, Laura 1962- *192*
  Earlier sketches in SATA *85, 146*
Leutscher, Alfred (George) 1913- *23*
Levai, Blaise 1919- *39*
Levchuk, Lisa *215*
Levenkron, Steven 1941- *86*
Leverich, Kathleen 1948- *103*
LeVert, (William) John 1946- *55*
Levert, Mireille 1956- *211*
Levete, Sarah 1961- *153*
Levin, Betty 1927- *201*
  Earlier sketches in SATA *19, 84, 137*
  See also SAAS 11
Levin, Ira 1929-2007 .... *66*
  Obituary *187*
Levin, Ira Marvin
  See Levin, Ira
Levin, Marcia Obrasky 1918- *13*
Levin, Meyer 1905-1981 .... *21*
  Obituary *27*
Levin, Miriam (Ramsfelder) 1962- *97*
Levine, Abby 1943- *54*
  Brief entry *52*
Levine, Anna *212*
Levine, Betty K(rasne) 1933- *66*
Levine, David 1926-2009 .... *43*
  Brief entry *35*
Levine, Edna S(imon) *35*
Levine, Ellen 1939- *190*
Levine, Evan 1962- *77*
  Earlier sketch in SATA *74*
Levine, Gail Carson 1947- *195*
  Earlier sketches in SATA *98, 161*
  See also CLR 85
Levine, I(srael) E. 1923-2003 .... *12*
  Obituary *146*
Levine, Joan Goldman *11*
Levine, Joseph 1910- *33*
Levine, Kristin 1974- *213*
Levine, Marge 1934- *81*
Levine, Rhoda *14*
Levine, Sarah 1970- *57*
Levine, Shar 1953- *131*
Levine-Freidus, Gail
  See Provost, Gail Levine
Levinson, Nancy Smiler 1938- *211*
  Earlier sketches in SATA *33, 80, 140*
Levinson, Riki *99*
  Brief entry *49*
  Earlier sketch in SATA *52*
Levithan, David 1972- *166*

Levitin, Sonia 1934- *192*
  Autobiography Feature *131*
  Earlier sketches in SATA *4, 68, 119, 131*
  See also CLR 53
  See also SAAS 2
Levitt, Sidney (Mark) 1947- *68*
Levon, O. U.
  See Kesey, Ken
Levoy, Myron 1930- *49*
  Brief entry *37*
Levy, Barrie *112*
Levy, Constance 1931- *140*
  Earlier sketch in SATA *73*
  See also SAAS 22
Levy, Elizabeth 1942- *169*
  Earlier sketches in SATA *31, 69, 107*
  See also SAAS 18
Levy, Janice *172*
Levy, Marilyn 1937- *67*
Levy, Nathan 1945- *63*
Levy, Robert 1945- *82*
Lewees, John
  See Stockton, Francis Richard
Lewin, Betsy 1937- *169*
  Autobiography Feature *115*
  Earlier sketches in SATA *32, 90*
Lewin, Hugh 1939- *72*
  Brief entry *40*
  See also CLR 9
Lewin, Ted 1935- *195*
  Autobiography Feature *115*
  Earlier sketches in SATA *21, 76, 119, 165*
Lewis, Alice C. 1936- *46*
Lewis, Alice Hudson 1895(?)-1971
  Obituary *29*
Lewis, Amanda 1955- *80*
Lewis, Anthony 1927- *27*
Lewis, Anthony 1966- *120*
Lewis, Barbara A. 1943- *73*
Lewis, Beverly 1949- *80*
Lewis, Brenda Ralph 1932- *72*
Lewis, Brian 1963- *128*
Lewis, C. S. 1898-1963 .... *100*
  Earlier sketch in SATA *13*
  See also CLR 109
Lewis, Claudia (Louise) 1907-2001 .... *5*
Lewis, Clive Staples
  See Lewis, C. S.
Lewis, Cynthia Copeland 1960- *111*
Lewis, E. M. *123*
  Earlier sketch in SATA *20*
Lewis, Earl Bradley
  See Lewis, E.B.
Lewis, E.B. 1956- *211*
  Earlier sketches in SATA *93, 124, 168*
Lewis, Elizabeth Foreman 1892-1958 .... *121*
  See also YABC 2
Lewis, Francine
  See Wells, Helen
Lewis, Harry Sinclair
  See Lewis, Sinclair
Lewis, Hilda (Winifred) 1896-1974
  Obituary *20*
Lewis, J. Patrick 1942- *205*
  Earlier sketches in SATA *69, 104, 162*
Lewis, Jack P(earl) 1919- *65*
Lewis, Jean 1924- *61*
Lewis, Jon Samuel
  See Lewis, J.S.
Lewis, Joseph Anthony
  See Lewis, Anthony
Lewis, J.S. 1972- *203*
Lewis, Julinda
  See Lewis-Ferguson, Julinda
Lewis, Kevin *173*
Lewis, Kim 1951- *217*
  Earlier sketch in SATA *84, 136*
Lewis, Linda (Joy) 1946- *67*
Lewis, Lucia Z.
  See Anderson, Lucia (Lewis)

Lewis, Marjorie 1929- 40
  Brief entry 35
Lewis, Mary 1907(?)-1988 64
  Obituary 56
Lewis, Mervyn
  See Frewer, Glyn (M.)
Lewis, Michael
  See Untermeyer, Louis
Lewis, Naomi 1911-2009 144
  Earlier sketch in SATA 76
Lewis, Paeony 1960- 173
Lewis, Paul
  See Gerson, Noel Bertram
Lewis, Richard 1935- 3
Lewis, Richard 1956- 209
Lewis, Rob 1962- 72
Lewis, Roger
  See Zarchy, Harry
Lewis, Rose 209
Lewis, Rose A.
  See Lewis, Rose
Lewis, Shannon
  See Llywelyn, Morgan
Lewis, Shari 1934-1998 35
  Brief entry 30
  Obituary 104
Lewis, Sylvan R.
  See Aronson, Virginia
Lewis, Thomas P(arker) 1936- 27
Lewis, Wendy A. 1966- 150
Lewis-Ferguson, Julinda 1955- 85
Lewison, Wendy Cheyette 177
Lewiton, Mina 1904-1970 2
Lew-Vriethoff, Joanne 186
Lexau, Joan M. 130
  Earlier sketches in SATA 1, 36
Ley, Willy 1906-1969 2
Leydon, Rita (Floden) 1949- 21
Leyland, Eric (Arthur) 1911- 37
L'Hommedieu, Dorothy Keasley 1885-1961
  Obituary 29
Li, Xiao Jun 1952- 86
Liao, Jimmy 1958- 202
Liatsos, Sandra Olson 1942- 103
Libby, Alisa M. 189
Libby, Barbara M. 153
Libby, Bill
  See Libby, William M.
Libby, William M. 1927-1984 5
  Obituary 39
Liberty, Gene 1924- 3
Lichtenheld, Tom 208
  Earlier sketch in SATA 152
Lichtman, Wendy 1946- 193
Liddell, Kenneth 1912-1975 63
Lidz, Jane 120
Lieberman, E(dwin) James 1934- 62
Liebers, Arthur 1913-1984 12
Lieblich, Irene 1923- 22
Liers, Emil E(rnest) 1890-1975 37
Lies, Brian 1963- 190
  Earlier sketch in SATA 131
Lieshout, Elle van
  See van Lieshout, Elle
Liestman, Vicki 1961- 72
Lietz, Gerald S. 1918- 11
Life, Kay (Guinn) 1930- 83
Lifton, Betty Jean 118
  Earlier sketch in SATA 6
Lifton, Robert Jay 1926- 66
Lightburn, Ron 1954- 91
Lightburn, Sandra 1955- 91
Lightner, A. M.
  See Hopf, Alice (Martha) L(ightner)
Lightner, Alice
  See Hopf, Alice (Martha) L(ightner)
Lignell, Lois 1911- 37
Liles, Maurine Walpole 1935- 81
Lillegard, Dee 184
Lilley, Stephen R. 1950- 97

Lilley, Stephen Ray
  See Lilley, Stephen R.
Lillington, Kenneth (James) 1916-1998 39
Lilly, Nate 182
Lilly, Ray
  See Curtis, Richard
Lim, John 1932- 43
Liman, Ellen (Fogelson) 1936- 22
Limb, Sue 1946- 203
  Earlier sketch in SATA 158
Limburg, Peter R(ichard) 1929- 13
Lin, Grace 1974- 198
  Earlier sketches in SATA 111, 162
Lincoln, C(harles) Eric 1924-2000 5
Lincoln, Christopher 1952- 208
Lincoln, Hazel 187
Lincoln, James
  See Bates, Katharine Lee
Lindbergh, Anne
  See Sapieyevski, Anne Lindbergh
Lindbergh, Anne Morrow 1906-2001 33
  Obituary 125
Lindbergh, Anne Spencer Morrow
  See Lindbergh, Anne Morrow
Lindbergh, Charles A(ugustus, Jr.)
  1902-1974 33
Lindbergh, Reeve 1945- 163
  Earlier sketch in SATA 116
Lindblom, Steven (Winther) 1946- 94
  Brief entry 39
  Earlier sketch in SATA 42
Linde, Gunnel 1924- 5
Lindenbaum, Pija 1955- 183
  Earlier sketches in SATA 77, 144
Lindgren, Astrid (Anna Emilia Ericsson)
  1907-2002 38
  Obituary 128
  Earlier sketch in SATA 2
  See also CLR 119
Lindgren, Barbro 1937- 207
  Brief entry 46
  Earlier sketches in SATA 63, 120
  See also CLR 86
Lindman, Maj (Jan) 1886-1972 43
Lindop, Edmund 1925- 5
Lindquist, Jennie Dorothea 1899-1977 13
Lindquist, Rowena Cory 1958- 98
Lindquist, Willis 1908-1988 20
Lindsay, Nicholas Vachel
  See Lindsay, Vachel
Lindsay, Norman Alfred William
  1879-1969 67
  See also CLR 8
Lindsay, Vachel 1879-1931 40
Lindsey, Kathleen D(orothy) 1949- 153
Line, David
  See Davidson, Lionel
Line, Les 1935-2010 27
Lines, Kathleen Mary 1902-1988
  Obituary 61
Linfield, Esther 40
Lingard, Joan (Amelia) 1932- 130
  Autobiography Feature 130
  Earlier sketches in SATA 8, 74, 114
  See also CLR 89
  See also SAAS 5
Link, Martin 1934- 28
Linn, Margot
  See Ziefert, Harriet
Linnea, Sharon 1956- 82
Lion, Melissa 1976- 176
Lionni, Leo(nard) 1910-1999 72
  Obituary 118
  Earlier sketch in SATA 8
  See also CLR 71
Lipinsky de Orlov, Lino S. 1908- 22
Lipkind, William 1904-1974 15
Lipman, David 1931-2008 21
Lipman, Matthew 1923- 14
Lipp, Frederick 204

Lippincott, Bertram 1898(?)-1985
  Obituary 42
Lippincott, Gary A. 1953- 119
  Earlier sketch in SATA 73
Lippincott, Joseph W(harton) 1887-1976 17
Lippincott, Sarah Lee 1920- 22
Lippman, Peter J. 1936- 31
Lipsyte, Robert 1938- 198
  Earlier sketches in SATA 5, 68, 113, 161
  See also CLR 76
Lipsyte, Robert Michael
  See Lipsyte, Robert
Lisandrelli, Elaine Slivinski 1951- 94
Lisker, Sonia O. 1933- 44
Lisle, Holly 1960- 208
  Earlier sketch in SATA 98
Lisle, Janet Taylor 1947- 150
  Brief entry 47
  Earlier sketches in SATA 59, 96
  See also SAAS 14
Lisle, Rebecca 162
Lisle, Seward D.
  See Ellis, Edward S.
Lisowski, Gabriel 1946- 47
  Brief entry 31
Liss, Howard 1922-1995 4
  Obituary 84
Lissiat, Amy
  See Thompson, Colin
Lisson, Deborah 1941- 110
  Earlier sketch in SATA 71
List, Ilka Katherine 1935- 6
Liston, Robert A. 1927- 5
Litchfield, Ada B(assett) 1916-1999 5
Litchfield, Jo 1973- 116
Lithgow, John 1945- 145
Lithgow, John Arthur
  See Lithgow, John
Litowinsky, Olga (Jean) 1936- 26
Littke, Lael J. 1929- 140
  Earlier sketches in SATA 51, 83
Little, A. Edward
  See Klein, Aaron E.
Little, Douglas 1942- 96
Little, (Flora) Jean 1932- 149
  Earlier sketches in SATA 2, 68, 106
  See also CLR 4
  See also SAAS 17
Little, Lessie Jones 1906-1986 60
  Obituary 50
Little, Mary E. 1912-1999 28
Littlechild, George 1958- 85
Littledale, Freya (Lota) 1929-1992 74
  Earlier sketch in SATA 2
Littlefield, Bill 1948- 83
Littlefield, Holly 1963- 97
Littlesugar, Amy 1953- 176
  Earlier sketch in SATA 122
Littleton, Mark R. 1950- 142
  Earlier sketch in SATA 89
Littlewood, Karin 211
Littman, Sarah Darer 175
Litty, Julie 1971- 181
Litzinger, Rosanne 1948- 196
Lively, Penelope 1933- 164
  Earlier sketches in SATA 7, 60, 101
  See also CLR 7
Lively, Penelope Margaret
  See Lively, Penelope
Liverakos, L. A.
  See Gilman, Laura Anne
Liversidge, (Henry) Douglas 1913- 8
Livesey, Claire (Warner) 1927- 127
Livingston, Carole 1941- 42
Livingston, (M.) Irene 1932- 150
Livingston, Myra Cohn 1926-1996 68
  Obituary 92
  Earlier sketch in SATA 5
  See also CLR 7
  See also SAAS 1
Livingston, Richard R(oland) 1922- 8

Livo, Norma J. 1929- 76
Liwska, Renata 199
Ljungkvist, Laura 180
Llerena Aguirre, Carlos 1952- 19
Llerena Aguirre, Carlos Antonio
    See Llerena Aguirre, Carlos
Llewellyn, Claire 1954- 196
    Earlier sketches in SATA 77, 143
Llewellyn, Grace 1964- 110
Llewellyn, Richard
    See Llewellyn Lloyd, Richard Dafydd Vivian
Llewellyn, Sam 1948- 185
    Earlier sketch in SATA 95
Llewellyn Lloyd, Richard Dafydd Vivian
    1906-1983 11
    Obituary 37
Llewelyn, T. Harcourt
    See Hamilton, Charles (Harold St. John)
Lloyd, Alan
    See Lloyd, A.R.
Lloyd, Alan Richard
    See Lloyd, A.R.
Lloyd, A.R. 1927- 168
    Earlier sketch in SATA 97
Lloyd, David
    See Lloyd, David T.
Lloyd, David T. 1954- 167
Lloyd, E. James
    See James, Elizabeth
Lloyd, Errol 1943- 22
Lloyd, Hugh
    See Fitzhugh, Percy Keese
Lloyd, James
    See James, Elizabeth
Lloyd, Megan 1958- 189
    Earlier sketches in SATA 77, 117
Lloyd, Norman 1909-1980
    Obituary 23
Lloyd, (Mary) Norris 1908-1993 10
    Obituary 75
Lloyd, Sam 183
Lloyd-Jones, Sally 1960- 179
Lloyd Webber, Andrew 1948- 56
Llywelyn, Morgan 1937- 109
Lo, Ginnie 165
Lo, Virginia M.
    See Lo, Ginnie
Lobato, Jose Bento Monteiro 1882-1948 ... 114
Lobel, Anita (Kempler) 1934- 162
    Earlier sketches in SATA 6, 55, 96
Lobel, Arnold (Stark) 1933-1987 55
    Obituary 54
    Earlier sketch in SATA 6
    See also CLR 5
Lobel, Gillian 181
Lobsenz, Amelia 12
Lobsenz, Norman M(itchell) 1919- 6
Lochak, Michele 1936- 39
Lochlons, Colin
    See Jackson, C(aary) Paul
Locke, Clinton W. 1
Locke, Elsie (Violet) 1912-2001 87
Locke, Gary 1963- 197
Locke, Lucie 1904-1989 10
Locke, Robert 1944- 63
    See also CLR 39
Locker, Thomas 1937- 109
    Earlier sketch in SATA 59
    See also CLR 14
Lockhart, E.
    See Jenkins, Emily
Lockridge, Hildegarde (Dolson)
    1908-1981 121
    Earlier sketch in SATA 5
Lockwood, Mary
    See Spelman, Mary
Lodge, Bernard 1933- 215
    Earlier sketches in SATA 33, 107
Lodge, Jo 1966- 173
    Earlier sketch in SATA 112
Loeb, Jeffrey 1946- 57

Loeb, Robert H., Jr. 1917- 21
Loefgren, Ulf 1931- 3
Loehfelm, Bill 1969- 153
Loehr, Mallory 184
Loehr, Patrick 1968(?)- 194
Loeper, John J(oseph) 1929- 118
    Earlier sketch in SATA 10
Loescher, Ann Dull 1942- 20
Loescher, Gil(burt Damian) 1945- 20
Loewer, Jean Jenkins
    See Jenkins, Jean
Loewer, (Henry) Peter 1934- 98
LoFaro, Jerry 1959- 77
Lofo
    See Heimann, Rolf
Lofthouse, Liz 199
Lofting, Hugh (John) 1886-1947 100
    Earlier sketch in SATA 15
    See also CLR 143
Lofts, Norah (Robinson) 1904-1983 8
    Obituary 36
Logan, Jake
    See Knott, William C(ecil, Jr.)
    and Krepps, Robert W(ilson)
    and Pearl, Jacques Bain
    and Riefe, Alan
    and Rifkin, Shepard
    and Smith, Martin Cruz
Logan, Mark
    See Nicole, Christopher (Robin)
Logan, Rochelle 1954- 169
Logston, Anne 1962- 112
Logue, Christopher 1926- 23
Logue, Mary 1952- 161
    Earlier sketch in SATA 112
Logue, Mary Louise
    See Logue, Mary
Loh, Morag 1935- 73
Lohans, Alison 1949- 101
Loizeaux, William 185
Loken, Newton Clayton 1919- 26
Lomas, Steve
    See Brennan, Joseph Lomas
Lomask, Milton (Nachman) 1909-1991 20
Lombard, Jenny 178
Lombino, Salvatore
    See Hunter, Evan
LoMonaco, Palmyra 1932- 102
London, Jack 1876-1916 18
    See also CLR 108
London, Jane
    See Geis, Darlene Stern
London, John Griffith
    See London, Jack
London, Jonathan (Paul) 1947- 157
    Earlier sketches in SATA 74, 113
Lonergan, (Pauline) Joy (MacLean) 1909- ... 10
Lonette, Reisie (Dominee) 1924- 43
Long, Cathryn J. 1946- 89
Long, Earlene (Roberta) 1938- 50
Long, Emmett
    See Leonard, Elmore
Long, Ethan 1968(?)- 182
Long, Helen Beecher 1
Long, Judith Elaine 1953- 20
Long, Judy
    See Long, Judith Elaine
Long, Kim 1949- 69
Long, Laura Mooney 1892-1967
    Obituary 29
Long, Laurel 203
Long, Loren 1966(?)- 188
    Earlier sketch in SATA 151
Long, Melinda 1960- 152
Long, Sylvia 1948- 179
    Earlier sketch in SATA 120
Longbeard, Frederick
    See Longyear, Barry B(rookes)
Longfellow, Henry Wadsworth 1807-1882 ... 19
    See also CLR 99
Longfellow, Layne 1937- 102

Longfellow, Layne A.
    See Longfellow, Layne
Longman, Harold S. 1919- 5
Longsworth, Polly 1933- 28
Longtemps, Kenneth 1933- 17
Longway, A. Hugh
    See Lang, Andrew
Longyear, Barry B(rookes) 1942- 117
Look, Lenore 180
Loomans, Diane 1955- 90
Loomis, Christine 160
    Earlier sketch in SATA 113
Loomis, Jennifer A. 1942- 101
Loomis, Robert D. 5
Lopez, Angelo (Cayas) 1967- 83
Lopez, Barry 1945- 67
Lopez, Barry Holstun
    See Lopez, Barry
Lopez, Jack 1950- 178
Lopez, Loretta 1963- 190
Lopez, Lorraine 1956- 181
Lopez, Lorraine M.
    See Lopez, Lorraine
Lopez, Rafael 1961(?)- 198
Lopshire, Robert M(artin) 1927- 6
Loraine, Connie
    See Reece, Colleen L.
Lorbiecki, Marybeth 1959- 172
    Earlier sketch in SATA 121
Lord, Athena V. 1932- 39
Lord, Beman 1924-1991 5
    Obituary 69
Lord, Bette Bao 1938- 58
    See also CLR 151
Lord, Cynthia 182
Lord, Doreen Mildred Douglas
    See Lord, Douglas
Lord, Douglas 1904-1992 12
Lord, Janet 204
Lord, John Vernon 1939- 21
Lord, Michele 201
Lord, Nancy
    See Titus, Eve
Lord, Patricia C. 1927-1988
    Obituary 58
Lord, Walter 1917-2002 3
Lorde, Diana
    See Reno, Dawn E(laine)
Lorenz, Albert 1941- 115
Lorenzini, Carlo
    See Collodi, Carlo
Lorey, Dean 1967- 193
Lorimer, Janet 1941- 60
Loring, Emilie (Baker) 1864(?)-1951 51
Lorkowski, Thomas V(incent) 1950- 92
Lorkowski, Tom
    See Lorkowski, Thomas V(incent)
Lorraine, Walter (Henry) 1929- 16
Lorrimer, Claire
    See Clark, Patricia Denise
Loss, Joan 1933- 11
Lothrop, Harriet Mulford Stone 1844-1924 . 20
Lottridge, Celia Barker 1936- 157
    Earlier sketch in SATA 112
LoTurco, Laura 1963- 84
Lotz, Wolfgang 1912-1981 65
Loughridge, Stuart 1978- 214
Louie, Ai-Ling 1949- 40
    Brief entry 34
Louis, Catherine 1963- 186
Louis, Pat
    See Francis, Dorothy
Louisburgh, Sheila Burnford
    See Burnford, Sheila (Philip Cochrane Every)
Louise, Anita
    See Riggio, Anita
Louise, Tina 1934- 191
Lourie, Helen
    See Storr, Catherine (Cole)
Lourie, Peter 1952- 183
    Earlier sketches in SATA 82, 142

Lourie, Peter King
  See Lourie, Peter
Love, Ann 1947- 168
  Earlier sketch in SATA 79
Love, D. Anne 1949- 180
  Earlier sketches in SATA 96, 145
Love, Douglas 1967- 92
Love, Judith Dufour
  See Love, Judy
Love, Judy 188
Love, Katherine (Isabel) 1907- 3
Love, Kathleen Ann
  See Love, Ann
Love, Sandra (Weller) 1940- 26
Lovegrove, James 1965- 216
Lovegrove, J.M.H.
  See Lovegrove, James
Lovejoy, Jack 1937- 116
Lovelace, Delos Wheeler 1894-1967 7
Lovelace, Maud Hart 1892-1980 2
  Obituary 23
Lovell, Ingraham
  See Bacon, Josephine Dodge (Daskam)
Lovelock, Brian 1956- 214
Loverseed, Amanda (Jane) 1965- 75
Lovett, Margaret (Rose) 1915- 22
Low, Alice 1926- 156
  Earlier sketches in SATA 11, 76
Low, Elizabeth Hammond 1898-1991 ... 5
Low, Joseph 1911-2007 14
Low, Penelope Margaret
  See Lively, Penelope
Low, William 177
Lowe, Helen 1961- 206
Lowe, Jay, Jr.
  See Loeper, John J(oseph)
Lowell, Pamela 187
Lowell, Susan 1950- 206
  Earlier sketches in SATA 81, 127
Lowenstein, Dyno 1914-1996 6
Lowenstein, Sallie 1949- 116
Lowery, Linda 1949- 151
  Earlier sketch in SATA 74
Lowitz, Anson C. 1901(?)-1978 18
Lowitz, Sadyebeth Heath 1901-1969 ... 17
Lowndes, Robert A(ugustine) W(ard)
  1916-1998 117
Lowrey, Janette Sebring 1892-1986 ... 43
Lowry, Lois 1937- 177
  Autobiography Feature 127
  Earlier sketches in SATA 23, 70, 111
  See also CLR 72
  See also SAAS 3
Lowry, Lois Hammersberg
  See Lowry, Lois
Lowry, Peter 1953- 7
Lowther, George F. 1913-1975
  Obituary 30
Loyie, Larry 1933- 150
Lozansky, Edward D. 1941- 62
Lozier, Herbert 1915- 26
Lubar, David 1954- 190
  Earlier sketch in SATA 133
Lubell, Cecil 1912-2000 6
Lubell, Winifred (A. Milius) 1914- 6
Lubin, Leonard
  See Lubin, Leonard B.
Lubin, Leonard B. 1943-1994 45
  Brief entry 37
Lubka, S. Ruth 1948- 154
Lubner, Susan 185
Luby, Thia 1954- 124
Lucado, Max (Lee) 1955- 104
Lucas, Cedric 1962- 101
Lucas, David 1966- 208
Lucas, E(dward) V(errall) 1868-1938 .. 20
Lucas, Eileen 1956- 113
  Earlier sketch in SATA 76
Lucas, George 1944- 56
Lucas, Jerry 1940- 33
Lucas, Margeaux 186

Lucas, Victoria
  See Plath, Sylvia
Lucashenko, Melissa 1967- 104
Luccarelli, Vincent 1923- 90
Luce, Celia (Geneva Larsen) 1914- 38
Luce, Willard (Ray) 1914-1990 38
Lucht, Irmgard 1937- 82
Lucke, Deb 202
Luckett, Dave 1951- 167
  Earlier sketch in SATA 106
Luckhardt, Mildred Corell 1898-1990 ... 5
Ludden, Allen (Ellsworth) 1918(?)-1981
  Obituary 27
Ludel, Jacqueline 1945- 64
Ludlow, Geoffrey
  See Meynell, Laurence Walter
Ludlum, Mabel Cleland
  See Widdemer, Mabel Cleland
Ludwig, Helen 33
Ludwig, Lyndell 1923- 63
Ludwig, Trudy 1959- 209
  Earlier sketch in SATA 166
Luebs, Robin 1949- 212
Lueders, Edward (George) 1923- 14
Luenn, Nancy 1954- 79
  Earlier sketch in SATA 51
Lufkin, Raymond H. 1897- 38
Lugard, Flora Louisa Shaw 1852-1929 ... 21
Luger, Harriett Mandelay 1914- 23
Luhrmann, Winifred B(ruce) 1934- 11
Luis, Earlene W. 1929- 11
Lujan, Jorge 201
Luke, Pauline 178
Luke, Pauline R.
  See Luke, Pauline
Lum, Peter
  See Crowe, (Bettina) Peter Lum
Lumry, Amanda (R.) 159
Lund, Deb 157
Lund, Doris Herold 1919- 12
Lunde, Darrin 202
Lundebrek, Amy 1975- 213
Lung, Chang
  See Jordan, Robert
Lunge-Larsen, Lise 1955- 184
  Earlier sketch in SATA 138
Lunn, Carolyn (Kowalczyk) 1960- 67
Lunn, Janet (Louise Swoboda) 1928- ... 110
  Earlier sketches in SATA 4, 68
  See also CLR 18
  See also SAAS 12
Lunsford, Cin Forshay
  See Forshay-Lunsford, Cin
Lupica, Michael
  See Lupica, Mike
Lupica, Michael Thomas
  See Lupica, Mike
Lupica, Mike 1952- 177
Lupoff, Dick
  See Lupoff, Richard A(llen)
Lupoff, Richard A(llen) 1935- 60
Lurie, Alison 1926- 112
  Earlier sketch in SATA 46
Lurie, Morris 1938- 72
Lussert, Anneliese 1929- 101
Lusted, Marcia Amidon 1962- 143
Lustig, Arnost 1926- 56
Lustig, Loretta 1944- 46
Lutes, Jason 1967- 210
Luthardt, Kevin 1973- 172
Luther, Frank 1905-1980
  Obituary 25
Luther, Rebekah (Lyn) S(tiles) 1960- ... 90
Luttmann, Gail
  See Damerow, Gail
Luttrell, Guy L. 1938- 22
Luttrell, Ida (Alleene) 1934- 91
  Brief entry 35
  Earlier sketch in SATA 40
Luttrell, William (J. III) 1954- 149
Lutz, John 1939- 180

Lutz, John Thomas
  See Lutz, John
Lutz, Norma Jean 1943- 122
Lutzeier, Elizabeth 1952- 72
Lutzker, Edythe 1904-1991 5
Luxbacher, Irene M. 1970- 153
Luzadder, Patrick 1954- 89
Luzzati, Emanuele 1921-2007 7
Luzzatto, Paola Caboara 1938- 38
Ly, Many 1977- 208
Lybbert, Tyler 1970- 88
Lydon, Michael 1942- 11
Lyfick, Warren
  See Reeves, Lawrence F.
Lyle, Katie Letcher 1938- 8
Lynch, Chris 1962- 209
  Earlier sketches in SATA 95, 131, 171
  See also CLR 58
Lynch, Jay 1945- 204
Lynch, Lorenzo 1932- 7
Lynch, Marietta 1947- 29
Lynch, Patricia (Nora) 1898-1972 9
Lynch, Patrick James
  See Lynch, P.J.
Lynch, P.J. 1962- 213
  Earlier sketches in SATA 79, 122
Lynds, Dennis 1924-2005 47
  Brief entry 37
Lyne, Alison Davis 188
Lyngseth, Joan
  See Davies, Joan
Lynn, Elizabeth A(nne) 1946- 99
Lynn, Mary
  See Brokamp, Marilyn
Lynn, Patricia
  See Watts, Mabel Pizzey
Lynn, Tracy 175
Lyon, Elinor 1921-2008 6
  Obituary 192
Lyon, Elinor Bruce
  See Lyon, Elinor
Lyon, George Ella 1949- 207
  Autobiography Feature 148
  Earlier sketches in SATA 68, 119, 148
Lyon, Lea 1945- 212
Lyon, Lyman R.
  See de Camp, L. Sprague
Lyons, Dorothy M(arawee) 1907-1997 ... 3
Lyons, Grant 1941- 30
Lyons, Marcus
  See Blish, James
Lyons, Mary E. 1947- 195
  Autobiography Feature 195
  Earlier sketches in SATA 93, 142
Lyons, Mary Evelyn
  See Lyons, Mary E.
Lystad, Mary (Hanemann) 1928- 11
Lytle, Elizabeth Stewart 1949- 79
Lytle, Robert A. 1944- 119
Lyttle, Richard B(ard) 1927- 23
Lytton of Knebworth, Baron
  See Bulwer-Lytton, Edward

M

Ma, Wenhai 1954- 84
Maar, Leonard (Frank, Jr.) 1927- 30
Maartens, Maretha 1945- 73
Maas, Selve -1997 14
Maass, Robert 195
Mabie, Grace
  See Mattern, Joanne
Mac
  See MacManus, Seumas
  and Maccari, Ruggero
Macalaster, Elizabeth G. 1951- 115
MacAlister, Katie 159
MacAlister, V. A.
  See McKernan, Victoria

MacAllan, Andrew
 See Leasor, James
MacAodhagain, Eamon
 See Egan, E. W.
MacArthur-Onslow, Annette Rosemary
 1933- 26
Macaulay, David (Alexander) 1946- 137
 Brief entry 27
 Earlier sketches in SATA *46, 72*
 See also CLR *14*
Macaulay, Teresa 1947- 95
Macauley, Theresa E.
 See Macaulay, Teresa
Macavinta, Courtney 176
MacBeth, George (Mann) 1932-1992 4
 Obituary 70
MacBride, Roger Lea 1929-1995 85
MacCarter, Don 1944- 91
MacClintock, Dorcas 1932- 8
MacCready, Robin Merrow 1959(?)- 190
MacCullough, Carolyn 174
MacDonald, Alan 1958- 192
MacDonald, Amy 1951- 156
 Autobiography Feature 156
 Earlier sketches in SATA *76, 136*
MacDonald, Anne Elizabeth Campbell Bard
 -1958
 See MacDonald, Betty
MacDonald, Anne Louise 1955- 217
MacDonald, Anson
 See Heinlein, Robert A.
MacDonald, Betty 1908-1958
 See YABC *1*
Macdonald, Blackie
 See Emrich, Duncan (Black Macdonald)
Macdonald, Caroline 1948- 86
 Obituary 111
 See also CLR *60*
Macdonald, Dwight 1906-1982 29
 Obituary 33
MacDonald, George 1824-1905 100
 Earlier sketch in SATA *33*
 See also CLR *67*
MacDonald, Golden
 See Brown, Margaret Wise
Macdonald, Guy 195
Macdonald, James D. 1954- 67
 Earlier sketches in SATA *81, 114, 165, 1*
Macdonald, Marcia
 See Hill, Grace Livingston
MacDonald, Margaret Read 1940- 194
 Earlier sketches in SATA *94, 164*
Macdonald, Marianne 1934- 113
Macdonald, Mary
 See Gifford, Griselda
Macdonald, Maryann 1947- 189
 Earlier sketch in SATA *72*
MacDonald, Ross 1957- 201
Macdonald, Shelagh 1937- 25
MacDonald, Suse 1940- 193
 Brief entry 52
 Earlier sketches in SATA *54, 109*
Macdonald, Wendy 217
Macdonald, Wendy M.
 See Macdonald, Wendy
Macdonald, Zillah K(atherine) 1885-1979 ... 11
MacDonnell, Megan
 See Stevens, Serita
MacDougal, John
 See Blish, James
Mace, Elisabeth 1933- 27
Mace, Varian 1938- 49
MacEachern, Stephen 206
MacEwen, Gwendolyn (Margaret)
 1941-1987 50
 Obituary 55
Macfarlan, Allan A. 1892-1982 35
MacFarlane, Iris 1922- 11
MacGill-Callahan, Sheila 1926-2000 78
MacGregor, Carol Lynn 153

MacGregor, Ellen 1906-1954 39
 Brief entry 27
MacGregor-Hastie, Roy (Alasdhair Niall)
 1929- 3
MacGrory, Yvonne 1948- 142
Machado, Ana Maria 1941- 150
MacHale, D.J. 1956- 175
MacHale, Donald James
 See MacHale, D.J.
Machetanz, Frederick 1908- 34
Machin, Sue
 See Williams, Sue
Machin Goodall, Daphne (Edith) 37
Macht, Norm
 See Macht, Norman L.
Macht, Norman L. 1929- 122
Macht, Norman Lee
 See Macht, Norman L.
Macht, Norman Lee
 See Macht, Norman L.
MacInnes, Helen (Clark) 1907-1985 22
 Obituary 44
Macintosh, Brownie 1950- 98
MacIntyre, Elisabeth 1916- 17
MacIntyre, Rod
 See MacIntyre, R.P.
MacIntyre, R.P. 1947- 203
MacIntyre, R.P. 1947- 203
MacIntyre, Wendy 1947- 196
Mack, Jeff 194
Mack, L.V.
 See Kimmelman, Burt
Mack, Stan(ley) 17
Mack, Todd 168
Mack, Tracy 1968- 183
 Earlier sketch in SATA *128*
Mackall, Dandi D.
 See Mackall, Dandi Daley
Mackall, Dandi Daley 1949- 182
 Earlier sketches in SATA *118, 177*
Mackay, Claire 1930- 97
 Autobiography Feature 124
 Earlier sketch in SATA *40*
 See also CLR *43*
Mackay, Constance D'Arcy (?)-1966 125
Mackay, Donald 1914-2005 81
 Obituary 173
Mackay, Donald Alexander
 See Mackay, Donald
MacKaye, Percy (Wallace) 1875-1956 32
Mackel, Kathryn 1950- 162
Mackel, Kathy
 See Mackel, Kathryn
MacKellar, William 1914- 4
Macken, JoAnn Early 1953- 201
Macken, Walter 1915-1967 36
Mackenzie, Anna 1963- 212
MacKenzie, Jill (Kelly) 1947- 75
Mackenzie, Robert 1974- 204
Mackey, Ernan
 See McInerny, Ralph
Mackey, Weezie Kerr 188
Mackie, Maron
 See McNeely, Jeannette
Mackin, Edward
 See McInerny, Ralph
MacKinnon, Bernie 1957- 69
MacKinnon Groomer, Vera 1915- 57
MacKinstry, Elizabeth 1879-1956 42
Mackler, Carolyn 1973- 156
MacLachlan, Emily
 See Charest, Emily MacLachlan
MacLachlan, Patricia 1938- 168
 Brief entry 42
 Earlier sketches in SATA *62, 107*
 See also CLR *14*
MacLane, Jack
 See Crider, Bill
MacLean, Alistair 1922(?)-1987 23
 Obituary 50

MacLean, Alistair Stuart
 See MacLean, Alistair
Maclean, Art
 See Shirreffs, Gordon D(onald)
MacLean, Christine Kole 1962- 177
MacLean, Glynne 1964- 150
MacLean, Jill 1941- 211
MacLeod, Beatrice 1910- 162
 Earlier sketch in SATA *10*
MacLeod, Beatrice Beach
 See MacLeod, Beatrice
MacLeod, Charlotte (Matilda) 1922-2005 28
 Obituary 160
MacLeod, Doug 1959- 201
 Earlier sketch in SATA *60*
MacLeod, Elizabeth 184
 Earlier sketch in SATA *158*
MacLeod, Ellen Jane (Anderson) 1916- 14
MacManus, James
 See MacManus, Seumas
MacManus, Seumas 1869-1960 25
MacMaster, Eve (Ruth) B(owers) 1942- 46
MacMillan, Annabelle
 See Quick, Annabelle
MacMillan, Dianne M(arie) 1943- 125
 Earlier sketch in SATA *84*
Macnaughton, Tina 182
Macneill, Janet
 See McNeely, Jeannette
MacPeek, Walter G. 1902-1973 4
 Obituary 25
MacPhail, Catherine 1946- 197
 Earlier sketch in SATA *130*
MacPherson, Margaret 1908-2001 9
 See also SAAS *4*
MacPherson, Thomas George 1915-1976
 Obituary 30
MacPherson, Winnie 1930- 107
MacRae, Tom 1980- 181
Macrae, Travis
 See Feagles, Anita MacRae
MacRaois, Cormac 1944- 72
Macumber, Mari
 See Sandoz, Mari(e Susette)
Macy, Sue 1954- 134
 Earlier sketch in SATA *88*
Madaras, Lynda 1947- 151
Madden, Don 1927- 3
Madden, Kerry 1961- 168
Madden-Lunsford, Kerry
 See Madden, Kerry
Maddern, Eric 1950- 166
Maddigan, Beth 1967- 174
Maddison, Angela Mary 1923- 10
 See also CLR *24*
Maddock, Reginald (Bertram) 1912-1994 15
Madenski, Melissa (Ann) 1949- 77
Madian, Jon 1941- 9
Madison, Alan 182
Madison, Arnold 1937- 6
Madison, Winifred 5
Madonna 1958- 149
Madsen, Gunnar 171
Madsen, Jim 1964- 202
Madsen, Ross Martin 1946- 82
Madsen, Susan A. 1954- 90
Madsen, Susan Arrington
 See Madsen, Susan A.
Maehlqvist, Stefan 1943- 30
Maestro, Betsy (Crippen) 1944- 106
 Brief entry 30
 Earlier sketch in SATA *59*
 See also CLR *45*
Maestro, Giulio 1942- 106
 Earlier sketches in SATA *8, 59*
 See also CLR *45*
Maeterlinck, Maurice 1862-1949 66
Magee, Doug 1947- 78
Magee, Wes 1939- 64
Maggio, Rosalie 1943- 69
Magid, Ken(neth Marshall) 65

Magnus, Erica 1946- 77
Magoon, Kekla 1980- 213
Magoon, Scott 182
Magorian, James 1942- 92
  Earlier sketch in SATA 32
Magorian, Michelle 1947- 128
  Earlier sketch in SATA 67
Magorian, Michelle Jane
  See Magorian, Michelle
Magovern, Peg 103
Magsamen, Sandra 1959- 213
Maguire, Anne
  See Nearing, Penny
Maguire, Gregory 1954- 200
  Autobiography Feature 200
  Earlier sketches in SATA 28, 84, 129
  See also SAAS 22
Maguire, Gregory Peter
  See Maguire, Gregory
Maguire, Jack 1920-2000 74
Maguire, Jesse
  See Smith, Sherwood
Maguire, Jessie
  See Smith, Sherwood
Maher, Ramona 1934- 13
Mahlqvist, Stefan
  See Maehlqvist, Stefan
Mahon, Julia C(unha) 1916- 11
Mahony, Elizabeth Winthrop
  See Winthrop, Elizabeth
Mahood, Kenneth 1930- 24
Mahy, Margaret 1936- 171
  Earlier sketches in SATA 14, 69, 119
  See also CLR 155
Mahy, Margaret May
  See Mahy, Margaret
Maiden, Cecil (Edward) 1902-1981 52
Maidoff, Ilka
  See List, Ilka Katherine
Maifair, Linda Lee 1947- 83
Maik, Henri
  See Hecht, Henri Joseph
Maillu, David G(ian) 1939- 111
Maine, Trevor
  See Catherall, Arthur
Mains, Randolph P. 1946- 80
Maione, Heather 189
Maiorano, Robert 1946- 43
Maisner, Heather 1947- 89
Maison, Della
  See Katz, Bobbi
Maitland, Antony Jasper 1935- 25
Maitland, Barbara 102
Mai-Wyss, Tatjana 1972- 187
Maizels, Jennie 210
Major, Kevin (Gerald) 1949- 134
  Earlier sketches in SATA 32, 82
  See also CLR 11
Majure, Janet 1954- 96
Makhijani, Pooja 188
Makie, Pam 1943- 37
Makowski, Silk
  See Sullivan, Silky
Makowski, Silvia Ann
  See Sullivan, Silky
Malam, John 1957- 152
  Earlier sketch in SATA 89
Maland, Nick 195
Malcolm, Dan
  See Silverberg, Robert
Malcolm, Jahnna N.
  See Beecham, Jahnna
Malcolmson, Anne
  See von Storch, Anne B.
Malcolmson, David 1899-1978 6
Maletta, Dr. Arlene
  See Feltenstein, Arlene
Maley, Carleen
  See Hutchins, Carleen Maley

Mali, Jane Lawrence 1937-1995 51
  Brief entry 44
  Obituary 86
Malkin, Nina 1959(?)- 179
Mallett, Jerry J. 1939- 76
Malley, Gemma 198
Malley, G.R.
  See Malley, Gemma
Mallory, Kenneth 1945- 185
  Earlier sketch in SATA 128
Mallowan, Agatha Christie
  See Christie, Agatha
Malmberg, Carl 1904-1979 9
Malmgren, Dallin 1949- 65
Malo, John W. 1911-2000 4
Malone, James Hiram 1930- 84
Malone, Nola Langner 1930-2003 8
  Obituary 151
Malone, Patricia 1932- 155
Malone, Peter 1953- 191
Maloney, Pat
  See Markun, Patricia Maloney
Malory, Sir Thomas 1410(?)-1471(?) 59
  Brief entry 33
Maltese, Michael 1909(?)-1981
  Obituary 24
Malvasi, Meg Greene 143
Malvern, Corinne 1905-1956 34
Malvern, Gladys (?)-1962 23
Mama G.
  See Davis, Grania
Mammano, Julie 1962- 202
  Earlier sketch in SATA 107
Mamonova, Tatyana 1943- 93
Manchel, Frank 1935- 10
Manchess, Gregory 1955- 203
Manchester, William (Raymond)
  1922-2004 65
Mandabach, Brian 1962(?)- 197
Mandel, Brett H. 1969- 108
Mandel, Peter 1957- 87
Mandel, Sally (Elizabeth) 1944- 64
Mandell, Muriel (Hortense Levin) 1921- 63
Manders, John 1957- 175
Manes, Stephen 1949- 99
  Brief entry 40
  Earlier sketch in SATA 42
Manfred, Frederick (Feikema) 1912-1994 30
Mangin, Marie France 1940- 59
Mangione, Gerlando 1909-1998 6
  Obituary 104
Mangione, Jerre
  See Mangione, Gerlando
Mango, Karin N. 1936- 52
Mangurian, David 1938- 14
Mania, Cathy 1950- 102
Mania, Robert 1952- 102
Mania, Robert C., Jr.
  See Mania, Robert
Maniatty, Taramesha 1978- 92
Maniscalco, Joseph 1926- 10
Manley, Deborah 1932- 28
Manley, Seon 1921- 15
  See also CLR 3
  See also SAAS 2
Mann, Elizabeth 1948- 153
Mann, Josephine
  See Pullein-Thompson, Josephine (Mary
  Wedderburn)
Mann, Kenny 1946- 91
Mann, Pamela 1946- 91
Mann, Patrick
  See Waller, Leslie
Mann, Peggy
  See Houlton, Peggy Mann
Mannetti, Lisa 1953- 57
  Brief entry 51
Mannheim, Grete (Salomon) 1909-1986 10
Manniche, Lise 1943- 31
Manning, Jane K. 185

Manning, Maurie
  See Manning, Maurie J.
Manning, Maurie J. 211
Manning, Maurie Jo
  See Manning, Maurie J.
Manning, Mick 1959- 176
Manning, Rosemary 1911-1988 10
Manning, Sarra 162
Manning-Sanders, Ruth (Vernon)
  1895(?)-1988 73
  Obituary 57
  Earlier sketch in SATA 15
Mannion, Diane
  See Paterson, Diane
Mannis, Celeste Davidson 173
Mannon, Warwick
  See Hopkins, (Hector) Kenneth
Manos, Helen 199
Mansir, A. Richard 1932- 170
Manson, Ainslie Kertland 1938- 115
Manson, Beverlie 1945- 57
  Brief entry 44
Mantha, John 1960- 217
Manthorpe, Helen 1958- 122
Mantinband, Gerda (B.) 1917- 74
Manton, Jo
  See Gittings, Jo (Grenville) Manton
Manuel, Lynn 1948- 179
  Earlier sketch in SATA 99
Manushkin, Fran 1942- 205
  Earlier sketches in SATA 7, 54, 93, 166
Manushkin, Frances
  See Manushkin, Fran
Man Without a Spleen, A
  See Chekhov, Anton
Many, Paul 1947- 210
Many, Paul A.
  See Many, Paul
Manzano, Sonia 1950- 167
Mapes, Mary A.
  See Ellison, Virginia H(owell)
Maple, Marilyn 1931- 80
Mappin, Strephyn 1956- 109
Mara, Barney
  See Roth, Arthur J(oseph)
Mara, Jeanette
  See Cebulash, Mel
Mara, Rachna
  See Gilmore, Rachna
Marais, Josef 1905-1978
  Obituary 24
Marasmus, Seymour
  See Rivoli, Mario
Marbach, Ethel
  See Pochocki, Ethel (Frances)
Marcal, Annette B.
  See Callaway, Bernice (Anne)
Marcelino
  See Agnew, Edith J(osephine)
Marcellino, Fred 1939-2001 118
  Obituary 127
  Earlier sketch in SATA 68
March, Carl
  See Fleischman, Sid
Marchant, Bessie 1862-1941
  See YABC 2
Marchant, Catherine
  See Cookson, Catherine (McMullen)
Marcher, Marion Walden 1890-1987 10
Marchesi, Stephen 1951- 114
Marchesi, Steve
  See Marchesi, Stephen
  and Older, Effin
  and Older, Jules
Marchetta, Melina 1965- 170
Marciano, John Bemelmans 1970- 167
  Earlier sketch in SATA 118
  See also CLR 93
Marco, Lou
  See Gottfried, Theodore Mark

Marcus, Leonard S. 1950- *187*
    Earlier sketch in SATA *133*
Marcus, Paul 1953- *82*
Marcus, Rebecca B(rian) 1907- *9*
Marcuse, Aida E. 1934- *89*
Marek, Margot L. 1934(?)-1987
    Obituary *54*
Maren, Julie 1970- *199*
Margaret, Karla
    See Andersdatter, Karla M(argaret)
Margolin, Harriet
    See Ziefert, Harriet
Margolis, Jeffrey A. 1948- *108*
Margolis, Leslie *187*
Margolis, Richard J(ules) 1929-1991 .... *86*
    Obituary *67*
    Earlier sketch in SATA *4*
Margolis, Vivienne 1922- *46*
Mariana
    See Foster, Marian Curtis
Marie, Geraldine 1949- *61*
Mariner, Scott
    See Pohl, Frederik
Marino, Dorothy Bronson 1912- *14*
Marino, Jan 1936- *114*
Marino, Nan *216*
Marino, Nick
    See Deming, Richard
Marino, Peter 1960- *179*
Mario, Anna
    See Odgers, Sally Farrell
Marion, Henry
    See del Rey, Lester
Maris, Ron *71*
    Brief entry *45*
Mark, Jan 1943-2006 .... *164*
    Obituary *173*
    Earlier sketches in SATA *22, 69, 114*
    See also CLR *11*
Mark, Janet Marjorie
    See Mark, Jan
Mark, Joan T. 1937- *122*
Mark, Pauline (Dahlin) 1913-1997 .... *14*
Mark, Polly
    See Mark, Pauline (Dahlin)
Mark, Ted
    See Gottfried, Theodore Mark
Markel, Michelle *169*
Marker, Sherry 1941- *76*
Markert, Jennifer 1965- *83*
Markert, Jenny
    See Markert, Jennifer
Markey, Kevin 1965- *215*
Markham, Lynne 1947- *102*
Markham, Marion M. 1929- *60*
Markham, Wendy
    See Staub, Wendy Corsi
Markins, W. S.
    See Jenkins, Marie M(agdalen)
Markle, Sandra L. 1946- *185*
    Brief entry *41*
    Earlier sketches in SATA *57, 92, 148*
Markle, Sandra Lee
    See Markle, Sandra L.
Marklew, Gilly *211*
Marko, Katherine D(olores) *28*
Markoosie
    See Patsauq, Markoosie
Marks, Alan 1957- *187*
    Earlier sketches in SATA *77, 151*
Marks, Burton 1930- *47*
    Brief entry *43*
Marks, Graham *158*
Marks, Hannah K.
    See Trivelpiece, Laurel
Marks, J.
    See Highwater, Jamake (Mamake)
Marks, J(ames) M(acdonald) 1921- *13*
Marks, Laurie J. 1957- *68*
Marks, Margaret L. 1911(?)-1980
    Obituary *23*

Marks, Mickey Klar -1986 .... *12*
Marks, Peter
    See Smith, Robert Kimmel
Marks, Rita 1938- *47*
Marks, Stan(ley) *14*
Marks-Highwater, J.
    See Highwater, Jamake (Mamake)
Markun, Patricia Maloney 1924- *15*
Markusen, Bruce (Stanley Rodriguez)
    1965- *141*
Marley, Louise 1952- *173*
    Earlier sketch in SATA *120*
Marlin, Hilda
    See Van Stockum, Hilda
Marlow, Layne *204*
Marlow, Max
    See Nicole, Christopher (Robin)
Marlow, Susan K. 1953- *178*
Marlowe, Amy Bell *67*
    Earlier sketch in SATA *1*
Marlowe, Jack
    See Deary, Terry
Marney, Dean 1952- *90*
Marokvia, Artur 1909- *31*
Marokvia, Mireille 1908-2008 .... *5*
    Obituary *197*
Marokvia, Mireille Journet
    See Marokvia, Mireille
Marol, Jean-Claude 1946- *125*
Marr, John S(tuart) 1940- *48*
Marr, Melissa 1972- *189*
Marric, J. J.
    See Butler, William Vivian
    and Creasey, John
Marrin, Albert 1936- *193*
    Brief entry *43*
    Earlier sketches in SATA *53, 90, 126*
    See also CLR *53*
Marriott, Alice Lee 1910-1992 .... *31*
    Obituary *71*
Marriott, Janice 1946- *134*
Marriott, Pat(ricia) 1920- *35*
Marriott, Zoe 1982- *216*
Marriott, Zoe Davina
    See Marriott, Zoe
Marroquin, Patricio
    See Markun, Patricia Maloney
Mars, W. T.
    See Mars, Witold Tadeusz J.
Mars, Witold Tadeusz J. 1912-1985 .... *3*
Marsden, Carolyn 1950- *212*
    Autobiography Feature *212*
    Earlier sketches in SATA *140, 175*
Marsden, John 1950- *146*
    Earlier sketches in SATA *66, 97*
    See also CLR *34*
    See also SAAS *22*
Marsh, Carole 1946- *127*
Marsh, Dave 1950- *66*
Marsh, J. E.
    See Marshall, Evelyn
Marsh, James 1946- *73*
Marsh, Jean
    See Marshall, Evelyn
Marsh, Joan F. 1923- *83*
Marsh, Paul
    See Hopkins, (Hector) Kenneth
Marsh, Valerie 1954- *89*
Marshall, Anthony D(ryden) 1924- *18*
Marshall, Bonnie C. 1941- *141*
    Earlier sketch in SATA *18*
Marshall, Bridget M(ary) 1974- *103*
Marshall, (Sarah) Catherine (Wood)
    1914-1983 .... *2*
    Obituary *34*
Marshall, Douglas
    See McClintock, Marshall
Marshall, Edmund
    See Hopkins, (Hector) Kenneth
Marshall, Edward
    See Marshall, James

Marshall, Evelyn 1897-1991 .... *11*
Marshall, Felicity 1950- *116*
Marshall, Garry 1934- *60*
Marshall, H. H.
    See Jahn, Michael
Marshall, James 1942-1992 .... *75*
    Earlier sketches in SATA *6, 51*
    See also CLR *21*
Marshall, James Edward
    See Marshall, James
Marshall, James Vance
    See Payne, Donald Gordon
Marshall, Janet (Perry) 1938- *97*
Marshall, Jeff
    See Laycock, George (Edwin)
Marshall, Kim
    See Marshall, Michael (Kimbrough)
Marshall, Michael (Kimbrough) 1948- *37*
Marshall, Percy
    See Young, Percy M(arshall)
Marshall, S(amuel) L(yman) A(twood)
    1900-1977 .... *21*
Marsoli, Lisa Ann 1958- *101*
    Brief entry *53*
Marsten, Richard
    See Hunter, Evan
Marston, Elsa 1933- *156*
Marston, Hope Irvin 1935- *127*
    Earlier sketch in SATA *31*
Marszalek, John F. 1939- *167*
Marszalek, John Francis, Jr.
    See Marszalek, John F.
Marszalek, John Francis 1939-
    See Marszalek, John F.
Martchenko, Michael 1942- *154*
    Earlier sketches in SATA *50, 95*
Martel, Aimee
    See Thurlo, Aimee
    and Thurlo, David
Martel, Suzanne 1924- *99*
Martignoni, Margaret E. 1908(?)-1974
    Obituary *27*
Martin, Ann M. 1955- *192*
    Brief entry *41*
    Earlier sketches in SATA *44, 70, 126*
    See also CLR *32*
Martin, Bill, Jr. 1916-2004 .... *145*
    Brief entry *40*
    Earlier sketches in SATA *40, 67*
    See also CLR *97*
Martin, Charles E(lmer)
    See Mastrangelo, Charles E(lmer)
Martin, Christopher
    See Hoyt, Edwin P(almer), Jr.
Martin, C.K. Kelly *207*
Martin, Claire 1933- *76*
Martin, Courtney Autumn 1984- *205*
Martin, David Stone 1913-1992 .... *39*
Martin, Del 1921-2008 .... *47*
Martin, Donald
    See Honig, Donald
Martin, Dorothy
    See Martin, Del
Martin, Dorothy L.
    See Martin, Del
Martin, Eugene *1*
Martin, Eva M. 1939- *65*
Martin, Frances M(cEntee) 1906-1998 .... *36*
Martin, Francesca 1947- *101*
Martin, Fred 1948- *119*
Martin, Fredric
    See Christopher, Matt(hew Frederick)
Martin, George Raymond Richard
    See Martin, George R.R.
Martin, George R.R. 1948- *118*
Martin, J(ohn) P(ercival) 1880(?)-1966 .... *15*
Martin, Jacqueline Briggs 1945- *188*
    Earlier sketches in SATA *98, 149*
Martin, Jane Read 1957- *84*
Martin, Jeremy
    See Levin, Marcia Obrasky

Martin, Les
  See Schulman, L(ester) M(artin)
Martin, Linda 1961- 82
Martin, Lynne 1923- 21
Martin, Marcia
  See Levin, Marcia Obrasky
Martin, Marvin 1926- 126
Martin, Melanie
  See Pellowski, Michael (Joseph)
Martin, Nancy
  See Salmon, Annie Elizabeth
Martin, Patricia 200
Martin, Patricia A.
  See Martin, Patricia
Martin, Patricia Miles 1899-1986 43
  Obituary 48
  Earlier sketch in SATA *1*
Martin, Peter
  See Chaundler, Christine
Martin, Rafe 1946- 175
Martin, Rene 1891-1977 42
  Obituary 20
Martin, Rupert (Claude) 1905- 31
Martin, S. R.
  See Mappin, Strephyn
Martin, Stefan 1936- 32
Martin, Vicky
  See Storey, Victoria Carolyn
Martin, Webber
  See Silverberg, Robert
Martin, Wendy
  See Martini, Teri
Martin, William Ivan, Jr.
  See Martin, Bill, Jr.
Martineau, Diane 1940- 178
Martineau, Harriet 1802-1876
  See YABC
Martinet, Jeanne 1958- 80
Martinez, Agnes 167
Martinez, Arturo O. 1933- 192
Martinez, Claudia Guadalupe 1978- 214
Martinez, Ed(ward) 1954- 98
Martinez, Elizabeth Coonrod 1954- 85
Martinez, Victor 1954- 95
Martini, Teri 1930- 3
Martini, Therese
  See Martini, Teri
Martino, Alfred C. 1964- 174
Martinson, Janis
  See Herbert, Janis
Marton, Jirina 1946- 144
  Earlier sketch in SATA *95*
Marton, Pierre
  See Stone, Peter
Martson, Del
  See Lupoff, Richard A(llen)
Martyr, Paula (Jane)
  See Lawford, Paula Jane
Maruki, Toshi 1912-2000 112
  See also CLR *19*
Marvin, Isabel R(idout) 1924- 84
Marx, Patricia Windschill
  See Marx, Trish
Marx, Robert F(rank) 1936- 24
Marx, Trish 1948- 202
  Earlier sketch in SATA *112, 160*
Marzani, Carl (Aldo) 1912-1994 12
Marzollo, Jean 1942- 190
  Autobiography Feature 190
  Earlier sketches in SATA *29, 77, 130*
  See also SAAS *15*
Masefield, John (Edward) 1878-1967 19
Masiello, Ralph 1961- 214
Masoff, Joy 1951- 118
Mason, Adrienne 1962- 163
Mason, Cherie 170
Mason, Edwin A. 1905-1979
  Obituary 32
Mason, Ernst
  See Pohl, Frederik

Mason, F(rancis) van Wyck 1901-1978 .... *3*
  Obituary 26
Mason, Frank W.
  See Mason, F(rancis) van Wyck
Mason, George Frederick 1904-2000 .... *14*
Mason, Miriam E(vangeline) 1900-1973 .... *2*
  Obituary 26
Mason, Prue 195
Mason, Simon 1962- 178
Mason, Tally
  See Derleth, August (William)
Mason, Van Wyck
  See Mason, F(rancis) van Wyck
Mass, Wendy 1967- 196
  Earlier sketch in SATA *158*
Mass, William
  See Gibson, William
Masselman, George 1897-1971 19
Massey, Misty 212
Massie, Dianne Redfield 1938- 125
  Earlier sketch in SATA *16*
Massie, Elizabeth 108
Massini, Sarah 213
Masson, Sophie 1959- 179
  Earlier sketch in SATA *133*
Masters, Anthony (Richard) 1940-2003 112
  Obituary 145
Masters, Kelly R(ay) 1897-1987 .... *3*
Masters, Mildred 1932- 42
Masters, William
  See Cousins, Margaret
Masters, Zeke
  See Bensen, Donald R.
  and Goulart, Ron
Mastrangelo, Charles E(lmer) 1910-1995 70
  Earlier sketch in SATA *69*
Masuda, Takeshi 1944- 56
Matas, Carol 1949- 194
  Autobiography Feature 112
  Earlier sketch in SATA *93*
  See also CLR *52*
Matchette, Katharine E. 1941- 38
Math, Irwin 1940- 42
Mathabane, Mark 1960- 123
Mather, Kirtley F(letcher) 1888-1978 65
Mathers, Petra 1945- 176
  Earlier sketch in SATA *119*
  See also CLR *76*
Matheson, Richard (Christian) 1953- 119
Matheson, Shirlee Smith 1942- 155
Mathews, Eleanor
  See Mathews, Ellie
Mathews, Ellie 1946(?)- 193
Mathews, Janet 1914-1992 41
Mathews, Judith
  See Goldberger, Judith M.
Mathews, Louise
  See Tooke, Louise Mathews
Mathiesen, Egon 1907-1976
  Obituary 28
Mathieu, Joe 1949- 185
  Brief entry 36
  Earlier sketches in SATA *43, 94*
Mathieu, Joseph P.
  See Mathieu, Joe
Mathis, Sharon Bell 1937- 58
  Earlier sketch in SATA *7*
  See also CLR *147*
  See also SAAS *3*
Matlin, Marlee 1965- 181
Matlin, Marlee Beth
  See Matlin, Marlee
Matloff, Gregory 1945- 73
Matott, Justin 1961- 109
Matranga, Frances Carfi 1922- 78
Matray, James I. 1948- 161
Matray, James Irving
  See Matray, James I.
Matson, Emerson N(els) 1926- 12
Matsui, Tadashi 1926- 8

Matsuno, Masako
  See Kobayashi, Masako Matsuno
Matsuoka, Mei 1981- 192
Matte, (Encarnacion) L'Enc 1936- 22
Mattern, Joanne 1963- 122
Mattheson, Jenny 180
Matthew, James
  See Barrie, J. M.
Matthews, Aline
  See De Wire, Elinor
Matthews, Andrew 1948- 138
Matthews, Caitlin 1952- 122
Matthews, Downs 1925- 71
Matthews, Elizabeth 1978- 194
Matthews, Ellen
  See Bache, Ellyn
Matthews, Ellen 1950- 28
Matthews, Harold Downs
  See Matthews, Downs
Matthews, Jacklyn Meek
  See Meek, Jacklyn O'Hanlon
Matthews, John (Kentigern) 1948- 116
Matthews, L. S. 183
Matthews, Laura S.
  See Matthews, L. S.
Matthews, Liz
  See Pellowski, Michael (Joseph)
Matthews, Morgan
  See Pellowski, Michael (Joseph)
Matthews, Nicola
  See Browne, N.M.
Matthews, Patricia 1927-2006 28
Matthews, Patricia Anne
  See Matthews, Patricia
Matthews, Tina 1961- 190
Matthews, Tom L.
  See Lalicki, Tom
Matthews, William Henry III 1919- 45
  Brief entry 28
Matthiessen, Peter 1927- 27
Mattingley, Christobel (Rosemary) 1931- 85
  Earlier sketch in SATA *37*
  See also CLR *24*
  See also SAAS *18*
Matulay, Laszlo 1912- 43
Matus, Greta 1938- 12
Maugham, W. S.
  See Maugham, W. Somerset
Maugham, W. Somerset 1874-1965 54
Maugham, William S.
  See Maugham, W. Somerset
Maugham, William Somerset
  See Maugham, W. Somerset
Maurer, Diane Philippoff
  See Maurer-Mathison, Diane V(ogel)
Maurer, Diane Vogel
  See Maurer-Mathison, Diane V(ogel)
Maurer-Mathison, Diane V(ogel) 1944- 89
Mauser, Pat Rhoads
  See McCord, Patricia
Mauser, Patricia Rhoads
  See McCord, Patricia
Maves, Mary Carolyn 1916- 10
Maves, Paul B(enjamin) 1913-1994 10
Mavor, Salley 1955- 125
Mawicke, Tran 1911- 15
Max 1906-1989
  See Diop, Birago (Ismael)
Max, Peter 1939- 45
Maxon, Anne
  See Best, (Evangel) Allena Champlin
Maxwell, Arthur S. 1896-1970 11
Maxwell, B.E. 1957- 211
Maxwell, Bruce E.
  See Maxwell, B.E.
Maxwell, Edith 1923- 7
Maxwell, Gavin 1914-1969 65
Maxwell, Katie
  See MacAlister, Katie
Maxwell, William (Keepers, Jr.) 1908-2000
  Obituary 128

Maxwell-Hyslop, Miranda 1968- *154*
May, Charles Paul 1920- *4*
May, Elaine Tyler 1947- *120*
May, J. C.
  See May, Julian
May, Julian 1931- *11*
May, Robert Lewis 1905-1976
  Obituary *27*
May, Robert Stephen 1929-1996 .... *46*
May, Robin
  See May, Robert Stephen
Mayall, Beth *171*
Mayberry, Florence V(irginia) Wilson *10*
Maybury, Richard J. 1946- *72*
Maybury, Rick
  See Maybury, Richard J.
Mayer, Agatha
  See Maher, Ramona
Mayer, Albert Ignatius, Jr. 1906-1994
  Obituary *29*
Mayer, Ann M(argaret) 1938- *14*
Mayer, Bill *200*
Mayer, Danuta 1958- *117*
Mayer, Hannelore Valencak 1929- *42*
Mayer, Jane Rothschild 1903-2001 .... *38*
Mayer, Marianna 1945- *132*
  Earlier sketches in SATA *32, 83*
Mayer, Mercer 1943- *137*
  Earlier sketches in SATA *16, 32, 73, 129*
  See also CLR *11*
Mayerson, Charlotte Leon *36*
Mayerson, Evelyn Wilde 1935- *55*
Mayfield, Katherine 1958- *118*
Mayfield, Sue 1963- *146*
  Earlier sketch in SATA *72*
Mayhar, Ardath 1930- *38*
Mayhew, James 1964- *204*
  Earlier sketches in SATA *85, 149*
Maynard, Olga 1920- *40*
Mayne, William 1928-2010 .... *122*
  Earlier sketches in SATA *6, 68*
  See also CLR *123*
  See also SAAS *11*
Mayne, William James Carter
  See Mayne, William
Maynes, J. O. Rocky, Jr.
  See Maynes, J. Oscar, Jr.
Maynes, J. Oscar, Jr. 1929- *38*
Mayo, Gretchen Will 1936- *163*
  Earlier sketch in SATA *84*
Mayo, Margaret 1935- *165*
  Earlier sketches in SATA *38, 96*
Mayo, Margaret Mary
  See Mayo, Margaret
Mayr, Diane 1949- *197*
Mays, Lucinda L(a Bella) 1924- *49*
Mays, (Lewis) Victor (Jr.) 1927- *5*
Mazellan, Ron *210*
Mazer, Anne 1953- *192*
  Earlier sketches in SATA *67, 105*
Mazer, Harry 1925- *167*
  Earlier sketches in SATA *31, 67, 105*
  See also CLR *16*
  See also SAAS *11*
Mazer, Norma Fox 1931-2009 .... *198*
  Earlier sketches in SATA *24, 67, 105, 168*
  See also CLR *23*
  See also SAAS *1*
Mazille, Capucine 1953- *96*
Mazza, Adriana 1928- *19*
Mazzio, Joann 1926- *74*
Mbugua, Kioi Wa 1962- *83*
McAfee, Carol 1955- *81*
McAllister, Amanda
  See Dowdell, Dorothy (Florence) Karns
  and Hager, Jean
  and Meaker, Eloise
McAllister, Angela *182*
McAllister, Margaret I. 1956- *169*
  Earlier sketch in SATA *117*

McAllister, M.I.
  See McAllister, Margaret I.
McArdle, Paula 1971- *198*
McArthur, Nancy *96*
McAvoy, Jim 1972- *142*
McBain, Ed
  See Hunter, Evan
McBain, Georgina *189*
McBratney, Sam 1943- *203*
  Earlier sketches in SATA *89, 164*
  See also CLR *44*
McBrier, Michael
  See Older, Effin
  and Older, Jules
McCafferty, Jim 1954- *84*
McCaffery, Janet 1936- *38*
McCaffrey, Anne 1926- *152*
  Autobiography Feature *152*
  Earlier sketches in SATA *8, 70, 116*
  See also CLR *130*
  See also SAAS *11*
McCaffrey, Anne Inez
  See McCaffrey, Anne
McCaffrey, Mary
  See Szudek, Agnes S(usan) P(hilomena)
McCain, Becky Ray 1954- *138*
McCain, Murray (David, Jr.) 1926-1981 .... *7*
  Obituary *29*
McCall, Bruce 1935(?)- *209*
McCall, Edith (Sansom) 1911- *6*
McCall, Virginia Nielsen 1909-2000 .... *13*
McCall, Wendell
  See Pearson, Ridley
McCall Smith, Alexander
  See Smith, Alexander McCall
McCallum, Phyllis
  See Koch, Phyllis (Mae) McCallum
McCallum, Stephen 1960- *91*
McCampbell, Darlene Z. 1942- *83*
McCann, Edson
  See del Rey, Lester
  and Pohl, Frederik
McCann, Gerald 1916- *41*
McCann, Helen 1948- *75*
McCannon, Dindga *41*
McCants, William D. 1961- *82*
McCarter, Neely Dixon 1929- *47*
McCarthy, Agnes 1933- *4*
McCarthy, Colin (John) 1951- *77*
McCarthy, Mary 1951- *203*
McCarthy, Meghan *199*
  Earlier sketch in SATA *168*
McCarthy, Ralph F. 1950- *139*
McCarthy-Tucker, Sherri N. 1958- *83*
McCarty, Peter 1966- *182*
McCarty, Rega Kramer 1904-1986 .... *10*
McCaslin, Nellie 1914-2005 .... *12*
McCaughrean, Geraldine 1951- *173*
  Earlier sketches in SATA *87, 139*
  See also CLR *38*
McCaughren, Tom 1936- *75*
McCauley, Adam 1965- *209*
  Earlier sketch in SATA *128*
McCay, (Zenas) Winsor 1869-1934 .... *134*
  Earlier sketch in SATA *41*
McClafferty, Carla Killough 1958- *137*
McClary, Jane Stevenson 1919-1990
  Obituary *64*
McCleery, Patsy R. 1925- *133*
  Earlier sketch in SATA *88*
McClelland, Susan *214*
McClements, George *196*
McClintock, Barbara 1955- *213*
  Earlier sketches in SATA *57, 95, 146*
McClintock, Marshall 1906-1967 .... *3*
McClintock, May Garelick
  See Garelick, May
McClintock, Mike
  See McClintock, Marshall
McClintock, Norah *178*
McClintock, Theodore 1902-1971 .... *14*

McClinton, Leon 1933- *11*
McCloskey, Kevin 1951- *79*
McCloskey, (John) Robert 1914-2003 .... *100*
  Obituary *146*
  Earlier sketches in SATA *2, 39*
  See also CLR *7*
McCloy, James F(loyd) 1941- *59*
McClung, Robert M(arshall) 1916- *135*
  Earlier sketches in SATA *2, 68*
  See also CLR *11*
  See also SAAS *15*
McClure, Gillian Mary 1948- *31*
McColley, Kevin 1961- *80*
  See also SAAS *23*
McConduit, Denise Walter 1950- *89*
McConnell, James Douglas Rutherford
  1915-1988 .... *40*
  Obituary *56*
McCord, Anne 1942- *41*
McCord, David (Thompson Watson)
  1897-1997 .... *18*
  Obituary *96*
  See also CLR *9*
McCord, Jean 1924- *34*
McCord, Pat Mauser
  See McCord, Patricia
McCord, Patricia 1943- *159*
  Earlier sketch in SATA *37*
McCord, Patricia Sue Rhoads Mauser
  See McCord, Patricia
McCormack, Caren McNelly *217*
McCormick, Brooks
  See Adams, William Taylor
McCormick, Dell J. 1892-1949 .... *19*
McCormick, (George) Donald (King)
  1911-1998 .... *14*
McCormick, Edith (Joan) 1934- *30*
McCormick, Kimberly A. 1960- *153*
McCormick, Patricia 1956- *181*
  Earlier sketch in SATA *128*
McCourt, Edward (Alexander) 1907-1972
  Obituary *28*
McCourt, Lisa 1964- *214*
  Earlier sketches in SATA *117, 159*
McCourt, Malachy 1931- *126*
McCoy, Glenn 1965- *212*
McCoy, Iola Fuller *3*
McCoy, J(oseph) J(erome) 1917- *8*
McCoy, Karen Kawamoto 1953- *82*
McCoy, Lois (Rich) 1941- *38*
McCrady, Lady 1951- *16*
McCrea, James (Craig, Jr.) 1920- *3*
McCrea, Ruth (Pirman) 1921- *3*
McCreigh, James
  See Pohl, Frederik
McCrumb, Sharyn 1948- *109*
McCue, Lisa 1959- *212*
  Earlier sketches in SATA *65, 177*
McCue, Lisa Emiline
  See McCue, Lisa
McCullen, Andrew
  See Arthur, Robert, (Jr.)
McCullers, Carson 1917-1967 .... *27*
McCullers, Lula Carson Smith
  See McCullers, Carson
McCulloch, Derek (Ivor Breashur) 1897-1967
  Obituary *29*
McCulloch, John Tyler
  See Burroughs, Edgar Rice
McCulloch, Sarah
  See Ure, Jean
McCullough, David 1933- *62*
McCullough, David Gaub
  See McCullough, David
McCullough, Frances Monson 1938- *8*
McCullough, Sharon Pierce 1943- *131*
McCully, Emily Arnold *210*
  See Arnold, Emily
McCune, Dan
  See Haas, Dorothy F.
McCunn, Ruthanne Lum 1946- *63*

McCurdy, Michael (Charles) 1942- *147*
  Earlier sketches in SATA *13, 82*
McCutcheon, Elsie (Mary Jackson) 1937- ... *60*
McCutcheon, John 1952- *97*
McDaniel, Becky Bring 1953- *61*
McDaniel, Lurlene 1944- *146*
  Earlier sketch in SATA *71*
McDaniels, Pellom III 1968- *121*
McDaniels, Preston 1952- *192*
McDearmon, Kay *20*
McDermott, Beverly Brodsky 1941- *11*
McDermott, Eleni *156*
McDermott, Gerald (Edward) 1941- *163*
  Earlier sketches in SATA *16, 74*
  See also CLR *9*
McDermott, Michael 1962- *76*
McDevitt, Jack 1935- *155*
  Earlier sketch in SATA *94*
McDevitt, John Charles
  See McDevitt, Jack
McDole, Carol
  See Farley, Carol (J.)
McDonald, Collin 1943- *79*
McDonald, Gerald D(oan) 1905-1970 .... *3*
McDonald, Jamie
  See Heide, Florence Parry
McDonald, Janet 1953-2007 .... *204*
  Earlier sketch in SATA *148*
McDonald, Jill (Masefield) 1927-1982 .... *13*
  Obituary *29*
McDonald, Joyce 1946- *164*
  Earlier sketch in SATA *101*
McDonald, Lucile Saunders 1898-1992 .... *10*
McDonald, Mary Ann 1956- *84*
McDonald, Megan 1958- *202*
  Autobiography Feature *151*
  Earlier sketches in SATA *67, 99, 148, 151*
  See also CLR *94*
McDonald, Meme 1954- *112*
McDonald, Mercedes 1956- *169*
  Earlier sketch in SATA *97*
McDonald, Rae A. 1952- *201*
McDonell, Chris 1960- *138*
McDonnell, Christine 1949- *115*
  Earlier sketch in SATA *34*
McDonnell, Flora (Mary) 1963- *146*
  Earlier sketch in SATA *90*
McDonnell, Kathleen 1947- *186*
McDonnell, Lois Eddy 1914-2001 .... *10*
McDonnell, Patrick 1956- *179*
McDonough, Yona Zeldis 1957- *73*
McDowell, Marilyn Taylor *217*
McElligott, Matt 1968- *196*
  Earlier sketch in SATA *135*
McElligott, Matthew
  See McElligott, Matt
McElmeel, Sharron L. 1942- *128*
McElmurry, Jill *198*
  Earlier sketch in SATA *159*
McElrath, William N. 1932- *65*
McElrath-Eslick, Lori 1960- *204*
  Earlier sketch in SATA *96*
McEntee, Dorothy (Layng) 1902- *37*
McEvoy, Anne *214*
McEwen, Katherine *183*
McEwen, Robert (Lindley) 1926-1980
  Obituary *23*
McFadden, Kevin Christopher
  See Pike, Christopher
McFall, Christie 1918- *12*
McFall, Gardner 1952- *183*
McFarlan, Donald M(aitland) 1915- *59*
McFarland, Henry "Hammer"
  See McFarland, Henry O.
McFarland, Henry O. 1934- *143*
McFarland, Kenton D(ean) 1920- *11*
McFarland, Martha
  See Smith-Ankrom, M. E.
McFarlane, Leslie 1902-1977 .... *100*
  Earlier sketches in SATA *31, 1, 65, 67*
  See also CLR *118*

McFarlane, Leslie Charles
  See McFarlane, Leslie
McFarlane, Peter 1940- *95*
McFarlane, Peter William
  See McFarlane, Peter
McFarlane, Sheryl P. 1954- *86*
McFarlane, Todd 1961- *117*
McGaw, Jessie Brewer 1913-1997 .... *10*
McGee, Barbara 1943- *6*
McGee, Marni *163*
McGhee, Alison 1960- *196*
McGhee, Alison R.
  See McGhee, Alison
McGhee, Holly M.
  See Durand, Hallie
McGiffin, (Lewis) Lee (Shaffer) 1908-1978 ... *1*
McGill, Alice *159*
McGill, Ormond 1913- *92*
McGinley, Jerry 1948- *116*
McGinley, Phyllis 1905-1978 .... *44*
  Obituary *24*
  Earlier sketch in SATA *2*
McGinnis, Lila S(prague) 1924- *44*
McGinty, Alice B. 1963- *202*
  Earlier sketch in SATA *134*
McGivern, Justin 1985- *129*
McGivern, Maureen Daly
  See Daly, Maureen
McGivern, Maureen Patricia Daly
  See Daly, Maureen
McGough, Elizabeth (Hemmes) 1934- *33*
McGovern, Ann 1930- *132*
  Earlier sketches in SATA *8, 69, 70*
  See also CLR *50*
  See also SAAS *17*
McGowen, Thomas E. 1927- *109*
  Earlier sketch in SATA *2*
McGowen, Tom
  See McGowen, Thomas E.
McGrady, Mike 1933- *6*
McGrath, Barbara Barbieri 1953- *169*
  Earlier sketch in SATA *108*
McGrath, Robin 1949- *121*
McGrath, Thomas (Matthew) 1916-1990 .... *41*
  Obituary *66*
McGraw, Eloise Jarvis 1915-2000 .... *67*
  Obituary *123*
  Earlier sketch in SATA *1*
  See also SAAS *6*
McGraw, William Corbin 1916-1999 .... *3*
McGreal, Elizabeth
  See Yates, Elizabeth
McGregor, Barbara 1959- *82*
McGregor, Craig 1933- *8*
McGregor, Iona 1929- *25*
McGrory, Anik *193*
McGuffey, Alexander Hamilton 1816-1896 . *60*
McGuigan, Mary Ann 1949- *106*
McGuire, Edna 1899- *13*
McGuire, Leslie (Sarah) 1945- *94*
  Brief entry *45*
  Earlier sketch in SATA *52*
McGuire, Robert *187*
McGuirk, Leslie (A.) 1960- *152*
McGurk, Slater
  See Roth, Arthur J(oseph)
McHargue, Georgess 1941- *77*
  Earlier sketch in SATA *4*
  See also CLR *2*
  See also SAAS *5*
McHenry, E.B. 1963(?)- *193*
McHugh, (Berit) Elisabet 1941- *55*
  Brief entry *44*
McIlvaine, Jane
  See McClary, Jane Stevenson
McIlwraith, Maureen Mollie Hunter
  See Hunter, Mollie
McInerney, Judith W(hitelock) 1945- *49*
  Brief entry *46*
McInerny, Ralph 1929-2010 .... *93*

McInerny, Ralph Matthew
  See McInerny, Ralph
McKaughan, Larry (Scott) 1941- *75*
McKay, Donald 1895- *45*
McKay, Hilary 1959- *208*
  Earlier sketches in SATA *92, 145*
  See also SAAS *23*
McKay, Hilary Jane
  See McKay, Hilary
McKay, Lawrence, Jr. 1948- *114*
McKay, Robert W. 1921- *15*
McKay, Sharon E. 1954- *165*
McKay, Simon
  See Nicole, Christopher (Robin)
McKean, Dave 1963- *197*
McKean, David Jeff
  See McKean, Dave
McKeating, Eileen 1957- *81*
McKee, David (John) 1935- *158*
  Earlier sketches in SATA *70, 107*
  See also CLR *38*
McKee, Tim 1970- *111*
McKeever, Marcia
  See Laird, Jean E(louise)
McKellar, Danica 1975- *213*
McKelvey, Carole A. 1942- *78*
McKelvy, Charles 1950- *124*
McKendrick, Melveena (Christine) 1941- *55*
McKendry, Joe 1972- *170*
McKenna, Colleen O'Shaughnessy 1948- .. *136*
  Earlier sketch in SATA *76*
McKenzie, Dorothy Clayton 1910-1981
  Obituary *28*
McKenzie, Ellen Kindt 1928- *80*
McKernan, Victoria 1957- *171*
McKie, Robin *112*
McKillip, Patricia A. 1948- *174*
  Earlier sketches in SATA *30, 80, 126*
McKillip, Patricia Anne
  See McKillip, Patricia A.
McKim, Audrey Margaret 1909-1999 .... *47*
McKimmie, Chris *194*
McKinley, Jennifer Carolyn Robin
  See McKinley, Robin
McKinley, Robin 1952- *195*
  Brief entry *32*
  Earlier sketches in SATA *50, 89, 130*
  See also CLR *127*
McKinney, Barbara Shaw 1951- *116*
McKinney, Nadine 1938- *91*
McKinty, Adrian *186*
McKissack, Fredrick L. 1939- *162*
  Brief entry *53*
  Earlier sketches in SATA *73, 117*
  See also CLR *55*
McKissack, Fredrick Lemuel
  See McKissack, Fredrick L.
McKissack, Patricia C. 1944- *195*
  Earlier sketches in SATA *51, 73, 117, 162*
  See also CLR *129*
McKissack, Patricia L'Ann Carwell
  See McKissack, Patricia C.
McKissack and McKissack
  See McKissack, Fredrick L.
  and McKissack, Patricia C.
McKown, Robin (?)-1976 .... *6*
McKy, Katie 1956- *184*
McLaren, Chesley *213*
McLaren, Clemence 1938- *158*
  Earlier sketch in SATA *105*
McLaughlin, Frank 1934- *73*
McLaughlin, Lauren *209*
McLaurin, Anne 1953- *27*
McLean, Andrew 1946- *172*
  Earlier sketch in SATA *113*
McLean, J. Sloan
  See Gillette, Virginia M(ary)
  and Wunsch, Josephine (McLean)
McLean, Jacqueline
  See Kolosov, Jacqueline
McLean, Janet 1946- *113*

McLean, Kathryn (Anderson) 1909-1966 .... *9*
McLean, Virginia Overton 1946- *90*
McLean-Carr, Carol 1948- *122*
McLeish, Kenneth 1940-1997 .... *35*
McLenighan, Valjean 1947- *46*
   Brief entry *40*
McLennan, Connie *171*
McLennan, Will
   See Wisler, G(ary) Clifton
McLeod, Bob 1951- *173*
McLeod, Chum 1955- *95*
McLeod, Emilie Warren 1926-1982 .... *23*
   Obituary *31*
McLeod, Kirsty
   See Hudson, (Margaret) Kirsty
McLeod, Margaret Vail
   See Holloway, Teresa (Bragunier)
McLerran, Alice 1933- *137*
   Earlier sketch in SATA *68*
McLimans, David 1949- *182*
McLoughlin, John C. 1949- *47*
McMahon, Bob 1956- *208*
McManus, Patrick F. 1933- *46*
McManus, Patrick Francis
   See McManus, Patrick F.
McMeekin, Clark
   See McMeekin, Isabel McLennan
McMeekin, Isabel McLennan 1895-1973 .... *3*
McMenemy, Sarah 1965- *156*
McMillan, Bruce 1947- *192*
   Earlier sketches in SATA *22, 70, 129*
   See also CLR *47*
McMillan, Naomi
   See Grimes, Nikki
McMorey, James L.
   See Moyer, Terry J.
McMorrow, Annalisa 1969- *104*
McMullan, Jim 1934- *150*
   Earlier sketch in SATA *87*
McMullan, K. H.
   See McMullan, Kate
McMullan, Kate 1947- *189*
   Brief entry *48*
   Earlier sketches in SATA *52, 87, 132*
McMullan, Kate Hall
   See McMullan, Kate
McMullan, Margaret 1960- *203*
McMurtrey, Martin A(loysias) 1921- *21*
McNabb, Linda 1963- *147*
McNair, Kate *3*
McNair, Sylvia 1924-2002 .... *74*
McNamara, Margaret C(raig) 1915-1981
   Obituary *24*
McNaught, Harry *32*
McNaughton, Colin 1951- *211*
   Earlier sketches in SATA *39, 92, 134*
   See also CLR *54*
McNaughton, Janet 1953- *162*
   Earlier sketch in SATA *110*
McNeal, Laura *194*
McNeal, Tom *194*
McNeely, Jeannette 1918- *25*
McNeer, May (Yonge) 1902-1994 .... *81*
   Earlier sketch in SATA *1*
McNeese, Tim 1953- *139*
McNeill, Janet
   See Alexander, Janet
McNicholas, Shelagh *191*
McNickle, D'Arcy 1904-1977
   Obituary *22*
McNickle, William D'Arcy
   See McNickle, D'Arcy
McNicoll, Sylvia (Marilyn) 1954- *113*
   See also CLR *99*
McNulty, Faith 1918-2005 .... *168*
   Earlier sketches in SATA *12, 84, 139*
McPhail, David 1940- *183*
   Brief entry *32*
   Earlier sketches in SATA *47, 81, 140*
McPhail, David M.
   See McPhail, David

McPhail, David Michael
   See McPhail, David
McPhee, Norma H. 1928- *95*
McPhee, Peter 1957- *214*
McPhee, Richard B(yron) 1934- *41*
McPherson, James M. 1936- *141*
   Earlier sketch in SATA *16*
McPherson, James Munro
   See McPherson, James M.
McQueen, Lucinda 1950- *58*
   Brief entry *48*
McQueen, Mildred Hark 1908-1978 .... *12*
McQuillan, Mary *200*
McRae, Russell (William) 1934- *63*
McShean, Gordon 1936- *41*
Mc Swigan, Marie 1907-1962 .... *24*
McTavish, Sandy
   See Eyerly, Jeannette
McVeity, Jen *148*
McVey, Vicki 1946- *80*
McVicker, Charles (Taggart) 1930- *39*
McVicker, Chuck
   See McVicker, Charles (Taggart)
McWhirter, A(lan) Ross 1925-1975 .... *37*
   Obituary *31*
McWhirter, Norris (Dewar) 1925-2004 .... *37*
McWilliams, Karen 1943- *65*
Mdurvwa, Hajara E. 1962- *92*
Meacham, Margaret 1952- *203*
   Earlier sketch in SATA *95*
Meachum, Virginia 1918- *133*
   Earlier sketch in SATA *87*
Mead, Alice 1952- *146*
   Earlier sketch in SATA *94*
Mead, Margaret 1901-1978
   Obituary *20*
Mead, Russell (M., Jr.) 1935- *10*
Mead, Stella (?)-1981
   Obituary *27*
Meade, Ellen
   See Roddick, Ellen
Meade, Holly *207*
Meade, Marion 1934- *127*
   Earlier sketch in SATA *23*
Meader, Stephen W(arren) 1892-1977 .... *1*
Meadmore, Susan
   See Sallis, Susan (Diana)
Meadow, Charles T(roub) 1929- *23*
Meadowcroft, Enid LaMonte
   See Wright, Enid Meadowcroft (LaMonte)
Meadows, Graham (W.) 1934- *161*
Meadows, Michelle *202*
Meaker, M. J.
   See Meaker, Marijane
Meaker, Marijane 1927- *160*
   Autobiography Feature *111*
   Earlier sketches in SATA *20, 61, 99*
   See also CLR *29*
   See also SAAS *1*
Meaker, Marijane Agnes
   See Meaker, Marijane
Means, Florence Crannell 1891-1980 .... *1*
   Obituary *25*
   See also CLR *56*
Mearian, Judy Frank 1936- *49*
Mebus, Scott 1974- *216*
Mecca, Judy Truesdell 1955- *127*
Mechling, Lauren 1978(?)- *194*
Mechling, Lauren 1978(?)- *194*
Mechner, Jordan 1964- *205*
Medary, Marjorie 1890-1980 .... *14*
Meddaugh, Susan 1944- *176*
   Earlier sketches in SATA *29, 84, 125*
Medearis, Angela Shelf 1956- *123*
   Earlier sketch in SATA *72*
Medearis, Mary 1915- *5*
Medina, Jane 1953- *167*
   Earlier sketch in SATA *122*
Medina, Meg 1963- *212*
Medina, Nico 1982- *193*
Medlicott, Mary 1946- *88*

Mee, Charles L., Jr. 1938- *72*
   Earlier sketch in SATA *8*
Meehl, Brian *204*
Meek, Jacklyn O'Hanlon 1933- *51*
   Brief entry *34*
Meek, S(terner St.) P(aul) 1894-1972
   Obituary *28*
Meeker, Clare Hodgson 1952- *96*
Meeker, Oden 1919(?)-1976 .... *14*
Meeker, Richard
   See Brown, Fornan
Meeks, Esther MacBain *1*
Meggs, Libby Phillips 1943- *130*
Mehdevi, Alexander (Sinclair) 1947- *7*
Mehdevi, Anne (Marie) Sinclair 1947- *8*
Meidell, Sherry 1951- *73*
Meier, Minta 1906- *55*
Meighan, Donald Charles 1929- *30*
Meigs, Cornelia Lynde 1884-1973 .... *6*
   See also CLR *55*
Meilach, Dona Z(weigoron) 1926- *34*
Meilman, Philip W(arren) 1951- *79*
Meinstereifel, Ronald L. 1960- *134*
Meisel, Paul *184*
Meister, Cari *204*
Melanson, Luc *198*
Melcher, Daniel 1912-1985
   Obituary *43*
Melcher, Frederic Gershom 1879-1963
   Obituary *22*
Melcher, Marguerite Fellows 1879-1969 ...... *10*
Meldrum, Christina *206*
Melendez, Francisco 1964- *72*
Melhuish, Eva *199*
Melin, Grace Hathaway 1892-1973 .... *10*
Mellersh, H(arold) E(dward) L(eslie)
   1897- *10*
Melling, David *186*
Melmed, Laura Krauss *212*
Melmoth, Sebastian
   See Wilde, Oscar
Melnikoff, Pamela (Rita) *97*
Meltzer, Amy 1968- *202*
Meltzer, Milton 1915-2009 .... *201*
   Autobiography Feature *124*
   Earlier sketches in SATA *1, 50, 80, 128*
   See also CLR *13*
   See also SAAS *1*
Melville, Anne
   See Potter, Margaret
Melville, Herman 1819-1891 .... *59*
Melwood, Mary
   See Lewis, E. M.
Melzack, Ronald 1929- *5*
Memling, Carl 1918-1969 .... *6*
Menchin, Scott *188*
Mendel, Jo
   See Bond, Gladys Baker
   and Gilbertson, Mildred Geiger
Mendelson, Steven T. 1958-1995 .... *86*
Mendelson-Stevens, Serita Deborah
   See Stevens, Serita
Mendes, Valerie 1939- *157*
Mendez, Raymond A. 1947- *66*
Mendez, Simon 1975- *215*
Mendonca, Susan
   See Smith, Susan Vernon
Mendoza, George 1934- *41*
   Brief entry *39*
   See also SAAS *7*
Menendez, Shirley (C.) 1937- *146*
Meng, Cece *194*
Meng, Heinz (Karl) 1924- *13*
Mennen, Ingrid 1954- *85*
Menotti, Gian Carlo 1911-2007 .... *29*
   Obituary *180*
Menuhin, Sir Yehudi 1916-1999 .... *40*
   Obituary *113*
Menville, Douglas 1935- *64*
Menzel, Barbara Jean 1946- *63*
Menzel, Peter 1948- *207*

Mercati, Cynthia 164
Mercati, Cynthia J.
  See Mercati, Cynthia
Mercer, Charles (Edward) 1917-1988 16
  Obituary 61
Mercer, Jessie 21
Mercer, Sienna 192
Meredith, Arnold
  See Hopkins, (Hector) Kenneth
Meredith, David William
  See Miers, Earl Schenck
Meringoff, Laurene Krasny
  See Brown, Laurene Krasny
Meriwether, Louise 1923- 52
  Brief entry 31
Merlin, Arthur
  See Blish, James
Merlin, Christina
  See Heaven, Constance (Christina)
Merriam, Eve 1916-1992 73
  Earlier sketches in SATA *3, 40*
  See also CLR *14*
Merrill, Jane 1946- 42
Merrill, Jane Merrill
  See Merrill, Jane
Merrill, Jean (Fairbanks) 1923- 82
  Earlier sketch in SATA *1*
  See also CLR *52*
Merrill, Phil
  See Merrill, Jane
Merriman, Alex
  See Silverberg, Robert
Merriman, Rachel 1971- 149
  Earlier sketch in SATA *98*
Merrit, Elizabeth
  See Goudge, Eileen
Merski, Patricia K.
  See Merski, P.K.
Merski, P.K. 172
Mertz, Barbara
  See Peters, Elizabeth
Mertz, Barbara Gross
  See Peters, Elizabeth
Merveille, David 200
Merz, Jennifer J. 196
Meschel, Susan V. 1936- 83
Meserve, Jessica 211
Messenger, Charles (Rynd Milles) 1942- 59
Messick, Dale 1906-2005 64
  Brief entry 48
Messier, Claire 1956- 103
Messieres, Nicole de
  See de Messieres, Nicole
Messinger, Carla 198
Messmer, Otto 1892(?)-1983 37
Mesta, Gabriel
  See Moesta, Rebecca
Metaxas, Eric 1963- 211
Metcalf, Doris H(unter) 91
Metcalf, Suzanne
  See Baum, L. Frank
Metos, Thomas H(arry) 1932- 37
Metter, Bert(ram Milton) 1927- 56
Metzenthen, David 1958- 167
  Earlier sketch in SATA *106*
Meunier, Brian 1954- 195
Meyer, Barbara 1939- 77
Meyer, Carolyn 1935- 142
  Autobiography Feature 142
  Earlier sketches in SATA *9, 70, 118*
  See also SAAS *9*
Meyer, Carolyn Mae
  See Meyer, Carolyn
Meyer, Edith Patterson 1895-1993 5
Meyer, F(ranklyn) E(dward) 1932- 9
Meyer, Jean Shepherd 11
Meyer, Jerome Sydney 1895-1975 3
  Obituary 25
Meyer, June
  See Jordan, June
Meyer, Kerstin 1966- 190

Meyer, L. A.
  See Meyer, Louis A(lbert), Jr.
Meyer, Louis A(lbert), Jr. 1942- 144
  Earlier sketch in SATA *12*
Meyer, Renate 1930- 6
Meyer, Stephenie 1973- 193
  See also CLR *142*
Meyer, Susan E. 1940- 64
Meyerhoff, Jenny 1972- 208
Meyers, Susan 1942- 164
  Earlier sketches in SATA *19, 108*
Meynell, Laurence Walter 1899-1989
  Obituary 61
Meynier, Yvonne (Pollet) 1908- 14
Mezey, Robert 1935- 33
Micale, Albert 1913- 22
Michael, James
  See Scagnetti, Jack
Michael, Jan 1947- 216
Michael, Livi 1960- 172
Michael, Manfred
  See Winterfeld, Henry
Michael, Olivia
  See Michael, Livi
Michaelis, Antonia 1979- 215
Michaels, Barbara
  See Peters, Elizabeth
Michaels, Jamie 195
Michaels, Joanne Louise
  See Teitelbaum, Michael
Michaels, Kristin
  See Williams, Jeanne
Michaels, Molly
  See Untermeyer, Louis
Michaels, Neal
  See Teitelbaum, Michael
Michaels, Rune 194
Michaels, Ski
  See Pellowski, Michael (Joseph)
Michaels, Steve 1955- 71
Michaels, William M. 1917- 77
Michalak, Jamie 1973- 217
Michel, Anna 1943- 49
  Brief entry 40
Michel, Francois 1948- 82
Michelin, Linda 183
Michelson, Richard 198
  Earlier sketch in SATA *173*
Micich, Paul 74
Mickelson, Scott 1963- 213
Micklish, Rita 1931- 12
Micklos, John, Jr. 1956- 173
  Earlier sketch in SATA *129*
Micklos J., John, Jr. 1956-
  See Micklos, John, Jr.
Micucci, Charles (Patrick, Jr.) 1959- 144
  Earlier sketch in SATA *82*
Middleton, Haydn 1955- 152
  Earlier sketch in SATA *85*
Miers, Earl Schenck 1910-1972 1
  Obituary 26
Migdale, Lawrence 1951- 89
Miglio, Paige 1966- 201
Mikaelsen, Ben 1952- 173
  Earlier sketches in SATA *73, 107*
Mikaelsen, Benjamin John
  See Mikaelsen, Ben
Miklowitz, Gloria D. 1927- 129
  Earlier sketches in SATA *4, 68*
  See also SAAS *17*
Mikolaycak, Charles 1937-1993 78
  Obituary 75
  Earlier sketch in SATA *9*
  See also SAAS *4*
Mild, Warren (Paul) 1922- 41
Milelli, Pascal 1965- 135
Miles, Betty 1928- 78
  Earlier sketch in SATA *8*
  See also SAAS *9*
Miles, Miska
  See Martin, Patricia Miles

Miles, (Mary) Patricia 1930- 29
Miles, Patricia A.
  See Martin, Patricia Miles
Miles, Victoria 1966- 188
Milgrim, David 187
  Earlier sketch in SATA *158*
Milgrom, Harry 1912-1978 25
Milhous, Katherine 1894-1977 15
Milich, Zoran 174
Milios, Rita 1949- 79
Militant
  See Sandburg, Carl
Millais, Raoul 1901- 77
Millar, Barbara F. 1924- 12
Millar, Margaret (Ellis Sturm) 1915-1994 61
  Obituary 79
Millard, Glenda 203
Millard, Kerry 204
Millbank, Captain H. R.
  See Ellis, Edward S.
Millen, C(ynthia) M. 1955- 114
Miller, Albert G(riffith) 1905-1982 12
  Obituary 31
Miller, Alice Ann 1958- 150
Miller, Alice P(atricia McCarthy) 22
Miller, Allan 1978- 216
Miller, Christopher 1976- 215
Miller, Debbie 1951- 160
  Earlier sketch in SATA *103*
Miller, Debbie S.
  See Miller, Debbie
Miller, Deborah Uchill 1944- 61
Miller, Don 1923- 15
Miller, Doris R.
  See Mosesson, Gloria R(ubin)
Miller, Eddie
  See Miller, Edward
Miller, Edna Anita 1920- 29
Miller, Edward 1905-1974 8
Miller, Edward 1964- 183
Miller, Elizabeth 1933- 41
Miller, Ellanita 1957- 87
Miller, Eugene 1925- 33
Miller, Frances A. 1937- 52
  Brief entry 46
Miller, Heather Lynn 1971- 214
Miller, Helen M(arkley) -1984 5
Miller, Helen Topping 1884-1960
  Obituary 29
Miller, Jane (Judith) 1925-1989 15
Miller, Jewel 1956- 73
Miller, John
  See Samachson, Joseph
Miller, Judi 117
Miller, Karen 1949- 210
Miller, Karen Hokanson
  See Miller, Karen
Miller, Kate 1948- 193
Miller, Kirsten 1973- 185
Miller, Louise (Rolfe) 1940- 76
Miller, M. L. 85
Miller, Madge 1918- 63
Miller, Margaret J.
  See Dale, Margaret J(essy) Miller
Miller, Marilyn (Jean) 1925- 33
Miller, Marvin 65
Miller, Mary
  See Northcott, (William) Cecil
Miller, Mary Beth 1942- 9
Miller, Mary Beth 1964- 185
Miller, Maryann 1943- 73
Miller, Natalie 1917-1976 35
Miller, Pat 1951- 214
Miller, Robert H. 1944- 91
Miller, Ron 1947- 185
Miller, Ruth White
  See White, Ruth
Miller, Sandra
  See Miller, Sandy
Miller, Sandra Peden
  See Miller, Sandy

Miller, Sandy 1948- *41*
  Brief entry *35*
Miller, Sarah 1969- *175*
Miller, Virginia
  See Austin, Virginia
Miller, William R. 1959- *116*
Miller Brothers
  See Miller, Allan
Milligan, Bryce 1953- *170*
Milligan, Spike
  See Milligan, Terence Alan
Milligan, Terence Alan 1918-2002 .... *29*
  Obituary *134*
  See also CLR 92
Millington, Ada
  See Deyneka, Anita
Millman, Isaac 1933- *140*
Mills, Adam
  See Stanley, George Edward
Mills, Claudia 1954- *191*
  Brief entry *41*
  Earlier sketches in SATA *44, 89, 145*
Mills, Elaine (Rosemary) 1941- *72*
Mills, G. Riley *196*
Mills, Joyce C. 1944- *102*
Mills, Judith Christine 1956- *130*
Mills, Yaroslava Surmach 1925- *35*
Millspaugh, Ben P. 1936- *77*
Millstead, Thomas E. *30*
Millward, Gwen *202*
Milne, A. A. 1882-1956 .... *100*
  See also YABC *1*
  See also CLR *108*
Milne, Alan Alexander
  See Milne, A. A.
Milne, Lorus J. *5*
  See also CLR *22*
  See also SAAS *18*
Milne, Margery *5*
  See also CLR *22*
  See also SAAS *18*
Milne, Terry
  See Milne, Theresa Ann
Milne, Theresa Ann 1964- *84*
Milnes, Irma McDonough 1924- *101*
Milonas, Rolf
  See Myller, Rolf
Milone, Karen
  See Dugan, Karen
Milone-Dugan, Karen
  See Dugan, Karen
Milord, Susan 1954- *200*
  Earlier sketches in SATA *74, 147*
Milotte, Alfred G(eorge) 1904-1989 .... *11*
  Obituary *62*
Milstein, Linda 1954- *80*
Milton, Ann *134*
Milton, Hilary (Herbert) 1920- *23*
Milton, John R(onald) 1924- *24*
Milton, Joyce 1946- *101*
  Brief entry *41*
  Earlier sketch in SATA *52*
Milusich, Janice *216*
Milverton, Charles A.
  See Penzler, Otto
Milway, Alex 1978- *215*
Milway, Katie Smith 1960- *203*
Minahan, John A. 1956- *92*
Minar, Barbra (Goodyear) 1940- *79*
Minard, Rosemary 1939- *63*
Minarik, Else Holmelund 1920- *127*
  Earlier sketch in SATA *15*
  See also CLR *33*
Miner, Jane Claypool 1933- *103*
  Brief entry *37*
  Earlier sketch in SATA *38*
Miner, Lewis S. 1909-1971 .... *11*
Mines, Jeanette 1948- *61*
Mines, Jeanette Marie
  See Mines, Jeanette

Minier, Nelson
  See Stoutenburg, Adrien (Pearl)
Minnitt, Ronda Jacqueline
  See Armitage, David
Minor, Wendell 1944- *199*
  Earlier sketches in SATA *78, 109, 164*
Minter, Daniel 1961- *176*
Mintonye, Grace *4*
Miranda, Anne 1954- *109*
  Earlier sketch in SATA *71*
Miranda, Inaki 1983(?)- *207*
Mirocha, Paul *192*
Mirsky, Jeannette 1903-1987 .... *8*
  Obituary *51*
Mirsky, Reba Paeff 1902-1966 .... *1*
Misako Rocks! *192*
Mishica, Clare 1960- *91*
Miskovits, Christine 1939- *10*
Miss Frances
  See Horwich, Frances R(appaport)
Miss Read
  See Saint, Dora Jessie
Mister Rogers
  See Rogers, Fred McFeely
Mitchard, Jacquelyn 1956- *168*
  Earlier sketch in SATA *98*
Mitchell, Adrian 1932-2008 .... *166*
  Obituary *200*
  Earlier sketch in SATA *104*
Mitchell, Allison
  See Griffin, W.E.B.
Mitchell, Betty Jo
  See Mitchell, B.J.
Mitchell, B.J. 1931- *120*
Mitchell, Clyde
  See Ellison, Harlan
  and Silverberg, Robert
Mitchell, Cynthia 1922- *29*
Mitchell, (Sibyl) Elyne (Keith) 1913- *10*
Mitchell, Gladys (Maude Winifred)
  1901-1983 .... *46*
  Obituary *35*
Mitchell, Jay
  See Roberson, Jennifer
Mitchell, Joyce Slayton 1933- *142*
  Brief entry *43*
  Earlier sketch in SATA *46*
Mitchell, K. L.
  See Lamb, Elizabeth Searle
Mitchell, Kathy 1948- *59*
Mitchell, Lori 1961- *128*
Mitchell, Margaree King 1953- *84*
Mitchell, Marianne 1947- *145*
Mitchell, Rhonda *89*
Mitchell, Saundra 1974(?)- *217*
Mitchell, Stephen 1943- *199*
Mitchell, Susan
  See Mitchell, Susan K.
Mitchell, Susan K. 1972- *210*
Mitchell, Todd 1974- *191*
Mitchell, Yvonne 1925-1979
  Obituary *24*
Mitchelson, Mitch
  See Mitchelson, Peter Richard
Mitchelson, Peter Richard 1950- *104*
Mitchison, Naomi (Margaret Haldane)
  1897-1999 .... *24*
  Obituary *112*
Mitchnik, Helen 1901-1982 .... *41*
  Brief entry *35*
Mitchum, Hank
  See Knott, William C(ecil, Jr.)
  and Murray, Stuart A. P.
  and Newton, D(wight) B(ennett)
  and Sherman, Jory (Tecumseh)
Mitgutsch, Ali 1935- *76*
Mitsuhashi, Yoko *45*
  Brief entry *33*
Mitton, Jacqueline 1948- *162*
  Earlier sketches in SATA *66, 115*
Mitton, Simon 1946- *66*

Mitton, Tony 1951- *203*
  Earlier sketches in SATA *104, 149*
Miura, Taro 1968- *181*
Mizner, Elizabeth Howard 1907- *27*
Mizumura, Kazue *18*
Mlynowski, Sarah 1977(?)- *180*
Mobin-Uddin, Asma *216*
  Earlier sketch in SATA *172*
Mobley, Joe A. 1945- *91*
Moche, Dinah (Rachel) L(evine) 1936- *44*
  Brief entry *40*
Mochi, Ugo (A.) 1889-1977 .... *38*
Mochizuki, Ken 1954- *146*
  Earlier sketch in SATA *81*
  See also SAAS *22*
Modarressi, Mitra 1967- *200*
  Earlier sketch in SATA *126*
Modell, Frank B. 1917- *39*
  Brief entry *36*
Modesitt, Jeanne 1953- *217*
  Earlier sketches in SATA *92, 143*
Modesitt, L.E., Jr. 1943- *164*
  Earlier sketch in SATA *91*
Modesitt, Leland Exton, Jr.
  See Modesitt, L.E., Jr.
Modrell, Dolores 1933- *72*
Moe, Barbara 1937- *20*
Moe, Jorgen (Ingebretsen) 1813-1882
  See CLR *104*
Moed-Kass, Pnina *169*
Moerbeek, Kees 1955- *98*
Moeri, Louise 1924- *93*
  Earlier sketch in SATA *24*
  See also SAAS *10*
Moesta, Rebecca 1956- *182*
Moffett, Jami 1952- *84*
Moffett, Mark W. 1957(?)- *203*
Moffett, Martha (Leatherwood) 1934- *8*
Mogensen, Suzanne A(ncher) 1946- *129*
Mohammed, Khadra *197*
Mohn, Peter B(urnet) 1934- *28*
Mohn, Viola Kohl 1914- *8*
Mohr, Nicholasa 1938- *97*
  Autobiography Feature *113*
  Earlier sketch in SATA *8*
  See also CLR *22*
  See also SAAS *8*
Mok, Esther 1953- *93*
Molan, Christine 1943- *84*
Molarsky, Osmond 1909- *16*
Moldon, Peter L(eonard) 1937- *49*
Mole, John 1941- *103*
  Earlier sketch in SATA *36*
  See also CLR *61*
Molesworth, Mary Louisa 1839-1921 .... *98*
Molin, Charles
  See Mayne, William
Molina, Silvia 1946- *97*
Molk, Laurel 1957- *162*
  Earlier sketch in SATA *92*
Mollel, Tololwa M. 1952- *88*
Molloy, Anne Baker 1907-1999 .... *32*
Molloy, Michael (John) 1940- *162*
Molloy, Paul (George) 1924- *5*
Moloney, James 1954- *202*
  Autobiography Feature *144*
  Earlier sketches in SATA *94, 144*
Molski, Carol *215*
Momaday, N. Scott 1934- *48*
  Brief entry *30*
Momaday, Navarre Scott
  See Momaday, N. Scott
Monaco, Octavia 1963- *169*
Monagle, Bernie 1957- *121*
Moncure, Jane Belk 1926- *23*
Monjo, F(erdinand) N(icholas III)
  1924-1978 .... *16*
  See also CLR *2*
Monk, Isabell 1952- *136*
Monks, Lydia *189*

Monroe, Lyle
 See Heinlein, Robert A.
Monroe, Marion
 See Cox, Marion Monroe
Monroy, Manuel 1970- *196*
Monsell, Helen Albee 1895-1971 .... *24*
Monson-Burton, Marianne 1975- *139*
Montana, Bob 1920-1975
 Obituary *21*
Montanari, Eva 1977- *209*
Montecalvo, Janet *177*
Montenegro, Laura Nyman 1953- *95*
Montero, Gloria 1933- *109*
Montes, Marisa 1951- *144*
Montgomerie, Norah (Mary) 1913- *26*
Montgomery, Constance
 See Cappel, Constance
Montgomery, Elizabeth
 See Julesberg, Elizabeth Rider Montgomery
Montgomery, Elizabeth Rider
 See Julesberg, Elizabeth Rider Montgomery
Montgomery, Hugh (Edward) 1962- *146*
Montgomery, L. M. 1874-1942 .... *100*
 See also YABC *1*
 See also CLR *145*
Montgomery, Lucy Maud
 See Montgomery, L. M.
Montgomery, Michael G. 1952- *208*
Montgomery, Raymond A. (Jr.) 1936- *39*
Montgomery, Rutherford George 1894-1985 . *3*
Montgomery, Sy 1958- *184*
 Autobiography Feature *132*
 Earlier sketches in SATA *114, 132*
Montgomery, Vivian *36*
Monthei, Betty *179*
Montijo, Rhode *179*
Montileaux, Donald F. 1948- *183*
Montpetit, Charles 1958- *101*
Montresor, Beni 1926-2001 .... *38*
 Earlier sketch in SATA *3*
 See also SAAS *4*
Montserrat, Pep *181*
Monty Python
 See Chapman, Graham
 and Cleese, John (Marwood)
 and Gilliam, Terry
 and Idle, Eric
 and Jones, Terence Graham Parry
 and Palin, Michael
Moodie, Craig 1956- *172*
Moodie, Fiona 1952- *133*
Moody, Minerva
 See Alcott, Louisa May
Moody, Ralph Owen 1898-1982 .... *1*
Moon, Carl 1879(?)-1948 .... *25*
Moon, Grace (Purdie) 1877(?)-1947 .... *25*
Moon, Lily
 See Warnes, Tim
Moon, Nicola 1952- *147*
 Earlier sketch in SATA *96*
Moon, Pat 1946- *113*
Moon, Sheila 1910-1991 .... *5*
 Obituary *114*
Moon, Sheila Elizabeth
 See Moon, Sheila
Mooney, Bel 1946- *95*
Mooney, Bill 1936- *122*
Mooney, Elizabeth C(omstock) 1918-1986
 Obituary *48*
Mooney, William
 See Mooney, Bill
Moor, Emily
 See Deming, Richard
Moorcock, Michael 1939- *166*
 Earlier sketch in SATA *93*
Moorcock, Michael John
 See Moorcock, Michael
Moorcock, Michael John
 See Moorcock, Michael
Moore, Anne Carroll 1871-1961 .... *13*

Moore, Cheri
 See Ladd, Cheryl (Jean)
Moore, Clement Clarke 1779-1863 .... *18*
Moore, Cyd 1957- *186*
 Earlier sketches in SATA *83, 133*
Moore, Don W. 1905(?)-1986
 Obituary *48*
Moore, Elaine 1944- *86*
Moore, Eva 1942- *103*
 Earlier sketch in SATA *20*
Moore, Ishbel (Lindsay) 1954- *140*
Moore, Jack (William) 1941- *46*
 Brief entry *32*
Moore, Janet Gaylord 1905-1992 .... *18*
Moore, Jim 1946- *42*
Moore, John Travers 1908- *12*
Moore, Lilian 1909-2004 .... *137*
 Obituary *155*
 Earlier sketch in SATA *52*
 See also CLR *15*
Moore, Liz
 See Moore, M. Elizabeth
Moore, M. Elizabeth 1959- *156*
Moore, Margaret R(umberger) 1903- *12*
Moore, Margie *176*
Moore, Marianne 1887-1972 .... *20*
Moore, Marianne Craig
 See Moore, Marianne
Moore, Patrick (Alfred Caldwell) 1923- *49*
 Brief entry *39*
 See also SAAS *8*
Moore, Patrick 1959- *184*
Moore, Perry *193*
Moore, Peter 1963- *175*
Moore, Peter G.
 See Moore, Peter
Moore, Raina 1970- *212*
Moore, Ray (S.) 1905(?)-1984
 Obituary *37*
Moore, Regina
 See Dunne, Mary Collins
Moore, Rosalie (Gertrude) 1910-2001 .... *9*
Moore, Ruth (Ellen) 1908-1989 .... *23*
Moore, Ruth Nulton 1923- *38*
Moore, S(arah) E. *23*
Moore, Sarah Margaret
 See Hodges, Margaret
Moore, Stephanie Perry 1969(?)- *214*
Moore, Tara 1950- *61*
Moore, Yvette 1958- *154*
 Earlier sketches in SATA *69, 70*
Moores, Dick
 See Moores, Richard (Arnold)
Moores, Richard (Arnold) 1909-1986
 Obituary *48*
Mooser, Stephen 1941- *75*
 Earlier sketch in SATA *28*
Mora, Francisco X(avier) 1952- *90*
Mora, Pat 1942- *186*
 Earlier sketches in SATA *92, 134*
 See also CLR *58*
Mora, Patricia
 See Mora, Pat
Morais, Flavio *207*
Morales, Yuyi *180*
 Earlier sketch in SATA *154*
Moran, Tom 1943- *60*
Moranville, Sharelle Byars *196*
 Earlier sketch in SATA *152*
Moray Williams, Ursula 1911-2006 .... *3*
 Obituary *177*
 See also SAAS *9*
Morden, Simon 1966(?)- *211*
Mordvinoff, Nicolas 1911-1973 .... *17*
More, Caroline
 See Cone, Molly (Lamken)
 and Strachan, Margaret Pitcairn
Moreno, Rene King *190*
Moreton, Andrew Esq.
 See Defoe, Daniel

Morey, Charles
 See Fletcher, Helen Jill
Morey, Walt(er Nelson) 1907-1992 .... *51*
 Obituary *70*
 Earlier sketch in SATA *3*
 See also SAAS *9*
Morgan, Alfred P(owell) 1889-1972 .... *33*
Morgan, Alison (Mary) 1930- *85*
 Earlier sketch in SATA *30*
Morgan, Anne 1954- *121*
Morgan, Christopher 1956- *199*
Morgan, Clay 1950- *198*
Morgan, Douglas
 See Macdonald, James D.
Morgan, Ellen
 See Bumstead, Kathleen Mary
Morgan, Geoffrey 1916- *46*
Morgan, Helen (Gertrude Louise)
 1921-1990 .... *29*
Morgan, Jane
 See Cooper, James Fenimore
 and Franklin, Jane (Morgan)
 and Moren, Sally M(oore)
Morgan, Lenore H. 1908-1976 .... *8*
Morgan, Mary 1957- *213*
 Earlier sketches in SATA *81, 114*
Morgan, McKayla
 See Basile, Gloria Vitanza
Morgan, Michaela
 See Basile, Gloria Vitanza
Morgan, Nicola 1961- *161*
Morgan, Nina 1953- *110*
Morgan, Pierr 1952- *122*
 Earlier sketch in SATA *77*
Morgan, Robin (Evonne) 1941- *80*
Morgan, Roxanne
 See Gentle, Mary
Morgan, Sarah (Nicola) 1959- *68*
Morgan, Shirley
 See Kiepper, Shirley Morgan
Morgan, Stacy T(owle) 1959- *104*
Morgan, Stevie
 See Davies, Nicola
Morgan, Tom 1942- *42*
Morgan, Wendy
 See Staub, Wendy Corsi
Morgan-Vanroyen, Mary
 See Morgan, Mary
Morgenstern, Susie Hoch 1945- *133*
Mori, Hana 1909-1990(?) *88*
Mori, Kyoko 1957- *122*
 Autobiography Feature *126*
 See also CLR *64*
 See also SAAS *26*
Moriarty, Jaclyn 1968- *162*
Moriarty, William J. 1930- *127*
Morice, Dave 1946- *93*
Morin, Isobel V. 1928- *110*
Morine, Hoder
 See Conroy, John Wesley
Morley, Taia *199*
Morley, Wilfred Owen
 See Lowndes, Robert A(ugustine) W(ard)
Morningstar, Mildred (Whaley) 1912-1997 .. *61*
 Obituary *114*
Morozumi, Atsuko *217*
 Earlier sketch in SATA *110*
Morpurgo, Michael 1943- *184*
 Earlier sketches in SATA *93, 143*
 See also CLR *51*
Morrah, Dave
 See Morrah, David Wardlaw, Jr.
Morrah, David Wardlaw, Jr. 1914-1991 .... *10*
Morreale-de la Garza, Phyllis
 See De la Garza, Phyllis
Morressy, John 1930-2006 .... *23*
Morrill, Leslie H(olt) 1934-2003 .... *48*
 Brief entry *33*
 Obituary *148*
 See also SAAS *22*
Morris, Carla *210*

Morris, Carla D.
    See Morris, Carla
Morris, Chris(topher Crosby) 1946- 66
Morris, Deborah 1956- 91
Morris, Desmond 1928- 14
Morris, Desmond John
    See Morris, Desmond
Morris, Don 1954- 83
Morris, Gerald 1963- 207
    Earlier sketches in SATA *107, 150*
Morris, Gerald Paul
    See Morris, Gerald
Morris, Gilbert (Leslie) 1929- 104
Morris, Jackie 202
    Earlier sketch in SATA *151*
Morris, Janet (Ellen) 1946- 66
Morris, Jay
    See Tatham, Julie Campbell
Morris, (Margaret) Jean 1924- 98
Morris, Jeffrey
    See Morris, Jeffrey Brandon
Morris, Jeffrey B.
    See Morris, Jeffrey Brandon
Morris, Jeffrey Brandon 1941- 92
Morris, Jennifer E. 1969- 179
Morris, Jill 1936- 165
    Earlier sketch in SATA *119*
Morris, Juddi 85
Morris, Judy K. 1936- 61
Morris, Oradel Nolen 128
Morris, Robert A(da) 1933- 7
Morris, William 1913-1994 29
Morrison, Bill 1935- 66
    Brief entry 37
Morrison, Chloe Anthony Wofford
    See Morrison, Toni
Morrison, Dorothy Nafus 29
Morrison, Frank 1971- 185
Morrison, Gordon 1944- 183
    Earlier sketches in SATA *87, 128*
Morrison, Joan 1922- 65
Morrison, Lillian 1917- 108
    Earlier sketch in SATA *3*
Morrison, Lucile Phillips 1896- 17
Morrison, Martha A. 1948- 77
Morrison, Meighan 1966- 90
Morrison, P.R. 196
Morrison, Richard
    See Lowndes, Robert A(ugustine) W(ard)
Morrison, Robert
    See Lowndes, Robert A(ugustine) W(ard)
Morrison, Roberta
    See Webb, Jean Francis (III)
Morrison, Susan Dudley
    See Gold, Susan Dudley
Morrison, Taylor 1971- 187
    Earlier sketches in SATA *95, 159*
Morrison, Toni 1931- 144
    Earlier sketch in SATA *57*
    See also CLR *99*
Morrison, Velma Ford 1909- 21
Morrison, Wilbur Howard 1915- 64
Morrison, William
    See Samachson, Joseph
Morriss, James E(dward) 1932- 8
Morrissey, Dean 183
Morrow, Barbara Olenyik 1952- 167
Morrow, Betty
    See Bacon, Elizabeth
Morse, C. Scott
    See Morse, Scott
Morse, Carol
    See Yeakley, Marjory Hall
Morse, C.S.
    See Morse, Scott
Morse, Dorothy B(ayley) 1906-1979
    Obituary 24
Morse, Flo 1921- 30
Morse, Scott 1973- 200
Morse, Tony 1953- 129

Mort, Vivian
    See Cromie, Alice Hamilton
Mortensen, Denise Dowling 179
Mortimer, Anne 1958- 206
    Earlier sketch in SATA *116*
Mortimer, Mary H.
    See Coury, Louise Andree
Morton, Alexandra (Hubbard) 1957- 144
Morton, Anthony
    See Arthur, Robert, (Jr.)
Morton, Christine
    See Morton-Shaw, Christine
Morton, Jane 1931- 50
Morton, Joseph C. 1932- 156
Morton, Lee Jack, Jr. 1928- 32
Morton, Miriam 1918(?)-1985 9
    Obituary 46
Morton-Shaw, Christine 1957- 211
Mosatche, Harriet 1949- 122
Mosatche, Harriet S.
    See Mosatche, Harriet
Moscow, Alvin 1925- 3
Mosel, Arlene (Tichy) 1921-1996 7
Moseley, James W(illett) 1931- 139
Moseng, Elisabeth 1967- 90
Moser, Barry 1940- 185
    Earlier sketches in SATA *56, 79, 138*
    See also CLR *49*
    See also SAAS *15*
Moser, Don(ald Bruce) 1932- 31
Moser, Laura 194
Moser, Lisa 192
Moses, Sheila P. 1961- 168
Moses, Will 1956- 178
    Earlier sketch in SATA *120*
Mosesson, Gloria R(ubin) 24
Mosher, Richard 1949- 120
Moskin, Marietta D(unston) 1928- 23
Moskof, Martin Stephen 1930- 27
Mosley, Francis 1957- 57
Moss, Don(ald) 1920- 11
Moss, Elaine (Dora) 1924- 57
    Brief entry 31
Moss, Jeff(rey) 1942-1998 73
    Obituary 106
Moss, Marissa 1959- 216
    Earlier sketches in SATA *71, 104, 163*
    See also CLR *134*
Moss, Miriam 1955- 202
    Earlier sketches in SATA *76, 140*
Moss, Thylias 1954- 108
Moss, Thylias Rebecca Brasier
    See Moss, Thylias
Most, Bernard 1937- 134
    Brief entry 40
    Earlier sketches in SATA *48, 91*
Mosz, Gosia 1972- 194
Mott, Evelyn Clarke 1962- 133
    Earlier sketch in SATA *75*
Motz, Lloyd 1909-2004 20
Mould, Chris 205
Mould, Edwin
    See Whitlock, Ralph
Moulton, Mark Kimball 212
Mouly, Francoise 155
Mountain, Robert
    See Montgomery, Raymond A. (Jr.)
Mountfield, David
    See Grant, Neil
Mourlevat, Jean-Claude 1952- 187
Mourning, Tuesday 206
Moussard, Jacqueline 1924- 24
Mowat, Claire 1933- 123
Mowat, Claire Angel Wheeler
    See Mowat, Claire
Mowat, Farley 1921- 55
    Earlier sketch in SATA *3*
    See also CLR *20*
Mowat, Farley McGill
    See Mowat, Farley
Mowll, Joshua 1970(?)- 188

Mowry, Jess 1960- 131
    Autobiography Feature 131
    Earlier sketch in SATA *109*
    See also CLR *65*
Moxley, Sheila 1966- 96
Moyer, Terry J. 1937- 94
Moyes, Patricia
    See Haszard, Patricia Moyes
Moyler, Alan (Frank Powell) 1926- 36
Mozelle, Shirley 179
Mozley, Charles 1915- 43
    Brief entry 32
Mphahlele, Es'kia 1919-2008 119
    Obituary 198
Mphahlele, Ezekiel
    See Mphahlele, Es'kia
Mphahlele, Zeke
    See Mphahlele, Es'kia
Mr. McGillicuddy
    See Abisch, Roslyn Kroop
Mr. Sniff
    See Abisch, Roslyn Kroop
Mr. Tivil
    See Lorkowski, Thomas V(incent)
Mr. Wizard
    See Herbert, Don
Mrs. Fairstar
    See Horne, Richard Henry Hengist
Muchamore, Robert 1972- 175
Muchmore, Jo Ann 1937- 103
Mude, O.
    See Gorey, Edward (St. John)
Mudgeon, Apeman
    See Mitchell, Adrian
Mueller, Jorg 1942- 67
    See also CLR *43*
Mueller, Miranda R. 201
Mueller, Virginia 1924- 28
Muggs
    See Watkins, Lois
Muir, Diana
    See Appelbaum, Diana Muir Karter
Muir, Frank (Herbert) 1920-1998 30
Muir, Helen 1937- 65
Mukerji, Dhan Gopal 1890-1936 40
    See also CLR *10*
Mulcahy, Lucille Burnett 12
Mulford, Philippa G. 1948- 112
    Earlier sketch in SATA *43*
Mulford, Philippa Greene
    See Mulford, Philippa G.
Mulgan, Catherine 1931- 24
Mulila, Vigad G.
    See Maillu, David G(ian)
Mull, Brandon 1974- 190
Mullen, Michael 1937- 122
Muller, Billex
    See Ellis, Edward S.
Muller, Birte 1973- 214
Muller, Jorg
    See Mueller, Jorg
Muller, (Lester) Robin 1953- 86
Mullin, Caryl Cude 1969- 130
Mullins, Edward S(wift) 1922- 10
Mullins, Hilary 1962- 84
Mulock, Dinah Maria
    See Craik, Dinah Maria (Mulock)
Mulvihill, William Patrick 1923- 8
Mumford, Ruth
    See Dallas, Ruth
Mumy, Bill 1954- 112
Mun
    See Leaf, (Wilbur) Munro
Munari, Bruno 1907-1998 15
    See also CLR *9*
Munce, Ruth Hill 1898- 12
Mundy, Simon 1954- 64
Mundy, Simon Andrew James Hainault
    See Mundy, Simon
Munger, Nancy 170
Munowitz, Ken 1935-1977 14

Munoz, Claudio 208
Munoz, William 1949- 92
 Earlier sketch in SATA 42
Munro, Alice 1931- 29
Munro, Alice Anne
 See Munro, Alice
Munro, Eleanor 1928- 37
Munro, Roxie 1945- 184
 Earlier sketches in SATA 58, 136
Munsch, Bob
 See Munsch, Robert (Norman)
Munsch, Robert (Norman) 1945- 120
 Brief entry 48
 Earlier sketches in SATA 50, 83
 See also CLR 19
Munsinger, Lynn 1951- 177
 Earlier sketches in SATA 33, 94
Munson, Derek 1970- 139
Munson, R. W.
 See Karl, Jean E(dna)
Munson-Benson, Tunie 1946- 15
Munsterberg, Peggy 1921- 102
Muntean, Michaela 182
Munthe, Nelly 1947- 53
Munves, James (Albert) 1922- 30
Munzer, Martha E. 1899-1999 4
Murawski, Darlyne A. 193
Murch, Mel
 See Manes, Stephen
Murdoch, David H(amilton) 1937- 96
Murdoch, Patricia 1957- 192
Murdock, Catherine Gilbert 185
Murhall, J(acqueline) J(ane) 1964- 143
Murphy, Barbara Beasley 1933- 130
 Earlier sketch in SATA 5
Murphy, Claire Rudolf 1951- 137
 Earlier sketch in SATA 76
Murphy, E(mmett) Jefferson 1926- 4
Murphy, Elizabeth Ann Maureen
 See Murphy, Liz
Murphy, Jill 1949- 214
 Earlier sketches in SATA 37, 70, 142
 See also CLR 39
Murphy, Jill Frances
 See Murphy, Jill
Murphy, Jim 1947- 185
 Brief entry 32
 Earlier sketches in SATA 37, 77, 124
 See also CLR 53
Murphy, Joseph E., Jr. 1930- 65
Murphy, Kelly 1977- 190
 Earlier sketch in SATA 143
Murphy, Liz 1964- 210
Murphy, Louise 1943- 155
Murphy, Mary 1961- 196
Murphy, Pat
 See Murphy, E(mmett) Jefferson
Murphy, Patricia J. 1963- 132
Murphy, Rita 180
Murphy, Robert (William) 1902-1971 10
Murphy, Shirley Rousseau 1928- 126
 Earlier sketches in SATA 36, 71
 See also SAAS 18
Murphy, Stuart J. 1942- 157
 Earlier sketch in SATA 115
Murphy, Thomas Basil, Jr. 1935- 191
Murphy, Tim
 See Murphy, Jim
Murphy, Tom
 See Murphy, Thomas Basil, Jr.
Murray, John 1923- 39
Murray, Kirsty 1960- 165
 Earlier sketch in SATA 108
Murray, Marguerite 1917- 63
Murray, Marian 5
Murray, Martine 1965- 125
Murray, (Judith) Michele (Freedman)
 1933-1974 7
Murray, Ossie 1938- 43
Murray, Peter
 See Hautman, Pete

Murrow, Liza Ketchum
 See Ketchum, Liza
Musgrave, Florence 1902-1999 3
Musgrove, Margaret W(ynkoop) 1943- 124
 Earlier sketch in SATA 26
Musgrove, Marianne 207
Mussey, Virginia Howell
 See Ellison, Virginia H(owell)
Mussey, Virginia T.H.
 See Ellison, Virginia H(owell)
Mussi, Sarah 206
Mutel, Cornelia F. 1947- 74
Muth, Jon J. 206
 Earlier sketch in SATA 165
Mutz
 See Kuenstler, Morton
Mwangi, Meja 1948- 174
My Brother's Brother
 See Chekhov, Anton
Myers, Anna 160
Myers, Arthur 1917- 91
 Earlier sketch in SATA 35
Myers, Bernice 81
 Earlier sketch in SATA 9
Myers, Caroline Elizabeth Clark
 1887-1980 28
Myers, Christopher 1975- 183
 See also CLR 97
Myers, Edward 1950- 172
 Earlier sketch in SATA 96
Myers, Elisabeth P(erkins) 1918- 36
Myers, (Mary) Hortense (Powner)
 1913-1987 10
Myers, Jack 1913-2006 83
 Obituary 178
Myers, Jack Edgar
 See Myers, Jack
Myers, Lou 1915-2005 81
 Obituary 171
Myers, Louis
 See Myers, Lou
Myers, R.E. 1924- 119
Myers, Robert Eugene
 See Myers, R.E.
Myers, Tim 1953- 176
 Earlier sketch in SATA 147
Myers, Timothy Joseph
 See Myers, Tim
Myers, Walter Dean 1937- 193
 Brief entry 27
 Earlier sketches in SATA 41, 71, 109, 157
 See also CLR 110
 See also SAAS 2
Myers, Walter M.
 See Myers, Walter Dean
Myller, Rolf 1926-2006 27
 Obituary 175
Myra, Harold L(awrence) 1939- 46
 Brief entry 42
Myracle, Lauren 1969- 204
 Earlier sketch in SATA 162
Myrus, Donald (Richard) 1927- 23
Mysterious Traveler, The
 See Arthur, Robert, (Jr.)

N

Na, An 149
Naaslund, Goorel Kristina 1940- 170
Nadel, Laurie 1948- 74
Naden, Corinne J. 1930- 166
 Earlier sketch in SATA 79
Nadimi, Suzan 188
Nagda, Ann Whitehead 199
Nagel, Andreas Fischer
 See Fischer-Nagel, Andreas
Nagel, Heiderose Fischer
 See Fischer-Nagel, Heiderose
Nagle, Shane 176

Nahoko, Uehashi
 See Uehashi, Nahoko
Naidoo, Beverley 1943- 180
 Earlier sketches in SATA 63, 135
 See also CLR 29
Nails, Jennifer 213
Nakae, Noriko 1940- 59
Nakata, Hiroe 205
Nakatani, Chiyoko 1930-1981 55
 Brief entry 40
 See also CLR 30
Nally, Susan W. 1947- 90
Namioka, Lensey 1929- 157
 Autobiography Feature 116
 Earlier sketches in SATA 27, 89
 See also CLR 48
 See also SAAS 24
Namovicz, Gene Inyart 1927- 6
Nance, Andrew 210
Nanji, Shenaaz 1954- 204
 Earlier sketch in SATA 131
Nanogak Agnes 1925- 61
Napier, Mark
 See Laffin, John (Alfred Charles)
Napoli, Donna Jo 1948- 190
 Earlier sketches in SATA 92, 137
 See also CLR 51
 See also SAAS 23
Napp, Daniel 1974- 204
Narahashi, Keiko 1959- 115
 Earlier sketch in SATA 79
Narayan, R. K. 1906-2001 62
Narayan, Rasipuram Krishnaswami
 See Narayan, R. K.
Nascimbene, Yan 1949- 173
 Earlier sketch in SATA 133
Nash, Bruce M(itchell) 1947- 34
Nash, Frederic Ogden
 See Nash, Ogden
Nash, Linell
 See Smith, Linell Nash
Nash, Mary (Hughes) 1925- 41
Nash, Ogden 1902-1971 46
 Earlier sketch in SATA 2
Nash, Renea Denise 1963- 81
Nast, Elsa Ruth
 See Watson, Jane Werner
Nast, Thomas 1840-1902 51
 Brief entry 33
Nastick, Sharon 1954- 41
Natale, Vince 196
Natarajan, Srividya 187
Nathan, Adele (Gutman) 1900(?)-1986
 Obituary 48
Nathan, Amy 155
 Earlier sketch in SATA 104
Nathan, Dorothy (Goldeen) (?)-1966 15
Nathan, Robert (Gruntal) 1894-1985 6
 Obituary 43
Nathanson, Laura Walther 1941- 57
Natti, Lee 1919- 67
 Earlier sketch in SATA 1
 See also SAAS 3
Natti, Susanna 1948- 125
 Earlier sketch in SATA 32
Nau, Thomas 186
Naughtie, Eleanor
 See Updale, Eleanor
Naughton, Bill
 See Naughton, William John (Francis)
Naughton, James Franklin 1957- 85
Naughton, Jim
 See Naughton, James Franklin
Naughton, William John (Francis)
 1910-1992 86
Navarra, John Gabriel 1927- 8
Naylor, Penelope 1941- 10
Naylor, Phyllis 1933-
 See Naylor, Phyllis Reynolds

Naylor, Phyllis Reynolds 1933- *209*
  Autobiography Feature *152*
  See also CLR *135*
  See also SAAS *10*
Nazarian, Nikki
  See Nichols, Cecilia Fawn
Nazaroff, Alexander I(vanovich) 1898-1981 .. *4*
Nazoa, Aquiles 1920-1976 .... *198*
Neal, Harry Edward 1906-1993 .... *5*
  Obituary *76*
Neal, Michael
  See Teitelbaum, Michael
Nearing, Penny 1916- *47*
  Brief entry *42*
Nebel, Gustave E. *45*
  Brief entry *33*
Nebel, Mimouca
  See Nebel, Gustave E.
Nee, Kay Bonner *10*
Needham, Kate 1962- *95*
Needle, Jan 1943- *98*
  Earlier sketch in SATA *30*
  See also CLR *43*
  See also SAAS *23*
Needleman, Jacob 1934- *6*
Neel, David 1960- *82*
Neel, Preston 1959- *93*
Negri, Rocco 1932- *12*
Negrin, Fabian 1963- *189*
Neidigh, Sherry 1956- *204*
Neier, Aryeh 1937- *59*
Neigoff, Anne *13*
Neigoff, Mike 1920- *13*
Neilan, Eujin Kim 1969- *200*
Neilson, Frances Fullerton (Jones)
  1910-2001 .... *14*
Neimark, Anne E. 1935- *145*
  Earlier sketch in SATA *4*
Neimark, Paul G. 1934- *80*
  Brief entry *37*
Neitzel, Shirley 1941- *134*
  Earlier sketch in SATA *77*
Nell
  See Hanna, Nell(ie L.)
Nelscott, Kris
  See Rusch, Kristine Kathryn
Nelson, Blake 1960- *177*
Nelson, Catherine Chadwick 1926- *87*
Nelson, Cordner 1918-2009 .... *54*
  Brief entry *29*
Nelson, Cordner Bruce
  See Nelson, Cordner
Nelson, D.A. 1970- *215*
Nelson, Dawn Ann
  See Nelson, D.A.
Nelson, Drew 1952- *77*
Nelson, Esther L. 1928- *13*
Nelson, Jim A.
  See Stotter, Mike
Nelson, Julie L. 1970- *117*
Nelson, Kadir *213*
  Earlier sketches in SATA *154, 181*
Nelson, Kris
  See Rusch, Kristine Kathryn
Nelson, Lawrence E(rnest) 1928-1977
  Obituary *28*
Nelson, Marilyn 1946- *60*
  Autobiography Feature *180*
Nelson, Mary Carroll 1929- *23*
Nelson, O. Terry 1941- *62*
Nelson, Peter N. 1953- *73*
Nelson, R. A. *197*
Nelson, Richard K(ing) 1941- *65*
Nelson, Robin Laura 1971- *141*
Nelson, Roy Paul 1923- *59*
Nelson, S.D. *181*
Nelson, Sharlene (P.) 1933- *96*
Nelson, Suzanne 1976- *184*
Nelson, Ted (W.) 1931- *96*

Nelson, Theresa 1948- *143*
  Autobiography Feature *143*
  Earlier sketch in SATA *79*
Nemeth, Sally *187*
Neri, G. *197*
Neri, Greg
  See Neri, G.
Neri, Gregory
  See Neri, G.
Nerlove, Miriam 1959- *53*
  Brief entry *49*
Nesbit, E. 1858-1924 .... *100*
  See also YABC *1*
  See also CLR *70*
Nesbit, Edith
  See Nesbit, E.
Nesbit, Troy
  See Folsom, Franklin (Brewster)
Nespojohn, Katherine V(eronica) 1912-1975 . *7*
Ness, Evaline (Michelow) 1911-1986 .... *26*
  Obituary *49*
  Earlier sketch in SATA *1*
  See also CLR *6*
  See also SAAS *1*
Ness, Patrick 1971- *207*
Nestor, Larry 1940- *149*
Nestor, William P(rodromos) 1947- *49*
Nethery, Mary *93*
Neubecker, Robert *214*
  Earlier sketch in SATA *170*
Neuberger, Julia (Babette Sarah) 1950- *142*
  Earlier sketch in SATA *78*
Neufeld, John (Arthur) 1938- *131*
  Autobiography Feature *131*
  Earlier sketches in SATA *6, 81*
  See also CLR *52*
  See also SAAS *3*
Neuhaus, David 1958- *83*
Neumeyer, Peter F(lorian) 1929- *13*
Neurath, Marie (Reidemeister) 1898-1986 ..... *1*
Neuschwander, Cindy 1953- *157*
  Earlier sketch in SATA *107*
Neusner, Jacob 1932- *38*
Neville, Charles
  See Bodsworth, (Charles) Fred(erick)
Neville, Emily Cheney 1919- *1*
  See also SAAS *2*
Neville, Mary
  See Woodrich, Mary Neville
Nevins, Albert (Francis) J(erome)
  1915-1997 .... *20*
Nevius, Carol 1955- *186*
Newberger, Devra
  See Speregen, Devra Newberger
Newberry, Clare Turlay 1903-1970 .... *1*
  Obituary *26*
Newbery, John 1713-1767 .... *20*
  See also CLR *147*
Newbery, Linda 1952- *184*
  Earlier sketch in SATA *142*
Newbigging, Martha *198*
Newbold, Greg *199*
Newcomb, Ellsworth
  See Kenny, Ellsworth Newcomb
Newcombe, Eugene A. 1923-1990 .... *45*
  Brief entry *33*
Newcombe, Jack
  See Newcombe, Eugene A.
Newcome, Robert 1955- *91*
Newcome, Zita 1959- *88*
Newell, Crosby
  See Bonsall, Crosby Barbara (Newell)
Newell, Edythe W(eatherford) 1910-1989 .... *11*
Newell, Hope Hockenberry 1896-1965 .... *24*
Newfeld, Frank 1928- *26*
Newgarden, Mark 1959- *194*
Newlon, (Frank) Clarke 1905(?)-1982 .... *6*
  Obituary *33*
Newman, Barbara Johansen *191*
Newman, C.J.
  See Newman, Coleman J.

Newman, Coleman J. 1935- *82*
Newman, Daisy 1904-1994 .... *27*
  Obituary *78*
Newman, Gerald 1939- *46*
  Brief entry *42*
Newman, Jerry
  See Newman, Coleman J.
Newman, Leslea 1955- *134*
  Earlier sketches in SATA *71, 128*
Newman, Margaret
  See Potter, Margaret
Newman, Marjorie *146*
Newman, Matthew (Harrison) 1955- *56*
Newman, Nanette 1934- *162*
Newman, Robert (Howard) 1909-1988 .... *87*
  Obituary *60*
  Earlier sketch in SATA *4*
Newman, Shirlee P(etkin) *144*
  Earlier sketches in SATA *10, 90*
Newsom, Carol 1948- *92*
  Earlier sketch in SATA *40*
Newsom, Tom 1944- *80*
Newth, Mette 1942- *140*
Newton, David E(dward) 1933- *67*
Newton, James R(obert) 1935- *23*
Newton, Jill 1964- *200*
Newton, Robert 1965- *191*
Newton, Suzanne 1936- *77*
  Earlier sketch in SATA *5*
Newton, Vanessa
  See Newton, Vanessa Brantley
Newton, Vanessa Brantley 1962(?)- *206*
Ney, John 1923- *43*
  Brief entry *33*
Nez, John *155*
Ng, Franklin *82*
Nguyen, Vincent *187*
Nichol, B(arrie) P(hillip) 1944-1988 .... *66*
Nicholas, Louise D.
  See Watkins, Dawn L.
Nicholls, Judith (Ann) 1941- *61*
Nicholls, Sally 1983- *209*
Nichols, Cecilia Fawn 1906-1987 .... *12*
Nichols, Grace 1950- *164*
  Earlier sketch in SATA *98*
Nichols, Janet (Louise) 1952- *67*
Nichols, Judy 1947- *124*
Nichols, Leigh
  See Koontz, Dean
Nichols, Michael 1952- *215*
Nichols, Michael Nick
  See Nichols, Michael
Nichols, Paul
  See Hawks, Robert
Nichols, Peter
  See Youd, Samuel
Nichols, (Joanna) Ruth 1948- *15*
  See also CLR *149*
Nichols, Travis *206*
Nicholson, C. R.
  See Nicole, Christopher (Robin)
Nicholson, Christina
  See Nicole, Christopher (Robin)
Nicholson, Joyce Thorpe 1919- *35*
Nicholson, Lois P. 1949- *88*
Nicholson, Robin
  See Nicole, Christopher (Robin)
Nicholson, William *180*
Nicholson, William 1872-1949
  See CLR *76*
Nickel, Barbara 1966- *188*
Nickell, Joe 1944- *167*
  Earlier sketch in SATA *73*
Nickelsburg, Janet 1893-1983 .... *11*
Nickerson, Betty 1922- *14*
Nickerson, Elizabeth
  See Nickerson, Betty
Nickl, Barbara (Elisabeth) 1939- *56*
Nicklaus, Carol *62*
  Brief entry *33*
Nickle, John *181*

Nickless, Will 1902-1979(?) 66
Nic Leodhas, Sorche
     See Alger, Leclaire (Gowans)
Nicol, Ann
     See Turnbull, Ann
Nicolas
     See Mordvinoff, Nicolas
Nicolay, Helen 1866-1954
     See YABC *1*
Nicole, Christopher (Robin) 1930- 5
Nicoll, Helen 1937- 87
Nicolson, Cynthia Pratt 1949- 141
Ni Dhuibhne, Eilis 1954- 91
Niehaus, Paddy Bouma
     See Bouma, Paddy
Nields, Nerissa 1967- 166
Nielsen, Kay (Rasmus) 1886-1957 16
     See also CLR *16*
Nielsen, Laura F. 1960- 93
Nielsen, Laura Farnsworth
     See Nielsen, Laura F.
Nielsen, Nancy J. 1951- 77
Nielsen, Susin 1964- 195
Nielsen, Virginia
     See McCall, Virginia Nielsen
Nielsen-Fernlund, Susin
     See Nielsen, Susin
Niemann, Christoph 1970- 191
Nieuwsma, Milton J(ohn) 1941- 142
Nightingale, Sandy 1953- 76
Nikolajeva, Maria 1952- 127
Nikola-Lisa, W. 1951- 180
     Earlier sketch in SATA *71*
Niland, Deborah 1951- 172
     Earlier sketch in SATA *27*
Niland, Kilmeny 75
Nilsen, Anna 1948- 174
     Earlier sketch in SATA *96*
Nilsson, Eleanor 1939- 117
     Earlier sketch in SATA *81*
     See also SAAS *23*
Nilsson, Per 1954- 159
Nimmo, Jenny 1944- 144
     Earlier sketch in SATA *87*
     See also CLR *44*
Nishimura, Kae 196
Niven, Larry 1938- 171
     Earlier sketch in SATA *95*
Niven, Laurence Van Cott
     See Niven, Larry
Niven, Laurence VanCott
     See Niven, Larry
Nivola, Claire A. 1947- 208
     Earlier sketches in SATA *84, 140*
Nix, Garth 1963- 210
     Earlier sketches in SATA *97, 143*
     See also CLR *68*
Nixon, Hershell Howard 1923- 42
Nixon, Joan Lowery 1927-2003 115
     Obituary 146
     Earlier sketches in SATA *8, 44, 78*
     See also CLR *24*
     See also SAAS *9*
Nixon, K.
     See Nixon, Kathleen Irene (Blundell)
Nixon, Kathleen Irene (Blundell)
     1894-1988(?) 14
     Obituary 59
Nobati, Eugenia 1968- 201
Nobisso, Josephine 1953- 121
     Earlier sketch in SATA *78*
Noble, Iris (Davis) 1922-1986 5
     Obituary 49
Noble, Marty 1947- 125
     Earlier sketch in SATA *97*
Noble, Trinka Hakes 1944- 197
     Brief entry 37
     Earlier sketch in SATA *123*
Nobleman, Marc Tyler 1972- 203
Noda, Takayo 1961- 168
Nodelman, Perry 1942- 101

Nodset, Joan L.
     See Lexau, Joan M.
Noel Hume, Ivor 1927- 65
Noestlinger, Christine
     See Nostlinger, Christine
Noguere, Suzanne 1947- 34
Nolan, Dennis 1945- 166
     Brief entry 34
     Earlier sketches in SATA *42, 92*
Nolan, Han 1956- 157
     Earlier sketch in SATA *109*
Nolan, Janet 1956- 191
     Earlier sketch in SATA *145*
Nolan, Jeannette Covert 1897-1974 2
     Obituary 27
Nolan, Lucy 215
Nolan, Paul T(homas) 1919- 48
Nolan, William F. 1928- 88
     Brief entry 28
Nolan, William Francis
     See Nolan, William F.
Nolen, Jerdine 1953- 157
     Earlier sketch in SATA *105*
Noll, Sally 1946- 82
Noonan, Brandon 1979- 184
Noonan, Diana 1960- 146
Noonan, Julia 1946- 148
     Earlier sketches in SATA *4, 95*
Norac, Carl 1960- 166
Norcross, John
     See Conroy, John Wesley
Nordan, Robert W(arren) 1934-2004 133
Nordhoff, Charles Bernard 1887-1947 23
Nordlicht, Lillian 29
Nordstrom, Ursula 1910-1988 3
     Obituary 57
Nordtvedt, Matilda 1926- 67
Norling, Beth 1969- 149
Norman, Charles 1904-1996 38
     Obituary 92
Norman, Howard
     See Norman, Howard A.
Norman, Howard A. 1949- 81
Norman, James
     See Schmidt, James Norman
Norman, Jay
     See Arthur, Robert, (Jr.)
Norman, Lilith 1927- 120
     Earlier sketch in SATA *86*
Norman, Mary 1931- 36
Norman, Steve
     See Pashko, Stanley
Norment, Lisa 1966- 91
Norris, Gunilla Brodde 1939- 20
North, Andrew
     See Norton, Andre
North, Anthony
     See Koontz, Dean
North, Captain George
     See Stevenson, Robert Louis
North, Captain George
     See Stevenson, Robert Louis
North, Howard
     See Trevor, Elleston
North, Joan 1920- 16
North, Milou
     See Erdrich, Louise
North, Robert
     See Withers, Carl A.
North, Sara
     See Bonham, Barbara Thomas
     and Hager, Jean
North, Sherry 201
North, Sterling 1906-1974 45
     Obituary 26
     Earlier sketch in SATA *1*
Northcott, (William) Cecil 1902-1987
     Obituary 55
Northeast, Brenda V(ictoria) 1948- 106
Northmore, Elizabeth Florence 1906-1974 . 122

Norton, Alice Mary
     See Norton, Andre
Norton, Andre 1912-2005 91
     Earlier sketches in SATA *1, 43*
     See also CLR *50*
Norton, Browning
     See Norton, Frank R. B(rowning)
Norton, Frank R. B(rowning) 1909-1989 10
Norton, Mary 1903-1992 60
     Obituary 72
     Earlier sketch in SATA *18*
     See also CLR *140*
Nosredna, Trebor
     See Anderson, Bob
Nostlinger, Christine 1936- 162
     Brief entry 37
     Earlier sketch in SATA *64*
     See also CLR *12*
Nourse, Alan E(dward) 1928-1992 48
     See also CLR *33*
Novak, Matt 1962- 204
     Brief entry 52
     Earlier sketches in SATA *60, 104, 165*
Novelli, Luca 1947- 61
Novgorodoff, Danica 1982(?)- 215
Nowell, Elizabeth Cameron 12
Noyes, Deborah 1965- 194
     Earlier sketch in SATA *145*
Nugent, Cynthia 1954- 205
Nugent, Nicholas 1949- 73
Numeroff, Laura 1953- 206
     Earlier sketches in SATA *28, 90, 142*
     See also CLR *85*
Numeroff Joffe, Laura
     See Numeroff, Laura
Nunes, Lygia Bojunga 1932- 154
     Earlier sketch in SATA *75*
Nunn, Laura (Donna) Silverstein 1968- 124
Nurenberg, Thelma
     See Greenhaus, Thelma Nurenberg
Nurnberg, Maxwell 1897-1984 27
     Obituary 41
Nussbaumer, Paul (Edmund) 1934- 16
Nutt, Ken 1951- 163
     Earlier sketch in SATA *97*
Nuttall-Smith, Margaret Emily Noel 1919- .. 26
Nuygen, Mathieu 1967- 80
Nuzum, K. A. 195
Nuzum, Kathy A.
     See Nuzum, K. A.
Nyberg, (Everett Wayne) Morgan 1944- 87
Nyce, (Nellie) Helene von Strecker
     1885-1969 19
Nyce, Vera 1862-1925 19
Nye, Naomi Shihab 1952- 198
     Earlier sketches in SATA *86, 147*
     See also CLR *59*
Nye, Robert 1939- 6
Nyeu, Tao 206
Nyikos, Stacy A. 1969- 164
Nystrom, Carolyn 1940- 130
     Earlier sketch in SATA *67*

O

O. Henry
     See Henry, O.
Oakes, Elizabeth H. 1964- 132
Oakes, Vanya 1909-1983 6
     Obituary 37
Oakley, Don(ald G.) 1927- 8
Oakley, Graham 1929- 84
     Earlier sketch in SATA *30*
     See also CLR *7*
Oakley, Helen (McKelvey) 1906- 10
Oana, Katherine 1929- 53
     Brief entry 37
Oates, Eddie H. 1943- 88
Oates, Joyce Carol 1938- 159

Oates, Stephen B(aery) 1936- *59*
Obed, Ellen Bryan 1944- *74*
Oberle, Joseph 1958- *69*
Oberman, Sheldon 1949-2004 .... *85*
   Autobiography Feature *114*
   Obituary *153*
   See also CLR 54
   See also SAAS 26
Obligado, Lilian (Isabel) 1931- *61*
   Brief entry *45*
Obrant, Susan 1946- *11*
O'Brian, E.G.
   See Clarke, Arthur C.
O'Brien, Anne Sibley 1952- *213*
   Brief entry *48*
   Earlier sketches in SATA *53, 80*
O'Brien, E.G.
   See Clarke, Arthur C.
O'Brien, Esse Forrester 1895(?)-1975
   Obituary *30*
O'Brien, Patrick 1960- *193*
O'Brien, Robert C.
   See Conly, Robert Leslie
O'Brien, Thomas C(lement) 1938- *29*
O'Callaghan, Julie 1954- *113*
O'Callahan, Jay 1938- *88*
O'Carroll, Ryan
   See Markun, Patricia Maloney
Ochiltree, Dianne 1953- *117*
Ockham, Joan Price
   See Price, Joan
O'Connell, Margaret F(orster) 1935-1977 .... *30*
   Obituary *30*
O'Connell, Peg
   See Ahern, Margaret McCrohan
O'Connell, Rebecca 1968- *212*
   Earlier sketch in SATA *130*
O'Connor, Barbara 1950- *193*
   Earlier sketch in SATA *154*
O'Connor, Francine M(arie) 1930- *90*
O'Connor, Genevieve A. 1914- *75*
O'Connor, George *183*
O'Connor, Ian 1965- *188*
O'Connor, Jane 1947- *186*
   Brief entry *47*
   Earlier sketches in SATA *59, 103, 150*
O'Connor, Karen 1938- *89*
   Earlier sketch in SATA *34*
O'Connor, Patrick
   See Wibberley, Leonard
O'Connor, Richard 1915-1975
   Obituary *21*
O'Conor, Jane 1958- *78*
Odaga, Asenath (Bole) 1937- *130*
   Earlier sketch in SATA *67*
   See also SAAS 19
O Danachair, Caoimhin
   See Danaher, Kevin
Odanaka, Barbara *159*
O'Daniel, Janet 1921- *24*
O'Day, Cathy
   See Crane, Barbara (Joyce)
O'Dell, Scott 1898-1989 .... *134*
   Earlier sketches in SATA *12, 60*
   See also CLR 126
Odenwald, Robert P(aul) 1899-1965 .... *11*
Odgers, Sally
   See Odgers, Sally Farrell
Odgers, Sally Farrell 1957- *139*
   Earlier sketch in SATA *72*
Odone, Jamison 1980- *209*
O'Donnell, Dick
   See Lupoff, Richard A(llen)
   and Thompson, Don(ald Arthur)
O'Donnell, Liam 1970- *209*
Odriozola, Elena *186*
Oechsli, Kelly 1918-1999 .... *5*
Oesterle, Virginia Rorby
   See Rorby, Ginny
Ofek, Uriel 1926- *36*
   See also CLR 28

Ofer, Avi 1975- *207*
Offenbacher, Ami 1958- *91*
Offill, Jenny 1968- *211*
Offit, Sidney 1928- *10*
Ofosu-Appiah, L(awrence) H(enry) 1920- ... *13*
Ogan, George F. 1912-1983 .... *13*
Ogan, M. G.
   See Ogan, George F.
   and Ogan, Margaret E. (Nettles)
Ogan, Margaret E. (Nettles) 1923-1979 .... *13*
Ogburn, Charlton (Jr.) 1911-1998 .... *3*
   Obituary *109*
Ogburn, Jacqueline K. *162*
Ogilvie, Elisabeth May 1917-2006 .... *40*
   Brief entry *29*
   Obituary *176*
Ogilvy, Gavin
   See Barrie, J. M.
Ogilvy, Ian 1943- *177*
Ogilvy, Ian Raymond
   See Ogilvy, Ian
Ogle, Lucille Edith 1904-1988
   Obituary *59*
Ogletree, Charles J. 1952- *175*
O'Green, Jennifer
   See Roberson, Jennifer
O'Green, Jennifer Roberson
   See Roberson, Jennifer
O'Hagan, Caroline 1946- *38*
O'Hanlon, Jacklyn
   See Meek, Jacklyn O'Hanlon
O'Hara, Elizabeth
   See Ni Dhuibhne, Eilis
O'Hara, Kenneth
   See Morris, (Margaret) Jean
O'Hara, Mary
   See Alsop, Mary O'Hara
O'Hara (Alsop), Mary
   See Alsop, Mary O'Hara
O'Hare, Jeff(rey A.) 1958- *105*
Ohi, Ruth 1964- *95*
Ohiyesa
   See Eastman, Charles A(lexander)
Ohlsson, Ib 1935- *7*
Ohmi, Ayano 1959- *115*
Ohtomo, Yasuo 1946- *37*
o huigin, sean 1942- *138*
   See also CLR 75
Oiseau
   See Moseley, James W(illett)
Oke, Janette 1935- *97*
O'Keefe, Susan Heyboer *176*
   Earlier sketch in SATA *133*
O'Keeffe, Frank 1938- *99*
O'Kelley, Mattie Lou 1908-1997 .... *97*
   Earlier sketch in SATA *36*
Okimoto, Jean Davies 1942- *103*
   Earlier sketch in SATA *34*
Okomfo, Amasewa
   See Cousins, Linda
olafsdottir, Gudrun Elin
   See Gunnella
Olaleye, Isaac O. 1941- *96*
   See also SAAS 23
Olcott, Frances Jenkins 1872(?)-1963 .... *19*
Old, Wendie C(orbin) 1943- *154*
Old Boy
   See Hughes, Thomas
Oldenburg, E(gbert) William 1936-1974 ...... *35*
Older, Effin 1942- *114*
Older, Jules 1940- *156*
   Earlier sketch in SATA *114*
Oldfield, Jenny 1949- *140*
Oldfield, Margaret J(ean) 1932- *56*
Oldfield, Pamela 1931- *86*
Oldham, June *70*
Oldham, Mary 1944- *65*
Olds, Elizabeth 1896-1991 .... *3*
   Obituary *66*
Olds, Helen Diehl 1895-1981 .... *9*
   Obituary *25*

Oldstyle, Jonathan
   See Irving, Washington
O'Leary, Brian (Todd) 1940- *6*
O'Leary, Chris *208*
O'Leary, Patsy B. 1937- *97*
O'Leary, Patsy Baker
   See O'Leary, Patsy B.
Oleynikov, Igor 1953- *202*
Oliphant, B.J.
   See Tepper, Sheri S.
Oliver, Burton
   See Burt, Olive Woolley
Oliver, Chad
   See Oliver, Symmes C.
Oliver, John Edward 1933- *21*
Oliver, Lin *202*
Oliver, Marilyn Tower 1935- *89*
Oliver, Mark *214*
   See Tyler-Whittle, Michael Sidney
Oliver, Narelle 1960- *197*
   Earlier sketch in SATA *152*
Oliver, Shirley (Louise Dawkins) 1958- *74*
Oliver, Symmes C. 1928-1993 .... *101*
Oliviero, Jamie 1950- *84*
Olmsted, Lorena Ann 1890-1989 .... *13*
Olney, Ross R. 1929- *13*
Olschewski, Alfred (Erich) 1920- *7*
Olsen, Barbara *148*
Olsen, Carol 1945- *89*
Olsen, Ib Spang 1921- *81*
   Earlier sketch in SATA *6*
Olsen, Violet (Mae) 1922-1991 .... *58*
Olson, Arielle North 1932- *67*
Olson, David J. 1974- *198*
Olson, Gene 1922- *32*
Olson, Gretchen *187*
Olson, Helen Kronberg *48*
Olson, Kay Melchisedech 1948- *175*
Olson, Marianne
   See Mitchell, Marianne
Olson-Brown, Ellen 1967- *183*
Olten, Manuela 1970- *197*
Olugebefola, Ademole 1941- *15*
Oluonye, Mary N(kechi) 1955- *111*
Om
   See Gorey, Edward (St. John)
O'Malley, Donough *208*
O'Malley, Kevin 1961- *191*
   Earlier sketch in SATA *157*
Oman, Carola (Mary Anima) 1897-1978 ..... *35*
O'Mara, Carmel 1965- *166*
O'Mara-Horwitz, Carmel
   See O'Mara, Carmel
O'Meara, Walter (Andrew) 1897-1989 .... *65*
Ommanney, F(rancis) D(ownes) 1903-1980 . *23*
O Mude
   See Gorey, Edward (St. John)
Oneal, Elizabeth 1934- *82*
   Earlier sketch in SATA *30*
   See also CLR 13
O'Neal, Katherine Pebley 1957- *204*
O'Neal, Reagan
   See Jordan, Robert
O'Neal, Regan
   See Jordan, Robert
Oneal, Zibby
   See Oneal, Elizabeth
O'Neill, Amanda 1951- *111*
O'Neill, Catharine *203*
O'Neill, Gerard K(itchen) 1927-1992 .... *65*
O'Neill, Judith (Beatrice) 1930- *34*
O'Neill, Mary L(e Duc) 1908(?)-1990 .... *2*
   Obituary *64*
O'Neill, Reagan
   See Jordan, Robert
Onslow, Annette Rosemary MacArthur
   See MacArthur-Onslow, Annette Rosemary
Onslow, John 1906-1985
   Obituary *47*
Onyefulu, Ifeoma 1959- *157*
   Earlier sketches in SATA *81, 115*

Opie, Iona (Margaret Balfour) 1923- *118*
   Earlier sketches in SATA *3, 63*
   See also SAAS 6
Opie, Peter (Mason) 1918-1982 .... *118*
   Obituary *28*
   Earlier sketches in SATA *3, 63*
Oppel, Kenneth 1967- *199*
   Earlier sketches in SATA *99, 153*
Oppel, Kenneth Kerry
   See Oppel, Kenneth
Oppenheim, Joanne 1934- *174*
   Earlier sketches in SATA *5, 82, 136*
Oppenheim, Shulamith Levey 1928- *177*
Oppenheimer, Joan L(etson) 1925- *28*
Oppong, Joseph Ransford 1953- *160*
Optic, Oliver
   See Adams, William Taylor
   and Stratemeyer, Edward L.
Oram, Hiawyn 1946- *101*
   Earlier sketch in SATA *56*
Orbach, Ruth Gary 1941- *21*
Orback, Craig *197*
Orczy, Emma
   See Orczy, Baroness Emmuska
Orczy, Emma Magdalena Rosalia Maria Josefa
   See Orczy, Baroness Emmuska
Orczy, Emmuska
   See Orczy, Baroness Emmuska
Orczy, Baroness Emmuska 1865-1947 .... *40*
Orde, A.J.
   See Tepper, Sheri S.
O'Reilly, Jackson
   See Jordan, Robert
Orenstein, Denise Gosliner 1950- *157*
Orgad, Dorit 1936- *199*
Orgel, Doris 1929- *148*
   Earlier sketches in SATA *7, 85*
   See also CLR *48*
   See also SAAS *19*
Orgill, Roxane *198*
Oriolo, Joe
   See Oriolo, Joseph D.
Oriolo, Joseph D. 1913-1985
   Obituary *46*
Orlean, Susan 1955- *209*
Orleans, Ilo 1897-1962 .... *10*
Orlev, Uri 1931- *135*
   Earlier sketch in SATA *58*
   See also CLR *30*
   See also SAAS *19*
Ormai, Stella *57*
   Brief entry *48*
Ormerod, Jan 1946- *210*
   Brief entry *44*
   Earlier sketches in SATA *55, 70, 132*
   See also CLR *20*
Ormerod, Janette Louise
   See Ormerod, Jan
Ormes, Jackie
   See Ormes, Zelda J.
Ormes, Zelda J. 1914-1986
   Obituary *47*
Ormondroyd, Edward 1925- *14*
Ormsby, Virginia H(aire) 1906-1990 .... *11*
Orona-Ramirez, Kristy 1964- *189*
Orozco, Jose-Luis 1948- *179*
Orr, Katherine S(helley) 1950- *72*
Orr, Wendy 1953- *206*
   Earlier sketches in SATA *90, 141*
Orris
   See Ingelow, Jean
Orth, Richard
   See Gardner, Richard (M.)
Ortiz Cofer, Judith
   See Cofer, Judith Ortiz
Orwell, George 1903-1950 .... *29*
   See also CLR *68*
Orwin, Joanna 1944- *141*
Os, Eric van
   See van Os, Erik
Osborn, Elinor 1939- *145*

Osborn, Jacob 1981(?)- *215*
Osborn, Kathy 1955(?)- *199*
Osborn, Lois D(orothy) 1915- *61*
Osborne, Charles 1927- *59*
Osborne, Chester G(orham) 1915-1987 .... *11*
Osborne, David
   See Silverberg, Robert
Osborne, George
   See Silverberg, Robert
Osborne, Leone Neal 1914-1996 .... *2*
Osborne, Linda Barrett 1949- *215*
Osborne, Mary Pope 1949- *144*
   Earlier sketches in SATA *41, 55, 98*
   See also CLR *88*
Osceola
   See Blixen, Karen
Osgood, William E(dward) 1926- *37*
O'Shaughnessy, Darren
   See Shan, Darren
O'Shaughnessy, Ellen Cassels 1937- *78*
O'Shea, Catherine Patricia Shiels
   See O'Shea, Pat
O'Shea, Pat 1931-2007 .... *87*
   See also CLR *18*
Osmond, Edward 1900- *10*
Ossoli, Sarah Margaret
   See Fuller, Margaret
Ostendorf, (Arthur) Lloyd, (Jr.) 1921-2000 .. *65*
   Obituary *125*
Osterweil, Adam 1972- *217*
Ostow, Micol 1976- *170*
Otfinoski, Steven 1949- *116*
   Earlier sketch in SATA *56*
Otis, James
   See Kaler, James Otis
O'Toole, Thomas 1941- *71*
O'Trigger, Sir Lucius
   See Horne, Richard Henry Hengist
Otten, Charlotte
   See Otten, Charlotte F.
Otten, Charlotte F. 1926- *98*
Otten, Charlotte Fennema
   See Otten, Charlotte F.
Ottley, Matt 1962- *171*
   Earlier sketch in SATA *102*
Ottley, Reginald Leslie 1909-1985 .... *26*
   See also CLR *16*
Otto, Margaret Glover 1909-1976
   Obituary *30*
Otto, Svend
   See Soerensen, Svend Otto
Oughton, Jerrie (Preston) 1937- *131*
   Earlier sketch in SATA *76*
Oughton, (William) Taylor 1925- *104*
Ouida
   See De La Ramee, Marie Louise
Ousley, Odille 1896-1976 .... *10*
Outcalt, Todd 1960- *123*
Overmyer, James E. 1946- *88*
Overton, Jenny (Margaret Mary) 1942- *52*
   Brief entry *36*
Owen, Ann
   See Qualey, Marsha
Owen, Annie 1949- *75*
Owen, Caroline Dale
   See Snedeker, Caroline Dale (Parke)
Owen, Clifford
   See Hamilton, Charles (Harold St. John)
Owen, Dilys
   See Gater, Dilys
Owen, (Benjamin) Evan 1918-1984 .... *38*
Owen, (John) Gareth 1936-2002 .... *162*
   Earlier sketch in SATA *83*
   See also CLR *31*
   See also SAAS *14*
Owen, James A. *185*
Owens, Bryant 1968- *116*
Owens, Dana Elaine
   See Queen Latifah
Owens, Gail 1939- *54*
Owens, Mary Beth *191*

Owens, Thomas S(heldon) 1960- *86*
Owens, Tom
   See Owens, Thomas S(heldon)
Oxenbury, Helen 1938- *149*
   Earlier sketches in SATA *3, 68*
   See also CLR *70*
Oxendine, Bess Holland 1933- *90*
Oz, Frank (Richard) 1944- *60*
Ozer, Jerome S. 1927- *59*

P

Paananen, Eloise (Katherine) 1923-1993 .... *9*
Pace, Lorenzo 1943- *131*
Pace, Mildred Mastin 1907- *46*
   Brief entry *29*
Pachter, Hedwig (?)-1988 .... *63*
Pack, Janet 1952- *77*
Pack, Robert 1929- *118*
Packard, Edward 1931- *148*
   Earlier sketches in SATA *47, 90*
Packer, Kenneth L. 1946- *116*
Packer, Vin
   See Meaker, Marijane
Pad, Peter
   See Stratemeyer, Edward L.
Page, Eileen
   See Heal, Edith
Page, Eleanor
   See Coerr, Eleanor (Beatrice)
Page, Gail 1950- *205*
Page, Jake 1936- *81*
Page, James Keena, Jr.
   See Page, Jake
Page, Lou Williams 1912-1997 .... *38*
Page, Mary
   See Heal, Edith
Page, Robin 1943- *154*
Pagliarulo, Antonio 1977(?)- *212*
Pagnucci, Susan 1944- *90*
Pahlen, Kurt 1907-2003
   Obituary *147*
Pahz, Cheryl
   See Pahz, Cheryl Suzanne
Pahz, Cheryl Suzanne 1949- *11*
Pahz, James Alon 1943- *11*
Paice, Margaret 1920- *10*
Paige, Harry W(orthington) 1922- *41*
   Brief entry *35*
Paige, Richard
   See Koontz, Dean
Paige, Robin
   See Albert, Susan Wittig
Paine, Penelope Colville 1946- *87*
Paine, Roberta M. 1925- *13*
Paisley, Tom 1932- *11*
   See also CLR *3*
Palatini, Margie *207*
   Earlier sketches in SATA *134, 174*
Palazzo, Anthony D.
   See Palazzo, Tony
Palazzo, Tony 1905-1970 .... *3*
Palder, Edward L. 1922- *5*
Palecek, Josef 1932- *56*
Palecek, Libuse 1937- *89*
Palen, Debbie *195*
Palin, Michael 1943- *67*
Palin, Michael Edward
   See Palin, Michael
Palladini, David (Mario) 1946- *40*
   Brief entry *32*
Pallas, Norvin 1918-1983 .... *23*
Pallister, John C(lare) 1891-1980
   Obituary *26*
Pallotta, Gerard Larry
   See Pallotta, Jerry
Pallotta, Jerry 1953- *186*
Pallotta-Chiarolli, Maria 1960- *117*
Palmer, Bernard (Alvin) 1914-1998 .... *26*

Palmer, C. Everard 1930- *14*
Palmer, (Ruth) Candida 1926- *11*
Palmer, Cyril Everard
  See Palmer, C. Everard
Palmer, Don
  See Benson, Mildred
Palmer, Hap 1942- *68*
Palmer, Heidi 1948- *15*
Palmer, Helen Marion
  See Geisel, Helen
Palmer, Jessica 1953- *120*
Palmer, Judd 1972- *153*
Palmer, Juliette 1930- *15*
Palmer, Kate Salley 1946- *97*
Palmer, Maria
  See Strachan, Ian
Palmer, Maria
  See Brennan, Herbie
Palmer, Robin 1909-2000 .... *43*
Palmero Caceres, Ana *198*
Palmisciano, Diane *202*
Paltrowitz, Donna 1950- *61*
  Brief entry *50*
Paltrowitz, Donna Milman
  See Paltrowitz, Donna
Paltrowitz, Stuart 1946- *61*
  Brief entry *50*
Pamela, Todd 1950- *124*
Pamintuan, Macky *214*
  Earlier sketch in SATA *178*
Panagopoulos, Janie Lynn *149*
Panati, Charles 1943- *65*
Panchyk, Richard 1970- *138*
Panetta, George 1915-1969 .... *15*
Panetta, Joseph N. 1953- *96*
Pang, YaWen Ariel *206*
Panik, Sharon 1952- *82*
Panowski, Eileen Thompson 1920- *49*
Pansy
  See Alden, Isabella (Macdonald)
Pantell, Dora (Fuchs) *39*
Panter, Carol 1936- *9*
Paolini, Christopher 1983- *157*
  See also CLR *102*
Papademetriou, Lisa *175*
Paparone, Pam *185*
Paparone, Pamela
  See Paparone, Pam
Papas, Bill
  See Papas, William
Papas, William 1927-2000 .... *50*
Papashvily, George 1898-1978 .... *17*
Papashvily, Helen (Waite) 1906-1996 .. *17*
Pape, D. L.
  See Pape, Donna (Lugg)
Pape, Donna (Lugg) 1930- *82*
  Earlier sketch in SATA *2*
Paperny, Myra (Green) 1932- *51*
  Brief entry *33*
Papp, Robert 1967- *205*
Paradis, Adrian A(lexis) 1912- *67*
  Earlier sketch in SATA *1*
  See also SAAS *8*
Paradis, Marjorie Bartholomew
  1886(?)-1970 .... *17*
Paradiz, Valerie 1963- *176*
Paratore, Coleen
  See Paratore, Coleen Murtagh
Paratore, Coleen Murtagh 1958- *200*
Pardo DeLange, Alex *211*
Parenteau, Shirley 1935- *199*
  Brief entry *40*
  Earlier sketch in SATA *47*
Parish, Margaret 1927-1988 .... *73*
  Obituary *59*
  Earlier sketch in SATA *17*
  See also CLR *22*
Parish, Margaret Holt
  See Holt, Margaret
Parish, Peggy
  See Parish, Margaret

Park, Barbara 1947- *123*
  Brief entry *35*
  Earlier sketches in SATA *40, 78*
  See also CLR *34*
Park, Bill
  See Park, W(illiam) B(ryan)
Park, Frances 1955- *171*
Park, Ginger *173*
Park, Janie Jaehyun *150*
Park, Jordan
  See Kornbluth, C(yril) M.
  and Pohl, Frederik
Park, Linda Sue 1960- *200*
  Earlier sketches in SATA *127, 173*
  See also CLR *84*
Park, Nick 1958- *113*
Park, (Rosina) Ruth (Lucia) 1923(?)- .. *93*
  Earlier sketch in SATA *25*
  See also CLR *51*
Park, W(illiam) B(ryan) 1936- *22*
Parke, Marilyn 1928- *82*
Parker, Barbara Keevil 1938- *157*
Parker, Daniel
  See Ehrenhaft, Daniel
Parker, Elinor Milnor 1906- *3*
Parker, Julie F. 1961- *92*
Parker, Kim 1963- *174*
Parker, Kristy 1957- *59*
Parker, Lois M(ay) 1912-1996 .... *30*
Parker, Margot M. 1937- *52*
Parker, Marjorie Blain 1960- *205*
  Earlier sketch in SATA *145*
Parker, Mary Jessie 1948- *71*
Parker, Nancy Winslow 1930- *132*
  Earlier sketches in SATA *10, 69*
  See also SAAS *20*
Parker, Richard 1915-1990 .... *14*
Parker, Robert
  See Boyd, Waldo T.
  and Parker, Robert Andrew
Parker, Robert Andrew 1927- *200*
Parker, Steve 1954- *213*
Parker, Tom S. *215*
Parker, Toni Trent 1947-2005 .... *142*
  Obituary *169*
Parker-Rees, Guy *193*
Parker-Rock, Michelle *214*
Parkes, Lucas
  See Harris, John (Wyndham Parkes Lucas)
  Beynon
Parkhill, John
  See Cox, William R(obert)
Parkins, David 1955- *176*
Parkinson, Ethelyn M(inerva) 1906-1999 .. *11*
Parkinson, Kathryn N. 1954- *71*
Parkinson, Kathy
  See Parkinson, Kathryn N.
Parkinson, Siobhan
  See Parkinson, Siobhan
Parkinson, Siobhan 1954- *178*
Parks, Deborah A. 1948- *133*
  Earlier sketch in SATA *91*
Parks, Edd Winfield 1906-1968 .... *10*
Parks, Gordon 1912-2006 .... *108*
  Obituary *175*
  Earlier sketch in SATA *8*
Parks, Gordon Roger Alexander
  See Parks, Gordon
Parks, Peggy J. 1951- *143*
Parks, PJ
  See Parks, Peggy J.
Parks, Rosa 1913-2005 .... *83*
  Obituary *169*
Parks, Rosa Louise Lee
  See Parks, Rosa
Parks, Van Dyke 1943- *62*
Parley, Peter
  See Goodrich, Samuel Griswold
Parlin, John
  See Graves, Charles Parlin
Parme, Fabrice 1966- *191*

Parnall, Peter 1936- *69*
  Earlier sketch in SATA *16*
  See also SAAS *11*
Paros, Jennifer *210*
Parotti, Phillip (Elliott) 1941- *109*
Parr, Ann 1943- *144*
Parr, Danny
  See Parr, Ann
Parr, Letitia (Evelyn) 1906-1985(?) ... *37*
Parr, Lucy 1924- *10*
Parr, Todd *179*
  Earlier sketch in SATA *134*
Parrish, Anne 1888-1957 .... *27*
Parrish, Mary
  See Cousins, Margaret
Parrish, Maxfield
  See Parrish, (Frederick) Maxfield
Parrish, (Frederick) Maxfield 1870-1966 .. *14*
Parry, Marian 1924- *13*
Parry, Rosanne *212*
Parson Lot
  See Kingsley, Charles
Parsons, Alexandra 1947- *92*
Parsons, Ellen
  See Dragonwagon, Crescent
Parsons, Garry *197*
Parsons, Martin 1951- *116*
Parsons, Martin Leslie
  See Parsons, Martin
Parsons, Tom
  See MacPherson, Thomas George
Parsons-Yazzi, Evangeline *172*
Partch, Virgil Franklin II 1916-1984 ... *39*
  Obituary *39*
Parton, Dolly 1946- *94*
Parton, Dolly Rebecca
  See Parton, Dolly
Partridge, Benjamin W., Jr. 1915-2005 ... *28*
  Obituary *163*
Partridge, Benjamin Waring, Jr.
  See Partridge, Benjamin W., Jr.
Partridge, Cora Cheney
  See Cheney, Cora
Partridge, Elizabeth *216*
  Earlier sketch in SATA *134*
Partridge, Jenny (Lilian) 1947- *52*
  Brief entry *37*
Pasachoff, Naomi 1947- *147*
Pascal, David 1918- *14*
Pascal, Francine 1938- *143*
  Brief entry *37*
  Earlier sketches in SATA *51, 80*
  See also CLR *25*
Paschal, Nancy
  See Trotter, Grace V(iolet)
Paschkis, Julie 1957- *177*
Pascudniak, Pascal
  See Lupoff, Richard A(llen)
Pashko, Stanley 1913-1982 .... *29*
Passailaigue, Thomas E.
  See Paisley, Tom
Pastel, Elyse *201*
Pateman, Robert 1954- *84*
Patent, Dorothy Hinshaw 1940- *162*
  Autobiography Feature *162*
  Earlier sketches in SATA *22, 69, 120*
  See also CLR *19*
  See also SAAS *13*
Paterson, A(ndrew) B(arton) 1864-1941 ... *97*
Paterson, Banjo
  See Paterson, A(ndrew) B(arton)
Paterson, Diane 1946- *177*
  Brief entry *33*
  Earlier sketch in SATA *59*
Paterson, John (Barstow) 1932- *114*
Paterson, Katherine 1932- *204*
  Earlier sketches in SATA *13, 53, 92, 133*
  See also CLR *127*
Paterson, Katherine Womeldorf
  See Paterson, Katherine
Patience, John 1949- *90*

Patneaude, David 1944- *159*
  Earlier sketch in SATA *85*
Paton, Alan 1903-1988 .... *11*
  Obituary *56*
Paton, Alan Stewart
  See Paton, Alan
Paton, Jane (Elizabeth) 1934- *35*
Paton, Priscilla 1952- *98*
Paton Walsh, Gillian
  See Paton Walsh, Jill
Paton Walsh, Jill 1937- *190*
  Autobiography Feature *190*
  Earlier sketches in SATA *4, 72, 109*
  See also CLR *128*
  See also SAAS *3*
Patricelli, Leslie *207*
Patrick, Susan
  See Clark, Patricia Denise
Patron, Susan 1948- *182*
  Earlier sketch in SATA *76*
Patsauq, Markoosie 1942-
  See CLR *23*
Patschke, Steve 1955- *125*
Patten, Brian 1946- *152*
  Earlier sketch in SATA *29*
Patterson, Charles 1935- *59*
Patterson, Geoffrey 1943- *54*
  Brief entry *44*
Patterson, James 1947- *197*
  Earlier sketch in SATA *164*
Patterson, James B.
  See Patterson, James
Patterson, Lillie G. -1999 .... *88*
  Earlier sketch in SATA *14*
Patterson, Nancy Ruth 1944- *148*
  Earlier sketch in SATA *72*
Pattison, Darcy (S.) 1954- *126*
  Earlier sketch in SATA *72*
Pattou, Edith *164*
Patz (Blaustein), Nancy *154*
Paul, Aileen 1917- *12*
Paul, Alison *196*
Paul, Ann Whitford 1941- *209*
  Earlier sketches in SATA *76, 110, 168*
Paul, David (Tyler) 1934-1988
  Obituary *56*
Paul, Dominique 1973- *184*
Paul, Elizabeth
  See Crow, Donna Fletcher
Paul, Hamish Vigne Christie 1951- *151*
  See also CLR *87*
Paul, James 1936- *23*
Paul, Korky
  See Paul, Hamish Vigne Christie
Paul, Robert
  See Roberts, John G(aither)
Paul, Tessa 1944- *103*
Pauley, Kimberly 1973- *208*
Pauli, Hertha (Ernestine) 1909-1973 .... *3*
  Obituary *26*
Paull, Grace A. 1898- *24*
Paulsen, Gary 1939- *189*
  Earlier sketches in SATA *22, 50, 54, 79, 111,
  158*
  See also CLR *82*
Paulson, Jack
  See Jackson, C(aary) Paul
Pauquet, Gina Ruck
  See Ruck-Pauquet, Gina
Pausacker, Jenny 1948- *72*
  See also SAAS *23*
Pausewang, Gudrun 1928- *165*
  Earlier sketch in SATA *104*
Pavel, Frances 1907- *10*
Paver, Michelle *215*
  Earlier sketch in SATA *170*
Paxton, Thomas R. 1937- *70*
Paxton, Tom
  See Paxton, Thomas R.
Paye, Won-Ldy *185*

Payne, Alan
  See Jakes, John
Payne, Bernal C., Jr. 1941- *60*
Payne, C. Douglas
  See Payne, C.D.
Payne, C.D. 1949- *133*
Payne, C.F. 1956- *179*
Payne, Chris Fox
  See Payne, C.F.
Payne, Donald Gordon 1924- *37*
Payne, Emmy
  See West, Emily Govan
Payne, Nina *135*
Payne, Rachel Ann
  See Jakes, John
Payson, Dale 1943- *9*
Payzant, Charles *18*
Paz, A.
  See Pahz, James Alon
Paz, Natalia Toledo
  See Toledo, Natalia
Paz, Zan
  See Pahz, Cheryl Suzanne
Peace, Mary
  See Finley, Mary Peace
Peacock, Louise *210*
Peacock, Shane 1957- *192*
Peake, Mervyn 1911-1968 .... *23*
Peale, Norman Vincent 1898-1993 .... *20*
  Obituary *78*
Pearce, Ann Philippa
  See Pearce, Philippa
Pearce, Emily Smith 1975- *199*
Pearce, Jacqueline 1962- *146*
Pearce, Margaret *104*
Pearce, Philippa 1920-2006 .... *129*
  Obituary *179*
  Earlier sketches in SATA *1, 67*
  See also CLR *9*
Peare, Catherine Owens 1911- *9*
Pearle, Ida *207*
Pearsall, Shelley 1966- *190*
Pearson, Gayle 1947- *119*
  Earlier sketch in SATA *53*
Pearson, Jean Mary
  See Gardam, Jane
Pearson, Kit 1947- *77*
  Autobiography Feature *117*
  See also CLR *26*
Pearson, Mary E. 1955- *211*
  Earlier sketch in SATA *134*
Pearson, Ridley 1953- *182*
Pearson, Susan 1946- *166*
  Brief entry *27*
  Earlier sketches in SATA *39, 91*
Pearson, Tracey Campbell 1956- *155*
  Earlier sketch in SATA *64*
Pease, (Clarence) Howard 1894-1974 .... *2*
  Obituary *25*
Peavy, Linda 1943- *54*
Peck, Anne Merriman 1884-1976 .... *18*
Peck, Beth 1957- *190*
  Earlier sketch in SATA *79*
Peck, Jan *159*
Peck, Jeanie J. 1967- *147*
Peck, Marshall III 1951- *92*
Peck, Richard 1934- *190*
  Autobiography Feature *110*
  Earlier sketches in SATA *18, 55, 97, 110, 158*
  See also CLR *142*
  See also SAAS *2*
Peck, Richard Wayne
  See Peck, Richard
Peck, Robert Newton 1928- *156*
  Autobiography Feature *108*
  Earlier sketches in SATA *21, 62, 111*
  See also CLR *45*
  See also SAAS *1*
Peck, Sylvia 1953- *133*
Peck-Whiting, Jeanie J.
  See Peck, Jeanie J.

Peddicord, Jane Ann *199*
Pedersen, Janet *193*
Pederson, Sharleen
  See Collicott, Sharleen
Pedler, Caroline *197*
Peebles, Anne
  See Galloway, Priscilla
Peek, Merle 1938- *39*
Peel, John 1954- *79*
Peel, Norman Lemon
  See Hirsch, Phil
Peeples, Edwin A(ugustus, Jr.) 1915-1994 ..... *6*
Peers, Judi 1956- *119*
Peers, Judith May West
  See Peers, Judi
Peet, Bill
  See Peet, William Bartlett
Peet, Creighton B. 1899-1977 .... *30*
Peet, Mal *171*
Peet, Malcolm
  See Peet, Mal
Peet, William Bartlett 1915-2002 .... *78*
  Obituary *137*
  Earlier sketches in SATA *2, 41*
  See also CLR *12*
Peguero, Leone *116*
Pelaez, Jill 1924- *12*
Pelham, David 1938- *70*
Pell, Ed(ward) 1950- *157*
Pelletier, Andrew T. *195*
Pelletier, Andrew Thomas
  See Pelletier, Andrew T.
Pellowski, Anne 1933- *20*
Pellowski, Michael (Joseph) 1949- *151*
  Brief entry *48*
  Earlier sketch in SATA *88*
Pellowski, Michael Morgan
  See Pellowski, Michael (Joseph)
Pelta, Kathy 1928- *18*
Peltier, Leslie C(opus) 1900-1980 .... *13*
Pemberton, Bonnie *191*
Pemberton, John Leigh
  See Leigh-Pemberton, John
Pembury, Bill
  See Groom, Arthur William
Pemsteen, Hans
  See Manes, Stephen
Pendennis, Arthur Esquir
  See Thackeray, William Makepeace
Pender, Lydia Podger 1907- *61*
Pendery, Rosemary (Schmitz) *7*
Pendle, Alexy 1943- *29*
Pendle, George 1906-1977
  Obituary *28*
Pendleton, Don
  See Cunningham, Chet
  and Garside, Jack
  and Jagninski, Tom
  and Krauzer, Steven M(ark)
  and Obstfeld, Raymond
Pendleton, Thomas 1965- *206*
Pendziwol, Jean E. 1965- *177*
Pene du Bois, William (Sherman)
  1916-1993 .... *68*
  Obituary *74*
  Earlier sketch in SATA *4*
  See also CLR *1*
Penn, Audrey 1947- *212*
Penn, Audrey 1950- *22*
Penn, Ruth Bonn
  See Rosenberg, Eth Clifford
Pennac, Daniel 1944- *155*
Pennage, E. M.
  See Finkel, George (Irvine)
Penner, Fred 1946- *169*
  Earlier sketch in SATA *67*
Penner, Frederick Ralph Cornelius
  See Penner, Fred
Penney, Grace Jackson 1904-2000 .... *35*
Penney, Ian 1960- *76*

Penney, Sue 1957- *152*
  Earlier sketch in SATA *102*
Pennington, Eunice 1923- 27
Pennington, Lillian Boyer 1904-2003 45
Pennypacker, Sara 1951- *187*
Penrose, Gordon 1925- 66
Penson, Mary E. 1917- 78
Penzler, Otto 1942- 38
Pepe, Phil 1935- 20
Pepe, Philip
  See Pepe, Phil
Peppe, Rodney (Darrell) 1934- 74
  Earlier sketch in SATA *4*
  See also SAAS *10*
Pepper, Frank S. 1910-1988
  Obituary 61
Percy, Charles Henry
  See Smith, Dorothy Gladys
Percy, Rachel 1930- 63
Perdrizet, Marie-Pierre 1952- 79
Perenyi, Constance 1954- 93
Perenyi, Constance Marie
  See Perenyi, Constance
Perera, Hilda 1926- *105*
Perera, Thomas Biddle 1938- 13
Peretti, Frank E. 1951- *141*
  Earlier sketch in SATA *80*
Perez, L. King 1940- *199*
Perez, Lana
  See Perez, Marlene
Perez, Lucia Angela 1973- *182*
Perez, Marlene *170*
Pericoli, Matteo 1968- *178*
Perkins, Al(bert Rogers) 1904-1975 30
Perkins, Lucy Fitch 1865-1937 72
Perkins, Lynne Rae 1956- *212*
  Earlier sketches in SATA *131, 172*
Perkins, (Richard) Marlin 1905-1986 21
  Obituary 48
Perkins, Mitali 1963- *188*
  Earlier sketch in SATA *88*
Perks, Anne-Marie 1955- *122*
Perl, Erica S. *188*
Perl, Lila 72
  Earlier sketch in SATA *6*
Perl, Susan 1922-1983 22
  Obituary 34
Perlman, Rhea 1948- *183*
Perlmutter, O(scar) William 1920-1975 8
Pernu, Dennis 1970- 87
Perrault, Charles 1628-1703 25
  See also CLR *134*
Perret, Delphine 1980- *190*
Perret, Gene (Richard) 1937- 76
Perriman, Cole
  See Perrin, Pat
Perriman, Cole
  See Coleman, Wim
Perrin, Pat *212*
Perrine, Mary 1913-1976 2
Perrins, Lesley 1953- 56
Perrow, Angeli 1954- *121*
Perry, Andrea 1956- *190*
  Earlier sketch in SATA *148*
Perry, Barbara Fisher
  See Fisher, Barbara
Perry, Elizabeth 1959- *174*
Perry, Elizabeth Goodwin
  See Perry, Elizabeth
Perry, Marie Fritz *165*
Perry, Patricia 1949- 30
Perry, Phyllis J(ean) 1933- *152*
  Earlier sketches in SATA *60, 101*
Perry, Ritchie (John Allen) 1942- *105*
Perry, Roger 1933- 27
Perry, Steve(n Carl) 1947- 76
Pershall, Mary K. 1951- *172*
  Earlier sketch in SATA *70*
Pershing, Marie
  See Schultz, Pearle Henriksen
Perske, Robert 1927- 57

Persun, Morgan Reed
  See Watkins, Dawn L.
Perversi, Margaret *213*
Petach, Heidi *149*
Peter
  See Stratemeyer, Edward L.
Peters, Alexander
  See Hollander, Zander
Peters, Andrew Fusek 1965- *169*
  Earlier sketch in SATA *107*
Peters, Bernadette 1948- *212*
Peters, Caroline
  See Betz, Eva Kelly
Peters, David
  See David, Peter
Peters, Elizabeth 1927- 49
Peters, Emma
  See Price, Karen
Peters, Gabriel
  See Matott, Justin
Peters, Julie Anne 1952- *197*
  Earlier sketches in SATA *82, 128*
Peters, Linda
  See Catherall, Arthur
Peters, Lisa Westberg 1951- *161*
  Earlier sketches in SATA *74, 115*
Peters, Patricia 1953- 84
Peters, Russell M. 1929- 78
Peters, S. H.
  See Henry, O.
  and Proffitt, Nicholas
Petersen, David 1946- *109*
  Earlier sketch in SATA *62*
Petersen, Gwenn Boardman 1924- 12
Petersen, P(eter) J(ames) 1941- *118*
  Brief entry 43
  Earlier sketches in SATA *48, 83*
Petersen, Palle 1943- 85
Petersham, Maud 1890-1971 17
  See also CLR *24*
Petersham, Maud Sylvia Fuller
  See Petersham, Maud
Petersham, Miska 1888-1960 17
  See also CLR *24*
Peterson, Cris 1952- *174*
  Earlier sketches in SATA *84, 145*
Peterson, Dawn 1934- 86
Peterson, Esther (Allen) 1934- 35
Peterson, Hans 1922- 8
Peterson, Harold L(eslie) 1922-1978 8
Peterson, Helen Stone 1910- 8
Peterson, Jean Sunde 1941- *108*
Peterson, Jeanne Whitehouse 1939- *159*
  Earlier sketch in SATA *29*
Peterson, Kathleen B. 1951- *119*
Peterson, Lorraine 1940- 56
  Brief entry 44
Peterson, Mary *215*
Peterson, Shelley 1952- *146*
Peterson, Will
  See Cocks, Peter
Petie, Haris
  See Petty, Roberta
Petricic, Dusan 1946- *176*
Petrides, Heidrun 1944- 19
Petrie, Catherine 1947- 52
  Brief entry 41
Petrone, Valeria *186*
Petrosino, Tamara *193*
Petroski, Catherine (Ann Groom) 1939- 48
Petrovich, Michael B(oro) 1922- 40
Petrovskaya, Kyra
  See Wayne, Kyra Petrovskaya
Petruccio, Steven James 1961- 67
Petrucha, Stefan 1959- *213*
Petry, Ann 1908-1997 5
  Obituary 94
  See also CLR *12*
Petry, Ann Lane
  See Petry, Ann
Pettit, Jayne 1932- *108*

Petty, J.T. 1977- *189*
Petty, Kate 1951-2007 .... *204*
Petty, Roberta 1915- 10
Pevsner, Stella *131*
  Earlier sketches in SATA *8, 77*
  See also SAAS *14*
Peyo
  See Culliford, Pierre
Peyton, K. M.
  See Peyton, Kathleen Wendy
Peyton, Kathleen Wendy 1929- *157*
  Earlier sketches in SATA *15, 62*
  See also CLR *3*
  See also SAAS *17*
Pfanner, (Anne) Louise 1955- 68
Pfeffer, Susan Beth 1948- *180*
  Earlier sketches in SATA *4, 83*
  See also CLR *11*
  See also SAAS *17*
Pfeffer, Wendy 1929- *204*
  Earlier sketches in SATA *78, 142*
Pfeiffer, Janet (B.) 1949- 96
Pfister, Marcus *207*
  Earlier sketches in SATA *83, 150*
  See also CLR *42*
Pfitsch, Patricia Curtis 1948- *148*
Pflieger, Pat 1955- 84
Pham, LeUyen 1973- *201*
  Earlier sketch in SATA *175*
Phelan, Mary Kay 1914- 3
Phelan, Matt 1970- *215*
  Earlier sketch in SATA *172*
Phelan, Terry Wolfe 1941- 56
Phelps, Ethel Johnston 1914-1984 35
Philbrick, Rodman 1951- *163*
Philbrick, W. Rodman
  See Philbrick, Rodman
Philbrick, W.R.
  See Philbrick, Rodman
Philbrook, Clem(ent E.) 1917- 24
Phillips, Aileen Paul
  See Paul, Aileen
Phillips, Betty Lou
  See Phillips, Elizabeth Louise
Phillips, Bob 1940- 95
Phillips, Douglas A. 1949- *161*
Phillips, Elizabeth Louise 58
  Brief entry 48
Phillips, Irv(ing W.) 1905-2000 11
  Obituary *125*
Phillips, Jack
  See Sandburg, Carl
Phillips, Leon
  See Gerson, Noel Bertram
Phillips, Loretta (Hosey) 1893-1987 10
Phillips, Louis 1942- *102*
  Earlier sketch in SATA *8*
Phillips, Mark
  See Garrett, Randall
  and Janifer, Laurence M(ark)
Phillips, Mary Geisler 1881-1964 10
Phillips, Michael
  See Nolan, William F.
Phillips, (Woodward) Prentice 1894-1981 10
Phillpotts, Eden 1862-1960 24
Phin
  See Thayer, Ernest Lawrence
Phipson, Joan
  See Fitzhardinge, Joan Margaret
Phiz
  See Browne, Hablot Knight
Phleger, Fred B. 1909-1993 34
Phleger, Marjorie Temple 1908(?)-1986 1
  Obituary 47
Piaget, Jean 1896-1980
  Obituary 23
Piatti, Celestino 1922- 16
Picard, Barbara Leonie 1917- 89
  Earlier sketch in SATA *2*
  See also SAAS *10*
Pichon, Liz *174*

Pickard, Charles 1932- *36*
Pickering, James Sayre 1897-1969 .... *36*
   Obituary *28*
Pickering, Jimmy *195*
Pickering, Robert B. 1950- *93*
Pielichaty, Helena 1955- *142*
Pienkowski, Jan (Michal) 1936- *131*
   Earlier sketches in SATA *6, 58*
   See also CLR *6*
Pierce, Edith Gray 1893-1977 .... *45*
Pierce, Katherine
   See St. John, Wylly Folk
Pierce, Meredith Ann 1958- *127*
   Brief entry *48*
   Earlier sketch in SATA *67*
   See also CLR *20*
Pierce, Ruth (Ireland) 1936- *5*
Pierce, Sharon
   See McCullough, Sharon Pierce
Pierce, Tamora 1954- *187*
   Brief entry *49*
   Earlier sketches in SATA *51, 96, 153*
Pierce, Terry *178*
Pierik, Robert 1921- *13*
Piernas-Davenport, Gail *199*
Piers, Robert
   See Anthony, Piers
Pig, Edward
   See Gorey, Edward (St. John)
Pike, Bob
   See Pike, Robert W.
Pike, Christopher 1954(?)- *156*
   Earlier sketch in SATA *68*
   See also CLR *29*
Pike, Deborah 1951- *89*
Pike, E(dgar) Royston 1896-1980 .... *22*
   Obituary *56*
Pike, R. William 1956- *92*
Pike, Robert
   See Pike, Robert W.
Pike, Robert W. 1931- *102*
Pike, Robert Wilson
   See Pike, Robert W.
Pilarski, Laura 1926- *13*
Pilgrim, Anne
   See Allan, Mabel Esther
Pilkey, Dav 1966- *166*
   Earlier sketches in SATA *68, 115*
   See also CLR *48*
Pilkey, David Murray, Jr.
   See Pilkey, Dav
Pilkington, Francis Meredyth 1907-1993 .... *4*
Pilkington, Roger (Windle) 1915-2003 .... *10*
   Obituary *144*
Pilutti, Deb *208*
Pin, Isabel 1975- *183*
Pinchot, David 1914(?)-1983
   Obituary *34*
Pincus, Harriet 1938- *27*
Pinczes, Elinor J(ane) 1940- *81*
Pine, Nicholas 1951- *91*
Pine, Tillie S(chloss) 1896-1999 .... *13*
Pini, Richard (Alan) 1950- *89*
Pini, Wendy 1951- *89*
Pinkerton, Kathrene Sutherland (Gedney)
   1887-1967
   Obituary *26*
Pinkett, Jada
   See Smith, Jada Pinkett
Pinkney, Andrea Davis 1963- *160*
   Earlier sketch in SATA *113*
Pinkney, Brian 1961- *206*
   Earlier sketches in SATA *74, 148*
   See also CLR *54*
Pinkney, Gloria Jean 1941- *212*
   Earlier sketch in SATA *85*
Pinkney, J. Brian
   See Pinkney, Brian

Pinkney, Jerry 1939- *198*
   Autobiography Feature *198*
   Brief entry *32*
   Earlier sketches in SATA *41, 71, 107, 151*
   See also CLR *43*
   See also SAAS *12*
Pinkney, John *97*
Pinkney, Sandra L. *193*
   Earlier sketch in SATA *128*
Pinkwater, D. Manus
   See Pinkwater, Daniel
Pinkwater, Daniel 1941- *210*
   Earlier sketches in SATA *8, 46, 76, 114, 158*
   See also CLR *4*
   See also SAAS *3*
Pinkwater, Daniel M.
   See Pinkwater, Daniel
Pinkwater, Daniel Manus
   See Pinkwater, Daniel
Pinkwater, Jill *188*
Pinkwater, Manus
   See Pinkwater, Daniel
Pinner, Joma
   See Werner, Herma
Pinto, Sara *200*
Pioneer
   See Yates, Raymond F(rancis)
Piowaty, Kim Kennelly 1957- *49*
Piper, Roger
   See Fisher, John
Pirner, Connie White 1955- *72*
Piro, Richard 1934- *7*
Pirot, Alison Lohans
   See Lohans, Alison
Pirotta, Saviour *184*
Pirsig, Robert M(aynard) 1928- *39*
Pita
   See Rendon, Maria
Pitcher, C.
   See Pitcher, Caroline
Pitcher, Caroline 1948- *214*
   Earlier sketch in SATA *128*
Pitcher, Caroline Nell
   See Pitcher, Caroline
Pitman, (Isaac) James 1901-1985
   Obituary *46*
Pitre, Felix 1949- *84*
Pitrone, Jean Maddern 1920- *4*
Pittman, Helena Clare 1945- *71*
Pitz, Henry C(larence) 1895-1976 .... *4*
   Obituary *24*
Pitzer, Susanna 1958- *181*
Piven, Hanoch 1963- *173*
Pixley, Marcella *194*
Pizer, Vernon 1918- *21*
Place, Marian T(empleton) 1910- *3*
Place, Robin (Mary) 1926- *71*
Plaidy, Jean
   See Hibbert, Eleanor Alice Burford
Plain, Belva 1919- *62*
Plaine, Alfred R. 1898(?)-1981
   Obituary *29*
Plant, Andrew *214*
Plath, Sylvia 1932-1963 .... *96*
Platt, Chris 1959- *185*
Platt, Kin 1911- *86*
   Earlier sketch in SATA *21*
   See also SAAS *17*
Platt, Randall 1948- *95*
Platt, Randall Beth
   See Platt, Randall
Platt, Richard 1953- *166*
   Earlier sketch in SATA *120*
Playfellow, Robin
   See Ellis, Edward S.
Playsted, James
   See Wood, James Playsted
Plecas, Jennifer 1966- *149*
   Earlier sketch in SATA *84*
Plimpton, George 1927-2003 .... *10*
   Obituary *150*

Plimpton, George Ames
   See Plimpton, George
Plomer, William Charles Franklin
   1903-1973 .... *24*
Plotz, Helen Ratnoff 1913-2000 .... *38*
Plourde, Lynn 1955- *168*
   Earlier sketch in SATA *122*
Plowden, David 1932- *52*
Plowden, Martha Ward 1948- *98*
Plowhead, Ruth Gipson 1877-1967 .... *43*
Plowman, Stephanie 1922- *6*
Pluckrose, Henry (Arthur) 1931- *141*
   Earlier sketch in SATA *13*
Plum, J.
   See Wodehouse, P. G.
Plum, Jennifer
   See Kurland, Michael
Plumb, Charles P. 1900(?)-1982
   Obituary *29*
Plume, Ilse *170*
   Brief entry *43*
Plumme, Don E.
   See Katz, Bobbi
Plummer, Margaret 1911- *2*
Plum-Ucci, Carol *184*
Pochocki, Ethel (Frances) 1925- *76*
Podendorf, Illa (E.) 1903(?)-1983 .... *18*
   Obituary *35*
Podwal, Mark 1945- *160*
   Earlier sketch in SATA *101*
Podwal, Mark H.
   See Podwal, Mark
Poe, Edgar Allan 1809-1849 .... *23*
Poe, Ty (Christopher) 1975- *94*
Pogany, William Andrew 1882-1955 .... *44*
   Brief entry *30*
Pogany, Willy
   See Pogany, William Andrew
Pohl, Frederik 1919- *24*
Pohlmann, Lillian (Grenfell) 1902-1997 .... *11*
Pohrt, Tom 1953- *195*
   Earlier sketches in SATA *67, 152*
Pointon, Robert
   See Rooke, Daphne
Points, Larry G. 1945- *177*
   Earlier sketch in SATA *133*
Points, Larry Gene
   See Points, Larry G.
Pokeberry, P.J.
   See Mitchell, B.J.
POLA
   See Watson, Pauline
Polacco, Patricia 1944- *212*
   Earlier sketches in SATA *74, 123, 180*
   See also CLR *40*
Polacco, Patricia Ann
   See Polacco, Patricia
Polak, Monique 1960- *178*
Polatnick, Florence T. 1923- *5*
Polcovar, Jane 1948- *211*
Polder, Markus
   See Kruss, James
Polese, Carolyn 1947- *58*
Polese, James 1914- *87*
Polette, Nancy (Jane) 1930- *42*
Polhamus, Jean Burt 1928- *21*
Polhemus, Coleman *210*
Policoff, Stephen Phillip 1948- *77*
Polikoff, Barbara G. 1929- *162*
   Earlier sketch in SATA *77*
Polikoff, Barbara Garland
   See Polikoff, Barbara G.
Polisar, Barry Louis 1954- *134*
   Earlier sketch in SATA *77*
Politi, Leo 1908-1996 .... *47*
   Obituary *88*
   Earlier sketch in SATA *1*
   See also CLR *29*
Polking, Kirk 1925- *5*
Pollack, Jill S. 1963- *88*

Pollack, Merrill S. 1924-1988
    Obituary 55
Polland, Barbara K(ay) 1939- 44
Polland, Madeleine A(ngela Cahill) 1918- ... 68
    Earlier sketch in SATA 6
    See also SAAS 8
Pollema-Cahill, Phyllis 1958- 123
Pollock, Bruce 1945- 46
Pollock, Mary
    See Blyton, Enid
Pollock, Penny 1935- 137
    Brief entry 42
    Earlier sketch in SATA 44
Pollowitz, Melinda Kilborn 1944- 26
Polner, Murray 1928- 64
Polonsky, Arthur 1925- 34
Polseno, Jo 17
Pomaska, Anna 1946- 117
Pomerantz, Charlotte 1930- 177
    Earlier sketches in SATA 20, 80
Pomeroy, Pete
    See Roth, Arthur J(oseph)
Pon, Cindy 1973- 216
Pond, Alonzo W(illiam) 1894-1986 5
Pontiflet, Ted 1932- 32
Poole, Gray Johnson 1906- 1
Poole, Josephine
    See Helyar, Jane Penelope Josephine
Poole, (Jane Penelope) Josephine
    See Helyar, Jane Penelope Josephine
Poole, Lynn 1910-1969 1
Poole, Peggy 1925- 39
Poortvliet, Rien 1932- 65
    Brief entry 37
Pope, Elizabeth Marie 1917-1992 38
    Brief entry 36
Pope, Kevin 1958- 183
Popescu, Christine
    See Pullein-Thompson, Christine
Poploff, Michelle 1956- 67
Popp, K. Wendy 91
Poppel, Hans 1942- 71
Porfirio, Guy 1958- 197
Portal, Colette 1936- 6
Porte, Barbara Ann 1943- 152
    Brief entry 45
    Earlier sketches in SATA 57, 93
Porter, A(nthony) P(eyton) 1945- 68
Porter, Connie (Rose) 1959(?)- 129
    Earlier sketch in SATA 81
Porter, Donald Clayton
    See Gerson, Noel Bertram
Porter, Eleanor H(odgman) 1868-1920
    See CLR 110
Porter, Gene Stratton
    See Stratton-Porter, Gene
Porter, Janice Lee 1953- 108
    Earlier sketch in SATA 68
Porter, Katherine Anne 1890-1980 39
    Obituary 23
Porter, Kathryn
    See Swinford, Betty (June Wells)
Porter, Pamela 1956- 193
Porter, Sheena 1935- 24
    See also SAAS 10
Porter, Sue
    See Limb, Sue
Porter, Sue 1951- 213
    Earlier sketch in SATA 76
Porter, Tracey 191
Porter, William Sydney
    See Henry, O.
Portis, Antoinette 189
Porto, Tony 1960- 153
Portteus, Eleanora Marie Manthei (?)-1983
    Obituary 36
Posada, Mia 187
Posell, Elsa Z(eigerman) -1995 3
Posesorski, Sherie 216
Posten, Margaret L(ois) 1915- 10
Postgate, Daniel 1964- 216

Posthuma, Sieb 1960- 150
Postier, Jim 1965- 202
Potok, Chaim 1929-2002 106
    Obituary 134
    Earlier sketch in SATA 33
    See also CLR 92
Potok, Herbert Harold
    See Potok, Chaim
Potok, Herman Harold
    See Potok, Chaim
Potter, Alicia 216
Potter, Beatrix 1866-1943 132
    Earlier sketch in SATA 100
    See also YABC 1
    See also CLR 73
Potter, Giselle 187
    Earlier sketch in SATA 150
Potter, Helen Beatrix
    See Potter, Beatrix
Potter, Katherine 217
Potter, Margaret 1926-1998 21
    Obituary 104
Potter, Marian 1915- 9
Potter, Miriam Clark 1886-1965 3
Poulin, Stephane 1961- 98
    See also CLR 28
Poulton, Kimberly 1957(?)- 136
Pournelle, Jerry (Eugene) 1933- 161
    Earlier sketches in SATA 26, 91
Povelite, Kay 1955- 102
Pow, Tom 1950- 163
Powe-Allred, Alexandra
    See Allred, Alexandra Powe
Powell, A. M.
    See Morgan, Alfred P(owell)
Powell, Consie 174
Powell, E. Sandy 1947- 72
Powell, E.S.
    See Powell, E. Sandy
Powell, Pamela 1960- 78
Powell, Patricia Hruby 1951- 136
Powell, Randy 1956- 118
Powell, Richard Stillman
    See Barbour, Ralph Henry
Powell, Robert (Stephenson Smyth) Baden
    See Baden-Powell, Robert (Stephenson
    Smyth)
Powell, Stephanie 1953- 93
Power, Margaret (M.) 1945- 125
    Earlier sketch in SATA 75
Powers, Anne
    See Schwartz, Anne Powers
Powers, Bill 1931- 52
    Brief entry 31
Powers, Daniel 1959- 164
Powers, J. L. 195
Powers, Jessica
    See Powers, J. L.
Powers, Jessica Lynn
    See Powers, J. L.
Powers, Margaret
    See Heal, Edith
Powers, Tim 1952- 107
Powers, Timothy Thomas
    See Powers, Tim
Powledge, Fred 1935- 37
Poydar, Nancy 190
Poynter, Margaret 1927- 27
Prachaticka, Marketa
    See Kolibalova, Marketa
Prachatika, Marketa
    See Kolibalova, Marketa
Prager, Arthur 44
Prager, Ellen J. 1962- 136
Prange, Beckie 172
Prap, Lila 1955- 177
Praprotnik-Zupancic, Lilijana
    See Prap, Lila
Pratchett, Terence David John
    See Pratchett, Terry

Pratchett, Terry 1948- 185
    Earlier sketches in SATA 82, 139
    See also CLR 64
Prater, John 1947- 149
    Earlier sketches in SATA 72, 103
Prato, Rodica 184
Pratt, Christine Joy 214
Pratt, (Murray) Fletcher 1897-1956 102
Pratt, Kristin Joy 1976- 87
Pratt, Pierre 1962- 208
    Earlier sketches in SATA 95, 166
Preiss, Byron 1953-2005 166
    Brief entry 42
    Earlier sketch in SATA 47
Preiss, Byron Cary
    See Preiss, Byron
Preller, James 1961- 209
    Earlier sketch in SATA 88
Prelutsky, Jack 1940- 171
    Earlier sketches in SATA 22, 66, 118
    See also CLR 115
Prentice, Amy
    See Kaler, James Otis
Prescott, Casey
    See Morris, Chris(topher Crosby)
Presnall, Judith (Ann) Janda 1943- 96
Pressler, Mirjam 1940- 155
Preston, Douglas 1956- 113
Preston, Edna Mitchell 40
Preston, Lillian Elvira 1918- 47
Preus, Margi 209
Preussler, Otfried 1923- 24
Prevert, Jacques 1900-1977
    Obituary 30
Prevert, Jacques Henri Marie
    See Prevert, Jacques
Prevost, Guillaume 1964- 192
Prevost, Mikela 203
Price, Beverley Joan 1931- 98
Price, Charlie 187
Price, Christine (Hilda) 1928-1980 3
    Obituary 23
Price, Garrett 1896-1979
    Obituary 22
Price, Jennifer
    See Hoover, Helen (Drusilla Blackburn)
Price, Joan 1931- 124
Price, Jonathan (Reeve) 1941- 46
Price, Karen 1957- 125
Price, Kathy Z. 1957- 172
Price, Lucie Locke
    See Locke, Lucie
Price, Olive 1903-1991 8
Price, Susan 1955- 128
    Earlier sketches in SATA 25, 85
Price, Willard 1887-1983 48
    Brief entry 38
Price-Groff, Claire 127
Priceman, Marjorie 1958- 168
    Earlier sketches in SATA 81, 120
Prichard, Katharine Susannah 1883-1969 66
Prideaux, Tom 1908-1993 37
    Obituary 76
Priestley, Alice 1962- 95
Priestley, Chris 1958- 198
Priestley, Lee (Shore) 1904-1999 27
Priestly, Doug 1954- 122
Priestly, Douglas Michael
    See Priestly, Doug
Prieto, Mariana Beeching 1912-1999 8
Priley, Margaret (Ann) Hubbard 1909-1992
    Obituary 130
Primavera, Elise 1954- 185
    Brief entry 48
    Earlier sketches in SATA 58, 109
Prime, Derek (James) 1931- 34
Prince, Alison (Mary) 1931- 86
    Earlier sketch in SATA 28
Prince, April Jones 1975- 180
Prince, J(ack) H(arvey) 1908- 17
Prince, Joshua 188

Prince, Maggie *102*
Prineas, Sarah *204*
Pringle, Eric *138*
Pringle, Laurence 1935- *201*
    Autobiography Feature *201*
    Earlier sketches in SATA *4, 68, 104, 154*
    See also CLR *57*
    See also SAAS *6*
Pringle, Laurence Patrick
    See Pringle, Laurence
Prinz, Yvonne 1960- *175*
Prior, Natalie Jane 1963- *106*
Pritchett, Elaine H(illyer) 1920- *36*
Pritchett, Laura 1971- *178*
Pritchett, Laura Rose
    See Pritchett, Laura
Pritts, Kim Derek 1953- *83*
Prochazkova, Iva 1953- *68*
Proctor, Everitt
    See Montgomery, Rutherford George
Proeysen, Alf 1914-1970 .... *67*
    See also CLR *24*
Professor Scribbler
    See Hollingsworth, Mary
Proimos, James 1955- *217*
    Earlier sketch in SATA *173*
Prose, Francine 1947- *198*
    Earlier sketches in SATA *101, 149*
Prosek, James 1975- *216*
Protopopescu, Orel *186*
Protopopescu, Orel Odinov
    See Protopopescu, Orel
Provensen, Alice 1918- *147*
    Earlier sketches in SATA *9, 70*
    See also CLR *11*
Provensen, Martin 1916-1987 .... *70*
    Obituary *51*
    Earlier sketch in SATA *9*
    See also CLR *11*
Provensen, Martin Elias
    See Provensen, Martin
Provenzo, Eugene (F., Jr.) 1949- *142*
    Earlier sketch in SATA *78*
Provist, d'Alain 1906-1989
    See Diop, Birago (Ismael)
Provost, Gail Levine 1944- *65*
Provost, Gary (Richard) 1944-1995 .... *66*
Proysen, Alf
    See Proeysen, Alf
Pruett, Candace (J.) 1968- *157*
Pryor, Bonnie H. 1942- *69*
Pryor, Boori (Monty) 1950- *112*
Pryor, Helen Brenton 1897-1972 .... *4*
Pryor, Michael 1957- *153*
Pucci, Albert John 1920- *44*
Pudney, John (Sleigh) 1909-1977 .... *24*
Pugh, Ellen (Tiffany) 1920- *7*
Pullein-Thompson, Christine 1925-2005 ...... *82*
    Obituary *172*
    Earlier sketch in SATA *3*
Pullein-Thompson, Diana
    See Farr, Diana
Pullein-Thompson, Joanna Maxwell
    1898-1961 .... *82*
Pullein-Thompson, Josephine (Mary
    Wedderburn) *82*
    Earlier sketch in SATA *3*
Pullen, Zachary *189*
Pullman, Philip 1946- *198*
    Earlier sketches in SATA *65, 103, 150*
    See also CLR *84*
    See also SAAS *17*
Pullman, Philip Nicholas
    See Pullman, Philip
Pulver, Harry, Jr. 1960- *129*
Pulver, Robin 1945- *208*
    Earlier sketches in SATA *76, 133*
Puner, Helen W(alker) 1915-1989 .... *37*
    Obituary *63*
Purdy, Carol 1943- *120*
    Earlier sketch in SATA *66*

Purdy, Susan G(old) 1939- *8*
Purkiss, Diane 1961- *194*
Purmell, Ann 1953- *206*
    Earlier sketch in SATA *147*
Purnell, Idella 1901-1982 .... *120*
Purscell, Phyllis 1934- *7*
Purtill, Richard L. 1931- *53*
Pushker, Gloria 1927- *162*
    Earlier sketch in SATA *75*
Pushker, Gloria Teles
    See Pushker, Gloria
Pushkin, Aleksandr Sergeevich
    See Pushkin, Alexander
Pushkin, Alexander 1799-1837 .... *61*
Putnam, Alice 1916- *61*
Putnam, Arthur Lee
    See Alger, Horatio, Jr.
Putnam, Peter B(rock) 1920-1998 .... *30*
    Obituary *106*
Puttapipat, Niroot *199*
Puttock, Simon *178*
Puvilland, Alex *205*
Puvilland, Alexandre
    See Puvilland, Alex
Puybaret, Eric 1976- *195*
Pyle, Howard 1853-1911 .... *100*
    Earlier sketch in SATA *16*
    See also CLR *117*
Pyle, Katharine 1863-1938 .... *66*
Pyne, Mable Mandeville 1903-1969 .... *9*
Pyrnelle, Louise-Clarke 1850-1907 .... *114*

Q

Quackenbush, Robert M(ead) 1929- *133*
    Autobiography Feature *133*
    Earlier sketches in SATA *7, 70*
    See also CLR *122*
    See also SAAS *7*
Qualey, Marsha 1953- *124*
    Earlier sketch in SATA *79*
Qualls, Sean *177*
Quammen, David 1948- *7*
Quark, Jason
    See Eldin, Peter
Quarles, Benjamin 1904-1996 .... *12*
Quarles, Benjamin Arthur
    See Quarles, Benjamin
Quatermass, Martin
    See Carpenter, John
Quattlebaum, Mary 1958- *185*
    Earlier sketches in SATA *88, 134*
Quay, Emma *173*
    Earlier sketch in SATA *119*
Queen, Ellery
    See Deming, Richard
    and Dannay, Frederic
    and Davidson, Avram (James)
    and Fairman, Paul W.
    and Flora, Fletcher
    and Holding, James (Clark Carlisle, Jr.)
    and Hoch, Edward D.
    and Kane, Henry
    and Lee, Manfred B.
    and Marlowe, Stephen
    and Powell, (Oval) Talmage
    and Sheldon, Walter J(ames)
    and Sturgeon, Theodore (Hamilton)
    and Tracy, Don(ald Fiske)
    and Vance, Jack
Queen Latifah 1970- *185*
Quennell, Marjorie Courtney 1884-1972 ...... *29*
Quentin
    See Sheldon, David
Quentin, Brad
    See Bisson, Terry
Quest, (Edna) Olga W(ilbourne) Hall
    See Hall-Quest, (Edna) Olga W(ilbourne)
Quick, Annabelle 1922-1986 .... *2*

Quigg, Jane (Hulda) (?)-1986
    Obituary *49*
Quill, Monica
    See McInerny, Ralph
Quin-Harkin, Janet 1941- *165*
    Earlier sketches in SATA *18, 90, 119*
Quin-Harkin, Janet Elizabeth
    See Quin-Harkin, Janet
Quinlan, Susan E. 1954- *88*
Quinlan, Susan Elizabeth
    See Quinlan, Susan E.
Quinn, Elisabeth 1881-1962 .... *22*
Quinn, Pat 1947- *130*
Quinn, Patrick 1950- *73*
Quinn, Rob 1972- *138*
Quinn, Susan 1940- *30*
Quinn, Susan Taft
    See Quinn, Susan
Quinn, Theodora K.
    See Kroeber, Theodora (Kracaw)
Quinn, Vernon
    See Quinn, Elisabeth
Quirk, Anne (E.) 1956- *99*
Quixley, Jim 1931- *56*
Quyth, Gabriel
    See Jennings, Gary

R

Ra, Carol F. 1939- *76*
Raab, Evelyn 1951- *129*
Rabb, Margo 1972- *188*
Rabb, M.E.
    See Rabb, Margo
Rabe, Berniece (Louise) 1928- *148*
    Autobiography Feature *148*
    Earlier sketches in SATA *7, 77*
    See also SAAS *10*
Rabe, Olive H(anson) (?)-1968 .... *13*
Rabin, Staton 1958- *162*
    Earlier sketch in SATA *84*
Rabinowich, Ellen 1946- *29*
Rabinowitz, Sandy 1954- *52*
    Brief entry *39*
Rachlin, Carol K(ing) 1919- *64*
Rachlin, Harvey 1951- *47*
Rachlin, Harvey Brant
    See Rachlin, Harvey
Rachlin, Nahid *64*
Rachlis, Eugene (Jacob) 1920-1986
    Obituary *50*
Rackham, Arthur 1867-1939 .... *100*
    Earlier sketch in SATA *15*
    See also CLR *57*
Racoma, Robin Yoko 1953- *207*
Raczka, Bob 1963- *191*
    Earlier sketch in SATA *163*
Radencich, Marguerite C. 1952-1998 .... *79*
Rader, Laura *197*
Radford, Ruby L(orraine) 1891-1971 .... *6*
Radin, Ruth Yaffe 1938- *107*
    Brief entry *52*
    Earlier sketch in SATA *56*
Radlauer, David 1952- *28*
Radlauer, Edward 1921- *15*
Radlauer, Ruth Shaw 1926- *98*
    Earlier sketch in SATA *15*
Radley, Gail 1951- *112*
    Earlier sketch in SATA *25*
Radunsky, Vladimir *177*
Radzinski, Kandy 1948- *212*
Rae, Gwynedd 1892-1977 .... *37*
Raebeck, Lois 1921- *5*
Rael, Elsa Okon 1927-
    See CLR *84*
Raffi
    See Cavoukian, Raffi
Raftery, Gerald (Bransfield) 1905-1986 .... *11*
Ragan-Reid, Gale 1956- *90*

Rahaman, Vashanti 1953- 98
Rahn, Joan Elma 1929- 27
Rai, Bali 1971- 152
Raible, Alton (Robert) 1918- 35
Raiff, Stan 1930- 11
Raines, Shirley C(arol) 1945- 128
Rainey, W. B.
    See Blassingame, Wyatt Rainey
Rake, Jody 1961- 157
Rallison, Janette 1966- 183
Ralston, Jan
    See Dunlop, Agnes M. R.
Rama, Sue 190
Ramal, Walter
    See de la Mare, Walter (John)
Ramanujan, A(ttipat) K(rishnaswami)
    1929-1993 86
Rame, David
    See Divine, Arthur Durham
Ramirez, Jose 1967- 198
Ramirez, Orlando L. 1972- 194
Ramos, Jorge 1958- 205
Ramstad, Ralph L. 1919- 115
Ramthun, Bonnie 214
Rana, Indi
    See Rana, Indira Higham
Rana, Indira Higham 1944- 82
Rana, J.
    See Bhatia, Jamunadevi
Ranadive, Gail 1944- 10
Rand, Ann (Binkley) 30
Rand, Gloria 1925- 156
    Earlier sketch in SATA 101
Rand, Paul 1914-1996 6
Randall, Carrie
    See Ransom, Candice F.
Randall, David 1972- 167
Randall, Florence Engel 1917-1997 5
Randall, Janet
    See Young, Janet Randall
    and Young, Robert W(illiam)
Randall, Robert
    See Garrett, Randall
    and Silverberg, Robert
Randall, Ruth (Elaine) Painter 1892-1971 3
Randell, Beverley
    See Price, Beverley Joan
Randle, Kristen D. 1952- 92
    Autobiography Feature 119
    See also SAAS 24
Randle, Kristen Downey
    See Randle, Kristen D.
Randolph, Boynton M.D.
    See Ellis, Edward S.
Randolph, Ellen
    See Rawn, Melanie
Randolph, Geoffrey
    See Ellis, Edward S.
Randolph, J. H.
    See Ellis, Edward S.
Randolph, Lieutenant J. H.
    See Ellis, Edward S.
Rands, William Brighty 1823-1882 17
Raney, Ken 1953- 74
Rankin, Joan 1940- 212
    Earlier sketches in SATA 88, 148
Rankin, Laura 1953(?)- 176
Ranney, Agnes V. 1916-1985 6
Ransom, Candice F. 1952- 183
    Brief entry 49
    Earlier sketches in SATA 52, 89, 135
Ransom, Jeanie Franz 1957- 187
Ransome, Arthur (Michell) 1884-1967 22
    See also CLR 8
Ransome, James E. 1961- 178
    Earlier sketches in SATA 76, 123
    See also CLR 86
Rant, Tol E.
    See Longyear, Barry B(rookes)
Raphael, Elaine
    See Bolognese, Elaine

Raposo, Joseph Guilherme 1938-1989
    Obituary 61
Rapp, Adam 1968- 148
Rappaport, Doreen 211
    Earlier sketch in SATA 151
Rappaport, Eva 1924- 6
Rappoport, Ken 1935- 167
    Earlier sketch in SATA 89
Rarick, Carrie 1911-2002 41
Raschka, Chris 1959- 207
    Earlier sketches in SATA 80, 117, 166
Raschka, Christopher
    See Raschka, Chris
Rascol, Sabina I. 159
Rash, Andy 162
Raskin, Edith Lefkowitz 1908-1987 9
Raskin, Ellen 1928-1984 139
    Earlier sketches in SATA 2, 38
    See also CLR 12
Raskin, Joseph 1897-1982 12
    Obituary 29
Rathjen, Carl Henry 1909-1984 11
Rathmann, Peggy 1953- 157
    Earlier sketch in SATA 94
    See also CLR 77
Ratliff, Thomas M. 1948- 118
Ratner, Sue Lynn
    See Alexander, Sue
Rattigan, Jama Kim 1951- 99
Ratto, Linda Lee 1952- 79
Rattray, Simon
    See Trevor, Elleston
Ratz de Tagyos, Paul 1958- 198
    Earlier sketch in SATA 76
Rau, Dana Meachen 1971- 167
    Earlier sketch in SATA 94
Rau, Margaret 1913- 168
    Earlier sketch in SATA 9
    See also CLR 8
Rauch, Mabel Thompson 1888-1972
    Obituary 26
Raucher, Herman 1928- 8
Raude, Karina 199
Rauh, Sherry
    See North, Sherry
Raum, Elizabeth 1949- 155
Raven, Margot Theis 184
RavenWolf, Silver 1956- 155
Ravielli, Anthony 1916-1997 3
    Obituary 95
Ravilious, Robin 1944- 77
Ravishankar, Anushka 1961- 200
Rawding, F(rederick) W(illiam) 1930- 55
Rawlings, Marjorie Kinnan 1896-1953 100
    See also YABC 1
    See also CLR 63
Rawlins, Donna 1956- 206
Rawlinson, Julia 212
    Earlier sketch in SATA 175
Rawls, (Woodrow) Wilson 1913-1984 22
    See also CLR 81
Rawlyk, George Alexander 1935- 64
Rawn, Melanie 1954- 98
Rawn, Melanie Robin
    See Rawn, Melanie
Rawson, Katherine 1955- 190
Ray, Carl 1943-1978 63
Ray, Deborah
    See Kogan Ray, Deborah
Ray, Delia 1963- 179
    Earlier sketch in SATA 70
Ray, Irene
    See Sutton, Margaret Beebe
Ray, Jane 1960- 196
    Earlier sketches in SATA 72, 152
Ray, JoAnne 1935- 9
Ray, Mary (Eva Pedder) 1932- 127
    Earlier sketch in SATA 2
Ray, Mary Lyn 1946- 154
    Earlier sketch in SATA 90
Rayban, Chloe 1944- 167

Rayevsky, Robert 1955- 190
    Earlier sketch in SATA 81
Raymond, James Crossley 1917-1981
    Obituary 29
Raymond, Robert
    See Alter, Robert Edmond
Rayner, Catherine 204
Rayner, Hugh 151
Rayner, Mary 1933- 87
    Earlier sketch in SATA 22
    See also CLR 41
Rayner, Shoo
    See Rayner, Hugh
Rayner, William 1929- 55
    Brief entry 36
Raynor, Dorka 28
Raynor, Gemma 1985- 216
Rayson, Steven 1932- 30
Rayyan, Omar 1968- 216
Razzell, Arthur (George) 1925- 11
Razzell, Mary (Catherine) 1930- 102
Razzi, James 1931- 10
Read, Elfreida 1920- 2
Read, Nicholas 1956- 146
Read, Piers Paul 1941- 21
Reade, Deborah 1949- 69
Reader, Dennis 1929- 71
Reading, Richard P(atrick) 1962- 161
Readman, Jo 1958- 89
Ready, Kirk L(ewis) 1943- 39
Reaney, James 1926-2008 43
Reaney, James Crerar
    See Reaney, James
Reardon, Joyce
    See Pearson, Ridley
Reaver, Chap 1935-1993 69
    Obituary 77
Reaver, Herbert R.
    See Reaver, Chap
Reaves, J. Michael
    See Reaves, (James) Michael
Reaves, (James) Michael 1950- 99
Reber, Deborah 189
Recorvits, Helen 191
Redding, Robert Hull 1919- 2
Redekopp, Elsa 61
Redlich, Ben 1977- 181
Redsand, Anna 1948- 184
Redway, Ralph
    See Hamilton, Charles (Harold St. John)
Redway, Ridley
    See Hamilton, Charles (Harold St. John)
Reece, Colleen L. 1935- 116
Reece, Gabrielle 1970- 108
Reed, Betty Jane 1921- 4
Reed, Dallas
    See Pendleton, Thomas
Reed, E.
    See Evans, Mari
Reed, Gwendolyn E(lizabeth) 1932- 21
Reed, Kit 1932- 184
    Autobiography Feature 184
    Earlier sketches in SATA 34, 116
Reed, Lynn Rowe 215
    Earlier sketch in SATA 171
Reed, Mike 1951- 211
Reed, Neil 1961- 99
Reed, Talbot Baines 1852-1893
    See CLR 76
Reed, Thomas (James) 1947- 34
Reed, William Maxwell 1871-1962 15
Reeder, Carolyn 1937- 97
    Earlier sketch in SATA 66
    See also CLR 69
Reeder, Colin (Dawson) 1938- 74
Reeder, Colonel Red
    See Reeder, Russell P(otter), Jr.
Reeder, Russell P(otter), Jr. 1902-1998 4
    Obituary 101
Reeder, Stephanie Owen 1951- 102
Reed-Jones, Carol 1955- 112

Reef, Catherine 1951- 189
  Earlier sketches in SATA 73, 128
Reekie, Jocelyn (Margaret) 1947- 145
Reeman, Douglas Edward 1924- 63
  Brief entry 28
Rees, Celia 1949- 124
Rees, David (Bartlett) 1936-1993 69
  Obituary 76
  Earlier sketch in SATA 36
  See also SAAS 5
Rees, Douglas 1947- 169
Rees, Ennis (Samuel, Jr.) 1925- 3
Rees, (George) Leslie (Clarence)
  1905-2000 105
  Obituary 135
Reese, Bob
  See Reese, Robert A.
Reese, Carolyn Johnson 1938- 64
Reese, Della 1931(?)- 114
Reese, Lyn
  See Reese, Carolyn Johnson
Reese, Robert A. 1938- 60
  Brief entry 53
Reese, (John) Terence 1913-1996 59
Reeve, Joel
  See Cox, William R(obert)
Reeve, Kirk 1934- 117
Reeve, Philip 201
  Earlier sketch in SATA 170
Reeve, Rosie 188
  Earlier sketch in SATA 186
Reeves, Faye Couch 1953- 76
Reeves, James
  See Reeves, John Morris
Reeves, Jeni 1947- 111
Reeves, John Morris 1909-1978 87
  Earlier sketch in SATA 15
Reeves, Joyce 1911- 17
Reeves, Lawrence F. 1926- 29
Reeves, Ruth Ellen
  See Ranney, Agnes V.
Regan, Dian Curtis 1950- 149
  Autobiography Feature 149
  Earlier sketches in SATA 75, 133
Regehr, Lydia 1903-1991 37
Reger, James P. 1952- 106
Reggiani, Renee 1925- 18
Rehm, Karl M. 1935- 72
Reibstein, Mark 211
Reich, Ali
  See Katz, Bobbi
Reich, Susanna 1954- 214
  Earlier sketch in SATA 113
Reiche, Dietlof 1941- 159
Reichel, Edwin C(lark) 1909-1988
  Obituary 57
Reichert, Mickey Zucker
  See Reichert, Miriam Zucker
Reichert, Miriam Zucker 1962- 85
Reichert, Renee 172
Reichhold, Jane(t E.) 1937- 147
Reid, Alastair 1926- 46
Reid, Barbara 1922- 21
Reid, Barbara (Jane) 1957- 93
  See also CLR 64
Reid, Desmond
  See Moorcock, Michael
  and McNeilly, Wilfred (Glassford)
Reid, Eugenie Chazal 1924- 12
Reid, John Calvin 21
Reid, (Thomas) Mayne 1818-1883 24
Reid, Meta Mayne 1905-1991 58
  Brief entry 36
Reid, Robin (Nicole) 1969- 145
Reid Banks, Lynne 1929- 165
  Earlier sketches in SATA 22, 75, 111
  See also CLR 86
Reider, Katja 1960- 126
Reid Jenkins, Debra 1955- 87
Reiff, Stephanie Ann 1948- 47
  Brief entry 28

Reig, June 1933- 30
Reigot, Betty Polisar 1924- 55
  Brief entry 41
Reilly, Joan 195
Reim, Melanie (K.) 1956- 104
Reinach, Jacquelyn (Krasne) 1930-2000 28
Reiner, Carl 1922- 151
Reiner, William B(uck) 1910-1976 46
  Obituary 30
Reinfeld, Fred 1910-1964 3
Reinhardt, Dana 1971- 175
Reinhart, Matthew 1971- 197
  Earlier sketch in SATA 161
Reiniger, Lotte 1899-1981 40
  Obituary 33
Reinsma, Carol 1949- 91
Reinstedt, Randall A. 1935- 101
Reinstedt, Randy
  See Reinstedt, Randall A.
Reisberg, Mira 1955- 82
Reisberg, Veg
  See Reisberg, Mira
Reiser, Lynn 1944- 180
  Earlier sketches in SATA 81, 138
Reiser, Lynn Whisnant
  See Reiser, Lynn
Reisgies, Teresa (Maria) 1966- 74
Reiss, Johanna 1929(?)- 18
  See also CLR 19
Reiss, Johanna de Leeuw
  See Reiss, Johanna
Reiss, John J. 23
Reiss, Kathryn 1957- 144
  Earlier sketch in SATA 76
Reit, Seymour Victory 1918-2001 21
  Obituary 133
Reit, Sy
  See Reit, Seymour Victory
Relf, Patricia 1954- 134
  Earlier sketch in SATA 71
Remi, Georges 1907-1983 13
  Obituary 32
  See also CLR 114
Remington, Frederic S(ackrider)
  1861-1909 41
Remkiewicz, Frank 1939- 217
  Earlier sketches in SATA 77, 152
Rempt, Fiona 1973- 198
Remy, Georges
  See Remi, Georges
Renaud, Anne 1957- 211
Renaud, Bernadette 1945- 66
Renault, Mary 1905-1983 23
  Obituary 36
Rendell, Joan 28
Rendina, Laura (Jones) Cooper 1902- 10
Rendon, Marcie R. 1952- 97
Rendon, Maria 1965- 116
Renee, Janina 1956- 140
Renfro, Ed 1924- 79
Renick, Marion (Lewis) 1905-1983 1
Renier, Aaron 1977- 202
Renken, Aleda 1907- 27
Renlie, Frank H. 1936- 11
Rennert, Richard Scott 1956- 67
Rennison, Louise 1951- 149
Reno, Dawn E(laine) 1953- 130
Rensie, Willis
  See Eisner, Will
Renton, Cam
  See Armstrong, Richard
Renvoize, Jean 5
Resau, Laura 1973- 190
Resciniti, Angelo G. 1952- 75
Resnick, Michael David
  See Resnick, Mike
Resnick, Mike 1942- 159
  Earlier sketches in SATA 38, 106
Resnick, Seymour 1920- 23
Retla, Robert
  See Alter, Robert Edmond

Rettig, Liz 199
Rettstatt, Chris
  See Ashland, Monk
Reuter, Bjarne (B.) 1950- 142
  Earlier sketch in SATA 68
Reuter, Carol (Joan) 1931- 2
Revena
  See Wright, Betty Ren
Revsbech, Vicki
  See Liestman, Vicki
Rex, Adam 186
Rex, Michael 191
Rey, H. A. 1898-1977 100
  Earlier sketches in SATA 1, 26, 69
  See also CLR 93
Rey, Hans Augusto
  See Rey, H. A.
Rey, Luis V. 1955- 201
Rey, Margret 1906-1996 86
  Obituary 93
  Earlier sketch in SATA 26
  See also CLR 93
Rey, Margret Elisabeth
  See Rey, Margret
Reyher, Becky
  See Reyher, Rebecca Hourwich
Reyher, Rebecca Hourwich 1897-1987 18
  Obituary 50
Reynold, Ann
  See Bernardo, Anilu
Reynolds, Aaron 1970- 197
Reynolds, Adrian 1963- 192
Reynolds, C. Buck 1957- 107
Reynolds, Dickson
  See Reynolds, Helen Mary Greenwood Camp-
  bell
Reynolds, Helen Mary Greenwood Campbell
  1884-1969
  Obituary 26
Reynolds, Jan 1956- 180
Reynolds, John
  See Whitlock, Ralph
Reynolds, Madge
  See Whitlock, Ralph
Reynolds, Malvina 1900-1978 44
  Obituary 24
Reynolds, Marilyn 1935- 121
  See also SAAS 23
Reynolds, Marilyn M.
  See Reynolds, Marilyn
Reynolds, Marilynn 1940- 141
  Earlier sketch in SATA 80
Reynolds, Pamela 1923- 34
Reynolds, Peter H. 1961- 128
Reynolds, Peter J. 1961- 179
Reynolds, Susan 179
Rhine, Richard
  See Silverstein, Alvin
  and Silverstein, Virginia B.
Rhoades, Diane 1952- 90
Rhodes, Bennie (Loran) 1927- 35
Rhodes, Donna McKee 1962- 87
Rhodes, Frank Harold Trevor 1926- 37
Rhue, Morton
  See Strasser, Todd
Rhyne, Nancy 1926- 66
Rhynes, Martha E. 1939- 141
Ribbons, Ian 1924- 37
  Brief entry 30
  See also SAAS 3
Ricciuti, Edward R(aphael) 1938- 10
Rice, Alice (Caldwell) Hegan 1870-1942 63
Rice, Bebe Faas 1932- 89
Rice, Charles D(uane) 1910-1971
  Obituary 27
Rice, Dale R. 1948- 42
Rice, Dale Richard
  See Rice, Dale R.
Rice, Dick
  See Rice, R. Hugh

Rice, Earle (Wilmont), Jr. 1928- *151*
  Earlier sketch in SATA *92*
Rice, Edward 1918-2001 .... *47*
  Brief entry *42*
Rice, Elizabeth 1913-1976 .... *2*
Rice, Eve 1951- *91*
  Earlier sketch in SATA *34*
Rice, Eve Hart
  See Rice, Eve
Rice, Inez 1907- *13*
Rice, James 1934- *93*
  Earlier sketch in SATA *22*
Rice, John F. 1958- *82*
Rice, R. Hugh 1929- *115*
Rice, Richard H.
  See Rice, R. Hugh
Rich, Anna 1956- *212*
Rich, Barbara
  See Graves, Robert
Rich, Elaine Sommers 1926- *6*
Rich, Josephine Bouchard 1912- *10*
Rich, Louise Dickinson 1903-1991 .... *54*
  Obituary *67*
Rich, Naomi *217*
Richard, Adrienne 1921- *5*
  See also SAAS *9*
Richard, James Robert
  See Bowen, Robert Sydney
Richards, Chuck 1957- *170*
Richards, Frank
  See Hamilton, Charles (Harold St. John)
Richards, Hilda
  See Hamilton, Charles (Harold St. John)
Richards, Jackie 1925- *102*
Richards, Jean 1940- *135*
Richards, Justin *169*
Richards, Kay
  See Baker, Susan (Catherine)
Richards, Laura E(lizabeth Howe) 1850-1943
  See YABC *1*
  See also CLR *54*
Richards, Leigh
  See King, Laurie R.
Richards, Marlee
  See Brill, Marlene Targ
Richards, Norman 1932- *48*
Richards, R(onald) C(harles) W(illiam)
  1923- *59*
  Brief entry *43*
Richards, Walter Alden (Jr.) 1907-1988
  Obituary *56*
Richardson, Andrew (William) 1986- *120*
Richardson, Carol 1932- *58*
Richardson, Frank Howard 1882-1970
  Obituary *27*
Richardson, Grace Lee
  See Dickson, Naida
Richardson, Jean (Mary) *59*
Richardson, Judith Benet 1941- *77*
Richardson, Nigel 1957- *187*
Richardson, Robert S(hirley) 1902-1981 .... *8*
Richardson, Sandy 1949- *116*
Richardson, V.A. *189*
Richardson, Willis 1889-1977 .... *60*
Richelson, Geraldine 1922- *29*
Richemont, Enid 1940- *82*
Richler, Mordecai 1931-2001 .... *98*
  Brief entry *27*
  Earlier sketch in SATA *44*
  See also CLR *17*
Richman, Sophia 1941- *142*
Rich-McCoy, Lois
  See McCoy, Lois (Rich)
Richmond, Robin 1951- *75*
Richoux, Pat(ricia) 1927- *7*
Richter, Alice 1941- *30*
Richter, Conrad (Michael) 1890-1968 .... *3*
Richter, Hans Peter 1925-1993 .... *6*
  See also CLR *21*
  See also SAAS *11*
Richter, Jutta 1955- *184*

Rickard, Graham 1949- *71*
Rico, Don(ato) 1917-1985
  Obituary *43*
Riddell, Chris 1962- *166*
  Earlier sketch in SATA *114*
Riddell, Christopher Barry
  See Riddell, Chris
Riddell, Edwina 1955- *82*
Ridden, Brian 1934- *123*
  See Ridden, Brian John
Riddle, Tohby 1965- *151*
  Earlier sketch in SATA *74*
Riddleburger, Sam *202*
Riddles, Libby 1956- *140*
Rideout, Sandy *194*
Ridge, Antonia (Florence) (?)-1981 .... *7*
  Obituary *27*
Ridge, Martin 1923-2003 .... *43*
Ridley, Philip *171*
  Earlier sketch in SATA *88*
Ridlon, Marci
  See Balterman, Marcia Ridlon
Riedman, Sarah R(egal) 1902-1995 .... *1*
Riehecky, Janet 1953- *164*
Ries, Lori *185*
Riesenberg, Felix, Jr. 1913-1962 .... *23*
Rieu, E(mile) V(ictor) 1887-1972 .... *46*
  Obituary *26*
Riffenburgh, Beau 1955- *175*
Rigg, Sharon
  See Creech, Sharon
Riggenbach, Holly
  See Black, Holly
Riggio, Anita 1952- *148*
  Earlier sketch in SATA *73*
Riggs, Shannon *190*
Riggs, Sidney Noyes 1892-1975
  Obituary *28*
Riggs, Stephanie 1964- *138*
Riglietti, Serena 1969- *189*
Rigney, James Oliver, Jr.
  See Jordan, Robert
Rikhoff, Jean 1928- *9*
Rikki
  See Ducornet, Erica
Riley, James A. 1939- *97*
Riley, James Whitcomb 1849-1916 .... *17*
Riley, Jocelyn 1949- *60*
  Brief entry *50*
Riley, Jocelyn Carol
  See Riley, Jocelyn
Riley, Linda Capus 1950- *85*
Riley, Martin 1948- *81*
Rimbauer, Steven
  See Pearson, Ridley
Rimes, (Margaret) LeAnn 1982- *154*
Rinaldi, Ann 1934- *202*
  Brief entry *50*
  Earlier sketches in SATA *51, 78, 117, 161*
  See also CLR *46*
Rinard, Judith E(llen) 1947- *140*
  Earlier sketch in SATA *44*
Rinck, Maranke 1976- *214*
Rinder, Lenore 1949- *92*
Ring, Elizabeth 1920- *79*
Ringdahl, Mark
  See Longyear, Barry B(rookes)
Ringgold, Faith 1930- *187*
  Earlier sketches in SATA *71, 114*
  See also CLR *30*
Ringi, Kjell (Arne Soerensen) 1939- *12*
Rinkoff, Barbara Jean (Rich) 1923-1975 .... *4*
  Obituary *27*
Rinn, Miriam 1946- *127*
Riordan, James 1936- *95*
Riordan, Rick *208*
  Earlier sketch in SATA *174*
Rios, Tere
  See Versace, Marie Teresa Rios
Ripken, Cal, Jr. 1960- *215*
  Earlier sketch in SATA *114*

Ripken, Calvin Edward, Jr.
  See Ripken, Cal, Jr.
Ripley, Catherine 1957- *82*
Ripley, Elizabeth Blake 1906-1969 .... *5*
Ripper, Charles L(ewis) 1929- *3*
Ripper, Chuck
  See Ripper, Charles L(ewis)
Riq
  See Atwater, Richard (Tupper)
Rish, David 1955- *110*
Riskind, Mary 1944- *60*
Rissinger, Matt 1956- *93*
Rissman, Art
  See Sussman, Susan
Rissman, Susan
  See Sussman, Susan
Ritchie, Barbara Gibbons *14*
Ritchie, Scot 1954- *217*
Ritter, Felix
  See Kruss, James
Ritter, John H. 1951- *215*
  Earlier sketches in SATA *129, 137*
Ritter, Lawrence S(tanley) 1922-2004 .... *58*
  Obituary *152*
Ritthaler, Shelly 1955- *91*
Ritts, Paul 1920(?)-1980
  Obituary *25*
Ritz, Karen 1957- *202*
  Earlier sketch in SATA *80*
Rivera, Geraldo (Miguel) 1943- *54*
  Brief entry *28*
Rivers, Elfrida
  See Bradley, Marion Zimmer
Rivers, Karen 1970- *131*
Riverside, John
  See Heinlein, Robert A.
Rivkin, Ann 1920- *41*
Rivoli, Mario 1943- *10*
Roach, Marilynne K. 1946- *9*
Roach, Marilynne Kathleen
  See Roach, Marilynne K.
Roach, Portia
  See Takakjian, Portia
Robb, Don 1937- *194*
Robb, Laura 1937- *95*
Robberecht, Thierry 1960- *182*
Robbins, Frank 1917-1994(?) *42*
  Brief entry *32*
Robbins, Ken 1945- *147*
  Brief entry *53*
  Earlier sketch in SATA *94*
Robbins, Raleigh
  See Hamilton, Charles (Harold St. John)
Robbins, Ruth 1917(?)- *14*
Robbins, Tony
  See Pashko, Stanley
Robbins, Wayne
  See Cox, William R(obert)
Robel, S. L.
  See Fraustino, Lisa Rowe
Roberson, Jennifer 1953- *72*
Roberson, John R(oyster) 1930- *53*
Robert, Adrian
  See St. John, Nicole
Roberts, Bethany *202*
  Earlier sketch in SATA *133*
Roberts, Bruce (Stuart) 1930- *47*
  Brief entry *39*
Roberts, Charles G(eorge) D(ouglas)
  1860-1943 .... *88*
  Brief entry *29*
  See also CLR *33*
Roberts, David
  See Cox, John Roberts
Roberts, David 1970- *191*
Roberts, Diane 1937- *184*
Roberts, Elizabeth 1944- *80*
Roberts, Elizabeth Madox 1886-1941 .... *33*
  Brief entry *27*
  See also CLR *100*

Roberts, Jim
  See Bates, Barbara S(nedeker)
Roberts, John G(aither) 1913-1993 .... *27*
Roberts, Judy I. 1957- *93*
Roberts, Katherine 1962- *152*
Roberts, M. L.
  See Mattern, Joanne
Roberts, Marion 1966- *212*
Roberts, Nancy Correll 1924- *52*
  Brief entry *28*
Roberts, Priscilla 1955- *184*
Roberts, Terence
  See Sanderson, Ivan T(erence)
Roberts, Willo Davis 1928-2004 .... *150*
  Autobiography Feature *150*
  Obituary *160*
  Earlier sketches in SATA *21, 70, 133*
  See also CLR *95*
  See also SAAS *8*
Robertson, Barbara (Anne) 1931- *12*
Robertson, Don 1929-1999 .... *8*
  Obituary *113*
Robertson, Dorothy Lewis 1912- *12*
Robertson, Ellis
  See Ellison, Harlan
  and Silverberg, Robert
Robertson, James I., Jr. 1930- *182*
Robertson, James Irvin
  See Robertson, James I., Jr.
Robertson, Janet (E.) 1935- *68*
Robertson, Jennifer Sinclair 1942-1998 .... *12*
Robertson, Jenny
  See Robertson, Jennifer Sinclair
Robertson, Keith (Carlton) 1914-1991 .... *85*
  Obituary *69*
  Earlier sketch in SATA *1*
  See also SAAS *15*
Robertson, Mark
  See Robertson, M.P.
Robertson, M.P. 1965- *197*
Robertson, Stephen
  See Walker, Robert W.
Robertus, Polly M. 1948- *212*
  Earlier sketch in SATA *73*
Robeson, Kenneth
  See Dent, Lester
  and Goulart, Ron
Robeson, Kenneth
  See Johnson, (Walter) Ryerson
Robinet, Harriette Gillem 1931- *104*
  Earlier sketch in SATA *27*
  See also CLR *64*
Robins, Deri 1958- *166*
  Earlier sketch in SATA *117*
Robins, Patricia
  See Clark, Patricia Denise
Robins, Rollo, Jr.
  See Ellis, Edward S.
Robins, Seelin
  See Ellis, Edward S.
Robinson, Adjai 1932- *8*
Robinson, Aminah Brenda Lynn 1940- *159*
  Earlier sketch in SATA *77*
Robinson, Barbara (Webb) 1927- *84*
  Earlier sketch in SATA *8*
Robinson, C(harles) A(lexander), Jr.
  1900-1965 .... *36*
Robinson, Charles 1870-1937 .... *17*
Robinson, Charles 1931- *6*
Robinson, Dorothy W. 1929- *54*
Robinson, Elizabeth Keeler 1959- *204*
Robinson, Eve
  See Tanselle, Eve
Robinson, Glen 1953- *92*
Robinson, Glendal P.
  See Robinson, Glen
Robinson, Jan M. 1933- *6*
Robinson, Jean O. 1934- *7*
Robinson, Joan (Mary) G(ale Thomas)
  1910-1988 .... *7*
Robinson, Kim Stanley 1952- *109*

Robinson, Lee 1948- *110*
Robinson, Lloyd
  See Silverberg, Robert
Robinson, Lynda S(uzanne) 1951- *107*
Robinson, Marileta 1942- *32*
Robinson, Maudie Millian Oller 1914- *11*
Robinson, Maurice R(ichard) 1895-1982
  Obituary *29*
Robinson, Nancy K(onheim) 1942-1994 ...... *91*
  Brief entry *31*
  Obituary *79*
  Earlier sketch in SATA *32*
Robinson, Ray 1920- *23*
Robinson, Raymond Kenneth
  See Robinson, Ray
Robinson, Shari
  See McGuire, Leslie (Sarah)
Robinson, Sharon 1950- *197*
  Earlier sketch in SATA *162*
Robinson, Spider 1948- *118*
Robinson, Sue
  See Robinson, Susan Maria
Robinson, Susan Maria 1955- *105*
Robinson, Susan Patricia
  See Gates, Susan
Robinson, Suzanne
  See Robinson, Lynda S(uzanne)
Robinson, T(homas) H(eath) 1869-1950 ...... *17*
Robinson, Tim 1963- *205*
Robinson, (Wanda) Veronica 1926- *30*
Robinson, W(illiam) Heath 1872-1944 .... *17*
Robison, Bonnie 1924- *12*
Robison, Nancy L(ouise) 1934- *32*
Robles, Harold E. 1948- *87*
Robottom, John 1934- *7*
Robson, Eric 1939- *82*
Roca, Francois 1971- *200*
Rocco, John 1967- *188*
Roche, A. K.
  See Abisch, Roslyn Kroop
  and Kaplan, Boche
Roche, Denis 1967- *196*
  Earlier sketch in SATA *99*
Roche, Denis Mary
  See Roche, Denis
Roche, Luane 1937- *170*
Roche, P(atricia) K. 1935- *57*
  Brief entry *34*
Roche, Terry
  See Poole, Peggy
Rochman, Hazel 1938- *105*
Rock, Lois
  See Joslin, Mary
Rock, Maxine 1940- *108*
Rocker, Fermin 1907- *40*
Rocklin, Joanne 1946- *134*
  Earlier sketch in SATA *86*
Rockwell, Anne F. 1934- *194*
  Earlier sketches in SATA *33, 71, 114, 162*
  See also SAAS *19*
Rockwell, Anne Foote
  See Rockwell, Anne F.
Rockwell, Bart
  See Pellowski, Michael (Joseph)
Rockwell, Harlow 1910-1988 .... *33*
  Obituary *56*
Rockwell, Lizzy 1961- *185*
Rockwell, Norman (Percevel) 1894-1978 .... *23*
Rockwell, Thomas 1933- *70*
  Earlier sketch in SATA *7*
  See also CLR *6*
Rockwood, Joyce 1947- *39*
Rockwood, Roy
  See McFarlane, Leslie
  and Stratemeyer, Edward L.
Rodanas, Kristina 1952- *155*
Rodari, Gianni 1920-1980
  See CLR *24*
Rodd, Kathleen Tennant
  See Rodd, Kylie Tennant

Rodd, Kylie Tennant 1912-1988 .... *57*
  Obituary *55*
  Earlier sketch in SATA *6*
Rodda, Emily 1948- *146*
  Earlier sketch in SATA *97*
  See also CLR *32*
Roddenberry, Eugene Wesley 1921-1991 ..... *45*
  Obituary *69*
Roddenberry, Gene
  See Roddenberry, Eugene Wesley
Roddick, Ellen 1936- *5*
Roddie, Shen *153*
Roddy, Lee 1921- *57*
Rodenas, Paula *73*
Rodgers, Frank 1944- *69*
Rodgers, Mary 1931- *130*
  Earlier sketch in SATA *8*
  See also CLR *20*
Rodman, Emerson
  See Ellis, Edward S.
Rodman, Eric
  See Silverberg, Robert
Rodman, Maia
  See Wojciechowska, Maia (Teresa)
Rodman, Mary Ann *185*
Rodman, (Cary) Selden 1909-2002 .... *9*
Rodowsky, Colby 1932- *164*
  Earlier sketches in SATA *21, 77, 120*
  See also SAAS *22*
Rodowsky, Colby F.
  See Rodowsky, Colby
Rodriguez, Alejo 1941- *83*
Rodriguez, Alex 1975- *189*
Rodriguez, Christina 1981- *177*
Rodriguez, Edel 1971- *196*
Rodriguez, Luis J. 1954- *125*
Rodriguez, Rachel *180*
Rodriguez, Rachel Victoria
  See Rodriguez, Rachel
Roeder, Virginia Marsh 1926- *98*
Roehrig, Catharine H. 1949- *67*
Roennfeldt, Robert 1953- *78*
Roessel-Waugh, C. C.
  See Waugh, Carol-Lynn Rossel
  and Waugh, Charles G(ordon)
Roets, Lois F. 1937- *91*
Roever, J(oan) M(arilyn) 1935- *26*
Rofes, Eric 1954-2006 .... *52*
Rofes, Eric Edward 1954-2006
  See Rofes, Eric
Roffey, Maureen 1936- *33*
Rogak, Lisa 1962- *80*
Rogak, Lisa Angowski
  See Rogak, Lisa
Rogan, S. Jones *199*
Rogan, Sally Jones
  See Rogan, S. Jones
Rogasky, Barbara 1933- *144*
  Earlier sketch in SATA *86*
Rogers, (Thomas) Alan (Stinchcombe)
  1937- *81*
  Earlier sketch in SATA *2*
Rogers, Bettye 1858-1919 .... *103*
Rogers, Cindy 1950- *89*
Rogers, Emma 1951- *74*
Rogers, Frances 1888-1974 .... *10*
Rogers, Fred McFeely 1928-2003 .... *33*
  Obituary *138*
Rogers, Gregory 1957- *211*
Rogers, Hal
  See Sirimarco, Elizabeth
Rogers, Jacqueline 1958- *213*
Rogers, Jean 1919- *55*
  Brief entry *47*
Rogers, Matilda 1894-1976 .... *5*
  Obituary *34*
Rogers, Pamela 1927- *9*
Rogers, Paul 1950- *98*
  Earlier sketch in SATA *54*
Rogers, Robert
  See Hamilton, Charles (Harold St. John)

Rogers, Sherry *193*
Rogers, W(illiam) G(arland) 1896-1978 .... *23*
Rohan, M. S.
   See Rohan, Michael Scott
Rohan, Michael Scott 1951- *98*
Rohan, Mike Scott
   See Rohan, Michael Scott
Rohmann, Eric 1957- *171*
   See also CLR *100*
Rohmer, Harriet 1938- *56*
Rohrer, Doug 1962- *89*
Rojan
   See Rojankovsky, Feodor (Stepanovich)
Rojankovsky, Feodor (Stepanovich)
   1891-1970 .... *21*
Rojany, Lisa *94*
Rokeby-Thomas, Anna E(lma) 1911- *15*
Roland, Albert 1925-2002 .... *11*
Roland, Mary
   See Lewis, Mary
Roleff, Tamara L. 1959- *143*
Rolerson, Darrell A(llen) 1946- *8*
Roll, Winifred 1909-1998 .... *6*
Rollins, Charlemae Hill 1897-1979 .... *3*
   Obituary *26*
Rollins, James 1961- *216*
Rollock, Barbara T(herese) 1924- *64*
Rolston, Steve 1978- *209*
Romack, Janice Reed
   See LeNoir, Janice
Romain, Trevor *134*
Romanenko, Vitaliy 1962- *101*
Romano, Christy
   See Romano, Christy Carlson
Romano, Christy Carlson 1984- *210*
Romano, Clare 1922- *111*
   Earlier sketch in SATA *48*
Romano, Louis G. 1921- *35*
Romano, Melora A. 1966- *118*
Romano, Ray 1957- *170*
Romano, Raymond
   See Romano, Ray
Romijn, Johanna Maria Kooyker
   See Kooyker-Romijn, Johanna Maria
Romyn, Johanna Maria Kooyker
   See Kooyker-Romijn, Johanna Maria
Rong, Yu 1970- *174*
Rongen, Bjoern 1906- *10*
Rongen, Bjorn
   See Rongen, Bjoern
Ronson, Mark
   See Alexander, Marc
Rood, Ronald (N.) 1920- *12*
Rook, Sebastian
   See Jeapes, Ben
Rooke, Daphne 1914-2009 .... *12*
Rooke, Daphne Marie
   See Rooke, Daphne
Rooney, Ronnie 1970- *212*
Roop, Connie 1951- *167*
   Brief entry *49*
   Earlier sketches in SATA *54, 116*
Roop, Constance Betzer
   See Roop, Connie
Roop, Peter 1951- *167*
   Brief entry *49*
   Earlier sketches in SATA *54, 116*
Roop, Peter G.
   See Roop, Peter
Roop, Peter Geiger
   See Roop, Peter
Roos, Stephen 1945- *128*
   Brief entry *41*
   Earlier sketches in SATA *47, 77*
Roose-Evans, James 1927- *65*
Roosevelt, Eleanor 1884-1962 .... *50*
Root, Barry *182*
Root, Betty *84*
Root, Kimberly Bulcken *192*

Root, Phyllis 1949- *184*
   Brief entry *48*
   Earlier sketches in SATA *55, 94, 145*
Root, Shelton L., Jr. 1923-1986
   Obituary *51*
Roper, Laura (Newbold) Wood 1911-2003 .. *34*
   Obituary *150*
Roper, Robert 1946- *142*
   Earlier sketch in SATA *78*
Roraback, Robin (Ellan) 1964- *111*
Rorby, Ginny 1944- *94*
Rorer, Abigail 1949- *85*
Rosaler, Maxine *208*
Rosamel, Godeleine de 1968- *151*
Roscoe, D(onald) T(homas) 1934- *42*
Rose, Anne *8*
Rose, Deborah Lee 1955- *185*
   Earlier sketches in SATA *71, 124*
Rose, Elizabeth (Jane Pretty) 1933- *68*
   Brief entry *28*
Rose, Florella
   See Carlson, Vada F.
Rose, Gerald (Hembdon Seymour) 1935- *68*
   Brief entry *30*
Rose, Malcolm 1953- *168*
   Earlier sketch in SATA *107*
Rose, Nancy A.
   See Sweetland, Nancy A(nn)
Rose, Ted 1940- *93*
Rose, Wendy 1948- *12*
Rosen, Elizabeth 1961- *205*
Rosen, Lillian (Diamond) 1928- *63*
Rosen, Marvin 1933- *161*
Rosen, Michael 1946- *181*
   Brief entry *40*
   Earlier sketches in SATA *48, 84, 137*
   See also CLR *45*
Rosen, Michael J. 1954- *199*
   Earlier sketch in SATA *86*
Rosen, Michael Wayne
   See Rosen, Michael
Rosen, Sidney 1916- *1*
Rosen, Winifred 1943- *8*
Rosenbaum, Maurice 1907-1987 .... *6*
Rosenberg, Amye 1950- *74*
Rosenberg, Dorothy 1906- *40*
Rosenberg, Eth Clifford 1915- *92*
   See also SAAS *22*
Rosenberg, Jane 1949- *58*
Rosenberg, Liz 1958- *129*
   Earlier sketch in SATA *75*
Rosenberg, Maxine B(erta) 1939- *93*
   Brief entry *47*
   Earlier sketch in SATA *55*
Rosenberg, Nancy (Sherman) 1931- *4*
Rosenberg, Sharon 1942- *8*
Rosenberry, Vera 1948- *144*
   Earlier sketch in SATA *83*
Rosenblatt, Arthur
   See Rosenblatt, Arthur S.
Rosenblatt, Arthur S. 1938- *68*
   Brief entry *45*
Rosenblatt, Lily 1956- *90*
Rosenbloom, Joseph 1928- *21*
Rosenblum, Richard 1928- *11*
Rosenburg, John M. 1918- *6*
Rosenfeld, Dina 1962- *99*
Rosenstiehl, Agnes 1941- *203*
Rosenthal, Amy Krouse 1965- *177*
Rosenthal, Betsy R. 1957- *178*
Rosenthal, Harold 1914-1999 .... *35*
Rosenthal, M(acha) L(ouis) 1917-1996 .... *59*
Rosenthal, Marc 1949- *193*
Rosenthal, Mark A(lan) 1946- *64*
Rosing, Norbert 1953- *196*
Rosman, Steven M 1956- *81*
Rosman, Steven Michael
   See Rosman, Steven M
Rosoff, Meg 1956- *209*
   Earlier sketch in SATA *160*

Ross, Alan
   See Warwick, Alan R(oss)
Ross, Christine 1950- *172*
   Earlier sketch in SATA *83*
Ross, Clare
   See Romano, Clare
Ross, Dana Fuller
   See Cockrell, Amanda
   and Gerson, Noel Bertram
Ross, Dave
   See Ross, David
Ross, David 1896-1975 .... *49*
   Obituary *20*
Ross, David 1949- *133*
   Earlier sketch in SATA *32*
Ross, Deborah J.
   See Wheeler, Deborah
Ross, Diana
   See Denney, Diana
Ross, Edward S(hearman) 1915- *85*
Ross, Eileen 1950- *115*
Ross, Frank (Xavier), Jr. 1914- *28*
Ross, Jane 1961- *79*
Ross, John 1921- *45*
Ross, Judy 1942- *54*
Ross, Katharine Reynolds
   See Ross, Kathy
Ross, Kathy 1948- *169*
   Earlier sketch in SATA *89*
Ross, Kent 1956- *91*
Ross, Lillian Hammer 1925- *72*
Ross, Michael Elsohn 1952- *170*
   Earlier sketches in SATA *80, 127*
Ross, Pat(ricia Kienzle) 1943- *53*
   Brief entry *48*
Ross, Ramon R(oyal) 1930- *62*
Ross, Stewart 1947- *134*
   Earlier sketch in SATA *92*
   See also SAAS *23*
Ross, Tom 1958- *84*
Ross, Tony 1938- *176*
   Earlier sketches in SATA *17, 65, 130*
Ross, Wilda 1915- *51*
   Brief entry *39*
Rossel, Seymour 1945- *28*
Rossell, Judith 1953- *187*
Rossel-Waugh, C. C.
   See Waugh, Carol-Lynn Rossel
Rossetti, Christina 1830-1894 .... *20*
   See also CLR *115*
Rossetti, Christina Georgina
   See Rossetti, Christina
Rossi, Joyce 1943- *116*
Rossotti, Hazel Swaine 1930- *95*
Rostkowski, Margaret I. 1945- *59*
Roth, Arnold 1929- *21*
Roth, Arthur J(oseph) 1925-1993 .... *43*
   Brief entry *28*
   Obituary *75*
   See also SAAS *11*
Roth, David 1940- *36*
Roth, Julie Jersild *180*
Roth, Matthue 1978(?)- *174*
Roth, Roger *190*
Roth, Ruby 1983(?)- *216*
Roth, Stephanie *202*
Roth, Susan L. *181*
   Earlier sketch in SATA *134*
Rothberg, Abraham 1922- *59*
Roth-Hano, Renee 1931- *85*
Rothkopf, Carol Z. 1929- *4*
Rothman, Joel 1938- *7*
Rotner, Shelley 1951- *169*
   Earlier sketch in SATA *76*
Rottman, S.L. 1970- *157*
   Earlier sketch in SATA *106*
Rottman, Susan Lynn
   See Rottman, S.L.
Roueche, Berton 1911-1994 .... *28*
Roughsey, Dick 1921(?)-1985 .... *35*
   See also CLR *41*

Roughsey, Goobalathaldin
  See Roughsey, Dick
Rounds, Glen (Harold) 1906-2002 .... *112*
  Obituary *141*
  Earlier sketches in SATA *8, 70*
Rourke, Constance Mayfield 1885-1941
  See YABC *1*
Rouss, Sylvia *211*
Rovetch, Gerda 1925(?)- *202*
Rovetch, L. Bob
  See Rovetch, Lissa
Rovetch, Lissa *201*
Rowan, Deirdre
  See Williams, Jeanne
Rowe, Jennifer
  See Rodda, Emily
Rowe, John A. 1949- *198*
  Earlier sketch in SATA *146*
Rowe, Viola Carson 1903-1969
  Obituary *26*
Rowh, Mark 1952- *90*
Rowland, Florence Wightman 1900-1997 ...... *8*
  Obituary *108*
Rowland-Entwistle, (Arthur) Theodore (Henry)
  1925- *94*
  Earlier sketch in SATA *31*
Rowling, J.K. 1965- *174*
  Earlier sketch in SATA *109*
  See also CLR *112*
Rowling, Joanne Kathleen
  See Rowling, J.K.
Rowsome, Frank (Howard), Jr. 1914-1983 .. *36*
Roy, Gabrielle 1909-1983 .... *104*
Roy, Jacqueline 1954- *74*
Roy, Jennifer
  See Roy, Jennifer Rozines
Roy, Jennifer Rozines 1967- *178*
Roy, Jessie Hailstalk 1895-1986
  Obituary *51*
Roy, Liam
  See Scarry, Patricia (Murphy)
Roy, Ron(ald) 1940- *110*
  Brief entry *35*
  Earlier sketch in SATA *40*
Roybal, Laura 1956- *85*
Roybal, Laura Husby
  See Roybal, Laura
Royds, Caroline 1953- *55*
Royston, Angela 1945- *169*
  Earlier sketch in SATA *120*
Rozakis, Laurie E. 1952- *84*
Rozen, Anna 1960- *206*
Rubel, Nicole 1953- *181*
  Earlier sketches in SATA *18, 95, 135*
Rubin, Eva Johanna 1925- *38*
Rubin, Susan Goldman 1939- *182*
  Earlier sketches in SATA *84, 132*
Rubin, Vicky 1964- *193*
Rubinetti, Donald 1947- *92*
Rubinstein, Gillian 1942- *158*
  Autobiography Feature *116*
  Earlier sketches in SATA *68, 105*
  See also CLR *35*
  See also SAAS *25*
Rubinstein, Gillian Margaret
  See Rubinstein, Gillian
Rubinstein, Patricia -2003
  See Forest, Antonia
Rubinstein, Patricia Giulia Caulfield Kate
  See Forest, Antonia
Rubinstein, Robert E(dward) 1943- *49*
Rublowsky, John M(artin) 1928- *62*
Rubright, Lynn 1936- *171*
Ruby, Laura *181*
  Earlier sketch in SATA *155*
Ruby, Lois 1942- *184*
  Autobiography Feature *105*
  Brief entry *34*
  Earlier sketches in SATA *35, 95*
Ruby, Lois F.
  See Ruby, Lois

Ruchlis, Hy(man) 1913-1992 .... *3*
  Obituary *72*
Ruckdeschel, Liz *214*
Rucker, Mike 1940- *91*
Ruckman, Ivy 1931- *93*
  Earlier sketch in SATA *37*
Ruck-Pauquet, Gina 1931- *40*
  Brief entry *37*
Ruddell, Deborah 1949- *210*
Ruditis, Paul *190*
Rudley, Stephen 1946- *30*
Rudolph, Marguerita 1908- *21*
Rudomin, Esther
  See Hautzig, Esther Rudomin
Rue, Leonard Lee III 1926- *142*
  Earlier sketch in SATA *37*
Rueda, Claudia *183*
Ruedi, Norma Paul
  See Ainsworth, Norma
Ruelle, Karen Gray 1957- *209*
  Earlier sketches in SATA *84, 126*
Ruemmler, John D(avid) 1948- *78*
Ruepp, Krista 1947- *143*
Ruffell, Ann 1941- *30*
Ruffins, Reynold 1930- *125*
  Earlier sketch in SATA *41*
Rugg, Jim *206*
Rugoff, Milton 1913- *30*
Ruhen, Olaf 1911-1989 .... *17*
Rui, Paolo 1962- *217*
Rukeyser, Muriel 1913-1980
  Obituary *22*
Rumbaut, Hendle 1949- *84*
Rumford, James 1948- *193*
  Earlier sketch in SATA *116*
Rumsey, Marian (Barritt) 1928- *16*
Rumstuckle, Cornelius
  See Brennan, Herbie
Runholt, Susan *216*
Runnerstroem, Bengt Arne 1944- *75*
Runyan, John
  See Palmer, Bernard (Alvin)
Runyon, Brent *217*
Runyon, Catherine 1947- *62*
Ruoff, A. LaVonne Brown 1930- *76*
Rupp, Rebecca *185*
Rusch, Elizabeth 1966- *198*
Rusch, Kris
  See Rusch, Kristine Kathryn
Rusch, Kristine Kathryn 1960- *113*
Rush, Alison 1951- *41*
Rush, Peter 1937- *32*
Rushdie, Ahmed Salman
  See Rushdie, Salman
Rushdie, Salman 1947-
  See CLR *125*
Rushford, Patricia H(elen) 1943- *134*
Rushmore, Helen 1898-1994 .... *3*
Rushmore, Robert (William) 1926-1986 .... *8*
  Obituary *49*
Ruskin, Ariane
  See Batterberry, Ariane Ruskin
Ruskin, John 1819-1900 .... *24*
Russ, Lavinia (Faxon) 1904-1992 .... *74*
Russell, Charlotte
  See Rathjen, Carl Henry
Russell, Ching Yeung 1946- *107*
Russell, Don(ald Bert) 1899-1986
  Obituary *47*
Russell, Franklin (Alexander) 1926- *11*
Russell, Gertrude Barrer
  See Barrer-Russell, Gertrude
Russell, Helen Ross 1915- *8*
Russell, James 1933- *53*
Russell, Jim
  See Russell, James
Russell, Joan Plummer 1930- *139*
Russell, P(hilip) Craig 1951- *162*
  Earlier sketch in SATA *80*
Russell, Patrick
  See Sammis, John

Russell, Paul (Gary) 1942- *57*
Russell, Sarah
  See Laski, Marghanita
Russell, Sharman Apt 1954- *123*
Russell, Solveig Paulson 1904-1985 .... *3*
Russo, Marisabina 1950- *188*
  Earlier sketches in SATA *106, 151*
Russo, Monica J. 1950- *83*
Russo, Susan 1947- *30*
Russon, Penni 1974- *179*
Rutgers van der Loeff, An
  See Rutgers van der Loeff-Basenau, An(na)
  Maria Margaretha
Rutgers van der Loeff-Basenau, An(na) Maria
  Margaretha 1910- *22*
Ruth, Rod 1912-1987 .... *9*
Rutherford, Douglas
  See McConnell, James Douglas Rutherford
Rutherford, Meg 1932- *34*
Ruthin, Margaret
  See Catherall, Arthur
Rutledge, Jill Zimmerman 1951- *155*
Rutz, Viola Larkin 1932- *12*
Ruurs, Margriet 1952- *215*
  Earlier sketches in SATA *97, 147*
Ruzicka, Rudolph 1883-1978
  Obituary *24*
Ruzzier, Sergio 1966- *210*
  Earlier sketch in SATA *159*
, Ryan
  See Ryan, John
Ryan, Betsy
  See Ryan, Elizabeth (Anne)
Ryan, Cheli Duran *20*
Ryan, Darlene 1958- *176*
Ryan, Elizabeth (Anne) 1943- *30*
Ryan, Jeanette
  See Mines, Jeanette
Ryan, John 1921-2009 .... *22*
Ryan, Margaret 1950- *166*
  Earlier sketch in SATA *78*
Ryan, Mary E. 1953- *61*
Ryan, Mary Elizabeth
  See Ryan, Mary E.
Ryan, Pam Munoz 1951- *197*
  Earlier sketch in SATA *134*
Ryan, Patrick 1957- *138*
Ryan, Peter (Charles) 1939- *15*
Ryan-Lush, Geraldine 1949- *89*
Rybakov, Anatoli (Naumovich) 1911-1998 .. *79*
  Obituary *108*
Rybakov, Anatolii (Naumovich)
  See Rybakov, Anatoli (Naumovich)
Rybolt, Thomas R. 1954- *62*
Rybolt, Thomas Roy
  See Rybolt, Thomas R.
Rybolt, Tom
  See Rybolt, Thomas R.
Rydberg, Ernest E(mil) 1901-1993 .... *21*
Rydberg, Lou(isa Hampton) 1908- *27*
Rydell, Katy 1942- *91*
Rydell, Wendell
  See Rydell, Wendy
Rydell, Wendy *4*
Ryden, Hope *91*
  Earlier sketch in SATA *8*
Ryder, Joanne (Rose) 1946- *163*
  Brief entry *34*
  Earlier sketches in SATA *65, 122*
  See also CLR *37*
Ryder, Pamela
  See Lamb, Nancy
Rye, Anthony
  See Youd, Samuel
Rylant, Cynthia 1954- *195*
  Brief entry *44*
  Earlier sketches in SATA *50, 76, 112, 160*
  See also CLR *86*
  See also SAAS *13*
Rymer, Alta May 1925- *34*
Rymond, Lynda Gene *199*

S

S. L. C.
See Twain, Mark
S., Svend Otto
See Soerensen, Svend Otto
Saaf, Donald W(illiam) 1961- 124
Saal, Jocelyn
See Sachs, Judith
Sabbeth, Carol (Landstrom) 1957- 125
Saberhagen, Fred 1930-2007 89
Obituary 184
Earlier sketch in SATA 37
Saberhagen, Fred T.
See Saberhagen, Fred
Saberhagen, Fred Thomas
See Saberhagen, Fred
Saberhagen, Frederick Thomas
See Saberhagen, Fred
Sabin, Edwin L(egrand) 1870-1952
See YABC 2
Sabin, Francene 27
Sabin, Lou
See Sabin, Louis
Sabin, Louis 1930- 27
Sabre, Dirk
See Laffin, John (Alfred Charles)
Sabuda, Robert (James) 1965- 120
Earlier sketch in SATA 81
Sabuda, Robert 1965- 170
Sabuda, Robert James
See Sabuda, Robert
Sachar, Louis 1954- 154
Brief entry 50
Earlier sketches in SATA 63, 104
See also CLR 79
Sachs, Elizabeth-Ann 1946- 48
Sachs, Judith 1947- 52
Brief entry 51
Sachs, Marilyn 1927- 164
Autobiography Feature 110
Earlier sketches in SATA 3, 68
See also CLR 2
See also SAAS 2
Sachs, Marilyn Stickle
See Sachs, Marilyn
Sackett, S(amuel) J(ohn) 1928- 12
Sackson, Sid 1920- 16
Sacre, Antonio 1968- 152
Saddler, Allen
See Richards, R(onald) C(harles) W(illiam)
Saddler, K. Allen
See Richards, R(onald) C(harles) W(illiam)
Sadie, Stanley 1930-2005 14
Sadie, Stanley John
See Sadie, Stanley
Sadiq, Nazneen
See Sheikh, Nazneen
Sadler, Catherine Edwards 1952- 60
Brief entry 45
Sadler, Marilyn (June) 1950- 79
Sadler, Mark
See Lynds, Dennis
Saffer, Barbara 144
Sagan, Carl 1934-1996 58
Obituary 94
Sagan, Carl Edward
See Sagan, Carl
Sage, Angie 1952- 197
Sage, Juniper
See Brown, Margaret Wise
and Hurd, Edith Thacher
Sagsoorian, Paul 1923- 12
Said, S.F. 1967- 174
Saidman, Anne 1952- 75
Saint, Dora Jessie 1913- 10
St. Anthony, Jane 175
St. Antoine, Sara L. 1966- 84
St. Clair, Byrd Hooper 1905-1976
Obituary 28

Saint-Exupery, Antoine de 1900-1944 20
See also CLR 142
Saint-Exupery, Antoine Jean Baptiste Marie
Roger de
See Saint-Exupery, Antoine de
St. George, Judith 1931- 161
Earlier sketches in SATA 13, 99
See also CLR 57
See also SAAS 12
St. George, Judith Alexander
See St. George, Judith
St. James, Blakely
See Gottfried, Theodore Mark
and Platt, Charles
St. James, Blakely
See Griffin, W.E.B.
St. James, Sierra
See Rallison, Janette
Saint James, Synthia 1949- 152
Earlier sketch in SATA 84
St. John, Lauren 1966- 214
St. John, Nicole 143
Autobiography Feature 143
Earlier sketches in SATA 29, 89
See also CLR 46
See also SAAS 7
St. John, Patricia Mary 1919-1993
Obituary 79
St. John, Philip
See del Rey, Lester
St. John, Wylly Folk 1908-1985 10
Obituary 45
St. Max, E. S.
See Ellis, Edward S.
St. Meyer, Ned
See Stratemeyer, Edward L.
St. Mox, E. A.
See Ellis, Edward S.
St. Myer, Ned
See Stratemeyer, Edward L.
St. Tamara
See Kolba, St. Tamara
Saito, Michiko
See Fujiwara, Michiko
Sakai, Komako 1966- 213
Sakaki, Ichiro 1969- 192
Sakamoto, Miki 198
Sakers, Don 1958- 72
Sakharnov, S.
See Sakharnov, Svyatoslav
Sakharnov, Svyatoslav 1923- 65
Sakharnov, Svyatoslav Vladimirovich
See Sakharnov, Svyatoslav
Saksena, Kate 148
Sakurai, Gail 1952- 153
Earlier sketch in SATA 87
Salamanca, Lucy
See del Barco, Lucy Salamanca
Salas, Laura Purdie 1966- 216
Salassi, Otto R(ussell) 1939-1993 38
Obituary 77
Salat, Cristina 82
Saldana, Rene, Jr. 186
Saldutti, Denise 1953- 39
Sale, Tim 1956- 153
Salem, Kay 1952- 92
Salerno, Steven 176
Salinger, J.D. 1919-2010 67
See also CLR 18
Salinger, Jerome David
See Salinger, J.D.
Salisbury, Graham 1944- 195
Earlier sketches in SATA 76, 108, 161
Salisbury, Joyce E(llen) 1944- 138
Salkey, (Felix) Andrew (Alexander)
1928-1995 118
Earlier sketch in SATA 35
Salley, Coleen 166
Sallis, Susan (Diana) 1929- 55
Salmieri, Daniel 1983- 208
Salmon, Annie Elizabeth 1899- 13

Salonen, Roxane Beauclair 1968- 184
Salsi, Lynn 1947- 130
Salsitz, R. A. V.
See Salsitz, Rhondi Vilott
Salsitz, Rhondi Vilott 115
Salten, Felix
See Salzmann, Siegmund
Salter, Cedric
See Knight, Francis Edgar
Saltman, Judith 1947- 64
Saltzberg, Barney 1955- 194
Earlier sketch in SATA 135
Saltzman, David (Charles Laertes)
1967-1990 86
Salvadori, Mario (George) 1907-1997 97
Earlier sketch in SATA 40
Salwood, F.K.
See Kilworth, Garry
Salzer, L. E.
See Wilson, Lionel
Salzman, Marian 1959- 77
Salzmann, Siegmund 1869-1945 25
Samachson, Dorothy (Mirkin) 1914-1997 3
Samachson, Joseph 1906-1980 3
Obituary 52
Sammis, John 1942- 4
Sampson, Emma (Keats) Speed 1868-1947 . 68
Sampson, Fay (Elizabeth) 1935- 151
Brief entry 40
Earlier sketch in SATA 42
Sampson, Michael 1952- 143
Earlier sketch in SATA 95
Samson, Anne S(tringer) 1933- 2
Samson, Joan 1937-1976 13
Samson, Suzanne M. 1959- 91
Samuels, Barbara 199
Samuels, Charles 1902-1982 12
Samuels, Cynthia K(alish) 1946- 79
Samuels, Gertrude 1910(?)-2003 17
Obituary 147
Sanborn, Duane 1914-1996 38
Sancha, Sheila 1924- 38
Sanchez, Alex 1957- 151
Sanchez, Anita 1956- 209
Sanchez, Sonia 1934- 136
Earlier sketch in SATA 22
See also CLR 18
Sanchez-Silva, Jose Maria 1911- 132
Earlier sketch in SATA 16
See also CLR 12
Sand, George X. 45
Sandak, Cass R(obert) 1950-2001 51
Brief entry 37
Sandberg, (Karin) Inger 1930- 15
Sandberg, Karl C. 1931- 35
Sandberg, Lasse (E. M.) 1924- 15
Sandburg, Carl 1878-1967 8
See also CLR 67
Sandburg, Carl August
See Sandburg, Carl
Sandburg, Charles
See Sandburg, Carl
Sandburg, Charles A.
See Sandburg, Carl
Sandburg, Helga 1918- 3
See also SAAS 10
Sandell, Lisa Ann 1977- 175
Sandemose, Iben 1950- 211
Sander, Heather L. 1947- 157
Sanderlin, George 1915- 4
Sanderlin, Owenita (Harrah) 1916- 11
Sanders, Betty Jane
See Monthei, Betty
Sanders, Nancy I. 1960- 141
Earlier sketch in SATA 90
Sanders, Scott Russell 1945- 109
Earlier sketch in SATA 56
Sanders, Winston P.
See Anderson, Poul
Sanderson, Irma 1912- 66
Sanderson, Ivan T(erence) 1911-1973 6

Sanderson, Margaret Love
   See Keats, Emma
   and Sampson, Emma (Keats) Speed
Sanderson, Ruth 1951- 172
   Earlier sketches in SATA *41, 109*
Sanderson, Ruth L.
   See Sanderson, Ruth
Sand-Eveland, Cyndi 211
Sandin, Joan 1942- 197
   Earlier sketches in SATA *12, 94, 153*
Sandison, Janet
   See Cameron, Elizabeth Jane
Sandler, Martin W. 216
   Earlier sketch in SATA *160*
Sandom, J. Gregory
   See Welsh, T.K.
Sandom, J.G.
   See Welsh, T.K.
Sandoz, Mari(e Susette) 1900-1966 5
Sanford, Agnes (White) 1897-1976 61
Sanford, Doris 1937- 69
Sanford, Rose
   See Simmonds, Posy
Sanger, Amy Wilson 1967- 205
Sanger, Marjory Bartlett 1920- 8
San Jose, Christine 1929- 167
Sankey, Alice (Ann-Susan) 1910- 27
San Souci, Daniel 192
   Earlier sketch in SATA *96*
San Souci, Robert D. 1946- 158
   Earlier sketches in SATA *40, 81, 117*
   See also CLR *43*
Santamaria, Benjamin 1955- 184
Santat, Dan 188
Santesson, Hans Stefan 1914(?)-1975
   Obituary 30
Santiago, Esmeralda 1948- 129
Santopolo, Jill 214
Santore, Charles 1935- 200
Santos, Helen
   See Griffiths, Helen
Santrey, Louis
   See Sabin, Louis
Santucci, Barbara 1948- 130
Sapergia, Barbara 1943- 181
Sapet, Kerrily 1972- 214
Sapieyevski, Anne Lindbergh 1940-1993 81
   Brief entry 32
   Earlier sketches in SATA *35, 78*
Saport, Linda 1954- 123
Sapp, Allen 1929- 151
Sarac, Roger
   See Caras, Roger A(ndrew)
Sarah, Duchess of York
   See Ferguson, Sarah
Sarasin, Jennifer
   See Sachs, Judith
Sarcone-Roach, Julia 215
Sardinha, Rick 192
Sarg, Anthony Frederick
   See Sarg, Tony
Sarg, Tony 1882-1942
   See YABC *1*
Sargent, Pamela 1948- 78
   Earlier sketch in SATA *29*
Sargent, Robert 1933- 2
Sargent, Sarah 1937- 44
   Brief entry 41
Sargent, Shirley 1927-2004 11
Sarnoff, Jane 1937- 10
Saroff, Phyllis V. 202
Saroyan, William 1908-1981 23
   Obituary 24
Sarton, Eleanor May
   See Sarton, May
Sarton, May 1912-1995 36
   Obituary 86
Sasaki, Chris 182
Sasaki, Ellen Joy 206
Saseen, Sharon (Dillon) 1949- 59

Sasek, Miroslav 1916-1980 16
   Obituary 23
   See also CLR *4*
Sasso, Sandy Eisenberg 1947- 162
   Earlier sketches in SATA *86, 116*
Sathre, Vivian 1952- 133
   Earlier sketch in SATA *79*
Satterfield, Charles
   See del Rey, Lester
   and Pohl, Frederik
Sattgast, L. J.
   See Sattgast, Linda J.
Sattgast, Linda J. 1953- 91
Sattler, Helen Roney 1921-1992 74
   Earlier sketch in SATA *4*
   See also CLR *24*
Sauer, Julia Lina 1891-1983 32
   Obituary 36
Sauerwein, Leigh 1944- 155
Saul, Carol P. 1947- 117
   Earlier sketch in SATA *78*
Saul, John III
   See Saul, John
Saul, John 1942- 98
Saul, John W.
   See Saul, John
Saul, John W. III
   See Saul, John
Saul, John Woodruff III
   See Saul, John
Saul, (Ellen) Wendy 1946- 42
Saulnier, Karen Luczak 1940- 80
Saunders, Caleb
   See Heinlein, Robert A.
Saunders, Dave 1939- 85
Saunders, Julie 1939- 85
Saunders, (William) Keith 1910-1994 12
Saunders, Rubie (Agnes) 1929- 21
Saunders, Steven
   See Jones, Allan Frewin
Saunders, Susan 1945- 96
   Brief entry 41
   Earlier sketch in SATA *46*
Saunders-Smith, Gail 1952- 169
Sauvain, Philip Arthur 1933- 111
Savadier, Elivia 1950- 164
   Earlier sketch in SATA *79*
Savage, Alan
   See Nicole, Christopher (Robin)
Savage, Blake
   See Goodwin, Harold L(eland)
Savage, Candace 1949- 142
Savage, Deborah 1955- 76
Savage, Jeff 1961- 97
Savage, Katharine James 1905-1989
   Obituary 61
Savage, Stephen 1965- 194
Savage, Thomas 1915-2003
   Obituary 147
Savageau, Cheryl 1950- 96
Savery, Constance (Winifred) 1897-1999 1
Saville, Andrew
   See Taylor, Andrew
Saville, (Leonard) Malcolm 1901-1982 23
   Obituary 31
Saviozzi, Adriana
   See Mazza, Adriana
Savitt, Sam 1917-2000 8
   Obituary 126
Savitz, Harriet May 1933-2008 72
   Earlier sketch in SATA *5*
   See also SAAS *26*
Sawicki, Mary 1950- 90
Sawyer, (Frederick) Don(ald) 1947- 72
Sawyer, Kem Knapp 1953- 84
Sawyer, Robert J. 1960- 149
   Earlier sketch in SATA *81*
Sawyer, Robert James
   See Sawyer, Robert J.
Sawyer, Ruth 1880-1970 17
   See also CLR *36*

Saxby, H.M.
   See Saxby, (Henry) Maurice
Saxby, (Henry) Maurice 1924- 71
Saxon, Andrew
   See Arthur, Robert, (Jr.)
Saxon, Antonia
   See Sachs, Judith
Say, Allen 1937- 161
   Earlier sketches in SATA *28, 69, 110*
   See also CLR *135*
Sayers, Frances Clarke 1897-1989 3
   Obituary 62
Sayles, Elizabeth 1956- 163
   Earlier sketch in SATA *108*
Saylor-Marchant, Linda 1963- 82
Sayre, April Pulley 1966- 191
   Earlier sketches in SATA *88, 131*
Sazer, Nina 1949- 13
Scabrini, Janet 1953- 13
Scagell, Robin 1946- 107
Scagnetti, Jack 1924- 7
Scaletta, Kurtis 1968- 215
Scamander, Newt
   See Rowling, J.K.
Scamell, Ragnhild 1940- 180
   Earlier sketch in SATA *77*
Scanlon, Marion Stephany 11
Scannel, John Vernon
   See Scannell, Vernon
Scannell, Vernon 1922-2007 59
   Obituary 188
Scarborough, Elizabeth
   See Scarborough, Elizabeth Ann
Scarborough, Elizabeth Ann 1947- 171
   Earlier sketch in SATA *98*
Scarf, Maggi
   See Scarf, Maggie
Scarf, Maggie 1932- 5
Scariano, Margaret M. 1924- 86
Scarlett, Susan
   See Streatfeild, Noel
Scarry, Huck
   See Scarry, Richard McClure, Jr.
Scarry, Patricia (Murphy) 1924- 2
Scarry, Patsy
   See Scarry, Patricia (Murphy)
Scarry, Richard (McClure) 1919-1994 75
   Obituary 90
   Earlier sketches in SATA *2, 35*
   See also CLR *41*
Scarry, Richard McClure, Jr. 1953- 35
Schachner, Judith Byron 1951- 178
   Earlier sketch in SATA *88*
Schachner, Judy
   See Schachner, Judith Byron
Schachtel, Roger 1949- 38
Schachtel, Roger Bernard
   See Schachtel, Roger
Schade, Susan 189
Schaedler, Sally 116
Schaefer, Carole Lexa 173
Schaefer, Jack (Warner) 1907-1991 66
   Obituary 65
   Earlier sketch in SATA *3*
Schaefer, Lola M. 1950- 183
   Earlier sketches in SATA *91, 144*
Schaeffer, Mead 1898- 21
Schaeffer, Susan Fromberg 1941- 22
Schaer, Brigitte 1958- 112
Schaller, George
   See Schaller, George B.
Schaller, George B. 1933- 30
Schaller, George Beals
   See Schaller, George B.
Schanzer, Rosalyn (Good) 1942- 138
   Earlier sketch in SATA *77*
Schatell, Brian 66
   Brief entry 47
Schechter, Betty (Goodstein) 1921- 5
Schechter, Simone
   See Elkeles, Simone

Schecter, Ellen 1944- 85
Scheeder, Louis 1946- 141
Scheer, Julian (Weisel) 1926-2001 8
Scheffer, Victor B(lanchard) 1906- 6
Scheffler, Axel 1957- 180
Scheffler, Ursel 1938- 81
Scheffrin-Falk, Gladys 1928- 76
Scheidl, Gerda Marie 1913- 85
Scheier, Michael 1943- 40
  Brief entry 36
Schell, Mildred 1922- 41
Schell, Orville (Hickok) 1940- 10
Scheller, Melanie 1953- 77
Schellie, Don 1932- 29
Schembri, Jim 1962- 124
Schembri, Pamela 1969- 195
Schemm, Mildred Walker 1905-1998 21
  Obituary 103
Schenker, Dona 1947- 133
  Earlier sketch in SATA 68
Scher, Paula 1948- 47
Scherer, Jeffrey 194
Scherf, Margaret 1908-1979 10
Schermer, Judith (Denise) 1941- 30
Schertle, Alice 1941- 192
  Earlier sketches in SATA 36, 90, 145
Schick, Alice 1946- 27
Schick, Eleanor 1942- 144
  Earlier sketches in SATA 9, 82
Schick, Joel 1945- 31
  Brief entry 30
Schields, Gretchen 1948- 75
Schiff, Ken(neth Roy) 1942- 7
Schiller, Andrew 1919- 21
Schiller, Barbara (Heyman) 1928- 21
Schiller, Pamela (Byrne) 127
Schindel, John 1955- 213
  Earlier sketches in SATA 77, 115
Schindelman, Joseph 1923- 67
  Brief entry 32
Schindler, S.D. 1952- 198
  Brief entry 50
  Earlier sketches in SATA 75, 118, 171
Schindler, Steven D.
  See Schindler, S.D.
Schinto, Jeanne 1951- 93
Schisgall, Oscar 1901-1984 12
  Obituary 38
Schlaepfer, Gloria G. 1931- 154
Schlee, Ann 1934- 44
  Brief entry 36
Schleichert, Elizabeth 1945- 77
Schlein, Miriam 1926-2004 130
  Obituary 159
  Earlier sketches in SATA 2, 87
  See also CLR 41
Schlesinger, Arthur M., Jr. 1917-2007 61
  Obituary 181
  See Schlesinger, Arthur Meier
Schlesinger, Arthur Meier 1888-1965
Schlesinger, Laura (Catherine) 1947- 160
  Earlier sketch in SATA 110
Schlitz, Laura Amy 184
Schloat, G. Warren, Jr. 1914-2000 4
Schmatz, Pat 197
Schmid, Eleonore 1939- 126
  Earlier sketches in SATA 12, 84
Schmid, Susan Maupin 208
Schmiderer, Dorothy 1940- 19
Schmidt, Annie M. G. 1911-1995 67
  Obituary 91
  See also CLR 22
Schmidt, C.A. 196
Schmidt, Diane 1953- 70
Schmidt, Elizabeth 1915- 15
Schmidt, Gary D. 1957- 193
  Earlier sketches in SATA 93, 135
Schmidt, James Norman 1912-1983 21
Schmidt, Karen Lee 1953- 185
  Earlier sketch in SATA 94
Schmidt, Lynette 1952- 76

Schmitz, Tamara 207
Schneider, Antonie 1954- 167
  Earlier sketch in SATA 89
Schneider, Christine M. 1972(?)- 171
  Earlier sketch in SATA 120
Schneider, Dick
  See Schneider, Richard H.
Schneider, Elisa
  See Kleven, Elisa
Schneider, Herman 1905-2003 7
  Obituary 148
Schneider, Howie -2007 181
Schneider, Josh 1980- 196
Schneider, Laurie
  See Adams, Laurie
Schneider, Nina 1913-2007 2
  Obituary 186
Schneider, Nina Zimet
  See Schneider, Nina
Schneider, Rex 1937- 44
Schneider, Richard H. 1922- 171
Schneider, Richard Henry
  See Schneider, Richard H.
Schneider, Robyn 1986- 187
Schnirel, James R. 1931- 14
Schnitter, Jane T. 1958- 88
Schnitzlein, Danny 134
Schnur, Steven 1952- 144
  Earlier sketch in SATA 95
Schnurre, Wolfdietrich 1920-1989
  Obituary 63
Schoberle, Cecile 1949- 80
Schock, Pauline 1928- 45
Schoell, William 1951- 160
Schoen, Barbara (Taylor) 1924-1993 13
Schoenherr, Ian 177
Schoenherr, John 1935-2010 66
  Earlier sketch in SATA 37
  See also SAAS 13
Schoenherr, John Carl
  See Schoenherr, John
Schofield, Sandy
  See Rusch, Kristine Kathryn
Scholastica, Sister Mary
  See Jenkins, Marie M(agdalen)
Scholefield, A. T.
  See Scholefield, Alan
Scholefield, Alan 1931- 66
Scholefield, Edmund O.
  See Griffin, W.E.B.
Scholey, Arthur 1932- 28
Scholz, Jackson Volney 1897-1986
  Obituary 49
Schone, Virginia 22
Schongut, Emanuel 1936- 184
  Brief entry 36
  Earlier sketch in SATA 52
Schoonover, Frank (Earle) 1877-1972 24
Schoor, Gene 1921- 3
Schories, Pat 1952- 164
  Earlier sketch in SATA 116
Schorr, Melissa 1972- 194
Schorr, Melissa Robin
  See Schorr, Melissa
Schott, Jane A. 1946- 172
Schotter, Roni 190
  Earlier sketches in SATA 105, 149
Schraff, Anne E(laine) 1939- 92
  Earlier sketch in SATA 27
Schram, Peninnah 1934- 119
Schrank, Joseph 1900-1984
  Obituary 38
Schrecengost, Maity 1938- 118
Schrecengost, S. Maitland
  See Schrecengost, Maity
Schreck, Karen
  See Schreck, Karen Halvorsen
Schreck, Karen Halvorsen 1962- 185
Schrecker, Judie 1954- 90
Schreiber, Elizabeth Anne (Ferguson)
  1947- 13

Schreiber, Ralph W(alter) 1942- 13
Schreiner, Samuel A(gnew), Jr. 1921- 70
Schroades, John 214
Schroeder, Alan 1961- 98
  Earlier sketch in SATA 66
Schroeder, Binette
  See Nickl, Barbara (Elisabeth)
Schroeder, Russell (K.) 1943- 146
Schroeder, Ted 1931(?)-1973
  Obituary 20
Schubert, Dieter 1947- 217
  Earlier sketches in SATA 62, 101
Schubert, Ingrid 1953- 217
  Earlier sketch in SATA 62
Schubert, Leda 1950(?)- 181
Schubert-Gabrys, Ingrid 1953- 101
  Earlier sketch in SATA 62
Schuelein-Steel, Danielle
  See Steel, Danielle
Schuelein-Steel, Danielle Fernande
  See Steel, Danielle
Schuerger, Michele R. 110
Schuett, Stacey 1960- 168
  Earlier sketch in SATA 75
Schulke, Flip Phelps Graeme 1930- 57
Schulman, Arlene 1961- 105
Schulman, Janet 1933- 208
  Earlier sketches in SATA 22, 137
Schulman, L(ester) M(artin) 1934- 13
Schulte, Elaine L(ouise) 1934- 36
Schultz, Betty K(epka) 1932- 125
Schultz, Gwendolyn 21
Schultz, James Willard 1859-1947
  See YABC 1
Schultz, Pearle Henriksen 1918- 21
Schulz, Charles M. 1922-2000 10
  Obituary 118
Schulz, Charles Monroe
  See Schulz, Charles M.
Schumacher, Julie 1958- 191
Schumaker, Ward 1943- 96
Schuman, Michael A. 1953- 134
  Earlier sketch in SATA 85
Schur, Maxine
  See Schur, Maxine Rose
Schur, Maxine Rose 1948- 135
  Autobiography Feature 135
  Brief entry 49
  Earlier sketches in SATA 53, 98
Schurfranz, Vivian 1925- 13
Schutzer, A. I. 1922- 13
Schuyler, Pamela R. 1948- 30
Schwabach, Karen 185
Schwager, Tina 1964- 110
Schwandt, Stephen (William) 1947- 61
Schwark, Mary Beth 1954- 51
Schwartz, Alvin 1927-1992 56
  Obituary 71
  Earlier sketch in SATA 4
  See also CLR 89
Schwartz, Amy 1954- 189
  Brief entry 41
  Earlier sketches in SATA 47, 83, 131
  See also CLR 25
  See also SAAS 18
Schwartz, Anne Powers 1913-1987 10
Schwartz, Carol 1954- 77
Schwartz, Charles W(alsh) 1914- 8
Schwartz, David M. 1951- 110
  Earlier sketch in SATA 59
Schwartz, David Martin
  See Schwartz, David M.
Schwartz, Elizabeth Reeder 1912- 8
Schwartz, Ellen 1949- 117
Schwartz, Jerome L.
  See Lawrence, Jerome
Schwartz, Joel L. 1940- 54
  Brief entry 51
Schwartz, Joyce R. 1950- 93
Schwartz, Julius 1907-2004 45
Schwartz, Perry 1942- 75
Schwartz, Sheila (Ruth) 1929- 27

Schwartz, Stephen (Lawrence) 1948- 19
Schwartz, Virginia Frances 1950- 184
  Earlier sketch in SATA 131
Schwarz, Silvia Tessa Viviane
  See Schwarz, Viviane
Schwarz, Viviane 1977- 204
Schwarz, (Silvia Tessa) Viviane 1977- 141
Schweitzer, Byrd Baylor
  See Baylor, Byrd
Schweitzer, Iris 59
  Brief entry 36
Schweninger, Ann 1951- 168
  Earlier sketches in SATA 29, 98
Schwerin, Doris H(alpern) 1922- 64
Schy, Yael 197
Scieszka, Jon 1954- 199
  Earlier sketches in SATA 68, 105, 160
  See also CLR 107
Scillian, Devin 199
  Earlier sketch in SATA 128
Scioscia, Mary (Hershey) 1926- 63
Sciurba, Katie 1957- 196
Scofield, Penrod 1933- 62
  Obituary 78
Scoggin, Margaret C(lara) 1905-1968 47
  Brief entry 28
Scoltock, Jack 1942- 141
  Earlier sketch in SATA 72
Scoppettone, Sandra 1936- 92
  Earlier sketch in SATA 9
Scot, Michael
  See Rohan, Michael Scott
Scot-Bernard, P.
  See Bernard, Patricia
Scotland, Jay
  See Jakes, John
Scott, Alastair
  See Allen, Kenneth S.
Scott, Ann Herbert 1926- 140
  Autobiography Feature 140
  Brief entry 29
  Earlier sketches in SATA 56, 94
Scott, Bill
  See Scott, William N(eville)
Scott, Bill 1920(?)-1985
  Obituary 46
Scott, Cora Annett (Pipitone) 1931- 11
Scott, Dan
  See Barker, S. Omar
Scott, Elaine 1940- 198
  Earlier sketches in SATA 36, 90, 164
Scott, Elizabeth 1972- 194
Scott, Jack Denton 1915-1995 83
  Earlier sketch in SATA 31
  See also CLR 20
  See also SAAS 14
Scott, Jane (Harrington) 1931- 55
Scott, Jessica
  See De Wire, Elinor
Scott, John 1912-1976 14
Scott, John Anthony 1916- 23
Scott, John M(artin) 1913- 12
Scott, Mary
  See Mattern, Joanne
Scott, Melissa 1960- 109
Scott, Michael 1959- 211
Scott, Mike
  See Scott, Michael
Scott, Richard
  See Rennert, Richard Scott
Scott, Roney
  See Gault, William Campbell
Scott, Sally 1909-1978 43
Scott, Sally 1948- 44
Scott, Sally Elisabeth
  See Scott, Sally
Scott, W. N.
  See Scott, William N(eville)
Scott, Sir Walter 1771-1832
  See YABC 2
  See also CLR 154

Scott, Warwick
  See Trevor, Elleston
Scott, William N(eville) 1923- 87
Scotti, Anna
  See Coates, Anna
Scotton, Rob 1960- 214
  Earlier sketch in SATA 177
Scribner, Charles, Jr. 1921-1995 13
  Obituary 87
Scribner, Joanne L. 1949- 33
Scribner, Kimball 1917- 63
Scrimger, Richard 1957- 164
  Earlier sketch in SATA 119
Scrimsher, Lila Gravatt 1897-1974
  Obituary 28
Scroder, Walter K. 1928- 82
Scroggs, Kirk 187
Scruggs, Sandy 1961- 89
Scudder, Brooke 1959- 154
Scudder, Mildred Lee 1908- 6
  See also SAAS 12
Scull, Marie-Louise 1943-1993 77
Scuro, Vincent 1951- 21
Seabrooke, Brenda 1941- 148
  Earlier sketches in SATA 30, 88
Seaman, Augusta Huiell 1879-1950 31
Seamands, Ruth 1916- 9
Searcy, Margaret Zehmer 1926- 54
  Brief entry 39
Searight, Mary W(illiams) 1918- 17
Searle, Kathryn Adrienne 1942- 10
Searle, Ronald (William Fordham) 1920- 70
  Earlier sketch in SATA 42
Sears, Stephen W. 1932- 4
Seaskull, Cecil
  See Castellucci, Cecil
Sebastian, Lee
  See Silverberg, Robert
Sebestyen, Igen
  See Sebestyen, Ouida
Sebestyen, Ouida 1924- 140
  Earlier sketch in SATA 39
  See also CLR 17
  See also SAAS 10
Sebrey, Mary Ann 1951- 62
Sechrist, Elizabeth Hough 1903-1991 2
Sederman, Marty 211
Sedges, John
  See Buck, Pearl S.
Sedgwick, Marcus 1968- 197
  Earlier sketch in SATA 160
Seed, Cecile Eugenie 1930- 86
  Earlier sketch in SATA 8
  See also CLR 76
Seed, Jenny
  See Seed, Cecile Eugenie
Seed, Sheila Turner 1937(?)-1979
  Obituary 23
Seeger, Elizabeth 1889-1973
  Obituary 20
Seeger, Laura Vaccaro 200
  Earlier sketch in SATA 172
Seeger, Pete 1919- 139
  Earlier sketch in SATA 13
Seeger, Peter R.
  See Seeger, Pete
Seeley, Laura L. 1958- 71
Seever, R.
  See Reeves, Lawrence F.
Sefozo, Mary 1925- 82
Sefton, Catherine
  See Waddell, Martin
Segal, John 178
Segal, Joyce 1940- 35
Segal, Lore 1928- 163
  Earlier sketches in SATA 4, 66
  See also SAAS 11
Segal, Lore Groszmann
  See Segal, Lore
Segar, E(lzie) C(risler) 1894-1938 61

Segovia, Andres 1893(?)-1987
  Obituary 52
Seguin, Marilyn W(eymouth) 1951- 91
Seguin-Fontes, Marthe 1924- 109
Seibold, J. Otto 1960- 196
  Earlier sketches in SATA 83, 149
  See also SAAS 22
Seidel, Ross 95
Seidelman, James Edward 1926- 6
Seiden, Art(hur) 107
  Brief entry 42
Seidensticker, John 1944- 200
Seidler, Ann (G.) 1925- 131
Seidler, Tor 1952- 149
  Brief entry 46
  Earlier sketches in SATA 52, 98
Seidman, Karla
  See Kuskin, Karla
Seidman, Laurence Ivan 1925- 15
Seigel, Kalman 1917-1998 12
  Obituary 103
Seignobosc, Francoise 1897-1961 21
Seinfeld, Jerry 1954- 146
Seitz, Jacqueline 1931- 50
Seixas, Judith S. 1922- 17
Sejima, Yoshimasa 1913- 8
Selberg, Ingrid (Maria) 1950- 68
Selden, George
  See Thompson, George Selden
Selden, Neil R(oy) 1931- 61
Self, Margaret Cabell 1902-1996 24
Selfors, Suzanne 1963- 193
Selick, Henry 1952- 183
Selig, Sylvie 1942- 13
Selkirk, Jane
  See Chapman, John Stanton Higham
Sellers, Naomi
  See Flack, Naomi John White
Sellier, Marie 1953- 212
Selman, LaRue W. 1927- 55
Selsam, Millicent E(llis) 1912-1996 29
  Obituary 92
  Earlier sketch in SATA 1
  See also CLR 1
Seltzer, Meyer 1932- 17
Seltzer, Richard 1946- 41
Seltzer, Richard Warren, Jr.
  See Seltzer, Richard
Selvadurai, Shyam 1965(?)- 171
Selway, Martina 1940- 169
  Earlier sketch in SATA 74
Selzer, Adam 1980- 192
Selznick, Brian 1966- 210
  Earlier sketches in SATA 79, 117, 171
Semel, Nava 1954- 107
Semloh
  See Holmes, Peggy
Sendak, Jack 1924(?)-1995 28
Sendak, Maurice 1928- 165
  Earlier sketches in SATA 1, 27, 113
  See also CLR 131
Sendak, Maurice Bernard
  See Sendak, Maurice
Sender, Ruth M(insky) 1926- 62
Sengler, Johanna 1924- 18
Senisi, Ellen B. 1951- 116
Senisi, Ellen Babinec
  See Senisi, Ellen B.
Senn, J(oyce) A(nn) 1941- 115
Senn, Steve 1950- 60
  Brief entry 48
Sensel, Joni 1962- 204
Serafini, Frank 201
Serage, Nancy 1924- 10
Seredy, Kate 1899-1975 1
  Obituary 24
  See also CLR 10
Serfozo, Mary 1925- 194
Seroff, Victor I(ilyitch) 1902-1979 12
  Obituary 26
Serra, Sebastia 1966- 202

Serraillier, Ian (Lucien) 1912-1994 .... *73*
Obituary *83*
Earlier sketch in SATA *1*
See also CLR *2*
See also SAAS *3*
Serros, Michele *175*
Serros, Michele M.
See Serros, Michele
Servello, Joe 1932- *10*
Service, Pamela F. 1945- *64*
Service, Robert
See Service, Robert W.
Service, Robert W. 1874(?)-1958 .... *20*
Serwadda, W(illiam) Moses 1931- *27*
Serwer-Bernstein, Blanche L(uria)
1910-1997 .... *10*
Sescoe, Vincent E. 1938- *123*
Seskin, Steve 1953- *211*
Seth, Mary
See Lexau, Joan M.
Seton, Anya 1904(?)-1990 .... *3*
Obituary *66*
Seton, Ernest (Evan) Thompson 1860-1946 . *18*
See also CLR *59*
Seton-Thompson, Ernest
See Seton, Ernest (Evan) Thompson
Seuling, Barbara 1937- *193*
Earlier sketches in SATA *10, 98, 145*
See also SAAS *24*
Seuss, Dr.
See Dr. Seuss
Severn, Bill
See Severn, William Irving
Severn, David
See Unwin, David S.
Severn, William Irving 1914- *1*
Sewall, Marcia 1935- *119*
Earlier sketches in SATA *37, 69*
Seward, Prudence 1926- *16*
Sewell, Anna 1820-1878 .... *100*
Earlier sketch in SATA *24*
See also CLR *17*
Sewell, Helen (Moore) 1896-1957 .... *38*
Sexton, Anne 1928-1974 .... *10*
Sexton, Anne Harvey
See Sexton, Anne
Seymour, Alta Halverson *10*
Seymour, Jane 1951- *139*
Seymour, Tres 1966- *164*
Earlier sketch in SATA *82*
Sfar, Joann 1971- *182*
Shachtman, Tom 1942- *49*
Shackleton, C.C.
See Aldiss, Brian W.
Shader, Rachel
See Sofer, Barbara
Shadow, Jak
See Sutherland, Jon
Shadyland, Sal
See Cooper, Louise
Shafer, Audrey *183*
Shafer, Robert E(ugene) 1925- *9*
Shaffer, Terea 1968- *79*
Shahan, Sherry 1949- *216*
Earlier sketches in SATA *92, 134*
Shahn, Ben(jamin) 1898-1969
Obituary *21*
Shahn, Bernarda Bryson
See Bryson, Bernarda
Shaik, Fatima *114*
Shalant, Phyllis 1949- *150*
Shan, Darren 1972- *199*
Earlier sketches in SATA *129, 168*
Shan, D.B.
See Shan, Darren
Shanahan, Lisa *199*
Shanberg, Karen
See Shragg, Karen (I.)
Shane, Harold Gray 1914-1993 .... *36*
Obituary *76*
Shange, Ntozake 1948- *157*

Shanks, Ann Zane (Kushner) *10*
Shannon, David 1959- *152*
Earlier sketch in SATA *107*
See also CLR *87*
Shannon, George 1952- *202*
Earlier sketches in SATA *35, 94, 143*
Shannon, George William Bones
See Shannon, George
Shannon, Jacqueline *63*
Shannon, Margaret
See Silverwood, Margaret Shannon
Shannon, Monica 1905(?)-1965 .... *28*
Shannon, Terry
See Mercer, Jessie
Shannon, Terry Miller 1951- *148*
Shapiro, Irwin 1911-1981 .... *32*
Shapiro, Jody Fickes 1940- *193*
Shapiro, Karen Jo 1964- *186*
Shapiro, Michelle 1961- *196*
Shapiro, Milton J. 1926- *32*
Shapiro, Tricia
See Andryszewski, Tricia
Shapiro, Zachary 1970- *213*
Shapp, Charles M(orris) 1906-1989
Obituary *61*
Shapp, Martha Glauber 1910- *3*
Sharenow, Robert *193*
Sharfman, Amalie *14*
Sharkey, Niamh *213*
Sharma, Partap 1939- *15*
Sharma, Rashmi
See Singh, Rashmi Sharma
Sharman, Alison
See Leonard, Alison
Sharmat, Marjorie Weinman 1928- *133*
Earlier sketches in SATA *4, 33, 74*
Sharmat, Mitchell 1927- *127*
Earlier sketch in SATA *33*
Sharp, Anne Wallace 1947- *144*
Sharp, Luke
See Alkiviades, Alkis
Sharp, Margery 1905-1991 .... *29*
Obituary *67*
Earlier sketch in SATA *1*
See also CLR *27*
Sharp, Zerna A. 1889-1981
Obituary *27*
Sharpe, Jon
See Duncan, Alice
and Knott, William C(ecil, Jr.)
and Messman, Jon
Sharpe, Mitchell R(aymond) 1924- *12*
Sharpe, Susan 1946- *71*
Sharratt, Nick 1962- *199*
Earlier sketches in SATA *104, 153*
Shasha, Mark 1961- *80*
Shattuck, Roger 1923-2005 .... *64*
Obituary *174*
Shattuck, Roger Whitney
See Shattuck, Roger
Shaw, Arnold 1909-1989 .... *4*
Obituary *63*
Shaw, Carolyn V. 1934- *91*
Shaw, Charles (Green) 1892-1974 .... *13*
Shaw, Evelyn S. 1927- *28*
Shaw, Flora Louisa
See Lugard, Flora Louisa Shaw
Shaw, Janet 1937- *146*
Earlier sketch in SATA *61*
See also CLR *96*
Shaw, Janet Beeler
See Shaw, Janet
Shaw, Lisa
See Rogak, Lisa
Shaw, Margret 1940- *68*
Shaw, Mary 1965- *180*
Shaw, Nancy 1946- *162*
Earlier sketch in SATA *71*
Shaw, Ray *7*
Shaw, Richard 1923- *12*

Shawn, Frank S.
See Goulart, Ron
Shay, Art
See Shay, Arthur
Shay, Arthur 1922- *4*
Shay, Lacey
See Shebar, Sharon Sigmond
Shea, Bob *188*
Shea, George 1940- *54*
Brief entry *42*
Shea, Pegi Deitz 1960- *172*
Earlier sketches in SATA *77, 137*
Shearer, Alex 1949- *204*
Shearer, John 1947- *43*
Brief entry *27*
See also CLR *34*
Shearer, Ted 1919- *43*
Shearing, Leonie 1972- *184*
Sheban, Chris *182*
Shebar, Sharon Sigmond 1945- *36*
Shecter, Ben 1935- *16*
Shedd, Warner 1934- *147*
Earlier sketch in SATA *87*
Sheedy, Alexandra Elizabeth 1962- *39*
Earlier sketch in SATA *19*
Sheehan, Ethna 1908-2000 .... *9*
Sheehan, Patty 1945- *77*
Sheehan, Sean 1951- *154*
Earlier sketch in SATA *86*
Sheen, Barbara 1949- *143*
Shefelman, Janice 1930- *205*
Earlier sketches in SATA *58, 129*
Shefelman, Janice Jordan
See Shefelman, Janice
Shefelman, Tom 1927- *204*
Earlier sketch in SATA *58*
Sheffer, H. R.
See Abels, Harriette S(heffer)
Sheffield, Charles 1935-2002 .... *109*
Sheffield, Janet N. 1926- *26*
Sheikh, Nazneen 1944- *101*
Sheinkin, Steve 1968- *204*
Sheinmel, Courtney 1977- *211*
Shekerjian, Regina Tor *16*
Shelby, Anne 1948- *85*
Autobiography Feature *121*
See also SAAS *26*
Sheldon, Ann
See Antle, Nancy
Sheldon, Ann *67*
Earlier sketch in SATA *1*
Sheldon, Aure 1917-1976 .... *12*
Sheldon, David *185*
Sheldon, Deyan *181*
Sheldon, John
See Bloch, Robert (Albert)
Sheldon, Muriel 1926- *45*
Brief entry *39*
Shell, Barry 1951- *176*
Shelley, Frances
See Wees, Frances Shelley
Shelley, John 1959- *202*
Shelley, Mary
See Shelley, Mary Wollstonecraft
Shelley, Mary Wollstonecraft 1797-1851 ..... *29*
See also CLR *133*
Shelton, William Roy 1919-1995 .... *5*
Obituary *129*
Shemie, Bonnie (Jean Brenner) 1949- *96*
Shemin, Margaretha (Hoeneveld) 1928- *4*
Shen, Michele 1953- *173*
Shenker, Michele
See Shen, Michele
Shenton, Edward 1895-1977 .... *45*
Shepard, Aaron 1950- *187*
Earlier sketches in SATA *75, 113*
Shepard, Ernest Howard 1879-1976 .... *100*
Obituary *24*
Earlier sketches in SATA *3, 33*
See also CLR *27*

Shepard, James R.
  See Shepard, Jim
Shepard, Jim 1956- 164
  Earlier sketch in SATA 90
Shepard, Mary
  See Knox, (Mary) Eleanor Jessie
Shephard, Esther 1891-1975 5
  Obituary 26
Shepherd, Amanda 201
Shepherd, Donna Walsh
  See Walsh Shepherd, Donna
Shepherd, Elizabeth 4
Shepherd, Irana 173
Shepherd, Roni
  See Shepherd, Irana
Sheppard, Kate 195
Shepperson, Rob 178
Sherburne, Zoa (Lillian Morin) 1912-1995 3
  See also SAAS 18
Sherk-Savage, Candace
  See Savage, Candace
Sherlock, Patti 71
Sherman, D(enis) R(onald) 1934- 48
  Brief entry 29
Sherman, Diane (Finn) 1928- 12
Sherman, Elizabeth
  See Friskey, Margaret (Richards)
Sherman, Harold (Morrow) 1898-1987 37
  Obituary 137
Sherman, Josepha 163
  Earlier sketch in SATA 75
Sherman, Michael
  See Lowndes, Robert A(ugustine) W(ard)
Sherman, Nancy
  See Rosenberg, Nancy (Sherman)
Sherman, Pat 174
Sherman, Peter Michael
  See Lowndes, Robert A(ugustine) W(ard)
Sherrard, Valerie (Anne) 1957- 141
Sherrod, Jane
  See Singer, Jane Sherrod
Sherry, Clifford J. 1943- 84
Sherry, (Dulcie) Sylvia 1932- 122
  Earlier sketch in SATA 8
Sherwan, Earl 1917- 3
Sherwood, Jonathan
  See London, Jonathan (Paul)
Sheth, Kashmira 186
Shetterly, Will 1955- 78
  Autobiography Feature 106
Shetterly, William Howard
  See Shetterly, Will
Shiefman, Vicky 1942- 22
Shields, Brenda Desmond (Armstrong)
  1914- 37
Shields, Carol Diggory 174
Shields, Charles 1944- 10
Shields, Gillian 203
Shiels, Barbara
  See Adams, Barbara Johnston
Shiffman, Lena 1957- 101
Shiina, Makoto 1944- 83
Shimin, Symeon 1902-1984 13
Shimko, Bonnie 1941- 191
Shine, Andrea 1955- 104
Shine, Deborah 1932- 71
Shinn, Everett 1876-1953 21
Shinn, Sharon 1957- 164
  Earlier sketch in SATA 110
Shippen, Katherine B(inney) 1892-1980 1
  Obituary 23
  See also CLR 36
Shippey, T. A. 1943- 143
Shippey, Thomas Alan
  See Shippey, T. A.
Shipton, Eric Earle 1907-1977 10
Shipton, Jonathan 1948- 215
Shipton, Paul 1963- 196
Shiraz, Yasmin 173
Shirer, William L(awrence) 1904-1993 45
  Obituary 78

Shirley, Debra 203
Shirley, Gayle C 1955- 96
Shirley, Gayle Corbett
  See Shirley, Gayle C
Shirley, Jean 1919- 70
Shirreffs, Gordon D(onald) 1914-1996 11
Shirts, Morris A(lpine) 1922- 63
Shlichta, Joe 1968- 84
Shmurak, Carole B. 1944- 118
Sholokhov, Mikhail 1905-1984
  Obituary 36
Sholokhov, Mikhail Aleksandrovich
  See Sholokhov, Mikhail
Shore, Diane Z. 215
  Earlier sketch in SATA 179
Shore, Diane ZuHone
  See Shore, Diane Z.
Shore, June Lewis 30
Shore, Nancy 1960- 124
Shore, Robert 1924- 39
Short, Michael 1937- 65
Short, Roger
  See Arkin, Alan
Shortall, Leonard W. 19
Shortt, Tim(othy Donald) 1961- 96
Shotwell, Louisa Rossiter 1902-1993 3
Shoulders, Michael 1954- 216
Shoup, Barbara 1947- 156
  Earlier sketch in SATA 86
  See also SAAS 24
Shoveller, Herb 184
Showalter, Jean B(reckinridge) 12
Showell, Ellen Harvey 1934- 33
Showers, Paul C. 1910-1999 92
  Obituary 114
  Earlier sketch in SATA 21
  See also CLR 6
  See also SAAS 7
Shpakow, Tanya 1959(?)- 94
Shpitalnik, Vladimir 1964- 83
Shragg, Karen (I.) 1954- 142
Shreeve, Elizabeth 1956- 156
Shreve, Susan
  See Shreve, Susan Richards
Shreve, Susan Richards 1939- 152
  Brief entry 41
  Earlier sketches in SATA 46, 95
Shriver, Jean Adair 1932- 75
Shriver, Maria 1955- 134
Shriver, Maria Owings
  See Shriver, Maria
Shrode, Mary
  See Hollingsworth, Mary
Shtainmets, Leon 32
Shub, Elizabeth 1915(?)-2004 5
Shuken, Julia 1948- 84
Shulevitz, Uri 1935- 165
  Earlier sketches in SATA 3, 50, 106
  See also CLR 61
Shulman, Alix Kates 1932- 7
Shulman, Dee 1957- 146
Shulman, Irving 1913-1995 13
Shulman, Lisa 202
Shulman, Mark 1962- 184
Shulman, Max 1919-1988
  Obituary 59
Shulman, Milton 1913-2004
  Obituary 154
Shulman, Neil B(arnett) 1945- 89
Shumsky, Zena
  See Collier, Zena
Shura, Mary Francis
  See Craig, Mary (Francis) Shura
Shusterman, Neal 1962- 201
  Autobiography Feature 140
  Earlier sketches in SATA 85, 121, 140
Shuter, Jane (Margaret) 1955- 151
  Earlier sketch in SATA 90
Shuttlesworth, Dorothy Edwards 3
Shwartz, Susan (Martha) 1949- 94
Shyer, Christopher 1961- 98

Shyer, Marlene Fanta 13
Siberell, Anne 29
Sibley, Don 1922- 12
Siburt, Ruth 1951- 121
Siculan, Daniel 1922- 12
Siddon, Barbara
  See Bradford, Barbara Taylor
Sidgwick, Ethel 1877-1970 116
Sidjakov, Nicolas 1924- 18
Sidman, Joyce 1956- 181
  Earlier sketch in SATA 145
Sidney, Frank
  See Warwick, Alan R(oss)
Sidney, Margaret
  See Lothrop, Harriet Mulford Stone
Siebert, Diane 1948- 189
Siegal, Aranka 1930- 88
  Brief entry 37
Siegel, Beatrice 36
Siegel, Helen
  See Siegl, Helen
Siegel, Robert 1939- 39
Siegel, Robert Harold
  See Siegel, Robert
Siegel, Siena Cherson 1967(?)- 185
Siegelson, Kim L. 1962- 114
Sieger, Ted 1958- 189
Siegl, Helen 1924- 34
Siepmann, Mary Aline
  See Wesley, Mary (Aline)
Sierra, Judy 1945- 195
  Earlier sketches in SATA 104, 162
Sieswerda, Paul L. 1942- 147
Sievert, Terri
  See Dougherty, Terri (L.)
Sigsawa, Keiichi 1972- 211
Silas
  See McCay, (Zenas) Winsor
Silcock, Sara Lesley 1947- 12
Silin-Palmer, Pamela 184
Sill, Cathryn 1953- 141
  Earlier sketch in SATA 74
Sill, John 1947- 140
  Earlier sketch in SATA 74
Sillitoe, Alan 1928-2010 61
Sills, Leslie (Elka) 1948- 129
Silly, E. S.
  See Kraus, (Herman) Robert
Silsbe, Brenda 1953- 73
Silva, Joseph
  See Goulart, Ron
Silver, Jago
  See Jago
Silver, Maggie 216
Silver, Ruth
  See Chew, Ruth
Silverberg, Robert 1935- 91
  Autobiography Feature 104
  Earlier sketch in SATA 13
  See also CLR 59
Silverman, Erica 1955- 165
  Earlier sketches in SATA 78, 112
Silverman, Janis L. 1946- 127
Silverman, Mel(vin Frank) 1931-1966 9
Silverman, Robin L. 1954- 96
Silverman, Robin Landew
  See Silverman, Robin L.
Silverstein, Alvin 1933- 124
  Earlier sketches in SATA 8, 69
  See also CLR 25
Silverstein, Herma 1945- 106
Silverstein, Robert Alan 1959- 124
  Earlier sketch in SATA 77
Silverstein, Shel 1932-1999 92
  Brief entry 27
  Obituary 116
  Earlier sketch in SATA 33
  See also CLR 96
Silverstein, Sheldon Allan
  See Silverstein, Shel

Silverstein, Virginia B. 1937- *124*
    Earlier sketches in SATA *8, 69*
    See also CLR *25*
Silverstein, Virginia Barbara Opshelor
    See Silverstein, Virginia B.
Silverthorne, Elizabeth 1930- *35*
Silverwood, Margaret Shannon 1966- *137*
    Earlier sketch in SATA *83*
Silvey, Diane F. 1946- *135*
Sim, David 1953- *162*
Sim, Dorrith M. 1931- *96*
Simak, Clifford D(onald) 1904-1988
    Obituary *56*
Simard, Remy 1959- *168*
Simmie, Lois (Ann) 1932- *106*
Simmonds, Posy 1945- *130*
    See also CLR *23*
Simmonds, Rosemary Elizabeth
    See Simmonds, Posy
Simmons, Andra 1939- *141*
Simmons, Elly 1955- *134*
Simmons, Michael 1970- *185*
Simms, Laura 1947- *117*
Simner, Janni Lee *113*
Simon, Charlie May
    See Fletcher, Charlie May Hogue
Simon, Francesca 1955- *111*
Simon, Gabriel 1972- *118*
Simon, Hilda Rita 1921- *28*
    See also CLR *39*
Simon, Howard 1903-1979 .... *32*
    Obituary *21*
Simon, Joe
    See Simon, Joseph H.
Simon, Joseph H. 1913- *7*
Simon, Martin P(aul William) 1903-1969 .... *12*
Simon, Mina Lewiton
    See Lewiton, Mina
Simon, Norma (Feldstein) 1927- *129*
    Earlier sketches in SATA *3, 68*
Simon, Seymour 1931- *202*
    Earlier sketches in SATA *4, 73, 138*
    See also CLR *63*
Simon, Shirley (Schwartz) 1921- *11*
Simon, Solomon 1895-1970 .... *40*
Simonetta, Linda 1948- *14*
Simonetta, Sam 1936- *14*
Simons, Barbara B(rooks) 1934- *41*
Simont, Marc 1915- *126*
    Earlier sketches in SATA *9, 73*
Simpson, Colin 1908-1983 .... *14*
Simpson, Harriette
    See Arnow, Harriette (Louisa) Simpson
Simpson, Jacynth Hope
    See Hope Simpson, Jacynth
Simpson, Lesley 1963- *150*
Simpson, Margaret 1943- *128*
Simpson, Myrtle L(illias) 1931- *14*
Sims, Blanche *168*
    Earlier sketch in SATA *75*
Sims, Blanche L.
    See Sims, Blanche
Simundsson, Elva 1950- *63*
Sinclair, Clover
    See Gater, Dilys
Sinclair, Emil
    See Hesse, Hermann
Sinclair, Jeff 1958- *77*
Sinclair, Olga 1923- *121*
Sinclair, Rose
    See Smith, Susan Vernon
Sinclair, Upton 1878-1968 .... *9*
Sinclair, Upton Beall
    See Sinclair, Upton
Singer, A.L.
    See Lerangis, Peter
Singer, Arthur 1917-1990 .... *64*
Singer, Isaac
    See Singer, Isaac Bashevis

Singer, Isaac Bashevis 1904-1991 .... *27*
    Obituary *68*
    Earlier sketch in SATA *3*
    See also CLR *1*
Singer, Jane Sherrod 1917-1985 .... *4*
    Obituary *42*
Singer, Julia 1917- *28*
Singer, Kurt D. 1911-2005 .... *38*
    Obituary *172*
Singer, Marilyn 1948- *201*
    Autobiography Feature *158*
    Brief entry *38*
    Earlier sketches in SATA *48, 80, 125, 158*
    See also CLR *48*
    See also SAAS *13*
Singer, Muff 1942-2005 .... *104*
    Obituary *160*
Singer, Nicky 1956- *194*
Singer, Susan (Mahler) 1941- *9*
Singh, Rashmi Sharma 1952- *90*
Singleton, Linda Joy 1957- *166*
    Earlier sketch in SATA *88*
Singleton, L.J.
    See Singleton, Linda Joy
Singleton, Sarah 1966- *214*
Sinykin, Sheri
    See Sinykin, Sheri Cooper
Sinykin, Sheri Cooper 1950- *142*
    Autobiography Feature *142*
    Earlier sketches in SATA *72, 133*
Sinykin, Sheril Terri Cooper
    See Sinykin, Sheri Cooper
Siomades, Lorianne *217*
Sipiera, Paul P., (Jr.) 1948- *144*
    Earlier sketch in SATA *89*
Siracusa, Catherine (Jane) 1947- *82*
Sirett, Dawn (Karen) 1966- *88*
Sirimarco, Elizabeth 1966- *158*
Sirof, Harriet 1930- *94*
    Earlier sketch in SATA *37*
Sirois, Allen L. 1950- *76*
Sirvaitis (Chernyaev), Karen (Ann) 1961- ... *79*
Sis, Peter 1949- *192*
    Earlier sketch in SATA *149*
    See also CLR *110*
Sisson, Rosemary Anne 1923- *11*
Sister Mary Terese
    See Donze, Mary Terese
Sita, Lisa 1962- *87*
Sitarski, Anita *200*
Sitomer, Alan Lawrence *174*
Sitomer, Harry 1903-1985 .... *31*
Sitomer, Mindel 1903-1987 .... *31*
Sittenfeld, Curtis 1975(?)- *164*
Sive, Helen R(obinson) 1951- *30*
Sivulich, Sandra (Jeanne) Stroner 1941- *9*
Siy, Alexandra *193*
Skarmeta, Antonio 1940- *57*
Skeers, Linda 1958- *207*
Skelly, James R(ichard) 1927- *17*
Skelton, Matthew 1971- *185*
Skinner, Constance Lindsay 1877-1939
    See YABC *1*
Skinner, Cornelia Otis 1901-1979 .... *2*
Skipper, G. C. 1939- *46*
    Brief entry *38*
Sklansky, Amy E(dgar) 1971- *145*
Sklansky, Amy E. 1971- *204*
Skofield, James *95*
    Brief entry *44*
Skold, Betty Westrom 1923- *41*
Skorpen, Liesel Moak 1935- *3*
Skott, Maria
    See Nikolajeva, Maria
Skrypuch, Marsha Forchuk 1954- *134*
Skultety, Nancy Laney 1960- *175*
Skurzynski, Gloria 1930- *145*
    Autobiography Feature *145*
    Earlier sketches in SATA *8, 74, 122*
    See also SAAS *9*

Skurzynski, Gloria Joan
    See Skurzynski, Gloria
Skutch, Robert 1925- *89*
Skye, Maggie
    See Werner, Herma
Skye, Obert *200*
    Earlier sketch in SATA *170*
Slack, Michael 1969- *189*
Slackman, Charles B. 1934- *12*
Slade, Arthur G. 1967- *149*
    Earlier sketch in SATA *106*
Slade, Arthur Gregory
    See Slade, Arthur G.
Slade, Christian 1974- *193*
Slade, Richard 1910-1971 .... *9*
Slangerup, Erik Jon 1969- *130*
Slate, Joseph 1928- *174*
    Earlier sketches in SATA *38, 122*
Slate, Joseph Frank
    See Slate, Joseph
Slater, Dashka 1963- *179*
Slater, David Michael 1970- *212*
Slater, Ray
    See Lansdale, Joe R.
Slaughter, Hope 1940- *84*
Slaughter, Jean
    See Doty, Jean Slaughter
Slaughter, Tom 1955- *152*
Slavicek, Louise Chipley 1956- *144*
Slavin, Bill 1959- *199*
    Earlier sketches in SATA *76, 148*
Slaymaker, Melissa Eskridge 1958- *158*
Sleator, William 1945- *208*
    Earlier sketches in SATA *3, 68, 118, 161*
    See also CLR *128*
Sleator, William Warner III
    See Sleator, William
Slegers, Liesbet 1975- *154*
Sleigh, Barbara 1906-1982 .... *86*
    Obituary *30*
    Earlier sketch in SATA *3*
Slepian, Jan 1921- *85*
    Brief entry *45*
    Earlier sketch in SATA *51*
    See also SAAS *8*
Slepian, Janice B.
    See Slepian, Jan
Slicer, Margaret O. 1920- *4*
Slier, Debby
    See Shine, Deborah
Sloan, Brian 1966- *172*
Sloan, Carolyn 1937- *116*
    Earlier sketch in SATA *58*
Sloan, Glenna 1930- *120*
Sloan, Glenna Davis
    See Sloan, Glenna
Sloane, Eric 1910(?)-1985 .... *52*
    Obituary *42*
Sloane, Todd 1955- *88*
Sloat, Teri 1948- *164*
    Earlier sketches in SATA *70, 106*
Slobodkin, Florence Gersh 1905-1994 .... *5*
    Obituary *107*
Slobodkin, Louis 1903-1975 .... *26*
    Earlier sketch in SATA *1*
Slobodkina, Esphyr 1908-2002 .... *1*
    Obituary *135*
    See also SAAS *8*
Sloggett, Nellie 1851-1923 .... *44*
Slonim, David 1966- *207*
Sloss, Lesley Lord 1965- *72*
Slote, Alfred 1926- *72*
    Earlier sketch in SATA *8*
    See also CLR *4*
    See also SAAS *21*
Slote, Elizabeth 1956- *80*
Small, Charlie
    See Ward, Nick

Author Index

Small, David 1945- *216*
   Brief entry *46*
   Earlier sketches in SATA *50, 95, 126, 183*
   See also CLR *53*
Small, Ernest
   See Lent, Blair
Small, Mary 1932- *165*
Small, Terry 1942- *75*
Smallcomb, Pam 1954- *159*
Smallman, Steve *197*
Smalls, Irene
   See Smalls-Hector, Irene
Smalls-Hector, Irene 1950- *146*
   Earlier sketch in SATA *73*
   See also CLR *103*
Smallwood, Norah (Evelyn) 1910(?)-1984
   Obituary *41*
Smaridge, Norah (Antoinette) 1903-1994 ...... *6*
Smath, Jerry 1933- *198*
Smee, Nicola 1948- *167*
   Earlier sketch in SATA *76*
Smiley, Virginia Kester 1923- *2*
Smit, Noelle 1972- *199*
Smith, Alexander McCall 1948- *179*
   Earlier sketch in SATA *73*
Smith, Andrew 1959- *209*
Smith, Andrew Anselmo
   See Smith, Andrew
Smith, Andy J. 1975- *207*
Smith, Anne Warren 1938- *41*
   Brief entry *34*
Smith, Barry (Edward Jervis) 1943- *75*
Smith, Beatrice S(chillinger) *12*
Smith, Betsy Covington 1937- *55*
   Earlier sketch in SATA *43*
Smith, Betty (Wehner) 1904-1972 .... *6*
Smith, Bradford 1909-1964 .... *5*
Smith, Brenda 1946- *82*
Smith, C. Pritchard
   See Hoyt, Edwin P(almer), Jr.
Smith, Caesar
   See Trevor, Elleston
Smith, Cat Bowman 1939- *201*
Smith, Charles R., Jr. 1969- *203*
   Earlier sketch in SATA *159*
Smith, Craig 1955- *172*
   Earlier sketches in SATA *81, 117*
Smith, Cynthia Leitich 1967- *215*
   Earlier sketch in SATA *152*
Smith, Danna *216*
Smith, Danna Kessimakis
   See Smith, Danna
Smith, Datus C(lifford), Jr. 1907-1999 .... *13*
   Obituary *116*
Smith, Debra 1955- *89*
Smith, Derek 1943- *141*
Smith, Dick King
   See King-Smith, Dick
Smith, Dodie
   See Smith, Dorothy Gladys
Smith, Doris Buchanan 1934-2002 .... *75*
   Obituary *140*
   Earlier sketch in SATA *28*
   See also SAAS *10*
Smith, Dorothy Gladys 1896-1990 .... *82*
   Obituary *65*
Smith, Dorothy Stafford 1905- *6*
Smith, Duane 1974- *202*
Smith, E(lmer) Boyd 1860-1943
   See YABC *1*
Smith, E(dric) Brooks 1917- *40*
Smith, Elwood H. 1941- *203*
Smith, Emily Wing 1980- *215*
Smith, Emma 1923- *52*
   Brief entry *36*
Smith, (Katherine) Eunice (Young)
   1902-1993 .... *5*
Smith, Frances C(hristine) 1904-1986 .... *3*
Smith, Gary R. 1932- *14*
Smith, Geof 1969- *102*
Smith, George Harmon 1920- *5*

Smith, Gordon 1951- *184*
Smith, Greg Leitich *152*
Smith, H(arry) Allen 1907-1976
   Obituary *20*
Smith, Helene 1937- *142*
Smith, Hope Anita *202*
Smith, Howard E(verett), Jr. 1927- *12*
Smith, Hugh L(etcher) 1921-1968 .... *5*
Smith, Imogene Henderson 1922- *12*
Smith, Jacqueline B. 1937- *39*
Smith, Jada Pinkett 1971- *161*
Smith, James D. 1955- *176*
Smith, James Noel 1950- *193*
Smith, Janet (Buchanan) Adam
   See Adam Smith, Janet (Buchanan)
Smith, Janice Lee 1949- *155*
   Earlier sketch in SATA *54*
Smith, Jean
   See Smith, Frances C(hristine)
Smith, Jean Pajot 1945- *10*
Smith, Jeff 1958- *161*
   Earlier sketch in SATA *93*
Smith, Jeff Allen
   See Smith, Jeff
Smith, Jenny 1963- *90*
Smith, Jessie
   See Kunhardt, Edith
Smith, Jessie Willcox 1863-1935 .... *21*
   See also CLR *59*
Smith, Joan (Mary) 1933- *54*
   Brief entry *46*
Smith, Johnston
   See Crane, Stephen
Smith, Jos A. 1936- *181*
   Earlier sketches in SATA *73, 120*
Smith, Joseph Arthur
   See Smith, Jos A.
Smith, Judie R. 1936- *80*
Smith, Kirsten 1970- *210*
Smith, Lafayette
   See Higdon, Hal
Smith, Lane 1959- *179*
   Earlier sketches in SATA *76, 131*
   See also CLR *47*
Smith, Lee
   See Albion, Lee Smith
Smith, Lendon H(oward) 1921- *64*
Smith, Lillian H(elena) 1887-1983
   Obituary *32*
Smith, Linda 1949- *177*
Smith, Linell Nash 1932- *2*
Smith, Lucia B. 1943- *30*
Smith, Maggie 1965- *190*
Smith, Margaret Emily Noel Nuttall
   See Nuttall-Smith, Margaret Emily Noel
Smith, Marion Hagens 1913- *12*
Smith, Marion Jaques 1899-1987 .... *13*
Smith, Mary Ellen *10*
Smith, Marya 1945- *78*
Smith, Mike
   See Smith, Mary Ellen
Smith, Nancy Covert 1935- *12*
Smith, Norman F. 1920- *70*
   Earlier sketch in SATA *5*
Smith, Patricia Clark 1943- *96*
Smith, Pauline C.
   See Arthur, Robert, (Jr.)
Smith, Pauline C(oggeshall) 1908-1994 .... *27*
Smith, Philip Warren 1936- *46*
Smith, R. Alexander McCall
   See Smith, Alexander McCall
Smith, Rebecca 1946- *123*
Smith, Robert Kimmel 1930- *77*
   Earlier sketch in SATA *12*
Smith, Robert Paul 1915-1977 .... *52*
   Obituary *30*
Smith, Roland 1951- *193*
   Earlier sketches in SATA *115, 161*
Smith, Rosamond
   See Oates, Joyce Carol
Smith, Ruth Leslie 1902- *2*

Smith, Samantha 1972-1985
   Obituary *45*
Smith, Sandra Lee 1945- *75*
Smith, Sarah Stafford
   See Smith, Dorothy Stafford
Smith, Sharon 1947- *82*
Smith, Sherri L. 1971- *156*
Smith, Sherwood 1951- *206*
   Autobiography Feature *206*
   Earlier sketches in SATA *82, 140*
Smith, Shirley Raines
   See Raines, Shirley C(arol)
Smith, Susan Carlton 1923- *12*
Smith, Susan Mathias 1950- *43*
   Brief entry *35*
Smith, Susan Vernon 1950- *48*
   Brief entry *45*
Smith, Tim(othy R.) 1945- *151*
Smith, Ursula 1934- *54*
Smith, Vian (Crocker) 1920-1969 .... *11*
Smith, Wanda VanHoy 1926- *65*
Smith, Ward
   See Goldsmith, Howard
Smith, William A. 1918- *10*
Smith, William Jay 1918- *154*
   Autobiography Feature *154*
   Earlier sketches in SATA *2, 68*
   See also SAAS *22*
Smith, Winsome 1935- *45*
Smith, Z.Z.
   See Westheimer, David
Smith-Ankrom, M. E. 1942- *130*
Smith-Griswold, Wendy 1955- *88*
Smith-Rex, Susan J. 1950- *94*
Smithsen, Richard
   See Pellowski, Michael (Joseph)
Smithson, Ryan 1985- *216*
Smits, Teo
   See Smits, Theodore R(ichard)
Smits, Theodore R(ichard) 1905-1996 .... *45*
   Brief entry *28*
Smolinski, Dick 1932- *86*
Smothers, Ethel Footman 1944- *149*
   Earlier sketch in SATA *76*
Smucker, Anna Egan 1948- *209*
Smucker, Barbara 1915-2003 .... *130*
   Earlier sketches in SATA *29, 76*
   See also CLR *10*
   See also SAAS *11*
Smucker, Barbara Claassen
   See Smucker, Barbara
Smyth, Iain 1959- *105*
Snedeker, Caroline Dale (Parke) 1871-1956
   See YABC *2*
Sneed, Brad *191*
Sneider, Marian 1932-2005 .... *197*
Snell, Nigel (Edward Creagh) 1936- *57*
   Brief entry *40*
Snellgrove, L(aurence) E(rnest) 1928- *53*
Snelling, Dennis (Wayne) 1958- *84*
Sneve, Virginia Driving Hawk 1933- *95*
   Earlier sketch in SATA *8*
   See also CLR *2*
Snicket, Lemony 1970- *215*
   Earlier sketches in SATA *126, 187*
   See also CLR *79*
Sniegoski, Thomas E. *195*
Sniegoski, Tom
   See Sniegoski, Thomas E.
Snodgrass, Mary Ellen 1944- *75*
Snodgrass, Quentin Curtius
   See Twain, Mark
Snodgrass, Thomas Jefferson
   See Twain, Mark
Snook, Barbara (Lillian) 1913-1976 .... *34*
Snow, Alan 1959- *190*
Snow, Carol 1965- *208*
Snow, Donald Clifford 1917-1979 .... *16*
Snow, Dorothea J(ohnston) 1909- *9*
Snow, Richard F(olger) 1947- *52*
   Brief entry *37*

Snyder, Anne 1922-2001 4
  Obituary 125
Snyder, Bernadette McCarver 1930- 97
Snyder, Carol 1941- 35
Snyder, Gerald S(eymour) 1933- 48
  Brief entry 34
Snyder, Jerome 1916-1976
  Obituary 20
Snyder, Laurel 1974- 209
Snyder, Midori 1954- 106
Snyder, Paul A. 1946- 125
Snyder, Zilpha Keatley 1927- 163
  Autobiography Feature 163
  Earlier sketches in SATA 1, 28, 75, 110
  See also CLR 121
  See also SAAS 2
Snyderman, Reuven K. 1922- 5
So, Meilo 162
Sobel, June 1950- 149
Soble, Jennie
  See Cavin, Ruth (Brodie)
Sobol, Donald J. 1924- 132
  Earlier sketches in SATA 1, 31, 73
  See also CLR 4
Sobol, Harriet Langsam 1936- 47
  Brief entry 34
Sobol, Richard 211
Sobol, Rose 1931- 76
Sobott-Mogwe, Gaele 1956- 97
Soderlind, Arthur E(dwin) 1920- 14
Soentpiet, Chris K. 1970- 159
  Earlier sketch in SATA 97
Soerensen, Svend Otto 1916- 67
Sofer, Barbara 1949- 109
Sofer, Rachel
  See Sofer, Barbara
Softly, Barbara Frewin 1924- 12
Sogabe, Aki 207
Soglow, Otto 1900-1975
  Obituary 30
Sohl, Frederic J(ohn) 1916- 10
Sohr, Daniel 1973- 190
Sokol, Bill
  See Sokol, William
Sokol, William 1923- 37
Sokolov, Kirill 1930- 34
Solbert, Romaine G. 1925- 2
Solbert, Ronni
  See Solbert, Romaine G.
Solheim, James 133
Solomon, Heather M. 188
Solomon, Joan 1930- 51
  Brief entry 40
Solomons, Ikey Esquir
  See Thackeray, William Makepeace
Solonevich, George 1915-2003 15
Solot, Mary Lynn 1939- 12
Soman, David 1965- 200
Somerlott, Robert 1928-2001 62
Somers, Kevin 205
Somervill, Barbara A(nn) 1948- 140
Sommer, Angela
  See Sommer-Bodenburg, Angela
Sommer, Carl 1930- 175
  Earlier sketch in SATA 126
Sommer, Elyse 1929- 7
Sommer, Robert 1929- 12
Sommer-Bodenburg, Angela 1948- 113
  Earlier sketch in SATA 63
Sommerdorf, Norma 1926- 131
Sommerdorf, Norma Jean
  See Sommerdorf, Norma
Sommerfelt, Aimee 1892-1975 5
Son, John 160
Sones, Sonya 131
Sonneborn, Ruth (Cantor) 1899-1974 4
  Obituary 27
Sonnenblick, Jordan 1969- 185
  See also CLR 144
Sonnenmark, Laura A. 1958- 73
Soo, Kean 201

Sopko, Eugen 1949- 58
Sorel, Edward 1929- 126
  Brief entry 37
  Earlier sketch in SATA 65
Sorensen, Henri 1950- 115
  Earlier sketch in SATA 77
Sorensen, Svend Otto
  See Soerensen, Svend Otto
Sorensen, Virginia 1912-1991 2
  Obituary 72
  See also SAAS 15
Sorenson, Jane 1926- 63
Sorenson, Margo 1946- 96
Sorley Walker, Kathrine 41
Sorra, Kristin 185
Sorrells, Walter 177
Sorrentino, Joseph N. 1937- 6
Sortor, June Elizabeth 1939- 12
Sortor, Toni
  See Sortor, June Elizabeth
Sosa, Hernan 1977- 203
Soskin, V. H.
  See Ellison, Virginia H(owell)
Soto, Gary 1952- 174
  Earlier sketches in SATA 80, 120
  See also CLR 38
Sotomayor, Antonio 1902-1985 11
Souci, Robert D. San
  See San Souci, Robert D.
Soudley, Henry
  See Wood, James Playsted
Souhami, Jessica 176
Soule, Gardner (Bosworth) 1913-2000 14
Soule, Jean Conder 1919- 10
Souster, (Holmes) Raymond 1921- 63
South, Sheri Cobb 1959- 82
Southall, Ivan 1921-2008 134
  Autobiography Feature 134
  Earlier sketches in SATA 3, 68
  See also CLR 2
  See also SAAS 3
Southall, Ivan Francis
  See Southall, Ivan
Southey, Robert 1774-1843 54
Southgate, Vera 54
Souza, Janet
  See Tashjian, Janet
Sovak, Jan 1953- 115
Sowden, Celeste
  See Walters, Celeste
Sowter, Nita 69
Spafford, Suzy 1945- 160
Spagnoli, Cathy 1950- 134
  Earlier sketch in SATA 79
Spain, Sahara Sunday 1991- 133
Spain, Susan Rosson 185
Spalding, Andrea 1944- 150
  Earlier sketch in SATA 101
Spalenka, Greg 1958- 198
Spanfeller, James J. 1930- 19
  See also SAAS 8
Spanfeller, Jim
  See Spanfeller, James J.
Spangenberg, Judith Dunn 1942- 5
Spangler, Brie 212
Spanyol, Jessica 1965- 206
  Earlier sketch in SATA 137
Spar, Jerome 1918- 10
Sparks, Barbara 1942- 78
Sparks, Beatrice (Mathews) 1918- 44
  Brief entry 28
  See also CLR 139
Sparks, Mary W. 1920- 15
Spaulding, Douglas
  See Bradbury, Ray
Spaulding, Leonard
  See Bradbury, Ray
Spaulding, Norma 107

Speare, Elizabeth George 1908-1994 62
  Obituary 83
  Earlier sketch in SATA 5
  See also CLR 8
Spearing, Judith (Mary Harlow) 1922- 9
Spears, Rick 182
Speck, Katie 196
Speck, Nancy 1959- 104
Specking, Inez 1890-1960(?) 11
Speed, Nell
  See Keats, Emma
  and Sampson, Emma (Keats) Speed
Speed, Nell (Ewing) 1878-1913 68
Speer, Bonnie Stahlman 1929- 113
Speer-Lyon, Tammie L. 1965- 89
Speicher, Helen Ross S(mith) 1915- 8
Speir, Nancy 1958- 210
  Earlier sketch in SATA 81
Spellman, John W(illard) 1934- 14
Spellman, Roger G.
  See Cox, William R(obert)
Spelman, Cornelia Maude 1946- 144
  Earlier sketch in SATA 96
Spelman, Mary 1934- 28
Spelvin, George
  See Lerangis, Peter
  and Phillips, David Atlee
Spence, Cynthia
  See Eble, Diane
Spence, Eleanor (Rachel) 1928- 21
  See also CLR 26
Spence, Geraldine 1931- 47
Spencer, Ann 1918- 10
Spencer, Britt 206
Spencer, Cornelia
  See Yaukey, Grace S(ydenstricker)
Spencer, Donald D(ean) 1931- 41
Spencer, Elizabeth 1921- 14
Spencer, Leonard G.
  See Garrett, Randall
  and Silverberg, Robert
Spencer, William 1922- 9
Spencer, Zane A(nn) 1935- 35
Sper, Emily 1957- 142
Speregen, Devra Newberger 1964- 84
Sperling, Dan(iel Lee) 1949- 65
Sperry, Armstrong W. 1897-1976 1
  Obituary 27
Sperry, Raymond
  See Garis, Howard R.
Sperry, Raymond, Jr. 1
Spetter, Jung-Hee 1969- 134
Spicer, Dorothy Gladys -1975 32
Spiegel, Beth 184
Spiegelman, Art 1948- 158
  Earlier sketch in SATA 109
Spiegelman, Judith M. 5
Spielberg, Steven 1947- 32
Spier, Peter (Edward) 1927- 54
  Earlier sketch in SATA 4
  See also CLR 5
Spilhaus, Athelstan (Frederick) 1911-1998 .. 13
  Obituary 102
Spilka, Arnold 1917- 6
Spillane, Frank Morrison
  See Spillane, Mickey
Spillane, Mickey 1918-2006 66
  Obituary 176
Spinelli, Eileen 1942- 186
  Earlier sketches in SATA 38, 101, 150
Spinelli, Jerry 1941- 195
  Earlier sketches in SATA 39, 71, 110, 158
  See also CLR 82
Spink, Reginald (William) 1905-1994 11
Spinka, Penina Keen 1945- 72
Spinner, Stephanie 1943- 132
Spinossimus
  See White, William, Jr.
Spiotta-DiMare, Loren 173
Spires, Ashley 1978- 183

Spires, Elizabeth 1952- *215*
Earlier sketches in SATA *71, 111*
Spiridellis, Gregg 1971(?)- *199*
Spirin, Gennadii
See Spirin, Gennady
Spirin, Gennadij
See Spirin, Gennady
Spirin, Gennady 1948- *204*
Earlier sketches in SATA *95, 134*
See also CLR *88*
Spiro, Ruth *208*
Spivak, Dawnine *101*
Spizman, Robyn Freedman *194*
Spohn, David 1948- *72*
Spohn, Kate 1962- *147*
Earlier sketch in SATA *87*
Spollen, Christopher 1952- *12*
Spooner, Michael (Tim) 1954- *92*
Spowart, Robin 1947- *177*
Earlier sketch in SATA *82*
Spradlin, Michael P. *204*
Sprague, Gretchen 1926-2003 .... *27*
Spranger, Nina 1969- *203*
Sprengel, Artie
See Lerangis, Peter
Sprigge, Elizabeth (Miriam Squire)
1900-1974 .... *10*
Spring, (Robert) Howard 1889-1965 .... *28*
Springer, Margaret 1941- *78*
Springer, Marilyn Harris 1931- *47*
Springer, Nancy 1948- *172*
Earlier sketches in SATA *65, 110*
Springstubb, Tricia 1950- *78*
Brief entry *40*
Earlier sketch in SATA *46*
Spudvilas, Anne 1951- *199*
Earlier sketch in SATA *94*
Spurll, Barbara 1952- *78*
Spurr, Elizabeth *172*
Spykman, E(lizabeth) C(hoate) 1896-1965 .. *10*
See also CLR *35*
Spyri, Johanna (Heusser) 1827-1901 .... *100*
Earlier sketch in SATA *19*
See also CLR *115*
Squires, Janet *215*
Squires, Phil
See Barker, S. Omar
Srba, Lynne *98*
Sreenivasan, Jyotsna 1964- *101*
S-Ringi, Kjell
See Ringi, Kjell (Arne Soerensen)
Staake, Bob 1957- *209*
Stacey, Cherylyn 1945- *96*
Stacy, Donald
See Pohl, Frederik
Stadler, John *204*
Stadtler, Bea 1921- *17*
Stafford, Jean 1915-1979
Obituary *22*
Stafford, Liliana 1950- *141*
Stafford, Paul 1966- *116*
Stahl, Ben(jamin) 1910-1987 .... *5*
Obituary *54*
Stahl, Hilda 1938-1993 .... *48*
Obituary *77*
Stahler, David, Jr. *162*
Staines, Bill 1949- *213*
Stainton, Sue *187*
Stair, Gobin (John) 1912- *35*
Stalder, Valerie *27*
Stamaty, Mark Alan 1947- *12*
Stambler, Irwin 1924- *5*
Stampler, Ann Redisch *209*
Standiford, Natalie 1961- *169*
Earlier sketch in SATA *81*
Stanek, Lou Willett 1931- *63*
Stang, Judit 1921-1977 .... *29*
Stang, Judy
See Stang, Judit
Stangl, (Mary) Jean 1928- *67*

Stanhope, Eric
See Hamilton, Charles (Harold St. John)
Stankevich, Boris 1928- *2*
Stanley, Diane 1943- *213*
Brief entry *32*
Earlier sketches in SATA *37, 80, 115, 164*
See also CLR *46*
See also SAAS *15*
Stanley, Elizabeth 1947- *206*
Stanley, George Edward 1942- *67*
Earlier sketches in SATA *53, 111, 157, 1*
Stanley, Jerry 1941- *127*
Earlier sketch in SATA *79*
Stanley, Mandy *165*
Stanley, Robert
See Hamilton, Charles (Harold St. John)
Stanley, Sanna 1962- *145*
Stanli, Sue
See Meilach, Dona Z(weigoron)
Stanstead, John
See Groom, Arthur William
Stanton, Karen 1960- *190*
Stanton, Schuyler
See Baum, L. Frank
Staples, Suzanne Fisher 1945- *207*
Earlier sketches in SATA *70, 105, 151*
See also CLR *137*
Stapleton, Marjorie (Winifred) 1932- *28*
Stapp, Arthur D(onald) 1906-1972 .... *4*
Starbird, Kaye 1916- *6*
See also CLR *60*
Stark, Evan 1942- *78*
Stark, James
See Goldston, Robert (Conroy)
Stark, Ken 1943- *199*
Stark, Ulf 1944- *124*
Starke, Ruth (Elaine) 1946- *129*
Starkey, Marion L(ena) 1901-1991 .... *13*
Starr, Ward
See Manes, Stephen
Starret, William
See McClintock, Marshall
Starr Taylor, Bridget 1959- *99*
Stasiak, Krystyna *49*
Staub, Frank 1949- *116*
Staub, Frank Jacob
See Staub, Frank
Staub, Wendy Corsi 1964- *114*
Stauffacher, Sue 1961- *199*
Earlier sketch in SATA *155*
Stauffer, Don
See Berkebile, Fred D(onovan)
Staunton, Schuyler
See Baum, L. Frank
Staunton, Ted 1956- *167*
Earlier sketch in SATA *112*
Stead, Judy *210*
Stead, Rebecca 1968(?)- *188*
Steadman, Ralph 1936- *123*
Earlier sketch in SATA *32*
Steadman, Ralph Idris
See Steadman, Ralph
Stearman, Kaye 1951- *118*
Stearns, Monroe (Mather) 1913-1987 .... *5*
Obituary *55*
Steckler, Arthur 1921-1985 .... *65*
Steding, Laurie 1953- *119*
Steel, Danielle 1947- *66*
Steel, Danielle Fernande
See Steel, Danielle
Steele, Addison II
See Lupoff, Richard A(llen)
Steele, Alexander 1958- *116*
Steele, Henry Maxwell
See Steele, Max
Steele, Mary 1930- *94*
Steele, Mary Q(uintard Govan) 1922-1992 .. *51*
Obituary *72*
Earlier sketch in SATA *3*
Steele, Max 1922-2005 .... *168*
Earlier sketch in SATA *10*

Steele, Philip 1948- *140*
Earlier sketch in SATA *81*
Steele, William O(wen) 1917-1979 .... *51*
Obituary *27*
Earlier sketch in SATA *1*
Steelhammer, Ilona 1952- *98*
Steelsmith, Shari 1962- *72*
Stefanik, Alfred T. 1939- *55*
Steffanson, Con
See Cassiday, Bruce (Bingham)
and Goulart, Ron
Steffens, Bradley 1955- *166*
Earlier sketch in SATA *77*
Steffensmeier, Alexander 1977- *195*
Stegeman, Janet Allais 1923- *49*
Brief entry *49*
Steggall, Susan 1967- *182*
Steig, William 1907-2003 .... *111*
Obituary *149*
Earlier sketches in SATA *18, 70*
See also CLR *103*
Steig, William H.
See Steig, William
Stein, David Ezra *211*
Earlier sketch in SATA *180*
Stein, M(eyer) L(ewis) 1920- *6*
Stein, Mathilde 1969- *195*
Stein, Mini *2*
Stein, R(ichard) Conrad 1937- *154*
Earlier sketches in SATA *31, 82*
Stein, Wendy 1951- *77*
Steinbeck, John 1902-1968 .... *9*
Steinbeck, John Ernst
See Steinbeck, John
Steinberg, Alfred 1917-1995 .... *9*
Steinberg, David 1962- *200*
Steinberg, D.J.
See Steinberg, David
Steinberg, Fannie 1899-1990 .... *43*
Steinberg, Fred J. 1933- *4*
Steinberg, Phillip Orso 1921- *34*
Steinberg, Rafael (Mark) 1927- *45*
Steinberg, Saul 1914-1999 .... *67*
Steincrohn, Maggie
See Davis, Maggie S.
Steiner, Barbara A(nnette) 1934- *83*
Earlier sketch in SATA *13*
See also SAAS *13*
Steiner, Charlotte 1900-1981 .... *45*
Steiner, George 1929- *62*
Steiner, Joan *199*
Earlier sketch in SATA *110*
Steiner, Jorg
See Steiner, Jorg
Steiner, Jorg 1930- *35*
Steiner, K. Leslie
See Delany, Samuel R., Jr.
Steiner, Stan(ley) 1925-1987 .... *14*
Obituary *50*
Steins, Richard 1942- *79*
Stem, Jacqueline 1931- *110*
Stemple, Heidi E.Y. 1966- *214*
Stemple, Jason *179*
Steneman, Shep 1945- *132*
Stengel, Joyce A. 1938- *158*
Stephanie, Gordon
See Gordon, Stephanie Jacob
Stephens, Alice Barber 1858-1932 .... *66*
Stephens, Casey
See Wagner, Sharon B.
Stephens, Henrietta Henkle 1909-1993 .... *6*
Stephens, J.B.
See Lynn, Tracy
Stephens, Mary Jo 1935- *8*
Stephens, Rebecca 1961- *141*
Stephens, Reed
See Donaldson, Stephen R.
Stephens, Suzanne
See Kirby, Susan E.
Stephens, William M(cLain) 1925- *21*

Stephensen, A. M.
    See Manes, Stephen
Stephenson, Lynda 1941- *179*
Stephenson, Lynda A.
    See Stephenson, Lynda
Stepp, Ann 1935- *29*
Stepto, Michele 1946- *61*
Steptoe, Javaka 1971- *213*
    Earlier sketch in SATA *151*
Steptoe, John (Lewis) 1950-1989 .... *63*
    Earlier sketch in SATA *8*
    See also CLR *12*
Sterling, Brett
    See Bradbury, Ray
    and Hamilton, Edmond
    and Samachson, Joseph
Sterling, Dorothy 1913-2008 .... *83*
    Autobiography Feature *127*
    Obituary *200*
    Earlier sketch in SATA *1*
    See also CLR *1*
    See also SAAS *2*
Sterling, Helen
    See Watts, Helen L. Hoke
Sterling, Philip 1907-1989 .... *8*
    Obituary *63*
Sterling, Shirley (Anne) 1948- *101*
Stern, Ellen Norman 1927- *26*
Stern, Judith M. 1951- *75*
Stern, Madeleine
    See Stern, Madeleine B.
Stern, Madeleine B. 1912-2007 .... *14*
Stern, Madeleine Bettina
    See Stern, Madeleine B.
Stern, Maggie 1953- *156*
Stern, Philip Van Doren 1900-1984 .... *13*
    Obituary *39*
Stern, Simon 1943- *15*
Sterne, Emma Gelders 1894- *6*
Steurt, Marjorie Rankin 1888-1978 .... *10*
Stevens, April 1963- *208*
Stevens, Bryna 1924- *65*
Stevens, Carla M(cBride) 1928- *13*
Stevens, Chambers 1968- *128*
Stevens, Diane 1939- *94*
Stevens, Franklin 1933- *6*
Stevens, Greg
    See Cook, Glen
Stevens, Gwendolyn 1944- *33*
Stevens, Helen *209*
Stevens, Jan Romero 1953- *95*
Stevens, Janet 1953- *193*
    Earlier sketches in SATA *90, 148*
Stevens, Kathleen 1936- *49*
Stevens, Leonard A. 1920- *67*
Stevens, Lucile Vernon 1899-1994 .... *59*
Stevens, Margaret Dean
    See Aldrich, Bess Streeter
Stevens, Patricia Bunning 1931- *27*
Stevens, Peter
    See Geis, Darlene Stern
Stevens, Serita 1949- *70*
Stevens, Serita Deborah
    See Stevens, Serita
Stevens, Serita Mendelson
    See Stevens, Serita
Stevens, Shira
    See Stevens, Serita
Stevenson, Anna (M.) 1905- *12*
Stevenson, Augusta 1869(?)-1976 .... *2*
    Obituary *26*
Stevenson, Burton Egbert 1872-1962 .... *25*
Stevenson, Drew 1947- *60*
Stevenson, Emma *207*
Stevenson, Harvey 1960- *148*
    Earlier sketch in SATA *80*
Stevenson, James 1929- *195*
    Brief entry *34*
    Earlier sketches in SATA *42, 71, 113, 161*
    See also CLR *17*
Stevenson, Janet 1913- *8*

Stevenson, Robert Louis 1850-1894 .... *100*
    See also YABC *2*
    See also CLR *107*
Stevenson, Robert Louis Balfour
    See Stevenson, Robert Louis
Stevenson, Sucie
    See Stevenson, Sucie
Stevenson, Sucie 1956- *194*
    Earlier sketch in SATA *104*
Stewart, A(gnes) C(harlotte) *15*
Stewart, Amber *181*
Stewart, Chantal 1945- *173*
    Earlier sketch in SATA *121*
Stewart, Charles
    See Zurhorst, Charles (Stewart, Jr.)
Stewart, Eleanor
    See Porter, Eleanor H(odgman)
Stewart, Elisabeth J(ane) 1927- *93*
Stewart, Elizabeth Laing 1907- *6*
Stewart, Gail B. 1949- *141*
Stewart, George Rippey 1895-1980 .... *3*
    Obituary *23*
Stewart, Jennifer J. 1960- *128*
Stewart, Jennifer Jenkins
    See Stewart, Jennifer J.
Stewart, Joel *211*
    Earlier sketch in SATA *151*
Stewart, John 1920- *14*
Stewart, Mary (Florence Elinor) 1916- *12*
Stewart, Mary Rainbow
    See Stewart, Mary (Florence Elinor)
Stewart, Melissa 1968- *209*
    Earlier sketches in SATA *111, 167*
Stewart, Paul 1955- *199*
    Earlier sketches in SATA *114, 163*
Stewart, Robert Neil 1891-1972 .... *7*
Stewart, Sarah *143*
Stewart, Scott
    See Zaffo, George J.
Stewart, Trenton Lee 1970- *216*
Stewart, W(alter) P. 1924- *53*
Stewart, Whitney 1959- *167*
    Earlier sketch in SATA *92*
Stewig, John Warren 1937- *162*
    Earlier sketches in SATA *26, 110*
Stickler, Soma Han 1942- *128*
Stidworthy, John 1943- *63*
Stiegemeyer, Julie *180*
Stier, Catherine *198*
Stiles, Martha Bennett *108*
    Earlier sketch in SATA *6*
Still, James 1906-2001 .... *29*
    Obituary *127*
Stille, Darlene R. 1942- *170*
    Earlier sketch in SATA *126*
Stille, Darlene Ruth
    See Stille, Darlene R.
Stillerman, Marci *104*
Stillerman, Robbie 1947- *12*
Stilley, Frank 1918- *29*
Stilton, Geronimo *158*
Stimpson, Gerald
    See Mitchell, Adrian
Stimson, James 1964- *213*
Stine, Catherine *165*
Stine, G(eorge) Harry 1928-1997 .... *136*
    Earlier sketch in SATA *10*
Stine, Jovial Bob
    See Stine, R.L.
Stine, R.L. 1943- *194*
    Earlier sketches in SATA *31, 76, 129*
    See also CLR *111*
Stine, Robert Lawrence
    See Stine, R.L.
Stinetorf, Louise (Allender) 1900-1992 .... *10*
Stinson, Kathy 1952- *98*
Stirling, Arthur
    See Sinclair, Upton
Stirling, Ian 1941- *77*
Stirling, Nora B(romley) 1900-1997 .... *3*
Stirnweis, Shannon 1931- *10*

Stobbs, William 1914-2000 .... *17*
    Obituary *120*
Stock, Carolmarie 1951- *75*
Stock, Catherine 1952- *214*
    Earlier sketches in SATA *65, 114, 158*
Stockdale, Susan 1954- *206*
    Earlier sketch in SATA *98*
Stockham, Peter (Alan) 1928- *57*
Stockton, Francis Richard 1834-1902 .... *44*
    Brief entry *32*
Stockton, Frank R.
    See Stockton, Francis Richard
Stockwell-Moniz, Marc J. 1954- *164*
Stoddard, Edward G. 1923- *10*
Stoddard, Hope 1900-1987 .... *6*
Stoddard, Sandol 1927- *98*
    Earlier sketch in SATA *14*
Stoehr, Shelley 1969- *107*
Stoeke, Janet Morgan 1957- *202*
    Earlier sketches in SATA *90, 136*
Stohner, Anu 1952- *179*
Stoiko, Michael 1919- *14*
Stojic, Manya 1967- *156*
Stoker, Abraham
    See Stoker, Bram
Stoker, Bram 1847-1912 .... *29*
Stokes, Cedric
    See Beardmore, George
Stokes, Jack (Tilden) 1923- *13*
Stokes, Olivia Pearl 1916- *32*
Stolarz, Laurie Faria *203*
Stolz, Mary 1920-2006 .... *133*
    Obituary *180*
    Earlier sketches in SATA *10, 71*
    See also SAAS *3*
Stolz, Mary Slattery
    See Stolz, Mary
Stone, Alan
    See Svenson, Andrew E(dward)
Stone, David K(arl) 1922- *9*
Stone, David Lee 1978- *166*
Stone, Eugenia 1879-1971 .... *7*
Stone, Gene
    See Stone, Eugenia
Stone, Helen V(irginia) *6*
Stone, Idella Purnell
    See Purnell, Idella
Stone, Ikey
    See Purnell, Idella
Stone, Irving 1903-1989 .... *3*
    Obituary *64*
Stone, Jeff *178*
Stone, Jon 1931-1997 .... *39*
    Obituary *95*
Stone, Josephine Rector
    See Dixon, Jeanne
Stone, Kyle M. 1972- *202*
Stone, Lesley
    See Trevor, Elleston
Stone, Peter 1930-2003 .... *65*
    Obituary *143*
Stone, Phoebe *205*
    Earlier sketch in SATA *134*
Stone, Raymond *1*
Stone, Rosetta
    See Dr. Seuss
Stone, Tanya Lee 1965- *217*
    Earlier sketch in SATA *182*
Stonehouse, Bernard 1926- *140*
    Earlier sketches in SATA *13, 80*
Stones, (Cyril) Anthony 1934- *72*
Stong, Phil(ip Duffield) 1899-1957 .... *32*
Stoops, Erik D(aniel) 1966- *142*
    Earlier sketch in SATA *78*
Stoppelmoore, Cheryl Jean
    See Ladd, Cheryl (Jean)
Stops, Sue 1936- *86*
Storace, Patricia *193*
Storad, Conrad J. 1957- *119*
Storey, Margaret 1926- *9*
Storey, Victoria Carolyn 1945- *16*

Stork, Francisco
  See Stork, Francisco X.
Stork, Francisco X. 1953- *210*
Storme, Peter
  See Stern, Philip Van Doren
Storms, Patricia 1963- *217*
Storr, Catherine (Cole) 1913-2001 .... *87*
  Obituary *122*
  Earlier sketch in SATA *9*
Story, Josephine
  See Loring, Emilie (Baker)
Stotko, Mary-Ann 1960- *154*
Stott, Dorothy (M.) 1958- *99*
  Earlier sketch in SATA *67*
Stott, Dot
  See Stott, Dorothy (M.)
Stotter, Mike 1957- *108*
Stout, William 1949- *132*
Stoutenburg, Adrien (Pearl) 1916-1982 .... *3*
Stoutland, Allison 1963- *130*
Stover, Allan C(arl) 1938- *14*
Stover, Jill (Griffin) 1958- *82*
Stover, Marjorie Filley 1914- *9*
Stowe, Harriet Beecher 1811-1896
  See YABC *1*
  See also CLR *131*
Stowe, Harriet Elizabeth Beecher
  See Stowe, Harriet Beecher
Stowe, Leland 1899-1994 .... *60*
  Obituary *78*
Stowe, Rosetta
  See Ogan, George F.
  and Ogan, Margaret E. (Nettles)
Stower, Adam *195*
Strachan, Bruce 1959- *205*
Strachan, Ian 1938- *85*
Strachan, Linda *167*
Strachan, Margaret Pitcairn 1908-1998 .... *14*
Strahinich, H. C.
  See Strahinich, Helen C.
Strahinich, Helen C. 1949- *78*
Strait, Treva Adams 1909-2002 .... *35*
Strand, Mark 1934- *41*
Strange, Philippa
  See Coury, Louise Andree
Stranger, Joyce
  See Wilson, Joyce M.
Strangis, Joel 1948- *124*
Strannigan, Shawn 1956- *93*
Strannigan, Shawn Alyne
  See Strannigan, Shawn
Strasser, Todd 1950- *215*
  Earlier sketches in SATA *41, 45, 71, 107, 153*
  See also CLR *11*
Stratemeyer, Edward L. 1862-1930 .... *100*
  Earlier sketches in SATA *1, 67*
  See Adams, Harrison
Stratford, Philip 1927- *47*
Stratton, Allan 1951- *178*
Stratton, J. M.
  See Whitlock, Ralph
Stratton, Thomas
  See Coulson, Robert S(tratton)
  and DeWeese, Thomas Eugene
Stratton-Porter, Gene 1863-1924 .... *15*
  See also CLR *87*
Strauss, Gwen 1963- *77*
Strauss, Joyce 1936- *53*
Strauss, Linda Leopold 1942- *127*
Strauss, Susan (Elizabeth) 1954- *75*
Strayer, E. Ward
  See Stratemeyer, Edward L.
Streano, Vince(nt Catello) 1945- *20*
Streatfeild, Mary Noel
  See Streatfeild, Noel
Streatfeild, Noel 1897(?)-1986 .... *20*
  Obituary *48*
  See also CLR *83*
Street, Janet Travell 1959- *84*
Street, Julia Montgomery 1898-1993 .... *11*
Streissguth, Thomas 1958- *116*

Strelkoff, Tatiana 1957- *89*
Stren, Patti 1949- *88*
  Brief entry *41*
  See also CLR *5*
Strete, Craig Kee 1950- *96*
  Earlier sketch in SATA *44*
Stretton, Barbara (Humphrey) 1936- *43*
  Brief entry *35*
Strickland, Brad 1947- *200*
  Earlier sketches in SATA *83, 137, 142*
Strickland, Craig (A.) 1956- *102*
Strickland, Dorothy S(alley) 1933- *89*
Strickland, Michael R. 1965- *144*
  Earlier sketch in SATA *83*
Strickland, Shadra *209*
Strickland, Tessa *173*
Strickland, William Bradley
  See Strickland, Brad
Striegel, Jana 1955- *140*
Striegel-Wilson, Jana
  See Striegel, Jana
Striker, Lee
  See Clark, Margaret (D.)
Striker, Susan 1942- *63*
Stringer, Lauren 1957- *183*
  Earlier sketch in SATA *129*
Stroeyer, Poul 1923- *13*
Stromoski, Rick 1958- *111*
Strong, Charles
  See Epstein, Beryl
  and Epstein, Samuel
Strong, David
  See McGuire, Leslie (Sarah)
Strong, Jeremy 1949- *175*
  Earlier sketches in SATA *36, 105*
Strong, J.J.
  See Strong, Jeremy
Strong, Pat
  See Hough, Richard (Alexander)
Strong, Stacie 1965- *74*
Stroud, Bettye 1939- *165*
  Earlier sketch in SATA *96*
Stroud, Jonathan 1970- *213*
  Earlier sketches in SATA *102, 159*
  See also CLR *134*
Stroyer, Poul
  See Stroeyer, Poul
Strug, Kerri 1977- *108*
Stryer, Andrea Stenn 1938- *192*
Stryker, Daniel
  See Morris, Chris(topher Crosby)
  and Stump, Jane Barr
Stuart, David
  See Hoyt, Edwin P(almer), Jr.
Stuart, Derek
  See Foster, John L(ouis)
Stuart, Forbes 1924- *13*
Stuart, Ian
  See MacLean, Alistair
Stuart, Jesse (Hilton) 1906-1984 .... *2*
  Obituary *36*
Stuart, Ruth McEnery 1849(?)-1917 .... *116*
Stuart, Sheila
  See Baker, Mary Gladys Steel
Stuart-Clark, Christopher (Anthony) 1940- .. *32*
Stubis, Talivaldis 1926- *5*
Stubley, Trevor (Hugh) 1932- *22*
Stuchner, Joan Betty *209*
Stucky, Naomi R. 1922- *72*
Stucley, Elizabeth
  See Northmore, Elizabeth Florence
Stultifer, Morton
  See Curtis, Richard
Sture-Vasa, Mary
  See Alsop, Mary O'Hara
Sturges, Philemon *174*
Sturtevant, Katherine 1950- *180*
  Earlier sketch in SATA *130*
Sturton, Hugh
  See Johnston, H(ugh) A(nthony) S(tephen)
Sturtzel, Howard A(llison) 1894-1985 .... *1*

Sturtzel, Jane Levington 1903-1996 .... *1*
Stutley, D(oris) J(ean) 1959- *142*
Stutson, Caroline 1940- *104*
Stuve-Bodeen, Stephanie
  See Bodeen, S. A.
Stux, Erica 1929- *140*
Styles, (Frank) Showell 1908- *10*
Stynes, Barbara White *133*
Suarez, Maribel 1952- *201*
Suba, Susanne *4*
Suber, Melissa *213*
Subond, Valerie
  See Grayland, Valerie (Merle Spanner)
Sudbery, Rodie 1943- *42*
Sudyka, Diana *208*
Sue, Majella Lue *209*
Suen, Anastasia 1956(?)- *157*
Sufrin, Mark 1925- *76*
Sugarman, Joan G. 1917- *64*
Sugarman, Tracy 1921- *37*
Sugita, Yutaka 1930- *36*
Suhl, Yuri (Menachem) 1908-1986 .... *8*
  Obituary *50*
  See also CLR *2*
  See also SAAS *1*
Suhr, Joanne *129*
Suid, Murray 1942- *27*
Sullivan, Edward T. *206*
Sullivan, George (Edward) 1927- *147*
  Earlier sketches in SATA *4, 89*
Sullivan, Jacqueline Levering *203*
Sullivan, Jody
  See Rake, Jody
Sullivan, Kathryn A. 1954- *141*
Sullivan, Mary Ann 1954- *63*
Sullivan, Mary W(ilson) 1907- *13*
Sullivan, Pat
  See Messmer, Otto
Sullivan, Paul 1939- *106*
Sullivan, Sarah G. 1953- *179*
Sullivan, Silky 1940- *101*
Sullivan, Sue
  See Sullivan, Susan E.
Sullivan, Susan E. 1962- *123*
Sullivan, Thomas Joseph, Jr. 1947- *16*
Sullivan, Tom
  See Sullivan, Thomas Joseph, Jr.
Sully, Tom 1959- *104*
Sumichrast, Jozef 1948- *29*
Sumiko
  See Davies, Sumiko
Summerforest, Ivy B.
  See Kirkup, James
Summers, Barbara 1944- *182*
Summers, Cassia Joy
  See Cowley, Joy
Summers, James L(evingston) 1910-1973 .... *57*
  Brief entry *28*
Summertree, Katonah
  See Windsor, Patricia
Summy, Barrie *208*
Sun, Chyng Feng 1959- *90*
Sunderlin, Sylvia (S.) 1911-1997 .... *28*
  Obituary *99*
Sung, Betty Lee *26*
Supeene, Shelagh Lynne 1952- *153*
Supplee, Suzanne *204*
Supraner, Robyn 1930- *101*
  Earlier sketch in SATA *20*
Supree, Burt(on) 1941-1992 .... *73*
Surface, Mary Hall 1958- *126*
Surge, Frank 1931- *13*
Susac, Andrew 1929- *5*
Susi, Geraldine Lee 1942- *98*
Sussman, Cornelia Silver 1914-1999 .... *59*
Sussman, Irving 1908-1996 .... *59*
Sussman, Michael 1953- *217*
Sussman, Michael B.
  See Sussman, Michael
Sussman, Susan 1942- *48*

Sutcliff, Rosemary 1920-1992 78
  Obituary 73
  Earlier sketches in SATA 6, 44
  See also CLR 138
Sutcliffe, Jane 1957- 138
Sutherland, Colleen 1944- 79
Sutherland, Efua (Theodora Morgue)
  1924-1996 25
Sutherland, Jon 1958- 167
Sutherland, Jonathan D.
  See Sutherland, Jon
Sutherland, Jonathan David
  See Sutherland, Jon
Sutherland, Margaret 1941- 15
Sutherland, Zena Bailey 1915-2002 37
  Obituary 137
Suttles, Shirley (Smith) 1922- 21
Sutton, Ann (Livesay) 1923- 31
Sutton, Eve(lyn Mary) 1906-1992 26
Sutton, Felix 1910(?)-1973 31
Sutton, Jane 1950- 52
  Brief entry 43
Sutton, Larry M(atthew) 1931- 29
Sutton, Margaret Beebe 1903-2001 1
  Obituary 131
Sutton, Myron Daniel 1925- 31
Sutton, Roger 1956- 93
Sutton, Sally 1973- 214
Suzanne, Jamie
  See Hawes, Louise
  and Lantz, Francess L(in)
  and Singleton, Linda Joy
  and Zach, Cheryl (Byrd)
Suzuki, David 1936- 138
Suzuki, David Takayoshi
  See Suzuki, David
Svendsen, Mark 1962- 181
  Earlier sketch in SATA 120
Svendsen, Mark Nestor
  See Svendsen, Mark
Svenson, Andrew E(dward) 1910-1975 2
  Obituary 26
Swaab, Neil 1978- 191
Swaim, Jessica 1950- 202
Swain, Carol 1962- 172
Swain, Gwenyth 1961- 134
  Earlier sketch in SATA 84
Swain, Ruth
  See Swain, Ruth Freeman
Swain, Ruth Freeman 1951- 161
  Earlier sketch in SATA 119
Swain, Su Zan (Noguchi) 1916- 21
Swallow, Pamela Curtis 178
Swamp, Jake 1941- 98
Swan, Susan 1944- 108
  Earlier sketch in SATA 22
Swann, Brian (Stanley Frank) 1940- 116
Swann, E.L.
  See Lasky, Kathryn
Swann, Ruth Rice 1920- 84
Swanson, Diane 1944- 203
Swanson, Helen M(cKendry) 1919- 94
Swanson, June 1931- 76
Swanson, Susan Marie 209
Swanson, Wayne 1942- 167
Swarner, Kristina 1965- 215
Swarthout, Glendon (Fred) 1918-1992 26
Swarthout, Kathryn 1919- 7
Swayne, Sam(uel F.) 1907- 53
Swayne, Zoa (Lourana) 1905- 53
Sweat, Lynn 1934- 168
  Earlier sketch in SATA 57
Swede, George 1940- 67
Sweeney, James B(artholomew) 1910-1999 . 21
Sweeney, Joyce 1955- 167
  Earlier sketches in SATA 65, 68, 108
Sweeney, Joyce Kay
  See Sweeney, Joyce
Sweeney, Karen O'Connor
  See O'Connor, Karen
Sweeney, Matthew (Gerard) 1952- 156

Sweet, Melissa 1956- 211
  Earlier sketch in SATA 172
Sweet, Sarah C.
  See Jewett, Sarah Orne
Sweetland, Nancy A(nn) 1934- 48
Swenson, Allan A(rmstrong) 1933- 21
Swenson, May 1919-1989 15
Swentzell, Rina 1939- 79
Swiatkowska, Gabi 1971(?)- 180
Swift, Bryan
  See Knott, William C(ecil, Jr.)
Swift, David
  See Kaufmann, John
Swift, Hildegarde Hoyt 1890(?)-1977
  Obituary 20
Swift, Jonathan 1667-1745 19
  See also CLR 53
Swift, Merlin
  See Leeming, Joseph
Swiger, Elinor Porter 1927- 8
Swinburne, Laurence (Joseph) 1924- 9
Swinburne, Stephen R. 1952- 188
  Earlier sketch in SATA 150
Swinburne, Steve
  See Swinburne, Stephen R.
Swindells, Robert (Edward) 1939- 150
  Brief entry 34
  Earlier sketches in SATA 50, 80
  See also SAAS 14
Swinford, Betty (June Wells) 1927- 58
Swinford, Bob
  See Swinford, Betty (June Wells)
Swithen, John
  See King, Stephen
Switzer, Ellen 1923- 48
Swope, Sam 156
Swope, Samuel
  See Swope, Sam
Sybesma, Jetske
  See Ironside, Jetske
Sydney, Frank
  See Warwick, Alan R(oss)
Sydor, Colleen 1960- 207
Sykes, Julie 1963- 202
Sylvada, Peter 1964- 202
Sylvester, Natalie G(abry) 1922- 22
Syme, (Neville) Ronald 1913-1992 87
  Earlier sketch in SATA 2
Symes, R. F. 77
Symes, Ruth Louise 1962- 179
Symons, (Dorothy) Geraldine 1909- 33
Symons, Stuart
  See Stanley, George Edward
Symynkywicz, Jeffrey B. 1954- 87
Symynkywicz, Jeffrey Bruce
  See Symynkywicz, Jeffrey B.
Synge, (Phyllis) Ursula 1930- 9
Sypher, Lucy Johnston 1907- 7
Szasz, Suzanne (Shorr) 1915-1997 13
  Obituary 99
Szekeres, Cyndy 1933- 157
  Autobiography Feature 157
  Earlier sketches in SATA 5, 60, 131
  See also SAAS 13
Szekessy, Tanja 98
Szpura, Beata 1961- 93
Szudek, Agnes S(usan) P(hilomena) 57
  Brief entry 49
Szulc, Tad 1926-2001 26
Szydlow, Jarl
  See Szydlowski, Mary Vigliante
Szydlowski, Mary Vigliante 1946- 94
Szymanski, Lois 1957- 91

T

Taback, Simms 1932- 170
  Brief entry 36
  Earlier sketches in SATA 40, 104
  See also CLR 100
Taber, Gladys (Bagg) 1899-1980
  Obituary 22
Tabor, Nancy Maria Grande 1949- 161
  Earlier sketch in SATA 89
Tabrah, Ruth Milander 1921- 14
Tacang, Brian 213
Tackach, James 1953- 123
Tackach, James M.
  See Tackach, James
Tadgell, Nicole 1969- 177
Tafuri, Nancy 1946- 192
  Autobiography Feature 192
  Earlier sketches in SATA 39, 75, 130
  See also CLR 74
  See also SAAS 14
Tagg, Christine Elizabeth 1962- 138
Tagliaferro, Linda 173
Taha, Karen T(erry) 1942- 156
  Earlier sketch in SATA 71
Tai, Sharon O. 1963- 153
Tait, Douglas 1944- 12
Takabayashi, Mari 1960- 156
  Earlier sketch in SATA 115
Takahashi, Hideko 209
Takahashi, Rumiko 1957- 163
Takakjian, Portia 1930- 15
Takashima, Misako
  See Misako Rocks!
Takashima, Shizuye 1928- 13
Takayama, Sandi 1962- 106
Takeda, Pete(r M.) 1964- 148
Tal, Eve 1947- 176
Talbert, Marc (Alan) 1953- 154
  Autobiography Feature 154
  Earlier sketches in SATA 68, 99
Talbot, Charlene Joy 1928- 10
Talbot, Toby 1928- 14
Talbott, Hudson 1949- 212
  Earlier sketches in SATA 84, 131
Taliaferro, Dorothy L.
  See Martin, Del
Talifero, Gerald 1950- 75
Talker, T.
  See Rands, William Brighty
Tallarico, Tony 1933- 116
Tallcott, Emogene 10
Tallec, Olivier 1970- 197
Tallis, Robyn
  See Smith, Sherwood
Tallon, Robert 1939- 43
  Brief entry 28
Talmadge, Marian 14
Tamaki, Jillian 1980- 201
Tamar, Erika 1934- 150
  Earlier sketches in SATA 62, 101
Tamarin, Alfred H. 1913-1980 13
Tamburine, Jean 1930- 12
Tames, Richard (Lawrence) 1946- 102
  Earlier sketch in SATA 67
Tamminga, Frederick W(illiam) 1934- 66
Tammuz, Benjamin 1919-1989
  Obituary 63
Tan, Amy 1952- 75
Tan, Amy Ruth
  See Tan, Amy
Tan, Shaun 1974- 198
Tanaka, Beatrice 1932- 76
Tanaka, Shelley 214
  Earlier sketch in SATA 136
Tanaka, Yoko 1947- 215
Tang, Charles 1948- 81
Tang, Greg 172
Tang, You-Shan 1946- 53
Tania B.
  See Blixen, Karen

Tankard, Jeremy 1973- *191*
Tannen, Mary 1943- *37*
Tannenbaum, Beulah Goldstein 1916- *3*
Tannenbaum, D(onald) Leb 1948- *42*
Tanner, Jane 1946- *74*
Tanner, Louise S(tickney) 1922-2000 .... *9*
Tanobe, Miyuki 1937- *23*
Tanselle, Eve 1933- *125*
Tapio, Pat Decker
    See Kines, Pat Decker
Tapp, Kathy Kennedy 1949- *88*
    Brief entry *50*
Tarbescu, Edith 1939- *107*
Tarkington, (Newton) Booth 1869-1946 .... *17*
Tarpley, Natasha A(nastasia) 1971- *147*
Tarr, Judith 1955- *149*
    Earlier sketch in SATA *64*
Tarry, Ellen 1906- *16*
    See also CLR *26*
    See also SAAS *16*
Tarshis, Jerome 1936- *9*
Tarshis, Lauren *187*
Tarsky, Sue 1946- *41*
Taschek, Karen 1956- *185*
Tashjian, Janet 1956- *151*
    Earlier sketch in SATA *102*
Tashjian, Virginia A. 1921-2008 .... *3*
Tasker, James 1908- *9*
Tate, Don(ald E.) *159*
Tate, Eleanora E. 1948- *191*
    Earlier sketches in SATA *38, 94*
    See also CLR *37*
Tate, Eleanora Elaine
    See Tate, Eleanora E.
Tate, Ellalice
    See Hibbert, Eleanor Alice Burford
Tate, Joan 1922- *86*
    Earlier sketch in SATA *9*
    See also SAAS *20*
Tate, Mary Anne
    See Hale, Arlene
Tate, Nikki *134*
Tate, Richard
    See Masters, Anthony (Richard)
Tate, Suzanne 1930- *91*
Tatham, Betty *142*
Tatham, Campbell
    See Elting, Mary
Tatham, Julie
    See Tatham, Julie Campbell
Tatham, Julie Campbell 1908-1999 .... *80*
Tavares, Matt *198*
    Earlier sketch in SATA *159*
Tavares, Victor 1971- *176*
Taves, Isabella 1915- *27*
Tayleur, Karen 1961- *213*
Taylor, Alastair 1959- *130*
Taylor, Andrew 1951- *70*
Taylor, Andrew John Robert
    See Taylor, Andrew
Taylor, Ann 1782-1866 .... *41*
    Brief entry *35*
Taylor, Audilee Boyd 1931- *59*
Taylor, Barbara J. 1927- *10*
Taylor, Ben
    See Strachan, Ian
Taylor, Brooke *205*
Taylor, Carl 1937-2010 .... *14*
Taylor, Cheryl Munro 1957- *96*
Taylor, Cora (Lorraine) 1936- *103*
    Earlier sketch in SATA *64*
    See also CLR *63*
Taylor, Dave 1948- *78*
Taylor, David
    See Taylor, Dave
Taylor, David 1900-1965 .... *10*
Taylor, Debbie A. 1955- *169*
Taylor, Eleanor 1969- *206*
Taylor, Elizabeth 1912-1975 .... *13*
Taylor, Florance Walton *9*

Taylor, Florence M(arian Tompkins)
    1892-1983 .... *9*
Taylor, Gage 1942-2000 .... *87*
Taylor, Geoff 1946- *204*
Taylor, G.P. 1958(?)- *216*
    Earlier sketch in SATA *156*
Taylor, Graham Peter
    See Taylor, G.P.
Taylor, Herb(ert Norman, Jr.) 1942-1987 ..... *22*
    Obituary *54*
Taylor, J. David
    See Taylor, Dave
Taylor, Jane 1783-1824 .... *41*
    Brief entry *35*
Taylor, Jerry D(uncan) 1938- *47*
Taylor, John Robert
    See Taylor, Andrew
Taylor, Judy
    See Hough, Judy Taylor
Taylor, Kenneth N. 1917-2005 .... *26*
Taylor, Kenneth Nathaniel
    See Taylor, Kenneth N.
Taylor, Kim *180*
Taylor, L(ester) B(arbour), Jr. 1932- *27*
Taylor, Lois Dwight Cole
    See Cole, Lois Dwight
Taylor, Louise Todd 1939- *47*
Taylor, Margaret 1950- *106*
Taylor, Mark 1927- *32*
    Brief entry *28*
Taylor, Mildred D. 1943- *135*
    See also CLR *144*
    See also SAAS *5*
Taylor, Mildred Delois
    See Taylor, Mildred D.
Taylor, Paula (Wright) 1942- *48*
    Brief entry *33*
Taylor, Peter Lane *210*
Taylor, Robert Lewis 1912-1998 .... *10*
Taylor, Sean 1965- *192*
Taylor, Sydney (Brenner) 1904(?)-1978 .... *28*
    Obituary *26*
    Earlier sketch in SATA *1*
Taylor, Theodore 1921-2006 .... *128*
    Obituary *177*
    Earlier sketches in SATA *5, 54, 83*
    See also CLR *30*
    See also SAAS *4*
Taylor, William 1938- *164*
    Earlier sketches in SATA *78, 113*
    See also CLR *63*
Tazewell, Charles 1900-1972 .... *74*
Tchana, Katrin
    See Tchana, Katrin Hyman
Tchana, Katrin H.
    See Tchana, Katrin Hyman
Tchana, Katrin Hyman 1963- *177*
    Earlier sketch in SATA *125*
Tchekhov, Anton
    See Chekhov, Anton
Tchen, Richard *120*
Tchudi, Stephen N. 1942- *55*
Teague, Bob
    See Teague, Robert
Teague, Mark 1963- *205*
    Earlier sketches in SATA *68, 99, 170*
Teague, Mark Christopher
    See Teague, Mark
Teague, Robert 1929- *32*
    Brief entry *31*
Teal, Val 1902-1997 .... *10*
    Obituary *114*
Teal, Valentine M.
    See Teal, Val
Teale, Edwin Way 1899-1980 .... *7*
    Obituary *25*
Teasdale, Sara 1884-1933 .... *32*
Tebbel, John (William) 1912-2004 .... *26*
Teckentrup, Britta 1969- *200*
Tedesco, P.R.
    See Naylor, Phyllis Reynolds

Teensma, Lynne Bertrand
    See Bertrand, Lynne
Tee-Van, Helen Damrosch 1893-1976 .... *10*
    Obituary *27*
Tegner, Bruce 1928- *62*
Teitelbaum, Michael 1953- *116*
    Earlier sketch in SATA *59*
Tejima
    See Tejima, Keizaburo
Tejima, Keizaburo 1931- *139*
    See also CLR *20*
Telander, Todd (G.) 1967- *88*
Teleki, Geza 1943- *45*
Telemaque, Eleanor Wong 1934- *43*
Telescope, Tom
    See Newbery, John
Tellis, Annabel 1967- *191*
Temkin, Sara Anne Schlossberg 1913-1996 . *26*
Temko, Florence *13*
Tempest, Margaret Mary 1892-1982
    Obituary *33*
Templar, Maurice
    See Groom, Arthur William
Temple, Arthur
    See Northcott, (William) Cecil
Temple, Charles 1947- *79*
Temple, Frances (Nolting) 1945-1995 .... *85*
Temple, Herbert 1919- *45*
Temple, Paul
    See McConnell, James Douglas Rutherford
Temple, William F(rederick) 1914-1989 .... *107*
Tenggren, Gustaf 1896-1970 .... *18*
    Obituary *26*
Tennant, Kylie
    See Rodd, Kylie Tennant
Tennant, Veronica 1947- *36*
Tenneshaw, S.M.
    See Beaumont, Charles
    and Garrett, Randall
    and Silverberg, Robert
Tenniel, John 1820-1914 .... *74*
    Brief entry *27*
    See also CLR *146*
Tepper, Sheri S. 1929- *113*
Terada, Alice M. 1928- *90*
Terban, Marvin 1940- *54*
    Brief entry *45*
Teresi, Judith M.
    See Goldberger, Judith M.
ter Haar, Jaap 1922- *6*
    See also CLR *15*
Terhune, Albert Payson 1872-1942 .... *15*
Terkel, Susan N(eiburg) 1948- *103*
    Earlier sketch in SATA *59*
Terlouw, Jan (Cornelis) 1931- *30*
Terrell, John Upton 1900-1988
    Obituary *60*
Terrill, Beth *198*
Terrill, Elizabeth
    See Terrill, Beth
Terris, Susan 1937- *77*
    Earlier sketch in SATA *3*
Terry, Luther L(eonidas) 1911-1985 .... *11*
    Obituary *42*
Terry, Margaret
    See Dunnahoo, Terry Janson
Terry, Walter 1913-1982 .... *14*
Terry, Will 1966- *205*
Terzian, James P. 1915- *14*
Tessendorf, K(enneth) C(harles) 1925-2003 . *75*
    Obituary *142*
Tessler, Manya *200*
Tessler, Stephanie Gordon
    See Gordon, Stephanie Jacob
Testa, Dom *208*
Tester, Sylvia Root 1939- *64*
    Brief entry *37*
Tether, (Cynthia) Graham 1950- *46*
    Brief entry *36*
Tetzner, Lisa 1894-1963 .... *169*
Thach, James Otis 1969- *195*

Thacher, Mary McGrath 1933- *9*
Thackeray, William Makepeace 1811-1863 .. *23*
Thaler, Michael C.
    See Thaler, Mike
Thaler, Mike 1936- *215*
    Brief entry *47*
    Earlier sketches in SATA *56, 93*
Thaler, Shmuel 1958- *126*
    Earlier sketch in SATA *72*
Thamer, Katie 1955- *42*
Thane, Elswyth 1900-1984(?) *32*
Tharp, Louise (Marshall) Hall 1898-1992 ...... *3*
    Obituary *129*
Tharp, Tim 1957- *189*
Thayer, Ernest Lawrence 1863-1940 .... *60*
Thayer, Jane
    See Woolley, Catherine
Thayer, Marjorie 1908-1992 .... *74*
    Brief entry *37*
Thayer, Peter
    See Wyler, Rose
Thelwell, Norman 1923-2004 .... *14*
Themerson, Stefan 1910-1988 .... *65*
Thermes, Jennifer 1966- *155*
Theroux, Paul 1941- *109*
    Earlier sketch in SATA *44*
Theroux, Paul Edward
    See Theroux, Paul
Thesman, Jean *124*
    Earlier sketch in SATA *74*
The Tjong-Khing
    See Khing, T.T.
Thieda, Shirley Ann 1943- *13*
Thiele, Colin 1920-2006 .... *125*
    Earlier sketches in SATA *14, 72*
    See also CLR *27*
    See also SAAS *2*
Thiele, Colin Milton
    See Thiele, Colin
Thiesing, Lisa 1958- *159*
    Earlier sketch in SATA *95*
Thimmesh, Catherine *189*
Thiry, Joan (Marie) 1926- *45*
Thistlethwaite, Miles 1945- *12*
Thollander, Earl 1922- *22*
Thomas, Abigail 1941- *112*
Thomas, Andrea
    See Hill, Margaret (Ohler)
Thomas, Art(hur Lawrence) 1952- *48*
    Brief entry *38*
Thomas, Carroll
    See Ratliff, Thomas M.
    and Shmurak, Carole B.
Thomas, Dylan 1914-1953 .... *60*
Thomas, Dylan Marlais
    See Thomas, Dylan
Thomas, Egbert S.
    See Ellis, Edward S.
Thomas, Estelle Webb 1899-1982 .... *26*
Thomas, Frances 1943- *171*
    Earlier sketch in SATA *92*
Thomas, Garen *213*
Thomas, H. C.
    See Keating, Lawrence A.
Thomas, Ianthe 1951- *139*
    Brief entry *42*
    See also CLR *8*
Thomas, J. F.
    See Fleming, Thomas
Thomas, Jan 1958- *197*
Thomas, Jane Resh 1936- *171*
    Earlier sketches in SATA *38, 90*
Thomas, Jerry D. 1959- *91*
Thomas, Joan Gale
    See Robinson, Joan (Mary) G(ale Thomas)
Thomas, Joyce Carol 1938- *210*
    Autobiography Feature *137*
    Earlier sketches in SATA *40, 78, 123, 137*
    See also CLR *19*
    See also SAAS *7*

Thomas, Lee
    See Floren, Lee
    and Pendleton, Thomas
Thomas, Lowell Jackson, Jr. 1923- *15*
Thomas, Margaret
    See Thomas, Peggy
Thomas, Meredith 1963- *119*
Thomas, Michael
    See Wilks, Michael Thomas
Thomas, Middy 1931- *191*
Thomas, Patricia 1934- *199*
    Earlier sketch in SATA *51*
Thomas, Peggy *174*
Thomas, Rob 1965- *97*
Thomas, Scott 1959- *147*
Thomas, Velma Maia 1955- *171*
Thomas, Vernon (Arthur) 1934- *56*
Thomas, Victoria
    See DeWeese, Thomas Eugene
    and Kugi, Constance Todd
Thomasma, Kenneth R. 1930- *90*
Thomason, Mark *215*
Thomassie, Tynia 1959- *92*
Thompson, Brenda 1935- *34*
Thompson, Carol 1951- *189*
    Earlier sketch in SATA *85*
Thompson, China
    See Lewis, Mary
Thompson, Colin 1942- *198*
    Earlier sketches in SATA *95, 163*
Thompson, David H(ugh) 1941- *17*
Thompson, Eileen
    See Panowski, Eileen Thompson
Thompson, George Selden 1929-1989 .... *73*
    Obituary *63*
    Earlier sketch in SATA *4*
    See also CLR *8*
Thompson, Harlan 1894-1987 .... *10*
    Obituary *53*
Thompson, Hilary 1943- *56*
    Brief entry *49*
Thompson, Joanna Maxwell Pullein
    See Pullein-Thompson, Joanna Maxwell
Thompson, Julian F(rancis) 1927- *155*
    Brief entry *40*
    Earlier sketches in SATA *55, 99*
    See also CLR *24*
    See also SAAS *13*
Thompson, K(athryn Carolyn) Dyble
    1952- *82*
Thompson, Kate 1956- *204*
Thompson, Kay 1912(?)-1998 .... *16*
    See also CLR *22*
Thompson, Lauren 1962- *200*
    Earlier sketches in SATA *132, 174*
Thompson, Lauren Stevens
    See Thompson, Lauren
Thompson, Megan Lloyd
    See Lloyd, Megan
Thompson, Richard 1951- *184*
Thompson, Ruth Plumly 1891-1976 .... *66*
Thompson, Sharon 1952- *119*
Thompson, Sharon Elaine
    See Thompson, Sharon
Thompson, Stith 1885-1976 .... *57*
    Obituary *20*
Thompson, Vivian L(aubach) 1911- *3*
Thomson, Bill 1963- *187*
Thomson, Celia
    See Lynn, Tracy
Thomson, David (Robert Alexander)
    1914-1988 .... *40*
    Obituary *55*
Thomson, Melissa 1979- *205*
Thomson, Pat 1939- *122*
    Earlier sketch in SATA *77*
Thomson, Peggy 1922- *31*
Thomson, Sarah L. *212*
    Earlier sketch in SATA *178*
Thon, Melanie Rae 1957- *132*
Thong, Roseanne *174*

Thorburn, John
    See Goldsmith, John Herman Thorburn
Thorn, John 1947- *59*
Thorndyke, Helen Louise
    See Benson, Mildred
Thorne, Ian
    See May, Julian
Thorne, Jean Wright
    See May, Julian
Thornhill, Jan 1955- *148*
    Earlier sketch in SATA *77*
Thornton, Hall
    See Silverberg, Robert
Thornton, W. B.
    See Burgess, Thornton Waldo
Thornton, Yvonne S. 1947- *96*
Thornton, Yvonne Shirley
    See Thornton, Yvonne S.
Thorpe, E(ustace) G(eorge) 1916- *21*
Thorpe, J. K.
    See Nathanson, Laura Walther
Thorvall, Kerstin 1925- *13*
Thorvall-Falk, Kerstin
    See Thorvall, Kerstin
Thrasher, Crystal (Faye) 1921- *27*
Threadgall, Colin 1941- *77*
Three Little Pigs
    See Lantz, Francess L(in)
Thum, Gladys 1920- *26*
Thum, Marcella *28*
    Earlier sketch in SATA *3*
Thundercloud, Katherine
    See Witt, Shirley Hill
Thurber, James 1894-1961 .... *13*
Thurber, James Grover
    See Thurber, James
Thurlo, Aimee *161*
Thurlo, David *161*
Thurman, Judith 1946- *33*
Thurman, Mark (Gordon Ian) 1948- *63*
Thwaite, Ann (Barbara Harrop) 1932- *14*
Tibbetts, Peggy *127*
Tibbles, Jean-Paul 1958- *115*
Tibo, Gilles 1951- *107*
    Earlier sketch in SATA *67*
Tiburzi, Bonnie 1948- *65*
Ticheburn, Cheviot
    See Ainsworth, William Harrison
Tichenor, Tom 1923-1992 .... *14*
Tichnor, Richard 1959- *90*
Tichy, William 1924- *31*
Tickle, Jack
    See Chapman, Jane
Tiegreen, Alan F. 1935- *94*
    Brief entry *36*
Tierney, Frank M. 1930- *54*
Tierney, Tom 1928- *113*
Tiffault, Benette W. 1955- *77*
Tildes, Phyllis Limbacher 1945- *210*
Tiller, Ruth L. 1949- *83*
Tilley, Debbie *190*
Tillman, Nancy *211*
Tilly, Nancy 1935- *62*
Tilton, Madonna Elaine 1929- *41*
Tilton, Rafael
    See Tilton, Madonna Elaine
Timberlake, Amy *156*
Timberlake, Carolyn
    See Dresang, Eliza (Carolyn Timberlake)
Timmers, Leo 1970- *190*
Timmins, William F(rederick) *10*
Tinbergen, Niko(laas) 1907-1988
    Obituary *60*
Tincknell, Cathy *194*
Tiner, John Hudson 1944- *32*
Tingle, Dolli (?)-
    See Brackett, Dolli Tingle
Tingle, Rebecca *174*
Tingle, Tim *208*
Tingum, Janice 1958- *91*
Tinkelman, Murray 1933- *12*

Tinkham, Kelly A. *188*
Tinkle, (Julien) Lon 1906-1980 .... *36*
Tinling, Marion (Rose) 1904- *140*
Tipene, Tim 1972- *141*
Tippett, James S(terling) 1885-1958 .... *66*
Tirone Smith, Mary-Ann 1944- *143*
Titlebaum, Ellen *195*
Titler, Dale M(ilton) 1926- *35*
    Brief entry *28*
Titmarsh, Michael Angelo
    See Thackeray, William Makepeace
Titus, Eve 1922- *2*
Tjia, Sherwin 1975- *204*
Tjong Khing, The 1933- *76*
Tobias, Katherine
    See Gottfried, Theodore Mark
Tobias, Tobi 1938- *82*
    Earlier sketch in SATA *5*
    See also CLR *4*
Todd, Anne Ophelia
    See Dowden, Anne Ophelia Todd
Todd, Barbara 1961- *173*
Todd, Barbara K(eith) 1917- *10*
Todd, Chuck *195*
Todd, H(erbert) E(atton) 1908-1988 .... *84*
    Earlier sketch in SATA *11*
Todd, Loreto 1942- *30*
Todd, Pamela *212*
Todd, Peter
    See Hamilton, Charles (Harold St. John)
Toews, Miriam 1964- *165*
Tofel, Richard J. 1957- *140*
Toft, Kim Michelle 1960- *170*
Tokunbo, Dimitrea *187*
Tolan, Stephanie S. 1942- *142*
    Earlier sketches in SATA *38, 78*
Toland, John (Willard) 1912-2004 .... *38*
Tolbert, Steve 1944- *143*
Toledo, Francisco 1940- *198*
Toledo, Natalia 1967- *197*
Tolkien, J. R. R. 1892-1973 .... *100*
    Obituary *24*
    Earlier sketches in SATA *2, 32*
    See also CLR *152*
Tolkien, John Ronald Reuel
    See Tolkien, J. R. R.
Toll, Emily
    See Cannon, Eileen E(mily)
Toll, Nelly S. 1935- *78*
Tolland, W. R.
    See Heitzmann, William Ray
Tolles, Martha 1921- *76*
    Earlier sketch in SATA *8*
Tolliver, Ruby C(hangos) 1922- *110*
    Brief entry *41*
    Earlier sketch in SATA *55*
Tolmie, Kenneth Donald 1941- *15*
Tolstoi, Lev
    See Tolstoy, Leo
Tolstoy, Leo 1828-1910 .... *26*
Tolstoy, Count Leo
    See Tolstoy, Leo
Tolstoy, Leo Nikolaevich
    See Tolstoy, Leo
Tomalin, Ruth *29*
Tomaselli, Rosa
    See Pausacker, Jenny
Tomecek, Steve *172*
Tomes, Margot (Ladd) 1917-1991 .... *70*
    Brief entry *27*
    Obituary *69*
    Earlier sketch in SATA *36*
Tomey, Ingrid 1943- *77*
Tomfool
    See Farjeon, Eleanor
Tomic, Tomislav 1977- *202*
Tomkins, Jasper
    See Batey, Tom
Tomline, F. Latour
    See Gilbert, W(illiam) S(chwenck)
Tomlinson, Heather *192*

Tomlinson, Jill 1931-1976 .... *3*
    Obituary *24*
Tomlinson, Reginald R(obert) 1885-1979(?)
    Obituary *27*
Tomlinson, Theresa 1946- *165*
    Earlier sketch in SATA *103*
    See also CLR *60*
Tommaso, Rich 1970(?)- *200*
Tompert, Ann 1918- *139*
    Earlier sketch in SATA *14, 89*
Tompkins, Troy
    See Cle, Troy
Toner, Raymond John 1908-1986 .... *10*
Tong, Gary S. 1942- *66*
Tong, Paul *188*
Took, Belladonna
    See Chapman, Vera (Ivy May)
Tooke, Louise Mathews 1950- *38*
Tooke, Susan *173*
Toonder, Martin
    See Groom, Arthur William
Toothaker, Roy Eugene 1928- *18*
Tooze, Ruth (Anderson) 1892-1972 .... *4*
Topaz, Ksenia *212*
Topek, Susan Remick 1955- *78*
Topping, Audrey R(onning) 1928- *14*
Tor, Regina
    See Shekerjian, Regina Tor
Torbert, Floyd James 1922- *22*
Torgersen, Don Arthur 1934- *55*
    Brief entry *41*
Torley, Luke
    See Blish, James
Torrecilla, Pablo 1967- *206*
Torres, Andres Segovia
    See Segovia, Andres
Torres, Daniel 1958- *102*
Torres, John A. 1965- *163*
    Earlier sketch in SATA *94*
Torres, John Albert
    See Torres, John A.
Torres, Laura 1967- *146*
    Earlier sketch in SATA *87*
Torres, Leyla 1960- *155*
Torrey, Rich
    See Torrey, Richard
Torrey, Richard *189*
Torrie, Malcolm
    See Mitchell, Gladys (Maude Winifred)
Toten, Teresa 1955- *99*
Totham, Mary
    See Breinburg, Petronella
Touponce, William F. 1948- *114*
Tournier, Michel 1924- *23*
Tournier, Michel Edouard
    See Tournier, Michel
Towle, Wendy 1963- *79*
Towne, Mary
    See Spelman, Mary
Townley, Rod
    See Townley, Roderick
Townley, Roderick 1942- *177*
Townsend, Brad W. 1962- *91*
Townsend, John Rowe 1922- *132*
    Autobiography Feature *132*
    Earlier sketches in SATA *4, 68*
    See also CLR *2*
    See also SAAS *2*
Townsend, Michael 1981- *194*
Townsend, Sue 1946- *93*
    Brief entry *48*
    Earlier sketch in SATA *55*
Townsend, Susan Lilian
    See Townsend, Sue
Townsend, Thomas L. 1944- *59*
Townsend, Tom
    See Townsend, Thomas L.
Townsend, Wendy 1962- *201*
Townson, Hazel *134*
Toye, William Eldred 1926- *8*

Traherne, Michael
    See Watkins-Pitchford, Denys James
Trahey, Jane 1923-2000 .... *36*
    Obituary *120*
Trapani, Iza 1954- *214*
    Earlier sketches in SATA *80, 116*
Trapp, Maria Augusta von
    See von Trapp, Maria Augusta
Travers, P(amela) L(yndon) 1899-1996 ...... *100*
    Obituary *90*
    Earlier sketches in SATA *4, 54*
    See also CLR *93*
    See also SAAS *2*
Travis, Lucille *133*
    Earlier sketch in SATA *88*
Treadgold, Mary 1910- *49*
Trease, (Robert) Geoffrey 1909-1998 .... *60*
    Obituary *101*
    Earlier sketch in SATA *2*
    See also CLR *42*
    See also SAAS *6*
Treat, Lawrence 1903-1998 .... *59*
Tredez, Alain 1926- *17*
Tredez, Denise 1930- *50*
Treece, Henry 1912-1966 .... *2*
    See also CLR *2*
Tregarthen, Enys
    See Sloggett, Nellie
Tregaskis, Richard 1916-1973 .... *3*
    Obituary *26*
Treherne, Katie Thamer 1955- *76*
Trell, Max 1900-1996 .... *14*
    Obituary *108*
Tremain, Ruthven 1922- *17*
Trembath, Don 1963- *168*
    Earlier sketch in SATA *96*
Tremens, Del
    See MacDonald, Amy
Trent, Robbie 1894-1988 .... *26*
Trent, Timothy
    See Malmberg, Carl
Treseder, Terry Walton 1956- *68*
Tresilian, (Cecil) Stuart 1891-(?) *40*
Tresselt, Alvin 1916-2000 .... *7*
    See also CLR *30*
Trevino, Elizabeth B(orton) de 1904- *29*
    Earlier sketch in SATA *1*
    See also SAAS *5*
Trevor, Elleston 1920-1995 .... *28*
Trevor, Frances
    See Teasdale, Sara
Trevor, Glen
    See Hilton, James
Trevor, (Lucy) Meriol 1919-2000 .... *113*
    Obituary *122*
    Earlier sketch in SATA *10*
Trewellard, J.M. *195*
Trewellard, Juliet
    See Trewellard, J.M.
Trez, Alain
    See Tredez, Alain
Trez, Denise
    See Tredez, Denise
Trezise, Percy 1923-
    See CLR *41*
Trezise, Percy James
    See Trezise, Percy
Triggs, Tony D. 1946- *70*
Trimble, Marshall I(ra) 1939- *93*
Trimby, Elisa 1948- *47*
    Brief entry *40*
Tring, A. Stephen
    See Meynell, Laurence Walter
Tripp, Eleanor B(aldwin) 1936- *4*
Tripp, Janet 1942- *108*
Tripp, Jenny *188*
Tripp, John
    See Moore, John Travers
Tripp, Nathaniel 1944- *101*
Tripp, Paul 1916-2002 .... *8*
    Obituary *139*

Tripp, Valerie 1951- 168
 Earlier sketch in SATA 78
Tripp, Wallace (Whitney) 1940- 31
Trivelpiece, Laurel 1926- 56
 Brief entry 46
Trivett, Daphne Harwood 1940- 22
Trivizas, Eugene 1946- 84
Trnka, Jiri 1912-1969 43
 Brief entry 32
Trollope, Anthony 1815-1882 22
Trost, Lucille W(ood) 1938- 149
 Earlier sketch in SATA 12
Trott, Betty 1933- 91
Trotter, Deborah W. 184
Trotter, Grace V(iolet) 1900-1991 10
Trottier, Maxine 1950- 175
 Earlier sketch in SATA 131
Troughton, Joanna (Margaret) 1947- 37
Trout, Kilgore
 See Farmer, Philip Jose
Trout, Richard E. 123
Trudeau, Garretson Beekman
 See Trudeau, G.B.
Trudeau, Garry
 See Trudeau, G.B.
Trudeau, Garry B.
 See Trudeau, G.B.
Trudeau, G.B. 1948- 168
 Earlier sketch in SATA 35
Trueit, Trudi
 See Trueit, Trudi Strain
Trueit, Trudi Strain 1963- 179
Trueman, Matthew 183
Trueman, Terry 1947- 178
 Earlier sketch in SATA 132
Truesdell, Judy
 See Mecca, Judy Truesdell
Truesdell, Sue 212
 See Truesdell, Susan G.
Truesdell, Susan G. 108
 Brief entry 45
 See Truesdell, Sue
Trumbauer, Lisa (Trutkoff) 1963- 149
Truss, Jan 1925- 35
Truss, Lynne 1955(?)- 194
Tryon, Leslie 194
 Earlier sketch in SATA 139
Tubb, Jonathan N. 1951- 78
Tubb, Kristin O'Donnell 1971- 209
Tubby, I. M.
 See Kraus, (Herman) Robert
Tucker, Allan James
 See James, Bill
Tucker, Caroline
 See Nolan, Jeannette Covert
Tucker, James
 See James, Bill
Tudor, Edward
 See Browne, Anthony
Tudor, Tasha 1915-2008 160
 Obituary 205
 Earlier sketches in SATA 20, 69
 See also CLR 13
Tuerk, Hanne 1951- 71
Tugeau, Jeremy 199
Tulloch, Richard 1949- 180
 Earlier sketch in SATA 76
Tulloch, Richard George
 See Tulloch, Richard
Tulloch, Shirley 169
Tully, John (Kimberley) 1923- 14
Tumanov, Vladimir A. 1961- 138
Tung, Angela 1972- 109
Tunis, Edwin (Burdett) 1897-1973 28
 Obituary 24
 Earlier sketch in SATA 1
 See also CLR 2
Tunis, John R(oberts) 1889-1975 37
 Brief entry 30
Tunnell, Michael
 See Tunnell, Michael O.

Tunnell, Michael O. 1950- 157
 Earlier sketch in SATA 103
Tunnell, Michael O'Grady
 See Tunnell, Michael O.
Tunnicliffe, C(harles) F(rederick)
 1901-1979 62
Turck, Mary C. 1950- 144
Turk, Hanne
 See Tuerk, Hanne
Turk, Ruth 1917- 82
Turkle, Brinton 1915- 79
 Earlier sketch in SATA 2
Turlington, Bayly 1919-1977 5
 Obituary 52
Turnbull, Agnes Sligh 1888-1982 14
Turnbull, Ann 1943- 160
 Earlier sketch in SATA 18
Turnbull, Ann Christine
 See Turnbull, Ann
Turner, Alice K. 1940- 10
Turner, Ann 1945- 188
 Autobiography Feature 188
 Earlier sketches in SATA 14, 77, 113, 178
Turner, Ann Warren
 See Turner, Ann
Turner, Bonnie 1932- 75
Turner, Elizabeth 1774-1846
 See YABC 2
Turner, Glennette Tilley 1933- 183
 Earlier sketch in SATA 71
Turner, Josie
 See Crawford, Phyllis
Turner, Megan Whalen 1965- 174
 Earlier sketch in SATA 94
Turner, Pamela S. 1957- 211
Turner, Philip (William) 1925- 83
 Earlier sketch in SATA 11
 See also CLR 89
 See also SAAS 6
Turner, Robyn 1947- 77
Turner, Sheila R.
 See Seed, Sheila Turner
Turngren, Annette 1902(?)-1980
 Obituary 23
Turngren, Ellen (?)-1964 3
Turska, Krystyna (Zofia) 1933- 31
 Brief entry 27
Turteltaub, H.N.
 See Turtledove, Harry
Turtledove, Harry 1949- 166
 Earlier sketch in SATA 116
Turtledove, Harry Norman
 See Turtledove, Harry
Tusa, Tricia 1960- 207
 Earlier sketches in SATA 72, 111
Tusiani, Joseph 1924- 45
Twain, Mark 1835-1910 100
 See also YABC 2
 See also CLR 66
Tweit, Susan J 1956- 94
Tweit, Susan Joan
 See Tweit, Susan J
Tweton, D. Jerome 1933- 48
Twinem, Neecy 1958- 92
Twohill, Maggie
 See Angell, Judie
Tworkov, Jack 1900-1982 47
 Obituary 31
Tyche
 See Papademetriou, Lisa
Tyers, Jenny 1969- 89
Tyers, Kathy 1952- 82
Tyler, Anne 1941- 173
 Earlier sketches in SATA 7, 90
Tyler, Linda
 See Tyler, Linda W(agner)
Tyler, Linda W(agner) 1952- 65
Tyler, Vicki 1952- 64
Tyne, Joel
 See Schembri, Jim
Tyrrell, Frances 1959- 107

U

Ubell, Earl 1926-2007 4
 Obituary 182
Uchida, Yoshiko 1921-1992 53
 Obituary 72
 Earlier sketch in SATA 1
 See also CLR 56
 See also SAAS 1
Udall, Jan Beaney 1938- 10
Uden, (Bernard Gilbert) Grant 1910- 26
Uderzo, Albert 1927-
 See CLR 37
Udovic, David 1950- 189
Udry, Janice May 1928- 152
 Earlier sketch in SATA 4
Uegaki, Chieri 1969- 211
 Earlier sketch in SATA 153
Uehashi, Nahoko 1962- 215
Ueno, Noriko
 See Nakae, Noriko
Ugliano, Natascia 196
Uhlberg, Myron 174
Uhlig, Richard 1970- 195
Uhlig, Susan 1955- 129
Ulam, S(tanislaw) M(arcin) 1909-1984 51
Ullman, Barb Bentler 210
Ullman, James Ramsey 1907-1971 7
Ulm, Robert 1934-1977 17
Ulmer, Louise 1943- 53
Ulmer, Wendy K. 1950- 201
Ulrich, Maureen 1958- 206
Ulriksen, Mark 1957- 210
Ulyatt, Kenneth 1920- 14
Umansky, Kaye 1946- 188
 Earlier sketch in SATA 158
Unada
 See Gliewe, Unada (Grace)
Uncle Carter
 See Boucher, (Clarence) Carter
Uncle Eric
 See Maybury, Richard J.
Uncle Gus
 See Rey, H. A.
Uncle Mac
 See McCulloch, Derek (Ivor Breashur)
Uncle Ray
 See Coffman, Ramon Peyton
Uncle Shelby
 See Silverstein, Shel
Underhill, Alice Mertie (Waterman)
 1900-1971 10
Underhill, Liz 1948- 53
 Brief entry 49
Underwood, Deborah 1962- 206
Unger, Harlow G. 1931- 75
Unger, Harlow Giles
 See Unger, Harlow G.
Unger, Jim 1937- 67
Ungerer, (Jean) Thomas 1931- 106
 Earlier sketches in SATA 5, 33
 See also CLR 77
Ungerer, Tomi 1931-
 See Ungerer, (Jean) Thomas
Unkelbach, Kurt 1913-1992 4
Unnerstad, Edith (Totterman) 1900-1982 3
 See also CLR 36
Unobagha, Uzo 139
Unrau, Ruth 1922- 9
Unstead, R(obert) J(ohn) 1915-1988 12
 Obituary 56
Unsworth, Walt(er) 1928- 4
Untermeyer, Bryna Ivens 1909-1985 61
Untermeyer, Louis 1885-1977 37
 Obituary 26
 Earlier sketch in SATA 2
Unwin, David S. 1918-2010 14
Unwin, David Storr
 See Unwin, David S.
Unwin, Nora S(picer) 1907-1982 3
 Obituary 49

Unzner, Christa 1958- *141*
Earlier sketch in SATA *80*
Unzner-Fischer, Christa
See Unzner, Christa
Updale, Eleanor 1953- *175*
Updyke, Rosemary K. 1924- *103*
Upitis, Alvis *109*
Urbain, Cat 1956- *211*
Urbain, Catherine
See Urbain, Cat
Urban, Helle (Denise) 1957- *149*
Urban, Linda *199*
Urbanovic, Jackie *189*
Urbigkit, Cat 1965- *196*
Urdahl, Catherine *215*
Ure, Jean 1943- *192*
Autobiography Feature *192*
Earlier sketches in SATA *48, 78, 129*
See also CLR *34*
See also SAAS *14*
U'Ren, Andrea 1968- *213*
Earlier sketch in SATA *142*
Uris, Leon 1924-2003 .... *49*
Obituary *146*
Uris, Leon Marcus
See Uris, Leon
Ursu, Anne *177*
Ury, Allen B. 1954- *98*
Uschan, Michael V. 1948- *129*
Usher, Margo Scegge
See McHargue, Georgess
Uslan, Michael E. 1951- *169*
Uston, Ken(neth Senzo) 1935-1987 .... *65*
Uttley, Alice Jane 1884-1976 .... *88*
Obituary *26*
Earlier sketch in SATA *3*
Uttley, Alison
See Uttley, Alice Jane
Utz, Lois (Marie) 1932-1986 .... *5*
Obituary *50*

V

Vaeth, J. Gordon 1921- *17*
Vaeth, Joseph Gordon
See Vaeth, J. Gordon
Vagin, Vladimir (Vasilevich) 1937- *142*
Vail, Rachel 1966- *201*
Earlier sketches in SATA *94, 163*
Vainio, Pirkko 1957- *123*
Earlier sketch in SATA *76*
Valen, Nanine 1950- *21*
Valencak, Hannelore
See Mayer, Hannelore Valencak
Valens, Amy 1946- *70*
Valens, E(vans) G(ladstone), Jr. 1920-1992 ... *1*
Valentine, Johnny *72*
Valerio, Geraldo 1970- *180*
Valgardson, W. D. 1939- *151*
Earlier sketch in SATA *101*
Valgardson, William Dempsey
See Valgardson, W. D.
Valleau, Emily 1925- *51*
Vamos, Samantha R. *215*
Van Abbe, Salaman 1883-1955 .... *18*
Van Allsburg, Chris 1949- *156*
Earlier sketches in SATA *37, 53, 105*
See also CLR *113*
Van Anrooy, Francine 1924- *2*
Van Anrooy, Frans
See Van Anrooy, Francine
Vanasse, Deb 1957- *170*
Van Buren, David *203*
Vance, Cynthia *207*
Vance, Eleanor Graham 1908-1985 .... *11*
Vance, Gerald
See Garrett, Randall
and Silverberg, Robert
Vance, Marguerite 1889-1965 .... *29*

Vance-Abrams, Cynthia
See Vance, Cynthia
VanCleave, Janice 1942- *116*
Autobiography Feature *123*
Earlier sketch in SATA *75*
Vandenburg, Mary Lou 1943- *17*
Vander Boom, Mae M. *14*
Vander-Els, Betty 1936- *63*
van der Heide, Iris 1970- *183*
van der Linde, Laurel 1952- *78*
van der Linden, Martijn 1979- *214*
van der Meer, Ron 1945- *98*
van de Ruit, John 1975- *199*
Van der Veer, Judy 1912-1982 .... *4*
Obituary *33*
Vanderwerff, Corrine 1939- *117*
Vander Zee, Ruth *199*
Earlier sketch in SATA *159*
Vande Velde, Vivian 1951- *211*
Earlier sketches in SATA *62, 95, 141*
See also CLR *145*
Vandivert, Rita (Andre) 1905-1986 .... *21*
Van Draanen, Wendelin *207*
Earlier sketch in SATA *122*
Van Dusen, Chris *173*
Van Duyn, Janet 1910- *18*
Van Dyne, Edith
See Baum, L. Frank
and Sampson, Emma (Keats) Speed
and van Zantwijk, Rudolf (Alexander
Marinus)
Vane, Mitch
See Vane, Mitchelle
Vane, Mitchelle *176*
van Frankenhuyzen, Gijsbert 1951- *132*
Van Genechten, Guido 1957- *165*
van Haeringen, Annemarie *193*
Van Hook, Beverly 1941- *99*
Van Hook, Beverly H.
See Van Hook, Beverly
Van Hook, Beverly Hennen
See Van Hook, Beverly
Van Horn, William 1939- *43*
van Hout, Mies 1962- *178*
Van Iterson, S(iny) R(ose) *26*
Van Kampen, Vlasta 1943- *163*
Earlier sketch in SATA *54*
Van Laan, Nancy 1939- *214*
Earlier sketch in SATA *105*
van Lawick-Goodall, Jane
See Goodall, Jane
Van Leeuwen, Jean 1937- *211*
Autobiography Feature *141*
Earlier sketches in SATA *6, 82, 132, 141*
See also SAAS *8*
van Lhin, Erik
See del Rey, Lester
van Lieshout, Elle 1963- *217*
van Lieshout, Maria *201*
Van Loon, Hendrik Willem 1882-1944 .... *18*
van Ommen, Sylvia 1978- *186*
VanOosting, James 1951- *170*
Van Orden, M(erton) D(ick) 1921- *4*
van Os, Erik 1963- *217*
Van Patter, Bruce *183*
Van Reek, Wouter *204*
Van Rensselaer, Alexander (Taylor Mason)
1892-1962 .... *14*
Van Riper, Guernsey, Jr. 1909-1995 .... *3*
van Rossum, Heleen 1962- *174*
Van Rynbach, Iris 1952- *102*
Vansant, Rhonda Joy Edwards 1950- *92*
Van Steenwyk, Elizabeth (Ann) 1928- *89*
Earlier sketch in SATA *34*
Van Stockum, Hilda 1908-2006 .... *5*
Obituary *179*
van Straaten, Harmen 1961- *195*
Van Tuyl, Barbara 1940- *11*
van Vogt, A(lfred) E(lton) 1912-2000 .... *14*
Obituary *124*
Van Wassenhove, Sue 1951- *202*

Van Woerkom, Dorothy (O'Brien)
1924-1996 .... *21*
Van Wormer, Joe
See Van Wormer, Joseph Edward
Van Wormer, Joseph Edward 1913-1998 ...... *35*
Van Wright, Cornelius *173*
Van Zwienen, Ilse Charlotte Koehn
1929-1991 .... *34*
Brief entry *28*
Obituary *67*
Van Zyle, Jon 1942- *176*
Earlier sketch in SATA *84*
Varela, Barry *180*
Varga, Judy
See Stang, Judit
Varley, Dimitry V. 1906-1984 .... *10*
Varley, Susan 1961- *134*
Earlier sketch in SATA *63*
Varon, Sara *195*
Vasileva, Tatiana
See Wassiljewa, Tatjana
Vasiliev, Valery 1949- *80*
Vasilieva, Tatiana
See Wassiljewa, Tatjana
Vasiliu, Mircea 1920- *2*
Vass, George 1927- *57*
Brief entry *31*
Vaughan, Carter A.
See Gerson, Noel Bertram
Vaughan, Harold Cecil 1923- *14*
Vaughan, Marcia (K.) 1951- *159*
Earlier sketches in SATA *60, 95*
Vaughan, Richard 1947- *87*
Vaughan, Sam(uel) 1928- *14*
Vaughn, Ruth 1935- *14*
Vaught, Susan 1965- *195*
Vaupel, Robin *198*
Vautier, Ghislaine 1932- *53*
Vavra, Robert James 1935- *8*
Vecsey, George Spencer 1939- *9*
Vedral, Joyce L(auretta) 1943- *65*
Vega, Denise *216*
Earlier sketch in SATA *174*
Vega, Denise B.
See Vega, Denise
Vega, Diego
See Adkins, Jan
Veglahn, Nancy (Crary) 1937- *5*
Vejjajiva, Jane 1963- *189*
Velasquez, Eric *192*
Velasquez, Gloria 1949- *113*
Velasquez, Gloria 1949-
See Velasquez, Gloria
Velthuijs, Max 1923-2005 .... *110*
Obituary *160*
Earlier sketch in SATA *53*
Venable, Alan (Hudson) 1944- *8*
Venezia, Mike 1945- *150*
Ventura, Anthony
See Pellowski, Michael (Joseph)
Ventura, Piero (Luigi) 1937- *61*
Brief entry *43*
See also CLR *16*
Vequin, Capini
See Quinn, Elisabeth
Verba, Joan Marie 1953- *78*
Verboven, Agnes 1951- *103*
verDorn, Bethea (Stewart) 1952- *76*
Vere, Ed *197*
Verissimo, Erico (Lopes) 1905-1975 .... *113*
Verne, Jules 1828-1905 .... *21*
See also CLR *88*
Verne, Jules Gabriel
See Verne, Jules
Verner, Gerald 1897(?)-1980
Obituary *25*
Verney, John 1913-1993 .... *14*
Obituary *75*
Verniero, Joan C. 1949- *181*
Vernon, (Elda) Louise A(nderson) 1914- *14*

Vernon, Rosemary
   See Smith, Susan Vernon
Vernon, Ursula 204
Vernor, D.
   See Casewit, Curtis W(erner)
Verr, Harry Coe
   See Kunhardt, Edith
Verral, Charles Spain 1904-1990 11
   Obituary 65
Verrillo, Erica 1953- 199
Verrillo, Erica F.
   See Verrillo, Erica
Verrone, Robert J. 1935(?)-1984
   Obituary 39
Versace, Marie Teresa Rios 1917- 2
Vertreace, Martha M(odena) 1945- 78
Vesey, A(manda) 1939- 62
Vesey, Mark (David) 1958- 123
Vesey, Paul
   See Allen, Samuel W(ashington)
Vess, Charles 1951- 215
Vestergaard, Hope 178
Vestly, Anne-Cath(arina) 1920- 14
   See also CLR 99
Vevers, (Henry) Gwynne 1916-1988 45
   Obituary 57
Viator, Vacuus
   See Hughes, Thomas
Viau, Nancy 208
Vicar, Henry
   See Felsen, Henry Gregor
Vick, Helen Hughes 1950- 88
Vicker, Angus
   See Felsen, Henry Gregor
Vickers, Sheena 1960- 94
Vickery, Kate
   See Kennedy, T.A.
Victor, Edward 1914- 3
Victor, Joan Berg 1942- 30
Vidrine, Beverly Barras 1938- 188
   Earlier sketch in SATA 103
Vieceli, Emma 1979- 210
Viereck, Ellen K. 1928- 14
Viereck, Phillip 1925- 3
Viertel, Janet 1915- 10
Vigliante, Mary
   See Szydlowski, Mary Vigliante
Vigna, Judith 1936- 102
   Earlier sketch in SATA 15
Viguers, Ruth Hill 1903-1971 6
Vila, Laura 207
Vilela, Fernando 1973- 216
Villareal, Ray 187
Villasenor, Edmund
   See Villasenor, Victor E.
Villasenor, Edmundo
   See Villasenor, Victor E.
Villasenor, Victor
   See Villasenor, Victor E.
Villasenor, Victor E. 1940- 171
Villasenor, Victor Edmundo
   See Villasenor, Victor E.
Villiard, Paul 1910-1974 51
   Obituary 20
Villiers, Alan (John) 1903-1982 10
Vilott, Rhondi
   See Salsitz, Rhondi Vilott
Vincent, Amy
   See Gray, Claudia
Vincent, Eric Douglas 1953- 40
Vincent, Erin 1969- 188
Vincent, Felix 1946- 41
Vincent, Gabrielle 1928-2000 121
   Earlier sketch in SATA 61
   See also CLR 13
Vincent, Mary Keith
   See St. John, Wylly Folk
Vincent, William R.
   See Heitzmann, William Ray
Vinegar, Tom
   See Gregg, Andrew K.

Vinest, Shaw
   See Longyear, Barry B(rookes)
Vinge, Joan (Carol) D(ennison) 1948- 113
   Earlier sketch in SATA 36
Vining, Elizabeth Gray 1902-1999 6
   Obituary 117
Vinson, Kathryn 1911-1995 21
Vinton, Iris 1906(?)-1988 24
   Obituary 55
Viola, Herman J(oseph) 1938- 126
Viorst, Judith 1931- 172
   Earlier sketches in SATA 7, 70, 123
   See also CLR 90
Vip
   See Partch, Virgil Franklin II
Vipont, Charles
   See Foulds, Elfrida Vipont
Vipont, Elfrida
   See Foulds, Elfrida Vipont
Viramontes, Helena Maria 1954-
   See CLR 285
Viscott, David S(teven) 1938-1996 65
Visser, W(illem) F(rederik) H(endrik)
   1900-1968 10
Vitale, Stefano 1958- 180
   Earlier sketch in SATA 114
Vivas, Julie 1947- 96
Vivelo, Jackie 1943- 63
Vivelo, Jacqueline J.
   See Vivelo, Jackie
Vivelo, Jacqueline Jean
   See Vivelo, Jackie
Vivian, Siobhan 1979(?)- 215
Vizzini, Ned 1981- 179
   Earlier sketch in SATA 125
Vlahos, Olivia 1924- 31
Vlasic, Bob
   See Hirsch, Phil
Voake, Charlotte 180
   Earlier sketch in SATA 114
Voake, Steve 1961- 178
Vo-Dinh, Mai 1933- 16
Vogel, Carole Garbuny 1951- 105
   Earlier sketch in SATA 70
Vogel, Ilse-Margret 1918- 14
Vogel, John H., Jr. 1950- 18
Vogt, Esther Loewen 1915-1999 14
Vogt, Gregory L. 94
Vogt, Marie Bollinger 1921- 45
Vohwinkel, Astrid 1969- 207
Voight, Virginia Frances 1909-1989 8
Voigt, Cynthia 1942- 160
   Brief entry 33
   Earlier sketches in SATA 48, 79, 116
   See also CLR 141
Voigt, Erna 1925- 35
Voigt-Rother, Erna
   See Voigt, Erna
Vojtech, Anna 1946- 108
   Earlier sketch in SATA 42
Vollstadt, Elizabeth Weiss 1942- 121
Volponi, Paul 175
Volting, Dr. R.E.
   See Lerangis, Peter
Von Ahnen, Katherine 1922- 93
von Buhler, Cynthia 185
Vondra, J. Gert
   See Vondra, Josef
Vondra, Josef 1941- 121
Vondra, Josef Gert
   See Vondra, Josef
Von Gunden, Kenneth 1946- 113
Von Hagen, Victor Wolfgang 1908-1985 29
von Klopp, Vahrah
   See Malvern, Gladys
von Schmidt, Eric 1931-2007 50
   Brief entry 36
   Obituary 181
von Storch, Anne B. 1910- 1
von Trapp, Maria Augusta 1905-1987 16

von Wodtke, Charlotte Buel Johnson
   1918-1982 46
von Ziegesar, Cecily 1970- 161
Vos, Ida 1931-2006 121
   Earlier sketch in SATA 69
   See also CLR 85
Vosburgh, Leonard (W.) 1912- 15
Votaw, Carol 1961- 201
Voyle, Mary
   See Manning, Rosemary
Vrettos, Adrienne Maria 187
Vriens, Jacques 1946- 151
Vugteveen, Verna Aardema
   See Aardema, Verna
Vulture, Elizabeth T.
   See Gilbert, Suzie
Vuong, Lynette Dyer 1938- 110
   Earlier sketch in SATA 60

W

Waas, Uli
   See Waas-Pommer, Ulrike
Waas-Pommer, Ulrike 1949- 85
Waber, Bernard 1924- 155
   Brief entry 40
   Earlier sketches in SATA 47, 95
   See also CLR 55
Wachtel, Shirley Russak 1951- 88
Wachter, Oralee (Roberts) 1935- 61
   Brief entry 51
Waddell, Evelyn Margaret 1918- 10
Waddell, Martin 1941- 129
   Autobiography Feature 129
   Earlier sketches in SATA 43, 81, 127
   See also CLR 31
   See also SAAS 15
Waddy, Lawrence 1912-2010 91
Waddy, Lawrence Heber
   See Waddy, Lawrence
Wade, Mary Dodson 1930- 151
   Earlier sketch in SATA 79
Wade, Suzanne
   See Kirby, Susan E.
Wade, Theodore E., Jr. 1936- 37
Wademan, Peter John 1946- 122
Wademan, Spike
   See Wademan, Peter John
Wadsworth, Ginger 1945- 157
   Earlier sketch in SATA 103
Wagenheim, Kal 1935- 21
Wagner, Michele R. 1975- 157
Wagner, Sharon B. 1936- 4
Wagoner, David (Russell) 1926- 14
Wahl, Jan (Boyer) 1933- 132
   Earlier sketches in SATA 2, 34, 73
   See also SAAS 3
Wahl, Mats 1945- 186
Waide, Jan 1952- 29
Wainscott, John Milton 1910-1981 53
Wainwright, Richard M. 1935- 91
Wainwright, Ruth
   See Symes, Ruth Louise
Wait, Lea 1946- 137
Waite, Judy 174
Waite, Judy Bernard
   See Bernard, Patricia
Waite, Michael
   See Waite, Michael P.
Waite, Michael P. 1960- 101
Waite, P(eter) B(usby) 1922- 64
Waites, Joan C. 187
Waitley, Douglas 1927- 30
Wakefield, Jean L.
   See Laird, Jean E(louise)
Wakin, Daniel (Joseph) 1961- 84
Wakin, Edward 1927- 37
Wakiyama, Hanako 1966- 192

Walck, Henry Z. 1908(?)-1984
  Obituary 40
Walden, Amelia Elizabeth 3
Walden, Mark 188
Waldherr, Kris 1963- 76
Waldman, Bruce 1949- 15
Waldman, Neil 1947- 203
  Earlier sketches in SATA *51, 94, 142*
Waldrep, Richard 198
Waldron, Ann Wood 1924-2010 16
Waldron, Kathleen Cook 176
Wales, Dirk 1931- 205
Walgren, Judy 1963- 118
Walker, Addison
  See Walker, (Addison) Mort
Walker, Alice 1944- 31
Walker, Alice Malsenior
  See Walker, Alice
Walker, Barbara (Jeanne) K(erlin) 1921- 80
  Earlier sketch in SATA *4*
Walker, Barbara M(uhs) 1928- 57
Walker, (James) Braz(elton) 1934-1983 45
Walker, David 1965- 197
Walker, David G(ordon) 1926- 60
Walker, David Harry 1911-1992 8
  Obituary 71
Walker, Diana 1925- 9
Walker, Diane Marie Catherine
  See Walker, Kate
Walker, Dick
  See Pellowski, Michael (Joseph)
Walker, Frank 1931-2000 36
Walker, Holly Beth
  See Bond, Gladys Baker
Walker, Kate 1950- 165
  Earlier sketch in SATA *82*
Walker, Kathrine Sorley
  See Sorley Walker, Kathrine
Walker, Lou Ann 1952- 66
  Brief entry 53
Walker, Louise Jean 1891-1976
  Obituary 35
Walker, Mary Alexander 1927- 61
Walker, Mildred
  See Schemm, Mildred Walker
Walker, (Addison) Mort 1923- 8
Walker, Pamela 1948- 142
  Earlier sketch in SATA *24*
Walker, Paul Robert 1953- 154
Walker, Robert W. 1948- 66
Walker, Sally M(acArt) 1954- 135
Walker, Stephen J. 1951- 12
Walker-Blondell, Becky 1951- 89
Wallace, Barbara Brooks 1922- 136
  Earlier sketches in SATA *4, 78*
  See also CLR *150*
  See also SAAS *17*
Wallace, Beverly Dobrin 1921- 19
Wallace, Bill 1947- 169
  Brief entry 47
  Earlier sketches in SATA *53, 101*
Wallace, Daisy
  See Cuyler, Margery
Wallace, Ian 1950- 141
  Earlier sketches in SATA *53, 56*
  See also CLR *37*
Wallace, John 1966- 155
  Earlier sketch in SATA *105*
Wallace, John A(dam) 1915-2004 3
  Obituary 155
Wallace, Karen 1951- 188
  Earlier sketches in SATA *83, 139*
Wallace, Nancy Elizabeth 1948- 186
  Earlier sketch in SATA *141*
Wallace, Nigel
  See Hamilton, Charles (Harold St. John)
Wallace, Paula S. 153
Wallace, Rich 1957- 196
  Earlier sketches in SATA *117, 158*
Wallace, Robert 1932-1999 47
  Brief entry 37

Wallace, Ruby Ann 1923(?)- 77
Wallace, William Keith
  See Wallace, Bill
Wallace-Brodeur, Ruth 1941- 169
  Brief entry 41
  Earlier sketches in SATA *51, 88*
Wallenta, Adam 1974- 123
Waller, Leslie 1923-2007 20
Walley, Byron
  See Card, Orson Scott
Wallis, Diz 1949- 77
Wallis, G. McDonald
  See Campbell, Hope
Wallner, Alexandra 1946- 156
  Brief entry 41
  Earlier sketches in SATA *51, 98*
Wallner, John C. 1945- 133
  Earlier sketches in SATA *10, 51*
Wallower, Lucille 11
Walrod, Amy 1973(?)- 182
Walsh, Ann 1942- 176
  Earlier sketch in SATA *62*
Walsh, Ellen Stoll 1942- 194
  Earlier sketches in SATA *49, 99, 147*
Walsh, George Johnston 1889-1981 53
Walsh, Gillian Paton
  See Paton Walsh, Jill
Walsh, Jill Paton
  See Paton Walsh, Jill
Walsh, Joanna 1970- 182
Walsh, Lawrence 1942- 170
Walsh, Marissa 1972- 195
Walsh, Mary Caswell 1949- 118
Walsh, Mitzy
  See Walsh, Marissa
Walsh, Rebecca 217
Walsh, Suella 170
Walsh, V. L.
  See Walsh, Vivian
Walsh, Vivian 1960- 120
Walsh Shepherd, Donna 1948- 78
Walter, Frances V. 1923- 71
Walter, Mildred Pitts 1922- 133
  Brief entry 45
  Earlier sketch in SATA *69*
  See also CLR *61*
  See also SAAS *12*
Walter, Villiam Christian
  See Andersen, Hans Christian
Walter, Virginia
  See Walter, Virginia A.
Walter, Virginia A. 134
Walters, Audrey 1929- 18
Walters, Celeste 1938- 126
Walters, Eric 1957- 205
  Earlier sketches in SATA *99, 155*
Walters, Eric Robert
  See Walters, Eric
Walters, Gregory 1964- 213
Walters, Helen B. (?)-1987
  Obituary 50
Walters, Hugh
  See Hughes, Walter (Llewellyn)
Walther, Thomas A. 1950- 31
Walther, Tom
  See Walther, Thomas A.
Waltner, Elma 1912-1987 40
Waltner, Willard H. 1909- 40
Walton, Darwin McBeth 1926- 119
Walton, Fiona L. M. 1959- 89
Walton, Richard J. 1928- 4
Walton, Rick 1957- 204
  Earlier sketches in SATA *101, 151*
Waltrip, Lela (Kingston) 1904-1995 9
Waltrip, Mildred 1911- 37
Waltrip, Rufus (Charles) 1898-1988 9
Walworth, Nancy Zinsser 1917- 14
Wang, Gabrielle 212
Wang, Shaoli 216

Wangerin, Walter, Jr. 1944- 98
  Brief entry 37
  Earlier sketch in SATA *45*
Waniek, Marilyn Nelson 1946-
  See Nelson, Marilyn
Wannamaker, Bruce
  See Moncure, Jane Belk
Warbler, J. M.
  See Cocagnac, Augustin Maurice(-Jean)
Warburg, Sandol Stoddard
  See Stoddard, Sandol
Ward, David 1967- 213
Ward, E. D.
  See Gorey, Edward (St. John)
  and Lucas, E(dward) V(errall)
Ward, Ed
  See Stratemeyer, Edward L.
Ward, Helen 1962- 206
  Earlier sketches in SATA *72, 144*
Ward, Jay 1920-1989
  Obituary 63
Ward, Jennifer 1963- 146
Ward, John (Stanton) 1917- 42
Ward, Jonas
  See Ard, William
  and Cox, William R(obert)
  and Garfield, Brian (Francis Wynne)
Ward, Lynd (Kendall) 1905-1985 36
  Obituary 42
  Earlier sketch in SATA *2*
Ward, Martha (Eads) 5
Ward, Melanie
  See Curtis, Richard
  and Lynch, Marilyn
Ward, Nicholas John
  See Ward, Nick
Ward, Nick 1955- 190
Ward, Tom
  See Stratemeyer, Edward L.
Wardell, Dean
  See Prince, J(ack) H(arvey)
Wardlaw, Lee 1955- 115
  Earlier sketch in SATA *79*
Ware, Cheryl 1963- 101
Ware, Chris 1967- 140
Ware, Leon (Vernon) 1909-1976 4
Wargin, Kathy-jo 1964- 210
  Earlier sketch in SATA *145*
Warhola, James 1955- 187
Warner, Frank A. 67
  Earlier sketch in SATA *1*
Warner, Gertrude Chandler 1890-1979 9
  Obituary 73
Warner, J(ohn) F. 1929- 75
Warner, Lucille Schulberg 30
Warner, Matt
  See Fichter, George S.
Warner, Oliver (Martin Wilson) 1903-1976 . 29
Warner, Sally 1946- 214
  Earlier sketch in SATA *131*
Warner, Sunny (B.) 1931- 108
Warnes, Tim 1971- 216
  Earlier sketches in SATA *116, 166*
Warnes, Timothy
  See Warnes, Tim
Warnick, Elsa 1942- 113
Warren, Andrea 1946- 98
Warren, Betsy
  See Warren, Elizabeth Avery
Warren, Billy
  See Warren, William Stephen
Warren, Cathy 1951- 62
  Brief entry 46
Warren, Elizabeth
  See Supraner, Robyn
Warren, Elizabeth Avery 1916- 46
  Brief entry 38
Warren, Jackie M. 1953- 135
Warren, Joshua P(aul) 1976- 107
Warren, Joyce W(illiams) 1935- 18
Warren, Mary Phraner 1929- 10

Warren, Robert Penn 1905-1989 .... *46*
  Obituary *63*
Warren, Scott S. 1957- *79*
Warren, William Stephen 1882-1968 .... *9*
Warrick, Patricia Scott 1925- *35*
Warriner, John 1907(?)-1987
  Obituary *53*
Warsh
  See Warshaw, Jerry
Warshaw, Jerry 1929- *30*
Warshaw, Mary 1931- *89*
Warshofsky, Fred 1931- *24*
Warshofsky, Isaac
  See Singer, Isaac Bashevis
Wartski, Maureen (Ann Crane) 1940- *50*
  Brief entry *37*
Warwick, Alan R(oss) 1900-1973 .... *42*
Wa-Sha-Quon-Asin
  See Belaney, Archibald Stansfeld
Wa-sha-quon-asin
  See Belaney, Archibald Stansfeld
Washburn, Bradford 1910-2007 .... *38*
  Obituary *181*
Washburn, Henry Bradford, Jr.
  See Washburn, Bradford
Washburn, Jan(ice) 1926- *63*
Washburn, Lucia *193*
Washburne, Carolyn Kott 1944- *86*
Washburne, Heluiz Chandler 1892-1970 ...... *10*
  Obituary *26*
Washington, Booker T. 1856-1915 .... *28*
Washington, Donna L. 1967- *159*
  Earlier sketch in SATA *98*
Wasserman, Robin 1978- *207*
Wasserstein, Wendy 1950-2006 .... *94*
  Obituary *174*
Wassiljewa, Tatjana 1928- *106*
Watanabe, Shigeo 1928- *131*
  Brief entry *32*
  Earlier sketch in SATA *39*
  See also CLR *8*
Waters, John F(rederick) 1930- *4*
Waters, Summer
  See Sykes, Julie
Waters, Tony 1958- *75*
Waterton, Betty 1923- *99*
  Brief entry *34*
  Earlier sketch in SATA *37*
Waterton, Betty Marie
  See Waterton, Betty
Watkins, Dawn L. *126*
Watkins, Gloria Jean
  See hooks, bell
Watkins, Lis
  See Watkins, Liselotte
Watkins, Liselotte 1971- *215*
Watkins, Lois 1930- *88*
Watkins, Peter 1934- *66*
Watkins, Yoko Kawashima 1933- *93*
Watkins-Pitchford, Denys James
  1905-1990 .... *87*
  Obituary *66*
  Earlier sketch in SATA *6*
  See also SAAS *4*
Watling, James 1933- *117*
  Earlier sketch in SATA *67*
Watson, Aldren A(uld) 1917- *42*
  Brief entry *36*
Watson, Amy Zakrzewski 1965- *76*
Watson, B. S.
  See Teitelbaum, Michael
Watson, Carol 1949- *78*
Watson, C.G. *193*
Watson, Clyde 1947- *68*
  Earlier sketch in SATA *5*
  See also CLR *3*
Watson, Helen Orr 1892-1978
  Obituary *24*
Watson, James 1936- *106*
  Earlier sketch in SATA *10*

Watson, Jane Werner 1915- *54*
  Earlier sketch in SATA *3*
Watson, Jesse Joshua *199*
Watson, John H.
  See Farmer, Philip Jose
Watson, Mary 1953- *117*
Watson, N. Cameron 1955- *81*
Watson, Nancy Dingman *32*
Watson, Pauline 1925- *14*
Watson, Richard F.
  See Silverberg, Robert
Watson, Richard Jesse 1951- *211*
  Earlier sketch in SATA *62*
Watson, Sally (Lou) 1924- *3*
Watson, Sasha *211*
Watson, Wendy (McLeod) 1942- *142*
  Earlier sketches in SATA *5, 74*
Watson Taylor, Elizabeth 1915- *41*
Watt, Melanie 1975- *193*
  Earlier sketch in SATA *136*
Watt, Thomas 1935- *4*
Wattenberg, Jane *174*
Watterson, Bill 1958- *66*
Watt-Evans, Lawrence 1954- *121*
Watts, (Anna) Bernadette 1942- *103*
  Earlier sketch in SATA *4*
Watts, Ephraim
  See Horne, Richard Henry Hengist
Watts, Franklin (Mowry) 1904-1978 .... *46*
  Obituary *21*
Watts, Helen L. Hoke 1903-1990
  Obituary *65*
Watts, Irene N(aemi) 1931- *111*
  Earlier sketch in SATA *56*
Watts, Isaac 1674-1748 .... *52*
Watts, James K(ennedy) M(offitt) 1955- *59*
Watts, Jeri Hanel 1957- *170*
Watts, Julia 1969- *103*
Watts, Leander 1956- *146*
Watts, Leslie Elizabeth 1961- *168*
Watts, Mabel Pizzey 1906-1994 .... *11*
Watts, Nigel 1957-1999 .... *121*
Waugh, C. C. Roessel
  See Waugh, Carol-Lynn Rossel
  and Waugh, Charles G(ordon)
Waugh, Carol-Lynn Rossel 1947- *41*
Waugh, Dorothy -1996 .... *11*
Waugh, Sylvia 1935- *169*
Waugh, Virginia
  See Sorensen, Virginia
Wax, Wendy A. 1963- *163*
  Earlier sketch in SATA *73*
Wayland, April Halprin 1954- *143*
  Earlier sketch in SATA *78*
  See also SAAS *26*
Wayland, Patrick
  See O'Connor, Richard
Wayne, (Anne) Jenifer 1917-1982 .... *32*
Wayne, Kyra Petrovskaya 1918- *8*
Wayne, Richard
  See Decker, Duane
Wayshak, Deborah Noyes
  See Noyes, Deborah
Waystaff, Simon
  See Swift, Jonathan
Weales, Gerald (Clifford) 1925- *11*
Weary, Ogdred
  See Gorey, Edward (St. John)
Weatherford, Carole Boston 1956- *181*
  Earlier sketch in SATA *138*
Weatherill, Cat *203*
Weatherly, Lee 1967- *192*
Weatherly, Myra 1926- *130*
Weatherly, Myra S.
  See Weatherly, Myra
Weaver, Harriett E. 1908-1993 .... *65*
Weaver, John L. 1949- *42*
Weaver, Robyn
  See Conley, Robyn
Weaver, Robyn M.
  See Conley, Robyn

Weaver, Tess *197*
Weaver, Ward
  See Mason, F(rancis) van Wyck
Weaver, Will 1950- *217*
  Earlier sketches in SATA *88, 109, 161*
Weaver, William Weller
  See Weaver, Will
Weaver-Gelzer, Charlotte 1950- *79*
Webb, Christopher
  See Wibberley, Leonard
Webb, Jacqueline
  See Pearce, Margaret
Webb, Jacquelyn
  See Pearce, Margaret
  and Pearce, Margaret
Webb, Jean Francis (III) 1910-1991 .... *35*
Webb, Kaye 1914- *60*
Webb, Lois Sinaiko 1922- *82*
Webb, Margot 1934- *67*
Webb, Sharon 1936-2010 .... *41*
Webb, Sophie 1958- *135*
Webber, Andrew Lloyd
  See Lloyd Webber, Andrew
Webber, Desiree Morrison 1956- *170*
Webber, Irma E(leanor Schmidt)
  1904-1995 .... *14*
Weber, Alfons 1921- *8*
Weber, Bruce 1942- *120*
  Earlier sketch in SATA *73*
Weber, Debora 1955- *58*
Weber, EdNah New Rider 1919(?)- *168*
Weber, Jill 1950- *209*
  Earlier sketch in SATA *127*
Weber, Judith E(ichler) 1938- *64*
Weber, Ken(neth J.) 1940- *90*
Weber, Lenora Mattingly 1895-1971 .... *2*
  Obituary *26*
Weber, Lisa K. *217*
Weber, Michael 1945- *87*
Weber, Sandra 1961- *158*
Weber, William J(ohn) 1927- *14*
Webster, Alice Jane Chandler 1876-1916 ..... *17*
Webster, David 1930- *11*
Webster, Frank V. *67*
  Earlier sketch in SATA *1*
Webster, Gary
  See Garrison, Webb B(lack)
Webster, James 1925-1981 .... *17*
  Obituary *27*
Webster, Jean
  See Webster, Alice Jane Chandler
Wechsler, Doug *189*
Wechsler, Herman J. 1904-1976
  Obituary *20*
Wechter, Nell (Carolyn) Wise 1913-1989 .. *127*
  Earlier sketch in SATA *60*
Weck, Thomas L. 1942- *62*
Wedd, Kate
  See Gregory, Philippa
Weddle, Ethel Harshbarger 1897-1996 .... *11*
Wedekind, Annie *204*
Weeks, Sarah *194*
  Earlier sketch in SATA *158*
Weems, David B(urnola) 1922- *80*
Wees, Frances Shelley 1902-1982 .... *58*
Weevers, Peter 1944- *59*
Wegen, Ronald 1946-1985 .... *99*
Wegman, William (George) 1943- *135*
  Earlier sketches in SATA *78, 129*
Wegner, Fritz 1924- *20*
Weidhorn, Manfred 1931- *60*
Weidt, Maryann N. 1944- *85*
Weigel, Jeff 1958- *170*
Weigelt, Udo 1960- *201*
  Earlier sketch in SATA *168*
Weihs, Erika 1917- *107*
  Earlier sketch in SATA *15*
Weik, Mary Hays 1898(?)-1979 .... *3*
  Obituary *23*
Weil, Ann Yezner 1908-1969 .... *9*
Weil, Lisl 1910- *7*

Weilerstein, Sadie Rose 1894-1993 .... *3*
  Obituary *75*
Weill, Cynthia 1959- *167*
Wein, Elizabeth E. 1964- *151*
  Earlier sketch in SATA *82*
Wein, Elizabeth Eve
  See Wein, Elizabeth E.
Weinberg, Larry
  See Weinberg, Lawrence (E.)
Weinberg, Lawrence (E.) *92*
  Brief entry *48*
Weinberger, Tanya 1939- *84*
Weiner, Sandra 1922- *14*
Weingarten, Lynn *217*
Weingarten, Violet (Brown) 1915-1976 .... *3*
  Obituary *27*
Weingartner, Charles 1922- *5*
Weinheimer, Beckie 1958- *186*
Weinstein, Ellen Slusky 1959- *200*
Weinstein, Muriel Harris *215*
Weinstein, Nina 1951- *73*
Weinstock, Robert 1967- *204*
Weir, Bob 1947- *76*
Weir, Diana (R.) Loiewski 1958- *111*
Weir, Joan S(herman) 1928- *99*
Weir, LaVada *2*
Weir, Rosemary (Green) 1905-1994 .... *21*
Weir, Wendy 1949- *76*
Weis, Margaret 1948- *164*
  Earlier sketches in SATA *38, 92*
Weisberger, Bernard A(llen) 1922- *21*
Weisburd, Stefi 1957- *202*
Weiser, Marjorie P(hillis) K(atz) 1934- *33*
Weisgard, Leonard (Joseph) 1916-2000 .... *85*
  Obituary *122*
  Earlier sketches in SATA *2, 30*
  See also SAAS *19*
Weiss, Adelle 1920- *18*
Weiss, Ann E(dwards) 1943- *69*
  Earlier sketch in SATA *30*
  See also SAAS *13*
Weiss, Edna
  See Barth, Edna
Weiss, Ellen 1953- *44*
Weiss, Harvey 1922- *76*
  Earlier sketches in SATA *1, 27*
  See also CLR *4*
  See also SAAS *19*
Weiss, Jaqueline Shachter 1926- *65*
Weiss, Malcolm E. 1928- *3*
Weiss, Margaret Edith
  See Weis, Margaret
Weiss, Miriam
  See Schlein, Miriam
Weiss, Mitch 1951- *183*
  Earlier sketch in SATA *123*
Weiss, Nicki 1954- *86*
  Earlier sketch in SATA *33*
Weiss, Renee Karol 1923- *5*
Weissberger, Ela 1930- *181*
Weissberger, Ela Stein
  See Weissberger, Ela
Weissenborn, Hellmuth 1898-1982
  Obituary *31*
Weissman, Elissa Brent *217*
Weitzman, David L. 1936- *172*
  Earlier sketch in SATA *122*
Wekesser, Carol A. 1963- *76*
Welber, Robert *26*
Welch, Amanda (Jane) 1945- *75*
Welch, D'Alte Aldridge 1907-1970
  Obituary *27*
Welch, Holly *206*
Welch, Jean-Louise
  See Kempton, Jean Welch
Welch, Pauline
  See Bodenham, Hilda Morris
Welch, Ronald
  See Felton, Ronald Oliver
Welch, Sheila Kelly 1945- *130*
Welch, Willy 1952- *93*

Weldin, Frauke 1969- *188*
Welford, Sue 1942- *75*
Weller, George 1907-2002 .... *31*
  Obituary *140*
Weller, George Anthony
  See Weller, George
Welling, Peter J. 1947- *135*
Wellington, Monica 1957- *157*
  Earlier sketches in SATA *67, 99*
Wellman, Alice 1900-1984 .... *51*
  Brief entry *36*
Wellman, Manly Wade 1903-1986 .... *6*
  Obituary *47*
Wellman, Paul I. 1898-1966 .... *3*
Wellman, Paul Iselin
  See Wellman, Paul I.
Wellman, Sam 1939- *122*
Wellman, Samuel
  See Wellman, Sam
Wells, H. G. 1866-1946 .... *20*
  See also CLR *133*
Wells, Helen
  See Campbell, Hope
Wells, Helen 1910-1986 .... *49*
  Earlier sketch in SATA *2*
Wells, Herbert George
  See Wells, H. G.
Wells, J. Wellington
  See de Camp, L. Sprague
Wells, June
  See Swinford, Betty (June Wells)
Wells, Robert
  See Welsch, Roger L(ee)
Wells, Robert E. *184*
Wells, Rosemary 1943- *207*
  Earlier sketches in SATA *18, 69, 114, 156*
  See also CLR *69*
  See also SAAS *1*
Wells, Susan (Mary) 1951- *78*
Wels, Byron G(erald) 1924-1993 .... *9*
Welsbacher, Anne 1955- *89*
Welsch, Roger L(ee) 1936- *82*
Welsh, David
  See Hills, C.A.R.
Welsh, Mary Flynn 1910(?)-1984
  Obituary *38*
Welsh, T.K. 1956- *184*
Weltner, Linda R(iverly) 1938- *38*
Welton, Jude 1955- *143*
  Earlier sketch in SATA *79*
Welty, S. F.
  See Welty, Susan F.
Welty, Susan F. 1905- *9*
Wemmlinger, Raymond *190*
Wendelin, Rudolph 1910-2000 .... *23*
Weninger, Brigitte 1960- *189*
Wentworth, Robert
  See Hamilton, Edmond
Werlin, Nancy 1961- *161*
  Earlier sketches in SATA *87, 119*
Werner, Elsa Jane
  See Watson, Jane Werner
Werner, Herma 1926- *47*
  Brief entry *41*
Werner, Jane
  See Watson, Jane Werner
Werner, K.
  See Casewit, Curtis W(erner)
Wersba, Barbara 1932- *58*
  Autobiography Feature *103*
  Earlier sketch in SATA *1*
  See also CLR *78*
  See also SAAS *2*
Werstein, Irving 1914(?)-1971 .... *14*
Werth, Kurt 1896-1983 .... *20*
Wesley, Alison
  See Barnes, Michael
Wesley, Kathryn
  See Rusch, Kristine Kathryn
Wesley, Mary (Aline) 1912-2002 .... *66*

Wesley, Valerie Wilson 1947- *168*
  Earlier sketch in SATA *106*
West, Andrew
  See Arthur, Robert, (Jr.)
West, Anna 1938- *40*
West, Barbara
  See Price, Olive
West, Betty 1921- *11*
West, Bruce 1951- *63*
West, C. P.
  See Wodehouse, P. G.
West, Dorothy
  See Benson, Mildred
West, Emily Govan 1919- *38*
West, Emmy
  See West, Emily Govan
West, James
  See Withers, Carl A.
West, Jerry
  See Svenson, Andrew E(dward)
West, (Mary) Jessamyn 1902-1984
  Obituary *37*
West, John
  See Arthur, Robert, (Jr.)
West, Owen
  See Koontz, Dean
West, Ward
  See Borland, Harold Glen
Westall, Robert (Atkinson) 1929-1993 .... *69*
  Obituary *75*
  Earlier sketch in SATA *23*
  See also CLR *13*
  See also SAAS *2*
Westaway, Jane 1948- *121*
Westcott, Nadine Bernard 1949- *130*
Westera, Marleen 1962- *187*
Westerberg, Christine 1950- *29*
Westerduin, Anne 1945- *105*
Westerfeld, Scott 1963- *161*
Westervelt, Virginia Veeder 1914-2005 .... *10*
Westheimer, David 1917-2005 .... *14*
  Obituary *170*
Westheimer, David Kaplan
  See Westheimer, David
Westmacott, Mary
  See Christie, Agatha
Westman, Barbara *70*
Westman, Paul (Wendell) 1956- *39*
Westmoreland, William C. 1914-2005 .... *63*
Westmoreland, William Childs
  See Westmoreland, William C.
Weston, Allen
  See Hogarth, Grace (Weston Allen)
  and Norton, Andre
Weston, Carol 1956- *135*
Weston, Carrie *190*
Weston, John (Harrison) 1932- *21*
Weston, Martha 1947- *119*
  Earlier sketch in SATA *53*
Weston, Robert Paul *209*
Westphal, Arnold Carl 1897- *57*
Westrup, Hugh *102*
Westwood, Jennifer 1940-2008 .... *10*
  Obituary *192*
Wexler, Jerome (LeRoy) 1923- *14*
Weyland, Jack 1940- *81*
Weyn, Suzanne 1955- *164*
  Earlier sketches in SATA *63, 101*
Weyr, Garret
  See Freymann-Weyr, (Rhoda) Garret (Michaela)
Wezyk, Joanna 1966- *82*
Whaley, Joyce Irene 1923- *61*
Whalin, W. Terry 1953- *93*
Wharf, Michael
  See Weller, George
Wharmby, Margot *63*
Wharton, Edith 1862-1937
  See CLR *136*
Wharton, Edith Newbold Jones
  See Wharton, Edith

Whatley, Bruce 1954- *213*
  Earlier sketch in SATA *177*
Wheatley, Arabelle 1921- *16*
Wheatley, Nadia 1949- *147*
Wheeler, Cindy 1955- *49*
  Brief entry *40*
Wheeler, Deborah 1947- *83*
Wheeler, Janet D. *1*
Wheeler, Jill C. 1964- *136*
  Earlier sketch in SATA *86*
Wheeler, Jody 1952- *148*
  Earlier sketch in SATA *84*
Wheeler, Lisa 1963- *200*
  Earlier sketch in SATA *162*
Wheeler, Opal 1898- *23*
Whelan, Elizabeth M(urphy) 1943- *14*
Whelan, Gloria 1923- *178*
  Earlier sketches in SATA *85, 128*
  See also CLR *90*
Whelan, Gloria Ann
  See Whelan, Gloria
Whipple, A(ddison) B(eecher) C(olvin)
  1918- *64*
Whipple, Cal
  See Whipple, A(ddison) B(eecher) C(olvin)
Whisp, Kennilworthy
  See Rowling, J.K.
Whistler, Reginald John 1905-1944 .... *30*
Whistler, Rex
  See Whistler, Reginald John
Whitaker, Zai *183*
Whitcher, Susan (Godsil) 1952- *96*
Whitcomb, Jon 1906-1988 .... *10*
  Obituary *56*
Whitcomb, Laura 1958- *214*
  Earlier sketch in SATA *171*
White, Anne Terry 1896-1980 .... *2*
White, Bessie (Felstiner) 1892(?)-1986
  Obituary *50*
White, Carolyn 1948- *130*
White, Dale
  See Place, Marian T(empleton)
White, Dori 1919- *10*
White, E. B. 1899-1985 .... *100*
  Obituary *44*
  Earlier sketches in SATA *2, 29*
  See also CLR *107*
White, Eliza Orne 1856-1947
  See YABC *2*
White, Elwyn Brooks
  See White, E. B.
White, Florence M(eiman) 1910- *14*
White, Laurence B(arton), Jr. 1935- *10*
White, Lee *176*
White, Martin 1943- *51*
White, Nancy 1942- *126*
White, Ramy Allison *67*
  Earlier sketch in SATA *1*
White, Robb 1909-1990 .... *83*
  Earlier sketch in SATA *1*
  See also CLR *3*
  See also SAAS *1*
White, Ruth 1942- *186*
  Autobiography Feature *186*
  Earlier sketches in SATA *39, 117, 165*
White, Ruth C.
  See White, Ruth
White, T(erence) H(anbury) 1906-1964 .... *12*
  See also CLR *139*
White, Tekla N. 1934- *115*
White, Timothy (Thomas Anthony)
  1952-2002 .... *60*
White, Tom 1923- *148*
White, William, Jr. 1934- *16*
Whitehead, Don(ald) F. 1908-1981 .... *4*
Whitehead, Jenny 1964- *191*
Whitehead, Kathy 1957- *176*
Whitehouse, Arch
  See Whitehouse, Arthur George Joseph

Whitehouse, Arthur George Joseph
  1895-1979 .... *14*
  Obituary *23*
Whitehouse, Elizabeth S(cott) 1893-1968 .... *35*
Whitehouse, Jeanne
  See Peterson, Jeanne Whitehouse
Whitelaw, Nancy 1933- *166*
  Earlier sketch in SATA *76*
Whitesel, Cheryl Aylward *162*
Whiting, Sue 1960- *205*
Whiting, Susan Allana
  See Whiting, Sue
Whitinger, R. D.
  See Place, Marian T(empleton)
Whitley, Mary Ann
  See Sebrey, Mary Ann
Whitley, Peggy 1938- *140*
Whitlock, Pamela 1921(?)-1982
  Obituary *31*
Whitlock, Ralph 1914-1995 .... *35*
Whitman, Alice
  See Marker, Sherry
Whitman, Candace 1958- *208*
Whitman, Sylvia (Choate) 1961- *135*
  Earlier sketch in SATA *85*
Whitman, Walt 1819-1892 .... *20*
Whitman, Walter
  See Whitman, Walt
Whitmore, Arvella 1922- *125*
Whitmore, Benette 1955- *203*
Whitney, Alex(andra) 1922- *14*
Whitney, David C(harles) 1921- *48*
  Brief entry *29*
Whitney, Kim Ablon *162*
Whitney, Phyllis A. 1903-2008 .... *30*
  Obituary *189*
  Earlier sketch in SATA *1*
  See also CLR *59*
Whitney, Phyllis Ayame
  See Whitney, Phyllis A.
Whitney, Sharon 1937- *63*
Whitney, Thomas P. 1917-2007 .... *25*
  Obituary *189*
Whitney, Thomas Porter
  See Whitney, Thomas P.
Whittington, Mary K(athrine) 1941- *75*
Whitworth, John 1945- *123*
Whybrow, Ian *202*
  Earlier sketch in SATA *132*
Whyte, Mal(colm Kenneth, Jr.) 1933- *62*
Whyte, Mary 1953- *148*
  Earlier sketch in SATA *94*
Whyte, Ron 1942(?)-1989
  Obituary *63*
Whytock, Cherry *177*
Wiater, Stanley 1953- *84*
Wibbelsman, Charles J(oseph) 1945- *59*
Wibberley, Leonard 1915-1983 .... *45*
  Obituary *36*
  Earlier sketch in SATA *2*
  See also CLR *3*
Wibberley, Leonard Patrick O'Connor
  See Wibberley, Leonard
Wiberg, Harald (Albin) 1908- *93*
  Brief entry *40*
Wick, Walter 1953- *148*
Wickberg, Susan
  See Rottman, S.L.
Wickens, Elaine *86*
Wicker, Ireene 1905(?)-1987
  Obituary *55*
Wickstrom, Sylvie 1960- *169*
Wickstrom, Thor 1960- *200*
Widdemer, Mabel Cleland 1902-1964 .... *5*
Widener, Terry 1950- *209*
  Earlier sketch in SATA *105*
Widerberg, Siv 1931- *10*
Wiebe, Rudy 1934- *156*
Wiebe, Rudy Henry
  See Wiebe, Rudy
Wieler, Diana (Jean) 1961- *109*

Wiener, Lori 1956- *84*
Wier, Ester (Alberti) 1910-2000 .... *3*
Wiese, Kurt 1887-1974 .... *36*
  Obituary *24*
  Earlier sketch in SATA *3*
  See also CLR *86*
Wiesel, Elie 1928- *56*
Wiesel, Eliezer
  See Wiesel, Elie
Wiesner, David 1956- *181*
  Earlier sketches in SATA *72, 117, 139*
  See also CLR *84*
Wiesner, Portia
  See Takakjian, Portia
Wiesner, William 1899-1984 .... *5*
Wiggers, Raymond 1952- *82*
Wiggin, Eric E. 1939- *167*
  Earlier sketch in SATA *88*
Wiggin, Eric Ellsworth 1939-
  See Wiggin, Eric E.
Wiggin (Riggs), Kate Douglas (Smith)
  1856-1923
  See YABC *1*
  See also CLR *52*
Wiggins, VeraLee (Chesnut) 1928-1995 .... *89*
Wight, James Alfred
  See Herriot, James
Wignell, Edel 1936- *69*
Wijnberg, Ellen *85*
Wikland, Ilon 1930- *93*
  Brief entry *32*
Wikler, Madeline 1943- *114*
Wilber, Donald N(ewton) 1907-1997 .... *35*
Wilbur, C. Keith 1923- *27*
Wilbur, Frances 1921- *107*
Wilbur, Helen L. 1948- *204*
Wilbur, Richard 1921- *108*
  Earlier sketch in SATA *9*
Wilbur, Richard Purdy
  See Wilbur, Richard
Wilburn, Kathy 1948- *68*
Wilcox, Charlotte 1948- *72*
Wilcox, Leah 1975(?)- *207*
Wilcox, R(uth) Turner 1888-1970 .... *36*
Wilcox, Roger
  See Collins, Paul
Wild, Jocelyn 1941- *46*
Wild, Kate 1954- *192*
Wild, Margaret 1948- *197*
  Earlier sketch in SATA *151*
Wild, Robin (Evans) 1936- *46*
Wild, Robyn 1947- *117*
Wilde, D. Gunther
  See Hurwood, Bernhardt J.
Wilde, Oscar 1854(?)-1900 .... *24*
  See also CLR *114*
Wilde, Oscar Fingal O'Flahertie Willis
  See Wilde, Oscar
Wilder, Buck
  See Smith, Tim(othy R.)
Wilder, Laura Elizabeth Ingalls
  See Wilder, Laura Ingalls
Wilder, Laura Ingalls 1867-1957 .... *100*
  Earlier sketches in SATA *15, 29*
  See also CLR *111*
Wildsmith, Brian 1930- *124*
  Earlier sketches in SATA *16, 69*
  See also CLR *52*
  See also SAAS *5*
Wiles, Deborah *171*
Wilhelm, Doug 1952- *190*
Wilhelm, Hans 1945- *196*
  Autobiography Feature *196*
  Earlier sketches in SATA *58, 135*
  See also CLR *46*
  See also SAAS *21*
Wilkie, Katharine E(lliott) 1904-1980 .... *31*
Wilkin, Eloise 1904-1987 .... *49*
  Obituary *54*
Wilkins, Frances 1923- *14*
Wilkins, Kim *147*

Wilkins, Marilyn (Ruth) 1926- *30*
Wilkins, Marne
  See Wilkins, Marilyn (Ruth)
Wilkins, Mary Huiskamp 1926- *2*
  See also CLR *42*
Wilkins, Mary Huiskamp Calhoun
  See Wilkins, Mary Huiskamp
Wilkins, Rose *180*
Wilkinson, (Thomas) Barry 1923- *50*
  Brief entry *32*
Wilkinson, Beth 1925- *80*
Wilkinson, Brenda 1946- *91*
  Earlier sketch in SATA *14*
  See also CLR *20*
Wilkinson, (John) Burke 1913-2000 .... *4*
Wilkinson, Carole 1950- *210*
Wilkinson, Sylvia 1940- *56*
  Brief entry *39*
Wilkon, Jozef 1930- *133*
  Earlier sketches in SATA *31, 71*
Wilkowski, Sue *193*
Wilks, Michael Thomas 1947- *44*
Wilks, Mike
  See Wilks, Michael Thomas
Will
  See Lipkind, William
Willard, Barbara (Mary) 1909-1994 .... *74*
  Earlier sketch in SATA *17*
  See also CLR *2*
  See also SAAS *5*
Willard, Elizabeth Kimmel
  See Kimmel, Elizabeth Cody
Willard, Mildred Wilds 1911-1978 .... *14*
Willard, Nancy 1936- *191*
  Brief entry *30*
  Earlier sketches in SATA *37, 71, 127*
  See also CLR *5*
Willcox, Isobel 1907-1996 .... *42*
Willems, Mo *180*
  Earlier sketch in SATA *154*
  See also CLR *114*
Willett, Edward 1959- *115*
Willett, Edward C.
  See Willett, Edward
Willey, Bee *184*
Willey, Margaret 1950- *86*
Willey, Robert
  See Ley, Willy
Willhoite, Michael A. 1946- *71*
William, Kate
  See Armstrong, Jennifer
Williams, Alex 1969- *209*
Williams, Arlene *171*
Williams, Barbara 1925- *107*
  Earlier sketch in SATA *11*
  See also CLR *48*
  See also SAAS *16*
Williams, Barbara 1937- *62*
Williams, Beryl
  See Epstein, Beryl
Williams, Brian (Peter) 1943- *54*
Williams, Carol Lynch 1959- *212*
  Earlier sketch in SATA *110*
Williams, Charles
  See Collier, James Lincoln
Williams, Clyde C. 1881-1974 .... *8*
  Obituary *27*
Williams, Coe
  See Harrison, C(hester) William
Williams, Colleen Madonna Flood 1963- .. *156*
Williams, Cynthia G. 1958- *123*
Williams, Dar 1967- *168*
Williams, Donna Reilly 1945- *83*
Williams, Dorothy
  See Williams, Marcia
Williams, Dorothy Snowden
  See Williams, Dar
Williams, Eric (Ernest) 1911-1983 .... *14*
  Obituary *38*
Williams, Ferelith Eccles
  See Eccles Williams, Ferelith

Williams, Frances B.
  See Browin, Frances Williams
Williams, Garth (Montgomery) 1912-1996 .. *66*
  Obituary *90*
  Earlier sketch in SATA *18*
  See also CLR *57*
  See also SAAS *7*
Williams, Guy R(ichard) 1920- *11*
Williams, Hawley
  See Heyliger, William
Williams, Helen 1948- *77*
Williams, J. R.
  See Williams, Jeanne
Williams, J. Walker
  See Wodehouse, P. G.
Williams, Jay 1914-1978 .... *41*
  Obituary *24*
  Earlier sketch in SATA *3*
  See also CLR *8*
Williams, Jeanne 1930- *5*
Williams, Jenny 1939- *60*
Williams, Karen Lynn 1952- *99*
  Earlier sketch in SATA *66*
Williams, Kit 1946(?)- *44*
  See also CLR *4*
Williams, L. E.
  See Williams, Laura E.
Williams, Laura E.
  See Williams, Laura Ellen
Williams, Laura Ellen *180*
Williams, Leslie 1941- *42*
Williams, Linda 1948- *59*
Williams, Louise Bonino 1904(?)-1984
  Obituary *39*
Williams, Lynn
  See Hale, Arlene
Williams, Marcia 1945- *159*
  Earlier sketches in SATA *71, 97*
Williams, Marcia Dorothy
  See Williams, Marcia
Williams, Margery
  See Bianco, Margery Williams
Williams, Mark
  See Arthur, Robert, (Jr.)
Williams, Mark London 1959- *140*
Williams, Maureen 1951- *12*
Williams, Michael
  See St. John, Wylly Folk
Williams, Patrick J.
  See Griffin, W.E.B.
Williams, Paulette Linda
  See Shange, Ntozake
Williams, Pete
  See Faulknor, Cliff(ord Vernon)
Williams, S. P.
  See Hart, Virginia
Williams, Sam *177*
  Earlier sketch in SATA *124*
Williams, Selma R(uth) 1925- *14*
Williams, Sherley Anne 1944-1999 .... *78*
  Obituary *116*
Williams, Sheron 1955- *77*
Williams, Shirley
  See Williams, Sherley Anne
Williams, Slim
  See Williams, Clyde C.
Williams, Sophy 1965- *135*
Williams, Sue 1948-2007 .... *208*
Williams, Susan
  See Beckhorn, Susan Williams
Williams, Suzanne
  See Williams, Suzanne Morgan
Williams, Suzanne 1953- *202*
  Earlier sketch in SATA *71*
Williams, Suzanne M.
  See Williams, Suzanne Morgan
Williams, Suzanne Morgan 1949- *207*
Williams, Ursula Moray
  See Moray Williams, Ursula

Williams, Vera B(aker) 1927- *102*
  Brief entry *33*
  Earlier sketch in SATA *53*
  See also CLR *9*
Williams-Andriani, Renee 1963- *98*
Williams-Ellis, (Mary) Amabel (Nassau
  Strachey) 1894-1984 .... *29*
  Obituary *41*
Williams-Garcia, Rita 1957- *160*
  Earlier sketch in SATA *98*
  See also CLR *36*
Williamson, Gwyneth 1965- *109*
Williamson, Henry (William) 1895-1977 ..... *37*
  Obituary *30*
Williamson, Joanne S(mall) 1926- *122*
  Earlier sketch in SATA *3*
Williamson, Kate T. 1979- *215*
Williamson, Melanie *196*
Willis, Charles
  See Clarke, Arthur C.
Willis, Connie 1945- *110*
  See also CLR *66*
Willis, Cynthia Chapman *215*
Willis, Jeanne 1959- *195*
  Earlier sketches in SATA *61, 123*
Willis, Jeanne Mary
  See Willis, Jeanne
Willis, Meredith Sue 1946- *101*
Willis, Nancy Carol 1952- *139*
  Earlier sketch in SATA *93*
Willis, Paul J. 1955- *113*
Willms, Russ *95*
Willoughby, Lee Davis
  See Avallone, Michael (Angelo, Jr.)
  and Brandner, Gary (Phil)
  and Deming, Richard
  and DeAndrea, William L(ouis)
  and Laymon, Richard (Carl)
  and Streib, Dan(iel Thomas)
  and Toombs, John
  and Webb, Jean Francis (III)
Willson, Robina Beckles
  See Beckles Willson, Robina
Wilma, Dana
  See Faralla, Dana
Wilsdorf, Anne 1954- *191*
Wilson, April *80*
Wilson, Barbara Ker
  See Ker Wilson, Barbara
Wilson, Beth P(ierre) *8*
Wilson, Budge 1927- *55*
  Brief entry *51*
Wilson, Carletta 1951- *81*
Wilson, Carter 1941- *6*
Wilson, Charles Morrow 1905-1977 .... *30*
Wilson, Christopher B. 1910(?)-1985
  Obituary *46*
Wilson, Darryl B(abe) 1939- *90*
Wilson, Diane Lee *172*
Wilson, Dirk
  See Pohl, Frederik
Wilson, Dorothy Clarke 1904-2003 .... *16*
Wilson, Edward A(rthur) 1886-1970 .... *38*
Wilson, Ellen (Janet Cameron) (?)-1976 .... *9*
  Obituary *26*
Wilson, Eric (H.) 1940- *34*
  Brief entry *32*
Wilson, Erica *51*
Wilson, Forrest 1918- *27*
Wilson, Gahan 1930- *35*
  Brief entry *27*
Wilson, Gina 1943- *85*
  Brief entry *34*
  Earlier sketch in SATA *36*
Wilson, (Leslie) Granville 1912- *14*
Wilson, Hazel (Hutchins) 1898-1992 .... *3*
  Obituary *73*
Wilson, J(erry) M. 1964- *121*
Wilson, Jacqueline 1945- *199*
  Brief entry *52*
  Earlier sketches in SATA *61, 102, 153*

Wilson, John 1922- 22
Wilson, John 1951- 182
Wilson, John Alexander
  See Wilson, John
Wilson, Johnniece Marshall 1944- 75
Wilson, Jonathan 1950- 181
Wilson, Joyce M. 84
  Earlier sketch in SATA 21
  See also SAAS 24
Wilson, Karma 174
Wilson, Leslie 1952- 166
Wilson, Linda Miller 1936- 116
Wilson, Lionel 1924-2003 33
  Brief entry 31
  Obituary 144
Wilson, Marjorie
  See Wilson, Budge
Wilson, Martin 1973- 205
Wilson, Maurice (Charles John) 1914- 46
Wilson, Nancy Hope 1947- 138
  Earlier sketch in SATA 81
Wilson, Nathan D.
  See Wilson, N.D.
Wilson, N.D. 1978- 194
Wilson, Nick
  See Ellis, Edward S.
Wilson, Phil 1948- 181
Wilson, Ron(ald William) 1941- 38
Wilson, Sarah 1934- 208
  Earlier sketches in SATA 50, 142
Wilson, Tom 1931- 33
  Brief entry 30
Wilson, Troy 1970- 169
Wilson, Walt(er N.) 1939- 14
Wilson-Max, Ken 1965- 170
  Earlier sketch in SATA 93
Wilton, Elizabeth 1937- 14
Wilton, Hal
  See Pepper, Frank S.
Wilwerding, Walter Joseph 1891-1966 9
Wimmer, Mike 1961- 194
  Earlier sketch in SATA 70
Winborn, Marsha (Lynn) 1947- 75
Winch, John 1944- 165
  Earlier sketch in SATA 117
Winchester, James H(ugh) 1917-1985 30
  Obituary 45
Winchester, Stanley
  See Youd, Samuel
Windawi, Thura al- 1983(?)- 165
Winders, Gertrude Hecker -1987 3
Windham, Basil
  See Wodehouse, P. G.
Windham, Kathryn T(ucker) 1918- 14
Windham, Sophie 184
Windling, Terri 1958- 151
Windrow, Martin
  See Windrow, Martin Clive
Windrow, Martin C.
  See Windrow, Martin Clive
Windrow, Martin Clive 1944- 68
Windsor, Claire
  See Hamerstrom, Frances
Windsor, Linda 1950- 124
Windsor, Patricia 1938- 78
  Earlier sketch in SATA 30
  See also SAAS 19
Wineman-Marcus, Irene 1952- 81
Winer, Yvonne 1934- 120
Winerip, Michael 175
Winfield, Arthur M.
  See Stratemeyer, Edward L.
Winfield, Edna
  See Stratemeyer, Edward L.
Winfield, Julia
  See Armstrong, Jennifer
Wing, Natasha 1960- 200
  Earlier sketch in SATA 82
Wingerter, Linda S. 1973(?)- 207
Winget, Susan 211
Winick, Judd 1970- 124

Winks, Robin William 1930-2003 61
Winn, Alison
  See Wharmby, Margot
Winn, Chris 1952- 42
Winn, Janet Bruce 1928- 43
Winn, Marie 1936(?)- 38
Winnick, Karen B. 1946- 211
Winnick, Karen B(eth) B(inkoff) 1946- 51
Winn-Lederer, Ilene 198
Winslow, Barbara 1947- 91
Winstead, Rosie 180
Winston, Clara 1921-1983 54
  Obituary 39
Winston, Richard 1917-1979 54
Winston, Sherri 1964(?)- 201
Winter, Janet 1926- 126
Winter, Jeanette 1939- 184
  Earlier sketch in SATA 151
Winter, Jonah 1962- 179
Winter, Milo (Kendall) 1888-1956 21
Winter, Paula Cecelia 1929- 48
Winter, R. R.
  See Winterbotham, R(ussell) R(obert)
Winter, Susan 182
Winterbotham, R(ussell) R(obert)
  1904-1971 10
Winterbotham, Russ
  See Winterbotham, R(ussell) R(obert)
Winterfeld, Henry 1901-1990 55
Winters, J. C.
  See Cross, Gilbert B.
Winters, Jon
  See Cross, Gilbert B.
Winters, Katherine
  See Winters, Kay
Winters, Kay 1936- 153
  Earlier sketch in SATA 103
Winters, Nina 1944- 62
Winters, Paul A. 1965- 106
Winterson, Jeanette 1959- 190
Winterton, Gayle
  See Adams, William Taylor
Winthrop, Elizabeth 1948- 164
  Autobiography Feature 116
  Earlier sketches in SATA 8, 76
  See also CLR 89
Winton, Ian (Kenneth) 1960- 76
Winton, Tim 1960- 98
Wintz-Litty, Julie
  See Litty, Julie
Wirt, Ann
  See Benson, Mildred
Wirt, Mildred A.
  See Benson, Mildred
Wirtenberg, Patricia Z. 1932-2007 10
Wirtenberg, Patricia Zarrella
  See Wirtenberg, Patricia Z.
Wirth, Beverly 1938- 63
Wirths, Claudine (Turner) G(ibson)
  1926-2000 104
  Earlier sketch in SATA 64
Wise, Bill 1958- 191
Wise, Lenny
  See Wise, Leonard
Wise, Leonard 1940- 167
Wise, Leonard A.
  See Wise, Leonard
Wise, Leonard Allan
  See Wise, Leonard
Wise, William 1923- 163
  Earlier sketch in SATA 4
Wise, Winifred E. 2
Wiseman, Ann (Sayre) 1926- 31
Wiseman, B(ernard) 1922-1995 4
Wiseman, David 1916- 43
  Brief entry 40
Wiseman, Eva 1947- 210
Wishinsky, Frieda 1948- 166
  Earlier sketches in SATA 70, 112

Wisler, G(ary) Clifton 1950- 103
  Brief entry 46
  Earlier sketch in SATA 58
Wismer, Donald (Richard) 1946- 59
Wisner, Bill
  See Wisner, William L.
Wisner, William L. 1914(?)-1983 42
Wisnewski, David 1953-2002
  See Wisniewski, David
Wisniewski, David 1953-2002 95
  Obituary 139
  See also CLR 51
Wister, Owen 1860-1938 62
Witham, (Phillip) Ross 1917- 37
Withers, Carl A. 1900-1970 14
Withers, Pam 1956- 182
Withrow, Sarah 1966- 199
  Earlier sketch in SATA 124
Witt, Dick 1948- 80
Witt, Shirley Hill 1934- 17
Wittanen, Etolin 1907- 55
Wittels, Harriet Joan 1938- 31
Wittig, Susan
  See Albert, Susan Wittig
Wittlinger, Ellen 1948- 189
  Autobiography Feature 128
  Earlier sketches in SATA 83, 122
Wittman, Sally (Anne Christensen) 1941- 30
Witty, Paul 1898-1976 50
  Obituary 30
Wodehouse, P. G. 1881-1975 22
Wodehouse, Pelham Grenville
  See Wodehouse, P. G.
Wodge, Dreary
  See Gorey, Edward (St. John)
Woelfle, Gretchen 1945- 145
Wohlberg, Meg 1905-1990 41
  Obituary 66
Wohlrabe, Raymond A. 1900-1977 4
Wohnoutka, Mike 195
Wojciechowska, Maia (Teresa) 1927-2002 ... 83
  Autobiography Feature 104
  Obituary 134
  Earlier sketches in SATA 1, 28
  See also CLR 1
  See also SAAS 1
Wojciechowski, Susan 126
  Earlier sketch in SATA 78
Wojnarowski, Adrian 1970- 190
Wojtusik, Elizabeth 208
Wolcott, Patty 1929- 14
Wold, Allen L. 1943- 64
Wold, Jo Anne 1938- 30
Woldin, Beth Weiner 1955- 34
Wolf, Allan 1963- 192
Wolf, Bernard 1930- 102
  Brief entry 37
Wolf, Erica (Van Varick) 1978- 156
Wolf, Gita 1956- 101
Wolf, J. M.
  See Wolf, Joan M.
Wolf, Janet 1957- 78
Wolf, Joan M. 1966- 193
Wolf, Sallie 1950- 205
  Earlier sketch in SATA 80
Wolfe, Art 1952- 76
Wolfe, Burton H. 1932- 5
Wolfe, Frances 216
Wolfe, Gene 1931- 165
  Earlier sketch in SATA 118
Wolfe, Gene Rodman
  See Wolfe, Gene
Wolfe, Gillian 199
Wolfe, Louis 1905-1985 8
  Obituary 133
Wolfe, Rinna (Evelyn) 1925- 38
Wolfenden, George
  See Beardmore, George
Wolfer, Dianne 1961- 167
  Autobiography Feature 117
  Earlier sketch in SATA 104

Wolff, Alexander (Nikolaus) 1957- *137*
　Earlier sketch in SATA *63*
Wolff, Ashley 1956- *203*
　Earlier sketches in SATA *50, 81, 155*
Wolff, Diane 1945- *27*
Wolff, Ferida 1946- *164*
　Earlier sketch in SATA *79*
Wolff, Jason 1972- *213*
Wolff, Jennifer Ashley
　See Wolff, Ashley
Wolff, Nancy *202*
Wolff, Robert Jay 1905-1977 .... *10*
Wolff, Sonia
　See Levitin, Sonia
Wolff, Virginia Euwer 1937- *137*
　Earlier sketch in SATA *78*
　See also CLR *62*
Wolfman, Judy 1933- *138*
Wolfson, Evelyn 1937- *62*
Wolitzer, Hilma 1930- *31*
Wolkoff, Judie (Edwards) *93*
　Brief entry *37*
Wolkstein, Diane 1942- *138*
　Earlier sketches in SATA *7, 82*
Wollheim, Donald A(llen) 1914-1990
　Obituary *69*
Wolny, P.
　See Janeczko, Paul B(ryan)
Wolters, Richard A. 1920-1993 .... *35*
Wondriska, William 1931- *6*
Wong, Jade Snow 1922-2006 .... *112*
　Obituary *175*
Wong, Janet S. 1962- *210*
　Earlier sketches in SATA *98, 148*
　See also CLR *94*
Wong, Nicole *214*
Woo, Howie 1974- *207*
Wood, Addie Robinson
　See Wiggin, Eric E.
Wood, Anne (Savage) 1937- *64*
Wood, Audrey *198*
　Brief entry *44*
　Earlier sketches in SATA *50, 81, 139*
　See also CLR *26*
Wood, Catherine
　See Etchison, Birdie L(ee)
Wood, David 1944- *212*
　Earlier sketch in SATA *87*
Wood, Don 1945- *50*
　Brief entry *44*
　See also CLR *26*
Wood, Douglas 1951- *180*
　Earlier sketches in SATA *81, 132*
Wood, Douglas Eric
　See Wood, Douglas
Wood, Edgar A(llardyce) 1907-1998 .... *14*
Wood, Esther
　See Brady, Esther Wood
Wood, Frances Elizabeth *34*
Wood, Frances M. 1951- *97*
Wood, Jacqueline
　See Wood, Jakki
Wood, Jakki 1957- *211*
Wood, James Playsted 1905- *1*
Wood, Jenny 1955- *88*
Wood, John Norris 1930- *85*
Wood, June Rae 1946- *120*
　Earlier sketch in SATA *79*
　See also CLR *82*
Wood, Kerry
　See Wood, Edgar A(llardyce)
Wood, Kim Marie *134*
Wood, Laura N.
　See Roper, Laura (Newbold) Wood
Wood, Linda C(arol) 1945- *59*
Wood, Marcia 1956- *80*
Wood, Marcia Mae
　See Wood, Marcia
Wood, Nancy
　See Wood, Nancy C.

Wood, Nancy C. 1936- *178*
　Earlier sketch in SATA *6*
Wood, Nuria
　See Nobisso, Josephine
Wood, Owen 1929- *64*
Wood, Phyllis Anderson 1923- *33*
　Brief entry *30*
Wood, Richard 1949- *110*
Wood, Tim(othy William Russell) 1946- *88*
Wood, Wallace 1927-1981
　Obituary *33*
Woodard, Carol 1929- *14*
Woodburn, John Henry 1914- *11*
Woodbury, David Oakes 1896-1981 .... *62*
Woodford, Peggy 1937- *25*
Woodhouse, Barbara (Blackburn)
　1910-1988 .... *63*
Woodhull, Ann Love *194*
Wooding, Chris 1977- *166*
Wooding, Sharon
　See Wooding, Sharon L(ouise)
Wooding, Sharon L(ouise) 1943- *66*
Woodman, Allen 1954- *76*
Woodrich, Mary Neville 1915- *2*
Woodruff, Elvira 1951- *211*
　Earlier sketches in SATA *70, 106, 162*
Woodruff, Joan Leslie 1953- *104*
Woodruff, Liza 1971(?)- *182*
Woodruff, Marian
　See Goudge, Eileen
Woodruff, Noah 1977- *86*
Woods, George A(llan) 1926-1988 .... *30*
　Obituary *57*
Woods, Geraldine 1948- *111*
　Brief entry *42*
　Earlier sketch in SATA *56*
Woods, Harold 1945- *56*
　Brief entry *42*
Woods, Lawrence
　See Lowndes, Robert A(ugustine) W(ard)
Woods, Margaret 1921- *2*
Woods, Nat
　See Stratemeyer, Edward L.
Woods, Titania
　See Weatherly, Lee
Woodson, Jack
　See Woodson, John Waddie Jr.
Woodson, Jacqueline 1964- *189*
　Earlier sketches in SATA *94, 139*
　See also CLR *49*
Woodson, Jacqueline Amanda
　See Woodson, Jacqueline
Woodson, John Waddie Jr. 1913- *10*
Woodtor, Dee
　See Woodtor, Delores Parmer
Woodtor, Dee Parmer 1945(?)-2002
　See Woodtor, Delores Parmer
Woodtor, Delores Parmer 1945-2002 .... *93*
Wood-Trost, Lucille
　See Trost, Lucille W(ood)
Woodward, (Landon) Cleveland 1900-1986 . *10*
　Obituary *48*
Woodworth, Chris 1957- *168*
Woodworth, Viki 1952- *127*
Woody, Regina Jones 1894-1983 .... *3*
Woodyadd, Charlotte
　See Hough, Charlotte
Woog, Adam 1953- *125*
　Earlier sketch in SATA *84*
Wooldridge, Connie Nordhielm 1950- *143*
　Earlier sketch in SATA *92*
Wooldridge, Frosty 1947- *140*
Wooldridge, Rhoda 1906-1988 .... *22*
Wooley, Susan Frelick 1945- *113*
Woolf, Paula 1950- *104*
Woolfe, Angela 1976- *169*
Woolley, Catherine 1904-2005 .... *3*
　Obituary *166*
Woolman, Steven 1969-2004 .... *163*
　Earlier sketch in SATA *90*

Woolsey, Janette 1904-1989 .... *3*
　Obituary *131*
Worcester, Donald E(mmet) 1915- *18*
Word, Reagan 1944- *103*
Work, Virginia 1946- *57*
　Brief entry *45*
Worline, Bonnie Bess 1914- *14*
Wormell, Christopher 1955- *154*
　Earlier sketch in SATA *103*
Wormell, Mary 1959- *96*
Wormser, Richard 1933- *106*
　Autobiography Feature *118*
　See also SAAS *26*
Wormser, Sophie 1897-1979 .... *22*
Worth, Richard
　See Wiggin, Eric E.
Worth, Richard 1945- *59*
　Brief entry *46*
Worth, Valerie 1933-1994 .... *81*
　Earlier sketches in SATA *8, 70*
　See also CLR *21*
Worthington, Leonie 1956- *200*
Wortis, Avi
　See Avi
Wortis, Edward Irving
　See Avi
Wosmek, Frances 1917- *29*
Woychuk, Denis 1953- *71*
Wrede, Patricia C(ollins) 1953- *146*
　Earlier sketch in SATA *67*
Wriggins, Sally Hovey 1922- *17*
Wright, Alexandra 1979- *103*
Wright, Betty Ren 1927- *109*
　Brief entry *48*
　Earlier sketch in SATA *63*
Wright, Cliff 1963- *168*
　Earlier sketch in SATA *76*
Wright, Courtni
　See Wright, Courtni C(rump)
Wright, Courtni C(rump) 1950- *84*
Wright, Courtni Crump
　See Wright, Courtni C(rump)
Wright, Dare 1914(?)-2001 .... *21*
　Obituary *124*
Wright, David K. 1943- *112*
　Earlier sketch in SATA *73*
Wright, Elinor
　See Lyon, Elinor
Wright, Enid Meadowcroft (LaMonte)
　1898-1966 .... *3*
Wright, Esmond 1915-2003 .... *10*
Wright, Frances Fitzpatrick 1897-1982 .... *10*
Wright, J. B.
　See Barkan, Joanne
Wright, Judith 1915-2000 .... *14*
　Obituary *121*
Wright, Judith Arundell
　See Wright, Judith
Wright, Katrina
　See Gater, Dilys
Wright, Kenneth
　See del Rey, Lester
Wright, Kit 1944- *87*
Wright, Leslie B(ailey) 1959- *91*
Wright, Michael 1954- *198*
Wright, Nancy Means *38*
Wright, R(obert) H(amilton) 1906- *6*
Wright, Rachel *134*
Wright, Susan Kimmel 1950- *97*
Wrightfrierson
　See Wright-Frierson, Virginia (Marguerite)
Wright-Frierson, Virginia (Marguerite)
　1949- *110*
　Earlier sketch in SATA *58*
Wrightson, Alice Patricia
　See Wrightson, Patricia
Wrightson, Patricia 1921-2010 .... *112*
　Obituary *215*
　Earlier sketches in SATA *8, 66*
　See also CLR *154*
　See also SAAS *4*

Wroble, Lisa A. 1963- *134*
Wrongo, I.B.
  See Katz, Alan
Wronker, Lili
  See Wronker, Lili Cassel
Wronker, Lili Cassel 1924- *10*
Wryde, Dogear
  See Gorey, Edward (St. John)
Wu, Donald *212*
Wu, Elizabeth
  See Wu, Liz
Wu, Liz *184*
Wu, Norbert 1961- *155*
  Earlier sketch in SATA *101*
Wulf, Linda Press *205*
Wulffson, Don 1943- *155*
  Earlier sketches in SATA *32, 88*
Wulffson, Don L.
  See Wulffson, Don
Wummer, Amy 1955- *201*
Wunderli, Stephen 1958- *79*
Wunsch, Josephine (McLean) 1914- *64*
Wunsch, Marjory 1942- *82*
Wuorio, Eva-Lis 1918- *34*
  Brief entry *28*
Wurts, Janny 1953- *98*
Wyatt, B. D.
  See Robinson, Spider
Wyatt, David 1968- *185*
Wyatt, Jane
  See Bradbury, Bianca (Ryley)
Wyatt, Melissa 1963- *177*
Wyatt, Valerie *209*
Wyeth, Betsy James 1921- *41*
Wyeth, N(ewell) C(onvers) 1882-1945 .... *17*
  See also CLR *106*
Wyler, Rose 1909-2000 .... *18*
  Obituary *121*
Wylie, Betty Jane *48*
Wylie, Laura
  See Matthews, Patricia
Wylie, Laurie
  See Matthews, Patricia
Wyllie, Stephen *86*
Wyman, Andrea *75*
Wyman, Carolyn 1956- *83*
Wymer, Norman (George) 1911- *25*
Wynard, Talbot
  See Hamilton, Charles (Harold St. John)
Wyndham, John
  See Harris, John (Wyndham Parkes Lucas)
    Beynon
Wyndham, Lee
  See Hyndman, Jane Andrews Lee
Wyndham, Robert
  See Hyndman, Robert Utley
Wynne, Patricia J. *210*
Wynne-Jones, Tim 1948- *186*
  Autobiography Feature *136*
  Earlier sketches in SATA *67, 96, 136*
  See also CLR *58*
Wynne-Jones, Timothy
  See Wynne-Jones, Tim
Wynter, Edward (John) 1914- *14*
Wynyard, Talbot
  See Hamilton, Charles (Harold St. John)
Wyss, Johann David Von 1743-1818 .... *29*
  Brief entry *27*
  See also CLR *92*
Wyss, Thelma Hatch 1934- *202*
  Earlier sketches in SATA *10, 140*

X

Xavier, Father
  See Hurwood, Bernhardt J.
Xuan, YongSheng 1952- *116*
  Autobiography Feature *119*

Y

Yaccarino, Dan *192*
  Earlier sketch in SATA *141*
Yadin, (Rav-Aloof) Yigael 1917-1984 .... *55*
Yaffe, Alan
  See Yorinks, Arthur
Yagher, Kevin 1962- *143*
Yakovetic, (Joseph Sandy) 1952- *59*
Yakovetic, Joe
  See Yakovetic, (Joseph Sandy)
Yamada, Utako 1963- *188*
Yamaguchi, Marianne (Illenberger) 1936- *7*
Yamaka, Sara 1978- *92*
Yamanaka, Lois-Ann 1961- *166*
Yamasaki, Katie *206*
Yancey, Diane 1951- *138*
  Earlier sketch in SATA *81*
Yancey, Richard *193*
Yancey, Rick
  See Yancey, Richard
Yang, Belle 1960- *170*
Yang, James 1960- *190*
Yang, Jay 1941- *12*
Yang, Mingyi 1943- *72*
Yarbrough, Camille 1938- *79*
  See also CLR *29*
Yarbrough, Ira 1910(?)-1983
  Obituary *35*
Yaroslava
  See Mills, Yaroslava Surmach
Yarrow, Peter 1938- *195*
Yashima, Taro
  See Iwamatsu, Jun Atsushi
Yates, Elizabeth 1905-2001 .... *68*
  Obituary *128*
  Earlier sketch in SATA *4*
  See also SAAS *6*
Yates, Janelle K(aye) 1957- *77*
Yates, John 1939- *74*
Yates, Kelly 1971- *208*
Yates, Philip 1956- *212*
  Earlier sketches in SATA *92, 149*
Yates, Raymond F(rancis) 1895-1966 .... *31*
Yaukey, Grace S(ydenstricker) 1899-1994 ... *80*
  Earlier sketch in SATA *5*
Yazzie, Johnson 1946- *205*
Ye, Ting-xing 1952- *106*
Yeahpau, Thomas M. 1975- *187*
Yeakley, Marjory Hall 1908- *21*
Yeatman, Linda 1938- *42*
Yeatts, Tabatha 1970- *215*
Yee, Brenda Shannon *133*
Yee, Lisa 1959- *160*
Yee, Paul 1956- *211*
  Earlier sketches in SATA *67, 96, 143*
  See also CLR *44*
Yee, Tammy *206*
Yee, Wong Herbert 1953- *172*
  Earlier sketches in SATA *78, 115*
Yeh, Chun-Chan 1914- *79*
Ye Junjian
  See Yeh, Chun-Chan
Yelchin, Eugene 1956- *196*
Yenawine, Philip 1942- *85*
Yensid, Retlaw
  See Disney, Walt(er Elias)
Yeo, Wilma (Lethem) 1918-1994 .... *81*
  Earlier sketch in SATA *24*
Yeoman, John 1934- *80*
  Earlier sketch in SATA *28*
  See also CLR *46*
Yep, Kathleen S. *203*
Yep, Laurence 1948- *213*
  Earlier sketches in SATA *7, 69, 123, 176*
  See also CLR *132*
Yep, Laurence Michael
  See Yep, Laurence

Yepsen, Roger B(ennet), Jr. 1947- *59*
Yerian, Cameron John *21*
Yerian, Margaret A. *21*
Yerxa, Leo 1947- *181*
Yetska
  See Ironside, Jetske
Yezerski, Thomas F. 1969- *190*
Yin *194*
Ylvisaker, Anne 1965(?)- *172*
Yoder, Carolyn P. 1953- *149*
Yoder, Carolyn Patricia
  See Yoder, Carolyn P.
Yoder, Dorothy Meenen 1921- *96*
Yoder, Dot
  See Yoder, Dorothy Meenen
Yoder, Walter D. 1933- *88*
Yolen, Jane 1939- *194*
  Autobiography Feature *111*
  Earlier sketches in SATA *4, 40, 75, 112, 158*
  See also CLR *149*
  See also SAAS *1*
Yolen, Jane Hyatt
  See Yolen, Jane
Yonezu, Yusuke *196*
Yonge, Charlotte 1823-1901 .... *17*
Yonge, Charlotte Mary
  See Yonge, Charlotte
Yoo, Paula 1969(?)- *174*
Yoo, Taeeun *191*
Yoon, Salina 1972- *204*
Yorinks, Adrienne 1956- *171*
Yorinks, Arthur 1953- *200*
  Earlier sketches in SATA *33, 49, 85, 144*
  See also CLR *20*
York, Alison
  See Nicole, Christopher (Robin)
York, Andrew
  See Nicole, Christopher (Robin)
York, Carol Beach 1928- *77*
  Earlier sketch in SATA *6*
York, Rebecca
  See Buckholtz, Eileen (Garber)
  and Glick, Ruth (Burtnick)
York, Simon
  See Heinlein, Robert A.
Yoshida, Toshi 1911- *77*
Yoshikawa, Sachiko *181*
Yost, Edna 1889-1971
  Obituary *26*
Youd, C. S.
  See Youd, Samuel
Youd, Samuel 1922- *135*
  Brief entry *30*
  Earlier sketch in SATA *47*
  See also CLR *2*
  See also SAAS *6*
Youme
  See Landowne, Youme
Young, Amy L. *185*
Young, Anne Mortimer
  See Mortimer, Anne
Young, Bob
  See Young, Robert W(illiam)
  and Young, James Robert
Young, Carol 1945- *102*
Young, Catherine
  See Olds, Helen Diehl
Young, Clarence
  See Garis, Howard R.
  and Stratemeyer, Edward L.
Young, Collier
  See Bloch, Robert (Albert)
Young, Dan 1952- *126*
Young, Dianne 1959- *88*
Young, Dorothea Bennett 1924- *31*
Young, Ed 1931- *211*
  Earlier sketches in SATA *10, 74, 122, 173*
  See also CLR *27*

Young, Ed Tse-chun
   See Young, Ed
Young, Edward
   See Reinfeld, Fred
Young, Elaine L.
   See Schulte, Elaine L(ouise)
Young, James
   See Graham, Ian
Young, Jan
   See Young, Janet Randall
Young, Janet 1957- 188
Young, Janet Randall 1919-1994 3
Young, Janet Ruth
   See Young, Janet
Young, Jeff C. 1948- 132
Young, John
   See Macintosh, Brownie
Young, Judy 1956- 207
   Earlier sketch in SATA *155*
Young, Judy (Elaine) Dockrey 1949- 72
Young, Karen Romano 1959- 168
   Earlier sketch in SATA *116*
Young, Ken 1956- 86
Young, Lois Horton 1911-1981 26
Young, Louisa 161
Young, Louise B. 1919- 64
Young, Margaret B. 1922-2009 2
Young, Margaret Buckner
   See Young, Margaret B.
Young, Mary 1940- 89
Young, Miriam 1913-1974 7
Young, Noela 1930- 89
Young, (Rodney Lee) Patrick (Jr.) 1937- 22
Young, Percy M(arshall) 1912-2004 31
   Obituary 154
Young, Richard Alan 1946- 72
Young, Robert W(illiam) 1916-1969 3
Young, Ross B. 1955- 150
Young, Ruth 1946- 67
Young, Sara
   See Pennypacker, Sara
Young, Scott A. 1918-2005 5
Young, Scott Alexander
   See Young, Scott A.
Young, Selina 1971-2006 201
Young, Vivien
   See Gater, Dilys
Younger, Barbara 1954- 108
Youngs, Betty 1934-1985 53
   Obituary 42
Younkin, Paula 1942- 77
Yount, Lisa (Ann) 1944- 124
   Earlier sketch in SATA *74*
Yourgrau, Barry 179
Yuditskaya, Tatyana 1964- 75
Yum, Hyewon 211
Yumoto, Kazumi 1959- 153

Z

Zach, Cheryl (Byrd) 1947- 98
   Brief entry 51
   Earlier sketch in SATA *58*
   See also SAAS *24*
Zacharias, Gary L. 1946- 153
Zaffo, George J. (?)-1984 42
Zagarenski, Pamela 1969(?)- 183
Zagwyn, Deborah Turney 1953- 138
   Earlier sketch in SATA *78*
Zahares, Wade 193
Zahn, Timothy 1951- 156
   Earlier sketch in SATA *91*
Zaid, Barry 1938- 51
Zaidenberg, Arthur 1908(?)-1990 34
   Obituary 66

Zalben, Jane Breskin 1950- 170
   Earlier sketches in SATA *7, 79, 120*
   See also CLR *84*
Zallinger, Jean (Day) 1918- 115
   Earlier sketches in SATA *14, 80*
Zallinger, Peter Franz 1943- 49
Zambreno, Mary Frances 1954- 140
   Earlier sketch in SATA *75*
Zanderbergen, George
   See May, Julian
Zappa, Ahmet 1974- 180
Zappa, Ahmet Emuukha Rodan
   See Zappa, Ahmet
Zappler, Lisbeth 1930- 10
Zarchy, Harry 1912-1987 34
Zarin, Cynthia 1959- 192
   Earlier sketch in SATA *108*
Zaring, Jane (Thomas) 1936- 40
Zarins, Joyce Audy
   See dos Santos, Joyce Audy
Zaslavsky, Claudia 1917- 36
Zaugg, Sandra L. 1938- 118
Zaugg, Sandy
   See Zaugg, Sandra L.
Zaunders, Bo 1939- 137
Zawadzki, Marek 1958- 97
Zebra, A.
   See Scoltock, Jack
Zebrowski, George 1945- 67
Zebrowski, George T.
   See Zebrowski, George
Zecca, Katherine 207
Zeck, Gerald Anthony 1939- 40
Zeck, Gerry
   See Zeck, Gerald Anthony
Zed, Dr.
   See Penrose, Gordon
Zei, Alki 1925- 24
   See also CLR *6*
Zeier, Joan T(heresa) 1931- 81
Zeinert, Karen 1942-2002 137
   Earlier sketch in SATA *79*
Zeises, Lara M. 1976- 184
   Earlier sketch in SATA *145*
Zelazny, Roger 1937-1995 57
   Brief entry 39
Zelazny, Roger Joseph
   See Zelazny, Roger
Zeldis, Malcah 1931- 146
   Earlier sketch in SATA *86*
Zelinsky, Paul O. 1953- 154
   Brief entry 33
   Earlier sketches in SATA *49, 102*
   See also CLR *55*
Zellan, Audrey Penn
   See Penn, Audrey
Zemach, Harve
   See Fischtrom, Harvey
Zemach, Kaethe 1958- 149
   Brief entry 39
   Earlier sketch in SATA *49*
Zemach, Margot 1931-1989 70
   Obituary 59
   Earlier sketch in SATA *21*
Zemach-Bersin, Kaethe
   See Zemach, Kaethe
Zeman, Ludmila 1947- 153
Zepeda, Gwendolyn 1971- 206
Zephaniah, Benjamin 1958- 189
   Earlier sketches in SATA *86, 140*
Zephaniah, Benjamin Obadiah Iqbal
   See Zephaniah, Benjamin
Zephaniah, Benjamin Pbadiah Iqubal
   See Zephaniah, Benjamin
Zerman, Melvyn Bernard 1930-2010 46
Zettner, Pat 1940- 70
Zevin, Gabrielle 176
Zhang, Christopher Zhong-Yuan 1954- 91

Zhang, Song Nan 1942- 170
   Earlier sketch in SATA *85*
Ziefert, Harriet 1941- 205
   Earlier sketches in SATA *101, 154*
Ziegler, Jack (Denmore) 1942- 60
Ziemienski, Dennis (Theodore) 1947- 10
Ziliox, Marc
   See Fichter, George S.
Zillah
   See Macdonald, Zillah K(atherine)
Zim, Herbert S(pencer) 1909-1994 30
   Obituary 85
   Earlier sketch in SATA *1*
   See also CLR *2*
   See also SAAS *2*
Zim, Sonia Bleeker 1909-1971 2
   Obituary 26
Zima, Gordon 1920- 90
Zimelman, Nathan 1921- 65
   Brief entry 37
Zimmer, Dirk 1943- 147
   Earlier sketch in SATA *65*
Zimmer, Tracie Vaughn 169
Zimmerman, Andrea 1950- 192
   Earlier sketch in SATA *123*
Zimmerman, Andrea Griffing
   See Zimmerman, Andrea
Zimmerman, H. Werner 1951- 101
Zimmerman, Heinz Werner
   See Zimmerman, H. Werner
Zimmerman, Naoma 1914-2004 10
Zimmermann, Arnold E. 1909- 58
Zimmermann, Karl 1943- 211
Zimmermann, Karl R.
   See Zimmermann, Karl
Zimmett, Debbie
   See Becker, Deborah Zimmett
Zimmy
   See Stratemeyer, Edward L.
Zimnik, Reiner 1930- 36
   See also CLR *3*
Zindel, Bonnie 1943- 34
Zindel, Lizabeth 187
Zindel, Paul 1936-2003 102
   Obituary 142
   Earlier sketches in SATA *16, 58*
   See also CLR *85*
Ziner, Feenie
   See Ziner, Florence
Ziner, Florence 1921- 5
Zingara, Professor
   See Leeming, Joseph
Zinger, Yitskhok
   See Singer, Isaac Bashevis
Zion, Eugene 1913-1975 18
Zion, Gene
   See Zion, Eugene
Zoehfeld, Kathleen Weidner 1954- 193
Zohorsky, Janet R. 1958- 148
Zolkower, Edie Stoltz 171
Zolkowski, Cathy (A.) 1969- 121
Zollars, Jaime 191
Zolotow, Charlotte 1915- 138
   Earlier sketches in SATA *1, 35, 78*
   See also CLR *77*
Zolotow, Charlotte Gertrude Shapiro
   See Zolotow, Charlotte
Zolotow, Ellen
   See Dragonwagon, Crescent
Zonderman, Jon 1957- 92
Zonia, Dhimitri 1921- 20
Zonta, Pat 1951- 143
Zubrowski, Bernard 1939- 90
   Earlier sketch in SATA *35*
Zubrowski, Bernie
   See Zubrowski, Bernard
Zucker, Miriam S.
   See Reichert, Miriam Zucker
Zuckerman, Amy 217

Author Index

Zuckerman, Linda *190*
Zudeck, Darryl 1961- *61*
Zug, Mark *204*
Zupa, G. Anthony
  See Zeck, Gerald Anthony
Zupancic, Lilijana Praprotnik
  See Prap, Lila
Zurbo, Matt(hew) 1967- *98*

Zurhorst, Charles (Stewart, Jr.) 1913-1989 .. *12*
Zurlo, Tony 1941- *145*
Zuromskis, Diane
  See Stanley, Diane
Zuromskis, Diane Stanley
  See Stanley, Diane
Zusak, Markus 1975- *149*
Zwahlen, Diana 1947- *88*

Zweifel, Frances W. 1931- *14*
Zwerger, Lisbeth 1954- *194*
  Earlier sketches in SATA *66, 130*
  See also CLR *46*
  See also SAAS *13*
Zwinger, Ann (H.) 1925- *46*
Zymet, Cathy Alter 1965- *121*